NTA UGC NET/JRF/SET

PAPER - 2

Education

Author
Nandini Sharma
Renu Kulshreshtha

arihant
SUCCESS AND NOTHING LESS

arihant
SUCCESS AND NOTHING LESS

ARIHANT PUBLICATION (INDIA) LIMITED

卐 Administrative & Production Offices

Regd. Office

'Ramchhaya' 4577/15, Agarwal Road, Darya Ganj, New Delhi -110002
Tele: 011- 47630600, 43518550

卐 Head Office

Kalindi, TP Nagar, Meerut (UP) - 250002
Tel: 0121-7156203, 7156204

卐 Sales & Support Offices

Agra, Ahmedabad, Bengaluru, Bareilly, Chennai, Delhi, Guwahati, Hyderabad, Jaipur, Jhansi, Kolkata, Lucknow, Nagpur & Pune.

卐 PRICE ₹725.00

卐 PO No : TXT-XX-XXXXXXX-X-XX

Published by Arihant Publications (India) Ltd.

For further information about the books published by Arihant, log on to www.arihantbooks.com or e-mail at info@arihantbooks.com

SYLLABUS

Applicable from June 2019, Examination

UNIT I Educational Studies

1 Contribution of Indian Schools of Philosophy (Sankhya, Yoga, Vedanta, Buddhism, Jainism) with special reference to Vidya, Dayanand Darshan and Islamic traditions towards educational aims and methods of acquiring valid knowledge.

2 Contribution of Western Schools of Thoughts (Idealism, Realism, Naturalism, Pragmatism, Marxism, Existentialism) and their contribution to education with special reference to information, knowledge and wisdom.

3 Approaches to Sociology of Education (symbolic Interaction, Structural Functionalism and Conflict Theory). Concept and types of Social Institutions and their functions (family, school and society), Concept of Social Movements, Theories of Social Movements (Relative Deprivation, Resource Mobilisation, Political Process Theory and New Social Movement Theory).

4 Socialisation and Education- Education and Culture; Contribution of Thinkers (Swami Vivekananda, Rabindranath Tagore, Mahatma Gandhi, Aurobindo, J Krishnamurthy, Paulo Freire, Wollstonecraft, Nel Noddings and Savitribai Phule) to the development of educational thought for social change, National values as Enshrined in the Indian Constitution - socialism, secularism, justice, liberty, democracy, equality, freedom with special reference to education.

UNIT II History, Politics an Economics of Education

1 Committees and Commissions' Contribution to Teacher Education Secondary Education Commission (1953), Kothari Education Commission (1964-66), National Policy of Education (1986,1992), National Commission on Teachers (1999), National Curriculum Framework 2005, National Knowledge Commission (2007), Yashpal Committee Report (2009), National Curriculum Framework for Teacher Education (2009), Justice Verma Committee Report (2012).

2 Relationship between Policies and Education, Linkage between Educational Policy and National Development, Determinants of Educational Policy and Process of Policy Formulation: Analysis of the Existing Situation, Generation of Policy Options, Evaluation of Policy Options, Making the Policy Decision, Planning of Policy Implementation, Policy Impact Assessment and Subsequent Policy Cycles.

3 Concept of Economics of Education: Cost Benefit Analysis v/s Cost Effective Analysis in Education, Economic returns to Higher Education Signaling Theory v/s Human Capital Theory, Concept of Educational Finance; Educational Finance at Micro and Macro Levels, Concept of Budgeting.

4 Relationship Between Politics and Education, Perspectives of Politics of Education Liberal, Conservative and Critical, Approaches to understanding Politics (Behaviouralism, Theory of Systems Analysis and Theory of Rational Choice), Education for Political Development and Political Socialisation.

UNIT III Learner and Learning Process

1 Growth and Development: Concept and principles, Cognitive Processes and stages of Cognitive Development , Personality: Definitions and theories (Freud, Carl Rogers, Gordon Allport, Max Wertheimer, Kurt Koffka) , Mental health and Mental hygiene.

2 Approaches to Intelligence from Unitary to Multiple: Concepts of Social intelligence, multiple intelligence, emotional intelligence. Theories of Intelligence by Sternberg, Gardner, Assessment of Intelligence, Concepts of Problem Solving, Critical thinking, Metacognition and Creativity.

3 Principles and Theories of Learning: Behaviouristic, Cognitive and Social theories of learning, Factors affecting social learning, Social competence, Concept of social cognition, Understanding social relationship and Socialisation goals.

4 Guidance and Counselling: Nature, Principles and Need, Types of guidance (educational, vocational, personal, health and social and directive, non-directive and eclectic), Approaches to counselling – Cognitive-Behavioural (Albert Ellis – REBT) and Humanistic, Person-centred Counselling (Carl Rogers) - Theories of Counselling (Behaviouristic, Rational, Emotive and Reality).

UNIT IV Teacher Education

1 Meaning, Nature and Scope of Teacher Education; Types of Teacher Education Programs, The Structure of Teacher Education Curriculum and its Vision in Curriculum Documents of NCERT and NCTE at Elementary, Secondary and Higher Secondary Levels, Organisation of Components of Pre-service Teacher Education Transactional Approaches (for foundation courses) Expository, Collaborative and Experiential learning.

2 Understanding Knowledge base of Teacher Education from the view point of Schulman, Deng and Luke and and Habermas, Meaning of Reflective Teaching and Strategies for Promoting Reflective Teaching, Models of Teacher Education - Behaviouristic, Competency-based and Inquiry Oriented Teacher Education Models.

3 Concept, Need, Purpose and Scope of In-service Teacher Education, Organisation and Modes of In-service Teacher Education, Agencies and Institutions of In-service Teacher Education at District, State and National Levels (SSA, RMSA, SCERT, NCERT, NCTE and UGC), Preliminary Consideration in Planning in-service teacher education programme (Purpose, Duration, Resources and Budget).

4 Concept of Profession and Professionalism, Teaching as a Profession, Professional Ethics of Teachers, Personal and Contextual factors affecting Teacher Development, ICT Integration, Quality Enhancement for Professionalisation of Teacher Education, Innovation in Teacher Education.

UNIT V Curriculum Studies

1 Concept and Principles of Curriculum, Strategies of Curriculum Development, Stages in the Process of Curriculum development, Foundations of Curriculum Planning - Philosophical Bases (national, democratic), Sociological Bases (socio cultural reconstruction), Psychological Bases (learner's needs and interests),Benchmarking and Role of National level Statutory Bodies - UGC, NCTE and University in Curriculum Development.

2 Models of Curriculum Design: Traditional and Contemporary Models (Academic / Discipline Based Model, Competency Based Model, Social Functions / Activities Model [social reconstruction], Individual Needs and Interests Model, Outcome Based Integrative Model , Intervention Model, C I P P Model (Context, Input, Process, Product Model).

3 Instructional System, Instructional Media, Instructional Techniques and Material in enhancing curriculum Transaction, Approaches to Evaluation of Curriculum : Approaches to Curriculum and Instruction (Academic and Competency Based Approaches), Models of Curriculum Evaluation: Tyler's Model, Stake's Model, Scriven's Model, Kirkpatrick's Model.

4 Meaning and types of Curriculum change, Factors affecting curriculum change, Approaches to curriculum change, Role of students, teachers and educational administrators in curriculum change and improvement, Scope of curriculum research and Types of Research in curriculum studies.

UNIT VI Research in Education

1 Meaning and Scope of Educational Research, Meaning and steps of Scientific Method, Characteristics of Scientific Method (Replicability, Precision, Falsifiability and Parsimony), Types of Scientific Method (Exploratory, Explanatory and Descriptive), Aims of research as a scientific activity: Problem-solving, Theory Building and Prediction, Types of research (Fundamental, Applied and Action), Approaches to Educational Research (Quantitative and Qualitative), Designs in Educational Research (Descriptive, Experimental and Historical).

2 Variables: Meaning of Concepts, Constructs and Variables, Types of Variables (Independent, Dependent, Extraneous, Intervening and Moderator), Hypothesis - Concept, Sources, Types (Research, Directional, Non-directional, Null), Formulating Hypothesis, Characteristics of a good hypothesis, Steps of Writing a Research Proposal, Concept of Universe and Sample, Characteristics of a good Sample, Techniques of Sampling (Probability and Non-probability Sampling), Tools of Research - Validity, Reliability and Standardisation of a Tool, Types of Tools (Rating scale, Attitude scale, Questionnaire, Aptitude test and Achievement Test, Inventory), Techniques of Research (Observation, Interview and Projective Techniques).

3 Types of Measurement Scale (Nominal, Ordinal, Interval and Ratio), Quantitative Data Analysis - Descriptive data analysis (Measures of central tendency, variability, fiduciary limits and graphical presentation of data), Testing of Hypothesis (Type I and Type II Errors), Levels of Significance, Power of a statistical test and effect size, Parametric Techniques, Non- Parametric Techniques , Conditions to be satisfied for using parametric techniques, Inferential data analysis, Use and Interpretation of statistical techniques: Correlation, t-test, z-test, ANOVA, chi-square (Equal Probability and Normal Probability Hypothesis). Qualitative Data Analysis - Data Reduction and Classification, Analytical Induction and Constant Comparison, Concept of Triangulation.

4 Qualitative Research Designs: Grounded Theory Designs (Types, characteristics, designs, Steps in conducting a GT research, Strengths and Weakness of GT) - Narrative Research Designs (Meaning and key Characteristics, Steps in conducting NR design), Case Study (Meaning, Characteristics, Components of a CS design, Types of CS design, Steps of conducting a CS research, strengths and weaknesses), Ethnography (Meaning, Characteristics, Underlying assumptions, Steps of conducting ethnographic research, Writing ethnographic account, Strengths and weaknesses), Mixed Method Designs: Characteristics, Types of MM designs (Triangulation, explanatory and exploratory designs), Steps in conducting a MM designs, Strengths and weakness of MM research.

UNIT VII Pedagogy, Andragogy and Assessment

1 Pedagogy, Pedagogical Analysis - Concept and Stages, Critical Pedagogy- Meaning, Need and its implications in Teacher Education, Organising Teaching: Memory Level (Herbartian Model), Understanding Level (Morrison teaching Model), Reflective Level (Bigge and Hunt teaching Model), Concept of Andragogy in Education Meaning, Principles, Competencies of Self-directed Learning, Theory of Andragogy (Malcolm Knowles), The Dynamic Model of Learner Autonomy.

2 Assessment – Meaning, nature, perspectives (assessment for Learning, assessment of learning and Assessment of Learning) - Types of Assessment (Placement, formative, diagnostic, summative) Relations between objectives and outcomes , Assessment of Cognitive (Anderson and Krathwohl), Affective (Krathwohl) and psychomotor domains (RH Dave) of learning.

3 Assessment in Pedagogy of Education: Feedback Devices: Meaning, Types, Criteria, Guidance as a Feedback Devices: Assessment of Portfolios, Reflective Journal, Field Engagement using Rubrics, Competency Based Evaluation, Assessment of Teacher Prepared ICT Resources.

4 Assessment in Andragogy of Education - Interaction Analysis: Flanders' Interaction analysis, Galloway's system of interaction analysis (Recording of Classroom Events, Construction and Interpretation of Interaction Matrix), Criteria for teacher evaluation (Product, Process and Presage criteria, Rubrics for Self and Peer evaluation (Meaning, steps of construction).

UNIT VIII Technology in/ For Education

1 Concept of Educational Technology (ET) as a Discipline: (Information Technology, Communication Technology and Information and Communication Technology (ICT) and Instructional Technology, Applications of Educational Technology in formal, non formal (Open and Distance Learning), informal and inclusive education systems, Overview of Behaviourist, Cognitive and Constructivist Theories and their implications to Instructional Design (Skinner, Piaget, Ausubel, Bruner, Vygotsky), Relationship between Learning Theories and Instructional Strategies (for large and small groups, formal and non formal groups).

2 Systems Approach to Instructional Design, Models of Development of Instructional Design (ADDIE, ASSURE, Dick and Carey Model Mason's), Gagne's Nine Events of Instruction and Five E's of Constructivism, Nine Elements of Constructivist Instructional Design, Application of Computers in Education: CAI, CAL, CBT, CML, Concept, Process of preparing ODLM, Concept of e learning, Approaches to e learning (Offline, Online, Synchronous, Asynchronous, Blended learning, mobile learning).

3 Emerging Trends in e learning: Social learning (concept , use of web 2.0 tools for learning, social networking sites, blogs, chats, video conferencing, discussion forum), Open Education Resources (Creative Common, Massive Open Online Courses; Concept and application), E Inclusion - Concept of E Inclusion, Application of Assistive technology in E learning , Quality of E Learning – Measuring quality of system: Information, System, Service, User Satisfaction and Net Benefits (D and M IS Success Model, 2003), Ethical Issues for E Learner and E Teacher - Teaching, Learning and Research.

4 Use of ICT in Evaluation, Administration and Research: E portfolios, ICT for Research - Online Repositories and Online Libraries, Online and Offline assessment tools (Online survey tools or test generators) – Concept and Development.

UNIT IX Educational Management, Administration and Leadership

1 Educational Management and Administration – Meaning, Principles, Functions and importance, Institutional building, POSDCORB, CPM, PERT, Management as a system, SWOT analysis, Taylorism, Administration as a process, Administration as a bureaucracy, Human relations approach to Administration, Organisational compliance, Organisational development, Organisational climate.

2 Leadership in Educational Administration: Meaning and Nature, Approaches to leadership: Trait, Transformational, Transactional, Value based, Cultural, Psychodynamic and Charismatic, Models of Leadership (Blake and Mouton's Managerial Grid, Fiedler's Contingency Model, Tri-dimensional Model, Hersey and Blanchard's Model, Leader-Member Exchange Theory).

3 Concept of Quality and Quality in Education: Indian and International perspective, Evolution of Quality: Inspection, Quality Control, Quality Assurance, Total Quality Management (TQM), Six sigma, Quality Gurus: Walter Shewart, Edward Deming, C K Pralhad.

4 Change Management: Meaning, Need for Planned change, Three-Step-Model of Change (Unfreezing, Moving, Refreezing), The Japanese Models of Change: Just-in-Time, Poka yoke, Cost of Quality: Appraisal Costs, Failure costs and Preventable costs, Cost Benefit Analysis, Cost Effective Analysis, Indian and International Quality Assurance Agencies: Objectives, Functions, Roles and Initiatives (National Assessment Accreditation Council [NAAC], Performance Indicators, Quality Council of India [QCI], International Network for Quality Assurance Agencies in Higher Education [INQAAHE].

UNIT X Inclusive Education

1 Inclusive Education: Concept, Principles, Scope and Target Groups (Diverse learners; Including Marginalised group and Learners with Disabilities), Evolution of the Philosophy of Inclusive Education: Special, Integrated, Inclusive Education, Legal Provisions: Policies and Legislations (National Policy of Education (1986), Programme of Action of Action (1992), Persons with Disabilities Act (1995), National Policy of Disabilities (2006), National Curriculum Framework (2005), Concession and Facilities to Diverse Learners (Academic and Financial), Rehabilitation Council of India Act (1992), Inclusive Education under Sarva Shiksha Abhiyan (SSA), Features of UNCRPD (United Nations Convention on the Rights of Persons with Disabilities) and its Implication.

2 Concept of Impairment, Disability and Handicap, Classification of Disabilities based on ICF Model, Readiness of School and Models of Inclusion, Prevalence, Types, Characteristics and Educational Needs of Diverse learners Intellectual, Physical and Multiple Disabilities, Causes and prevention of disabilities, Identification of Diverse Learners for Inclusion, Educational Evaluation Methods, Techniques and Tools.

3 Planning and Management of Inclusive Classrooms: Infrastructure, Human Resource and Instructional Practices, Curriculum and Curricular Adaptations for Diverse Learners, Assistive and Adaptive Technology for Diverse learners: Product (Aids and Appliances) and Process (Individualised Education Plan, Remedial Teaching), Parent-Professional Partnership: Role of Parents, Peers, Professionals, Teachers, School.

4 Barriers and Facilitators in Inclusive Education: Attitude, Social and Educational, Current Status and Ethical Issues of inclusive education in India, Research Trends of Inclusive Education in India.

CONTENTS

UGC NET/JRF/SET

Education (Paper-2)

Solved Paper, August 2024

General Instructions

1. There are total one hundred questions in this paper. Each question carries 2 marks.
2. All questions are compulsory.

---

1. Choose the correct order for the steps involved in the process of construction of a standardised test.

A. Writing the items
B. Pre-try out
C. Dress-rehearsal
D. Planning of the test
E. Final try out

Choose the correct answer from the options given below.

(1) A, D, B, C,E
(2) A, D, C, B, E
(3) D, A, B, E, C
(4) D, A, C, B, E

2. Which of the following statement is correct about null hypothesis?

(1) The null hypothesis relates to a statistical method of interpreting conclusions about sample characteristics that are inferred from the variable relationships observed in samples.
(2) The null hypothesis relates to a statistical method of interpreting conclusions about population characteristics that are inferred from the variable relationships observed in samples.
(3) The null hypothesis relates of a statistical method of interpreting conclusions about population characteristics that are inferred from the variable relationships observed in populations.
(4) The null hypothesis related to a statistical method of interpreting conclusions about sample characteristics that are inferred from the variable relationships observed in population.

3. Which of the following statements are incorrect?

A. Thorndike's theory is atomistic theory of intelligence.
B. Evaluation is the primary mental process which means retention of what is recognised.
C. Group of specific abilities known as 'S' factor is universal in born ability.
D. According to Faculty theory of intelligence, mind is made up of different faculties like reasoning, memory, discriminations and imagination, etc.
E. Structure of Intellect Model of Intelligence was given by Spearman.

Choose the correct answer from the options given below.

(1) A, B and C
(2) B, C and E
(3) B, C and D
(4) A, C and D

4. Which of the following statements are TRUE?

A. Bismillah-a ritual was performed at the age of 4 years, 4 months and 4 days in Muslim Education.
B. Pabbaja-a ritual performed at the age of 8 years in Buddhist education
C. Upasampada-a ritual post-education for permanent membership of a Sangh in Buddhist education

D. Upanayana-a ritual to begin education at the 8, 11, 12 and 15 years of age for brahmins, kshatriyas, Vaisyas and Shudras.

E. Ballabhi and Jagdalla Centres of Vedic education.

Choose the correct answer from the options given below.

(1) A, B and C (2) A, B, D and E
(3) D and E (4) B, C, D and E

5. The Dave Committee report is especially focused on

(1) Minimum Levels of Learning (MLL) at Secondary Level
(2) Minimum Levels of Learning (MLL) at Primary Level
(3) Art and Craft Education at Primary Level
(4) Early Childhood Education

6. Pick the INCORRECT match.

A. Education and Schooling are ideological state apparatuses - Althusser

B. Education is for Cultural and Social Reproduction- Bourdieu

C. School is a miniature society Parsons

D. Education helps the individual to grow and achieve her potentials -Marx

E. Education for democracy is thus education freed from the authoritarian relationships-Dewey

Choose the correct answer from the options given below.

(1) Only A (2) Only D
(3) B and C (D) C and E

7. Which of the following is true regarding 'grounded theory' research?

A. Axial coding is the process of relating sub-categories to a category.

B. It includes.continuous comparative analysis of cases.

C. Selective coding continues the axial coding at a higher level of abstraction.

D. The size of sample is determined by the theoretical saturation of categories.

E. It is a substitute of experimental research.

Choose the correct answer from the options given below.

(1) A, B and C (2) A, B, C and D
(3) B, C and D (4) A, C and D

8. Which of the following are not steps of Instructional Technology?

A. Selection of Instructional material

B. Suggestions for improvements

C. Selection of Appropriate Alternative

D. Reinforced Practice

E. Description of Restrictions

Choose the correct answer from the options given below.

(1) A, B and C (2) B, C and D
(3) A, C and D (4) C, D and E

9. The correct hierarchy of needs given by Maslow is

A. safety needs

B. prestige needs

C. physiological needs

D. self Actualization needs

E. needs for belongingness

Choose the correct answer from the options given below.

(1) A, C, E, D, B (2) C, A, E, B, D
(3) A, C, B, E, D (4) A, B, C, D, E

10. It is a learning platform that brings together an integrated environment, a range of resources that enable the learners and teachers to. interact online and includes content delivery and tracking.

(1) SPSS (2) META AI
(3) SWAYAM (4) R

11. The correct sequence of the five steps of Morrison's teaching model is

A. recitation B. organisation
C. assimilation D. presentation
E. exploration

Choose the correct answer from the options given below.

(1) D, C, A, B, E (2) B, A, C, D, E
(3) E, D, C, B, A (4) E, D, C, A, B

12. Match List-I with List-II.

	List-I		List-I
A.	Taxonomy of Education Objectives: The classification of Educational Goals, Handbook I: Cognitive Domain	I.	Krathwohl et al.
B.	Taxonomy of Educational objectives: The classification of Educational Goals Handbook II: Affective Domain	II.	Anderson and Krathwohl
C.	Developing and Writing Behavioural Objectives	III.	Bloom et al.

D.	A Taxonomy for Learning, Teaching and Assessing. A Revision of Bloom's Taxonomy of Educational Objectives	IV.	Dave

Codes

	A	B	C	D		A	B	C	D
(1)	IV	II	III	I	(2)	III	I	IV	II
(3)	III	II	I	IV	(4)	II	I	IV	III

13. Which component is not a part of RMSA initiative?
(1) Construction of new classrooms
(2) Provision of scholarships
(3) Establishment of laboratories
(4) Appointment of additional teaching faculties

14. A teacher conducts an assessment in her class and then adjusts the next lesson to meet the students' needs. She is doing
(1) assessment of learning
(2) assessment for learning
(3) assessment as learning
(4) assessment through learning

15. The congruence-contingency model of curriculum evaluation was given by
(1) Tyler (2) Stake
(3) Scriven (4) Kirkpatrick

16. "Core Design" is an example of
(1) learner-centered curriculum
(2) problem-centred curriculum
(3) subject-centred curriculum
(4) core-curriculum

17. Which of these accurately reflect the limitations of cost benefit analysis in education?
A. Difficulty in quantifying non-monetary benefits.
B. Short-term focus on costs.
C. Overemphasis on quantitative data.
D. Inclusion in intangible cost.
E. Lack of consideration for long-term outcomes.
Choose the correct answer from the options given below.
(1) A, B and E (2) A, D and E
(3) A, C and E (4) A, B and D

18. Which of the following in not a principle of guidance?
(1) Holistic development of an individual
(2) Recognition of individual needs and differences
(3) Non-cognisance of individual differences
(4) Acceptance of individual needs

19. The correct sequence of consequential leadership style of Managerial Grid is:
A. country club
B. team management
C. impoverished management
D. authority - compliance
E. middle-of-the road
Choose the correct answer from the options given below.
(1) A, B, E, C, D (2) B, C, D, A, E
(3) D, A, B, C, E (4) C, A, D, E, B

20. Curriculum was defined by .... as "a plan for action, or a written document, which includes strategies for achieving desired goals or ends".
(1) Galen Saylor (1970)
(2) Tanner & Tanner (1980)
(3) Tyler and Hilda Taba (1962)
(4) Oliva (1982)

21. Which of the following is not true about critical thinking/critical pedagogy?
(1) The focus is to understand the oppressions of the individual, group and society which might be self-imposed.
(2) The focus is to understand the oppressions of the individual, group and society which might be created via external forces.
(3) According to Freire dialogue is capable of generating critical thinking
(4) According to Freire dialogue does not need any pre-requirement in the classroom.

22. Which of the following statements are true?
A. Medical Model of disabilities find its base in psychology.
B. Human Rights Model of Disabilities talks about equity.
C. Charity Model of Disabilities treats people with disabilities as incapable.
D. Economic Model of Disabilities considers disabilities as burden.
E. Religions Model of Disabilities relates disabilities with God's Wrath.
Choose the correct answer from the options given below.
(1) A, B and D
(2) B,C and D
(3) B, C and E
(4) C, D and E

23. What leads to curriculum change?
A. National priorities
B. Placement in jobs
C. Socio-cultural contexts
D. Availability of effective teachers
E. Ideology of the government.

Choose the correct answer from the options given below.

(1) B, C and E (2) B, C and D
(3) A, C and E (4) A, B and E

24. The term 'Andragogy' was coined by

(1) Malcolm Shepherd Knowles
(2) Edward C. Linderman
(3) Jobann Heinrich Pestalozzi
(4) Alexander Kapp

25. This theory affirms that education is a sequence of selection between binary options of available long-term utility End short-term risk of failure.

(1) Rational choice theory
(2) Systems analysis theory
(3) Signalling theory
(4) Human capital theory

26. Match the List-I with List-II.

List-I	List-II
A. External Criticism	I. Pre-Experimental design
B. The time series design	II. Quasi Experimental design
C. Internal criticism	III. Accuracy or worth of the source
D. The static-group comparison design	IV. Authenticity or genuineness of data

Codes

	A	B	C	D
(1)	IV	II	III	I
(2)	III	I	IV	II
(3)	I	II	IV	I
(4)	IV	I	II	II

27. Which amongst the following is not a Marxist theorist of Sociology of Education?

(1) Emile Durkheim (2) Althusser
(3) Gramsci (4) Bowles and Gintis

28. Following are significant milestones in the field of inclusive education. Arrange them chronologically.

A. National Education Policy
B. Salamanca Statement
C. United Nations Convention on Rights of the Persons with Disabilities (UNCRPD)
D. Sarva Shiksha Abhiyan
E. National Policy on Disabilities

Choose the correct answer from the options give in below.

(1) B, C, A, E, D
(2) B, E, C, A, D
(3) B, D, E, C, A
(4) B, C, A, D, E

29. Which of the following is not a part of curriculum development?

(1) Choosing appropriate transaction strategy
(2) Exploring relevant learning experiences
(3) Identifying effective teachers
(4) Progressive testing of the achievement of objectives

30. Match the List-I with List-II.

List-I	List-II
A. Contextual competency	I. Including various concepts of Education and Learning
B. Conceptual competency	II. As regarded general, subject-wise, state-wise, dimensions
C. Evaluation competency	III. Comprising a wider view of the development of education in society and teacher's role in it
D. Transactional competency	IV. Preparation, selection and use of tools and tests

Codes

	A	B	C	D
(1)	II	IV	II	I
(2)	II	I	IV	II
(3)	III	II	I	IV
(4)	III	I	II	IV

31. Among the following which is not an advantage of SWOT.

(1) It is easy to understand
(2) It is easy to communicate
(3) Data collection, evaluation and decision-making are easily confused
(4) Applicable to many levels in an organization

32. The correct sequence of the steps for developing an Instructional Design is

A. assessment
B. delivery of instructions
C. deciding instructional goals
D. need analysis
E. task analysis

Choose the correct answer from the options given below.

(1) A, C, D, B, E (2) C, A, D, E, B
(3) D, C, E, B, A (4) A, B, D, C, E

33. Which of the following statements are true about 'hypothesis'?

A. The minor premise of the older deductive method was gradually replaced by hypothesis.
B. Snow (1973) described six levels of theory, with the first level being hypothesis formation.

C. For the hypothesis to be testable, the variables most be operationally defined.

D. The most common use of hypothesis is to test whether an existing theory can be used to solve a problem.

E. The hypothesis focuses the investigation on indefinite targets.

Choose the correct answer from the options given below.

(1) A, B, C and D
(2) B, C, D and E
(3) B, C and D
(4) C and D

34. Which of the following statements are true as per functionalist perspective on sociology of education?

A. The major function of education is the transmission of society's norms and values.

B. School serves a function that cannot be provided either by family or peers.

C. School is a focal socializing agency.

D. Educational system is a part of superstructure and reproduces ruling ideology.

E. Mass education began in industrial society and is an established requirement of an industrial society.

Choose the correct answer from the options given below.

(1) C, D and E (2) A, C and D
(3) B, C, D and E (4) A, B, C and E

35. Schooling reproduces norms and values. Norms and values are simply chipenomenal expressions of the ruling class. This idea can be associated with

(1) Realism (2) Pragmatism
(3) Maxism (4) Post modernism

36. The tenth category of Flander's Interaction analysis is related to

(1) Teacher talk
(2) Public talk
(3) Accepting the ideas of pupil
(4) Silence on pause on confession

37. According to which commission, a majority of stand-alone teacher education Institutions - over 10,000 in numbers- are not even attempting serious teacher education but are essentially selling degrees for a price?

(1) Radhakrishnan Commission
(2) Mudaliar Commission
(3) Kothari Commission
(4) J. S. Verma Commission

38. What is the primary focus of Poka-Yoke model in educational leadership?

(1) Eliminating financial inefficiencies
(2) Preventing errors in educational process
(3) Enhancing student-teacher communication
(4) Developing innovative teaching materials

39. Match the List-I with List-II.

List-I		List-II
A. Type of curriculum change.	I.	Systems
B. Factor affecting curriculum change	II.	Perturbations
C. Approach to curriculum change	III.	Learning communities
D. Strategy for curriculum change	IV.	Aspirations of people

Codes

	A	B	C	D		A	B	C	D
(1)	II	IV	I	III	(2)	I	II	IV	III
(3)	IV	III	II	I	(4)	III	II	I	IV

40. The Dynamic Model of Learner Autonomy is

A. a tool for self-assessment

B. a tool for choosing appropriate pedagogy by the teacher in classroom

C. given by Tassinari

D. to be followed in fixed ascending order.

Choose the correct answer from the options given below.

(1) A and B (2) A and C
(3) B and C (4) B and D

41. Those who are soft and round, such personalities are categorised by Sheldon as

(1) Ectomorphic (2) Mesomorphic
(3) Asethetic (4) Endomorphic

42. The correct sequence of functions of management is

A. directing B. organising
C. planning D. controlling
E. staffing

Choose the correct answer from the options given below.

(1) C, B, A, E, D (2) C, B, E, A, D
(3) A, C, B, E, D (4) A, D, B, E, C

43. A class teacher administered Thematic Apperception Test (TAT) to a group of students to assess their.

(1) achievement (2) awareness
(3) attitude (4) personality

44. Who is known as the Father of Management Process?
(1) Elton Mayo
(2) Abraham H. Maslow
(3) Henry Fayol
(4) Edger Henry Schein

45. Islamic philosophers divide natural/universal expressions in five types.
A. common accident
B. species
C. property
D. difference
E. genus
Choose the correct answer from the options given below.
(1) E, A, C, B, D (2) E, B, D, C, A
(3) A, B, D, E, C (4) E, D, C, B, A

46. Which of the following is not a quadrant of MOOCs?
(1) e-Tutorial
(2) e-Content
(3) Web resources
(4) Assessment by the Tutor

47. Match the List-I with List-II.

List-I		List-II	
A.	Existentialism	I.	Reality is ultimately mental
B.	Idealism	II.	Education as a means of proletariat emancipation
C.	Critical Thinking	III.	Essence preceedes in natural world
D.	Marxism	IV.	All education is concerned with reason and logic

Codes

	A	B	C	D
(1)	III	IV	I	II
(2)	II	IV	III	I
(3)	III	I	IV	II
(4)	II	I	III	IV

48. Which of the following statements are true for Signalling theory of economics of education?
A. Michael Spence is one of the theorist.
B. Individuals have different levels of inate productivity.
C. Education helps to enhance the innate levels of productivity.
D. Education helps to identify different levels of productivity.
E. More years of schooling lead to more productivity.
Choose the correct answer from the options given below.
(1) A, B and D
(2) C and E
(3) B, C, D and E
(4) A, B, C and D

49. Mass education, or the idea that anybody and everybody can learn owes its genesis to:
(1) colonialism
(2) modernism
(3) postmodernism
(4) reformism

50. According to Hackney and Cormier (2005), the correct sequence of steps of counselling process is
A. goal setting
B. problem assessment
C. evaluation, terimination or Referral
D. relationship building
E. counselling intervention
Choose the correct answer from the options given below.
(1) D, B, A, E, C (2) B,A, D,C,E
(3) A, B, D, C, E (4) A,D, B, E, C

51. When for a particular degree of freedom, a null hypothesis could not be rejected at the .05 level of significance then
(1) it will definitely be rejected at the .01 level of significance.
(2) it may or may not be rejected at the .01 level of significance
(3) it will definitely not be rejected at the .01 level of significance
(4) the given information is insufficient to decide upon.

52. Match the List-I with List-II.

List-I		List-II	
A.	Pre-Scientific Management Era	I.	Frederik W. Taylor
B.	Classical Management Era	II.	George Elton Mayo
C.	Neo-Classical Era	III.	Ernest Dale
D.	Modern Management Era	IV.	Charles Babbage and Robert Oven

Codes

	A	B	C	D
(1)	I	III	IV	II
(2)	IV	I	II	III
(3)	II	I	III	IV
(4)	I	II	IV	III

53. Match the List-I with List-II.

List-I		List-II	
A.	Cutcome-based Integrative Model	I.	Evaluating quality of education at school
B.	CIPP Model	II.	Systematic and Comprehensive evaluation
C.	Scriven's Model	III.	Clear learning Outcomes.
D.	Tyler's Model	IV.	Objective Four-step process

Codes

	A	B	C	D		A	B	C	D
(1)	I	II	III	IV	(2)	I	III	IV	II
(3)	IV	I	II	III	(4)	III	I	II	IV

54. Identify the impact of C.K. Prahlad's theory on curriculum design in teacher education.

A. Enhancing value through innovative curriculum elements.

B. Aligning curriculum with the long-term goals of Educational Institution.

C. Focusing on high-income student populations to maximise returns.

D. Integrating core competencies into curriculum development.

E. Addressing the needs of under served student groups within the curriculum.

Choose the correct answer from the options given below.

(1) A, B, D and E (2) A, C, D and E
(3) A, B, C and D (4) A, B,C and E

55. Correct sequence of five quality indicators used in Education given by Ogawa and Collum.

A. Description B. Monitoring
C. Policy Relevance D. Evaluation
E. Value Judgement

Choose the correct answer from the options given below.

(1) A, D, B, E, C (2) A, B, E, C, D
(3) A, C, B, D, E (4) A, E, D, B, C

56. The Paideia Proposal by Mortimer Adler involves

A. providing all children with the same quality of schooling.

B. a school curriculum that is primarily liberal and humanistic.

C. having different objectives for different students.

D. the curriculum consisting of only one kind of learning.

E. remedial and compensatory interventions for individual differences.

Choose the correct answer from the options given below.

(1) B, C and E (2) B, C and D
(3) A, B and D (4) A, B and E

57. These are dominant trait of one's personality which may dominate personality to such an extent that the person, may become known for those traits only

(1) secondary traits
(2) learning traits
(3) cardinal traits
(4) central traits

58. Match the List-I with List-II.

List-I		List-II	
A.	Children with Learning Disabilities	I.	Associated speech problems
B.	Children with hearing Impairment	II.	Braille
C.	Children with Intellectual Disabilities	III.	Achievement Potential Discrepancy
D.	Children with Visual Impairment	IV.	Intelligence Quotient

Codes

	A	B	C	D		A	B	C	D
(1)	I	III	IV	II	(2)	III	IV	II	I
(3)	IV	II	III	I	(4)	III	I	IV	II

59. Which of the following statements are incorrect?

A. Asynchronous interaction takes place in real time.

B. A blog offers interaction with reflective comments and also the ability to interlink related ideas.

C. Synchronous Interaction gives freedom to the learner to learn at his/her own pace and as per the availability of time at his/her disposal.

D. Question Mark Perception is a software which provides scope for submission of answers to multiple choice questions.

E. Calibrand Marker is an Intranet based workflow application through which assessment can be carried out for formative tests.

Choose the correct answer from the options given below.

(1) B, C and D (2) A, C and D
(3) C, D and E (4) A, B and C

60. In his work during nineteenth century, Charles Darwin,

(1) used the inductive method of Bacon.
(2) used the deductive method of Aristotle.
(3) integrated the deductive method of Aristotle and the inductive method of Bacon.
(4) discarded the deductive method and the inductive method completely.

61. Choose the correct order of event fora true experimental design.

A. Random selection of total sample units
B. Exposure to the treatment
C. Identification of population
D. Random assignment of treatment to one group
E. Random division of sampled units into two (one for experimental and one for control) groups

Choose the correct answer from the options given below.

(1) C, A, E, D, B (3) C, E, A, B, D
(3) C, E, A, D, B (4) B, C, E, A, D

62. Problem-based Learning (PBL) approach is used for curriculum development as it results in

(1) reducing the gap between curriculum and syllabus.
(2) enhancing the employability of learners.
(3) filling the gap between academics and practioners.
(4) economic growth of the country.

63. Identify the challenges involved in service teacher education programme.

A. Resistance to change
B. High motivation among teachers
C. Insufficient time allocation
D. Strong institutional support
E. Lack of Resources

Choose the correct answer from the options given below.

(1) A, C and E (2) A, B and E
(3) A, C and D (4) A, B and D

64. Which of the following is not correct about ANOVA?

(1) The F-ratio is computed in ANOVA.
(2) It is a ratio between 'between-groups variance' and 'within-group variance'.
(3) The 'between-groups variance' represents the sampling error in the distributions.
(4) F-ratio is named after Sir Ronald Fisher.

65. Match the List-I with List-II.

	List-I		List-II
A.	Linear Programming	I.	Wrong response also helps in diagnosis of weaknesses of the learner
B.	Branching Programming	II.	Science of control and communication
C.	Mathetics Programming	III.	Based on operant conditioning learning theory
D.	Cybernatics	IV.	Based on connectionist theory of learning

Codes

	A	B	C	D		A	B	C	D
(1)	III	I	IV	II	(2)	I	III	II	IV
(3)	III	II	IV	I	(4)	IV	III	I	II

66. Which of the following are the assumptions of Knowles' theory of Andragogy?

A. Readiness to learn
B. Internally motivated (Motivation to learn)
C. Self-concept
D. Mandatory guidance

Choose the correct answer from the options given below.

(1) A, B and C (2) B, C and D
(3) A, C and D (4) A and B

67. Negative reinforcement is

(1) the same as punishment
(2) not generally liked by the organism
(3) meant for decreasing the probability of the occurrance of a behaviour
(4) resulting indirectly opposite behaviours

68. Identify those which best represent the benefits of implementing six-sigma in teacher education?

A. Improved teacher effectiveness,
B. Enhanced student-learning outcomes.
C. Increased Administrative work load
D. More efficient use of Resources.
E. Greater standardisation of teaching practices.

Choose the correct answer from the options given below.

(1) A, C, B and E
(2) A, B and E
(3) A, B and D
(4) A, C, D and E

69. Match the List-I with List-II.

	List-I		List-II
A.	Method of Difference	I.	Assumption of experimental research
B.	Law of single variable	II.	Threat for experimental validity
C.	While individual events cannot be predicted with accuracy, aggregate events can	III.	Assumption of randomization
D.	Interaction effect of testing	IV.	Mill's Canon

Codes

	A	B	C	D
(1)	II	I	IV	III
(2)	III	I	IV	II
(3)	IV	I	III	II
(4)	I	IV	III	II

70. Which of the following does not come under the updated D & M is Success Model (2003)?

(1) Information quality
(2) System quality
(3) Net benefits
(4) Organisational impact

71. Match the List-I with List-II.

	List-I		List-II
A.	Permissive style	I.	The 9.9 Managerial Style
B.	Most desirable leadership behaviour	II.	Scientific Management
C.	Replacement of old rules to thumb method	III.	Laissez Faire
D.	Principle of span of control	IV.	Ian Hamilton

Codes

	A	B	C	D
(1)	III	I	II	IV
(2)	I	II	III	IV
(3)	IV	III	II	I
(4)	III	I	II	IV

72. Which of the following have direct relevance for inclusive education?

A. UNCRPD
B. Project on Integrated Education for the Disabled (PIED)
C. NEP 2020
D. NPE, 1986
E. Universal Design for Learning

Choose the correct answer from the options given below.

(1) A, B and C (2) A, C and E
(3) A, B and D (4) A, D and E

73. Arrange the following theorists chronologically.

A. Functionalist- Durkheim
B. Open System Theory Bertanlaffy
C. Symbolic Interactionist - Mead
D. Conflict Theorist- Weber
E. Conflict Theorist - Marx

Choose the correct answer from the options given below.

(1) E, B, C, A, D (2) A, B, C, D, E
(3) A, D, B, C, E (4) E, A, D, C, B

74. The function of search engine to scour tie internet for content, looking over the code/content for each URL they find, is called

(1) indexing (2) crawling
(3) ranking (4) URL

75. Match the List-I with List-II.

	List-I		List-II
A.	Classical Conditioning	I.	The response is made first, then reinforcement follows
B.	Operant Conditioning	II.	When learners have difficulty with new material, go back to the concrete anchors (Advance organisers)
C.	Discovery Learning	III.	A stimulus is presented in order to get a response
D.	Meaningful Verbal Learning	IV.	Anybody can learn anything at any age, provided it is stated in terms they can understand

Codes

	A	B	C	D
(1)	II	IV	I	III
(2)	I	III	IV	II
(3)	I	II	III	IV
(4)	III	I	IV	II

76. Which of the following statements are correct?

A. Gagne bas classified learning into Six (06) types in a hierarchical order.
B. The study of instrumental conditioning started from the puzzle box experiments on cats by Skinner.
C. The law of disuse states that other things being equal, when a modifiable connection between stimulus-response (S-R) is not made over a period of time, the strength of that connection is weakened.

D. Hull's theory of learning is called Drive-Reduction Theory.

E. Shaping is the most important mechanism used in classical conditioning.

Choose the correct answer from the options given below.

(1) A and C (2) B and D
(3) A and E (4) C and D

77. Which of the following CC licenses of OER allows others to distribute, change, remix and build upon your work, even commercially, as long as they credit you for the original work?

(1) CC BY -NC -SA (2) CC BY-NC
(3) CC BY (4) CC BY- SA

78. Arrange following categories of children in order of increasing IQ.

A. Slow learners
B. Moderate mental retardation
C. Mild mental retardation
D. Profound mental retardation
E. Severe mental retardation

Choose the correct answer from the options given below.

(1) D, E, B, C, A (2) E, D, C, B, A
(3) D, B, C, E, A (4) E, C, A, D, B

79. Which model of leadership relies on reward and punishments to motivate followers?

(1) Transformational (2) Democratic
(3) Transactional (4) Servant

80. The main difference between Galloway's system of interaction analysis and Flauder's interaction analysis is

(1) augmentation and integration of non-verbal communication aspects by Galloway.
(2) removal of verbal communication aspects by Galloway.
(3) removal of non-verbal communication aspects by Galloway,
(4) augmentation and integration of non-verbal communication aspects by Flander.

81. Select the correct statement in the following.

(1) The state spends six percent of GDP on education.
(2) Education is a subject matter of the state government.
(3) The State of Karnataka has established its own State Education Policy Commission to review NEP and give alternative policy for the state.
(4) Education Cess levied goes to the accounts of the State Government.

82. Match the List-I with List-II.

List-I	List-II
A. A Hierarchically structured chronologically graded education system	I. De-schooling
B. Set of learning experiences free of time and space limitations	II. Non-formal Education
C. Lifelong process whereby, every individual learns from daily experiences	III. Formal education
D. Education out of the confines of school for diverse needs and interests.	IV. Informal Education

Codes

	A	B	C	D
(1)	I	I	II	IV
(2)	IV	I	III	I
(3)	II	III	I	IV
(4)	III	II	IV	I

83. 3 × 3 factorial design of experiment represents

(1) three independent variables with three dependent variables
(2) two independent variables with three conditions of each
(3) three independent variables with three conditions of each.
(4) three independent variables with two conditions of each.

84. Match the List-I with List-II.

List-I	List-II
A. Web conferencing	I. Asynchronous Interaction
B. Formative Assessment	II. As a learning and assessment tool, it may comprise artifacts and also expresses a reflective dimension
C. Digitalised Course Material	III. Synchronous Interaction
D. e-Portfolios	IV. Typically conducted during the development of a programme

Codes

	A	B	C	D
(1)	III	IV	I	II
(2)	II	III	IV	I
(3)	I	II	III	IV
(4)	III	IV	II	I

85. Arrange the following chronologically.
A. Hunter Commission
B. The Education Dispatch
C. Grant's Plan
D. Establishment of Universities at Calcutta, Bombay and Madras
E. Charter allocating one lakh rupees
Choose the correct answer from the options given below.
(1) C, B, E, D, A (2) A, C, D, E, B
(3) A, E, C, B, D (4) C, E, B, D, A

86. Organise sequentially the components of an effective curriculum development process.
A. Defining course goals.
B. Developing assessment items to measure student progress.
C. Identifying key issues and trends in the content area.
D. Determining the success of the programme.
E. Identifying resource materials.
Choose the correct answer from the options given below.
(1) C, B, A, E, D (2) B, A, E, D, C
(3) A, B, C, D, E (4) C, A, E, B, D

87. Match the List-I with List-II.

	List-I		List-II
A.	Functions of school and universities should be different.	I.	Kothari Commission
B.	Schools should play a crucial role in developing democratic citizenship.	II.	University Education Commission
C.	Education plays a crucial role in national development.	III.	Yashpal Committee Report
D.	Learning must not be a burden of the leaner.	IV.	Secondary Education Commission

Codes

	A	B	C	D
(1)	III	I	IV	I
(2)	III	I	II	IV
(3)	II	I	IV	III
(4)	II	IV	I	III

88. Who was the Chairperson of National Commission on Teachers (1983)?
(1) Prof. Yashpal
(2) Dr. Ram Murti
(3) Sam Pitroda
(4) Prof. D P Chattophadhyay

89. Which of the following is related to Web 2.0 ?
(1) Read only pages
(2) Semantic integration and data interoperability
(3) Social networking and user generated content
(4) Advance virtual reality

90. According to Gutherie which is not an important characteristic of strategic leadership?
(1) Vision
(2) Inspiration
(3) Symbolic
(4) Strategic orientation

Directions **(Q. Nos. 91-95) Read the passage carefully and answer the questions that follows.**

Freedom does not exist without order. The two go together. If you cannot have order, you cannot have freedom. The two are inseparable. If you say: "I will do what I like. I will turn up for my meals when I like I will come to the class when I like"—you create disorder. You have to take into consideration what other people want. To run things smoothly, you have to come on time. If I had come ten minutes late this morning, I would have kept you waiting. So I have to consideration. I have to think of others. I have to be polite, considerate, be concerned about other people. Out of that consideration, out of that thoughtfulness, out of that watchfulness, both outward and inward, comes order and with that order there comes freedom.

You know soldiers all over the world are drilled every day, they are told what to do, to walk in line, They obey orders implicitly without thinking. Do you know what that does to man? When you are told what to do, what to think, to obey, to follows, do you know what it does to you? Your mind becomes dull, it loses its initiative, its quickness. This external, outward imposition of discipline makes the mind stupid, it makes you conform, it makes you imitate. But if you discipline yourself by watching, listening, being considerate, being very thoughtful-out of that watchfulness, that listening, that consideration for others, comes order. Where there is order, there is always freedom. If you are shouting, talking, you cannot hear what others have to say. You can only hear clearly when you sit quietly, when you give your attention.

91. If a teacher wants her students to obey orders without thinking, she is making her students
(1) rationalists (2) conformists
(3) progressives (4) authoritarian

92. According to the given paragraph, Freedom without order is
(1) invaluable (2) indiscipline
(3) invalid (4) non-existent

93. Being on time, punctuality brings
(1) discipline (2) inward imposition
(3) order (4) conformity

94. Conformism and imitation are the learning outcomes of the pedagogy that believes in
(1) external discipline (2) internal discipline
(3) freedom of learners (4) individual difference

95. A teacher shouts, 'Pindrop Silence in the Class', She is
(1) making her students considerate of orders
(2) making the students thoughtful and watchful
(3) making outward imposition of discipline
(4) making order in the class to make her students free

Directions (Q. Nos. 96-100) Read the passage carefully and answer the questions that follows.

Inclusive education means that all people-regardless of their gender, religion, cultural and social origin, cognitive, physical and physical and psychological preconditions - are entitled to equal access to higher education and that existing entry barriers have to be removed. This broad understanding of inclusive education is fixed to the Curriculum Framework as a cross-cutting theme.

As a pedagogical approach with the essential principle of appreciation and acknowledgment of diversity, the scientific foundation and acceptance of inclusive education has increased since the 1990s. At school it is about "the appropriate non*-hierarchical and democratic response to the existing heterogeneity of students" (see Boban; Hinz, 2003; Index for Inklusion).

The implementation of inclusive education is one of the big challenges to our education system and its stakeholders. Institutions of formal and non-formal education and their activities should be designed in a way that the learning environment adjusts to the students and respects the individual personalities with their different preconditions. Such an orientation towards the students requires a high personal commitment but also differentiated material and activating methods of education which support the individual and at the same time cooperation.

96. Inclusive education
(1) negates cultural diversity
(2) celebrates teacher's authority
(3) celebrates heterogeneity of students
(4) negates social needs

97. It is necessary for these institutions to be inclusive
(1) institutions of formal education only
(2) institutions of informal education only
(3) both the institutions of formal and informal education
(4) institutions of non-formal education only

98. In inclusive education, an orientation towards the students requires
(1) a high personal commitment only
(2) non-differentiated materials.
(3) passive methods of education
(4) high personal commitment along with differential material

99. Inclusive education mainly focuses on education of
(1) children with disabilities
(2) children with challenging behaviours
(3) children with learning difficulties
(4) all children

100. Inclusive education is a pedagogical approach having a principle of
(1) acceptance of learning difficulties only
(2) appreciation of diversity
(3) acceptance of group dynamics
(4) appreciation of singularity

ANSWERS

1	(3)	2	(2)	3	(2)	4	(1)	5	(2)	6	(2)	7	(2)	8	(4)	9	(2)	10	(3)
11	(1)	12	(2)	13	(2)	14	(2)	15	(2)	16	(2)	17	(3)	18	(3)	19	(4)	20	(3)
21	(4)	22	(3)	23	(3)	24	(4)	25	(1)	26	(1)	27	(1)	28	(3)	29	(3)	30	(2)
31	(3)	32	(3)	33	(3)	34	(4)	35	(3)	36	(4)	37	(4)	38	(2)	39	(1)	40	(2)
41	(4)	42	(2)	43	(4)	44	(3)	45	(2)	46	(4)	47	(3)	48	(1)	49	(2)	50	(1)
51	(3)	52	(2)	53	(4)	54	(1)	55	(1)	56	(4)	57	(3)	58	(4)	59	(2)	60	(3)
61	(1)	62	(3)	63	(1)	64	(3)	65	(1)	66	(1)	67	(*)	68	(3)	69	(3)	70	(4)
71	(4)	72	(2)	73	(4)	74	(2)	75	(4)	76	(4)	77	(3, 4)	78	(1)	79	(3)	80	(1)
81	(3)	82	(4)	83	(2)	84	(1)	85	(4)	86	(4)	87	(4)	88	(4)	89	(3)	90	(3)
91	(2)	92	(4)	93	(3)	94	(1)	95	(3)	96	(3)	97	(3)	98	(4)	99	(4)	100	(2)

UGC NET/JRF/SET

Education (Paper-2)

Solved Paper, December 2023

General Instructions

1. There are total one hundred questions in this paper. Each question carries 2 marks.
2. All questions are compulsory.

1. **We are caught in narratives and metanarratives and they sit on our judgements. We must be incredulous towards metanarratives. This sentence can be associated with**

(1) Idealism
(2) Structuralism
(3) Post-modernism
(4) Realism

2. **Erotetic teaching relies on .... as a central pedagogic technique.**

(1) questioning
(2) homework
(3) activity
(4) lecturing

3. **Which of the following can not be associated with 'Discipline'?**

(1) Authority
(2) Punishment
(3) Reward
(4) Child Centredness

4. **Which of the following is not a social function of Schooling as understood by the Deschooling Movement?**

(1) Custodial Care
(2) Social Role Selection
(3) Indoctrination
(4) Social Change

5. **According to Thorndike, following is one of the secondary laws of learning.**

(1) Law of Readiness
(2) Law of Exercise
(3) Principle of Partial Activity
(4) Principle of Effect

6. **Following is not a category of learning as per Gagne's classification of learning**

(1) Stimulus response learning
(2) Chain learning
(3) Ideational learning
(4) Verbal associate learning

7. **Which of the following is not an aspect of 4P model of creativity as given by Rhodes?**

(1) Person (2) Peers (3) Process (4) Press

8. **...... is the stable body of information that we know about ourselves and other people as thinkers.**

(1) Self-regulations
(2) Meta cognitive knowledge
(3) Knowledge about self (4) Self-cognition

9. **The University Education Commission is also known as**

(1) Mudaliar Commission
(2) Radhakrishnan Commission
(3) Kothari Commission
(4) Secondary Education Commission

10. Which policy suggested to confer autonomous status to SCERT, NCTE and set-up State Board of Teacher Education?
(1) Programme of Action on NPE, 1986
(2) National Policy on Education, 1986
(3) National Education Policy, 2020
(4) National Commission on Teacher, 1983

11. Professional norms of teacher education are developed by
(1) NCTE (2) IGNOU
(3) UGC (4) NCERT

12. Which apex body is regulating integrated education programme country?
(1) NCERT (2) NCTE (3) NIEPA (4) UGC

13. This theory of intelligence consist of one factor - a fund of intellectual competency, which is universal for all the activities of an individual.
(1) Anarchic Theory
(2) Monarchic Theory
(3) Sampling Theory
(4) Hierarchical Theory

14. Under the heuristics, which of the following is a strategy for the solution of the problems stands for the identification of the difference between the current state and the one that is desired in relation to the nature and solution of the problems and then taking action to reduce this difference for arriving at the solution of the problem?
(1) Means-end analysis (2) Using an analogy
(3) Sub-goal analysis (4) Working backward

15. Creativity emphasises more on testing of
(1) similar thinking (2) progressive thinking
(3) convergent thinking (4) divergent thinking

16. When judgements are based on the information present in our memories, we are using the
(1) heuristic
(2) confirmation bias
(3) representative heuristic
(4) availability heuristic

17. If a phenomenon changes over time, what kind of research should be undertaken to study it?
(1) Experimental research
(2) Longitudinal research
(3) Ex-post facto research
(4) Ethnographic research

18. "Students of high intelligence will significantly do better in their academic achievement", which type of hypothesis is it?
(1) Directional hypothesis
(2) Non-directional hypothesis
(3) Null-hypothesis
(4) Concurrent hypothesis

19. The difference between the values of 'Parameter' and 'Statistics' is called as
(1) Type-I error (2) Type-II error
(3) Sampling error (4) Error in calculation

20. In an educational research, variable under study are being manipulated and controlled, what kind of research it is?
(1) Quasi-experiential research
(2) Experimental research
(3) Ex-post facto research
(4) Mixed method research

21. If a teacher through her teaching enables the students to learn, comprehend, understand the related concepts and perform behavioural actions based on learning, the teaching level is
(1) Memory level teaching
(2) Understanding level teaching
(3) Application level teaching
(4) Reflective level teaching

22. 'Assessment for learning' emphasises
(1) assessment to enhance learning.
(2) assessment to know the mastery of the content.
(3) assessment to certify the learners.
(4) assessment to grade the learners.

23. Which is not a benefit to use reflective journal as an assessment tool in pedagogy of education?
(1) Reflective writing can enable students to demonstrate complex learning outcomes including critical thinking.
(2) Students can demonstrate analysis, creativity and originality.
(3) Students may not fully understand what is required of them in reflective writing.
(4) Reflection in and of itself can be a powerful learning process.

24. Which is not true in case of Flander's Interaction analysis?
(1) Interaction means participation of teacher and students in the process of teaching.
(2) Teacher evaluates the students through assignment.
(3) It helps to know whether the teacher is effective or not.
(4) Teacher influences students through lecture, asking questions, criticising, giving directions, etc.

25. Which of the following is most important for inclusive teaching learning?
(1) Educational technologies
(2) Teaching technologies
(3) Assistive technologies
(4) Communication technologies

26. The Virtual University for Small States of Commonwealth (VUSSC) in 2000 was initiated by
(1) Inflibnet
(2) Commonwealth of Learning
(3) Delnet
(4) IGNOU

27. Reactive change
(1) is a change brought about by a sudden or unplanned event.
(2) involves reimplementation of a change in the same organisational unit.
(3) involves changes that are generally new and familiar.
(4) is a systematic deliberate change in the way part or all of an organisation function.

28. Light, sound, love, truth are all examples of
(1) tangibles (2) intangibles
(3) innovations (4) goal orientation

29. Disability represents
(1) disturbance in perception.
(2) disturbance at a personal level.
(3) disturbance in social functions.
(4) disturbance in medical conditions.

30. A Zero Rejection Policy was adopted under
(1) National Policy of Education, 1986
(2) Persons with Disability Act, 1995
(3) Sarva Shiksha Abhiyan, 2001
(4) National Curriculum Framework, 2005

31. A six sigma process is one in which too much percentage of the products manufactured are statistically expected to be free of defects
(1) 95.99966% (2) 99.99966%
(3) 98.99966% (4) 96.99966%

32. Taylor Postcard Frame is used for
(1) writing large character Braille on one side of the paper.
(2) writing large character Braille on both side on the paper.
(3) writing small character Braille on one side of the paper.
(4) writing small character Braille on both side of the paper.

33. Teaching-learning process and learning strategy in adult education should be based on
A. experience based learning
B. self-directed learning
C. readiness to learn
D. as per the formal education system
E. rigid learning environment
Choose the correct answer from the options given below.
(1) A, B and C (2) A, B, C and E
(3) B, C, D and E (4) C and D

34. Which is a correct statement relating to the types of assessment?
A. Criterion referenced test is related to formative assessment.
B. Criterion referenced test is related to summative assessment.
C. Norm referenced test is related to formative assessment.
D. Norm referenced test is related to summative assessment.
E. Summative assessment is terminal in nature.
Choose the correct answer from the options given below.
(1) B and E (2) B and C
(3) A and D (4) A, D and E

35. Which is the component of affective domain as per Krathwohl et al?
A. Comprehension B. Emotion
C. Feeling D. Attitude
E. Values
Choose the correct answer from the options given below.
(1) A, B and C (2) B, C, D and E
(3) B and C (4) D and E

36. What is the nature of educational research?
A. Educational research is empirical in nature.
B. Educational research should be systematic.
C. Educational and physical science research findings are measured in the same scale.
D. Educational research should be valid.
E. Educational research should be reliable.
Choose the correct answer from the options given below.
(1) A and B (2) A, B and C
(3) D and E (4) A, B, D and E

37. Which are correct facts relating to reliability and validity of research tool?
A. Consistency is necessary for reliability.
B. Validity is the pre-condition for reliability.
C. A reliable test is always valid.
D. A valid test is always reliable.
E. There is no relationship between reliability and validity of a test.

Choose the correct answer from the options given below.

(1) A and B (2) A and C
(3) A and D (4) A and E

38. Which statements are correct in relation to scales of measurement?

A. Ratio scale is having an absolute zero point.
B. Interval scale is having an absolute zero point.
C. Ratio scale is used in mental measurement.
D. Interval scale is mental measurement.
E. All the characteristics of ratio scale are included in the interval scale.

Choose the correct answer from the options given below.

(1) A and C (2) B and D
(3) A and D (4) D and E

39. The advantages of digital libraries as compared to traditional libraries are

A. effective use of technology
B. difficult cataloguing
C. accessible anytime anywhere
D. easily linked to other resources
E. a resource can be simultaneously used by multiple users.

Choose the correct answer from the options given below.

(1) A, B, C, D (2) A, C, D, E
(3) A, B, D, E (4) C, E, B, A

40. What is not related to education?

A. Direct benefit
B. Indirect benefit
C. Investment in people
D. Human resource development
E. Public funding

Choose the correct answer from the options given below.

(1) Only A (2) B and C
(3) C and D (4) B and E

41. Which of the following are post-independence commissions on education?

A. Kothari Commission
B. Hunter Commission
C. Calcutta University Commission
D. Nai Talim
E. National Knowledge Commission

Choose the correct answer from the options given below.

(1) B and C (2) A and E
(3) A, C and E (4) B, C and D

42. Which of the following can be associated with Gandhi?

A. Sabarmati Ashram B. Nai Talim
C. Geetanjali D. Santiniketan
E. Craft based education

Choose the correct answer from the options given below.

(1) A, B and E (2) C and D
(3) A and E (4) B and D

43. Which of the following are 'Astik' schools of Indian philosophy?

A. Buddhism B. Jainism
C. Samkhya D. Nyaya
E. Charvaka

Choose the correct answer from the options given below.

(1) A and B (2) A, B and E
(3) C and A (4) C and D

44. Which of the following are method of knowing according to Nyaya philosophy?

A. Perception B. Inference
C. Arthapatti D. Smriti
E. Abhava

Choose the correct answer from the options given below.

(1) C and E (2) C and D
(3) A and B (4) B and E

45. Which of the following are associated with Rouessau?

A. Emile B. Social contract
C. Back of nature D. Man is born as slave
E. Knowledge is based on reason only

Choose the correct answer from the options given below.

(1) A, B and C (2) Only D
(3) A and D (4) Only E

46. According to Thurston, the primary factor in intelligence is

A. Spatial ability B. Associative memory
C. Problem solving D. Perceptual speed
E. Reasoning

Choose the correct answer from the options given below.

(1) Only B (2) A and C
(3) A and E (4) Only E

47. Which of the following affects curriculum change?

A. Placement in jobs
B. Religious sentiments
C. Availability of competent teachers

D. Important to nation
E. Socio-cultural context
Choose the correct answer from the options given below.
(1) A ad D
(2) B and C
(3) D and E
(4) C and E

48. Which of the following is correct?
A. CIPP model for curriculum evaluation is developed by Daniel Mento in 1949.
B. Tayler's curriculum model is a four part linear model.
C. CIPP model for curriculum evaluation is based on "how can we determine whether the purposes are being attained?".
D. CIPP model for curriculum evaluation involves the steps and resources needed to meet the new goals and objectives and might include indentifying successful external programmes and materials as well as gathering information.
E. Tayler's model for curriculum evaluation provides decision makers with information about how well the programme is being implemented.
Choose the correct answer from the options given below.
(1) B and E (2) Only A
(3) Only E (4) B and D

49. Carl Rogers proposed the following types of Counselling
A. Rehabilitation counselling
B. Substance abuse counselling
C. Non-directive counselling
D. Education counselling
E. Directive counselling
Choose the correct answer from the options given below.
(1) A and B
(2) C and E
(3) Only C
(4) Only D

50. Which of the following is are correct?
A. Intellectual academic approach to curriculum propagates for curriculum areas in arts, music, literature, etc.
B. Behavioural-rational approach to curriculum is also known as logical positivist, conceptual, rational-scientific and technocratic approach.
C. Humanistic aesthetic approach to curriculum also refers to as traditional encyclopedic or knowledge oriented approach.
D. Systems Managerial Approach to curriculum focuses on programmes, schedules, materials, personnel and resource.
E. Reconceptionalist Approach to curriculum looks at schooling and education from a broader perspective and discusses education from a historical and philosophical angle.
Choose the correct answer from the options given below.
(1) A and B (2) Only E
(3) B and D (4) B and C

51. The International Classification of Functioning, Disability and Health (ICF) conceptualise a persons' level of functioning as a dynamic interaction between his or her
A. health conditions
B. environmental factors
C. personal factors
D. economic factors
E. innovative factors
Choose the correct answer from the options given below.
(1) A and B (2) A, B and C
(3) C, D and E (4) D and E

52. The types of cerebral palsy are
A. Diplegia
B. Rickets
C. Orthotics
D. Hemiplegia
E. Ataxia
Choose the correct answer from the options given below.
(1) A, D and E
(2) D and E
(3) C and D
(4) A, B, C and D

53. Screening measures that can assist in the diagnosis of Autism Spectrum Disorder (ASD) include
A. Autism Behaviour Checklist (ABC)
B. Development Behaviour Checklist (DBC)
C. Self Confidence Checklist
D. Psycho Educational Profile Revised (PEP-R)
E. Hand Flapping
Choose the correct answer from the options given below.
(1) A, B, and D (2) Only A
(3) B, C and D (4) B, C, D and E

54. Which one is not an example of learning management systems?

A. Moodle B. Canvas

C. Edupuzzle D. Schoology

Choose the correct answer from the options given below.

(1) A, C, B (2) A, B, D

(3) C, A, D (4) B, C, D

55. Identify the situation involving sychronous and asychronous communication.

A. Taking to someone in your room

B. Checking email

C. Reading an email

D. Participating in web conferencing

Choose the correct answer from the options given below.

(1) sychronous A, D asychronous B, C

(2) sychronous A, B asychronous D, C

(3) sychronous C, A asychronous D, B

(4) sychronous D, A asychronous B, C

56. Important approaches of cost analysis in education are

A. cost benefit B. cost feasibility

C. cost utility D. cost empire

E. cost counting

Choose the correct answer from the options given below.

(1) C, D and E only

(2) A, B and C only

(3) A and C only

(4) B, C, D and E only

57. The foundational principles of cost benefit analysis in education includes

A. Explicit valuation

B. Intrinsic value of freedom

C. Consequential evaluation

D. Pricing the intangible

E. Additive accounting

Choose the correct answer from the options given below.

(1) Only C (2) A and B

(3) A, C and E (4) B, C and D

58. The types of planning techniques are

A. critical path method

B. cost benefit analysis

C. planning, programming and budgeting system

D. managerial quality

E. programme evaluation review technique

Choose the correct answer from the options given below.

(1) A and D

(2) C, D and E

(3) B, D and E

(4) A, B, C and D

59. Match List-I with List-II.

List-I	List-II
A. Stratified random sampling	I. Error in sampling
B. Purposive sampling	II. Sample
C. A representative proportion of the population	III. Non-probability sampling
D. Difference between the estimate of parameter and statistics	IV. Probability sampling

Codes

	A	B	C	D
(1)	IV	III	I	II
(2)	III	IV	II	I
(3)	IV	III	II	I
(4)	III	IV	I	II

60. Match List-I with List-II.

List-I	List-II
A. Measurement	I. Value judgement
B. Assessment	II. Standardised test
C. Evaluation	III. Quantitative description
D. Norm	IV. Qualitative description

Codes

	A	B	C	D
(1)	IV	I	II	III
(2)	III	IV	II	I
(3)	II	I	IV	III
(4)	III	IV	I	II

61. Match List-I with List-II.

List-I	List-II
A. Shaikshik Gyan Aur Varchasva	I. Gijubhai Badheka
B. Shiksha Mein Badlav Ke Sawal	II. Sadhna Saxena
C. Shiksha Aur Jan Andolan	III. Krishna Kumar
D. Divaswapn	IV. Anil Sadgopal

Codes

	A	B	C	D		A	B	C	D
(1)	IV	III	I	II	(2)	II	IV	III	I
(3)	III	II	IV	I	(4)	III	IV	II	I

62. Match List-I with List-II.

List-I	List-II
A. Pedagogy of Oppressed	I. John Dewey
B. Deschooling Society	II. Paulo Freire
C. Democracy and Education	III. Bertrand Russell
D. Education and Social Order	IV. Ivan Illich

Codes

	A	B	C	D		A	B	C	D
(1)	II	IV	I	III	(2)	I	II	III	IV
(3)	II	I	IV	III	(4)	III	IV	I	IV

63. Match List-I with List-II.

List-I	List-II
A. Choleric type	I. Active, cheerful and optimistic
B. Melancholic type	II. Humble, sad depressed
C. Sanguine type	III. Slow, dull and unemotional
D. Phlegmatic type	IV. Energetic, full of ambition and courage but easily excitable to anger

Codes

	A	B	C	D		A	B	C	D
(1)	I	II	III	IV	(2)	III	I	II	IV
(3)	IV	II	I	III	(4)	IV	I	III	II

64. Match List-I with List-II.

List-I (Books)	List-II (Authors)
A. Emotional Intelligence : Why It can Matter More Than IQ	I. C. Darwin
B. Emotion, Obesity and Crime	II. PT Young
C. Emotion in Man and Animal	III. D. Goleman
D. The Expression of the Emotions in Man and Animals	IV. S. Schachter

Codes

	A	B	C	D		A	B	C	D
(1)	II	I	IV	III	(2)	III	IV	II	I
(3)	I	II	III	IV	(4)	IV	III	II	I

65. Match List-I with List-II.

List-I	List-II
A. Anxiety reduction	I. Direct, spontaneous expression of feeling in social situations
B. Assertive training	II. Social behaviour, skills
C. Managing behaviour	III. Substitution of relaxtation for anxiety in social situations
D. Relaxation	IV. Reduction of stress

Codes

	A	B	C	D
(1)	I	III	II	IV
(2)	IV	I	III	II
(3)	III	I	II	IV
(4)	III	II	IV	I

66. Match List-I with List-II.

List-I	List-II
A. E Learning	I. Hyper media based instruction programme which utilises the attributes and resources of the World Wide Web to create a meaningful learning environment where learning is fostered and supported.
B. Virtual Learning	II. It is synonymous to web based learning where learning is fostered *via* hypertext transfer protocol (http) in internet or intranet.
C. Web Based Instruction	III. A wide set of application and processes including computer based learning, web based learning, virtual classroom and digital collaboration.
D. Online Learning	IV. The educational process of learning over the internet without having face to face contact.

Codes

	A	B	C	D		A	B	C	D
(1)	I	III	II	IV	(2)	III	IV	I	II
(3)	IV	I	III	IV	(4)	IV	III	II	I

67. Match List-I with List-II.

List-I (Leadership Styles)	List-II (Characteristics)
A. Autocratic leadership	I. Inspires and motivates followers to achieve a shared vision
B. Democratic leadership	II. Leader provides little guidance or structure, allowing subordinates to make most decisions
C. Laissez fairer leadership	III. Leader makes decisions without input from subordinates
D. Transformation al leadership	IV. Encourages participation and input from group members in decision making

Codes

	A	B	C	D
(1)	III	I	IV	II
(2)	III	IV	II	I
(3)	III	IV	I	II
(4)	III	II	I	IV

68. Match List-I with List-II.

List-I (Concepts)	List-II (Explanations)
A. Mainstreaming	I. A legal requirement specifying that students with disabilities should be educated in typical classrooms to the maximum extent possible.
B. Full Inclusion	II. A document outlining educational goals and services for a student with a disability.
C. Least Restrictive Environment (LRE)	III Placing students with disabilities in regular education classes for a portion of the day
D. Individualised Education Programme (IEP)	IV. Inclusive education model where students with disabilities are fully integrated into regular classrooms

Codes

	A	B	C	D
(1)	III	IV	I	II
(2)	III	I	IV	II
(3)	IV	III	I	II
(4)	II	III	IV	I

69. Arrange the following in chronological order.

A. University Education Commission

B. Secondary Education Commission

C. Acharya Ramamurti Committee

D. National Education Commission

E. Birla Ambani Report

Choose the correct answer from the options given below.

(1) A, B, D, C, E (2) B, A, C, D, E
(3) A, D, B, E, C (4) B, E, C, D, A

70. Arrange the following in chronological order.

A. Post-modernism

B. Transcendentalism

C. Empiricism

D. Analytical Philosophy

E. Rationalism

Choose the correct answer from the options given below.

(1) E, B, C, A, D (2) B, D, A, C, E
(3) B, C, E, A, D (4) E, C, B, D, A

71. The correct sequences of stages of curriculum evaluation is

A. Planning B. Regular Monitoring

C. Goal Specification D. Validation

E. Field Testing

Choose the correct answer from the options given below.

(1) A, B, D, C, E (2) E, D, A, C, B
(3) C, D, A, B, E (4) C, A, D, E, B

72. Arrange the steps involved in scientific procedure of problem solving behaviour in correct order.

A. Collection of relevant information about problem

B. Problem understanding

C. Problem awareness

D. Verification of the concluded solution

E. Hunch for possible solution

Choose the correct answer from the options given below.

(1) A, B, C, D, E (2) B, C, A, D, E
(3) C, B, A, E, D (4) B, E, C, A, D

73. Order the sequence of steps followed in educational research.

A. Selection of research problem

B. Selection of research method

C. Formulation of research question

D. Data collection and analysis

E. Reporting the results

Choose the correct answer from the options given below.

(1) A, B, C, D, E
(2) A, C, B, D, E
(3) A, D, B, C, E
(4) B, A, C, D, E

74. Which is the sequence of taxonomy of cognitive domain as per Anderson and Krathwohl's taxonomy (2001)?

A. Remembering B. Understanding
C. Analysing D. Applying
E. Evaluating

Choose the correct answer from the options given below.

(1) A, B, C, D, E (2) A, C, B, D, E
(3) A, B, D, C, E (4) A, B, D, E, C

75. Arrange the following steps of AADIE model framework in the correct sequence.

A. Design B. Analysis
C. Implementation D. Evaluation
E. Development

Choose the correct answer from the options given below.

(1) C, B, A, E, and D (2) B, A, E, C, and D
(3) B, C, E, A, and D (4) B, D, E, A, and C

76. Mention the correct sequence of the following education commissions in post-Independent India.

A. The Secondary Education Commission
B. National Commission on Teachers
C. Acharya Ramamurti Committee
D. The University Education Commission
E. The Kothari Commission

Choose the correct answer from the options given below.

(1) D, A, E, B, and C (2) A, C, D, E, and B
(3) D, B, A, C, and E (4) A, C, D, B, and E

77. Arrange the leadership styles in the Blake and Mouton's managerial grid in order of their concern for people from the least concern to the most concern.

A. Country club management
B. Authority obedience management
C. Impoverished management
D. Team management
E. Middle of the road management

Choose the correct answer from the options given below.

(1) C, D, B, A, E (2) D, A, B, C, E
(3) B, E, C, A, D (4) B, C, D, A, E

78. According to WHO statistics (2011), arrange the following from most prevalent to least prevalent communication related disabilities.

A. Communication related disabilities
B. Mobility related disabilities
C. Hearing related disabilities
D. Vision related disabilities
E. Cognition related disabilities

Choose the correct answer from the options given below.

(1) E, A, C, D, B
(2) B, D, C, A, E
(3) A, C, E, B, D
(4) C, A, B, E, D

79. Arrange the following in traditional manner of writing lesson plan.

A. Previous knowledge B. Specific aims
C. Home work D. Content delivery
E. Recapitulation

Choose the correct answer from the options given below.

(1) B, A, D, E, C (2) A, C, E, D, B
(3) C, A, D, B, E (4) D, E, A, B, C

80. Given below are two statements.

Statement (I) The entire process of teacher education lies in its curriculum, designs and transaction modes as well as the extent and its appropriateness.

Statement (II) The curriculum is essential component for every stream.

In the light of the above statements, choose the correct answer from the options given below.

(1) Both Statement I and Statement II are correct.
(2) Both Statement I and Statement II are incorrect.
(3) Statement I is correct, but Statement II is incorrect.
(4) Statement I is incorrect, but Statement II is correct.

81. Given below are two statements.

Statement (I) Nai Talim was suggested by the Zakir Hussain Committee at Wardha.

Statement (II) Nai Talim suggested that all education must be in English to make independent citizens.

In the light of the above statements, choose the correct answer from the options given below.

(1) Both Statement I and Statement II are correct.
(2) Both Statement I and Statement II are incorrect.
(3) Statement I is correct, but Statement II is incorrect.
(4) Statement I is incorrect, but Statement II is correct.

82. Given below are two statements.

Statement (I) According to realists, curriculum follows a hierarchical order with the abstract subjects at the top and the transitory subjects at the bottom.

Statement (II) Pragmatist curriculum would focus on experiences and subjects that land themselves to philosophical dialogue and acts of the choice making

In the light of the above statements, choose the correct answer from the options given below.

(1) Both Statement I and Statement II are correct.
(2) Both Statement I and Statement II are incorrect.
(3) Statement I is correct, but Statement II is incorrect.
(4) Statement I is incorrect but Statement II is correct.

83. Given below are two statements.

Statement (I) All valid tests are reliable but all reliable tests are not valid.

Statement (II) Split-half method is used to determine reliability of a test.

In the light of the above statements, choose the correct answer from the options given below.

(1) Both Statement I and Statement II are correct.
(2) Both Statement I and Statement II are incorrect.
(3) Statement I is correct, but Statement II is incorrect.
(4) Statement I is incorrect but Statement II is correct.

84. Given below are two statements.

Statement (I) Collection of learner's work on a variety of tasks is meant for keeping a record of their performance and is known as Portfolio.

Statement (II) Portfolio is an essential part of learner's performance.

In the light of the above statements, choose the correct answer from the options given below.

(1) Both Statement I and Statement II are correct.
(2) Both Statement I and Statement II are incorrect.
(3) Statement I is correct, but Statement II is incorrect.
(4) Statement I is incorrect, but Statement II is correct.

85. Given below are two statements.

Statement (I) The concept of quality in education is solely determined by the availability of modern technology and resources.

Statement (II) Quality in education encompasses a broad range of factors including curriculum teaching methods, assessment and learning environment in addition to technology and resources.

In the light of the above statements, choose the correct answer from the options given below.

(1) Both Statement I and Statement II are correct.
(2) Both Statement I and Statement II are incorrect.
(3) Statement I is correct, but Statement II is incorrect.
(4) Statement I is incorrect, but Statement II is correct.

86. Given below are two statements, one is labelled as Assertion (A) and the other is labelled as Reason (R).

Assertion (A) Psychomotor domain of learning helps the children to acquire skills on certain aspects to create something by their own.

Reason (R) Psychomotor domain of learning is very much linked with cognitive and affective domains as it helps the children to understand the concept and to develop a right attitude for working on that concept for developing skills.

In the light of the above statements, choose the correct answer from the options given below.

(1) Both A and R are true and R is the correct explanation of A.
(2) Both A and R are true, but R is not the correct explanation of A.
(3) A is true, but R is false.
(4) A is false, but R is true.

87. Given below are two statements, one is labelled as Assertion (A) and the other is labelled as Reason (R).

Assertion (A) Counselling is a face to face relationship between the guidance worker and the person who seeks a special kind of guidance.

Reason (R) Counselling is an intimate interpersonal relationship in which one person by virtue of this special training and skills is recognised as the helper while the other person is recognised as an individual or group with a problem who can benefit from the former.

In the light of the above statements, choose the correct answer from the options given below.

(1) Both A and R are true and R is the correct explanation of A.
(2) Both A and R are true but R is not the correct explanation of A.
(3) A is true, but R is false.
(4) A is false, but R is true.

88. Given below are two statements, one is labelled as Assertion (A) and the other is labelled as Reason (R).

Assertion (A) Buddhism is a nastik school of philosophy.

Reason (R) Astik-nastik in Indian philosophy is about faith in vedas.

In the light of the above statements, choose the correct answer from the options given below.
(1) Both A and R are true and R is the correct explanation of A.
(2) Both A and R are true but R is not the correct explanation of A.
(3) A is true, but R is false.
(4) A is false, but R is true.

89. Given below are two statements, one is labelled as Assertion (A) and the other is labelled as Reason (R).

Assertion (A) Ethical leadership is not relevant in education as ethical standards are not applicable to administrative roles.

Reason (R) Ethical leadership in educational administration is essential because it emphasises making morally sound decisions and serving as a role model for ethical behaviour.

In the light of the above statements, choose the correct answer from the options given below.
(1) Both A and R are true and R is the correct explanation of A.
(2) Both A and R are true but R is not the correct explanation of A.
(3) A is true, but R is false.
(4) A is false, but R is true.

90. Given below are two statements, one is labelled as Assertion (A) and the other is labelled as Reason (R).

Assertion (A) Teacher should use a wide variety of online assessment tools and technique to assess children.

Reason (R) No single online tool is capable of providing information about a child's progress and learning in different areas of development.

In the light of the above statements, choose the correct answer from the options given below.
(1) Both A and R are true and R is the correct explanation of A.
(2) Both A and R are true but R is not the correct explanation of A.
(3) A is true, but R is false.
(4) A is false, but R is true.

Directions (Q. Nos. 91-95) *Read the passage carefully and answer the questions that follows.*

What passes for knowledge is of two kings : first, knowledge of facts; second, knowledge of the general connection between facts very closely connected with this distinction is another : there is knowledge which may be described as 'mirroring', and knowledge which consists in capacity to handle Leibinitz's monads 'mirror' the universe, and in this sense know it; but since monads never interact they cannot handle any thing external to themselves. This is the logical extreme of one conception of 'knowledge'. The logical extreme of the other conception is pragmatism which was first promulgated by Marx in his Thesis on Feuerbach (1845) the question whether objective truth belongs to human thinking is not a question of theory, but a practical question, the truth, i.e., the reality and power of though must be demonstrated in practice ...... philosophers have only interpreted the world in various ways, but the real task is to alter it.

91. Philosophers have only interpreted the world in various ways ..... this sentence closely sounds akin to
(1) Satyameva Jayate
(2) Ekam Sat Vipra Bahudha Vadanti
(3) Asato Ma Sadgamaya
(4) Jnanam Param Balam

92. According to the paragraph, the real aim for knowledge is to
(1) interpret the world
(2) alter the world
(3) practice the power in world
(4) know facts and general connections

93. Leibinitz's monads know the universe as they ...... it.
(1) reflect (2) image
(3) mirror (4) analyse

94. There is smoke on the hill, there must be the fire. This knowledge is
(1) knowledge of facts
(2) knowledge of reality
(3) knowledge of truth
(4) knowledge of general connections

95. In Philosophy of education, who is considered as the father of pragmatism.
(1) Betrand Russell (2) Leibinitz
(3) Karl Marx (4) John Dewey

Directions (Q. Nos. 96-100) *Read the passage carefully and answer the questions that follows.*

The Education Commission (1964-66) reviewed Indian education in its totality and gave special attention to women's education. It said, "The problem of women's education has been examined by a number of committees-the National Committee on Education of Women 1959, the committee on differentiation of curricula between boys and girls 1961, the Bhaktvatsalam Committee 1963 which studied the problem in six states where the education of girls is less developed". "We fully endorse the recommendations of these committees". Inspite of this it made following recommendations (i) education of women should be regarded as a major programme for some years to come to close the existing gap between men and women in this regard (ii) special schemes should be prepared for this purpose and funds should be provided on priority basis and (iii) both the centre and in the states there should be special machinery to look after the education of girls and women.

96. The biggest hindrance in women and girls education is

(1) lack of interest in education by women
(2) household work
(3) economic loss
(4) patriarchy and its implications

97. Girls and women's education must be given priority for

(1) companionable wives
(2) empowerment of women
(3) teaching daily economics of home
(4) to teach own children

98. The paragraph mentions a committee on differentiation of curricula between boys and girls (1961), this committee was headed by

(1) Durgabai Deshmukh
(2) Vijaya Lakshmi Pandit
(3) Hansa Mehta
(4) Rajkumari Amrit Kaur

99. The National Committee on Education of women was set-up in 1959. It was chaired by

(1) Indira Gandhi
(2) Durgabai Deshmukh
(3) Hansa Mehta
(4) Sarojini Naidu

100. The Education Commission (1964-66) was headed by

(1) S. Radhakrishnan
(2) Prof. Yashpal
(3) UKRV Rao
(4) Daulat Singh Kothari

ANSWERS

1	*(3)*	2	*(1)*	3	*(4)*	4	*(4)*	5	*(3)*	6	*(3)*	7	*(2)*	8	*(2)*	9	*(2)*	10	*(1)*
11	*(1)*	12	*(2)*	13	*(2)*	14	*(1)*	15	*(4)*	16	*(4)*	17	*(2)*	18	*(1)*	19	*(3)*	20	*(2)*
21	*(4)*	22	*(1)*	23	*(3)*	24	*(2)*	25	*(3)*	26	*(2)*	27	*(1)*	28	*(2)*	29	*(2)*	30	*(3)*
31	*(2)*	32	*(3)*	33	*(1)*	34	*(4)*	35	*(2)*	36	*(4)*	37	*(3)*	38	*(3)*	39	*(2)*	40	*(1)*
41	*(2)*	42	*(1)*	43	*(4)*	44	*(3)*	45	*(1)*	46	*(*)*	47	*(3)*	48	*(4)*	49	*(3)*	50	*(3)*
51	*(2)*	52	*(1)*	53	*(3)*	54	*(2)*	55	*(1, 4)*	56	*(2)*	57	*(3)*	58	*(4)*	59	*(3)*	60	*(4)*
61	*(4)*	62	*(1)*	63	*(3)*	64	*(2)*	65	*(3)*	66	*(2)*	67	*(2)*	68	*(1)*	69	*(1)*	70	*(4)*
71	*(4)*	72	*(3)*	73	*(2)*	74	*(3)*	75	*(2)*	76	*(1)*	77	*(*)*	78	*(2)*	79	*(1)*	80	*(1)*
81	*(3)*	82	*(3)*	83	*(1)*	84	*(3)*	85	*(4)*	86	*(1)*	87	*(1)*	88	*(1)*	89	*(4)*	90	*(1)*
91	*(2)*	92	*(2)*	93	*(3)*	94	*(4)*	95	*(4)*	96	*(4)*	97	*(2)*	98	*(3)*	99	*(2)*	100	*(4)*

Solved Paper
2022

UGC NET/JRF/SET

Education (Paper-2)
Solved Paper, October 2022

General Instructions

1. There are total one hundred questions in this paper. Each question carries 2 marks.
2. All questions are compulsory.

---

1. Jung has classified human beings according to their

(1) social behaviour (2) body built
(3) energy level (4) mood

2. Given below are two statements.

Statement I Assessment is a systematic process of identifying, collecting and interpreting information about the students' learning.

Statement II Assessment results must be communicated in a clear and transparent way.

In the light of the above statements, choose the correct answer from the options given below

(1) Both statement I and statement II are true.
(2) Both statement I and statement II are false.
(3) Statement I is true, but statement II is false.
(4) Statement I is false, but statement II is true.

3. Who amongst the following coined the terms 'Formative' and 'Summative' evaluation ?

(1) Michael Sadler (2) Michael Scrieven
(3) Knut (4) Alken Howard

4. What is the exact title of Justice Verma Commission Report on Teacher Education ?

(1) Vision of Teacher Education in India : Regulatory Perspective
(2) Vision of Teacher Education in India : Quality and Regulatory Perspective
(3) Vision of Teacher Education in : Quality Perspective
(4) Vision of Teacher Education in India : Status and Quality Perspective

5. The basic principles of ethics in using open educational resources have been laid down by

(1) British Education Research Association (BERA)
(2) Massachusetts Institute of Technology (MIT)
(3) Creative Commons (CC)
(4) Open Educational Resources (OER) Commons

6. The duration of Master of Education (M.Ed.) programme has been increased to two years by

(1) 2014 year
(2) 2013 year
(3) 2012 year
(4) 2015 year

7. Which aspect of CIPP model of curriculum involves material, time, physical and human resources needed for the effective working of the school?

(1) Context (2) Input
(3) Process (4) Product

8. Programme learning is based on the principle of

A. Conditioned Learning Theory
B. Cognitive Learning Theory
C. Gestalt Learning Theory
D. Operant Conditioning Theory

Choose the correct answer from the options given below.

(1) A and B (2) B and C
(3) A and C (4) Only D

9. The emphasis of Learning Outcome-based Curriculum Framework (LOCF) is on

A. application of knowledge.
B. providing holistic educational experiences to students.
C. designing a national common syllabus for a particular programme of study.
D. changing most of books in a college or university library.

Choose the correct answer from the options given below.

(1) A and B (2) C and D
(3) Only C (4) Only D

10. Arrange the following Indian Philosophers in choronological order of their year of birth

(A) Aurboindo Ghose
(B) Swami Vivekananda
(C) J Krishnamurti
(D) Rabindra Nath Tagore

Codes

(1) A, B, C, D (2) D, C, B, A
(3) D, B, A, C (4) D, C, A, B

11. According to National Council for Teacher Education (NCTE), which of the following is a composite institution ?

(1) an institution offering a single undergraduate programme.
(2) an institution offering a single postgraduate programme.
(3) an institution offering multi-teacher education programmes.
(4) an institution offering a single diploma programme.

12. In Andragogy

A. learning of adults is there within its scope.
B. learners are independent and strive for self direction in learning.
C. teacher decides what, how and when anything is to be learned.
D. motivation stems from self esteem, confidence and recognition that comes from successful performance.

Choose the correct answer from the options given below.

(1) A, C and D (2) A, B and D
(3) A, B and C (4) B, C and D

13. Given below are two statements. One is labelled as Assertion (A) and the other is labelled as Reason (R).

Assertion (A) Though ex-post facto research examines cause and effect but it is not part of experimental research.

Reason (R) In ex-post facto research, effect of independent variable has already taken place.

In the light of the above statements, choose the most appropriate answer from the options given below.

(1) Both A and R are true and R is the correct explanation of A.
(2) Both A and R are true, but R is not the correct explanation of A.
(3) A is true, but R is false.
(4) A is false, but R is true.

14. The test-retest, the split half, the equivalent/parallel form and the rational equivalance methods are used for the assessment of

(1) validity of a test
(2) usability of a test
(3) reliability of a test
(4) validity and reliability of a test

15. Which of the following is false about the concept of 'Blended Learning'?

A. It is Mix Web based Technology.
B. It is Mix Instructional Technology.
C. It is Mix Pedagogical Approach.
D. It is related to Assignments of the Students.

Choose the correct answer from the options given below.

(1) Only D (2) Only A
(3) B and C (4) Only C

16. Match List I with List II.

List I (Theory/Concept)	List II (Description)
A. Development of theories	I. Assessment studies
B. Finding solution of immediate problems in a particular setting without generalisation of findings beyond the situation studied	II. Applied Research
C. Adaptation of theories	III. Action Research
D. No hyphotheses are proposed or tested	IV. Basic Research

Codes

	A	B	C	D		A	B	C	D
(1)	I	II	III	IV	(2)	II	III	I	IV
(3)	II	III	IV	I	(4)	II	I	III	IV

17. Which of the following programmes are related to quality improvement in in-service education?

A. Foundation course in teacher education.

B. Skill development programmes.

C. Courses on Pedagogy in specific subjects.

D. Induction Meeting.

E. Micro simulation for competency development.

Choose the most appropriate answer from the options given below.

(1) A, B and C (2) B and D
(3) B and E (4) D and E

18. Which of the following is/are not principle(s) of inclusive education?

(A) Segregated education

(B) Zero rejection

(C) Appreciation of student diversity

(D) Professional collaboration

Choose the correct answer from the options given below.

(1) Only A (2) C and D
(3) Only B (4) B and D

19. ICF framework for classification of health and disability related domains is given by

(1) UNICEF (2) UNCRPD
(3) WHO (4) UNESCO

20. A teacher is explaining about a model of change by giving an example of converting a cube of ice into a cone of ice. The teacher is talking about

(1) Kurt Lewin's model (2) Kotter's model
(3) Kubler-Ross's model (4) Jeff Hiatt's model

21. The programmes on Teacher Education recognised by National Council for Teacher Education (NCTE) are

(A) Diploma in Pre-school Education (DPSE)

(B) Diploma in Elementary Education (D.El.Ed)

(C) Diploma in Arts Education (Performing Arts)

(D) Master of Physical Education (M.P.Ed)

(E) Bachelor of Arts in education (B.A—Education)

Choose the correct answer from the options given below.

(1) A and B (2) B and C
(3) D and E (4) A, B, C and D

22. Aristotle's teaching became the philosophical foundations for

(1) Realism (2) Idealism
(3) Naturalism (4) Existentialism

23. The National Council for Teacher Education (NCTE) is headed by

(1) Chairperson (2) Director
(3) Co-ordinator (4) Secretary

24. 'SWAYAM' stands for

(1) Study Websites for Automated Young Active Minds.

(2) Study Webs of Active Learning for Young Aspiring Minds.

(3) Study Website for Actual Learning.

(4) Study Webs for Action Learning of Attentive Minds.

25. What is the correct order of the process of portfolio development ?

(A) Collection (B) Display
(C) Reduction (D) Reflection

Codes

(1) A → B → C → D
(2) D → A → C → B
(3) D → C → B → A
(4) A → D → C → B

26. Which of the following is/are example(s) of alternative assessment ?

(A) Response Journals

(B) Portfolio

(C) Typical end term examination

Choose the correct answer from the options given below.

(1) Only A (2) A and B
(3) Only B (4) B and C

27. Arrange the below listed requirements of an Individualised Education Plan (IEP) in sequence from beginning to end

A. Statement of current level of performance.

B. Statement of assessment of student's achievement.

C. Statement of preliminary information about the student.

D. Statement of aids, services, modifications and supports to be provided to the child.

E. Statement of Academic and Functional goals.

Choose the correct answer from the options given below.

(1) C, E, A, D, B (2) C, A, E, D, B
(3) A, C, B, E, D (4) B, E, A, D, C

28. Arrange the following scales of measurement in a descending order from higher scale to lower scale

A. Ordinal B. Ratio
C. Nominal D. Interval

Codes

(1) A → C → D → B
(2) C → A → D → B
(3) B → D → A → C
(4) B → D → C → A

29. Which of the following institutions has been entrusted the responsibility of in-service teacher education for primary /elementary schools as per National Policy on Education, 1986 ?
(1) Institute of Advanced Studies in Education (IASE)
(2) Colleges for Teacher Education (CTEs)
(3) District Institute of Education and Training (DIET)
(4) State Colleges of Education

30. Which of the following techniques is not covered under non-probability sampling ?
(1) Stratified random sampling technique
(2) Purposive sampling technique
(3) Incidental sampling technique
(4) Quota sampling technique

31. Match List I with List II.

List I (Theories of the States)	List II (Area of Focus)
A. The Classical Liberal Theory	I. Emphasis on individualism and general welfare
B. The Maxist-Socialist Theory	II. Emphasises the supermacy of the State
C. The Nationalist -Totalitarian Theory	III. Propagation of Socialist conception of the State
D. Progressive-Liberal Theory	IV. Propagates that State is a promoter of social welfare and protector of individual rights

Codes

	A	B	C	D
(1)	I	II	III	IV
(2)	II	III	I	IV
(3)	II	III	IV	I
(4)	II	I	III	IV

32. A Projective technique is used for the assessment of
(1) Aptitude
(2) Academic Achievement
(3) Intelligence
(4) Personality

33. Choose the correct year of Publication of National Curriculum Frameworks out of the following and arrange in sequential order.
A. 1972
B. 1975
C. 1987
D. 2000
E. 2005

Codes
(1) A → D → E
(2) B → D → E
(3) B → C → E
(4) C → D → E

34. Match List I With List II.

List I (Quality Enhancement Programme)	List II (Mandate)
A. Deeksharambh	I. Faculty Development
B. Jeevan Kaushal	II. Induction programme for students
C. Guru Dakshata	III. Preventing publication in predatory,dubious and sub-standard journals
D. Consortium for Academic Research and Ethics	IV. Imparting life skills to students

Codes

	A	B	C	D
(1)	I	II	III	IV
(2)	II	III	I	IV
(3)	II	III	IV	I
(4)	II	I	III	IV

35. Arrange the following committees and commissions in order of their establishment.
A. Justice Verma Committee
B. National Knowledge Commission
C. National Commission on Teachers
D. Secondary Education Commission

Choose the correct answer from the options given below.
(1) A, B, C, D
(2) B, C, A, D
(3) D, C, B, A
(4) D, B, A, C

36. Match List I with List II.

List I	List II
A. Blended Learning	I. A learner learns where computers smart phone with Internet connectivity are available.
B. Online Learning	II. A learner learns in a classroom as well as at distance through online learning.
C. Wiki	III. A learner learns face to face in a classroom situation.
D. Offline learning	IV. It is a website for reference.

Codes

	A	B	C	D
(1)	I	II	III	IV
(2)	II	III	I	IV
(3)	II	III	IV	I
(4)	II	I	III	IV

37. Pedagogy
A. is a method and practice of teaching.
B. encompasses teaching style, teaching theory and feedback assessment.
C. involves the style of transacting the curriculum content in class room.
D. requires teachers not to get influenced due to difference in the age of students and nature of content to be delivered.

Choose the correct answer from the options given below.
(1) A, B and C (2) B, C and D
(3) A and D (4) B and D

38. Learning
A. implies change in behaviour.
B. takes place through experience and maturation.
C. also implies changes due to growth and maturation.
D. implies that change must be relatively permanent.
Choose the correct answer from the options given below.
(1) A, B and C (2) B, C and D
(3) A, B and D (4) A, C and D

39. Identify the barriers to effective communication,
A. Noise B. Negative attitude
C. Unclear graphics D. Slang language
E. Positive behaviour
Choose the correct answer from the options given below.
(1) B, C, D (2) A, B, C, D (3) A and E (4) C, D, E

40. Terms of Reference of National Knowledge Commission were to
A. build excellence in the educational system to meet the knowledge challenges of the 21st century.
B. promote creation of knowledge in Science and Technology Laboratories.
C. promote knowledge application in preservation of environment.
D. improve the management of institutions engaged in intellectual property rights.
Choose the correct answer from the options given below.
(1) A, B and C (2) A, B and D
(3) A, C and D (4) B, C and D

41. Which of the following has recommended that an Independent Regulatory Authority for Higher Education (IRAHE) should replace NCTE, AICTE, UGC and others ?
(1) National Knowledge Commission
(2) YashPal Committee
(3) National Policy on Education — 1986
(4) Kothari Education Committee

42. Bandura's 'Social Learning Theory', is considered as the bridge between
(1) Behaviourism and Gestalt Psychology
(2) Functionalism and Gestalt Psychology
(3) Behaviourism and Cognitivism
(4) Structuralism and Functionalism

43. Which of the following is not a platform of MOOCs ?
A. Coursera B. Edx
C. Future Learn D. MIT (Massachussetts)
E. SWAYAM
Choose the correct answer from the options given below.
(1) A and B (2) C and A
(3) C and D (4) Only D

44. Who amongst the following is considered as father of Sociology?
(1) George Payne (2) Max Weber
(3) Auguste Comte (4) Maciver

45. Which of the following is not a correct statement with regard to Indian Philosophy?
(1) Indian philosophy denotes the philosophical speculation of ancient and modern Indian thinkers.
(2) Indian philosophy denotes the philosophical speculation of Indian thinkers who are essentially Hindus.
(3) Indian philosophy denotes the philosophical speculation of Indian thinkers-theists or atheists.
(4) Indian philosophy is marked with its devotion to the search for truth.

46. 'Shiksha Vaani' is an audio based learning initiative started by
(1) National Council for Teacher Education (NCTE)
(2) Rehabilitation Council of India (RCI)
(3) University Grants Commission (UGC)
(4) Central Board of Secondary Education (CBSE)

47. The 'banking concept of education' is coined by
(1) Paulo Freire
(2) Ivan Illich
(3) JF Herbert
(4) Johann Pestalozzi

48. According to Sankhya Philosophy, the mind or the intellect is
(1) unconscious material entity
(2) sub conscious material entity
(3) conscious material entity
(4) consciousness or intellect (Chaitanya)

49. In India, the statutory body to set norms and standards for teacher education in special education is
(1) Rehabilitation Centre of India
(2) Rehabilitation Council of India
(3) National Council of Rehabilitation Education
(4) National Council for Teacher Education

50. A secondary source of a particular historical research
(1) will always be a secondary source for all the historical researches.
(2) will always be a primary source for all other historical researches.
(3) may be a primary source for another historical research.
(4) cannot be used as a source in any other historical research.

51. Choose the visual conditions which are types of refractive disorders.
A. Myopia B. Amblyopia
C. Hyperopia D. Astigmatism
E. Strabismus
Choose the correct answer from the options given below.
(1) A and D (2) B, C and E
(3) B and E (4) A, C and D

52. Arrange the following stages of cognitive development as recommended by Piaget.
A. Sensorimotor stage
B. Concrete operational stage
C. Pre-operational stage
D. Formal operational stage
Choose the correct answer from the options given below.
(1) A, C, D, B
(2) A, B, C, D
(3) B, C, A, D
(4) A, C, B, D

53. The term UNCRPD is associated with
(1) United Nations Convention on Regulations for Persons with Disabilities.
(2) United Nations Confederation on Rights of People with Disabilities.
(3) United Nations Convention on the Rights of Persons with Disabilities.
(4) United Nations Conclave on the Rights for People with Disabilities.

54. Given below are two statements.
Statement I All educators are potentially leaders, in that all may create followers by influencing those around them, whether as heads of departments, teacher leaders, principal or Vice-Chancellor.
Statement II Leaders in educational administration are concerned with responding to diversity among learners.
In the light of the above statements, choose the correct answer from the options given below.
(1) Both statement I and statement II are true.
(2) Both statement I and statement II are false.
(3) Statement I is true, but statement II is false.
(4) Statement I is false, but statement II is true.

55. Who was the main proponent of Understanding Level of Teaching ?
(1) Morrison (2) Hunt
(3) Herbart (4) Robert Glaser

56. Arrange the following stages of Total Quality Management in a sequence proposed by Dahlgaard, Kristensen and Kanji (2002)
A. Quality Control
B. Total Quality Management
C. Quality Inspection
D. Quality Assurance
Codes
(1) A, B, C, D (2) D, C, B, A
(3) C, A, D, B (4) B, C, D, A

57. In which year the Persons with Disabilities (PWD) Act was enacted?
(1) 1992 (2) 1995 (3) 1998 (4) 2006

58. Match List I with List II.

List I (Psychological Theory)	List II (Developer)
A. Psychoanalytic theory	I. Tolman
B. Field theory	II. Allport
C. Sign theory of learning	III. Lewin
D. Trait theory	IV. Freud

Codes

	A	B	C	D		A	B	C	D
(1)	I	II	III	IV	(2)	II	III	I	IV
(3)	II	III	IV	I	(4)	II	I	III	IV

59. 'NISTHA' is
A. a national mission to improve learning out comes at elementary level.
B. a programme launched by Rehabilitation Council of India for its staff.
C. a capacity building programme for improving quality of school education through integrated teacher training.
D. a programme launched by University Grants Commission.
Choose the correct answer from the options given below.
(1) A and B (2) B and D (3) A and C (4) A and D

60. The National Institute of Educational Planning and Administration (NIEPA) is located in
(1) Mumbai (2) Hyderabad
(3) New Delhi (4) Chennai

61. Which of the following was not the aim of craft based education recommended by Mahatma Gandhi ?
(1) Meeting the expenses of the teachers' salaries.
(2) Creation of a speacilised class of craftsmen.
(3) Dignity of labour.
(4) Minimisation of drift of rural youth to the cities in search of jobs.

62. The strategy for the education and development of human resources for any nation should be based on
A. the character and traditions of its people.
B. the stage of the country's development.
C. the wealth of its students and teachers.
D. the opportunities available for its development.
Choose the most appropriate answer from the options given below.
(1) A and B (2) A, B and D
(3) C and D (4) Only D

63. The National Council for Teacher Education (NCTE), as a regulatory body came into existence on
(1) 17th August, 1992 (2) 17th August, 1994
(3) 17th August, 1995 (4) 17th August, 1996

64. Match List I with List II.

List I	List II
A. Demonstrative Model of Curriculum Development	I. It proposes that curriculum should be developed by the administration and implemented by Teachers in classroom.
B. Grassroot Model of Curriculum Development	II. In this model, Top-Down approach is followed.
C. Administrative Model of curriculum Development	III. In this model, Bottom-up approach is followed.
D. Hilda Taba Model of Curriculum Development	IV. This model is used to enhance the thinking skills of students.

Codes

	A	B	C	D
(1)	I	II	III	IV
(2)	II	III	I	IV
(3)	II	III	IV	I
(4)	II	I	III	IV

65. Given below are two statements.
Statement I Rather than just focusing on what learners are expected to learn in terms of traditionally defined subject content, competency based curriculum emphasises the various outcomes of a learning process such as skills knowledge and attitudes to be applied by learners.
Statement II Competency based curriculum allows students to take responsibility for their education.
In the light of the above statements, choose the correct answer from the options given below.
(1) Both statement I and statement II are true.
(2) Both statement I and statement II are false.
(3) Statement I is true, but statement II is false.
(4) Statement I is false, but statement II is true.

66. Broad functions of the State Council of Educational Research and Training (SCERT) are
(1) design and development of integrated teacher education programmes of 4 year duration.
(2) preparation of code of professional ethics for teachers.
(3) development of curriculum, text books, training, research and innovation.
(4) accrediation of teacher education institutions and their monitoring.

67. Planning, as the basic function of educational management, invokes certain steps. Arrange these in sequential order:
A. Developing planning premises
B. Establishing goals
C. Charting out various alternatives and choosing from among them the most suitable alternative for reaching the desired goals.
D. Determining and allocating the resources required.
E. Ensuring that plans are communicated to all the concerned.
Choose the correct answer from the options given below.
(1) A, D, B, E, C (2) A, B, E, C, D
(3) B, A, C, D, E (4) B, C, D, A, E

68. Organisational climate
A. determines work performance of an individual.
B. does not affect sentiments of an individual employee.
C. affects the level of job satisfaction of an individual/employee.
D. affects work efficiency of an individual/ employee.
Choose the correct answer from the options given below.
(1) A, B and C (2) B, C and D
(3) A, C and D (4) A and D

69. Discipline based model of curriculum design is basically
(1) learner centred (2) teacher centred
(3) subject centred
(4) social reconstruction centred

70. Which of the following is not a type of budgeting ?
(1) Formula budgeting
(2) Programme budgeting
(3) Performance budgeting
(4) Planned budgeting

71. Davis has characterised which of the following as the main social functions of the family?
A. Reproduction
B. Maintenance
C. Placement
D. Socialisation of the young ones
E. Marrying the kids
Choose the correct answer from the options given below.
(1) A and B (2) B and C
(3) A and D (4) A, B, C and D

72. Which of the following Sustainable Development goals (SDG) ensures 'inclusive and equitable quality education?
(1) SDG 3 (2) SDG 4 (3) SDG 5 (4) SDG 6

73. Match List I with List II.

List I (Philosophy)	List II (Source of Knowledge)
A. Jain Philosophy	I. Perception is the only valid source of knowledge
B. Carvaka Philosophy	II. Perception, inference and testimony are sources of valid knowledge
C. Nyaya	III. Perception, inference comparison and testimony are valid source of knowledge
D. Prabhakara	IV. Perception, inference, comparison, testimony and postulation are valid source of knowledge

Codes

	A	B	C	D
(1)	I	II	III	IV
(2)	II	III	I	IV
(3)	II	III	IV	I
(4)	II	I	III	IV

74. Competency based assessment
A. should be done just after the end/completion of the programme.
B. should take into its scope all measurable components/aspects that need to be assessed.
C. does not demand flexibility with regard to use of different tools/approaches.
D. should be fair and objective.
Choose the correct answer from the options given below.
(1) A, B and C (2) B, C and D
(3) A, B and D (4) A and B

75. Match List I with List II.

List I (Programmes on Education)	List II (Focus Area)
A. Kasturba Gandhi Balika Vidyalaya	I. In this programme, the women's groups are themselves allowed to set up their agenda and priorities.
B. Mahila Samakhya	II. In this programme, residential schools are set up for girls in educationally backward blocks.
C. Rashtriya Madhyamic Shiksha Abhiyan	III. In this programme the focus is no enhancing the access to secondary education as well as its quality.
D. Ek Bharat Shreshtha Bharat Abhiyan	IV. In this programme, the focus is on celebrating the unity in diversity of the country.

Codes

	A	B	C	D
(1)	I	II	III	IV
(2)	II	III	I	IV
(3)	II	III	IV	I
(4)	II	I	III	IV

76. What in your opinion, is an Individualised Educational Plan (IEP)?
A. Rehabilitation and Career Plan for a student.
B. Family Support Plan.
C. Statement of Instructional Supports and Services required by a student.
D. Transition statement for a student with disability from home to school.
Choose the correct answer from the options given below.
(1) Only A (2) A and B
(3) Only C (4) C and D

77. Match List I with List II.

List I (Impairments)	List II (Aids/Appliances)
A. Aural Impairments	I. White canes
B. Skeletal Abnormalities	II. Communication Boards
C. Ocular Impairments	III. Hearing Aids
D. Language Impairments	IV. Wheel Chairs

Codes

	A	B	C	D
(1)	I	II	III	IV
(2)	II	III	I	IV
(3)	II	III	IV	I
(4)	II	I	III	IV

78. The standard error of mean

A. has a greater value than the standard deviation of individual scores.

B. decreases with the increase in sample size.

C. is less for the samples drawn from heterogeneous group.

Choose the correct answer from the options given below.

(1) Only A (2) Only B
(3) A and B (4) A and C

79. In the context of a Path (marga) to reach a state free from misery, as recommended by Buddha, which of the following is not amongst those eight steps or rules (also called astangika-marga)?

(1) Right conduct (2) Right effort
(3) Right knowledge (4) Right speech

80. The first and second step of Dick and Carey Instructional Design Model is

A. Development of instructional strategy.

B. Instructional/learning goals.

C. Instructional analysis.

D. Performance Objectives.

Codes

(1) A and B (2) B and D
(3) B and C (4) C and D

81. Match List I with List II.

List I	List II
A. Educational Guidance	I. It assists students to make a detailed study of careers they intend to pursue and also acquainting them regarding different avenues of work.
B. Vocational Guidance	II. It assists in developing study habits, for selecting curricular/co-curricular activities and also helps in knowing about the availability of scholarships.
C. Personal Guidance	III. It assists the students in certain issues related to health, moral ideals, and interpersonal relationships.
D. Counselling	IV. It is a face to face relationship for the purpose of helping the counsellee.

Codes

	A	B	C	D
(1)	I	II	III	IV
(2)	II	III	I	IV
(3)	II	III	IV	I
(4)	II	I	III	IV

82. Which of the following best illustrates an example of a mixed-methods research study?

(1) Sahil conducts interviews and observations in his study of transitional students.

(2) Rekha interviews parents and their children regarding transition.

(3) Sameer looks at percentages of successful transitions from the district and class grades.

(4) Reshma conducts observations and supplements her findings with class grades.

83. Arrange the following stages for developing and implementing a curriculum framework

A. Preparation

B. Development

C. Evidence gathering

D. Implementation

E. Monitoring and Evaluation

Choose the correct answer from the options given below.

(1) A, B, C, D, E (2) C, A, B, D, E
(3) A, C, B, D, E (4) A, B, C, E, D

84. Portfolio development is basically a

(1) spontaneous process

(2) static process

(3) dynamic process

(4) teacher centred process

85. Which of the following constitutional provisions is made to eliminate discrimination of caste, creed or colour in any government aided school?

(1) Article 16 (2) Article 29
(3) Article 30 (4) Article 32

86. Given below are two statements.

Statement I Rubrics can be used for peer feedback.

Statement II Rubrics can be used only for paired-peer feedback.

In the light of the above statements, choose the correct answer from the options given below.

(1) Both statement I and statement II are true.

(2) Both statement I and statement II are false.

(3) Statement I is true, but statement II is false.

(4) Statement I is false, but statement II is true.

87. Equal educational opportunity means

A. equal accessibility to have suitable education.

B. free education for girls only.

C. equality of educational standards for minorities and disabled only.

D. Both A and B are correct.

E. Both B and C are correct.

Choose the correct answer from the options given below.

(1) Only A (2) Only B
(3) Only D (4) Only E

88. In India, the National Curriculum Framework for Teacher Education (NCFTE). 2009 was prepared by
(1) National Curriculum Committee of India
(2) National Commission for Teacher Education
(3) National Council of Educational Research and Training
(4) National Council for Teacher Education

89. Who rejected the ideas of mind and consciousness as subject matter of Psychology ?
(1) Sadler (2) Watson
(3) James (4) Wundt

90. Learning through informal education is called
(1) open learning
(2) formal learning
(3) insightful learning
(4) learning by chance or incidental learning

Direction *(Q. Nos. 91-95) Read the following paragraph carefully and answer the following five questions.*

As with any change, regardless of advantages and dis-advantages. There are several barriers to the successful implementation of inclusion. These include organisational barriers, attitudinal barriers and knowledge barriers.

Organisational barriers include the way schools and classrooms are organised. This could include physical organisation as well as how the schedules are developed and how classes are assigned to teachers. Attitudinal barriers focus on the beliefs of teachers administrators and other school personnel about students with disabilities and inclusion.

Knowledge barriers are simply the limited knowledge about students with disabilities and inclusive teaching strategies. While all of these barriers could make it difficult to have a successful inclusive education programme, each one can be overcome with various strategies. It is the school's role to overcome these barriers so that students with disabilities can receive an appropriate education with their non-disabled peers.

91. In this paragraph, the attitudinal barriers to inclusion refer to
(1) limited knowledge of teachers about inclusive pedagogy.
(2) attitude of parents of students with disabilities.
(3) attitude of non- disabled peers.
(4) beliefs of the school teachers and administrators about students with disabilities.

92. Which of the following is not indicated a barrier to the successful implementation of inclusion ?
(1) Knowledge barrier
(2) Technological barrier
(3) Attitudinal barrier
(4) Organisational barrier

93. The most appropriate title for the given paragraph would be
(1) Implementation Regarding Inclusive Education
(2) Implementation of Inclusive Education
(3) Barriers to Inclusion
(4) Barriers about Inclusion

94. Organisational barriers to inclusion do not relate to
(1) family members of students with disabilities
(2) teachers
(3) classrooms
(4) schedules

95. Why should the schools overcome barriers to inclusion?
(1) Because students with disabilities do better when served in inclusive education.
(2) To fulfill the legal obligations.
(3) To ensure that students with disabilities and without disabilities receive education together.
(4) To meet the demands of the society.

Directions *(Q. Nos. 96-100) Read the following paragraph carefully and answer the following five questions.*

In a ninth standard class of 50 students, the teacher administered test to measure achievement of students in Physics and Chemistry, respectively. The mean and SD of the class for the achievement scores in Physics were 50 and 20, respectively whereas, the mean and SD of the class for the achievement scores in Chemistry were 20 and 5 respectively. One student Rekha scored 30 marks in Physics and 26 marks in Chemistry. Another student Reshma scored 56 marks in Physics and 22.5 marks in Chemistry. Another student Sameer scored 46 marks in Physics and 19 marks in Chemistry. The summary of these scores is given below

Subject	Mean of the Class	SD of the class	Rekha	Reshma	Sameer
Physics	50	20	30	56	46
Chemistry	20	5	26	22.5	19

96. Who had the least consistent scores in both tests ?
(1) Rekha (2) Reshma
(3) Sameer (4) Reshma and Sameer both

97. Who had the most consistent scores in both tests ?
(1) Rekha (2) Reshma
(3) Sameer (4) Reshma and Sameer both

98. Who had the best mean score in both tests ?
(1) Rekha (2) Reshma
(3) Sameer (4) Reshma and Sameer both

99. Who had the best score in either test ?
(1) Rekha
(2) Reshma
(3) Sameer
(4) Reshma and Sameer both

100. Who had the poorest score in either test ?
(1) Rekha
(2) Reshma
(3) Sameer
(4) Reshma and Sameer both

ANSWERS

1	*(1)*	2	*(1)*	3	*(2)*	4	*(2)*	5	*(1)*	6	*(1)*	7	*(2)*	8	*(4)*	9	*(1)*	10	*(3)*
11	*(3)*	12	*(2)*	13	*(1)*	14	*(3)*	15	*(1)*	16	*(2)*	17	*(3)*	18	*(1)*	19	*(3)*	20	*(1)*
21	*(4)*	22	*(1)*	23	*(1)*	24	*(2)*	25	*(4)*	26	*(2)*	27	*(2)*	28	*(3)*	29	*(3)*	30	*(1)*
31	*(1)*	32	*(4)*	33	*(2)*	34	*(1)*	35	*(3)*	36	*(2)*	37	*(1)*	38	*(3)*	39	*(2)*	40	*(2)*
41	*(1)*	42	*(3)*	43	*(4)*	44	*(3)*	45	*(2)*	46	*(4)*	47	*(1)*	48	*(1)*	49	*(2)*	50	*(3)*
51	*(4)*	52	*(4)*	53	*(3)*	54	*(1)*	55	*(1)*	56	*(3)*	57	*(2)*	58	*(1)*	59	*(3)*	60	*(3)*
61	*(2)*	62	*(2)*	63	*(3)*	64	*(*)**	65	*(1)*	66	*(3)*	67	*(3)*	68	*(3)*	69	*(3)*	70	*(4)*
71	*(4)*	72	*(2)*	73	*(3)*	74	*(3)*	75	*(*)**	76	*(3)*	77	*(4)*	78	*(2)*	79	*(3)*	80	*(3)*
81	*(2)*	82	*(4)*	83	*(2)*	84	*(3)*	85	*(2)*	86	*(3)*	87	*(1)*	88	*(4)*	89	*(2)*	90	*(4)*
91	*(4)*	92	*(2)*	93	*(3)*	94	*(1)*	95	*(3)*	96	*(1)*	97	*(3)*	98	*(2)*	99	*(1)*	100	*(1)*

Solved Paper

2021

UGC NET/JRF/SET

Education (Paper-2)
Solved Paper, November 2021

General Instructions

1. There are total one hundred questions in this paper. Each question carries 2 marks.
2. All questions are compulsory.

1. Which of the following terms best indicates the intent of a qualitative research study?

(a) Explanation (b) Prediction
(c) Exploration (d) Estimation

2. A variable which potentially influences the outcome of a research study, but cannot be directly observed and controlled, is known as

(a) Attribute variable
(b) Confounding variable
(c) Moderator variable
(d) Concomitant variable

3. A teacher gave a test to 50 students of his class and awarded letter grades A, B, C, D and E to indicate their level of performance in hierarchical order from best to the poorest. Which of the following combinations of scales of measurement has been used?

(a) Ordinal and Ratio scales
(b) Nominal and Interval scales
(c) Nominal and Ordinal scales
(d) Interval and Ratio scales

4. A historian conducts a research study to develop biography of a social reformer and publishes it in the form of a book. The study conducted by him may be called

(a) An ethnographic research
(b) A phenomenological study
(c) A grounded theory research
(d) A narrative study

5. The essential element of distinction between the concepts of 'pedagogy' and 'andragogy' is

(a) Methods and approaches used in teaching
(b) Role of previous life-experiences in learning
(c) Socio-economic background of learners
(d) Degree of growth and maturation

6. Continuous and Comprehensive Internal Evaluation (CCIE) and feedback mechanism are the essential components of

(a) Summative Evaluation
(b) Diagnostic Testing
(c) Formative Evaluation
(d) Placement Decisions

7. The most important instrument used in the process of competency based evaluation is

(a) A norm-referenced interpretation of scores
(b) A face to face interview with the examinee
(c) A Standardised achievement test
(d) A criterion-referenced interpretation of scores

8. If the lowest score in a distribution is increased by a small quantity and the highest one is decreased by the same quantity such that their relative rankings are not changed, then, in the new distribution, which of the following measures will not change?

1. Mean
2. Median
3. Mode
4. Variance
5. Quartile Deviation

Choose the correct answer from the options given below

(a) 1, 3 and 5 (b) 2, 4 and 5
(c) 1, 3 and 4 (d) 1, 2 and 5

9. A statistical measure based on the entire population is called parameter. Which of the following are the characteristics of a parameter?

1. It varies from sample to sample.
2. It can be practically computed for a finite population.
3. It has a fixed value for a given population under given conditions.
4. It changes with the size of population
5. It can be estimated by using sampling variance.

Choose the correct answer from the options given below

(a) 2, 3 and 5
(b) 1, 3 and 4
(c) 2, 3 and 4
(d) 3, 4 and 5

10. Which of the following statements are true for reliability of a measuring instrument?

1. It is fixed for a given instrument.
2. It is correlation of scores on measuring instrument with themselves.
3. It varies from sample to sample.
4. Its value can vary from -1 to +1.
5. It is affected by size of the sample used for its determination.

Choose the correct answer from the options given below

(a) 1, 3 and 4 (b) 2, 3 and 5
(c) 2, 4 and 5 (d) 3, 4 and 5

11. Which of the following are the key processes in designing an experimental research study?

1. Manipulation of changes in the outcome variable.
2. Random assignment of subjects to experimental and control groups.
3. Exercising control over extraneous variables.
4. Observation of changes in the treatment variable.
5. Random assignment of treatments to groups.

Choose the correct answer from the options given below

(a) 1, 3 and 5
(b) 2, 3 and 5
(c) 1, 4 and 5
(d) 2, 4 and 5

12. Which of the following statements about adult learners help an instructor while developing his andragogy?

1. Learning process is self-directed and independent.
2. Previous life experiences have limited role in learning process.
3. Desire of self-development to cope with changes in lifestyle and work-environment.
4. What and how to learn is decided by the instructors or other authorities.
5. Motivation to learn is guided by desire to enhance self-esteem, self-confidence and recognition.

Choose the correct answer from the options given below

(a) 1, 3 and 5
(b) 1, 2 and 4
(c) 2, 4 and 5
(d) 2, 3 and 4

13. "What is not said may be more meaningful than what is said," is an idea that led to the development of

(a) Flander's Interaction Analysis of Teaching Behaviour.
(b) Guilford's Structure of Intellect Model of Intelligence.
(c) Galloway's System of Interaction Analysis of Communication.
(d) Piaget's Theory of Cognitive Development.

14. Before gathering data for his research, an investigator asks himself the following questions. What should be the right order of asking/answering these questions?

1. How will data be collected?
2. How will the sample of subjects be selected?
3. What information will be collected?
4. Who will be the subjects to give information?

Choose the correct answer from the options given below

(a) 2, 3, 1, 4 (b) 1, 4, 2, 3
(c) 3, 4, 2, 1 (d) 4, 3, 2, 1

15. The steps involved in the pedagogical analysis of syllabus of a teaching subject are listed below

1. Formulation of instructional objectives and stating them in behavioural terms
2. Selection of teaching method, classroom activities and needed equipment
3. Content analysis of subject matter in terms of units, sub-units, concepts and sub-concepts

4. Choice of appropriate method of evaluation of learning outcomes

Place these steps in a correct order. Choose the correct answer from the options given below

(a) 2, 1, 4, 3 (b) 4, 2, 3, 1
(c) 3, 1, 2, 4 (d) 1, 3, 2, 4

16. Match List I with List II.

List I		List II
A. Purposeful collection of a student's work sample, self-assessment statements for assessing his progress in learning	1.	Triangulation
B. Process of corroborating data from different individuals or sources	2.	Rubric
C. Detailed reconstruction of a person's life stories, experiences and achievements	3.	Portfolio
D. A scoring tool that lists the criteria at various levels of quality for assessing a piece of work	4.	Vignette
	5.	Biography

Choose the correct answer from the options given below.

	A	B	C	D		A	B	C	D
(a)	2	5	3	1	(b)	3	1	5	2
(c)	1	3	2	4	(d)	5	2	1	3

17. Match List I with List II.

List I		List II
A. Content Validity	1.	Extent to which the test scores correlate with a criterion variable after some gap of time
B. Concurrent Validity	2.	Extent to which a test measures some identified basic psychological trait
C. Predictive Validity	3.	Extent to which a test samples the learning material of the curriculum
D. Construct Validity	4.	Degree to which a test-scores correlate with a presently available criterion
	5.	Extent to which different measures of the same trait correlate with one another

Choose the correct answer from the options given below.

	A	B	C	D		A	B	C	D
(a)	4	2	1	3	(b)	1	3	2	5
(c)	5	1	3	2	(d)	3	4	1	2

18. Given below are two statements, one is labelled as Assertion (A) and the other is labelled as Reason (R).

Assertion (A) In the case of small samples, use of non-parametric statistical tests is recommended for analysis of research data.

Reason (R) The sampling errors are large in the case of small samples due to which parametric tests do not give dependable results.

In light of the above statements, choose the correct answer from the options given below.

(a) Both (A) and (R) are true and (R) is the correct explanation of (A)
(b) Both (A) and (R) are true, but (R) is not the correct explanation of (A)
(c) (A) is true, but (R) is false
(d) (A) is false, but (R) is true

19. An investigator commits Type II error in his research when he

(a) rejects null hypothesis when it is true
(b) rejects null hypothesis when it is false
(c) accepts null hypothesis when it is false
(d) accepts null hypothesis when it is true

20. In the process of collecting data for a quantitative research the following steps are followed in a certain order. Place them in correct order.

1. Identification of research instruments
2. Administering the research instrument to sampling units
3. Seeking permission of appropriate authority
4. Selecting a sample by appropriate method
5. Approaching the sampling frame

Choose the correct answer from the options given below:

(a) 1, 4, 3, 5, 2 (b) 1, 5, 4, 3, 2
(c) 3, 1, 2, 5, 4 (d) 4, 3, 1, 5, 2

21. Which of the following is a mandatory requirement to receive grants from University Grants Commission?

(a) Shall be a Grant-in-aid institution
(b) Established by a Central or State Government
(c) Recognised by an international quality control body like ISO
(d) Accredited by National Assessment and Accreditation Council

22. What is the score needed by an institution of higher education to get an A+ Grade from NAAC?

(a) 2.56-3.25 (b) 3.26-3.50
(c) 4.00-4.50 (d) 4.51-5.00

23. Which of the theories of leadership explains the crucial relationship between productivity and concerns for employees?
(a) Managerial Grid
(b) Field theory
(c) Transformational theory
(d) Transactional theory

24. Which of the following points states the concept of the Japanese Model of 'Just in Time Model'?
(a) Minimise time from within production to supply to customers
(b) Minimise time to produce good in limited time
(c) Procure and supply of materials to citizens for consumption
(d) Prompt service delivered by employees in an organisation

25. What is the main disadvantage of Bureaucratic management?
(a) Employees get irritated
(b) Productivity gets affected
(c) It is time taking
(d) Leader has a lot of risk

26. Among the types of disabilities in our population, which can be found more in terms of its percentage?
(a) Mental disability
(b) Locomotor disability
(c) Hearing disability
(d) Visual disability

27. How many types of disabilities are listed in the PWD Act 2016?
(a) Five (b) Fourteen
(c) Sixteen (d) Twenty-one

28. How are the normal children affected in inclusive education?
(a) Proper social and emotional development take place
(b) Their cognitive development get hampered
(c) Developed negative attitude towards the disabled
(d) Their interest in study affected negatively

29. Which of the following statements represents the meaning of inclusive education?
(a) A system of education where the disabled children are given special care
(b) A system where the special children are taught by trained professionals
(c) A system where normal children and children with special needs are taught together
(d) A system where normal children are asked to teach the special children

30. As a Teacher, which of the following act shall be your prime duty to make education inclusive?
(a) Plan lesson effectively
(b) Have positive attitude towards inclusion
(c) Identify children with special needs and adapt pedagogy accordingly
(d) Develop competency to teach in inclusive classroom

31. Match List I with List II by considering the types of disability and its percentage.

List I (Types of disability)	List II (Percentage of disability in India)
A. Mental disability	1. 1.0
B. Locomotor disability	2. 0.1
C. Visual disability	3. 0.2
D. Hearing disability	4. 0.6

Choose the correct answer from the options given below

	A	B	C	D
(a)	4	2	3	1
(b)	3	4	1	2
(c)	2	4	1	3
(d)	3	1	4	2

32. Match List I with List II by considering the concepts with its founders.

List I (Concepts/theories of management)	List II (Founder name)
A. Management by objectives (MBO)	1. Mac Gregor
B. POSDCORB	2. Edward Deming
C. Theory X and Y	3. Peter Drucker
D. PDCA	4. Luther Gulick

Choose the correct answer from the options given below

	A	B	C	D
(a)	1	3	2	4
(b)	2	3	1	4
(c)	3	4	1	2
(d)	4	2	1	3

33. Which criteria can be followed to judge the effectiveness of inclusive education?
1. Identification and enrolment of children with special needs in school.
2. Participation of CWSN children in teaching-learning process.
3. Parents get relieved from their responsibility.
4. Development of children as per their potentialities.
5. Political interference in school activities.

Choose the correct answer from the options given below:

(a) 1, 2 and 4 (b) 1, 3 and 4
(c) 2, 3 and 5 (d) 4, 3 and 5

34. What are the basic principles of Total Quality Management (TQM) as a process?

1. Customer satisfaction
2. Total employee involvement
3. Salary to employee
4. Effective Communication
5. Fact-based decision

Choose the correct answer from the options given below

(a) 1, 2, 3 and 4 (b) 1, 3, 4 and 5
(c) 2, 3, 4 and 5 (d) 1, 2, 4 and 5

35. Given below are two statements, one is labelled as Assertion (A) and the other is labelled as Reason (R).

Assertion (A) PWD Act, 2016 is based on the principles of respect for inherent dignity, individual autonomy including the freedom to make one's own choices, and independence of persons.

Reason (R) In India, a child has the right to get admission to any school as per his/her choice.

In light of the above statements, choose the correct answer from the options given below

(a) Both (A) and (R) are true and (R) is the correct explanation of (A)
(b) Both (A) and (R) are true, but (R) is not the correct explanation of (A)
(c) (A) is true, but (R) is false
(d) (A) is false, but (R) is true

36. Given below are two statements, one is labelled as Assertion (A) and the other is labelled as Reason (R).

Assertion (A) The main concern of a Manager is to make profit for his/her organisation.

Reason (R) Leader has to work as per peoples' requirements.

In light of the above statements, choose the correct answer from the options given below.

(a) Both (A) and (R) are true and (R) is the correct explanation of (A)
(b) Both (A) and (R) are true, but (R) is not the correct explanation of (A)
(c) (A) is true, but (R) is false
(d) (A) is false, but (R) is true

37. What steps are followed logically to recruit people?

1. Advertisement
2. Job-analysis
3. Interview
4. Orientation/Induction
5. Agreement for work/job

Choose the correct answer from the options given below

(a) 1, 2, 5, 4, 3 (b) 5, 1, 4, 2, 3
(c) 2, 1, 3, 5, 4 (d) 4, 5, 1, 2, 3

38. Which type of higher education institution in India has the highest percentage of students' enrolment?

(a) Government institution
(b) Private institution
(c) Public-private institution
(d) Central government institution

39. Match List I with List II.

List I (Concept in Management)	List II (Meaning of Concept)
A. Scalar Principle	1. Administrator works only as per given rulebook
B. Human Relation Approach	2. Freezing, Moving, Unfreezing
C. Bureaucracy	3. A manager can control five/six people effectively
D. Change Model	4. Facility and leisure enhance work

Choose the correct answer from the options given below

	A	B	C	D
(a)	4	1	3	2
(b)	2	3	1	4
(c)	3	4	1	2
(d)	1	3	2	4

40. Given below are two statements, one is labelled as Assertion (A) and the other is labelled as Reason (R).

Assertion (A) Proximity between people enhances communication.

Reason (R) Face to face communication does not ensure effective communication.

In light of the above statements, choose the correct answer from the options given below.

(a) Both (A) and (R) are true and (R) is the correct explanation of (A)
(b) Both (A) and (R) are true, but (R) is not the correct explanation of (A)
(c) (A) is true, but (R) is false
(d) (A) is false, but (R) is true

41. Attention, perception, language, thought, memory and learning are part of

(a) Cognitive processes
(b) Understanding processes
(c) Developmental processes
(d) Visualisation processes

42. Match List I with List II

List I (Stage)	List II (Age Group)
A. Sensorimotor stage	1. Elementary and early adolescence
B. Pre-operational stage	2. Toddlerhood and early childhood
C. Concrete operational stage	3. Infancy
D. Formal operational stage	4. Adolescence and adulthood

Choose the correct answer from the options given below

	A	B	C	D		A	B	C	D
(a)	1	2	3	4	(b)	2	3	4	1
(c)	3	2	1	4	(d)	4	1	2	3

43. Which among the following statements are correct?

1. Mental health is a part of mental hygiene
2. Mental hygiene prevents an individual from psychosis
3. Mental hygiene promotes neurosis in an individual
4. Mental hygiene helps in treating mental disorders

Choose the correct answer from the options given below

(a) 1, 2 and 4 (b) 1, 2 and 3
(c) 2, 3 and 4 (d) 3, 4 and 1

44. Among the following which intelligences are associated with Howard Gardner's theory of multiple intelligences?

1. Linguistic intelligence
2. Musical intelligence
3. Spatial intelligence
4. Social intelligence

Choose the correct answer from the options given below

(a) 1, 2 and 4 (b) 1, 2 and 3
(c) 2,3 and 4 (d) 1, 3 and 4

45. The term emotional intelligence was created by

(a) Howard Gardner
(b) Daniel Goleman
(c) Robert Sternberg
(d) Peter Salovey and John Mayer

46. Among the following which activities are a part of the metacognitive strategy?

1. Writing a reflective journal
2. Self-praising
3. Self-questioning
4. Awareness of self-learning style

Choose the correct answer from the options given below

(a) 1, 2 and 4 (b) 2, 3 and 4
(c) 1, 3 and 4 (d) 1, 2 and 3

47. Experiential learning theories that situate experience at the core of the learning process are based on

(a) Constructivist theories of learning
(b) Social theories of learning
(c) Cognitive theories of learning
(d) Both Social and Constructivist theories of learning

48. The process of helping individuals discover and develop their educational, vocational, and psychological potentialities and thereby to achieve an optimal level of personal happiness and social usefulness is named as

(a) Guidance
(b) Counselling
(c) Counselling and guidance
(d) Career counselling

49. Any counselling theory or practice that incorporates and combines doctrines, findings, and techniques selected from diverse theoretical systems is termed as

(a) Non-directive counselling
(b) Directive counselling
(c) Eclectic counselling
(d) Vocational counselling

50. Match List I with List II.

List I (Theory)	List II (Characteristic)
A. Psychodynamic theory of counselling	1. is used to identify irrational beliefs and negative thought patterns that may lead to emotional or behavioural issues.
B. Behaviouristic theory of counselling	2. explains personality in terms of unconscious psychological processes
C. Rational emotive theory of counselling	3. focuses on improving present relationships and circumstances, while avoiding discussion of past events.
D. Reality theory of counselling	4. is used for those with behavioural problems or mental health conditions

Choose the correct answer from the options given below

	A	B	C	D		A	B	C	D
(a)	1	2	3	4	(b)	2	3	4	1
(c)	2	4	1	3	(d)	3	4	2	1

51. Given below are two statements.

Statement I The curriculum principles should reflect the school's values, context, pedagogy and needs.

Statement II Schools need to identify the resources required to bring their curriculum to life and ensure its coherence. A good curriculum needs good quality resources.

In light of the above statements, choose the most appropriate answer from the options given below

(a) Both Statement I and Statement II are correct
(b) Both Statement I and Statement II are incorrect
(c) Statement I is correct, but Statement II is incorrect
(d) Statement I is incorrect, but Statement II is correct

52. The National Curriculum Framework 2005 begins with a quotation from an essay titled 'Civilisation and Progress'. This essay was written by

(a) Mahatma Gandhi
(b) Gijubhai Badheka
(c) Rabindranath Tagore
(d) Gopal Krishna Gokhale

53. The following are some steps for curriculum development. Arrange them in a sequential order

1. Produce curriculum product
2. Implement curriculum
3. Test and revise curriculum
4. Design evaluation strategies
5. Form curriculum development team

Choose the correct answer from the options given below

(a) 1, 2, 3, 4, 5 (b) 2, 3, 4, 5, 1
(c) 5, 1, 3, 2, 4 (d) 3, 4, 5, 1, 2

54. Given below are two statements.

Statement I Stake's Model of curriculum evaluation is based explicitly on the assumption that the concerns of the stakeholders-those for whom the evaluation is done-should be paramount in determining the evaluation issues

Statement II The Eisner Model is built on two closely related constructs: connoisseurship and criticism.

In light of the above statements, choose the most appropriate answer from the options given below.

(a) Both Statement I and Statement II are correct
(b) Both Statement I and Statement II are incorrect
(c) Statement I is correct, but Statement II is incorrect
(d) Statement I is incorrect, but Statement II is correct

55. Match List I with List II.

List I (Curriculum Evaluation Model)	**List II** (Given by)
A. Effectiveness Model	1. Kirkpatrick
B. Goal-Free Model	2. Scriven
C. Four-Level Training Evaluation Model	3. Tyler
D. Countenance Model	4. Stake
	5. Bradley

Choose the correct answer from the options given below

	A	B	C	D		A	B	C	D
(a)	1	2	3	4	(b)	2	4	3	5
(c)	5	2	1	4	(d)	3	1	2	4

56. Finding solution of problems by creating proper environment is the main essence of which philosophy?

(a) Idealism
(b) Naturalism
(c) Biological Pragmatism
(d) Existentialism

57. "God, the great giver, can open the whole Universe to our gaze in the narrow space of a single land" was said by

(a) Plato
(b) Rabindranath Tagore
(c) Swami Vivekananda
(d) Mahatma Gandhi

58. Match the given theme in List I with most suitable School of Philosophy given in List II.

List I (Theme)	**List II** (School of Thought)
A. Recognises ideals and beliefs on the basis of experiments	1. Idealism
B. Recognises truth beauty and goodness of self-consciousness	2. Existentialism
C. Recognises no clear-cut difference between matter and consciousness.	3. Pragmatism
D. Recognises the inner and immediate realisation	4. Naturalism

Choose the correct answer from the options given below

	A	B	C	D
(a)	1	2	3	4
(b)	3	1	4	2
(c)	3	4	2	1
(d)	1	4	2	3

59. Which of the following statements are true?

1. According to Sankhya both Spirit and Matter are Infinite and External.
2. Upanishad dispels ignorance and takes the person desirous of emancipation near God and frees the bondage of birth and death.
3. Kain is one of the Chief Upanishads.
4. Shankaracharya has supported Bhaktiyoga of Gita.
5. According to Mahayana a man should strive for his own emancipation.

Choose the correct answer from the options given below

(a) 1, 2 and 4 (b) 2, 3 and 5
(c) 1, 2 and 3 (d) 2, 3 and 4

60. Maharshi Patanjali has spoken about Five kinds of *Chiitavriti* or Mental Processes. Arrange them sequentially.

1. Enables us to get true knowledge of things
2. Remembrance of the subject retained in memory
3. In dream an object is not present, seems to be present
4. Which depends on words in the absence of the concerned object
5. False knowledge that does not allow one to get true picture of anything or situation

Choose the correct answer from the options given below

(a) 1, 2, 3, 4, 5 (b) 1, 5, 3, 4, 2
(c) 1, 4, 5, 3, 2 (d) 3, 4, 2, 1, 5

61. Match List I with List II.

List I (Chief-Tenets)	List II (Respective Forum)
A. Provides a framework of virtual repository of learning resources with a single window search facility	1. Virtual Labs
B. The training for teachers and students is imparted through workshops where participants are taught basics of embedded systems and programming	2. Swayam Prabha
C. Provides a fully interactive simulation environment to perform experiments, collect data, and answer questions to assess the understanding of the knowledge acquired	3. E-Yantra
D. An initiative to provide 32 high quality educational channels through DTH to deliver education in a most cost effective and inclusive manner	4. National Digital Library

Choose the correct answer from the options given below

	A	B	C	D
(a)	3	1	4	2
(b)	4	3	1	2
(c)	2	3	1	4
(d)	4	3	2	1

62. Which of the following online learning destination founded by Harvard and MIT in 2012, which offers courses from the world's best universities and institutions to learners everywhere?

(a) Moodle (b) edX
(c) CEMCA (d) LinkedIn

63. Match List I with List II.

List I (Chief characteristic)	List II (Learning school)
A. Learning happens when a learner obtains new or changed behaviour as a result of a stimulus	1. CONSTRUCTIVISM
B. Learning is about internal cognitive processes or the handling of symbols in the mind.	2. HUMANISTIC THEORY
C. Focuses on individuals and the mental structures they possess, and how those structures and past experiences/knowledge speak to and influence the construction of various things	3. CONNECTIVISM
D. Students learn best when their natural desires and inclinations to be creative, to grow, to learn etc. are harnessed rather than changed or suppressed	4. COGNITIVISM
	5. BEHAVIOURISM

Choose the correct answer from the options given below

	A	B	C	D
(a)	5	3	1	2
(b)	2	1	4	5
(c)	5	3	4	2
(d)	5	4	1	2

64. Arrange the first five instructional strategies used in learning in sequential order.

1. Information Presentation: The web pages display textual as well as graphical information for the learners.
2. Guidance and Collaboration: E-mail and online asynchronous discussion group facilitate collaboration on the web.
3. Decision-Making: Computer and web technologies allow learners to take their own decision to follow links provided on the pages.

4. Drill and Practice: As in computer assisted learning, the web also provides drill and practice opportunities. Using formative assessment techniques in the course content presented in small web pages can lead to optimised learning.
5. Feedback: Learners can receive automated feedback to their assignments, and interaction with formative assessment tools in the web pages.

Choose the cqorrect answer from the options given below

(a) 1, 3, 2, 4, 5 (b) 3, 1, 2, 4, 5
(c) 1, 3, 4, 2, 5 (d) 1, 2, 3, 4, 5

65. Which of the following options are correct for Synchronous learning?
1. Synchronous learning refers to a learning event in which a group of participants is engaged in learning at the same time
2. Participants can learn in their own time and schedule
3. Real-time feedback for the instructor
4. Self paced learning

Choose the correct answer from the options given below

(a) 1 and 2 (b) 1 and 3
(c) 1, 2 and 3 (d) 2, 3 and 4

66. Which of the following theory may support this statement "The teacher should encourage the student to discover their own connections between seemingly discrete information, using different means (e.g. Twitter, wikis, blogs, open educational resources)"

(a) Cognitivist (b) Constructivist
(c) Connectivism (d) Humanistic

67. Which of the following are the Asynchronous Learning Platforms?

1. Webex 2. Moodle
3. Canvas 4. Google meet

Choose the correct answer from the options given below

(a) 1 and 2 (b) 2 and 3
(c) 1 and 3 (d) 2 and 4

68. Match List I with List II.

List I (Social Theories)	List II (Key features)
A. Symbolic Interactionism	1. Use symbols, face to face interactions
B. Structuralism	2. Aspects of society and its functions
C. Functionalism	3. Competition for scarce resources
D. Conflict Theory	4. Breaking down mental processes into small components

Choose the correct answer from the options given below

	A	B	C	D		A	B	C	D
(a)	1	4	2	3	(b)	2	4	1	3
(c)	3	1	2	4	(d)	1	4	3	2

69. Which of the following are key components of Care Model of Nel Noddings?

1. Modeling 2. Dialogue
3. Practice 4. Confirmation
5. Originality

Choose the correct answer from the options given below

(a) 1, 2, 3 and 4 (b) 1, 3, 4 and 5
(c) 2, 3, 4 and 5 (d) 1, 2, 4 and 5

70. Who coined the term 'Sociological Imagination'?

(a) Giddens (b) Michael Young
(c) Nicolas Sarkozy (d) Wright Mills

71. The most difficult part in doing cost benefit analysis is to determine

(a) Tangible benefits and costs
(b) Intangible benefits and costs
(c) Private economic costs
(d) Total monetary expenditure

72. Yashpal Committee report is titled as

(a) ICT in teacher education
(b) Education and national development
(c) School without walls
(d) Learning without burden

73. Which one of the following is not involved in policy making decisions?

(a) Analysis of the existing policy
(b) Generation of policy options
(c) Policy impact assessments
(d) Evaluation of policy options

74. Which one of the following is emphasised in the NEP-2020?

(a) What to learn
(b) When to learn
(c) Where to learn
(d) How to learn

75. 'Deschooling Society' is written by

(a) Ivan Illich
(b) Jerome K Bruner
(c) David Hartley
(d) Robert Sherman

76. Pedagogical content knowledge in the field of teacher education was first put forward by

(a) Habermas (b) Le Shulman
(c) Deng-Xio-Ping (d) Luke

77. The centrally sponsored scheme of Samagra Shiksha subsumes which of the following schemes?

(a) SSA, RMSA and TE schemes
(b) KGBV, Mahila Samakhya and ICT@ Schools
(c) MDM, VE and Eklavya Model Schools
(d) IEDSS, SPQEM and Setting of model schools at block level

78. Dr. *X*, a teacher in school always takes time to analyse her classroom process, to identify more than just what went in the classroom, what worked and what did not. She is practicing

(a) inquiry oriented teaching
(b) reflective teaching
(c) competency based teaching
(d) expository teaching

79. Match List I with List II.

List I (Subject)	List II (Article of the Constitution)
A. Education of Minorities	1. Article 21 A
B. Instruction in Mother tongue at a primary stage	2. Article 29
C. Right to Education	3. Article 30
D. Right of Minorities to establish Educational Institutions	4. Article 46
	5. Article 350 A

Choose the correct answer from the options given below

	A	B	C	D		A	B	C	D
(a)	2	5	4	3	(b)	3	5	1	4
(c)	1	3	2	5	(d)	2	5	1	3

80. The guiding principles for curriculum development in NCF-2005 are

1. Connecting knowledge to life outside school
2. Ensuring that learning shifts from rote methods
3. Nurturing an over-riding identity informed by caring concerns within the democratic polity of the country
4. Emphasis on examinations
5. Teacher-centered education

Choose the correct answer from the options given below

(a) 1, 2 and 5 (b) 2, 3 and 5
(c) 1, 2 and 4 (d) 1, 2 and 3

81. An institution wishes to apply for the assessment and accreditation from NAAC. Which of the following performance indicators it should focus on as per NAAC requirements.

1. Teaching learning and evaluation
2. Curricular aspects
3. Election of students union members
4. Infrastructure and learning resources
5. Students support and progression

Choose the correct answer from the options given below

(a) 1, 2, 3 and 4
(b) 1, 3, 4 and 5
(c) 1, 2, 4 and 5
(d) 2, 3, 4 and 5

82. The new pedagogical and curricular structure envisaged for ECCE in NEP-2020 is

(a) preparatory
(b) foundational
(c) early childhood and care education
(d) middle

83. PARAKH is proposed to be set up as

(a) National Training Centre for Teachers
(b) Nasdtional Assessment Centre
(c) National Testing Agency
(d) National Digital Repository

84. The sequence of steps taken by policy makers using Rational choice theory is

1. discover all the alternative policies available to accomplish the values.
2. identify all the value preferences currently existing in a society and assign each value a relative weight.
3. involves only small number of persons to allocate values for society and not the masses.
4. know the total cost and consequences of each alternative policy.
5. select the best alternative which is also the most efficient in terms of costs and benefits of social values.

Choose the correct answer from the options given below

(a) 2, 1, 4 and 5 (b) 4, 2, 1 and 3
(c) 1, 2, 3 and 5 (d) 3, 1, 4 and 5

85. Arrange the following in the chronological order of formation.

1. Wardha or Basic scheme of Education
2. Rammurthy Report
3. Mudaliyar Commission
4. Kothari Commission
5. University Education Commission

Choose the correct answer from the options given below

(a) 1, 2, 3, 4, 5 (b) 1, 5, 2, 4, 3
(c) 2, 3, 5, 4, 1 (d) 1, 5, 3, 4, 2

86. Match List I with List II.

List I (Verticals of HECI)	List II (Functions)
A. NHERC	1. Funding
B. NAC	2. Regulation
C. HEGC	3. Academic standard setting
D. GEC	4. Accreditation
	5. Professional development

Choose the correct answer from the options given below

	A	B	C	D		A	B	C	D
(a)	2	4	1	3	(b)	2	4	5	1
(c)	1	2	4	5	(d)	4	3	2	1

87. Given below are two statements, one is labelled as Assertion (A) and the other is labelled as Reason (R).

Assertion (A) The regulatory system of higher education should ensure that the distinct function of regulation, accreditation, funding and academic standards setting are done by independent bodies.

Reason (R) This will help to redistribute workload with ever increasing number of institutions.

In light of the above statements, choose the correct answer from the options given below.

(a) Both (A) and (R) are true and (R) is the correct explanation of (A)
(b) Both (A) and (R) are true, but (R) is not the correct explanation of (A)
(c) (A) is true, but (R) is false
(d) (A) is false, but (R) is true

88. Given below are two statements, one is labelled as Assertion (A) and the other is labelled as Reason (R).

Assertion (A) The revision and revamping of all aspects of the educational structure, including its regulation and governance is necessary.

Reason (R) Education system is facing unprecedented challenges.

In light of the above statements, choose the most appropriate answer from the options given below

(a) Both (A) and (R) are correct and (R) is the correct explanation of (A)
(b) Both (A) and (R) are correct but (R) is not the correct explanation of (A).
(c) (A) is correct, but (R) is not correct
(d) (A) is not correct, but (R) is correct

89. Given below are two statements.

Statement I The school complex/cluster aimed at greater resource efficiency and more effective functioning, coordination, leadership, governance and management of schools in the cluster.

Statement II The Kothari commission recommendation on school complexes could not be implemented since the school leaders, teachers, students, supporting staff, parents, and local citizens of different schools grouped in school complex/cluster objected to it.

In light of the above statements, choose the correct answer from the options given below.

(a) Both Statement I and Statement II are true
(b) Both Statement I and Statement II are false
(c) Statement I is true, but Statement II is false
(d) Statement I is false, but Statement II is true

90. Given below are two statements.

Statement I Covid-19 has led to potential opportunities for disruptive technologies to offer solutions which, aside from their long-term interest, can potentially maintain business continuity, enhance health-care outcomes and avoid service disruptions.

Statement II Disruptive technology will make certain jobs redundant, and hence approaches to skilling and deskilling that are both efficient and ensure quality will be of increasing importance to create and sustain employment.

In light of the above statements, choose the correct answer from the options given below.

(a) Both Statement I and Statement II are true
(b) Both Statement I and Statement II are false
(c) Statement I is true, but Statement II is false
(d) Statement I is false, but Statement II is true

Directions (Q. Nos. 91-95) *Read the paragraph given below and answer the question that follows :*

Narration (with the teacher as narrator) leads the students to memorise mechanically the narrated content. Worse yet, it turns them into 'containers,' into 'receptacles' to be "filled" by the teacher. The more completely she fills the receptacles, the better a teacher she is. The more meekly the receptacles permit themselves to be filled, the better students they are.

Education thus becomes an act of depositing, in which the students are the depositories and the teacher is the depositor. Instead of communicating, the teacher issues communiques and makes deposits which the students patiently receive, memorise, and repeat. This is the 'banking' concept of education, in which the scope of action allowed to the students extends only as far as receiving, filing, and storing the deposits. They do, it is true, have the opportunity to become collectors or cataloguers of the things they store. But in the last analysis, it is the people themselves who are filed away through the lack of creativity, transformation, and knowledge in this (at best) misguided system. For apart from inquiry, apart from the praxis, individuals cannot be truly human. Knowledge emerges only through invention and re-invention, through the restless, impatient, continuing, hopeful inquiry human beings pursue in the world, with the world, and with each other.

In the banking concept of education, knowledge is a gift bestowed by those who consider themselves knowledgeable upon those whom they consider to know nothing. Projecting an absolute ignorance onto others, a characteristic of the ideology of oppression, negates education and knowledge as processes of inquiry. The teacher presents himself to his students as their necessary opposite; by considering their ignorance absolute, he justifies his own existence. The students, alienated like the slave in the Hegelian dialectic, accept their ignorance as justifying the teachers existence-but, unlike the slave, they never discover that they educate the teacher.

91. This passage depicts exiting education systems as
(a) Teacher-centered
(b) Learner-centered
(c) Democratic
(d) Laissez-faire

92. The main characteristic of the banking concept of education is
(a) The teacher tells and students listen
(b) Students speak and the teacher listens
(c) Both teacher and students discuss with each other
(d) Students raise questions for answers

93. Knowledge has to emerge mainly through
(a) Listening to teachers
(b) Reading the books
(c) Memorising the content
(d) Reflection and action

94. According to this passage, knowledge must be acquired through
(a) Transfer of content by knowledgeable to less knowledgeable
(b) A process of inquiry about content
(c) Mechanical memorisation of the content
(d) Receiving, memorising, and storing content

95. The main criticism of the banking system of education is
(a) Emphasis on memorisation
(b) Process of knowledge transfer
(c) Not developing individuals as human beings
(d) Treating students as slaves

Directions (Q. Nos. 96-100) *Read the paragraph below and answer the question that follows :*

NEP leads with three radical changes that will bring much-needed relief from the tunnel vision of restricted student potential. The first is the exit and re-entry of students in universities. We all live with uncertainty-but this should not be a reason to lose out on one's degree. Combined with the ability to transfer credits across universities, this gives true freedom to students to find their best fit. The second is multi-disciplinarity, across schools and higher education. Students can choose any subjects, all subjects are equal, and the concept of streams has been disbanded.

This truly frees up students to work to their talents rather than to an administrators diktat. The third is the flexibility given in board exams. Again, more choice, more chances to get it right. This is to support students to be their best selves in a way that had not been enabled before. NEP has also recognised the urgency of foundational learning and upgraded it to a mission.

There are many other things that NEP gets right, such as focus on teacher training for schools, the fund for educating girls, and the freedom for university course length, among others. Creating a framework for teachers to only teach and not co-opted for other duties is good, as is the emphasis on supporting the less able. The intent is to breach gaps that have been untended for too long. There is so much to be said and done here, and it is already too little too late-but every effort mut be appreciated. The challenge is to get it right.

96. Which of the following is not under radical changes?
(a) Exit and re-entry of students
(b) Multi-disciplinarity
(c) Incentivising teachers
(d) Flexibility

97. Which of the following is a wrong statement?
(a) Credit transfer will give freedom to the students
(b) Students can choose any subject within a discipline
(c) Disciplinary boundaries will be broken
(d) Foundational literacy is an utmost urgency

98. Multi-disciplinarity will be ensured
(a) Across school education level
(b) Across higher education level
(c) Across technical education level
(d) Irrespective of levels of education

99. Which of the following statements is not wrong?
(a) Greater possibility for relief from the tunnel vision of restricted student potential
(b) Restricted possibility for relief from the tunnel vision of restricted student potential
(c) Choice-based possibility for relief from the tunnel vision of restricted student potential
(d) No possibility for relief from the tunnel vision of restricted student potential

100. Which of the following statements is not incorrect?
(a) Credit transfer will be done within Central Universities
(b) Credit transfer will be done within State Universities
(c) Credit transfer will be done within Central and State Universities
(d) Credit transfer will be done within Universities and HEIs

ANSWERS

1 (c)	2 (b)	3 (c)	4 (d)	5 (b)	6 (c)	7 (d)	8 (d)	9 (a)	10 (b)
11 (b)	12 (a)	13 (c)	14 (c)	15 (c)	16 (b)	17 (d)	18 (b)	19 (c)	20 (a)
21 (d)	22 (b)	23 (a)	24 (a)	25 (c)	26 (d)	27 (d)	28 (a)	29 (c)	30 (c)
31 (b)	32 (c)	33 (a)	34 (d)	35 (a)	36 (b)	37 (c)	38 (b)	39 (c)	40 (c)
41 (a)	42 (c)	43 (a)	44 (b)	45 (d)	46 (c)	47 (d)	48 (c)	49 (c)	50 (c)
51 (a)	52 (c)	53 (c)	54 (a)	55 (c)	56 (c)	57 (b)	58 (b)	59 (c)	60 (b)
61 (b)	62 (b)	63 (d)	64 (a)	65 (b)	66 (c)	67 (b)	68 (a)	69 (a)	70 (d)
71 (b)	72 (d)	73 (c)	74 (d)	75 (a)	76 (b)	77 (a)	78 (b)	79 (d)	80 (d)
81 (c)	82 (b)	83 (b)	84 (a)	85 (d)	86 (a)	87 (b)	88 (b)	89 (c)	90 (a)
91 (a)	92 (a)	93 (d)	94 (b)	95 (c)	96 (c)	97 (b)	98 (d)	99 (a)	100 (d)

SOLVED PAPER
2020 & 2019

UGC NET/JRF/SET

Education (Paper-2)
Solved Paper, November 2020

General Instructions

1. There are total one hundred questions in this paper. Each question carries 2 marks.
2. All questions are compulsory.

---

1. In the, 'Developmental stages of Reading' when the child becomes aware of the ways in which letters are combined leading to distinct sounds, is referred to as

(a) Symbolic stage
(b) Orthographic stage
(c) Blending stage
(d) Pictorial stage

2. Which of the following mentioned inclusive education as, "to integrate the handicapped with general community at all levels as equal partners, to prepare them for normal growth and to enable them to face life with courage and confidence"?

(a) World Declaration on Education for All (1990)
(b) Rehabilitation Council of India Act (1992)
(c) National Policy of Education (1986)
(d) Scheme of Integrated Education for Disabled Children (1974)

3. Sarva Shiksha Abhiyan (SSA) adopted which of the following?

(a) Zero Resource Room Policy
(b) Zero Rejection Policy
(c) Zero Acceptance Policy
(d) Zero Home-based Education Policy

4. In United Nations Convention as the Right of Persons with Disability (UNCRPD) Report, the right to Education has been discussed in which Article?

(a) 40 (b) 20
(c) 42 (d) 24

5. For education of CWSN (Children With Special Needs), the concept of Inclusive Education as laid down in SSA was based upon

(a) Integration Model
(b) Medical Model
(c) Multi-Option Model
(d) International Model

6. Which of the following Open Educational Resources (OER) comes under the ambit of Indian Initiatives?

(a) Coursera (b) Edse
(c) E-Gyan Kosh (d) Open Stax

7. An inquiry oriented activity in which the information comes from resources on the internet, optimally supplemented with video conferencing is called

(a) Digital Technology
(b) Bring Your Own Device (BYOD)
(c) Virtual Learning
(d) Web Quest

8. When teaching learning material is introduced offline, so that learners can access the content anytime before the class starts and can write down their questions/problems which can be asked during the classroom is called

(a) Virtual classroom (b) Google classroom
(c) Flipped classroom (d) Traditional Classroom

9. WBL stands for

(a) Wide Based Learning (b) Web Based Learning
(c) Web Biased Learning (d) Web Based Listening

10. For a group of adult learners, a trainer provides information to enable them to understand the information for indicating acceptability or non-acceptability of their responses. This will be technically called providing

(a) prompt for emission of correct behaviour.
(b) feedback of the given response.
(c) judging the value of information.
(d) information linkage device.

11. Who has proposed that "Organisation shall eliminate the need of quality control after the process"?

(a) Edward Deming
(b) Walter Shewart
(c) C K Prahalad
(d) Poka Yoke

12. Which of the following statements, represents the rationale underlying "Span of Control"?

(a) One can work effectively for a period of time.
(b) One can work with a small number of people.
(c) One can make a small group of people to work effectively.
(d) One can control a large group of workers.

13. The main limitation of Bureaucratic management is that

(a) work efficiency gets questioned.
(b) work procedure gets thwarted.
(c) workers have no choice in work procedure.
(d) Observing rules and regulations without emphasising work procedure.

14. Which among the following is best suited for assessment of social skills?

(a) Checklist (b) Rating scale
(c) Numerical scale (d) Rubrics

15. During the course of teaching, a teacher very often uses probing questions to clarify student's ideas and concepts. This may be linked with which of the following assessment procedures?

(a) Diagnostic assessment
(b) Predictive assessment
(c) Formative assessment
(d) Summative assessment

16. "Automated, unconscious mastery of activities and related skills at strategic level" with reference to classification of objectives of learning in the psychomotor domain proposed by R H Dave means

(a) Manipulation (b) Articulation
(c) Naturalisation (d) Precision

17. Who of the following developed the concept of Behaviour shaping through the use of principle of successive approximation?

(a) Thorndike (b) Watson
(c) Skinner (d) Piaget

18. Which of the following schemes have been subsumed in Samagra Shiksha?

(a) SSA and RMSA
(b) RMSA and RUSA
(c) RUSA, SSA, RMSA and TE
(d) SSA, RMSA and TE

19. Which theory of Habermas is useful way to explore knowledge and its impact on student engagement?

(a) Knowledge-Constitutive Interest Theory
(b) Critical Theory
(c) Social Theory
(d) Theory of Communicative Action

20. What are the three concepts of knowledge proposed by Deng and Luke?

(a) Disciplinary, practical, experiential
(b) Procedural, meta-cognitive, practical
(c) Disciplinary, procedural, experiential
(d) Factual, practical, experiential

21. Which of the following institutions is directly responsible for the professional growth of school teachers in India?

(a) CSIR (b) NAAC
(c) NCERT (d) EMMRC

22. Which method of the qualitative research focuses on language and meanings that are given to texts, for the purpose of creating and shaping knowledge and behaviour?

(a) Discourse analysis (b) Narrative research
(c) Trend analysis (d) Grounded theory

23. Given below is a summary of ANOVA for four groups of students tested in a research project.

Source of Variance	SS (Sum of Squares)	DF (Degree of Freedom)	MS (Means Sum of Squares)
Between Groups	76	3	23.33
Within Groups	122	16	7.62

What will be the value of 'F' for the above data?

(a) 76/122 (b) 3/16
(c) 23.33/7.62 (d) 7.62.23.33

24. A teacher finds that the distribution of scores for a self made test is positively skewed. What inference he/she should make about the difficulty level of this test?

(a) The test is difficult.
(b) The test is easy.
(c) The test is of moderate difficulty.
(d) The test is moderately of low difficulty.

25. A university teacher has conducted a survey of achievement of students in chemistry through a self made test. The distribution of scores has been studied in terms of mean and standard deviation for a sample of 100 students. The results are as follows

Mean = 50 Standard deviation = 10 and N = 10
Assuming that the distribution of scores is normal, what will be the Percentile Rank (PR) of a student whose scores is 60?
(a) 70 (b) 75 (c) 80 (d) 84

26. The observation "What the curriculum neglects is as important as what it advocates for" is related to which of the following types of curriculum?
(a) Overt Curriculum (b) Hidden Curriculum
(c) Core Curriculum (d) Null Curriculum

27. Which of the following approaches to Curriculum objectives provides scope for meeting the self-actualisation needs?
(a) Behavioural–Rational Approach
(b) Intellectual–Academic Approach
(c) Systems–Managerial Approach
(d) Humanistic–Aesthetic Approach

28. The Congruence-Contingency Model of Curriculum evaluation was developed by
(a) Ralph Tyler (b) Malcolm Provus
(c) Robert Stake (d) Daniel Stufflebean

29. Which of the following dimensions of curriculum design focuses on interrelatedness of various aspects of curriculum?
(a) Scope (b) Sequence
(c) Articulation (d) Continuity

30. Empathetic understanding of the client's problem is stressed in which type of counselling?
(a) Rational-problem analysis based counselling.
(b) Person-centred humanistic approach dominated counselling.
(c) Reality-based directive counselling.
(d) Behaviouristic–modification based counselling.

31. A student has graduated from a university. He/she wants help in making the choice of stream of education. The type of guidance to be put in place for such a case will be called
(a) Personal guidance (b) Educational guidance
(c) Vocational guidance (d) Social guidance

32. Who among the following behaviourist theorists of learning, advocated the role of cognitive and molar concepts?
(a) C L Hull (b) E L Thorndike
(c) E C Tolman (d) J B Watson

33. The techniques in respect of 'human learning context' advocated by Carl Rogers were given the caption
(a) Self-regulated learning (b) Reception learning
(c) Self-initiated learning (d) Discovery learning

34. Developing brand and enhancing marketing is emphasised by
(a) Theory of System Analysis (b) Signal Theory
(c) Theory of Rational Choice (d) Human Capital Theory

35. The essential components of a budget are
(a) Building and Infrastructure
(b) Income and Expenditure
(c) Policy and Programmes
(d) Fees and Salary

36. The right to free and compulsory education at primary education level is ensured by the constitution of India through
(a) Article 45 of directive principles
(b) Article 21 B, 2002
(c) Article 21 A, 2009
(d) Article 21 A, 2002

37. Establishment of DIETs was a result of one of the recommendations of
(a) Education Commission–1966
(b) University Education Commission 1948-49
(c) Secondary Education Commission 1952-53
(d) National Policy of Education 1986

38. The recommendation to reduce the burden of school bags was given by
(a) Yashpal Committee
(b) National Commission for Women
(c) Ramamurti Committee
(d) National Education Policy 1986

39. Who among the following contributed the book entitled "Savitri : A Legend and a Symbol"?
(a) Mahatma Gandhi (b) Savitribai Phule
(c) Sri Aurobindo (d) Swami Vivekananda

40. In Sankhya Philosophy, 'Evolution' is considered to be a
(a) Teleological Process (b) Linear Process
(c) Mechanical Process (d) Novel Change

41. Which school of Western Philosophy endorses the following metaphysical assertion?
"Since the universe exists independent of us and is governed by laws over which we have little control, it is necessary to know certain definite things about this universe in order to adopt to it".
(a) Idealism (b) Pragmatism
(c) Existentialism (d) Realism

42. According to NCF (2005), the salient guiding principles of curriculum development include
1. connecting knowledge to life outside the school.
2. ensuring that the learning shifts away from rote methods.
3. enriching curriculum beyond textbooks.
4. interfacing with medical model of disability.
5. focusing on the dominant culture.

Choose the most appropriate answer from the options given below.
(a) 4, 1 and 3 (b) 5, 2 and 1
(c) 3, 2 and 5 (d) 1, 2 and 3

43. Which of the following conditions of disabilities have been identified according to the 'Persons with Disability Act 1995'?
1. Blindness and Low Vision
2. Hearing Impairment
3. Mental Retardation and Mental Illness
4. Autism Spectrum Disorder
5. Specific Learning Disabilities

Choose the most appropriate answer from the options given below.
(a) 5, 4 and 2 (b) 4, 1 and 5
(c) 1, 2 and 3 (d) 5, 3 and 2

44. Creative common licensing allows the users to
1. Use the Educational Context
2. Remix the Educational Content
3. Remember the Educational Content
4. Redistribute the Educational Content

Choose the most appropriate answer from the options given below.
(a) 1, 3 and 4 (b) 3, 4 and 1
(c) 1, 2 and 4 (d) 2, 3 and 4

45. Which of the following statements exemplify the characteristic features of Linear-Programmed style of Instructional Technology?
1. Small step presentation
2. Treatment of errors to promote understanding
3. Active responding
4. Demonstrate, prompt and release
5. Immediacy of feedback

Choose the most appropriate answer from the options given below.
(a) 1, 2 and 3 (b) 1, 2 and 5
(c) 1, 3 and 5 (d) 2, 4 and 5

46. The implications of constructivist theory for Instructional design is reflected through which of the statements given below?
1. Instructional design should be specific and learning outcome related.
2. Instructional design should promote participatory approaches leading to creation of meaning giving processes.
3. Instructional designs should be specific so that learning outcomes are measured accurately.
4. Instructional designs should provide scope for challening learning contexts and proactive moves.
5. Instructional designs promote cognitive rather than meta-cognitive process.

Choose the most appropriate answer from the options given below.
(a) 1 and 2 (b) 2 and 4
(c) 3 and 4 (d) 4 and 1

47. Which of the following are the types of Mobile Application?
1. Native 2. Mobile Web
3. Hybrid 4. Immigrants

Choose the most appropriate answer from the options given below
(a) 1, 2 and 4 (b) 1, 2 and 3
(c) 1, 3 and 4 (d) 2, 3 and 4

48. Which of the following have been identified as performance indicators for assessment and accreditation of institution by NAAC?
1. Curricular aspects
2. Research, Innovations and Extension
3. Governance, Leadership and Management
4. Election of students union members and their interest
5. Institutional values and best practices

Choose the most appropriate answer from the options given below.
(a) 2, 3, 4 and 5 (b) 1, 2, 4 and 5
(c) 1, 3, 4 and 5 (d) 1, 2, 3 and 5

49. For describing teaching as a profession, which of the following statements are most appropriate?
1. Long or short duration of training has effect on making teaching skill repertoire representative.
2. A well defined performance standard facilitates professional acquisition.
3. Teaching means an activity aimed at influencing others.
4. An organised body of knowledge brings sophistication in a procession.
5. Teaching and learning are like selling-buying transactions.

Choose the most appropriate answer from the options given below.
(a) 1, 4 and 5 (b) 1, 2 and 3
(c) 4, 3 and 5 (d) 1, 2 and 4

50. Which of the following are presage related criteria for teacher evaluation?
1. Teacher's personality pattern and motivational disposition.
2. Teacher's method of providing feedback and follow up action during instruction.
3. Extent of learning and motivation ensured by the teacher while teaching.
4. Social competence and self-esteem of a teacher.
5. Mangement and mentoring technique employed by the teacher.

Choose the most appropriate answer from the options given below.
(a) Both 1 and 4 (b) Both 2 and 3
(c) Both 4 and 5 (d) Both 3 and 1

51. Which of the following programmes are related to quality improvement in in-service education?

1. Foundation course in teacher education
2. Skill development programmes
3. Courses on pedagogy in specific subejcts
4. Induction training
5. Micro simulation for competency development

Choose the most appropriate answer from the options given below.

(a) 1, 2 and 3 (b) 2, 3 and 4 (c) 2, 4 and 5 (d) 3, 4 and 5

52. Which of the following sampling methods are probability based?

1. Cluster sampling
2. Quota sampling
3. Systematic sampling
4. Dimensional sampling
5. Stratified sampling

Choose the most appropriate answer from the options given below.

(a) 2, 3 and 4 (b) 1, 3 and 5
(c) 1, 4 and 5 (d) 3, 4 and 5

53. Identify from the list of characteristics given below those which are related to a good hypothesis in a research?

1. Simplicity of explanation
2. Plausibility of explanation
3. Highly difficult to verify the postulated relations
4. Not related to an existing theory
5. Relationship formulated among variables having conceptual clarity

Choose the most appropriate answer from the option given below.

(a) 1, 2 and 3 (b) 2, 3 and 4
(c) 3, 4 and 5 (d) 1, 2 and 5

54. Which of the following is the correct order of human needs as formulated in Maslow's hierarchy of needs?

1. Safety needs
2. Love and belonging needs
3. Physiological needs
4. Self-actualisation needs
5. Esteem needs

Choose the most appropriate answer from the options given below.

(a) 3, 1, 2, 5 and 4 (b) 1, 3, 2, 4, and 5
(c) 2, 1, 3, 4 and 5 (d) 3, 2, 1, 5 and 4

55. Which is the correct sequence of tasks involved in the development of curriculum?

1. Formulating goals and objectives
2. Assessing needs
3. Selecting appropriate instructional strategies
4. Selecting and organising content
5. Evaluating effectiveness of learning and instruction

Choose the most appropriate answer from the options given below.

(a) 1, 2, 4, 3 and 5 (b) 2, 1, 4, 3 and 5
(c) 2, 1, 3, 4 and 5 (d) 1, 3, 2, 4 and 5

56. In the statements given below, identify those which are related to competency-based curriculum design?

1. The abilities and learning styles of individuals get a support
2. Individuals memory based knowledge is stressed
3. Individuals are helped to achieve their potential
4. Domain specific proficiency of individuals is focused
5. Curriculum gets designed with an idealist perspective

Choose the most appropriate answer from the options given below.

(a) 1, 2 and 3 (b) 2, 4 and 5
(c) 1, 3 and 4 (d) 4, 5 and 1

57. For training in behaviour modification using Skinner's operant conditioning model in which of the following types of procedures, negative reinforcement is made contingent on making or with holding of a response in the presence or absence of cues?

1. Reward learning
2. Escape learning
3. Punishment learning
4. Active avoidance learning
5. Discriminated operant learning

Choose the most appropriate answer from the options given below.

(a) 1, 2 and 3 (b) 2, 4 and 5
(c) 3, 4 and 5 (d) 2, 3 and 4

58. Which of the following statements describe the major purposes of mental hygiene?

1. Prevention of mental disorders
2. Preservation of the mental health of the individual and the group
3. Satisfaction of security and esteem needs of a person
4. Discovery and utilisation to therapeutic measures to cure mental illness
5. Promoting between interpersonal relationship in a group

Choose the most appropriate answer from the options given below.

(a) 1, 2 and 3 (b) 1, 2 and 4
(c) 2, 3 and 4 (d) 3, 4 and 5

59. Which of the following shifts have been suggested by NCF-2005 for teachers?

1. Knowledge disbursed to knowledge owned
2. Disciplinary to multidisciplinary focus
3. Learners autonomy to teacher directions
4. Teacher centric to learner centric designs
5. From four walls of classrooms to surroundings and outside the classroom

Choose the most appropriate answer from the options given below.

(a) 1, 2 and 5
(b) 2, 4 and 5
(c) 2, 1 and 3
(d) 4, 5 and 1

60. The concepts of education which will be assented to by Vedant Philosophy are

1. Awakening of intelligence with all the three Q's – IQ, Eq, and SQ
2. Vocationalisation of education
3. Inclusive education
4. Reptilian leadership model
5. Education for all

Choose the most appropriate answer from the options given below.

(a) 1, 2 and 3
(b) 2, 3 and 4
(c) 3, 4 and 5
(d) 1, 3 and 5

61. Savitribai Phule is known for her contribution in which of the following listed areas?

1. Peace education
2. Art education
3. Education of the scheduled castes
4. Women education
5. Child care education

Choose the most appropriate answer from the options given below.

(a) Both 1 and 4
(b) Both 2 and 3
(c) Both 1 and 3
(d) Both 3 and 4

62. Identify from the following list those factors that help in social mobility?

1. Education
2. Caste
3. Income
4. Occupation
5. Religion

Choose the most appropriate answer from the options given below.

(a) 1, 2 and 5
(b) 3, 4 and 5
(c) 1, 3 and 5
(d) 1, 3 and 4

63. Match the disability in List I with its description in List II.

List I (Disabilities)	List II (Descriptions)
A. Dyspraxia	1. Difficulty in paying attention and action without knowing consequences
B. Dyslexia	2. Difficulty in development of literacy and language related skills
C. ADHD	3. Difficulty in writing associated with usage of wrong word during communication
D. Dysgraphia	4. Difficulty in motor coordination resulting in poor or out of order movements

Choose the correct answer from the options given below.

	A	B	C	D
(a)	1	3	4	2
(b)	3	1	2	4
(c)	4	1	2	3
(d)	4	2	1	3

64. List I embodies situational leadership style and List II indicates the power resource which supports them.

List I (Situational leadership styles)	List II (Power resources)
A. Directive style (HT/LR)	1. Expert power
B. Supportive style (HT/HR)	2. Information power
C. Participative style (LT/HR)	3. Reward power
D. Delegating style (LT/LR)	4. Coercive power

Choose the correct answer from the options given below.

	A	B	C	D
(a)	1	2	4	3
(b)	3	4	1	2
(c)	4	3	2	1
(d)	2	1	4	3

65. List I presents names of organisations and List II is about their functions.

List I (Organizations)	List II (Functions)
A. UGC	1. To formulate new policy and programmes of education
B. NAAC	2. To maintain and regulate standards of higher education
C. CABE	3. To regulate standards of the institutions of teacher education
D. NCTE	4. To give accreditation to institutions of higher learning

Choose the correct answer from the options given below.

	A	B	C	D
(a)	4	2	3	1
(b)	3	1	4	2
(c)	2	4	1	3
(d)	2	3	1	4

66. List I gives levels of teaching and List II provides teacher learner activities.

List I (Levels of Teaching)		**List II** (Activities)
A. Autonomous Development Level	1.	Problem raising and problem solving by teachers and students in a participatory mode
B. Memory Level	2.	Feeling of autonomy with little or no scope for teacher intervention-a kind of negative education
C. Understanding Level	3.	Emphasis on positive and negative examples with a view to promote concept attainment
D. Reflective Level	4.	Clear and systematic presentation of facts and their description with an eye on correct retention

Choose the correct answer from the options given below

	A	B	C	D		A	B	C	D
(a)	3	1	4	2	(b)	4	3	2	1
(c)	1	2	3	4	(d)	2	4	3	1

67. Match the models of teacher education in List I with the description in List II.

List I (Models of teacher education)		**List II** (Descriptions)
A. Compentency based	1.	Participants explore academic content by posing and investigating question.
B. Behaviouristic	2.	Knowledge and skills are developed by observation.
C. Inquiry oriented	3.	Principle of operant conditioning used for teacher training.
	4.	Participants become proficient through demonstrating mastery.

Choose the correct answer from the options given below.

	A	B	C		A	B	C
(a)	4	3	1	(b)	3	1	4
(c)	3	2	1	(d)	1	3	2

68. Match the types of research in List I with the features in List II.

List I (Types of research)		**List II** (Features)
A. Exploratory	1.	Quantitative and qualitative data are gathered. and integrated
B. Cross-sectional	2.	Qualitative data is gathered first and the same predominates later.
C. Explanatory	3.	Retrospective analysis of history of a unit.
D Triangulation	4.	Quantitative data is gathered first and the same predominates later.
E Longitudinal	5.	Macro level analysis attempted for the data

Choose the correct answer from the options given below.

	A	B	C	D	E
(a)	5	3	1	2	4
(b)	2	5	4	1	3
(c)	4	3	1	2	5
(d)	1	2	3	4	5

69. List I consists of kinds of curriculum change according to complexity and List II comprises examples of such curriculum change.

List I (Types of Curriculum Change)		**List II** (Examples)
A. Substitution	1.	Emphasis on personal growth of students than academic growth
B. Alteration	2.	Change in time allowed for teaching a particular subject
C. Perturbation	3.	New text book replaces the old text book
D. Value orientation	4.	Introduction of new content into existing learning materials

Choose the correct answer from the options given below.

	A	B	C	D
(a)	4	2	1	3
(b)	1	3	4	2
(c)	3	4	2	1
(d)	2	1	3	4

70. List I consists of types of evaluation in CIPP model and List II comprises the objectives to be achieved through these evaluation.

List I (Types of Evaluation)		**List II** (Objectives)
A. Context evaluation	1.	To identify defects in the procedural design or its implementation plan
B. Input evaluation	2.	To communicate information regarding objectives achieved and contents covered
C Process evaluation	3.	To determine the needs and opportunities present and diagnose the problem
D Product evaluation	4.	To identify and assess the school system capacities

Choose the correct answer from the options given below.

	A	B	C	D
(a)	2	3	4	1
(b)	3	4	1	2
(c)	4	1	2	3
(d)	1	2	3	4

71. List I gives the names of intelligence theories and List II indicates the proponents of theories.

	List I (Intelligence Theories)		List II (Promoters)
A.	Multiple Factor theory	1.	Daniel Golemen
B.	Structure of Intellect Model	2.	Howard Gardner
C.	Multiple Intelligence	3.	L.L. Thurstone
D.	Emotional Intelligence Theory	4.	J.P. Guilford

Choose the correct answer from the options given below.

	A	B	C	D		A	B	C	D
(a)	3	4	2	1	(b)	1	2	3	4
(c)	4	3	1	2	(d)	2	1	4	3

72. List I includes the name of Indian thinkers and List II mention books authored by them.

	List I (Indian thinkers)		List II (Name of Books)
A.	Mahatma Gandhi	1.	A life Devine
B.	Rabindranath Tagore	2.	Bartaman Bharat
C.	Sri Aurobindo	3.	The Home and the World
D.	Swami Vivekananda	4.	My Experiment with Truth

Choose the correct answer from the options given below.

	A	B	C	D		A	B	C	D
(a)	3	4	1	2	(b)	2	4	1	3
(c)	1	3	4	2	(d)	4	3	1	2

73. List II gives twenty five metaphysical categories of Sankhya and List II provides their types.

	List I (Types)		List II (Metaphysical categories)
A.	Cause only	1.	Purusa
B.	Effect only	2.	Mahat, Ahankara and five subtle essences
C.	Both cause and effect	3.	Five sensory organs, Five motor organs, Manas and five gross bodies
D.	Neither cause nor effect	4.	Prakriti

Choose the correct answer from the options given below.

	A	B	C	D		A	B	C	D
(a)	4	3	2	1	(b)	2	1	4	3
(c)	3	4	1	2	(d)	1	2	3	4

74. Which of the following are included under ICF model of classification and disabilities?

1. Body function and structures
2. Participation or involvement in all areas of life
3. Environmental factors
4. Policies framed for the disabled
5. Funding from the government

Choose the correct answer from the options given below.

(a) 2, 3, 4 (b) 1, 2, 3 (c) 3, 4, 5 (d) 1, 3, 5

75. Identify the statements which indicate the needed actions for a change process of an organisation.

1. The organisation must go through an "Unfreezing"
2. Anxiety one – fear of change should be decreased
3. Anxiety two – fear of not changing must be increased
4. Adoption of any innovative procedure leading to trial
5. Discussion based on the analysis of forces – restraing and driving

Choose the correct answer from the options given below.

(a) 1, 3 and 4 (b) 2, 4 and 5
(c) 3, 4 and 5 (d) 1, 2 and 3

76. Which of the following are proposed by Edward Deming for quality assurance.

1. Adopt new philosophy
2. Cease dependence on inspection
3. Coerce for poor performance
4. Institute training on the job
5. Drive out fear

Choose the correct answer from the options given below.

(a) 1, 2, 3 and 4
(b) 2, 3, 4 and 5
(c) 1, 2, 4 and 5
(d) 1, 3, 4 and 5

77. Identify the sequence in generating a grounded theory.

1. Coding and memoing
2. Deciding about the needed sampling design and data collection
3. Identification of the core variable leading to its saturation
4. Categorisation and comparison
5. Theory verification and generalisation emerging

Choose the correct answer from the options given below.

(a) 1, 2, 4, 3 and 5 (b) 3, 1, 4, 2 and 5
(c) 4, 1, 3, 2 and 5 (d) 2, 1, 4, 3 and 5

78. Human capital theory gives emphasis on

1. Security of staff
2. Staff motivation
3. Investment on education
4. Inservice education of the staff
5. Staff recruitment

Choose the correct answer from the options given below.

(a) 1, 2 and 5 (b) 2, 3 and 5
(c) 2, 3 and 4 (d) 3, 4 and 5

79. While preparing a budget, which of the following points are considered to be mandatory?

1. Revenue
2. Objectives of the institution
3. Expenditure
4. Community involvement
5. Teacher's salary

Choose the correct answer from the options given below.

(a) 1, 3 and 4 (b) 1, 2 and 3 (c) 2, 3 and 5 (d) 3, 4 and 5

80. Which of the following features explain the concept of dependent origination in Buddhist Philosophy?

1. Everything in this world is conditional and relative.
2. From the ultimate stand point, there is no difference between "Sanasara and Nirvana".
3. All appearances have real orgination.
4. Appearances are not devoid of ultimate reality.
5. All appearances (dharmas) being relative have no real origination.

Choose the correct answer from the options given below.

(a) 1, 2 and 3 (b) 2, 3 and 4 (c) 1, 2 and 5 (d) 3, 4 and 5

81. Given below are two statements, one is labelled as Assertion (A) and the other is labelled as Reason (R).

Assertion (A) Information systems support promotion of research, development and innovation related growth of a country.

Reason (R) Information is the basic input to the development.

In the light of the above statements, choose the most appropriate answer from the options given below.

(a) Both A and R are true and R is the correct explanation of A
(b) Both A and R are true, but R is not the correct explanation of A
(c) A is true, but R is false
(d) A is false, but R is true

82. Given below are two statements, one is labelled as Assertion (A) and the other is labelled as Reason (R).

Assertion (A) Planning for instructions refers to the decisions made about organising, implementing and evaluating instruction.

Reason (R) Planning gives a sense of direction and through this a feel of confidence to the teacher. It helps the teacher to become a reflective decision maker about instruction.

In the light of the above statements, choose the most appropriate answer from the options given below.

(a) Both A and R are true and R is the correct explanation of A
(b) Both A and R are true, but R is not the correct explanation of A
(c) A is true, but R is false
(d) A is false, but R is true

83. Given below are two statements, one is labelled as Assertion (A) and the other is labelled as Reason (R).

Assertion (A) Tests with larger number of items have hither reliability.

Reason (R) Each test item adds to test reliability.

In the light of the above statements, choose the most appropriate answer from the options given below

(a) Both A and R are true and R is the correct explanation of A
(b) Both A and R are true, but R is not the correct explanation of A
(c) A is true, but R is false
(d) A is false, but R is true

84. Given below are two statements, one is labelled as Assertion (A) and the other is labelled as Reason (R).

Assertion (A) Concurrent validity coefficients are generally higher than predictive validity coefficient.

Reason (R) This does not mean that the test with higher validity coefficient is more suitable for a given purpose.

In the light of the above statements, choose the most appropriate answer from the options given below.

(a) Both A and R are true and R is the correct explanation of A
(b) Both A and R are true, but R is not the correct explanation of A
(c) A is true, but R is false
(d) A is false, but R is true

85. Given below are two statements, one is labelled as Assertion (A) and the other is labelled as Reason (R).

Assertion (A) The quality of reflection is determined by the ability to match teaching behaviour to the established codes.

Reason (R) In technical approach to reflection propositional knowledge is reflected upon and then applied to practice.

In the light of the above statements, choose the most appropriate answer from the options given below.

(a) Both A and R are true and R is the correct explanation of A
(b) Both A and R are true, but R is not the correct explanation of A
(c) A is true, but R is false
(d) A is false, but R is true

86. Given below are two statements.

Statement I Scientific management theory of F W Taylor gives a mechanical explanation of work and workers.

Statement II Human relations, leisure and emotion are given prime importance by F.W. Taylor to enhance productivity of an organisation.

In the light of the above statements, choose the most appropriate answer from the options given below.

(a) Both Statement I and Statement II are correct.
(b) Both Statement I and Statement II are incorrect.
(c) Statement I is correct, but Statement II is incorrect.
(d) Statement I is incorrect but Statement II is correct.

87. Given below are two statements.

Statement I To improve preservice teacher education programme, the aspirants for teaching profession be screened for their aptitude in teaching.

Statement II Faculty improvement programme for teachers should be regularised to improve preservice teacher education.

In the light of the above statements, choose the most appropriate answer from the options given below.

(a) Both Statement I and Statement II are true.
(b) Both Statement I and Statement II are false.
(c) Statement I is true, but Statement II is false
(d) Statement I is false, but Statement II is true.

88. Given below are two statements.

Statement I As the alpha level becomes more stringent – goes from 0.05 to 0.01 the power of a statistical test decreases.

Statement II A directional hypothesis leads to more power than a non – directional hypothesis.

In the light of the above statements, choose the most appropriate answer from the options given below.

(a) Both Statement I and Statement II are true.
(b) Both Statement I and Statement II are false.
(c) Statement I is true, but Statement II is false.
(d) Statement I is false, but Statement II is true.

89. Given below are two statements.

Statement I In Freud's postulation

Id is the original system of personality and is the reservoir of psychic energy. It uses the mechanism of pleasure principle and is a tension reduction mechanism.

Statement II All decence mechanism have two qualities. They deny, distort or falsify reality and they operate unconsciously.

In the light of the above statements, choose the most appropriate answer from the options given below.

(a) Both Statement I and Statement II are true.
(b) Both Statement I and Statement II are false.
(c) Statement I is true, but Statement II is false.
(d) Statement I is false, but Statement II is true.

90. Given below are two statements.

Statement I In addition to the fact that growth is continuous, it can be relatively rapid in certain stages of development.

Statement II The process of development follows a pattern in terms of physical development –Cephalo – Caudal sequence while in the case of mental development, it shows an increase in the capacity of concrete level thinking to abstract thinking.

In the light of the above statements, choose the most appropriate answer from the options given below

(a) Both Statement I and Statement II are true.
(b) Both Statement I and Statement II are false.
(c) Statement I is true, but Statement II is false.
(d) Statement I is false, but Statement II is true.

Directions *(Q. Nos. 91-95) Read the following paragraph and answer the five questions which as follows.*

Communication is much more difficult when there is a difference of opinion between employee and supervisor, or between any colleague at work, than when they agree. Laura Carrol has outlined a series of steps for employees to use when they wish to communicate a problem to an employer or coworker or to get a negative situation resolved.

The central idea is the idea of creating a thought process that fosters an understanding of what the problem is and how it can best be resolved. She suggests that the employee see the problem from the other person's point of view and make certain that the "facts" of the situation are true from both view points.

If this can be done, then there exists a level non judgemental playing field from which solution can arise without hurt feelings and misgivings. This is what the communication process is all about : respect for yourself, your ideas and those of the other person. Under the stress of differences, however it is all too easy for empathy to disappear and judgement to take the centre state. Any difficult conversation is really three conversations in one all operating at the same time.

The first is the "What happened?" conversation in which you describe "My story" and the other person defends theirs, instead of exploring each other's stories and acknowledging what each party contributed to the issue. Second is the "feelings" conversation–which is often regarded as unprofessional and may be discouraged in the work place.

However, emotions are always present they are normal and they are data that can more fully inform the nature of the conflict. Finally there is the "identity" conversation in which there involved may feel that some of their identity is threatened. Leaders with social competence can navigate these three conversations and transform them into one learning conversation at a time.

91. Communication becomes difficult in which of the following situations?

1. Difference of opinion between employee and employer.
2. Difference in the nature of work allotted and done.
3. Difference of opinion between employees at work.
4. Difference of treatment given to employees.
5. Difference of language spoken by employees.

Choose the most appropriate answer from the options given below.

(a) 1, 2, 4 only
(b) 1, 2, 3 only
(c) 1, 3, 5 only
(d) 1, 3, 4 only

92. Which of the following steps are needed to communicate in a negative situation?

1. Create a thought process to foster understanding.
2. Enable people to see the problem from other's perspective.
3. Speak loudly and clearly.
4. Create a non-judgemental playing field for both parties.
5. Understand the language of the receiver.

Choose the most appropriate answer from the options given below.

(a) 1, 3, 5 only (b) 1, 4, 5 only
(c) 1, 2, 3 only (d) 1, 2, 4 only

93. Which of the following statements describe the meaning of communication?

(a) Respect for culture community and nation.
(b) Respect for self, one's ideas and other's ideas.
(c) Respect for family self and other ideas.
(d) Communication is a two way process.

94. Under which of the following circumstances empathy is replaced by judgement?

(a) In case of same opinion between sender and receiver.
(b) In case of large number of people to be communicated.
(c) In case of in-formal communication.
(d) In case of difference of opinion between sender and receiver.

95. Which competency is needed in a leader to navigate a difficult conversational situation to a meaningful learning conversation?

(a) Social intelligence
(b) Emotional intelligence
(c) Multiple language
(d) Manipulative skills

Directions *(Q. Nos. 96-100) Read the following paragraph and answer the five questions which as follows.*

Organisational change is a complex and continuous process, having several sequential aspects. In the process of planned change, several actors are involved – the corporate management the external consultant(s), the counterpart, implementation team the, chief implementer and the task forces.

Every actor performs specific functions.The investment of time and energy in the process work in the beginning helps to smoothen progress on task achievement later. The implementation of change is itself a complex process and requires a great deal of attention. Planning is followed by action leading to the institutionalisation and stabilisation of change. The monitoring of progress is necessary and forms a small feedback loop in correcting action.

There is always resistance to any change being introduced. Sometimes resistance plays a positive role in warning the organisation of possible consequences. Generally, resistance is caused by various kinds of fear and lack of attention to the actual process. Effective strategies for coping with resistance can be achieved by understanding and dealing with the sources of resistance.

96. In the process of planned change who plays in important role?

1. Corporate Management
2. Consumers
3. External consultant
4. Implementation team
5. Chief implementer

Choose the correct answer from the options given below

(a) 2, 3, 4 and 5
(b) 1, 2, 4 and 5
(c) 1, 3, 4 and 5
(d) 1, 2, 3 and 4

97. **Change can be stabilised in an organisation by**

(a) Systematic planning and implementation
(b) Providing regular feedback
(c) Closely monitoring the change process
(d) Providing financial support to implement change

98. **For an organisational change to be successful what is essential?**

(a) Motivation of employee
(b) Decentralisation of power
(c) Monitoring of progress made
(d) Support of the society

99. **Organisational change is resisted because of**

(a) fear of different kinds and uncertainty
(b) no financial benefit to employees
(c) social pressure
(d) change in international scenario

100. **How can an organisation cope with resistance to change?**

(a) Adhere to strict rules of the organisation
(b) Motivate employees to work
(c) Convey to the employees that it is needed for organisational development.
(d) Work – strategy after understanding the source of resistance.

ANSWERS

1	*(b)*	2	*(c)*	3	*(b)*	4	*(d)*	5	*(c)*	6	*(c)*	7	*(d)*	8	*(c)*	9	*(b)*	10	*(b)*
11	*(d)*	12	*(c)*	13	*(b)*	14	*(d)*	15	*(c)*	16	*(c)*	17	*(c)*	18	*(d)*	19	*(a)*	20	*(a)*
21	*(c)*	22	*(a)*	23	*(c)*	24	*(a)*	25	*(d)*	26	*(d)*	27	*(d)*	28	*(c)*	29	*(c)*	30	*(b)*
31	*(b)*	32	*(c)*	33	*(c)*	34	*(b)*	35	*(b)*	36	*(d)*	37	*(d)*	38	*(a)*	39	*(c)*	40	*(a)*
41	*(d)*	42	*(d)*	43	*(c)*	44	*(c)*	45	*(c)*	46	*(b)*	47	*(b)*	48	*(d)*	49	*(d)*	50	*(a)*
51	*(c)*	52	*(b)*	53	*(d)*	54	*(a)*	55	*(b)*	56	*(c)*	57	*(d)*	58	*(b)*	59	*(b)*	60	*(d)*
61	*(d)*	62	*(d)*	63	*(d)*	64	*(c)*	65	*(c)*	66	*(d)*	67	*(a)*	68	*(b)*	69	*(c)*	70	*(b)*
71	*(a)*	72	*(d)*	73	*(a)*	74	*(b)*	75	*(d)*	76	*(c)*	77	*(d)*	78	*(c)*	79	*(b)*	80	*(c)*
81	*(a)*	82	*(a)*	83	*(c)*	84	*(a)*	85	*(b)*	86	*(c)*	87	*(c)*	88	*(a)*	89	*(a)*	90	*(a)*
91	*(b)*	92	*(d)*	93	*(b)*	94	*(d)*	95	*(a)*	96	*(c)*	97	*(a)*	98	*(c)*	99	*(a)*	100	*(d)*

UGC NET/JRF/SET

Education (Paper-2)
Solved Paper, December 2019

General Instructions

1. There are total one hundred questions in this paper. Each question carries 2 marks.
2. All questions are compulsory.

---

1. In the eight fold noble paths given by Buddha, which of the following is the basis of 'Right Knowledge'?

(a) Right Speech and Right Action
(b) Right Action and Right Living
(c) Right Thought and Right Concentration
(d) Right Faith and Right Resolve

2. 'Rapport Building' will be emphasised in which of the counselling paradigm?

(a) Person-centred counselling
(b) Directive counselling
(c) Behaviouristic counselling approach
(d) Rational counselling

3. Preamble to the Constitution of India mentions different types of liberty for the people of India. Which types of liberty, out of these, have a direct bearing on the practitioners in the field of education?

(a) Liberty of belief and faith
(b) Liberty of thought and expression
(c) Liberty of faith and worship
(d) Liberty of expression and belief

4. According to Jain philosophy, when by the possession and practice of right faith, knowledge and conduct, the influx of fresh Karmic matter is blocked, this state is called

(a) Flow (Ashrava)
(b) Bondage (Bandha)
(c) Stoppage (Sanvar)
(d) Wearing out (Nirjara)

5. Nearest 'Kosha' to Atman according to Vedanta philosophy is called

(a) Pranmaya Kosha
(b) Manomaya Kosha
(c) Vigyanmaya Kosha
(d) Anandmaya Kosha

6. Islamic tradition in education lays stress on inculcation of which of the values?

(a) Humility and nobility
(b) Equality and equity
(c) Freedom and discipline
(d) Quality and excellence

7. According to Sternberg, which one of the following is the most important goal in learning intelligent behaviour?

(a) Presenting and structuring of thoughts and ideas.
(b) Probing and eliciting ideas.
(c) Confronting novel tasks and situations of learning to deal with them.
(d) Analysing the issues involved in a situation.

8. In the six basic types of learning as given by Tolman in his later theoretical articles, which one is similar to Skinner's conditioned reinforcers?

(a) Formation of Cathexis
(b) 'Equivalence beliefs' learning
(c) Field expectancies
(d) Drive discrimination learning

9. Which of the following subordinate laws in Thorndike's Theory of Learning is equivalent to Watson of Pavlov's Classical Conditioning Theory?

(a) Multiple response
(b) Set or attitude
(c) Prepotency of elements
(d) Associative shifting

10. A student of class X approaches the class teacher and informs him/her that the schedule of examination, when announced, makes him/her uneasy. What type of guidance does this situation warrant?
(a) Educational guidance (b) Vocational guidance
(c) Personal guidance (d) Health guidance

11. Which of the following commissions/committees was required exclusively to address Teacher Education in India?
(a) Yashpal Committee
(b) Justice Verma Commission
(c) Chattopadhyaya Commission-I
(d) Kothari Commission

12. The 'Internship programme' in teacher education has been provided to help
(a) the teachers in school.
(b) the student teachers in the training programme.
(c) the teacher educators in the training institutions.
(d) the principals of the school where internship is conducted.

13. Which of the following assessment area of learning outcomes will belong to the category of lower level?
(a) Ability of analyse the facts and information.
(b) Ability to create and synthesise various facts together.
(c) Mastery of facts and information as shown in reproducing them when asked for.
(d) Ability to use standards and arriving at decisions.

14. At the district level, which of the following institution has been entrusted with the responsibility of in-services teacher-education for primary and elementary schools?
(a) CTEs (b) IASEs
(c) SCERTs (d) DIETs

15. RUSA aims at
(a) providing strategic funding to eligible state higher educational institutions.
(b) faculty development programmes.
(c) funding the central universities for innovative research project.
(d) preparing a blue print for higher education system.

16. Broad functions of the SCERT are
(a) design and development of integrated teacher education courses of four year duration.
(b) preparation of a code of professional ethics for teachers.
(c) accreditation of teacher education institutions and their monitoring.
(d) development of curriculum, textbooks, training, research and innovation.

17. Which branch of philosophy has a direct relevance for deciding transactional strategies of curriculum?
(a) Metaphysics (b) Ontology
(c) Epistemology (d) Axiology

18. In developing 'learning-outcome based curriculum', the formulation of objectives in behavioural terms poses challenge for which of the learning types given below?
(a) Learning of facts and information
(b) Learning of concepts and principles
(c) Learning of application and use
(d) Learning of critical and creative thinking

19. In a research study, the variable which is not directly observable but whose effect is inferred on the dependent variable is termed as
(a) Extraneous variable (b) Moderate variable
(c) Intervening variable (d) Treatment variable

20. The combination of different approaches to validate information, strategies and results in a research study is technically known as
(a) Meta analysis (b) Triangulation
(c) Trend analysis (d) Cross validation

21. An investigator commits type II error when he/she
(a) rejects a null hypothesis when it is true.
(b) accepts a null hypothesis when it is true.
(c) rejects a null hypothesis when it is false.
(d) accepts a null hypothesis when it is false.

22. Which of the following research designs utilises data from individuals, autobiographies and personal talks/discussions?
(a) Grounded theory design (b) Narrative research design
(c) Case study design (d) Ethnographic design

23. In which of the following, the main purpose of research is to formulate generalisations leading to theory building?
(a) Phenomenology with subjective frame of reality.
(b) Participant observation with focus on perspective.
(c) Symbolic interaction with emphasis on social interaction.
(d) Experimentation with controls and manipulation of variables.

24. Which of the following research designs is the most appropriate for depicting lived experiential realities?
(a) Phenomenological designs
(b) Case study designs
(c) Grounded theory designs
(d) Narrative research designs

25. Investigator wants to study the functioning of a school meant for tribal children. The most appropriate research design for this context would be classified as
(a) Narrative Research (b) Phenomenology
(c) Grounded Theory (d) Ethnography

26. An investigator wants to conduct a study on politically active student-leaders in educational institutions. Which of the following methods of sampling would be most appropriate?
(a) Simple random sampling (b) Quota sampling
(c) Purposive sampling (d) Snow-ball sampling

27. A weighing machine mostly over measures the weight of individuals. It will be said to be indicative of

(a) Random error (b) Systematic error
(c) Standard error (d) Probable error

28. Which of the following are the assumptions underlying the use of parametric statistics?

1. The variable being studied is continuous.
2. Measurements are based on nominal/ordinal scale.
3. Scores are normally distributed.
4. Variances over all groups are equal.

Select the answer from the options given below.

(a) 2, 3 and 4 (b) 1, 3 and 4
(c) 1, 2 and 4 (d) 1, 2 and 3

29. A standard of performance for a defined domain is termed as

(a) Portfolio (b) Blue Print
(c) Rubrics (d) Achievement

30. On the basis of Flanders' Interaction Analysis Categories (FIAC) in a 10×10 observation matrix, the cells which indicate a sustained level of verbal interchange are known as

(a) Content Cross Ratio (CCR)
(b) Teacher Talk Ratio (TTR)
(c) Pupil Talk Ratio (PTR)
(d) Steady State Ratio (SSR)

31. A teacher intends to conduct remedial classes for some students who are not responding satisfactorily. Which type of evaluation she/he would undertake for choosing students for her/his remedial classes?

(a) Summative Evaluation
(b) Diagnostic Evaluation
(c) Assessment of Portfolios
(d) Competency Based Evaluation

32. In Portfolio assessment, which of the following should be given priority?

(a) The specific nature of activities to be performed.
(b) The norms following which the activities have to be regulated.
(c) The duration of time allowed for completion of portfolio.
(d) The rubrics in terms of which Portfolio will be judged.

33. A teacher educator offers immediate comments in the following form for classroom behaviour as being practiced by the student teacher
"No, you should do it rather this way"
This is an example of

(a) Negative feedback
(b) Corrective feedback
(c) Positive feedback
(d) Evaluative feedback

34. For classroom discussion sessions which of the following is the most appropriate in encouraging reflection amongst learners?

(a) Individual and Group Interaction Sessions
(b) Think, Pair and Share Sessions
(c) Question and Answer Sessions
(d) Individual-Work Assignment Based Sessions

35. In the instructional design based on Skinner's Theory of Reinforcement, which of the following set of activities are appropriate?

(a) Step by step presentation of learning material, student response and immediacy of feedback
(b) Planning, acting and observing
(c) Instructional objectives, planning of teaching-learning systems and evaluation
(d) Asking question, guiding and evaluating

36. Combination of both face to face and traditional classroom methods with e-learning is used to create a hybrid approach to teaching which is called as

(a) Distance learning
(b) Blended learning
(c) Synchronous learning
(d) Asynchronous learning

37. What describes a virtual classroom?

(a) Learners using technology in a classroom environment led by a tutor.
(b) A training course done using you-tube tutorials.
(c) On-line learning environment accessed through the Webinars.
(d) On-line live learning course.

38. Use of Educational Technology in open and distance learning is helpful in

1. promoting learner interest.
2. ensuring cost effectiveness of the system.
3. facilitating learners to benefit from varied learning resources.
4. determining learner status in teaching-learning processes.
5. making learners active participants in teaching learning processes.

Select the answer from the options given below.

(a) 2, 3, 4 and 5
(b) 1, 3, 4 and 5
(c) 1, 2, 3 and 5
(d) 1, 2, 4 and 5

39. Which of the following has the high potential for empirical validation in using Educational Technology?

(a) Text book
(b) Printed lectures of distance education
(c) Modular reading materials
(d) Programmed instructional material

40. Which of the following statements explains the management principle "Span of control" propounded by Fayol?

(a) One can work effectively for limited hours.
(b) One can work with limited number of people.
(c) One can make 4-6 people work effectively under him/her.
(d) Only 4-6 people can make an effective group.

41. Which of the following averments constitute 'Critical Pedagogy' of Paulo Freire?

1. Teaching is inherently political.
2. Teaching implies absence of neutrality of knowledge.
3. Teaching is pro-establishment.
4. Issues of social justice and democracy are integral part of teaching.
5. Teaching is away from social reality.

Choose your answer from the options below.

(a) 1, 2 and 3 (b) 2, 3 and 4
(c) 1, 2 and 4 (d) 3, 4 and 5

42. Strengths of "Behaviourism" as learning theory are

1. It provides clear predictions.
2. It has real life application.
3. It is too deterministic.
4. It has reductionist approach.
5. It emphasises objective measurement.

Choose the answer from the following options.

(a) 1, 2 and 3 (b) 2, 3 and 4
(c) 1, 2 and 5 (d) 3, 4 and 5

43. Disadvantages of Bottom up approach of Budgeting are that the budget

1. may not be synchronous with the overall objectives of the organisation.
2. will be more realistic.
3. can be quite accurate.
4. preparation may be slow.

Select the answer from the options given below.

(a) 1 and 2 (b) 3 and 4
(c) 1 and 4 (d) 2 and 3

44. What are the reasons of negligible number of studies of Cost-Effectiveness Analysis (CEA) of projects in the field of Education?

1. Evaluator's inadequate background in CEA
2. Lack of requisite exposure in CEA
3. Lack of familiarity of the decision-makers with CEA
4. Less weightage assigned to educational concepts in CEA

Select your answer from the options given below.

(a) 1, 2 and 3 (b) 2, 3 and 4
(c) 3, 4 and 5 (d) 1, 3 and 4

45. The basic competencies needed for an effective teacher education programme have to be related to which of the following personality and attitude related domains?

1. Locus of control
2. Communication
3. Managing
4. Monitoring
5. Self-efficacy
6. Positive expectancy

Select the answer from the options given below.

(a) 1, 2 and 3 (b) 2, 3 and 4
(c) 4, 5 and 6 (d) 1, 5 and 6

46. Which of the following action words, when emphasised in Teacher Education will form a part of reflective teaching styles?

1. Plan, act and improve
2. Design, deliver and evaluate
3. Engage, explore and evaluate
4. Explain, clarify and elaborate
5. Praise, encourage and influences

Choose the correct option from the following lists.

(a) 1 and 2 (b) 3 and 4
(c) 4 and 5 (d) 2 and 3

47. Professionalisation of Teacher Education is needed to

1. enrich teacher's knowledge of subjects being taught.
2. sharpen teaching skills in the classroom.
3. generate and contribute new knowledge for the profession.
4. train the students to be tech-savy.
5. help teachers to open coaching centers.

Select the correct option from the following.

(a) 1, 2 and 3 (b) 2, 3 and 4
(c) 3, 4 and 5 (d) 4, 5 and 1

48. In planning In-service Teacher Education Programs in India, which of the following are most important?

1. Making in-service teaching-learning systems as an integral part of teacher preparation.
2. Focusing on human resource development.
3. Enhancing financial budget and infrastructure.
4. Increasing the duration of In-service Teacher Education Program.
5. Emphasis on building commitment and confidence level of teachers.

Choose the correct option from the following.

(a) 1, 2 and 3 (b) 2, 3 and 4
(c) 1, 2 and 5 (d) 3, 4, and 5

49. For addressing needs of learners through a curriculum design, which of the following bases have to be relied upon and given consideration?

1. Developmental stage of the learner
2. Socio-cultural background of the learner
3. Dominant caste structure from which learners hail
4. Mobility of the learner's family
5. Cognitive characteristics of the learner

Choose the answer from the options given below.

(a) 1, 2 and 5 (b) 2, 3 and 4
(c) 2, 3 and 5 (d) 3, 4 and 5

50. The Academic and Administrative Reforms Committee of U.G.C. has given recommendations in respect of curriculum development suggesting some needed steps.

Identify them from the following lists.

1. Development of model curriculum.
2. Updation/revision of curriculum to a limited extent every year and substantially every three years.
3. Updation of curriculum to be carried out in terms of current knowledge, national and international developments.
4. Fresh entrants to be given induction training.
5. Curricular transactions and synergies of all faculty members.

Choose the answer from the options given below.

(a) 1, 2 and 3 (b) 2, 3 and 5
(c) 2, 3 and 4 (d) 3, 4 and 5

51. Which of the following factors influence curriculum change?

1. Growth in knowledge
2. Technology change
3. Needs and aspirations of people
4. Job-placement
5. Availability of competent teachers

Choose the answer from the options given below.

(a) 1, 2 and 5 (b) 1, 2 and 3
(c) 1, 3 and 4 (d) 2, 3 and 5

52. Curriculum change envisages which of the following?

1. Change in aims and objectives
2. Change in contents
3. Change in infrastructure
4. Change in methods of teaching
5. Change in evaluation process

Choose the answer from the following.

(a) 1, 2, 3 and 4 (b) 1, 3, 4 and 5
(c) 2, 3, 4 and 5 (d) 1, 2, 4 and 5

53. Which of the following statements are true for a historical research design?

1. Mostly based on qualitative data.
2. Testing hypothesis is an integral part.
3. Findings can be generalised to other situations.
4. Data are examined for validity and authenticity.
5. Content-analysis is used for data treatment.

Choose the correct options.

(a) 1, 2 and 5 (b) 2, 3 and 5
(c) 1, 4 and 5 (d) 2, 3 and 4

54. Which of the following statement are true from reliability of a research tool?

1. Reliability is fixed for a given testing tool.
2. It is correlation of scores on the testing tool itself.
3. Reliability can have negative value.
4. It varies from sample to sample.
5. It is affected by variance of scores.

Choose the correct options.

(a) 1, 3 and 4 (b) 2, 4 and 5
(c) 1, 2 and 4 (d) 3, 4 and 5

55. In Flanders Interaction Analysis Categories (FIAC), which of the following are related to Indirect Teacher Talk (ITT)?

1. Lecturing
2. Giving directions
3. Acceptance of feelings
4. Criticising or justifying authority by the teacher
5. Praising or encouraging
6. Using student's ideas in his/her talk by the teacher

Select the correct answer from the following options.

(a) 1, 2 and 3 (b) 3, 5 and 6
(c) 4, 5 and 6 (d) 2, 3 and 4

56. Which of the following learning outcomes based behaviours belong to the category of being high in terms of taxonomic categories in cognitive domain?

1. Analysis 2. Application
3. Comprehension 4. Creation
5. Critical thinking
6. Knowledge

Select the correct answer from the following options.

(a) 1, 3 and 5 (b) 1, 4 and 5
(c) 2, 4 and 6 (d) 3, 4 and 5

57. In which of the following sets is stipulated the highest level category of taxonomies in cognitive, affective and psycho-motor domains respectively?
(a) Synthesis; Valuing; Articulation
(b) Analysis; Receiving; Manipulation
(c) Application; Organisation; Precision
(d) Evaluation; Characterisation; Naturalisation

58. Which of the following statements are indicative of formative assessment mode?
1. The teacher encourages students to answer.
2. The teacher asks questions to motivate students.
3. The teacher assesses the comprehension of students towards the end of the unit transaction.
4. The teacher judges the level of performance after the unit test.
5. The teacher provides prompts to help students to avoid incorrect responses.

Select the correct answer from the following options.
(a) 1, 2 and 3 (b) 1, 2 and 5
(c) 2, 3 and 4 (d) 3, 4 and 5

59. According to Robert M. Gagne, which learning types precede concept learning?
1. Rule learning 2. Sign learning
3. Problem solving learning
4. Verbal association learning
5. S-R learning

Choose the correct options.
(a) 1, 2 and 5 (b) 2, 3 and 5
(c) 2, 4 and 5 (d) 3, 4 and 5

60. The ethical and social issues of information systems are becoming more important these days because of the increased
1. use of the internet.
2. use of learning new technology.
3. monitoring of employees in the institutions.
4. cost of information systems.
5. use of interconnected information systems.

Select the correct answer from the options given below.
(a) 1 and 5 (b) 1 and 2 (c) 2 and 3 (d) 4 and 5

61. From the following list of statements, identify those which describe the characteristics of transactional leadership style?
1. Role and goal clarity
2. Raising commitment and motivational level
3. Emphasis on competency building
4. Monitoring people
5. Counselling people and inspiring

Choose the right answer from the following options.
(a) 1, 2 and 3 (b) 3, 4 and 5
(c) 1, 3 and 4 (d) 2, 4 and 5

62.* How would you as a teacher identify students with mild learning impairment in the class?
1. The learner keeps hand near his/her ear when you speak to him/her.
2. The learner leans towards you in an attempt to hear better.
3. The learner squeezes his/her eyes and looks at you.
4. The learner does not respond to your calling unless someone tells him/her.

Choose the correct answer from the following options given below.
(a) 1, 2 and 4 (b) 1, 2 and 3
(c) 2, 3 and 4 (d) 1, 3 and 4

63. Which of the following are barriers in the way of Education to be inclusive?
1. Parents do not send children with special needs to schools.
2. Non-availability of suitably trained teachers.
3. Children with special needs get legal protection.
4. Scarce financial provision from the government.

Select the correct answer from the options given below.
(a) 1, 2 and 4 (b) 1, 3 and 4
(c) 1, 2 and 3 (d) 2, 3 and 4

64. What are the measures suggested by United Nations Convention on the Rights of Persons with Disabilities (UNCRPD)?
1. Ensure full and equal enjoyment of human rights.
2. Ensure fundamental freedom to all persons with disabilities.
3. Ensure legal actions for parents not sending children to school.
4. Promote respect for inherent dignity of such children.

Choose correct answer from the following.
(a) 1, 3 and 4 (b) 1, 2 and 4
(c) 2, 3 and 4 (d) 1, 2 and 3

65. Which of the following are needed for inclusive education to be successful?
1. Availability of trained teachers in schools.
2. Availability of infrastructure in schools.
3. Asking parents of children with special needs to send their wards to special schools.
4. Appointment of trained Counsellors in schools.

Choose the correct answer from the options given below.
(a) 1, 2 and 3 (b) 2, 3 and 4
(c) 1, 2 and 4 (d) 1, 3 and 4

* Answer not given in official answer key.

66. In the two sets given below, Set I mentions some of the evolutes of Prakiti, while Set II indicates their nature and function in term of Sankhya Philosophy. Match the two sets.

Set I (Evolution of Prakiti)	Set II (Nature and Function)
A. Mahat, the great	1. Are neither the qualities nor the differentia of gross elements nor the functions.
B. Ego (Ahankar)	2. It is cosmic in nature and functions as a psychological aspect of knowing.
C. Mind (Manas)	3. It is the principle of individuation and its function is to generate self-sense.
D. Subtle essences (Tanmatras)	4. It is the subtle and central sense organ which synthesises sense data into determinate perception.

Select the correct answer from the following options.

	A	B	C	D
(a)	1	4	3	2
(b)	4	3	2	1
(c)	2	3	4	1
(d)	3	2	1	4

67. In the two sets given below, Set I mentions the Western schools of thought, while Set II offers their visualisation of teacher's role. Match the two sets.

Set I (Western School of Thought)	Set II (Teachers's Role Visualised)
A. Idealism	1. To assist each student personally in his/her journey towards self-realisation
B. Realism	2. To function as a consultant in problem situation
C. Pragmatism	3. To be a role model to be emulated
D. Existentialism	4. To impart knowledge

Choose the correct answer from the options given below.

	A	B	C	D
(a)	1	2	3	4
(b)	3	4	2	1
(c)	4	3	2	1
(d)	4	3	1	2

68. Under Set I are given the names of Indian thinkers and under Set II are their outstanding works. Match the two sets.

Set I (Thinkers)	Set II (Works)
A Swami Vivekananda	1. Gitanjali
B. Rabindranath Tagore	2. The First and Last Freedom
C. M K Gandhi	3. Modern India
D. J Krishnamurti	4. My Experiments with Truth

Choose your answer from the options given below.

	A	B	C	D
(a)	2	3	4	1
(b)	4	2	3	1
(c)	3	1	4	2
(d)	1	3	2	4

69. Given below are two sets. Set I mentions some terms from the Preamble to the Constitution of India and Set II gives their explanation. Match the item from Set I with explanation from Set II.

Set I (Terms)	Set II (Explanations)
A. Socialism	1. State has no religion, it is neither pro nor against any religion.
B. Secularism	2. A system in which government is elected and managed by the people of the country.
C. Democracy	3. Political idea that all people are equal and resources should be equally shared.
D. Republic	4. A nation state that has an elected government and elected leader.

Select the correct answer from the following options.

	A	B	C	D
(a)	3	1	2	4
(b)	4	2	3	1
(c)	2	3	4	1
(d)	1	4	2	3

70. Match the following two sets, in which Set I indicate the underlying purpose and Set II status the levels of teaching.

Set I (Underlying Purpose)	Set II (Levels of Teaching)
A. The main objective is to know the subject in depth and developing insight leading to clarity of structures.	1. Autonomous development level
B. The main emphasis is on orderly presentation of thoughts leading to their longer retention.	2. Memory level
C. The basic purpose is to engage students in clear, coherent and critical thinking leading to patterns of thought.	3. Understanding level
D. Purpose is to promote self-feelings leading to a sense of freedom.	4. Reflective level

Select the correct answer from the following options.

	A	B	C	D
(a)	1	3	2	4
(b)	2	4	1	3
(c)	4	1	3	2
(d)	3	2	4	1

71. Given below are two sets in which Set I gives the named theory of Intelligence and Set II indicates their main proponents and contentions associated with the theory. Match the two sets.

	Set I (Theory of Intelligence)		Set II (The main Proponents and Contentions)
A.	Multiple Factor Theory	1.	Sternberg, intelligence can be taught and the classroom is the logical place to teach it.
B.	Theory of Multiple Intelligence	2.	Cattell, intelligence is neither completely monarchic, nor oligarchic, nor anarchic.
C.	Theory of Fluid and Crystallised Intelligence	3.	Thurstone, intelligence is oligarchic in nature.
D.	Coping Theory of Intelligence	4.	Gardner, intelligence is a capacity with component processes and should not be confused with a learning or cognitive style.

Choose the correct answer from following.

	A	B	C	D
(a)	3	4	2	1
(b)	1	2	3	4
(c)	4	3	1	2
(d)	2	1	4	3

72. Given below are two sets in which Set I provides the dimensions of Emotional Intelligence (EI) and Set II offers their characteristics. Match the two sets.

	Set I (EI dimensions)		Set II (Characteristics)
A.	Self awareness	1.	Ability to guide others' emotions and the way they act
B.	Self management	2.	Being able to sense what others feel and want
C.	Self motivation	3.	Knowledge of true feeling at the moment
D.	Empathy	4.	Handling one's emotions to facilitate rather than hinder the tasks at hand
E.	Social skills	5	Staying in the course towards desired goal

Choose the correct answer from the following options.

	A	B	C	D	E
(a)	1	2	3	5	4
(b)	5	4	2	1	3
(c)	3	4	5	2	1
(d)	2	3	4	5	1

73. Given below are two sets in which Set I provides the five steps of Morrison's Teaching Model and Set II gives their description. Match the following sets.

	Set I (Steps of Morrison's Teaching Model)		Set II (Description of Steps)
A.	Exploration	1.	Asking students to present their acquired ideas without help of teacher
B.	Presentation	2.	Helping students to relate presented material to their internal self
C.	Assimilation	3.	Ascertaining the previous task-related behaviour of students
D.	Organisation	4.	Revisiting the material
E.	Recitation	5.	Describing the theme to be taken up for discussion

Select the correct option.

	A	B	C	D	E
(a)	2	3	4	5	1
(b)	4	3	5	1	2
(c)	3	5	2	1	4
(d)	1	5	4	2	3

74. Given below are two sets in which Set I gives the names of proponents of constructivist approach, while Set II offers the recommended procedures for knowledge construction.

	Set I (Proponents)		Set II (Knowledge Construction Procedure)
A.	Jean Piaget	1.	Activation, maintenance and direction based exploratory learning approach
B.	Gerome Bruner	2.	Advanced organiser, expository organiser and comparative organisers based learners approach
C.	David Ausubel	3.	Peer group based interactive and social learning approach
D.	Lev Vygotsky	4.	Assimilation, accommodation and adoption based cognitive approach

Select the correct option from the following.

	A	B	C	D
(a)	4	1	2	3
(b)	3	4	1	2
(c)	2	3	4	1
(d)	1	2	3	4

75. **In the following two sets, Set I indicates various components of teacher education programme and Set II gives the rationale for providing such components. Match the two sets.**

	Set I (Various components of Teacher Education)		**Set II** (Rationale for Providing such Components)
A.	Foundation courses	1.	For promoting application of knowledge and skills
B.	Elective courses	2.	For enabling the students to understand the basic principles underlying teaching-learning process
C.	Practical and Practicum courses	3.	For providing situations of applying pedagogical knowledge of skills
D.	Enhancing professional competencies courses	4.	For broad basing the competencies of teaching

Select the correct options from the following.

	A	B	C	D		A	B	C	D
(a)	2	1	3	4	(b)	1	2	4	3
(c)	4	3	2	1	(d)	3	4	1	2

76. **Which is the correct sequence in formulation of behavioural objectives?**
(a) Criteria of acceptability of behaviour, conditions in which behaviour will occur, the behaviour
(b) The behaviour, the criteria of acceptability, the conditions in which behaviour will occur
(c) The condition of behaviour, behaviour, criteria of acceptability
(d) Behaviour to be specified, conditions in which behaviour will occur and criteria of acceptability of the behaviour

77. **Which is the correct sequence in the development of learning theories?**
(a) Thorndike's Connectionism, Pavlov's Classical Conditioning, Skinner's Operant Conditioning. Tolman's Sign Gestalt, Cognitivist Theory and Constructivist Theory
(b) Skinner's Operant Conditioning, Classical Conditioning, Constructivist Theory and Cognitivist Theory
(c) Thorndike's Connectionism, Skinner's Operant Conditioning, Social Theory and Cognitive Theory
(d) Classical Conditioning, Operant Conditioning, Gestalt Theory, Connectionism and Constructivist Theory

78. **Which of the following is the correct order of measurement scales in increasing order of accuracy, precision and number of operations used?**
(a) Ratio, interval, nominal, ordinal
(b) Ordinal, ratio, interval, nominal
(c) Interval, ordinal, ratio, nominal
(d) Nominal, ordinal, interval, ratio

79. **The correct sequence in the development of educational technology in India is reflected by which of the following?**
(a) Audio aids, Video aids, Audio-visual aids, ICT supported aids
(b) ICT aids, Audio aids, Audio-visual aids, Video aids
(c) Video aids, Audio-visual aids, Audio aids, ICT aids
(d) Audio-visual aids, Video aids, Audio aids, ICT aids

80. **Which one of the following indicates Deming's "system of profound knowledge" consisting of four interrelated theories?**
(a) Optimisation, variation, knowledge and psychology
(b) Optimisation, variation, knowledge and need hierarchy
(c) Variation, knowledge, need hierarchy and participation
(d) Knowledge, need hierarchy, participation and goal setting

81. **The acronym DMAIC of Six Sigma method stands for**
(a) Design-Measure-Assess-Integrate-Control
(b) Define-Measure-Analyse-Improve-Control
(c) Demonstrate-Measure-Aggregate-Implement-Connect
(d) Define-Match-Assume-Improve-Communicate

82. **Keeping in view the continuous cycle of process improvement, which of the following is in proper sequence?**
(a) Do-Check-Act-Plan (b) Check-Do-Act-Plan
(c) Plan-Do-Check-Act (d) Act-Check-Do-Plan

83. **What is the correct sequence of actions in conducting an intervention-based action research in Education?**
(a) Act, observe, plan and reflect
(b) Plan, act, observe and reflect
(c) Observe, plan, reflect and act
(d) Reflect, observe, plan and act

84. **Which of the following is the correct sequence for staff recruitment?**
(a) Testing cum interview, Job-analysis, Advertisement and Issue of appointment
(b) Interview, Job-analysis, Appointment order, Advertisement
(c) Job-analysis, Advertisement, Interview, Selection and Appointment order
(d) Advertisement, Job-analysis, Interview, Selection and Appointment order

85. **In the process of drawing a random sampling, which of the following process is in order of sequence?**
(a) Define target population, decide sample size, list all the units of target population and drawing the sample by randomisation
(b) Decide sample size, define the target population, list the units of target population and select the sample by randomisation
(c) List all the units of target population decide sample size, define the population and apply randomisation
(d) Drawing sample by randomisation, decide sample size, define target population and list all units of target population.

86. Given below are two statements one is labelled as Assertion (A) and the other is labelled as Reason (R).

Assertion (A) There have been conscious efforts to bring together all teacher education programmes at various stages, leading to stage-specific and programme specific different forms of knowledge base.

Reason (R) NCTE acquired statutory status and brought a discussion document on teacher education. In the light of the above two statements, choose the correct option.

(a) Both A and R are true and R is the correct explanation of A
(b) Both A and R are true, but R is not the correct explanation of A
(c) A is true, but R is false
(d) A is false, but R is true

87. Given below are two statements one is labelled as Assertion (A) and the other is labelled as Reason (R).

Assertion (A) You can find people with fixation, obsessions and compulsions who put work ahead of health and family but this is not normal; work after all is only work.

Reason (R) The key to success as a manager is intervening effectively, doing the right things at the right time. In the light of the above two statements, choose the correct option

(a) Both A and R are true and R is the correct explanation of A
(b) Both A and R are true, but R is not the correct explanation of A
(c) A is true, but R is false
(d) A is false, but R is true

88. Given below are two statements, one is labelled as Assertion (A) and the other is labelled as Reason (R).

Assertion (A) Effective leader motivates people.

Reason (R) People may be self-motivated to give their best. In the light of the above two statements, choose the correct option.

(a) Both A and R are true and R is the correct explanation of A
(b) Both A and R are true, but R is not the correct explanation of A
(c) A is true, but R is false
(d) A is false, but R is true

89. Given below are two statements one is labelled as Assertion (A) and the other is labelled as Reason (R).

Assertion (A) A budget is a balanced estimate of expenditure and receipts of a given period of time.

Reason (R) In the hands of an educational administrator, the budget is a record of past performance, a method of current control and a projection of future plans.

In the light of the above two statements, choose the correct option.

(a) Both A and R are true and R is the correct explanation of A
(b) Both A and R are true, but R is not the correct explanation of A
(c) A is true, but R is false
(d) A is false, but R is true

90. Given below are two statements one is labelled as Assertion (A) and the other is labelled as Reason (R).

Assertion (A) In ancient India, the development of the inner nature of character of the student was deemed as one of the essential objects of education.

Reason (R) Mere intellectual development without the development of character will defeat the very ends of studentship.

In the light of the above two statements, choose the correct option.

(a) Both A and R are true and R is the correct explanation of A
(b) Both A and R are true, but R is not the correct explanation of A
(c) A is true, but R is false
(d) A is false, but R is true

Directions *(Q. Nos. 91-95) Read the following paragraph and answer the five questions which as follows :*

There is no short cut to knowledge. Just because Reality is a creative activity, knowledge to correspond to it, must in turn be a creative activity. Hence, I must deny the revelation of any reality transcending the process. That is not deny all value to such experience, but only cognitive value-truth. At its lowest, it gives men the assurance necessary to enable them to maintain the strenuous activity of participation in the creative process that is reality itself. At its highest it is as members of an imaginary society that human being may become the creators of new values and originate new ideals of the good and of beauty, but I still deny any absolute or eternal value to the ideals thus imagined, because they are imagined. Imagination like any other kind of creation, is not making something out of nothing, but reshaping and recombining in a new way what is already known. Imagination is thus conditioned by experience and can only just advance the boundaries of knowledge a small step.

Society is the repository of all values, the ultimate arbiter of Truth, Goodness and Beauty. The Good the True or the Beautiful is just what society establishes as the standard. We know in history only societies and therefore there are different standards of Goodness, Truth and Beauty and these may conflict. We can of course imagine a single society embracing all men. Toward such an imaginary society, men conceive themselves bound by obligations.

It is possible to see why the humanist ideal is not absolute or final. It is possible to imagine a society comprising more than humanity. Indeed scientists have hinted that humanity may owe a duty to non human nature and that not only in the generally recognised utilitarian sense of conserving natural resources for more economical human exploitation.

91. The correspondence between knowledge and reality implies

(a) making of value (b) a mechanical act
(c) a creative process (d) a cognitive value truth

92. Participation in the creative process at its highest

(a) gives men a certainity to maintain it.
(b) the process of participation is full of tension.
(c) leads to creation of values of absolute nature.
(d) is originator of new ideals.

93. The function of imagination is

(a) recombining two things already known.
(b) making something out of nothing.
(c) reforming and recombining.
(d) reforming and recombining in a new way.

94. Standards of value differ because of

(a) difference in society.
(b) conflicting value in society.
(c) conflict in personal values.
(d) obligations of societies.

95. According to the author "Humanistic ideals" are

(a) fixed and final. (b) relative and challenging.
(c) absolute and final. (d) broad and encompassing.

Directions *(Q. Nos. 96-100) Read the following paragraph and answer the five questions which as follow :*

Leaders have always played a primordial emotional role. No doubt humankind's original leader-whether tribal chieftains or shamanesses–earned their place in large part because their leadership was emotionally compelling. Throughout history and in cultures everywhere, the leader in any human group has been the one to whom others look for assurance and clarity when facing uncertainity or threat, or when there's a job to be done.

The leader acts as the group's emotional guide. In the modern organisation, this primordial emotional task-though by no largely invisible remains foremost among the many jobs of leadership : driving the collective emotions in a positive direction and clearing the smog created by toxic emotions. The task applies to leadership everywhere, from the boardroom to the shop floor. Quite simply, in any human group the leader has maximal power to sway everyone's emotions. If people's emotions are pushed towards the range of enthusiasm, performance can soar; if people are driven towards rancor and anxiety, they will be thrown off stride.

This indicates another important aspect of primal leadership. Its effects extend beyond ensuring that a job is well done. Followers also look to a leader for supportive emotional connection for empathy. All leadership includes this primal dimension, for better or for worse. When leaders drive emotions positively, they bring out everyone's best. We call this effect resonance. When they drive emotions negatively, leaders spawn dissonance, undermining the emotional foundations that let people shine. Whether an organisation whithers or flourishes depends to a remarkable extent on the leader's effectiveness in the primal emotional dimension.

96. According to the passage, leaders have become popular due to

(a) their power of knowledge about needs of people in the society.
(b) their emotional power to guide.
(c) their dominating nature.
(d) their ability to let people go astray.

97. The emotional quality to influence other is

(a) confined to specific workplace.
(b) largely invisible.
(c) largely visible.
(d) creating toxic emotions.

98. The power of leader to influence can result in

(a) raising expectations.
(b) supportive emotional connection of followers.
(c) enhancing stress.
(d) enhancing self-perception.

99. The best caption by which the key/focal idea of the passage may be represented is

(a) Human emotions. (b) Shamanic leadership.
(c) Leadership styles. (d) Resonant leadership.

100. An effective leader is one who

(a) creates change (b) directs change
(c) transforms others (d) inspires others

ANSWERS

1	(d)	2	(d)	3	(b)	4	(c)	5	(d)	6	(a)	7	(c)	8	(b)	9	(d)	10	(c)
11	(b)	12	(b)	13	(c)	14	(d)	15	(a)	16	(d)	17	(c)	18	(d)	19	(c)	20	(b)
21	(d)	22	(b)	23	(d)	24	(a)	25	(d)	26	(c)	27	(b)	28	(b)	29	(c)	30	(d)
31	(b)	32	(d)	33	(b)	34	(b)	35	(a)	36	(b)	37	(c)	38	(c)	39	(d)	40	(c)
41	(c)	42	(c)	43	(c)	44	(a)	45	(d)	46	(b)	47	(a)	48	(c)	49	(a)	50	(b)
51	(b)	52	(d)	53	(c)	54	(b)	55	(b)	56	(b)	57	(d)	58	(b)	59	(c)	60	(a)
61	(c)	62	(*)	63	(a)	64	(b)	65	(c)	66	(c)	67	(b)	68	(c)	69	(a)	70	(d)
71	(a)	72	(c)	73	(c)	74	(a)	75	(a)	76	(d)	77	(a)	78	(d)	79	(a)	80	(a)
81	(b)	82	(c)	83	(b)	84	(c)	85	(a)	86	(b)	87	(b)	88	(b)	89	(a)	90	(b)
91	(c)	92	(d)	93	(d)	94	(b)	95	(d)	96	(b)	97	(b)	98	(b)	99	(d)	100	(d)

UGC NET/JRF/SET

EDUCATION

Solved Paper, July 2018 (Paper-2)

General Instructions

1. There are total one hundred questions in this paper. Each question carries 2 marks.
2. All questions are compulsory.

1 Which one of the following combinations gives a correct reason for including philosophy of education in Teacher Education Curriculum?

1. Philosophy is an oldest discipline
2. Philosophy helps in understanding educational concepts in a holistic way
3. Philosophy and education are two sides of the same coin
4. Philosophy helps in developing a better personality of prospective teachers
5. Philosophical analysis of educational concepts helps in developing a rational view point

Codes

(a) 1, 2, 3 and 5 (b) 2, 3 and 5
(c) 2, 3, 4 and 5 (d) 1, 2, 3 and 4

2 Which of the following reflects the stance to be taken by a teacher advocating existentialist education?

(a) Values cannot be taught
(b) Values are subjective and personal
(c) Values are essentially contextual but objective
(d) Values are derived from market forces

3 "Prayer cannot be offered with an empty stomach". This statement will get support from ....

(a) Idealism (b) Naturalism
(c) Pragmatism (d) Logical positivism

4 Assertion (A) Maya takes a contrary view to Brahman.

Reason (R) Maya creates an illusory world.

Codes

(a) Both A and R are true and R is the correct explanation of A.
(b) Both A and R are true, but R is not the correct explanation of A.
(c) Both A and R are not true.
(d) A is false, but R is true.

5 Select the correct combination of concepts which will represent Buddhism.

1. Anekantvada
2. Vaibhashik
3. Pabajja
4. Sanskar
5. Sautantrik
6. Syadvada

Codes

(a) 1, 2, 3 and 5 (b) 1, 2, 3 and 4
(c) 2, 3, 4 and 6 (d) 2, 3, 4 and 5

6 Match the following two lists. List-I provides the form of causation while List-II gives the name of metaphysical entities as postulated by Sankhya Philosophy.

List I (Form of Causation)	List II (Metaphysical Entities)
A. Cause only	1. Purusha
B. Effect only	2. Tanmatras
C. Both cause and effect	3. Sensory and Motor organs
D. Neither cause nor effect	4. Ishwar
	5. Prakriti

Codes

	A	B	C	D
(a)	5	2	4	3
(b)	4	1	5	3
(c)	4	1	5	2
(d)	5	3	2	1

7 The ultimate purpose of Gandhian education is the
(a) creation of a classless society
(b) promotion of human beings
(c) development of a human and awakened society
(d) salvation for all

8 Sri Aurobindo's idea of supermind implies that
(a) Darwinian theory is relevant, hence education cannot do much
(b) The task of a teacher is to uplift the awakened consciousness of human beings
(c) A teacher has to integrate psychology, biology and education in his/her teaching techniques
(d) Education can achieve its divine purpose through meditation

9 Below are two lists. List I mentions thinkers while List II consists of schools of thought associated with them. Match the two and choose from the codes to indicate your answer.

List I (Thinkers)	List II (Schools of Thought)
A. A J Ayer	1. Linguistic Analysis
B. Wittgenstein	2. Logical Positivism
C. Bertrend Russel	3. Neorealism
D. G E Moore	4. Positive Relativism
	5. Logical Empiricism
	6. Logical Atomism

Codes

	A	B	C	D		A	B	C	D
(a)	1	2	5	4	(b)	1	2	3	5
(c)	2	1	6	3	(d)	2	1	3	5

10 Which of the following will not be assented to by Indian Constitution ?
1. Liberty, equality, fraternity and justice
2. Republic and a Democratic society
3. Religion, God and Salvation
4. Racialism and Regionalism
5. Vasudhaiv Kutumbkam and Universal brotherhood

Codes
(a) 1, 2 and 5 (b) 1, 2 and 4
(c) 3 and 4 (d) 3, 4 and 5

11 By modernization is meant
(a) Shifting to western mode of life
(b) Following the current fashion and modes of living
(c) Disassociation with traditions and traditional mode of living
(d) The process of adaptation in terms of current needs and life styles

12 Which combination of the following factors tends to slow down the progress in education in India ?
1. High interest rates on educational loans
2. Regionalism
3. Urban way of life
4. Ethnicity
5. Less emphasis on training of teachers
6. Scarcity of ICT resources in schools

Codes
(a) 1, 2, 3 and 4 (b) 2, 3, 4 and 5
(c) 3, 4, 5 and 6 (d) 2, 4, 5 and 6

13 Which one of the following is an example of social mobility ?
(a) En masse withdrawal of learners from school by their parents
(b) Shifting school to a far off place
(c) Weekend visits to villages by city dwellers
(d) Deputising village youths in Indian Army

14 The concept of equalization of educational opportunities implies
(a) Providing books and uniform to learners
(b) Providing resources to learners as per their ability
(c) Encouraging learners to study as many subjects as they can
(d) Optimising learning conditions for success in school board examinations

15 Which of the following combinations will represent the disadvantaged section of Indian society?
1. Tribes
2. Religious groups
3. Slum dwellers
4. Contractual labourers
5. Scheduled Castes
6. City dwellers

Codes
(a) 1, 3, 4 and 5 (b) 1, 2, 3 and 4
(c) 1, 2, 4 and 5 (d) 1, 2, 5 and 6

16 Which of the following aspects focuses more on physical dimensions ?
(a) Concept of development
(b) Concept of growth
(c) Concept of change
(d) Concept of learning

17 Identify from the list given below the correct sequence of concept formation. Select from the codes to answer
1. Analysing the problem
2. Facing the problem
3. Identifying the common elements
4. Perceiving the differences
5. Abstracting the common and non-common elements
6. Understanding the critical features

Codes
(a) 6, 5, 4, 3, 2 and 1 (b) 2, 3, 4, 5, 1 and 6
(c) 4, 5, 6, 1, 2 and 3 (d) 2, 1, 3, 4, 5 and 6

18 For ensuring effectiveness in organizing educational programmes which areas of individual differences in students will be of optimal value ?

(a) Physical characteristics of students
(b) Racial characteristics of students
(c) Psychological characteristics of students
(d) Moral characteristics of students

19 Below is given a list of five types of learning indicated in a hierarchical arrangement as mentioned by Robert M. Gagne. From the codes given select the correct hierarchy to show your answer.

1. Signal learning
2. Chain learning
3. Rule learning
4. Concept learning
5. S - R learning

Codes

(a) 1, 5, 2, 4 and 3 (b) 1, 2, 4, 5 and 3
(c) 3, 2, 1, 5 and 4 (d) 3, 4, 5, 1 and 2

20 Which of the following forms part of the revised basic types of Learning in Tolman's system?

(a) Latent learning
(b) Field cognition modes
(c) Reward expectancy
(d) Place learning

21 Who developed the concept of 'Functional Autonomy of Motives'?

(a) Mcdougal (b) Atkinson
(c) Maslow (d) Allport

22 Which of the following principles is used in shaping behaviour in Skinner's Operant Conditioning?

(a) Principle of keeping the response simple and specific
(b) Principle of keeping the response soft and sweet
(c) Principle of successive approximation
(d) Principle of reward and punishment

23 The list given below embodies a number of statements in the context of adjustment and use of defence mechanisms. Identify those which highlight the role of defence mechanism? Select from the code to give your answer.

1. Giving time to solve problems that might otherwise may overwhelm us.
2. Ensuring 'wellness life style'.
3. Sidetracking the issues.
4. Unconscious use to promote comfort level in life situations.
5. Facing the challenges straightway.
6. Offering explanations which are plausible.

Codes

(a) 1, 2, 4, 5 and 6 (b) 3, 4, 5, 1 and 2
(c) 1, 3, 4 and 6 (d) 5, 2, 1 and 3

24 Given below are two listss which describe the Indian model of personality. List-I provides the list of 'Sheaths of body' called 'Kosha' and List-II indicates names of various types of body with the associated principal element. Match the two and indicate your answer by choosing from the codes.

List I (Sheath of Body)		List II (Name of Body and the Principal Element)
A. Vigyanmaya Kosh	1.	The concrete body + Earth
B. Manomaya Kosh	2.	The state in body between subtle and concrete body + Water
C. Pranmaya Kosh	3.	Subtle body + Fire
D. Annmaya Kosh	4.	Causal body + Air
	5.	Absolute causal body + Akash

Codes

	A	B	C	D		A	B	C	D
(a)	1	2	3	4	(b)	2	1	4	3
(c)	4	3	2	1	(d)	5	4	3	2

25 In Hull's 'Reinforcement theory' which of the following was postulated as intervening variable?

(a) Drive condition (b) Reaction latency
(c) Reaction amplitude (d) Excitatory potential

26 In the two lists given below, List I provides operant conditioning procedures and List II offers their descriptions in terms of cue being present or absent, the mode of reinforcement - positive or negative and response made/withheld. Match the two and indicate your answer by selecting the code given.

List I (Operant Conditioning Procedures)		List II (Descriptions in Terms of Cue and Reinforcement Modality Response Made/ Withheld)
A. Reward training	1.	Cue absent, response withheld and positive reinforcement
B. Escape training	2.	Cue present, response made and negative reinforcement
C. Active Avoidance training	3.	Cue absent, response made and negative reinforcement
D. Omission training	4.	Cue absent, response made and positive reinforcement
	5.	Cue present, response made and positive reinforcement

Codes

	A	B	C	D		A	B	C	D
(a)	4	3	2	1	(b)	1	2	3	4
(c)	2	3	4	5	(d)	5	2	1	3

27 For arriving at classical conditioning paradigm, which of the following was used as the independent variable?

(a) Magnitude of response
(b) Resistance to extinction
(c) Spontaneous recovery
(d) Number of CS - US pairings

28 Which of the laws of learning given by Thorndike had to be revised ?
(a) Law of Exercise (b) Law of Readiness
(c) Law of Effect (d) Law of Belongingness

29 In measurement of which of the following types of intelligence an optimal age level is considered pertinent ?
(a) Cultural Intelligence (b) Emotional Intelligence
(c) Spiritual Intelligence (d) Cognitive Intelligence

30 Who developed the concept of group factors in intelligence ?
(a) Burt (b) Spearman (c) Thurstone (d) Guilford

31 Which of the following set of statements is correct in the context of Guidance ?
1. Guidance is a personal help
2. Guidance leads to self-regulation
3. Guidance focuses on problems rather than on individual
4. Guidance considers individual differences as a basic starting point
5. Guidance service can be organised with various time lags
6. Guidance is panacea for all ills

Codes
(a) 1, 2 and 3 (b) 3, 4 and 5
(c) 2, 4 and 5 (d) 1, 2 and 4

32 A teacher discusses in depth the problems and challenges being faced by a student with a view to help him/her to arrive at a decision. Which of the following modality of Guidance will designate this situation appropriately ?
(a) Counselling type
(b) Vocational Guidance type
(c) Educational Guidance type
(d) Information, Exploration Technique type

33 Which of the following tools at a Guidance Centre can be used for ascertaining prospective success in a chosen occupation?
(a) Achievement test
(b) Interest inventory
(c) Differential aptitude test
(d) Personality inventory

34 For an effective non-directive counselling session, which one of the following will be most essential ?
(a) Training of the counsellor
(b) Establishing a rapport with the client
(c) Expertise in using tests
(d) Conversational fluency

35 Match the following two lists. In List I the different Guidance Services are given and in List II the Role/Functions of these Guidance Services are described. Select the correct answer from the given alternatives.

List I (Guidance Services)	List II (Role / Function)
A. Occupational Information Service	1. Gives information about the characteristics - strength and weaknesses of a person
B. Placement Service	2. Provides information about world of work
C. Follow-up Service	3. Provides suitable engagement as per the vocational preparedness
D. Individual Inventory Service	4. Takes up a view of how things are going on after entry into the specific job
	5. Provides opportunity for understanding oneself in a realistic way

Codes

	A	B	C	D
(a)	2	3	4	1
(b)	3	2	4	5
(c)	1	3	5	2
(d)	2	4	5	1

36 A college librarian plans the purchase of books keeping in view the demand of different books among students. Which of the following measures of central tendency would be suitable for this purpose ?
(a) Mean (b) Median
(c) Mode (d) Geometric Mean

37 The main difference between 'Laboratory Experiment' and 'Field Experiment' is in :
(a) Precision in measurement of variables
(b) Degree of control of extraneous variables
(c) Use of data analysis techniques
(d) Application of research instruments

38 An investigator wants to conduct a study to ascertain the progress of implementation of RTE Act, 2009. Which of the following research tools would be most suitable for this purpose ?
(a) Rating scale (b) Questionnaire
(c) Observation (d) Sociometry

39 A researcher used t-test to compare two means based on independent samples and found the t-value to be significant at .05 level. This means that :
(a) Chances are 5 out of 100 that the difference between means has occurred due to sampling errors.
(b) Chances are 95 out of 100 that the difference between means has occurred due to sampling errors.
(c) If experiment is repeated 100 times, it would give the obtained result only 5 times.
(d) If the experiment is repeated 5 times, it would give the same result every time.

40 A researcher uses both t-test and F-test on the same data obtained from two groups. The functional relationship between values of t and F if calculated would be :
(a) t=F (b) t^2=F (c) t=F^2 (d) $t^2 = F^2$

41 Below are given two lists of statistical tests of significance. List I lists the parametric tests while List II provides their non-parametric counterparts. Match the two and give your answer by selecting from the given codes.

List I (Parametric Tests)	List II (Non-parametric Tests)
A. Independent t-test	1. Chi-square test
B. Dependent t-test	2. Kruskal Wallis H-test
C. ANOVA F-test	3. Mann Whitney 'U' test
	4. Willeoxon T-test

Codes

	A	B	C		A	B	C
(a)	2	1	4	(b)	3	1	2
(c)	3	4	2	(d)	2	1	3

42 In a normal distribution of scores, the percentile rank of a students scoring at -1Z is :

(a) 16 (b) 34
(c) 48 (d) 68

43 In a sample distribution with N=300, M=60 and SD=12, the number of cases falling above the score 48 will be :

(a) 252 (b) 204
(c) 184 (d) 48

44 If two variables X and Y have significant negative correlation, which of the following statement is true ?

(a) X causes variation in Y
(b) Y causes variation in X
(c) X and Y vary together
(d) X and Y cause each other to vary

45 Match the items of List I with items of List II and select the correct code from the given options.

List I	List II
A. Nominal Scale	1. Superior performance in musical events
B. Ordinal Scale	2. Performance scores on a spelling test
C. Interval Scale	3. Listing students according to participation in co-curricular activities
D. Ratio Scale	4. Speed of students in writing words per minute

Codes

	A	B	C	D		A	B	C	D
(a)	3	1	2	4	(b)	1	3	2	4
(c)	2	1	4	3	(d)	4	2	3	1

46 Two variables X and Y have a negative correlation coefficients of -.48. The proportion of variance common to both the variables will be :

(a) 0.23 (b) 0.27
(c) 0.48 (d) 0.52

47 In a negatively skewed curve obtained after testing students, the correct inference about the difficulty of the test would be :

(a) The test was easy.
(b) The test was difficult.
(c) The test was neither easy nor difficulty.
(d) No statement about difficulty of the test can be made.

48 A method of sampling that ensures proportional representation of all sections of a population is technically called :

(a) Quota Sampling
(b) Systematic Sampling
(c) Snow-ball Sampling
(d) Stratified Sampling

49 For estimating maximum value of multiple correlation, which of the following conditions should be met?

1. Independent variables should correlate high with the dependent variable.
2. The Independent variables should correlate low with one another.

Select the correct alternative from the following :

(a) Only condition I should be met
(b) Only condition II should be met
(c) Both conditions I and II should be met
(d) Neither condition I nor II is necessary

50 Using equivalent samples, a researcher obtained a significant correlation 95 times out of 100 trials. He/She decided to reject the null hypothesis. The alpha level would be :

(a) .01 (b) .02
(c) .05 (d) .001

51 Approaches to sampling commonly used in qualitative research design are given in List I and their characteristics in List II. Match List I and List II and select appropriate code.

List I (Approaches to Sampling in Qualitative Research)	List II (Characteristics)
A. Extreme case sampling	1 Seeks cases that are typical
B. Purposive sampling	2 Seeks cases that are highly similar to each other
C. Snowball sampling	3 Seeks cases that are unusual
	4 Seeks help from participants to identify additional participants
	5. Seeks cases according to his/her judgements about the appropriateness

Codes

	A	B	C		A	B	C
(a)	1	4	3	(b)	2	4	1
(c)	3	5	4	(d)	4	2	3

52 When you read a research article published in a journal which is not peer reviewed, what aspect of the report should you be most concerned about?
(a) author's sincerity and skill in writing
(b) rigour reflected in reporting the research
(c) length of the report
(d) practical importance of the research question

53 Which of the following decisions will tend to decrease sampling error?
(a) Obtaining representative sample
(b) Decreasing the sample size
(c) Homogeneous grouping of individuals
(d) Possibility of reduction of the sample size

54 A group of 10 students was randomly drawn from Class 12 and was given yoga training for three weeks. Their wellness life style was compared with another similarly selected group which did not undergo such training. Which type of statistical test will be appropriate for testing the tenability of Null Hypothesis ?
(a) Independent t-test (b) Dependent t-test
(c) Wilcoxon t-test (d) Sign test

55 Given a Mean=100 ; S.D=20 ; and N =100. Which one of the following will be the correct statement for indicating the possibility of population mean at 0.01 level of confidence?
(a) Population mean falls between 93 to 107
(b) Population mean falls between 96.08 to 103.9
(c) Population mean falls between 97.2 to 102
(d) Population mean falls between 94.8 to 105.2

56 "While assessing the attitude of administrators towards a 'Women Empowerment Programme', a researcher had no preconceived notions about what she might discover and she continued interviewing until key themes emerge". Indicate the paradigm of research being followed.
(a) Ethnographic Study approach
(b) Grounded Theory approach
(c) Phenomenological Study approach
(d) Case Study approach

57 A researcher compares two sets of curricular materials in order to determine which set is more pedagogically sound. In the study, which of the following factors may act as source of error?
(a) Attrition (b) Content choice bias
(c) History (d) Subject effects

58 For the purpose of highlighting the characteristics of a particular group of children, which of the following may be considered as the primary source?
(a) A review of research published in the last 5 years
(b) A critical explanation of the psychological characteristics of children suffering from Autism
(c) Findings of case studies of a group of children with Autism
(d) List of books on special education

59 A teacher prepares a test for measuring socially acceptable behaviour of participants in the school programme. What type of reliability would be considered to be important ?
(a) Internal consistency reliability
(b) Split-half reliability
(c) Equivalent forms reliability
(d) Inter-rater reliability

60 In the two lists given below, List I provides a list of attributes based scientific criteria and List II offers their brief description. Match the two lists and select appropriate code for correct matching.

List I (Attribute Based Scientific Criteria)	List II (Description)
A. Parsimony	1. Knowledge should remain open to revision
B. Empiricism	2. Interpretation of research should not reflect personal biases
C. Precision	3. Knowledge should be grounded in observation
D. Objectivity	4. Explanations should be as simple as possible
	5. Research statement should be based on accurate measurements

Codes

	A	B	C	D
(a)	2	4	3	5
(b)	4	3	5	2
(c)	3	5	2	4
(d)	1	2	4	5

61 The Right to Free and Compulsory Education at primary education level is ensured by our Constitution under
(a) Article 21 A of 2009 Act
(b) Article 21 B of 2002 Act
(c) Article 45 of directive principles
(d) Article 21 A of 2002-Act

62 Which of the following set of factors pose hurdle in achieving targets of Universalization of Elementary Education in India?
1. Materials to ensure minimum levels of learning
2. Poverty of parents
3. Slackness in implementing related provisions
4. Availability of boundary walls and safe drinking water
5. Mindset of parents and teachers
6. Shortage of teachers

Codes
(a) 2, 3, 4 and 5 (b) 2, 3, 5 and 6
(c) 1, 2, 3 and 4 (d) 2, 3, 4 and 6

63 Which of the following set of features represent the functions of Community Colleges of USA?
1. Low fee structure
2. Locally situated
3. International quality education
4. Helping the deprived sections

5. Helping the urban poor

Codes

(a) 2, 3 and 4 (b) 1, 2, 3 and 4
(c) 1, 2 and 4 (d) 2, 3, 4 and 5

64 **Which of the following systems tends to practice utmost centralization in educational administration?**

(a) Primary education in USA
(b) Higher education in Ireland
(c) Primary education in UK
(d) Navodaya Vidyalayas in India

65 **Which of the following combinations of learning resources gives a comprehensive concept of distance education?**

1. Mobile learning
2. Opportunity for teacher taught interactions
3. Mass media
4. Use of creative instructional procedures
5. ICT
6. Print material

Codes

(a) 1, 3, 5 and 6 (b) 1, 2, 3 and 5
(c) 1, 2, 3 and 6 (d) 3, 4, 5 and 6

66 **Which one of the following is an essential part of the curricular designing process ?**

(a) Demographic features of the community
(b) Development index of the parents
(c) Consideration of inputs, process and output of instruction
(d) Affiliation of the school to a particular school board

67 **There is a maximum scope of change in curricular contents by the state boards of school education in ________.**

(a) Demonstration model (b) Administrative model
(c) System Analysis model (d) Grassroot model

68 **In which Curricular model a school teacher enjoys maximum autonomy ?**

(a) Demonstration model (b) Administrative model
(c) System Analysis model (d) Grassroot model

69 **In which of the following approaches to curriculum design, constructivist orientation will be manifest ?**

(a) Job analysis of learning tasks
(b) Evaluation approach to curriculum design
(c) Concept mapping as a tool for curricular choice
(d) Input process emphasis on curriculum

70 **The concept of formative evaluation implies that**

(a) benchmarking data should be considered essential
(b) learning should be assessed at terminal stages
(c) learning should be managed and monitored continuously
(d) there should be emphasis on gradation of students in terms of learning outcome

71 **In the two lists which follow, List I contains the names of leaders of modern concepts of educational administration and List II indicates their theories. Match the two and indicate your answer from the codes given.**

List I (Leaders of Modern Concepts of Educational Administration)	List II (Specific Theory Contributed)
A. Frederick Winslow Taylor	1. Theory X and Theory Y
B. Elton Mayo	2. Management systems
C. Rennis Likert	3. Human Relations movement
D. Douglas Mc Gregor	4. Scientific Management movement
	5. SOAR Peak Performance model

Codes

	A	B	C	D
(a)	1	2	3	4
(b)	5	4	3	2
(c)	4	3	2	1
(d)	2	4	3	5

72 **Which combination of following characteristics correctly describes the Bureaucratic Administration?**

1. Well defined rules
2. Established hierarchy
3. Standard operating procedures
4. Good interpersonal relationships
5. Combined responsibility of completing work

Codes

(a) 1, 2 and 4 (b) 1, 2 and 5
(c) 2, 3 and 4 (d) 1, 2 and 3

73 **In the two lists given below, List I specifies the type of power exercised by an educational administrator and List II gives the description of these powers. Match the two and select your answer from the codes.**

List I (Type of Power)	List II (Description)
A. Coercive power	1. The perception that the administrator has relevant education and experience
B. Reward power	2. The perceived attractiveness of interaction
C. Legitimate power	3. The perceived ability to provide things liked by the members
D. Expert power	4. The perception that decisions taken by the administrator are appropriate in terms of role assigned
	5. Perceived ability to provide consequences for not performing

Codes

	A	B	C	D
(a)	1	2	3	5
(b)	5	3	4	1
(c)	2	1	3	4
(d)	2	3	4	5

74 There are two lists given below. List I describes Leader behaviour in terms of task and relationship orientation while List II mentions the leadership style. Match the two lists and give your answer by selecting an appropriate code.

List I (Leader Behaviour)	List II (Style of Leadership)
A. High task and low relationship	1. Consulting style
B. High task and high relationship	2. Delegating style
C. High relationship and low task	3. Selling style
D. Low relationship and low task	4. Telling style

Codes

	A	B	C	D
(a)	1	2	3	4
(b)	2	3	4	1
(c)	1	3	2	4
(d)	4	3	1	2

75 A school principal plans the targets of activities and programmes to be undertaken in next five years. This is an example of :

(a) Grassroot planning
(b) Perspective planning
(c) System's approach to planning
(d) Micro planning

76 The basic purpose of educational supervision is to:

(a) Ensure better result of students in the board examination
(b) Ensure effective teaching-learning ambieance in the school
(c) Ensure maximum attendance of learners in the school
(d) Ensure compliance of set rules and procedures

77 If the deviation of a score from the mean is given as 10 and standard deviation as 5, what will be the T-score for the concerned raw score?

(a) 50 (b) 75 (c) 70 (d) 80

78 Categories of tests are given as List I and their description as List II. Match List I with List II and select appropriate code

List I (Categories of Test)	List II (Description)
A. Standardized test	1. Developed by teachers for local purposes to measure achievement
B. Norm referenced test	2. Used for comparing individuals in terms of their relative position
C. Diagnostic test	3. Analysis of strength and weakness of students for further help
D. Criterion referenced test	4. Developed by experts, administered and scored by using an objective procedure
	5. Raw scores are compared with some pre-determined standard

Codes

	A	B	C	D
(a)	3	5	1	4
(b)	4	2	3	5
(c)	2	3	4	1
(d)	4	5	3	2

79 A multiple choice test consists of 50 test items. The difficulty values of items vary in a narrow range with an average value of 0.48. The test gave a variance of 81 when administered to a group of students. The reliability co-efficient of the test would be :

(a) 0.91 (b) 0.86 (c) 0.78 (d) 0.67

80 The percentile rank of a student on a test was found to be 67. This means that :

(a) the student scored 67% marks.
(b) 33% students scored below his score.
(c) 67% students scored above his score.
(d) 67% students scored below his score.

81 A test having 20 items has a reliability coefficient of 0.60. If 80 more similar items are added, the new reliability coefficient would be :

(a) 0.81 (b) 0.86 (c) 0.88 (d) 0.92

82 Which of the following term is closely related to the meaning of the term 'aptitude' ?

(a) Ability (b) Achievement
(c) Capability (d) Potential

83 In the following list of statements, identify those which are related to interactive stage of teaching. For indicating your answer select from the codes.

1. The teacher decides what to teach.
2. The teacher organizes learning tasks and monitors them.
3. The teacher takes a planned repetition.
4. Learning outcomes are determined.
5. The teacher keeps students maximally 'on task' and minimally 'off task'.
6. The teacher assesses the learning outcomes.

Codes

(a) 2, 3 and 5 (b) 1, 2 and 3
(c) 4, 5 and 6 (d) 1, 3 and 6

84 In programmed learning, who is said to be the proponent of 'Adaptive programming' ?

(a) Skinner (b) Gilbert
(c) Crowder (d) Mager

85 In the two lists which follow, List I indicates the specific devices and List II mentions the stage of programme development. Match the two on the basis of their appropriateness. Choose from the codes to give your answer.

List I (Devices Used)	List II (Stage of Programme Development)
A. Writing of behavioural objectives	1. For introductory frames
B. Priming	2. During withdrawl of prompts
C. Prompting	3. For shaping behaviour in steps
D. Testing	4. Prior to development of a programme
	5. During small group try-out

Codes

	A	B	C	D
(a)	1	2	3	4
(b)	2	3	4	5
(c)	1	2	4	5
(d)	4	1	3	2

86 From the list of statements given below, which of them indicate the meaning, purpose and scope of Educational Technology. Give your answer by selecting from the codes.

1. ET optimises learning outcomes.
2. ET reduces the cost of education.
3. ET is user friendly.
4. ET ensures effectiveness of learning outcomes.
5. ET has a tremendous role in rendering teaching-learning systems effort effective.
6. ET is the outcome of communication's network.

Codes

(a) 1, 2 and 3 (b) 4, 5 and 6
(c) 2, 3 and 6 (d) 1, 4 and 5

87 In which of the following Communication model, there is optimum scope for encoding and decoding messages ?

(a) International model based on learner participation
(b) Distance Learning model based on use of Information and Communication Technology support
(c) Discussion-cum-Lecture session model conducted by the teacher
(d) Transactional model based on collaborative projects

88 Optimum use of the 'Principle of Successive Approximation' has been empirically demonstrated through which model of instruction?

(a) Model of School Learning
(b) Programmed Instructional model
(c) Concept Attainment model
(d) Basic Teaching model

89 The Duchenne is the most common type of

(a) spina bifida
(b) multiple sclerosis
(c) muscular dystrophy
(d) traumatic brain injury

90 Which of the following statements is correct in the context of students with learning disabilities?

(a) They show perceptual impairment affecting perceptual skills, such as thinking and reasoning.
(b) They learn in the same way as efficiently as their classmates.
(c) They display academic performance higher than expected.
(d) They have the emotional problem which is one of the primary cause of their learning disabilities.

91 Match the following two lists given below. List I consists of terms related to specific deviations and List II consists of resultant impairments.

List I (Terms Denoting Nature of Deviations)	List II (Resultant Impairments)
A. Cerebral Palsy	1. Problems related to reading words and letter
B. Congenital Cytomegalovirus	2. Characterised by rapid, involuntary movements of eyes which make it difficult to focus on objects and causes dizziness
C. Dyslexia	3. Disorder related to movements and posture
D. Nystagmus	4. Herpes - related viral infection causes hearing loss
	5. Disorder related to farsightedness

Codes

	A	B	C	D		A	B	C	D
(a)	3	2	1	5	(b)	2	5	1	4
(c)	4	3	1	5	(d)	3	4	1	2

92 Match the following two lists. List I consists of terms related to refractive disorders, retinal and optic nerve problems. List II provides description of those terms. Select the correct code for indicating your answer.

List I (Terms)	List II (Description)
A. Astigmatism	1. It occurs when the flow of fluids in the eye is restricted
B. Glaucoma	2. It is a hereditary disorder that causes degeneration of retina
C. Hyperopia	3. It is the result of improper functioning of muscles of eye(s)
D. Retinitis Pigmentosa	4. It is most commonly known as farsightedness, results from the failure of cornea
	5. Result in blurred vision, caused by an uneven curve of cornea or lens of eye

Codes

	A	B	C	D		A	B	C	D
(a)	5	1	4	2	(b)	4	5	1	2
(c)	3	4	5	1	(d)	2	3	4	5

93 Morfan syndrome is a kind of

(a) genetic disorder
(b) viral infection
(c) degenerative neuromuscular disease
(d) muscular contraction

94 Which of the following provisions is most appropriate for addressing the learning needs of the students having disabilities/impairments?

(a) Individualised Transition Programme (ITP)
(b) Pre-school Programmes for Children
(c) Individualised Education Programme (IEP)
(d) Free and Appropriate Education (FAPE)

95 Which of the following has relatively greater promise for professionalisation of teacher education in India?

(a) Forming of teacher associations
(b) Developing teacher code for transaction of teaching-learning systems
(c) Special packages to teachers offered
(d) Enhancing the period of pre-service teacher education programme

96 Below are given a few programmes for enhancing teacher quality. Which of these are specially related to in-service teacher education? Select the correct code to indicate your answer.

1. Induction training
2. Skill development training
3. Pedagogy courses in specific subjects
4. Foundation courses in teacher education
5. Micro-simulation for particular competencies

Codes
(a) 1, 3, 4 (b) 1, 2, 5 (c) 3, 4, 5 (d) 2, 3, 4

97 For application of Total Quality Management (TQM) in teacher education, which of the following measures will be considered helpful? Select the correct code to indicate your answer.

1. Finding out the needed number of teachers in various states-demand and supply of teachers
2. 'Can do', Will do' analysis for specified groups of teacher educators
3. Finding out the number of teacher education institutions
4. SWOC analysis by teacher educators
5. Action research projects to improve school practices

Codes
(a) 1, 2, 4 (b) 2, 4, 5
(c) 3, 4, 5 (d) 1, 3, 4

98 Which of the following set of statements is relevant for describing teaching as a Profession? For your answer select the correct code.

1. Teaching Profession has an organised body of knowledge
2. Teaching Profession implies a set of attitudes
3. Duration of Teacher Training Programme is not a professional pre-requisite
4. Teaching Profession has its own code of moral ethics

Codes
(a) 2, 3, 4 (b) 1, 3, 4
(c) 1, 2, 4 (d) 1, 2, 3

99 Which of the following arrangements is an effective supplement for providing teacher education through distance mode?

(a) EDUSAT
(b) Smart classrooms
(c) Virtual universities
(d) MOOC

100 Which of the following has been found to be effective for modifying teacher behaviour in terms of the evidences supported by research?

(a) Interaction analysis procedure for classroom teaching behaviour
(b) Participation in seminars
(c) Undergoing training in research methodology
(d) Teacher consultation

ANSWERS

1 (b)	2 (b)	3 (c)	4 (b)	5 (d)	6 (d)	7 (b)	8 (b)	9 (c)	10 (c)
11 (d)	12 (d)	13 (d)	14 (b)	15 (a)	16 (b)	17 (d)	18 (c)	19 (a)	20 (b)
21 (d)	22 (c)	23 (c)	24 (c)	25 (d)	26 (a)	27 (d)	28 (c)	29 (d)	30 (a)
31 (d)	32 (a)	33 (c)	34 (b)	35 (a)	36 (c)	37 (b)	38 (b)	39 (a)	40 (b)
41 (c)	42 (a)	43 (a)	44 (c)	45 (a)	46 (a)	47 (a)	48 (d)	49 (c)	50 (c)
51 (c)	52 (b)	53 (a)	54 (a)	55 (d)	56 (b)	57 (b)	58 (c)	59 (d)	60 (b)
61 (d)	62 (b)	63 (c)	64 (d)	65 (a)	66 (c)	67 (b)	68 (d)	69 (c)	70 (c)
71 (c)	72 (d)	73 (b)	74 (d)	75 (b)	76 (b)	77 (c)	78 (b)	79 (b)	80 (d)
81 (c)	82 (d)	83 (a)	84 (c)	85 (d)	86 (d)	87 (d)	88 (b)	89 (c)	90 (a)
91 (d)	92 (a)	93 (a)	94 (c)	95 (b)	96 (b)	97 (b)	98 (c)	99 (d)	100 (a)

NTA
UGC
NET/JRF/SET

EDUCATION

CHAPTER 01

Contribution of Indian Schools of Philosophy

Almost every school of Indian philosophy is associated with practical life. Theory does not exists without practical implications. To have a better understanding of the contribution of Indian schools, the chapter deals with Sankhya, Yoga, Vedanta, Buddhism, Jainism, Dayanand Darshan and Islamic philosophy.

In this Chapter

- Education
- Philosophy
- Indian Philosophy
- Indian Schools of Philosophy
  - Sankhya
  - Yoga
  - Vedanta
  - Buddhism
  - Jainism
  - Dayanand Darshan
  - Islamic Philosophy

Education

Education plays a vital role in the overall development of a person. Education and philosophy are two disciplines, which are very closely related and in some way both overlap each other.

Education is a process of initiating the child into the way of life. An educator not only holds certain beliefs and ideals of life, but also rise to convert his pupil to his own views and his own way of life. The influence of a person, holding a vital belief, brought to bear upon another person with the object of making him also to hold that belief is **education**.

The term 'education' is derived from the following three latin words:

Educare : This means to bring up, to nourish, to rear and to train.

Educere : This implies to draw out and to lead out.

Educo : The letter 'E' means 'out of' and 'duco' means 'to lead'. This denotes to extract out and to lead forth.

Definitions of Education

Several great educators and thinkers have explained the meaning of education are as follows

According to **Plato**, "Education develops in the body and soul of the pupil, all the beauty and all the perfection he is capable of".

According to **Pestalozzi**, "Education is the natural, harmonious and progressive development of man's innate powers".

According to **Froebel**, "Education is unfoldment of what is already enfolded in the germ".

According to **Aristotle** "Education is the creation of sound mind in a sound body".

According to **Aurobindo**, "Education means helping the growing soul to draw out that is in itself".

According to **Swami Vivekananda**, "Education is the manifestation of divine perfection already existing in man".

According to **Gandhiji**, "By education I mean all round drawing out the best in child and man body and mind and spirit".

According to **John Dewey**, "Education is the process of continuous reconstruction of experience".

Thus, we can say that education is the process of facilitating learning, or the acquisition of knowledge, skills, values, beliefs and habits which teaches us to be a true human being.

Nature of Education

Following are the important characteristics of the nature of education

Education is Purposive There is a definite purpose of all the educational activities.

Education is Planned Education is systematic and needs planning.

Education is Life Long Education starts from the time of conception and goes on till death. It is the process of development from infancy to maturity. It includes the effect of everything which influences human personality.

Education is Overall Development Education is concerned with the overall development of the personality.

Education is Bi-Polar Both the teacher and the pupil influence each other.

Education is Tri-Polar Education involves the teacher, the pupil and the environment.

Education is Psychological as well as Social The capacities, needs, interest of the child, etc. must be interpreted in relation with his/her social environment.

Scope of Education

Education has a vast scope in the life of human beings. Some of them are as follows

- All the aspects and dimensions of life are covered under education. It is a life long process.
- It is concerned with the overall development of the individual, which includes physical, mental, aestheic, cultural, ethical, intellectual, social, spiritual and vocational development.
- It focuses on the maximum development of the innate abilities and powers of the individual.
- It also helps in the development of character and personality of the individual.

Philosophy

Philosophy is the study of general and fundamental problems, such as those connected with reality, existence, knowledge, values, reasons, mind and language.

Philosophy is concerned with the understanding of the life and the universe. It aims at comprehending the nature of existence. Philosophy is human endeavour that reads to the ultimate truth.

The English word *'Philosophy'* has its root in the Greek term 'philo-sophia'. The term 'philo' refers 'to love' and 'sophia' refers to 'human reason'. The Greek word can be literally translated in English as love of reason or love of human judgement and discrimination.

From the Indian view point, the word 'Philosophy' suggests observing and surveying the existence.

In Sanskrit, the *'Philosophy'* is referred to as *'Darshana'*. The Sanskrit word 'Darshana' has its root in the word 'drs' that means to see, to look or to view. Seeing or viewing the reality and facts of experience forms the basis of philosophy. In other words, Darshana is a whole view related to the inner self, what we term as the soul or the spirit or the inner being. Philosophy or Darshana is concerned with the vision of six ways to the truth and reality.

In Sanskrit, the 'Philosophy' is also referred to as 'Tatva'. The word 'Tatva' is concerned with the nature of reality.

The history of philosophy deals with the study of philosophical ideas and concepts through time. All cultures be they pre-historic, medieval or modern, eastern, western, religious or secular have their own unique schools of philosophy, arrived through both heritance and through independent discovery.

According to **John Grier Hibben**, "Philosophy is concerned with that, which is in contrast with that which seems to be. Its aim is to reveal the reality which underlines appearance".

According to **Plato**, "Philosophy is aquisition of knowledge".

Branches of Philosophy

Philosophy is traditionally divided into several branches i.e.

- **Metaphysics** It inquires into the nature and ultimate significance of the universe.
- **Logic** It is concerned with the laws of valid reasoning.
- **Epistemology** It investigates the nature of knowledge and the process of knowing.
- **Ethics** It deals with the problems of right conduct.
- **Aesthetics** It attempts to determine the nature of beauty and the criteria of artistic judgement.
- In order to understand more about philosophy, it is necessary to divide it into two traditions *i.e.* 'Indian Philosophy' and 'Western Philosophy'.

Philosophy of Education

Philosophy is a search for a general understanding of values and reality by chiefly speculative other than observational means. It signifies a natural and necessary urge in human beings to know themselves and the world in which they live and move and have their being.

Education like philosophy is also closely related to human life. Therefore, being an important life activity, education is also greatly influenced by philosophy.

In the modern times, education has acquired two different shades of meaning, namely :

- an institutional instruction given to students in schools and colleges, formally.
- a pedagogical science studied by the student of education.

Scope of Philosophy of Education

Scope of philosophy of education includes following

Aims and Ideals of Philosophy of Education Education as a discipline critically evaluates the different aims and ideals of education. These aims and ideals have been propagated by various philosophers in different times. They are character building, man-making, harmonious human development, preparation for adult life, development of citizenship and achieving social and national integration.

Interpretation of Human Nature A philosophical picture of human nature is a result of the synthesis of the facts borrowed from all the human science with the values discussed in different normative science. The philosophical picture, therefore is more broad as compared to the picture of man drawn by Biology, Sociology, Psychology, Economics, Anthropology and other Human Science.

Educational Values Value is typically-a philosophical subject, since it is more abstract, integral and universal.

Theory of Knowledge Education is related to knowledge. It is determined by the source, limits, criteria and means of knowledge.

Relationship Between Education and National Components of System of Education The most important contribution of the philosophy of education to the cause of education is the provision of criteria for deciding the relationship of state and education, economic system and education, curriculum and school, organisation and management discipline.

Relationship Between Philosophy and Education

Education and philosophy are inseparable. It can be explained by the following points

- The main aim of education is the all round development or promotion of life while philosophy also aims at the understanding of life and it's nature. Therefore, education and philosophy are related to the concept of life.
- To lead a harmonious life, the philosophy provides a direction and education takes help from it. There is a constant mutual agreement and interaction between the two. In short, philosophy deals with the end result and education with the means.
- Education and philosophy are the two sides of the same coin. Education is nothing but the dynamic side of philosophy. It is the practical means of realising ideals of life.

The study of philosophy of education can be exciting and challenges that encounter great and enduring ideas of human thought. It enables in understanding the past of education and to develop the kinds of perspectives and intellectual tools that can help in dealing with the educational problems.

Indian Philosophy

Indian philosophy primarily begins with the later part of the Rig Veda, which was compiled before 1100 BC. Most of the philosophy of the Rig Veda is contained in the sections of the Purusha Sukta and Nasadiya Sukta. The Vedas are followed by the Upanishads; the oldest, such as the Brihadaranyaka and Chandogya Upanishads, have been dated to around the 8th century BC.

The philosophical edifice of Indian religion *viz.* the Hinduism, the Jainism and the Buddhism is built on the foundation laid by the Upanishads. The Upanishad's thoughts were followed by the Buddhist and the Jain philosophies. **Webster's dictionary** defines philosophy as "the rational investigation of questions about existence, knowledge and ethics".

The main schools of Indian philosophy were formalised chiefly between 1000 BC to the early centuries AD. Subsequent centuries produced commentaries and reformulations continuing up to as late as the 20th century by Sri Aurobindo Ghosh and Swami Prabhupada among others. Competition and integration among the various schools were intense during their formative years, especially between 800 BC to AD 200 .

History of Indian Philosophy

The philosophies develop over long spells of time. It is difficult for the historians to ascertain the period for the development of a particular philosophy. The historian go on debating about the origin of the Aryans and the time period when the Vedic civilisation developed in India.

It is believed by the Western scholars that the Aryans descended from the regions of the North Central Asia sometime around 15000 BC. Though this has been challenged by some other learned scholars, some of the eminent Indian scholars also differ from their Western counter parts, saying that the Aryans were natives of India for long and that the Vedic civilisation developed about 4000 to 8000 years ago.

The renowned Indian scholar Lokmanya Tilak contends that the first Vedic hymns could have been composed nearly 6000 years ago and the later works like the Upanishads themselves could be nearly 3000 years old.

According to **Dr. Radhakrishanan,** *the outline of the history of Indian philosophies is as follows*

- The Vedic period (1500 BC to 600 BC)
- The Epic period (600 BC to AD 200)
- The Sutra period (AD 200 to AD 1700)
- The Scholastic period (from Sutra period to 17th century)

Characteristics of Indian Philosophy

The system of Indian philosophies with a singular exception of **Charvakism**, have certain common characteristics. Charvakism, remarkably differs from other system as it promotes materialism.

The following characteristics are common to all other systems

- All schools emphasise on the fact that philosophy must have positive impact on the life of a man.
- All the systems believe that philosophy leads man from darkness and ignorance to light and knowledge.
- There must be a general agreement among the systems that the truth and reality should be verifiable. They should be substantiated by reasoning and experience.
- It is accepted by all the schools that man's suffering results from his ignorance. Man can conquer ignorance and other total freedom *i.e.* Moksha in their bodily existence.
- There is a general agreement on man's essential spirituality or spiritual unity.

Classification of Indian Schools of Philosophy

The system of Indian philosophy is classified into two groups i.e.

(i) **Orthodox System** upholds the supermacy of the Vedas as Vaisheshika, Nyaya, Sankhya, Yoga, Purva Mimamsa and Uttar Mimamsa.

(ii) **Unorthodox System** rejects the authority of the Vedas as Charvaka, Jainism and Buddhism. Very often, Purva Mimamsa is referred to as Mimamsa only and Uttar Mimamsa as Vedanta. The four systems like Nyaya, Vaisheshika, Sankhya and Yoga actually are infact neither orthodox nor unorthodox.

The following are widely acknowledged as proponents of the systems:

Proponents of the Indian Systems of Philosophy

Orthodox System		Unorthodox System	
System	**Proponents**	**System**	**Proponents**
Nyaya	Gautama	Charvakism	Charvaka
Vaisheshika	Kanada	Jainism	Vardhamana Mahavira
Yoga	Patanjali		
Sankhya	Kapila	Buddhism	Gautama Buddha
Purva Mimamsa	Jamini		
Uttar Mimamsa	Shankara		

Indian Schools of Philosophy

We must look for better understanding of education in Indian schools. Here, we are especially dealing with Sankhya, Yoga, Vedanta, Buddhism, Jainism, Dayananda Darshan and Islamic Philosophy. *They can be explained as follows*

Sankhya

Sankhya is one of the most prominent and one of the oldest school of Indian philosophy. The word *'Sankhya'* is based upon the Sanskrit word 'Sankhya', which means 'number'. The school specifies the number and the nature of the ultimate constituents of the universe and thereby imparts knowledge of reality. Infact, the term Sankhya also means perfect knowledge. Hence, it is a system of perfect knowledge.

Sankhya is one of the six Orthodox schools of Hindu philosophy and classical Indian philosophy. Sage Kapila is traditionally credited as the founder of the Sankhya school. It is regarded as one of the oldest philosophical systems in India. Based on the Upanishads, two schools of philosophies developed in India and they are

(i) The Realistic (*e.g.* Sankhya)

(ii) The Idealistic (*e.g.* Vedanta)

The Sankhya philosophy combines the basic doctrines of Sankhya and Yoga. However, it should be remembered that the Sankhya represents 'the theory' and Yoga represents 'the application or the practical aspects'.

Sankhya denies the existence of Ishvara (God) or any other exterior influence. Sankhya philosophy regards the universe as consisting of two realities *i.e.* Purusha (Consciousness) and Prakriti (Phenomenal realm of matter).

Metaphysics of Sankhya

Sankhya is a dualistic realism. It is dualistic because of its doctrine of two ultimate realities *i.e.* Prakriti (Matter) and Purusha (Self-spirit). Sankhya is realist as it holds that both matter and spirit are equally real. With regard to self, Sankhya is pluralistic because of its teaching that Purusha is not one but many.

Purusha

Purusha is transcendental self or pure consciousness. It is absolute, independent, free, imperceptible and unknowable, through other agencies, above any experience by mind or senses and beyond any words or explanations. Purusha is neither produced nor it produce anything.

Prakriti

Prakriti is the first cause of the manifest material universe of everything except the Purusha. Prakriti accounts for whatever is physical, both mind and matter. It is composed of three essential characteristics. *They are :*

- **Sattva** pose, fineness, lightness, illumination and joy
- **Rajas** dynamism, activity, excitation and pain
- **Tamas** heaviness, obstruction and inertia

Sankhya philosophy offers a framework for all the levels of manifestation, from the subtlest to the gross. Sankhya comes from Samyag Alchyate, which literally means that which explains the whole.

The Sankhya system held that the creation cannot be made of one entity alone and that it is the union of two entities, *viz.* nature and God. One cannot clap with one hand, one needs two hands to clap.

There is an important role of causation in all branches of Indian philosophy, where we try to develop the concept on the basis of casual relations.

The two important views on the Theory of Causation in the Indian philosophy are :

(i) **Satkaryavada** (Pre-existence of the effect in the cause) It maintains that Karya (effect is real). It is present in the Karana (cause) in a potential form, even before its manifestation.

(ii) **Asatkaryavada** It literally means the theory of non-existent effect. The Theory of Asatkaryavada is also known as Arambhavada. It means something has a new beginning. If the cause now transfer into a different phenomenon or effect, then the effect is a new creation. It is a new Arambha.
It is a beginning when there is a milk, it is a material cause, when there is a curd is an effect right. If the effect is that, this is a new creation, it is a new beginning. The Sankhya as well as Vedanta uphold the Satkaryavada, but their interpretations are different.

Idea of Evolution in Sankhya

The idea of evolution in Sankhya revolves around the interaction of Prakriti and Purusha. Prakriti remains unmanifested as long as the three Gunas are in equilibrium. This equilibrium of the Gunas is disturbed when Prakriti comes into proximity with consciousness or Purusha. The disequilibrium of the Gunas triggers an evolution that leads to the manifestation of the world from unmanifest Prakriti. The metaphor of movement of iron in the proximity of a magnet is used to describe this process. Some evolutes of Prakriti can cause further evolution and are labelled evoluents. *e.g.* intellect while itself created out of Prakriti causes the evolution of ego-sense or ahamkara and is therefore an evoluent.

While, other evolutes like the five elements do not cause further evolution. It is important to note that an evoluent is defined as a principle, which behaves as the material cause for the evolution of another principle.

The intellect is the first evolute of Prakriti and is called *Mahat* or the great one. It causes the evolution of ego-sense or self-consciousness. Evolution from self-consciousness is affected by the dominance of Gunas. So, dominance of sattva causes the evolution of the five organs of perception, five organs of action and the mind. Dominance of Tamas triggers the evolution of five subtle elements *i.e.* sound, touch, sight, taste, smell from self-consciousness. These five subtle elements are themselves evoluents and cause the creation of the five gross elements space, air, fire, water and Earth. Rajas is cause of action in the evolutes. Purusha is pure consciousness absolute, eternal and subject to no change. It is neither a product of evolution nor the cause of any evolute. Evolution in Sankhya is thought to be purposeful. The two primary purposes of evolution of Prakriti are the enjoyment and the liberation of Purusha.

Historical Development of Sankhya

Sankhya thought to be evolved into a cohesive philosophical system in early centuries as such there is a little evidence of existence of the Sankhya school before this time. However, the ideas that were developed and assimilated into the classical Sankhya text, Sankhya karika, are visible in earlier Hindu scriptures such as Vedas, Upanishads and Bhagavad Gita.

The hymn of Purusha Sukta may also have influenced Sankhya. It contains the easiest conception of Purusha, a cosmic being from whom the manifestation arises. The sankhya notion of Buddhi or Mahat is similar to the notion Hiran Yagarbha, which appears in both the Rig Veda and the Shvetashvatara Upanishad.

Educational Implications

According to the principles of Sankhya philosophy, an action (karma) is already inherent in a cause, so it is true to remark that the development of man is already inherent in him (man). Hence, the work of education is to bring out the development of man to the fullest extent.

Sankhya accepts the Prakriti (Matter) and Purusha (Spirit) as the fundamental elements, but it has very clearly pointed out the basic difference between the two. According to Sankhya, true education is that which acquaints one with the difference between Prakriti and Purusha.

Sankhya has great relevance for contemporary education. If we consider the modern view of education as development, then Sankhya's postulate that development is only the unfolding of what already has potential existence needs no modification to suit today's world. Sankhya's psychological views also reflect modern learning theories.

If knowledge leads to the modification of Buddhi in the Sankhya system, then modern education aims at the modification of behaviour. If cognition is a function of Buddhi or intellect in Sankhya, it is the formation of intellectual structure in modern education. Sankhya's theory states that generalisation is the result not only of observation of elements, but also non-observation of non-elements reflect the modern view of concept formation.

Fundamentals of Education

To Sankhya philosophy, man's body is made of senses (Gyanendriya) and organs of action (Karmendriya). The inner-self (Antahkaran) of man is a harmonious assemblage of Man (Mind), Ahankar (Ego or self-consciousness) and Buddhi (Intellect). The Purusha (Soul) is the enlightener of these three elements. Education should develop from the three basic elements. According to Sankhya, Mukti or deliverance or liberation of the soul is the ultimate purpose of one's life.

This Mukti may be obtained through releasing the difference between the Prakriti and Purusha (Matter and spirit). Therefore, the development of man should be so guided that he may distinguish between matter and spirit, and may obtain freedom from the miseries of life.

According to Sankhya philosophy, End (Saddhya) is the basic purpose of education. For realisation of this end, the practice of Yoga is necessary. For the practice of Yoga (Yoga-Sadhana), moral conduct is the first requisite. In the modern language, the above purpose of education may be further analysed in the following manner.

To get freedom from the three fold miseries (Dukha Traya) i.e.

- the miseries pertaining to soul, mind and body, in other words, the miseries pertaining to the spiritual realm *i.e.* Adhyatmik.
- the miseries relating to external world *i.e.* Adhibhautik.
- the miseries due to divine disorder *i.e.* Dam Peakop.

Aims of Education

Sankhaya states the ultimate aims as attaining the perfection of Purusha through discrimination, leading to its salvation. Thus, the objective of education should be to create discerning individuals capable of attaining the perfection that exists within them.

Methods of Teaching

- Through study of authorities but keeping an open mind and using reason to validate their theories.
- Experiential learning with maximum involvement of the senses.
- Activity based learning include projects, practical work, etc. enabling the development of observation and logical reasoning.

Curriculum

The curriculum will involves the study of all disciplines, with stress on the natural sciences, since to understand Prakriti is to discriminate between Purusha and Prakriti and the art, so as to develop an appreciation and understanding of the work of authorities. Physical Science and Yoga will also form part of the curriculum, since Sankhya believes that only a healthy and focused individual can attain salvation.

Discipline

Sankhya recommends a high degree of discipline. One can deduce that it should be self-imposed.

Role of a Teacher

The teacher is to be a facilitator of the development of the innate potentiality of the child.

Place of Student

Since, Sankhya believes in the multiplicity of Purusha, it follows that education must be individualised and child-centred.

Religious and Moral Education

It can be deduced that religious education will not have much importance but moral education involving the teaching of ethical values will definitely hold a central place in any system of education based on Sankhya.

Yoga

'Patanjali' is regarded as founder of Yoga System. The word 'Yoga' literally means 'Union' *i.e.* spiritual union of the individual soul with the universal soul and is used in this sense in the Vedanta. According to **Patanjali**, Yoga does not mean union but spiritual effort to attain perfection through the control of the body, sense and mind and through right discrimination between Purusha and Prakriti.

Patanajali's Theory of Pramana

Sankhya and Yoga are said to be the aligned system of thoughts. The theory of knowledge according to Yoga school is similar to that of Sankhya theory. As according to **Sankhya**, it accepts only three independent source of valid knowledge (Pramanas). These are perception, inference and verbal testimony (Sabda). The other source of knowledge like comparison, postulation (Arthapatti), and non-cognition (Anupalabdhi) are included under these three only, not recognise as a separate source of knowledge.

Perception

It is the direct cognition of an object through its contact with some sense. When an object like table come in contact with the range of eyes, it produces certain impression of modification in the sense organ which are analysed and synthesise by the mind. According to **Sankhya**, the knowledge of an object takes place when there is reflection of the self in the intellect which have been modified into the form of object.

According to him, there are two kinds of perception 'Nirvikalpaka' or the indeterminate and 'Sanikalpaka' or the determinate. The Nirvikalpaka pratyaks arises at the first moment. It is the moment of contact between a sense and its object and is antecedent to all mental analysis and synthesis of sense data. And the Sanikalpaka's perception is result of the analysis, synthesis and interpretation of sense data by the manas or the mind.

Inference

It is regarded as the knowledge of one term of relation, which is not perceived, through the other which is perceived and known to be invariable related to the first. In inference, what is perceived lead us to the knowledge of what is unperceived through the knowledge of the universal relation (invariable concomitance) between the two. We get the knowledge of Vyapti between the two things through the repeated observation of their concomitance.

According to **Sankhya**, Inference is further divided into two kinds *i.e.* 'Vita' and 'Avita'.

'Vita' is based on universal affirmative propositions and 'Avita' is based on a universal negative proposition. Vita is further sub-divided into **Purvavat** and **Samanyatdrasta**.

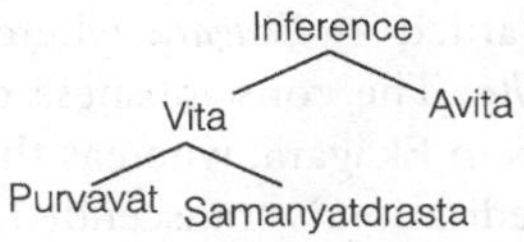

Purvavat's inference is that which is based on the observed uniformity of concomitance between two things. While Samanyatdrasta is not based on any observation of the concomitance between the middle and major term.

Verbal Testimony (Sabda)

Verbal statement and verbal testimony of the knowledge of object derived through words is known as **Sabda**. It is also defined as valid testimony *i.e.* the testimony of trust worthy person (apta) who knowns the truth and convey it correctly. Sabda literally means sound (dhwani) but epistemologically it means meaningful sound or word. It is an important source of knowledge because a major portion of our knowledge of the objects of this world is derived from words.

Eight Fold Path of Yoga

Yoga's main function is to control the body, the senses and the mind. It recommends only perfection. Yoga also overcomes sensual attachment and passion.

According to **Yoga System**, there are eight-fold path of discipline known as 'Astanga Yoga', *which are as follows*

(i) **Yama** It is regarded as abstention. It includes the five vows of Jainism *i.e.* Ahimsa, Satya, Asteya, Brahmacharya and Aparigraha.

(ii) **Niyama** It is regarded as self-culture. It includes external and internal purification.

(iii) **Asana** It is regarded as steady and comfortable postures. Various kinds of postures provides physical help to meditation.

(iv) **Pranayama** It is regarded as control of breath. It also deals with regulation of inhalation and exhalation of breath. It is very important for the concentration of the mind.

(v) **Pratyahara** It is regarded as the control of the senses. It is referred as the process of introversion.

(vi) **Dharana** It is regarded as the fixation of the mind on the object of meditation. Here, the mind is regarded as the steadfast.

(vii) **Dhyana** It is regarded as meditation. It is also referred as the steadfast contemplation without any break.

(viii) **Samadhi** It is regarded as concentration. The mind is completely absorbed in the object of meditation.

It is regarded as of two kinds which are as follows :

- Conscious
- Supra-conscious

The former is regarded as *Ekagara* whereas the latter is regarded as *Nirudha*. The consciousness of the object of meditation persists in Ekagara, whereas the consciousness of the object of meditation is transcended in Nirudha.

Patanjali's Concept of Chitta and Chitta-Vrtti

The cessation of the modifications of Chitta is known as Yoga. This cessation occurs only through meditation. Chitta is defined as the three internal organs of Sankhya. The three internal organs includes **Buddhi**, **Ego** and **Manas**.

Antahkarana and Chitta means the same. Chitta is regarded as the first evolute of Prakriti. Chitta has the predominance of Sattva. It is regarded as unconscious. It is nearest to Purusha also. It also reflects the Purusha.

Vrtti is known as modification. When Chitta gets related to any object, then it assumes the form of the object. Chitta is referred as the physical medium for the manifestation of the spirit.

There are five kinds of the modification of the Chitta, which are as follows

- Right cognition
- Wrong cognition
- Verbal cognition
- Absence of cognition
- Memory

Right cognition includes perception, inference and verbal testimony. Wrong cognition means positively wrong knowledge. Verbal cognition means imagination. Nidra means absence of cognition. Smrti is regarded as the recollection of past experience. It requires the impressions.

Ignorance, egoism, attachment, aversion, clinging to life and instinctive fear of death are the main sufferings of life.

Yoga in Education

Education in the Yoga is also a spirituous-social necessity because the system aims at attaining the highest evolution of human-self. The aim of entire education, formal and informal is to attain God head or bliss that comes after the empirical self is merged in the transcendental self or God. But the process of self-discipline implies that without the well-being of human body and moral preparation on the part of man, Yoga is not possible. This aspect makes education a social necessity.

Aims of Education

The aim of education according to the Yoga is the comprehensive development of human personality and also to make human child, free from bodily, mental and super natural miseries. This implies that education must care for the physical, mental, intellectual and spiritual growth of the pupil. The aim of education according to the Yoga is the moral preparation of the pupil, spiritual attainment, the development of scientific attitude and logical and intellectual faculties. It further means is to evolve a society of person who is noblest in their thoughts and actions.

The teacher is not only a theoretician but, also a demonstrator in a scientific notion, power of knowledge, power of will and power of action. The method of education believes in discriminative method in acquiring knowledge in terms of concentration. The disciplining of body and mind is the core of educational process and modern educators must know the inevitability of this factor any kind of education.

Methods of Education

- 'Cittavrthinirodha' (Concentration/meditation) involves right cognition, wrong cognition, imagination, memory.
- Concentration as the most essential method.
- Scientific attitude development method.
- Yoga adopts not only the scientific attitude but also the programmatic one.
- The system also believes in discriminative method in acquiring knowledge.
- The law of association in education constitutes great importance in the Yoga.

Role of a Teacher

- Great importance to teacher.
- Not only a theoretician but also a demonstrator.
- Give practical demonstration to the student (scientific notion).
- Teacher has power of knowledge, power of will and power of action.

Role of a Student

- Surrender to his teacher for his total cure.
- Without teacher nothing can be obtained by the student.

Curriculum

- System stands for psycho-physical training of human child.
- Provides literature which arouses interest amongst students in moral life.

- Embodies such specific sciences as medicine, clinical psychology, social sciences.
- Yoga approves all those subjects which deal with human physiology, true human nature and hidden laws of nature.
- Most appropriate to the evolution of individual and society.
- If society are highly evolved divine culture can be happily fostered.

Discipline

- Education and discipline are identical.
- Discipline is the means of which Yoga is the aim.
- One has to discipline oneself physically and intellectually.
- Disciplining of body and mind is the core of educational process.

Education system not only in India, but the modern globalising world also really is in great need of taking help of Yoga System. Therefore, it is high time to think seriously on inclusion of Yoga and Yogic values in education system.

Self-Education (Education of Self-Realisation)

Yoga renders self-education. It is nothing but education of self-awareness. Yoga teaches us how to live with wisdom, not with the worldly orientations, present education system should inculcate this yogic value intensively. Yoga system can impart progressive training for the development of self-awareness and educate us about the realities of our being and becoming.

Vedanta

The most pervasive philosophical tradition in India is the Vedanta in its different forms. The reason for this is that the schools of Vedanta trace their origin to the Upanishads, which have justly been called the Himalayas of the soul. The **Upanishads** themselves are called **Vedanta**, because they constitute the end of Veda, both in the sense of constituting, mostly the concluding portion of the Veda.

Vedanta was originally a word used in Hindu Philosophy as a synonym for that part of which we mark it's end and this end is said to be Upanishads.

In respect to Vedanta, it is also said to be the *Uttar Mimamsa*. The theory of Vedanta is often paired with *Purva Mimamsa*. It is believed that Vedanta school is more Orthodox because of their close adherence and philosophical sections of the Veda.

Classification of Vedanta School

Advaita Vedanta It is the most influential school of all, and many philosophers, both Indian and Western have been influenced by it. It was propounded by *Adisankara*, a great Hindu reformer. According to this, Brahman is the only ultimate reality and the world is an illusion. Ignorance is the cause of all suffering in the world and only upon true knowledge of Brahman can liberation be attained. Upon liberation, there is no difference between the individual soul Jivatman and Brahman.

"The Guru is Brahma, the Guru is Vishnu, the Guru is Shiva, the God of Gods, the Guru is verily the supreme Brahman. Salutations to the adorable Guru".

Vishishtadvaita It is propounded by Ramanuja and says that the Jivatman is a part of Brahman and hence is similar, but not identical. It also propounds Bhakti or devotional form of worship of God visualised as Vishnu. Maya is seen as the creative power of God.

Dvaita It is propounded by Madhva. It identifies God with Brahman completely and in turn with Vishnu or his incarnation Krishna. It regards individual soul as separate from Brahman and also advocated Bhakti. There is no concept of Maya.

Dvaitadvaita It is propounded by Nimbarka. According to this, Brahman-Jiva relation may be regarded as Dvaita from one point of view and Advaita from another.

Shuddhadvaita It is propounded by Vallabha. This system also encourages Bhakti as the only means of liberation to go to Goloka (The world of cows). The world is said to be the sport (Leela) of Krishna, who is Sat-Chit-Ananda.

Achintya Bhedabheda It is propounded by Chaitanya Mahaprabhu. A Bhakti oriented devotees of Krishna, this doctrine is followed by the world famous ISKCON movement.

Vedanta Philosophy and practice provides contemplative methods of self-inquiry leading to the realisation of one's true nature, that which is not subject to death, decay or decomposition. A major key of these practices is contemplation on the Mahavakyas.

The teachings of the Vedanta are best captured in the books of the Upanishads. The text Vivekachudamani (Crest jewel of discrimination) by Adi Shankaracharya is an excellent source.

Vedanta in Education

Education during Vedic period was the third eye, the third eye of insight and source of illumination. The system of education generally advocated emanated from the Vedas and was called Vedic System of Education.

Vedanta is nothing but a teachings of the Upanishads, the Brahma Sutras and Bhagwat Gita. The essence of the teachings of Vedanta is that Brahman (God) which is existence, consciousness and bliss absolute is the only reality and that the universe is an illusionary appearance like a mirage seen in a desert or rope mistakenly seen as a snake and that the individual being (self) is essentially Brahman or God himself. This oneness of the self (Jiva) with absolute consciousness (Brahman or God) is the goal of Vedanta.

Aims of Education

Tamso-ma-Jyotirgamaya One of the aim of education is this, in which knowledge should dispel doubts, dogmas and darkness.

Individual-Centred Education Education should aims at overall development of an individual.

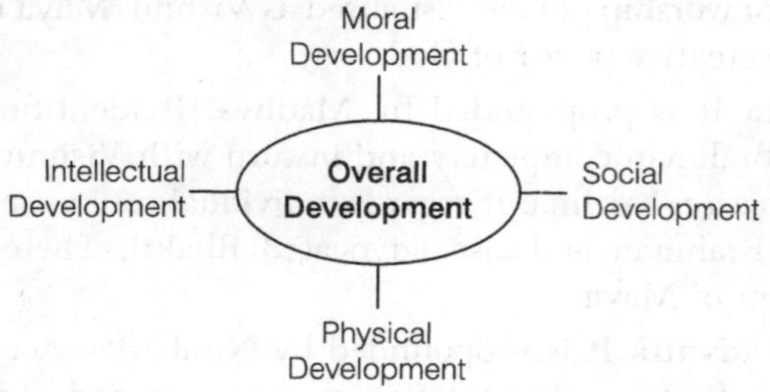

Nature-Oriented Education The centres of education were located from the populated and crowded areas, more in natural and serene surroundings. Education should make man one with nature.

Religion-Centered Education Religion dominated every aspects of life i.e. national, personal, social and educative procedures and practices, hence education should be wedded to religion.

Education of Mind Education should provide knowledge for creativity and pursuit of culture and civilisation.

Educational Implications

All Round Development of Child All round development of a child's personality was the chief aim of education. The nature of education was much more individualistic rather than in groups.

Equality of Opportunity There was no discrimination on the basis of caste, creed and colour and the students of a strata of society received education on an equal footing. In modern India too, the Constitution has adopted the principle of equality in the field of education.

Education for Self-Sufficiency Apart from the intellectual aspects of education, its practical side was not lost sight of and along with art, literature and philosophy, students got a working knowledge of agriculture and other vocations of life.

Discipline and Pupil-Teacher Relationship The sense of discipline and cordial relation between teacher and pupil of Vedic age is well known to the world.

Subject of Studies Vedic literature is enriched by the sense of peace, humanity, universal brotherhood, which is also vital part of our curriculum.

Commercial Education and Vedic Mathematics This is one of chief feature of Vedic period. Vedic mathematics have become more popular now.

Methods of Teaching

During the Vedanta or Upanishadic period, the teacher imparted education to his pupils. The pupils were to listen to their teacher's words attentively. But the teacher and pupil were very much involved in the teaching and learning process.

The first step of studying was hearing, second step to practice or recitation of the taught text, the third step was to understand the meaning *i.e.* comprehension and fourth was inference *i.e.* understanding the result. After this, the fifth step comes in which the semantic was related to the explanatory subject matter and Brahmanic subjects of study. The sixth step was that of evidence or proofs which meant arriving at conclusions. Thus, the method of study had six points of development. The teacher explained the subject matter with the help of stories, proverbs and other illustrations.

Role of Teacher

The teacher is not merely a teacher but also a guide, mentor, a surrogate, parent, a role model and a friend.

Curriculum

In Vedanta, it has been mentioned that student should receive knowledge of various subjects. Thus, the major division of education is one where we are concerned with the supreme in which we deals with the knowledge about the soul, the universe and God. In other words, the efforts are made to know the universal truth.

On the other side, the focus is on the subjects like Vedas, Vedang, sound system, knowledge of religious rites, grammar, astronomy, commentary history, Purans, ethics and military science etc. were studied.

Discipline

- Rules of conduct should be listed down for both teacher and student.
- Rules also for respect due from pupils to teacher were framed.
- Rigid rules were laid for conduct of pupils.
- Code of dress was observed.
- Observation of Brahmacharya or Celibacy was compulsory for all pupils.

Buddhism

The religious background, in which Buddhism grew up in India was that of Brahmanism. The supremacy of Brahmanical religion coupled with social inequalities and economic disparities created a condition that helped the rise of the protestant movements in India during 6th century BC. Buddhism was the most remarkable among them.

Buddhism is a religion indigenous to the Indian sub-continent that encompasses a variety of traditions, beliefs and practices largely based on teachings attributed to **Siddhartha Gautama**, who is commonly known as the **Buddha**, meaning the awakened one. Buddha was a Kshatriya prince from small Shakya kingdom in the Himalayan foothills. Buddhism is unusual among the world religions in that it does not centre upon a God. Its supreme purpose was to achieve liberation from suffering through the renunciation of desire, known as 'Nirvana'.

Buddhism gives importance to the impermanence of existence and the sufferings associated with it. All existence, animate and inanimate, being in a state of flux, undergo changes incessantly. Nothing is permanent; existence is the source of all sufferings. Life is suffering the impermanence itself is the greatest Dukha. Ignorance leads to sufferings and bondage. Karma is born out of ignorance. Karmic impressions are carried from this birth to the next birth. This means that the present conditions of life are the results of the past Karma. Every thought, word or action of the past existence has a bearing on the present existence.

Principles of Buddhism

The most striking feature of Buddhism is the Doctrine of Non-Self (Anatta). In a glaring and sharp contrast to the major philosophies, Buddhism does not accept the permanent entity such as *Soul* or the *Atman*. It maintains that there is no permanent and enduring entity in man. There is no distinct entity as the self or the soul. Buddhism advances the theory of Nirvana. Nirvana is a state of total freedom and no sufferings, with perfect knowledge, perfect peace and perfect wisdom, man is free from all bondage in the state of Nirvana Lord Buddha taught his followers four 'Noble Truths' or 'Aryasatya', which he realised during his enlightenment.

The four noble truths presented by Buddha are

(i) The truth of suffering (Dukkha).
(ii) The truth of the origin of suffering (Samudaya).
(iii) The truth of the cessation of suffering (Nirodha).
(iv) The truth of the path to the cessation of suffering (Marga).

The eight fold path to Nirvana suggested by the Buddha are

- Right to Belief
- Right to Memory
- Right to Speech
- Right to Thought
- Right to Meditate
- Right to Effort
- Right to Conduct
- Right to Action

Classification of Buddhism School

Hinayana School (i.e. the lesser vechicle)

- Its followers believed in the original teaching of Buddha.
- They sought individual salvation through self-discipline and meditation.
- They did not believe in idol worship.
- They favour Pali language.
- It is known as 'Southern Buddhist Religion' because it prevailed in South India. eg. Sri Lanka, Burma, etc.
- There were two sub-sects of Hinayana *i.e.* Vaibhasika and Sautrantika

Mahayana School (i.e. the greater vehicle)

- Its followers belived in the heavenliness of Buddha.
- They sought the salvation of all through the grace and help of Buddha and Bodhisattva.
- They believe in idol worship.
- They favoured Sanskrit language.
- It is known as 'Northern Budhhist Religion' because it prevailed in North India and religions like China, Korea, Japan, etc.

Educational Philosophy

Buddhist education offered to impart education for all. Many people shifted to Buddhist educational system. It was for the first time in India that education was institutionalised on a large scale during Buddhist movement.

It is also a historic fact that with the arrival of Buddhist era, great international centres of education like Nalanda, Takshashila, Vikramshila, Ballabhi, Odantapuri, Nadia, Amravati, Nagahalla and Sarnath were in prominence. Educational centres in Buddha period developed in Viharas and Sanghas.

Aims of Education

The Buddhist educational aims were comprehensive based on knowledge, social development, vocational development, religious development, character development, *which are as follows*

- To follow the moral values of Buddhist religion.
- To eradicate Vedic Karmakanda or Ritualism.
- To provide education in the language of masses *i.e.* Pali.

- To emphasise the progress and development of the society rather than the individual.
- To provide education through the new system and this was stated by Buddha.
- To give up caste system.
- To achieve the final goal of Nirvana.

Methods of Teaching

The following are methods adopted in Buddhist Philosophy for teaching

Methods of Teaching
- Agra Shishya Pranali (Monitorial System)
- Preaching and Conference Method
- Travelling and Nature Study Method
- Mostly Verbal with Discussions and Debates

The ***two-tier system*** *was adopted in education system as follows:*

Two-Tier System of Education
- Popular Elementary Education
  - Curriculum of Elementary Education
    - Hetu Vidya (Logic)
    - Nyaya (Science and reasoning)
    - Adyatma Vidya (Philosophy)
    - Shilpasthan (Art and crafts)
    - Chikitsya Vidya (Medicine)
- Higher Education
  - Curriculum of Higher Education
    - Buddhism
    - Hinduism
    - Astrology
    - Medicine
    - Administration
    - Tantrik Philosophy
    - Logic
    - Meta physics

Educational Implications

Total Development of Personality Buddhist education laids much emphasis on physical, mental and spiritual development. Even today the aim of education is integration of personality that can develop the various aspects of the individual which are inter-linked.

Positivism Buddhist philosophy is positivistic and has a careful logical systematisation of idea.

Ethical It is ethical, the eight fold path to Nirvana makes a universal appeal.

Cosmopolitan Buddhist education was free from communal narrowness, there was no favouritism on the basis of caste, creed in the centres.

No Corporal Punishment Corporal punishments were absolutely forbidden, which is also very true in the present scenario of education.

Development of Good Conduct The entire techniques of Buddhism provide directions to develop good conduct and which is also the essence of a sound system of education.

Moral Discipline Character was the basis of moral discipline. The monk took the vows of chastity and of poverty.

Emphasis on Manual Skills Training of manual skills like spinning and weaving was emphasised to enable men to earn for living.

Educational Implications of Buddhism
- Emphasis on simple life and high thinking
- Emphasis on values
- Emphasis on mass education
- Emphasis on spread of higher education
- Emphasis on development of art and literature
- Emphasis on state patronage of education
- Emphasis on higher standard of education
- Emphasis on ideal relationship between teacher and the taught

Symbols of Buddhism

Buddhist's symbols have special meanings that remind us of Buddha's teachings. The main room or building is called a *Shrine* or a *Buddha Hall*. In front of this room, there is an *Altar*.

There are many symbols and beautiful things on the Altar, which are as follows

Buddhist's Symbols
- Images of the Buddha
- Traditional Offerings
- Dharma Instruments

Images of the Buddha There are many different kinds of Buddha and Bodhisattva images that show different qualities. *e.g.*, a statue of the Buddha with his hand resting gently on his lap reminds us to develop peace within overselves. A statue with the Buddha's right hand touching the ground shows determination.

Traditional Offerings Traditional offerings are to show respect to the Buddha.

Traditional Offerings
- Flowers — These are offered as reminders of how quickly things changes
- Light from lamps or candles — These symbolises wisdom
- Incense — These remind one to be peaceful
- Water — This represents purity
- Food — This represents us to give our best to the Buddha

Dharma Instruments The instruments, which used in ceremonies and meditation are called Dharma instruments Each instrument has a specific use, for instance, the wooden fish is hit to keep rhythm.

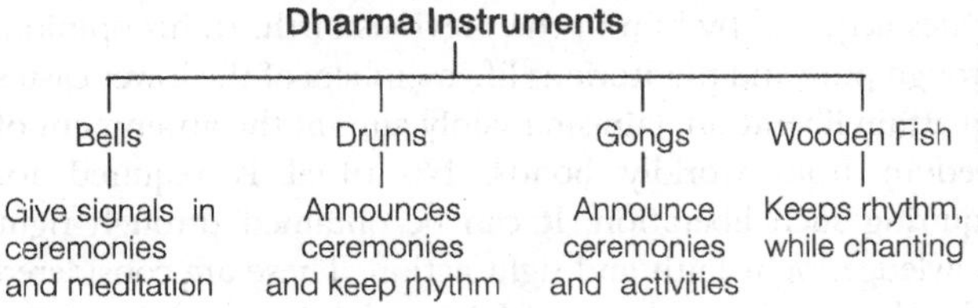

Curriculum

- As Buddha stressed actions, so curriculum of Buddhistic education includes practical activities. These practical activities include physical, intellectual, moral and social actions.
- For achieving salvation, moral education, meditation, and intelligence have been considered necessary. Although, Buddha usually avoids long discussions, yet towards superstitions, orthodox views, and useless rituals he had the approach of a modern scientist.
- Training of senses was emphasised in Buddhistic education which helps in detachment, destruction of passion, end of miseries, achievement of mental peace, knowledge, wisdom and Nirvana.
- Everything remains in this world for some time and then it meet's its end in the same way as one wave goes. By illusion, we consider the continuity of sequence as permanent.
- Thus, he suggested social science, moral education, ethics, science etc. and co-curricular activities includes social service, welfare of all, non-violence and behaviour of the student should be according to the vows emphasised by Buddhist thoughts.

Discipline

Buddha teaching contains three major points *i.e.* discipline, meditation and wisdom. Wisdom is the goal and deep meditation is the crucial process towards achieving wisdom. Discipline through observing the precepts is the method that helps one to achieve deep meditation, wisdom will then be realised naturally. Buddha's entire teaching as conveyed in the Sutra never depart from these three points.

After getting education in the Buddhist schools, colleges and universities one cannot do any injustice, tell a lie, commit theft, cannot kill, cannot be addicted in wine and make himself free from moral turpitude. In this way, students become free from greed, lust, enmity and ignorance.

The monk and the students in Buddhist period were following the simple living and high thinking principle. Their lives were full of purity, dutifulness and are suppose to follow the **Astang Marg**.

Role of a Teacher

The duties of the teachers were imparting education to the students, writing books, propagation of religion, discussion, and arrangement of debate for the clarification of serious subjects. The teachers were responsible for physical, mental, spiritual and moral development of the students. Teachers loved the students and helped them in every affair. They also took care of them during their diseases and agony.

During Buddhist period, the place of teacher in the scheme of education was very important. There were the categories of teachers *i.e.* Acharyas and Upadhayas. The teachers were responsible for their food, accommodation and other necessities of livelihood. They kept eyes on the all round development of the students. Especially, they were serious about the obedience of the rules, meditation and concentration to their learning.

Both the teacher and the student were responsible to the Buddhist's order. But regarding education, clothes , food and residence of the student monk, the teacher was wholly responsible. The teacher was also responsible for any treatment of the student whenever he fell ill. The teacher used to bestow all the affection to his student and used to educate him through lecture and question- answer method. The teacher was regarded as spiritual father or intellectual father of the student.

Jainism

Jainism is one of the major religions that flourished in India prior to Buddhism and Christianity. This is a transethnic religion of India, which believes that human beings to conquer the worldly passions through physical and mental control. Jainism left remarkable impact on Indian civilisation. Jains are extremely rich and extensive with huge number of epics, texts and stories.

The Jainas believe in **24 Tirthankaras**. They are said to be Tirthankaras because they serve as the ferry men across the river of transmigration. The 24th Tirthankara was *Vardhman Mahavira*. The philosophical outlook of Jainism is the common sense, realism and pluralism.

The objects perceived by us are real and they are many.

Jainism traditionally known as 'Jaina Dharma' that prescribes a path of non-violence towards all living beings and emphasises spiritual independence and equality between all forms of life. Thus, this religion is marked as the oldest religion of the world.

Core Principles of Jainism

- **Non-violence** The principle of non-violence or ahimsa is the most distinctive and well known aspect of Jaina religious practice. The Jaina's understanding and implementation of ahimsa is more radical, scrupulous and comprehensive than in other religions. Non-violence is seen as the most essential religious duty for everyone.

  A scrupulous and thorough application of non-violence to everyday activities and especially to food, is the most significant hall mark of Jaina's identity. The strictest forms of Jaina's diet are practised by the ascetics, for Jains lacto-vegetarianism represents the minimal obligation *i.e.* food which contains even small particles of the bodies of dead animal or eggs is absolutely unacceptable. Jains make considerable efforts in every day life not to injured plants any more than necessary.
- **Self-control** Jainism encourages spiritual development through cultivation of personal wisdom and through reliance on self-control through vows. Jains accept different levels of compliance for ascetics and lay followers.
- **Soul and Karma** According to Jains, souls are intrinsically pure and possess the qualities of infinite knowledge, infinite perception, infinite bliss and infinite energy.

  In contemporary experience, however these qualities are found to be obstructed, on account of the soul's association with a substance called Karma over an eternity of beginning less time.

Doctrine of Jaina

Jaina metaphysics deals with *Anekantavada* or the Doctrine of Manyness of Reality. All objects of knowledge are manifold or multiform (Anekanta). They have infinite qualities and relations which distinguishes them from the other objects. Every object is what it is because of its positive and negative characteristics. Therefore, only the omniscient can know an object fully.

Every object possesses innumerable characteristics but it is impossible for ordinary people to know all the qualities of a thing. An ordinary person can know only some qualities of something. Human knowledge is necessarily relative and limited and so are all our judgements. This epistemology and logical theory of Jainas is called *Syadvada*.

As a matter of fact, both Anekantavada and Syadvada are the two aspects of the same teaching relativistic pluralism and realistic. The metaphysical side that reality has innumerable character is called *Anekantavada*, while the epistemological and logical side that we can know only some aspects of reality is called *Syadvada*.

Jainism recognised the existence of the Gods, but placed them lower than the Jina. It did not condemn the Varna system, as Buddhism did. According to **Mahavira**, a person is born in a high or in a lower varna in consequence of the sins or the virtues acquired by him in the previous birth. In his opinion, through pure and meritorious life members of the lower castes can attain liberation. Jainism mainly aims at the attainment of freedom from worldly bonds. No ritual is required for acquiring such liberation. It can be obtained through right knowledge, right faith and right action. These are considered to be *three jewels* or *triratna of Jainism*. Jainism prohibited the practice of war and even agriculture for its followers because both involve the killing of living beings.

Path of Liberation for Jaina

The Jaina's teacher urges that right faith, right knowledge and right conduct are the three indispensable paths to self-realisation or liberation. All the three should be practised simultaneously. Hence, these three taken together have been called *three Jewels*. (Triratna)

Liberation is joint effort of these three i.e.

(i) **Right Faith** (Samyak-Darshana) It is the attitude of respect towards truth. Right faith is sincere belief in the essential principle of Jainism.

(ii) **Right Knowledge** (Samyak-Jnana) It is the state of detailed cognition of the real nature of the soul and non-soul. Right knowledge is free from doubt, error and uncertainty. For the attainment of perfect knowledge, the removal of Karmas that hinder in the way of attaining knowledge should be removed. Perfection of this process ends in the attainment of absolute omniscience (Kevaljnana).

(iii) **Right Conduct** (Samyak-Charitra) Right conduct is what helps the soul to get rid of the Karmas and lead him to bondage. For the stoppage of the influx of new Karmas and for the wearing out of the Karmas that have already entered the soul, the aspirant must practice extreme carefulness (Samiti) in walking, speaking, etc.

Teaching of Jainism

Thus, in order to attain liberation, Jaina talked about five great vows (Pancha-Mahavrata).

The Panch-Mahavrata of Jain includes

Ahimsa or Non-Injury to Life It is based on the idea of potential equality of all souls. It is not only simply to take life but also one should not even think and speak of taking life nor even permit, nor encourage others to take life.

Satyam or Abstinence from Falsehood It consists in not only what is true, but also what is good and pleasant.

Asteyam or Abstinence from Stealing It consists in not taking what is not given. It is based on the idea of the sanctity of property.

Brahmacharyam or Abstinence from Self-Indulgence It consists in abstaining from all forms of self-indulgence *i.e.* external and internal, subtle and gross, mundane and extra mundane, direct and indirect.

Aparigraha or Abstinence from all Attachment It consists in abstaining from all attachment of the five senses *i.e.* pleasant sound, touch, colour, taste and smell.

Aims of Education

- Teaching should give necessary Jnana and penance to help Jiva.
- Believe in transmigration of soul, hence, education may partly be the preparation for the next world.
- Education should leads to self-enlightenment and restore the full potentials of Jiva.
- Self-realisation as Jiva is divine. Education must focus on his divinity and remove the material bonds of soul.
- Education should helps student to do Karma which leads towards Moksha.

Educational Implications

Law of Karma (Cause and effect) Universe is ruled by moral law, which punishes all sins and rewards good deeds. Belief that our character creates its own heaven and hell is significant in nearly all schools of philosophy.

Highest State of Knowledge The highest state of knowledge is intuition through which man achieves a realisation of oneness of the universe.

Integrated Education The contribution of Jain Philosophy in the development of Indian Philosophy has been significant. Jain Philosophical concepts like Ahimsa, Karma, Moksha, Sansara and the like have been assimilated into philosophies of other Indian religions like Hinduism and Buddhism.

Aim of Education The main objective of education in India, since earliest days of civilisation had been man-making ,who is capable of self-realisation.

Concept of Compassion Sense of sympathy extends to all living being, even to animals as stated in both Jainism and Buddhism.

Emphasis on Non-violence The feature of Philosophy is its strong emphasis on non-violence, accent on multiple facts of truth, morality and ethics.

Contribution to the Strain of Pacifism Absolute respect for living beings is stressed and the best way to resist evil is through non-violence.

Methods of Teaching

The following are the methods of teaching used in Jaina's education

- Teaching through senses and meditation.
- Teaching should be social and tolerant.
- Teaching should be action based and ideally oriented.

Curriculum

- Jaina system stressed that the Jiva has to face the consequences of its deeds. Its colour, physical beauty, age and other senses are according to its deeds. Whatever gets in his life are the fruit of his own deeds not the grace of God. Hence, Jaina curriculum includes those subjects which lead students towards different actions or activities. And thus, the Jaina curriculum is activity-centered.
- A person dependent on others cannot practice his religion or duties in its true sense. Thus, one's own actions have been emphasised. Therefore, education should provide such environment which is helpful in developing social and moral values in the students.
- The ultimate end of education is to attain salvation. If it is possible to repel our attachment from wordly pleasures many of our strong and unhealthy desires will disappear. Then we shall devote ourselves for attaining salvation. As a result, one should have more faith in doing good to others.
- The ways suggested in Jainism to attain salvation will help us in achieving the aims of education. True education liberates the soul from bondage. This aim can be achieved through different subjects, co-curricular activities and different cultural activities.
- Apart from this, Jaina curriculum also emphasised on vocational education. For this education of different vocations should be provided to the students. This will help in equipoising economic conditions in the country and in developing manpower also.
- Thus, Jaina curriculum includes social sciences, natural science, moral education, vocational education and various co-curricular activities and yoga exercise.

Discipline

- Student should respect the teacher and treat them as God.
- Emulate all the ideal character from their Gurus.
- One should be careful in the walk of life.
- Follow five vows to attain good conduct.
- Practice ten different Dharmas like, non-attachments, forgiveness, self-restraint, austerity, etc.

Role of a Teacher

- He/she should be the role model.
- A living exemplary will all vows.
- Gurus are considered as Gods.
- Train rigorously to liberate the soul from bondage.

Dayanand Darshan

Among the contemporary Indian philosophers, **Swami Dayanand** may be called to be the greatest rationalist. While on the one hand, he was a great supporter of Vedas and other holy texts, his approach everywhere was that of a rationalist. He never accepted anything without meditating upon its advantages and disadvantages.

His magnum opus Satyartha Prakash is an eloquent testimony to his rationalism. Pointing out the object of this great work Dayanand wrote, "there is not the remotest idea to hurt the feelings of any person either directly or indirectly, but on the contrary, the book proposes that men should distinguish truth from falsehood. Thus, since none but the practicing of truth is the cause of the improvement of the human family".

These words express both his rationalism and humanism. As is clear by the above object of the chief work of Dayanand, like a true humanist, he aimed at the progress of humanity on the path of happiness. Thus, it was in keeping with this aim that Dayanand presented his Philosophy.

Nature of Education

According to **Swami Dayanand**, education imparts true and real knowledge about master, self-development and welfare of all living beings. In other words, it should inculcate a spirit of service and help to others.

In this way, according to **Swami Ji**, education is a supreme and most important moral process for the development of mankind. **Swami Dayanand** says, "A man without education is only a man in name. It is bound in duty of a man to get education, become virtuous, be free from malice and preach for all well-being of people advancing the cause of righteousness".

Contribution of Dayanand

Education for Perfection

The discussion of the Philosophy of Education presented by Dayanand, leads one to the conclusion that his aim was education for perfection.

He sought this aim most vigorously, even sometimes presenting schemes which were far from practicable and demanding standards and virtues which could not be attained even by the selected person. He demanded very high standard of character and conduct. He wanted to realise all round perfection.

Multi-Sided Curriculum

A perusal of the curriculum given in Satyartha Prakash amply clarifies the fact that Dayanand aimed at perfection of man through education.

It is due to his anxiety about achieving an all round and most comprehensive perfection of man that he prescribed such a detailed curriculum which may appear too wide in the modern age of specialisation and yet if one remembers the fact that specialised knowledge always creates a one sided personality and never a total perfection, one may be able to appreciate Dayanand's stand point. It is undeniable that the scheme of education presented by Dayanand is too rigorous and beyond the capacity of most of the males and females in the present time.

Humanism and Rationalism

Besides the ideal of perfection as a humanist ideal, Dayanand showed his humanistic tendency in his strong condemnation of all superstitions, unscientific beliefs, immoralities and deceptions. In his support of science and the scientific outlook, he was more positive than many contemporary positivists.

He was among the foremost rationalists to emphasis upon the use of reason in every field of human life. While on the one hand, he had absolute respect for the Vedas, whom he considered to be divine, on the other hand, he advised everyone to distinguish truth and untruth, use rational criteria and accept only that which is supported by sound logic. Thus, if something appears to be out of date in his scheme of education that hardly detracts its value, since what is important is not the detailed scheme but the insight behind it.

Dayanand's educational philosophy is as kin to Vedic Philosophy, although his interpretation of Vedic Philosophy is unique. When he first preached his lesson, there was the greatest need to protect Hindu religion and Philosophy from the onslaughts of Muslim and Christian religions. He saved Hindu society. He protected the ancient Hindu values from the influence of Muslim and Christian cultures and tried to maintain the traditional modes of thinking. His ideas on education have great significance for contemporary educational Philosophy. The contribution of Swami Dayanand towards the Philosophy and practice of education is noteworthy. There is no gain saying, the fact that the history of education of modern India cannot be complete without mention of his glorious contribution.

Aims of Education

Aims of education, according to Indian Tradition is imparting Vidya, which is real knowledge. Dayanand considered that true education removes ignorance and increases knowledge and spiritual values like religiousity and self-control.

According to Dayanand, education has five characteristics, *viz* provision of right knowledge, cultivation of culture, increase of religiousity, increase of self-control and liberation from ignorance, such education is for the welfare in this world and also the other world.

In his book, **Vyavahar Bhanu**, Dayanand maintained that education is that by which man attains happiness and knowledge. It is through knowledge that one can attain happiness.

The function of education is to provide this vidya. Prior to defining right knowledge or Vidya, Dayanand pointed out the following characteristics of Avidya or ignorance.

Education aims at removing the above mentioned fourfold ignorance. Besides this negative aspect, education has a positive aspect in the provision of right knowledge.

Role of a Teacher

Great importance is given to the role of the teacher by Swami Dayanand. The teachers are to be learned, of good character and devoted to their task. There is no room for arrogant teachers who are not dedicated to their task. There has to be a close relationship, like that of a father and son, between the teacher and his pupil.

Discipline

Dayanand was a strict disciplinarian and believes in taking strong action against teachers and pupils, who broke the rules of the school.

Curriculum

In his scheme of education, Dayanand prescribed almost similar types of education for males and females. Besides a general curriculum for educand from the four Varnas, Dayanand also prescribed some special studies for each Varna. He pointed out that only those books should be recommended for deep study which passes all scrutiny.

Methods of Teaching

Dayanand not only prescribed a detailed curriculum but also pointed out the impediments which should be avoided by the teachers and students, in order to achieve the aims of education. Describing these impediments, he wrote "Both the teachers and their scholars should avoid all those things that act as hindrances in the way of the acquisition of knowledge such as the company of the wicked people, contraction of bad habits (such as the use of intoxications), fornication, child-marriage, want of perfect Brahmacharya, want of love on the part of the rulers, parents and learned men for the dissemination of knowledge of the Vedas and other Satras, over-eating".

He prescribed some teaching methods that are given below

- He says that the curriculum should be such which takes man to the path of truth.
- He pointed out the impediments which should be avoided by the teachers and students in order to achieve the aims of education.
- Both teachers and students must avoid hindrance such as company of wicked people, dishonesty, etc.
- Teacher should have good memory and sound logic. He was supporting Vedic philosophy of education.

Educational Implications

Swami Dayanand brought into light about constructive, comprehensive character of scheme of education. He tries to materialise the moral and spiritual welfare and upliftment of humanity irrespective of caste, creed, nationality or time.

Islamic Philosophy

Islamic Philosophy is a branch of Islamic studies, and is a longs tanding attempt to create harmony between Philosophy (Reason) and the religious teachings of Islam (Faith). Islamic Philosophy, as the name implies, refers to Philosophical activity within the Islamic milieu.

The main sources of classical or early Islamic Philosophy are the religion of Islam itself (especially ideas derived and interpreted from the Quran). In early Islamic thought, two main currents may be distinguished *i.e.* **Kalam**, dealing mainly with theological questions, and **Falsafa**, founded on interpretation of Aristotelian and Neoplatonic Philosophy.

Concept of Islamic Education

Islamic philosophy concerned with the matters such as the problem of unity and multiplicity, the relationship between God and the world. One of the most important principles in Islamic philosophy is the Principle of Divinity. Islamic philosophy was largely concerned with defining and elaborating God's attributes. God's attributes were enumerated, but his essence was deemed to lie beyond human knowledge.

Islamic philosophy reconciles revelation with intellect, knowledge with faith and religion with philosophy.

So, in Islamic philosophy, the result of revelation, intellect, faith, knowledge and religion matches and confirms each other.

Islam accounts for a great following in India, after Hinduism. Ideologically, it is a continuation of the ancient Mesopotamian tradition and recrystallisation of Judaism and Christianity, but does not support inter-religious borrowing. Islam means total submission to Allah or God.

Educational Implications

Islam is a religion for all mankind and is relevant to both spiritual and mundane life. Islam does not recognise the differences on the basis of caste, creed, wealth, language, race, region, etc.

Islam means peace through the submission to God. Islam essentially stands for deep religious life and at the same time defines a good living for the mankind. The object of Islamic education was attainment of worldly prosperity and social distinction. The main aim of education is to understand the relation of man with God as revealed in the Holy Quran.

Aims and Objectives

- To provide experiences which are based on fundamentals of Islam.
- To foster great consciousness of the divine presence in the universe.
- To provide the teachings of Holy Quran as the first step of education.
- To provide experiences in the form of knowledge and skills with clear understanding that these experiences are likely to be changed in the light of changes in society.
- To encourage international brotherhood, irrespective of differences in generations, occupation and social class.

Methods of Teaching

- Recitation, learning Kalama and collective repetition.
- Writing, reading and oral methods and also monitor methods in Maktabs and Madarsa.
- Oral and monitorial .
- Akbar stressed on effective teaching by writing letters.
- Due to the Purdah system, women's education was totally neglected. Young girls were secluded and so education was a matter of great difficulty.
- There were no annual exams in the examination system.
- Evaluation was a continuous process.
- Promotion was based upon assessment by the teacher.

Basic Principles

Free Education Education in Maktabs and Madarsa was free and compulsory up to elementary level for all Muslim children.

Patronage of Education Almost all Muslim rulers setup Maktabs and Madarsa and showed their generosity, favour and love for education.

Promotion of Cultural Unity No restriction of caste and religion to get admissions in Maktabs and Madarsa.

Development of Literature and History Great attention was given to the growth of history and art of writing history, in fact, tradition of writing history had its root in this period. Various forms of literature also underwent significant growth.

Monitorial System Monitorial system was also more commonly used.

Practical and Useful Education Education was for preparation for the practical life. Education achieved more objectivity.

Encouragement to Persian Language and Science Persian language was the media of education, so special emphasis was given on the teaching of Arabic and Persian language and the study of science subject was emphasised.

Curriculum

- Reading, writing, arithmetic and religious education, at elementary stage.
- Astronomy, physics, medicine, algebra, geometry, law, history, economics, etc, at higher stage.
- Hindus were taught their own religious books and they were allowed at the Madarsas. Many of the Hindus, also read Persian and acquired mastery.
- Science and art/craft was getting more of importance.
- Theological curriculum, Dare-E-Nizami were followed in India.

EXAM BASED QUESTIONS

1 Education is made from three latin words *i.e.*
(a) Edictive, Educare, Educo (b) Edio, Edicto, Educere
(c) Educare, Educere, Educo (d) None of these

2 Which of the following statement(s) is/are correct?
(a) Education is an art.
(b) Education is a science.
(c) It is neither an art nor science.
(d) To some extent, it is art and to some extent, it is science.

3 What are the three components of the educational process?
(a) Education, teacher and book
(b) Teacher, student and environment
(c) Teaching, learning and practice
(d) Direction, instruction and skill

4 The need for teaching Philosophy of education is based on
(a) all pupils are not alike
(b) different systems of education, found in different countries
(c) different philosophies expressed different points of view, on every aspect of education
(d) different ways of teaching-learning

5 Which is not the nature of philosophy?
(a) It is a science of knowledge.
(b) It is collective assemble of various view points.
(c) It is a planned attempt on search for the truth.
(d) It is totality of man's creative ideas.

6 What does the individual aim of education imply?
(a) Education must secure for everyone, the conditions under which the individuality is most completely developed.
(b) It must contribute to the peace and happiness of the whole society.
(c) It should have more and more institutions every year
(d) It should be by and large the concern of the private sector.

7 Which one of the following sentence(s) is/are correct about the nature of teaching?
(a) It is diagnostic.
(b) It is remedial.
(c) Both a and b
(d) All of the above

8 Which of the following statement(s) does not goes in favour of the individual aims of education?
(a) The individual is an asset to the society, his development and growth are necessary.
(b) The society is strong if the individual is strong.
(c) Society is supreme and all individuals are only part of it.
(d) Every individual is unique, development of his potentialities is essential.

9 What marked the beginning of Indian Philosophy?
(a) Rig Veda (b) Sama Veda
(c) Yajur Veda (d) Atharva Veda

10 Which among the following Indian religions is laid by the Upanishad?
(a) Hinduism (b) Jainism
(c) Buddhism (d) Sufism

11 What is the most important and first period of the history of Indian Philosophy?
(a) Epic period (b) Sutra period
(c) Scholastic period (d) Vedic period

12 Which school promotes materialism?
(a) Nyaya (b) Charvaka
(c) Jainism (d) Buddhism

13 What according to various schools of Indian Philosophy is the main cause of man's suffering?
(a) Ideology (b) Ignorance
(c) Intelligence (d) Emancipation

14 Teachers should study educational philosophy because
(a) they may improve their work by clarifying their own philosophy
(b) they do not have their own philosophy
(c) they do not know it
(d) philosophy is the backbone of disciplines

15 Educational philosophy should be
(a) able to determine the education from a theoretical point of view
(b) concerned with determining the aim of education only
(c) a determining factor in the context of education
(d) concerned with the relation between mind and matter

16 Which philosophy developed the monitorial system in classrooms?
(a) Vedic (b) Islam
(c) Vedanta (d) Buddhism

17 A teacher can adopt methods to realise the objectives of education with the help of
(a) suitable technology
(b) suitable material for infraction
(c) Both a and b
(d) None of the above

18 In the ancient Indian educational tradition, education was regarded as
(a) tool for successful living
(b) tool for self-realisation
(c) means of social service
(d) None of the above

19 Which school upholds the supremacy of Vedas?
(a) Atheistic (b) Theistic
(c) Orthodox (d) Unorthodox

20 Which of the following belongs to Unorthodox System of philosophy?
(a) Sankhya (b) Yoga (c) Jainism (d) Nyaya

21 Who among the following is the founder of Nyaya?
(a) Mahavira (b) Gautama
(c) Kanada (d) Jaimini

22 Who is the founder of Yoga?
(a) Patanjali (b) Kapila
(c) Jaimini (d) Shankara

23 Who is the founder of Sankhya school?
(a) Patanjali (b) Shankara
(c) Kanada (d) Kapila

24 How many schools come under the heading of Unorthodox system?
(a) Three (b) Two
(c) Four (d) Seven

25 'Kanada' is the founder of
(a) Nyaya (b) Vaisheshika
(c) Jaimini (d) Mahavira

26 What is the etymological meaning of the word 'Sankhya'?
(a) Peace (b) Time
(c) Number (d) Space

27 What is said to be the nature of Sankhya based on Upanishad?
(a) Naturalistic (b) Platonic
(c) Idealistic (d) Realistic

28 Whose philosophy is idealistic in nature?
(a) Sankhya (b) Vedanta
(c) Shankara (d) Jainism

29 "It denies the existence of Ishvara (God) or any other exterior influence. It regards the universe as consisting of two realities *i.e.* Purusha and Prakriti."
The above statement belongs to
(a) Nyaya (b) Yoga
(c) Sankhya (d) Vedanta

30 Which school among the following represents the practical aspect of the theory?
(a) Sankhya (b) Yoga (c) Vedanta (d) Nyaya

31 Purusha and Prakriti belongs to system of Indian School of Philosophy.
(a) Vedanta (b) Buddhism
(c) Sankhya (d) Jainism

32 When three qualities of Prakriti come in contact with Purusha, universe was created. This is the belief of
(a) Buddha (b) Mimamsa
(c) Sankhya (d) None of these

33 Which is not among the three Gunas by Sankhya?
(a) Sattva (b) Rajas
(c) Tamas (d) Tejas

34 Which of the following statement(s) is/are correct about the change of Gunas?
(a) Change doesn't describe the equilibrium.
(b) Change disturbs equilibrium.
(c) Change disturbs in some manner while in some manner does not.
(d) None of the above

35 Which type of change in Gunas causes the starting of evolution?
(a) Heterogeneous (b) Homogeneous
(c) Inter-related (d) None of these

36 Which among the following theories of causation is accepted by Sankhya?
(a) Asatkaryavada (b) Arambhavada
(c) Satkaryavada (d) Vivartavada

37 The theory that the effect is pre-existent in its material cause, is known as
(a) Asatkaryavada (b) Satkaryavada
(c) Arambhavada (d) None of these

38 Sankhya's Satkaryavada is also known as
(a) Prakriti-Parinamavada (b) Brahma-Parinamavada
(c) Vivartavada (d) Arambhavada

39 What is already present in man, according to Sankhya for better future?
(a) Emotions (b) Intelligence
(c) Development (d) Philosophy

40 What is the basic purpose of Sankhya educational philosophy?
(a) Knowledge (b) Belief
(c) Happiness (d) End

41 How one can reach 'end' (saddhya), according to Sankhya educational philosophy?
(a) Yoga (b) Dialectic
(c) Education (d) Meeting people

42 What is the role of a teacher, according to Sankhya?
(a) Development of educational theories
(b) Development of inner potency of child
(c) Making techniques for easy learning
(d) None of the above

43 What should come under the ideal educational system of Sankhya?
(a) Education must be in group.
(b) Education should be child-centered.
(c) Education should be given in gaps.
(d) Education should be in game form.

44 Which theory or school deals with the concluding part of Vedas?
(a) Mimamsa (b) Sankhya
(c) Yoga (d) Vedanta

45 Yoga mostly accepts the metaphysics and epistemology of
(a) Nyaya (b) Vaisheshika
(c) Sankhya (d) Mimamsa

46 Which among the following are the five types of Yama by Yoga?
(a) Ahimsa, Asteya, Satya, Brahmacharya, Asana
(b) Ahimsa, Satya, Asteya, Brahmacharya, Aparigraha
(c) Satya, Asteya, Brahmacharya, Aparigraha, Dhyana
(d) Asteya, Brahmacharya, Satya, Dhyana, Asana

47 According to Yoga, which of the following is/are regarded as the first evolute of Prakriti?
(a) Ahankara (b) Chitta
(c) Both a and b (d) None of these

48 According to Yoga, which of the following Gunas is/are said to be predominance in Chitta?
(a) Sattva (b) Rajas
(c) Tamas (d) None of these

49 Whose discipline is important for educational process?
(a) Body and mind (b) Body and spirit
(c) Subject and object (d) Student and teacher

50 What leads by Samadhi *i.e.* transcendental state, according to Jaina?
(a) Faith (b) Belief
(c) Knowledge (d) Wisdom

51 Advaita and Dvaita are the sub-schools of which school of Philosophy?
(a) Vedanta (b) Sankhya
(c) Vaisheshika (d) Nyaya

52 Who is the pro-founder of Dvaitadvaita?
(a) Vallabha (b) Gautama Buddha
(c) Nimbarka (d) Madhva

53 Which school is profounded by Madhva?
(a) Dvaita (b) Vishishtadvaita
(c) Advaita (d) Dvaitadvaita

54 Who founded Shuddhadvaita school?
(a) Madhva (b) Nimbarka
(c) Vallabha (d) Buddha

55 Aim(s) of education, according to Vedantic philosophy is/are
(a) material gain
(b) liberation from the worldly life
(c) moral development of the child
(d) Both b and c

56 What is the highest goal of Vedanta philosophy?
(a) Liberation (b) Oneness of the self
(c) Conscious spirit (d) Attainment of Mahat

57 "Tamso Ma Jyotirgmaya" means
(a) Bringing from darkness to light
(b) Bringing from disbelief to faith
(c) Both a and b
(d) None of the above

58 The root meaning of the term 'Buddha' comes from
(a) Siddhartha's past lives
(b) overcoming temptation
(c) having super human abilities
(d) waking up to reality

59 The first two main divisions of Buddhism were
(a) Mahayana and Vajrayana
(b) Theravada and Mahayana
(c) Theravada and Vajrayana
(d) Mahayana and Tantra

60 Which of the following does not belong to the four noble truths identified by the Buddha?
(a) Salvation is necessary.
(b) Life is suffering.
(c) Suffering can be extinguished.
(d) Desire is the cause of suffering.

61 Buddhist philosophy is mainly aimed at
(a) coping with only physical problems of the world
(b) ending the suffering of the people
(c) making a caste free society
(d) All of the above

62 Which of the following statement belongs to Buddhism?
(a) Harmonious development of personality
(b) The Doctrine of Karma
(c) Child is more important than all kinds of books.
(d) The Doctrine of Dharma

63 The enlightened disciples of the Buddha in the Thervada tradition are called
(a) Bodhidharmas (b) Bodhisattvas
(c) Arhats (d) House holders

64 Mahayana Buddhism
(a) spread South to Ceylon and East to Thailand
(b) continued in India until modern times
(c) spread North to China and Japan
(d) replaced Daoism in China

65 Which classification of Buddhism doesn't believe in idol worship?
(a) Hinayana (b) Yogachara
(c) Mahayana (d) Madhyamika

66 Aim of education, according to Buddhism is
(a) pleasing God
(b) extinction of sufferings
(c) Nirvana through eight fold paths
(d) None of the above

67 The aim of Buddhist education was
(a) cultural development
(b) religious development
(c) scientific development
(d) All of the above

68 What is said about those instruments, which are used for Buddhist ceremonies?
(a) Dharma instrument (b) Table
(c) Tomb (d) Tower

69 What is the correct option, with regard to the teachings of Buddha?
(a) Appetite, Dukha and Yoga
(b) Discipline, Philosophy and Knowledge
(c) Discipline, Meditation and Wisdom
(d) Wisdom, Equality and Belief

70 According to Jainism, knowledge is obtained through
(a) meditation (b) senses
(c) Both a and b (d) None of these

71 Who was the 24th Trithankara of Jainism?
(a) Mahavira (b) Jinasena
(c) Risabhanatha (d) Kshemendra

72 Non-violence as a belief is accepted mainly by
(a) Jainism (b) Christianity
(c) Buddhism (d) All of these

73 Regular practices of Jains include
(a) alms giving and animal sacrifice
(b) fasting and pilgrimage
(c) deity worship and meditation
(d) wearing orange or white robes

74 According to which, absolute affirmation and absolute negation both are wrong?
(a) Anekantvada (b) Syadvada
(c) Hinayana (d) Mahayana

75 Which of the following is the first Tirthankaras of Jainism?
(a) Mahavira (b) Parshwanath
(c) Padmaprabhu (d) Rishabha

76 Jaina's metaphysics is referred as what?
(a) Syadvada (b) Manyness of reality
(c) Duality of reality (d) Awareness of reality

77 Jaina's epistemology side means
(a) Syadvada (b) Nothingness
(c) Everything (d) Rationality

78 What is the possible quality of soul for Jaina?
(a) Intrinsically pure (b) External
(c) Impure (d) Emancipation

79 Aim(s) of education, according to Jainism is/are
(a) attainment of triratna
(b) development of personality
(c) to enable the child to discriminate Pap and Punya
(d) All of the above

80 Liberation, according to Jainism is
(a) freedom from life and death
(b) freedom from Karma
(c) freedom from Matter
(d) All of the above

81 The correct sequence is
(a) Samyaka Darshan, Samyaka Jnana, Samyaka Charitra
(b) Samyaka Jnana, Samyaka Darshan, Samyaka Charitra
(c) Samyaka Charitra, Samyaka Jnana, Samyaka Darshan
(d) Samyaka Darshan, Samyaka Charitra, Samyaka Jnana

82 What is highest state of education in Jaina philosophy?
(a) Faith (b) Intuition
(c) Intelligence (d) Belief

83 Which ideology is followed by Swami Dayanand?
(a) Representationalist (b) Idealist
(c) Empiricalist (d) Rationalist

84 Why education is important for Swami Dayanand?
(a) Development of mankind
(b) Welfare of mankind
(c) Self-realisation
(d) All of the above

85 Which religious value did Dayanand support?
(a) Hinduism (b) Muslim
(c) Christianity (d) All of these

86 Which is the important feature of Dayanand philosophy?
(a) Subjective ideology
(b) Whole part relation
(c) Multi-sided curriculum
(d) Casual relation

87 Islamic philosophy attempts to create harmony between
(a) Philosophy (Reason)
(b) Religious teaching of Islam (Faith)
(c) Both a and b
(d) None of the above

88 What does the word 'Kalam' mainly deals with?
(a) Theological questions
(b) Interpretation of Aristotelian
(c) Neoplatonic Philosophy
(d) All of the above

89 What does 'FIQH' referred in Islamic philosophy?
(a) Conjunction (b) Jurisprudence
(c) Both a and b (d) None of these

90 Islamic Philosophy concerned with
(a) problem of unity and multiplicity
(b) relationship with God and world
(c) both a and b
(d) None of the above

91 'Metaphysics' means
(a) a branch of physics
(b) exploring the nature of ultimate reality
(c) physics of metals
(d) physics of weather

92 The two basic divisions in schools of Indian Philosophy are
(a) Vedanta and Buddhism
(b) Advaita and Dvaita
(c) Theistic and Atheistic
(d) Orthodox and Heterodox

93 The ultimate goal of education in Jainism is
(a) non-violence (b) renunciation
(c) liberation (d) philanthropy

94 The ceremony of initiation of education in Buddhism is called
(a) Vidyarambam (b) Upananyanam
(c) Pabajja (d) Uparampada

95 A common feature of Hinduism, Buddhism and Jainism is belief about
(a) the unreality of the world
(b) the existence of God
(c) the soul
(d) Karma and rebirth

96 'Epistemology' means
(a) stem cell research
(b) study of the nature of knowledge
(c) study of the nature of values
(d) study of the nature of the world

97 In Indian Philosophy 'Pramana' means
(a) oath (b) measurement
(c) assurance (d) source of knowledge

98 Which of the following is the source material about the Jain way of life?
(a) Dhammapada (b) Karma Kanda
(c) Tripitaka (d) Tri-Ratna

99 The schools of Vedanta are
(a) Dharma, Artha and Moksha
(b) Advaita, Dvaita and Visishtadvaita
(c) Hinduism, Buddhism and Jainism
(d) Orthodox and Heterodox

100 Which philosophy says, "Don't care to know various theories about body and soul, do good and be good, that will take you to whatever truth there is"?
(a) Vedanta (b) Sankhya
(c) Buddhism (d) All of these

101 Epistemology is the branch of Philosophy, which deals with the theories of
(a) reality (b) existence
(c) knowledge (d) values

102 Choose the correct or the best answer, among the following. 'Philosophy' means
(a) consoling oneself while facing disappointments in life
(b) a form of religion
(c) attempts to find answer to fundamental and ultimate questions
(d) sophisticated arguments

103 Four noble truths frame the basic tenets of the Philosophy of
(a) Sankhya (b) Vedanta
(c) Buddhism (d) Jainism

104 The Vedas teach us that
(a) creation is without beginning
(b) creation is without an end
(c) creation is without beginning and without an end
(d) creation has a definite beginning and also an end

105 According to Sankhya Philosophy, the sequence of creation is as under
(a) Purusha, Prakriti, Ahankar, Mahat
(b) Prakriti, Purusha, Ahankar, Mahat
(c) Prakriti, Purusha, Mahat, Ahankar
(d) Purusha, Prakriti, Mahat, Ahankar

106 'Hinayana' is the name of which school of Buddhism?
(a) Theravada (b) Vajrayana
(c) Tantric (d) Esoteric

107 Purpose of creation of the universe and it's relation to man and God is discussed in
(a) metaphysics (b) ethics
(c) epistemology (d) None of these

108 Which philosophy developed the monitorial system in classrooms?
(a) Vedic (b) Vedanta
(c) Islam (d) Buddhism

109 Which of the following does not go in favour of the individual aims of education?
(a) The individual is an asset to the society, his development and growth are necessary.
(b) The society is strong if the individual is strong.
(c) Every individual is unique, development of his potentialities is essential.
(d) Society is supreme and all individuals are only part of it.

110 "Rising knowledge to wisdom is real education" was said by
(a) Rigveda
(b) Chhandogya Upanishad
(c) Samaveda
(d) Bhagwad Gita

111 What is the educational implication of the Vedant Sutra: Brahma Satya Jagat Mithya?
(a) Search for individual truth is the ultimate goal of education.
(b) Spirituality is the ultimate purpose of all education.
(c) The students should be instructed to renounce worldly life.
(d) The disciples should follow the Guru's example.

112 Which of the following is the belief of Islamic epistemology?
(a) True knowledge is temporal.
(b) Intuitional knowledge is not real until substantiated by the scripture.
(c) Personal experience is the main source of knowledge.
(d) The knowledge based on reasoning is universally true.

113 "Education according to interest rather than the caste, creed, race or religion" was propagated by
(a) Vedantic education (b) Islamic education
(c) Jainistic education (d) Buddhistic education

114 According to Quran, education is compulsory for
(a) all men (b) all women
(c) all men and women (d) None of these

115 'Astamarg' has been practised by the philosophy of
(a) Vedanta (b) Islam
(c) Jainism (d) Buddhism

116 Match the following

	List I		List II
A.	Ahimsa	1.	Non-injury
B.	Satya	2.	Chastity
C.	Aparigraha	3.	Non-possession
D.	Brahmacharya	4.	Non-laying

Codes

	A	B	C	D		A	B	C	D
(a)	1	2	3	4	(b)	4	3	2	1
(c)	1	2	4	3	(d)	2	1	3	4

117 Match the following

	List I (Buddhist Concepts)		List II (Meanings/Examples)
A.	Arya Satya	1.	Namrupa
B.	Dwadash Nidan	2.	Samadhi
C.	Ashtanga Marg	3.	Samyaka Vyayam
D.	Nirvana	4.	Controlling of breath
		5.	Sorrow in life

Codes

	A	B	C	D		A	B	C	D
(a)	2	4	1	3	(b)	5	1	3	2
(c)	5	1	4	2	(d)	1	5	4	3

118 The most ascetic school of Indian philosophy is
(a) Buddhism (b) Jainism
(c) Vedanta (d) Sankhya

119 'Vinaya Pitaka' deals with
(a) rules of conduct for the Buddhist Samga
(b) rules for polite behaviour for Jain Monks
(c) rules for polite behaviour for Hindu Sannyasins
(d) Emperor Ashoka's edicts

120 The pathway to liberation in Buddhism consists of
(a) two steps (b) four steps
(c) six steps (d) eight steps

Directions (Q. Nos. 121-129) *Given below are two statements labelled as Assertion (A) and Reason (R). In the context of the two statements, which of the following is correct?*

Codes
(a) Both A and R are true
(b) Both A and R are false
(c) A is true, but R is false
(d) A is false, but R is true

121 **Assertion** (A) Jains are Atheist.
Reason (R) Jains reject the Vedas.

122 **Assertion** (A) Philosophy of education is the criticism of the general theory of education.
Reason (R) Philosophy consists of critical evaluation and systematic reflection upon general theories.

123 **Assertion** (A) Buddhist propounded Astan Marga.
Reason (R) Buddhist propounded Madhyam Marga.

124 **Assertion** (A) Jainism believes in the Doctrine of Anekantvada.
Reason (R) Anekantvada belongs to the 'doctrine of may be.'

125 **Assertion** (A) Philosophy signifies a natural and necessary urge in human being.
Reason (R) It is because of to know themselves and the world.

126 **Assertion** (A) Jainism and Buddhism Philosophy emphasis upon humanism.
Reason (R) Both Mahavira and Buddha endeavoured to improve the life of common man.

127 **Assertion** (A) There is nothing wrong in getting attached to Maya.
Reason (R) Though opposite to Brahma, Maya had been created by Brahma only.

128 **Assertion** (A) Philosophy helps in determining aims of education.
Reason (R) Education depends mostly on Philosophy.

129 **Assertion** (A) All Muslim women need to go to school.
Reason (R) Muslim Philosophy lays emphasis on the equality of all men or women.

130 Arrange the four noble truths given by Lord Buddha in proper sequence.
1. Misery is the reality of life.
2. Every misery has cause.
3. Freedom from misery is possible.
4. There is a remedy for every misery.

Codes
(a) 1, 3, 4, 2 (b) 1, 2, 4, 3
(c) 2, 4, 3, 1 (d) 3, 2, 4, 1

131 Which statement(s) is/are true as per Buddhist philosophy?
1. Maya is root cause of all troubles.
2. Sorrow is the root cause of all troubles.
3. Birth and death are causes of troubles.
4. Getting involved in worldly pursuits, is the cause of all troubles.

Which of the statement(s) given above is/are correct?
(a) 1, 2, 3 and 4 (b) 1 and 2
(c) 2 and 3 (d) 2, 3 and 4

132 Which among the following are neither orthodox nor unorthodox?
1. Nyaya 2. Vaisheshika
3. Sankhya 4. Yoga

Codes
(a) 2 and 3 (b) Only 2 (c) 1 and 4 (d) 1, 2, 3, 4

133 According to Sankhya, ... is known as spirit.
(a) Purusha (b) Prakriti
(c) Perception (d) Inference

134 Prakriti serves .... end.
(a) perception (b) inference
(c) Purusha (d) verbal testimony

135 Purusha is regarded as .... and devoid of qualities.
(a) inactive (b) active
(c) error theory (d) asatkaryavada

136 The original Sankhya was regarded as ...... and atheistic.
(a) monistic (b) pluralist
(c) relativist (d) None of these

137 The community influences the child's growth and development
(a) formally (b) informally
(c) Both a and b (d) None of these

138 Which institution has maximum control over education?
(a) Religion (b) State
(c) Family (d) Economy

139 The nature of world as illusion has been accepted in Indian Philosophy by
(a) Advaita Philosophy
(b) Mimamsa
(c) Viashishtadvaita
(d) All of the above

140 Theory of Representative Knowledge was accepted by
(a) Yoga
(b) Sankhya
(c) Advaita Vedanta
(d) All of the above

141 Match the following

List I	List II
A. Madhyamika	1. Hinayana
B. Yogocara	2. Mahayana
C. Sautrantika	
D. Vaisheshika	

Codes

	A	B	C	D
(a)	1	2	1	2
(b)	2	2	1	1
(c)	1	1	2	2
(d)	2	1	2	1

142 Match the following

List I (Philosophy)	List II (Thinkers)
A. Nyaya	1. Buddha
B. Yoga	2. Kapila
C. Sankhya	3. Patanjali
D. Buddhism	4. Gautama

Codes

	A	B	C	D		A	B	C	D
(a)	4	3	1	2	(b)	4	3	2	1
(c)	1	2	3	4	(d)	3	1	2	4

143 Match the following

List I (Guna)	List II (Features)
A. Sattva	1. Pain
B. Rajas	2. Heaviness
C. Tamas	3. Lightness

Codes

	A	B	C		A	B	C
(a)	2	3	1	(b)	1	2	3
(c)	3	1	2	(d)	3	2	1

144 Match the following

List I	List II
A. Yama	1. Steady and comfortable posture
B. Niyama	2. Self-culture
C. Asana	3. Control of breath
D. Pranayama	4. Abstention

Codes

	A	B	C	D		A	B	C	D
(a)	1	2	3	4	(b)	2	3	4	1
(c)	4	2	1	3	(d)	3	2	1	4

145 Match the following

List I (Principles)	List II (Meanings)
A. Ahimsa	1. Not stealing
B. Satya	2. Abstention from all kinds of injury to any life
C. Asteya	3. Non-acceptance of unnecessary gifts from other people
D. Aparigraha	4. Truthfulness in thought and speech.

Codes

	A	B	C	D		A	B	C	D
(a)	2	4	1	3	(b)	1	2	3	4
(c)	3	2	1	4	(d)	4	3	2	1

PREVIOUS YEARS' QUESTIONS

July 2018

1 Select the correct combination of concepts, which will represent Buddhism?

1. Anekantvada
2. Vaibhashik
3. Pabajja
4. Sanskar
5. Sautantrik
6. Syadvada

Codes

(a) 1, 2, 3 and 5
(b) 1, 2, 3 and 4
(c) 2, 3, 4 and 6
(d) 2, 3, 4 and 5

2 Match the following

List I (Forms of Causation)	**List II** (Metaphysical Entities)
A. Casue only	1. Purusha
B. Effect only	2. Tanmatras
C. Both cause and effect	3. Sensory and motor organs
D. Neither cause nor effect	4. Ishwar
	5. Prakriti

Codes

	A	B	C	D
(a)	5	2	4	3
(b)	4	1	5	2
(c)	4	1	5	2
(d)	5	3	2	1

November 2017

3 Which of the following combinations of statements, justify the study of educational philosophy in a teacher education course?

1. Philosophy helps in developing relationships between terms and concepts.
2. Philosophy clarifies the meaning of concepts underlying education.
3. Philosophy is a tool for use in various subjects.
4. Philosophy develops holistic perception of educational issues.

Codes

(a) 1, 2 and 3
(b) 2, 3 and 4
(c) 1, 2 and 4
(d) 1, 2, 3 and 4

4 "This universe is constantly evolving through the cycles of Sarg and Pralay". This statement would be endorsed by the philosophy of

(a) Sankhya
(b) Vedanta
(c) Buddhism
(d) Jainism

5 "Which of the following mandates will be supported by a teacher with learnings in Buddhist philosophy?

(a) Teacher is greater than God, so follow him
(b) Always strive for attaining the best in life
(c) Be your own guide in life
(d) Experiences are great teachers

6 A line of Indian film song runs like this. "You are in me and I am in you". This can be interpreted to accord with the views of which philosophy?

(a) Vedanta
(b) Sankhya
(c) Jainism
(d) Yoga

7 A school got grade A in a ranking. Four teachers reacted differently as under. Which one of the following observations shall be in conformity with the epistemology of Jainism?

(a) This was all a design of God
(b) This was the natural consequence of our environmental awareness
(c) This incident is an expression of fulfilment within me and you
(d) There can be many causes for this, I cannot be sure.

January 2017

8 Select a proper combination for the answer. The study of philosophy by a teacher helps him/her to

1. learn the concepts of education easily.
2. think in holistic perspective.
3. take a logical view of the world and reality.
4. attain confidence in planning how to teach.
5. develop a critical framework.

Codes

(a) 1, 2, 4 and 5
(b) 1, 2, 3 and 5
(c) 2, 3, 4 and 5
(d) 2, 3 and 5

9 In the framework of Sankhya stipulation, which of the following will not be considered acceptable?

(a) Prakriti is trigunțmak
(b) Prakriti is subtle
(c) Prakriti is directly visible
(d) Prakriti is by nature evolutionary

10 Which Indian school of thought considers all knowledge as relative?

(a) Buddhism
(b) Vedanta
(c) Jainism
(d) Islam

11 Select the most appropriate combination of the following, which may be used to describe the relation between philosophy and education.

1. Goals of life
2. Study of human behaviour
3. Needed knowledge and skills for jobs
4. Patterns of human interactions
5. Life values
6. History of human growth

Codes

(a) 1, 3 and 5
(b) 1, 3 and 4
(c) 3, 4 and 5
(d) 1, 2 and 4

12 In terms of which of the following epistemological approaches, knowledge is considered to be multifaceted?
(a) Principles of Islamic knowledge
(b) Anuman of Vedanta
(c) Dwadash Nidan of Buddhism
(d) Syadvad of Jainism

13 In Buddhism, which school advocates attainment of 'Nirvana' through practical and wordily reality considerations?
(a) Hinyana (b) Mahayana
(c) Soutantrik (d) Yogachara

July 2016

14 Match the following.

List I (Forms)	List II (Metaphysical Entities)
A. Both cause and effect	1. Prakriti
B. Cause only	2. Mahat
C. Effect only	3. Sensory organs
D. Neither cause nor effect	4. Subtle essences
	5. Mind
	6. Purusha

Codes

	A	B	C	D
(a)	6	5	3 and 4	1
(b)	2 and 4	6	3	5
(c)	3 and 4	1	3 and 5	6
(d)	4	5	3	6

15 The Jain philosophy propounds which of the following epistemological principle for arriving at true knowledge?
(a) Ankantvada (b) Syadvada
(c) Naya (d) Mati Gyan

16 In the terms of Vedanta philosophy, the concept of Maya is used to represent
(a) transcendent reality
(b) immanent reality
(c) inherent reality
(d) temporary power of the absolute

17 As per Jain philosophy, a disciple cannot attain definitive knowledge because
(a) the truth is fleeting in nature
(b) the truth is multifaceted
(c) the truth is bound by workings as pudgal
(d) the truth is out of the reach of human mind

18 The Islamic educational practice of combining knowledge of skills along with the knowledge of 'gone God' runs parallel to the thesis of
(a) Advait Vedanta (b) Bhedabhed Vedanta
(c) Vishisht Vedanta (d) Poorva Mimamsa

December 2015

19 The study of philosophy should be considered important for prospective teachers because
(a) philosophy gives a broader perpective of educational issues and concepts
(b) philosophy helps in making a wise person
(c) philosophy brings clarity in educational concepts
(d) philosophy provides a framework for viewing educational problems in true perspective

20 In Jain epistemology, which one is the basis for true knowledge?
(a) Inductive reasoning
(b) Deductive reasoning
(c) Dialectic reasoning
(d) Naya based reasoning

21 A Vedantist teacher will teach the following
1. Maya
2. Science and Technology
3. World History
4. Educational Technology
Codes
(a) 1, 2, 3 and 4 (b) 2, 3 and 4
(c) 1, 3 and 4 (d) 1, 2 and 4

22 The school of Indian philosophy which states that there are six distinct Pramanas (source of knowledge) is
(a) Sankhya (b) Buddhism
(c) Jainism (d) Advaita Vedanta

23 Education as a social sub-system
(a) can promote normative social change
(b) cannot promote normative social change
(c) has nothing to do with social change
(d) will retard social change

24 Which one of the following is broadest in its scope?
(a) The school as a social system
(b) Social foundations of Education
(c) Educational sociology
(d) Sociology of education

25 Madhyama Pratipada is a cardinal principle of
(a) Jainism (b) Buddhism
(c) Vedanta philosophy (d) Sankhya

26 Integral education is a concept given by
(a) Aurobindo (b) J Krishnamurti
(c) M A Kalam Azad (d) Annie Beasant

27 The Jain epistemology considers a five stage hierarchy of knowledge. Which of the following is the proper order of different levels of knowledge?
(a) Mati, Shruti, Manahparyava, Avadhi, Kaivalya
(b) Shruti, Mati, Avadhi, Manahparyava, Kaivalya
(c) Mati, Shruti, Avadhi, Manahparyava, Kaivalya
(d) Kaivalya, Avadhi, Manahparyava, Shruti, Mati

28 Match the following

	List I		List II
A.	Kaivalya	1.	Panchkosh
B.	Jivan Mukti	2.	Buddhism
C.	Nirvana	3.	Jainism
D.	Ananda	4.	Vedanta
		5.	Islamic traditions

Codes

	A	B	C	D		A	B	C	D
(a)	2	3	1	5	(b)	3	5	2	4
(c)	5	3	2	1	(d)	3	4	2	1

December 2014

29 Which of the following statement is correct?

(a) Maktab is a place where pupils learn reading and writing and Madarsa is where lectures are delivered

(b) The two concepts are the same, there is no actual difference

(c) Madarsa is where literacy is provided and Maktab where higher education is given

(d) Maktabs care educational institutions means for religious (Islamic) education, but Madarsas are institutions where non-religious secular edcation is provided

30 Which of the following is the proper order of the levels of knowledge (hierarchy) as propounded by Jaina's thinkers?

(a) Shrutijnana, Avadhijnana, Matijnana, Kalvalya, Manahparyava

(b) Shrutijnana, Matijnana, Manahparyava, Avadhijnana, Kalvalya,

(c) Matijnana, Shrutijnana, Avadhijnana, Manahparyava, Kalvalya

(d) Avadhijnana, Matijnana, Shrutijnana, Kalvalya, Manahparyava

June 2014

31 Which of the following is not the purpose of educational philosophy?

(a) To professionalise the job of teaching

(b) To increase the teacher's love of and control over the students

(c) To critically examine assumptions behind educational practice

(d) To clarify values and aims in teaching

ANSWERS

Exam Based Questions

1 (c)	2 (d)	3 (b)	4 (c)	5 (d)	6 (a)	7 (d)	8 (c)	9 (a)	10 (c)
11 (d)	12 (b)	13 (b)	14 (a)	15 (a)	16 (a)	17 (b)	18 (b)	19 (c)	20 (c)
21 (b)	22 (a)	23 (d)	24 (a)	25 (b)	26 (c)	27 (d)	28 (b)	29 (c)	30 (b)
31 (c)	32 (c)	33 (d)	34 (a)	35 (a)	36 (c)	37 (b)	38 (a)	39 (c)	40 (d)
41 (a)	42 (b)	43 (b)	44 (d)	45 (c)	46 (b)	47 (b)	48 (a)	49 (a)	50 (d)
51 (a)	52 (c)	53 (a)	54 (c)	55 (d)	56 (b)	57 (a)	58 (d)	59 (b)	60 (a)
61 (d)	62 (d)	63 (a)	64 (a)	65 (a)	66 (c)	67 (b)	68 (a)	69 (c)	70 (c)
71 (a)	72 (d)	73 (b)	74 (b)	75 (d)	76 (b)	77 (a)	78 (a)	79 (d)	80 (d)
81 (a)	82 (b)	83 (d)	84 (d)	85 (a)	86 (c)	87 (c)	88 (a)	89 (b)	90 (c)
91 (b)	92 (d)	93 (c)	94 (c)	95 (d)	96 (b)	97 (d)	98 (d)	99 (b)	100 (c)
101 (c)	102 (d)	103 (c)	104 (c)	105 (d)	106 (c)	107 (a)	108 (c)	109 (d)	110 (b)
111 (a)	112 (b)	113 (a)	114 (c)	115 (d)	116 (c)	117 (b)	118 (c)	119 (a)	120 (d)
121 (a)	122 (a)	123 (c)	124 (a)	125 (a)	126 (a)	127 (d)	128 (a)	129 (d)	130 (b)
131 (d)	132 (d)	133 (a)	134 (c)	135 (a)	136 (a)	137 (a)	138 (b)	139 (d)	140 (d)
141 (c)	142 (b)	143 (c)	144 (c)	145 (a)					

Previous Years' Questions

1 (d)	2 (d)	3 (c)	4 (a)	5 (c)	6 (a)	7 (d)	8 (a)	9 (c)	10 (c)
11 (a)	12 (d)	13 (b)	14 (c)	15 (b)	16 (c)	17 (b)	18 (b)	19 (d)	20 (d)
21 (a)	22 (d)	23 (b)	24 (b)	25 (d)	26 (a)	27 (c)	28 (d)	29 (a)	30 (c)
31 (b)									

CHAPTER
02

Contribution of Western Schools of Philosophy

The spirit of idealism, the real world of realism, the natural laws of naturalism, the facts of pragmatism, the world of senses of existentialism, and the materialistic interpretations of marxism, all these somehow influence education.

Introduction

It is quite often said that the philosophy and education are the two sides of the same coin. Education is the dynamic side of philosophy. Education is practical in nature and philosophy is theoretical. Education is a sacred necessity of the life, both from the biological and the sociological point of view. In other words, we can say that the philosophy provides the purpose or the aim and education makes it practical.

We have seen that the importance of education is discussed in both the major division of philosophy *i.e.* the Indian philosophy and the Western philosophy. Both the areas in philosophical domain play a significant role in trasforming the overall thought process. Here, we will talk about education in the light of Western philosophy.

Western Philosophy

The Western philosophy is a line related to philosophical thinking, beginning in ancient Greece and including the predominant philosophical thinking of Europe and its former colonies up to the present day. The concept of the philosophy, itself is originated in the West, derived from ancient Greek word 'Philosophia' literally 'the love of wisdom' (philein = 'to love' + 'sophia' = 'wisdom' is in the sense of theoretical or the cosmic insight).

The Western philosophy refers to the philosophical thinking in the Western world, as opposed to Eastern or Oriental philosophies (comprising Indian, Chinese, Persian, Japanese and Korean philosophies) and the varieties of indigenous philosophies.

In this Chapter

The Western philosophy has a tremendous influence on and has been greatly influenced by Western religion, science and politics. Indeed, the central concepts of these fields can be thought of elements or the branches of the Western philosophy. To an ancient Greek, these fields were often one and the same. Thus, in the West, philosophy is an expansive and ambiguous concept. Today, however, what generally distinguishes philosophy from other Western disciplines is the notion that philosophy is a 'deeper' and more rational, fundamental, and the universal form of the thoughts than other disciplines.

Branches of Western Philosophy

As with any field of the academic study, philosophy has many sub-disciplines, but few fields are as vast as philosophy. Generally, the sub-disciplines can be organised under the major branches given below, much as Aristotle divided the philosophy originally. There is now a philosophical sub-discipline for nearly all other major fields of the study and the most are concerned with the interpretations of those fields.

Aesthetics The axiological study of the basic philosophical questions about art and the beauty, art, history, value theory, bridging with epistemology.

Epistemology The theory and the study of the knowledge, consciousness and intelligence, including the mind and body problem in the philosophy of mind and artificial intelligence.

Ethics The axiological study of the moral problems, including the right action, metaethics, value theory, theory of conduct, bioethics, applied ethics and political philosophy, which is concerned with the justice and the punishment, the human rights and the role of the state or the government, bridging with metaphysics is the philosophy of religion, studying the rationality of the faith.

Logic The study of the meaning and the truth through argumentation (or argument), deduction, induction and reasoning, including propositional logic and computation, the philosophy of language and the philosophy of mathematics, bridging with the epistemology and the metaphysics is the philosophy of science, concerned with the problems of induction, scientific method and progress.

Metaphysics The study of the most basic categories of things in Ontology and the Teleology, such as existence, the objects, properties and causality, including free will and determinism, bridging with the logic. The epistemology is the philosophy of science, including the philosophy of physics, concerned with physical laws, space, time and force. The philosophy of Biology and the other sciences is like analytical Chemistry and the cosmology, the philosophy of religion, which studies the meaning of the concept of the God and of the rationality of the faith.

History of Philosophy The study of what the philosophers have written, their interpretations and the influences, metaphilosophy is the study of the philosophical methods and the goals of philosophy, philosophy of the history, philosophy of education, and the other issues linking with the history and the value.

Western Schools of Thought

Philosophies of education are reflected not only on the accepted ideals and beliefs of society at a particular time, but also on all those principles that have a bearing on the practices of education. The philosophical throughts of idealism, realism, naturalism, pragmatism, marxism and existentialism are discussed here.

Idealism

The name 'Idealism', arose from 'idea-ism'. Idealism, contends that the spiritual aspects are the chief aspects of human life. Natural or scientific facts of life are subordinate to spiritual ones. In the Western world, idealism begans with Socrates and Plato. It was Plato, who wrote that ideas are real. Some of the linkage names that may be cited are Descartes, Spinoza, Kant, Berkeley, Hegel and Leibnitz.

The word 'Idealism' has been derived from the word 'ideas', According to this doctrine, ultimate supremacy is 'ideas'. The philosophy of idealism gives much emphasis on ideas, the feelings and ideals than the material things.

Forms of Idealism

Idealism can be understood with the viewpoints of different philosophers.

The interpretations are given below

Platonic Idealism The 'Plato' was a Greek philosopher, who started as a disciple of Socrates and remained ardent admires throughout his life. Two of his most famous works are the **Republic** and the **Laws**. According to **Plato**, "People should concern themselves primarily with the search for truth". As the truth is perfect and eternal, it cannot be found in the world of matter, which is imperfect and constantly changing. Plato saw the dialectic, as a vehicle, for assisting people in moving from a concern with the material world to concern with world of ideas.

Religious Idealism Idealism has exerted considerable influence on Christianity. It contained many beliefs compatible with idealism. Idea of one God, as pure spirit and the universal God can be readily recognised as compatible with idealism. Augustine referred the two worlds as the 'World of God' and the 'World of Man'. The world of God is the world of spirit and the good. The world of man is the material world of darkness, sin, ignorance and suffering. Augustine believed that one should release oneself from the world of man and enter into the world of God.

Modern Idealism With the rise of scientific revolution, idealism had come to be largely identified with systemisation and subjectivism. This identification was encouraged in writings of Rene Descartes, George Berkeley, Immanuel Kant, George WF Hegel and Josiah Royce.

Main Philosophical Ideas of Idealism

Idealists hold that mind or spirit, as each man experiences, it in himself is fundamentally real and the total of the universe is spirit in essence. The physical world is just a manifestation of this great spirit behind it. The physical world is destructible and changeable. An idea behind it, which is the essence or the spirit of the universe cannot be destroyed. Ideas are expressions of the mind. The mind is able to create them and they are not perishable. The ultimate reality can be understood and expressed only in terms of ideas.

According to an idealist, every person has a 'mind' or 'self' or 'spirit', which is spiritual. An individual 'mind' is part of the 'universal mind'. The whole has a quality of its own, which the parts do not have by themselves. Another very significant aspect is that idealist believes in about the nature of knowledge. For them, knowledge of the heart of spiritual reality is the highest and worthiest knowledge. This knowledge can be obtained only through intuition unlike the knowledge of the physical universe, which is dependent on the senses. The external world around is a perceived world and not a real world. What is the real idea behind it?

Idealist says that the knowledge of the ultimate reality is not possible through the methods of observation, experimentation, reasoning, etc. which are true guides to the knowledge of physical universe. Idealist advocates the use of intuition, for knowing the ultimate reality. However, they would use both deductive and inductive logic for understanding the physical universe.

The knowledge of the physical universe is basic to the knowledge of the ultimate. Idealism believes in three spiritual values, they are the truth, beauty and goodness. The truth is an intellectual value, the beauty is aesthetic value and the goodness is a moral value together, they constitute the good. These values are already existing and the purpose of man is to discover them. Man cannot create values. Values are the essences, essence preceedes existence.

Idealism and Education

The most important contribution of idealism, to the field of education is that it has provided human life with high aims. It has set out aims of education very clearly. Idealist very rightly point out that the aim of education that is not merely to enable individual to produce more material goods, but to exalt human personality.

Idealism forwards two types of aims in education *i.e.* one for the welfare of individual and other for the good of the society. The ultimate aim of education is self-realisation or spiritual becoming. Self-realisation is the goal of life and hence, the aim of education.

A self-realised man is an ideal man. He will have internalised the spiritual values. Professor **Hiriyana** says that "A self-realised man will not be realising virtue, but will be revealing it". The aim of education is to develop the natural man into ideal man. Ideal man will be possessing physical, intellectual, emotional, moral and spiritual perfection and all round integrated and complete development.

Idealist includes physical development also as a laudable aim, but they reckon it only as an instrumental to the health of the mind or the spirit. They believe that a sound mind can exist only in a sound body.

According to idealism, aims of education may be summed up as under

- Exaltation of human personality unfolding the divine in man.
- Development of rational attitude.
- Transmission of spiritual and cultural heritage.
- Universal education for universal individual.
- Moral education, *which falls into two categories i.e.*
  - (i) Duties to self, which includes physical fitness, self-culture, industriousness, etc.
  - (ii) Duties-to others, which includes respect and appreciation for the opinion of others, cooperativeness, generosity, liberality, etc.
- To cultivate the values of truth, beauty and goodness.

Idealism and Curriculum

Idealist likes to give children such knowledge that is of permanent value. They attach a higher importance to humanities than physical and biological sciences. They would like to teach about culture, art, morality, history, philosophy and literature. They would advocate the teachings of all those subjects that centre around man and aid his moral and spiritual development. They would not like object to the teaching of science and technology, but are only eager to caution that they must be humanised before they are taught *i.e.* organised and directed towards goals of human welfare.

Idealism stresses on three values *i.e.* truth, goodness and beauty. These three values determine three types of human activities *i.e.* intellectual, moral and aesthetic. Each type of activity is represented by studies or subjects that should form a part of the curriculum.

The following arrangement of the curriculum is recommended by idealism

Value	Subject /Activity
Truth	It is represented by an intellectual subjects or activities like humanities, languages, social sciences and physical sciences.
Goodness	This includes subjects like ethics, metaphysics, religion, etc.
Beauty	Aesthetic subjects or activities, like an art, the poetry, etc. relate to this part of the curriculum.

Idealism and Pupil

Idealist looks at the child as a *self*, a spiritual being. He is also a social being. He is not just organismic reality, but basically a spiritual reality. **Horne** writes "our philosophy dares to suggest that learner is a finite person, growing when properly educated into the image of an infinite person that his real origin is deity, that his nature is freedom and that his destiny is immortality". The pupil is in a process of self-actualisation. Education is a necessary condition of the process.

According to an **Idealist**, pupil is also a social being. He can actualise himself only through the service of themselves. Such a belief is the foundation of a modern off shoot of an idealism known as **humanistic idealism**. Unlike **Rousseau**, who considered the child as good by nature and hobbies, who considered man as base by nature.

An Idealist looks at the child as neither good nor bad by nature. They think that he has the potential either to be good or bad, which depends for its actualisation upon environment and education. The teacher and the pupil are equal as both of them are spiritual in nature and have a common goal, self-realisation. The teacher because of his age, has gone ahead of the pupil towards the goal. He is just like the member of an advance party in a mountaineering expectation.

Idealism and Teaching Methods

Idealism advocates the use of ideal-centered methods of teaching *i.e.* while teaching any subject, emphasis is placed upon the dignity of man, grandeur, worth of human life and the goals of living.

Idealist also believes in self-education of the child, but as distinct from naturalists, they would not consider just over activity as self-activity. Rather, they would say that even speculation, meditation and other mental activities are also self-activities. **Horne** describes self-activity as "power of self-directed pursuit of consciously conceived ends".

For classroom practice, idealists would encourage the use of the discussion and the lecture methods. The discussion method of learning, which is popularly known as the **Socratic Method** involves questioning and discussion. It was the method of learning in the Upanisadic period of Indian education. It is also known as an **Informal Dialectic Method**. Idealist values the use of well prepared and presented lectures. Lecture should not be a phonographic recitation of facts, but a scholarly exposition. It should also not be delivered in autocratic way. It should be participatory.

Idealism and Teacher

The position of the teacher in idealist scheme of education is focal. It is the teacher who provides the key to educative process. He decides the opportunities for learning and growing for the students and also sets an environment congenial for that.

A child is greatly influenced by his conduct *i.e.* his way of speech, his etiquette, etc. Idealism considers the teacher a friend, philosopher and guide to his pupils. Character development and value development are the most important concerns of the teacher. Froebel's metaphor of the Kindergarten perhaps explains the best, the function of an educator. The school is regarded as a garden and teacher as the gardener, whose function is to tend the little human plants in his charge, carefully and to help them to grow to beauty and perfection.

According to idealism, main functions of a teacher are

- The teacher must assume the role of a Guru.
- The teacher must understand his pupils thoroughly.
- The teacher should present high standard of behaviour and conduct them before his pupils.
- The teacher should have a deep knowledge of his subject.
- The teacher should aim at inculcating in the pupils, a desire to work hard.
- The teacher should employ thought provoking techniques and thereby, encourage his pupils to think for themselves in his subjects.

Idealism and Discipline

Idealist likes to give freedom to children, but that will be a qualified freedom. It should be for activity. Freedom does not mean license or a way wardness, rather it implies responsibility. It should be regulated, guided freedom, and restrained freedom. Their emphasis is on self-discipline.

They believe that human behaviour should have internal controls, rather than such external controls as praises and punishments. The teacher should win over the child through *impression i.e.* good personal examples of behaviour and conduct.

Idealist strongly believes that participation in social service activities develops spirit of sacrifice, an important feature of the life of an ideal person.

Limitations of Idealism

- Concepts like 'spirit', 'mind', 'soul', 'the cosmos', etc are inherent in an idealism, have little relevance in classroom teaching.
- Idealism in education stresses limitation of models, but younger generation prefers invention and originality rather than imitation.
- Idealism emphasis on gaining knowledge is likely to turn educational institutions as information monger's workshops. School curriculum becomes overloaded with obsolete knowledge sometimes.
- Idealistic scheme of education by and large, pays less attention to physical, industrial, social and electronic environment of today.

Realism

Aristotle is regarded as the '*Father of Realism*'. To understand the philosophy of the realism, it is necessary to examine the conditions prevalent in the middle ages.

In the middle ages, the bookish and unreal knowledge was the order of the day in Europe. Consequently, there was a wide gap between the real life and education.

As a philosophy, realism is opposed to the subjective idealism of **Berkely** and **Kant**. According to them, physical world has an appearance of phenomenal existence. The perfect triangle or circle exists in our mind in idea and not on the board or on the paper. While, realism asserts that there is a true reality outside the mind for responding to our conception and perception. The complete and particular is not real than the abstract and the universal. Thus, for realism, reality is objective rather than subjective. Realism regards the world of physical reality as truely fundamental thing is experience.

The physical world is objective and factual. The realism regards the personal wants as subjective, subordinate and secondary, realism is not prepared to accept the existence of an infinite or absolute mind as idealism does. According to realist, mind has been in the course of evolution and is also a part of the universe. Realism is a philosophy of common sense and also the philosophy of science. Realists does not believe in idealist's unreal theory, which has no relation to present life. They opine the truth of life and aim of life is the development from the present systematic life.

In other words, realist says that the world around us is the reality. It is a world of objects and not an ideas. It is a pluralistic world, a world of materials, a world of ideas and a world of experiences. The world is a mechanism. There is an order and design in the world, man is a part of this order. The world is self-caused and ruled by the laws of cause and effect relationships. According to realism, as reality is outside the mind and the world around is an objective reality, knowledge of the surrounding world is the most desirable knowledge. The best method to acquire knowledge is the experimental or the scientific method. Realists does not believe in an ideal values. They would like to discover values in immediate social life.

Forms of Realism

The realism can be understood with the viewpoints of different philosophers.

The interpretations are given below

Aristotelian Realism According to **Aristotle**, ideas or forms, such as idea of God or idea of a tree can exist without matter, but no matter can exist without form. Each piece of matter has universal and particular properties.

Religious Realism Thomas Aquinas connected with an idea of Christian revelation and maintained that we are the children of God and our best thinking should agree with Christian tenets. Aquinas believed that God created matter out of nothing and God gives meaning and purpose to the universe.

Modern Realism Modern realism developed an adequate method of inductive thinking. **Francis Bacon** and **John Locke** were involved in developing systematic methods of thinking and ways to increase human understanding. Induction is the logic of arriving at generalisations on the basis of systematic observations of particulars.

Humanistic Realism Humanistic realism is a form of realism, which emphasises the general human welfare through education by saying that human beings are the fundamental realities in the material world. So, realities of the material objects must be examined in terms of human realities. Irasmus, Rabelias and John Milton have given this aspect of realism, where, there is no place for logic, grammar or literature in curriculum.

Realism and Education

Education for the realists is a preparation for life. Realists, does not believe in general or common aims of education. Aims are specific to individual and his perspectives. Realism emphasises scientific tendencies in education and accords prominence to experiments in education. They point out the importance of practical aspects of learning.

Realism asserts that education should contribute to individual as well as social development. It says that mental and physical faculties of the child should be developed and senses of the child should be developed through an appropriate experiences. Education should provide the child with the knowledge of both the society and external nature. Child should be trained for a vocational pursuit.

Realism and Teacher

The teacher in a realist school must be a scholar. They want men of high character and integrity, still they believe that they would be of no avail to children unless, coupled with mastery of information. The teacher is only a guide to children. He must neither be a pessimist nor optimist, but guide the children towards the hard realities of life. He must expose children to the problems of life and the world around them.

Realism and Curriculum

Curriculum for the realists is a means of forming desirable habits. These habits are to be acquired not through conditioning, but through the mastery of subject matter. However, mastery of the subject matter does not mean memorisation of facts. It is rather the understanding and application of knowledge in planning, deciding and executing actions. Realists, prefer a system of general education over a period of time at the earlier stages and specialisation to come later. At later stages, they would like to give a vocational bias to the curriculum. Subjects of the curriculum would include courses in physics, chemistry, mathematics, life sciences and their applications, social sciences in an integrated way and literature, biography, philosophy, psychology and art. They do not advocate a separate curriculum for moral education.

Realism insists that practical utility of the subjects should be the main consideration in the inclusion of subjects in the curriculum. There should be no gap between what is learnt in the school and what is actually there in the daily life.

Realism and Teaching Methods

Realists encourage the use of lectures, discussions and symposia. They believe in the Socratic method of learning. They do not object to memorisation at the earlier stages. They advocate profuse employment of an audio-visual methods in teaching. An audio-visual aids enable the teacher to develop sensory powers in children. Children would have clear feel of reality through them. Realist, values insight learning as of superior quality.

Realism and Discipline

To realists, the discipline implies to an act, according to rules and regulations of an educational institutions. The purpose of discipline is to make the people submit himself to the directions of the physical world, because he himself is its physical part. But, they were not in the favour of using any punishment for maintaining the discipline. They advocate discipline, by providing a good physical environment.

Limitations of Realism

- Realism lays undue stress on the needs of the material world.
- Realism neglects the spiritual world.
- Curriculum suggested by the realism is lopsided.
- By placing more emphasis on material aspect realism neglects the human aspect.
- Realism does not accept the importance of an eternal value without which, it is not possible to attain real happiness.

Naturalism

Contrary to an idealism, there is another school of the philosophy, called the **Naturalism** which has greatly influenced the educational theory and practice.

According to **Rusk**, "Naturalism is a philosophical position adopted by those who approach's philosophy, from purely scientific point of view". This philosophy believes that nature alone represents the entire reality. There is nothing beyond nature, behind nature and other than nature. Nature justifies all existence including human beings. According to this philosophy, human life is a part of the scheme of nature. It is a self-sufficient entry having its own natural matter, natural force and natural laws.

Naturalism, applies natural laws to the entire human experience material, rational or spiritual. It emphasise, on matter and the physical world.

This material world is governed by certain laws, man, who is creature of the material world, must submit to those laws.

Forms of Naturalism

Naturalism as a philosophic doctrine, has three distinct forms. *They are*

Physical Naturalism This form believes that the laws of physical nature govern the laws of human life. Reality does not exist within an individual. It is rather outside him, in the natural universe. Tagore calls 'nature' as the 'manuscript of God'. Since human life is moulded and controlled by external nature, it should be in accordance with the natural laws. Such a philosophy throws man into the background and as such, it has not influenced an educational theory and practice.

Mechanical Naturalism This form regards man as a mere machine. There is no spirit or soul. Only matter is everything. Mind is also matter, which is made up of atoms, empty space and motion. Matter keeps on moving and changing and this change is governed by the laws of physical science. Man is also matter, he is a mere machine, governed by mechanical laws. He has no creative capacity, purpose or direction. This philosophy, therefore, aims at training man as a good machine, and keeping it in good working conditions.

Biological Naturalism This form seeks to explain man in terms of the lower form of life from which he has evolved. According to this philosophy, body which he has in common with other animals, is the real man. Man's natural endowments, including his instinct emotions and temperament, are the real signs of his behaviour. If our behaviour is according to our instincts, we feel happy, if not, we feel unhappy, and disappointed. Education should try to sublimate these natural impluses for socially desirable ends. It is that form of naturalism which has made the most significant contribution to the development of educational theory and practice.

Naturalism and Education

Naturalists, believe that nature is ultimate reality and is propelled by her own laws. For them reality and nature are identical. They have no belief in a supernatural reality. As **Hocking** writes, "Naturalism denies the existence of anything beyond nature, behind nature, other than nature such as the supernatural or other worldly".

The method of acquiring knowledge advocated by the naturalists is an inductive method. It involves the stages like meticulous observation, exhaustive collection, careful classification, accurate description, intelligent interpretation and cautioned generalisation. So, naturalist believe that knowledge gained primarily through observation is of utmost importance. They would like to see nature as it is, makes specific observations, accumulate and then generalise about the world inductively.

For naturalists, an education is a process of development of the natural life. The process of development must be natural and integrated. Education is for both body and mind. The whole being of the child must be unfolded as a unit. As **Ross**, puts it, "Education is merely the fostering of natural development and true education takes place when the nature, power and inclinations of the child are allowed to develop freely with a minimum of guidance".

The dictum of naturalist education is to follow nature of the pupil and of environment as the personality of the child is fashioned by both. An eminent naturalist educator, Rousseau likes to look at the child as he is than as he would be.

Aims of Education

According to **Herbert Spencer**, "The aim of education is to enable individual to lead a complete life". It is the general aim, which comprises of five specific objectives. These objectives must be guiding posters of education.

They are as follows

- Self-preservation
- Securing the necessities of life
- Upbringing children
- Maintaining social and political relations
- Enjoyment of leisure

Naturalists, strongly believe that, "Senses are the gateway of knowledge". They are very emphatic that all knowledge comes through the senses. The senses are eye, ear, nose, tongue and skin. Knowledge gathered through these is more lasting.

Naturalism and Pupil

The naturalist looks at the child as a little animal. Therefore, his first requirement is to be healthy and vigorous animal able to stand the wear and tear of living. He depends upon others for his physical nourishment and mental nurture during his infancy, childhood and adolescence.

The infant educates himself to a great extent. His education should be based upon his spontaneous activities. His impromptu activities are the guides of his education. What the child likes to do is important index to the kind of activity, which is educative for him at a given stage of development.

The child is very important in the system of naturalist education. He is the centre of an educational system. It is child himself rather than an educator, the school, the text book or the subject of study *i.e.* the focus of educational activity.

Education should be geared to the needs of the child. According to naturalists, an educational activities should be anchored in the child's experiences, needs and not guided by ideals of adult life. As **Monroe**, puts it an "Education finds its purpose, its process and the means wholly within the child's life and child's experience". This attitude of holding the child as the focus of an educational activity is called as the paedocentric attitude.

According to naturalists, child should be given a negative education instead of a positive education. Positive education attempts to mould the child disregarding his natural inclinations. Negative education is not idleness. As **Rousseau** describes, "It does not give him virtue, it protects from vice, it does not inculcate truth, it protects from error". It helps the child to discover things by himself.

Naturalism and Curriculum

The naturalist conceives the curriculum under two stages–earlier stage and later stage. In the earlier stage, they prefer to give sensory training as they believe that senses are the gateways of knowledge and the key to experiences. Sensory training is an essential and integral part of the Modern Pre-school Education Movement. The Montessori Schools through their didactic apparatus and the Kindergarten Schools through Froebel's provide for sensory training.

At the later stage, naturalists would like to include in the curriculum such subjects as Physiology, Physical and Natural Sciences, so much of Mathematics and languages as is necessary to understand the above subjects, psychology of child development, social studies, anatomy etc. It lays stress on the subjects, which are helpful in the self-preservation of man.

Naturalism and Teacher

The place of the teacher in a naturalist school is behind the scenes. His duty is just to observe the child rather than to pour information, ideas and ideals or mould character.

He has to set the stage, supply the learning materials and opportunities, provide an ideal environment and create conditions under which natural development takes place.

As the method of education involves intelligent direction the teacher should help pupils to select such experiences, which contributes to growth and contain potentialities for further growth.

Learning experiences should be selected, organised and coordinated. A teacher is not a positive but a negative educator. He is a mere observer. He should be one among children and not make his presence felt.

Naturalism and Teaching Methods

Naturalistic methods of teaching emerged out of a revolt against the old, traditional and bookish methods of teaching. Naturalist, believes that an exhaustive observation is essential for effective learning. Methods of teaching should be inductive. They advise the teachers to tell the childrens as little as possible and allow them to discover as much as possible.

The emphasis in methods of teaching should be direct experience. **Rousseau**, said "Give your scholar no verbal lessons, he should be taught by experience alone". He also said, "Burn the books and break the walls, throw the child into the bounty of nature". According to naturalists, all knowledge must emerge out of actual situations and experiences. Observation and experimentation should replace the chalk and talk methods.

The play-way method of teaching is advocated by naturalists. All learning should take place in the spirit of and by the method of play because play reveals the child's nature and the lines of his natural development. Naturalist talks about the 'art of delay' during the process of learning for children. They must not be in a haste and hurry as by doing, so they ignore and contradict the natural rhythms of development. Delay helps for discovering these rhythms and provides an opportunity for joining hands with maturation.

Naturalism and Discipline

Naturalists advocate a free discipline. They disapprove the practice of punishment to children. According to them, punishment should be determined by natural consequences of wrong deeds. If the child breaks the windowpane of his room, he should not be punished physically as Rousseau did imagine for Emile. Instead, allow the child to suffer the cold for a night, so that he learns through the consequences.

The proverb, '*a burnt child dreads fire*', very well fits in an illustration of nature's punishment. The spirit behind free discipline is that the child must learn through a process of trial and error, by his own mistakes. The school should be organised as a free and natural society. The children should learn about the rights and duties of citizenship through participation in such a society and not through lectures.

Limitations of Naturalism

- Naturalism does not offer definite aims of education.
- It neglects books, which are treasure of knowledge contained in the printed materials.
- Absolute freedom advocated by naturalism does not exist. It never existed and will never exist in a civilised society. Child cannot be given a long rope to hang himself.
- Naturalism minimises the role of the teacher in an educative process. Even in the electronic age, a teacher occupies an important place in the teaching and learning process.
- Naturalism does not give due importance to the moral and spiritual development of the child.

Pragmatism

The term 'pragmatism' is derived from the Greek word 'Pragma', which means action from which words like practice and practical have been derived. Charles Pierce introduced these words into philosophy. The contributions of Charles Pierce, William James and especially John Dewey in America are regarded as making up the modern philosophy of pragmatism.

In his book **Pragmatism**, James described it as "The pragmatistic method is primarily a method of solving metaphysical disputes, which are unending". Pragmatism is a method wherein one looks away from first principles and looks towards last things or consequences of action. It welcomes an idea, which is testable and which leads to favourable consequences. If an idealism speaks of ideas and ideals, pragmatism is concerned only with facts. Other equivalent names for pragmatism are instrumentalism and experimentalism. Pragmatism is also known by various names such as, practical philosophy, utilitarian philosophy and philosophy of consequentialism.

In the words of **John Dewey**, "Values are as unstable as the forms of clouds". They keep on changing from time to time and reality is still in the process of making. An ideal ends are remotely connected with an immediate and urgent conditions. Men naturally devote themselves to the present conditions rather than the remote. A bird in hand is worth than two in the bush. This is the Pragmatic Philosophy of life. Its chief exponents are William James, John Dewey and S. Kilpatrick.

Forms of Pragmatism

Forms of pragmatism are as follows

Humanistic Pragmatism According to it, whatever fulfill our purpose, satisfies our desire, develops our life is true.

Experimental Pragmatism An experimental pragmatist believes, whatever can be experimentally verified is true.

Biological Pragmatism A biological pragmatists believe that by this type of pragmatism, best is found in the function of thought, in adopting the human and organism to its environment.

Fundamental Principles of Pragmatism

Fundamental principles of pragmatism are as follow

No Ultimate Values The main principle of pragmatic philosophy is that man creates his own values during the course of activity. There are no fixed values for all times to come. Even truths are man made products. There is nothing like absolute truth.

Emphasis on Experimentation Pragmatism lays a special stress on the value of experimentation. It stands for testing every statement by finding out its practical implications. Man is always carrying out various experiments in his life.

Only that thing is good and beautiful which emerges our useful after experimentation. **John Dewey** says, "I affirm that the term 'pragmatic' means only the rule of referring all thinking, all reflective consideration to consequences for final meaning and test".

Belief in Practical Philosophy Pragmatism believes that philosophy is not simply a wisdom of the past. True philosophy is one that helps in the solution of practical problems of life.

According to **Pragmatism**, "Philosophy is the thinking of what to do in a life situation and it is brought into existence when problems occcur".

Human Development according to Environment Pragmatism believes that growth of human personality takes place because of interaction with environment. Man tries to adjust himself to his environment and this results in his growth. During the process of adjustment, man not only adapts himself to his environment but he also tries to mould the environment according to his needs, purposes and desires.

Faith in Democracy Pragmatism has deep faith in democracy. It is only through democracy that an individual can realise the maximum development of his personality. This development is possible only in a social context.

An individual development also leads to the development of society. Thus a democratic social order is considered essential for the healthy growth of an individual.

Revolt Against Traditionalism Pragmatism belives that reality is in the making. Truth is that which works in practical situation. Whatever fulfills one's purpose and develops his life, is true. So, it is a revolt against traditionalism and absolutism.

Emphasis on the Principle of Utility Pragmatism is an utilitarian philosophy which holds that the reality of a principle lies in its utility. An idea or thing which is useful to us is proper and right. In case it is of no use, it is improper, wrong and untrue. In other words, only those ideas and things are true which have a utility for man. In the words of **William James**, "It is true because it is useful".

Importance of Man Power Pragmatism emphasises to the power of man to a great extent. By virtue of this power, a man can create an environment useful, beneficial and conducive to his own development and welfare of society.

Faith in Flexibility Pragmatism believes that nothing is fixed and final in this world. Everything grows, changes and develops. In other words, the world is changing and every thing is under a process of change. Human life is also changing. Therefore, they discard rigidity.

Reality Still in the Making To pragmatists, future is more helpful and bright in comparison with the present. The world is still in the process of formation and development. Man is to aid this process of formation to such an extent that all the needs and requirements of human beings are fully satisfied. In this sense, pragmatic attitude is optimistic, developing and progressive.

Importance of Activity Pragmatism lays great emphasis on activity rather than ideas. Pragmatists holds the view that ideas are born out of activities. Man is active being. Thus, the greatest contribution of pragmatism to an education is the principle of 'Learning by doing'.

Pragmatism and Education

- Education should enable the child to learn new techniques to cope with new situations.
- Values are created through experimentation.
- Child learns by doing more than by reflection.
- Education is a continuous process. It is a constant reorganising or reconstructing of experience.

- Educational practices have to be experimental.
- Curriculum is activity centred.
- Curriculum is integrated.
- Life situations should be made on the basis of education.
- Education is a social necessity. It is the means by which it renews itself.
- Freedom should be given to the child for the development of his all round personality.

Pragmatism and Curriculum

Pragmatists neither approve of a rigid, traditional pattern of curriculum where in there would be watertight compartmentalisation of knowledge into different subjects nor do they support a Laissez Faire Policy in curriculum organisation. They believe in a certain degree of organisation of the curriculum.

They would like to integrate the curriculum with the life and experiences of children. To quote **Dewey**, "The child and the curriculum are simply two limits, which define a single process". Pragmatists prefer to give integrated knowledge around particular and significant problems of life rather than divide knowledge into various subjects of instructions.

A study of social, economical and political institutions, current, social, economical and political problems, natural resources and such other similar studies can form the curriculum. Life and experiences of the pupil should be integrated with the activities of the school.

According to pragmatists, curriculum should include tools of knowledge as reading, writing, counting, nature study, drawing, hygiene, physical training, history, geography, science, domestic science for girls and agricultural sciences for boys. Vocational training is an indispensable part of the curriculum.

Pragmatism and Teaching Methods

The focus of pragmatic methods of teaching is on the 'child-in-society' and his activities there in rather than the book, the teacher, the subject or exclusively the child of nature. Learning always occurs as a result of movement and activity. The teacher has to capitalise upon the activities of children to direct the teaching learning process. Activity is the basis of all teaching. Children should be encouraged to discover and investigate the facts of life. Education must develop the 'laboratory habit of mind'. The method of teaching should be experimental.

Dewey, feels that methods of teaching should develop reflective thinking in children.

They must ask the 'why' of things and not merely the 'how' of things. To speak of the actual methods employed in classrooms, pragmatists lean on creative and constructive projects.

As **WH Kilpatric** has defined it, "A project is a whole-hearted purposeful activity proceeding in a social environment". Projects may be worked outside the school also. They take note of the constructive efforts of children. There are four stages in the project method. They are purposing, planning, executing and evaluating. Student participates in all four stages. Projects may be worked by any individual or a group. However, pragmatists would prefer group projects as they allow for cooperation, participation in group life and sharing of responsibilities.

Pragmatism also encourages discussion as a method of learning. It also encourages laboratory work, personal reference in the library, educational tours and excursions. The basic principle of education is that child is ever active. While doing he is learning, while learning he is doing. Pragmatists tells us to confront the child with real situations not by a passive surrender, but by a constant, dynamic interaction between himself and the changing situations.

Pragmatism and Teacher

Pragmatism regards the teacher as a helper and guide. The teacher assumes the role of 'arranger of experience'. According to **Dewey**, "The teacher is a guide and director, he steers the boat, but the energy that propels it must come from those who are learning".

The teacher's job is to keep the child alive to

- his purposes
- his capacities
- his limitations

So that, he

- evolves his own discipline
- develops his own values
- makes his own adjustment
- and thus, realises himself

According to pragmatists, teacher is not a dictator but only a leader of group activities. He has to plan and organise the teaching-learning situation, provide learning experiences and opportunities for experimentation. He must not impose himself on children. The teacher should treat the pupils as his own equals in regard to social life.

Pragmatism and Discipline

Pragmatism condemns enforced discipline and advocates social discipline based on child's interests, activities and a sense of social responsibility. Free, purposeful and cooperative activities organised in the school lead to social discipline. These activities inculcate attitudes of cooperation and consideration. Moral development takes place through such activities and student develops a sense of self-control.

Pragmatist believes that work can become a play, if it is rooted in the interest of the child. If the activities of children are rooted in the interests, specific needs, capabilities and preferences of children then there is no problem of discipline.

Limitations of Pragmatism

- It by and large ignores internal values.
- It pays little attention to spiritual values.
- It advocates a utilitarian approach only.
- It provides very insignificant place to cultural values.
- It believes that experience is all in all. It ignores the knowledge accumulated through the ages.
- It does not give due importance to regular and systematic instructions.
- The entire knowledge and experience needed by child cannot be obtained through projects.
- It does not indicate fixed educational goals.

Marxism

The 'Marxist' ideas about man and matter are generally known as **Marxism**. Marxism constitutes the general views about the world and the human society. Marxism developed as a protest against an idealist conception of man and the world as represented by Hegel (1770-1831).

Marxist was influenced by Hegelian dialectics, French socialism and english economics. But marxism is a fundamental and total philosophy of life.

Karl Marx's conflict theory is plain and simple. Class struggle constitutes the central theme of Marx's theoretical scheme, which is based on three premises related to his theory of class struggle.

These are :

- The history of the hitherto existing society is the history of class struggles.
- The social learning of man determines his consciousness.
- The class, which is dominant material force in society, is dominant in intellectual sphere.

Marx is said to be founder of conflict perspective. He has helped through his ideas in understanding of nature of society specifically from conflict perspective. He gave the concept of dialectical materialism that consist of two words 'dialectic' and 'materialism'; idea of dialectic derived from Hegeal and idea of materialism from Feverbach. But Marx rejected the earlier ideas and presented this concept of dialectic materialism, as a new idea/method of study of social reality.

The main tenents of Marxian dialectical materialism are :

- All the phenomena of nature are part of an integrated whole.
- Nature is in a continuous state of movement and change.
- The development process is a product of qualitative advances, which culminate in abrupt qualitative change.
- Contradictions are inherent in all realms of the nature but particularly in human society.

Marxism and Education

Education helps in the development of military and economic power of the state to establish a classless society, the communist society. Because of this, an education system in the erstwhile USSR was given utmost importance, it was highly centralised, strategically organised and controlled by the trusted leaders of the communist party of the USSR.

Marxism and Goals of Education

- Education should propose the citizens to obey the state and law.
- Education should be compulsory for all citizens.
- The state should bear the burden of education.
- The state should emphasise on imparting objective knowledge.
- The state should promote the physical and mental development of all its citizens.
- Though vocational and trade education dignity of manual labour should be established in society.
- Education should create full employment situation.
- The underprivileged should be given priority.
- Education should develop national and progressive temperament.
- There is no place for religion in an education system because it cannot solve the problems of material world.

Different Levels of Education

Primary Education Marxism emphasises on eight years of compulsory free and universal primary education. It should continue till the age of fifteen.

Secondary Education After the completion of compulsory primary education, the competent adolescents should be selected for three years of vocational & technical education.

Higher Education After the completion of secondary education the competent youths should be selected for three years of university education.

Marxism and Teaching Methods

The Marxists have followed the following methods of teaching

- Lecture and texbooks
- Tutorials and seminars
- Projects and problem-solving

Main ideas involved in Marxism theory are

- Nature as material in Marxian theory in character everything derived from it.
- Nature develops in a dialectical pattern, where struggle exists between opposing factors.
- Dialectical method applied to human social organisation, struggle of social class leads to social change.
- The social relations are the basic factors of economic production.

Marxism and Teaching Methodology

- Emphasis is laid on the practical aspects of education instead of theoretical aspects.
- Marxist education is based on the principle of learning by doing. Student should work both in agricultural farms and factories.
- Education should not be confined within the four walls of the school. The natural environment and the community at large will also serve as great books and teachers.
- Marxist education emphasises learning through personal experience of the child.
- It emphasises group activity instead of an individual activity. Marxist education intends to promote cooperative spirit instead of competitive spirit among students.

Marxism and Curriculum

- Marxist philosophy and doctrines will be taught at all levels of education on compulsory basis. The students should be made conscious about class division, unequal distribution of wealth, exploitation of the working class by the capitalist class, etc.
- Those subjects are included in the curriculum, which tends to develop skill instead of abstract knowledge.
- Marxism lays stress on respect for labour and as such, work-experience is regarded as an integral part of education.
- The curriculum includes the socially useful subjects such as science, mathematics, geography, life sciences, geology, astronomy, etc. The history of communist movement and political economy should also be included in the curriculum.
- At the primary level, only the mother-tongue should be taught. But at the secondary level, the curriculum should include foreign language.
- Creative work and co-curricular activities have been given an important place in Marxist curriculum. These includes physical exercise, music, painting, games and sports, etc.

Marxism and Role of Teacher

The role of the teacher is significant and crucial in Marxist education. He must be fully equipped not only with the content of an education but also the Marxist methodology of teaching as well as Marxist aims of education.

A Marxist teacher must entirely be different in attitude and temperament from a bourgeois teacher. His philosophy of teaching will be the Marxist philosophy. He must be an active member of the Marxist social order.

According to **Lenin**, a best Marxist worker can only be a best Marxist teacher. Both in thought and action he must be a true Marxist. He should not have only mastery on the content of an education but also have consciousness about life, social environment and communist ideology. He should possess sound health, respect for cultural heritage, deep practical sense, socialistic bent of mind and true patriotism.

Limitations of Marxism

- Marxist education is absolutely state-controlled education. It attaches too much importance to the role of state in education.
- The role of teacher in Marxist education is insignificant.
- Marxist educational philosophy believes that economics lies at the root of every human activity. But this is not absolutely true as principal aims of Marxist education is to acquire productive skill.
- Competition is absent in Marxist education, as a result initiative is not taken by an individual.
- There is no scope of religious and world education in Marxism system of education.

Existentialism

Existentialism may be described as the modern and youngest philosophy. This theory gives prominence to man's passionate, aeshetic nature and to his feelings, like anguish, love, guilt and sense of inner freedom in the tradition of romanticism, emerging from the 19th century, which is centered upon the analysis of existence and of the way humans find themselves existing in the world. The notion is that humans exist first and then each individual spends a lifetime in their essence or nature.

Chief Exponent of Existentialism, **Soren Kierkegaard** (1913-1855) is regarded as the **Father of Modern Existentialism** and is the first European philosopher who bears the existentialist label. In his view, subjectivity and intensity should be priced as the criteria of truth and genuineness. We touch reality in intense moments of existence, especially moments of painful decision. These moments are characterized by deep anxiety and life is known in such moments and cannot be reduced to just system of ideas.

Friedrich Nietzsche (1844-1900) is regarded as a key figure in the rise of existentialism. According to him, Christianity is to be overcome by putting in its place the doctrine of superman *i.e.* man surpassing himself.

Martin Heidgger (1889-1976) in his book **Being and Time**, gave a very impressive analysis of human existance, the prominence of the important themes of existentialism, like care, anxiety, guilt and above all death is brought out here.

Jean Paul Sarte stressed that man's existence preceedes his essence. Man is nothing else but what he purpose, he exists only in so far as he realizes himself, he is therefore nothing else but the sum of his actions, nothing else but what his life.

One of the fundamental, foundational concepts of existentialism is that 'existence preceedes essence'. It was **Plato**, who said that the surrounding world is a world of essences-ideas and the purpose of life is to discover these essences. Essences are already there and they precede existence. Even existence is an embodiment of an essence-the self, which is a part of an universal essence, the self.

The other Western philosophers carried forward this theory such as Descartes even affirmed the reality of existence because of its essence-thinking, as he said, 'I think' therefore, 'I am'. Bergson even went to the extreme of saying that "I do not think, it (essence) thinks in me", there, striking transcendental, desperately deterministic note on human existence. As such, existentialism is a revolt against any kind of determinism and an affirmation of the free nature of man. They not only affirm that existence is prior to essence, that man is fundamentally free to create his essence, but think that this is the tragedy about man.

As Sartre, himself explains that first of all, man exists, turns up, appears on the scene and only afterwards define himself.

Existentialist says that man is nothing other than what he makes himself. Such is the first principle of existentialism.

Therefore, it can be easily observed that, when an idealist believes in trancendental values, naturalists believe that values are resident in nature, pragmatists believe that values arise out of social life, existentialist affirms that individual alone creates values. Reality is a state of becoming affirm, that existence increases with every moment of life and essence is a consequence of this perpetual becoming.

Basic Concepts of Existentialism

Basic concepts of existentialism are as follows

- Existence preceedes essence.
- Contingency of human life, the 'giveness' or 'throwness'.
- Their view of man 'free will v/s determinism.' Man is free and he has no other alternative, but to be free *i.e.* he is not only free, but is condemned to be free.

Existentialist believes in human being's personal choices and he is considered as an end in himself. They also believe that man is responsible for all the deals and consequences. He, though free, should bear his own responsibility.

Main Philosophical Themes

The main philosophical themes of existentialism are

Truth It is not introduced by an individual, but it is there in himself all the time. Such thinking explores hypothetical knowledge, achieves truth about the actual concrete individual.

Existentialists thinking, according to an individual, is abstract speculative. Truth is passionate, inner commitment, objective and theoretically uncertain. Highest truth can only be attainable by an individual and according to existentialist truth is equivalent to faith.

Choice Choice *i.e.* either/or *i.e.* decision between two ways of life.

Aesthetic Life Devoted to an art, music and dance.

Ethical Life Seeks happiness in marriage, business or a profession. In this, no more description of choice is possible. Character of choice can only be sketching outline, its qualities or individual, subjective, momentary, absolute and free irrevocable. The choice of an individual in this philosophy is a lead over the abyss (bottomless).

God Culminating of existentialist thinking in the knowledge of God. An individual inner experience may have a choice of achieving eternal God. There is a possibility of union of individual with God, where individual is not obliterated (mystic men). Individual man exists in the sense of having a unique dimension of being characterised by choice.

Educational Implications of Existentialism

The whole philosophy of existentialism rests on providing freedom to the child individual and realise his existence as individual and realise the best that he can. Human beings should be able to face the contingency of human life and world. Contrary to the happy learning at school or joyful learning and playful experiences suggested by Pestalozzi, Montessori and Froebel, existentialist feels that there is nothing without experiencing pains and sufferings.

Significant educational implications of existentialism are given as

- The school should provide an atmosphere where individual develops in a healthy way. Children learn better when relieved from an intense competition, harsh discipline and fear from failure.

- The teacher is in a position to foster individual growth. They can facilitate the development of an originality and the creativity by providing a climate as well as basic skills and the tools which makes exploration possible. School grades or the rewards and punishments do not foster the growth.
- The teacher is in the foreground and is the centre of attention. Students resistance is often manifested during the process of an instruction, but as resistance is natural and necessary in order that the student may retain his over being. The teacher welcomes the challenges to his ideas from the students.
- The mechanisation and impersonality should be counteracted in the school. Concern and respect for individual student should be a feature of the school. Education in the contemporary, industrial and technological society may well be cleansed and strengthened by emphasis on man for himself.

Existentialism and Aims of Education

- Education should aims at imparting knowledge to an individual, pertaining to human nature, especially, from the existentialist point of view. Education should helps an individual to make him/her a good human.
- The development of an introspective powers should also be the aim of education. It should develop powers like self observation among pupils.
- Education must also develop in the pupil, a scale of values consistent with the absolute freedom. The pupil must develop a commitment to these values and act for them.
- Education must foster the growth of uniqueness in man. This should be the primary aim of education because existentialists are not intersted in the universal man.
- Education must make pupil aware of an infinite possibilities of his freedom and the responsibilities, he must discharge in his/her life. Education must foster the capacity for self-direction.

Existentialism and Curriculum

Existentialists do not believe in prescriptive curriculum. It should be based on child's needs and abilities, related to immediate social, political, economical and related problems of the child.

The main features of the curriculum are

- It should not be examination oriented.
- Appropriate to the student.
- Not lay stress on mere studying of the subjects.
- Emphasises on living, enacting and experiencing the values.
- Enable the child to learn about the human suffering, anguish, anxiety and death.
- Helps to acquire self-knowledge.
- It should be child-centered.
- Utilitarian
- Elective based
- Realistic

Existentialism and Teaching Methods

The most favoured method is the Socratic method, which involves, personal, intimate relation and helps in acquiring knowledge and wisdom by bringing teacher and taught together closely. More preference is given to education at home than at school.

However the methods preferred are

- Socratic method
- Individualised method
- Informal method
- Discussion method
- Method of induction
- Methods to develop creativity
- Methods which can test inner life

Existentialism and Discipline

Freedom is central to existentialism, freedom to cultivate children's experiences in the free atmosphere. Children need not to conform. A child has its own personal choice and action. No restriction should laid from outside. Instead, a child should realise its own responsibility and act.

Existentialism and Teacher

Teacher should not impose their ideas, ideals and values on children. Teacher should allow the children to think about the problems of life and make them think critically and understand the meaning and purpose of existence. Teachers should be sympathetic to that child, who is rebellious in nature. A teacher should not think about children as problem children. Instead, the teacher should empathise with problem children by entering in the emotional life and expressing concern.

Limitations of Existentialism

- More emphasis on the subjectivity and negligence of objectivity cannot be practically followed in this material world.
- There is no uniqueness in this theory as many of its ideas have been covered under naturalism and idealism.

EXAM BASED QUESTIONS

1 Which along with education is said to be the same side of a coin ?
(a) Philosophy (b) Logic (c) Asthetic (d) Mathematics

2 What is the characteristic of education?
(a) Illusionary (b) Pervasive
(c) Dynamic (d) Transparent

3 What is the kind of discipline philosophy ?
(a) Mathematical (b) Experimental
(c) Practical (d) Theoretical

4 What is the meaning of the word 'Philosophy'?
(a) Love of wisdom (b) Love of knowledge
(c) Love of faith (d) All of these

5 What is the other name used for the Eastern Philosopher?
(a) Greek Philosopher (b) Sophists
(c) Oriental Philosophers (d) None of these

6 Which branch of the philosophy have an 'art and the beauty' as the major field of the study?
(a) Asthetic (b) Epistemology
(c) Ethics (d) Logic

7 Which branch of the philosophy deals with the knowledge, structure, method and validity?
(a) Logic (b) Ethics
(c) Metaphysics (d) Epistemology

8 Which domain contains political philosophy?
(a) Logic (b) Ethics (c) Asthetic (d) All of these

9 What is the goal of an education, according to an idealism?
(a) Perfect adaptation to an environment
(b) Realisation of moral values
(c) Satisfaction of human wants
(d) Cultivation of dynamic, adaptable mind, which will be resourceful and enterprising in all situations

10 On what, depends the values of an educational experience in the eyes of idealist?
(a) Whether or not the pupil has been properly motivated
(b) Whether or not it preserves accepted institutions
(c) The extent to which it satisfies pupil desires
(d) The manner in which it affects future experience

11 Which philosophy advocates the role of a teacher as a strict disciplinarian?
(a) Idealism (b) Naturalism
(c) Realism (d) Existentialism

12 The religious education is strongly advocated by
(a) Pragmatists (b) Idealists
(c) Realists (d) Existentialists

13 Which philosophy of an education consider psychology as incomplete study of and inadequate basis of an educational theory?
(a) Realism (b) Pragmatism
(c) Idealism (d) Naturalism

14 Which among the following does not fit the scheme of educational goals of idealist?
(a) Care of body (b) Moral values
(c) Skills (d) Self-expression

15 Which of the following does not emphasise on individualisation?
(a) Idealism (b) Realism
(c) Pragmatism (d) Naturalism

16 The realist's aim of education is
(a) self-realisation
(b) spiritual and the moral development
(c) happy and the moral development
(d) total development of the personality

17 In the light of the relevant past events, contemporary events and their understandings should find a place in the teaching of history. Who maintained this principle?
(a) Marxists (b) Idealists
(c) Realists (d) Naturalists

18 What is the ultimate reality for realism?
(a) Thoughts (b) Feelings
(c) Social relations (d) Objective world

19 Realism in education was born out of
(a) an enthusiam of the renaissance.
(b) the great religious movements of the 17th century.
(c) a cleavage between the work of the school and the life of the outside world that occured during the 19th century.
(d) the degeneration of humanism after renaissance.

20 As Huxley, pleaded for the introduction of "a complete and through the scientific culture into the schools", he is claimed to be
(a) an Idealist (b) a Realist
(c) a Pragmatist (d) a Naturalist

21 The most important thing to keep in mind for a teacher, according to Realism in education is
(a) the method of teaching
(b) the value and significance of what is taught
(c) the nature of the child
(d) the organisation of the content to be taught

22 Which of the following is not criticised by realism in education?
(a) Teachers denying the value of the school co-curricular activities
(b) Pupils cramming for the knowledge from the books for reproducing in an examination
(c) Organising schools in a way that is conductive to practical training in the citizenship
(d) Teaching, drifts away from the life of the child

23 Which one of the following education systems supports the scientific progress?
(a) Idealistic education (b) Realistic education
(c) Naturalistic education (d) All of these

24 Identify that which of the following is promoted by the realism.
(a) Empirical truths (b) Scientific truths
(c) Cognitive knowledge (d) All of these

25 Who believes that the objects have a reality independent of the mental phenomena ?
(a) Idealists (b) Realists
(c) Naturalists (d) Existentialists

26 Which is not an aspect of mind according to the Realist's Theory of Knowing?
(a) Awareness (b) Consciousness
(c) Behaviour (d) Process of awareness

27 Who raised the slogan 'Back to Nature'?
(a) Realism (b) Pragmatism
(c) Naturalism (d) Existentialism

28 Who was the supporter of the naturalism in education?
(a) Frobel (b) Armstrong (c) John Locke (d) Rousseau

29 Which statement is not correct about the naturalism?
(a) A reaction against the degenerated humanism of the renaissance period
(b) A reaction against the sophistication, artificiality and paraphernalia in the education
(c) A reaction against a more study of books and linguistic forms
(d) None of the above

30 Which is not the naturalism's aim of education?
(a) An education is the notion of man's evolution from the lower forms of the life.
(b) To equip, an individual or the nation for the struggle for the existence, so as to ensure survival.
(c) To help the pupils to learn to be in harmony with and well-adapted to their surroundings.
(d) To inculcate an ethical and the moral values in the pupils.

31 Which school held the view, "The God makes all the things good, the man meddles with and they become evil"?
(a) Marxism (b) Existentialism
(c) Naturalism (d) Pragmatism

32 Which school maintained self-expression with the accompanying cries of 'no interference, no restraints'?
(a) Extreme form of the naturalism
(b) Most widely accepted form of naturalism
(c) Truest form of the naturalism
(d) Most valid form of naturalism

33 Who played the method of teaching has been emphasised in the scheme of education?
(a) Naturalist (b) Realist
(c) Pragmatists (d) Existentialist

34 'Emile' is the first treatise on
(a) Naturalism (b) Idealism
(c) Realism (d) Existentialism

35 Naturalist's conception of the man is
(a) man's very essence of being is his spiritual nature.
(b) it is the spirit rather than the animality that is most truly man.
(c) there exists in the nature of the things, a perfect pattern of an individual.
(d) nature would have them children before they are men.

36 According to which Philosophy of education, the childhood is something desirable for its own sake and the children should be the children?
(a) Idealism (b) Pragmatism
(c) Naturalism (d) Existentialism

37 Which educational activity is the most desirable to the pragmatist?
(a) Approximates the goals which an educational scientists have set up.
(b) Results from the indiscrimination of the pupil in the Democratic Theory.
(c) That is the beneficial effect upon the future experiences of the pupil.
(d) That characterises by spontaneous, active, continuously pleasurable and practical for the pupil.

38 The term 'progressive education' is related to
(a) Realism (b) Pragmatism
(c) Idealism (d) Existentialism

39 The pragmatists are against
(a) the external examinations
(b) the specialist teachers
(c) the breakdown of knowledge into separate subjects
(d) the eternal spiritual teachers

40 Which is the most widely accepted method of education, according to the pragmatists?
(a) Lecturing by the teacher
(b) Leaving the child free to learn
(c) Learning by doing
(d) The Heuristic Method

41 Which of the following claims of the Pragmatists are not acceptable?
(a) The free activity of the pupil is likely to result in the permanent attitudes of initiative, independence and moral discipline.
(b) Training in citizenship is possible through school and community activities.
(c) Training in character through school's co-curricular activities is possible.
(d) Child's own experience is valuable for an adequate development of child's personality.

42 Education, according to Pragmatist is
(a) wholly pupil oriented (b) wholly societal oriented
(c) wholly purposive (d) wholly inter-disciplinary

43 Which of the following schools of philosophy integrates students, capacities, interests, habits with social participation?
(a) Pragmatism (b) Realism
(c) Naturalism (d) Idealism

44 Today, there is lot of emphasis on an ICT in education, it is the implication of
(a) Realism (b) Logical analysis
(c) Pragmatism (d) Marxism

45 Fine arts and aesthetics are given top priority in the curriculum of
(a) Naturalism (b) Existentialism
(c) Idealism (d) Pragmatism

46 Which school of philosophy of education, advocated 'Project Method' of teaching?
(a) Realism (b) Pragmatism
(c) Idealism (d) Naturalism

47 Which of the following characteristics is common to pragmatism, naturalism and existentialism?
(a) Emphasis on spiritual aims of education
(b) Emphasis on an individual
(c) Emphasis on physical environment
(d) Emphasis on value education

48 Who was the 19th century founder of existentialism?
(a) Hegel (b) Soren Kierkegaard
(c) Rousseau (d) DJO Connor

49 Who was the 20th century existentialist?
(a) Soren Kierkegaard (b) Jean Paul Sartre
(c) Kant (d) Hegel

50 According to existentialists, the essence of existence means
(a) unity with the ultimate reality
(b) spiritual good and happiness
(c) tensions and contradictions which condition loneliness and anxiety
(d) continuous growth and development

51 What is the aim of education, according to existentialists?
(a) Humanitarian and humanist self realisation
(b) Adaptation to practical life
(c) Objective knowledge
(d) A good understanding of the world outside

52 Which among the following statements is not a characteristic of marxism?
(a) It pre-supposes a reality independent of man's mind.
(b) Its educational philosophy is essentially materialistic.
(c) Its major objective is the development of child's personality.
(d) It asserts that physical environment can definitely change the nature of the child.

53 Which of the following has been asserted about schools by marxist educational philosophy?
(a) They should stand above politics
(b) They should disinterestedly serve society as a whole
(c) They should function as a deliberate instruments of state policy
(d) There should not be a more weapons in the hands of the ruling class

54 Which school of philosophy of education regrets dualism between cultural and vocational curriculum?
(a) Marxism (b) Idealism
(c) Existentialism (d) Naturalism

55 According to which educational philosophy, socially useful labour must form the central pivot of the entire school?
(a) Idealism (b) Marxism
(c) Existentialism (d) Naturalism

56 Marxism, does not believes in
(a) education for productivity
(b) religious education
(c) education for equality and equity
(d) mass education

57 Marxist educational philosophy is closer to
(a) Idealism (b) Realism
(c) Naturalism (d) Pragmatism

58 Who said that "Mode of productions, the sole determinate of the culture of people"?
(a) Karl Marx (b) Max Weber (c) MacIver (d) Lundberg

59 Who is the ultimate concern of ' what is existence'?
(a) Idealist only (b) Realist only
(c) Existentialist and Idealist both
(d) Existentialist only

60 Who was the 19th century founder of existentialism?
(a) Hegel (b) Soren Kierkegaard
(c) Rousseau (d) D J O Connor

61 Who was 20th century existentialist?
(a) Soren Kierkegaard (b) D J O Connor
(c) Jean Paul Sartre (d) Hegel

62 Which of the following is said about idealist ?
(a) They are content with 'briars'
(b) They like 'roses'
(c) They are satisfied neither with 'briars' nor with 'roses'
(d) They want 'roses' and 'briars' both

63 The advocates of philosophy of pragmatism believe that reality is
(a) imagination (b) stagnant
(c) constantly changing (d) related to mind

64 Playway method of teaching has been emphasised in the scheme of an education of
(a) naturalist (b) realist
(c) pragmatist (d) existentialist

65 **Statement I** Pragmatists prefer to give integrated knowledge around particular and significant problems of life.
Statement II The believe in a certain degree of organisation of the curriculum.
(a) Only statement I is correct
(b) Both the statements, I and II are correct
(c) Only statement II is correct
(d) Neither statement I nor II is correct

66 "A project is a whole hearted purposeful activity preceeding in a social environment". Who said this?
(a) John Dewey (b) Karl Jaspers
(c) W H Kilpatric (d) Hegel

67 Which of the following statement(s) is/are incorrect regarding the limitations of realism?
(a) They neglects the spiritual world
(b) Curriculum suggested is lopsided
(c) It neglects books, which are treasure of knowledge contained in the printed material
(d) Lays under stress on the needs of the material world

68 Who strongly believes that "senses are the gateway of knowledge"?
(a) Realists (b) Idealists
(c) Pragmatists (d) Naturalists

69 Which philosophy of education consider Psychology, as incomplete study of an inadequate basis of educational theory?
(a) Realism (b) Pragmatism
(c) Idealism (d) Naturalism

70 Which branch of philosophy, examines issues pertaining to the nature of 'reality'?
(a) Ontology (b) Metaphysics
(c) Axiology (d) Epistemology

71 "No disinterested pursuit of knowledge and no intellectual education for its own sake", was the slogan of the
(a) Realist (b) Idealist
(c) Pragmatist (d) Naturalist

72 The process of attaining one's existence as per existentialism is
(a) essence, struggle, pain and pleasure, lonliness
(b) lonliness, pain and pleasure, struggle, essence
(c) lonliness, struggle, pain and pleasure, essence
(d) essence, pain and pleasure, struggle, lonliness

73 "All systems of an ideas are subject to verification by consequences" is the core of the philosophy of
(a) Idealism (b) Existentialism
(c) Pragmatism (d) Realism

74 Pre-existent values are not accepted by
(a) Idealists and Existentialists
(b) Idealists and Pragmatists
(c) Idealists and Realists
(d) Pragmatists and Existentialists

75 According to existentialists, the teacher should allow the children ....
(a) to think about the problems of life
(b) to think critically
(c) to understand the meaning and purpose of existence
(d) All of the above

76 The statement an "Education is the dynamic side of philosophy" means
(a) no education can proceed without having an ideological basis.
(b) the ultimate aim of an education is to teach philosophical wisdom.
(c) an education keeps philosophy moving.
(d) theoretical tenets are translated into practice by education.

77 Pragmatism is instrumentalist by nature, because
(a) it considers an education as an instrument to social change.
(b) it insists on using lot of teaching aids for enhancing student's learning.
(c) education is used by democracy as its instrument.
(d) it considers knowledge and values as means and not as ends.

78 What will a teacher who believes in naturalism not do ?
(a) Allow her students to venture freely
(b) Give instructions for developing higher values
(c) Expose her students to experiences leading to sense development
(d) Wait for students to get mature before teaching the prescribed content

79 'Things as they are and as they are likely to be encountered in life rather than words", was the slogan of the
(a) pragmatist (b) realist
(c) idealist (d) existentialist

80 Fine arts and aesthetics are given top priority in the curriculum by
(a) naturalism (b) existentialism
(c) idealism (d) pragmatism

81 Epistemology is the branch of philosophy which deals with theories of
(a) reality (b) existence
(c) knowledge (d) values

82 Purpose of creation of the universe and its relation to man and God is discussed in
(a) Metaphysics (b) Ethics
(c) Epistemology (d) None of these

83 The Oriental School of Thought is related to
(a) knowledge of science (b) classical literature
(c) conservation of fashion (d) learning of natives

84 Which of the following is an epistemological tenet of existentialism ?
(a) Knowledge is in things and thoughts
(b) Knowledge is affective and inter-subjective
(c) Knowledge is temporal and cognitive
(d) Nothing can be known

85 'Principle of independence' is a fundamental tenet of
(a) idealism (b) pragmatism
(c) realism (d) existentialism

86 Which of the following is not an existentialistic thinker?
(a) Kierkegaard (b) Frederic Nietzsche
(c) Bertrand Russell (d) Jean Paul Sartre

87 "Man is nothing but what he makes of himself" is the fundamental viewpoint of
(a) idealism (b) naturalism
(c) pragmatism (d) existentialism

88 Individual aim of education aims at making a child
(a) cooperative individual
(b) self-realised individual
(c) isolated individual
(d) follower of God

89 The word 'Pragmatism' has been derived from the word 'Pragma' which means
(a) action (b) reaction
(c) passive behaviour (d) thoughtless behaviour

90 Which one of the following is the main source of educational progress?
(a) Educational theory
(b) Educational practice
(c) Educational philosophy
(d) Educational history

91 Functions of educational philosophy is
(a) normative (b) critical
(c) speculative (d) All of these

92 Weakest point of an idealistic education is
(a) aim (b) curriculum
(c) methods of teaching (d) discipline

93 Which of the following is not a task of philosophy?
(a) Speculation (b) Description and Analysis
(c) Prescription (d) Observation

94 The founder of pragmatism was
(a) John Dewey (b) William James
(c) Kilpatrick (d) Charles Sanders Peirce

95 'Intuitive knowledge' is attained through
(a) external experiences (b) internal experiences
(c) Both (a) and (b) (d) None of these

96 Which branch of philosophy, does examine the issue pertaining to the nature of reality ?
(a) Axiology (b) Aesthetics
(c) Metaphysics (d) Epistemology

97 "The child is an integral part of the ultimate universe" is the view point of
(a) realism (b) pragmatism
(c) existentialism (d) idealism

98 Which book was written by 'Plato' on education?
(a) The Republic
(b) Educational Philosophy
(c) Education of Plato
(d) Emile

99 Education is .... aspect of philosophy and philosophy is the ...... aspect of an education.
(a) theoretical, practical (b) practical, theoretical
(c) dynamic, dormant (d) dormant, dynamic

100 Pragmatism professes for .... as a School of Philosophy.
(a) an idea (b) action
(c) reality (d) programme

101 Existentialism believes more in ...... than in.....
(a) essence, existence
(b) existence, essence
(c) action, intuition
(d) intuition, action

102 Identify the function(s) of educational Philosophy.
1. To integrate divinity into an education of man.
2. To provide theoretical basis for teacher's behaviour.
3. To generate the principles of curriculum framework.
4. To answer all ultimate 'why' questions regarding educational practices.

Select the correct answer using the codes given below.
(a) 2 and 3 (b) 1 and 4
(c) 1, 2 and 4 (d) 2, 3 and 4

103 An existentialist teacher should emphasise on
1. freedom 2. responsibility
3. subjective feelings 4. cooperative living

Select the correct answer using the codes given below.
(a) 1 and 2 (b) 1 and 3
(c) 1, 2 and 3 (d) 2, 3 and 4

104 Match the following

	List I (Philosophy)		List II (Methods)
A.	Idealism	1.	Heuristic Approach
B.	Realism	2.	Deductive Method
C.	Pragmatism	3.	Experiential learning
D.	Naturalism	4.	Inductive Method

Codes

	A	B	C	D		A	B	C	D
(a)	3	4	1	2	(b)	4	3	1	2
(c)	2	4	3	1	(d)	2	3	4	1

105 Match the following

List I (Characteristics)	List II (Philosophy)
A. Learning by doing	1. Naturalism
B. Education through an environment	2. Idealism
C. Realisation of truth, beauty and goodness	3. Pragmatism
D. "World as it is here and now"	4. Realism
	5. Existentialism

Codes

	A	B	C	D		A	B	C	D
(a)	3	1	2	4	(b)	1	4	2	3
(c)	1	3	2	4	(d)	3	2	4	5

106 Match the following

List I (Philosophy)		List II (Characteristics)	
A.	Existentialism	1.	Idea
B.	Pragmatism	2.	Reality
C.	Idealism	3.	Self
D.	Realism	4.	Action

Codes

	A	B	C	D		A	B	C	D
(a)	3	4	1	2	(b)	1	2	3	4
(c)	4	3	2	1	(d)	3	4	2	1

107 Match the following

List I (Philosophers)		List II (Philosophy)	
A.	Marx	1.	Realism
B.	Plato	2.	Existentialism
C.	Aristotle	3.	Idealism
D.	Sartre	4.	Marxism

Codes

	A	B	C	D		A	B	C	D
(a)	1	2	3	4	(b)	4	3	2	1
(c)	4	3	1	2	(d)	3	2	4	1

108 The most important outward factor is the formation of nationalities in state. To which philosophy, do you attribute this statement?

(a) Marxism
(b) Capitalism
(c) Fascism
(d) Socialism

109 Who wrote the book 'School and Society'?

(a) Auguste Comte
(b) John Dewey
(c) Emile Durkheim
(d) Robert Merton

Directions (Q. Nos. 110-120) *Given below are two statements, one labelled as Assertion (A) and other labelled as Reason (R). Select the correct code for the following.*

Codes

(a) Both A and R are true
(b) Both A and R are false
(c) A is true, but R is false
(d) A is false, but R is true

110 Assertion (A) Philosophy helps in determining aims of education.

Reason (R) Education depends mostly on philosophy.

111 Assertion (A) To realist, the discipline implies to an act according to rules and regulations of educational institutions.

Reason (R) They advocate discipline by providing a good physical environment.

112 Assertion (A) The naturalist looks at a the child as a little animal.

Reason (R) They believed that child should be trained for a vocational pursuit.

113 Assertion (A) Idealism stresses on three values truth, goodness and beauty.

Reason (R) These values determine three types of activities, such as intellectual, moral and asthetic.

114 Assertion (A) Pragmatist believes that curriculum should not be integrated.

Reason (R) They ignore internal values.

115 Assertion (A) Marxist believes that education should be compulsory for all citizens.

Reason (R) Education should create full employment.

116 Assertion (A) In Marxist education, a teacher must be entirely different in attitude and temperament from a bourgeoise teacher.

Reason (R) His philosophy of teaching to Marxist philosophy.

117 Assertion (A) The idealist for classroom practice should encourage the use of play way method.

Reason (R) They believe in socratic method of teaching.

118 Assertion (A) Realists do not believe in general or common aims of education.

Reason (R) They believe that education should contribute to individual as well as social development.

119 Assertion (A) Mechanical naturalism regards man as a machine.

Reason (R) Man is a matter, he is more machine governed by mechanical laws.

120 Assertion (A) Existentialist believes that teacher should impose their ideas and values on teacher.

Reason (R) Teacher should not allow the children to think about problem of life.

PREVIOUS YEARS' QUESTIONS

July 2018

1 "Prayer cannot be offered with an empty stomach". This statement will get support from ....

(a) idealism (b) naturalism
(c) pragmatism (d) logical positivism

November 2017

2 Which of the following combinations of statements would be associated with a naturalistic stance?

1. Museums and Zoos orient man to learn about nature.
2. Life is ultimately governed by the laws of nature.
3. The aim of education is to help a child realise his/her goals.
4. Sciences are the gateways of learning.

Codes

(a) 1, 2 and 3 (b) 1, 2 and 4
(c) 2, 3 and 4 (d) 1, 2, 3 and 4

3 Which school of philosophy would favour the statement, "Since both pain and pleasure are the wealth of man, they are his good teachers"?

(a) Existentialism (b) Naturalism
(c) Idealism (d) Pragmatism

4 In dealing with the problems of education, which of the following combinations will be supported by a teacher of Marxist orientation?

1. The aim of education is to help in the creation of a classless society.
2. Science and technology help in the development of society.
3. Individual freedom accelerates the progress of society.
4. Progress of society implies subsequent changes in the means of educaiton.

Codes

(a) 1, 2 and 3 (b) 2, 3 and 4
(c) 1, 3 and 4 (d) 1, 2 and 4

5 'Honesty is the best policy'. This statement will be assented to

(a) idealism (b) naturalism
(c) pragmatism (d) realism

6 The schools should focus on the teaching of contents drawn from pure sciences would be an imperative of which school of philosophy?

(a) Idealism (b) Naturalism
(c) Realism (d) Existentialism

7 Which of the following school of philosophy regards education as a means for social growth and economic production?

(a) Idealism (b) Realism
(c) Naturalism (d) Marxism

July 2016

8 Match the following.

List I (Points of Accent)	List II (Schools of Philosophy)
A. Education for eternal values	1. Idealism
B. Education for democracy	2. Realism
C. Emphasis on mass production	3. Naturalism
D. Scientific method	4. Pragmatism
	5. Existentialism
	6. Marxism

Codes

	A	B	C	D
(a)	1	6	2	4
(b)	3	4	2	1
(c)	5	4	6	3
(d)	1	4	6	2

9 Which school of philosophy in education will plead affinity with Darwinian Theory of Evaluation?

(a) Existentialism (b) Naturalism
(c) Idealism (d) Pragmatism

10 Which of the following features are a pointer toward similarity among existentialist and idealistic's education?

1. Emphasis on self.
2. Valuing human potential.
3. Striving for the goal of freedom and responsibility.
4. Struggle for survival.

Codes

(a) 1 and 2 (b) 1, 2 and 3
(c) 2, 3 and 4 (d) 3 and 4

December 2015

11 Which subject of study will be emphasised by idealist teacher?

1. Science 2. Mathematics
3. Literature 4. History and Culture

Choose the correct answer from the following.

(a) 1, 3 and 4 (b) 2, 3 and 4
(c) 1, 2 and 3 (d) 1, 2 and 4

12 Which philosophy favours the statement that "Man is the measure of all things"?

(a) Realism (b) Pragmatism
(c) Idealism (d) Naturalism

13 Idealism states that

(a) mind alone is real (b) matter alone is real
(c) Both (a) and (b) (d) Neither (a) nor (b)

14 Realism views knowledge as generated by

(a) the mind alone
(b) matter alone
(c) the interaction of matter and mind
(d) reality

15 Which one of the following is not related to realist idelogy?
(a) Herbert Spencer (b) Bertrand Russell
(c) Henry Bergson (d) G.E. Moore

16 Which one of the following advice an existantialist teacher did not offer to his/her students?
(a) Do self-analysis
(b) You should take your own decisions
(c) For your development use your miseries and sorrows
(d) Listen to the voice of your inner-self

June 2015

17 When a teacher says that the delinquent behaviour of my students is an expression of evil in me, he is following
(a) idealism (b) Vedantic philosophy
(b) realism (d) pragmatism

18 One major difference between Tagorian and Rousseau's ideas on nature is
(a) Tagore gave less emphasis on nature
(b) Tagore did not believe in negative education
(c) Tagore regarded God as the creator of nature
(d) Tagore believed that nature will punish erring human

19 Which one of the following is not correct?
(a) Gandhi did not appreciate Tagorian practice of having services of non-teaching class IV employees
(b) Tagore did not appreciate Gandhian emphasis on Ram Rajya
(c) Vivekananda advocated reading of indigenous texts
(d) Aurobindo did not oppose worldly pursuits

20 Which one of the following thinkers has been described as "idealist in aim, naturalist in content and pragmatist in method"?
(a) Swami Vivekananda
(b) Rabindranath Tatore
(c) Mahatma Gandhi
(d) Sri Aurobindo

June 2014

21 Of Froebel's idealism it can be said that
(a) education is not a process of unfoldment
(b) education unites knowledge, feelings and doing
(c) education cannot be a process of self-realisation
(d) the notion of self-activity is limited to manual activity

22 Concerning the nature of truth
(a) the idealist says it is absolute discovered through reasoning and intuition
(b) the realist says is is constantly changing and is a concept that it is man-made
(c) the pragmatist says it consists of laws governing the physical world of man
(d) the rationalist and humanist says it is whatever the individual in his/her society makes it

23 Whose educational philosophy is based on pragmatism, will
(a) reject the scientific method of experimentation
(b) accept that complete objectivity is possible
(c) accept the Stimulus Response Theory of Learning
(d) claim that knowledge is tentative, truth is relative

ANSWERS

Exam Based Questions

1 *(a)*	2 *(c)*	3 *(d)*	4 *(a)*	5 *(c)*	6 *(a)*	7 *(d)*	8 *(b)*	9 *(b)*	10 *(b)*
11 *(a)*	12 *(b)*	13 *(c)*	14 *(a)*	15 *(a)*	16 *(c)*	17 *(c)*	18 *(d)*	19 *(c)*	20 *(b)*
21 *(b)*	22 *(c)*	23 *(b)*	24 *(b)*	25 *(b)*	26 *(c)*	27 *(c)*	28 *(c)*	29 *(c)*	30 *(d)*
31 *(c)*	32 *(a)*	33 *(a)*	34 *(a)*	35 *(d)*	36 *(c)*	37 *(a)*	38 *(b)*	39 *(c)*	40 *(c)*
41 *(a)*	42 *(c)*	43 *(a)*	44 *(c)*	45 *(d)*	46 *(b)*	47 *(b)*	48 *(b)*	49 *(b)*	50 *(c)*
51 *(a)*	52 *(c)*	53 *(b)*	54 *(a)*	55 *(b)*	56 *(b)*	57 *(b)*	58 *(a)*	59 *(c)*	60 *(b)*
61 *(c)*	62 *(c)*	63 *(b)*	64 *(a)*	65 *(b)*	66 *(c)*	67 *(c)*	68 *(d)*	69 *(c)*	70 *(b)*
71 *(c)*	72 *(c)*	73 *(d)*	74 *(d)*	75 *(d)*	76 *(d)*	77 *(b)*	78 *(d)*	79 *(b)*	80 *(d)*
81 *(c)*	82 *(a)*	83 *(b)*	84 *(b)*	85 *(c)*	86 *(c)*	87 *(d)*	88 *(a)*	89 *(a)*	90 *(c)*
91 *(d)*	92 *(c)*	93 *(c)*	94 *(d)*	95 *(c)*	96 *(c)*	97 *(c)*	98 *(a)*	99 *(b)*	100 *(d)*
101 *(b)*	102 *(d)*	103 *(c)*	104 *(c)*	105 *(a)*	106 *(a)*	107 *(c)*	108 *(d)*	109 *(b)*	110 *(a)*
111 *(a)*	112 *(b)*	113 *(a)*	114 *(c)*	115 *(a)*	116 *(a)*	117 *(d)*	118 *(a)*	119 *(a)*	120 *(b)*

Previous Years' Questions

1 *(c)*	2 *(b)*	3 *(a)*	4 *(d)*	5 *(c)*	6 *(c)*	7 *(d)*	8 *(d)*	9 *(b)*	10 *(a)*
11 *(b)*	12 *(b)*	13 *(a)*	14 *(c)*	15 *(c)*	16 *(d)*	17 *(b)*	18 *(c)*	19 *(b)*	20 *(c)*
21 *(b)*	22 *(a)*	23 *(d)*							

CHAPTER 03

Approaches to Sociology of Education

Sociology has been concerned with the units of social life. An important area which sociology deals with is social institutions. The institutions provide a structure for the society and perform functions which enables a society to meet it's demands. In any society, there are social institutions namely, family, school, society, political institutions, economic institutions, etc.

Education and Sociology

The word 'education' is a broad concept, referring to all the experiences in which learner can learn something. It is a social endeavour designed to get the maximum from the ability of each of the member of the society. Education covers both the learning and teaching of values and knowledge in the individual. Education consists of systematic instruction, teaching and training by professional teachers. This consists of the application of pedagogy.

It thus, focuses on the cultivation of skills be it communication, intellectual, or any specialised skills, advancement of knowledge and spreading of secular view (values). Teachers depend on many different disciplines for their lessons like psychology, philosophy, information technology, linguistics, biology and sociology.

On the other hand, the word 'sociology' originates from Latin prefix 'societus' which means 'society' and the suffix 'ology' means 'the study of', from Greek logos it means 'knowledge'. Thus, the word sociology means a systematic study of society. It encompasses all the elements of society *i.e.* social relation, social stratification, social interaction, culture. Perhaps, sociology can be best regarded as an attempt to name that which secretly keeps society going.

Sociology is concerned with social relations in general and with social groups and institutions in particular. It is the study of society of human interactions, inter-relations and patterns of social relationship and it fundamentally deals with the network of social relationship which is called a society.

In this Chapter

- Education and Sociology
- Sociology of Education
  - Theoretical Approaches to Sociology of Education
- Social Institutions
- Social Movement
  - Theories of Social Movement

Definitions of Sociology

According to **Ginsberg**, "Sociology is a study of society, that is of the web or tissue of human interactions and inter relations".

According to **Simmel**, "Sociology asks what happens to man and by what rules they behave, no in so far as they unfold their understandable individual existences in their totality, but in so far as they form groups and are determined by their group existence because of interaction".

According to **Ogburn**, "Sociology is a body of learning about society. It is a description of ways to make society better. It's social ethics, a social philosophy, generally, is defined as a science of society".

Nature of Sociology

- It is the study of social life.
- It is an independent science.
- It is a science of society's reactions.
- It is both rational and empirical science.
- It is a pure science, not an applied science.

Relationship Between Sociology and Education

The relationship between sociology and education has always been a subject of debate. Education and sociology are mutually inter-related and inter-dependent disciplines. They are so closely intertwined and inter-connected that their subject matter and method of study are often overlapped to a great extent.

The following are the arguments, which highlight the relationship between education and sociology

- Sociology is the science of society and education is an implicit aspect of any social system.
- Sociology studies the structure and functions of social system, while education is one of the important function of any social system.
- The prime concern of sociology is socialised individuals, while education is the process of socialising individuals.
- Education is the means for achieving the goals of sociology.
- Sociology develops methods and techniques to be utilised by educational system to attain its goals.
- Sociology contributes greatly to the planning, execution, monitoring and evaluation of educational process.
- Sociology attempts to ascertain the functions performed by the educational system, while education adopts the principles of sociology to improve its functioning.
- Sociology develops laws and principles which are adopted by the educational system for its improvement.
- Sociology provides the principles and education practices them.
- Sociology put forth the ideals and values which education has to achieve.
- Education preserves the social and cultural heritage which is owned by sociology.
- Education brings about reforms and changes in the field of sociology.

Sociology of Education

It is defined as a study of the relation between education and society. It is an investigation of the sociological processes involved in educational institution. It is concerned with educational aims, methods, institutions, administration and curricula in relation to the economical, political, religious, social and cultural forces of the society, in which they function. It emphasises sociological aspects of educational phenomena and institutions.

It is a philosophical as well as a sociological concept, indicating ideologies, curricula and pedagogical techniques of the inculcation and management of knowledge and the social reproduction of personalities and cultures. It is concerned with the relationships, activities and reactions of the teachers and students in the classroom and highlights the sociological problems in the realm of education.

Theoretical Approaches to Sociology of Education

Historically, American education served both political and economic needs, which dictated the function of education. Today, sociologists and educators debate over the function of education. The three main theories represent their views *i.e.* Symbolic Interactionism, Structural Functionalism and Conflict theory.

Symbolic Interactionism

Symbolic interactionism is a school of thought in sociology that explains social behaviour in terms of how people interact with each other *via* symbols. In this view, social structures are best understood in terms of such individual interactions. It was developed by thinkers, such as **George Herbert Mead** and **Herbert Blumer** in the **20th century**. **Mead** believed that one self develops through social interactions.

George Herbert Mead is considered a founder of symbolic interactionism. Mead's student, Herbert Blumer, coined the term 'symbolic interactionism' and outline these basic premises *i.e.* humans interact with things based on meaning ascribed to those things, the ascribed meaning of things comes from our interactions with others and society and the meaning of things are interpreted by a person when dealing with things in specific circumstances.

Moreover, how people communicate and interact with each other depends on how they interpret factors such as language, actions and status (potential symbols). *e.g.,* one might interpret a handshake as either a friendly greeting or cool farewell, depending on context the symbolism of a handshake varies. Sometimes symbols change, long hair in males once symbolised rebellion, but now does not.

Concept of Symbolic Interactionism

According to the symbolic interactionist perspective, people attach meanings to symbols and then they act according to their subjective interpretation of these symbols. Verbal conversations, in which spoken words serve as the predominant symbols, make this subjective interpretation especially evident. The words have certain meanings for the 'sender' during effective communication, they hopefully have the same meaning for the 'receiver.' In other terms, words are not static things, but they require intention and interpretation. Conversation is an interaction of symbols between individuals, who constantly interpret the world around them. Of course, anything can serve as a symbol as long as it refers to something beyond itself. Written music serves as an example. The black dots and lines become more than mere marks on the page, they refer to notes organised in such a way as to make musical sense. Thus, symbolic interactionists give serious thought to how people acts and then seeks to determine what meanings individuals assign to their own actions and symbols, as well as to those of others.

Symbolic interactionism reflects the micro-sociological perspective and was largely influenced by the work of early sociologists and philosophers, such as George Simmel, Charles Cooley, George Herbert Mead and Erving Goffman. Symbolic interactionism emphasises that human behaviour is influenced by definitions and meanings that are created and maintained through symbolic interaction with others. Symbolic interactionism also suggests that our identity or sense of self is shaped by social interaction. We develop our self-concept by observing how others interact with us and label us. By observing how others view us, we see a reflection of ourselves that cooley calls the 'looking glass self'.

Structural Functionalism

The Structural Functionalist theory focuses on the ways that universal education serves the needs of society. Functionalists first see education in its manifest role, conveying basic knowledge and skills to the next generation. **Durkheim** (the founder of Functionalist Theory) identified the latent role of education as one of socialising people into society's mainstream. This **moral education** as he called it, helped form a more cohesive social structure by bringing together people from diverse backgrounds, which echoes the historical concern of people.

Structured functionalism interprets each part of society in terms of how it contributes to the stability of the whole society. Society is more than the sum of its parts, rather, each part of society is functional for the stability of whole. Durkheim actually envisioned society as an organism and just like within an organism, each component plays a necessary part, but none can function alone and one experiences a crises or failure, other parts must adapt to fill the void in same way.

The Structured Functionalist theory shows that different parts of social institutions are primarily composed of social factors, each of which is designed to fill different needs, and each of which has particular consequences for the form and shape of society. The parts are all dependent on each other. The core institutions defined by sociology and which are important to understanding for this theory includes family, government, economy, media, education and religion.

According to functionalism, an institution only exists because it serves a vital role in the functioning of society. If it no longer serves a role, an institution will die away. When new needs evolve or emerge, new institutions will be created to meet them.

Conflict Theory

Conflict theory is based upon the educational system which reinforces and perpetuates social inequalities that arise from differences in class, gender, race and ethnicity. Some conflict theorists believe education is controlled by the state which is controlled by those with the power. Its purpose is to reproduce the inequalities already existing in the society as well as legitimise 'acceptable' ideas which actually work to reinforce the privileged positions of the dominant group. Conflict theorists believe this social reproduction continues to occur because the whole education system is overlain with ideology provided by the dominant group. In effect, they perpetuate the myth that education is available to all to provide a means of achieving wealth and status. Anyone who fails to achieve this goal continues the myth, has only themselves to blame.

This perspective has been criticised for being deterministic, pessimistic and allowing nothing for the agency of individuals to improve their situation. Conflict theorists are interested in how those who possess more power in society, exercise control over those with less power.

According to conflict theorists, competition over scarce resources is the basis of society conflict. Because resources such as power and wealth are limited in supply, people must compete with one another for them. Once particular group gain control of society resources, they tend to establish rules and procedures that protect their interests at the expense of other groups. This inequality between groups leads to social conflict as those with less power gain access to desired resources and those with power attempt to keep it. Conflict in turn leads to social change. The conflict theorists see social change as an inevitable feature of society.

Implications of Conflict Theory on Education

- Reforms in education should be preceeded by changes in the economy and other social structure.
- Education should be reviewed constantly to accomodate all the interested groups.
- Performance in different schools is different due to unequal allocation of resources and necessarily due to intellectual endowment and hard work.
- Significant improvements in education can only be achieved if they are accompanied by wider social changes.
- Everybody should be given a chance to continue with education.

Social Institutions

A social institution consists of a group of people who have come together for a common purpose. Social institutions have been created by man from social relationships in the society. To meet such basic needs, as stability, law and order and clearly defined roles of authority and decision-making. These institutions are a part of the social order of society and they govern behaviour and expectations of individuals. Social institutions are important structural components of modern societies that address one or more fundamental activity and/or specific function. Without social institutions, modern societies could not exist. Societies consist of a range of institutions that play myriad specific roles in facilitating human social life, and which themselves are dependent upon one another for the performance of their respective functions. A given institution can also perform different functions at once and/or over time.

A social institution is a complex and integrated set of social norms, organised around the preservation of a basic societal value. Obviously, the sociologist does not defines institutions, in the same way, as does the person on the streets. Lay persons are likely to use the term **institution** very loosely, for churches, jails, hospitals and many other things as institutions.

Sociologists agree that institutions arises and persists because of a definite felt need of the members of the society. While, there is an essential agreement on the general origin of institutions, sociologists have differed about the specific motivating factors.

In every society, there are certain basic social needs. It is must for the society to meet these needs for the survival and satisfaction of its members. The sociological concept of the term is different from its common usage. An institution is not a building, not a group of people, and not an organisation. An institution is a system of norms to achieve some goals or activities that person feels is important, or more formally, an organised cluster of folkways and more centered around a major human activity.

Institutions are structured processes through which people carry on their activities. Institutions do not have members, they have followers. This is a subtle but important distinction. Let's illustrate that a religion is not a group of people but a religion is a system of ideas, beliefs, practices, and relationships. A mosque is an association of people who accepts the beliefs and follows the practice of Islam. The clear cut distinction between an institution and association is that the institution is always an organised system of ideas and behaviour, and association is the organised group of people engaging in the behaviour.

Definitions of Social Institutions

According to **Horton**, "Social institution is an organised system of social relationships which embodies certain common values and procedures and meets certain basic needs of the society".

According to **Landis**, "Social institutions are formal cultural structures devised to meet basic social needs".

Characteristics of Social Institutions

- Social institutions have some definite objectives and multiple functions to meet goals and to fulfil primary needs.
- They have definite procedures which are based on customs and traditions.
- They depend upon the collective activities of people.
- They are inter-dependent within a society as no institution can exist by itself.
- They are patterns of behaviour grouped, about the central needs of human beings in society.
- Institutions are connected through status and role of the members.

Functions of Social Institutions

- Simplify the actions and work of an individual.
- Provides a means to control the society and people who constitute it.
- Every individual is assigned a role depending on which he can achieve and regulates his status.
- Helps to maintain the order in the society.
- Act as stimulants by giving the required freedom.
- Creates harmony and unity among the members of the society.
- Establishes permanent patterns of social behaviour.
- Satisfies the basic needs of society.

Types of Social Institutions

Every society has a social institution. These aren't some places but the structure of relationship, obligation and function. Many members in society have their own concept of right and wrong, relationship, values and norms.

Here, we will discuss about family, school and society as social institutions.

Family as Social Institution

The family is the most basic of all social institutions. It existed among our ancestors long before the human species evolved to its present physical form and it remains in the basic social unit in every society.

Even though, family is an important social institution, but the question is what is the future of this social institution?

Several modern sociologists believe that the functions that family performs in the society are very important. With such functions, the existence of the family cannot be vanished. There seems little variations in the functions, but are sure about the need of the family to the society. But, on the other hand, **Tofler**, in his book, **The Future Shock**, writes that keeping in view the changing trends in the values and norms of the society, some institutions will be no more required. Particularly, about marriage as an institution, he perceives, 'Perhaps we are the last married generation'.

Characteristics of the Family

- Family consists of a group of people who are in some way related to one another.
- Its members lives together for long period.
- The adults in the group, assumes responsibility for any off-spring.
- The members of the family form an economic unit, often for the production of foods and services.

We may say that the family is a relatively permanent group of people related by ancestry, marriage or adaptation, who lives together and forms an economic unit, whose adult members assume responsibility for the young ones.

We lead our life in two kinds of families. **One** is the family of orientation, into which we are born and the **other** is the family of procreation, which we later create ourselves. In every society, marriage is the foundation of family.

Functions of the Family

The family performs several basic social functions which are imperative for the maintenance of the entire social order. *They are :*

Regulation of Sexual Behaviour No society allows people to be mate at random, and no society regards sexual behaviour purely as a matter of private choice. The marriage and family system provides a means of regulating sexual behaviour by specifying who may mate with whom under what circumstances they may do so.

Replacement of Members A society cannot survive unless it has a system for replacing members from generation to generation. The family provides a stable, institutionalised means through which this replacement can takes place, with specific individuals, occupying the social roles of mother and father and assuming defined responsibilities.

Socialization New born infants do not become fully human, until they are socialised and the primary context for this socialisation is the family. Because the child is their, the parents normally take particular care to monitor its behaviour and to transmit the language, values, norms and beliefs of the culture. Although, many of these socialisation functions have been taken over by other institutions in modern society, such as education, religion and entertainment, the family remains the earliest and the most significant agency of socialisation.

Social Placement Legitimates birth into a family, gives the individual a stable place in society. We inherit from our family of orientation, not only material goods but also our social status. We belongs to the same racial or ethnic group and usually to the same religion and social class as our parents belongs to. Our family background is the most significant single determinant of our status in society.

Care and Protection The family is able to offer the care, protection, security and love that are vital to its members. Infant need warmth, food, shelter, and affection. The family provides an intimate atmosphere and an economic unit in which these needs can be provided. The adult family members too provide one another with material and emotional support that cannot be readily obtained outside the family context. The productive members take care of those who owing to reasons of age or other incapacity, cannot care for themselves.

School as Social Institution

In modern industrial society, the school system has emerged as one of the most potent agencies of socialisation. The school is an artificial institutional setup for the purpose of socialisation and cultural transmission. The school can be regarded as a formally constituted community as opposed to mutual communities.

The school is the first large scale organisation of which the child becomes a member. The school is a miniature, reflecting what goes on in the wider society. School offers two context of educational cum socialising ability to students. The **first** is the formal context of the classroom, wherein the context of socialisation is decided by the prescribed curriculum. The **second** context is informal and can be perceived in the inter-personal relationships of students with teachers and those among the students.

Thus, we see that school is said to be next to the family in terms of importance as far as socialisation is concerned. The school combines the formal (*e.g.* classroom teaching, suspension expulsions, official mention, prices) and informal (*e.g.* peer group influences) approaches in its socialising function.

Functions of Schools

- Through curriculum, the school in a formal way provides the child with :
  - (i) cultural achievements of one's society.
  - (ii) opportunities to acquire social and vocational abilities, which are necessary in order to make one a social, useful and economically productive member of the society.
  - (iii) knowledge of basic intellectual skills such as reading, writing, verbal expressions, quantitative and other cognitive abilities. Education teaches languages and allows people to communicate with each other, according to positions in the society.
  - (iv) gender roles as perceived as suitable role by the society.
- Educational systems socialise students to become members of society, to play meaningful roles in the complex network of independent positions.
- Education helps in shaping values and attitudes to the needs of the contemporary society.
- Education widens the mental horizon of pupils and teaches them the new ways of looking at themselves and their society.
- Education offers opportunities to young people for intellectual, emotional and social growth. Thus, education can be influential in promoting new values and stimulating adaption of changing conditions.
- Informally and especially through social clubs, the school enables the child to learn a number of other social roles and skills which are also important for his/her overall development as a member of society.

Society as Social Institution

The term 'society' has been derived from the latin word 'socius' which means 'a companion', 'association' or 'fellowship'. It is because man always lives in the company of his fellow beings. In sociology, society refers not to group of people but to the complex pattern of the norms or interaction or relationships that arise among them. People exist only as an agent of social relationships. Mere congregation of individuals does not constitute society. Rather society refers to the complicated network of social relationships by which every individual is inter-related with his fellow men.

Definitions of Society

According to **MacIver and Page**, "Society is a system of usages and procedures, authority and mutual aid, of many groupings and divisions, of controls of human's behaviour and of liberties".

According to **Cooley**, "Society is a complex of forms or processes, each of which is living and growing by interaction with others, the whole being so unfied that what takes place in one part affects all the rest".

According to **Parsons**, "Society may be defined as the total complex of human relationships in so far as they grow out of action in terms of mean end relationship, intrinsic or symbolic".

From such definitions, we can divide the perspective of society into **two** categories *i.e.* **structural perspective** and **functional perspective**. From structural perspective, society is a whole of various attibutes like folkways mores, institutions of various categories etc. From functional perspective, society is viewed as a complex whole of the reciprocal relationships and various interactions that take place due to such relationships.

Characteristics of Society

Society has following characteristics

Likeness MacIver believes that society means likeness. Hence, one of the characteristic is likeness. Through the meaning of likeness has changed from traditional to modern societies, whereas in traditional societies, the attribute of likeness was defined by family, kinship or blood relationship. In modern societies, social likeness has broadened its attribute to the Principle of Vasuadhev Kutumbham or one world.

Difference Though likeness is the basic feature of society, the feature of difference cannot be ignored. Difference here means diversity or reciprocality in relations. It is a society all are alike, then their will be very less interaction and society would not be diverse.

The difference or diversity compliments opposite or reciprocal relationships. There are various differences or diversity on the basis of sex, interest, nature, etc. Such difference brings diversity to society and hence, gives different aspect to society.

Inter-dependence In a society, one unit depends on another hence, all are inter-dependent. One institution of society cannot fulfils all the requirements of society. Hence, it is inter-dependence, which fulfils the needs of society and its goals. In modern society, not only countries, but several countries are inter-dependent on one another.

Various organisations, like United Nations, SAARC, etc shows the visibility and existence of such inter-dependence.

Cooperation For a society to be in harmony and proper functioning, proper cooperation is a necessary aspect.

No society can exist without cooperation. *e.g.* in a family and marriage, cooperation is an essential feature for a harmonious life.

Hence, these are various features of a society. Society cannot be treated as a means of fulfilment of social needs, but it is a whole system of complex social relationships. Various institutions of society interact with each other to have a harmonious functioning of society.

Functions of Society

Provision for Satisfaction of Basic Needs Food, clothing and shelter are the basic needs of every individual living in the society. Besides these man needs security for protection of its members.

Socialization The newborn children are expected to learn the social values, norms and systems of behaviour. Society provides its members with a mechanism through which they learn the ways of social living. So socialisation is an important pre-requisite of society.

Inter-dependence In all societies, there is social relationship. As there is mutual awareness among individuals in a society, there is also mutual dependence and cooperation. Individuals are bound together in a web of inter-dependence.

Social Control There are some people in a society who do not act, according to the desire of the society. In order to bring these people into line, every society devises a mechanism called social control. By social control, every society regulates anti-social activities of its members.

Goal Attainment Goal attainment is another functional pre-requisite. It includes the determination of goals, the motivation of the members of the society to attain these goals and the mobilising of the members and their energies for the achievement of goals.

Replacement It is another vital condition for the society to survive. Old members die. New members usually take their place. Otherwise, society may die. The replacement is done through procreation.

Division of Labour As there is inter-dependence in society,there is division of labour too. If one function is performed by one individual, the other by other individual. In simple societies, division of labour was simply based on sex, age and ability. In modern societies, division of labour has become complex.

A System of Role Allocation In every society, there must be a proper process for determining which persons will occupy what role at what time and for what purpose. This process is called **role allocation**. Proper allocation of roles between members, minimises problems for the society. Otherwise, society may face disintegration.

A System of Production No society can function in the absence of a system of production. It involves techniques and organisation. Human beings learn these techniques of production through observation, participation, and instruction. Production has both individual and collective aspect. Man achieves many things through collective effort.

A System of Distribution Production is closely associated with distribution. In simple societies, producers were the consumers. In complex societies, this is not so. There are some persons who cannot produce, but only consume. For instance children, the diseased and the disabled. For these people, society also makes provision for consumption. Improper distribution may lead to conflict in society.

Hence, society is abstract, not concrete, in nature. We can't touch it but feel it. Because society resides in the minds of individual. Society is a process of living not a thing, a motion rather than structure. A system of social relationships is the most important aspect of society. Not all relationships are social. A social relationship implies reciprocal awareness among individuals. This reciprocal awareness, direct or indirect is the characteristic of every social relationship.

Social Movement

Defining what exactly a social movement is, can be difficult. It is not the political party or interest group, which are having stable political entities that have regular access to political power and political elities, nor it is a mass fad or trend, which are unorganised, fleeting and without goals. Instead, they are somewhere in between (Freeman and Johnson, 1999).

Social movements are purposeful and organised groups that strive to work toward a common social goal. Social movements are broad alliances of people who are connected through their shared interest in social change. Social movements can advocate for a particular social change, but they can also organise to oppose a social change that is being advocated by another entity. These movements do not have to be formally organised and to be considered social movements. Different alliances can work separately for common causes and still be considered a social movement. Social movements occur when large groups of individuals or organisations work for or against change in social and/or political matters.

Lundberg defines social movement as "A voluntary association of people engaged in concerted efforts to change attitude, behaviour and social relationships in a larger society".

Some characteristics of social movements are that they are involved in conflictual relations with clearly identified opponents, that are linked by dense informal networks and they share a distinct collective identity.

Then, social movements can be thought of as organised, yet informal social entities that are engaged in extra-institutional conflict that is oriented towards a goal. These goals can be either aimed at a specific and narrow policy or be more broadly aimed at cultural change. To early, scholar's collective action was inherently oriented towards change.

Some of the earliest works on social movements were attempts to understand why people got caught up in collective action or what conditions were necessary to foment social movements. These works were rooted in theories of mass society. **Mass Society theory** was concerned with the increasing industrialisation of society, which many felt led to a sense of alienation among individuals as traditional and social structures and support networks broke down.

Features of Social Movement

- It is an effort by a group.
- It's aim is to bring or resist a change in society.
- It may be organised or unorganised.
- It may be peaceful or violent.
- It may continue for a long period or it may die out soon.

Types of Social Movements

Reform Movements They are organised to carry out reforms in some specific areas. The reformers endeavour to change elements of the system for better. For example, Civil Right's Movement, Women's Liberation Movement, Arya Samaj Movement, Brahmo Samaj Movement, etc.

Revolutionary Movements The revolutionary movements denies that the system will even work. These movements are deeply dissatisfied with the social order and work for radical change. They advocate replacing the entire existing structure. Their objective is the reorganisation of society in accordance with their own ideological blueprint. Generally, revolutionary movements become violent as they progress. For example, The Protestant Reformation Movement, the Socialist Movement, The Communist Revolution of China, etc.

Reactionary or Revivalist Movements Some movements are known as reactionary or regressive movements. These aim to reverse the social change. They highlight the importance and greatness of traditional values, ideologies and institutional arrangements. They strongly criticise the fast moving changes of the present.

Resistance Movements These movements are formed to resist a change that is already taking place in society. These can be directed against social and cultural changes, which are already happening in the country.

Utopian Movement These are attempts to take the society or a section of it towards a state of perfection. These are loosely structured collectivities that envision a radically changed and blissful state, either on a large scale, at some time in the future or on a smaller scale in the present. The utopian ideal and the means of it are often vague, but many utopian movements have quite specific programmes for social change. The Communists and Socialists pronouncement of a movement towards the classless and casteless society, free from all kinds of exploitation.

Theories of Social Movement

Sociologists have developed several theories related to social movements.

Some of the better known theories are

Relative Deprivation Theory

Deprivation Theory argues that social movements have their foundations, among people who feel deprived of some good(s) or resource(s). According to this approach, individuals who are lacking some good service or comfort are more likely to organise a social movement to improve (or defend) their conditions (Morrison 1978).

Social scientists have citied 'relative deprivation' as a potential cause of social movements and deviance.

Relative deprivation is the experience of being deprived of something to which one feels to be entitled. It refers to the discontent that people feel, when they compare their positions to those around them and realise that they have less of that which they believe themselves to be entitled. This theory of relative deprivation has a potential to lead political violence such as rioting, terrorism, civil wars and other instances of social deviance such as crime.

Feelings of deprivation are relative, as they come from a comparison to social norms that are not absolute and usually differ from time and place. This differentiates relative deprivation from objective deprivation (also known as absolute deprivàtion or absolute poverty), a condition that applies to all underprivileged people. This leads to an important conclusion, while the objective deprivation (poverty) in the world may change over time, relative deprivation will not, as long as social inequality persists and some humans are better off than others. Relative deprivation may be temporal *i.e.*, it can be experienced by people that experience expansion or rights or wealth, followed by stagnation or reversal of those gains. Such phenomena are also known as unfulfiled rising expectations.

Some sociologists, for instance, **Karl Polanyi** argued that relative differences in economic wealth are more important than absolute deprivation, and that this is a more significant determinate of human quality of life. This debate has important consequences for social policy, particularly on whether poverty can be eliminated simply by raising total wealth or whether egalitarian measures are also needed. A specific form of relative deprivation is relative poverty. A measure of relative poverty defines poverty as being below some relative poverty line, such as household, who earns less than 20% of the median income. Notice that if everyone's real income in an economy increases, but the income distribution stays the same, the number of people living in relative poverty will not change.

There are two significant problems with this theory. **First**, since most people feels deprived at one level or the other almost all the time, the theory has a hard time, explaining why the groups that form social movements do when other people are also deprived. **Second**, the reason behind this theory is circular, often the only evidence for deprivation in the social movement.

Resource Mobilisation Theory

It emphasises the importance of resources in social movement development and success. Resources are understood here to include knowledge, money, media, labour, solidarity, legitimacy and internal and external support from power elite. The theory argues that social movements develop when individuals with grievances are able to mobilise sufficient resources to take action. The emphasis on resources offers an explanation why some discontented/deprived individuals are able to organise while others are not.

It also divides social movements, according to their position among other social movements. This helps sociologists to understand them in relation to other social movements, for example, how much influence does one theory or movement have on another.

Features of Resource Mobilisation

- There will always be grounds for protest in modern, politically and pluralistic societies because there is constant discontent (*i.e.* grievances or deprivation); this de-emphasises the importance of these factors as it makes them ubiquitous.
- Actors are rational and they are able to weigh the costs and benefits from movement's participation.
- Members are recruited through networks, commitment is maintained by building a collective identity and continuing to nurture inter-personal relationships.
- Movement organisation is contingent upon the aggregation of resources.
- Social movement organisations require resources and continuity of leadership.
- Social movement entrepreneurs and protest organisations are the catalysts, which transforms collective discontent into social movements, social movement organisation form the backbone of social movement.
- The form of the resources, shapes the activities of the movement (*e.g.* access to a T.V. station will result in the extensive use of T.V. media).

Critics of this theory, emphasises the importance of resources, especially financial resources. Some movements are effective without an influx of money and are more dependent upon the movement of members for time and labour legislation, The Civil Right's Movement.

New Social Movement Theory

It is a theory of social movement that attempts to explain the plethora of movements that have come up in various Western societies, roughly since the mid 1960s, which are claimed to depart significantly from the conventional Social Movement's paradigm. This movement focuses on issues related to human rights, rather than on materialistic concerns, such as social and economical development.

*There are **two** central claims of this movements and they are :*

- The rise of the post industrial economy is responsible for a new wave of social movements.
- These movements are significantly different from previous social movements of the industrial economy.

The primary difference is their goals, as the new movements focus not on issues of materialistic qualities, such as economic well-being, but on issues related to human rights.

Characteristics

The most noticeable feature of new social movement is that they are primarily social and cultural and only secondarily, if at all, political. Departing from the worker's movement, which was central to the political aim of gaining access to citizenship and representation for the working class, new social movements concentrate on bringing about social mobilsation, though cultural innovations, the development of new lifestyles and the transformation of identities.

Habermas has elaborated that new social movements are the **new politics**, which is about quality of life, individual self-realisation and human rights, whereas the **old politics** focused on economical, political and military security. The concept of new politics can be exemplified in gay liberation, the focus of which transcends the political issue of gay rights to address the need for a social and cultural acceptance of homosexuality. Hence, new social movements are understood as new because they are first and foremost social, unlike older movements, which mostly have an economical basis.

New social movements also emphasise the role of post-material values in contemporary and post-industrial society, as opposed to conflicts over material resources.

According to **Melucci**, "One of the leading new social movement theorists, these movements arise not from relations of production and distribution of resources, but within the sphere of reproduction and the life world". Consequently, the concern has shifted from the production of economical resources as a means of survival or for reproduction to cultural production of social relations, symbols and identities.

The contemporary social movements reject the materialistic orientation of consumerism in capitalist societies by questioning the modern idea that links the pursuit of happiness and success closely to growth, progress and increased productivity and by instead, promoting alternative values and understandings in relation to the social world. For example, the environmental movement that had appeared in the late 1960s, throughout the world with its strong points in the United States and Northern Europe, has significantly brought about a dramatic reversal, in the ways we consider the relationship between economy, society and nature.

Political Process Theory

The way in which Political Process Theory is similar to resource mobilisation in many regards, but tends to emphasise a different component of social structure that is important for Social Movement's development *i.e.* political opportunities. It argues that there are **three** vital components for movement's formation *i.e.* insurgent consciousness, organisational strength and political opportunities.

Insurgent Consciousness refers back to the ideas of deprivation and grievances. The idea is that certain members of society feels like they are being mistreated or somehow the system is unjust. The insurgent consciousness is the collective sense of injustice that movement members (or potential movement members) feels and serves as the motivation for movement's organisation.

Organisational Strength falls inline with Resource Mobilisation Theory, arguing that in order for a Social Movement to organise it must have strong leadership and sufficient resources.

Political Opportunity refers to the receptivity or vulnerability of the existing political system to challenge.

This vulnerability can be the result of any of the following (or a combination thereof):

- Growth of political pluralism.
- Decline in effectiveness of repression.
- Elite disunity; the leading factions are internally fragmented.
- A broadening of access to institutional participation in political processes.
- Support of organised opposition by elites.

One of the advantage of the Political Process Theory is that it addresses the issue of timing or emergence of social movements. Some groups may have the insurgent consciousness and resources to mobilise, but because political opportunities are closed, they will not have any success. Then, the theory argues that all three of these components are important.

Critics of the Political Process Theory and Resource Mobilisation Theory points out that neither theory discusses movement's culture to any great degree. This has presented culture's theorists an opportunity to expound on the importance of culture.

One advance on the Political Process Theory is the Political Mediation Model, which outlines the way in which the political context facing movement actors intersects with the strategic choices that movements make. An additional **strength** of this model is that it can look at the outcomes of social movements not only in terms of success or failure, but also in terms of consequences (whether intentional or unintentional or positive or negative) and in terms of collective benefits.

The chief characteristic of Political Process Theory is that it is related to Social Movement's mobilisation, political opportunities, mobilising structures and framing processes.

EXAM BASED QUESTIONS

1 **What is the basic concept of term 'Education'?**
(a) Experience which gives no knowledge.
(b) Experience where knowledge is one sided.
(c) Experience in which learner can learn something.
(d) All of the above

2 **Which disciple application is related to the education?**
(a) Geology (b) Pedagogy
(c) Humanities (d) Arts

3 **Is it correct to say that philosophy spreads secular values?**
(a) Absolutely true (b) Absolutely false
(c) Can't say (d) May be

4 **What is the meaning of the word 'Socius'?**
(a) Educate (b) Knowledge
(c) Theory (d) Companion

5 **Which among the following is correct with reference to meaning of the word 'Education'?**
(a) Synchronisation of knowledge
(b) Systematic study of society
(c) Organisation of common knowledge
(d) None of the above

6 **Who said that in a society, moral education is necessary?**
(a) Emile Durkheim (b) BF Skinner
(c) Pavlov (d) Tolman

7 **What is the basis of Durkhein's Educational Theory?**
(a) Integrity (b) Culture
(c) Social Solidarity (d) All of these

8 **Applications of principles of sociology of education is known as**
(a) sociology of education
(b) educational sociology
(c) social foundation of education
(d) social science of education

9 **Whose analysis for education is directly based on the activities, happening in the classroom?**
(a) Symbolic transformation
(b) Symbolic interactionism
(c) Repetative guidance
(d) Conflict Theory

10 **Who plays a major role in student's performance?**
(a) Peer (b) Parents
(c) Culture (d) Teacher

11 **Which study was performed by Robert Rosenthal and Lenore Jacobson?**
(a) Blue Star Theory (b) Landmark study
(c) Descriptive study (d) Analytics

12 **.......... is considered to be the founder of symbolic interactionism.**
(a) Durkheim (b) George Herbart Mead
(c) Morrison (d) Horton

13 **What is the procedure, through which Structural Functionalist theory focuses on the needs of the society?**
(a) Primary education (b) Secondary education
(c) Elementary learning (d) Universal education

14 **Who is marked as the founder of Functional theory?**
(a) Durkheim (b) Skinner
(c) Ray Rist (d) Rosenthal Jacobson

15 **What term is used by Durkheim, which brings in people from various diverse backgrounds and historical concerns under the same roof?**
(a) Equal education (b) Psychological education
(c) Moral Education (d) Education

16 **Which theory prevents the social inequality?**
(a) Preventive theory (b) Reformative theory
(c) Deterrent theory (d) Conflict theory

17 **What is said to the role of education for conflict theorists?**
(a) Fragmented beliefs (b) Hidden curriculum
(c) Mobilisation (d) None of these

18 **What type of test is performed by school to sort students?**
(a) IQ test
(b) Syllabus test
(c) Reasoning test
(d) Verbal and vocabulary test

19 **What is required for the formation of the integrated set of values, to be implemented on the society?**
(a) Social institutions (b) Family
(c) Values (d) Schools

20 **"An enduring cultural structure that meets certain fundamental needs of the society and establishes social control" is the definition of**
(a) religion (b) economical system
(c) social institution (d) school

21 Social institution have
(a) physical structure
(b) non-physical structure
(c) psychological structure
(d) None of these

22 If we say that institution doesn't have members, than what does it have?
(a) Students (b) Family
(c) Religion (d) Followers

23 What lies in the contrast with institution?
(a) Association (b) Followers
(c) Society (d) None of these

24 How many types of basic institutions are described by sociologists?
(a) Three (b) Five
(c) Seven (d) Six

25 Who of the following has said that "a social institution is a functional configuration of culture pattern"?
(a) Kinball Young
(b) Gillin and Gillin
(c) MacIver
(d) Ginsberg

26 Which of the following statement is true about family?
(a) Family is an old institution.
(b) Family's origin can be traced.
(c) Family is a new institution.
(d) Family is an old institution and it's origin is in obsecurities.

27 Mark out the primary group among the following.
(a) Members of a trade union.
(b) Family
(c) Students of History
(d) Social workers

28 Which of the following is not a purpose of a family institution?
(a) To nurture and socialise children
(b) To pass on generational traditions
(c) To increase the population in a society
(d) To provide a sense of belongingness and identity

29 Schools are social institutions because they
(a) preserve and instill in future generations, the knowledge, ideas and customs of our culture.
(b) suggest ways and means of social progress.
(c) suggest solutions to social problems.
(d) are established by the society.

30 Which of the following is not correct about the school?
(a) They are affected by the social and economical situations and changes in our civilisation.
(b) They are powerful instruments of social change.
(c) They are potential agents of conflicts and disintegration.
(d) They are social agencies of cultural transmission.

31 What type of education, the family imparts to the child?
(a) Formal (b) Informal
(c) Deliberate (d) Regular

32 Education provided to the child, by the school is
(a) formal (b) informal
(c) highly standardised (d) traditional

33 Which of the following can serve as the suitable example of the primary group?
(a) School (b) Family
(c) Church (d) Community

34 "Social institution is an organised system of social relationships which embodies certain common values and procedures and meets certain baisc needs of the society". Who said this?
(a) Landis (b) Horton
(c) Parsons (d) Ginsberg

35 Function of social institutions are
(a) helps to maintain the order in the society
(b) satisfies the basic needs of society
(c) creates harmony and unity among the members of the society
(d) All of the above

36 Which of the following statement(s) regarding Conflict theory is/are correct?
(a) The purpose of education is maintaining social inequality
(b) Preserving the power of those who dominate society
(c) Conflict theorists see education not as a social benefit
(d) All of the above

37 What is the basic trait of social movement in education?
(a) Formal (b) Informal
(c) Materialist (d) Platonic

38 The theory of relative deprivation is an example of what?
(a) Macro Sociological theory
(b) Feminist Sociological theory
(c) Micro Sociological theory
(d) Middle Range Sociological theory

39 What is the major cause of 'relative deprivation'?
(a) Lack of resources
(b) Performance of people
(c) Lack of goods, services and comforts
(d) No culture

40 Which theory talks about the movement transformation?
(a) Conflict theory
(b) Performance theory
(c) Resource Mobilisation theory
(d) All of the above

41 Which theory focuses on the political opportunities?
(a) Political Progress theory
(b) Conflict theory
(c) Derivative theory
(d) New Social Movement theory

42 Identify the type of social movement. "These movements are formed to resist a change that is already taking place in society".
(a) Reform Movement
(b) Revolutionary Movement
(c) Revivalist Movement
(d) Resistance Movement

43 Relative deprivation means
(a) the experience of being deprived to which one feels to be entitled
(b) the discontent the people have when they compare their position to those around them
(c) Theory of Relative Deprivation has a potential to lead political violence, such as rioting, civil wars, etc
(d) All of the above

44 Following are the major elements of society.
1. Social relation
2. Social stratification
3. Social interaction
4. Social culture

Which among the following is the correct code?
(a) Only 1
(b) 1, 2 and 4
(c) 2, 3 and 4
(d) 1, 2, 3 and 4

45 In his sociological explanation of religion, Durkheim made certain observations that
1. religion is mental illness.
2. god is only society personified.
3. religion brings salvation for the suffering humanity.
4. the kingdom of heaven is a glorified society.

Codes
(a) 1 and 2 (b) 2 and 3
(c) 1 and 3 (d) 2 and 4

46 Which of the following statement is not true about the family?
(a) It is only socially recognised relationship for child-bearing.
(b) It is the only institution of society, which caters to the development of child's personality.
(c) It is seen as an essential agency for socialising and rearing the child.
(d) It is only important agency that introduces the child to the culture of the society.

47 Which of the following influenced the Theoretical approach known as Symbolic Interactionism?
(a) George Hegel
(b) George Herbert Mead
(c) Talcott Parsons
(d) Ralf Dahrendorf

48 Which of the following is not associated with functionalism?
(a) Talcott Parsons (b) Ralf Dahrendorf
(c) Emile Durkheim (d) Robert Merton

49 The features of Resource Mobilisations theory are
(a) Develops when individuals with grievance are able to mobilise sufficiet resources to take action
(b) Members are recruited through networks
(c) Social Movement entrepreneurs and protest organisations are the catalysts which transform collective discontent into social movements
(d) All of the above

50 Match the following

	List I (Approaches)	List II (Founders)
A.	Symbolic Interactionism	1. Bummer
B.	Social action	2. Pareto
C.	Conflict	3. Marx
D.	Functionalism	4. Durkheim

Codes

	A	B	C	D		A	B	C	D
(a)	1	2	3	4	(b)	2	1	3	4
(c)	2	1	4	3	(d)	1	3	2	4

51 Match the following.

	List I (Concepts)	List II (Sociologists)
A.	Organic solidarity	1. Herbert Spencer
B.	Religious ethics	2. Emile Durkheim
C.	Mode of production	3. Vifredo Parito
D.	Social evolution	4. Karl Marx
		5. Max Weber

Codes

	A	B	C	D		A	B	C	D
(a)	1	3	4	2	(b)	2	1	5	3
(c)	5	3	4	1	(d)	2	5	4	1

52 Basic principles of symbolic interactionism include
1. human capacity for throught.
2. social institutions and social interactions.
3. mind and social consciousness.
4. meanings and symbols that facilitate action and interaction.

Select the correct answer using the codes given below
(a) 1 and 2 (b) 2 and 3 (c) 3 and 4 (d) 1 and 4

53 Functionalism constitutes an important element in the social theories of
(a) E Durkheim and C Levi Strauss
(b) E Durkheim and Max Weber
(c) Talcott Parsons and Karl Marx
(d) AR Radciffe Brown and RK Merton

54 Who among the following has emphasised the positive functions of the conflict in society?
(a) Lewis A Coser (b) Karl Marx
(c) Max Weber (d) Emile Durkheim

55 The advancement of society is based on differention in their functions of
(a) individual (b) society
(c) organism (d) None of these

56 The most important feature of symbolic interactionism is that human interactions are based on
(a) sociability
(b) the meaning given to one another's action
(c) social order
(d) reciprocal relationships

57 Symbolic interactionism is a
(a) a continual process of interpreting the social world around us
(b) a way of looking at the stars
(c) a famous research method book
(d) a branch of research philosophy which refers to the study of material artifacts

58 Who coined the term symbolic interactionism?
(a) Herbert Blumer (b) Charles Cooley
(c) George Simmel (d) Erving Goffman

59 Political Process theory emphasis the role of
(a) political opportunities (b) mobilising structure
(c) framing policies (d) All of these

Directions (Q. Nos. 60-76) *In the questions given below are two statements, labelled as Assertion (A) and Reason (R). In the context of the two statements, select the correct code.*

Codes
(a) Both A and R are true and R is the correct explanation of A
(b) Both A and R are true, but R is not the correct explanation of A
(c) A is true, but R is false.
(d) A is false, but R is true.

60 **Assertion** (A) Man becomes the kind of work he does.
Reason (R) The work he does, his thinking and senses becomes accordingly.

61 **Assertion** (A) Education is the broad concept.
Reason (R) It refers to the over all experience in which learner can learn anything.

62 **Assertion** (A) Education is the application of pedagogy.
Reason (R) Education consists of systematic instruction, teaching and training by professional teacher.

63 **Assertion** (A) Sociology is the study of social life.
Reason (R) It is guided by rational and empirical science.

64 **Assertion** (A) Sociology provides principles that helps in education.
Reason (R) Education practices these principles.

65 **Assertion** (A) Emile Durkheim was marked as a greatest French sociologist.
Reason (R) He gave importance to the social function of education.

66 **Assertion** (A) 'Self' is important for the development of society.
Reason (R) 'Self' is a social concept.

67 **Assertion** (A) 'Moral Education' was the outcome of Durkheim's structural functions.
Reason (R) Durkheim believed that moral education brings in the people from various social structure into one society.

68 **Assertion** (A) Family holds the relations, among the people.
Reason (R) In family, we have certain groups of people, who are inter-related and co-related to each other.

69 **Assertion** (A) In nuclear or individualistic family, husband-wife and their children, live together.
Reason (R) Modern industrial urban system has encouraged this type of family.

70 **Assertion** (A) Institutions are necessary to maintain social harmony.
Reason (R) Without institutions, society would be chaotic and anarchistic, which is a terrible condition to live.

71 **Assertion** (A) Family life is not always happy and harmonious.
Reason (R) Most sexual abuse of children and domestic violence occurs within it.

72 **Assertion** (A) According to symbolic interactionalist perspective, people do not attach meanings to symbols and act according to objective's interpretation.

Reason (R) Symbolic interactionalism explain's social behaviour in terms of how people interact with each other via symbol.

73 **Assertion** (A) Social institutions consist of group of people who have come together for a common purpose.

Reason (R) Social institutions cannot exist with modern societies.

74 **Assertion** (A) Institutions are structured process through which people carry on their activities.

Reason (R) Institutions do not have members, they have followers.

75 **Assertion** (A) In modern industrial society, the school system has emerged as one of the most potent agencies of socialism.

Reason (R) The school is an miniature, reflecting what goes on in wider society.

76 **Assertion** (A) Social movements are purposeful and organised groups that strive to work toward a common goal.

Reason (R) Social movements can advocate for a particular social change.

PREVIOUS YEARS' QUESTION

January 2017

1 The concept of sociology of education implies

(a) use of sociology for making learning socially relevant

(b) devising ways and means of education to reach all sections of society

(c) consideration on the uses of education from sociological perspective

(d) discussion on the implications of sociology for education

ANSWERS

Exam Based Questions

1 (c)	2 (b)	3 (a)	4 (d)	5 (b)	6 (a)	7 (c)	8 (a)	9 (b)	10 (d)
11 (b)	12 (b)	13 (a)	14 (a)	15 (c)	16 (d)	17 (b)	18 (a)	19 (a)	20 (c)
21 (b)	22 (d)	23 (a)	24 (b)	25 (b)	26 (d)	27 (b)	28 (c)	29 (a)	30 (a)
31 (b)	32 (a)	33 (d)	34 (b)	35 (d)	36 (d)	37 (b)	38 (d)	39 (c)	40 (c)
41 (a)	42 (d)	43 (d)	44 (d)	45 (d)	46 (b)	47 (b)	48 (b)	49 (d)	50 (a)
51 (d)	52 (d)	53 (d)	54 (a)	55 (a)	56 (b)	57 (a)	58 (a)	59 (d)	60 (a)
61 (a)	62 (d)	63 (b)	64 (a)	65 (a)	66 (a)	67 (a)	68 (b)	69 (b)	70 (a)
71 (b)	72 (d)	73 (b)	74 (b)	75 (a)	76 (b)				

Previous Years' Question

1 (c)

CHAPTER 04

Socialisation and Contribution of Educational Thinkers

Education is a social process which prepares individuals to lead a successful and meaningful life. Socialisation is the process of cultural learning, whereby a new person acquires necessary skills and education to play a regular part in a social system. Thus, to understand the relationship between education and socialisation we need to study about the contribution of various educational thinkers.

In this Chapter

- Socialisation
- Culture and Education
- Contribution of Educational Thinkers
  - Swami Vivekananda
  - Rabindranath Tagore
  - Mahatma Gandhi
  - Sri Aurobindo Ghosh
  - Jiddu Krishnamurti
  - Paulo Freire
  - Marry Wollstonecraft
  - Nel Noddings
  - Savitribai Phule
- National Values of Constitution with Reference to Education

Socialisation

Socialisation is the process, whereby an individual learns to adjust to a group and behave in a manner, approved by the group. It is the process by which individuals acquire language, knowledge, skills and values, that makes him/her well adjusted in family, neighbourhood, social groups and society. It is of prime importance for individual, as he/she is prepared and moulded with belief's personality and behaviour by various social agents *i.e.* family, peer group, school, etc, through the process of socialisation. It is a transmission process, where knowledge and skills are transmitted either formally or informally. It is a process where a person learns about role, status and value that should have in a society. It leads to the interaction of child with others, in order to make the environment adaptable with respect to current society.

Definitions of Socialisation

According to **AW Green**, "Socialisation is the process by which the child acquires a cultural content along with selfhood and personality".

According to **Drever**, "Socialisation is a process by which an individual has adapted his social environment and becomes a recognised, cooperating and efficient member of it".

Process of Socialisation

Socialisation is the process by which children acquire the values, standards, behaviour, attitudes and skills that are viewed as appropriate to the culture in which the child resides.

Rearing The upbringing of a child plays a significant role in the process of socialisation of a child. The key factors associated with child rearing includes warmth, rules, behaviour control, supportive responsiveness and expectations. Parenting style, affects children's traits such as achievement, independence, curiosity, self-reliance, self-control and friendliness.

It means that improper upbringing of a child, leads to the growth of anti-social tendencies in him because of social maladjustment. Therefore, for child socialisation, healthy and proper upbringing is essential.

Cooperation Society makes the child social.The cooperation of society plays an important role to socialise the child. Paying attention and expressing your appreciation to your children for not only complying with your request, but doing it in a cooperative manner will impact them in a way that makes them feel good about themselves.

Suggestion It is the psychological process by which one person guides the thoughts, feelings or behaviour of another. In the child socialisation, suggestion plays a significant role. It is a natural fact that a child acts according to the suggestion received from his/her well wishers. Thus, suggestion determines the direction of social behaviour.

Social Teaching It also plays an important role in socialisation of child. It includes, family, friends and relations, who guides the child in one way or the other.

Recognition Sympathy, love and suggestion of parents and well wishers develops a feeling of recognition in the child with others. Those who behave well with the child, the child consider them as his/her well wishers.

Imitation It is an advanced behaviour where an individual observes and replicate another's behaviour. It is also a form of social learning that leads to the development of traditions and ultimately our behaviour.

In the socialisation of the children, it plays an important role. It imitates the behaviour, impulses and feelings of family members. So, learning by imitation is the most powerful means of socialising a child.

Sympathy It is a feeling and concern or it can be the perception, understanding and reaction to the distress or need of another human being. During infancy, child is fully dependent on his family for the fulfilment of all his needs and requirements. It is the sympathy, which develops oneness in the child and he learns to discriminate between his real well-wishers and other members of the society.

Controlling Factors of Socialisation

- The child's behaviour is to be controlled through reward and punishment, praise or blame, etc.
- The child should be exposed to good social behaviour.
- The child should be taught to follow the rules of games.
- Emphasis is given to the qualities like cooperation, respect, obedience, etc.
- Child should be taught to be affectionate towards his peers and friends.

Relationship Between Socialisation and Education

Both socialisation and education are processes of learning. At one time in the past, the difference between the two was very distinct, but as the time passes that boundary becomes more blurred. Socialisation is the process of internalising the norms and ideologies of society, it encompasses both learning and teaching and is thus the means by which social and cultural continuity are attained. On the other hand, education is the process of facilitating learning or the acquisition of knowledge, skills, values, beliefs and habits. Through education, society imparts its knowledge to its younger generation.

Thereby, ensuring self-preservation and continuity. In this sense, education is a process of socialisation. At the same time, changes in society, mould the education system itself and it acquires complexity. Education in this sense is a process, which prepares the members of the society to adapt to the constantly changing conditions of society.

Thus, it can said that education is a social process and education is the process of socialisation.

Culture and Education

Originally, the word 'culture' means 'the cultivation of the soul or mind'. It also signifies man's moral, spiritual and intellectual achievement. Culture is the stock, in trade of group. It is a medium through which individual develops and matures. The word 'culture' was first appeared in Europe to connote a process of cultivation and improvement, in agriculture.

In 19th century, the word developed to refer, first to the betterment on the refine of the individual and then to the fulfilment of national aspirations or ideals. In the 19th century, some scientists used the word 'culture' to refer to a universal human capacity. In the 20th century, culture emerged as a central concept, encompassing the range of human phenomena that cannot be attributed to genetic inheritance.

According to **Bogardus**, "Culture is composed of an integrated customs, traditions and current behaviour patterns of human group".

According to **Hobe**, "Culture acts as an integrated system of learned behaviour patterns, which are characteristics of the members of a society and which are not a result of biological behaviours".

Characteristics of Culture

Following are the characteristics of culture

Culture is Social Culture does not exist in isolation. It is a product of society. It develops through social interaction. No man can acquire culture without association with others. Man becomes a man only among men.

Culture is Shared Culture is not something that an individual alone can possess. Culture in sociological sense is shared. *e.g.*, customs, traditions, beliefs, ideas and morale, etc, are all shared by people of a group or society.

Culture is Learnt Culture is not inborn, it is learnt. Culture is often called 'learned ways of behaviour.' Unlearned behaviour is not culture. But, shaking hands, saying thanks or namaskar, dressing sense, etc, are all cultural behaviour.

Culture is Transmissive Culture is transmissive as it is transmitted from one generation to another. Language is the main vehicle of culture. Language in different forms, makes it possible for the present generation to understand the achievement of earlier generation. Transmission of culture may take place by imitation as well as by instruction.

Culture is Continuous and Cumulative Culture exists as a continuous process. In its historical growth it tends to become cumulative. Sociologist, **Linton** called culture 'the social heritage of man.' It becomes difficult for us to imagine, what society would be without culture.

Culture Varies from Society to Society Every society has its own cutture. It differs from society to society. It is unique. There elements like customs, traditions, morale, values and beliefs are not uniform everywhere. It varies from time to time.

Culture is Dynamic No culture ever remains constant or changeless, it keeps on changing. It is subject to slow, but constant change. It peeps n changing is responsive to the changing conditions of the physical world.

Culture is Gratifying It provides proper opportunities for the satisfaction of our needs and desires. Our needs both biological and social are fulfiled in the cultural ways. It determines and guides various activities of man. Thus, culture is defined as the process through which human beings satisfy their wants.

From the above discussion, it is clear that each and every society has a culture of its own. It is not only diverse, but also unequal, and is found in different societies throughtout the world.

Association of Education and Culture

Culture is closely related to education, in which educational system of any society has a clear impact on its culture. The basis of educational system of a society are its need and they are fulfiled by education. Culture has its impact on education *e.g.*, in a communistic culture, materialism is more powerful than spiritualism. It means the mode of education is towards material progress.

Culture Based Education (CBE) positively impacts students socio-emotional well being *e.g.*, identity, self-efficacy, social relationship, etc. It also affects cultural affiliation, civic engagement and school motivation.

Culture Based Education is also more likely to put cultural skills to use in their communities and report higher levels of trusting relationship with teacher and staff, underscoring a deeper sense of belonging at school. The strength of these connections is critical for producing engaged and successful learners, as they prepare for future.

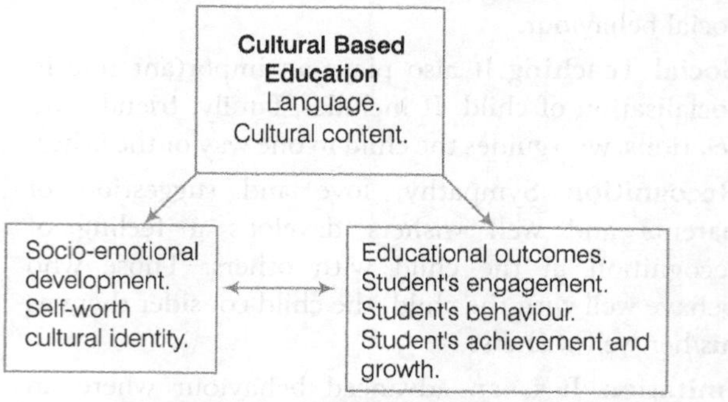

Relationship Between Culture Based Education and Its Outcome

The ultimate relationship between culture and education is evident from the fact that one of the major aims of education is to educate the child about his cultural heritage. In any human group, the various elements and parts of culture evolve after thousand of years of experience and these are handed down as a whole to the succeeding generations. Hence, every individual is born into a particular culture, which provides him definite pattern of behaviour and values, which guides his conduct in different walks of life. Culture plays an important role in man's life in the adaptation to the natural environment, in the adaptation to the social environment and in the development of personality and socialisation.

Education as a part of culture has the twin functions of conservation and modification or renewal of the culture. Education is conceived as a systematic effort to maintain a culture. In its technical sense, "education is the process by which society, through schools, colleges, universities and other institutions, deliberately transmit its cultural heritage, its accumulated knowledge, values and skills from one generation to another". Education is an instrument of cultural change.

Education can impart knowledge, training and skills as well as inculcate new ideas and attitude among the young. It is culture in which education germinates and flowers. It is the culture, also upon which education exerts, in turn, a nourishing influence. The intimate relationship between culture and education is to impart to the child cultural heritage and social heritage. Every individual is born into a particular culture which provides him with definite patterns of behaviour and values which guide his/her conduct in different walks of life. Thus, culture plays an important role in the life of a person.

Influence of Culture on Education

As mentioned above, culture and education have give and take relationship. Both are compliment to each other in various aspects.

The following are some of the influences of culture on education

Aim and Ideals of Education They are mostly determined by the values and patterns of society.

Curriculum It is conditioned according to the culture of society. It is framed according to the ideals and needs of the society to realise the cultural values.

Method of Teaching and Culture They are intimately connected to each other. The changing cultural patterns of a society exerts powerful influence upon the method of teaching also. The shift from the old-centred teaching to child-centred education is an example. Socialised Method like Project Method, seminar, symposium, discussion, etc are widely used in the teaching-learning process because of the influence of culture.

Discipline It is also influenced by the cultural values. The present cultural patterns of thinking and living are directly linked to our concept of discipline. The concept of repressive discipline of ancient and middle ages has been replaced by the modern values of life.

Textbooks They are written according to the formulated curriculum. Only these books are welcomed which promotes and fosters cultural ideals and values are welcomed.

Teacher He/she is one who has imbibed the cultural ideals and values of the society to achieve his mission successfully. Only such teacher is able to infuse higher ideals and moral values in children.

School It is a miniature of society. The total activities and programmes of the school are organised according to the cultural ideals and values of the society. Hence, school is the centre of promoting, moulding, reforming and developing the cultural pattern of the society.

Influence of Education on Culture

Just as culture influences education, in the same way education also exerts a powerful influence upon the culture of a country.

Following are the various ways by which education influences the culture of a country

Preservation of Culture Each country believes and flaunts the superiority of its own culture over the rest. Hence, it tries to preserve its culture in its original form. Education is the only means, to complete this task. Thus, education preserves the culture of the society.

Transmission of Culture The process of preservation includes the process of transmission as well. Transmission of culture from one generation to another is the best guarantee of its preservation.

The famous sociologist, **Ottaway** says that "The function of education is to transmit the social values and ideals to the young and capable members of the society".

Development of Culture The function of education is to bring about the needed and desirable changes in the cultural ideals and values for the progress and continued development of society, without which social progress cannot take place.

Continuity of Culture Culture is the life and blood of society. Without culture a society is bound to decay and die sooner or later. Education upholds the continuity of culture through its diverse activities and programmes. A society establishes schools to preserve and transmit its culture from generation to generation.

Development of Personality Education employs diverse cultural patterns of thinking behaviours and items of cultural values, so that children are physically, mentally, socially and emotionally developed to the maximum extent. Thus, education aims at developing the personality of the child.

Removal of Cultural Lag Material culture develops at a fast pace due to scientific researches and innovations, whereas non-material culture consisting of ideals, values and norms lags behind creating a gulf between the two. Education is the only means to bridge this cultural lag by its activities and programmes of development.

Contribution of Educational Thinkers

Educational thinkers love to dwelt on the Philosophy of Education and its related aspects like knowledge, intelligence, mind and the function of teaching and learning. Among others, we will discuss about the few renowned thinkers from Indian origin to Western thinkers.

Swami Vivekananda

Swami Vivekananda's original name was Narendranath Dutt. He was born in an affluent family in Calcutta (Kolkata) on 12th January, 1863. He acquired his new name in 1886, when he took sanyasa. He was an Indian Hindu monk and chief disciple of the 19th century saint Ramakrishna. He belonged to a traditional Bengali Kayastha (caste of Hindus) family and was one of the nine siblings. His father Vishwanath Dutta, was a successful practicing lawyer at Calcutta High Court. His mother Bhuvaneshwari Devi, was endowed with deep devotion, strong character and other qualities. The progressive rational approach of Narendranath's father and the religious temperament of his mother helped in shaping his thinking and personality.

Swamiji graduated with honours from Calcutta University, He was deeply interested in the study of Philosophy and. religion. Swamiji first introduction to saint Ramakrishna was held at Dakshineswar. The meeting with Ramakrishna Paramhansa was a turning point in his life. Swami Ramakrishna was an enlightened soul. In 1888, two years after his master's death he set out to the Himalayas. He wandered for two years through deserts and forests.

On **1st May, 1897** at **Calcutta**, Vivekananda founded the Ramakrishna Mission, the organ for social service. In this mission, monks undertake propagation of practical Vedanta. The ideals of the Ramakrishna Mission are based on Karmayoga. The headquarter of Ramakrishna Mission was at Belur Math.

Swami Vivekananda was a staunch individualist. He believed in dignity of humanity and had faith in man. He believed in immortality of soul and God. Swamiji showed four paths i.e., path of work, worship, contemplation and knowledge. He believed in religion, which is science based and urged for the rights of women.

Philosophy of Swami Vivekananda

"All the power is within you, you can do anything and everything. Believe in that, don't believe that you are weak. Stand-up and express the divinity within you". **—Swami Vivekananda**

Teachings and Philosophy of Swami Vivekananda stressed on different aspects of religion, education, character building as well as social issues pertaining to India.

Swami Vivekananda's teachings propagated the advaitic principles as far more reaching on the social and political front, apart from its philosophical aspect.

Rabindranath Tagore commented on Swami Vivekananda and his teachings that "If you want to know India, study Vivekananda. In him, everyone is positive and nothing negative. Vivekananda realised a country's future depends on its people, so he mainly stressed on man, 'man making is my mission', that's how he described his teachings".

Vivekananda was a Hindu monk from India, who played significant role in introducing **Vedanta** to the Western world and also reviving and re-defining certain aspects of the religion within India. To him, the emerging compassion that transforms into a strong determination to help others, who are unaware of the oneness, is the true mark of an enlightened person are the keynote of Philosophy of Vivekananda.

It can be represented as follows :

Essence of Education

To Vivekananda, education was not only collection of information, but something more meaningful. He felt education should be man making, life giving and character building. To him, education was an assimilation of noble ideas *i.e.* "Education is not the amount of information that you put into your brain and runs not there, undigested, all your life.

We must have life building, man making, character making assimilation of ideas. If you have assimilated five ideas and made them your life and character, you have more education than any man, who has got by heart a whole library".

Positive Education

Vivekananda stressed on giving the positive education only because negative thoughts weaken men. He told, if young boys and girls are encouraged and are not unnecessarily criticised all the time, they are bound to improve in time.

Religion

He was a follower of Vedanta. He received an important teaching from Ramakrishna was that 'Jiva is Shiva' (each individual is divinity itself). According to him, man is potentially divine, so service to man is indeed service to God.

Vivekananda told that we must not only tolerate other religions but positively embrace them and that the truth is the basis of all religions.

National Integration

According to Swami Vivekanand, Sectarian violence and growing intolerance are threatening the social harmony and national security. Intolerance of all kinds, be it religious tolerance, caste intolerance all have been on the rise for sometime, threatening the integrity of the nation.

Human Mind

Swamiji suggested that not to do anything which disturbs the mind or make it restless. Swamiji compared human mind with a monkey who is always restless and incessantly active by his own nature.

Women Development

It is completely unfair to discriminate between sexes. He suggested not to think that there are men and women, but only that there are human beings. According to **Swami Vivekananda**, "The ideal of womenhood in India is motherhood, the marvellous, unselfish, all suffering, ever forgiving mother". He felt two evils in India *i.e.* trampling on the women and grinding the poor through caste restriction.

Philosophy of Education

On the Philosophy of Education, Swami Vivekananda said that "all knowledge *i.e.* secular or spiritual, is in the human mind". In many cases, it is not discovered, but remains covered and when the covering is being slowly taken off, we say that 'we are learning and the advance of knowledge is made by this process of uncovering". What Swamiji means is not any sectarian religion, but qualities like truthfulness, justice, selflessness and concern for others. The learner must be free from all prejudices and pre-conceived notions and receive from his teacher learning, which is a trust.

Implications of Vivekananda's Philosophy

Swami Vivekananda looked upon education from two view points and they are

- Transcendental view
- Empirical view

From the **transcendental point** of view, "Education is defined as manifestation of the perfection already in man". This is in consonance with the teaching of Advaita Vedanta.

From the **empirical point** of view, "Education is defined as that kind of training and skill by which man's will power is brought under control and become conductive to the good of humanity as a whole".

So far, the first definition is concerned about that one cannot fail to notice the implications of the Advaita Vedanta, contained in the definition. According to **Advaita Vedanta**, "Man is potentially divine, he is identical with the supreme reality, which is Brahman or existence consciousness bliss". Only on account of the cloud of ignorance, which covers his nature, he cannot realise his divine nature. Education helps him to manifest his own potential divinity. While the second definition is concerned about that Swami Vivekananda looks upon education as an instrument of social change.

"Education should aim at character building of an individual and promote selflessness and courage".

During his time, Vivekananda insisted that our education should be conducted on national lines through national methods. It was he, who inspired his countrymen to develop a sense of pride in their cultural heritage yet was not a blind follower of the ancient cultural heritage of our country. All what he wanted is to provide a synthesis between tradition and modernity.

What he wanted to emphasise, was that emotional attachment to and reverence for traditional values is not enough. One has to examine how far traditional values are relevant in the modern context. He had this in mind, when he insisted on a synthesis of **Vedanta** and **Western Science** as a model of our educational planning and programme.

Fortunately, India has believed in such education and knowledge, since the days of the **Upanishads**. Only Upanishads are the literature in the world which teaches man to find and realise within himself the implications of the word **Abhih** (fearlessness). It urges a person to believe in himself and believe in the oneness of the universe. Religion underlines that man has to live for all beings. All are one and invisible.

Vivekananda had warned that a major shortcoming of Eastern Civilisation (for which he had great admiration in many other ways) was that it thought intellectual education alone was enough, without taking care of the heart. Only that kind of education can made a mind more selfish.

Today, India along with the rest of the world, has to give the topmost priority of the dissemination of an education that will inspire every human being to work for amity and fellowship to have internal peace and search for revolving all conflicts. Spiritual education seeks to bring home the message that "He alone sees, who sees all beings as himself".

For the world, a time has come to realise, more than ever before, a value education makes a man realise his spiritual nature. Only a man conscious of his spiritual self can be truly secular in his conviction and outlook. Religious education brings out the spirituality of man and that is the only life giving force.

Aims of Education

According to Swami Vivekananda, the following should be the main aims of education :

Creation of Self-Confidence and Self-Realisation All through his life, Swamiji exhorted the individuals to keep full confidence upon their powers. They should inculcate a spirit of self-surrender, sacrifice and renunciation of material pleasures for the good of others. Education should inculcate all these qualities in an individual. In Swamiji's own words, "Faith in us and faith in God, this is the secret of greatness."

Formation of Character Character is the aggregate of a man's tendencies, the sum total of the best of his mind. We are what our thoughts have made us. Education must build-up character and manifest our real nature.

Development of Personality Personality is the influence of the impression that one creates on the others. It is the personality of a man that counts.

According to **Vivekananda**, "Personality is two-third and his intellect and words are only one-third in making the real man".

Reaching Perfection The prime aim of education is to achieve fullness of perfection, already present in the child. According to **Swamiji**, "All material and spiritual knowledge is already present in man covered by a curtain of ignorance"

Physical and Mental Development The main aim of education is that the child should able to promote national growth and advancement as a fearless and physically well developed citizen of tomorrow. Stressing the mental development of the child, Swamiji wished education to enable the child to stand on his own feets economically, rather than becoming a parasite on others.

Moral and Spiritual Development According to Swami Vivekananda, "A nation's greatness is not only measured by its parliamentary institutions and activities, but also by the greatness of its citizens. But, the greatness of citizens is possible only through their moral and spiritual development, which education should foster".

Religious Development Each individual should be able to search out and to develop the religious seed, embedded in him and thus, find the absolute truth or reality. Swamiji advocated the training of feelings and emotions, so that the whole life is purified and sublimated.

Searching Unity in Diversity The true aim of education is to develop insight into the individuals, so that they are able to search out and realise unity in diversity.

Curriculum

He was not in favour of the prevalent system of education in the county, as the education in India was influenced by the British system of education. Curriculum should synthesise the knowledge and wisdom of the east and the west. He also attached great importance to the physical development of the individual, for which he wanted to include physical education as an integral part of the curriculum.

Discipline

According to him, "Discipline is an important aspect of a person's character, each of us teach ourselves". The external teacher offers suggestions and the internal teacher starts working. If you don't allow a child to become a lion, he will become a fox. Do's and don'ts have to be reduced and right environment must be created.

Role of Teacher and Student in Education

According to **Swami Vivekananda**, a person with an attitude of renunciation, influence children through his ideal examples, love his students, sympathise at their difficulties, teaches according to the needs, abilities and interest of them, contributes to their spiritual development so that they can be good teacher.

A student should have an inclination and eagerness to learn. He should be an observer of celibacy, have control over his senses, follow the ideals laid down by his teacher.

He laid stress on the following qualities, that a teacher should have :

- He should be sinless.
- He should know the spirit of scriptures.
- The spiritual force of the teacher should be based on love for his students.
- The teacher should think that he is only helping the child to grow. He is the external teacher and he offers the suggestion, which arouses the internal teacher, *i.e.,* the mind of the child.

Methods of Teaching

With regard to teaching methods, Swamiji was of the view that children should be made to learn themselves. As all knowledge is within them and learning is only a function of their mind, to made them active.

Methods like self-learning, discussion method and meditation and concentration are used for teaching.

Rabindranath Tagore

Rabindranath Tagore was born in a family of Brahmo Samajists. He studied law. He was a born poet, a versatile genius, with his multi-splendoured personality, he shines like a morning star on the intellectual firmament of the globe and received Nobel Prize for Literature in November, 1913 for his world famous classic 'Gitanjali'. He was a great artist, and he founded his own school of art and music. He was well versed in Sanskrit language and Indian Philosophy, religion and culture. He was a rishi, a saint and a guru also called as prophet and educationist.

Philosophy of Rabindranath Tagore

His philoscphy of life was based on the ideals of dedication, patriotism and naturalism. He was an ideal philosopher, but the thoughts of naturalism, pragmatism and individualism are aslo reflected in his philosophy.

Like **Rousseau,** Tagore was an individualist and naturalist. He believed in the rights and freedom of an individual to shape his life in his own way. But in an individual's development, he ultimately wanted the unity of mankind. He said that every individual is different from another and everyone is unique.

"Experience of the spiritual world, religion as the right centre of life's activities and the unity of thought and truth" was the keynote of Tagore's great philcsophy.

The following are the values enriched as a philosopher, according to Tagore :

As an Individualist He believed in giving right type of freedom to an individual.

As an Idealist He believed that the man should live for the ultimate truth, which liberates us from the cycle of birth and death. He should had faith in absolute values.

As a Spiritualist He believed that every individual should try to attain spiritual perfection.

As a Humanist He preached human brotherhood, having faith in fundamental unity of mankind. He remarked that "even God depends upon man, for perfecting his universe".

As a Naturalist He considered nature as a great teacher. God revealed himself through various forms, colours and rhythm of nature.

As a Vedantist He had a firm belief in the Philosophy of Veda. He believed in 'I am Brahma'.

Educational Philosophy of Rabindranath Tagore

The basic principles of Tagore's philosophy of education are as follows

- **Harmony with All Things** Tagore's philosophy of education is based on naturalism, humanism, internationalism and idealism. Harmony with all things means harmony with nature, human surroundings and harmony in international relations.
- Principle of freedom.
- Principle of creative self-expression.
- Active communion with nature and man.

According to **Tagore**, "Education is to produce good thinkers and achievers in all aspects of life, physical, intellectual, moral, spiritual. An educated person is ready to serve society and country at all times".

He was fully aware of education's innumerable implications. According to **Tagore**, "Education is a permanent part of the adventure of life, it is not like a painful hospital treatment for curing them of the congenial melody of their ignorance, but is a function of the health, the natural expression of their mind's vitality".

To him, the object of education is freedom of mind through the path of freedom, though it had its risk and responsibility too. Education should be natural in content and quality. Through contact with nature, the child will be introduced to the great world of reality easily and jointly.

Factors Influencing Tagore's Philosophy of Education

- Influence of the home environment
- Influence of the school environment
- Love for nature
- His extensive visits

Tagore's Literary Works

Poetry Tagore's poems are varied in style and subject matter.

Gitanjali His most known collection, winning him Nobel Prize in the year. This collection replicates the true Indian Philosophy in all its glory.

Novels Tagore wrote novels, such as Gora Chaturanga, Shesher Kobita, Char Adhyay, Noukadubi and The Home and The World.

Story Books Tagore composed some beautiful stories, which are worthy to read. The **Hungry Stones** is one of importance.

Kabuliwala It depicts the friendship of a fruit seller from Kabul and little mini instead of their age difference.

Aims of Education

Moral and Spiritual Aims Tagore said that the principal's aim of education should be the development of moral and spiritual aspects of the child's personality. For this, he emphasized upon inner development, attainment of inner freedom, inner power and enlightenment. One of the important objectives of starting **Shantiniketan** was 'to give spiritual culture to our boys.

Education should enable the child to realize self and help them to develop the self-force. He wanted to develop an unflinching faith in the spiritual force. Further, he stressed moral training and development of character through austere devotion and development of inner-discipline .

Physical Development Tagore emphasized the physical well-being of the children. In order to achieve this, he said that education in nature, play activities, dancing, exercise, body and sensory training were the tools. Education of the body is necessary for acquiring the capacity to adjust itself to all sorts of weather conditions and health hazards.

Intellectual Development Condemning the prevailing system of education as bookish, methodical, monotonous, examination oriented, where intellect was starved of intellectual nourishment and where we adorned the cage but the parrot within lays starving. Tagore wanted education should aim at cultivating the power of acquiring ideas through independent effort, curiosity and alertness of mind and the potentiality of critically appraising the ideas, of assimilating them and of using what we learn. Education should develop thinking and imagination rather than mere memory or storage of scattered information.

International Brotherhood Being a lover of humanity, Tagore wanted to make a synthesis between Eastern culture and Western culture by education. He wanted to promote inter-cultural and inter-social understanding for the unity and harmony of mankind. He said that since Brahman manifests himself through men and he is the source of all the creations, all are equal and are brothers and sisters. Therefore, he prescribed social service for realization of self. He believed in the dictum that "Service to man is service to God".

Education for Fullness According to **Tagore**, "The aim of education should be harmonious development of all human faculties". In other words, education should aims at making a man full or complete without neglecting one at the cost of other.

Discipline

According to **Tagore**, "An educational institution is an open house, in which students and teachers are one, they must live their compact life together".

He observed that "an educational institution must not be a dead cage, in which living minds are fed with food artificially prepared". About the discipline of the educational institution, Tagore founded and states that "I never said to them that don't do this, or don't do that. The boys are encouraged to managed their own affairs".

Curriculum

Tagore was in favour of comprehensive curriculum, which should satisfy child's aesthetic, creative, spiritual and vocational needs.

In Tagore's experimental school at Shanti Niketan, children was taught in various classes. These schools had a very well equipped laboratory for performing experiments. The study of nature is also taught here.

Methods of Teaching

Rabindranath Tagore believed in activity and dynamic methods of teaching based upon the interst, need, ability and mental development of the child. He labelled the then system of teaching as bookish, mechanical, stereotyped, dull and uninteresting. He strongly suggested independent study and efforts. Learning should proceed from familiar to unfamiliar, hear to far and known to unkown.

Learning should be linked with joy and ecstasy. He wanted to give education in natural surroundings characterised by freedom and creativity. He said that teaching while walking is the best method of teaching. He favoured discussion, activity or learning by doing method.

Role of the Teacher

Rabindranath Tagore has placed high premium upon the role of teacher. The teacher is cardinal embodiment of all cardinal values and ideas. According him, the teacher should not be hard task master rather a friend, philosopher and guide. he advocated that the relationship between teacher and pupil should be friendly in nature.

Tagore laid great emphasis on the attitude of the teacher. He said that "I have found that little children learn more quickly, the attitude of the teacher than the knowledge imparted by him". Tagore concept of good teacher is stated in these words that "A teacher can never truely teach, unless he is still learning himself" *i.e.* "A lamp can never light another lamp unless it continues to burn its own flame". The teacher, who has come to the end of his subject, who has no living traffic with his knowledge, but merely repeats his lesson to his students, can only load their minds, he cannot quicken them. Truth, not only informs but also inspires. Tagore never liked the school master, moulding the child's mind according to his readymade doctrines.

According to **Tagore**, the first important lesson for children would be that of improvisation. They should be provided constant opportunities to explore their capacities through surprises of achievement. It is not the subject of study, organisation and equipment in the school that is important, but the living contact between the mind of the teacher and the mind of the taught that is important.

Visvabharati and Shantiniketan

The word 'Visvabharati' is composed of two words. In Sanskrit, the word 'Visva' means 'world' and 'bharti' means 'culture'. Thus, Visvabharati means world culture. The motto of this university is Yatra Visvam Bhavati Ekamidam *i.e.* where the world meets at one place. Through the Visvabharati as a whole, the poet and the seer sought to establish a relationship between East and West, to promote inter-cultural and inter-social amity and understanding and to fulfil the highest mission of the present age and the unification of mankind.

Shantiniketan is a small town near Bolpur in the district of West Bengal. It was established by Maharshi Debendranath Tagore and later expanded by his son Rabindranath Tagore whose vision became what is now a university town 'Visvabharati University', Shantiniketan means 'the abode of peace'.

Mahatma Gandhi

According to him, "Strength does not come from physical capacity. It comes from an indomitable will".

Biography

Mohandas Karamchand Gandhi was born at Porbander, Kathiawar, Western India on 2nd October, 1869. Gandhiji was popularly known as Bapu out of affection and reverence by the people. His father, Karamchand Gandhi served as the Dewan of Porbander State, a small princely state in the Kathiawar Agency of British India. His mother, Putlibai, who was from a Pranami Vaishnava family.

He was sent to a local high school, but as a student, he was slow, shy and hesitant. He was married to Kasturba at the age of 13. At 18, Gandhiji matriculated at Ahmedabad. He was sent to London to study law, where he remained for three years. After returning from South Africa, he started his law practice at Bombay. However, he was not very successful. He returned to his native place, Rajkot. Here, he received an offer from an Indian firm, which had a branch in South Africa, to go to that country to help them in an important case.

In April, 1893, he sailed for Durban. Although, his case was over, he continued to stay in Africa. There, he saw a series of insulting events of disgracing Indians and his political feeling was awakened. He founded the Natal Indian Congress in 1894. This was the turning point in his life. He found that the Indians in South Africa were treated very cruelly and infact like animals. They had no political rights.

He gave up his legal practice. He completely devoted himself to the service of the people. He put himself into practice of Satyagraha and Ahimsa. Mahatma Gandhi is considered as 'Father of the Indian Independence Movement'. Gandhiji spent 20 years in South Africa, working to fight discrimination. He spent his remaining years, working diligently to both i.e. to remove British rule from India as well as to better the lives of India's poorest classes. He was a modern **Messiah**, whose life became the message to the world.

Philosophy of Gandhiji

According to **Mahatma Gandhi**, "Man is the maker of his own destiny and I therefore, ask you to become makers of your own destiny". He was a great thinker and experimenter. He formulated his own views about everything in the world.

Gandhiji's philosophy of life can be described as follows

Truth and Ahimsa (Non-Violence) According to **him**, "Truth and Ahimsa are the two sides of a coin. They are interwined and it is practically impossible to separate them".

Satyagraha It implies holding of truth through love and purity.

Supreme God According to him, "God is indefinable, mysterious power that pervades every thing. God's presence is proved not by extraneous evidence but in the transformed conduct and character of those who have felt the real presence of God within".

Righteousness and Truth as the Highest Religion Gandhiji was of the firm view that "true religion and true morality are inseparably bound up with each other."

Service of Humanity The immediate service of all human being becomes a necessary part because it is the only way to see him in his creation.

Ram Rajya as the Concept of a Society He identified society with justice, peace, happiness and welfare of all.

Fundamental Principles of Education Proposed by Mahatma Gandhi

The following are the fundamental principles of education

Indian Control on Education British control over Indian education policies was resented. National education must be controlled, shaped and carried by Indians only.

Fostering of Patriotism Education should not cultivate loyalty to British rule. Instead, it should promote national consciousness and a love of the motherland.

No Servile Imitation of the West Although, many lessons were to be learnt from foreign cultures, Indian education should be based on its own cultural and intellectual traditions.

Domination of English Language to Go The use of English as the medium of instruction was considered a serious defect of the official system. The media of instruction should be the modern vernaculars.

Vocational Education to be Emphasised The failure of the prevailing system to improve living standards for India's masses were deplored. National education should have a vocational emphasis and focus on the economic development of the country.

Basic Education

The origin of Basic System of Education may be traced back to July, 1937, when Gandhiji wrote in Harijan (a journal started by him) that "By education, I mean an all round development drawing out of the best in child and man-body, mind and spirit. Literacy itself is not education. I would, therefore, begin the child's education by teaching it a useful handicraft and enabling it to produce from the moment it begins its training. Thus, every shcool can be made self-supporting, the condition being the state takes over the manufacture of these schools." In October, 1937, a Conference of National Workers were held at Wardha, under the Chairmanship of Mahatma Gandhi.

Educational Implications of Gandhian Philosophy

The real education has to draw out the best from the boys and girls to be educated.

According to **him**, "By education I mean an all round drawing out of the best in child and man-body, mind and spirit".

There are several factors that determined the educational philosophy of Gandhiji and they are

- His educational experiments at Tolstoy Farm, at Sabarmati and Sewagram Ashrams.
- His philosophy of life.
- His dissatisfaction with the prevailing system of education.
- A new social order.

The chief tenets of Gandhiji's new educational philosophy were as follows

Free and Compulsory Education According to **Gandhiji,** within the age of 7 and 14, there should be free and compulsory primary education for childrens.

Craft-Centered Education Gandhiji believed that the highest development of mind and the soul was possible only through handicraft. He did not want to teach the handicraft side by side with the liberal education. It was his wish that the whole process of education should be imparted through some handicraft or industry.

Self-Supporting Element By advocating the self-supporting aspect, he never wanted the craft to be made the be-all and end-all of instruction, thus, sacrificing the educative and cultural objectives of education. He believed that right kind of teachers would teach the children, the dignity of labour and those children would regard the craft as an integral part and means of their intellectual growth.

Education should be in Mother Tongue He believed that mother tongue would enable the children not only to understand clearly the rich heritage of people's ideas, emotions and aspiration, but also enable the children to express themselves effectively, clearly and lucidly.

Education should be Based on Non-Violence Gandhiji had firm conviction in non-violence, so he wanted that it should be based on non-violence. Society's politics, economics and education must stand on non-violence, truth and justice.

Aims of Education

All Round Development of Personality By all round development, he means, development of body, mind and spirit. All round development implies harmonious development of human personality in a balanced manner *i.e.* hand, head and heart. This emphasizes 3 Rs instead of 3 Rs *i.e.* reading, writing and arithmetic. Development of either two, neglecting the one aspect of personality leads to lop-sided education or incomplete education.

Harmonious development of all powers and faculties was the chief goal of his scheme of education. He emphasized this type of development as the child could adjust himself to self, his occupation and his environment adequately.

The Utilitarian Aim He advocated self-supporting education, taking into account the basic needs of man's life which was meant in two different senses *i.e.*

(i) Education that will help one to be self-supporting in later life which implies that the child of tomorrow's adult would not be a drag on the society. This type of education will turn him into a self-sufficient entity and this education will be a kind of insurance against unemployment.

(ii) In the second, he wanted that teacher's salaries should be met out of the productive work of the children, provided that the state takes over the manufacture of the school.

Cultural Aim Gandhiji attached greater importance to the cultural aspect of education than to the literacy. Culture is a quality of mind which may be reflected in his daily conduct.

He said, "It should show itself in smallest details of your conduct and personal behaviour, how you sit, how you walk, how you dress, etc. Inner culture must be reflected in your speech, the way in which you treat visitors and guests, and behave towards one another and your teachers and elders".

According to him, "Culture is not the product of intellectual work, but the quality of the soul, permeating all aspects of human behaviour". It is, therefore, an important function of education that children must be taught to have winsome conduct and to career and our pupils must not remain alien in their native lands with rich cultural tradition and ethos.

Character Building He made character-building as the central purpose of education. Character development, for him, implies the cultivation of such moral virtues as courage, strength of conviction, purity of heart and personal life, righteousness, self-restraint, inner-discipline, subordination of one's interest to the greater interest of society and service of mankind.

This character is too built up in terms of universal love and non-violence. He said that character as the expression of the whole personality including its ethical and spiritual aspect. Thus, if character is well built, the society would evolve itself in a new form and fashion without dependence upon others.

Preparation for Complete Living Like Herbert Spencer, he stressed preparation for complete living as one of the aim of education. Since life is very complex and beset with a plethora of problems and difficulties, education should aim at preparing the future citizens to face the problems of life, here and there. A child was considered prepared for complete living if he could adjust himself to self, his occupation and his society.

Training for Citizenship He aimed at producing useful citizens for a democracy by means of education. The future citizens should understand their problems, rights and duties in proper perspectives and know the democratic institutions that work for the good of all. Education should aim at building citizens imbued with all cardinal qualities of good citizen.

Therefore, he spearheaded a silent revolution by education to cover all the sections and segments of people by eliminating all sorts of discrimination. He believed that for a success of democracy, it was the need of training the pupils, the budding citizens in citizenship qualities. Therefore, he made a slogan, 'Educate your masters'.

Individual and Social Aim He synthesized the individual and social aims of education. He wanted a society in which all individuals will have to play their part for the good of the whole, without losing their individual characters and identities. He does not want to damp down the individuality. He strikes a balance between the ideals of social service and individual development.

Discipline

He was critical of free discipline and strongly favoured inner-discipline through self-control and not by being free to follow stray impulses. He thought that freedom embedded in self-discipline or inner-discipline that arises spontaneously from the inner springs of life rather than that which is clamped from without is called true freedom.

This self-discipline is voluntary discipline which emanates from the following *i.e.* pure life, self-restraint, fearlessness, sacrifice, usefulness and practice of non-violent conduct.

Further, he favoured social discipline through some productive works based upon cooperation, initiative, accuracy and individual responsibility. This form of social discipline can emerge out of the living mutually in the society by cultivating ideals of citizenship necessary for a vibrant and living democracy.

Role of Teacher

He thought that only the right type of teacher could help in achieving the objectives of education. He should be a lover of truth and non-violence and he should possess a sound base of knowledge, skill, enthusiasm, patriotism, dedication, love for children and labour, respect for the dignity of individuals and special training in the basic education.

He should be a man of action, not a man of slogan and should have a good moral character and a social bent of mind. He should lead a pure and simple life and be a man of ideals and a saga of examples.

Curriculum

Gandhiji advocated complete overhauling of the curriculum. He suggested a broad-based and integrated curriculum for realising the objectives of education and developing the whole man.

He included the following aspects in his scheme of studies

Basic Craft Agriculture, spinning and weaving, cardboard, wood and metal work, tailoring, gardening, business practice, book-keeping, etc.

Mother Tongue As opposed to teaching of English and other foreign languages.

Mathematics Concerning numerical and geometrical problems connected with craft and community life. Besides, learning of four basic rules by sincerely working out the problems arising out of craft work and gardening.

Social Studies History, Civics and Geography.

General Science Nature's study, Zoology, Physics Chemistry, Astronomy, Physiology, Hygiene, etc.

Drawing and Music For the development of artistic talents.

Methods of Teaching

Correlation He advocated the Principle of Correlation in teaching different subjects. Craft is the pivot round which all other subjects should revolve. He wanted all subjects need to be correlated with craft. Craft should be the starting point of other subjects and a meeting point of both physical and social environment. Therefore, craft is the medium of instruction.

Learning by Doing He said that learning would be permanent if it is permeated by doing. It can be possible if children are given opportunities to undertake a host of productive activities. So, in his scheme, learning by doing was the important method of teaching.

Learning by Living Learning takes place by actually participation in community life and rendering selfless service to the cause of goodness of all. This makes learning social.

Lecture Questioning and Disvision Methods These methods were followed in his scheme of education.

Thus, it can be said that Gandhiji philosophy of education still hold a promise for better tomorrow in the modern scenario of rapid, scientific and technological advancement.

Sri Aurobindo Ghosh

According to **Sri Aurobindo Ghosh**, "The aim of (my) Yoga is an inner-self development, by which each one who follows it, can discover it on time. The oneself in all evolves a higher consciousness, than the mental, a spiritual and supra-mental consciousness which will transform and divinise human nature".

Biography

Aurobindo was an Indian nationalist, a freedom fighter, a Philosopher, a Yogi and a Poet. He was born in an educated middle class family of Calcutta (Kolkata) in Bengal on 15th August, 1872. At the age of 7, he went to England and lived there for 14 years. He received his education at Cambridge. Besides English, he mastered Latin and Greek and learnt French, German, Italian and Spanish. He knew all the classical languages and modern European languages and could read Dente and Goethe in the original.

His father, Krishnadhan Ghosh, was district surgeon at Rangapur, Bengal. His mother Swarnalata Devi was the daughter of Brahm religious and social reformer, Rajnarayan Basu. Between 1880 and 1884, while his brothers were studying at Manchester Grammar School, Drewett coached Aurobindo in Latin and his wife coached him in French, Geography and Arithmetic, until he joined St. Paul's School. On his return to India in 1893, he joined service in the Princely State of Baroda (Vadodara). During his work in Baroda, he started working as a part-time French teacher at Baroda College. He devoted himself to cultural and literary activities.

Philosophy of Sri Aurobindo

"True knowledge is not attained by thinking. It is what you are, it is what you become". **—Sri Aurobindo**

His unique contribution to human potential and growth, developed through his integration of Western and Eastern cultures. He brought the energy and vision of the West, with its focus on the perfection of the physical, material and mental areas of human life together with the spiritual development and philosophical directions developed over thousands of years in the East. His life began with political, poetic and philosophical experiences.

He said that the truth of spiritualism, science and religion were already contained in the Vedas. The Gita contains vedic values, which is essential for the elevation of human life.

He has been considered as one of the foremost philosophers of the 20th century, but he was far more than just a philosopher. The great philosophy of **Sri Aurobindo** can be summed up in one phrase *i.e.* "Realisation of the sublime truth, which can be achieved through the integral view of life".

According to him, "The divine truth is greater than any religion or creed or scripture or idea or philosophy".

His philosophy is based on an **integralism**. It is the synthesis of idealism, realism, pragmatism and spiritualism. According to him, yoga transforms the mankind, life and body to superman. Wholesome or an integral development is possible through the practice of yoga. Usually, transformation takes place on a supramental stage, where diverse elements get transferred and then integrated. It changes the nature of man and lead to realise the divine power and divine perfection.

He also believed that there is Brahma in everybody, there is an innate power inside the man and education, would enable man to discover the same. Since, both matter and spirit are necessary for the welfare of mankind, education should help in bringing about a balanced development in both.

He argues that man is born as an ignorant, divided, conflicted being a product of the original inconscience (*i.e.* unconsciousness) inherent in matter that he evolved out of. As a result, he does not know the nature of reality, including its source and purpose, his own nature, including the parts and integration of his being, what purpose he serves and what his individual and spiritual potential is, amongst others.

To overcome these limitations, man must embark on a process of self-discovery, in which he uncovers his divine nature. To that end, he undertakes a three step process, which Aurobindo calls the triple transformation.

Psychic Transformation With the psychic transformation, he sees the oneness and unity of creation and the harmony of all opposites, experienced in life.

Spiritual Transformation As a result of making the psychic change, his mind expands and he experience knowledge not through the hard churning of thought, but through light, intuition and revelation of knowledge, culminating in supramental perception.

Supramental Transformation After making the psychic and spiritual change, he makes the supramental and most radical change. It is basically a complete transformation of the mind, the heart, the emotions and the physical body.

He considered mind as the sixth sense and asserted that "the first business of the educationist is to develop in the child, the right use of the six senses, to see that they are not stunted or injured by disuse, but trained by the child himself under the teacher's direction to that perfect accuracy and keen subtleness of which they are capable".

According to him, "Mind must be perfectly trained to the highest possible limit, otherwise the education of the child will remain incomplete and one sided". He wanted to reform our mind first before reforming the world. Education cannot be a machine-made fabric. It should aims at building the powers of the mind.

He recognised three minds as

- the individual mind
- the mind of a nation
- the universal mind

He wanted the teacher to understand the human mind at all the stages of development *i.e.* infancy, childhood, adolescence and adulthood.

He recognises two qualities of mind and they are

- Well disciplined or well structured mind.
- Individualised or well textured mind.

A person whose mind has these two qualities, is a complete and integrated man. That person can observe accurately and discriminatively, to think clearly and to criticise judiciously and to remain well informed.

Important Publications of Sri Aurobindo

Important publications on education and allied subjects of Aurobindo are

- The Mind of Light
- Ideal of Human Unity
- Riddle of This World
- Essay on the Gita
- Upanishads
- The Human Cycle
- Life Divine
- The Savitri
- The Secret of the Vedas

Features of Aurobindo's Philosophy

- Everyone have something divine in himself. The task is to find it, develop it and use it. This divine can be obtained by a spiritual discipline, called **Yoga**.
- Aurobindo's concept of yoga is not that of a sanyasi, who moves away from life in order to move towards God.
- Yoga is for the ordinary man, while he carries on his worldly pursuits.
- If a merchant wishes to follow yoga, he regards his work as divine, he does not use unfair practices to earn money.
- If a student looks for higher values, he must observe Brahmacharya (self-control).
- According to him, complete surrender of man to God, creates a superman, who transcends his own nature by rising above the qualities of Sattva, Rajas and Tamas. Such a man attains union with God in body, mind and soul and becomes a Jnani.
- He feels the presence of divine in every centre of his consciousness. All beings are to him and his ownselves.
- When a man attains union with God, in body, mind and soul, the divine power descends on him and this helps him to fulfil his cosmic purpose and divine energy radiates from him into the world.
- An integral view of life culminates in synthetic yoga, which Aurobindo defines as "A methodised effort towards self-perfection by the expression of the potentialities talent in the being".
- He envisages a world, in which life and mind work harmoniously and achieve the truth by transformation and transmutation of them in the light of the highest.
- According to **Aurobindo**, the main instrument of thought is mind, which has immense and diverse powers.
- He considered mind as having four layers, which he defined as chitta, manas, intellect and institution.

(i) The **first** layer or **chitta** is that of passive memory. It is a storehouse of memories or past impressions.

(ii) The **second** layer of the mind is called the **manas** (or the proper mind). This receives the images coming from the five senses (touch, smell, taste, sight and sound) and transforms those images into thought perceptions.

(iii) The **Intellect** of Buddhi is the **third** layer, where the elements of the knowledge are arranged and re-arranged. The intellect has comprehensive, creative, synthetic and analytical faculties.

(iv) The **fourth** layer of the mind, is **intuition**, which brings man to those brilliant messages from the unknown, which are the beginning of his higher knowledge.

Integral Education

According to **Sri Aurobindo**, "It is one which helps to bring out to full advantage, makes ready for the full purpose of life and scope of all that is in the individual man, which at the same time helps him to enter into his right relation with life, mind and soul of the people to which he belongs and with the great total life, mind, soul of humanity of which he himself is a unit and his people or nation, a separate and yet inseparable member".

It will recognise the individual not as a vague combination of matter (body) and spirit, but a personality having four distinct aspects, *i.e.* physical, vital, mental and psychic. An ideal system of education must open up avenues for the best possible development of each of these faculties of the student.

Two fold basis of integrated education are

- Individuality is one whole.
- Humanity is one.

Individuality is One Whole

It includes:

Harmonious Development of Three Dimensions of Individuality Body, mind and soul have their significance when they are harmoniously developed as they constitute the whole individuality.

According to **Sri Aurobindo,** "There should be a balanced and harmonious development of all the aspects of human personality i.e. cognitive (knowledge), conative (skills) and affective (attitude and values). Thus, an individual becomes an integrated individual".

Social Economico-Politico Integration Sri Aurobindo said that "India has always seen man as individual soul, a portion of the divinity enwrapped in mind and body".

Different Aspects of the Self, but Self is One Man is the conscious manifestation of the universal spirit.

No Concentration on Academic Perfection Alone The study of mind is fundamental in education. Any system of education, which concentrates on academic perfection of the child with disregard to his mind is destined to fail.

Humanity is One

Sri Aurobindo immersed himself in **Vedanta** and **Yoga**. Instead of seeing conflict or find inconsistencies between the East and the West, he evolved a synthesis of both. He also synthesised **spirit** and **matter, science** and **Vedanta**.

Stages or Phases of Integral Education

Education to be complete must have five principle aspects relating to five principal activities of the human being, *which are discussed below*

Physical Education

It means education of the body. The body is the pedestal of our terrestial existence. The body is the means, the expression of life, mind and soul. The physical is our base and even the highest spiritual values to be effective on the Earth must express themselves through the life. Our body which is the dwelling place of consciouness should be beautiful as well as strong enough to receive spiritual energy for it's perfection. Sri Aurobindo further said that "Even a highest and completest education of the mind is not enough without the education of the body".

All education of the body must be rigorous, detailed and methodical. The physical education to be effective must be based upon a minimum knowledge of the human body its structure and its functions. In physical education, the basic qualities to be evolved should be courage, certitude, vision and strength not fear, doubt, stupidity or weakness.

Vital Education

According to **Sri Aurobindo**, where there is life in plant and animal or man there is life force and without the vital can be not life in matter and no living action. He says that the vital is the life nature made up of desires, sensations, feelings, passions, energies of action, will of desires, reaction of the desire soul in man and of all that play of possessive and other related instincts, anger, fear, greed, lust, etc. However, the vital is taken as the seat of impulses and desires for acting and reacting upon one another. One has to begin his education with the primary sources of the sensations because vital is the storehouse of life energy of will power. The building of character and the training of the aesthetic beings are two parts of vital education. The vital education of the child should begin as early as possible indeed as soon as he is able to use his senses in order to avoid bad habits and to eliminate many harmful influences. Various competitions in constructive creative activities should be organised to use the the vital energy properly.

Moral Education

The moral education is an important component of vital education. It is essential for an individual to lead harmonious life in the society. Sri Aurobindo declared that few principles are required for effective moral training. **Firstly**, moral training is to suggest and invite not command or impose and the best method of suggestion is by personal experience.

Secondly, good company *i.e.* reading books, attending study circle for live discussions about the ideals of the great souls.

Thirdly, if one does wish to be respected by his child, he should have respect for himself and be and every moment worthy of respect. Even telling lie, loosing temper and displaying other weaknesses are bad examples for the child. **Fourthly**, one must not scold a child except with a definite purpose and only when it is felt quite indispensable.

Lastly, one should not allow any fear to slip in between he and his child otherwise it will give birth to pretence and falsehood. Moral education is the best instrument for the formation of character.

Mental Education

Man is primarily a mental being, so the education of human being should centres around the education of his mind. According to Sri Aurobirdo, mind is the through driven chariot of the soul. Mental education is a process of training the mind of the student to arrive at such central conception around which the widest and the complex and subtle ideas can be assimilated and integrated. Besides mind has many faculties and possibilities those need a special education so that they can express the light. Thus, the aim of mental education is to develop the various possibilities and faculties of the mind to receive the light for the perfection of the mind.

Psychic Education

Psychic education is most essential aspect. It is because the physic inspiration alone is true. All that comes from the vital and the mind is necessarily mixed with egoism and is arbitrary. The psychic education leads towards the discovery of psychic being. Its purpose is to bring psychic being to the forefront so that it can act upon the mind, vital and body, purifying thought, perception, emotion, sensation, action and everything else in the human being and preparing them to be divine movements. In this context, the aim of psychic education is to manifest and develop in the outer being new capacities, which actually are not in one's present outer.

Psychic education is a life long process and it must be the point of all education. All spontaneous turning to love, truth, beauty, knowledge, nobility and heroism is a sure sign of the psychic influence. To recognise their reactions on the pupils to encourage them wisely would be the first indispensable step towards psychic education.

Spiritual Education

Man is evolving soul and all life is a growth of the soul from darkness to light. Education is that light which removes darkness of ignorance. Spiritual education aims at the growth of consciousness and to bring down the higher consciousness into the lower. It is solely concerned with the inner-awakening and realisation of the self and helps a person to become a perfect instrument of divine manifestation.

In the spiritual education, the help of a Guru is indispensable. The Guru is generally a Yogi who put his influence for the growth of a pupil. All education without the education of the spirit is incomplete. Hence, the education of the self or spiritual education is a must to achieve the highest aim of life and education. Education which can bring the total change of consciousness is spiritual education.

Functions of Education

- To bring out the real man.
- To build the powers of the human mind and spirit *i.e.* the evoking of knowledge, character and culture.
- To enable an individual to establish a clear continuity between the past, present and the future.
- To enable the individual, to establish right relations with life.

Principles of Teaching

Aurobindo suggests three principles of teaching as

- The **first** principle of true teaching is that nothing can be taught. The teacher is not an instructor or task master, he is a helper and guide.
- The **second** principle is that the mind has to be consulted in its growth.
- The **third** principle of teaching is to work from the near to the far, from the known to the unknown.

Educational Implications of Aurobindo's Philosophy

Education being the dynamic side of philosophy, every philosopher is ultimately an educator. Philosophy determines the fundamental postulates of life *i.e.* its meaning and aims. Education becomes an instrument of realising those aims. Aurobindo was thoroughly disgusted with the prevailing system of education, which ignored the psychology of the learner, whose mind was laboriously loaded with numerous little packets of information, carefully tied with red tape.

Aurobindo wanted a system of education which sought immensely to enlarge the field of knowledge of the student and activised his memory, judgement and creative power, *i.e.* which laid stress on experiment and observation and encouraged the play of thought on the subject of study, which corrected the habit of spoiling the instruments of knowledge and employed, the natural and easy instrument of mother tongue. He was an idealistic to the core. His idealistic Philosophy of Life was based on Vedantic Philosophy of Upanishad.

He maintains the kind of education that we need in our country, is an education "Proper to the Indian soul and need temperament and culture that we are in quest of, not indeed something faithful merely to the past, but to the developing soul of India, to her future need, to the greatness of her coming self-creation, to her eternal spirit".

Sri Aurobindo's concept of education is not only acquiring information, but the acquiring of various kinds of information.

Aims of Education

According to **Sri Aurobindo**, "Indeed if the education is to have its maximum result, it must begin even before birth".

Sri Aurobindo emphasised that education should be in accordance with the needs of our real modern life. In other words, education should create dynamic citizens, so that they are able to meet the needs of modern complex life. According to him, "The chief aim of education should be to help the growing soul, to draw out that in itself which is best and makes it perfect for a noble use".

According to **Aurobindo**, physical education and holiness are the main aims of education. As such, he not only emphasised mere physical development but physical purity also, without which no spiritual development is possible. In this sense, physical development and purification are the two basis, on which the spiritual development is built.

Another important aim of education is to train all the senses *i.e.* hearing, speaking, listening, touching, smelling and testing, to achieve mental development of the child. This mental development means the enhancement of all mental faculties.

The development of morality is also an important aim of education. **Sri Aurobindo** has emphasised that without moral and emotional development, only mental development becomes harmful to human process. The heart of a child should be developed in such a way that it shows extreme love, sympathy and consideration for all living beings. This is real moral development. The human race is composed of people and nation and a nation is composed of individuals. The nation makes the universal humanity.

Methods of Teaching

Nothing can be Taught It means that the pupil has to acquire new knowledge by his own attempt and the teacher is to work as helper or guide to the pupil. The pupil is allowed to study by his own capacity and interest.

Self-Pacing Learning According to the method of teaching, the teacher should not impose on the child from the above if the child is not prepared to receive the knowledge. Once the mother said that a child wants to remain ignorant, we may explain to him consequences or remaining ignorant but we should not pressurise the child for learning. The child to be allowed to learn, according to his interest.

Teaching from Near to Far This means that the child should be led from near to for. That is all education should be built upon the day to day experience of the learners.

Role of Teacher

The teacher is the king pin in the educational machinery. No system improves and rises without the teacher. Actually, teacher does not trains the pupil's mind, but shows him, how to perfect his instruments of knowledge and helps him and encourages him in the process. Aurobindo laid great stress on the intuitive power, he considered that teacher as ideal or liberal encourged the development of this power by eliminating the add mixture of error, caprice and biased fancifulness and allows the child to grow into the way of his own perfection. The teacher is only a guide and not an imposer.

The individual is a self-developing soul. The duty of the parents and the teacher is to enable the child to educate himself, to develop his own practical, intellectual, moral and aesthetical capacities and to grow independently as an organic being.

Curriculum Transaction

***Aurobindo** describes curriculum for following different stages of education*

Different Stages of Education

- Primary Stage
  - Subject taught
    - Mother Tongue
    - English
    - Literature
    - Natural History
    - General Science
    - Social Studies
    - National History
- Secondary Stage
  - Subject taught
    - Mother Tongue
    - English
    - Literature
    - Art
    - Chemistry
    - Physiology
    - Health Education
- University Stage
  - Subject taught
    - Indian and Western Philosophy
    - History of Civilisation
    - English Literature
    - Psychology
    - Botany
- Vocational Stage
  - Subject taught
    - Art
    - Painting
    - Photography
    - Scriptural
    - Drawing
    - Cottage Industries
    - Engineering

Instead of shallowness and superficiality in many subjects, he wants an intensive knowledge in a few subjects. He wanted the study of Indian History and culture to be an essential ingredient of the curriculum. He assumes that every child has a sense of History. He prescribed the free environment for the child to develop, all his latent faculties to the maximum and suggested all those subjects and activities should possess elements of creativity and educational expression. He wished to infuse a new life and spirit into each subject and activity, through which the development of super human can becomes possible.

He laid down the following principles for curriculum

- Curriculum should be interesting.
- It should include those subjects, which promotes mental and spiritual development.
- It should motivates children, towards the attainment of knowledge of whole world.
- It should certain, creativity of life and constructive capacities.

Discipline

Purification of the mental and moral habits should be the basis of discipline. This means to discriminate between right and wrong impressions and to absorb right ones in the mind. Children should be provided with a free environment, so that they are able to gain more and more knowledge by their own efforts. **Aurobindo** propagated the concept of self-discipline, which was the cure of impressionistic discipline. The goal aimed by Aurobindo was not merely the liberation of the individual from the chain that letters him and realisation of the self, but to workout the will of the divine in the world, to effect a spiritual transformation and to bring down the divine nature and a divine life into the mental, vital and physical nature and life of humanity.

Jiddu Krishnamurti

He was born on 11th May, 1985 in Andhra Pradesh. His father was an official in the revenue department. In the early years, he underwent through the training and educational, befiting a budding world teacher. He developed an independent perspective both about the nature of inquiry and about his role in the pursuit of the good society. He rejected the view that the teaching is something that has to be first studied and then translated into action. Infact, he spent his entire life talking about education as being the agent not only of inner-renewal, but also of social change.

Krishnamurti's perspective on education says that education should be towards the fullest development of the human being.

Major points of Krishnamurti's education are

- Educating the whole person (all parts of the person).
- Educating the person as a whole (not as an assemblage of parts).
- Educating the person within a whole (as a part of society, humanity, nature, etc.) from which it is not meaningful to extract that person.

So, it can be said that education is not about preparation for only a part of life (like work) but is about preparation for the whole of life and the deepest aspect of living.

Aims of Education

According to **Jiddu Krishnamurti**, the aim of education should be to understand the life and constant searching of the mystery of life. The materialistic achievements can only be a source and not the aim of life, so the role of education should not be making people materialistic.

- Education does not mean only acquiring the knowledge of subjects, but to develop complete and responsible human being. By complete education, he means love and compassions which can tranforms the present situation in its totality.
- Education should help to discover lasting values so that we do not merely cling to formulas or repeat slogans, it should help us to break down our national and social barriers, instead of emphasising them for they breed, antagonism between human beings.
- The aim of education should not be to produce mere scholars, technicians and job hunters but integrate men and women who are free of fear, for only between such human beings can there enduring peace.

- Education should not encourage the individual to confirm to society or to be negatively harmonious with it, but help him to discover the true values which come unbiased investigation and self-awareness.
- He further said that education should be a life transforming process.

Role of a Teacher

The teacher himself should be a properly integrated human being. According to him, the teacher has to be careful, thoughtful and affectionate in the creation of the right environment for the development of understanding to enable the child to deal intelligently with human problem. In order to achieve all this, the education needs to understand himself. In order to deal with children, great deal of patience and understanding are needed. For a teacher, teaching was not a technique but a way of life. He further said that education is a dual responsibility of parents and teachers.

Curriculum

- Curriculum should develop the working efficiency.
- Development of curriculum should encourage the patriotism in students.
- Curriculum should give the knowledge to find the solution of problems.
- Curriculum should encourage the interest for research and development in students.
- Curriculum should develop the self expression ability in the students.
- Curriculum should encourage national integrity and harmony in the students.
- Curriculum should raise curiosity in the students.
- Teachers should use interactive resources for methods, while transacting curriculum.
- Curriculum should be able to develop, praise and aesthic opinion in students.

Further that, Jiddu Krishnamurti said that "The highest function of education is to bring about an integrated individual who is capable or dealing with life as a whole". Education according to him, was a transformation of human mind and creation of new culture.Education must free the mind and spirit of children.

Education should encourage self-observation and experiencing of life as a whole not 'me' and 'mine' but to go above and beyond to discover the real. That's why education should be concerned with the immediate response to immediate challenges. The function of education is to help each pupil to discover inner- psychological resources and develop his own individual strengths, as well as to realise his weaknesses, without imposing upon him the teachers notion what he should be.

Paulo Freire

He was a famous philosopher and educationalist of Brazil. He was born on 19 September, 1921 in a middle class family. In March, 1934, his father died, due to which he had to face financial difficulties. In 1934, he took admission in University of Recife and studied Philosophy and Language psychology. He worked as educationalist, reformer and consultant. By joining the Labour Party in the city of Freire Sao Paulo (1980-1988), he worked as an adult supervisor in literacy project and had an adult literacy mission. In 1988, he was appointed as educational secretary in Sao Paulo. He made his special contribution in education and delivered education to the general public. He died on 2 May, 1997 due to a heart attack in Sao Paulo.

He was the most significant educational thinker of the 20th century. His most famous educational texts were the 'Pedagogy of the Oppressed' and 'Cultural Action for Freedom'. He made a considerable impact on the development of educational practices, informal education and in adult educational programme.

Aim of Education

According to Freire, aim of education is to break the culture of silence among the oppressed and conscientize them in order to make them fully human. Freire believed that the goal of education should be freedom to speak, think and act in an authentic way. His educational thoughts were based on developing a dialectical perception of reality. His contribution analyses how to be with the people so that they can develop the way of thinking.

Educational Philosophy of Paulo Freire

According to **Freire**, education should not only deposit information for future used only. It should open minds to higher stages of consciousness. His concern with conscientisation was an important element of learning process.

The developing consciousness understood to have the power to transform reality. Paulo Freire was concerned with praxis. Praxis involves analysis, discussion and action to change the situation. It creates a new situation for true learning. Dialogue is a cooperative activity. It can be seen as enhancing community and social welfare. It helps us in leading for justice and human flourishing. According to **Freire**, children should be aware about the abilities of their learning.

Children should learn by interacting with the environment. Through dialectical process, means asking questions, problem-posing, interacting with each other child will learn better. According to Freire, in the class, teacher should divide the students into a small group. Questions should be asked to that group. By doing this, the students get chance to interact with each other and able to discover new ideas. Freire believed that this education pedagogy was a democratic approach of learning. Freire argues that education process cannot be neutral.

It could be an instrument of domination or liberation. Education process domesticates the people where there exists a dominant culture of silence. Freire believed that education must begin with the solution of the teacher-student contradiction. Freire wants us to think in terms of teacher-student and student-teacher i.e., a teacher who learns and a learner who teaches, as the basic roles of classroom's participation.

Teachers must recognize that "Their fundamental objective is to fight alongside the people for the recovery of the people's stolen humanity not to win the people over to their side". Paulo Freire's views on Education Philosophy came from classical, modern and anti-colonialist thinkers. According to **Freire**, "Education is the cultural action for freedom. Education as practice of freedom opposed as the practice of domination. Liberating education consists in acts of cognition. Education is a knowing process rather than memorizing process".

*According to **Freire**, concept of education maintains the following attitudes and practices*

- The teacher teaches and the students are taught.
- The teacher knows everything and the students know nothing.
- The teacher thinks and the students are thought about.
- The teacher talks and the students listen meekly.
- The teacher disciplines and the students are disciplined.
- The teacher chooses and enforces his choice, and the students comply.
- The teacher acts and the students have the illusion of acting through the action of the teacher.
- The teacher chooses the program content and the students (who were not consulted) adapt to it.
- The teacher confuses the authority of knowledge with his or her own professional authority, which she and he sets in opposition to the freedom of the students.
- The teacher is the subject of the learning process, while the pupils are mere objects.

His theory of education closely linked with issues, such as oppression and struggle with social relation that center round with ideology and material domination. Freire maintained that from reflection by the oppressed on the oppression will come engagement in the struggle for the liberation. For this struggle and liberation pedagogy will be made and remade. According to **Freire**, education is the cultural action for freedom, an act of knowing and not the act of memorization. He also said that education is the practice of liberation because it frees the educator from slavery of silence.

Major Works

- Pedagogy of the oppressed.
- Cultural actions for freedom.
- Education for consciousness.
- Pedagogy in process.
- The politics of education in culture, power and literacy.
- Pedagogy of liberation.
- Pedagogy of freedom.
- Pedagogy of the city.

Marry Wollstonecraft

She was an English writer, modern feminist, philosopher and an advocate of female rights. She was born in **London** on 27th April, 1759. Throughout her life, she challenged the authority of such conferences, which are against women's rights and against any anti-women norms. Therefore, she was considered to be the forerunner of feminist movement and major figure in the Feminist Philosophy.

In the contradiction of popular social gatherings in society, she started her career as a writer. Her most famous book was 'The Vindication of The Rights of Man' is a reaction to the criticism of the French Revolution by Edmund Burke of the British Parliament. She advocated against republicanism and attacked the support of logic for hereditary privileges.

In 1792, an article on women's right was published on political and ethical subjects. Their work enhanced the argument that women should be given equal rights with respect to men. She continued her effort to honour and empower women throughout her life. On 10th September, 1797, she died at the age of 38. After death, her husband Godwin wrote articles on contradiction in the rights of women, in her memory which was a celebration of his wife's work. She was known as a ground breaking thinker and forerunner of modern racist movement.

Wollstonecraft's Views on Education

According to her, education is an essential element for the people of the society. During her short career, she wrote novels and books in which she gave special emphasis on the education of children, youth and women. For this, she believed that **'The Vindication of The Rights of Women'** is most important. In this book, she argued that woman is naturally weaker than man in intellectual basis. Thus, to overcome this, we need to give proper education to women as well. In **1700s**, girl's education was limited but by the end of the 18th century various schools came into force, in which emphasis was on the art, drawing and basic skills.

She gave special emphasis on girl's education and established short-term schools for women. Apart from this, emphasis was also given on child's emerging confidence, discipline, honesty and social satisfaction. She believed that with the motivation of learning, to read with logic, education is important and helpful for person's development. Therefore, if we promote education among the women in the society than will have great grandmothers and wives who can contribute positively, to the development of nation.

In this way, she described the need for education as important in the context of men and women. Simultaneously, she also talked about the parliamentary representation of women like men. Hence, she paved the way for the education of women, which is focused on encouraging women in society.

Major Works

- Thought of the Education of Daughters (1787)
- Marie and Fiction (1788)
- Vindication of the Rights of the Women (1792)
- Marry and Marie (1791)

Nel Noddings

Nel Noddings is Amercia's best known philosopher and educationalist. She was born on 13th January, 1929 in United States. She received a bachelor's degree from Montcl State College in New Jersey and completed Phd in Education from Standford Graduate School of Education. She worked for 17 years in primary school and High School where she taught Mathematics.

She was a professor and dean of the Stanford University and after retirement, joined Columbia University. She developed some of the important roles of educational development and worked for the upliftment of education.

Educational Philosophy of Nel Noddings

Nel Noddings (1929) has made a significant contribution to our appreciation of education. In particular, her explorations of the ethics of care and their relationship to schooling, welfare and to learning and teaching within families and local communities came at a especially opposite moment. She has been able to demonstrate the significance of caring and relationship both as an educational goal and as a fundamental aspect of education. As a result, Nel Noddings' work has become a key reference point for those wanting to re-affirm the ethical and moral foundations of teaching, schooling and education more broadly.

She defines education as "A constellation of encounters, both planned and unplanned, that promote growth through the acquisition of knowledge, skills, understanding and appreciation with punishment or humiliation".

In the field of moral education, it is Nel Noddings who has consistently critiqued the prevalence of character education and moral instruction in schools, and instead proposed her theory in caring, a feminine approach to ethics and moral education, the challenge to care in schools and educating moral people, a caring alternative to character education.

For Noddings, moral education has been of great importance throughout her work on care ethics, which she has developed over three decades. She feels any debate on practical ethics will have to naturally include the educational aspect. Moreover, education is a community wide enterprise and not a task exclusively reserved for home, church, or school (2013: 171) and therefore has to be understood in a broader perspective.

Nel Noddings has argued that education from the care perspective has four key components *i.e.* modelling, dialogue, practice and confirmation. **Modelling** is the **first** component, which highlights the centrality of exemplary action for the student to learn from live examples. Instead of merely teaching through direct instruction about the importance of caring behaviour, Noddings argues that it is much more effective to teach through exemplary action. Embodying care in our engagement with student can inspire them to cultivate caring habits in their own behaviour.

The **second** and the most fundamental component of care ethics education, according to Noddings is **dialogue**, where she draws the Freierian Model of Dialogue as open-ended. In this understanding of dialogue, the teacher and student are not teleologically moving towards a set goal of moral education but open to discovering differences in their views, even if they are ideologically opposite.

The **third** component of the framework is the **centrality of practice** in developing habits of care. Noddings argues that more than the obligation it is the practice of care which can dispose the student to act in compassionate ways. Thus, developing care giving activities are far more crucial rather than giving and taking of reasons for utility of care ethics.

The **fourth** component in care ethics education is that of **confirmation** which implies that we need to constantly encourage the student to nurture his caring attitude even when he/she fails to do so in her relationships. In the Caring model it is through confirmation that the teacher can express disappointment as well as direct the student towards her own better side. By creating a conducive environment for practicing care, the students can be constantly drawn towards ethical action rather than being disciplined. It is acknowledged that different sides of the student can surface based on its immediate surroundings.

Noddings also believed that students should learn the knowledge and skills necessary to help them to navigate the world around them, while simultaneously caring for children, the elderly, the animals and the environment. She reflects on the two ways themes of care that can exist in schools. In one arena, subjects in schools to be organised around the thematic units of care. In the other arena, she says that subject in school remains the standard modern day disciplines but incorporate themes of care throughout.

Noddings stress the importance of adapting curriculum to fit the personal interest of students and making core subjects applicable to real life situations. Students should not be forced into learning from specific curriculum, but rather to be given the practical life skills to make well-informed choices.

Noddings believed that the main aim of education should be to produce competent, caring and loveable people. Thus, it can said that her contribution is of great significance as an educator, philosopher and writer.

Major Works

- Philosophy of Education (1965)
- Caring, The Feminine Approach of Ethics (1984)
- Women and Evil (1989)
- Educating Moral Police (2002)

Savitribai Phule

She was a prominent Indian social reformer, educationist and poet who played an instrumental role in women's education and empowerment during the 19th century. Counted among few literate women of those times, Savitribai is credited for founding the first girl's school in Pune in Bhide Wada with her husband Jyotirao Phule. She took great efforts towards educating and emancipating child, widows campaigned against child marriage and sati pratha, and advocated for widow re-marriage.

A leading figure of Maharashtra's social reform movement, she is considered an icon of Dalit Mang caste along with B R Ambedkar and Annabhau Sathe. She campaigned against untouchability and worked actively in abolishing caste and gender based discrimination.

Role in Women Education and Empowerment

The first indigenously run school for girls in Pune (at that time Poona) was started by Jyotirao and Savitribai in 1848 when the later was still in her teens. Although, they were ostracised by both family and community for this step. Savitribai became the first teacher of the school. Later, Jyotirao and Savitribai started schools for children from the Mang and Mahar castes, who were regarded as untouchables. Three Phule schools were in operation in 1852. On November 16,1852, the British government honoured the Phule's family for their contribution in the field of education while Savitribai was named the best teacher. In 1852, she also started the Mahila Seva Mandal with the objective of creating awareness among women, regarding their rights, dignity and other social issues. She was successful in organising a barber's strike in Mumbai and Pune to oppose the prevailing custom of shaving heads of widows.

All the three schools that were run by the Phule, were closed in 1858. There were many reasons for this, including drying up of private European donations, post the Indian Rebellion of 1857, resignation of Jyotirao from the school management committee due to difference of opinion on curriculum, and withdrawal of support from the government. Undeterred by the circumstances Jyotirao and Savitribai along with Fatima Sheikh, took charge of educating people from the oppressed communities as well.

Over the years, Savitribai opened 18 schools and taught children from different castes. Savitribai and Fatima Sheikh began teaching women, as well as other people from downtrodden castes.

This was not taken well by many, particularly the upper caste of Pune, who were against Dalit's education. Savitribai and Fatima Sheikh were threatened by the locals and were also harassed and humiliated socially. Cow dung, mud and stones were thrown at Savitribai when she walked towards the school. However, such atrocities could not discourage the determined Savitribai from her goal and that's why she carried two sarees. Later, Savitribai and Fatima Sheikh joined by Saguna Bai, who also eventually became a leader in the educational movement. Meanwhile, a night school was also opened by the Phule couple in 1855 for agriculturist and labourers, so that they can work in day time and can attend school at night.

To check the school dropout rate, Savitribai started the practice of giving stipends to children for attending school. She remained an inspiration for the young girls. She encouraged them to take up activities like writing and painting. One of the essay, written by a student of Savitribai called Mukta Salve became the face of dalit feminism and literature during that period. She conducted parent-teacher meetings at regular intervals to create awarenes among parents on the significance of education, so that they can send their childrens to school regularly.

In 1863, Jyotirao and Savitribai also started a care centre called 'Balhaty Pratibandhak Griha' possibly the first ever infanticide prohibition home founded in India. It was setup, so that pregnant Brahmin widows and rape victims can deliver their children in a safe and secure place, thus preventing the killing of widows as well as reducing the rate of infanticide. In 1874, Jyotirao and Savitribai, went on to adopt a child from a Brahmin widow called Kashibai, thus, sending a strong message to the progressive people of the society. The adopted son, Yashavantrao, grew up to become a doctor.

While, Jyotirao advocated widow remarriage, Savitribai worked tirelessly against social evils like child marriage and Sati pratha, two of the most sensitive social issues that were gradually weakening the very existence of women. She also made efforts in bringing the child widows into mainstream by educating and empowering them and advocated for their re-marriage. Also, such pursuits met with strong resistance from the conservative upper caste society.

Her Writings and Valuable Contribution

Savitribai Phule's poems and writings is an inspiration for many and remain pioneering in the struggle against India's caste system. Together, she has put some very valuable writings.

They are :

- Kavyaphule, Collection of Poems, 1854
- Jyotirao's Speeches, Edited by Savitribai Phule, 25th December, 1856
- Savitribai's Letters to Jyotirao
- Speeches of Matoshree Savitribai, 1892
- Bavankashi Subodh Ratnakar, 1892

National Values of Constitution with Reference to Education

Education, its values and relevance, finds an important place in the Constitution of India. It provides the conception of the economic and social order for which youth of the country should be educated. Its preamble has reflects the National echoes and the objectives of national policy. Every constitution has a philosophy of its own which embodies the ideals, values, hopes and aspirations of its people. So, education should find an important place in this constitution. This fact underlined the vital role of education in the national development.

The values expressed in the Preamble are expressed as objectives of the Constitution. These are sovereignity, socialism, secularism, democracy, republican character of Indian state, justice, liberty, equality, fraternity, human dignity and the unity and integrity of the nation.

Socialism

The word 'Socialism' has been used in the context of economic planning. It signifies major role in the economy. It also means commitment to attaint ideals, like removal of inequalities, provision of minimum basic necessities to all and equal pay for equal work.

Socialism is a socio-economic political doctrine which arose as a revolt against the capitalism, in **Europe**. **Karl Marx** and **Lenin** in **Russia** and **Mao** in **China** were the chief architects of socialism. Socialism aims in establishing a classless society based on the total supremacy of the state and total submission of the individual to the state.

Aims of Socialism

- Establishing a classless society.
- Social justice, equality and the complete supremacy of the state.
- Abolishing the capitalist system.
- The active participation of the individual in the productive process of the society.
- It ignores spiritual values.

Socialism and Aims of Education

- Development of democratic outlook.
- Development of socialist values.
- Development of secular values.
- Providing equal opportunites to all, for their all round development and welfare.
- Rapid expansion of educational facilities in all areas.
- Developing values like dharma, dignity of labour, non-violence, unselfishness and selfless service.

Socialism and Curriculum and Methods of Teaching

- Topics like democracy, duties of citizens, equality, freedom, rights, secularism, socialism, social reform movements, non-violence, etc, should be taught.
- Group activities like debates, discussion, social service camps, social surveys, shramadhan, etc, to be organised.
- Inclusion of socially useful productive work as an essential component of the social curriculum, to be the key note of the curriculum.
- Emphasise should be laid on polytechinc vocational and professional courses.
- Introduction of information technology. It's effective use would enable students to do well age of modernisation.

- Emphasise should be given to group method, like teaching, seminars, projects, etc.
- Self-Discovery Method should be encouraged.

Secularism

In the context of secularism in India, it is said that "India is neither religious nor irreligious nor anti-religious". It implies that there will be no 'state' religion *i.e.* the state will not support any particular religion out of public funds. This has two aspects *i.e.* every individual is free to believe in and practice, any religion he/she belongs to and state will not discriminate against any individual or group on the basis of religion.

Characteristics of Secular Education

- Moral outlook.
- Development of wider vision.
- Pluralistic outlook.
- Democratic values.
- Cultural development.
- Synthesis of spiritual and material.
- Humanitarianism.

Education for Secularism in India

India presents educational system that promotes secular attitude and values through its broad based aims, curriculum, enlightened teachers and appropriate activities, progressivism, rationality, freedom from bigotry and equal respect for all religion.

The following traits characterise education for secularism in India :

- Secular aims.
- Democratic organisation of educational institutions.
- Multiple curriculum.
- Science teaching.
- Enlightened teachers.

The present Indian educational system is trying to create a social climate in the country, in which secular values are sought to be promoted effectively and enthusiastically.

Reason for Imparting Secular Education

- It develops a moral outlook.
- It helps in the development of liberal attitudes and values.
- It develops wider vision.
- It develops an attitude of appreciation and understanding of other's point of view.
- It develops democratic values and humanistic outlook.
- It synthesises materialism and spiritualism.
- It serves as an antidote to religious fanaticism and hatred.

Educational Implications

Many positive steps have been taken to promote secularism in the country. It is laid down in the constitution that religious minorities are free to establish their educational institutions from grant. Secularism is a philosophy of moral education. Secular behaviour springs in the school from the influence of school through the conduct and behaviour of teachers themselves and life in the school community as a whole. All the activities and programs of school must strive for the inculcation of values of love, truth and tolerance.

Democracy

Democracy refers both to a political system and a political aspiration. Democracy refers not only to system of government but also to general way of life itself. It has ethical, political, social and economic aspects. It is the form of government in which the supreme power is vested in the people and exercised by them directly or indirectly through a system of representation.

Education for Democracy

For the success of democracy, it is essential that each individual owns his responsibilities, consciously and this will be possible only when the individual's power of understanding is high and he is of good character. It is the duty of the society that it should prepare an individual from intellectual, moral and physical point of view to discharge his duties of citizenship, so that the society may remain happy and rich.

The main features of education are usually sited as two folds. **Firstly**, to transmit the social and cultural heritage to the new generation (example, through schools). **Secondly**, to create a feeling of adjustment among the students, towards the environment. The school should develop all the qualities among the children which are desirable as a good citizen.

These includes :

- Self-realisation
- Human relationship
- Economic efficiency
- Civic responsibility

True education for democracy should help the people to appreciate an urgent necessity of acquiring knowledge to discriminate between facts and prejudices, to weigh and judge efficiencies, to arrive at conclusion.

Responsibility of Formal and Informal Agencies

A person learns the first principle of democratic life from his/her home. An individual learns the best methods for his socialisation by spending a wholesome life in his family and by gaining experiences from the social life of other persons.

We know that the school is a formal agency of education. In the school, proper arrangement can be made for the education of democracy. The people through the personal efforts and through group activities can learn the responsibilities of a future citizen. The state should ensure that there are available opportunities for universal free primary education.

The informal agencies are also helpful in developing desirable public consciousness. Education does not end with school education but it is a continuous process. The informal agencies take the responsibility of education about the rights and duties to an individual, even after their formal schooling. Democracy will become successful only, if the citizens are intellectually advanced and educated. In democracy, the opinion of the people influences governmental policies.

Relationship Between Democracy and Aims of Education

Harmonious development of the individual citizen is the main aim of education in all democratic countries. In democracy, there must be a capacity to understand the social, economical and political problems in an effective way. One should think in a creative way. The education should give importance to both individual and social development.

Education should develop socialism, both in thought and action of the people. According to the **Secondary Education Commission** (1952-53), three aims fit in democracy. **Firstly**, the framing of the character to fit the students to participate creatively as the citizens in the democratic social order. **Secondly**, the improvement of their practical and vocational efficiency, so that they can play their part in building up the economical prosperity of their country.

Curriculum and Democracy

In order to achieve democratic ideals, the curriculum should be well planned.

Role of curriculum in creating democratic ideals are as follows

- Different activities like play, school education, co-curriculur activities, etc, should be included in curriculum.
- There should be an ample scope for individual freedom and it should be flexible in nature.
- While selecting a course, intelligence, capabilities and necessities of individual must be considered.
- It should give importance to local needs.
- It should be social oriented.
- Importance should be given to efficient utilisation of the leisure time.
- Vocational needs should also be considered, while framing the curriculum.

Role of School in Democracy

Every school is established in the society, for the welfare of the people. In democracy, the school should propagate democratic ideals.

Some important demoratic ideals of schools are

- The school should make the students capable of living in democracy.
- Steps should be taken, to develop secularism and religious neutrality.
- Teachers should have freedom, to select their own methods and textbooks.
- Democratic feeling should be given to the teachers.
- Creating desirable environment for developing friendship among teachers, principals and inspectioners.
- Cooperation, sympathy, love, etc, should be given special emphasis.

Teacher and Democracy

In a democratic society, the teachers should be given high status to bring desirable changes in the society and this will lead towards the progress of the society. They should have an adequate training and must have competency of developing the feelings of democracy, among the children. They should be able to understand the potentialities of each child. He should have ability to provide education for good citizenship and must be a man of high character.

Teaching Methods and Democracy

The method of teaching can influence in developing democratic setup in every nation.

The teaching methods must follow the given facts

- They must be flexible.
- They must be based on dynamisms and progressivism.
- They must be activity-centered.
- There must be an individual freedom (use methods, like Dalton's plan, project method, montessory).
- They should emphasise the intellectual and social development of the child.

Self-discipline also has importance in democracy. It should be emphasised in democracy. For this, children should be given opportunity for self-governance. It is essential to remember that democracy whether in the school or society can be only successful when it's members have proper approach towards it.

We can conclude by quoting the words of **Alexander Meikeljohn**, who says that "The art of democracy is the art of thinking independently, together".

Justice

It is the concept of basic rights. It holds an important position in the life of an individual and society. It is basically centered on the good relations between the people and the state.

It is divided into following three sections

Social Justice It means the place of equality in society. It assures everyone, to get the proper place in the society and to overcome difficulties.

Economical Justice It assures that everyone has the right to property.

Political Justice It states that anyone who attained the age of 18 and is the citizen of India, should have the power to vote.

If there is educational inequality in schools, it demonstrates a case of social justice. This inequality prevails everywhere in the world. Social justice in education prevails bright and deserving students to reach their potential because the wealthy not so bright, students take over and leave them behind using their resources. Schools can promote social justice by giving social justice education to their teachers and changing their educational policy by practicing social justice principles.

Equality

'Equality of educational opportunity' has assumed different connotations. It can be taken as the application of the principle of distributive justice in respect of the good of education. At the **primary level**, it means provision of free, compulsory education of an adequate duration and content to all without any discrimination, at the **secondary level**. It implies provision of diversified curricula to suit the differing needs and interests of individuals, at the higher education level, it can only mean provision of opportunities, to all those who have the required ability to profit from such education and make proper social contribution in return.

Despite large scale expansion of educational facilities during the six decades after independence, glaring inequalities still remains in the education of the poor and the rich, of the SCs STs and other backward classes on the one hand and the forward groups on the other, and between boys and girls. While, the goal of universal education is far from being reached, beneficiaries of expansion at the secondary and higher levels have been mostly drawn from the relatively affluent sections of the society.

Universal Education

In society like ours, where 70% of the people are illiterate, equality of educational opportunity at higher levels will have any meaning at all only if the constitutional directive of universalising education to all children in the age group of 6 to 14 is effectively realised. As you know, the staggering rate of dropout leading to huge wastage of educational resources and expenditure has foiled national efforts in this direction.

In order to reduce this wastage and to fulfil the target of universalising education, several programmes have been launched in recent years. This includes giving priority consideration to primary education in the matter of allocation of financial resources, allowing for multiple entry, using the service of part-time for multiple entry, using the service of part-time and locally available non-professional teachers, wherever necessary for continuing non-formal education.

Liberty

Education gives you the tools to be able to think and learn and liberty gives you the ability to find truth. Liberty is basically freedom from restraint. However, it is not the freedom to do whatever you want, being irresponsible and denying basic truths and morals.

Education is dependent on liberty because of two main reasons. **First**, without liberty, you will be taught what to think, instead of how to think. That is not true education, it is indoctrination. If you are taught, what to think instead of how to think, then your mind is not being enlightened in understanding, you are simply being programmed like a robot, to think in a certain way.

Secondly, education is dependent on liberty because without liberty, you cannot truly learn. Education is about expanding your knowledge and abilities, and that is impossible without the liberty to search for truth. Just as education is dependent on liberty, liberty is dependent upon education. Without education, you will be confined to the realm of your limited knowledge.

Freedom

The ideas of freedom in education were an expression of the dissatisfaction of democratically minded, petit bourgeois intellectuals and some bourgeois intellectuals with the status quo in society. The anarchist educational theorists presented freedom in education as a means or restructuring society, by ensuring the comprehensive development of children's creativity and intellectual and physical powers, as well as the free, creative educational practice of the teacher.

EXAM BASED QUESTIONS

1 Socialisation requires
(a) teachers (b) rewards
(c) reinforcement (d) All of these

2 One of the most needed requirements of socialisation, learning and education is
(a) cooperation (b) competition
(c) conflict (d) discipline

3 The process of socialisation is similar to that of teaching because
(a) both require interactions.
(b) both are an automatic processes.
(c) both start from the family.
(d) Both a and b

4 Process of socialisation of a child will become slow if
(a) he is not allowed to go to neighbourhood due to social evils, rampant there.
(b) child cannot communicate due to language barrier.
(c) child is handicapped and he is hated by the society.
(d) All of the above

5 The process by which an individual learns to behave in accordance with social norms and culture is called
(a) acculturation (b) socialisation
(c) assimilation (d) None of these

6 Which of the following is not the means of socialisation?
(a) Segregation (b) Imitation
(c) Counselling (d) Association

7 Which of the following, plays a vital role in the process of socialisation?
(a) Group activities in the school
(b) Cooperation
(c) Competition
(d) All of the above

8 Process of socialisation increases, when the child is brought to
(a) participate in the co-curricular activities
(b) attend classes
(c) do experiment in the laboratory
(d) All of the above

9 "Socialisation is a process as a result of which children take on themselves the various social roles." Who said this?
(a) Cook (b) Redcliffe
(c) Linton (d) Krober

10 Which of the following is/are the characteristic(s) of culture?
(a) Culture is social
(b) Culture is dynamic
(c) Culture is learnt
(d) All of the above

11 Who said that "Culture is composed of integrated customs, traditions and current behaviour patterns of human groups"?
(a) Drever (b) Hobe (c) Bogardus (d) AW Green

12 How is education related to culture?
(a) Education preserves old culture
(b) Education creates new culture
(c) Education sustains old culture and usher in new ones
(d) Education and culture are mutually supporting each other

13 The cultural lag is removed by
(a) law (b) education
(c) lecture (d) revolution

14 Which of the following factor(s) influence(s) the culture of a country?
(a) Removal of cultural lag
(b) Continuity of culture
(c) Transmission of culture
(d) All of the above

15 Discipline is must to maintain
(a) individual study (b) rules and regulations
(c) social setup (d) All of these

16 Analysis of the sociological processes involved in the educational institutions could be known as the
(a) social foundation of education
(b) educational sociology
(c) sociology of education
(d) social science of education

17 Which of the following factor(s) help(s) in the process of socialisation ?
(a) Rear and care
(b) Strict control on children by peers
(c) Limitation of elders on children
(d) All of the above

18 Culture based education positively impacts student's
(a) identity
(b) self-efficacy
(c) social relationship
(d) All of the above

19 Which of the following is/are the part(s) of socialisation process?
(a) Rearing
(b) Cooperation
(c) Imitation
(d) All of the above

20 Through socialisation of an individual, we
(a) develop affiliative tendencies towards other individuals and groups
(b) develops hostile attitude towards other groups
(c) saves an individual, from the prejudices of other people and groups
(d) Both a and b

21 Culture may be defined as
(a) uncodified ideology of people
(b) sum total of collective behaviour
(c) pattern of arrangements, material and behavioural, adopted by a society
(d) typical habit patterns of people

22 Standard of living has maximum relationship with which one of the following factors?
(a) Culture (b) Environment
(c) People (d) None of these

23 The term 'sub culture' is used to indicate
(a) the culture of the lower state of the society
(b) the beliefs and customs of traditional social groups
(c) the culture of different groups of societies
(d) the traditions and ideas of tribal groups of a society

24 In a culturally pluralistic country, which type of the education is suitable?
(a) Education free from culture
(b) Education developing tolerance to other cultures
(c) Education emphasising national culture
(d) Both a and b

25 Which of the following is/are the characteristic(s) of culture?
(a) Continuity
(b) Unconscious adaptation
(c) Growth and change
(d) All of the above

26 Which of the following comes under non-material culture?
(a) Group behaviour pattern i.e. dance, music, drama, etc.
(b) Literary and scientific progress
(c) Ideals of life and moral values
(d) All of the above

27 Which of the following is not included in the material culture of a country?
(a) Warfare technology
(b) Houses
(c) Software technology
(d) Industrial growth

28 Which of the following is/are an important characteristic(s) of culture?
(a) Culture is cumulative form of all non-material aspects.
(b) Culture is the cumulative product that people have acquired in centuries.
(c) Culture can be preserved and transmitted.
(d) All of the above

29 The difference between the pace of progress of material and non-material culture, in which pace material culture is much more developed, is known as
(a) cultural lag (b) social lag
(c) technological lag (d) social and cultural lag

30 The book, 'Races and Culture of India' was written by
(a) DN Majumdar (b) MN Prabhu
(c) TB Bottomore (d) KM Kapadia

31 They are important characteristics of culture, except
(a) culture is inherited from forefathers
(b) culture varies from place to place and from race to race
(c) culture varies from person to person
(d) culture is both revealed and man made

32 A cultural area is a
(a) segment of a particular society's culture
(b) geographical area characterised by distinguishing cultural traits
(c) segment of culture, which cuts score of particular society
(d) geographical area characterised by a high level of cultural development, distinguishing cultural traits

33 Which of the following is not an attribute of culture ?
(a) Shared (b) Transmittable
(c) Innate (d) Learnt

34 Which of the following statement is true?
(a) Culture is a borrowed behaviour.
(b) Superior culture is always adopted.
(c) Western culture has become universal.
(d) Only culture traits of other cultures are adopted, as they can be assimilated.

35 Which is not a form of culture?
(a) Material culture (b) Non-material culture
(c) Intellectual culture (d) Industrial culture

36 Who said that "Education is man-making. It is that by which character is formed, strength of mind is increased, intellect is expended and by which man can stand on his own feet"?
(a) Swami Vivekannanda
(b) Rabindranath Tagore
(c) Dayanand Saraswati
(d) All of the above

37 Who said that "Material and spiritual knowledge is already present in man, covered by a curtain of ignorance"?
(a) Plato (b) Mahatma Gandhi
(c) Tagore (d) Swami Vivekananda

38 Which of the following concept(s) is/are emphasised by Swami Vivekananda?
(a) Integral education (b) Man-making education
(c) Education for harmony (d) Citizenship education

39 Which of the following is not an aim of education, according to Swami Vivekananda?
(a) To bring about the innate perfection
(b) To integrate spirituality and science
(c) To develop national character
(d) To prepare the young students as social beings

40 Which of the following is not a unique feature of education, envisaged by Swami Vivekananda?
(a) Cultivation of heart and physical strength
(b) Residential Programme of Education
(c) Intelligent and productive manual labour
(d) Importance of concentration

41 'Learning in communion with nature' was propagated by
(a) Swami Vivekananda (b) Sri Aurobindo Ghosh
(c) Rabindranath Tagore (d) Mahatma Gandhi

42 Who said that "Education is the manifestation of divine perfection that already exists in man"?
(a) Mahatma Gandhi (b) Swami Vivekananda
(c) Tagore (d) Sri Aurobindo

43 "Stand up, be bold, be strong. Take the whole responsibility on your own shoulders and know that you are the creator of your own destiny. All the strength and success you want are within yourself". Who said this statement?
(a) Swamiji (b) Tagore
(c) Rousseau (d) Gandhiji

44 "His childhood name is Narendranath. He is the disciple of Swami Ramakrishna Paramhansa. He realised that truth is in every religion and there are different paths to reach one goal". Who is he?
(a) R N Tagore
(b) Swami Dayanand Saraswati
(c) M K Gandhi
(d) Swami Vivekananda

45 'Sons of the morning' is the poem written by
(a) Aurobindo (b) Swamiji
(c) Gandhiji (d) Tagore

46 Which of the following is not an aim of education according to Tagore?
(a) Moral development
(b) Unity of truth
(c) Women's education
(d) Perfection of man

47 The school of Shantiniketan, upholds in many respects of the chief principle of pragmatism. To whom, this school is associated with?
(a) Swami ji (b) Tagore
(c) Aurobindo (d) Gandhiji

48 Which among the following is not the publication of Tagore?
(a) Shiksar Milan
(b) Young India
(c) Dharma Shiskha
(d) Abaran

49 Rabindranath Tagore was awarded with the Nobel Prize for the contribution to
(a) the message of ancient Indian education
(b) the cause of humanity through Sevasadans
(c) literature, for the English version of his Gitanjali
(d) education is started with Shantiniketan

50 According to Tagore, knowledge should be communicated to children in
(a) an environment of nature
(b) a social and friendly environment
(c) an environment where free actions are permitted
(d) All of the above

51 The development of physical, mental, moral and spiritual potentialities of the child, in a balanced manner means
(a) development through man-making education
(b) development through integral education
(c) all round development of child
(d) harmonious development of child

52 We can call Gandhiji an idealist because
(a) he believed that truth is the ultimate value
(b) he emphasised on character building
(c) for him education means bringing out the best
(d) he saw education as a tool of social revolution

53 Who has formally initiated the concept of Naturalism in modern Indian education?
(a) Tagore (b) Swamiji
(c) Gandhiji (d) Sri Aurobindo

54 Which of the following is not a specific characteristic of Gandhian education?
(a) Community living and teacher as a model
(b) Intelligent productive manual labour
(c) Raise up non-violent men and non-violent society
(d) Mastery over material science and technology

55 What does Gandhiji meant by 'drawing out the best'?
(a) religion (b) truth
(c) inner-voice (d) Both b and c

56 Who said that "Man's ultimate aim is the realisation of God"?
(a) Tagore (b) Gandhiji
(c) Sri Aurobindo (d) Swamiji

57 Which among the following is the ashram, where Gandhiji helped children in their all round development?
(a) Sabarmati
(b) Transwal
(c) Sevagram
(d) Ashram at Puducherry

58 According to 'My Experiment with Truth'
(a) there is little significance of Hinduism
(b) caste and classes are baseless
(c) caste and classes are useless
(d) caste and classes have significance in Hinduism

59 Mahatma Gandhi's Basic Education Scheme was characterised by
(a) secret discipline and punishment for wrongs
(b) opposition to control and punishment
(c) education of children through sense training
(d) strict supervision and control of activities

60 Which of the following is not a chief tenet of Gandhi's new educational philosophy?
(a) There should be a free and compulsory primary education.
(b) The education should be man-making.
(c) The education should be craft-centered.
(d) The education should be given in the mother tongue.

61 "The community should be the hub activity. The community-centred activity in the villages should be mainly the craft of the community. Thus, he believed in craft-centered activity". These lines are associated with
(a) MK Gandhi (b) Tagore
(c) Swami Vivekananda (d) Aurobindo

62 Why is Aurobindo's educational thinking called an integral education?
(a) Because it integrates Indian and Western education.
(b) Because it does not neglect any physical, psychic and spiritual dimensions.
(c) Because it believes that truth is innate.
(d) It teaches us to live in harmony with nature and God.

63 Who has suggested the concept of integral education for Indian people?
(a) Gandhiji
(b) Tagore
(c) Swami Vivekananda
(d) Sri Aurobindo

64 'A system of national education' is the book written by
(a) Sri Aurobindo (b) Swami Vivekananda
(c) Tagore (d) Gandhiji

65 "Integralism is the synthesis of idealism, realism, pragmatism and spiritualism". Whose philosophy is this ?
(a) Tagore (b) Sri Aurobindo
(c) Gandhiji (d) Swami Vivekananda

66 Concept of yoga in education was introduced by
(a) Gandhiji (b) Sri Aurobindo
(c) Tagore (d) Swami Vivekananda

67 Who said that "A civilisation is to be judged by the power of it's ideas"?
(a) Gandhi ji (b) Sri Aurobindo
(c) Tagore (d) Swami Vivekananda

68 According to whom, the purification of the mental and moral habits should be the basis of discipline ?
(a) Swami Vivekananda (b) Tagore
(c) Sri Aurobindo (d) Gandhiji

69 Which of the following is not associated with Sri Aurobindo?
(a) Vital education (b) Physical education
(c) Man-making education (d) International education

70 Who among the following, favoured development of senses as aim of education?
(a) Swami Vivekananda (b) Tagore
(c) Gandhi ji (d) Sri Aurobindo

71 Who profounded that teaching is not something that one should study first and later translates it into action?
(a) Swami Vivekananda (b) Gandhiji
(c) Tagore (d) Krishnamurti

72 What is the characteristic of education for Krishnamurti?
(a) Performer (b) Agent
(c) Doer (d) All of these

73 "We can understand education as a whole", this view was held by
(a) Krishnamurti (b) Radhakrishnan
(c) Gandhi ji (d) Tagore

74 Apart from students, who plays an important role in education?
(a) Parents (b) Peers
(c) Staff (d) Teachers

75 Who said that "the highest function of education is to bring about an integrated individual, who is capable or dealing with life as a whole"?
(a) Paulo Freire (b) Jiddu Krishnamurti
(c) Nel Noddings (d) Savitribai Phule

76 What 'Education' means to Paulo Freire?
(a) It facilitates self-confidence.
(b) It removes inequality.
(c) It facilitates the integration in the logic of current system.
(d) None of the above

77 Who was marked as the founder of 'Critical Pedagogy'?
(a) Sri Aurobindo (b) Tagore
(c) Paulo Freire (d) Marry Wollstonecraft

78 **Whose philosophical idea influenced Freire for his Theory of Philosophy of Education?**
(a) Socrates (b) Plato and Aristotle
(c) Kant and Marx (d) Plato and Marx

79 **Who was marked as a 'Feminist Philosopher'?**
(a) Swami Vivekananda (b) Wollstonecraft
(c) Freire (d) All of these

80 **Who wrote the book, 'The Vindication of the Rights of Women'?**
(a) Simon de Beaviour (b) Marry Mighlie
(c) Carol Gilligon (d) Marry Wollstonecraft

81 **According to whom, Wollstonecraft should be given more priority in education?**
(a) Women and poor
(b) Children, youth and women
(c) Children and women
(d) Only Children

82 **Apart frop-m social representation, which representation is focused by Wollstonecraft?**
(a) Constitutional representation
(b) Religious representation
(c) Superiority of sex
(d) None of the above

83 **Who among the following worked for the upliftment of education?**
(a) Paulo Freire (b) Marry Wollstonecraft
(c) Nel Nodding (d) All of these

84 **What kind of learning is promoted by Nel Nodding?**
(a) Audio (b) Visual
(c) Both a and b (d) Neither a nor b

85 **Which among the following book was written by Nodding?**
(a) Meditation (b) Educational Ethics
(c) Marry and Marlie (d) Philosophy of Education

86 **"Good use of vocabulary, plays an important role in education". Who said this?**
(a) Nel Nodding (b) Voltaire
(c) Gandhiji (d) Paulo Freire

87 **Who marked as a founder of first girl's school in Pune?**
(a) Swami Vivekananda (b) Savitribai Phule
(c) Gandhiji (d) Sri Aurobindo

88 **What is the objective of 'Mahila Seva Mandal'?**
(a) To create feminist movement
(b) To fight against man
(c) To create awareness among women
(d) All of the above

89 **What is the name of care centre for infanticide, which was started by Savitribai Phule ?**
(a) Balhatya Pratibandhak Griha
(b) Pratibandhak Griha Balhatya
(c) Balhatya Griha
(d) None of the above

90 **'Kavyaphule, Collection of Poems' was written by?**
(a) Savitribai Phule
(b) Gandhiji
(c) Wollstonecraft
(d) Krishnamurti

91 **Who said that "True Knowledge is not attained by thinking. It is what you are, it is what you become"?**
(a) Savitribai Phule
(b) Sri Aurobindo
(c) Tagore
(d) Mahatma Gandhi

92 **What is the aim of socialism in education?**
(a) Having social advocacy
(b) Having non-secular values
(c) Favouring anarchy
(d) Development of democratic outlook

93 **Which of the following was not suggested as a method of education by Vivekananda?**
(a) Lecture-cum discussion
(b) Yoga
(c) Meditation
(d) Guided teachings

94 **Which of the following types represents Aurobindo's contribution to education?**
(a) Integral education
(b) Basic education
(c) Education for man-making
(d) Education for international understanding

95 **........... favoured social discipline through some production works based on coaperation, initiative, accuracy and individual's responsibility.**
(a) Mahatma Gandhi
(b) Rabindranath Tagore
(c) Sri Aurobindo
(d) Vivekananda

96 **Which is the least important aim of education in the context of Indian democracy?**
(a) Development of leadership qualities
(b) Development of democratic citizenship
(c) Teaching democracy in the class
(d) Increasing the vocational efficiency of students

97 **In how many parts the term 'justice' is divided?**
(a) Three (b) Two (c) Five (d) Seven

98 **Who said that to be the most eligible for the equality of educational opportunity?**
(a) One who follows social institution
(b) One who follows democratic principles
(c) One who follows principles of distributive justice
(d) None of the above

99 **What is regarded as freedom from restraints?**
(a) Fraternity (b) Liberty
(c) Justice (d) Equality

100 What is required to make oneself free from bourgeois intellectuals?
(a) Secularity (b) Justice
(c) Power (d) Freedom

101 Which of the following reason(s) is/are correct with regard to the imparting of secular education?
(a) It develops a moral outlook
(b) It develops democratic values and humanistic outlook
(c) It helps in the development of liberal attitudes and values
(d) All of the above

102 **Statement I** Secularism is the philosophy of moral education.
Statement II It helps in the development of liberal attitudes and values.
(a) Statement I is correct
(b) Statement II is correct
(c) Both the statements, I and II are correct
(d) Neither a nor b

103 Aims of socialism are
(a) establishing a classless society
(b) abolishing the capitalist society
(c) The active participation of the individual in the productive process of the society
(d) All of the above

104 Match the following

List I (Thinkers)	List II (Philosophy)
A. Tagore	1. Harmonious development of personality
B. Swami Vivekananda	2. The Doctrine of Karma
C. Mahatma Gandhi	3. Child is more important than all kinds of books.
D. Buddhism	4. Yoga as a method of education
	5 The Doctrine of Dharma

Codes

	A	B	C	D
(a)	5	1	2	4
(b)	3	4	1	2
(c)	3	4	2	5
(d)	4	2	1	3

105 Match the following

List I (Thinkers)	List II (Types of Education)
A. Gandhi ji	1. Shantiniketan
B. Tagore	2. Integral yoga
C. Sri Aurobindo	3. Gurukul
D. Swami Vivekananda	4. Man-making education
	5. Wardha scheme

Codes

	A	B	C	D
(a)	5	1	2	4
(b)	5	1	4	2
(c)	3	4	2	5
(d)	4	2	3	5

106 Match the following

List I	List II
A. Chitta	1. Intuition
B. Manas	2. Intellect
C. Buddhi	3. Mind
D. Abhaas	4. Passive memory

Codes

	A	B	C	D
(a)	1	2	4	3
(b)	2	1	3	4
(c)	1	2	3	4
(d)	4	3	2	1

107 Match the following

List I (Philosophers)	List II (Characteristics)
A. Gandhiji	1. Character development
B. Swami Vivekananda	2. Craft
C. Tagore	3. Yoga
D. Sri Aurobindo	4. Active communion

Codes

	A	B	C	D
(a)	1	3	2	4
(b)	2	1	4	3
(c)	4	3	2	1
(d)	2	1	3	4

108 Match the following

List I (Thinkers)	List II (Types of Education)
A. Swami Vivekananda	1. Shantiniketan
B. Tagore	2. Man-making education
C. Gandhiji	3. Integral yoga
D. Sri Aurobindo	4. Wardha scheme

Codes

	A	B	C	D
(a)	1	2	4	3
(b)	1	2	3	4
(c)	2	1	4	3
(d)	4	3	2	1

109 Match the following

List I (Name of philosophers)	List II (Philosophies)
A. Mahatma Gandhi	1. Child is more important than all kinds of books.
B. Buddhism	2. Yoga as a method of education
C. Vivekananda	3. The Doctrine of Dharma
D. Tagore	4 Harmonious development of personality

Codes

	A	B	C	D
(a)	1	2	4	3
(b)	2	1	4	1
(c)	4	3	2	1
(d)	1	2	3	4

110 Match the following

List I (Features of Education)	List II (Thinkers)
A. Education through craft	1. Tagore
B. Man-making education	2. Sri Aurobindo
C. Integral education	3. Vivekananda
D. Self-expression	4. Gandhiji

Codes

	A	B	C	D
(a)	4	3	2	1
(b)	2	1	3	4
(c)	1	2	4	3
(d)	1	2	3	4

111 Match the following

List I (Philosophers)	List II (Books /Journals)
A. Mahatma Gandhi	1. Advaita Vedanta
B. Tagore	2. The Life Divine
C. Aurobindo	3. Gitanjali
D. Vivekananda	4. Young India

Codes

	A	B	C	D
(a)	1	2	3	4
(b)	4	3	2	1
(c)	1	2	4	3
(d)	2	1	3	4

112 Match the following

List I	List II
A. Navodaya Vidyalaya	1. Culturally decided
B. Home	2. Socialisation
C. Changing way of life	3. Equality of educational opportunities
D Social stratification	4. Modernisation

Codes

	A	B	C	D
(a)	1	2	3	4
(b)	1	3	4	2
(c)	3	2	4	1
(d)	3	4	2	1

113 Match the following

List I	List II
A. Socialisation	1. Religion
B. Collaborative activities	2. School
C. Democratic practices	3. Home
D. Cultural practices	4. State
	5 Village

Codes

	A	B	C	D
(a)	1	2	3	4
(b)	4	2	5	1
(c)	3	2	4	5
(d)	5	4	1	2

114 The aim of basic education, as per the dream of Gandhiji is to

1. create a classless society.
2. create a sarvodaya society
3. create a society, respecting all religions.
4. create a society, where rich and poor can live together.

Codes

(a) 1, 2, 3 and 4 (b) 1, 2 and 3
(c) 2, 3 and 4 (d) 1, 2 and 4

115 In Tagore's education system, the child learns better by

1. debates and discussions.
2. reading, writing and speaking
3. dance, drama and music
4. travelling and interacting with nature.

Codes

(a) 1, 2, 3 and 4 (b) 1, 3 and 4
(c) 1, 2 and 3 (d) 2, 3 and 4

116 The aim(s) of education, according to Jiddu Krishnamurti is/are

(a) education does not mean only acquiring the knowledge of the subject.
(b) education should help discover lasting values so that one does not cling merely to formulas or repeating values.
(c) education should not be making people meterialistic.
(d) All the above

117 Which of the following statement (s) is/are true about Jiddu Krishnamurti's views on curriculum?

Statement I Curriculum should encourages national integrity and harmony in the students.

Statement II It should give the knowledge to final solution to problems.

(a) Only I (b) Both I and I
(c) Only II (d) Neither I nor II

118 .... Theory of Education is closely linked with issues such as oppression and struggle with social relation that centre round with ideology and material domination.

(a) Wollstonecraft's (b) Nel Noddings'
(c) Krishnamurti's (d) Paulo Freire's

119 According to Nel Nodding, education from care perspectives should have .... key components.

(a) two (b) three
(c) four (d) five

120 Arrange the following in sequential order to describe complete socialisation.

1. Man to society, man to country
2. Man to relatives, man to friends
3. Man to mankind, man to universe
4. Man to self, man to family

Codes
(a) 3, 1, 2 and 4 (b) 4, 1, 3 and 2
(c) 2, 3, 1 and 4 (d) 4, 2, 1 and 3

121 Arrange the following books in the chronological order in which they appeared.
1. Education and Sociology
2. School and Society
3. Principles of Educational Sociology, an outline
4. Dynamic Sociology

Codes
(a) 4, 2, 1, 3 (b) 1, 3, 4, 2
(c) 3, 2, 4, 1 (d) 2, 1, 3, 4

122 "Your country requires heroes, be heroes, your duty is to go on work and then everything will follow of itself". Who said this statement?
(a) Gandhiji (b) Sri Aurobindo
(c) Swami Vivekananda (d) Tagore

123 "All the power is within you, you can do anything and everything. Believe in that, don't believe that you are weak. Stand up and express the divinity within you". Who said this statement?
(a) Tagore
(b) Swami Vivekananda
(c) Gandhiji
(d) Aurobindo

124 Who said that "The greatest sin is to think yourself weak"?
(a) Swami Vivekananda (b) Tagore
(c) Gandhiji (d) Aurobindo

125 "You must have an iron will, if you want cross the ocean. You must be strong enough to pierce mountains". Who said this?
(a) Tagore (b) Gandhiji
(c) Swami Vivekananda (d) Sri Aurobindo

126 Aim of complete living in education was propounded by
(a) F. Herbert (b) Herbert Spencer
(c) John Dewey (d) Plato

127 "The most important outward factor is the formation of nationalities in the state". To which philosophy do you attribute this statement?
(a) Marxism (b) Capitalism
(c) Fascism (d) Socialism

128 Some sociologists have importance to the functioning factors of social interaction. These factors are concerned with
(a) the proximity and similarity of the societies
(b) the purpose and common facts of societies
(c) the needs and past experiences of the societies
(d) goodness, common cause and economy of the societies

129 "Freedom of choice is the highest value for a person". What does this mean?
(a) If you are not free, you cannot have your choice.
(b) A good life is impossible without independence of thought.
(c) Only free choice is a real choice.
(d) In human life, nothing is greater than man's freedom from all ignorance.

130 Which of the following is the common belief held by Tagore, Gandhiji and Sri Aurobindo?
(a) Self-reliance (b) International harmony
(c) Socialisation of children (d) National character

131 In which of the following layers, were the elements of the knowledge are arranged and re arranged?
(a) Chitta (b) Manas
(c) Intuition (d) Intellect

132 Which among the following is not included in the 'Trinity of the Indian Genius'?
(a) Spirituality (b) Creativity
(c) Intellectuality (d) Comparatively

133 **Statement I** In 1864, Jyotirao and Savitribai started a care centre called Balhaty Pratibhandak Griha.

Statement II Savitribai founded the first girl's school in Pune in Bhide Wada.
(a) Only Statement I is correct
(b) Only Statement II is correct
(c) Both the Statements, I and II are incorrect
(d) Both the Statements, I and II are correct.

Directions (Q. Nos. 134-148) *Given below are two statements, one labelled as Assertion (A) and other labelled as Reason (R). Select the correct code from the following.*

Codes
(a) Both A and R are true and R is the correct explanation of A
(b) Both A and R are true, but R is not the correct explanation of A
(c) A is true, but R is false
(d) A is false, but R is true

134 **Assertion** (A) Purification of the mental and moral habits should be the basis of discipline.

Reason (R) It means to distinguish between right and wrong impression and to absorb the right ones in the mind.

135 **Assertion** (A) The end point of social development is social maturity.

Reason (R) A socially matured person is fully adjusted person in the society.

136 Assertion (A) Swamiji was a rationalist and a man must develop rational attitude in life.
Reason (R) His concept of man, transcends the cultural boundaries of the East and the West.

137 Assertion (A) Perfection is the true aim of education and physical development is an integral part of perfection.
Reason (R) Without physical development, Dharma can be performed.

138 Assertion (A) Tagore pleaded for bringing the child into direct contact with nature.
Reason (R) Such a contact will make the child homely with the real world.

139 Assertion (A) The human race is composed of people or nation and nation is composed of individuals.
Reason (R) The nation makes the universal humanity.

140 Assertion (A) The Brahman is the absolute. It is called Sat Chit Anand.
Reason (R) Pure existence, pure knowledge and pure bliss, merges all houses in one.

141 Assertion (A) Machines had killed all sense of art and hand work.
Reason (R) Gandhiji wanted craft which should have rich educative possibilities.

142 Assertion (A) Tagore is one of the very few educational philosophers, whose philosophy is the outcome of his educational experiments.
Reason (R) Tagore gave a practical shape to his ideology.

143 Assertion (A) Literacy is not the end of education, not even the beginning.
Reason (R) It it the only means, whereby men and women can be educated. Literacy in itself is not education.

144 Assertion (A) Swamiji believed in the unity of all religions.
Reason (R) It leads to the rational development of man.

145 Assertion (A) By teaching craft, Gandhiji objective was to produce craftsmen.
Reason (R) He wanted that the craft should be learnt to serve as a means for intellectual work and economical self-sufficiency.

146 Assertion (A) The educational aims, contents and methods of teaching and infact, the entire process of education must be based on the pillars like secularism, socialism and democracy.
Reason (R) Educational needs of modern India are reflected in the Preamble of our Constitution.

147 Assertion (A) Savirtibai Phule worked actively in abolishing caste and gender based discrimination.
Reason (R) Savitribai started schools for children from Mang and Mahar castes, who were regarded as untouchables.

148 Assertion (A) The first principle of true teaching is that nothing can be taught.
Reason (R) The teacher is not an instructor or task master, he is a helper and a guide.

PREVIOUS YEARS' QUESTIONS

July 2018

1 The ultimate purpose of Gandhi's education is the
(a) creation of a classless society
(b) promotion of human beings
(c) development of a human and awakened society
(d) salvation for all

2 Sri Aurobindo's idea of supermind implies that
(a) Darwinian Theory is relevant, hence education cannot do much
(b) The task of a teacher is to uplift the awakened consciousness of human beings
(c) A teacher has to integrate psychology, biology and education in his/her teaching techniques
(d) Education can achieve its divine purpose through mediation

November 2017

3 Match the following.

List I (Educational Thinkers)	List II (Works)
A. Gandhiji	1. Savitri
B. Tagore	2. Geeta Rahasya
C. Sri Aurobindo	3. Brahma Sutra
D. Vivekananda	4. Practical Vedant
	5 My experiments with Truth
	6. Universal Man

Codes

	A	B	C	D
(a)	5	6	1	4
(b)	5	3	2	1
(c)	6	3	4	2
(d)	2	6	3	4

4 A teacher cannot truely teaches unless he is learning himself, is a viewpoint articulated particularly by

(a) Gandhiji (b) Tagore
(c) Sri Aurobindo (d) Vivekananda

5 The value of liberty in Indian Constitution implies that

(a) a teacher will advocate full liberty and freedom
(b) a teacher should help students to be free from influence of dogmas and fears in life
(c) a teacher can teach anything, even outside the syllabus
(d) a teacher should inspire his students to feel good

6 According to Sri Aurobindo, the human mind

(a) has evolved to its maximum limit
(b) is still in the process of evolution
(c) has evolved to the level of 'Sat-Chit-Anand'
(d) is in need of proper education for evolving

7 The concept of 'Equality of educational opportunity' implies

(a) identical educational opportunity to each and every child, irrespective of differences
(b) everybody to be given his/her due
(c) providing educational facilities to all
(d) education on the basis of ability neutralising negative factors

January 2017

8 Match the following

List I (Thinkers)		List II (Premier Organisations)	
A.	Gandhiji	1.	Rishi Valley School
B.	Tagore	2.	Tolstoy Farm
C.	Aurobindo	3.	Saraswati Vidya Mandir
D.	Vivekananda	4.	Mirambika
		5	Ram Krishna School
		6.	Shri Niketan

Codes

	A	B	C	D
(a)	2	6	4	5
(b)	1	6	3	5
(c)	2	4	3	6
(d)	6	2	4	3

9 Which of the following core content will not confirm to Gandhiji's views?

(a) Language (b) Social studies
(c) Vocational skills (d) Genetic engineering

10 Which of the following constitutional value gets endorsed through reservation policy in education?

(a) Liberty (b) Equality
(c) Fraternity (d) Humanity

11 The main purpose of education should be the integrated development of the person. Who has offered a model in this regard?

(a) Aurobindo (b) Tagore
(c) Gandhiji (d) Vivekananda

12 Which combination of measures in the list given below is likely to ensure social equity and equality of educational opportunity?

1. The education of girl child should be organised separately.
2. Each child should be provided an opportunity to grow, develop and flourish.
3. Education of tribal children should be given priority as against the non-tribals.
4. Curriculum at the school level should be diversified to cater the diverse needs of students.
5. Moral education should form a part of every school curriculum.
6. The multiplicity of methods and approaches should be emphasised in school system.

Codes

(a) 1, 2 and 3 (b) 4, 5 and 2
(c) 2, 4 and 6 (d) 3, 4 and 5

13 Match the following

List I (Disciplines)		List II (Focus of Concerns)	
A.	Politics	1.	Promoting human values
B.	Culture	2.	Encouraging a sense of equity and justice
C.	Democracy	3.	Sustaining power
D.	Religion	4.	Imbibing modes of behaviour and values
		5.	Transforming people

Codes

	A	B	C	D
(a)	2	1	5	3
(b)	1	4	3	2
(c)	5	2	1	4
(d)	3	4	2	1

14 Which one of the following statements appropriately describes the position of Sri Aurobindo?

(a) Life has been evolving to a higher level
(b) Art is long and time is short
(c) Life has a purpose
(d) Man is a divine animal

July 2016

15 Match the following.

List I (Thinkers)	List II (Title of the Books)
A. Gandhiji	1. Geeta Pravachan
B. Tagore	2. Practical Vedanta
C. Aurobindo	3. Geeta Rahasya
D. Vivekananda	4. Savitri
	5 My Experiment with Truth
	6. Universal Man

Codes

	A	B	C	D		A	B	C	D
(a)	5	6	3	2	(b)	6	4	3	1
(c)	1	2	4	6	(d)	5	6	4	2

16 According to Gandhiji, which of the following aims can be achieved through basic education?

1. Ram Rajya
2. Freedom and autonomy
3. Natural justice
4. Sarvodya
5. Equality
6. Democracy

Codes

(a) 1, 2, 3 and 4 (b) 2, 3, 4 and 5
(c) 1, 3, 4 and 5 (d) 2, 3, 4 and 6

17 The phrase, 'equality of educational opportunity' implies

1. giving equal opportunity for educational advancement to all irrespective of differences.
2. the state to provide adequate educational facilities for all children upto certain level.
3. no child should remain educationally unserved owing to poor economic conditions.
4. giving identical educational opportunity to all children irrespective of differences.

Codes

(a) 1, 2 and 4 (b) 1, 2, 3 and 4
(c) 1, 2 and 3 (d) 1, 3 and 4

18 Which of the following is not a characteristic feature of culture?

(a) Culture is social inheritance
(b) Culture is cumulative
(c) Culture is in constant flux
(d) Culture is biological inheritance

19 Which of the following statement does not imply that education is an instrument of cultural diffusion?

(a) Preserves culture through formal and informal ways
(b) Transmits cultural norms, values and ideas to young generation
(c) Preaches cultural norms, values and ideas to younger generation
(d) Interprets culture and perpetuates the social heritage

20 Which of the following is not a basic need of every social system?

(a) Democracy (b) Adaptation
(c) Integration (d) Goal attainment

21 Which one of the following combinations represent Tagore's vision of education?

1. Education is means of attaining self-sufficiency and confidence by man
2. Education can be attained through the study and practice of art, literature, drama and music
3. Nature is a creation of God
4. The nature of man allover the globe is one only

Codes

(a) 1, 2 and 3 (b) 2, 3 and 4
(c) 1, 2 and 4 (d) 1, 2, 3 and 4

December 2015

22 Which of the following thinker(s) does not give priority to modern science and technology in education?

(a) Gandhiji
(b) Tagore
(c) Aurobindo
(d) Vivekananda

23 Sri Aurobindo's concept of supermind implies

1. constant evolution of human mind
2. synthesis of sat, chit and anand
3. realising self through yoga
4. attainment of perfect intuition

Select the correct answer using the codes given below.

Codes

(a) 1, 2 and 4
(b) 1, 2 and 3
(c) 1, 2, 3 and 4
(d) 2, 3 and 4

24 The true value of democratic education as per Indian Constitution lies in

(a) imparting education to all Indians
(b) attaining 100% literacy in India
(c) making all Indians good citizens of tomorrow
(d) modernisation and spiritualisation of all Indians

June 2015

25 Match the following.

List I	List II
A. Gandhiji	1. Integral education
B. Tagore	2. Naturalistic education
C. Aurobindo	3. Negative education
D. Vivekananda	4. Basic education
	5 Man-making education
	6. Instinctive education

Codes

	A	B	C	D
(a)	3	6	2	5
(b)	4	2	3	5
(c)	4	2	1	5
(d)	5	6	1	3

26 **The modern sociologist is more concerned with**

(a) study of the social development of man and institutions
(b) study of the impact of science and Industrial Revolution on social and economical conditions
(c) study of social life of its members
(d) study of the contemporary societies and the current problems

27 **It is well established by thinkers, philosophers and academicians that ideals like 'Social Justice' etc. are to be achieved by education. Here, 'Social Justice' implies**

1. to remove economic unequalities
2. to provide decent standards of living to the people
3. to protect the interest of the weaker sections of society
4. to end inequality of the opportunities

Select the correct answer using the codes given below.

(a) 1 and 4 (b) Only 2
(c) 1, 3 and 4 (d) All of these

December 2014

28 **Gandhi's Philosophy of Education is**

(a) naturalistic in its aims, pragmatic in setting and idealistic in its methods
(b) naturalistic in its methods, idealistic in its setting and pragmatic in its aims
(c) naturalistic in its setting, idealistic in its aims and pragmatic in its methods
(d) realistic in its methods, idealistic in its setting and pragmatic in its aims

June 2014

29 **In socialisation, the teacher should play the role of**

(a) an agent (b) an administrator
(c) a counsellor (d) All of these

30 **'Pedagogy of the Oppressed' is authored by**

(a) Paulo Freire (b) Bertrand Russell
(c) J Krishnamurti (d) John Dewey

31 **The phrase 'equal educational opportunities' in India means**

(a) equal opportunities for all children to have access to higher education
(b) equalities of educational opportunities for each child
(c) equality of the type of education available for each child
(d) equal opportunities to have the type of education for which one is suited

ANSWERS

Exam Based Questions

1	(d)	2	(a)	3	(d)	4	(d)	5	(b)	6	(a)	7	(d)	8	(a)	9	(a)	10	(d)
11	(c)	12	(b)	13	(b)	14	(d)	15	(d)	16	(b)	17	(b)	18	(d)	19	(d)	20	(a)
21	(b)	22	(a)	23	(b)	24	(d)	25	(d)	26	(d)	27	(c)	28	(c)	29	(a)	30	(a)
31	(a)	32	(a)	33	(c)	34	(d)	35	(d)	36	(a)	37	(d)	38	(b)	39	(d)	40	(b)
41	(a)	42	(b)	43	(a)	44	(d)	45	(d)	46	(c)	47	(b)	48	(b)	49	(c)	50	(d)
51	(d)	52	(b)	53	(c)	54	(d)	55	(d)	56	(b)	57	(b)	58	(d)	59	(b)	60	(b)
61	(a)	62	(b)	63	(d)	64	(a)	65	(b)	66	(b)	67	(b)	68	(c)	69	(c)	70	(d)
71	(d)	72	(b)	73	(a)	74	(c)	75	(b)	76	(c)	77	(c)	78	(d)	79	(b)	80	(d)
81	(b)	82	(a)	83	(c)	84	(b)	85	(d)	86	(a)	87	(b)	88	(c)	89	(a)	90	(a)
91	(b)	92	(d)	93	(d)	94	(b)	95	(a)	96	(c)	97	(a)	98	(c)	99	(b)	100	(d)
101	(d)	102	(c)	103	(d)	104	(b)	105	(a)	106	(d)	107	(b)	108	(c)	109	(c)	110	(a)
111	(b)	112	(c)	113	(b)	114	(c)	115	(b)	116	(a)	117	(c)	118	(d)	119	(c)	120	(d)
121	(d)	122	(c)	123	(b)	124	(a)	125	(c)	126	(b)	127	(d)	128	(c)	129	(d)	130	(d)
131	(d)	132	(d)	133	(d)	134	(c)	135	(c)	136	(a)	137	(c)	138	(a)	139	(a)	140	(a)
141	(a)	142	(a)	143	(a)	144	(a)	145	(d)	146	(a)	147	(a)	148	(a)				

Previous Years' Questions

1	(b)	2	(b)	3	(c)	4	(b)	5	(b)	6	(b)	7	(d)	8	(a)	9	(d)	10	(b)
11	(a)	12	(c)	13	(d)	14	(a)	15	(d)	16	(a)	17	(d)	18	(c)	19	(b)	20	(a)
21	(b)	22	(a)	23	(c)	24	(a)	25	(c)	26	(a)	27	(d)	28	(b)	29	(a)	30	(a)
31	(d)																		

CHAPTER 05

Committees and Commissions on Education

With the intention to revamp the educational scenario, the Government of India appointed a good number of committees and commissions, namely Secondary Education Commission, Kothari Commission, Yashpal Committee, National Policy on Education, Justice Verma Committee during the post-independence period.

Educational Committees and Commissions

In India, teacher education has always been recognised as one of the most crucial means of social and national development. A large number of teachers were found untrained and attempt was made to clear the backlog. The main concerns of teacher education were pertaining to both quality and quantity. After independence, efforts were made to tackle the emerging problem of access, quality and relevance of teacher education system in the country. This view has been reflected by several commissions and committees, after independence. The Government of India set up many commissions and committees time to time for addressing different issues of general education as well as teacher education.

After independence, the Government of India appointed the 'University Education Commission' under the chairmanship of Dr. S Radhakrishnan which was known as 'Radhakrishnan Commission.' It submitted its report on University Education in 1949. But, the commission reviewed the position of secondary education in India and gave certain notable suggestions. It remarked that our secondary education in India remains the weakest link in our educational machinery and needs urgent reforms. Thus to solve this problem, Government of India in 1952 appointed the Secondary Education Commission under the chairmanship of AL Mudaliar.

In this Chapter

Secondary Education Commission (1953)

The Secondary Education Commission was appointed by the Government of India in terms of their resolution number F-9-5/52B-1 dated 23rd September, 1952.

The Secondary Education Commission (1952-53) had a far reaching effect on India's secondary education. The Government of India setup the Secondary Education Commission, under the Chairmanship of **Dr. A Lakshmanaswami Mudaliar,** the Vice-Chancellor of Madras University. So, this commission is also known as **Mudaliar's Commission**.

It prepared a questionnaire dealing with the various aspects of secondary education. This was sent out to various educational experts, teachers and educational institutions of India. On the basis of their replies, some important informations were collected. The members of the commission took an extensive tour of the various parts of India and acquired first-hand knowledge of the various educational problems and presented its report in August, 1953.

Aims of Secondary Education Commission

The commission has suggested the aims of secondary education in the following ways

To Produce Ideal Citizens The commission realised that no nation can progress without a national feeling along with social feeling. Thus, the aim of secondary education should be to produce such ideal citizens, who are responsible citizens and can easily offer any sacrifice for the sake of their motherland.

To Develop Capacity for Earning Money After receiving secondary education, one should be able to earn enough for maintaining himself. For developing the capacity, vocational subjects should be introduced.

Quality of Leadership Secondary education should develop the quality of leadership in students which is very necessary for the overall development of the country.

To Develop Human Virtues Being social animal, man should have the spirit of cooperation, discipline, love, kindness, feeling of brotherhood, etc. The curriculum of secondary education must include science, literature, fine arts, humanities, music and dance, through which students can gain these virtues.

Important Recommendations

The commission has suggested the following recommendations

- Secondary education should be for children of 11 to 17 years.
- It suggested to end intermediate college and merge class 11th with secondary schools and class 12th with B.A.
- Multi-purpose schools should be established to take care of various abilities of students.
- Degree course should be of three years.
- One year Pre-University course for high school students, to enter in university.
- Students who passed Pre-University course should be allowed to enter in professional courses.
- Vocational or practical courses should be introduced.
- Technical institutions should be opened near factories so that students can take practical training.

*Recommendations regarding **teacher education** are as follows :*

- There should be two years course for non-graduates and one year training course for graduates.
- The teachers should be trained in one or two extra-curricular activities also.
- The commission also stressed on the importance of refresher courses, short-term intensive courses and specialised courses, workshops, conferences for in-service teacher.
- Training colleges should conduct research work.
- Special part-time courses were recommended for untrained teachers.
- Trained graduates with at least three years teaching experience should be admitted to M.Ed course.
- There should be only two types of institutions for teacher training.
- Training colleges should organise refresher courses, start intensive courses in special subjects, practical training in workshops.
- Teacher trainees should receive training in one or more of various extra-curricular activities.
- During the period of training, all student teachers should be given suitable stipend by the state and no fees should be charged in training colleges.
- The training institutions should advocate methods and training that are practicable and realistic.

A L Mudaliar

Sir Arcot Lakshmanswami Mudaliar was an Indian educationist and physician with notable international and academic roles. He was the longest serving vice-chancellor of University of Madras for 27 years. He was elected as a chairman of **WHO** executive board in 1949 and 1950. He was awarded with **Padma Bhushan** in 1954 and **Padma Vibhushan** in 1963.

Kothari Education Commission (1964-66)

National Education Commission (1964-66), popularly known as **Kothari Commission** was formed in July, 1964, under the chairmanship of **Daulat Singh Kothari**. It pointed out major weakness in the existing system of professional education in India.

The commission pointed out the following deficiencies in India's education system

- Standards of teacher education were poor and mediocre.
- The teacher education was isolated from the main stream academic life.
- Training colleges lacked competent staffs.
- Teacher training in India was very traditional *i.e.* set patterns and rigid techniques were followed in practice teaching.

Important Recommendations

Visualising such weakness in teacher training programmes, the commission made many recommendations. They are :

- Removing isolation of teacher training from the main academic life.
- Expansion of teacher training facilities.
- Making adequate provision for continuing professional education of all teachers.
- Creating appropriate agencies for the maintenance of standards, both of the centres and the states.
- Education should be treated as independent academic discipline and should be introduced as an optional subject at B A and M A levels.
- Schools of education should be started in the universities.
- Integrated courses of general and professional education should be introduced, so that teacher prospects are not narrowed.
- Along with practice teaching, there should be internship programme also as it exposes the teacher to all such environment, which a person faces when he is an actual teacher.
- Increasing the number of working days.
- Abolishing fees, give scholarships and loans to student teacher.
- Demonstration school should be established, so that pupil-teacher can get an opportunity to work as a teacher, what is taught them in training colleges.
- To organise special courses for graduates, entering in primary teaching.
- To improve the quality of teacher training institutions.
- To establish a State Board of Teacher Education that should be responsible for all functions related to teacher education at all levels and in all fields.

Kothari Commission, the fourth education commission in the independent India recommended many changes, of which most of them were implemented.

As a result of this recommendation, four years courses were started at different Regional Institutes of Education in 1963. These RIEs were set up in different parts of India covering various regions.

Regional Institute of Education (RIE)

- It was earlier known as **Regional College of Education.**
- It is a constitutional unit of **NCERT.**
- RIEs were set-up in 1963 by Government of India in different regions of India.
- At present, RIEs are situated in Ajmer, Bhopal, Bhubaneshwar, Mysore and Shillong.
- The regional institutes were started with the objectives of qualitative improvement of school education through innovative pre-service and in-service teacher education programmes.
- RIEs run four years integrated course like B.Sc B.Ed, B.A. B.Ed.

National Policy of Education (1986)

In the post-independence period, reconstruction of educational system was the major concern of the Government of India. The National Policy of Education (NPE) is a policy formulated by the Government of India to promote education among Indians, both in urban and rural area. Based on the report and recommendations of the Kothari Commission, the Government of India announced the National Policy of Education. The **first** NPE was promoted by **Indira Gandhi** in **1968** and the **second** by **Rajiv Gandhi** in **1986**.

The new National Policy of Education called for "special emphasis on the removal of disparities and to equalise educational opportunity" especially for Indian women, Scheduled Tribes (STs) and Scheduled Castes (SCs) communities. The National Policy of Education (NPE) was adopted by Parliament in May, 1986.

NPE, 1986 recommended a **National System of Education**. The concept of national system of education implies that upto a given level, all students, irrespective of caste, creed, location or sex have access to education of a comparable quality. To achieve this, government will initiate appropriately funded programmes.

Effective measures have been taken in the direction of the common school system recommended in the 1968 policy. The Curricular Framework of NSE promotes values such as India's common culture heritage, democracy, equality of the sexes, protection of the environment, removal of social barriers and inculcation of the scientific temper.

All educational programmes will be carried on in strict conformity with secular values. Minimum level of learning will be laid down for each stage of education. Steps will also be taken to foster among students an understanding of the diverse culture and social systems of the people living in different parts of the country. In higher education, in general and technical education, in particular steps will be taken to facilitate inter-regional mobility by providing equal access to every Indian of requisite merit, regardless of his origins.

Opportunities will be provided to the youth, housewives, agricultural and industrial workers and professionals to continue the education of their choice at the pace suited to them. The future thrust will be in the direction of open and distance learning.

The institutions which will be strengthened to play an important role in giving shape to the National System of Education are the University Grants Commission (UGC), All India Council of Technical Education (AICTE), Indian Council of Agricultural Research (ICAR) and the Indian Medical Council (IMC).

It also recommended that these together with the National Council of Education Research and Training (NCERT) and the National Institute of Educational Planning and Administration (NIEPA), the National Council of Teachers Education (NCTE) and the National Institute of Adult Education (NIAE) will be involved in implementing the educational policy.

Important Recommendations

Recommendations regarding teacher education are as follows :

- Orientation of teachers should be a continuous process of teacher education.
- To upgrade selected secondary teacher training institutions.
- Emphasising inseparability to pre-service and in-service components of teacher education.
- To establish District Institutes of Education and Training (DIET) with the capability to organise pre-service and in-service courses for elementary school teachers and for the personnel working in non-formal and adult education sectors.
- To establish, the National Council for Teacher Education (NCTE) at the national level, which will have the power to accredit institutions of teacher education, provide guidance regarding curriculum and methods.
- Upgrading of selected teacher training colleges to complement the work of SCERT.
- Networking arrangements should be created between institutions of teacher education and university departments of education.

Acharya Ramamurti Committee was appointed by the Government of India in **1990**, reviewed the National Policy of Education (1986).

The major suggestions regarding teacher education are

- The first degree course on teacher education should not be given on correspondence mode.
- More institutions should be encouraged to introduce four years integrated courses in the pattern of Regional Colleges of Education.

Pioneer Institutions of Education in India

- **NCERT** It was established by Government of India in 1961 to advise and assist the central and state government on academic matters related to school education. It's important functions are implementation of National Curriculum Framework (NCF), vocational education and development of teaching-learning material.
- **NCTE** It was setup by Government of India under the NCTE Act, 1993 in 1995. It was established to oversee standards, procedures and processes in the Indian education system. Before this, it had existed since 1973, as a government advisory body to look after the development and progress of teacher education.
- **NUEPA** National University of Educational Planning and Administration was established by Government of India for research and development in education. Like any Central University, NUEPA is fully maintained by the Government of India. It offers M Phil, Phd and part-time P.hd programmes in educational policy, planning and administration from a broader **inter-disciplinary** social science perspectives.

Key Highlights of NPE (1986)

- Expand scholarships to all category.
- Promote adult education all over India.
- Employing more teachers from the SCs and STs communities.
- Provide incentives for poor families to send their children to school regularly.
- Develop the new institutions for all.
- Provide housing and services facilities.
- For primary education, the NPE called for a 'Child-Centered approach', and 'Operation Blackboard' was launched to expand primary schools nationwide.
- Under this policy, the Open University system was expanded with the Indira Gandhi National Open University (1985).
- The policy was also recognised as 'Rural University Model', based on the philosophy of 'Mahatma Gandhi'. It encourages economical and social development at the grassroot levels in rural India.

The National Policy of Education (1986) was modified in 1992. This new policy was based on the 'Common Minimum Programme' of the government. According to this policy, common national level tests were introduced. This helps in maintenance of professional standards. This solves problems of overlaps and reduces physical, mental and financial burden on students and their parents due to multiplicity of entrance examination.

National Policy of Education (1992)

The National Policy of Education (NPE) was adopted by Parliament in May, 1986. A committee was set up under the chairmanship of **Acharya Ramamurti** in May, 1990 to review NPE and to make recommendations for its modifications. That Committee submitted its report in December, 1990.

At the request of the Central Advisory Board of Education (CABE), a committee was set up in July, 1991, under the chairmanship of **Shri N. Janardhana Reddy**, chief minister of Andhra Pradesh, to consider modifications in NPE, taking into consideration the report of the Rammurti Committee and other relevant developments having a bearing on the policy and to make recommednations regarding modifications to be made in the NPE, 1986. The committee submitted its report in 1992.

Key Highlights of NPE (1992)

The following modifications have been suggested by the committee

- Making availability of non-formal education for the girl child especially from the age group of 15-35 years.
- Special provisions were made for the students from weaker sections like SCs, STs, OBCs and minorities in the form of mid-day-meal, stationary, books and free education.
- Efforts were made for the backward minorities for giving them hostel facilities, polytechnic education, coaching and removal of difficulties coming in the way of education.
- Provisions for the NGO were made to come forward in this sector for opening new special schools and give students vocational training.
- Efforts were made to make them self-dependent by imparting education through National Literacy Mission.
- Relating to Early Childhood Care and Education, provisions were made for establishing the **Anganwadis** and **Balwadis**.
- Relating to elementary education, provisions of schools were made for low density areas. Minimum numbers of teachers were suggested for the school as per the enrollment of the school.
- Provisions were made for the improvement of quality education with the enhancement of Secondary School Education till +2 level.
- Emphasizing quality enhancement in **Navodaya Vidyalaya** schools and setting a role model for all other schools.
- Provisions were made in vocational education to meet the requirements of industry and employment.
- In higher education, provisions were made for self-financed universities.
- Provision was made to open at least one Open University in each state and IGNOU had to give technical assistance and Distance Education Council to regulate them.
- Provision was made to delink job with degree. More focus was given to attain skill and competencies for youth.
- Provision was made to open rural universities and institutes. It was suggested to provide technical and financial support to the NGOs and government institutions.
- Suggestions were made to establish All India Council of Technical Education (AICTE).
- Establishing culture bond was also emphasized in education from the regional to national level and from national level to global level.
- Research must not be confined to just obtaining the degree but its result must influence the society too.
- For development of languages, three language formula was promoted and it was recommended to develop Hindi as the national language.
- To include the media, radio, computers and new technologies as a part of education process.
- Emphasis was laid on sports and other physical activities.
- Suggestions were given to motivate students to participate in the NCC and NSS.
- Recommendation was made to attain minimum level of learning in each subject making evaluation process more flexible, and avoid unfair means in the evaluation process.
- To give constitutional status to NCTE, to establish DIETs, CTEs, and IASEs.
- To decentralize education and to allow the NGOs to participate in this sector.

National Commission on Teachers (1983-85)

According to National Policy Statement on Education (1968), of all the factors which determine the quality of education, teacher is undoubtedly the most important. Their salary and other service condition should be satisfactory with respect to their qualifications and responsibilities.

This commission was appointed by Government of India in 1983, under the Chairmanship of Prof. D P Chattopadhyaya; made a number of recommendations for the improvement of educational process. Regarding the selection of trainees for the teaching profession, *the commission suggested that the following factors may be taken into consideration:*

- Good physique.
- Linguistic ability and communication skills.
- A fair degree of mental ability.
- General awareness of the world.
- A positive outlook on life and capacity of good human relations.

The commission further recommended that the selection of trainees should be made through a combination of objective tests, rating scales, group discussion and personal interviews. *The commission also suggested the professional preparation with:*

- Study of education as a discipline including educational psychology, sociology of education and educational philosophy.
- Practice teaching and its content-cum-methodology.
- Learning a variety of skills related to the role of a teacher; including educational technology and preparation of software.

National Curriculum Framework (2005)

This is one of the important National Curriculum Framework prepared and developed by the National Council of Educational Research and Training (NCERT) in India. Other National Curriculum Frameworks were published in 1975, 1988 and 2000. The Framework (2005) gives suggestions about the changing syllabii, textbooks and teaching practices within the school education programmes in India. It has made the suggestion on the basis of earlier government's report on education as learning without burden, National Policy of Education (1986-1992) and different group discussions that took place. The main aim of NCF is to bring about reforms in the education system by introducing a curriculum that is learner centric, has a flexible process and making teacher's role as a facilitator who supports and encourages the students.

Objectives of NCF

- Connecting knowledge to life, outside the school.
- Shifting learning from rote learning.
- Enriching the curriculum so that it goes beyond text books.
- Making examinations more flexible and integrated into life.
- Nurturing an over-riding identity informed by caring concerns within democratic polity of the country.

The main focus of NCF are :

- Ensuring that irrespective of caste, creed, religion and sex, all are provided with a standard curriculum.
- Making learning a joyful experience without stress, it recommends major changes in the design of syllabus.
- Ensuring quality education for all children.
- Reducing the curriculum load based on insights provided in 'learning without burden'.
- Developing a sense of self-reliance and dignity of the individual which would develop a sense of non-violence and oneness across the society.
- Developing a Child Centered Approach which would promote universal enrollment.
- Promoting national identity among students which would help to re-evaluate the new generation.
- Building commitment to democratic values of equality, justice, secularism and freedom.

The draft of NCF was translated into 22 languages listed in the VIII Schedule of the Constitution. The NCF was approved by Central Advisory Board on Education in September, 2005.

Thus, the NCF (2005), seeks to provide a framework within which teachers and school can choose and plan experiences that they think the children should have. It addresses four issues such as educational purpose, educational experience, an organisation of experience and assessing learner. NCF differs from curriculum and syllabus. It provides guidelines on different aspects of education. Earlier NCFs were based on Behaviourist Psychology but NCF (2005) is based on Constructivist Theory.

National Knowledge Commission (2007)

The National Knowledge Commission (NKC) was constituted on 13th June, 2005 by the Prime Minister of India, Dr. Manmohan Singh. The commission introduced policy related to education, research institutes and reforms that made India competitive in the field of education. **Sam Pitroda** was the chairman. Other prominent members were Dr. Ashok Sekhar Ganguly, Nandan Nilkeni, Dr. Deepak Nayyar, Dr. Jayati Ghosh, etc. In 2014, it was discontinued by the BJP government.

The vision of the National Knowledge Commission (NKC) was constituted as an advisory body to the Prime Minister. It helped to restructure knowledge related institutions and infrastructure to meet the challenges of the 21st century.

Aims of NKC

- To promote knowledge applications in agriculture and industry.
- To build excellence in the educational system.
- To improve the management of institutions engaged in intellectual property rights.
- To promote the use of knowledge capabilities in making government an effective, transport and accountable service provider.
- To promote creation of knowledge in Science & Technology laboratories.

Important Recommendations

Recommendations submitted in 2007 by NKC are

Heath Information Network It recommended that extensive use of IT in health care will promote the delivery of efficient health care in the country. India needs to develop a web-based network connecting all health care establishment in both private and public sector. This will help in improving public health planning, medical education, cost control, medical research, drug development, prevention of fraud, disaster management and improved patient care.

Portals The NKC recommended the creation of web portals to aggregate, organise and present relevant and useful content in local languages, in a highly uniform, customisable, user friendly and personalised way for serveral key areas related to basic human needs. The portals should be translated into all Indian languages to reach a wider audience. Interactive applications and e-learning content must be made available in local languages.

Legal Education The NKC recognises legal education as an important constituent of professional education. The vision of legal education is to provide justice-oriented education essential to the realisation of values enshrined in the Constitution of India. The NKC constituted a working group of experts, to suggest necessary measures to improve the quality of education in India.

Medical Education The quality, the quantity distribution and availability of human resources for the health sector in India at present, need to be improved substantially to deliver care-driven, rural oriented and equitable health services. Thus, the NKC considered it imperative to carry out a comprehensive appraisal of the system and took the important steps.

Management Education Management education has seen phenomenal growth in the last decade in our country. The NKC constituted a working group of experts from academia and industry and proposed some rules like, new regulatory framework, grading the institutions, faculty development, introduction of non-traditional management education, etc.

Apart from these, the NKC also took important initiatives in the field of open and distance education, intellectual property rights, legal framework for public funded research and traditional health system.

Yashpal Committee Report (2009)

The Yashpal Committee was chaired by **Prof. Yashpal** and other eminent scholars gave suggestions on 'Renovation and Rejuvenation of Higher Education'. They help the authorities to improve the quality of higher education and to rectify the defects that has crept into the system.

Objectives of Yashpal Committee Report

- All universities must be teaching cum research universities. All research bodies must connect with universities in their vicinity and create teaching opportunities for their researchers.
- We must prevent isolation of study of engineering or management. We should look forward to the day when IITs and IIMs also produce scholars in areas like literature, linguistics and politics. Institutions must be given the freedom to expand and diversify as they see fit rather than thrusting a uniform diktat on all institutions.
- All syllabi should require teachers and students to apply what they have learnt in their courses, on studying a local situation, issue or problem. There should be sufficient room for the use of local data and resources to make the knowledge covered in the syllabus come alive as experience.

- Minimum set of occupational exposure to be made compulsory for all students, irrespective of discipline, in the form of summer jobs or internships, with evaluation of the students on this front.
- Need to expose students at the undergraduate level to various disciplines like humanities, social sciences, aesthetics, irrespective of the discipline they would like to specialise in subsequently.
- Teacher training for all levels of school education (from primary to higher secondary) must be carried out by institutions of higher education. The absence of university-level interest in teacher training has resulted in poor academic quality.
- We need to build strong bridges between different fields of professional education and the disciplines of science, social sciences and humanities. All professional institutions must be a part of a comprehensive university in a complete administrative and academic sense. We must abolish intermediary bodies that have been set up solely to issue licenses to professional colleges alone and inspect them. This will also help new inter-disciplinary courses and research to evolve in the comprehensive universities.
- All vocational institutions must also be a part of universities.
- It should be mandatory for all universities to have undergraduate programmes. All teachers in universities must teach at the undergraduate level.
- Universities must take steps to reduce gender, class and caste asymmetries.

Important Recommendations

- Universities to be self-regulatory bodies to be assisted by hassle-free and transparent regulatory processes.
- Universities to be made responsible regarding the academic content of professional courses.
- Creation of an all encompassing commission for higher education, a central statutory body to replace the existing regulatory bodies including the UGC, AICTE, NCTE, etc.
- Institutions of excellence like the IITs and IIMs to be converted into full-fledged universities, while keeping intact their unique features, which shall act as pace-setting and model governance systems for all universities.
- Undergraduate programmes to be restructured to enable students to have opportunities to access all curricular areas with fair degree of mobility.
- All universities to have the full range of knowledge areas. No single discipline or specialised university to be created.

National Curriculum Framework for Teacher Education (2009)

After independence, number of commissions and committees have focused on curricular content along with the role of teacher and their education programmes.

The National Curriculum Framework for Teacher Education, 2009 was developed by an expert committee comprising of eminent scholars, teacher educators, teachers, representatives of NGOs, faculty of RIEs, NCERT, SCERTs, DIETs, IASEs, CTEs, University departments of education, state departments of education, etc. Two previous significant developments particularly, NCF (2005) and the Right of Children to Free and Compulsory Education Act, 2009 as well as the fundamental tenets enshrined in the Constitution of India have guided the development of this framework.

Main Features of National Curriculum Framework

The National Curriculum Framework for Teacher Education (NCFTE, 2009) elaborates the context, concerns and vision underscoring that teacher education and school education have a symbiotic relationship and developments in both these sectors mutually reinforce the concerns necessary for qualitative improvements of the entire spectrum of education including teacher education as well. The new concerns of school curriculum and the expected transactional modalities have been emphasized in designing this framework for all stages of school education. Issues related to inclusive education, perspectives for equitable and sustainable development, gender perspectives, role of community knowledge in education and ICT in schooling as well as e-learning become the centre-stage in the framework.

- NCFTE acknowledges the diversity of learning spaces and curriculum sites, apart from the classroom. It also trusted that pedagogical knowledge has to constantly undergo adaptation to meet the need of diverse context through critical reflection by the teacher of individuals' practices.
- Teacher education is a long and continuous process in which pre-service, in-service and continuing professional development of the teachers are the in separatable part.
- Shifting towards the use of critical pedagogy was suggested.
- Suggestions were made to integrate theory and practice in the subjects in curriculum.

- In the process of education and training observation, story-telling, analysis critical enquiry, self-learning, reflection on practices, linking practices to concepts, etc, are highlighted.
- Need for enhancing language competence and communication skill is also felt.
- Emphasis has been given on teacher as a reflective practitioner.
- Both qualitative and quantitative evaluation and measurement procedures are highlighted.
- Modern teaching approaches such as constructivism, comprehensive learning, contextual pedagogy and ICT integration need to be highlighted.

The Education Commission says, "the destiny of India is not being shaped in its classrooms". Teachers can play their role significantly if they are properly prepared or trained, The National Curriculum Framework for Teacher Education (2009) was made to achieve this goal properly.

Justice Verma Committee Report (2012)

Education is the basic tool for development of consciousness and reconstruction of society. Teacher is the medium to achieve this goal. Hence, the quality of teacher education to provide quality teachers is an important component for the success of this programme. The National Council of Teacher Education (NCTE) setup a Teacher Education Assessment Committee under Justice J S Verma. This committee proposed that NCTE should setup a national level academic body by the name of National Institute for Policy and Research in Teacher Education (NIPRTE).

Functions of NIPRTE

- Continual reflection and analysis of teacher education programmes.
- Continual reflection and analysis of norms and standards.
- Development of reading material.
- Faculty development of teacher educators.

Objectives of NIPRTE

- To examine and review norms, guidelines and standards laid down by the NCTE for Teacher Education Programmes for all levels (including ECCE) and recognition of institutions, and to provide appropriate feedback to the NCTE periodically.
- To undertake surveys and studies/research relating to various aspects of teacher education at all levels.
- To function as an institutional platform for ensuring coordination and collaboration amongst all stakeholders in teacher education. This institutional platform shall advise on policy and academic decisions on standards, procedures and quality parameters and shall review the implementation of such decisions.
- To design a framework for the accreditation of teacher education institutions is to undertake the process of accreditation.
- To review curricula of existing teacher education programmes and design Model Curriculum/ Curricular Framework for them including ECCE. The duration of Bachelor of Education (B.Ed) programme has been raised to two years.
- To prepare a comprehensive framework of accreditation of teacher education institutions and to undertake process of accreditation through outsourcing or using its own resources.
- To evolve academic accountability norms to be applied on all the institutions of teacher education of all levels including ECCE.
- To develop, collate, translate and disseminate reading material and other material (audio and visual) and academically and financially support institutions of teacher education.
- To conduct short-term (3-5 days) orientation programmes for individuals who get empanelled to serve as 'inspectors' in order to carry out the work of giving recognition and recommending upgradation of the institutions.
- To encourage research by Indian scholars on teacher education in other countries, especially, countries with which India's links have not been fully explored namely, Europe (Germany, France, Scandinavia,) East Asia (Japan, China), SAARC countries, countries of the Commonwealth and the CIS.

EXAM BASED QUESTIONS

1 What is the ideal role played by a teacher?
(a) He should play the role of a leader inside and outside the classroom.
(b) He should initiate action for the transformation of the society as an agent of social change.
(c) He should help in achieving the goal of national development.
(d) All of the above

2 Who was the first chairman of 'University Education Commission'?
(a) Dr. S Radhakrishnan
(b) Jawaharlal Nehru
(c) Maulana Abul Kalam Azad
(d) None of the above

3 Secondary Education Commission was started in
(a) 1950 (b) 1952 (c) 1953 (d) 1955

4 Name the first chairman of the Secondary Education Commission.
(a) JC Verma (b) BN Kashyap
(c) AL Mudaliar (d) None of these

5 The aim of secondary education suggested by the Secondary Education Commission is
(a) to produce ideal citizens
(b) to develop capacity for earning money
(c) to develop quality of leadership and human virtues
(d) All of the above

6 Secondary education should be for children of
(a) 10 to 16 years (b) 11 to 17 years
(c) 4 to 15 years (d) 5 to 18 years

7 Sir AL Mudaliar was the longest serving Vice Chancellor of University of
(a) Calcutta (b) Madras (c) Bombay (d) Lucknow

8 Which of the fact(s) is/are correct for AL Mudaliar?
(a) He was an educationist and physician with notable international and academic roles.
(b) He was the longest serving Vice Chancellor of University of Madras.
(c) He elected as chairman of WHO Executive Board twice.
(d) All of the above

9 Technical institutions should be opened near factories so that
(a) students can take practical training
(b) instructors are easily available
(c) other facilities are easily availed
(d) None of the above

10 National Education Commission is popularly known as
(a) Kothari Commission (b) Ganguly Commission
(c) Verma Commission (d) None of these

11 Kothari Commission was formed in
(a) 1960 (b) 1962 (c) 1964 (d) 1965

12 Who was the first chairman of Kothari Commission?
(a) Daulat Singh Kothari (b) Uday Singh Kothari
(c) Sanjay Singh Kothari (d) Brij Bhushan Kothari

13 **Statement I** Kothari Commission pointed out major weakness in the existing system of professional education in India.
Statement II Tranining colleges have sufficient staff.
Which of the above statement is true?
(a) Only I (b) Only II
(c) Both I and II (d) None of these

14 Regional Institutes of Education were set up in .... by Government of India.
(a) 1963 (b) 1964 (c) 1965 (d) 1966

15 The first two National Policy on Education (NPE) was formulated in
(a) 1968 and 1986 (b) 1968 and 1985
(c) 1960 and 1965 (d) 1966 and 1990

16 In 1986, a National System of Education was recommended by
(a) National Policy on Education (NPE)
(b) Kothari Commission
(c) National Knowledge Commission
(d) None of the above

17 Effective measures have taken in the direction of common school system in 1968 recommended by
(a) National Policy on Education
(b) National Knowledge Commission
(c) Kothari Commission
(d) None of the above

18 NCERT was established by Government of India in
(a) 1960 (b) 1961 (c) 1962 (d) 1965

19 The important function(s) of NCERT is /are
(a) Implementation of National Curriculum Framework (NCF)
(b) Vocational education
(c) Development of teaching-learning material
(d) All of the above

20 Indira Gandhi National Open University was started in
(a) 1980 (b) 1982 (c) 1989 (d) 1985

21 Rural University Model was based on the philosophy of
(a) Dr. S Radhakrishnan (b) Rabindranath Tagore
(c) Mahatma Gandhi (d) None of these

22 The minimum qualification for a teacher educator is
(a) graduate with honours
(b) post graduate
(c) post graduate with B.Ed degree
(d) None of the above

23 The main responsibility of National Council of Teacher Education is
(a) to coordinate and monitor teacher education and its development in the country.
(b) to understand survey's and studies relating to various aspects of teacher education and publish the result.
(c) to take all necessary steps to prevent commercialisation of teacher education.
(d) All of the above

24 The phrase 'the practice teaching of the teacher' should be replaced by the word
(a) Internship (b) Course-time
(c) Practical Knowledge (d) None of these

25 The National Curriculum Framework, 2005 gives suggestion about
(a) the changing syllabii.
(b) textbooks of particular classes.
(c) teaching practices within school education programmes
(d) All of the above

26 The main aim(s) of National Curriculum Framework is / are
(a) to bring about reforms in the education system
(b) to introduce learner centric curriculum
(c) to make teacher's role as a facilitator
(d) All of the above

27 The main objective(s) of National Curriculum Framework is/are
(a) connecting knowledge to life outside the school.
(b) shifting learning from rote learning.
(c) enriching curriculum so that it goes beyond text books
(d) All of the above

28 The National Knowledge Commission (NKC) was constituted in
(a) 2000 (b) 2002 (c) 2004 (d) 2005

29 Who was the chairman of the National Knowledge Commission (2007)?
(a) Sam Pitroda (b) Dr. Ashok Sekhar Ganguly
(c) Dr. Deepak Nayyar (d) None of the above

30 The main aim(s) of National Knowledge Commission (2007) is/are to
(a) promote knowledge applications in agriculture and industry.
(b) build excellence in the education system.
(c) improve the management of institutions engaged in intellectual property rights.
(d) All of the above

31 India needs to develop a web-based network connecting all health care establishment in
(a) private sector
(b) public sector
(c) government specialised hospitals
(d) Both a and b

32 Renovation and rejuvenation of higher education is the main objective of
(a) Yashpal Committee Report
(b) Justice Verma Committee Report
(c) Kothari Education Commission Report
(d) None of the above

33 "Institutions must be given the freedom to expand the diversity as they see fit rather than thrusting a uniform diktat on all institutions". In which committee report this was emphasised by the experts?
(a) Justice Verma Committee Report
(b) Kothari Education Commission Report
(c) Yashpal Committee Report
(d) None of the above

34 The National Curriculum Framework for teacher education was started in
(a) 2010 (b) 2008 (c) 2009 (d) 2007

35 Basic features of National Curriculum Framework consist of
(a) social and personal needs of children
(b) emerging needs of the school
(c) the Integrated and Inter-disciplinary Approach
(d) All of the above

36 Why flexibility of education in our education system becomes necessary?
(a) Advancement of knowledge in science and technology
(b) Changing socio-economic conditions of our country
(c) Both (a) and (b)
(d) None of the above

37 NCTE was established by an Act of Parliament in
(a) 1995 (b) 1975 (c) 1986 (d) 1996

38 National Institute for Policy and Research in Teacher Education (NIPRTE) was set up by
(a) NCTE (b) NCERT
(c) UGC (d) None of these

39 Main function(s) of the NIPRTE would be
(a) Continual reflection and analysis of teacher education programmes.
(b) Continual reflection and analysis of norms and standards.
(c) Faculty development of teacher educators.
(d) All of the above

40 Which of the following commission(s) first decentralised the primary education?
(a) Hunter Commission
(b) Mudaliar Commission
(c) Kothari Commission
(d) Sadlar Commission

41 The policy recommended by the Kothari Commission, vis-a-vis language is
(a) three language formula (b) two language formula
(c) Hindi (d) mother tongue

42 The first National Policy of Education in free India was launched in the year
(a) 1947 (b) 1964 (c) 1968 (d) 1986

43 **The title of the Report of Education Commission (1964-66) is**
(a) learning without burden
(b) an enlightened and human society
(c) education and the people of India
(d) education and national development

44 **The first committee to be constituted after independence by the Government of India on women's education was**
(a) Dr. Radhakrishnan Commission
(b) Mudaliar Commission
(c) Shri Prakasha Committee
(d) Dr. Durga Bhai Deshmukh Committee

45 **National Curriculum Framework for Teacher Education in India (2009) was developed by (2014)**
(a) NCERT (b) NUEPA (c) NCTE (d) NAAC

46 **The purpose of establishing the NCTE is to**
(a) universalisation of education
(b) to improve the quality of teacher education
(c) empowerment of teachers in India
(d) to encourage educational research

47 **Vocationalisation of education in India was first recommended by**
(a) Dr. Radhakrishnan Commission
(b) Mudaliar Commission
(c) Kothari Commission
(d) New Education Policy

48 **The duration of Bachelor of Education (B.Ed) programmme of the country has been raised to two years w.e.f. 2015-16 academic session on the basis of the recommendation of**
(a) Kothari Commission, 1964-66
(b) Justice Verma Commission, 2012
(c) National Curriculum Framework, 2005
(d) Right to Education Act, 2009

49 **A review of NPE (1986), Programme of Action (POA) was done by**
(a) National Commission for Teachers
(b) Yashpal Committee
(c) Rama Murti Committee
(d) Hansa Mehta Committee

50 **In helping students to make educational plans, it is unwise for them to**
(a) mix general with vocational subjects
(b) select all their subjects from one field
(c) take typing with college preparatory subjects
(d) plan their programmes more than a year ahead

51 **Three domains of a child's personality which teacher of contemporary society should be able to tackle are**
(a) affective, cognitive and psychomotor domain
(b) working dynamics, thinking and emotions
(c) personality traits
(d) affective domain only

52 **Which of the following agency regulates education?**
(a) Church (b) State (c) School (d) Library

53 **Which of the following is/are the part of teachers' education process?**
1. Initial teacher education stage
2. Induction stage
3. Continuous professional development stage
4. Deductive stage

Select the correct answer using the codes given below.
(a) 1, 2 and 3 (b) 3, 2 and 4 (c) 1, 3 and 4 (d) 1, 2 and 4

54 **Teaching is a profession that is branded as the**
(a) resort of even the last competent persons
(b) most peaceful job
(c) most challenging job
(d) most lucrative job because of the scope for private tution

55 **A teacher should play the role of a**
(a) leader (b) authority (c) philosopher (d) facilitator

56 **Which of the following skills are needed for present day teacher to adjust properly with the classroom teaching?**
1. Knowledge of technology
2. Use of technology in teaching-learning
3. Knowledge of student's needs
4. Content mastery

Select the correct answer using the codes given below.
(a) 1 and 3 (b) 2 and 3 (c) 2, 3 and 4 (d) 2 and 4

57 **DPEP was started in**
(a) 1990 (b) 1994 (c) 1998 (d) 1996

58 **Education falls under the**
(a) Concurrent List (b) Fundamental Rights
(c) Constitution of India (d) State List

59 **The 'Indian Education Commission' is name of**
(a) The Hunter Commission (b) Wood's Despatch
(c) Dellar's Report (d) Education Commission

60 **The most important challenge for teacher is**
(a) to maintain discipline in the classroom
(b) to make students to do their homework
(c) to prepare the question bank
(d) to make teaching process enjoyable

61 **Which one of the following qualities of a teacher will be liked most by you?**
(a) Idealistic philosophy (b) Compassion
(c) Discipline (d) Entertaining

62 **The principle's function of the NCERT is an extension work with the state education departments centering around the improvement of**
(a) higher education (b) school education
(c) secondary education (d) technical education

63 **The fundamental national values have been given in**
(a) Preamble of our Constitution
(b) Articles of our Constitution
(c) Enteries of the lists of subjects
(d) All of the above

64 The National Policy on Teacher Education (1968) adopted by the Indian Government laid stress on which of following aspects of teacher education?
(a) Adequate emoluments and academic freedom for teachers
(b) Travel allowance and family passion for teachers
(c) In-service training and correspondence education for teachers
(d) Promotion and retirement facilities for teachers

65 Techno pedagogic competency is
(a) a science of using technology in teaching.
(b) a technique of combining principles of technology and principles of teaching.
(c) a set of skills of inter-weaving technology into teaching and learning both scientifically and aesthetically
(d) a competence to develop techno pedagogic systems in education

66 Article 45 under the Directive Principles of State Policy in the Indian Constitution provides for
(a) right of minorities to establish educational institutions
(b) free and compulsory education
(c) education for weaker sections of the country
(d) giving financial assistance to less advanced states

67 Which of the following commission(s) is/are also known as 'Calcutta University Commission'?
(a) Mudaliar Commission
(b) Education Commission
(c) Sadler Commission
(d) Hunter Commission

68 Which part of Indian Constitution allows every citizen to impart education as per one's own religion?
(a) Directive principles
(b) Concurrent list of central and states
(c) Democratic rights
(d) Fundamental rights

69 Educational institutions are basically those who
(a) preserve and instill values of our culture in future generations
(b) suggest ways and means for social progress
(c) suggest solutions to social problems
(d) are established by the society only

70 "There cannot be educated people without educated women." This was indicated by
(a) The Resolution of the National Policy of Education (1968)
(b) The United Nations Declaration on the Elimination of Discrimination Against Women (1967)
(c) The University Education Commission (1948-49)
(d) New Policy on Education (1986)

71 Teacher's primary responsibility lies in
(a) planning educational experiences
(b) keeping students' record
(c) implementing policies
(d) All of the above

72 A good teacher should have
(a) inter-personal skills (b) communication skills
(c) conceptual clarity (d) All of these

73 During the days of informal education children used to get
(a) some kind of education first through the process of living
(b) education without any specific purpose
(c) professional education through non-professional schools
(d) education only at an advanced age through schools

74 In which year, NCF was approval by Central Advisory Board?
(a) 2004 (b) 2009 (c) 2005 (d) 2007

75 Which of the following does not go in favour of the individual aims of education?
(a) The individual is an asset to the society, his development and growth is necessary.
(b) The society is strong, if the individual is strong.
(c) Every individual is unique, development of his potentialities is essential.
(d) Society is supreme and all individuals are only part of it

76 In the teaching of any subject, a unit means
(a) a part of lesson plan such as introduced of assignment
(b) the portion covered by the teacher in the class period
(c) a topic which may require several lessons to be completed
(d) the post of a presentation requiring demonstration

77 The Secondary Education Commission, 1952-53, took the lead for introduction of technical education in the country from
(a) the Abbot-Wood Report of 1936-37
(b) the Sergeant Report of 1944
(c) the Hunter Commission Report of 1882
(d) the Hertog Committee Report of 1929

78 One of the following statement is correct, identify it.
(a) A scholar in his/her subject need not prepare and go to the class.
(b) Preparation for the class is not needed for well experienced teachers.
(c) Irrespective of his/her experience or scholarship, a teacher needs to prepare and enter the class every time.
(d) A skilled teacher can manage class even without preparation.

79 A teacher is strict in maintaining discipline in class in curricular and extra-curricular activities. But there is always a room for discussion regarding clarification of doubts in teaching-learning and conducting other activities, what is the approach of teacher towards students?
(a) Authoritative (b) Flexible
(c) Democratic (d) Rigid

80 Which commission pointed out major weaknesses in existing system of professional education?
(a) Mudaliar Commission
(b) National Education Commission
(c) Radhakrishnan Commission
(d) Sadler Commission

81 Who recommended that "Integrated courses of general and professional education should be introduced, so that teacher prospects are not narrowed"?
(a) Mudaliar Commission
(b) Dr. Radhakrishnan Commission
(c) Wood's Despatch
(d) Kothari Commission

82 As a result of recommendations given by Kothari Commission for four years integrated courses were started by
(a) RIE (c) CIE (c) IASE (d) SCERT

83 Match the following.

List I (Commissions)	List II (Years)
A. University Education Commission	1. 1952-53
B. Secondary Education Commission	2. 1968, 1986
C. NPE	3. 1948,49
D. Ecucation Commission	4. 1964-66

Codes

	A	B	C	D		A	B	C	D
(a)	1	2	3	4	(b)	3	2	4	1
(c)	2	3	1	4	(d)	3	1	2	4

84 Which committee or report promoted work experience and national service?
(a) Kothari Commission (b) Sergeant Report
(c) NPE (1968) (d) Abott-Wood Report

85 Who recommended a 'National System of Education'?
(a) NPE (1986) (b) IGNOU
(c) NCTE (d) Kothari Commission

86 Which of the following is the most important quality of a teacher?
(a) Punctuality (b) Content mastery
(c) Content mastery and communication competency
(d) Sociability

87 Regarding co-education at the secondary stage, the 1952-53, Education Commission has suggested
(a) to start resource, in several states could not afford
(b) there should be objection to extend co-educational school
(c) to maintain separate schools for boys and girls
(d) an institution in our country warrants establishment of more boys schools than co-educational school.

88 Adult education's main objective is to
(a) enable the adults to read and write
(b) teach adults to be able to understand what they need
(c) help adults to achieve literacy among with personal development.
(d) socialise the adults to move around freely

89 In relation with the Education Commission of 1882, the Government of India was recommended
(a) to centralise the authority of management of institutions of higher education.
(b) to withdraw gradually from the support and management of institutions of higher education.
(c) separate answers for pursuit of vocational and technical education.
(d) Both (b) and (c)

90 Which policy refers teacher education as a continuous process?
(a) NPE (1986)
(b) NPE (1968)
(c) NCFTE (2009)
(d) University Education Commission

91 Modernisation of educational programmes has posted many issues in the society. Which one of the following is not applicable?
(a) Increasing numbers of crimes in teenagers
(b) Increasing numbers of suicides in students
(c) Misuse of media by youngsters
(d) Reduced status of teachers

92 According to recommendations of the Mudaliar Secondary Education Commission, the maximum number of pupils in a class at this secondary stage
(a) should not exceed 50
(b) should committed to 30 only
(c) should not exceed 60
(d) should not exceed 40

93 The draft of National Policy on Education (1997) recommended the language formula for which of the following non-Hindi speaking areas?
(a) English as a link language along with mother tongue and a modern Indian language.
(b) a modern Indian language along with a regional language and English.
(c) Hindi as a link language along with mother tongue and English.
(d) regional language and English in addition to Hindi.

94 Which of the following was not a scheme offered by the government in the National Education Policy of 1986?
(a) Expansion of scholarship
(b) Incentives to poorer families
(c) Creation of 'Rural University Model'
(d) None of the above

95 The Kothari Commission Report was entitled as
(a) education and national development
(b) learning to be
(c) diversification of education
(d) education and social change in democracy

96 According to National Curriculum Framework of Teacher Education (NCFTE, 1988), what are the teacher's functions and roles?
1. Organise learning resources
2. Evaluate outcomes of learning
3. Plan effective curricular transaction strategies
4. Maintain silence to proceed teaching-learning process

Select the correct answer using the codes given below.
(a) 1, 2 and 3 (b) 2, 3 and 4
(c) 2, 4 and 1 (d) 3, 4 and 2

97 The National Policy of Education, 1986 also emphasised on
(a) national understanding (b) international understating
(c) social understanding (d) All of the above

98 The National Policy of Teacher Education, 1968, was adopted by the Indian Government to laid stress on which of the following aspects of teachers education?
(a) Adequate emoluments and academic freedom for teachers
(b) Travel allowance and family precision for teachers
(c) In-service training and correspondence education for teachers
(d) Promotion and retirement facilities for teachers

99 The Secondary Education Commission (1952-53) in India recommended which of the following pattern of education?
(a) 10 + 2 + 3 Scheme (b) 12 + 3 Scheme
(c) 10 + 3 + 2 Scheme (d) 11 + 2 + 3 Scheme

100 The Indian Educational Commission (1964-66) recommended that
(a) the system of streaming in schools of general education at class IX stage should be given up.
(b) specialisation of courses should commence at the class X stage.
(c) the effort that class IX is the proper stage to start specialisation.
(d) None of the above

101 The provisions of better and expanded programmes for the education of minorities have been given priority by
(a) Ramamurti Report, 1990
(b) National Policy of Education, 1986
(c) Both (a) and (b)
(d) None of the above

Directions (Q. Nos. 102-106) *In each of the questions given below, there are two statements marked as Assertion (A) and Reason (R). Mark your answer as per the codes given below.*

Codes
(a) Both A and R are true and R is the correct explanation of A.
(b) Both A and R are true, but R is not the correct explanation of A.
(c) A is true, but R is false.
(d) A is false, but R is true.

102 **Assertion** (A) The basic tenentes of National Curriculum framework is to ensure that learning shifts away from rote methods.
Reason (R) Making examinations more flexible and integrating them with classroom life.

103 **Assertion** (A) All Muslim womens need to go to school.
Reason (R) In Indian educational policies education is right of every individual.

104 **Assertion** (A) Learning principles have to be given utmost importance in the classroom.
Reason (R) Knowledge of principles facilitates transfer of learning to a greater extent.

105 **Assertion** (A) Early admission to school is not scientific.
Reason (R) It is against demonstratic principles.

106 **Assertion** (A) Classroom instruction should involve variety of strategies.
Reason (R) There are individual styles among students.

PREVIOUS YEARS' QUESTIONS

January 2017

1 Which of the following institution is the apex body for controlling, guiding and monitoring the activities and programmes of DIETs and other centrally sponsored schemes for teacher education?
(a) National Council for Teacher Education (NCTE)
(b) National Council for Educaiton Research and Training (NCERT)
(c) University Grants Communication (UGC)
(d) State Council of Educaitonal Research and Training (SCERT)

July 2016

2 Establishment of DIETs was the result of one of the recommendations of
(a) Indian Educaiton Commission (1882)
(b) University Education Commission (1948-49)
(c) Secondary Educaiton Commission (1952-53)
(d) National Policy on Education (1986)

3 A review of NPE (1986) Programme Of Action (POA) was done by
(a) National Commission for Teachers
(b) Yashpal Committee
(c) Ramamurti Committee
(d) Hansa Mehta Committee

December 2015

4 Implementation of curricular of teacher education is the direct responsibility of
(a) NCERT
(b) UGC
(c) NCTE
(d) Teacher education institutions

5 Vocationalisation of education in India was first recommended by
(a) Dr. Radhakrishnan Commission
(b) Mudaliar Commission
(c) Kothari Commission
(d) New Education Policy

June 2015

6 India has taken a move to ensure that there would be no untrained teacher at elementary school level by the end of August, 2015. This is in the wake of
(a) Verdict of Supreme Court
(b) Right to Education Act, 2009
(c) Rule made by NCTE
(d) Recommendation of NPE, 1986

7 District Institutes of Education and Training (DIETs) were created in pursuance of the recommendation of
(a) National Policy of Education, 1968
(b) National Policy of Education, 1986
(c) Kothari Commission, 1964-66
(d) 42nd Constitutional Amendment Act, 1976

8 The duration of Bachelor of Education (B.Ed) programme of the country has been raised to two years *w.e.f.* 2015-16 academic session on the basis of the recommendation of
(a) Kothari Commission, 1964-66
(b) Justice Verma Commission, 2012
(c) National Curriculum Framework, 2005
(d) Right to Education Act, 2009

December 2014

9 Arrange the following policies/reports in order in which they appeared.
1. Report of National Commission on Teachers-I (Chairperson, Professor DP Chattopadhyaya).
2. Towards an Enlightened and Humane Society (Chairperson, Acharaya Ramamurti).
3. Challenge of Education : A Policy Perspective.
4. National Policy of Education, 1986 : Revised Policy Formulations.

Codes
(a) 3, 1, 2, 4 (b) 1, 3, 2, 4
(c) 3, 4, 1, 2 (d) 4, 2, 3, 1

10 The purpose of establishing the NCTE is to
(a) universalisation of education
(b) to improve the quality of teacher education
(c) empowerment of teachers in India
(d) to encourage educational research

11 National Curriculum Framework for Teacher Education in India (2009) was developed by
(a) NCERT (b) NUEPA
(c) NCTE (d) NAAC

June 2014

12 National Education Day is observed on 11th November, every year in memory of
(a) Sarvapalli Radhakrishnan
(b) Maulana Abul Kalam Azad
(c) Zakir Hussain
(d) Mahatma Gandhi

13 "Destiny of India is being shaped in her classroom". This is stated in
(a) Education Commission (1964-1966)
(b) National Policy of Education (1986)
(c) National Knowledge Commission (2005)
(d) University Education Commission (1948-49)

ANSWERS

Exam Based Questions

1 (d)	2 (a)	3 (b)	4 (c)	5 (d)	6 (b)	7 (b)	8 (d)	9 (a)	10 (a)
11 (c)	12 (a)	13 (a)	14 (a)	15 (a)	16 (a)	17 (a)	18 (b)	19 (d)	20 (d)
21 (c)	22 (c)	23 (d)	24 (a)	25 (d)	26 (d)	27 (d)	28 (d)	29 (a)	30 (d)
31 (d)	32 (a)	33 (c)	34 (c)	35 (d)	36 (c)	37 (a)	38 (a)	39 (d)	40 (a)
41 (a)	42 (c)	43 (d)	44 (d)	45 (c)	46 (b)	47 (b)	48 (b)	49 (c)	50 (b)
51 (a)	52 (b)	53 (a)	54 (c)	55 (d)	56 (c)	57 (b)	58 (a)	59 (a)	60 (d)
61 (b)	62 (b)	63 (a)	64 (c)	65 (c)	66 (b)	67 (c)	68 (d)	69 (a)	70 (d)
71 (a)	72 (d)	73 (a)	74 (c)	75 (d)	76 (b)	77 (a)	78 (c)	79 (b)	80 (b)
81 (d)	82 (a)	83 (d)	84 (c)	85 (a)	86 (c)	87 (a)	88 (c)	89 (b)	90 (a)
91 (c)	92 (a)	93 (c)	94 (d)	95 (a)	96 (a)	97 (b)	98 (a)	99 (a)	100 (a)
101 (c)	102 (c)	103 (a)	104 (c)	105 (a)	106 (a)				

Previous Years' Questions

1 (d)	2 (d)	3 (c)	4 (d)	5 (b)	6 (b)	7 (b)	8 (b)	9 (c)	10 (b)
11 (c)	12 (b)	13 (a)							

CHAPTER

06

Education and Educational Policies

Education is a pre-requisite to national development. India since the early days of independence has always focused on improving the literacy rate in our country, for which India has formulated a number of educational policies. Policies are part and parcel of almost all the countries across the globe. Educational policy consists of the principles in the educational sphere to govern the operation of education systems.

Policies and Education

In a democratic society, the goal lies in the various aspects of the welfare of the people. For the well being of the people, definite stress must be given on education. In order to achieve education for all, many attempts and initiatives are taken by the Government of India. A nation's progress and development depends on the availability of the basic civil rights of education to all its citizens.

A policy is a deliberate system of principles to guide decisions and achieve rational outcomes. Policies are important because they help an educational department to establish rules and procedures and to create standards of quality for learning. Ultimately, policies are necessary for the success of educational goals. On the other hand, education sector also suggests a scheme or series of steps through which sound and workable policies can be formulated and then an effective planning, puts into effect, evaluated and re-designed.

Education is the basic foundation of awakening to any society and nation. Therefore, the main purpose of education should be qualitative education and its usefulness to life. For the development of nation or society, the formulation of good educational policies is essential. The education policy implies a lot of good work in education, it is related to future generation.

Relationship Between Policies and Education

There is a direct relationship between policies and education. The effective improvement in education can be made through effective policies as this would benefit the future generation. Our government has always valued the importance of education and this is reflected in our policies. After independence, various types of commissions and committees were formed and through these great success was

In this Chapter

achieved. In this context, the basic education vision of Mahatma Gandhi proved to be more effective and important. As a result of these policies of Gandhi ji, the basic schools were started in India. In 1953-54, the Government of India considered the edu cation system seriously and constituted the Secondary Education Committee. It is also called the Mudaliar Committee. Accordingly, primary education was increased from fourth to fifth grade. Similarly, in 1964, 1966, 1968 and 1975 several Committees were set up to determine education related policies.

Policies are attached to the basic improvement in education process. The consequences of the policies are made by the changes made at the basic level of education. Under this, in the education sector various types of specific tools and applications are applied. The use of modern resources in education sector, effective changes in uniformity reflect the effect of the policies. Therefore, there is an interdependence of relationship between policies and education.

Linkage Between Educational Policy and National Development

An organised education has a long history in our country. Famous **Gurukul** system of India is one of the oldest educational system of Earth, which is dedicated to the highest level of all round human development. Although, at that time, an education was often limited to the higher castes, students stayed at teacher's house or monastery for their education.

After the completion of their study, they paid **Gurudakshina** to their teacher which was a voluntary contribution. At the Gurukul, the student learned religion, philosophy, warefare, medicine, scripture, literature, statecraft, astrology and history. There was an intimate relationship between the teacher and the disciple or student.

In **modern period**, the European missionaries first started schools and later introduced teacher training institutions in India. In the beginning, the East India Company felt no responsibility for an education in India. Only some British intellectuals felt the need. Later, Christian missionaries made attempts to revive an outdated system of education by introducing Christian religion and Western literature through English medium.

Gradually, Indians wanted a system of education which could help them to earn their livelihood. Progressive Indians favoured the spread of Western learning and English education. The British government encouraged the study of an oriental language as well as English. Various committees which looked into the system of teacher education and training were instituted.

The beginning of the **20th century**, under the colonial supremacy of British in India witnessed numerous changes and initiatives in terms of an educational administration. From the grassroot level of policy-making, everywhere an infrastructure based and policy based decisions were taken which made an education progressive.

After independence, education became the responsibility of the states. The central government's only obligation was to coordinate in technical and higher education to specify standards. The Government of India introduced some important commissions like University Education Commission (1948), Mudaliar Commission or Secondary Education Commission (1952-53), Kothari Commission (1964-66), etc.

Education is a vital investment for human and economic development of a country. Tradition, culture and faith, all reflects upon education system and at the same time are also affected by education system. Changes in technology, labour market, general global environment, all are changing rapidly in the 21st century. To prepare the youth and the children to cope with the present scenario, modern education is utmost needed.

Educational policy plays an extremely crucial role in long term growth and productivity of a nation. It brings the positivity in our lives. It teaches us not only theoretical material but also the practical and successful way to lead lives as a responsible citizen.

The social and economical development of a nation is fundamentally an education process in which people learn to create new institutions, utilize new technologies, cope with their environment, and alter their patterns of behaviour. Education in a broad sense improves the capabilities of an individual and the capacity of institutions, and becomes a catalyst for the closely inter-related economical, social, cultural, and demographical changes that become defined as national development.

The greatest need of the hour is to redesign curriculum, textbooks, teaching methodology and children's literature, formal and non-formal education systems. Curriculum plays a crucial role in national integration and harmony. It should enable the learners to learn knowledge, develop conceptual and an intellectual skills, attitudes, values and amplitudes conducive to the all round development. Thus, education policy plays a very important role in the national development of a country.

Determinants of Educational Policy

The determinants of educational policy depends upon the qualitative policy framed by the government during its policy planning. The qualitative education, New Education Policy, new development and innovative ideas are the base of good education policy. There are other factors, like social, economical, political and religion also affects the educational policy of a country.

Following are the important determinants of educational policy

Parental Education Levels of parental education is an important determinant of children completing their education. The importance of parental education prompts questions about how policy makers can support parents with lower levels of education to support their children and help them through school.

Socio-Economic Problems The socio-economic problems of a country is also a significant determinant of educational policy and it also determines the aims of education. For instance, the Indian Education Commission (1964-66) put emphasis on "increasing productivity as one of the national objectives of education".

Cultural Differentiation Another determinant is cultural differentiation which affects the educational policies in Indian education system. Existing cultural differences should be taken into account in the structure for education or training programmes.

Physical Facilities Education and training should take place in a specific physical space. When we plan an educational policy, attention should be given to the availability of the necessary facilities, distribution of facilities and the use of available facilities with the costs of the capital.

Process of Policy Formulation

Policy formulation is the development of an effective and acceptable courses of action for addressing what has been placed on the policy agenda. It involves discussion among scholars about possible solutions followed by adoption of a new policy or an amendment of an existing policy. It is an integral part of the process of planning and a comprehensive process is involved in creating the most suitable policies.

Every policy formulation process involves different kinds of phases.

They are

- Selecting the desired objective.
- Identifying the target of objective.
- Determining the pathway to reach that objective.
- Designing the specific programme or measures in respect of that goal.
- Implementing the measures and assessing its impact on the target subjects.

Analysis of the Existing Educational Policy

Educational policy consists of the principles and governmental policies in an educational sphere. An educational policy consists of the analysis of the requirement of the contermpary educational field. Every country has different social and economical structure, thus, the requirement of an education is also different.

Government of the relevant country appoints scholars or an eminent personalities to make an educational policy. Educational policy seeks to answer questions about the purpose of education, objectives, aims and the required methods for attaining them. It also makes tools for measuring the success and failures of the process. Research on educational policies is carried on several academic disciplines or different fields like, psychology, economics, sociology and human development.

Thus, it is necessary to understand our existing educational policy mainly with the RTE Act, 2009. India's main educational policy is **Right to Education** (RTE) under article 21A (2002) of the Indian Constitution, which covers the Right to Education Act, 2009. This act describes the modalities of the importance of free and compulsory education for children between 6 to 14 years. India became one of the 135 countries to make an education a fundamental right of every child, when the Act came into force on 1 April, 2010.

The title of the RTE Act, incorporates the words 'free and compulsory'. Free education means that no child, other than a child who has been admitted by his or her parents to a school which is not supported by an appropriate government, shall be liable to pay any kind of fees or charges or expenses which may prevent him or her from pursuing and completing an elementary education.

India has moved forward to the rights based framework that casts a legal obligation on the central and state governments to implement this fundamental right.

Main Features of Right to Education (RTE) Act (2009)

- Free and compulsory education to all children's of India of the age group of 6 to 14 years.
- No child shall be held back, expelled or required to pass a board examination, until he/she completes an elementary education.
- Proof of age for the purpose of an admission to an elementary education, the age of a child shall be determined on the basis of the birth certificate. But no child shall be denied to an admission in a school for lack of age proof.
- A child who completes an elementary education shall be awarded a certificate.
- 25% reservation for an economically disadvantaged communities in all private schools should be done.
- Improvement in the quality of an education is important.
- School teachers should have adequate professional degree within five years or else will loose his/her job.
- School infrastructure needs to be improved in every 3 years.
- Financial burden of responsibilities will be shared between the state and the central governments.

Implications of the Right to Education Act (2009)

The Right to Education Act has various positive, social and economical implications. *They are*

- It resulted an increase in an enrollment of number of students. Free uniforms, textbooks and writing materials encouraged the students to attend school and has also encouraged parents to send their children to school, rather than making them to work as child labour.
- An educational policy also tends to look at reducing the gap between different communities by giving reservation for socially and economically deprived classes.
- The purpose of the **Mid-Day Meal** is to make sure that the students who are enrolled are able to attain basic amount of nutritions in their meals during school hours. The act also ensures that no person availing the mid-day meal shall be discriminated.

Challenges to RTE in India

According to **Amartya Sen**, the basic problem with an education in India exists in education setup of the country. Here, the importance is given to higher education and the neglection of primary education has been intolerably large. This is the main reason for not being able to develop a proper base that would help students to cope with higher educational standards. Thus, it cannot gives the expected result.

This leads to following developments

- Students, who do not receive sufficient education, fails to cope up, they end up by dropping out. The dropout rates in government schools are very high.
- The dropout rates for students coming from reserved categories is more, as compared to general categories. This reveals an inequality between various communities while availing an education. The dropout rates are high among SCs, STs and OBCs, as most of them come from low income background.
- Lack of teachers or lack of good teachers results in an inequality of an educational attainments. The person who has attained education from a government school, is in disadvantaged position, in comparision to that person who has attained an education from private school.
- Mid-Day Meal Scheme has faced a certain flaws in its implementation.
- The automatic promotion of students in the Right to Education Act, hampers a very high quality of education. There is no formal form of examination, which is mandatory to clear in order to reach the next grade.

Infact, the educational policy of India does not lack anything. It satisfies all the objectives that any educational policy would wants to achieve. This also matches global standards. The unsuccessful outcomes, reveals an ugly depiction of its faulty implementation.

Generation of Policy Options

The policy process is a crucial element in an educational planning. It is essential to clarify the concepts of 'policy' and 'policy-making' before proceeding further. Policy-making is the first step in any planning cycle. Policies differ in terms of their scope, complexity, decision environment, range of choices and decision criteria. New policies are usually generated when the present situation of the sector and its context is disturbed by a problem, a political decision or a reorganisation scheme.

Types of Policies

Issue Specific Policies These policies are short-term decisions involving day-to-day management or as the term implies, a particular issue.

Multi-Programme Policies These policies are concerned with different fields like general education, vocational education, diversified education, etc.

Large Scale Policies These policies are made for large number of peoples. These policies mainly covers the general or basic requirement in the field of an education.

Evaluation of Policy Options

Evaluation is a systematic and an impartial assessment of activity, project, programme, policy, topic, etc.

When we evaluate a policy, it suggests the following steps

- It focuses on expected and achieved accomplishment, examine the result, processes in order to understand achievements.
- It aims at determining the relevance, impact, effectiveness, efficiency and sustainability of an interventions and contributions of the policies.
- It provides evidence based information that is credible, reliable and useful.
- It is an integral part of each stage of the programming cycle.

Thus, policy options can be evaluated only if alternative scenarios are developed to allow estimations of the likely implications of the options considered. The 'imaginary' situation that would be created if the policy options were implemented is compared with the present situation and the scenario of transition from the existing to the imaginary case is evaluated in terms of desirability, affordability and feasibility.

Decision Making Policy

It is the conclusion of a process during which all information, relevant to the decision was gathered and carefully analysed, so that a total optimal policy might be designed and selected.

Being a welfare state, all the policies in India relates to the benefit of the citizens and the development of our society and an economy. The process of policy formation starts with identifying the problems and coming up with the solutions. Poverty and illiteracy are the main hindrance of progress in our society. Thus, government has taken many important steps to promote an education in our country.

Policies are a collection of ideas. Decisions initiates the actions to be taken to implement the policy. The government insists that the policy framework is clear and an unambiguous and it requires proper implementation. Maximum members of the committee should express same opinion and then only important decision-making takes place.

Decision-making is an integral part of our everyday life. It is sometimes difficult to tell where decision-making starts and ends. Policies are plans, courses of action or procedures that are intended to influence decisions. As such, they form a part of the context for decision-making. A policy decision tells us how to make choices in order to act in an alignment with own purposes and goals.

Planning of Policy Implementation

Policy implementation is a purposeful and multi-directional change process, aiming to put a specific policy into practice which may affect an educational system on several levels.

Policy's decisions are made with the consent of the people who will put the policy into operation. Requiring consent ensures equal consideration of each member of the group. Each member's objection to a policy must be resolved before the policy can be adopted. But the implementation of policy is not an easy job. There are many local level problems in our society. To implement national level policies on an education is a tough task. Studies shows that what has happened in an implementation stage, influences the actual outcome of the policy. It cannot be anticipated early.

Conversely, the livelihood of a successful outcome will be increased, if thought is given at the policy design stage to potential the problems of the society, instead of facing problems. Later, through an evaluation research, attempts can be made to modify the policy prior. It is regarded as a good alternative.

The policy implementation process theoretically includes an attempt to assess as many areas of potential policy impact as possible, to lessen the chances that a given will have unexpected consequences.

Applications or Implementation of the Educational Policy

Policy implementation is what happened after a law is passed. Educational policy implementation is the transformation of an educational policy into action.

Here, are some important facts about the implementation of the policy

- While applying the policy, we must observe who is the beneficiary and who are negatively affected.
- Time required to completely implement the policy is also observed.
- Calculating the associated cost and financing of the policy is mostly needed phenomenon.
- We should examine the political complexities of a federal structure while applying the new policy.

Rules for Educational Policy Implementation

- Planning related to implementation of new policy must include policy assessment.
- Feedback should be obtained during implementation, reassessment of aspects of policy's decisions and modification by policy's makers.
- Concrete implementation of policies causes reassessment of the policies.

Strategies for Implementation of Educational Policy

- Involving those who play some roles or supporting roles in the process of providing certain necessities and services.
- Using community leaders, religious leaders, political leaders, academicians for mobilising people around it.
- Using people and various groups that are beneficiary.
- The mass media is the greatest means of reaching the far and near people.

Policy Impact Assessment

The ability to evaluate which project or policy will have the most impact is truly commendable. This policy impact assessments are formal, evidence-based procedures that access economical, social and environmental effects of the public policy.

The policy impact assessment can be improved, if we follow these steps:

- Informing policy's makers about potential, economical, social and environmental ramifications.
- Increasing public participation in order to reflect a range of considerations.
- Improving transparency and special interest lobbying is discouraged.
- Clarifying how public policy helps to achieve its goals.
- Contributing to continuous learning in policy development.

Today, many methods are accepted for the policy impact assessment. These includes scoping, aggregation, comparison of options, analysing coherence, data presentation, involvement, monitoring, evaluation, etc.

Subsequent Policy Cycle

Policy is considered as a deliberate system of principles to guide decisions and to achieve rational outcome. The policy cycle is a tool used for analysing of the development of a policy item. It also refers to as 'Stages Approach'.

***James E Anderson** suggests the following stages in policy cycle*

- Agenda setting
- Policy formulation
- Decision-making
- Implementation
- Evaluation

It was later developed by **Peter Bridgman** and **Glyn David**. *According to them, policy cycle includes eight steps. They are*

- Issue identification
- Policy analysis
- Consultation
- Policy instrument development
- Building coordination and coalitions
- Program design or decision-making
- Policy implementation and
- Policy evaluation

EXAM BASED QUESTIONS

1 Name the oldest education system of Earth which is dedicated to the all round human development.
(a) Gurukul system
(b) Schools in monastery
(c) Education given by institution patronised by the king
(d) None of the above

2 In modern period, the European missionaries first started school and later introduced
(a) School for Arts
(b) School for Music and Dance
(c) Teacher Training Institution
(d) None of the above

3 Indians in pre-independence era wanted a system of education
(a) which could help them to earn their livelihood.
(b) which could make them modern.
(c) which could satisfy their thirst for knowledge.
(d) None of the above

4 Statement I After independence, an education became the responsibility of the states.

Statement II The central government's only obligation was to co-ordinate in technical and higher education and specify standards.

Codes
(a) Both statements, I and II are true, but II is not the cause of I
(b) Only I is true
(c) Only II is true
(d) Both I and II are true and II is the cause of I

5 University Education Commission was established in ....
(a) 1945 (b) 1946
(c) 1948 (d) 1950

6 Generally, educational policy consists of
(a) the principles and governmental policies in an educational sphere.
(b) the collection of laws and rules that governs an operation of an education system.
(c) Both a and b
(d) None of the above

7 What are unwritten educational policies?
(a) They contain rules and regulations.
(b) They contain norms and traditions.
(c) These are acts of Parliament.
(d) All of the above

8 Educational policies are
(a) normative
(b) persuasive
(c) coercive
(d) Both a and b

9 Policy formulation process involves
(a) selecting the desired objective
(b) identifying the target of an objective
(c) Both a and b
(d) None of the above

10 While applying the policy, we must observe
(a) who is beneficiary and who are negatively affected.
(b) calculating the associated cost and financing of the policy is mostly needed.
(c) that we should not examine the political complexities
(d) Both a and b

11 For the implementation of new educational policies, the people for mobilisation, are
(a) community leaders
(b) religious leaders
(c) political leaders and academicians
(d) All of the above

12 What is regarded as proof of age for an elementary education?
(a) Birth certificate
(b) Bills of hospital or health care centre
(c) Doctor's certificate
(d) None of the above

13 A child who completes an elementary education, according to RTE is awarded with
(a) a certificate (b) ₹ 10,000
(c) ₹ 25,000 (d) None of these

14 .... reservation for an economically disadvantaged comminutees in all private schools is to be done.
(a) 25% (b) 30%
(c) 20% (d) 40%

15 Financial burden of responsibility for education will be shared by
(a) The state government
(b) The central government
(c) The authority of the school
(d) Both a and b

16 The Right to Education Act, tends to look at reducing the gap between different communities, by giving reservation for socially and economically deprived classes. This is the .... implication of the Act.
(a) social (b) psychological
(c) economical (d) Both a and c

17 Statement I According to Amartya Sen, the basic problem with an education in India exists in the education set up of the country.
Statement II In India, the importance is given to higher and primary education is largely neglected.
Codes
(a) Only I is true
(b) Only II is true
(c) Both statements, I and II are true and II is the cause of I
(d) Both statements, I and II are false and II is not the cause of I

18 The dropout rates in schools are high among
(a) SCs (b) STs
(c) OBCs (d) All of these

19 Expert thinks that an automatic promotion of students in the Right to Education Act
(a) hampers very high quality of education.
(b) inspire the students to get admission.
(c) encourages the students to study seriously .
(d) None of the above

20 What is the first step in any planning cycle?
(a) Observing the factors responsible for an event
(b) Policy-making
(c) Concept-making
(d) Both a and b

21 Policies are of
(a) issue specific (b) multi-programme
(c) large scale (d) All of these

22 The policies which are short-term decisions, involving day-to-day management are known as
(a) issue specific policies (b) open-to-run policies
(c) short-term policies (d) None of these

23 The National Policy of Education (1968) was further modified in
(a) 1982 (b) 1985
(c) 1992 (d) Both a and c

24 Major emphasis on women's education was given by the National Policy of Education to
(a) overcome poor rate of literacy among womens.
(b) encourages womens to be an economically independent.
(c) to encourage womens for taking part in social activities.
(d) None of the above

25 .... is a systematic and impartial assessment of an activity, project , programme, policy, topic, etc.
(a) Evaluation (b) Result
(c) Decision (d) None of these

26 Policy decision tells us how to make choices in order to
(a) act in an alignment with our purposes and goals.
(b) take actions properly.
(c) makes decisions for course of action.
(d) All of the above

27 Why the implementation of policy is not an easy job?
(a) Because there are many local level problems in a society.
(b) Because people are not prepared to accept the national policy.
(c) Because people wants to modify the policy.
(d) None of the above

28 Policy impact assessments are procedures that access
(a) economical effects of public policy
(b) social effects of public policy
(c) environmental effects of public policy
(d) All of the above

29 The .... is a tool used for analysing of the development of a policy item.
(a) policy decision (b) policy assessment
(c) policy cycle (d) None of these

30 James E Anderson suggests that the stages in policy cycle should consists of agenda setting, policy formulation, decision-making and
(a) implementation (b) evaluation
(c) Both (a) and (b) (d) None of these

31 **Statement I** Policy implementation sometimes faces problems.
Statement II Evaluation of policy can be made through research and modification of policy will make the policy more acceptable.
Codes
(a) Both statements, I and II are true and II is the cause of I
(b) Only I is true
(c) Only II is true
(d) Both statements, I and II are true, but II is not the cause of I

32 Peter Bridgman and Glyn David suggests that policy cycle includes .... steps.
(a) 7 (b) 8 (c) 9 (d) 10

33 The future of an education in India, depends on
(a) government (b) economy
(c) family (d) society

34 The purpose of basic education scheme is
(a) universalisation of primary education.
(b) to vocationalise an education.
(c) to fulfill basic needs of persons through an education.
(d) to make education compulsory for all.

35 RTE Act was implemented in India with effect from
(a) 1st April, 2009 (b) 1st May, 2010
(c) 1st April, 2008 (d) 1st April, 2010

36 The Right to Free and Compulsory Education for Children between age group of 6 to 14 years has been inserted in an Indian Constitution as
(a) Article 46 (b) Article 16
(c) Article 45A (d) Article 21A

37 The Mid-Day Meal Programme for pre-schools was initiated with a view to
(a) increase enrollment
(b) involve community
(c) engage teachers
(d) increase in employment

38 The main distinct between aims and outcomes of education is that
(a) aims are a matter of insight, whereas outcomes are a matter of foresight
(b) aims are a matter of foresight, while outcomes are a matter of insight
(c) aims are guided by outcomes, whereas the outcomes are guided by experiences
(d) aims are a matter of impulse, whereas the outcomes are a matter of determination

39 The social aim of an education implies that
(a) the state is above an individual citizen.
(b) the state is an idealised meta-physical entity.
(c) the state is superior to an individual, transcending all his desires and aspirations.
(d) the state has to give and not to take anything from an individual.

40 The quality of teaching is reflected
(a) by the attendance of students in the class.
(b) by the pass percentage of students.
(c) by the quality of questions asked by students.
(d) by the duration of silence maintained in the class.

41 The most important instrument of the development is
(a) an education
(b) will power
(c) religion
(d) None of the above

42 Government's policy on education regards a unique
(a) consumption (b) investment
(c) source of income (d) expenditure

43 Match the following

List I	List II
A. Teacher	1. Community part
B. Student	2. Administrator
C. Principal	3. Facilitator
D. Parents	4. Active learner

Codes

	A	B	C	D		A	B	C	D
(a)	1	2	3	4	(b)	3	2	1	4
(c)	3	4	2	1	(d)	2	3	4	1

44 ……… policies are short term decisions involving day-to-day management.

(a) Multi-programme (b) Issue specific
(c) Large scale (d) Both a and b

45 Which of the following statements regards making policy decision is incorrect.

Statement I Decision-making is an integral part of our everyday life.

Statement II All the policies in India relates to the benefit of the citizens and development of the society.

Codes

(a) Statement I is true
(b) Statement II is false
(c) Both statements, I and II are true
(d) Neither a nor b

Directions (Q. Nos. 46-55) *Given below are two statements. One labelled as Assertion (A) and other labelled as Reason (R). Select the correct code from the following.*

Codes

(a) Both A and R are true and R is the correct explanation of A
(b) Both A and R are true, but R is not the correct explanation of A
(c) A is true, but R is false
(d) A is false, but R is true

46 **Assertion** (A) Educational policy consists the principles and governmental policies in an educational sphere.

Reason (R) Educational policy seeks to answer the questions about the purpose of education.

47 **Assertion** (A) Multi-programme policies are concerned with different fields.

Reason (R) These policies are made for large number of people.

48 **Assertion** (A) The National Policy of Education (NPE) was prepared to improve the quality of education.

Reason (R) It was focused on providing educational facilities to all the citizens.

49 **Assertion** (A) Evaluation is a systematic and impartial assessment of an activity.

Reason (R) It provides evidence based information that is reliable.

50 **Assertion** (A) Poverty and illiteracy are the main hindrances of progress in our society.

Reason (R) India is a welfare country which helps in development of society.

51 **Assertion** (A) Decision-making is a part of policy making.

Reason (R) A policy decision tells how to make choices.

52 **Assertion** (A) Policy implementation is a purposeful and multi-directional change process.

Reason (R) Implementation of policy is an easy job.

53 **Assertion** (A) Policy decisions are not made with the consent of the people.

Reason (R) Consent ensures equal consideration of each member of the group.

54 **Assertion** (A) Many methods are accepted for the policy impact assessment.

Reason (R) It includes scoping, aggregation, data presentation, etc.

55 **Assertion** (A) Policy cycle is a tool used for analysing the development of a policy item.

Reason (R) James E Anderson has suggested stages in policy cycle.

ANSWERS

1	(a)	2	(c)	3	(a)	4	(d)	5	(c)	6	(c)	7	(d)	8	(d)	9	(c)	10	(d)
11	(d)	12	(a)	13	(a)	14	(a)	15	(d)	16	(d)	17	(c)	18	(d)	19	(a)	20	(b)
21	(d)	22	(a)	23	(d)	24	(a)	25	(a)	26	(a)	27	(a)	28	(d)	29	(c)	30	(c)
31	(d)	32	(b)	33	(a)	34	(c)	35	(d)	36	(d)	37	(a)	38	(a)	39	(d)	40	(c)
41	(a)	42	(b)	43	(c)	44	(b)	45	(c)	46	(c)	47	(b)	48	(a)	49	(a)	50	(b)
51	(a)	52	(b)	53	(d)	54	(a)	55	(a)										

CHAPTER 07

Economics of Education

The study of economics of education includes private and social returns to education, human capital and Signaling theory to education, education finance at micro and macro level in India. The budgeting plays an important role as it is helpful in better coordination between different functions/activities. It also enables its organisation to prefix its goals and push up the forces towards their achievement.

Educational Economics

The economics of education is a rapidly growing and evolving field. It covers a diverse area of Economic Theories, Models and Quantitative Methodologies. All these helps to understand, analyse and improve the performance of education system.

Economics is a social science, that studies how society chooses to allocate its scarce resources, which have alternative uses, to provide goods and services for present and future consumption. Economics of education is the application of economic principles, concepts and laws to the process of education.

It studies human behaviour (in terms of human decisions), actions and reactions about schooling. It further looks into how human behaviour affects economical development. It is one of the branches of ordinary economics. Though, it is the study of how educational managers makes official or approved choices from scare available resources which is meant for the realisation of the best possible educational outcomes. It employs the use of some elementary concepts commonly used in labour economics, public sector economics, welfare economics, etc. Economists like **Adam Smith**, **Alfred Marshall**, **John Stuart Mill** had discussed education and development extensively.

The fundamental problem of economics of education is how the society, institution and the household makes use of the limited human and material resources they have, to best satisfy their unlimited wants for education. The solution to the fundamental problem requires the application of certain economical concepts. The study of economics of education includes private and social rates of return to education, human capital and signaling theory of education, non-pecuniary benefits of education, educational and economical development, contribution of education to the economy, measuring educational expenditure, man-power

In this Chapter

planning, educational planning and human resource development, educational cost, cost analysis, educational production, educational efficiency and effectiveness, cost efficiency and effectiveness, cost benefit analysis and economics of teacher supply, education and equity.

Today, education is considered as a form of investment in human beings, which yields economical benefits and contributes to a country's future wealth by increasing the productive capacity of its people. So, the expenditure on education can be partially justified in terms of the potential contribution of education to economical growth.

The evaluation of investment in human capital began in mid-fifties by economists like, **TW Schultz**, **GS Becker**, **Jacob Mincer**, **HP Miller**, etc. The extensive use of Cost-Benefit Analysis or CBA in the field of education started in sixties by the economists like **M Blaug**, **M Woodhall**, **R Layard**, **Lee Hansen**. The findings of their studies have facilitated to adopt the technique of CBA to evaluate educational investment projects.

Cost Benefit Analysis in Education

The term 'Cost Benefit Analysis' implies a systematic comparison of the magnitude of the costs and benefits of some form of investment in order to assess economical profitability. All forms of investment involve a sacrifice of the present consumption, in order to secure future benefits in the form of higher levels of output or income. It provides a means of appraising these future benefits in the light of the costs that must be incurred at present. The purpose of such analysis is to provide a measure of the expected yield of the investment, "Of all the techniques of investment appraisal which in recent years have come to be applied to the public sector, none has attracted more than Cost Benefit Analysis (Blaug, 1970)".

A general definition of Cost Benefit Analysis states that "It is a practical way of assessing the desirability of projects, where it is important to take a long view (in the sense of looking at repercussions in the further, as well as in the nearer future) and a wide view (in the sense of allowing for side-effects of many kinds on many persons, industries, regions, etc.), *i.e.* it implies the enumeration and evaluation of all the relevant costs end benefits (Press end Turvey, 1965)."

This is a technique that has been used for the purpose of choosing a project from among a number of projects on the basis of a consideration of their Cost Benefit relationship. In applying this technique, one has to be careful about both the concepts of cost and benefit as well as their measurement. It provides a measure of the profitability of education as an investment for society, or for the individual student or his/her family. It will act as a general guide for resource allocation and enable the comparison of the profitability of different types of education. One has to be clear about the social and private benefits of education, and its social and private costs. Essentially, it relates the educational cost with the benefits measured in monetary terms.

Cost Benefits Analysis is useful for decision-making in education, in the following ways

- It may point out the need for change in resource allocation in favour of those types of education which can offer the highest rates of return.
- It may suggest ways of increasing the profitability of education, either by increasing benefits or by lowering the costs.
- Finally, it provides a conceptual framework for the examination of the costs of education in relation to the relative earnings of the educated man-power.
- It plays a great role in educational policy-making. It has been applied to people as human capital, to assess the rates of return to investment in education.

In 1981, **Segun Adesina** noted that Cost Benefit Approach looks at each level of education as investment in human beings with the purpose that the returns will help to improve the whole economy. Assumptions, the wages/salaries paid to worker reflects differences in their productivity, variations in productivity results from different amount and kind of education people receives.

Cost Benefit Analysis in education is perceived from two angles, namely

- The social rates of return
- The private rates of return

Social Rates of Return

This rates of the benefit is to be derived by the state of investing in a particular form of education. The cost of education is usually borne by the society as a whole and can be calculated by equating the total present value, earning of an average educated person before tax with benefits to be gained from alternative investments, in physical capital.

Private Rates of Return

This is the investment by private individual and the expected benefit for acquiring a particular type of education. This is calculated by equating the direct and out of pocket costs of student plus earning done by them while studying.

Advantages of Cost Benefit Analysis

- By looking at the age earnings structure of the educated person, it is possible to measure or quantify the increase in productivity of an educated person.
- The analysis can show or suggest the directions in which education system in a society should expand, so as to maximise the earning capacity of their product.
- It shows the relationship between the cost of gaining more education and the increase in payment, which results from additional education.

Disadvantages of Cost Benefit Analysis

- It is difficult to measure the benefits, which derives from investing in any type of education.
- In developing countries, differential in earnings of workers cannot be attributed to additional education acquired, but to other things such as habits, customs, family background, etc.
- Primary education gives the highest return to society, according to some studies done on the calculation of the social rates of return for all levels of education which seems to be vague.
- The salaries of civil servants are more influenced by economic variables than by productivity consideration.

Over the years and across many countries, various approaches to educational planning have been developed.

Cost Effective Analysis in Education

It is a technique for measuring the relationship between the total inputs, or cost of a project or activity and its outputs or objectives.

It is the comparison of the cost of implementing a new information system or upgrading an existing one to the cost that would be involved in retaining the existing ones of doing things. A measure of the cost effectiveness is obtained by measuring costs against outcomes. In education, the effects may include quantity measures such as school enrollment, attendance, completion or overall years, or degree attained, and quality measures such as cognitive development, academic achievement or non-cognitive skills.

It is closely related to Cost Benefit Analysis. They both represents economic evaluations of alternative resource use and measure costs in the same way. However, cost-benefit analysis is used to address only those types of alternative where the outcomes can be measured in terms of their monetary values. For *e.g.*, vocational education is judged according to Cost Benefit Analysis.

The purpose of Cost Effective Analysis in education is to judge which programme or combination of programmes can achieve particular objectives at the lowest cost. By choosing those with the least cost for a given outcome, society can use its resources properly. Those resources that are saved through using more Cost Effective Approaches can be devoted to expand programmes or can be applied to other important and social endeavours.

Thus, we can say that, Cost Effective Analysis is a form of economic analysis that compares the relative costs and outcomes (effects) of two or more courses of action. It is distinct from Cost Benefit Analysis, which assigns a monetary value to the measure of effect. It is often used in the field of health services, where it may be inappropriate to monetize health effect. Typically, the CEA is expressed in terms of a ratio where the denominator is a gain in health from a measure (years of life, premature births averted, sight-years gained) and the numerator is the cost associated with the health gain.

The most commonly used outcome measure is Quality Adjusted Life Years (QALY). Cost Utility Analysis is similar to Cost Effective Analysis. The concept of Cost Effective Analysis is applied to the planning and management of many types of organized activity. In education, CEA can be utilized in the form of investment done in the education sector and its subsequent result, for example, allocation of Rs 21000 crore on SSA. Now, an analysis has to be done so that whatever money has been invested had it been yielding the desired result, or not has to be examined. If the returns are not favourable then rethinking, replanning and reconsideration has to be done.

Difference Between Cost Benefit Analysis and Cost Effective Analysis

Cost Benefit Analysis (CBA)	**Cost Effective Analysis** (CEA)
It an economic evaluation technique that compares the cost of the intervention with the benefit incurred, where the benefit is measured by monetary units.	It is an economic evaluation technique that compares cost per consequence of two or more interventions, where the consequences are measured by natural units (life years gained, saved years of life).
It focuses on the monetary outcomes.	It focuses on non-monetary outcomes.
Here, both costs and consequences are measured in monetary unit.	Here, consequences are measured by natural units.
As it is based on the monetary terms, it is quantitative project evaluation technique.	It is a mixed of both qualitative and quantitative evaluation techniques.
It adopts broad societal perspective as it includes all costs and all benefits.	It has its limitation on outcomes related to monetary value.

Cost Benefit Analysis (CBA)	Cost Effective Analysis (CEA)
The results are presented in terms of ratio of benefit to cost and return on investment.	The results are presented in terms of incremental cost per unit of effectiveness for interventions.
It helps to identify the best ways to achieve given outcome.	It helps to identify ways to redirect resources to achieve more.
It is suitable for evaluation of industrial projects, since monetary value can be easily calculated.	It is more suitable for the service-oriented organisations.

Higher Education Signaling Theory

The Signaling theory of education, usually attributed to **Michael Spence** (1973). It suggests that individual workers innate productivity levels that are identified by their years of schooling rather than enhanced by them. This suggests that more educated workers receives higher pays as education provides them a credential than the workers who has acquired skills. It was developed by **Arrow** (1973), **Layard** and **Psacharopoulos** (1974), **Riley** (1975, 1979), **Spence** (1974,1976), **Stiglitz** (1975) and **Wolpin** (1977).

Signaling theory is based on the following assumptions

- Every individual have different innate levels of productivity. These are not affected by their education.
- Additional education demands additional costs. This helps to differ for high and low productivity of workers. Those who can learn easily can acquire the signal more cheaply than others. Thus, they need to spend less time for study.
- There is always asymmetric information with respect to worker's productivity. Individual workers know their skill levels, but the employers often do not know.
- Schooling levels can be observed without incurring a cost. Employers always use educational qualifications to predict productivity, making hiring decisions, and set wages. This is based on the fact that individuals are rational and they invest in education as long as the benefit of an additional year of schooling exceeds the cost. The benefit of an additional year of schooling is the same for high and low-productivity workers, but the costs are higher for low productivity workers.

The Signaling model is attached on the assumption that worker's productivity is negatively related to the cost of acquiring the signal. As long as cost differences across workers result from differences in cognitive ability or tastes for learning, they may be indicative of differences in the job productivity. If cost of education vary because of differences in family contributions towards school fees, tuition, etc., then the students who face higher schooling costs may be no less productive than those who face lower schooling costs and education will not allow employers to distinguish between high and low productivity workers.

Human Capital Theory

It claims that education and training are investments that make individuals genuinely more productive. These individuals earn high salary and become more employable. The gain of the individual can be measured by the net gain in life-time earning accumulated as a result of their investment in education or training. Policy's makers around the world admit that investment in education and training is a good thing.

They suggests that Vocational Education and Training (VET) is a means of securing higher economical growth and national prosperity. Some economists have argued that individuals who are more able and productive also tends to invest in more education (Spence and Arrow, 1973). In other words, education does not necessarily makes an individual more productive, rather it simply acts as expensive sorting device which enables employers to identify more able individuals.

Wolf (2002) suggests that the policy emphasises on education and skills as the main driver of economic growth, overstates the importance of human capital investments and the major function of education as a social discriminator. The separating out the genuine impact of education on productivity and earning from its role as a sorting device is very difficult.

Recent researchers like **Carneiro** and **Heckman** (2003), **Cunha and Heckman** (2009), and **Carneiro** (2009) argues that it is also crucial that we understand the technology of skill formation over the life cycle. We need to know how different types of people can effectively acquire skills at different stages of the life cycle and the economic returns to those skills once acquired. This is particularly important in the area of VET. Some international evidences suggests that the economic returns to some VET are low.

Finally, even if we accept that education and training genuinely do enhance individual's productivity in the labour market, it is not clear that focusing on earning is enough. It is not clear whether wages always accurately reflect individual's productivity level. Education is far more than an economic investment as it yields various non-economic benefits like reduced crime, better parenting skills, better healtchare outcomes for the individual. These wider benefits also play a crucial role in policy development for education, particularly in the area of VET.

Difference Between Signaling Theory and Human Capital Theory

Signaling Theory	Human Capital Theory
It claims that education raises wages simply because educational level is a signal of the worker's ability.	It claims that education raises wages by increasing productivity.
It suggests that education does not improve the student's ability.	It suggests that education has a positive causal effect on student's ability, which in a competitive which in a competitive labour market translates into higher earnings. Those with education earn more because they learn.
It can similarly be defined using mediating variables. It could be limited to measures of potential employer's beliefs about ability.	It assumes that education improves individual and aggregate outcomes because it improves the broadly defined job, relevant skills of the student.

Educational Finance

Educational finance means the financing of private and public educational institutions. It refers to governmental and organisational process by which revenues are generated through taxation, tuition fees, philanthropy, etc.

It is not a technical field, dominated by financial formulas and budget categories but it involves public policy issues at the dynamic core of any society regarding equity, efficiency and freedom of choice.

Improvement of education should be made within the financial and human resources available in the country. Through careful analysis, allocation of money should be made to important educational sectors, according to the requirements.

Attempts should be made to provide education free or at a much lower cost than the real one, to help the young members of our society. As a result, maximum returns will be ensured and the wastage of human and physical resources of the country will be eliminated.

For encouraging educational opportunities in our country, a large number of scholarships, stipends and free studentship should be given to the students. Also special grants for physical activities, libraries, reading rooms, expenses on special programmes should be given to all institutions. Different commissions recommend several grants in the field of education which will enhance the over all standard and prestige of our education system.

Educational institutions are mainly funded by students and their parents, employers from the private sector, government tax revenue or they rely mostly on private donors. Funding can be direct, that is through recurrent grants, capital grants and taxes or through student's tuition fees and other charges which are the main source of revenue for institutions. A small number of institutions are funded through loans. A school or university can choose between one or more of those funding sources.

Public institutions are usually funded by national governments through direct transfers of tax revenues. Therefore, public universities are either absolutely free or charge low tuition fees regulated by the state of federal governments. Often such institutions are owned and administered by the state, but in some cases they maintain their institutional autonomy to decide on governance, tuition and student enrollment. Some private universities may also receive public funding in the form of tax breaks and government loans and grants for students from disadvantaged backgrounds. Similarly, private donations are given to students who choose to attend public educational institutions.

Sources of Finance

In India, the sources of finance for education can broadly be classified into external and internal or domestic sources.

Sources of Educational Financing in India

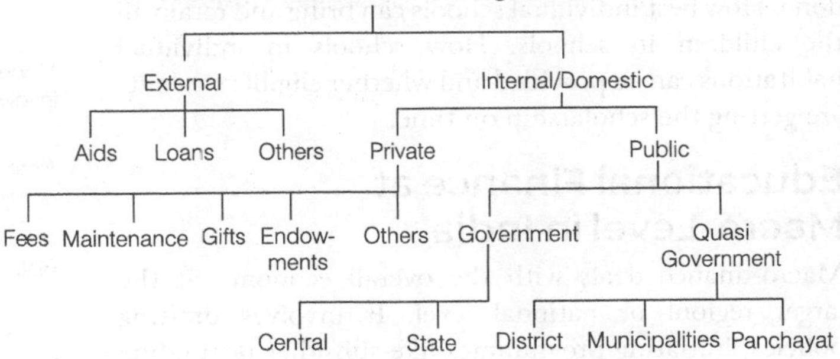

Principles of Educational Finance

- All allocations of funds to education should be determined by the educational budget and priorities to various sectors should be made within the sphere of education itself.
- An improvement of education should be made within the financial and human resources available in the country.
- Through careful analysis, allocations should be made to important educational sectors in accordance with the projected man-power requirements.
- Education cannot be purchased like a commodity, attempts should be made to provide education free or at a much lower cost than the real one.
- Education should be duly financed to provide equality of opprotunity for the development of the individuals.

- Special grants for physical activities, libraries and reading rooms, expenses on special programmes like mid-day meal, etc. should be given.
- For craft, cottage industry, finance should be introduced in schools. Teachers should be given incentives.

Educational Finance at Micro-Level in India

Micro-finance services are providing financial assistance to an individual or an eligible client, either directly or through a group mechanism. It is a powerful tool to fight poverty. It means building financial systems that serves the poor. It promotes socio-economic development at the grass root level through Community-Based Approach.

Micro Planning Theory analysis consumption and investment of households, prices of particular goods, output, sales and purchase decision of individual firms and industries. Micro-planning in education starts from grass root level.

For instance, the head of an institution has to plan how best he/she should bring all the children to school in his/her area. Here, planning at the village level has to be done. How best individual schools can bring and retain all the children in schools. How schools in individual habitations can be provided and whether eligible students are getting the scholarship on time.

Educational Finance at Macro-Level in India

Macro-finance deals with the overall economy at the larger regionl or national level. It involves drafting policies, initiating programmes like subsidies or funding and operating multi-year development plans with an aim to generate employment. Macro-finance aims for overall economical development more broadly.

Educational finance supports not only individual well being, but also the economical health of our nation. At the time of financial crisis, consumers not only take important decisions about financial products and services for their own best interests, but collectively, they also help to promote broader economical stability.

The main aim of macro-finance is to help an economy to grow and to generate employment and expand an economy. A government provides macro-finance in any form to the business like tax benefits or a subsidy because it will benefit the economy in future. Here, the amount of money involved is in a large proportion.

A macro-finance is for a specific time period like 2 or 3 years. It means it has a pre-defined tenure. **Sarva Shiksha Abhiyan, Mid-Day Meal**, etc. are important Indian Government programmes which aims at universalisation of elementary education and the improvement of nutritional status of school age children nation wide. All these plannings are designed for realisation of educational aims and objectives for both individual and social development. These plannings of India in macro level helps to become India, a country of super power.

Difference Between Micro Finance and Macro Finance

Basis	Micro Finance	Macro Finance
Meaning	It is an individual based concept to furnish financial services to low income individuals who have no access to finance in a conventional way.	It is a whole economy based concept, which is not framed for any particular group, to grow the economy at a national level.
Concept	It is a narrow concept and focuses on the need of an individual.	It is a broad concept and focuses the whole nation.
By whom	It is provided by micro-finance companies, self-help groups and non-governmental organisations.	It involves a large entity like governments, big corporations, banks, and some big private lenders.
Money involved	In micro-finance, the money involved is in a small amount.	The amount of money involved is in a large portion.
Time-period	It is an endless activity which goes on and on.	It is for a specific-time period like 2 to 3 years. It means it has a pre-defined tenure.
Risk level	There is a risk of default that an individual may not pay.	There is no risk at all because the main aim is to give benefit to the economy.
Effect	It has a direct effect on an individual.	It has a direct effect on the whole economy, which indirectly affects the whole population.

Budgeting

The word 'budget' came from a French word 'bougette' meaning **little bag**. Budget is an estimation of probable future income (revenue) and expenditure for a programme or project form a period of time. It is also defined as "a financial and quantitative statement prepared and approved prior to defined period of time, of the policy to be pursued during that period for the purpose of attaining given objective. It may include income, expenditure and the employment of capital".

A major element of financial data activity rests in the act of budgeting. Budgeting is the process of allocating finite resources to the prioritised needs of an organisation. A carefully planned budget is needed for educational policies taken by the government. Educational policies like distribution policies, curriculum policies, pedagogical policies or resource policies makes funding imperative.

The school budget may be described as the process of preparing a statement of anticipated revenue and for the proposed expenditure for a period of time. In school, the budget is the financial dimension of the school improvement plan.

So, budget is regarded as a plan that informs and empowers spending decisions and facilities for the achievement of the school's educational aims. Colleges and universities and other research institutes follow a balanced budget which best suited for them. Their budget should be approved by the state government and sometimes by the central government when the institute is directly financed by the central government.

Principles of Budgeting

Certain principles must be kept in mind while making budget

Management Support Top management's support and cooperation is essential for successful implementation of the budget. It is necessary to monitor the actual performer and reward the good performer.

Employee's Involvement Participation of employees in budgeting process, motivates them to strive hard to achieve budget levels of an efficiency and activity.

Statement of Organisational Goal An organisational goal should be quantified and clearly stated and this policy is a pre-requisite for budgeting.

Responsibility Accounting Management should inform the employees about the expectations from them. The cost over which an individual has pre-dominant control should be used in evaluating perfomance of that individual.

Organisational Structure There should be a well planned organisational structure comprising of Budget Committee and its President who are responsible to make the budget.

Flexibility The budget can be changed during a year, according to the performance of the employee.

Communication of Results Proper communication should be maintained so that remedial actions can be taken wherever necessary.

Sound Accounting System Every organisation should have good accounting system so as to generate precise, accurate, reliable and prompt information which is regarded essential for successful implementation of budget system.

Objectives of Budgeting

- To control the cost and increase revenue and thereby maximise profit, so as to know profit at different level of production and best production level.
- To run production activities in efficient manner by lay behind the chances of interruption in production process due to lack of material, labour etc.
- To bring about coordination between different functions of an enterprise, which is essential for the success of any enterprise.
- To incorporate measures of calculation of deviations from budgeted results and analysis of the same, whereby responsibility can be fixed and controlling measures/ action can be taken.
- To ensure that actions taken are in accordance with the targets and if required, to take suitable corrective-action.
- To predict short and long term financial positions for better financial position and management of working capital in better manner.

Essentials of Effective Budgeting

A good budgeting system requires good organisational system with lines of authority and responsibility clearly mentioned. There must be perfect co-ordination among different functions as well as participation of responsible managers/ supervisors in the decision-making process.

Thus, the main essentials of effective budgeting are as follows :

- There should be well-planned organisational setup authority and responsibility clearly defined, Budget Committee should be formed consisting of all top executives.
- There should be a good accounting system which provides accurate and timely information.
- Variations should be reported promptly and clearly to the appropriate levels of management.
- Budgets have no meaning unless they lead to control action as a consequence of feedback provided.
- The whole system should enjoy the support and cooperation of top management.
- Staff should be strongly and properly motivated towards the systems.
- Budget should be prepared on the basis of clearly defined business policies, after discussion held with the head of individual department so that they may provide their suggestions in this regard.

Advantages of Budgeting

- It leads to maximum utilisation of resources with a view to ensuring maximum return.
- It increases the awareness about business enterprise at all levels of management in process of fulfilment of targets.
- It is helpful in better coordination between different functions/activities of business/organisation and hence, better understanding between different functions.
- It is a process of self-examination and self-criticism which is essential for the success of any organisation.
- It makes a path for active participation and support of top management.
- It enables the organisation to prefix its goals and push up the forces towards their achievements.
- It stimulates the effective use of resources and creates an attitude of cost consciousness throughout the organisation.
- It creates the base for measuring performances of different departments as well as different functions of the production activities.

Disadvantages of Budgeting

- Forecasting, planning or budgeting is not an exact science and a certain amount of judgement is present in any budgeting plan.
- The basic requirement for the success of budgeting is the absolute support and enthusiam provided by the top management. If it is lacking at any time, the whole system will collapse.
- It should be followed-up by effective control action, this is often lacking in many organisations, which defeats the very purpose of budgeting.
- The installation of budgeting system is an elaborate process and it takes time.
- It is only a source and not a target and hence, cannot take the place of management, while it is only a tool of management. Thus, the budget should be regarded not as a master, but as a servant.
- It requires the experienced man-power, technical staff, analysis, control etc, hence, it is costly affair.

EXAM BASED QUESTIONS

1 Economics of education is the application of
(a) economic principles (b) concepts
(c) laws (d) All of these

2 Education is perceived from
(a) the social rates of return
(b) the economic rates of return
(c) the private rates of return
(d) Both a and c

3 In the mid-fifties the evaluation of investment in human capital was began by the economists.
(a) Adam Smith (b) GS Becker
(c) Jacob Mincer (d) Both b and c

4 Name the economist who started Cost Benefit Analysis (CBA) in the field of educaton.
(a) M Blaug (b) M Woodhall
(c) Both a and b (d) None of these

5 Cost Benefit Approach looks at each level of education as
(a) investment in human beings
(b) the purpose that the return will help to improve the whole economy
(c) Both a and b
(d) None of the above

6 **Statement** I Cost Benefit Approach looks at each level of education as investment in human beings.
Statement II Salaries of the persons depends on the productivity which is a result of their education.
Codes
(a) Both I and II are true, but are not related to each other
(b) Only II is true
(c) Both I and II are true and II is the cause of I
(d) None of them is true

7 Which one is not the advantage of Cost Benefit Analysis Approach?
(a) It is possible to measure or quantify the increase in productivity of an educated person.
(b) Education system should be expanded, so that it can maximise the earning capacity.
(c) The relationship between the cost of gaining should be more than the education.
(d) None of the above

8 Cost Benefit approach in education emphasises
(a) expenditure on education should be thought of as a form of national investment
(b) the investment in education should be based on the benefits of return.
(c) the level of earning of educated people must be high
(d) Both a and b

9 According to Adesina (1981), Cost Benefit Approach assumes education as an
(a) investment (b) profit
(c) loss (d) All of these

10 Cost Benefit Analysis emphasises the investment in education that should be based on
(a) the benefits (b) return
(c) Either (a) or (b) (d) None of these

11 **Statement I** Cost Benefit Analysis focus on the monetary outcomes.
Statement II It is more suitable for the service oriented organisation.
(a) Both the statements are correct, but statement II is not related to statement I
(b) Only I is correct
(c) Both I and II are incorrect
(d) Both the statements are correct and statement I is related to statement II.

12 "Of all the techniques of investment appraisal which in recent years have come to be applied to the public sector, home has attracted more attention than Cost Benefit Analysis". Who said this?
(a) Arrow (b) Blang (c) Spence (d) Walpin

13 Which of the following statement with regard to Cost Benefit analysis is useful for decision-making in education?
(a) Cost Benefit Analysis may suggest ways of increasing the profitability of education, either by increasing its benefit or by lowering the costs.
(b) It may point out the need for change in resource allocation in favour of these types of education which can offer the highest rates of return
(c) Cost Benefit Analysis provides a conceptual framework for the examination of the costs of education in relation to the relative earnings of the educated man-power.
(d) All of the above

14 What is the purpose of Cost Effective Analysis in education?
(a) The outcomes can be measured in terms of their monetary values.
(b) To measure the relationship between the total inputs, or cost of a project or activity and its outputs or objectives.
(c) To judge which programme or combination of programmes can achieve particular objectives at the lowest cost.
(d) None of the above

15 Consider the following statement(s) with regard to Cost Effective Analysis is/are incorrect.
1. It is suitable for evaluation of industrial projects, as monetary value can be easily calculated.
2. It helps to identify ways to redirect resources to achieve more.

Codes
(a) Only 1 (b) Both 1 and 2
(c) Only 2 (d) Neither 1 nor 2

16 Cost Effective approach is also known as
(a) Rate of Return Approach (b) Social Demand Approach
(c) Both a and b (d) None of these

17 Which of the following statement(s) with regard to Cost Effective Analysis is/are correct?
(a) It adopts broad societal perspectives as it includes all costs and all benefits
(b) It focuses on non-monetary outcomes.
(c) It has its limitation on outcome related to monetary value.
(d) Both b and c

18 Match the following

List I (Principles of Analysis)	List II (Related Facts)
A. Cost Benefit Analysis in education	1. Optimal instrument re-occurrence
B. Cost Effective Analysis in education	2. Cost Benefit Analysis
C. Notation Theory	3. Education, a capital investment
D. Human Capital Theory	4. Sheepskin's Impact Code

Codes

	A	B	C	D		A	B	C	D
(a)	1	2	3	4	(b)	2	1	3	4
(c)	1	2	4	3	(d)	3	2	1	4

19 Which of the following statement(s) with regard to Cost Effective Analysis is/are true?
Statement I The purpose of Cost Effective Analysis of education is to ascertain which programme or combination of programmes can achieve particular objectives at the lower cost.
Statement II Cost Effective Analysis relates the cost of education with various measures of educational objectives, not expressed in terms of money.
(a) Only I
(b) Only II
(c) Both statements, I and II are true
(d) Neither I nor II

20 Education raises wages simply because education level is a signal of the worker's ability.
Name the theory which suggests the above statement.
(a) Signaling theory (b) Human Capital theory
(c) Performance test (d) None of these

21 Match the following

List I (Names of the Philosophers)		List II (Years of the Signaling Theory)
A. Arrow	1.	1975
B. Riley	2.	1974
C. Spence	3.	1977
D. Wolpin	4.	1973

Codes

	A	B	C	D		A	B	C	D
(a)	4	1	3	2	(b)	4	1	2	3
(c)	3	2	1	4	(d)	2	3	4	1

22 Layard and Psacharopoulos have developed the Signaling Theory in the year

(a) 1970 (b) 1972
(c) 1974 (d) 1975

23 Rearrange the following statements according to their correct sequence.

1. Employers set wages for the workers.
2. Employers makes the hiring decision through analysis.
3. Employers predict productivity by using the educational qualification of the employee.
4. Employers select the candidate on the basis of the educational qualification for interview.

Codes

	A	B	C	D		A	B	C	D
(a)	4	3	2	1	(b)	4	2	3	1
(c)	3	4	2	1	(d)	1	2	3	4

24 Education and training are investments that make individuals genuinely more productive. Name the theory which claims this.

(a) Signaling theory
(b) Human Capital theory
(c) Cognitive Development theory
(d) None of the above

25 **Statement I** In Signaling theory, there is always asymmetrical information with respect to worker's productivity.

Statement II Individual workers know their skill levels, but the employers often do not know.

Codes

(a) Both statements, I and II are true and II is the cause of I
(b) Only I is true
(c) Only II is true
(d) None of the above

26 .... in education suggests productivity is independent of education, but education acts as a credential for greater ability.

(a) Human Capital theory (b) Signaling theory
(c) Investment (d) Expenditure

27 Consider the following statements and select the correct answer from the codes given below.

1. The Signaling theory of education, usually attributed to Michael Spence (1971).
2. The Signaling theory is developed by Arrow, Riley, Wolpin, Spence and Layard.
3. The theory claims that education and training are investments that make individuals genuinely more productive.
4. The theory assumes that every individual have different innate levels of productivity. These are not affected by their education.

Codes

(a) 1 and 2 (b) 1, 2 and 3
(c) 1 and 4 (d) 3 and 4

28 According to the Signaling principle, which of the following is considered as the main qualification?

(a) Degree in higher education
(b) Qualification
(c) Investment in education
(d) Research and development

29 Human Capital theory claims that education and training are investments that make individuals

(a) genuinely more productive
(b) genuinely more intelligent
(c) genuinely more limited
(d) None of the above

30 Human capital investment consists of

(a) any activity that enhances the quality of labour
(b) expenditure from formal schooling only
(c) expenditure from on the job training
(d) any activity that leads to the substitution of physical capital for labour

31 "Individuals who are more able and productive also tends to invest in more education", who said this?

(a) Spence and Arrow
(b) Arrow
(c) Wolf
(d) None of the above

32 Vocational Education and Training (VET) is a means of securing

(a) higher economic growth
(b) national prosperity
(c) Both a and b
(d) None of the above

33 Consider the following.

1. Capital investment
2. National investment
3. Spiritual investment

Which of the above mentioned, has been adopted in a form of education as per Human Capital theory?

(a) Only 1 (b) 1 and 2
(c) Only 3 (d) 1, 2 and 3

34 Who among the following were the advocates of Human Capital theory?

1. Adam Smith
2. Spencer
3. Schultz
4. Mincer

Codes

(a) 1, 2, 3 (b) 2, 3, 4
(c) 1, 3, 4 (d) 1, 2, 3, 4

35 Which of the following statement(s) is/are true about the strengths of Human Capital theory.

1. It helps policy's makers and researchers to evaluate the relationship between education and training as inputs and economical and social benefits as outputs.
2. It helps to provide a usefulness for understanding how policy can be developed to incentives individual investment in their own education.

Codes

(a) Only 1 (b) 1 and 2
(c) Only 2 (d) Neither 1 nor 2

36 "Take into account the innate and acquired skills. Those are important and may invest to expand, will form the human", who gave this definition?

(a) A Smith (b) W Petty
(c) Schultz (d) G Becker

37 Education is far more than an economic investment as it

(a) reduces crime
(b) develops better parenting skills
(c) gives better healthcare
(d) All of the above

38 Which of the following statement(s) is/are correct with regard to macro finance?

(a) It is a broad concept and focuses the whole nation.
(b) There is no risk at all because the main aim is to give benefit to the economy.
(c) It has a direct effect on an individual
(d) Only a and b

39 Micro finance is a powerful tool to fight against

(a) poverty (b) illiteracy
(c) superstition (d) None of these

40 Micro planning in education starts from

(a) primary school level (b) grass root level
(c) secondary level (d) None of these

41 Macro finance deals with the overall economy at the larger

(a) regional level (b) national level
(c) Both a and b (d) None of these

42 What is/are the main aim(s) of macro finance?

(a) Helps an economy to grow
(b) To generate employment
(c) To expand an economy
(d) All of the above

43 Government provides macro finance in any form to the business like

(a) tax benefit
(b) announcing subsidy
(c) Both a and b
(d) None of the above

44 Which of the following statement(s) is/are true about the educational finance at micro level?

1. It promotes socio-economic development at grassroot level.
2. There is no risk at all because the main aim is to give benefit to the economy.

Codes

(a) Only 1
(b) Only 2
(c) Both 1 and 2
(d) Neither 1 nor 2

45 Which of the following statement is incorrect about macro finance?

(a) There is a risk of default
(b) The amount of money involved is in large portion
(c) There is a direct effect on the whole economy which indirectly affects the whole population
(d) It aims for overall economic development

46 Educational finance refers to governmental and organisational process by which revenues are generated through

(a) taxation and tuition
(b) fees and philanthropy
(c) Both a and b
(d) None of the above

47 For enhancing educational opportunities, which of the following step(s) is/are necessary?

(a) introducing scholarships and stipends
(b) introducing free studentship
(c) Both a and b
(d) None of the above

48 "It is the process of allocating finite resources to the prioritised needs of an organisation". Here 'it' stands for

(a) budgeting
(b) loan
(c) Both a and b
(d) None of the above

49 Which of the following statement(s) is/are true about the advantage(s) of budgeting?

1. Budgeting retard the effective use of resources and creates an attitude of cost consciousness throughout the organisation.
2. It creates the base for measuring performances of different departments as well as different functions of production activities.

(a) Only 1 (b) Only 2
(c) Both 1 and 2 (d) Neither 1 nor 2

50 Statement I Economics of education is the application of economic principles, concepts and laws to the process of education.

Statement II Today, education is considered as a form of investment in human beings.

(a) Both the statements, I and II are correct but not related to each other.
(b) Only I is true
(c) Only II is true
(d) Both the statements, I and II are incorrect

51 Arrange the following stages, which are important in budget development in schools.

1. Study the budgeting guidelines issued by the Ministry of Education.
2. Identify and list activities to be carried out in the school within the session.
3. Give an estimated cost of human and physical resources.
4. Identify and list the resources, both human and physical that will be required.
5. Using the guidelines, prepare the budget and seek approval of it by the authorities.

Codes
(a) 2, 4, 3, 1, 5 (b) 1, 3, 4, 2, 5
(c) 3, 2, 1, 5, 4 (d) 1, 2, 4, 3, 5

52 .... is the process of allocating finite resources to the prioritised needs of an organisation.
(a) Signaling-Theory (b) Researching
(c) Budgeting (d) None of these

53 The budget of the college or university should be reviewed by .... and submitted to the .... of the institution.
(a) staff, dean (b) registrar, principal
(c) teacher, vice-chancellor (d) None of the above

54 A good institutional plan should be
(a) specific
(b) conducive to development
(c) scientific and task-oriented
(d) All of the above

55 Which of the following approach becomes impossible to forecast?
(a) Man-Power Approach
(b) Cost Benefit Approach
(c) Both a and b
(d) None of the above

56 The budget can be changed during the year, according to the performance of the employee, it means
(a) flexibility (b) discipline
(c) rules (d) None of these

57 A budget is prepared for ....
(a) indefinite period (b) definite period
(c) period of one year (d) six months

58 Which of the following is not an advantage of budgeting?
(a) It promotes study, research and focus on the future
(b) It is a source of motivation
(c) It will prevent net losses from occurring
(d) It is a means of coordinating business activities

59 Which of the following statement(s) is/are true about budget, budgeting and budgetary control?

1. Budgetary control is a wider concept, whereas budget and budgeting are narrow concepts.
2. Budgeting is the process of preparing business estimates.

Codes
(a) Only 1 (b) Both 1 and 2
(c) Only 2 (d) Neither 1 nor 2

60 Which of the following is not the principle of budget making?
(a) The budget must be balanced one
(b) Budgeting should be not and not gross
(c) Estimating should close
(d) The rule of Lapse

61 Which of the following statement(s) is/are correct about the budget?

1. It is an Instrument of policy.
2. Budget estimate should be on a departmental basis.
3. It is a tool of people's control over administration.

Codes
(a) 1 and 2 (b) 2 and 3 (c) 1, 2, 3 (d) 1 and 3

62 Statement I The budget administration in colleges and universities must support the mission of the institution.

Statement II Each budgetory unit must be in keeping with the institution's goals and planning priorities.

(a) Only statements, I is correct
(b) Both the statements, I and II are correct, but are not related to each other
(c) Only statement II is correct
(d) None of them is true

63 Which of the following is not a function of budgeting?
(a) Motivating (b) Decision-making
(c) Controlling (d) Planning

64 The term budgetary period refers to
(a) The sub-division of the main budget
(b) The period in which the budget is finalised
(c) The period for which the budget is prepared
(d) A specific year for which the budget has been prepared

65 A fixed budget is
(a) A budget that itemises the fixed cost of a department
(b) A budget that never changes
(c) A budget that is set for a specified level of activity
(d) A budget that ignores inflation

66 While preparing the budget, which certain principles must be kept in mind?

(a) Management support
(b) Employee's involvement
(c) Statement of organisational goal
(d) All the above

67 The budgeting process in any educational institution should

(a) study carefully educational needs of the school and make estimate of the revenue necessary to meet these needs.
(b) identify and list activities you want to be carried out in your school within a year.
(c) give an estimated cost of these sources and study the budgeting guidelines issued by government.
(d) All the above

Directions (Q. Nos. 68-70) *Given below are two statements, one labelled as Assertion (A) and other labelled as Reason (R). In the context of the two statements, which of the following is correct?*

Codes

(a) Both A and R are correct and R is the correct explanation of A
(b) Both A and R are correct, but R is not correct explanation of A
(c) Both A and R are incorrect
(d) A is incorrect, while R is correct

68 **Assertion** (A) Educational finance means the financing of private and public educational institutions.

Reason (R) It refers to governmental and organisational process which revenues are generated through taxation.

69 **Assertion** (A) In school, the budget is the financial dimension of the school improvement plan.

Reason (R) It is regarded as a plan that informs and empowers spending decisions and facilities for the achievement of the school's educational aims.

70 **Assertion** (A) Micro finance enables financial self-reliance for individuals, providing them with money and education.

Reason (R) It is usually a continuous ongoing activity without any defined end.

ANSWERS

1	(d)	2	(d)	3	(c)	4	(c)	5	(c)	6	(c)	7	(d)	8	(d)	9	(a)	10	(c)
11	(c)	12	(c)	13	(a)	14	(c)	15	(c)	16	(a)	17	(c)	18	(a)	19	(a)	20	(a)
21	(b)	22	(c)	23	(a)	24	(b)	25	(a)	26	(d)	27	(a)	28	(c)	29	(a)	30	(a)
31	(a)	32	(c)	33	(c)	34	(a)	35	(a)	36	(c)	37	(a)	38	(b)	39	(a)	40	(b)
41	(a)	42	(c)	43	(d)	44	(b)	45	(a)	46	(b)	47	(c)	48	(c)	49	(c)	50	(d)
51	(a)	52	(c)	53	(d)	54	(d)	55	(b)	56	(b)	57	(b)	58	(c)	59	(a)	60	(b)
61	(b)	62	(b)	63	(b)	64	(b)	65	(c)	66	(d)	67	(d)	68	(d)	69	(d)	70	(c)

CHAPTER

08

Education and Politics

Education and politics enjoy a symbiotic relationship *i.e.* education affects politics and vice-versa. Although education is expected to be free from politics, yet many times the educational policies followed by government may be influenced by political ideology. In addition to its various approaches, political development and political socialisation should also be studied.

Introduction

Education is a pre-requisite for the acquisition of knowledge, enhancement of skills, development of attitudes and values. We need education because it provides us knowledge and skills to lead a meaningful life. During the British era, education was only available to some selected persons, who were mainly engaged in service of the colonial rule. After independence, importance was given to all forms of education for promoting the welfare of the citizens of the country.

An urgent need is felt to make education accessible and possible to all the citizens of the country. Thus, by introducing Right to Education Act (RTE), 2009, India provides free and compulsory education to all children in the age group of six to fourteen years as a fundamental right. It is vital for every society to develop a system of education for the survival of the society and individual.

Education is the method by which a society transmits from one generation to the next, its knowledge, culture and values. Education is the process by which a person learns facts, acquires skills and develop abilities and attitudes necessary for the livelihood and survival. Thus, education is necessary for economical and social development.

Relationship Between Politics and Education

In the past, politicians and educators perceived their roles as completely separate and independent. There was a common myth that politics and education did not mix. But, the reality is that no educational system can be separated from political system. Considering the societal responsibilities and objectives, education and politics are inextricably related.

In this Chapter

The educational policies are generally taken by the government in power. Educational policies are therefore those guidelines which expedient both for political socialisation and for national socio-economic and cultural development. Every government is conscious to ensure its political, social and economical success, the education system must be involved in the promotion of the interests of the governing power. Some common examples of how the political system used the education system to promote the political ambition of it are found in Hitler's Germany, the French Revolution and some military governments in Africa, etc.

On the other hand, the education system and educator needs the support and patronage of the ruling political system. They also need the public and other governmental agencies in order to carry out their functions of socialisation and training of the people. No educational system can survive without the financial support and protection of the government in power. Thus, by having this unavoidable dependence on successive governmental support and protection, education finds itself used for the promotion of political beliefs and social views of the government and its political leaders.

Impact of Politics on Indian Education System

India is one of the largest democracy in the world. India has number of political problems which remain without any solution for decades. Some are national level and some are regional level problems. Some demands autonomous states within Indian Union, others demand independence. With all its problems, India still survives as a single democratic country.

Like other fields, Indian education system faces many problems. Education system is undoubtedly the foundation of a nation which makes man and country more civilised. If we have a well balanced education system then a large portion of problems can be solved. The problem we are facing today is political corruption in an education system. Political corruption is the use of power by government officials for an illegitimate private gain. Forms of corruption vary, but include bribery, nepotism, patronage, etc. Ideally, the education system should just have the motto of providing proper education and knowledge, but now it is developing more. Education has become a business. Politicians and businessmen see it as an another industry where money flows uninterrupted, irrespective of any recession.

A lot has to be done to make Indian education system flawless and at par with those of developed countries. India is a developing country which is known for its varied cultures and traditions. Education has become a remedy for every state and its tradition. Some states have well developed education system, some states do not have. Indian government should look into such problems and make sure that these inconveniences are covered up sufficiently. It is the duty of the government to promote new policies and amendments in education. While doing this, we must not forget the words of **Dr. Abdul Kalam Azad** that "When learning is purposeful, creativity blossoms, when creativity blossoms, thinking emanates, when thinking emanates, knowledge is fully lit, when knowledge is lit, economy flourishes". Thus, we must join our hands in placing our country and its economy as a 100% educated citizen's nation.

Perspectives of Politics of Education

The main motive of education is to promote quality education for the good of the society. In this context, *the perspectives of liberal, conservative and critical are discussed below*

Liberal View of Education

Liberal education is an approach to learning that empowers individuals and prepares them to deal with complexity, diversity and change. This provides students with broad knowledge of wider world, viz, science, culture and society and also indepth study in specific area of interest. It helps students to develop a sense of social responsibility and also helps to develop strong intellectual and practical skills that span all major fields of study.

Today, liberal education in a sense is quite different from its traditional usage in the history of education. Some have taken the adjective 'Liberal' to refer to the kind of pedagogy built upon the free choices and initiatives of individual learners. In this respect, we hardly distinguish it from progressive learning.

Liberal education is the attempt to make the whole of human knowledge available to the learner. The various categorisation of the liberal curriculum as 'forms of knowledge', 'realms of meaning', 'disciplines' or 'voices' are a reminder that the assimilation of knowledge must be structured, significant, critical and concerned with understanding.

This kind of education is often considered as 'elitist'. 'Elite education' is an educational arrangement which appears designed to set for selected individuals apart from the population at large in order to recruit and train them for social, professional and political eminence. It is clear that this process of educational provision applies mainly to those belonging to the upper social classes, or to those from other social classes who display a high degree of measured intelligence. To claim that liberal education is elitist is to say that it is only good for the selection and training of those who are destined to be members of the managerial or social elites and of no use to ordinary people.

Some proponents of liberal education suggests that it is a life irrelevant activity, having no extrinsic value, being merely the pursuit of knowledge for its own sake. But, this defence of knowledge for its own sake in the curriculum have to be made in the context of two other imperative.

First, there is an argument that knowledge must also be for the learner's sake, that individual idiosyncratic interests, capacities, social and ethnic backgrounds and personal life histories, as well as aspirations for the future must figure in our curricular calculations. No individual can learn everything that could be learned for its own sake, and from an encyclopedic knowledge, potentially available to student's choice have to be made.

Second, since individual learners live in a particular time and places, which colour their own interests and aspiration, the cultural significance of knowledge in a particular society should also affect our calculation of what knowledge is of most valuable.

The liberal education also brings political and economical power. The better educated are better fed, clothed, housed, healthier and have a longer life expectations and much lower rates of infant mortality rate. Liberal education has proposed for political efficacy, economic prosperity and cultural enrichment of the majority of citizens.

Conservative's View of Education

Conservatism is a political and social philosophy promoting traditional and social institutions in the context of culture and civilisation. The conservatives are promising old fashioned discipline in educational system. Conservatism is the belief that institutions should function according to their intended original purpose and that any concepts that have not been maintained should be restored.

Conservatives maintain certain core principles. **First** is that all humans are imperfect by nature, and there is no way to create a perfect society on earth. **Second**, the past is the basis for our social sensitivity and human relationships. **Finally**, tradition provides stability and cohesion to our society and its culture. A conservative education preserves the traditional curriculum, aiming to transmit to the students as a means of bringing them into an already established culture. They believe that the primary role of education is academics and that schools should not assumes non-academic, custodial, therapeutic and social functions, such functions are believed to weaken education.

According to conservatives, education and the society are closely related and we cannot think of the one, without the other. Education is required to preserve a particular society, its culture, value system, religion, faiths, beliefs, languages and life styles. These are transmitted from one generation to another, through ages.

Thus, every society has its own pattern of life and mode of living. For example, India's secular and democratic education ideals and traditions are maintained and fostered by their system. Similarly, Pakistan and Iran maintain their Muslim Philosophy and spirit by their educational process. USSR and USA tries to promote their Socialistic and Capitalistic Models, through their education.

Every society has its own life with peculiar features. Education system adopted in a society is to reflect an idea of that particular society. Thus, education is grown from within as the society grows. Such growth is slow, steady and natural. No specific change is experienced so quickly or promptly. The difference of education in different types of society is very prominent. The young generation adapts the changes in the way of life, habits of food and dress, values and customs easily than the older generation who are in favour of traditional values and customs of the society.

Critical Perspective

The critical perspective on education is different from both the liberal and the conservative perspectives in several ways. While liberals and conservatives conceive of culture as a series of texts and knowledge to be passed on to new generations, critical pedagogy emphasizes culture as a matter of the unequal exchange of meanings through meaning-making practices.

In the view of critical perspective, all meaning-making practices need to be scrutinized for the kinds of authority they secure, the sorts of social relationships they foster and the material and symbolic interests they affirm or contest. While in the view of critical pedagogy, culture is inherently political and struggled over, for cultural conservatives culture is closer to dogma.

While cultural conservatives put the greatest emphasis on individual codes of conduct, despite different circumstances and critical perspective emphasize the importance of social context in the moral choices that people make. The critical perspective is also distinguished by its emphasis on theory.

The liberal and cultural conservative perspectives on education tend to devalue the necessity for students and teachers to have the theoretical tools to interpret their experiences in schools and outside of schools. Criticalists make the theoretical tools of interpretation a starting point for teachers and students to interpret individual and social reality as the basis for community and collective social intervention. For criticalists, theory always undergrids practices.

Approaches to Understand Politics

Political scientists have adopted several approaches to the study of politics. *Scholars have also used different approaches to study comparative politics which are as follows*

Behaviouralism

Behaviouralism is an Approach in political science that emerged in the 1930s. Behaviouralists used strict methodolgoy and empirical research to validate their study as a social science. **Edward Thorndike**, **JB Watson**, **BF Skinner** are the famous Behaviourist Psychologists.

Behaviouralism is defined as "It is a movement in political science that insists on analysing only observable behaviour of political actors." In this definition, two things are mentioned. **First**, Behaviouralism is a movement and is based on the observable behaviour of individuals who are regarded as 'political actors'. **Second**, Behaviouralism gives an indepth analysis by scrutinising the political behaviour of individuals.

It can be defined in another way as "It is a belief which insists that Social theory can be and should be constructed only on the basis of observable behaviours because only such behaviour provides measurable or quantifiable data for research".

The exponent of Behaviouralism suggests that neglecting the behaviour of individuals, who are real actors of social and political events *i.e.* plausible political, Social Theory cannot be constructed. It asserts that for an acceptable Scientific Theory of Social Science, it is essential that the political behaviour of individuals is to be studied and not the units and organisations which deals with political questions and principles.

The political behaviour of individuals constitutes the central aspect of politics. From the view point of an education, learning is nothing more than an acquisition of new behaviour based on environmental conditions. Thus, with this new behaviour we always try to adjust with our environment.

Thus, Behavioural Approach to politics or behaviouralism denotes that it is an attempt to improve our understanding of politics by seeking to explain the empirical aspects of political life by means of methods, theories and criteria of proof that are acceptable according to the canons, conventions and assumptions of modern empirical science.

Theory of System Analysis

Theory of System Analysis was part of the behaviouralist movement in political science. **David Easton** was the first to think and analysing politics from the view point of System Analysis in his work, **Political System**, (1953). According to **Easton**, political system is an interaction in any society through which authoritative and binding allocations of values are made and implemented.

He suggested political system as a unit of analysis and concentrated on intra-system behaviour. He holds that all political systems are both open and adaptive. He studied the nature of exchanges and transactions that takes place in closed circuit. It is made because of the demand from the society or environment. *This demand can be* :

- for allocation of goods and services such as wages, working conditions, education, health, etc.
- regulations of behaviour *i.e.* public safety, control over market, etc.
- participation in the political system *i.e.* right to vote from political associations.
- communication and information regarding policies of the government.

Demand cannot be satisfied without support and this support can be of various types. *They are*

- material support like payment of taxes,
- obedience of laws and rules,
- participatory support-voting, political discussion, etc.
- paying attention to government's communication like advertisements, ceremonies, symbols, etc.

Gabriel Almond is another prominent American political scientist who has adopted the Method of System Analysis in comparative politics. He said that a system of interaction to be found in all independent societies, which performs the functions of integration and adaptation by mean of the employment or threat of employment of more or less legitimate physical compulsion.

He suggests that functions of political system performs function at three levels, *viz.* capability level, conversion level and the system level. The idea of political development is central in **Almond's Functional Analysis**. This is popularly known to the students as Structural Functionalism.

This new system approach has influenced the educational administration and organisation to a great extent. The teaching-learning process has become quiet complex. The System Approach can be used to systematise this process.

The System Approach to design and analysis of teaching and training situations is the basis of great majority of modern technology related developments.

Education is a systematic way of designing an effective and economical educational system in the society.In the teaching-learning process, the System Approach takes into consideration all available learning resources, content, learning experiences, methods, etc, to achieve the learning objectives.

The importance of system approach in education is

- framework for planning, decision-making, controlling and problem-solving.
- throws light on dynamic nature of management.
- provides a unified focus to institutional efforts.
- helps to look at institution as a whole and not as a part.
- helps the manager to identify the critical sub-system and their interaction with each other.
- helps in improving institution.
- helps in bringing efficiency in school administration and management.
- helps in systematic educational planning.
- maximum utilisation of resources.
- helps in improving examination and evaluation system.
- maintaining, controlling and improving the guidance services.
- designing, controlling and improving non-formal and adult education system.
- improving quality of education.
- improving the teacher training programmes *i.e.* in-servie as well as pre-service.

Theory of Rational Choice

The theory of rational choice suggests that individuals rely on rational calculations to achieve outcomes that are in line with their personal objectives. These decisions give people the greatest benefit or satisfaction. Here, the choices are for their highest self-interest. Most mainstream academic assumptions and theories are based on this theory.

It assumes that all people tries to actively maximise their advantage in any situation and therefore, consistently try to minimise their losses. We must remember rationality is the driving force when making a choice whose outcome will be maximising the individual's pleasure or profit.

It declares that all complex social phenomena are driven by individual human actions. This theory is used to model human decision-making, especially in the context of micro-economics. Here, it helps economists to better understand the behaviour of a society in terms of individual actions as explained through rationality. It is also applied to Evolutionary Theory, political science, sociology, etc.

The Rational Choice theory also known as Choice theory or Rational Action theory. It has certain strengths and weaknesses. The strength lies in its simplicity. It is clear straight forward theory that is not only easy to understand but allows us to evaluate and consider other's decisions. Its weakness is that real life isn't simple, clear or straight forward. Thus, the rational choice theorists do not claim that the theory describes the choice process, but rather that it predicts the outcome and pattern of choices.

Education for Political Development and Political Socialisation

Education plays a very prominent role in the political development and political socialisation of the child. As the child acquires various societal norms, traditions, values, etc. through home, family and society; help to develop the feeling of socialisation in him/her. At the same time, child through school curriculum/subjects learns the administrative functioning of the government at various levels. This helps him/her to understand the process of political development. Thus, it can be said that both are related to each other and in an effective way these are discussed below.

Political Development

Nowadays, educational system and processes have assumed a significant place in political science research. In political science, notion of political development is reviewed. The notion of political development becomes more meaningful when it is assessed at the individual level, where it relates to express needs and values. The historical review is made about the role of education in development.

At the time of freedom movement, people having Western education had played a significant role. They took initiatives to educate the masses and tried to unite them for the struggle against the Britishers. They believe that only proper education can motivate the people against the foreign rulers. After independence, our Constitution gives fundamental rights to all its citizens to enjoy all the rights and to do the duties for motherland, it is also very necessary to become educated.

Proper polices of government are the ways in which India has achieved its growth. How can a leader who is not exposed to global politics, economics and other facts of policy-making, do anything for his country? With educated person, at least there is some hope that exposure to the world through the media of education that will help, in some positive thinking and proper identification and resolution of problems.

Society has made a great effort to modernise the world by education, communication, travel, health, commerce, etc. To increase the standard of living, modernisation has transferred the responsibility of education from the family to public institutions. As a result, crime rate, drug addiction, corruption are increasing.

Modern schools, colleges and universities do not give much emphasis upon transmitting a way of life to the students as was given earlier. This is due to the fact that traditional education was meant for an unchanging and static society, a society not marked by rapid change associated with industrialisation.

Modern society is a changing society. In such a society, education aims at communicating empirical knowledge, *i.e.*, knowledge about science and technology and types of specialised knowledge. A transformation in the contents and methods of education has taken place to meet the demands of modern society.

Political Socialisation

Political socialisation includes the ways in which people acquire values and opinions that shape their political stance and ideology. It is regarded as a study of the developmental process by which people of all ages acquire political cognition, attitude and behaviour. Here, the family educational system, peer groups and mass-media plays a very significant role.

It can be explained as given below

Family

Our first political ideas and values are developed within our family. Often parents and elder siblings discuss about the politics infront of the younger members of the family. All these conversations have a great impact on them and they develop generally a similar view of their elderly members.

Schools

Children are introduced to elections and voting, when they choose their class monitors. Later, in high school and colleges, they learn more advanced form of politics through campaigning, when they are encouraged to criticise government's policies. Schools and colleges often arrange debate that involves students, teachers, parents and other larger communities.

Peer Groups

Peer pressure certainly affects teenager's viewpoint and lifestyle. Sometimes, it also affects their political views when the peers are politically conscious. For example, at the time of freedom movement, many school's students joined and took active role in it.

Mass Media

Much of our political information comes from the mass-media, like, newspapers, magazines, radio, television and the internet. It gives us not only political information, but also influences our political values and beliefs.

Besides, these political parties, different religious views, legal system of the states are also playing as important agents of socialisation.

Political education plays an important role in socialising people. As political education helps members of society either to form or change their political views. Through political education, the views of new generation can easily be changed. The educational system provides all the procedures and methods, where by the large society (the socio-political system) gives its members organised and controlled socialisation in the various fields and institutions of human endeavours. Formal education plays the role of political socialisation of citizens. Educational policies are the guidelines expedient both for political socialisation and for national socio-economic and cultural development.

EXAM BASED QUESTIONS

1 Education is process, through which a person
(a) acquires skills
(b) develops abilities and attitudes
(c) learn facts
(d) All of the above

2 What kind of relationship exist between education and politics?
(a) closeness (b) wholeness
(c) collaboralous (d) All of these

3 To promote its political, social and economical success, every government in power wants
(a) education system must be involved to promote its power.
(b) education system must be informative and rationalistic.
(c) education system must be open for all in the society.
(d) All of the above

4 Political of education is
(a) democracy
(b) secularism
(c) cosmopolitanism
(d) constitutionalism

5 The education system was used to fulfil the political ambition of the government in
(a) Hitler's Germany
(b) the French Revolution
(c) some military governments in Africa
(d) All of the above

6 No educational system can survive without the .... support and protection of the government in power.
(a) social (b) financial
(c) psychological (d) None of these

7 Large portion of problems can be solved in a country if it has
(a) a well balanced education system
(b) state controlled education system
(c) centrally controlled education system
(d) None of the above

8 Education system in India has become a business as
(a) politicians and businessmen see it as an another industry.
(b) politicians and businessmen used education for their own gain.
(c) it is only limited to upper class of the society.
(d) All of the above

9 Education is an approach of learning that empowers individuals and prepares them to deal with complexity, diversity and change. It is the .... view of education.
(a) liberal (b) empirical
(c) conservative (d) None of these

10 Which type of education, helps students to develop a sense of social responsibility, strong intellectual and practical skills?
(a) Empirical (b) Rational
(c) Liberal (d) Moral

11 Liberal education refers to the kind of pedagogy built upon an individual's
(a) free choice (b) initiatives
(c) interest (d) Both a and b

12 Liberal education has proposed for the majority of citizen's
(a) political efficacy (b) economical prosperity
(c) cultural enrichment (d) All of these

13 Who believes that the primary role of education is academic and the school should not assume non-academic, custodial and social functions?
(a) Liberalists (b) Rationalists
(c) Behaviourists (d) None of these

14 Which of the following is not included in the type of liberation?
(a) Contemporary
(b) Modern liberalism
(c) Conventional liberalism
(d) Neutral liberalism

15 Tradition provides .... and .... to our society and its culture.
(a) stability, cohesion (b) truth, stability
(c) freedom, stability (d) None of these

16 Education is required to preserve some features of a particular society, these are
(a) culture and value system
(b) religions, faiths and beliefs
(c) language and life style
(d) All of the above

17 Which one is not correct?
(a) India – Secular and democratic education system
(b) Pakistan – Muslim Philosophy in education system
(c) Iran – Liberal views on an education
(d) USA – Capitalistic Model of Education

18 Conservatism is a political and social philosophy, which promotes
(a) traditional social institutions
(b) old fashioned disciplines
(c) Both a and b
(d) None of the above

19 Behaviourism emerged in the
(a) 1930s (b) 1940s
(c) 1950s (d) 1920s

20 Famous behaviourist psychologist(s) is/are
(a) Edward Thorndike
(b) JB Watson
(c) BF Skinner
(d) All of the above

21 Behaviourism insists that Social Theory should be constructed on the basis of
(a) political behaviour
(b) social behaviour
(c) observable behaviour
(d) All of the above

22 Who among the following is the famous Behaviourist Psychologist?
(a) BF Skinner (b) JB Watson
(c) David Easton (d) Both a and b

23 Who among the following have been noted for their strident criticism of behaviourism?
(a) Edward Thorndike
(b) BF Skinner
(c) John B Watson
(d) Noam Chomsky

24 Which one of the following has been wrongly listed as a Traditional Approach?
(a) Historical approach
(b) Behavioural approach
(c) Historical approach
(d) Both b and c

25 .... was the first, who gave System Analysis in political system.
(a) JS Mill (b) JB Watson
(c) David Easton (d) None of these

26 Education adopts Systematic Approach, which judges
(a) available learning resources and contents
(b) learning experiences and methods
(c) Both a and b
(d) None of the above

27 Gabriel Almond suggested that the function of political system perform at these levels.
(a) Capability
(b) Conversion
(c) System
(d) All of the above

28 .... assumes that all people try to actively maximise their advantage in any situation and consistently tries to minimise their losses.
(a) Rational Choice theory
(b) Empirical theory
(c) System Analysis theory
(d) None of the above

29 Rational Choice Theory is also known as ......
(a) Choice theory
(b) Rational Action theory
(c) General System theory
(d) Both a and b

30 Political socialisation, as a study of the developmental process includes
(a) family and schools
(b) peer-group and mass-media
(c) Both a and b
(d) None of the above

31 Which of the following are agencies of social change?
1. Family
2. School
3. National army
4. National calamity

Select the correct answer using the codes given below
(a) 1 and 2 (b) 2 and 3
(c) 3 and 4 (d) 4 and 1

32 The process by which an individual learns to behave in accordance with social norms and culture is called
(a) acculturation (b) socialisation
(c) assimilation (d) None of these

33 Which of the following is not the means of socialisation?
(a) Segregation (b) Imitation
(c) Counselling (d) Association

34 By the process of socialisation, we make the child
(a) cultured
(b) acceptable to the society
(c) aware of the social norms
(d) All of the above

35 Which of the following plays a vital role in the process of socialisation?
(a) Group activities in the school
(b) Cooperation
(c) Competition
(d) All of the above

36 Process of socialisation increases, when the child is brought to
(a) participate in co-curricular activities
(b) attend classes
(c) do experiments in the laboratory
(d) All of the above

37 The school socialised the child by providing social control through
(a) social values (b) regulation
(c) rulers (d) All of these

38 Which of the following helps in the process of socialisation?
(a) Printed material
(b) Meditation process
(c) Playmates
(d) Self-centered living

39 One of the most needed requirement of socialisation, learning and education is
(a) cooperation (b) competition
(c) conflict (d) discipline

40 The process of socialisation is similar to that of teaching because
(a) both requires interactions
(b) both are an automatic process
(c) both starts from the family
(d) Both a and b

41 Process of socialisation of a child will become slow if
(a) child is not allowed to go to neighbourhood, due to social evils rampant there
(b) child cannot communicate due to language barriers
(c) child is handicapped and he/she is hated by the society
(d) All of the above

42 Socialisation requires
(a) teachers (b) rewards
(c) reinforcement (d) All of these

43 In a democratic country, school should reflects
(a) national aspirations
(b) community related local aspirations
(c) Both a and b
(d) None of the above

44 Who is responsible for providing the education in India?
(a) Family (b) Society
(c) State (d) All of these

45 Liberal ideology ....
(a) was invested in the 18th century to serve the interest of the British liberal party
(b) developed as a positive response, to the emergence of industrial capitalism
(c) is a compromise between socialism and conservatism
(d) is a long established creed, which focuses on an individual freedom

46 The family imparts education to the child
(a) formally (b) informally
(c) deliberately (d) regularly

47 What is the modern method of acquiring knowledge?
(a) Authority
(b) Personal experience
(c) Scientific Method
(d) Expert's opinion

48 Which is the pattern of modernisation, through education?
(a) Capitalist
(b) Non-capitalist
(c) Both a and b
(d) Neither (a) nor (b)

49 Except ...., all of the following are important agencies of modernisation.
(a) religious institutions
(b) adult education centres
(c) universities and colleges
(d) primary schools

50 The sociological effect of technology in education will be
(a) alienation in students
(b) modernisation of the society
(c) cultural invasion
(d) collaboration in classroom's learning

51 Through socialisation of individual, we
(a) develops affiliative tendencies towards other individuals and groups.
(b) develops hostile attitude towards other groups.
(c) both a and b
(d) saves an individual, from the prejudices of other people and groups

52 The process of socialisation
(a) is a life long process
(b) intensities in the old age
(c) begins with adulthood
(d) lasts only till the student's life

53 Socialisation is a process by which an individual is adapted to his
(a) classroom's environment
(b) social environment
(c) political environment
(d) cultural environment

54 Which of the following is not a characteristic of modernisation?
(a) Religious faith (b) Participation
(c) Empathy (d) Mobility

55 Schools are basically considered as social institutions because
(a) they preserve and instill in future generations values of our culture
(b) they suggests ways and means of social progress
(c) they suggests solutions to social problems
(d) they are established by the society

56 What is meant by the term 'socialisation'?
(a) Participation in social services.
(b) Teaching rural masses that how to keep their homes and streets clean.
(c) Process of interaction, among members of the society and imbibing social values.
(d) Influence exerted on the illiterate rural masses by social organisations to send their children to schools.

57 Socialisation is entirely based on
(a) political interaction
(b) economical interaction
(c) social interaction
(d) universal interaction

58 School as an agent of socialisation is a
(a) primary agent (b) secondary agent
(c) tertiary agent (d) None of the above

59 **Statement I** No educational system can be separated from political system.
Statement II Considering the societal responsibilities and objectives, education and politics are inextricably related.
Codes
(a) Both statements are true, but II is not the cause of I
(b) Statement I is true, but II is false
(c) Both statements are false
(d) Both statements are true and II is the cause of I

60 **Statement I** The political ideas and values are develop within our family.
Statement II At times, if affects their political views.
Codes
(a) Both statements are true, but II is not the cause of I
(b) Only II is true
(c) Only I is true
(d) Both statements are true and I is the cause of II

61 **Statement I** Indian states have well developed education system.
Statement II It is the duty of the government to promote new policies and amendments in education.
Codes
(a) Both I and II are true
(b) I is true, but II is false
(c) I is false, but II is true
(d) Both I and II are false

62 **Statement I** Liberal education sometimes considered as 'elitist' education system.
Statement II Elite education is an educational arrangement for selected few to train them for social, professional and political eminence.
(a) Only I is true
(b) Only II is true
(c) I is true, but II is false
(d) Both I and II are true

63 **Statement I** In the past politicians perceived their role as completely separate and independent.
Statement II But in reality, no educational system can be separated from political system.
Codes
(a) Both statements, I and II are false
(b) Both statements, I and II are true
(c) Only I is true
(d) Neither I nor II is true

64 Which of the following statement(s) is/are correct about the Principles of Conservatism.
Statement I They believe that all humans are imperfect by nature and these is no way to create a perfect society on the earth.
Statement II Tradition provides stability and cohesion to our society and its culture.
(a) Only statement I is true
(b) Both statements, I and II are false
(c) Both statements, I and II are true
(d) Only statement II is true

65 **Statement I** Education is known as a potential instrument of social change.
Statement II To achieve national integration, education must be critical and modern.
(a) Only I is true
(b) Only II is true
(c) Both I and II are true
(d) I is true, but II is false

Directions (Q. Nos. 66-69) *Given below are two statements. One labelled as Assertion (A) and other labelled as Reason (R). Choose the correct code from the following.*
Codes
(a) Both A and R are true and R is the correct explanation of A
(b) Both A and R are true, but R is not the correct explanation of A
(c) A is true, but R is false
(d) A is false, but R is true

66 **Assertion** (A) Peer groups socialise children towards politics.
Reason (R) Peer groups have the most impact when they get involved with political discussions and activities.

67 **Assertion** (A) An individual acquires three types of basic orientations, related to functioning or polity during the process of political socialisation.
Reason (R) Political socialisation helps in learning of political attitudes and social preferences which is crucial for stable government and democracy.

68 **Assertion** (A) The end point of social development is social maturity.
Reason (R) A socially matured person is fully adjusted person in the society.

69 Assertion (A) Socialisation is a continuous process.
Reason (R) Social learning never ends.

70 A classroom teacher enhances the process of learning by all methods, except
(a) controlling the behaviour of learners
(b) dealing with the learners, individually
(c) applying Learning Theories in the class
(d) teaching the students, by disregarding their maturity level

71 Analysis of the sociological processes, involved in educational institutions, could be known as
(a) social foundations of education
(b) educational sociology
(c) sociology of education
(d) social science of education

72 In the history of education in India, the pre-dominant influence was of the following.
1. Democracy
2. Religion
3. Politics
4. Modernisation

Codes
(a) 1, 2, 3, 4 (b) 2, 3, 1, 4
(c) 3, 2, 4, 1 (d) 4, 1, 2, 3

73 Characteristically conservatives are
(a) opposed to rationalism
(b) supportive of their tried and trusted preference to the experiment
(c) believes in organic society
(d) All of the above

74 Match the following

List I		List II	
A.	Liberal	1.	It suggests that individual rely on rational calculations to achieve outcomes
B.	Conservative	2.	It was a part of the Behaviourist Movement in political science
C.	System analysis	3.	They are old fastioned in educational system
D.	Rational Choice theory	4.	An approach to learning which empowers individual and prepares then to deal with complexity, diversity and change

Codes

	A	B	C	D
(a)	4	3	2	1
(b)	1	2	3	4
(c)	2	3	1	4
(d)	4	3	2	1

ANSWERS

1 *(d)*	2 *(d)*	3 *(a)*	4 *(a)*	5 *(d)*	6 *(b)*	7 *(a)*	8 *(a)*	9 *(a)*	10 *(c)*
11 *(d)*	12 *(d)*	13 *(a)*	14 *(d)*	15 *(a)*	16 *(d)*	17 *(c)*	18 *(c)*	19 *(c)*	20 *(a)*
21 *(d)*	22 *(d)*	23 *(d)*	24 *(b)*	25 *(c)*	26 *(c)*	27 *(d)*	28 *(a)*	29 *(d)*	30 *(c)*
31 *(a)*	32 *(b)*	33 *(a)*	34 *(d)*	35 *(d)*	36 *(a)*	37 *(d)*	38 *(b)*	39 *(a)*	40 *(d)*
41 *(d)*	42 *(d)*	43 *(c)*	44 *(c)*	45 *(d)*	46 *(d)*	47 *(c)*	48 *(c)*	49 *(a)*	50 *(b)*
51 *(a)*	52 *(a)*	53 *(b)*	54 *(c)*	55 *(a)*	56 *(c)*	57 *(c)*	58 *(b)*	59 *(d)*	60 *(d)*
61 *(c)*	62 *(d)*	63 *(b)*	64 *(b)*	65 *(a)*	66 *(c)*	67 *(d)*	68 *(b)*	69 *(d)*	70 *(d)*
71 *(b)*	72 *(b)*	73 *(d)*	74 *(a)*						

CHAPTER 09

Growth and Development

Growth is the progressive increase in the size of a child or parts of a child while development is a progressive acquisition of various skills such as speaking, learning, expressing and relating with other people. Growth and development go together but at different rates. Both processes highly depend on genetic, nutritional and environmental factors.

Concept of Growth and Development

It is a process that starts with a single cell. It is created by joining together of one special cell with another cell, which comes from each parent. Growth refers to the specific body changes and increase in child's size (such as height, weight, body mass index). These size changes can be easily measurable. Whereas, development refers to an increase in complexity (a change from simple to more complex). Basically, it involves a progression along a continuing pathway on which child acquires more refined knowledge, behaviour and skills.

Human development is a lifelong process of physical, behavioural, cognitive and emotional growth and change. It describes the growth of humans throughout the life span, from conception to death. A lot of changes take place at various stages of life; infancy, childhood, adolescence and adulthood. Throughout the stages, each individual develops attitude, values that guide choices, relationships and understanding. The scientific study of human development seeks to understand and explain how and why people change throughout the life. This includes all aspects of human growth and development including physical, emotional, intellectual, social, perceptual and personality development.

Human development is the basic fact of human existence and each person develops uniquely. It occurs in an orderly sequence, involving physical, cognitive and emotional development. Although, there are universally accepted principles of development, but they occur with difference in the rate or timing of the changes from one person to another.

In this Chapter

Growth and development are oftenly used interchangeably in terminologies, but both are different from each other.

The difference between growth and development is discussed below:

Difference Between Growth and Development

Growth	Development
Growth is physical changes in the organism.	Development is overall and progressive changes in the organism.
Growth is cellular.	Development is organisational.
Growth is change in shape, form, structure and size of the body.	Development is structural and functional changes in body.
Growth stops at maturation.	Development continues till death.
Growth is a part of development.	Development includes growth.
Growth is quantitative in nature.	Development is qualitative in nature.

Both growth and development are correlated and dependent on each other.

Definitions of Growth and Development

According to **Hurlock**, "Growth refers to change in size, in proportion, disappearance of old features and acquisition of new ones".

According to **Crow and Crow**, "Growth refers to structural and physiological changes".

According to **Hurlock, Development** means "a progressive series of changes that occur in an orderly predictable pattern as a result of maturation and experience".

According to **Crow and Crow**, "Development is concerned with growth as well as those changes in behaviour which results from environmental situations".

Principles of Development

All children develops at different rates and therefore, the notion of individual differences exists. A child can show more rapid changes in some developmental areas than in others. Regardless of the perspective, *there are certain principles of development that apply to all the children*

Development is a Never Ending Process The process of development is continuous, as human beings continue to develop, change and to be affected by experience throughout the life. Most of the growth and noticeable changes take place in childhood. The rate of development is higher in the first few years than in any period of life. Yet humans of all ages continue to grow, to learn and to change.

Rate of Development can be Different, for Different Individuals Each individual is a unique package of emotional, mental and physical traits. The time-table of development does not always provide evenly spaced starts and stops. A child may show growth in one area before another. The rate of development can be different for different individuals.

All Growth are Related Every aspect of human growth influences every other aspect. Despite occassional time lags, physical, emotional and mental growth are related. There is a positive correlation, a direct relationship among physical, emotional, social and mental development. Improvement in physical status improves self-concept and positive self-concept is related to academic achievement. Social development influences the behaviour of individual. So, all the growth are inter-related.

Development Proceeds in Stages There are four stages of development : infancy, childhood, adolescence and adulthood that are common in all the humans.

Development is Influenced by Both Heredity and Environment The final outcome of growth and development is a result of the dynamic interplay of genetic potential and environmental factors.

Development has Direction Every individual develops at an different rate, but each one goes through same stages. The sequences are predictable and same for all individuals. Babies first crawl, then stand and then walk. Each stage, each task is successfully mastered, makes the next stage and task more complex.

Some of the major directions of development are listed below

(i) **Cephalocaudal and Proximodistal** Every human being develop from head to feet (cephalocaudal) and from center of the body towards outer (proximodistal). The head develops first, then the trunk, then arms and legs. Large muscles develops before small ones.

(ii) **Structure Precedes Function** Muscles must be ready to perform specific functions. An individual cannot use his/her body, until the body is capable of being used.

(iii) **General to Specific** Development precedes from general to specific. Young children see only the whole unit until they are mature enough to be able to focus on parts of the whole.

(iv) **Concrete to Abstract** Mental growth preceeds from an ability to think only about things that are physically present to an ability to visualise that are not present and to conceptualise and understand them.

(v) **Egocentrism to Perspectivism** A very young child is the center of the universe and sees the events as related to his/her needs. As the child grows and interacts with people, he or she can begin to see things from others point of view and then form the perspective of abstract principle.

(vi) **Outer Control to Inner Control** Young children are dependent on others for physical care as well as for values and principles. As they grow, they develop their own value system and own set of inner control.

(vii) **Absolutism to Relativism** Children see everything as absolute and unchangeable. As they grow, they understand that everything is changeable to meet the specific situation.

(viii) **Spiraling** The same task is mastered at varying degrees of complexity like walk, run, etc, at different stages of development.

Continuous and Discontinuous Development

Some psychologists believe that development is smooth and continuous process. Children gradually add more of the same type of skills. Other psychologists think that development is a discontinuous process. Children change rapidly as they step up to a new level of development and then change very little for a while. With each step, the child interprets and responds to the world in a qualitatively different way.

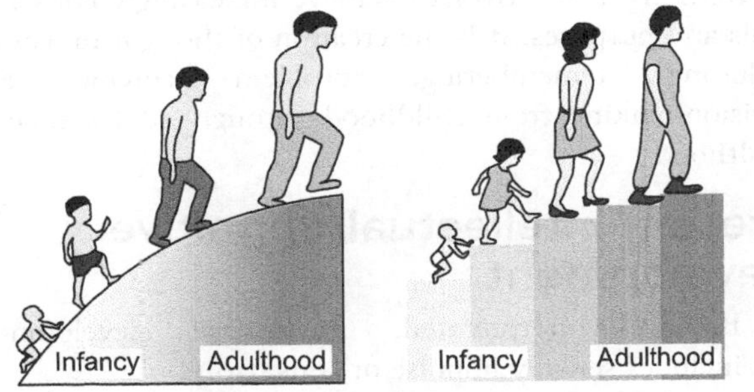

(a) Continuous Development (b) Discontinuous Development

Cognitive Processes

The word cognition derives from Latin Word 'cognosco' means 'to recognize'. Cognitive process refers to the process of thinking involved in obtaining and storing knowledge. It encompasses many aspects of intellectual functions and processes such as attention, formation of knowledge, judgement, evaluation, reasoning, problem solving and decision-making. It is the process by which existing knowledge is used to create new knowledge. It is a demonstration of the central ability human posses that define us.

Cognitive processes are analyzed from different sciences including sociology, linguistics, neurology, anthropology and philosophy. As for psychology, cognitive psychology is the field in charge of studying cognitive processes. The cognitive psychologists study the various cognitive processes that make up this branch. These processes include attention, the process through which we focus on some stimulus; perception, the process through which we interpret sensory information and memory, the process through which information is stored for later retrieval. Each of these cognitive functions work together to integrate the new knowledge and create an interpretation of the world around us.

The cognitive processes can happen naturally or artificially, consciously or unconsciously, but they usually happen fast.

In the 60's, a new psychological perspective emerged that lead to the cognitive revolution and the study of cognitive processes. They are now even applied not only to explain disorders but to areas such as marketing and sales. Neuro imaging has been of great help in how we process information and what parts of the brain are related to what cognitive processes.

Types of Cognitive Processes

There are various types of cognitive processes which are given below

Basic Cognitive Processes

Basic cognitive processes are classified into three parts such as

(i) **Sensation and Perception** Sensations are the result of different stimuli in our environment. The stimuli first reach our senses and allow us to filter information from the outside world. Once we receive this information, perception takes over and we start interpreting these stimuli.

Human beings continuously use their perception without even noticing it. We are conscious of other people's movements, food flavours, our posture, etc. Our past experiences also plays an important part in the interpretation of different stimuli.

Gestalt psychologists were the main researchers in perception.

"The whole is greater than the sum of the parts"-Gestalt

They believed that we are active human beings that process reality as a whole comprised of different parts. They also explained how different types of perception can happen including illusions.

(ii) **Attention** Attention is the cognitive process that makes it possible to position ourselves towards relevant stimuli and consequently respond to it. In life, we experience many stimuli happening at the same time but we are capable of centering our attention on the stimuli that interest us. For *e.g.* we give little attention on actions such as walking and chewing but the activities such as speaking and body language requires focus, especially when we are giving a lecture.

We have different types of attention including arousal, focused attention, sustained attention, selective attention, alternating attention and divided attention. Through these types of attention we make our life possible.

(iii) **Memory** Our memory has the answers to the questions we think. It allows too many processes happen such as to encode the data we receive from the environment, consolidate and retrieve it later.

We have different types of memory such as sensory memory, short-term memory, working memory, semantic memory and so on. All these types of memories interact together but they do not all depend on the same brain areas. Memory includes three main processes like encoding, storage, and retrieval. Encoding is the mechanism where information is changed from the moment it reaches us to a form that our brain can store. Storage refers to how long the memory lasts for or duration and how much can be stored at any time (capacity) and what kind of information is held. Finally, retrieval refers to getting information out storage.

High or Complex Cognitive Processes

High or complex cognitive processes are divided into three parts such as

(i) **Intelligence** According to Gardner's multiple bits of intelligence, there is not only one intelligence but several different bits of intelligence. Examples of higher cognitive processes are intrapersonal intelligence, linguistic intelligence, logical-mathematical intelligence, and musical intelligence. Emotional intelligence has got people's attention, which is the ability to manage the difficulties we face daily.

(ii) **Thought** Our thoughts have many complexity and heterogeneity. Through our thoughts we are able to do our tasks related to problem-solving, reasoning, decision-making, creative thinking, divergent thinking and many more things.

Our brain creates concepts to simplify these functions like ideas, objects, people or any other kind of elements that come to our mind. Usually, this helps streamline our cognitive processes. Sometimes we take shortcuts to process information faster not taking into account the details that might be important. This can lead to cognitive biases which can lead to cognitive distortions which are extremely negative and irrational thoughts. Thus, it is important that we should stop these types of thoughts and work on them.

(iii) **Language** Language is a means of communication. Through cognitive processes we are capable of producing and comprehending different sounds and words and combine them to understand language and communicate with others. We even use our body language to communicate.

Language development is a process which continues throughout our life. The communicative skills of each person vary significantly and can be improved by practice.

Cognitive Development

Cognitive development comprehends the development of intellect, mental capabilities, imagination, thinking, emotion and other mental processes. Functions of brain (to know, to experience and to make decisions), play an important role in the intellectual development. Therefore, intellectual/cognitive development refers to development in the ability to adapt behaviour to environmental conditions as the individual strives to achieve increasingly conscious goals and purposes. It is the creation of thought processes, including remembering, problem solving and decision-making from childhood through adolescence to adulthood.

Areas of Intellectual/Cognitive Development

- Broadly interpretated, intellectual development includes sensory impulse or **sensation**.
- The interpretation of sensations or **perception** includes the power to build upon perceptual material, not present to the senses.
- And also the ability to recall the experience with the help of **memory**.
- And lastly, the highest form of mental/intellectual development is **reasoning**, that helps in formulating generalisations from the experiences and dealing with abstractions.

Piaget's Cognitive Development Theory

Jean Piaget was a Swiss developmental psychologist who studied children in the early 20th century. His theory of intellectual or cognitive development, was published in 1936, which is still in use in some branches of education and psychology.

It focuses on children from birth through adolescence & characterises different stages of cognitive development.

Stages of Cognitive Development

Piaget's stages of cognitive development are age-specific and marked by important characteristics of thought processes. They also include goals, children should achieve as they move through a given stage.

The important stages of cognitive development are given below

Sensorimotor Stage (Infancy-birth until 2 years) In this period, which has six sub-stages, intelligence is demonstrated through motor activity without the use of symbols. Knowledge of the world is limited, but developing, because it is based on physical interactions and experiences. Children acquires object permanence at about seven months of age (memory). Physical development (mobility) allows the child to begin developing non-intellectual abilities. Some symbolic (language) abilities are developed at the end of this stage.

Pre-Operational Stage (2 years until 6 or 7 years) In this period, which has two sub-stages, intelligence is demonstrated through the use of symbols, language, memory and imagination which are developed, but thinking is done in a non-logical, non-reversible manners. Egocentric thinking predominates.

Concrete Operational Stage (7 to 11 years) In this stage, which is characterised by seven types of conservations (number, length, liquid, mass, weight, area and volume), intelligence is demonstrated through logical and systematic manipulation of symbols related to concrete objects. In this stage, operational thinking develops (mental actions that are reversible) and egocentric thought diminishes.

Formal Operational Stage (11 or 12 years through adulthood) At this stage, children develops the ability of abstract reasoning, hypothetical and contrary to fact information. They also begin to understand the concept of proportion, and become capable of thinking about their own thought processes. They also become capable of evaluating the quality and logic of those thoughts.

As we have seen that cognitive development is an important aspect of life, which proceeds through different stages. Thus, it is important for parents and teachers to help their youngsters in their growth period and provide them positive environment to develop their mental abilities.

Terms Used by Piaget

There are a variety of terms Piaget used in his theory to explain cognitive development and how it's achieved at different stages.

These are discussed below

Schema is a term Piaget used to represent the building blocks of knowledge. You may think of schemas as different index cards inside the brain. Each one informs an individual on how to react to new information or situations.

In the same way, when a new baby borns he/she has few practical instincts and reflexes such as sucking, looking, reaching and grasping. Piaget named these abilities or potentials as schemas.

Thus, these various schemas form the basic structure of the human mind. The earlier schemas represent those reflexes and instincts that are biologically inherited. However, as a child grows, with the interaction of physical and social environment, he is able to form different schemas, resulting in changes and modifications in his cognitive structure.

Assimilation is using an existing schema and applying it to a new situation or object.

Accommodation is changing approaches when an existing schema does not work in a particular situation.

Equilibration is the driving force that moves all development forward. He asserted that the process of assimilation or accommodation helps the organism to adjust or maintain a harmonious relationship between himself and his environment. This adjustment mechanism was called equilibration by Piaget.

Personality

The term 'personality' is often used in our day-to-day discussion. For a **Layman**, personality is often understood in terms of physical or external appearance of the individual. People generally, go by the impression created by the other person. The ability to talk, interact with other pleasantly in addition to being good looking, would make others say that the person has a charming personality. This notion of personality is based on superficial impressions, which may not be correct. Scientifically, this is not the true concept of personality.

Psychologists does not consider personality in terms of social attractiveness. It is because of two reasons, firstly, it limits the number and types of behaviour considered important in study of personality. And secondly, such notion carries the absurd implication that some people, who have unique abilities are devoid of having personalities.

The literal meaning of the term 'personality' is derived from the Latin word 'persona'. 'Persona' originally denotes the 'theatrical mask', first used in Greek drama and adopted about a 100 years before Christ by Roman players. It was the mask used by actors in Roman theatres for changing their facial make up. After putting on the mask, audience expected the person to perform a role in a particular manner.

In **psychological** terms, personality refers to our characteristics, ways of responding to individuals and situations. People can describe the way in which they respond to a particular situation. There are certain words or traits associated with the personality. These words are used to describe the personality. Words like shy, quite, sensitive, warm, concerned are used to refer the different components of personality. In this sense, personality refers to unique and relatively stable qualities that characterise an individual's behaviour across different situations over period of time.

Definitions of Personality

There are lot of definitions of personality. Each and every definition, suggests a different approach towards personality. *Some of the definitions given by renowned psychologists are given below*

According to **Allport**, "Personality is the dynamic organisation within the individual of those psychological systems that determine his unique adjustment to his environment".

According to **Morton Prince**, "Personality is the sum total of all the biological innate disposition, impulses, tendencies, appetities and instincts of the individual and the acquired dispositions and tendencies".

According to **Kemph**, "Personality is the integration of those systems of habits that represents one's individual characteristic adjustment to his environment".

Personality characterises individuals as they appear in maximum circumstances. Consistency in behaviour, thought, emotion of an individual across situations and time periods characterise a person's personality. *e.g.*, an honest person will remain honest in all the situations. However, there can be some variation in the behaviour according to the change in the environment.

Therefore, in brief, the personality can be defined by the following features

- It comprises of both physical and psychological components.
- Every individual poseses a unique set of behaviour. Therefore, its expression in terms of behaviour is different for different individuals.
- It is dynamic in nature. Change can occur due to the internal or external situations.
- It is adaptive to situations.
- It is greatly infuenced by social interactions.

Character and temperament are important part of the personality. Character refers to value judgement. These are made about a person's moral values or ethical behaviour. Temperament refers to the inborn enduring characteristics such as adaptability, irritability, etc.

Factors Affecting Personality Development

Right from the time, the term *personality development* came into existence, it has become the topic of interest for the personality psychologists. Psychologists have tried to identify the factors, which directly or indirectly influence the growth and development of the individual personality.

Factors influencing development of personality can be classified into the following categories:

Biological Factors	*It includes* Body building Physical attractiveness Homeostasis Physical defects Health conditions
Psychological Factors	*It includes* Intellectual determinants Emotional determinants Self-disclosure Aspiration and achievements
Environmental Factors	*It includes* Social acceptance Social deprivation Educational factors Family determinants Ordinal position Size of family

Theories of Personality

There are various theories of personality which are discussed below

Freudian Psychoanalytic Theory of Personality

Sigmund Freud (1856-1939) is considered to be the 'Father of Psychiatry'. He gave Psychoanalytic Theory of Personality. According to him, human personality is complex and has more than a single component. The aim of Psychoanalytic theory is to release repressed emotions and experiences, i.e. make the unconscious, conscious. Psychoanalytic is commonly used to treat depression and anxiety disorders.

He described the personality is composed of three elements of minds. These three elements of personality are known as the id, the ego, and the super ego which work together to create complex human behaviours. This theory is also known as **Freud's Structural Theory of Personality** which places great emphasis on the role of unconscious psychological conflicts in shaping behaviour and personality. He also described different stages of development.

Stages of Development

Freud emphasised five stages of psychosexual development believing that most human suffering is determined during childhood development. As a child passes through these stages unresolved conflicts between physical drives and social expectation may arise.

These stages are given below

Oral Stage (0 to 1.5 years of age) In this stage, the main focus is pleasure seeking through the infant's mouth. Oral stimulation is crucial during this stage. If the infant's needs are not met during this time frame, he or she will be fixated in the oral stage. This fixation can lead to adult habits such as thumb-sucking, over-eating, and nail-biting.

Anal Stage (1.5 to 3 years of age) At this stage, the infant's pleasure seeking centres are located in the bowles and bladder. This stage is primarily related to developing healthy toilet training habits. Fixation in this stage may lead to anal-retention or anal-expulsion.

Anal retention includes being overly neat, precise and orderly. While being anal expulsive involves being disorganised messy, and destructive.

Phallic Stage (3 to 5 years of age) At this stage, development of healthy substitutes for the sexual attraction for boys and girls have toward a parent of the opposite gender.

Latency Stage (5 to 12 years of age) At this stage, children do not have any pleasure seeking region in the body, instead all sexual feelings are repressed. During this stage, children are able to develop social skills and find comfort through peer and family interaction.

Genital Stage (12 to adulthood) All tasks from the previous four stages are integrated into the mind allowing for the onset of healthy sexual feeling and behaviours.

Freud's Structure of the Human Mind

In his theory, he stated three levels of human mind which filter the experiences of human beings during the given stages. From these structures and the inherent conflicts, a person's personality gets shaped. According to him, while there is interdependence among the three levels i.e. id, ego and superego, each level also serves a purpose in personality development.

These levels are described below

Id The id, the most primitive of the three structures and is present from birth. It is concerned with instant gratification of basic physical needs and urges. It is childish, selfish, pleasure-oriented part of the personality with no ability to delay gratification. It operates entirely unconsciously means outside of conscious thought. For example, if your id walked past a stranger eating ice cream, it would most likely take the ice cream for itself. It doesn't know, or care, that it is rude to take something belonging to someone else; it would care only that you wanted the ice-cream.

Ego Ego is responsible for creating balance between pleasure and pain. It is less primitive than the id and is partly conscious and partly unconscious. Freud considered this to be the 'self' and its job is to balance the demands of the id and superego in the practical context of reality. The ego functions in conscious, and unconscious mind. The ego operates based on the reality principle which strives to satisfy the id's desires in realistic and socially appropriate ways.

Superego This develops around age four or five which is a conscious level and is concerned with social rules and morals. Freud believed that the superego is what allows the mind to control its impulses that are looked down upon morally. At this level, society and parental guidance is weighed against personal pleasure and gain as directed by ones id. At this level, children learn what their culture considers right and wrong. This level acts to perfect and civilise our behaviour. The superego is present in the conscious and unconscious mind.

Thus, in many cases the id's impulses can be satisfied through a process of delayed gratification, the ego will eventually allow the behaviour, but only in an appropriate time and place.

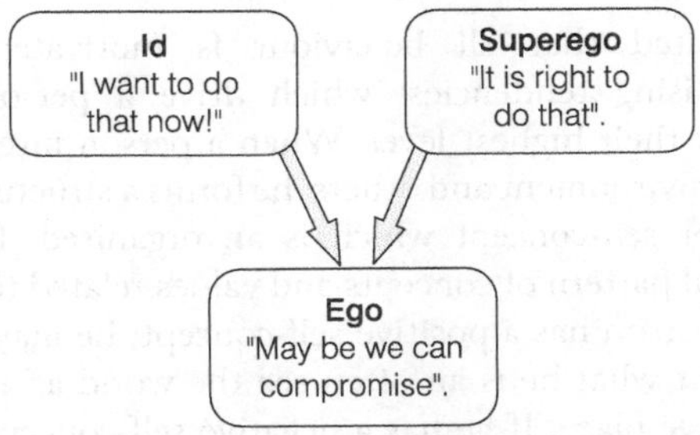

Carl Rogers Humanistic Theory of Personality

Carl Rogers (1902-1987) was a humanistic psychologist. He is well known by his personality theory that emphasised the importance of the self-actualising tendency in shaping human personalities.

He greatly contributed to our understanding of the self and personality. According to him, human is an active, creative, experiencing being that lives in the present and subjectively responds to current perceptions and relationships.

He is credited to coin the term **actualising tendency**, which refers to a person's basic instinct to succeed at his or her highest possible capacity. His theory of personality development is based on person-centered counseling and scientific theory research. This theory highlights free will and the great reservoir of human potential for goodness.

Personality Development and the Self-Concept

Rogers based his theories of personality development on humanistic psychology and theories of subjective experience. According to him, everyone exists in a constantly changing world of experiences that they are at the centre of. He believed that a person reacts to changes in their phenomenal field, which includes external objects, people, internal thoughts and emotions.

The Phenomenal Field

Carl Rogers described the phenomenal field as a person's subjective reality. Motivations and environment of a person act on his phenomenal field.

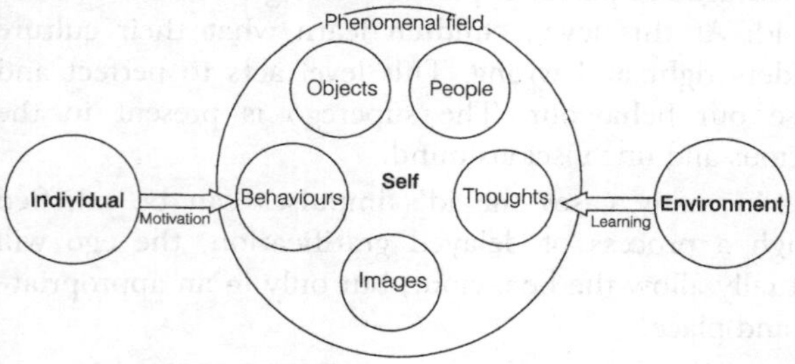

Roger stated that all behaviour is motivated by self-actualising tendencies, which drive a person to achieve at their highest level. When a person interacts with the environment and others, he forms a structure of the self or self-concept which is an organised, fluid, conceptual pattern of concepts and values related to the self. If a person has a positive self-concept, he may feel good about what he is an often see the world as a safe and positive place. If he has a negative self-concept, he may feel unhappy with who he is.

Ideal Self v/s Real Self

He divided the self into the ideal self and the real self. The ideal self is the person that you would like to be whereas the real self is the person you actually are. He stressed that we need to achieve consistency between these two selves. We experience congruence when our thoughts about our real self and ideal self are very similar. Greater sense of self-worth and a healthy and productive life is the result of high congruence.

Conversely, when there is a great discrepancy between our ideal and actual selves, we experience a state of incongruence. Consequently, it may lead to maladjustment.

Unconditional Positive Regard

In his theory of personality, Rogers gave more importance to unconditional positive regard, or unconditional love. According to him, when people are raised in an environment of unconditional positive regard, where no preconceived conditions of worth are present, have the opportunity to fully actualise. When people are raised in an environment of conditional positive regard, where worth and love are only given under certain conditions, they must achieve those conditions to receive the love or positive regard they yearn for. This contributes to incongruence and a greater gap between the real self and the ideal self.

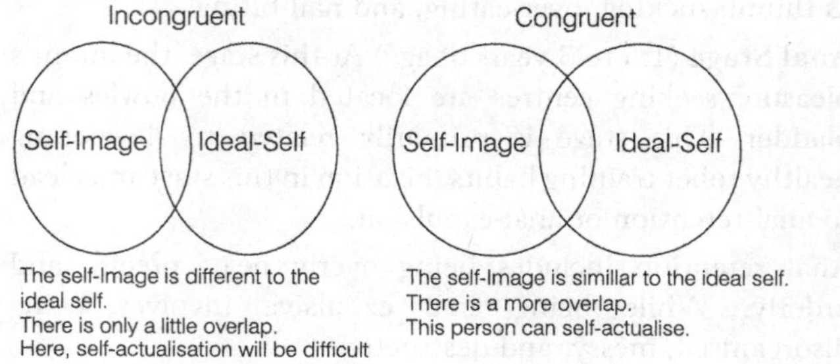

The self-Image is different to the ideal self.
There is only a little overlap.
Here, self-actualisation will be difficult

The self-Image is simillar to the ideal self.
There is a more overlap.
This person can self-actualise.

The Good Life

According to him, life is described in terms of principles rather than stages of development. These principles exist in fluid processes rather than static states.

He claimed that to achieve "the good life", a fully functioning person would continuously work to fulfill his or her potential in each of these processes. He stated several traits or tendencies about the fully functioning individuals.

These are as follows

A growing openness to experience These people move away from defensiveness.

An increasingly existential lifestyle These people live each movement fully, rather than distorting the moment to fit personality or self-concept.

Increasing organismic trust These people trust their own judgement and their ability to choose behaviour that is appropriate in life.

Freedom of choice These people are not restricted by incongruence and are able to make a wide range of choices more fluently. They themselves responsible for their own behaviour.

Higher levels of creativity These people are more creative.

Gordon Allport's Trait Theory of Personality

Gordon Willard Allport was one of the pioneer trait theorists who attempted to list the traits that make an individual's personality. He founded the trait theory in 1936.

Allport's Personality Theory separates all traits into three basic sub-categories that are cardinal, secondary and central traits. This theory suggests that individual personalities are composed of broad dispositions. It is also based mainly on difference between individuals. The combination and interaction of various traits forms a personality that is unique to each individual, this theory focused on identifying and measuring these individual personality characteristics.

"The basic principle of behaviour is its continuous flow". —**Allport**

Motivation is an important personality concept in Allport's theory. At the same time, a person stream of activity has both a variable portion and a constant portion. The constant portion is described with the concept of trait and the variable portion is described with the functional autonomy or the tendency for a behaviour to continue to be performed for reasons that differ from the reasons that originally motivated it.

Both, the trait and functional autonomy are motivational. Many traits have motive power and functional autonomy explains adult motivation.

Concept of Trait and Personal Dispositions

Allport defines trait as neuro psychic structure having the capacity to render many stimuli functionally equivalent and to initiate and guide equivalent (meaningfully consistent) forms of adaptive and expressive behaviour. In simpler terms, a trait is a predisposition to act in the same way in a wide range of situations.

Traits are psychological entities that render many stimuli as well as many responses functionally equivalent. Many stimuli may evoke the same responses or many responses. *e.g* feelings, perceptions, interpretations, actions have the same functional meaning in terms of traits.

Common Traits v/s Individual Traits

Common Traits	Individual Traits
It includes any generalised disposition to which most people within a given culture can be reasonably compared.	It includes those characteristics of individual, which are unique or peculiar to individual.
Majority of people within the particular culture could be measurably compared with one another on those common traits or dimensions.	These traits operate in unique ways within each person. It pinpoints the personality structure of any given individual.
e.g., social attitude, anxiety, value.	*e.g.* shy, introvert.

Types of Traits

Allport proposed that trait may be classified into a three-fold and somewhat overlapping category system. These are:

Cardinal Traits These are traits that dominate an individual's entire personality. Allport suggested that these traits are developed later in life, and are infact quite rare.

Central Traits Common traits that make up our personalities. Traits such as kindness, honesty and friendliness are all examples of central traits.

Secondary Traits These are traits that are only present under certain conditions and circumstances. An example of secondary trait would be getting nervous before delivering a speech to a large group of people.

Characteristics of Traits

In 1966, Allport published an article entitled, **'Traits Revisited'** in which he proposed eight basic characteristics of traits. *They are as follows*

A Trait has more than Normal Existence Personality traits are real and important part of everyone's existence. *e.g.,* honesty, punctuality, aggressiveness, etc. Everyone possesses certain generalised action tendencies.

A Trait is more Generalised than a Habit Trait is relatively permanent and general features of our behaviour. While habits are more specific tendencies and are less generalised in terms of situation. *e.g.,* brushing the teeth twice is a habit and cleanliness is a trait.

A Trait is Dynamic or atleast Determinative in Behaviour Traits are not dormant waiting to be aroused by external stimuli. Traits guides and directs a person's actions.

A Trait's Existence may be Established Empirically Traits cannot be observed directly. Their existence can be verified.

A Trait is only Relatively Independent of other Traits Traits are not independent of other. There is no specific boundary separating one trait from another. The personality is compromised of a network of overlapping traits only relatively independent of one another.

A trait is not synonymous with moral and social judgement.

- A trait may be viewed in light of either the personality that contains it or its distribution in the population at large.
- Acts or habits that are in consistent with a trait are not proof of the non-existence of the trait.

Functional Autonomy

Allport believed in looking at the person's present, rather than exploring the past. This belief is strongly evident in the concept of functional autonomy, in which person's motives are independent of their origins.

The concept of functional autonomy of motives provides the necessary base for a theory of motivation. It simply means that adult motives are not related to past motives. In other words, the reasons why an adult engages in some behaviour are independent of whatever reasons that might have originally caused him/her to engage in that behaviour.

Types of Functional Autonomy

Preservative functional autonomy is the feedback mechanism in the nervous system that are governed by simple neurological principles.

These mechanisms become neurologically self-maintaining over time and help to keep an organism on track. *e.g.* eating, brushing at the same time.

Propriate functional autonomy refers to the acquired interest, values and attitudes of the person. It represents the striving for values and goals, the sense of responsibility that people take for their lives.

Gestalt Theory of Learning

The Gestalt theorists were the first group of psychologists to systematically study perceptual organisation around the 1920's in Germany. This theory was developed by the research work of Max Wertheimar, Wolfgang Kohler, Kurt Koffka and Kurt Lewin.

In this theory, the psychologists tried to see learning as a more deliberate and conscious effort of the individual rather than a mere product of habit formation or a machine-like stimulus response connection. According to them, the learner does not merely respond to a stimulus, but mentally processes what he receives or perceives. Gestalt's theory focused on the mind's perspective.

Educational Implications of Gestalt Theory

Problem Solving Approach This theory emphasizes that as the learner is able to solve problems by his insight, meaningful learning, learning by understanding, reasoning, etc must be encouraged in the school.

From Whole to Part The teacher should present the subject matter as a whole to facilitate insight learning.

Integrated Approach While planning curriculum, Gestalt principles should be given due consideration. A particular subject should not be treated as a mere collection of isolated facts. It should be closely integrated into a whole.

Goal Orientation As learning is purposeful and goal oriented task, the learner has to be well acquainted with these objectives.

Emphasis on Understanding It has made learning an intelligent task requiring mental abilities than a stimulus response association.

Kurt Koffka

Kurt Koffka (1886-1941) was a German Psychologist who developed Gestalt Psychology along with other psychologists. Koffka's interests were wide ranging and they included : perception, hearing impairments in brain-damaged patients, interpretation, learning and extension of Gestalt theory to developmental psychology. His work on Gestalt Psychology is an attempt to understand the laws behind the ability to acquire and maintain meaningful perceptions in an apparently chaotic world.

The central principle of Gestalt psychology is that the mind forms a global whole with self organizing tendencies. However, the assumed physiological mechanisms on which Gestalt theory rests, are poorly defined and support for their existence in lacking. Contrary to behaviourist approach focussing on stimulus and response, Gestalt Psychologists sought to understand the organization of cognitive processes.

Max Wertheimer's Views on Gestalt Theory

Max Wertheimer (1880-1943) was born in the Czech Republic. He was one of the trio of psychologists who founded the Gestalt Theory of Learning along with his collaborators namely Wolfgang Kohler and Kurt Koffka. In 1910, Wertheimer developed his Gestalt theory which emphasised higher-order cognitive processes in the midst of behaviourism. According to Wertheimer, the focus of Gestalt theory was an idea of 'grouping', i.e. characteristics of stimuli causes us to structure or interpret a visual field or problem in a certain way.

Factors Determining Grouping

He proposed primary factors which determined grouping. These factors were called the laws of organisation and were explained in the context of perception and problem-solving.

These factors were

Proximity elements tend to be grouped together according to their nearness.

Similarity items similar in some respect tend to grouped together.

Closure items are grouped together if they tend to complete some entity.

Simplicity items will be organised into simple figures according to symmetry, regularity, and smoothness.

The main focus of Wertheimer was concerned with the problem-solving. In 1959, Wertheimer provides a Gestalt interpretation of problem-solving episodes of famous scientists (*e.g.* Galileo, Einstein) as well as children presented with mathematical problems.

He believed that the essence of successful problem-solving behaviour is being able to see the overall structure of the problem. Gestalt theory applies to all aspects of human learning, although it applies most directly to perception and problem-solving. The work of Gibson was strongly influenced by Gestalt theory.

Principles

Wertheimer formulated principles in his Gestalt theory. *Some of important principles are given below*

- The learner should be encouraged to discover the underlying nature of a topic or problem (*i.e.* the relationship among the elements.)
- Gaps, incongruities, or disturbances are an important stimulus for learning.
- Instruction should be based upon the laws of organisation *i.e.* proximity, closure, similarity and simplicity.

Example The classical example of these principles can be seen when children try to find the area of parallelograms. As long as the parallelograms are regular figures, a standard procedure can be applied (make lines perpendicular from the corners of the base).

However, if a parallelogram with a novel shape or orientation is provided, the standard procedure will not work and children are forced to solve the problem by understanding the true structure of a parallelogram *i.e.* the figure can be bisected anywhere if the ends are joined.

Mental Health

Mental health is state of well-being, in which an individual realises his or her own abilities, can cope with the normal stresses of life, can work productively and fruitfully and is able to make a contribution to his or her community. In this positive sense, mental health is the foundation for well-being and an effective functioning for an individual and for a community. It is more than the absence of mental illness, for the states and capacities noted in the above meanning and has value in themselves.

Mental, physical and social functioning are interdependent. Furthermore, health and illness may co-exist. They are mutually exclusive only, if health is defined as a state of balance including the self. The environment helps communities and individuals to understand, how to seek its improvement. Mental health is an integral part of health, which is ultimately connected with physical health and behaviour.

Meaning of Mental Health

The concept of mental health is as old as human evolution. Our ancient scriptures are full of reference to mental diseases. But this concept is comparatively new. Mental health emphasises the importance of integration or wholeness of personality is "A mentally healthy person is one, who has a balanced personality, free from schism and inconsistencies, emotional and nervous tensions, discords and conflicts, a well adjusted person can deal with his potentialities as well as he can accept his limitations".

Generally a person, who likes himself may be regarded as mentally healthy. Conversely, strong dislikes of one's self is a typical symptom of maladjustment. A mentally healthy individual feels that he is an accepted member of a social group and they in turn liked by him. But the maladjusted person may react in totally different ways.

Definitions of Mental Health

According to **PV Lewkan**, "Mentally healthy individual is one, who is himself satisfied, live peacefully with his neighbours, become healthy citizen of the country and even after performing these fundamental duties has enough energy left to do something of benefit to society".

According to **KA Menninger**, "Mental health refers to adjustment of human beings to the world and to each other with a maximum of effectiveness and happiness. It is the ability to maintain an even temper, an alert intelligence, socially considerate behaviour and happy disposition".

Problematic Areas of Mental Health and their Solutions

Mental health resources	On average, the higher the number of psychiatrists, psychologists and social workers per capita in a state, the lower the suicide rate.
Barriers to treatment	The lower the percentage of the population reporting that they could not obtain healthcare because of costs, the lower the suicide rate, the better the state's depression status.
Mental health treatment utilisation	The lower the percentage of the population that reported unmet mental healthcare needs, the better the state's depression status. When mental health treatment is utilised more, while holding the baseline level of depression in the state constant, the higher the number of anti-depressant prescriptions per capita in the states, the lower the suicide rates.
Socio-economic characteristics	The more educated the population, the greater the percentage with health insurance, the lower the suicide rate. The more educated the population, the better the state's depression status.
Mental health policy	The more generous a state's mental health policy coverage, the greater the number of people in the population that receive mental health services.

Concept of Mental Health by WHO

Since, the founding of the United Nations, the concepts of mental health and hygiene has achieved international acceptance. As defined in the 1946, Constitution of the World Health Organisation, "Health is a state of complete physical, mental and social well-being and not merely the absence of disease or infirmity." In this, mental health is represented as a variety of human aspirations and prevention of mental disorder.

Characteristics of Mental Health

Indian concept of mental health is available in the Atharva Veda, which provides detailed information on mental disorder and their treatment.

Atharva Veda says that mentally ill personality consists of three gunas or characteristics: Satya, Rajas and Tamas. The imbalance of these gunas causes mental disorder, they exist in the mind since birth, but they keep certain equilibrium in a normal person. In 1963, Jadhoda proposes six criteria's of the mentally healthy individual.

These are :

- The ability to love adequacy in interpersonal relationship, efficiency in problem-solving.
- Undistorted perception of reality including empathy and social sensitivity.
- Possessing a balance of psychic forces in the individual and a unifying outlook on life and resistance to stress.
- Can make decisions his or her own.
- Growth, self development and self-actualisation including conception of self, etc.
- Attitude towards self concept and sense of identity.

Difference Between Mentally Healthy and Unhealthy

Mentally Healthy	Mentally Unhealthy
Aware about self and have respect for others.	Not aware about their own self and have no respect for others.
Understand one's own limitations and can also tolerate.	Can't understand the cause of behaviour.
They can understand the basic needs that motivates behaviour.	They can't understand the basic needs that motivates behaviour.

Factors affecting Mental Health

Mental health plays a crucial role in the development of the personality, but there are many factors, which helps in developing positive and negative development of mental health. Mental ill-health is caused by different factors, which have been described by different authors in different ways. *These are*

Heredity Traits of the parents and ancestors are transmitted to the children through their genes. Intelligence and feeble mindedness are inherited. Heredity is the passing of traits from parents to off spring. It is the factor that shapes one's personality and behaviour.

Socio-Cultural Through this factor children develops attitudes and behavioural patterns from past experiences. The community in which an individual belongs may contribute to the development of his/her mental health. School and religious institutions may also help in moulding child's personality.

Family Breakup or Loss Separation or loss of a parent or sibling is extremely painful. Finding ways to cope and adjust to the changes by these events is critical for everyone.

Physical Ill Health Diseases, injuries and other physical problem often contribute to poor mental health and sometimes mental illness. Some physical causes can directly affect brain and contribute to mental illness.

Abuse The mental health of the abused children is at great risk. Abused children are more likely to experience mental disorders or mental illness during childhood and into adulthood.

Principal Areas for Action in Mental Health Policy

- Financing
- Legislation and human rights
- Organisation of services
- Human resources and training
- Promotion, prevention, treatment and rehabilitation
- Essential drug procurement and distribution
- Advocacy
- Quality improvement
- Information systems
- Research and evaluation of policies and services
- Inter-sectoral collaboration

Education and Mental Health

How can mental aberrations be prevented in school? It mostly happens that many students, particularly children and adolescents, cannot clarify their parents, teachers and psychologists. It is for, the guide to understand the adolescent and to sympathise with them and to offer them affectionate advice. Scolding or punishing them is not very effective. They should be given an opportunity of expressing their desires and mental tendencies.

Importance of School

It is the school that has the greatest influence, after the home, in forming the child's personality. And even in schools, the most important factor is the atmosphere existing there. In a healthy atmosphere, the children adopt discipline and other qualities on their own. The greatest need is for providing each child with work, adequate and proper to the needs of his personality. Hence, it is essential that the backward and the brilliant children should be given special treatment. Teachers presents an ideal to the children in their charge. Hence, their character and conduct could be such as can be profitably imitated by the children.

Factors of Mental Health in School

In school, the teacher should keep the following factors vividly in mind, if he wants to preserve mental health and prevent mental disturbance among his students.

They are

Discipline It should be exercised not through creating fear of punishment, but through arousing feeling of responsibility and the desire to be law abiding among the students. True-discipline is self-discipline.

Affectionate Behaviour A teacher should maintain the same loving attitude towards all his students. Any discrimination in this treatment injures the feelings of students.

Play and Recreation Students should be given opportunities for healthy expression through games and other forms of recreation.

Educational Guidance It is essential that some subjects should given to their requirements and abilities so that their educational problems can be solved out.

Balanced Curriculum Develop all aspects of the student's personality, to increase his fund for necessary knowledge and to avoid all unnecessary strains on the mind.

Formation of Good Habits It is desirable for the teachers to help students in the formation of good habits regarding a regular life, balanced diet, exercise, good behaviour and high-thinking, etc.

Preservation of Mental Health

- Developing total potentialities of the individual.
- Attaining emotional maturity and stability.
- Achieving personal and social security and adequacy.
- Developing healthy human relationships and interactions.
- Helping the individual is acquiring sound body and normal mental health.

Mental Hygiene

It is a science, which deals with the process of attaining mental health and preserving mental health in the society. The term mental health is closely related with the term mental hygiene as the main objective of mental hygiene is to attain mental health.

In other words, mental hygiene is a means of mental health. That is why, we can say that mental hygiene is the means and mental health is an end. Apart from the treatment of mental disease, one important function of mental hygiene is the creation of favourable conditions.

Definitions of Mental Hygiene

Mental hygiene is the science, which studies the principles and practices of preventing mental disorders and promoting mental health.

"Mental hygiene is that approach to human adjustment and achievement, which is related to the prevention of emotional maladjustment and preparation of the individual for skilled working".

According to **Ryan**, "Mental hygiene means the discovery of mental aberrations in their developmental stages, prevention of as many diseases of this kind as possible in society and provision of a mentally healthy life in society for the greatest number of individuals".

According to **Rivillin**, "Mental hygiene is the application of a body of hygiene information and technique. It cares for the purpose of the preservation and improvement of mental health of the individual and community".

Aims of Mental Hygiene

The aims and objectives of mental hygiene is not merely the prevention and curing of mental disease, but the development of a personality of each individual in society that makes for good adjustment with the environment.

It should attain a proper synthesis between the intellectual, emotional and physical aspects, that is satisfied and optimistic, and experiences minimum tensions and conflicts in its conduct with other individuals in society. The aim of mental hygiene is the evolution and development of a properly adjusted and balanced personality. Thus, we can say that approach of mental hygiene is positive rather than negative.

The aims and objectives of the mental hygiene can be summarised as shown below

- To help to realises one's potential.
- To develop self-respect and respect for others.
- To understand one's limitations and tolerate the limitations of others.
- To prevent personality complications.
- To treat and remedying of mental defects.
- To enable one to know his/her own self.

From the description of above points, it is apparent that mental hygiene has two prominent aspects, **curative** and **preventive**. In its curative aspect, it indicates ways and means of curing mental deviations, defects and imbalances, ways and means of preventing them or counteracting them are suggested by it, following which any and every individual can ensure his mental health.

In preventive aspect, mental health and hygiene problems can be prevented by developing some programmes such as counselling and psychotherapy to treat an individual.

Functions of Mental Hygiene

Mental hygiene has four functions. These are

Prevention The most important function of mental hygiene is to prevent mental health problems by developing some programmes.

Creative To develop programmes like counselling, psychotherapy to treat an individual or a group or to treat a mental patient.

Preservative Not all people are mentally ill; rather some of them possess sound mental health. So, third function is to develop programme through education for preserving mental health.

Training Another function of mental hygiene is to train a set of personnel who can help the people with psychological problems by trying to understand the problems and then helping them.

Whatever can be done to develop an emotionally stable citizenry must begin by an evaluation of

- the potential strength of young people as this is measured indirectly through their heritage.
- the educational and other environmental interests, attitudes and activities.

Principles of Mental Hygiene

To formulate general principles of mental hygiene is a difficult task as there is a wide range of differences among the individuals.

Some of the reasons for this are

- Human beings have multiple needs which grow in the course of development. These needs are contradictory in nature.
- There is no single, also absolute standard to judge, human behaviour or action. However, inspite of these difficulties, we can formulate some general principles.

These are

Adjustment in Home Every child should develop such type of behaviour at home so that he can adjust himself in any type of situation. Parents should take utmost care because the behaviour patterns that develop in early childhood leave permanent impression on the child. Parents should try to develop competence, security, adequacy, self-esteem and discipline by catering to their basic needs.

Adjustment in School The school through its various activities can go a long way in creating an environment for the children to preserve and to develop their mental health.

Adjustment in Society Man is a social animal and he has to adjust himself with the society. Without proper social interaction, harmonious development of personality cannot occur. Hence, parents, teachers and society must provide socially acceptable channels for the release of pent up emotional feeling so that the children and adolescents can develop healthy personality.

Adjustment in Work According to **Freud**, one is mentally healthy, if one can work successfully. School through its programme, should develop the proper mental state towards work in child.

Limitations of Mental Hygiene

Though, mental hygiene is an important aspect in our educational system, yet there are many limitations in implementing the principles of mental hygiene.

Some of these are

- Majority of parents are not aware about mental hygiene. Hence, they does not give any importance on how to keep their children's mental health preserved and unimpaired.
- Teachers in our school system are so overloaded with work that they cannot devote time to organise different types of programmes which would help the students in curing their mental health intact.
- There is also a dearth of trained personnel to deal with the mental health problems of our population.

EXAM BASED QUESTIONS

1 Growth and development are
(a) not related to each other
(b) independent of each other
(c) correlated and dependent on each other
(d) None of the above

2 The child's development takes place
(a) fast (b) slow
(c) gradually (d) None of these

3 The limit of growth is fixed by
(a) internal factors of organism
(b) nutrition and exercise
(c) Both a and b
(d) None of the above

4 Which of the following is not true?
(a) Growth is a biological process
(b) Development is a quantitative process
(c) Education is a goal-oriented process
(d) Learning is a process of behavioural change

5 The main element of growth is
(a) it affects behaviour
(b) it is measurable
(c) Both a and b
(d) it is also mental

6 Development takes place when
(a) environmental forces work on an organism
(b) environmental forces interact with the heredity forces in an organism
(c) Both a and b
(d) None of the above

7 Which of the following statement about development is correct?
(a) Process of development can be improved by health.
(b) Development may be positive and negative both.
(c) Development proceeds from general to specific.
(d) All of the above

8 Which indicates the change in the quality or character of the child?
(a) Growth (b) Development
(c) Learning (d) Environment

9 Development is
(a) maturation
(b) learning
(c) synthesis of abilities
(d) All of the above

10 Understanding human growth and development enables a teacher to
(a) not to be emotionally affected by their work
(b) to tell people how they can improve their lives
(c) to be intellectually clear of their works
(d) All of the above

11 Which of the following is true for the processes of growth and development?
(a) Both are natural processes.
(b) Growth is natural while development needs external intervention.
(c) If growth is satisfactory, development follows.
(d) Both the process go together without any external intervention.

12 The main principles of development are
(a) individual difference (b) continuity
(c) same pattern (d) All of these

13 Identify the wrong statement from the following.
(a) Growth does not continue throughout life.
(b) Heredity sets the limit for development.
(c) Development proceeds from specific to general.
(d) Correlation and not compensation is the rule in development.

14 DNA test helps us to know
(a) the genetic traits of a person
(b) nature of personality and its composition
(c) Both a and b
(d) None of the above

15 Which statement best resolves the nature-nurture controversy?
(a) Nature is clearly more important in development.
(b) The interaction between nature and nurture is most important in development.
(c) Nurture is clearly more important in development.
(d) Neither plays a particularly strong role in development.

16 Rozee is 86 years old. She continues to learn phrases in new languages, she writes poetry and she enjoys going to museums to see the latest up-coming artists. These examples of her adaptive capacities demonstrates
(a) chronological age (b) biological age
(c) psychological age (d) social age

17 According to Piaget's Theory of Cognitive Development, the concrete operational stage starts at the age of
(a) 1 year (b) 3 year
(c) 5 year (d) 7 year

18 Which of the following is/are cognitive processes?
(a) Attention (b) Memory
(c) Sensation and perception (d) All of these

19 High or complex cognitive processes includes
(a) intelligence (b) thoughts
(c) language (d) All of these

20 Concept of inherited developmental tendencies was advanced by Piaget in
(a) 1950 (b) 1951
(c) before 1950 (d) after 1950

21 "Ideas on inherited developmental tendencies" was proposed by
(a) Piaget (b) Binet (c) Crown (d) Freud

22 Piaget's Theory of Cognitive Development is essentially about
(a) influence of social world on growing child
(b) the development of the ability to think
(c) procedure to correct incorrect cognitions
(d) problems in sensory motor development

23 According to Piaget, the third stage of cognitive development is
(a) concrete operational (b) sensory motor
(c) pre-operational (d) formal operational

24 The stage during which an individual is able to think in abstract and general terms is
(a) early childhood (b) adulthood
(c) adolescence (d) late childhood

25 When does an individual makes serious efforts to pattern his/her behaviour according to social acceptance?
(a) 13-20 years (b) 14-21 years
(c) 10-21 years (d) 15-23 years

26 According to Piaget, at what stage does abstract thinking begans to develop?
(a) Sensory motor (b) Pre-operational
(c) Concrete operational (d) Formal operational

27 Allan spends a great deal of time working and trying to establish his career. He also has been thinking about how his personal relationship is going and considering whether it could be long-term and lead to establishing a family. Allan is most likely in
(a) late adolescence (b) early adulthood
(c) middle adulthood (d) late adulthood

28 Which period of development is characterised by establishing independence, developing an identity and thinking more abstractly?
(a) Middle childhood (b) Late childhood
(c) Adolescence (d) Early adulthood

29 Ankit depends completely on his parents. He is just learning to recognise things that he wants and how to get them. Ankit is in the development period called
(a) late childhood (b) infancy
(c) middle childhood (d) early childhood

30 Contrary to the view held centuries ago, today we believe that
(a) children are miniature adults.
(b) childhood is a unique and important period in life
(c) children ought to be treated as small adults in need of training but little else.
(d) children are autonomous and may be expected to grow and develop with very little parental support.

31 The period of development during which school readiness skills are developed and most free time is spent playing with friends is called
(a) infancy (b) early childhood
(c) middle childhood (d) late childhood

32 In a child develops logical operations from simple associations and add, subtract, multiply and divide, then the stage of development he has reached is
(a) sensory motor (b) pre-operational
(c) concrete operational (d) formal operational

33 The rate of physical growth of children is more
(a) in early childhood than in later childhood
(b) in later childhood than in adolescence
(c) in adolescence than in early childhood
(d) in adulthood than in adolescence

34 Which of the following is not a feature of adolescence period?
(a) Faster physical development
(b) Clear stable self-concept
(c) Increased interest in opposite sex
(d) Heightened emotional tendencies

35 Piaget reasoned that before the individual can organise and interpret experience, they must first
(a) represents it mentally
(b) create schemas
(c) receive appropriate tuitions
(d) intellectualise it

36 "In this stage, the children do more abstract thinking." This stage is
(a) childhood (b) infancy
(c) adolescence (d) None of these

37 The following change is observed in adolescence
(a) increasing in understanding
(b) growth in muscles
(c) generalisation
(d) Both a and b

38 The traditional and life-span perspectives are contrasting views of developmental change. According to the life-span perspective, when do developmental changes occur?
(a) During infancy and early childhood
(b) During adolescence and early adulthood
(c) During middle and late adulthood
(d) Throughout the entire life cycle

39 Children are usually ego-centric during .... and .... stages.
(a) sensorimotor, pre-operational
(b) formal operational, sensorimotor
(c) pre-operational, concrete operational
(d) concrete operational, formal operational

40 Personality has been derived from the latin word
(a) personal (b) persona
(c) person (d) personnel

41 The ideal personality should be
(a) emotionally stable
(b) socially acceptable
(c) Both a and b
(d) None of the above

42 For harmonious development of the personality of the child, parents should
(a) over protect the child
(b) regularly compare the child with other children
(c) provide conducive environment at home
(d) engage qualified teachers for the child

43 In the context of the role of heredity and environment in personality development, which of the following is true?
(a) Good heredity can make up for poor environment.
(b) Heredity and environment have equal contribution.
(c) Poor environment can supress good heredity.
(d) Good environment can make up for poor heredity.

44 Who held that "Personality is the dynamic organisation within the individual of those psychological systems that determine his unique to his environment"?
(a) GW Allport (b) Morton Prince
(c) Sigmund Freud (d) Kurt Koffka

45 Human behaviours are largely determined by
(a) internal factors
(b) environmental factors
(c) Both a and b
(d) None of these

46 Which of the following are regarded as component of behavioural identity of personality?
(a) Thoughts (b) Feelings
(c) Actions (d) All of these

47 Personality has been understood as largely the combination of
(a) trait and temperament
(b) consistency and individuality
(c) value and attitude
(d) character and temperament

48 The fundamental units of personality is referred as
(a) interest (b) abilities
(c) motives (d) traits

49 Personality is determined by
(a) non-verbally communicated attitudes between the parent and the child
(b) the behaviour of parents
(c) the relationship between child and parents
(d) All of the above

50 The personality of an individual is
(a) a psychological term for character
(b) a dynamic and continuous process
(c) a fixed state of one's behaviour
(d) a concept developed by psychologists

51 A personality is a/an
(a) category used to describe personality
(b) interrelated system of concepts used to explain personality
(c) relatively permanent set of behaviour patterns
(d) subjective evaluation of a person

52 Which of the following things can have an effect on the development of an individual's personality?
(a) Physical and mental capabilities
(b) Health and physical appearance
(c) Skin colour, gender and sexual orientation
(d) All of the above

53 Which of these are part of psychological factors?
(a) Physical defects
(b) Emotional determinants
(c) Social deprivation
(d) None of the above

54 The ancient Greeks hypothesised that there were four different personality characteristics. These are
(a) irritability, optimism, pessimism, calmness
(b) calmness, depression, pessimism, irritability
(c) depression, irritability, pessimism, optimism
(d) irritability, depression, optimism, calmness

55 What is the trait approach to personality?
(a) Assumes that people are motivated by unconscious emotional conflicts.
(b) Assumes that each individual has stable personality characteristics.
(c) Assumes that people's thoughts and beliefs are central to personality.
(d) Assumes that people have an innate tendency to become self-actualised.

56 The gland which plays a key role in the development of personality is
(a) pituitary (b) thyriod
(c) adrenal (d) thymus

57 Which of the following is not a personality trait?
(a) Intelligence (b) Interest
(c) Emotionality (d) Honesty

58 A personality trait is a
(a) particular ability
(b) distinct way of behaving in a specific situation
(c) specific motive
(d) the whole individual

59 The most predominant aspect of the personality picture is the
(a) cultural aspect (b) social aspect
(c) physical aspect (d) intellectual aspect

60 Which of the following is not the property of traits?
(a) Traits are directly observable
(b) Traits are quantifiable
(c) Traits change with time
(d) Traits are higher order habits

61 Which is not a physical determinants of personality?
(a) Homeostasis (b) Physical attractiveness
(c) Gender (d) Body builds

62 Character could be distinguished from personality in the following sense.
(a) Personality deals with over all disposition a person only.
(b) Personality includes physical and social aspects, whereas character stresses on the intellectual and spiritual aspects.
(c) Character is a patent objective of education for the society whereas personality is popular among education.
(d) All of the above

63 The search for primary traits personality uses the techniques of
(a) holistic assessment
(b) projective test
(c) content analysis
(d) factor analysis

64 Personality traits are characterised by
(a) consistency and distinctiveness
(b) charm and wit
(c) changes as function of the situation
(d) lack of individual differences

65 Most social scientists believes that an individual personality is influenced by two main factors. They are
(a) Inherited characteristics and social environment
(b) Education and genetic make-up
(c) Social class and family environment
(d) Local environment and family traits

66 Behavioural theories of personality are often criticised for their
(a) inability to test or verify concepts
(b) limited recognition of temperament, emotion and subjective factors
(c) ability to explain behaviour after the fact only
(d) emphasis on the conditions under which behaviours occurs

67 To understand personality, trait theorists attempted to
(a) create traits that fit people.
(b) increase the number of basic traits that have been identified.
(c) classify traits and discover how they are related to behaviour.
(d) reduce the common traits to measures of temperament.

68 One problem psychologists have with personality type is that they
(a) are hypothetical construct.
(b) over simplify personality.
(c) describe character, not personality.
(d) are not observable or measurable.

69 If you know the personality of an identical twin, you can expect the personality of the other twin to be
(a) unrelated (b) similar
(c) identical (d) conflicting

70 At what age does personality quite stable?
(a) 20 (b) 30 (c) 40 (d) 50

71 Which of the following theories considers personality as the product of environmental factors?
(a) Traits theories (b) Learning theories
(c) Both a and b (d) None of these

72 Which theory of personality was developed by Sigmund Freud?
(a) Psychoanalytic (b) Behaviouristic
(c) Humanistic (d) Psychosocial

73 Who among the following psychologists developed first systematic theory of personality?
(a) Erikson (b) Freud (c) Sullivan (d) Jung

74 Freud became interested in the study of personality when he realised that
(a) his patients lacked physical causes for their problems.
(b) the treatment of psychological disorders was more advanced that those for physical disorders.
(c) many of his patients were faking symptoms.
(d) no comprehensive theories of the mind were widely accepted.

75 Reference to an individual as 'introvert' and 'extrovert' were first during
(a) Freud (b) Adler (c) Jung (d) Allport

76 According to Freud, super ego is properly developed during
(a) latency period (b) anal period
(c) phallic period (d) None of these

77 Normal requirements of society are satisfied by
(a) id (b) superego
(c) ego (d) None of these

78 Demand of outside world, the task will best accomplished by development of a
(a) id (b) superego
(c) ego (d) All of these

79 The id is
(a) primitive unreasonable man
(b) primitive reasonable man
(c) developed reasonable man
(d) developed unreasonable man

80 The child starts with
(a) id (b) ego
(c) superego (d) All of these

81 According to psychoanalytical thinkers, the process of socialisation is closely identified with
(a) ego development (b) id development
(c) superego development (d) None of these

82 **According to Freud, what is the function of the 'ego'?**
(a) To boost a person's self-confidence
(b) To push for the fulfilment of one's self-interests
(c) To mediate between impulsive drives and the moral conscience
(d) All of the above

83 **What did Freud consider to be the role of 'Id'?**
(a) To represent innate, instinctive desires and impulses
(b) To be aware of the needs and feelings of those around us
(c) To moderate our impulses, acting as the moral conscience of the mind
(d) None of the above

84 **The first four and most crucial of Freud's stages of psychosexual development are**
(a) Anal, Oral, Latency and Phallic
(b) Oral, Anal, Phallic and Latency
(c) Oral, Anal, Genital and Latency
(d) Anal, Latency, Phallic and Genital

85 **The right order of the structure of mind according to Freud is**
(a) superego-id-ego (b) id-ego-superego
(c) ego-superego-id (d) id-superego-ego

86 **Which of the following works upon 'reality principle', according to Freudian Theory?**
(a) Id (b) Ego
(c) Superego (d) None of these

87 **Carl Roger was a**
(a) Humanistic Psychologist
(b) Cognitive Psychologist
(c) Behaviouristic Psychologist
(d) None of the above

88 **Allport emphasised more upon**
(a) common trait (b) individual trait
(c) proprium (d) None of these

89 **Personality was beautifully remarked as "The same fire which melts the butter hardens the egg" by**
(a) Watson (b) Lindzey
(c) Hull (d) Allport

90 **Allport believed that traits could be organized into three levels *i.e.***
(a) primary, secondary and tertiary
(b) cognitive, emotional and physiological
(c) id, ego and superego
(d) cardinal, central and secondary

91 **"The basic principle of behaviour is its continuous flow". Who gave this statement?**
(a) Allport (b) Cattell (c) Rogers (d) Eysenck

92 **Who developed the Gestalt Psychology Theory of learning?**
(a) Kurt Koffka (b) Max Wertheimer
(c) Wolfgang Kohler (d) All of these

93 **'Growth of Mind' is a work of**
(a) Max Wertheimer (b) Kurt Koffka
(c) Wolfgang Kohler (d) Carl Rogers

94 **The diagnostic and statistical manual of mental disorders is an example of a**
(a) biological typology (b) psychological typology
(c) multi-trait typology (d) Both a and c

95 **Which of the following is an important cause of mental ill-health of the teacher in the school?**
(a) Poor service conditions
(b) Hostile attitude of students
(c) Prejudices against him
(d) All of the above

96 **Which one of the following is not a characteristic of mentally healthy being?**
(a) Aware about self
(b) Can't understand the cause of behaviour
(c) Understand one's limitations
(d) Understand the basic needs that motivates behaviour

97 **Which of these are the principle areas for action in Mental Health Policy?**
(a) Quality improvement (b) Research and evaluation
(c) Financing (d) All of these

98 **Which of the following is an important symptom(s) of mental ill- health?**
(a) He is irritated to pity situations.
(b) The person demands more from others he pays to them.
(c) He considers himself a perfect person.
(d) All of the above

99 **A science, which deals with the process of attaining mental health and preventing mental illness is called**
(a) adjustment psychology (b) mental hygiene
(c) social medicine (d) None of these

100 **The purpose of mental hygiene is**
(a) to make the individual healthy and happy.
(b) to help the individual to adjust in the environment.
(c) to enable the individual to use his potentialities effectively to achieve to the maximum.
(d) All of the above

101 **Which of the following is/are the Principles of Development?**
1. Development is a never ending process.
2. Rate of Development can be different for different individuals.
3. All growths are related.
4. Development has direction.
Codes
(a) 1 and 2 (b) 2 and 3
(c) 3 and 4 (d) All of these

102 **Which of the following statement(s) is/are correct about growth?**
1. Growth is the physical change in an organism.
2. Growth is cellular.
3. Growth stops at maturation.
4. Growth is qualitative.

Codes
(a) 1 and 2 (b) 1, 2 and 3
(c) 3 and 4 (d) All of these

103 Which of the following is/are included in the direction of development?
1. Cephalocaudal and Proximodistal
2. Structure precedes function
3. General to specific
4. Concrete to abstract
5. Egocentrism to perspectivism

Codes
(a) 1 and 2 (b) 2 and 3
(c) 4 and 5 (d) All of these

104 Cognitive processes are analysed from
1. Anthropology 2. Sociology
3. Philosophy 3. Neurology
5. Linguistic

Codes
(a) 1 and 2 (b) 3 and 4
(c) 1, 2 and 5 (d) All of these

105 Arrange the following cognitive stages in sequential order:
1. Concrete Operational Stage
2. Sensory Motor Stage
3. Formal Operational Stage
4. Pre-operational Stage

Codes
(a) 2, 4, 1 and 3 (b) 1, 2, 3 and 4
(c) 2, 3, 1 and 4 (d) 4, 1, 2 and 3

Directions (From Q. Nos. 106 to 115) *In the following questions, the Assertion (A) and Reason (R) have been put forward. Read both the statements carefully and choose the correct alternative from the following.*

(a) Both A and R are true and R is the correct explanation of A
(b) Both A and R are true, but R is not the correct explanation of A
(c) A is true, but R is false
(d) A is false, but R is true

106 **Assertion** (A) A child, who is not taught to walk will nevertheless begin to do so when strength and ability permit.
Reason (R) It is a natural consequence of human maturation.

107 **Assertion** (A) The notion of individual differences exists in human life.
Reason (R) All the children develops at different rates.

108 **Assertion** (A) Development proceeds in stages.
Reason (R) There are four stages of development i.e. infancy, childhood, adolescence and adulthood.

109 **Assertion** (A) Mental health status is associated with behaviour at all stages of life.
Reason (R) Diseases, injuries and other physical problems contribute to poor mental health.

110 **Assertion** (A) Mental awareness is viewed as a positive attribute.
Reason (R) A person can reach enhanced level of mental health.

111 **Assertion** (A) Sigmund Freud is considered to be the 'Father of Psychiatry'.
Reason (R) He gave the humanistic theory of personality.

112 **Assertion** (A) Wertheimer held that the focus of Gestalt theory was on idea of 'grouping'.
Reason (R) Psychology can point the way where science and life will meet.

113 **Assertion** (A) Development is a never ending process.
Reason (R) Human beings continue to develop, change and affected by experience throughout life.

114 **Assertion** (A) Jean piaget was a swiss developmental psychologist.
Reason (R) He characterises different stages of cognitive development.

115 **Assertion** (A) Accomodation is a stagnant approach.
Reason (R) Accomodation is a term used by Piaget.

116 Match the following

List I (Thinkers)	List II (Theories)
A. Jean Piaget	1. Humanistic theory
B. Sigmund Freud	2. Trait theory
C. Carl Rogers	3. Cognitive development
D. Gordon Allport	4. Psychoanalytic theory

Codes

	A	B	C	D		A	B	C	D
(a)	3	4	1	2	(b)	1	2	3	4
(c)	2	1	4	3	(d)	4	1	2	3

117 Match the following

List I (Stages)	List II (Goals)
A. Sensorimotor	1. Abstract concepts
B. Pre-operational	2. Operational thought
C. Concrete operational	3. Symbolic thought
D. Formal operational	4. Object permanence

Codes

	A	B	C	D		A	B	C	D
(a)	2	4	3	1	(b)	3	1	4	2
(c)	1	2	3	4	(d)	4	3	2	1

PREVIOUS YEARS' QUESTIONS

July 2018

1 **Which of the following aspects focuses more on physical dimensions?**
(a) Concept of development
(b) Concept of growth
(c) Concept of change
(d) Concept of learning

2 **For ensuring effectiveness in organizing educational programmes which areas of individual differences in students will be of optimal value?**
(a) Physical characteristics of students
(b) Racial characteristics of students
(c) Psychological characteristics of students
(d) Moral characteristics of students

November 2017

3 **According to Piaget, in which stage of development the child shows attainment of concept of reversibility as a cognitive capacity?**
(a) Sensory motor stage
(b) Preoperational stage
(c) Concrete operational stage
(d) Formal operational-stage

4 **In the following statements, given below are some indicators of development during various stages of development. Select the set of statements, from the code which points out most appropriately these developmental features :**
1. There appears change in the size of the person.
2. There is a change manifest in the personal relationship of the individuals.
3. The bodily organisation and various organs of the person show change in proportion.
4. The thinking of the person changes.
5. There occurs disapperance in the old features of the person.
6. There is perceptible change in the attitude of the person.
7. There develops acquisition of new features.
8. The language of the person undergoes a change.

Codes
(a) 2, 2, 3 and 4
(b) 5, 6, 7 and 8
(c) 1, 3, 5 and 6
(d) 3, 4, 5 and 6

5 **Which of the following in Tolman's revision of his system represents motivational principle of Freud?**
(a) Equivalence beliefs
(b) Drive Discrimination
(c) Cathexis
(d) Field Cognition Mode

6 **Two lists are given below, list I and list II. Match the two lists and select the correct code to give your answer.**

List I (Personality Theorists)	List II (Concepts of Personality Advocated)
A. Cattel	1. The Anima and the Animus
B. Allport	2. Striving for superiority
C. Freud	3. Cardinal, central and secondary Traits
D. Jung	4. Surface and source traits
E. Adler	5. Id, Ego and Superego
	6. Endomorph and Ectomorph

Codes

	A	B	C	D	E
(a)	1	2	3	4	6
(b)	2	3	4	5	6
(c)	1	2	4	5	6
(d)	4	3	5	1	2

7 **Which of the following tools is most appropriate for assessing deeper aspects of personality?**
(a) Sentence Completion Test
(b) Summated Rating Scale
(c) Vocational Interest Inventory
(d) Verbal Aptitude Test

8 **What is the 'Gestalt word' for transfer of learning?**
(a) Stimulus discrimination
(b) Transposition of understanding
(c) Stimulus generalisation
(d) Response generalisation

9 **Assertion** (A) Adolescence is a period of storm and stress.
Reason (R) There is intensity in the expression of emotions coupled with absence of consistency

Codes
(a) Both A and R are true, but R is not the correct explanation of A
(b) Both A and R are true and R is the correct explanation of A
(c) A is correct, but R is false
(d) A is false, but R is true

10 Which of the following of statements most appropriately conveys the process of adjustment? Choose from the code for your answer

1. Adjustment is a two-dimensional process.
2. Mental health of a person is indicative of his/her adjustment.
3. Adjustment implies satisfying one's needs in a given environment.
4. Conflicts and tensions are a part of the adjustment process.
5. Adjustment is the goal of life.
6. Adjustment and mental health are one and the same thing.

Codes

(a) 1, 2 and 3 (b) 2, 3 and 4
(c) 1, 3 and 4 (d) 4, 5 and 6

11 **Assertion** (A) Adolescence is a period of storm and stress

Reason (R) There is intensity in the expression of emotions coupled with absence of consistency

Codes

(a) Both A and R are true, but R is not the correct explanation of A
(b) Both A and R are true and R is the correct explanation of A
(c) A is correct, but R is false
(d) A is false, but R is true

January 2017

12 In the context of social development which of the following stages is characterised by 'Intense Self Awareness'?

(a) Infancy (b) Childhood
(c) Adolescence (d) Adulthood

13 Match the two lists by selecting the correct code.

List I (Stages of Cognitive Development)	List II (Main Features of Cognitive Growth)
A. Sensory Motor Stage	1. Ability to comprehend reversibility
B. Peroperational Stage 3	2. Hypothesis making and hypothesis testing
C. Concrete Operational Stage	3. Object permanence
D. Formal Operational Stage	4. Transductive reasoning
	5. Critical thinking

Codes

	A	B	C	D
(a)	1	2	3	5
(b)	3	4	1	2
(c)	2	3	1	5
(d)	5	4	3	2

14 Match the two lists and choose the correct answer from the codes given below.

List I (Theory of Personality Advocated by)	List II (The Main Concepts Stressed)
A. Psychoanalytic Theory of Freud	1. Traits of personality are influenced by both environment and inheritance.
B. Psychological types of Jung	2. Traits of personality are indicative of a neuropsychic structure expressed through modes of behaviour.
C. Allport's Theory of Personal Disposition	3. Traits represent two extreme points on a scale rather than two types.
D. Cattle's Theory of Surface and Source Traits	4. Traits are expressive of a life style.
	5. Personality traits represents a cathexix of either 'life urge' or 'death urge'.

Codes

	A	B	C	D
(a)	1	2	3	4
(b)	2	3	4	5
(c)	4	5	3	1
(d)	5	3	2	1

15 Peer group membership has high educational implications during

(a) Childhood (b) Later childhood
(c) Adolescence (d) Adulthood

16 Who advanced the concept of 'creative self' as the most essential aspect of one's personality?

(a) Allport (b) Adler
(c) Freud (d) Jung

17 Match the two lists and choose the code to give your answer.

List I (Stages)	List II (Goals)
A. Sensorimotor Stage	1. Logical reasoning and ability to think in terms of abstract concepts.
B. Pre-operational Stage	2. Transductive reasoning.
C. Formal Operational Stage	3. Object constancy.
D. Concrete Operational Stage	4. Reversibility.

Codes

	A	B	C	D
(a)	2	3	4	1
(b)	3	2	4	1
(c)	3	2	1	4
(d)	4	1	3	2

18 A school programme is directed at ensuring a satisfactory level of cleanliness with a view to organise 'Yoga Camps' for wellness life style in children. Which aspect of the programme may lead to 'mental health' of children?

(a) The school programme itself
(b) Cleanliness of a satisfactory level
(c) Organising cleanliness drive
(d) Yoga camps for wellness life style

July 2016

19 Match the following two lists in order to render them meaningful in terms of psychology of growth and development and select the right answer from the given codes.

List I (Aspects of Development)	List II (Characteristics)
A. Language Development	1. The child is able to walk.
B. Cognitive Development	2. The parents take care of child's toilet habits.
C. Emotional Development	3. The child holds conversation with peers.
D. Physical Development	4. The child starts asking questions.
	5. The child feels shy.
	6. The child attacks another child.

Codes

	A	B	C	D		A	B	C	D
(a)	5	4	2	6	(b)	3	4	5	1
(c)	1	3	4	5	(d)	2	1	4	3

20 Who is an arch advocate of trait theory of personality?

(a) Sheldon (b) Kretschmer
(c) Jung (d) Allport

21 Which of the following intimately associated with mental health?

(a) Absence of anxiety
(b) Keeping one's desires in abeyance
(c) Resources for gratifying needs
(d) Ability to defer gratification of needs

22 Match the two lists and select the correct code to give your answer.

List I (Stages of Development)	List II (Characteristics Associated)
A. Sensory Motor stage	1. Transductive reasoning
B. Pre-operational Stage	2. Reversibility
C. Concrete Operational Stage	3. Object permanence
D. Formal Operational Stage	4. Repetitive acts
	5. Intense self-awareness
	6. Concept formation

Codes

	A	B	C	D		A	B	C	D
(a)	5	3	1	2	(b)	3	1	2	5
(c)	4	5	1	2	(d)	1	2	3	4

23 Which of the following features belongs to intellectual development during adolescence stage?

(a) Moral development
(b) Conflict in motivation
(c) Capacity for convergent and divergent thinking
(d) Hero-worship

24 The concept of functional autonomy of motive was advanced by

(a) D C Mclelland (b) Frederick Herzberg
(c) Harrry F Harlow (d) Gordon W Allport

25 Match the two lists by selecting the appropriate answer from the codes given below.

List I (Personality Theory)	List II (Chief Proponents)
A. Psychological personality type	1. Adler
B. Personality based on personal disposition	2. Freud
C. Surface and source traits based personality	3. Eysenck
D. Psycho-analytic theory of personality	4. Jung
	5. Allport
	6. Cattel

Codes

	A	B	C	D		A	B	C	D
(a)	4	5	6	2	(b)	1	2	3	4
(c)	2	1	5	4	(d)	5	4	3	2

26 Which of the statements is respect of adjustment process will find favour in the psychoanalytic model of adjustment?

1. Adjustment is objective and action oriented process.
2. Learning plays an important role in adjustment.
3. Adjustment process can be explained in terms of schedules of reinforcement.
4. Ego mechanisms play an important role in adjustment.
5. Shaping forms part of the adjustment process.
6. Adjustment of a person with his/her environment is based on his/her personal and racial unconscious.

Codes

(a) 1 and 4 (b) 1 and 2 (c) 3 and 4 (d) 5 and 6

December 2015

27 Which stage of development is said to be overpowered with a tendency for 'hero worship'?

(a) Early childhood (b) Later childhood
(c) Early adolescence (d) Later adolescence

28 According to Piaget, the most important cognitive outcome of the Sensori-Motor Stage of development is

(a) object permanence (b) identification
(c) language (d) reasoning

29 The idea of 'Unconscious motivation' is one of the major contributions of the psychologist

(a) Adler (b) Allport (c) Freud (d) Jung

30 An individual tends to show immature, self centred, seductive and attention getting behaviour. The type of personality implied here is

(a) Antisocial personality (b) Histrionic personality
(c) paranoid personality (d) Compulsive personality

31 A mentally healthy person will show which of the following behaviour?
(a) Repenting over the mistakes committed by him/her
(b) Pointing out the mistakes of others
(c) Exploring means of correcting his/her mistakes
(d) Finding out weaknesses of others

32 The overall changes in shape, form or structure resulting in the improved quality functioning refer to the ....
(a) growth
(b) quality of growth
(c) development
(d) quality of growth

33 Which of the following statement is correct with regard to growth and development?
(a) Growth is psychological and development is physical
(b) Growth is physical while development is psychological
(c) Both growth and development are psychological
(d) Both growth and development are physical

34 Development of creative thinking begins at what stage?
(a) Infancy (b) Childhood
(c) Adolescence (d) Adulthood

35 **Assertion** (A) Heredity influences the process of growth and development.
Reason (R) The living conditions-physical, social and cultural do not affect growth and development.
Codes
(a) Both A and R are true and R is the correct explanation
(b) Both A and R are ture, but R is not the correct explanation
(c) A is true, but R is false
(d) A is false, but R is true

36 In which stage of a person's life emotions and their control become crucial for professional and personal wellness of life style?
(a) Later childhood (b) Early adolescent
(c) Later adolescent (d) Adulthood

37 Which of the following statements is correct?
(a) Mental Hygiene is the process and Mental Health is the product.
(b) Mental Health is the process and Mental Hygiene is the product.
(c) Mental Hygiene and Mental Health are one and the same.
(d) Mental Hygiene has nothing to do with Mental Health.

June 2015

38 In view of Piaget, the stage of development from the age 7 to 12 years is called
(a) Sensori Motor
(b) Preoperational
(c) Concrete Operational
(d) Formal Operational

39 In Freud's psycho-analytic concept of personality, which one of the following is indicative of psychic-energy?
(a) Ego (b) Id
(c) Superego (d) Conscious level of psyche

40 Defence mechanisms are used to protect the person's
(a) 'ego' consciously (b) 'id' unconsciously
(c) 'superego' unconsciously (d) 'ego' unconsciously

41 In Piaget's view, which of the following stages of development is the highest stage in terms of cognitive development?
(a) Childhood (b) Adolescence
(c) Adulthood (d) Old age

42 'Object permanence' is the characteristic of which age group in Piaget's research evidence of growth and development?
(a) Upto the age of 8 to 9 months
(b) Between 2 to 7 years
(c) Between 9 to 11 years
(d) Between 11 to 14 years

43 Who in the following list proposed the concept of the 'Anima' and the 'Animus' in explaining the concept of personality ?
(a) Freud (b) Jung
(c) Adler (d) Eric Fromm

44 Who was the chief proponent among the type theorists of personality to advance a psychological personality type?
(a) Sheldon (b) Jung
(c) Allport (d) Eysenck

45 Match the following.

List I (Characteristics)	List II (Stages at Which This Features appear)
A. Ability to understand symbols from concrete situations	1. In emotional development of adolescence
B. Tendency of being away from parents	2. In the social development of adolescence
C. Development of self concept	3. In the intellectual development during childhood
D. Hero worship	4. In the social development during childhood
E. Conflict in motivation	5. In the intellectual development of adolescence
	6. In the process of adjustment during adolescence

Codes

	A	B	C	D	E
(a)	3	4	5	2	1
(b)	1	2	4	5	3
(c)	6	5	3	2	1
(d)	2	1	6	5	4

46 **Which theory of transfer of learning suggests that it is the understanding developed by the learner which transfers from one situation to the other?**
(a) Theory of Identity of Elements
(b) Mental Faculty Theory
(c) Theory of Generalisation
(d) Gestalt Theory

December 2014

47 **Defence mechanisms are used by the**
(a) ego of a person knowingly
(b) superego of a person knowingly
(c) id of a person unknowingly
(d) ego of a person unknowingly

48 **Which one of the following statements best describes the mental health of a teacher?**
(a) A teacher handles student problems without creating fuss.
(b) A teacher deals with students in a friendly manner.
(c) A teacher controls his/her emotions in the class.
(d) A teacher persuades his/her students to follow the rules.

49 **In differentiating growth from development, which one of the following is not the basis?**
(a) Physical (b) Qualitative
(c) Quantitative (d) Emotional

50 **According to Jean Piaget, the formal operation stage is during the**
(a) infancy (b) childhood
(c) adolescence (d) adulthood

51 **Which one of the following statements appropriately describes personality?**
(a) Personality is a physiological concept.
(b) Personality is a molecular concept.
(c) Personality is a dynamic concept.
(d) Personality is a popular concept.

52 **In the study of personality, which sequence is most appropriate?**
(a) Personality type, Personality trait, Psychoanalytic
(b) Personality trait, Personality type, Psychoanalytic
(c) Psychoanalytic, Personality type, Personality trait
(d) Psychoanalytic, Personality trait, Personality type

53 **Which of the following traits can be measured effectively through projective techniques of personality ?**
(a) Extraversion-Introversion
(b) Conscientious
(c) Mental inhibitions
(d) Balanced approach

June 2014

54 **Which of the following best describes the process of growth and development?**
(a) It is entirely physical and physiological
(b) It is pre determined by heredity
(c) All of its aspects are highly inter-related
(d) It is essentially an individual phenomenon, different from person to person

ANSWERS

Exam Based Questions

1 *(c)*	2 *(c)*	3 *(c)*	4 *(b)*	5 *(c)*	6 *(c)*	7 *(d)*	8 *(b)*	9 *(d)*	10 *(c)*
11 *(b)*	12 *(d)*	13 *(c)*	14 *(c)*	15 *(b)*	16 *(c)*	17 *(d)*	18 *(d)*	19 *(d)*	20 *(c)*
21 *(a)*	22 *(a)*	23 *(a)*	24 *(c)*	25 *(b)*	26 *(d)*	27 *(b)*	28 *(c)*	29 *(a)*	30 *(b)*
31 *(b)*	32 *(c)*	33 *(c)*	34 *(b)*	35 *(a)*	36 *(c)*	37 *(d)*	38 *(d)*	39 *(a)*	40 *(b)*
41 *(c)*	42 *(c)*	43 *(b)*	44 *(a)*	45 *(c)*	46 *(d)*	47 *(b)*	48 *(d)*	49 *(d)*	50 *(b)*
51 *(b)*	52 *(d)*	53 *(b)*	54 *(d)*	55 *(b)*	56 *(a)*	57 *(a)*	58 *(b)*	59 *(c)*	60 *(a)*
61 *(c)*	62 *(a)*	63 *(d)*	64 *(a)*	65 *(a)*	66 *(b)*	67 *(c)*	68 *(c)*	69 *(b)*	70 *(b)*
71 *(c)*	72 *(a)*	73 *(b)*	74 *(a)*	75 *(a)*	76 *(a)*	77 *(b)*	78 *(b)*	79 *(a)*	80 *(a)*
81 *(c)*	82 *(c)*	83 *(a)*	84 *(b)*	85 *(b)*	86 *(b)*	87 *(a)*	88 *(b)*	89 *(d)*	90 *(d)*
91 *(a)*	92 *(d)*	93 *(b)*	94 *(b)*	95 *(d)*	96 *(b)*	97 *(d)*	98 *(d)*	99 *(b)*	100 *(d)*
101 *(d)*	102 *(b)*	103 *(d)*	104 *(d)*	105 *(a)*	106 *(a)*	107 *(a)*	108 *(a)*	109 *(b)*	110 *(a)*
111 *(c)*	112 *(c)*	113 *(a)*	114 *(a)*	115 *(d)*	116 *(a)*	117 *(d)*			

Previous Years' Questions

1 *(b)*	2 *(c)*	3 *(c)*	4 *(c)*	5 *(c)*	6 *(d)*	7 *(a)*	8 *(b)*	9 *(b)*	10 *(c)*
11 *(b)*	12 *(c)*	13 *(b)*	14 *(d)*	15 *(c)*	16 *(b)*	17 *(c)*	18 *(d)*	19 *(b)*	20 *(d)*
21 *(d)*	22 *(b)*	23 *(c)*	24 *(d)*	25 *(a)*	26 *(d)*	27 *(c)*	28 *(a)*	29 *(c)*	30 *(b)*
31 *(c)*	32 *(c)*	33 *(b)*	34 *(b)*	35 *(c)*	36 *(d)*	37 *(a)*	38 *(c)*	39 *(b)*	40 *(d)*
41 *(b)*	42 *(a)*	43 *(b)*	44 *(b)*	45 *(a)*	46 *(d)*	47 *(d)*	48 *(b)*	49 *(d)*	50 *(c)*
51 *(c)*	52 *(c)*	53 *(c)*	54 *(c)*						

CHAPTER

10

Approaches to Intelligence and Problem-Solving

Intelligence is a complex thing to define but it can be broadly thought of as the measure of a person's ability to master a specific cognitive function such as problem solving, logical reasoning and self-awareness. We are going to explore competing theories of intelligence to understand the cognitive strengths a person possess.

Intelligence

Intelligence is the ability to acquire and apply knowledge and skills. It has been defined in many different ways including, abstract thought, understanding, self-awareness, communication, reasoning, learning, having emotional knowledge, retaining, planning and problem solving.

The term **intelligence** means the ability to have benefit from experience, which implies the ability to behave adaptively, to function successfully within particular environments. The word 'intelligence' derives from the Latin word **'interleggere'** which means to pick out or discern. It is a general mental capability that, among other things, involves the ability to reason, plan, solve problems, think abstractly, comprehend complex ideas, learn quickly and learn from experience. It is not merely learning, or narrow academic skill, rather it reflects a broader and deeper capability for comprehending our surroundings—'catching on', 'making sense' of things or 'figuring out' what to do.

Individuals differ from one another in their ability to understand complex ideas, to adapt effectively to the environment, to learn from experience, to engage in various forms of reasoning, to overcome obstacles by taking thought. Although, these individual differences can be substantial, they are never entirely consistent. A given person's intellectual performance will vary on different occasions, in different domains, as judged by different criteria. Concepts of intelligence are attempts to clarify and organise this complex set of phenomena. Although, considerable clarity has been achieved in some areas, no such conceptualisation has yet answered all the important questions and none commands universal assent.

In this Chapter

- *Intelligence*
- *Problem-Solving*
- *Critical Thinking*
- *Metacognition*
- *Creativity*

Few concepts in psychology have received more devoted attention and few have resisted clarification so thoroughly. Despite many efforts over the years to develop some independent definition of the term, its connotations have remained intimately interwined with the techniques developed for its measurement.

Binet, the inventor of the individual intelligence test, felt that intelligent behaviour would be manifested in such abilities as reasoning, imagination, insight, judgement and adaptability, so he designed his tests to evaluate just these functions. Still others have argued that all such abilities are only manifestations of a single underlying factor (the so called general factor), which is presumed to be at the root of all intellectual functioning.

Intelligence may be regarded as a sort of mental energy (in the form of mental or cognitive abilities) available with an individual to enable him to handle his environment in terms of adaptation and facing novel situations as effectively as possible.

Thus, we can conclude that

- It is the ability to learn.
- It is the ability to deal with abstraction.
- It is the ability to make adjustment or to adapt to new situations.
- It is the ability or power of making appropriate responses to certain stimuli in a given situation.

Definitions of Intelligence

According to **David Wechsler**, Intelligence is defined as "The aggregate or global capacity of the individual to act purposefully, to think rationally and to deal effectively with his environment".

According to **Cyril Burt**, "Intelligence is an innate generate cognitive ability".

According to **Howard Gardner**, "To my mind a human intellectual competence must entail a set of skills of problem solving enabling the individual to resolve genuine problems or difficulties that, he or she encounters and when appropriate, to create an effective product and must also entail the potential for finding or creating problems and thereby laying the ground work for the acquisition of new knowledge".

According to **Woodworth** and **Marquis**, "Intelligence means intellect put to use. It is the use of intellectual abilities for handling a situation or accomplishing any task".

Approaches to Intelligence

There are many views regarding what constitutes intelligence. Different psychologists have given different viewpoints and formulated their own theories of intelligence.

Some important approaches to intelligence are as follows

Modern Approach

The modern approaches of intelligence call into questions the following, such as

- Meta issues that are related to understanding a person's own thinking.
- Aspects which take into consideration knowledge.
- Specific behaviour of oriented adaptations towards achieving goals and multiple intelligences.

So, modern approach integrates the concept of intelligence in the context of information processing.

System Approach

System approach to intelligence is related to Gardner Theory of Multiple Intelligence in which intelligence is not just a single, unitary construct. He used converging operations, gathering evidence from multiple sources and types of data. Instead of speaking of multiple abilities that together constitute intelligence, Gardner speaks of eight distinct intelligences that are relatively independent of each other.

Contextual Approaches

According to contextualists, intelligence cannot be understood outside its real-world context. The context of intelligence may be viewed at any level of analysis, focusing narrowly, on the home and environment or on entire cultures. Contextualists are particularly intrigued by the effects of cultural context on intelligence.

Cognitive Approaches

Cognitive theorists are interested in studying how people or other organisms mentally represent and process what they learn and know about the world. The ways in which various cognitive investigators study intelligence differ primarily in terms of complexity of the processes being studied. This approach was advocated by Ted Nettelbeck, Arthur Jensen, Earl Hunt and Herbert Simon.

Social Intelligence

Social intelligence is a major component to make healthy social relations with people in a society. The concept of social intelligence was given by **Edward Thorndike** in the year 1920. Through it, people connects with each other and understands about facts and phenomenas. It includes an awareness of situations and the social dynamics that govern them and a knowledge of interaction styles and strategies that can help a person to achieve his or her objectives in dealing with others. In other words, it is the capacity to effectively negotiate complex social relationships and environment.

Definitions of Social Intelligence

In **1920**, **Thorndike** states that "Social intelligence is the ability to understand and manage men and women, boys and girls to act wisely in human relations".

In **1945**, **Cater V. Good** states that "Social intelligence can be define as the ability to adjust oneself to the social environment and to act for its improvement it is an individual's ability to deal effectively with social relationships and with noval social situations".

In **1983**, **Howard Gardner** states that "Social intelligence is the capacity to know oneself and to know other is an inalienable part of the human condition as is the capacity to know objects or sounds and it observes to be investigated no less than these other less charged forms".

In **1984**, **M. Goldenson Robert** states that "Social intelligence is the degree of ease and effectiveness displayed by a person in social relationships".

Elements of Social Intelligence

Knowledge Related to Society Socially intelligent people know how to live and behave in the society. They are well-versed in social relations.

Effective Listening Skills It is seen that socially intelligent persons are good listeners. They leaves a good impression on others.

Word Fluency and Conversational Skills Socially intelligent persons can be easily identified by others as they have good conversational skills. They are highly socially intelligent person who can carry on conversations with a wide variety of people.

Effective in Classroom Management Socially intelligent teachers have skills to deal with individual differences. They know effective elements which are useful in classroom discipline management. Social intelligence is a key tool for teachers to remove the educational problems related to self and society.

Multiple Intelligence

Multiple intelligence is a combination of distinct types of intelligences and each of these intelligences are independent to each other.

In multiple intelligence, each person poseses each intelligence to an extent, but there is always a primary or more dominant intelligence. The Theory of Multiple Intelligence was given by **Howard Gardner** in the year 1983, who formulated the term of multiple intelligence. As per his theory, the traditional method to assess human intelligence i.e. I.Q. test is far too limited and there are eight different types of intelligence which a human poseses. *Such as*

- Linguistic Intelligence (Word smart)
- Logical-Mathematical Intelligence (Number /reasoning smart)
- Spatial Intelligence (Picture smart)
- Bodily-Kinesthetic Intelligence (Body smart)
- Musical Intelligence (Music smart)
- Inter-personal Intelligence (People smart)
- Intrapersonal Intelligence (Self-smart)
- Naturalist Intelligence (Nature smart)

Definitions of Multiple Intelligence

According to **Hattie**, "Multiple intelligence provides students with multiple ways to access content improves learning".

According to **Hammond**, "Multiple intelligence provides students with multiple ways to demonstrate knowledge and skills increases engagement and learning and provides teachers with more accurate understanding of students' knowledge and skills".

Elements of Multiple Intelligence

Here are some elements that would help if they were introduced to classrooms

Visuals Visual media can make complex concepts easier to comprehend so it helps make learners' lives easier.

Realia These are physical tangible objects that learners can touch and feel. These objects are very effective in teaching motor skills. For instance, in some subjects students have to attend lab and workshop sessions for better understanding.

Colour On the subjects that will need multi-media, colour is important if the object's colour is relevant to what is being learned.

Learning Ability Some learners are not as good readers as others. For these learners, the concept will be hard to grasp if the lesson is primarily delivered using written materials. Incorporating some visuals in the teaching materials will help a big deal.

More Emphasis on Identifying Strengths There is a bigger need to identify the strengths and weaknesses of the students. With this understanding, the teacher can pick the teaching materials that work best for the learners.

Emotional Intelligence

In Psychology, emotional intelligence is the ability to identify and manage your emotions, as well as other people's emotions. The concept of emotional intelligence was propounded by **Daniel Goleman** (1998), an American psychologist, in his book, **'Working with Emotional Intelligence.'** In his book, he stated that emotional intelligence accounts for 67% of the abilities needed to be a successful leader. He further suggested that it is twice as important as techinical proficiency or IQ. This research has subsequently been supported by a number of studies. He also identified five main components of emotional intelligence.

Definitions of Emotional Intelligence

According to **Peter Salovey and John Mayer**, "Emotional intelligence is the ability to perceive emotions, to access and generate emotions so as to assist thought, to understand emotions and emotional meanings, and to reflectively regulate emotions in ways that promote emotional and intellectual growth".

According to **Hein**, "Emotional intelligence is the innate potential to feel, use, communicate, recognise, remember, learn from manage, understand and explain emotions".

Components of Emotional Intelligence

Daniel Goleman determined that there are five fundamental components of emotional intelligence which are follows

Self Awareness As per this component, people with high emotional intelligence understand their emotions, strengths and weaknesses and they don't let their feeling rule them. They continuously work on these areas so that they can perform better.

They can also recognise the effect of their moods and motivations on others. To become a self-aware person, one must monitor his/her emotional state and identify his/her own emotions.

Self-Regulation As per this component, people have the ability to control their emotions and impulses. These people think before they act. They typically don't allow themselves to become too angry or jealous, and they don't make impulsive, careless decisions.

According to **Goleman**, emotional maturity is seen in this component where people are able to take responsibility for their actions, being able to adapt to change, and also have the ability to respond appropriately to other people's irrational emotions or behaviour.

Internal Motivation According to **Goleman**, people who have an interest in learning and self improvement, set their goals and follow them. He also stated that an emotionally mature individual in this category has traits such as having initiative and the commitment to complete a task, and having perseverance in the face of adversity. These people are highly productive who love challenges and are effective in whatever they do.

Empathy According to **Goleman**, empathetic people have the ability to identify with and understand the wants, needs and view points of people around them. These people avoid stereotyping and judging too quickly and they live their lives in an open, honest way. He stressed that empathy can only be achieved if self-awareness is achieved. He believed that one must be able to understand themselves before they can understand others.

Social Skills People with strong social skills have the ability to manage relationships in a way that benefits others. They are always ready to help others rather than focus on their own success. According to **Goleman**, these people have emotional maturity who can easily manage disputes, are excellent communicators and are excellent at building and maintaining relationships.

Theories of Intelligence

There are different theories about intelligence in educational psychology. Different psychologists have given different viewpoints and formulated their own theories of intelligence. The main theories are Sternberg's Triarchic Theory and Gardner's Theory of Multiple Intelligence *which are discussed below*

Gardner Theory of Multiple Intelligence

The Theory of Multiple Intelligence was proposed by **Howard Gardner.** He put forth on new and re-defined view of human intellectual competencies in his book, **"Frames of Mind : The Theory of Multiple Intelligence"** (1983). According to **Gardner**, intelligence is not a single entity, rather distinct types of intelligences exist. Each of these intelligences are independent of each other. This means that, if a person exhibits one type of intelligence, it does not necessarily indicate being high or low on other types of intelligence.

He also put forth that different types of intelligence interact and work together to find a solution to a problem. He studied extremely talented persons, who had shown exceptional abilities in their respective areas and described eight types of intelligence.

Types of Intelligence

The eight types of intelligence according to Gardner are as follows

Linguistic It is a kind of skill involved in the production and use of language. It is related to reading, writing, listening, talking, understanding, etc. This is the capacity to use language fluently and flexibly to express one's thinking and understand others. Persons high on this intelligence are ***word-smart***, *i.e.* they are sensitive to different word meanings, are articulate and can create linguistic images in their mind. *e.g.* poets and writers are very strong in this component of intelligence.

Logical Mathematical This type of skill is involved in scientific thinking and problem solving. This type of intelligence deals with abstract reasoning and manipulation of symbols involved in numerical problems. Persons high on this type of intelligence can think logically and critically. It is exhibited in scientific work. *e.g.* scientists and Nobel prize winners are likely to be strong in this component.

Spatial This type of intelligence have skills which are used in forming visual images and visual patterns. The kinds of skills used while navigating in space, forming, transforming and using mental images. The person high on this intelligence can easily represent the spatial world in the mind. Pilots, sailors, sculptors, painters, architects, interior decorators and surgeons are likely to have developed visual spatial intelligence.

Musical This type of intelligence gives sensitivity to musical rhythms and patterns. It is the capacity to produce, create and manipulate musical patterns. Persons high on this intelligence are very sensitive to sounds and vibrations and in creating new patterns of sounds *e.g.* singers are likely to be strong in this component.

Bodily Kinesthetic In this type of intelligence, the whole or portion of the body is used flexibly and creatively. This consists of the use of the whole body or portion of it for display or construction of products and problem solving. It requires the skills and dexterity for fine coordinated motor movements such as those required for dancing, athletics, surgery, craft making and so on.

Interpersonal It is the sensitivity to subtle aspects of others behaviours. This is the skill of understanding the motives, feelings and behaviour of other people so as to bond into a comfortable relationship with others *e.g.* psychologists, counsellors, politicians, social workers and religious leaders have high degree of this intelligence.

Intrapersonal It is an awareness of one's own feelings, motives and desires. This refers to the knowledge of one's internal strengths and limitations and using that knowledge, to effectively relate to others. Persons high on this ability have finer sensibilities regarding their identity, human existence and meaning of life *e.g.* philosophers and spiritual leaders having strong intrapersonal skills.

Naturalistic It is the sensitivity to the features of the natural world. It is related to recognising the flora and fauna and making a distinction in the natural world. It is more possessed by hunters, farmers, tourists, students of biological sciences and the like.

Although Gardener's theory was widely popular over the last two decades but it was also criticised by other psychologists.

Some Psychlogists argued that his theory was too much based on his own intuition rather than any empirical data, while others felt that the intelligence described by Gardner were synonymous for personality type.

Triarchic Theory of Intelligence

Triarchic Theory of Intelligence is another important modern theory of intelligence. It was proposed by **Robert Sternberg** in 1985. It attempts to understand the cognitive processes involved in solving problems.

According to **Sternberg,** "Intelligence is the ability to adapt, to shape and select environment to accomplish one's goals and those of one's society and culture".

According to this theory, there are three basic types of human intelligence

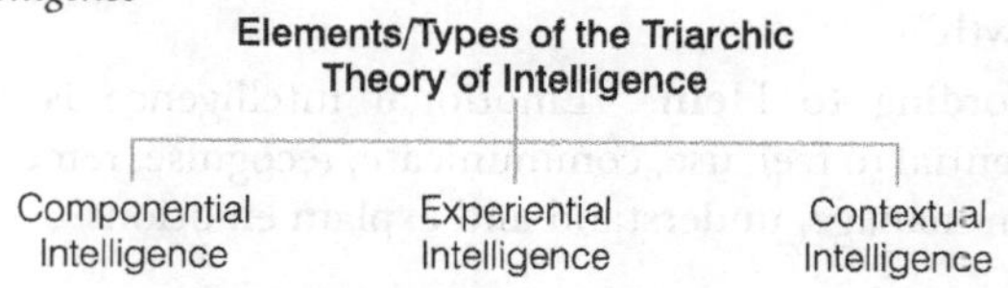

Componential Intelligence

Componential intelligence or analytical intelligence involves the ability to think critically and analytically. Persons high on this dimension usually excel on standard tests of academic potential and make excellent students. It consists of internal mental mechanisms that are responsible for intelligent behaviour.

This intelligence has three components, each serving a different functions :

Knowledge Acquisition Component This refers to the meaningful acquisition of new information and relating that information (relation between onion and vegetable or jasmine and flower) to the prior knowledge (meanings of onion, vegetable, jasmine and flower) existing in the memory.

Meta Component refers to how one directs ones own thinking *i.e.* performance and knowledge acquisition components. It means the way in which one's thinking to understand the problem and choose the strategy to solve the problem using the performance components. It is the knowledge about one's own thinking.

Meta-components are higher-order mental processes that determine which performance and learning components will be used as well as the sequence in which they will be used. These components are common for all tasks; they plan, monitor and evaluate what one is doing. Furthermore, they activate performance and knowledge acquisition components.

Performance Component includes basic operations which are involved in any cognitive act/process. These are the processes that are used to perform a task or solve a problem. This component is the one that is measured best by existing intelligence tests.

Experiential Intelligence

The second type of intelligence is experiential or creative intelligence, which emphasises insight and the ability to formulate new ideas. Persons who are high on this dimension have excellent mind and are able to find out which information/facts are crucial and which are not.

This is the kind of intelligence shown by many scientific geniuses and inventors, such as **Einstein**, **Newton** and some would say **Freud**. It focuses on the relationship between the person's inner, mental world and the outer external world.

This aspect is concerned with the effect of intelligence on one's experiences as well as the effect of person's interaction with the environment on intelligence. This view adds creativity (or novelty and originality) to the overall conception of intelligence.

A creatively intelligent person may not particularly perform well on a test of intelligence, but is able to combine different experiences in uniquely original ways. A second aspect of experiential intelligence is the ability to automatise or make routine tasks that are encountered repeatedly. An example of automatising is reading, which is carried out largely without conscious thought. Playing music is another example of this type of activity.

Contextual Intelligence

Sternberg states the third type of intelligence as contextual or practical intelligence and in some ways, it is the most interesting of all. Persons high on this dimension are intelligent in a practical, adaptive sense, they have what many would term ***street smarts*** and are able to solve the problems of everyday life. People high on contextual sense remains practical or down to Earth in life. Such people remains involved in activities such as implementing, using, applying and seeking relevance.

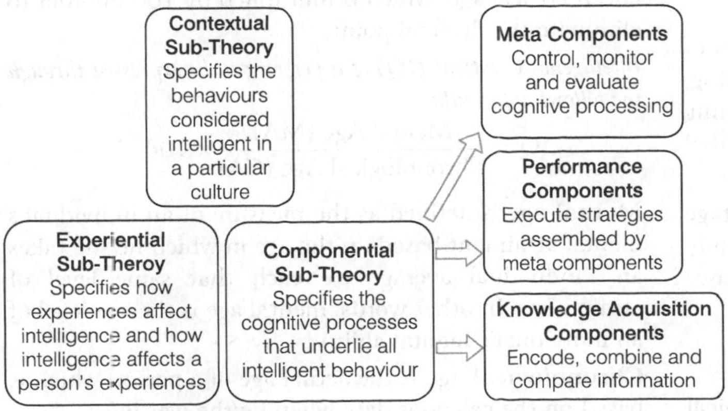

Elements of Triarchic Theory of Intelligence

Assessment of Intelligence

Generally, it is seen that intelligence of a person is different from the others. The intelligence of people are assess by a number of intelligence scales/tests which have been devised by many psychologists.

Intelligence Tests

Intelligence tests are psychological tests that are designed to measure a variety of mental functions, such as reasoning, comprehension and judgement. Intelligence tests assess the characteristics of human intelligence. Western psychologists discovered various methods to measure human intelligence. In this direction, the first attempt was made by **Wilhelm Wundt**, who established a laboratory in 1879 which was dedicated to Psychology to assess intelligence.

In 1900, **Cattell** used some measures of intelligence such as, strength of grip, colour discrimination and rote memory.

However, the major effort was made by **Alfred Binet**, who was French Psychologist and also known as the 'Father of Mental Testing' and pioneer of intelligence test.

Types of Intelligence Tests

Intelligence tests are of several types. They can be classified as either verbal or performance tests on the basis of the nature of items used.

Some of the tests are as follows

Individual or Group Tests An Individual intelligence test is one which can be administered to one person at a time. A group intelligence test can be administered to several persons simultaneously. Individual tests allow people to answer orally or in a written form while the group tests generally seek written answers usually in a multiple choice format.

Verbal, Non-verbal or Performance Tests An intelligence test may be fully verbal, fully non-verbal or fully performance based, or it may consist of a mixture of items from each category. Verbal tests are presented in words and languages and can be administered only to literate people whereas non-verbal tests use pictures or illustrations as test items. Performance tests require subjects to manipulate objects and other materials to perform a task.

Culturally Biased Tests Psychologists have tried to develop tests that are culture-fair or culturally appropriate, *i.e.* one that does not discriminate against individuals belonging to different cultures. In such tests, items are constructed in a manner that they assess experiences common to all cultures.

Some of the important types of intelligence scales/tests are given below

Binet-Simon Intelligence Scale/Test

This general test of mental ability was devised by **Alfred Binet** and his collegue, **Theodore Simon** in 1905. At first, he gave a very crude scale of 30 items to assess mental age. This scale was revised in the year 1908, and he prepared a scale of 59 items for the age group 3 to 13 years along with a method of finding out the mental age. He again revised his scale in the year 1911 and prepared a scale which contained tests for age group 3 to 16 years.

With the help of this scale, Binet could identify whether a person is average, above or below, depending upon his mental age.

According to his test, if a person gives all the answers as per his age is considered '**Average**', if gives all the answers set for people above his age is considered '**above average**' and if does not give answer as per his age is considered '**below the average**'.

Stanford-Binet Intelligence Scale/Test

The Binet-Simon Intelligence test was further revised and expanded by **Lewis Terman** in the year 1916 at **Stanford University**. This scale is known as **Stanford-Binet Intelligence Scale**. This scale had 90 items. In the year 1937, two higher age groups were added in this scale i.e. Superior adult mental age is 19 years and very superior adult mental age is 22 years.

In this type of test, intelligence is analysed by five factors of cognitive ability. These five factors are fluid reasoning, knowledge, quantitative reasoning, visual spatial processing and working memory. In this test, both verbal and non-verbal responses are measured.

During this test, each of the five factors is given a weightage and the combined score is often reduced to a ratio commonly known as IQ. It is the most commonly used test of intelligence today.

Wechsler Intelligence Scale/Test

It is an intelligence test which was developed by a clinical psychologist, **Dr. David Wechsler**, in the year 1939. This test was developed for both children and adults. It is an individual test which has the unique quality of being simultaneously a verbal as well as a performance scale.

This scale/test consists of 11 tests, out of which 6 are verbal scale and 5 are performance scale. *Such as*

Verbal Scale

- Test of general information
- Test of general comprehension
- Test of arithmetic reasoning
- Test of distinction between similarities
- Test of memory/digit span
- Test of vocabulary

Performance Scale

- Digit symbol test
- Picture completion test
- Block design test
- Picture arrangement test
- Object assembly test

The scores on these sub-tests are added together to assess the individual's intelligence.

It is of two types

(i) **The Wechsler Intelligence Scale for Children** (WISC) It covers children between the age of 6 to 16 years,.

(ii) **The Wechsler Intelligence Scale for Adults** (WISA) It covers adults and elder adolescents.

Intelligence Quotient

When intelligence is assessed by intelligence tests than it is expressed in terms of Intelligence Quotient (IQ).

The concept of Intelligence Quotient was introduced by **William Stem** in the year 1912.

Intelligence Quotient (IQ) is the ratio of mental age and chronological age, which is multiplied by 100 in order to eliminate the decimal point.

Intelligence Quotient (IQ) of a person can be expressed through the following formula:

$$IQ = \frac{\text{Mental Age (MA)}}{\text{Chronological Age (CA)}} \times 100$$

Mental age is defined as the measure of an individual's mental attaiment based on the age in which he/she takes an individual average to reach that same level of attainment. In other words, mental age is the age level of an individual's mental ability.

Chronological age is the actual age of a person which is based on the calendar date when he/she was born.

For *e.g.*

If the mental age of a child is 12 years and his/her chronological age is 10 years, then what IQ level he / she possess?

According to the formula,

$$IQ = \frac{12}{10} \times 100 = 120$$

Hence, he/she possess IQ level 120.

Intelligence Quotient given by Wechsler

Classification of People on the Basics of IQ

IQ Range	Descriptive Label
Above 130	Very superior
120-129	Superior
110-119	High average
90-109	Average
80-89	Low average
70-79	Borderline
Below 70	Mentally challenged/Retarded

Problem-Solving

In Cognitive Psychology, the term **problem-solving** refers to the mental process that people go through to discover, analyse and solve problems. The ultimate goal of the problem-solving is to overcome obstacles and to find a solution that best revolves around the issue.

This is an essential exercise for individual advancement and also for the advancement of society.

Definitions of Problem-Solving

In **1968**, **Skinner** states that "Problem solving is a process of overcoming difficulties that appear to interfere with the attainment of a goal. It is a procedure of making adjustment in spite of interferences".

In **1948**, **Woodworth and Marquis** states that "Problem-solving behaviour occurs in normal or difficult situations in which a solution is not obtainable by the habitual methods of applying concepts and principles derived from the past experiences which are very similar to the present situations".

Nature of Problem-Solving

- The problem-solving behaviour involves quite deliberate, conscious and serious efforts on the part of the problem-solver.
- One has to utilise one's thinking and reasoning powers and engage in serious mental work by systematically following some well-organised steps for the removal of the difficulties and obstacles.
- Problem-solving behaviour helps in the removal of or adjustment with, interferences and ultimately helps an individual to reach his goal and satisfy his motives.
- Problem-solving behaviour helps an individual in the growth and development of his personality, making his life happier and wiser by appropriate adjustment. It also contributes significantly to the progress and development of society.

Steps in Problem-Solving

In order to solve a problem, it is important to follow a series of steps. These steps are known as problem solving cycle, which includes developing strategies and organising knowledge.

The major steps of problem-solving process are given below

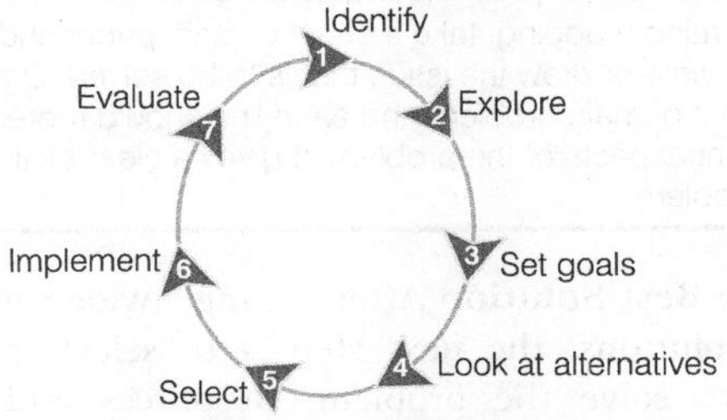

Steps of Problem-Solving Process

Identifying the Problem The first step in the problem-solving process is to identify the problem, by sizing up the situation. It may seem an obvious and simple step, but it is the most important step in the problem-solving process. It is the base of the whole process. If a wrong problem is identified, the whole process gets futile.

Some useful techniques for identifying the problem includes

- comparison with others
- monitor weak signals
- checklist
- brain storming
- comparison of current performance with last performance
- listing complaints
- role playing

Exploring the Problem After identifying the problem, its root cause should be find. Often people focus on symptoms or effects of the problem, but ignore the real cause. The point here is to focus on analysing the problem for the real cause. It also helps in fully defining the problem, so that it can be solved.

Setting Goals After exploring and analysing the problem, the focus should be on making a goal statement that emphasises on the successful end of the problem. Making a goal statement, helps in clarifying the direction to take in solving the problem and gives definite focus on the solution of the problem. It is a way of addressing the problem and fixing the gap between the problem and the goal.

Look at Alternatives After analysing and setting up goals, the next step is to develop possible solutions. This is a creative as well as practical step, where every possible solution is identified.

Various alternative solutions are identified through the following techniques :

- Analysis of past solutions
- Researching
- Asking questions
- Brain storming
- Reading
- Thinking
- Discussing

Mind Mapping

- **Mind mapping** is another technique that can be used for identifying alternative solutions. It was developed by **Tony Buzan** in 1970.
- Mind mapping uses pictures and word phrases to organise and develop thoughts in a non-linear fashion. It helps the people to see the problem and its solution.
- To do mind mapping, take a sheet of plain paper and in center write or draw the issue that is to be solved. Draw lines out of main problem and each line should represents different aspects of the problem. It gives a clear picture of the problem.

Select the Best Solution After getting a wide variety of possible solutions, the next step is to select the best solution to solve the problem. Resources and other considerations like money, time, policy, people, rules, procedures that can affect the solution are also selected.

Implementation It is the most crucial part of the problem-solving process. Action plan is developed in order to implement the solution of the problem. Action plan confirms the plans and events of solving the problem.

Evaluation This is the final step in the problem-solving process. The effectiveness of the solution is reviewed against the desired outcomes. In this stage, careful analysis of solution is done.

Factors Affecting Problem-Solving

Problem-solving is not a flawless process. There are a number of factors which can interfere in the problem-solving process. *These are as follows:*

Functional Fixedness It is the tendency to view problems only in their customary manner. It prevents people from fully seeing all of the different options that might be available to find a solution.

Assumption While dealing with the problem, people often make assumptions about the constraints and obstacles that prevent certain solutions.

Irrelevant or Misleading Information In the problem-solving process, it is important to distinguish between relevant and irrelevant information. When the problem is complex, it becomes easier to focus on misleading or irrelevant information and it should be avoided.

Mental Set It is the tendency of people to use only solutions that have worked in the past rather than looking for alternative solutions. It can often work as heuristic by making a useful problem solving technique. or it can also lead to inflexibility, making it more difficult to find effective solutions.

Critical Thinking

Critical thinking is a type of thinking that helps a person in stepping aside from his own personal beliefs, pre-judices and opinions to sort out the facts and identify the truth.

Critical thinking represents challenging thought process which leads a person to new avenues of knowledge and understanding. Infact, it is a sructural approach of thinking to find ways and means for the improvement of thinking process itself. For critical thinking, a person must have higher cognitive abilities and skills for the proper interpretation, analysis, evaluation and interference as well as explanation of the gathered information resulting in a purposeful, unbiased and self-regulatory judgement.

Definitions of Critical Thinking

Edward Glaser *defines critical thinking as follows*

- An attitude of being disposed to consider in a thoughtful way and the problems and subjects that came within the range of one's experiences.
- Knowledge of the methods of logical inquiry and reasoning.
- Some skill in applying those methods.

Critical thinking calls for a persistent effort to examine any belief or supposed form of knowledge in the light of evidence that supports it and further concludes to which it tends.

According to **Michael Scriven and Richard Paul**, "Critical thinking is the intellectually disciplined process of actively and skillfully conceptualizing, applying, analyzing, synthesizing, reasoning or communication as a guide to belief and action".

Nature of Critical Thinking

- It is a higher order well-disciplined thought process. It involves the use of cognitive skills like conceptualisation, interpretation, analysis, synthesis and evaluation for arriving at an unbiased, valid and reliable judgement of the gathered or communicated information or data as a guide to one's belief and action.
- The value of critical thinking lies in its quality of being most skillful and responsible thinking that facilitates good judgement.
- It is self-correcting and sensitive to the contemporary issues and circumstances.

- It is the basis and reliable support for carrying out the process of problem-solving.
- It discourages the child to merely adopt things without proper understanding. Rather it makes him/her a self-reliant, conscious, independent enquirer and discoverer to find out the reality beyond assumptions.

Thus, it is our responsibility to encourage our youngsters to have the required critical thinking which is essential to discover the realities of the world.

Importance of Critical Thinking

- It helps to understand the logical connections between ideas.
- It helps to identify, construct and evaluate arguments.
- It helps to solve a problem critically without loosing any important fact.
- It helps a person to identify the relevance and importance of ideas.
- It also helps to detect inconsistencies and common mistakes in reasoning.

Metacognition

The term '**metacognition**' was first coined by **John Flavell**, an American Developmental Psychologist, in the year **1979**. The word 'meta' means 'beyond' and 'cognition' means 'thinking', so the term 'metacognition' refers to '**beyond thinking**'.

According to him, *"metacognition is a cognition about cognitive phenomenon, or basically thinking about thinking"*.

Definitions of Metacognition

In **1988, Cross and Paris** states that "Metacognition is the knowledge and the control that children have over their own thinking and learning activities".

In **1999, Hennessey** states that "Metacognition is the awareness of one's own thinking, awareness of the content of one's conception, as active monitoring of one's cognitive processes, an attempt to regulate one's cognitive processes in relationship to further learning, and an application of a set of heuristics as an effective device for helping people to organize their methods of attacks in general".

Nature of Metacognition

- It highlights in-depth thinking in which cognitive processes are actively controlled.
- It focuses on planning which includes how a task can be accomplished. It monitors, understands and estimates progress towards the completion of a particular task.
- With the help of metacognition, a student can be aware of how dedicated he is to reach his goals, of how strong his trait of perseverance is, and of how focused his attention is to a task that involves thinking or writing. He can also regulate his dedication, disposition, and attention.

Components of Metacognition

John Flavell identified two components of metacognition which are given below

Metacognitive Knowledge

It is the awareness individuals possess about themselves and other people as cognitive processors.

It has three types such as

Declarative Knowledge It means person's knowledge or understanding one's own capabilities.

Procedural Knowledge It means task knowledge, including content and length.

Strategy Knowledge It means conditional knowledge or one's ability to use strategies to learn information as well as for adapting these strategies to new situations.

Metacognitive Regulation

It has the sequential process that one uses to control cognitive activities and to ensure that a cognitive goal has been achieved. This process helps to regulate and oversee learning and consists of planning and monitoring cognitive activities. These processes also check the outcomes of those activities.

It has three skills such as

Planning It involves suitable selection of strategies and the right assignment of resources.

Monitoring It includes awareness of understanding and task performance.

Evaluating It refers to the assessment of the final result of a task and the efficiency carried out during that particular task performance.

Creativity

Creativity is a mental process involving the generation of new ideas or concepts, or new associations of the creative mind between existing ideas or concepts. It is simply the act of making something new.

As we know that no two individuals are alike. Humans are made by God, thus, every one of us is a unique creation, but does not possess the same creative abilities as others have.

Some of us have creative talents and contributes to advancement in the fields of an art, literature, science, business, and other spheres of human activity. Abraham Lincolon, Homi Bhabha, Mahatma Gandhi, Einstein, Shakespere and many others are the examples of having creative thinking abilities. With the help of creativity, people creates something new and lead a unique life which is different from others.

Definitions of Creativity

In 1973, **Stagner and Karwoski** states that "Creativity is the production of a 'totally or partially' novel identity".

In 1931, **Pearman** states that "Creativity is the power of the human mind to create new contents by transforming relations and thereby generating new correlates".

In 1978, **MJ Levin** states that "Creativity is the ability to discover new solutions to problems or to produce new ideas, inventions or work of an art. It is a special form of thinking, a way of viewing the world and interacting with it in a manner different from that of the general population".

In 1974, **Wilson, Guilford and Christensen** states that "The creative process is any process by which something new is produced *i.e.*, an idea or an object including a new form or arrangement of old elements. The new creation must contribute to the solution of some problems".

Nature of Creativity

- It is not confined to any individual, groups of individuals, caste, colour or creed. It is universal. Everyone of us possesses it and is capable of demonstrating creativity to some extent.
- It is a God given gift as well as is the result of influence of cultural background, experiences, education and training.
- It produces something new or novel.
- It is a kind of adventurous thinking, calling a person to come out in the open to experess himself according to his/her will and to function unrestricted by routine or previous practice.
- It has a wide scope which is not restricted by any limits or boundaries or scientific inventions or production of work.
- It covers multifarious human aspects like writing stories, composition of poems, performance in the field of dance and music and so on.

EXAM BASED QUESTIONS

1 Who said that "Intelligence is an innate general cognitive ability"?
(a) David Wechsler (b) Cyril Burt
(c) Cattell (d) Guilford

2 Intelligence is the ability
(a) to learn
(b) to adjust oneself to new situations
(c) to think in terms of ideas
(d) All of the above

3 The intelligence of an individual can be rightly defined as
(a) a natural gift, which is inherent in a person
(b) a quality of his learned behaviour
(c) a constant and unmodifiable quality of behaviour
(d) a potentially fixed quality of the genes

4 When did spearman proposed Two Factor Theory of Intelligence?
(a) 1901 (b) 1903 (c) 1904 (d) 1905

5 Who said that "Social intelligence is the ability to understand and manage men and women, boys and girls to act wisely in human relations"?
(a) Howard Gardner (b) Cater V. Good
(c) Thorndike (d) M. Goldenson Robert

6 Consistent low achievement leads to low intelligence because
(a) learning develops thinking and reasoning power
(b) 50% of intellectual ability is expressed in verbal form
(c) Both a and b
(d) None of the above

7 It is normally distributed in nature, it is a joint product of both heredity and environment, it grows with age and its vertical growth ceases at the age of 16 to 20. The above passage is related to
(a) growth (b) development
(c) intelligence (d) interaction

8 Who suggested the components of emotional intelligence?
(a) Guilford (b) Gardner (c) Goleman (d) Cattell

9 Which of the following is not related to 'emotional intelligence'?
(a) Understanding emotions (b) Using emotions
(c) Reducing emotions (d) Perceiving emotions

10 Which of the following is not a major components of emotional intelligence?
(a) Managing your own emotions
(b) Motivating ourselves
(c) Knowing your own emotions
(d) Plan your day to day activities

11 According to Indian view, which of the following is not a competency of intelligent person?
(a) Cognitive competence (b) Social competence
(c) Economic competence (d) Emotional competence

12 The term 'emotional intelligence' was coined by
(a) JP Das (b) Lewis Terman
(c) Stanford Binet (d) Daniel Goleman

13 Which among the following is not a type of multiple intelligence?
(a) Linguistic (b) Spatial
(c) Interpersonal (d) Analysis

14 The Theory of Multiple Intelligence was given by
(a) Gardner (b) Sternberg (c) Thorndike (d) Guilford

15 The theories of intelligence like the 'Two Factor Theory' and the 'Multiple Factor Theory' are related to which of the following approaches?
(a) Abstract thought
(b) Conceptual thought
(c) Psychometric approach
(d) Information processing approach

16 'Great athletic skill' is an example of which of the following theories?
(a) Cattell's theory (b) Sternberg's theory
(c) Gardner's theory (d) Thorndike's theory

17 In Multi Factor Theory, range is related to
(a) general intelligence of learners
(b) number of tasks that a person can do in a limited period of time
(c) difficulty level of items
(d) None of the above

18 Who said that "Multiple intelligence provides students with multiple ways to access content improving learning"?
(a) Gardner (b) Terman (c) Hattie (d) Hammond

19 Which of the following is not a type of Gardner's Theory of Multiple Intelligence?
(a) Bodily Kinesthetic (b) Musical
(c) Practical (d) Mathematical

20 Which of the following refers to 'street smart' or 'situationally smart'?
(a) Contextual (b) Experiential
(c) Knowledge (d) Understanding

21 Bodily Kinesthetic Intelligence is one of the component of which of the following?
(a) Guildford's Structural Model of Intellectual
(b) Cattell's Theory of Fluid
(c) Triarchic Theory of Intelligence
(d) Theory of Multiple Intelligence

22 Triarchic Theory of Intelligence is proposed by
(a) Sternberg (b) Thorndike
(c) Stanford Binet (d) Guilford

23 Triarchic Theory of Intelligence is proposed by Robert Sternberg in the year
(a) 1980 (b) 1982 (c) 1985 (d) 1975

24 Who said that, "Intelligence is the ability to adopt, to shape and to select environment to accomplish one's goals and those of one's society and culture"?
(a) Guilford (b) William Stern
(c) Sternberg (d) David Wechsler

25 Which among the following is not a component of componential intelligence?
(a) Knowledge acquisition component
(b) Understanding component
(c) Meta component
(d) Performance component

26 Which of the following is not a component of Triarchic Theory of Intelligence?
(a) Analytical (b) Componential
(c) Experiential (d) Contextual

27 The Robert Sternberg's Triarchic Theory of Intelligence using which of the following approaches?
(a) Information Processing approach
(b) Psychometric approach
(c) Abstract approach
(d) Learning approach

28 Contextual intelligence is also known as
(a) analytical intelligence (b) componential intelligence
(c) practical intelligence (d) fluid intelligence

29 Which among the following is also known as creative intelligence?
(a) Experiential intelligence (b) Contextual intelligence
(c) Componential intelligence (d) Practical intelligence

30 "It specifies the cognitive processes that underline all intelligent behaviour." It refers to
(a) Contextual Sub-Theory (b) Componential Sub-Theory
(c) Experiential Sub-Theory (d) Performance Components

31 Control, monitor and evaluate cognitive processing are the functions of which of the following?
(a) Meta components
(b) Performance components
(c) Knowledge aquisition components
(d) Practical components

32 Single Factor Theory of Intelligence was given by
(a) Thorndike (b) Pavlov (c) Alfred Binet (d) Freeman

33 In the pre-Binet period, intelligence was considered as
(a) associative ability of the individual
(b) sensory activity of the individual
(c) verbal ability of the individual
(d) All of the above

34 **Which among the following is considered as 'The Father of Mental Test'?**
(a) Francis Galton (b) William Stern
(c) Raymond Cattell (d) Stanford Binet

35 **Score on intelligence tests cannot be fully relied because**
(a) cultural factors can influence the score
(b) they generally do not reveal all the mental abilities of a person
(c) fatigue level can influence the performance
(d) All of the above

36 **Name the first Psychologist, who worked on intelligence?**
(a) Alfred Binet (b) Gardner (c) Sternberg (d) Thorndike

37 **Intelligence testing is useful for knowing**
(a) mental retardation (b) educational backwardness
(c) individual difference (d) All of the above

38 **Binet Simon scale of intelligence measures**
(a) mental growth of the individual over a period of time
(b) the aptitude or level of an examinee, not his speed
(c) general mental abilities, not specific ones
(d) All of the above

39 **The concept of 'divergent thinking' and 'convergent thing' are given by**
(a) Thorndike (b) Sternberg (c) Guilford (d) Cattell

40 **Binet with his student Simon developed the first test of intelligence in**
(a) 1905 (b) 1917 (c) 1925 (d) 1977

41 **The first psychological laboratory was established by**
(a) Galton (b) Cattell (c) Pestalozzi (d) Wundt

42 **The first person to devise a workable series of intelligence tests was**
(a) Binet (b) Raven (c) Wechsler (d) Spearman

43 **Stanford Binet scale measures the attribute of an individual**
(a) intelligence (b) creativity (c) aptitude (d) personality

44 **Which of the following types of intelligence tests can be categorised on the basis of nature of items used?**
(a) Individual or Group tests
(b) Verbal, Non-Verbal or Performance tests
(c) Culture-fair or Culture-biased tests
(d) Binet and Wechsler tests

45 **Who said that, "The aggregate or global capacity of an individual is to act purposefully, to think rationally and to deal effectively with his environment?"**
(a) Cyril Burt (b) David Wechsler
(c) Guilford (d) William Stern

46 **Which of the following is not an example of verbal tests?**
(a) Digit span (b) Picture arrangement
(c) Comprehension (d) Vocabulary

47 **Wechsler Test of Intelligence is a type of**
(a) Individual test (b) Verbal test
(c) Performance test (d) Culture-fair test

48 **Wechsler developed an intelligence test for children in**
(a) 1935 (b) 1939 (c) 1949 (d) 1936

49 **Find out the mental age of a 12 years old child with an IQ level of 90.**
(a) 10.8 (b) 10.5 (c) 10.9 (d) 11.2

50 **In the IQ level range (50-70), which of the following levels of mental retardation lies?**
(a) Moderate (b) Mild (c) Severe (d) Profound

51 **Stanford Binet and Wechsler scales are examples of which of the following?**
(a) Verbal test (b) Non-verbal test
(c) Individual test (d) Performance test

52 **"It requires constant supervision and help". Under which of the following IQ levels, the above degree of mental retardation occurred?**
(a) IQ level under 20 (b) IQ level 20 to 34
(c) IQ level 35 to 49 (d) IQ level 40 to 60

53 **If the mental age of a child is 5 years and his chronological age is 4 years then, what would be the IQ level of the child?**
(a) 175 (b) 125 (c) 155 (d) 100

54 **Maximum number of individuals possess an average of IQ level between**
(a) 80-89 (b) 70-79 (c) 120-130 (d) 90-110

55 **If the mental age of a child is 5 years and his chronological age is 6 years, then what would be the IQ level of that child?**
(a) 56 (b) 83 (c) 183 (d) 65

56 **Intelligence is expressed as a quotient and the formula used to express IQ is**
(a) $\frac{MA}{CA} \times 100$ (b) $\frac{CA}{MA} \times 100$
(c) $MA \times CA$ (d) $MA + CA \times 100$

57 **Which among the following is derived by dividing an individual's mental age by his or her chronological age?**
(a) EQ (b) IQ (c) MR (d) RMT

58 **Under which IQ level, a person can reach to level-II and can contribute to own support?**
(a) IQ level 40 to 60 (b) IQ level under 20
(c) IQ level 35 to 49 (d) IQ level 20 to 34

59 **Calculate the IQ level of a 12 year old child, whose mental age is 9 years?**
(a) 85 (b) 70 (c) 75 (d) 100

60 **The concept of Intelligence Quotient (IQ) was proposed by Psychologist named**
(a) William Stern (b) Sternberg
(c) Goleman (d) Binet and Terman

61 Find out the mental age of a 16 year old student, who has an IQ level of 125.

(a) 30 (b) 20 (c) 25 (d) 18

62 Mind mapping uses .... and ...... to organise and develop thoughts in non-linear fashion.

(a) pictures, word phrases (b) word phases, situations
(c) pictures, counselling (d) None of these

63 Skinner gave definition of problem-solving in the year

(a) 1805 (b) 1895 (c) 1900 (d) 1968

64 Who developed the concept of mind mapping?

(a) Jean Piaget (b) BF Skinner
(c) Hilda Taba (d) Tony Buzan

65 Who coined the concept of metacognition?

(a) Skinner (b) Thorndike
(c) Sternberg (d) John Flavell

66 Who said that "metacognition is the knowledge and the control that children have over their own thinking and learning activities"?

(a) Skinner (b) John Flavell
(c) Cross and Paris (d) Hennessey

67 Creativity increases with

(a) age (b) education (c) practice (d) experience

68 In creativity, ability always

(a) fosters it (b) inhibits it
(c) stops it (d) cultivates it

69 Who said that "creativity implies the production of a 'totally or partially' novel identity"?

(a) Stagner and Karwoski (b) Skinner
(c) Piaget (d) John Flowell

70 Identify the true statement from the following.

(a) A certain level of intelligence is essential for being creative.
(b) A highly intelligent person is highly creative.
(c) A person with low intelligence can be creative.
(d) Intelligence and creativity are not related to each other.

71 Which of the following is/are the component(s) of social intelligence?

1. Knowledge related to society
2. Effective listening skills
3. Word fluency and conversational skills
4. Effective in classroom management

Codes

(a) Only 1 (b) 1 and 2 (c) 3 and 4 (d) All of these

72 Which of the following is/are the steps of problem-solving?

1. Exploring the problem
2. Setting goals
3. Look at alternatives
4. Evaluation

Codes

(a) 1 and 2 (b) 2 and 3
(c) 3 and 4 (d) All of these

73 Consider the following statements.

1. Gardner has proposed seven kinds of inter-related intelligence.
2. Sailors are high on spatial intelligence.
3. Street smart persons are high on experiential intelligence.
4. Solving logical puzzles requires bodily kinesthetic intelligence.

Which of the following is true?

(a) 1 and 2 (b) 2, 3 and 4
(c) Only 3 (d) All of these

74 Which of the following is not an example of performance tests?

1. Picture completion 2. Picture arrangement
3. Block design 4. Digit span

Codes

(a) Only 1 (b) 1 and 2 (c) 3 and 4 (d) Only 4

75 Consider the following statements.

1. We can also know one's intelligence on the basis of his/her reaction time.
2. Culture-fair tests can only be administered to the persons of a particular culture.
3. Wechsler scales of intelligence have both verbal and performance sub-tests.
4. Mental age is obtained on the basis of the individual's performance on a test of intelligence.

Which of the above statements is / are not correct?

(a) Only 1 (b) 2, 3 and 4
(c) Only 3 (d) All of these

76 Consider the following statements about the nature of Metacognition.

1. Metacognition highlights in-depth thinking in which cognitive processes are actively controlled.
2. Metacognition focuses on planning whch includes how a task can be accomplished. It monitors, understands and estimates progress towards the completion of a particular task.
3. With the help of metacognition, a student can be aware of how dedicated he is to reaching his goals, of how strong his trait of perseverance is, and of how focused his attention is to a task that involves thinking or writing. He can also regulate his dedication, disposition, and attention.

Which of the above statements is / are correct?

(a) Only 1 (b) Only 2
(c) 2 and 3 (d) All of these

77 Match the following

List I (Concepts)	**List II** (Years)
A. Mind mapping	1. 1970
B. Theory of Multiple Intelligence	2. 1979
C. Triarchic Theory of Intelligence	3. 1985
D. Metacognition	4. 1879

Codes

	A	B	C	D		A	B	C	D
(a)	1	2	3	4	(b)	2	3	1	4
(c)	3	1	4	2	(d)	1	4	3	2

78 Match the following

List I (IQ Ranges)	List II (Descriptive Labels)
A. 130 and above	1. Average
B. 120-129	2. Bright normal/High average
C. 110-119	3. Superior
D. 90-109	4. Very superior

Codes

	A	B	C	D		A	B	C	D
(a)	1	2	3	4	(b)	1	2	4	3
(c)	4	3	1	2	(d)	4	3	2	1

79 Match the following

List I (Meanings)	List II (Sub-Theories)
A. Control, monitor and evaluate cognitive processing.	1. Contextual Sub-Theory
B. Execute strategies assembled by meta components.	2. Knowledge acquisition components
C. Encode, combine and compare information.	3. Performance components
D. Specifies the behaviours considered intelligent in a particular culture.	4. Meta components

Codes

	A	B	C	D		A	B	C	D
(a)	1	2	3	4	(b)	1	2	4	3
(c)	4	3	2	1	(d)	4	3	1	2

80 Match the following.

List I (Descriptive Lables)	List II (IQ Ranges)
A. Superior	1. 55-69
B. Mildly mentally retarded	2. 120-129
C. Border line	3. 110-119
D. High average	4. 70-79

Codes

	A	B	C	D		A	B	C	D
(a)	1	2	3	4	(b)	4	3	2	1
(c)	2	1	4	3	(d)	1	2	3	4

81 Match the following.

List I	List II
A. Picture completion	1. Examinees attempt to duplicate designs made with red and white blocks.
B. Picture arrangement	2. Examinees attempt to solve picture puzzles.
C. Object assembly	3. Examinees arrange pictures to make a sensible story.
D. Block design	4. Examinees indicates which part of each picture is missing.

Codes

	A	B	C	D
(a)	1	2	3	4
(b)	1	2	4	3
(c)	4	3	1	2
(d)	4	3	2	1

Directions (Q. Nos. 82-86) *Given below are two statements, one is labelled as Assertion (A) and the other is labelled as Reason (R). Read the statements and choose the correct answer using the code given below.*

(a) Both A and R are true and R is the correct explanation of A
(b) Both A and R are true and R is not the correct explanation of A
(c) A is true, but R is false
(d) A is false, but R is true

82 **Assertion** (A) Critical thinking represents challenging thought process which leads a person to new avenues of knowledge and understanding.
Reason (R) It is a higher order well-disciplined thought process.

83 **Assertion** (A) Intelligence is the ability to learn in an abstract manner or to think or adapt to his or her environment.
Reason (R) This represents a psychometric approach of intelligence, which focuses on measuring differences in intellectual abilities.

84 **Assertion** (A) Intelligence is the result of the interaction of a person's genes and environment.
Reason (R) Intelligence does not help in the abstract thinking of a person.

85 **Assertion** (A) If a person has high IQ level, will also gets high achievements in life.
Reason (R) A person's success and achievements are based on his/her IQ level.

86 **Assertion** (A) A person's intelligence is different from the other person's intellegence.
Reason (R) Only heredity is responsible for the development of intelligence.

87 Arrange the following theories/concepts in a sequential order.
1. Social intelligence
2. Theory of Multiple Intelligence
3. Triarchic Theory of Intelligence
4. Mind mapping

Codes
(a) 1, 4, 2, 3 (b) 1, 2, 3, 4
(c) 2, 3, 4, 1 (d) 2, 1, 3, 4

PREVIOUS YEARS' QUESTIONS

July 2018

1 In measurement of which of the following types of intelligence an optimal age level is considered pertinent?

(a) Cultural intelligence (b) Emotional intelligence
(c) Spiritual intelligence (d) Cognitive intelligence

2 Who developed the concept of group factors in intelligence?

(a) Burt (b) Spearman
(c) Thurstone (d) Guilford

November 2017

3 Which of the following types of intelligence reaches an optimal development ceiling ?

(a) Emotional intelligence
(b) Social intelligence
(c) Cognitive intelligence
(d) Spiritual intelligence

4 There are two sets given below, List I mentions the theories of intelligence while List II provides the chief proponents of the theories of intelligence. Match the two lists and indicate your answer by selecting from the code.

List I (Theories of Intelligence)	List II (Proponents of the Theories of Intelligence)
A. Group factor theory	1. Daniel Goleman
B. Hierarchical structure theory	2. Guilford
C. Structure of intellect model	3. Burt
D. Emotional intelligence theory	4. Vernon
	5. Spearman

Codes

	A	B	C	D		A	B	C	D
(a)	3	4	2	1	(b)	1	2	3	4
(c)	2	3	4	5	(d)	1	4	3	5

5 In the following list some general conclusions based on intelligence testing have been indicated. Select those which relate to academic intelligence testing. For your answer choose from the following code.

1. The optimum point in one's mental development is reached during adulthood.
2. As one advances in age, intelligence also advances.
3. In terms of functions, the rate of mental development changes.
4. Empathy forms an important component of intelligence.
5. On the basis of intelligence we are able to address problems of meaning and value.
6. By placement of an individual in socially and culturally advanced environment, the intelligence quotient can increase but not his/her classification on the basis of intellectual capacity.

Codes

(a) 1, 2 and 3 (b) 2, 3 and 4
(c) 3, 4 and 5 (d) 1, 3 and 6

6 Below given are two lists, list I and list II. Match the two lists and answer the following.

List I (Types)	List II (Emphasis)
A. Cognitive Intelligence (IQ)	1. Unitive Thinking
B. Emotional Intelligence (EQ)	2. Serial Thinking
C. Spiritual Intelligence (SQ)	3. Associative Thinking
D. Cultural Intelligence (CQ)	4. Symbolic Thinking
	5. Trans - Situational Thinking

Codes

	A	B	C	D		A	B	C	D
(a)	1	2	3	4	(b)	2	3	1	4
(c)	3	4	2	1	(d)	3	2	4	5

January 2017

7 Brainstorming procedures are helpful specially for which category of children ?

(a) Gifted children (b) Backward children
(c) Creative children (d) Mentally retarded children

8 Creativeness and originality are processes of arranging well known facts and principles in new relationships so that whatever is intended may be achieved more effectively. In other words, this means

(a) new knowledge has been applied in a traditional way to achieve a purpose.
(b) common knowledge has been applied in a new way to achieve a new purpose.
(c) known knowledge has been applied in a traditional way to achieve a purpose.
(d) new knowledge has been applied in a traditional existing way to achieve a purpose.

9 Choose the appropriate sequence of steps involved in problem-solving.

1. Confronting the problem
2. Collection of evidences
3. Formulating possible solutions of hypothesis
4. Testing the possible solutions
5. Arriving at conclusions
6. Evaluating the sustainability of solutions

Codes

(a) 1, 2, 3, 4, 5 and 6 (b) 1, 3, 2, 6, 5 and 4
(c) 1, 3, 2, 4, 5 and 6 (d) 1, 2, 4, 3, 5 and 6

10 **Which concept of intelligence addresses the problem of meaning and value?**
(a) Academic Intelligence (IQ)
(b) Emotional Intelligence (EQ)
(c) Spiritual Intelligence (SQ)
(d) Cultural Intelligence (CQ)

11 **Match the two lists, list I and list II and choose the correct code for indicating your answer.**

List I (Theories)	**List II** (Concepts)
A. Guilford's Structure of Intellect Theory	1. Associative thinking and self-motivation
B. Vernon's Hierarchical Structure Theory	2. Capacity to transcend
C. Gardner's Multiple and Emotional Intelligence Theory	3. General, broad and specific factors linked with ability
D. Daniel Goleman's Emotional Intelligence Theory	4. Abilities can be nurtured and developed
	5. Abilities can be explained through basic mental processes, specific contents and products

Codes

	A	B	C	D		A	B	C	D
(a)	5	3	4	1	(b)	1	2	3	4
(c)	2	3	4	5	(d)	1	3	4	5

July 2016

12 **In the list given below, a few theories of intelligence have been indicated. What is the correct sequence of their historic formulation ? Give your answer by selecting the appropriate alternative from the code.**
List **Burt's group factor theory, Spearman's two factor theory, Guilford's Structure of intellect, Daniel Goleman's theory of Emotional intelligence, Zohar and Marshall's theory of spiritual intelligence**
Codes
(a) Guilford's structure of intellect, Spearman's two factor theory, Daniel Goleman's theory of Emotional intelligence, Zohar and Marshall's theory of spiritual intelligence, Bart's group factor theory
(b) Spearman's two factor theory, Burt's group factor theory, Guilford's structure of intellect, Daniel Goleman's theory of emotional intelligence, Zohar and Marshall's theory of spiritual intelligence
(c) Bart's group factor theory, Guilford's structure of intellect, Spearman's two factor theory, Zohar and Marshall's theory of spiritual intelligence, Daniel Goleman's theory of emotional intelligence
(d) Guilford's structure of intellect, Spearman's two factor theory, Zohar and Marshall's theory of spiritual intelligence, Burt's group factor theory, Daniel Goleman's theory of Emotional intelligence

13 **In explaining the development of 'problem-solving' capability, which of the combination is most appropriate ?**
(a) discrimination, generalisation and logical thinking
(b) memorisation, conceptualisation and assimilation
(c) discrimination, conceptualisation and assimilation
(d) convergent thinking skills, divergent thinking skills, seeing of relation between means and end

14 **For the concept of emotional intelligence, which theory of intelligence is considered to be the fore-runner ?**
(a) Thurstone's Multiple Factor Theory
(b) Vernon's hierarchical Structure Theory
(c) Burt's Group Factor Theory
(d) Gardner's Theory of Multiple Intelligence

15 **Assertion** **(A) All gifted children are creative.**
Reason **(R) Creativity is not necessarily related to giftedness.**
Codes
(a) Both A and R are true, but R is not the correct reason for A
(b) Both A and R are true and R is the correct reason for A
(c) Both A and R are false
(d) R is true, but R is not be the correct reason for A

December 2015

16 **Which one of the following concepts of intelligence uses associative thinking ?**
(a) Academic intelligence
(b) Emotional intelligence
(c) Spiritual intelligence
(d) Numerical intelligence

17 **Which of the following intelligence does not stop increasing with age of a person ?**
(a) Academic intelligence (b) Spatial intelligence
(c) Verbal intelligence (d) Emotional intelligence

18 **In emotional intelligence, which will not be considered a component ?**
(a) Self management (b) Self analysis
(c) Self motivation (d) Empathy

19 **The problem solving ability depends upon the ……… .**
(a) growth in height and weight
(b) development of vocabulary
(c) development of thinking and reasoning
(d) development in size and shape

June 2015

20 **Which one of the following statements is correct?**
(a) A gifted child may be creative also
(b) Creativity implies giftedness
(c) Giftedness and creativity are related concepts
(d) Creativity has nothing to do with giftedness

21 Which one of the following will be most correct order in the development of Theory of Intelligence?

1. Spearman's Two Factor Theory
2. Burt's Group Factor Theory
3. Goleman's Emotional Intelligence Theory
4. Guilford's Structure of Intellect

Codes

(a) 1, 2, 3, 4 (b) 1, 2, 4, 3
(c) 2, 1, 2, 4 (d) 2, 1, 3, 4

22 In chronological order, which theory of intelligence is the latest?

(a) Two Factor Theory
(b) Group Factor Theory
(c) Theory of Multiple Intelligence
(d) Multiple Factor Theory

23 Which of the following determinants of individual differences will not contribute to the development of emotional intelligence in Daniel Goleman's formulation even after the age of 25?

(a) Interactive experiences (b) Educational exposure
(c) Technical expertise (d) Genetic potential

December 2014

24 While measuring intelligence, which tests assume that upto a certain chronological age, intelligence reaches a peak ?

(a) Verbal and non-verbal tests
(b) Emotional and social intelligence tests
(c) Spiritual and ethical intelligence tests
(d) Social and emotional intelligence tests

25 Arrange the following concepts of intelligence in the order in which they appeared.

1. Academic intelligence
2. Emotional intelligence
3. Spiritual intelligence
4. Ethical intelligence

Codes

(a) 4, 1, 2 and 3 (b) 1, 3, 4 and 2
(c) 1, 2, 3 and 4 (d) 4, 3, 1 and 2

June 2014

26 The theory of level-I and level-II intelligence was propounded by

(a) Jenson (b) Guilford
(c) Cattel (d) Eysenck

27 Structure of Intellect (SI model) is evolved by

(a) Thurstone (b) Guilford
(c) Spearman (d) Gardner

28 An intelligent child is characterised by

(a) creative and divergent thinking
(b) critical and convergent thinking
(c) critical, creative and convergent thinking
(d) All of the above

29 The formula for calculation of Intelligence Quotient (IQ) is

(a) $\frac{CA}{MA} \times 100$ (b) $\frac{MA}{CA} \times 100$
(c) $\frac{CA}{100} \times MA$ (d) $\frac{100}{MA} \times CA$

ANSWERS

Exam Based Questions

1 (b)	2 (d)	3 (b)	4 (c)	5 (c)	6 (c)	7 (c)	8 (b)	9 (c)	10 (d)
11 (c)	12 (d)	13 (c)	14 (d)	15 (a)	16 (c)	17 (c)	18 (c)	19 (b)	20 (c)
21 (a)	22 (d)	23 (a)	24 (c)	25 (c)	26 (b)	27 (a)	28 (a)	29 (c)	30 (a)
31 (b)	32 (a)	33 (c)	34 (b)	35 (d)	36 (d)	37 (a)	38 (d)	39 (d)	40 (c)
41 (a)	42 (d)	43 (a)	44 (a)	45 (b)	46 (b)	47 (b)	48 (a)	49 (b)	50 (a)
51 (b)	52 (c)	53 (a)	54 (b)	55 (d)	56 (b)	57 (a)	58 (b)	59 (c)	60 (c)
61 (a)	62 (a)	63 (d)	64 (d)	65 (d)	66 (d)	67 (c)	68 (c)	69 (a)	70 (a)
71 (a)	72 (d)	73 (d)	74 (c)	75 (d)	76 (c)	77 (d)	78 (a)	79 (d)	80 (c)
81 (d)	82 (a)	83 (b)	84 (c)	85 (c)	86 (c)	87 (a)			

Previous Years' Questions

1 (d)	2 (a)	3 (c)	4 (a)	5 (b)	6 (c)	7 (b)	8 (a)	9 (c)	10 (a)
11 (d)	12 (b)	13 (d)	14 (b)	15 (b)	16 (d)	17 (b)	18 (c)	19 (b)	20 (a)
21 (d)	22 (c)	23 (b)	24 (a)	25 (c)	26 (a)	27 (b)	28 (b)	29 (b)	

CHAPTER 11

Principles and Theories of Learning

Learning is an active process influenced by many factors. There are some significant learning theories such as behaviouristic, cognitive and social theories which are based on observations and experiments.

Learning

When we hear the word 'learning', most of us think of studying in school. We think about subjects or skills we intend to master, such as Mathematics, English, Science, etc. But, learning is not limited to schools only. We learn everyday in our lives. For e.g. Babies learns to kick, crawl, teenagers learns to cycle or lyrics of their favourite songs, middle-aged people learns to change their diet patterns, etc.

So, in the broadest sense, learning occurs when experience causes a relatively permanent change in an individual's knowledge and behaviour. The change may be delibrate or unintentional, for better or for worse, correct or incorrect and conscious or unconscious.

Therefore, learning can be defined as any relatively permanent change in behaviour that occurs as a result of practice or experience.

Learning has three important elements

- It is a change in behaviour for better or worse.
- It is a change that takes place through practice or experience, changes due to growth or maturation.
- Before it can be called learning, the change must be relatively permanent; it must be for a long time.

Learning is an active process that needs to be stimulated and guided towards desirable outcomes. External stimuli that induces learning includes particularly, the influence of the teacher through the assignments he/she makes, the questions he she asks, the visual aids and other procedures that he/she utilises to arouse learning interest and activity among students.

Learning is the acquisition of habits, knowledge and attitudes. It involves new ways of doing things and it operates in an individual's attempts to overcome obstacles or to adjust to new situations. When learning takes place, it can be expected that a more or less permanent change will be evidenced in the learner's behaviour.

In this Chapter

- *Learning*
  - *Theories of Learning*
- *Social Competence*
- *Social Cognition*
- *Society and Social Relationship*
- *Socialisation*

Definitions of Learning

According to **Woodworth,** (1945) "An activity may be called learning in so for as it develops an individual in anyway, good or bad and makes his environment and experiences different from what it would otherwise have been".

According to **Kingsley and R Gary** (1957), "Learning is the process by which behaviour in the broader sense is originated or changes through practice or training".

According to **Hilgard** (1958), "Learning is the process by which an activity originates or is changed through reading to an encountered situation, provided that the characteristics of the changes in activity cannot be explained on the basis of native response, tendencies, maturation or temporary states of the organism (e.g. fatigue or drugs, etc)".

According to **Kimble** (1961), "Learning is a relatively permanent change in behavioural potentiality that occurs as a result of reinforced practice."

According to **Henry P Smith** (1962), "Learning is the acquisition of new behaviour or the strengthening or weakening of old behaviour as the result of an experience".

According to **Pressey, Robinson and Horrocks** (1967), "Learning is an episode in which a motivated individual attempts to adapt his behaviour so as to succeed in a situation which he perceives as requiring action to attain a goal".

According to **Gardner Murphy** (1968), "The term 'learning', covers every modification in behaviour to meet environmental requirements".

According to **Crow and Crow** (1973), "Learning is an acquisition of habits, knowledge and attitudes. It involves new ways of doing things and it operates in an individual's attempts to overcome obstacles or to adjust to new situations. represents progressive changes in behaviour. It enables him to satisfy interests to attain goals".

Principles of Learning

Learning principles are laws of learning. They provide a research-based and conceptual foundation for how people learn. Learning principles add insight into what makes people learn most effectively.

Some of the principles of learning are discussed below

- Learning is an active process in which learners use sensory input to construct meaning. People learn best when they can take in information using a variety of sensory inputs.
- Learners link new information with prior knowledge and experiences in meaningful ways. Prior knowledge and experiences are primary factors in a persons ability to learn new information.
- Learning requires the use of various forms of language (*e.g.* words, symbols, numbers and images) to capture and develop thinking.
- Learning is influenced by many contextual factors including differences in background, knowledge, thinking patterns; and cultural, linguistic and social backgrounds. Teachers should create learning contexts that maximize student's learning opportunities.
- Learning is influenced by emotional state, social interactions, interpersonal relations and communication with others. Learning is dependent on positive social interactions, communication and relationships.
- Learner's motivation both extrinsic and intrinsic, a key component to ensure engagement and learning. Motivation is the activation of goal-oriented behaviour. Because the learning process is based on establishing and achieving learning goals, figuring out how to motivate students is a key to effective learning experiences.
- Learner's persistent effort, developmentally appropriate challenges and instructional support results in rigorous learning. Students need both support and challenge to achieve rigorous learning.
- Learners need multiple opportunities over time to practice in supportive, respectful environments. Significant learning takes time and must be supported in a safe learning environment. Teacher must support through close monitoring of progress toward achieving the learning goals.
- Learners need regular, specific and timely feedback with opportunities to use the feedback to maximize learning experiences.
- Learners reflect, monitor and adjust their thinking and reasoning to achieve learning goals (metacognition). The ability to self-assess and monitor one's own work accelerates learning.

Theories of Learning

Theories of learning are organised set of principles, explaining how individuals acquires, retains and recalls their knowledge. There are number of theories of learning which have been formulated to answer the questions like, what goes into the process of learning?, How does an individual learns a set of facts and figures, skills, habits, attitudes and similar other things in his/her life?

These theories may be broadly classified as follows

Behaviouristic Theory Behaviourism is a learning theory that only focuses on objectively observable behaviours and discounts any independent activities of the mind. Behavioural theorists define learning as nothing more than the acquisition of new behaviour based on environmental conditions.

Cognitive Theory Cognitive Learning theory is a broad theory that explains thinking and differing mental process and how they are influenced by internal and external factors in order to produce learning in individuals.

Social Learning Theory Social learning theory is the view that people learn by observing others. This theory explains how people learn new behaviours, values and attitudes. It requires attention to the person(s) observed, remembering the observed behaviour, the ability to replicate the behaviour and a motivation to act, in the same way.

Behaviouristic Theories of Learning

Behaviouristic theories of learning are as follows

Thorndike Connectionism or Behaviourial Theory or Trial and Error Theory

Edward Lee 'Ted' Thorndike (31st August, 1874- 9th August, 1949) was an American Behaviourial Psychologist, who developed Learning Theory on the basis of behaviourism. Skinner Theory of operant conditioning was built on the ideas of Edward Thorndike. Thorndike was a pioneer not only in behaviourism and in studying learning, but also in using animals in psychological experiments.

Connectionism is a learning theory based on the concept of bonds formed between stimulus and response *i.e.* natural connections between **Situations** (S) and **Responses** (R) are formed and strengthened. The stimulus affects the organism which responds to it.

Thus, S-R bonds are formed which are considered as physical conditions. This theory of learning is related to conditioning, that utilises the concept of association of connection. It emphasises that the behaviour begins with conditioned reflexes and natural responses and new behaviours result from the acquisition of new bonds through experience. Thorndike formulated the major laws of learning on the basis of his belief in connectionism.

EL Thorndike had a powerful impact on both psychology and education. He was a strong supporter of educational research and helped in creating the intelligence and aptitude tests.

Thorndike's Puzzle Box

One of Thorndike's major contributions to the study of psychology was his work with animals. He believed that learning occured through trial and error. The animal made many responses, many of them were wrong and ineffective and eventually learned to repeat those that got desirable results.

Thorndike felt that the learning was a matter of creating associations between stimuli and response and no speculation about mind was necessary or useful. Through long, extensive research with these animals, he constructed a device called **'puzzle box'**.

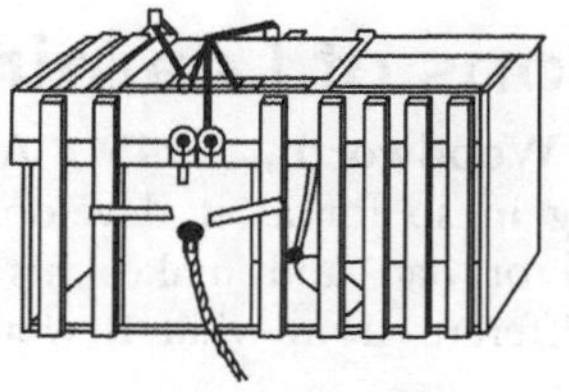

Puzzle Box

The puzzle box was approximately 20 inches long, 15 inches wide and 11 inches tall. The box had a door that was pulled open by a weight attached to a string that ran over a pulley and was attached to the door. The string attached to the door led to a lever or button inside the box. When the animal pressed the bar or pulled the lever, the string attached to the door would cause the weight to lift and the door to open.

Experiment by Thorndike on Cat

In one of his experiments, he put a hungry cat in a puzzle box (Cage). There was only one door which could be opened by correctly manipulating a latch.

A fish was placed outside the box. The smell of the fish acted as a strong motive for the hungry cat to come out of the box.

Thorndike described this situation in his words as:

"It tries to squeeze through every opening, it claws and bits at the bars or wires, it thrusts it paws through any opening and claws at everything it reaches. "

In this way, the cat made a number of random movements and in one of the random movements, the latch was manipulated accidentlly. The cat came out and got her reward (fish). Gradually, in subsequent trials, the cat learned the art of opening the door.

Cat in the Puzzle Box

The experiment sums up the following stages in the process of learning

Drive In the above experiment, she was hungry and was intensified by the sight of the food.

Goal To get the food (fish) by getting out of the box.

Black The cat was confined in the box with a closed door.

Random Movements The cat persistently tried to come out of the box without knowing how.

Chance of Success As a result of this striving and random movements, the cat, by chance succeeded in opening the door.

Selection (of proper movement), Gradually, the cat recognised the correct way to manipulate the latch. She selected the proper way of manipulating the latch out of its random movements.

Fixation At last, the cat learned the proper way to open the door by eliminating all the incorrect responses and fixing only the right one. Then, she was able to open the door without any error or in other words, learned the correct way of opening the door.

Thorndike explained learning with his 'law of effect'. Animals tended to repeat a behaviour that resulted in a pleasing effect. This was an early version of the concept of positive reinforcement that Skinner has used effectively. Behaviour was varied during a trial and error phase. Thorndike believed that the animal stumbled upon a behaviour that produced a desirable effect.

This created a link between stimulus (cage) and a response (stepping on switch or pulling the lever). Later, in the same stimulus situation, that response occurred faster. Thorndike compared the performance of, chickens, cats, dogs and monkeys in similar task.

He produced a graph called a '**learning curve**' showing the number of seconds the animal took to escape on each trial.

Thorndike concluded that all animals learn, solely by trial and error or reward and punishment. He observed the cat's behaviour in the puzzle box and described what happens when all the beings learned together. All learning involves the formation of connections and connections are strengthened according to the '**law of effect**'.

Thorndike's Laws

Thorndike presented laws of learning on the basis of his belief in Connectionism Theory. Originally, these laws are the outgrowth of experiments in the field of animal psychology. He first presented his theory in his book **'Animal Learning'** published in 1898.

His major laws are Primary and Subordinate Laws. Primary Laws include Law of Readiness, Law of Exercise and Law of Effect. Whereas, Subordinate Laws are composed of Law of Multiple Response, Law of Attitude, Prepotency of Elements, Law of Response by Analogy and Law of Associative Shifting.

With the subject of the importance of these laws in learning, Thorndike points out, "Both theory and practice need emphatic and frequent reminders that man's learning is fundamentally the action of laws of readiness, exercise and effect". Thus, in Thorndike's opinion man's learning takes place according to these laws.

Primary Laws

Law of Readiness

"*When a bond is ready to act, act gives satisfaction and not to act gives annoyance*". If a person is ready to learn, he/she can learn quickly. The law of readiness describes those situations in which the person, who learns or either invites the object of his/her learning or rejects it. Readiness means a preparation of action. If a person is not prepared to learn, then learning cannot be instilled in him/her. Readiness includes all those preparatory adjustments which immediately preceeds the activity. Reminding the learner of his/her past experiences, the understanding of new things, diverting attention towards the subject to be learned, changing the environment to suit the learning, are all included in readiness. The readiness creates a mental set for learning.

Law of Exercise

It has two important aspects. It is based on the law of use and disuse. The law of use states that "when a modifiable connection is made between a situation and a response, that connection's strength is being increased".

Similarly, the law of disuse states, that "when a modifiable connection is not made between a situation and a response over a length of time, the connection's strength is decreased".

The repeated application of an activity fixes it firmly in the mind, while on the other hand, the relation is weakened through continuous disuse. Drill and practice helps in increasing efficiency and durability of learning.

According to **Thorndike's** S-R bond or Connectionism Theory, the connections are strengthened with trial and practice.

Whenever, there is an appropriate situation, the activity which is firmly entrenched, might takes place. It is the experience that whenever any action is repeated, it becomes easy and prompt. Learning and re-learning helps in mastering the activity.

Repetitions of activities fix knowledge and skills to be learned. Practice makes it perfect. Lack of practice weakens memory and skills. It may be said that longer is the period of disuse, greater is the loss of memory and weakening of skills.

Law of Effect

The 'law of effect' is the 'effect of learning.' The trial or steps leading to satisfaction stamps in the bond or connection. Satisfying states lead to consolidation and strengthening of connection, whereas dissatisfaction, annoyance or pain lead to the weakening or stamping out of the connection. Success brings with it satisfaction and along with it a strengthening of the relation of the experiences. Failure increases dissatisfaction and the absence of the relation among the experiences weakens them. The success can be compared to reward and failure to punishment, and the desire to repeat success avoids failures as the inevitable antecedents.

Subordinate Laws

Other five subordinate laws were also mentioned by Thorndike in relation to the three major ones. *The five subordinate laws are:*

Law of Multiple Response

A person varies or changes his/her response till an appropriate behaviour is succeeded. A person solves a problem with his instinctive and learned behaviour. There are multiple responses in the behaviour, which guides a person in achieving success and making learning possible. The learner reaches the solution by variation in the response.

Law of Set or Attitude

Learning is conditioned or guided by the attitude or set of the person which determines not only what the person will do, but what will satisfy or annoy the person. The response of a person is dependent upon his/her attitude towards the situation. Learning is affected more in the individual if he/she is set to learn more or to excel.

Prepotency of Elements

According to this law, the learner reacts selectively to the important or essential in the situation and neglects the other features or elements which may be irrelevant or non-essential. The ability to deal with the essential or relevant part of the situation, makes analytical and insightful learning possible. In this law, Thorndike is really anticipating insight in learning which was more emphasized by the Gestaltions.

Law of Response by Analogy

The person uses old experiences in responding to a new situation. A person will respond in a manner similar to the one in which he/she has behaved previously, if he/she finds some similarity between the situations.

Law of Associative Shifting

The response of person/learner shifts in respect to the basic or associative stimulus. The learner's response is shifted from one stimulus to another.

Educational implications of the theory are:

- A task can be started from the easier aspect towards its difficult aspect, which will help the children to learn properly.
- Trial and error method can be used in teaching.
- Rewards and punishment affects the learning of the child.
- Habits are formed as a result of repetition. With the help of this theory the wrong habits can be modified and good habits can be strengthened.
- Practice is the main feature of trial and error method. It helps in reducing errors committed by children in learning a concept.

Pavlov's Classical Conditioning Theory

Classical conditioning gets its name from the fact, that it is the kind of learning situation that existed in the early 'classical' experiments of Ivan P Pavlov. In late 1920, this famous Russian Psychologist began to establish many of the basic principles of conditioning. It is also sometimes called **respondent conditioning** or **Pavlovian conditioning**.

It focuses on the learning of involuntary emotional or psychological responses such as fear, increased muscle tension, salivation or sweating. These sometimes are called respondents because they are automatic responses to stimuli. Through the process of classical conditioning, humans and animals can be trained to react involuntarily to a stimulus that previously had no effect or a very different effect on them.

Pavlov did experiments on the digestive systems of dogs. He was trying to determine how long it took a dog to secrete digestive juices after it had been fed, but the intervals of time kept changing. At first, the dogs salivated in the expected manner while they were being fed.

Then the dogs began to salivate as soon as they saw food. Finally, they salivated as soon as they saw the scientist in the room. Pavlov decided to make a detour from his original experiments and examine these unexpected interferences in his work.

Acquisition or Learning of Conditioned Responses

For studying the digestive system in dogs, Pavlov had designed an apparatus, that could accurately measures the amount of saliva produced by the dogs in response to food or other things in his environment. Normally, when food is placed in the mouth of any animal, the salivary glands automatically start releasing saliva to help with chewing and digestion. This is a normal reflex or involuntary response in both animals and humans.

The food causes a particular reaction, the salivation. A stimulus can be defined as any object, event or experience that causes a response, the reaction of an organism. In case of Pavlov's dogs, the **food** is the **stimulus** and **salivation** is the **response**.

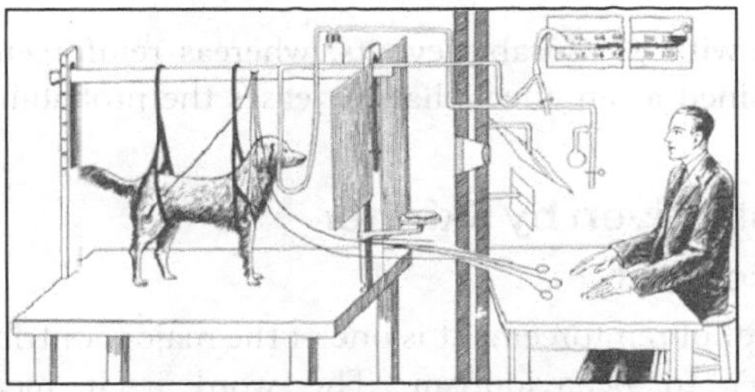

Pavlov's Apparatus for Studying the Conditioned Salivary Response

At the beginning of his experiments, Pavlov began by a sound of bell and recording a dog's response. As expected, there was no salivation. At this point, the bell was a **Neutral Stimulus** because it brought forth no salivation. Then Pavlov fed the dog, the response was salivation. The food was an **Unconditioned Stimulus (US)** because no prior training or conditioning was needed to establish the natural connection between food and salivation. The salivation was an **Unconditioned Response (UR)**, because it occurred automatically without any conditioning.

Using these three elements—**the food, the salivation** and **the bell**, Pavlov demonstrated that a dog could be conditioned to salivate after hearing the bell. He did this by pairing of sound of bell with food. At the beginning of the experiment, he sounded the bell and then quickly fed the dog. After Pavlov repeated this several times, the dog began to salivate after hearing the sound of bell, but before receiving the food. Now, the sound had became a **Conditioned Stimulus (CS)** that could bring forth salivation by itself. The response of salivating after the tone was now a **Conditioned Response (CR)**.

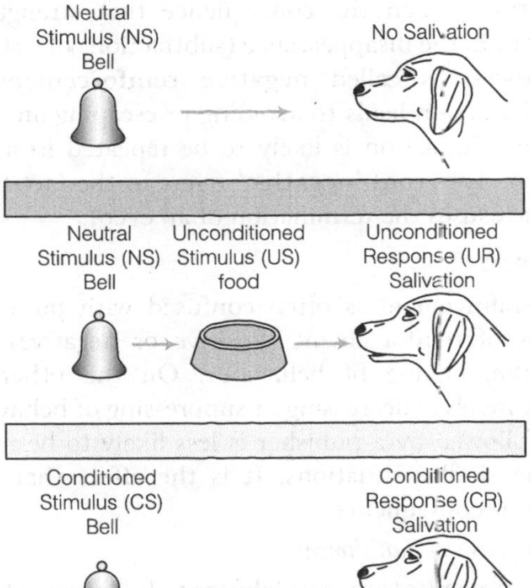

Elements of Classical Conditioning

Pavlov eventually identified several key elements that must be present and experienced in a particular way, for conditioning to take place.

Unconditioned Stimulus It is original, naturally occurring stimulus, that leads to reflex or involuntary response. In case of Pavlov's dogs, food is the unconditioned stimulus.

Unconditioned Response The reflex response to the unconditioned stimulus is called unconditioned response. In case of Pavlov's experiment, salivation to food is the unconditioned response.

Conditioned Stimulus Pavlov determined that almost any kind of stimulus could become associated with the unconditioned stimulus, often enough. In case of Pavlov's experiment, bell was the neutral stimulus because it had no effect on salivation. After being paired with food, so many times, the bell came to produce the same salivation response. The neutral stimulus can now be called conditioned stimulus.

Conditioned Response It is a learned response to the previously neutral stimulus, that has changed into conditioned stimulus. In case of Pavlov's experiment, the salivation on hearing the sound of bell is conditioned response.

Skinner's Operant Conditioning Theory

B F Skinner (1904-1990) was the behaviourist, who gave the **Theory of Operant Conditioning**. It is the learning in which voluntary behaviour is strengthened or weakened by consequences or antecedents. Skinner began with the belief that the principles of classical conditioning accounts for only a small proportion of learned behaviours.

Many human behaviours are operants, not respondents. Respondents are elicited by specific stimuli such as **Pavlov's bell**. In a respondent situation, an individual learns merely by being in the situation and responding to it. But not all behaviour are of this type. Most of human behaviours are operant behaviours, which are emitted not elicited.

Classical conditioning describes only how existing behaviours might be paired with new stimuli, it does not explains, how new operant behaviours are acquired. Behaviour, like response or action, is simply a word for what a person does in a particular situation. It lies between the antecedents and consequences. Antecedents are the events that preceeds a behaviour or action, and consequence is the event that follow an action or behaviour. There is a relationship in antecedent, behaviour and consequence.

A—B—C

Research in operant conditioning shows that operant behaviour can be altered by changes in the antecedents, the consequences or both.

Skinner's Experiment

In 1930s, **BF Skinner** began his influential experiments on operant conditioning. He wanted to study reinforced responding without breaking the experiment in discrete trials. To do all this, he invented the **Skinner box** or it is often called the **operant chamber**. It is a simple box with device at one end that can be worked by the animal in the box. For rats, cats and monkeys the device is a lever, for pegion the device is a small panel, called a *key* which can be pecked. The lever and key are switches that activates when positive reinforcement is being used. Thus, positive reinforcement is contingent upon pressing a lever or pecking a key.

The first step in the operant conditioning of a hungry rat is to get food pellets when they are delivered by the experimenter, who operates the pellet, delivery mechanism from a push button switch outside the operant chamber. The pellets are delivered one by one, after a time the rat eats each pellet as soon as it drops. Then the experimenter stops releasing the pellets and the rat is left alone in the box with the lever, which will release the pellets. After an initial period of inactivity the rat being hungry, begins to explore the box. Eventually, it presses the lever accidently. A pellet of food is released *i.e.* the reinforcement is contingent upon pressing the lever.

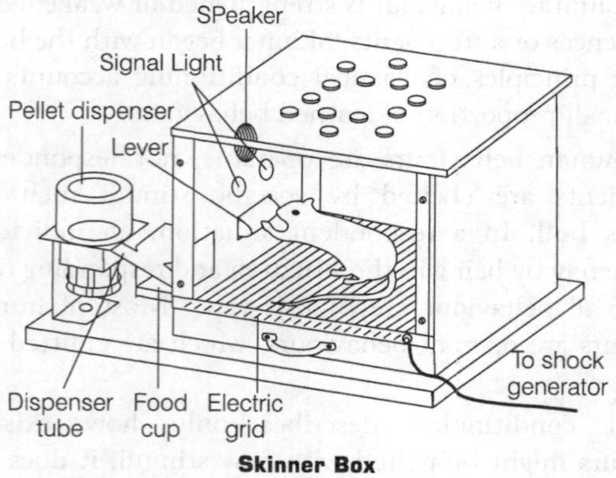

Skinner Box

After eating the food pellet, the rat continues exploring and after a while, it presses the lever again and again and the pellet is released, when it presses the lever third time. Usually, after the fourth or fifth press, the rat begins to press the lever more rapidly and operant behaviour is developed. Skinner preferred the term '**reinforcement**' to reward. **According to Skinner**, "reward is a subjective interpretation of behaviour associated with pleasurable events, whereas reinforcement is simply defined as an effect that increases the probability of a response".

Concepts Given by Skinner

Reinforcement

The concept of reinforcement is one of the major contributions by Skinner to behaviourism. The word itself means to strengthen. A reinforcer is any consequence that strengthens the behaviour it follows. Reinforced behaviours increases in frequency or duration.

The reinforcement process can be diagrammed as follows

	Consequence	Effect
Behaviour ⟶	Reinforcer ⟶	Strengthened or Repeated Behaviour

Therefore, reinforcement can be defined as the environmental event that is the consequence of an instrumental response and that makes the response more likely to occur again.

There are two types of reinforcement

- The first is called positive reinforcement which occurs when the behaviour produces new stimulus. It is a stimulus or event, which, when it follows a response, increases the livelihood that the response will occur again. Response results in the occurrence of the reinforce. *e.g.* food for hungry animals, praise from parents, reward from teachers and many other stimuli or events will serve as positive reinforcers, when they are contingent on some behaviour. When the consequence that strengthens a behaviour in the appearance (addition) of a new stimulus, the situation is defined as **positive reinforcement**.
- In contrast, when the consequence that strengthens a behaviour in the disappearance (subtraction) of a stimulus, this process is called **negative reinforcement**. If a particular action leads to avoiding or escaping an aversive situation, the action is likely to be repeated in a similar situation. The word '**negative**' refers to the fact that the response causes the termination of an event.

Punishment

Negative reinforcement is often confused with punishment. The process of reinforcement (Positive or negative) always involves strengthening of behaviour. On the other hand, punishment involves decreasing or suppressing of behaviour. A behaviour followed by a punisher is less likely to be repeated again in the similar situations. It is the effect that defines punishment as consequence.

There are two forms of punishment

The first is **presentation punishment**. It occurs when the appearance of a stimulus following the behaviour supresses or decreases the behaviour. *e.g.* running laps, extra work, etc.

The second is the **removal punishment**. It involves removing a stimulus. e.g. taking away the privileges from children. It decreases the chances of behaviour occurence again by removing a pleasant stimulus following the behaviours.

Schedules of Reinforcement

It refers to the time plan of when and how often a response is reinforced. Reinforcement may be continuous or intermittent. When people are learning a new behaviour, they will learn it faster if they are reinforced for every correct response. This is continuous reinforcement schedule. Initially, it is used during the initial operant conditioning. Then, the new behaviour in mastered that can be maintained by reinforcing intermittently rather than every time.

An **intermittent reinforcement schedule** helps people to maintain skills without expecting constant results. There are two basic types of intermittent reinforcement schedules. One is called an interval schedule, that is based on the amount of time that passes between reinforcement. The second is a ratio schedule, that is based on the number of responses, learners give between reinforcement. Interval and ratio schedules may be either fixed or variable.

All the reinforcement schedules are summarised in the table given below

Reinforcement Schedules

Schedule	Meaning	Example	Response Pattern	Reaction When Reinforcement Stops
Continuous	Reinforcement after every response.	Turning on the television	Rapid learning response.	Very little persistence rapid disappearance of response.
Fixed Interval	Reinforcement after set period of time.	Weekly Quiz	Response rate increases as time for reinforcement approaches then drops after reinforcement.	Little persistence rapid drop in response rate when time for reinforcement passes and no reinforcer appears.
Variable Interval	Reinforcement after varying lengths of time.	Pop quizzes	Slow, steady rate of responding very little pause after reinforcement.	Greater persistence slow decline in response rate.
Fixed ratio	Reinforcement after a set number of responses .	Piece work	Rapid response rate pause after reinforcement.	Little persistence, rapid drop in response rate, when expected number of responses are given and no reinforcer appears.
Variable Ratio	Reinforcement after varying number of responses .	Slot Machines	Very high response rate little pause after reinforcement .	Greatest persistence response rate stay high and gradually drops off.

Hull's Reinforcement Theory and Drive Reduction Model

Clark Hull was majorly influenced by the work of **Pavlov, Darwin, Thorndike and Tolman. Hull** is best known for his Drive Reduction Model and Reinforcement Theory which postulated that behaviour occurs in the response to drives. He was an influential behaviourist, American psychologist and learning theorist.

Hull's theory was first presented in 1943, in his book 'Principles of Behaviour'. This theory was extended in 1952 through his last book 'A Behaviour System'.

Hull used the term **'drive'** to refer to the state of tension or arousal caused by biological or physiological needs. Thirst, hunger, need for warmth are the example of drives. A drive creates an unpleasant state, a tension that needs to be reduced.

When the goal of the drive is attained (food, water, warmth) the drive is reduced, atleast temporarily. He did not include cognitive aspects such as purpose, ideas, intelligence, values or knowledge as a part of his theoretical constructs as these cannot be directly observed.

Drive Reduction Model

Hull's model was Drive Reduction Model. He mentioned two types of drives. **Primary drives** are tied to innate biological needs, such as food, water, sex, etc. They are internal stimuli that compel the organism to act in a certain way. **Secondary drives**, also called learned drives, are those that develops through association of stimuli with the reduction of primary drives. Once developed, the secondary drives can also impel the organism into action. *e.g.* the need to acquire money is the secondary drive. Primary and secondary drives constitutes motivation and motivation is a major factor of behaviour.

In Hull's model, the reduction in drive constitutes reinforcement of S-R association (Stimulus- Response). Through repetition of the reinforcement, the probability of the occurrence of the response, *i.e.* its habit strength increases. Thorndike's law of effect appears in Hull's model as the law of primary reinforcement. The reinforcement is the reduction of the drive state and any behaviour associated with such reinforcement. Secondary reinforcement operates in a similar manner.

Hull developed version of behaviourism in which

The response depends on the characteristics of stimulus and organism. Hull was interested in studying intervening variables that affected behaviour such as initial drive, incentives, etc. The Hull's drive reduction or need satisfaction model plays an important role.

Hull Theoretical Framework consisted of many postulates, which are as follows

- Organism possess a hierarchy of needs which are aroused under conditions of stimulation and drive.
- Habit strength increases with activity that is associated with primary and secondary reinforcement.
- Habit strength aroused by a stimulus, other than the one originally conditioned, depends upon the closeness of the second stimulus.
- Stimuli associated with cessation of a response becomes conditioned inhibitors.

Reinforcement Theory

Clark Hull presented the Reinforcement Theory to explain learning. He gave no importance to consciousness in learning. He has presented behaviourist and instrumentalist explanation of learning. According to him, in learning, an organism learns to respond to a stimulus. An organism learns gradually by practice. His theory is also called goal gradient or reinforcement gradient, which can be said the refined form of the Thorndike's law of effect.

Hull gave an important place to motivation in the learning process. It is a kind of drive in organism. It helps in the formation of habits resulting from practice and also it is a source of practice. An organism cannot learn anything in absence of motivation. As soon as the motivation arises, the organism becomes active and the actions are also goal directed.

The organism repeats the same action and out in a particular way to get reward, in the form of motivation. On the other hand, the tendency of repeating the responses, which are not rewarded, decreases. Reward strengthens the relationship between stimulus and response in an organism. Reward is also called reinforcement.

Goal gradient or **reinforcement gradient** is the central point of Hull's theory. Therefore, his theory is called reinforcement theory. The attainment of goal brings stability to the relation between stimulus and response. It reduces the tension of the organism, which helps it in learning the specific response.

Hull accepts the importance of practice in learning. Hull suggested that animals and humans repeats any behaviour that reduces the drives. This reduction of drive serves as a reinforcer for learning. This reinforcement increases the livelihood that the same behaviour will occur again in the future, when the same need arises. Thus, learning involves dynamic interplay between survival drives and their attainment. The bonding of the drive with the goal of the drive is a type of reinforcement and his theory is a reinforcement theory of learning.

Physiological and physical reinforcement are also important in learning process. Hull's theory began to fall out of favour in middle part of 20th century. His theory lacks generalisation due to emphasis on quantifying of variables. Also, it does not show that how secondary reinforcers reduces drive, as they do nothing directly to reduce physiological and biological needs. Also, it does not explain that why people engage in behaviours that do not reduce drives.

Gagne's Hierarchical Theory of Learning

Robert Gagne was an American Educational Psychologist, best known for his writings, 'Conditions of Learning' and 'Instructional Technology Foundations.' His focus was on intentional or purposeful learning, which is a type of learning that occurs in school or specific training programmes. He believed that events in the environment influence the learning process. This theory identifies the general type of human capabilities that are learned, in terms of behavioural changes. Once the learning outcomes are identified, an analysis of conditions of learning is done.

There are four elements of Gagne's theory, which are as follows

- Learning
- Types of learning
- Hierarchial Step Model
- Designing of instruction

Learning

According to Gagne, learning is

- cumulative, human intellectual development which is the building of increasing complex structures of human capabilities.
- the mechanism by which an individual becomes a complete functioning member of the society.
- the result of different kinds of human behaviour. Different human capabilities are required both from the stimulation, from the environment and the cognitive processing undertaken by the learners.

Types of Learning

Gagne identifies five major types of learning *i.e.* verbal information, intellectual skills, cognitive strategies, motor skills and attitude. Different internal and external conditions are necessary for each type of learning.

Types, Conditions and Principles of Human Capabilities/Learning

Types of Human Capabilities/ Learning	Conditions	Principles for Instructional Events
Verbal Information	Retrieving stored information : The internal conditions to support this learning includes: ▪ Pre-existing of organised knowledge ▪ Strategies for processing the new information	▪ Provide meaningful context of information for encoding. ▪ Provide elaborations, imagery, or other encoding cues. ▪ Organise information, so that it can be learned in chunks.
Intellectual Skills	Mental operations that permits individuals to respond to conceptualisations of the environment. ▪ Discrimination ▪ Concrete and defined concepts ▪ Using rules ▪ Problem-solving: combining subordinate rules in order to solve a problem. The, internal conditions to facilitate this type of learning includes: ▪ Recalling pre-requisite skills ▪ Interacting in a variety of ways with the new learning	▪ Provide varied concrete examples and rules . ▪ Provide opportunities for interacting with examples in different ways . ▪ Assess learners in new situations.
Cognitive Strategies	An internal process by which the learners plans, controls and monitors his/her own ways of thinking and learning, including ▪ Task specific ▪ General ▪ Executive	▪ If task is specific, it describes the strategy, if task is general, it demonstrates the strategy. ▪ Provides opportunities for strategy specific practice with support and feedback.
Attitude	An internal state, *i.e.*, pre-disposition that affects an individual's choice of action.	▪ Provides respected models who enact positive behaviour and reinforce the model . ▪ When learner enacts the behaviour, provide reinforcement.
Motor Skills	Capability to perform a sequence of physical movements. *It involves three stages:* ▪ Learning the sequence of the movement. ▪ Practicing the movement . ▪ Refining the movement from the feedback from the environment.	▪ Establish executive sub-routine and provides for mental rehearsal. ▪ Arrange several repetitions of skills with correct feedback.

Hierarchical Step Model of Learning

Gagne identified eight basic steps and arranged them in the hierarchical order. According to **Gagne**, the higher orders of learning in the hierarchy build upon the lower levels, requiring progressively to greater amount of previous orders for their success. The lowest four orders tends to focus on the behavioural learning and highest four on cognitive learning simple tasks function as real components of a more complex tasks. The underlying assumption of the hierarchy is that the basic skills are necessary to perform the most complex skill (problem-solving).

These steps are as follows

Signal Learning This is the simplest form of learning and consist Pavlov's classical conditioning response, where the individual learns to carry out a general conditioned response towards a given signal. The subject is conditioned to emit a desired response as a result of stimulus.

Stimulus Response Learning This form of learning is also known as *Skinner's operant conditioning*. The individual shows a certain Response (R) to a discriminated Stimulus (S).

Psychomotor Connection Learning/Chaining This is a more advanced form of learning in which the subject develops the ability to connect two or more previously-learned stimulus response bonds into a linked sequence.

Verbal Association Learning It is a form of chaining in which the links between the items being connected are verbal in nature. Verbal association is one of the important process in the development of language skills.

Multiple Discrimination Learning Separate associations which have been learnt are connected to form multiple discrimination. This involves developing the ability to make appropriate (different) responses to a series of similar stimuli that differ in a systematic way.

Concept Learning It is the learning to respond to a stimulus according to abstract characteristics such as position, shape, colour and not according to the concrete physical characteristics.

Principle Learning A principle is a chain of two or more concepts. In principle learning, one needs to associate more than one concept.

Problem-Solving This is the highest level of cognitive process according to Gagne. It involves developing the ability to invent a complex rule, algorithm for the purpose of solving the problem.

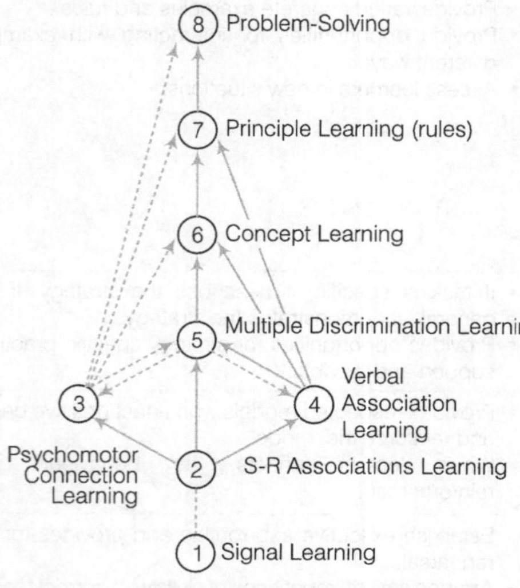

Hierarchical Step Model

Designing Instruction

In designing instruction, the skills are to be learned at the lowest level and mastered before proceeding. The instructor should use positive reinforcement and repetition, with each new skill building upon previously acquired skills.

Steps of Instruction

Gain Attention The first event or step of instruction is to gain attention to get the reception of stimuli.

Informing Learners of the Objective It is important to inform the learner of the purpose and expected outcome of the learning to provide the motivation to learners.

Stimulating Recall of Prior Learning The learners are asked to recall the existing relevant knowledge.

Presenting the Stimulus Relevant stimulus to the subject matter should be presented.

Providing Learning Guidance It requires the instructor to make the stimulus as meaningful as possible.

Eliciting Performance The learners are asked to demonstrate the newly learned behaviour.

Providing Feedback Giving informative feedback to learner's performance is important.

Assessing Performance It consists of assessments to verify that learning has occurred.

Enhancing Retention and Transfer It refers to retaining the learned capability over a long period of time and transferring it to new situations outside the learning environment.

Events of Instruction

Internal Process	Instructional Event	Action Example
Reception	Gaining attention	Use abrupt stimulus change
Expectancy	Informing learners of the objective	Tell learners what they will be able to do after learning
Retrieval to Working Memory	Stimulating recall of prior knowledge	Ask for recall of previously learned knowledge of skills
Selective Perception	Presenting the stimulus	Display the content with distinctive features
Semantic Encoding	Providing learning guidance	Suggest a meaningful organisation
Responding	Eliciting performance	Ask learner to perform
Reinforcement	Providing feedback	Give informative feedback
Retrieval and Reinforcement	Assessing performance	Require additional learner performance, with feedback
Retrieval and Generalisation	Enhancing retention and transfer	Provide varied practice and spaced reviews

Cognitive Theories of Learning

Cognitive theories of learning are discussed below

Kurt Lewin's Field Theory

"Learning is more effective, when it is an active rather than a passive process". **— Kurt Lewin**

Lewin, as a Neo-Gestaltist, transferred the Gestalt Model to everyday situations. He presented his theory in 1917. He was highly influenced by **Einstein** and applied the idea of Einsteinian field physics to psychology. For **Kurt Lewin**, behaviour was determined by totality of an individual's situation. Human behaviour is a function of both the person and the environment in which the behaviour takes place, including the social parameters. Lewin viewed the social environment as a dynamic field which impacted in an interactive way with human consciousness.

In the field theory, a **field** is defined as the totality of co-existing facts, which are concieved of as mutually interdependent. The needs of individual organise perception of the field and acting within the field. There is a dynamic interaction of elements in the field. The behaviour of individual was purposeful and visualised the forces in the field, which included positive forces, which attract people and negative valence forces which repel people. The blending of these forces produced dynamic interactions.

The psychological field as **life-space**, within which people had to be viewed in order to understand the behaviour. In this, the individual and groups could be seen in topological terms (using map for representation).

According to **Lewin's theory**, learning is essential in coping with opposing force fields. Changes in valances and values are important for an individual to deal with the ongoing situations. Also, a holistic investigation of human behaviour should also include the environment in which the learning is taking place. It includes the psychological environment of the learners and others with whom he/she interacts.

Lewin's field theory lead to field research on human behaviour. Lewin believed that it was possible to study social and psychological phenomena experimentally. He conducted experiments in natural settings, where he manipulated complex situational variables and observed the effects.

Features of Kurt Lewin's Field Theory

- Behaviour is the function of the field that exists at the time behaviour occurs.
- Analysis begins with the situation as a whole from which component parts are differentiated.
- The concrete person in a concrete situation can be represented mathematically.
- Topology (life space), Psychology (need, aspiration) and Sociology (force, fields, motives), comprises of well integrated system.

Lewin's field theory is the "proposition that human behaviour is the function of both the person and the environment". Symbolically, it can be represented as:

$$\boxed{B = f(P, E)}$$

Where, B = Behaviour
F = Field (Life space)
P = Person
E = Environment

It means that behaviour is the function of the person in their environment.

Lewin's field theory leads to the development of actual field research on human behaviour. His approach has guided experiments in the field of social cognition, social motivation and group processes. Most importantly, Lewin helped in the development of action research.

> **Action Research**
>
> Kurt Lewin first coined the term 'action research' in *1944*. In his paper, " **Action Research and Minority Problems** "(1946), he described action research as a comparative research on the conditions and effects of various forms of social action and research that uses a spiral of steps. Each of which is composed of a circle of planning, action and fact finding about the result of the action.
>
> Action research is a research initiated to solve an immediate problem or a reflective process of progressive problem-solving led by individuals working in teams or as a part of community of practice to improve the way they address issues and solves problems.

Tolman's Sign Learning Theory or Sign Gestalt Learning Theory

Edward Tolman made significant contributions to the field of psychology. He developed a Cognitive Theory of Learning, which came in the year **1932** with the publication of his work **Purposive Behaviour in Animals and Men**, which became his trademark to the field of psychology. He thought learning as developing from bits of knowledge and cognitions about the environment and how an organism relates to it. This idea was in contrast to the theories of Thorndike and Hull, who thought of learning as a strict stimulus response connection. His theory is also known as 'Sign Learning' or 'Sign Gestalt Learning Theory'.

Experiment

To study learning, Tolman conducted several classical rat experiments. One of his most well known experiments involved maze running. He examined the role of reinforcement that rats learn to find their way through complex mazes. These experiments eventually led to the concept of latent learning, which describes learning that occurs in the absence of an obvious reward. It is the learning which is not apparent in learner's behaviour at the time of learning, but which manifests later, when a suitable motivation and circumstances appear.

In one of his experiment, he illustrated purposive behaviour in rats. *For this, Tolman used the apparatus shown in the figure drawn below*

A was the starting point of the box and **B** was the goal. The hungry rat learned to run to **B** very quickly. Tolman wondered, what was the learning of rats in this process. One explanation was that the rat has learned the response of turning right, which led to food. But, Tolman said that the rat had developed a cognitive map of the maze, where the place of the reward was located. A test was developed to determine the right answer. Once the rat learned to run from A to B, it was started from C. The stimulus response explanation predicted the rat would **turn right** and reach **D**.

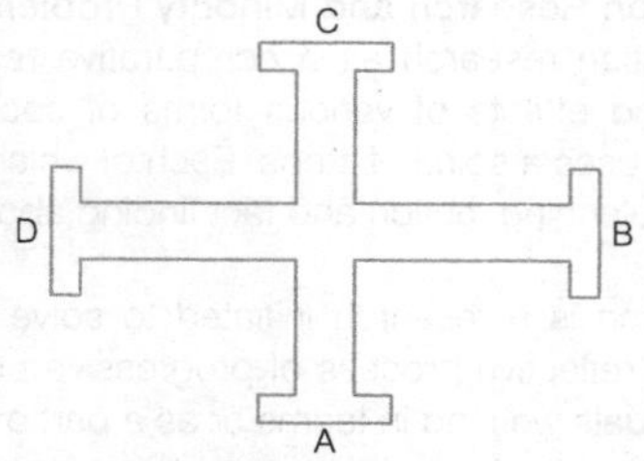

The cognitive map explanation predicted that the rat would reach the reward **B**. The test showed that most of the rats reached **B**, leading Tolman to conclude that a cognitive map was most likely developed by the rats in maze running.

Tolman's termed his system of psychology as 'purposive behaviourism'. He started as a behaviourist but acquired an interest in Gestalt theories. He believed that individuals do more than merely responding to stimuli. They act on beliefs, attitudes, changing conditions and strive towards goal. Tolman believed that reinforcement is not the only factor, that is important for learning to occur. He believed that behaviour is holistic, purposive and cognitive. Behaviour is not just a response to a stimulus, but is cognitive coping with a pattern of stimuli.

Tolman advocated his theory in explaining the process of learning. *The main features of his theory are given below:*

Molar Theory Tolman's theory is molar. According to him, although group behaviour is made of individual's behaviour, yet in defining behaviour, group should be emphasised, not individual.

Goal Directed Behaviour Every behaviour has some aim and the form of it is established by the means of reaching the goal and passing the obstacles. The group behaviour is group directed.

Changing Behaviour The group behaviour of an individual is not stable and fixed. It keeps on changing.

Cognitive Map

> **Cognitive Map** was coined by Tolman. It is an internal perceptual representation of external environmental features and landmark. Individuals acquire large number of cues from environment and build-up expectancies about their permanence or changeable characteristics. By using this internal representation of a physical space, the individual could get to the goal. Shortcuts and variable routes are also possible with the cognitive maps.

Tolman, in **Sign Gestalt Theory**, has put forth the three parts to learning, which work together as a Gestalt Theory.

The three parts of learning are:

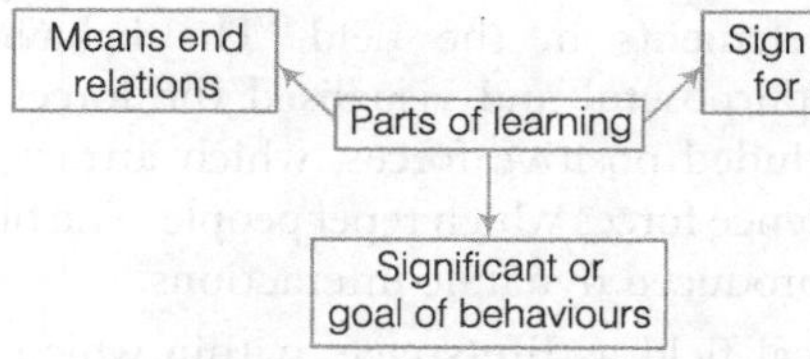

He believed that learning is an accumulation of these Sign Gestalts and these are configured into cognitive maps. Input about the environment also influences the behaviour. It causes certain Gestalts to be selected or not, in relation to individual's purpose or goal and other factors. Therefore, learning is unique to each individual.

Tolman also introduced **intervening variables** into the roman culture of learning psychology. In Tolman's system there were three classes of variables. *They are*

- Dependent variables (behaviours or responses being observed and measured)
- Independent variables (Environmental and Individual)
- Intervening variables (These are hypothetical constructs. They are definable and measurable, but not observable. They have functional relationships with both independent and dependent variables.)

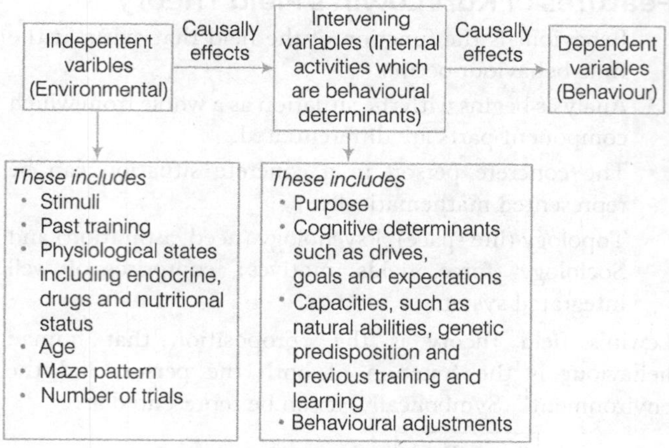

Function of Variables

Types of Learning

Tolman identified six types of learning

Learning by Cathexes It is connecting or associating basic drives with desired goals with the end results of developing preferences for certain types of food, drink.

Equivalence Beliefs These are the sub goals leading to major ones. It acquires similar attractiveness as the end goals.

Field Expectancies Cognitive maps enables an individual to route himself/herself based on these maps.

Field Cognition Modes The perceptions, memories and inferences function influences the learning of an individual.

Drive Discrimination It is the learning to discriminate between competing or more refined drives.

Motor Patterns It is the learning and refinement of sensory motor skills.

Social Learning Theory

Social theory of learning is discussed below

Albert Bandura's Social Learning Theory

Albert Bandura was a prominent American Learning Theorist, who gave the **Social Learning Theory**, which plays the role of a bridge between behaviourist and cognitive learning theories because it encompasses attention, memory, and motivation. His theory explains that people learn from one another through observation, imitation and modelling.

He stated that "*Most human behaviour is learned observationally through modelling, by observing others, one forms an idea of how new behaviours are performed and on later occasions this coded information serves as a guide for action.*"

Unlike traditional behavioural theories, which were dominant during 20th century and were based on the concept that learning is a result of direct experience with the environment through the process of association and reinforcement.

Bandura's theory explained that direct reinforcement could not account for all types of learning. Rather, he believed that learning can also occur simply by observing the actions of others. He further explained that people can learn new information and behaviours by simply watching other people's actions.

Bobo Doll Experiment by Albert Bandura

To explain his theory, Bandura demonstrated that children learn and imitate behaviour that they have observed in other people. For this, he did a Bobo Doll Experiment, where he watched children who were observed adults attacking Bobo Dolls. When hit, the dolls fell over and then bounced back up again.

After this, the children were allowed to play in a room with the Bobo doll, then they began to imitate the same aggressive behaviour of the adults, they had previously observed. However, when they observed adults, acting aggressively and then being punished, Bandura noted that the children were less willing to imitate an aggressive behaviour themselves.

Besides observations, learning can also take place while hearing verbal instructions, reading or watching the actions of characters in books and films. Bandura stated that the person, whose behaviour a person observes and often imitates are known as **'model'** and observational learning is referred to as **'modelling'**.

Principles of Social Learning

Bandura formulated four principles of social learning

Attention Bandura stated that a person cannot learn if he/she/is not focused on the task. If we see something as important or different in some way, we are more likely to make it the focus of our attention. Social context helps to reinforce these perceptions. It includes modelled events such as distinctiveness, affective valence, complexity, prevalence, functional value and observer characteristics, such as sensory capacities, arousal level, perceptual set, past reinforcement.

Retention In this principle of learning people learn by internalising information in their memories. They recall that information later when required to respond to a situation that is similar to the situation within which they first learned the information. It includes symbolic coding, cognitive organisation, symbolic rehearsal, motor rehearsal and so on.

Reproduction As per this principle, people reproduce previously learned information i.e. behaviour, skills and knowledge when required. It includes physical capabilities, self-observation of reproduction, accuracy of feedback and so on.

Motivation Bandura stated that in order for observational learning to be successful, we have to be motivated to imitate the behaviour that has been modelled. Reinforcement and punishment plays an important role in motivation. For example, if a child sees another student rewarded with extra credit for being in the class on time, he might starts to show up a few minutes early each day.

It is seen that Social Learning Theory of Bandura has been applied extensively to understanding of aggression and psychological disorders, particularly in the context of behaviour modification. It is also considered as the theoretical foundation for the technique of behaviour modelling which is widely used in training programs.

Factors Affecting Social Learning

There are various factors which affect social learning of people. *These are as follows*

Personal Factors

Physical and Mental Health Social learning is greatly affected by the learner's physical and mental health maintained by him/her, particularly at the time of learning. A tense, emotionally, mentally, physically disturbed learner can not show satisfactory results in social learning.

Personal Inadequacy A nervous sense of inadequacy is a factor which affects the social learning. Suppose a student is not so brilliant, but his/her parents are very ambitious and sets high goals for him/her. This well lead him/her to frustration and as a result, he/she may develops problems of maladjustment.

Parental Attitude If a child is rejected by his / her parents from an early childhood, the child may develops the feeling of insecurity, hopelessness and loneliness. Rejection and lack of affection may affect the social learning of the child.

Environment at Home If a child comes from a family which encourages him/her to learn new things and does not become a hurdle in his/her life, this kind of environment leads effective social learning. Whereas, if a child comes from a broken family (death of parents, divorce and separation), it may badly affect the social learning of a child.

Goals of Life The goals of life of a person affect the process and product of social learning. A learner's mode and ways of looking towards things, his inclination towards learning a particular subject and patience and persistence in pursuing his/her learning, despit the heavy odds, all depends on his/her goals and principles of life.

Readiness and Will Power Both of these are important in social learning. It is true that no power on Earth can help a learner if he/she is not ready to learn. In the same way, if he/she has a will to learn a new thing, then automatically, he/she will find way for himself/herself in effective learning.

Social Factors

Religious Beliefs In this era of modernisation, adolescents, often gets confused about the traditional religious beliefs for which they do not find any rational basis and as a result they suffer from a lack of positive attitude and get frustrated. This ultimately, affects social learning of children and an adolescents.

Mobility of Parents Children, whose parents moves from one place to another very frequently, face different types of problems. This may lead to maladjustment on the part of the children, who suffers from a feeling of insecurity. Thus, it is also a major factor which affects social learning.

School's Environment

Inadequate Curriculum Our present curriculum is not meeting the psychological, social as well as the physical needs of our children at different stages. This creates frustration in our children, as a result of which the children find themselves maladjusted in their real life situations.

Lack of Proper Recreational Facilities Children who are not getting space for extra curricular activities like play, library, debate, discussion, etc, may suffer from maladjustment problems.

Improper Classroom Environment If there is no good relationship between students and teachers, as well as among the peers, the students may suffer from an emotional problems, which in turn will affect the social learning of children.

Social Competence

Social competence or interpersonal competence is the condition of possessing the social, emotional, and an intellectual skills and behaviours need to become a member of society and to act wisely. It is one of the most widely investigated areas of human social behaviour. It is needed for the successful social adaptation. In other words, it is a set of positive social skills which helps a person to:

- show respect and express appreciation for others.
- being able to work and communicate well with others and listen to other's ideas.
- demonstrates an appropriate behaviour that is accepted as per the social norms.
- use a range of skills or processes which aimes at resolving conflicts.

When we talk about a child's social competence, it depends upon a number of factors such as the child's social skills, social awareness, and self-confidence. When the above mentioned human skills develops appropriately, then, these facilitates the growth of a variety of social abilities among people.

In the early stage of life of a children, parents are the primary source of social and emotional support for them. Gradually, when children reaches to maturity, peers begin to play a significant role in a child's social-emotional development as they become a source of an entertainment and support. Young children engage in fantasy play that allows them to assume different roles, learns to take another person's perspective and develops an understanding of the social rules and conventions of their culture. This give and take relationship with peers provides an opportunity for the development of social competencies such as cooperation and negotiation.

Definitions of Social Competence

According to **Schneider** (1993), "Social competence is enabling one to engage in an appropriate social behaviour, thus, enhancing one's interpersonal relationships, in a way that are not harmful to others."

According to **Argyle** (1999), "Social competence is an ability, the mastery of social skills, which makes it possible to generate the desired effect in social relationships."

Social Cognition

Social cognition is a multi-faceted topic of psychology that can be broadly defined by what an individuals know about their social environment. It is a process through which people thinks about others, interacts with them and also thinks about the world, in which they live. Cognitive processes are important in social interactions like perception, attention, memory and action planning which helps to attain social cognition.

Social cognition involves

- those processes which helps in perceiving other people and how we get to know about the other people around us.
- such mental processes that involved in perceiving, remembering, thinking about and attending to the other people in our social world.
- the concepts of Psychologists through which they understand why people attend to certain information about the social world,how this information is stored in memory and how it is used to interact with other people.

Social cognition is not merely a simple topic within social psychology but it is an approach to study any subject with social psychology. When researchers use a social-cognitive perspective, they can study different human-related topics such as self-concept, attitudes, person's perception, prejudice, stereotypes, discrimination, persuasion, decision-making and other areas.

Role of Social Cognition

The role of social cognition can be seen through the given example. Imagine, that a person is going to meet an unknown person. Not only he/she would worry about an impression and signals like facial expressions (fear or disgust, happy, etc.) of him but would also concern about the receiving responses from that individual. How does he/she forms an impression on this person?, What meaning does he/she reads into the other person's behaviour? It helps a person to understand the other persons, one can identify how to deal with such kind of situations. Thus, we can say that social cognition is a level of analysis that aims to understand social psychological phenomena by investigating the cognitive processes that underlie within them. It mainly focuses on how people process, store and apply information about other people and social situations in a positive way.

Society and Social Relationship

A society is a group of people who lives together and follows some set of rules which are made by these people in order to maintain social harmony and fraternity among them. A society shares the same geographical or social territory, subject to the same political authority and dominant cultural expectations. Human societies are characterised by patterns of relationships between individuals who shares distinctive cultures and institutions.

Definitions of Society

According to **Talcott Parsons**, "It may be regarded as the most general term referring to the whole complex of relations of man to his fellows".

According to **Maciver and Charles Page**, "It is a system of usages and procedures of authority and mutual aid, of many groupings and divisions, of controls of human behaviour and of liberties. This ever changing complex system we call it society".

According to **Prof Wright**, "Society is a system of relationships that exists among the individuals of the groups".

According to **Adam Smith**, "Society is an artificial device of natural economy".

According to **AW Green**, "Society is the largest group in which an individual have relationships".

Social Relationship

Social relationship is any relationship between two or more individuals which is formed by humans to achieve a set goal. For e.g. if a person interacts with other person in order to fulfill his biological or societal needs, thus, the relation created by this interaction process is known as 'social relationship'. Thus, social relations are formed by interaction process among people.

These interactions takes place at three levels such as

- Individual- between individuals
- Individual-between groups
- Group -between groups

The interactions which takes place at these three levels will ultimately, form social relationships and through these relationships society is formed.

Without an interaction and awareness, no relationship can be formed and without social relationship no society can be formed. Where people are aware and do interaction process and take care of feelings and expectations of each other, that is called a society.

Types of Social Relationships

There are different types of social relationships such as of husband- wife, mother-father, brother-sister, friend - friend, teacher- student, servant- owner, customer-shopkeeper, voter-candidate and so on. Some of these relations are based on an economy, religion, blood, political, and so on.

These relationships are created with the reciprocal interaction and awareness. Some of the social relations are also based on enmity or conflict, but most of the relationships have mutual companionship, communalism, participation and basic elements of simple life. Social arrangements are based on social relationships which leads to the formation of a healthy society.

Socialisation

When a child borns, he lacks all the types of social traits. When he comes into the contact of his parents and family he learns to smile, talk, recognising people, and in the later ages he learns the special traits of the society like norms,customs, values, etiquettes and roles of the society in which he lives. In sociology, when a child is developed into a social being, then this process is known as socialisation.Through this process, people are taught to be proficient members of a society.

Definitions of Socialisation

According to **DMacionis**, "The life long process by which an individual becomes the proper member of society and develops human characteristics".

According to **Horton and Hunt**, "Socialisation is a learning process in which groups interact and learn social norms to develop themselves".

According to **Ogburn**, "Socialisation is the process of learning the norms of the group and society".

According to **Maclver**, "Socialsiation is the process through which social beings develops relationships and associations with each other".

According to **Bogardus**, "A process of learning to live and work together is called socialisation".

Goals of Socialisation

With the help of socialisation, a child learns to make adjustment in the community and society. He becomes aware about the things he must take care of for such adjustment and how he can develop his strengths.

The important aims/goals of socialisation are as follows

Develop the Basic Discipline Socialisation aims to inculcate basic disciplines among children, ranging from etiquettes to behave with others to the methods of science. Through socialisation, an individual can be taught about the accepted ways by which he/she may express his/her emotions.

Teach Appropriate Social Roles We have many social roles throughout our life. For instance, many people takes the social role of child, sibling, partner, parent, friend, and worker at some point in their lives.Thus, socialisation helps to play such role in an effective way.

Enable Self-Regulation Socialisation helps to develop self-regulation which involves an ability to control one's impulses, behaviour, and emotions until an appropriate time or place is available for an expression. In other words, self-regulation is the routing of our feelings through our brains before acting on them according to a situation. Through self-regulated behaviour, a person often postpones or modifies the immediate gratification for the sake of a future goal. In such situation, the person becomes able to tolerate frustration. Thus, socialisation helps to develop strategies for coping with disappointment, frustration, rejection, and anger in life.

Empower Achievement Socialisation helps to find out goals for life that what a child wants to become in the future (adulthood). In this sense, the child works to achieve his/her goals by following society's rules and gives purpose to his/her adulthood and to that long process which the child has to go through to achieve those set goals. Thus, with the help of socialisation,the child acquires an important skills like motivation, to achieve the goals and the ability to explain success and failure.

Implement Developmental Skills Socialisation aims to provide social, emotional and cognitive skills to children, so that they can function successfully in the society.These skills depend on the culture of the society and are important to develop among children to live an effective life. Hence, socialisation is extremely important to children's well-being. It results in the development of values, qualities, attitudes and morals among people that are important for their life.

EXAM BASED QUESTIONS

1 Which of the following statements about learning is not true?
(a) Learning is another word for maturation
(b) Learning is relatively permanent
(c) Learning involves changes in behaviours
(d) Learning involves experiences

2 Learning can be best defined as change in
(a) behaviour (b) personality
(c) habits (d) aptitudes

3 For effective learning, the goal must be meaningful in terms of
(a) curricular objectives
(b) the learner's needs and purposes
(c) an intellectual ideas involved
(d) None of the above

4 The result of learning is
(a) storing new knowledge in the mind
(b) acquiring more information
(c) utility to use old experiences
(d) modification and development

5 Which of the following is not a method of learning?
(a) Imitation (b) Trial and error
(c) Cramming (d) Conditioned response

6 Who is the best motivator at school?
(a) The class teacher
(b) The head master
(c) The class fellows
(d) The subject teacher

7 The best way to motivate a child is
(a) to appeal to his/her sense of pride and self-respect
(b) to rechannel the motives he/she already has
(c) to threaten him/her with failure and punishment
(d) to tempt him/her with praise

8 Identify the most important process involved in learning concepts.
(a) Specification (b) Categorisation
(c) Generalisation (d) Experimentation

9 Experiential learning is advocated by
(a) humanists
(b) behaviourists
(c) cognitive psychologists
(d) gestaltians

10 Which of the following is not a behaviourist?
(a) Watson (b) Skinner
(c) Pavlov (d) Lewin

11 Which theory was given by Thorndike?
(a) Operant Conditioning Theory
(b) Connectionism Theory
(c) Reinforcement Theory
(d) Gestalt Theory

12 Behavioural learning theories apply best to
(a) observable behaviour
(b) young children
(c) non-observable behaviour
(d) None of the above

13 In Thorndike's Puzzle Box experiment, the cat was rewarded by
(a) getting out of the box
(b) getting food
(c) being petted and praised
(d) Both a and b

14 In his theory of learning, Thorndike stressed most on the importance of
(a) law of effect (b) law of exercise
(c) law of frequency (d) law of readiness

15 An animal learns by trial and error, when
(a) there is a strong motivation
(b) the goal is clear
(c) the problem cannot be solved
(d) All of the above

16 The device used by Thorndike in his experiment with cats, who learned to escape for food reward is called a
(a) maze (b) skinner box
(c) pavolvian apparatus (d) puzzle box

17 Thorndike and Skinner do not differ at all in
(a) law of effect (b) law of readiness
(c) law of contiguity (d) All of these

18 'Learning is direct not mediated by ideas'. This statement is associated with
(a) Thorndike (b) Watson
(c) Pavlov (d) Kohler

19 In his explanation of behaviour, Thorndike has most in common with
(a) Pavlov (b) Tolman (c) Bandura (d) Skinner

20 To be an effective punisher, an unpleasant consequence
(a) reduces the behaviour, but causes other problems
(b) reduces the behaviour at least once
(c) does not reduces the frequency of the behaviour
(d) reduces the frequency of the behaviour

21 Learning by insight is similar to some extent, to which of the following theories?
(a) Need Reduction Theory
(b) R Type of Learning
(c) Trial and Error Theory
(d) None of the above

22 Which of the following is not an essential requirement in trial and error learning?
(a) Drive
(b) Barrier
(c) Chance of success
(d) Selective movement of an organism

23 The principle of learning is an act which has a satisfying effect to learn more quickly then one, to which has a classifying effect was put forth by
(a) Watson (b) Thorndike
(c) Skinner (d) Gulthrie

24 Verbal skills are acquired on the basis of
(a) trial and error (b) an imitation
(c) reflex vocalisation (d) All of these

25 When a question is answered wrongly the teacher should
(a) punish the student for giving wrong answer
(b) correct the fault in the answer and tell the student
(c) correct the answer with the help of student
(d) leave that question and proceed to the next question

26 In the process of teaching a lesson, Thorndike's law of readiness finds applications in
(a) introduction (b) recapitulation
(c) presentation (d) home work

27 In learning theory, the naturally occurring response is called the
(a) conditioned stimulus (b) unconditioned response
(c) conditioned response (d) None of these

28 A snake learns to dance to the tune of a flute. Which of the following theories is applicable in this case?
(a) Skinner's Operant Conditioning
(b) Thorndike's Connectionism
(c) Kurt Lewin's Field theory
(d) Pavlov's Classical Conditioning

29 Contingency in classical conditioning refers to
(a) the amount of time that passes between the conditioned and the unconditioned stimulus.
(b) the frequency with which the conditioned and the unconditioned stimulus occur together.
(c) the pairing of the conditioned response with the unconditioned response.
(d) the weakening of the conditioned response, when the unconditioned stimulus is absent.

30 Much learning in human beings takes place by
(a) trial and error
(b) imitation and insight
(c) insight and conditioning
(d) conditioning and imitation

31 The use of pleasant and unpleasant consequences to change behaviour is known as
(a) operant conditioning
(b) pavlovian conditioning
(c) stimulus generalisation
(d) the conditioned reflex

32 What is the other name for operant conditioning?
(a) Classical conditioning
(b) Instrumental conditioning
(c) Reinforcement conditioning
(d) None of the above

33 BF Skinner is important in psychology because he
(a) developed the principles of classical conditioning
(b) formulated the law of effect
(c) conducted research which suggests a cognitive component to learning
(d) developed the principles of operant conditioning

34 A rat learns that it will be reinforced only by a red light in its cage. This is an example of
(a) generalisation
(b) stimulus control
(c) continuous reinforcement
(d) backward conditioning

35 An example of a negative reinforcement is, when a teacher says
(a) if you get an 'A' on tomorrow's test, you will be the member of the 'A' club.
(b) if you do your homework, you will get a prize.
(c) if you get an 'A' on tomorrow's test, you won't have to do homework in the rest of the week.
(d) if you do your homework, you may be very successful.

36 Consequences that discourages repetition of a particular behaviour are called
(a) negative reinforcement (b) extinction
(c) operant conditioning (d) punishment

37 Development of language in children, according to BF Skinner, is the result of
(a) training in grammar
(b) imitation and reinforcement
(c) innate abilities
(d) maturation

38 'Negative reinforcement' means
(a) not presenting any stimulus
(b) presenting an unpleasant stimulus
(c) punishment
(d) terminating an unpleasant stimulus

39 ……… occurs, when a response is followed by experiencing something pleasurable.
(a) Positive reinforcement (b) Negative reinforcement
(c) Punishment (d) Generalisation

40 The term 'learning' includes
(a) all changes in behaviour
(b) changes in behaviour, resulting from practice
(c) all permanent changes in behaviour
(d) improvement in behaviour pattern

41 The connectionism theory was presented in Thorndike book 'Animal Learning' in ....
(a) 1898 (b) 1897
(c) 1899 (d) 1890

42 Reinforcement can be
(a) negative only
(b) positive only
(c) both a and b
(d) None of the above

43 "Children construct their own understanding through an interaction with their environment," who gave this statement?
(a) Skinner (b) Pavlov
(c) Piaget (d) Burt

44 Operant conditioning mainly emphasis on the role of
(a) the teacher (b) the learning material
(c) the reinforcement (d) an environment

45 The principles of reinforcement are most similar to the ideas expressed in
(a) the law of effect
(b) discrimination training
(c) latent training
(d) vicarious training

46 The role of responding is rapid in
(a) variable interval schedule
(b) fixed ratio schedule
(c) variable ratio schedule
(d) both b and c

47 Maladaptive behaviour may be treated by applying the principles of
(a) conditioning (b) deconditioning
(c) learning (d) adjustment

48 Children learn new words for specific objects mostly by
(a) imitation (b) conditioning process
(c) insight (d) trial and error

49 Programmed learning is based on
(a) Field Theory
(b) Operant Conditioning Theory
(c) Gestalt learning Theory
(d) Classical Conditioning Theory

50 Social approval works as
(a) primary reinforcement
(b) secondary reinforcement
(c) non contigent reinforcement
(d) discriminative stimulus

51 When the rat presses a lever, the mild electric shock on the cage floor is turned on. What procedure is being used here?
(a) Punishment
(b) Escape
(c) Discrimination training
(d) Avoidance

52 Punishment results in the response being
(a) weakened
(b) suppressed
(c) unlearned
(d) substituted always by more desirable response

53 The following reinforcement schedule is more resistant to extinction of
(a) fixed and variable interval schedule
(b) fixed and variable ratio schedule
(c) continuous reinforcement schedule
(d) Both a and b

54 Behaviour pattern that increases in frequency, when followed by a reward is known as
(a) shaping
(b) classical conditioning
(c) generalisation
(d) operant conditioning

55 Programmed learning is based on the principles of
(a) Conditioned Learning Theory
(b) Cognitive Learning Theory
(c) Gestalt Learning Theory
(d) Operant Conditioning Theory

56 From which time period Ivan Pavlov started establishing his principles of conditioning?
(a) Early 1920's (b) Late 1920's
(c) Early 1930's (d) Late 1930's

57 The classical and operant conditioning do not differ in which of the following aspect?
(a) In classical conditioning the animal is passive whereas in operant conditioning the animal is active.
(b) The conditioned behaviour in classical conditioning is called respondent behaviour whereas in operant conditioning it is called operant behaviour.
(c) In classical conditioning the reinforced behaviour is similar to the behaviour normally elicited by the reinforcing stimulus, whereas in operant conditioning it is not.
(d) By classical conditioning, a subject can be mode to alter his autonomic and muscular responses whereas in operant conditioning it is not possible.

58 In the Conditioning Approach to learning
(a) the subject should be in readiness requires to be reinforced.
(b) the unnatural stimulus follows the natural stimulus
(c) response to natural stimulus required to be reinforced
(d) the natural stimulus follows the unnatural stimulus

59 Which of the following is not the element of classical conditioning?
(a) Unconditioned stimulus
(b) Unconditioned response
(c) Conditioned stimulus and response
(d) Negative reinforcement

60 Sensory stimuli can arouse the following drive states
(a) hunger (b) pain
(c) sexual drive state (d) All of these

61 A student working hard and solving mathematical problems as his father has promised to give him a cycle, if he gets good marks. This means that student has
(a) intrinsic motivation
(b) extrinsic motivation
(c) mathematical motivation
(d) Both a and b

62 For maximum reinforcement effect, a given reward should
(a) be applied immediately proceeding the response
(b) be applied immediately upon the response
(c) be applied simultaneously with response
(d) follow the response only after a substantial delay

63 What schedule of reinforcement produces behaviour that is very consistent over time and most resistant to extinction?
(a) Fixed interval schedules of reinforcement.
(b) Continuous reinforcement.
(c) Fixed ratio schedules of reinforcement.
(d) Variable ratio schedules of reinforcement, such as those associated with gambling behaviours.

64 A supervisor comes into the work place to check his/her employees every hour and a half. An observer notices that the workers increase their work behaviour about 10 minutes before the supervisor arrives and then decrease their work behaviour after he/she leaves. On what type of reinforcement schedule are the workers?
(a) A fixed - ratio schedule
(b) A variable - ratio schedule
(c) A fixed - interval schedule
(d) A variable-interval schedule

65 According to operant conditioning
(a) behaviour is controlled by consequences
(b) punishment can strengthen behaviour
(c) punishment is some as negative reinforcement
(d) once a behaviour is learned, it is forgotten

66 What would be a practical and appropriate use of punishment in the classroom?
(a) Loss of privileges contingent upon an unacceptable behaviour such as having to stay in during recess for talking out of turn.
(b) Loss of privileges for unspecified behaviour.
(c) Corporeal punishment.
(d) Providing a positive reinforcer for stopping an unacceptable behaviour.

67 In Drive Reduction theory, habit formation is a function of
(a) stimulus potential (b) stimulus generalisation
(c) reaction potential (d) All of these

68 Which of the following theories is most quantitatively measurable?
(a) Hull (b) Pavlov
(c) Skinner (d) None of these

69 Which of the following theories is most quantitatively measurable and valid?
(a) Pavlov (b) Skinner
(c) Hull (d) None of these

70 Hull may be considered superior to other S-R theorist in the sense that he was able to measure
(a) latency of response
(b) reinforcement potential
(c) Both a and b
(d) None of the above

71 Reinforcement in Skinner's theory is similar to drive reduction, it comes under which theory?
(a) Hull's theory
(b) Guthrie's theory
(c) Lewin's theory
(d) None of the above

72 In Gagne's hierarchy learning has been divided into
(a) eight parts (b) nine parts
(c) seven parts (d) None of these

73 A learner is faced with an unique problem. To solve the problem, he/she applied a combination of rules that already known to her. She is displaying the learning outcomes of an intellectual skills suggested by Gagne as
(a) concrete concepts (b) rules
(c) higher order rules (d) defined concepts

74 Which of the following is the Neo- Gestaltist?
(a) Tolman (b) Skinner
(c) Kurt Lewin (d) Pavlov

75 Eclectic theory of learning was propouned by
(a) Gagne (b) Tolman
(c) Skinner (d) Hull

76 The type of learning explained by Albert Bandura is also known as
(a) insight learning
(b) observational learning
(c) sign learning
(d) verbal learning

77 Who said that "People can learn new information and behaviours by simply watching other's people's action"?
(a) Albert Bandura (b) Edward Tolman
(c) Kurt Lewin (d) Clark Hull

78 When it comes to applying learning theory to the classroom, the most pressing problem for educators is
(a) presenting students with the right stimuli on which to focus their attention and mental effort
(b) finding age-appropriate learning materials
(c) presenting the learning material in a gender-neutral manner
(d) getting students to learn

79 According to Gestalt, psychologist's behaviour cannot be quantified because

(a) it is always changeable
(b) it is governed by the configuration produced in mind
(c) it is rarely overt
(d) All of the above

80 Which of the following factors affects the social learning of a person?

(a) Personal Inadequacy (b) Parental Attitude
(c) Goals of Life (d) All of these

81 Maladjustment may arise from

(a) inadequate curriculum
(b) lack of proper recreational facilities
(c) Improper classroom environment
(d) All of the above

82 A society consists of

(a) group of people (b) set of rules
(c) social harmony (d) All of these

83 Who said "society is an artificial device of natural economy"?

(a) AW Green (b) Adam Smith
(c) Prof. Wright (d) Talcott Parsons

84 Who said "Socialisation is the process of learning the norms of the group and society"?

(a) Horton and Hunt
(b) Ogburn
(c) Dmacionis
(d) Bogardus

85 Which of the following is/are the goals of socialisation?

(a) Enable self-regulation
(b) Empower achievement
(c) Teach appropriate social roles
(d) All of the above

86 Socialisation develops skills like

(a) social skills (b) emotional skills
(c) cognitive skills (d) All of these

87 The other name of social competence is

(a) cognitive competence
(b) interpersonal competence
(c) emotional competence
(d) None of the above

88 Who said "social competence is an ability, the mastery of social skills, which makes it possible to generate the desired effect in social relationship"?

(a) Rose-Krasnor (b) Schneider
(c) Argyle (d) None of these

89 In the social cognition

(a) people think about others
(b) people interact with others
(c) people know about their surrounding environment
(d) All of the above

90 When a researcher uses a social cognitive perspective, he can study human related topics such as

(a) Person's perception
(b) Prejudice
(c) Stereotypes
(d) All of the above

91 Match the following

List I (Theories)	List II (Thinkers)
A. Classical conditioning	1. Hull
B. Drive reduction	2. Pavlov
C. Sign Gestalt learning	3. Skinner
D. Operant conditioning	4 Tolman

Codes

	A	B	C	D
(a)	4	2	3	1
(b)	2	1	4	3
(c)	4	2	1	3
(d)	3	2	1	4

92 Match the following

List I	List II
A. Generalisation	1. Reaction to differences
B. Discrimination	2. Repetition of the conditioned stimulus without reinforcement
C. Acquisition	3. Association between CS and US
D. Extinction	4. Reaction to similarities

Codes

	A	B	C	D
(a)	1	2	3	4
(b)	4	1	3	2
(c)	1	3	4	2
(d)	1	2	3	4

93 How can principles of stimulus generalisation be used to aid learning in the classroom?

1. By using it in conjunction with punishment.
2. By using multiple choice tests in the classroom .
3. By using too many examples from different contexts *e.g.* teaching the relationship between supply and demand (and how it affects price) can be taught by using examples from grocery shopping, the value of natural resources and the values of collectibles (such as Beanie Babies which are produced in small numbers in order to keep up the price).
4. By rehearsing the same material over and over until the students get it right.

Codes

(a) Only 1 (b) Only 3
(c) 2 and 4 (d) All of these

94 Pavlov's example 'the Unconditioned Stimulus' was

1. tone or bell
2. salivation
3. hunger
4. food placed in mouth

Codes
(a) Only 1 (b) 2 and 3
(c) 3 and 4 (d) All of these

95 Which of the following statements is correct ?

1. Classical conditioning focuses on involuntary responses, while operant conditioning focuses on voluntary behaviours.
2. Classical conditioning is involved with negative outcomes, while operant conditioning is involved with positive outcomes.
3. Extinction occurs in classical conditioning, but not in operant conditioning.
4. Shaping occurs in classical conditioning, but not in operant conditioning.

Codes
(a) Only 1 (b) 2 and 3
(c) 3 and 4 (d) All of these

96 Which is the most effective reinforcement schedule according to Operant Conditioning Theory of Learning for stable learning?

1. Continuous reinforcement
2. Fixed ratio reinforcement
3. Variable ratio reinforcement
4. Fixed interval reinforcement

Codes
(a) Only 1 (b) 1, 2 and 4
(c) Only 3 (d) All of these

97 .... is an example of a primary reinforces, whereas .... is an example of a secondary reinforces.

(a) A Candy bar, a gold star
(b) A gold star, money
(c) Food, a drink
(d) A gold star, candy

98 The concept of self-regulated learning derives from

1. Bandura's work
2. Thorndike's law of effect
3. Pavlov's work
4. Skinner's work

Codes
(a) Only 1 (b) 2 and 3
(c) 3 and 4 (d) All of these

99 Which of the following is not a problem with punishment?

1. The effect of punishment is often temporary.
2. Severe punishment creates fear and anxiety.
3. Mild punishment can be paired with reinforcement punishment of the correct behaviour.
4. Aggressive punishment can model aggressive behaviour in child.

Codes
(a) Only 1 (b) 2 and 3
(c) Only 3 (d) All of these

100 Arrange the principles given by Albert Bandura in sequential order

1. Attention
2. Retention
3. Motivation
4. Reproduction

Codes
(a) 1, 2, 4, 3 (b) 2, 3, 4, 1
(c) 1, 2, 3, 4 (d) 4, 3, 1, 2

101 Arrange in sequential order, the stages in the process of learning given by Thorndike during his experiment.

1. Fixation
2. Goal
3. Drive
4. Block
5. Random movement

Codes
(a) 3, 2, 4, 5, 1 (b) 2, 3, 4, 5, 1
(c) 1, 2, 3, 4, 5 (d) 2, 3, 4, 1, 5

102 Arrange in sequence the Hierarchical Step Model of Learning given by Robert Gagne.

1. Signal Learning
2. Stimulus-Response Learning
3. Psychomotor Connection
4. Verbal Association Learning

Codes
(a) 1, 2, 3, 4 (b) 2, 1, 4, 3
(c) 3, 1, 2, 4 (d) 4, 1, 2, 3

Directions (Q. Nos. 103 to 111) *In each of the questions given below, there are two statements marked as Assertion (A) and Reason (R). Mark your answer as per the codes given below*

(a) Both A and R true and R is the correct explanation of A
(b) Both A and R true, but R is not the correct explanation of A
(c) A is true but R is false
(d) A is false but R is true

103 **Assertion** (A) Secondary reinforcement has important practical implications.

Reason (R) Secondary reinforcement has wide degree of generalisation.

104 **Assertion** (A) Hull presented Drive Reduction Model.

Reason (R) His model was based on primary drives and secondary drives.

105 **Assertion** (A) Cognitive map was coined by Tolman.

Reason (R) Cognitive map is an internal perceptual representation of external environmental features and landmark.

106 **Assertion** (A) If a child is rejected by his/her parents from an early childhood, the child may develop the feeling of insecurity, hoplessness and lonelines.

Reason (R) Parental attitude affects social learning and behaviour of a child.

107 **Assertion** (A) A society is a group of people who live together and follow same set of rules.

Reason (R) According to Charles Page and Maclver, society is ever changing and complex system.

108 **Assertion** (A) Social arrangements are based on social relationships.

Reason (R) Social relationships lead to the formation of a healthy society.

109 **Assertion** (A) Socialization is important for all human beings.

Reason (R) Socialisation helps a child to learn that how to adjust in the community and society.

110 **Assertion** (A) Social competence or interpersonal competence is the condition of possessing the social emotional, and intellectual skills and behaviours needed to become a member of society and act wisely.

Reason (R) It is one of the most widely investigated areas of human social behaviour.

111 **Assertion** (A) Learning is associated with change in behaviour.

Reason (R) Learning is a change that takes place through practice or experience and changes due to growth.

PREVIOUS YEARS' QUESTIONS

July 2018

1 In Hull's Reinforcement Theory, which of the following was postulated as intervening variable ?

(a) Drive Condition
(b) Reaction Latency
(c) Reaction Amplitude
(d) Excitatory Potential

2 Which of the following forms part of the revised basic types of learning in Tolman's system ?

(a) Latent learning
(b) Field cognition modes
(c) Reward expectancy
(d) Place learning

3 Below is given a list of five types of learning indicated in a hierarchical arrangement as mentioned by Robert M. Gagne. From the code given below, select the correct hierarchy to show your answer.

List

1. Signal learning
2. Chain learning
3. Rule learning
4. Concept learning
5. S - R learning

Codes

(a) 1, 5, 2, 4, 3
(b) 1, 2, 4, 5, 3
(c) 3, 2, 1, 5, 4
(d) 3, 4, 5, 1, 2

4 Which of the laws of learning given by Thorndike had to be revised?

(a) Law of Exercise
(b) Law of Readiness
(c) Law of Effect
(d) Law of Belongingness

5 For arriving at classical conditioning paradigm, which of the following was used as the independent variable?

(a) Magnitude of response
(b) Resistance to extinction
(c) Spontaneous recovery
(d) Number of CS and US pairings

6. The two lists are given below as list I and list II Match the two sets and indicate your answer by selecting the code given.

List I	List II
A. Reward training	1. Cue absent, response withheld and positive reinforcement
B. Escape training	2. Cue present, response made and negative re inforcement
C. Active Avoidance training	3. Cue absent response made and negative reinforcement
D. Omission training	4. Cue absent, response made and positive reinforcement
	5. Cue present, response made and positive reinforcement

Codes

	A	B	C	D
(a)	4	3	2	1
(b)	1	2	3	4
(c)	2	3	4	5
(d)	5	2	1	3

November 2017

7 **For fostering creativity among children, which of the following methods have been given a trial ?**
(a) Acceleration approach
(b) Enrichment approach
(c) Brainstorming procedures
(d) Special education approach

8 **A trainer so designs the training procedure that in the presence of cue, negative reinforcement is made contingent on making of a response by the trainee. The operant conditioning procedure so used is called by the name of**
(a) escape training
(b) punishment training
(c) discriminated punishment training
(d) active - avoidance training

9 **Who among the following cognitive learning promoters developed the concept of meaningful learning ?**
(a) Jean Piaget
(b) David Ausubel
(c) Jerome S Bruner
(d) Ference Merton

10 **Which of the following laws/principles of learning of Thorndike anticipated the classical conditioning paradigm of Pavlov ?**
(a) Law of exercise
(b) Law of effect
(c) Principle of prepotency of elements
(d) Principle of associative shifting

11 **In which of the following Classical Conditioning procedures, Unconditioned Stimulus (UCS) is presented after the termination of the Conditioned Stimulus (CS) ?**
(a) Forward conditioning
(b) Backward conditioning
(c) Trace conditioning
(d) Simultaneous conditioning

12 **Which of the following is a subordinate law in Thorndike's system of learning ?**
(a) Response by analogy
(b) Law of exercise
(c) Law of readiness
(d) Law of effect

13 **Which of the following is designated as an independent variable in classical conditioning ?**
(a) Choice of Conditioned and Unconditioned Stimulus (CS and US)
(b) Strength of Conditioned Response (CR)
(c) Number of pairings as CS and US (conditioned and unconditioned stimulus)
(d) Amplitude or latency of response

14 **Below given are two lists, List I and List II. Match the two lists and indicate your answer by choosing from the code.**

List I	List II
A. Reward training	1. Positive reinforcement, response made, with cue present.
B. Escape training	2. Positive reinforcement, response withheld with cue absent.
C. Discriminated omission training	3. Positive reinforcement, response made with cue absent.
D. Active avoidance	4. Negative reinforcement, response made with training cue absent.
E. Punishment training	5. Positive reinforcement, response withheld with cue present.
	6. Negative reinforcement, response withheld with cue absent.

Codes

	A	B	C	D	E
(a)	3	4	5	1	6
(b)	3	2	3	4	5
(c)	2	3	4	5	6
(d)	1	3	4	5	6

15 **Which of the following statements indicates the features of social development during adolescence? Select from the code to indicate your answer.**
1. The adolescent develops a norm for evaluation of one's own conduct.
2. There is a manifest capacity for both convergent and divergent thinking in the adolescent.
3. There is an expansion in the vocabulary of the adolescent.
4. The adolescent girl or boy shows tendency for hero worship.
5. The adolescents are usually moody.
6. Formation of cliques takes place during adolescence.

Codes
(a) 1, 2, 4 (b) 2, 3, 5
(c) 3, 4, 5 (d) 1, 4, 5

January 2017

16 **In which of the following operant conditioning procedures, the training arrangement insists the presence of a cue and making of a response to get negatively reinforced ?**
(a) Escape training
(b) Punishment training
(c) Omission training
(d) Active avoidance training

17 Skinner viewed secondary reinforces are derived when associated with
(a) neutral stimulus
(b) positive stimulus
(c) negative stimulus
(d) Either b or c

18 The evidence on latent learning became the basis of formulating which theory/model of learning ?
(a) Bruner's Discovery Learning Model
(b) Tolman's Sign Gestalt Theory
(c) Lewin's Cognitive Field Theory
(d) Kohler's Theory of Insight Learning

19 Which of the following set of statements appropriately differentiates between classical and operant conditioning paradigm ?
1. Classical conditioning involves stimulus-stimulus substitution whereas operant conditioning is S-R conditioning where S is made contingent on R.
2. Classical conditioning is related to psycho-somatic behaviour while operant conditioning deals with reflexes.
3. In classical conditioning, reinforcement preceeds a response while in operant conditioning it follows a response.
4. Subject is relatively active in classical conditioning whereas it is a passive responder in operant conditioning.
5. The association between two stimuli is a critical factor in learning through classical conditioning while the response and reinforcement contingency is important for learning in operant conditioning.

Codes
(a) 1, 2 and 3 (b) 1, 3 and 5
(c) 2, 3 and 4 (d) 1, 4 and 5

20 Which of the following subordinate laws of learning developed by Thorndike is related to classical conditioning of Pavlov ?
(a) Multiple response
(b) Pre-potency of elements
(c) Associative shifting
(d) Response by analogy

21 Match the two lists by selecting the correct code.

List I	List II
A. Forward conditioning	1. US precedes CS
B. Simultaneous conditioning	2. CS and US commence and terminate at the same time
C. Trace conditioning	3. CS precedes US
D. Backward conditioning	4. US is presented after the termination of CS
	5. US is presented with delay

Codes

	A	B	C	D		A	B	C	D
(a)	1	2	3	4	(b)	2	3	1	4
(c)	2	1	4	5	(d)	3	2	4	1

July 2016

22 What is the critical difference between Pavlovian and Skinnerian conditioning ? From the code, select the combination which is most appropriate.
1. Stimulus-Stimulus substitution.
2. Elicited Vs Emitted class of responses.
3. Reinforcement comes before the response in one while in the other reinforcement follows the response.
4. In one, the number of pairings of two stimuli is critical while in the other response reinforcement contingency is critical.
5. In one, the learner is passive while in the other learner is active.
6. Elapsed time between two stimuli or two responses is not important.

Codes
(a) 1, 2, 3, 4 (b) 2, 3, 4, 5
(c) 2, 3, 4, 6 (d) 2, 4, 5, 3

23 Pavlov's conditioning paradigm was developed originally in which of the following, was used as independent variable ?
(a) Response magnitude
(b) Response latency
(c) Number of CS-US pairing
(d) Presentation of CS alone

24 Match the following two lists and choose the correct code which follows.

List I	List II
A. Reward training	1. Positive reinforcement with making of a response in the absence of cue.
B. Escape training	2. Negative reinforcement with holding of response in the presence of cue.
C. Discrimination training	3. Positive reinforcement with making of response in the presence of a cue.
D. Active-avoidance training	4. Negative reinforcement with making of a response in the presence of a cue.
	5. Negative reinforcement with making of a response in the absence of a cue.

Codes

	A	B	C	D		A	B	C	D
(a)	1	5	3	4	(b)	5	1	2	3
(c)	1	3	5	4	(d)	3	5	4	2

June 2015

25 **Thorndike's law of effect in learning, anticipated in which of the following paradigms?**

(a) Pavlovian conditioning
(b) Operant conditioning
(c) Contiguous conditioning
(d) Insight learning

26 **In which of the following operant conditioning procedures, the learner is able to avoid an aversive stimulus in the absence of a cue?**

(a) Active avoidance training
(b) Discriminated punishment training
(c) Punishment training
(d) Escape training

27 **In which conditioning paradigm of learning reinforcement follows rather than preceeds a response?**

(a) Classical conditioning
(b) Operant conditioning
(c) Contiguous conditioning
(d) Backward conditioning

December 2014

28 **Which of the following learning theories is intimately related to Thorndike's law of effect ?**

(a) Guthrie's Contiguity Theory
(b) Pavlov's Reflex Conditioning
(c) Skinner's Operant Conditioning
(d) Kohler's Gestalt Theory

June 2014

29 **Latent learning is a concept enunciated by**

(a) Hull (b) Piaget
(c) Tolman (d) Skinner

ANSWERS

Exam Based Questions

1 (a)	2 (a)	3 (b)	4 (d)	5 (c)	6 (d)	7 (b)	8 (d)	9 (c)	10 (d)
11 (b)	12 (a)	13 (d)	14 (d)	15 (d)	16 (d)	17 (a)	18 (a)	19 (d)	20 (d)
21 (c)	22 (c)	23 (b)	24 (d)	25 (c)	26 (a)	27 (b)	28 (d)	29 (a)	30 (d)
31 (a)	32 (b)	33 (d)	34 (b)	35 (c)	36 (a)	37 (b)	38 (c)	39 (a)	40 (b)
41 (a)	42 (c)	43 (a)	44 (c)	45 (b)	46 (a)	47 (a)	48 (b)	49 (b)	50 (b)
51 (b)	52 (b)	53 (d)	54 (d)	55 (d)	56 (b)	57 (d)	58 (b)	59 (d)	60 (d)
61 (b)	62 (b)	63 (d)	64 (a)	65 (a)	66 (a)	67 (a)	68 (a)	69 (c)	70 (a)
71 (a)	72 (a)	73 (c)	74 (c)	75 (b)	76 (b)	77 (a)	78 (a)	79 (b)	80 (d)
81 (d)	82 (d)	83 (b)	84 (b)	85 (d)	86 (d)	87 (b)	88 (c)	89 (d)	90 (d)
91 (b)	92 (b)	93 (c)	94 (a)	95 (a)	96 (c)	97 (a)	98 (a)	99 (c)	100 (a)
101 (a)	102 (a)	103 (a)	104 (a)	105 (a)	106 (a)	107 (b)	108 (b)	109 (a)	110 (b)
111 (a)									

Previous Years' Questions

1 (d)	2 (b)	3 (a)	4 (c)	5 (d)	6 (a)	7 (c)	8 (d)	9 (b)	10 (d)
11 (c)	12 (a)	13 (c)	14 (a)	15 (d)	16 (d)	17 (d)	18 (b)	19 (b)	20 (c)
21 (d)	22 (b)	23 (c)	24 (a)	25 (b)	26 (d)	27 (b)	28 (c)	29 (c)	

CHAPTER

12

Guidance and Counselling

Guidance and counselling are important part of life which helps a person to take good decisions in a situation where he/she feels confusion to take an appropriate action. Guidance is an important part of education which helps to develop identity of a person. Whereas, counselling is a process, which helps to find out the unhealthy reason that affects a person to take a decision.

Guidance

Human life is a long series of struggle. On the one side, human works to achieve his/her goal by continuous process and on the other side, he/she keeps on struggling with his/her environment-related situations. This struggle continues from the birth till the death and human works to achieve his/her aim by removing the difficulties of life.

For this, human develops his strengths and capabilities and prepare plans. But sometimes such situation arises where he faces difficulties to fulfill his/her aim. Then, he/she needs such a guide, who can give him/her an appropriate guidance, which may help him/her to overcome that particular situation and to achieve his/her goal. Generally, guidance is a process, through which a person gets an appropriate help to achieve the desirable aims in life.

Literally, 'Guidance' means 'to direct', 'to point out' or 'to show the path'. It is the assistance or help rendered by a more experienced person to a less experienced person to solve certain major problems of the individual (less experienced) *i.e.* educational, vocational, personal, etc.

Guidance is considered a concept as well as a process. As a concept, it is concerned with the optimal development of the individual. As a process, it helps an individual in self-understanding and in self-direction

In this Chapter

Definitions of Guidance

According to **Chisholm** "Guidance seeks to help each individual become familiar with a wide range of information about himself, his abilities, and his previous development in the various areas of living and his plans or ambitions for the future".

According to **A J Jones** "Guidance is an assistance, given to an individual in making intelligent choices and adjustments".

According to **Dunsmoor & Miller** "Guidance is a means of helping individuals to understand and use wisely the educational, vocational and personal opportunities, they have or can develop and as a form of systematic assistance, whereby students are aided in achieving satisfactory adjustments to school and life".

According to **Crow and Crow** "Guidance is not giving directions. It is not the imposition of one person's point of view upon another person. It is not making decisions for an individual, which he should make for himself. It is not carrying the burdens of another life".

According to the **Secondary Education Commission (1964-66)** "Guidance involves the difficult art of helping boys and girls to plan their own future wisely in the full light of all the factors that can be mastered about themselves and about the world, in which they are to live and work".

Thus, from the above definitions, we can say that guidance helps an individual to make his own selection and solution out of varied type of opportunities and problems. It helps a person to adjust with different environments and situations, according to his own capacities.

Nature of Guidance

- It is a helping service, whether is given to an individual or a group. Its aim is to provide assistance to individuals.
- It is a self-oriented, problem-solving and multi-faceted activity.
- It can be given to any individual who needs that scope of guidance is very wide which includes individuals of any age, any interest, and of any nature.
- It cannot be given by any person. It is a work of experts. In the field of psychology, it is work of techniques which needs expert guides, career experts, psychologists and counsellors.
- It helps a person to adjust in the environment where he/she lives and also adjust with oneself and others.
- It helps to develop self-dependence and self-determination in the person, to solve his difficulties and problems by himself.

Principles of Guidance

Principle of All-Round Development of the Individual Guidance must take into account the all-round development of the individual when bringing about desirable adjustment in any particular area of his personality.

Principle of Human Uniqueness No two individuals are alike. Individuals differ in their physical, mental, social and emotional development. Guidance service must recognise these differences and guide each individual according to their specific need.

Principle of Holistic Development Guidance has to be imparted in the context of total development of personality. The child grows as a whole and even if one aspect of personality is in focus, the other areas of development which are indirectly influencing the personality have also to be kept in mind.

Principle of Cooperation No individual can be forced into guidance. The consent and cooperation of the individual is a pre-requisite for providing guidance.

Principle of Continuity Guidance should be regarded as a continuous process of service to an individual in different stages of his life.

Principle of Extension Guidance service should not be limited to a few persons, who give observable evidence of its need, but it should be extended to all persons of all ages, who can benefit from it directly or indirectly.

Principle of Elaboration Curriculum materials and teaching procedures should be elaborated according to the view point of guidance.

Principle of Adjustment While it is true that guidance touches every aspect of an individual's life, it is chiefly concerned with an individual's physical or mental health, with his adjustment at home, school, society and vocation.

Principle of Individual Needs The individual and his needs are of utmost significance. Recognition of individual freedom, worth, respect and dignity is the hallmark of guidance. Freedom to make a choice and take a decision needs to be respected and encouraged.

Principle of Expert Opinion Specific and serious guidance problems should be referred to persons who are trained to deal with particular area of adjustment for their expert opinion.

Principle of Evaluation The guidance programme should be evaluated in terms of its effectiveness and improvement. Evaluation is essential for the formulation of new goals or re-drafting the existing goals.

Principle of Responsibility Parents and teachers have great responsibility in the execution of the work of guidance. The responsibility for guidance should be centred on a qualified and trained person, who is the head of the guidance centre.

Principle of Periodic Appraisal Periodic appraisal should be made of the existing guidance programme so that requisite changes, if any can be carried out for its improvement.

Need of Guidance

Guidance is important in today's world in almost every sphere of life.

The need of guidance can be seen through the following points

- It helps a person to develop his/her capabilities and prepares him/her to cope up with different situations.
- There are many examples of individual differences among people who face difficulties performing in different situations. Some are shy, social, kind, etc., by nature. Thus, guidance helps individuals, to adjust in his/her environment and act accordingly.
- It helps students to choose which stream and career is best for them. Usually, this situation arises at the time of career selection and after board exams. Thus, guidance plays a very important role at this time and helps youths to opt best career plan which gives meaning to their life.
- It plays an important role to prepare an individual as per the objectives of the ever-changing curriculum. Today, the scope of curriculum is not limited to only intellectual and physical development of students but it has changed as per the need of the society. The goal of the present curriculum is the all-round development of the youth of the nation and attach to the need of industrial development which also aims to prepare future generation who could get the better option in career. In other words, today's curriculum is career- oriented.
- It is necessary to help the individual to attain the maturity of judgement, stability of emotions and volitional control which are characteristics of true self-direction.
- It helps to understand oneself, one's talents, abilities and potentialities and also the limitations.
- It also helps to recognise and develop favourable attitudes and habits and the elimination of undesirable traits.
- It plays a crucial role to help those students who do not complete their education, due to various reasons like due to fear of failure, bad conduct of peers and teachers, home's environment, poverty and so on. Thus, an appropriate guidance is very essential for such students, which will encourage them to complete their education and become successful in their life. Thus, guidance plays a very important role in every sphere of life.

Types of Guidance

There are different types of guidance which are important in human life.

These are given below

Educational Guidance

It is the most important among various types of guidance. It is that specific area of guidance, which identifies and takes care of students problems that pertain to their educational progress and experiences.

It is directly concerned with the students, thus, it is important for student's life. The chief aim of educational guidance is to develop the ability of coordinating with the school environment in the students to create necessary awareness, so that they may select themselves, proper learning objectives and situations.

It is seen that students often face difficulties in understanding what is taught in the classroom and their work place thus, expected change in behaviour is not fully achieved. Failures in examinations and tests, poor standards and unsatisfactory involvement in the academic work by students, are some of the often-noticed problems. Thus, these problems needs to be solved to the maximum extent by assisting them. Here, it plays a very crucial role to identify and rectify such types of problems.

Objectives of Educational Guidance

- To monitor the academic progress of the students.
- To identify the gifted, creative, backward, and other category of special learners.
- To assist the students, to understand themselves i.e., to understand their potentialities, strengths and limitations.
- To help students, to adjust with the school's environment, its rules and regulations, and social life connected with it.
- To help students, to participate in the educational activities, in which they can develop leadership, etiquettes and other social qualities.
- To help students, to make educational plans consist with their abilities, interests and goals.

Guidance at Different Educational Levels

At Elementary Level As, it is the first level of education, where children are only a beginner, thus, guidance programme should be planned in such a manner, which must help the students to make good beginning, to plan intelligently, to get the best out of their education and prepares them for secondary level. Educational guidance should be used in diagnosing difficulties, which will arise at this level and also for identifying the special needs of children.

At Secondary Level At this level, children are at the adjustment stage, thus, educational guidance should be planned in such a manner which can help the students to understand themselves better, to understand different areas of education, to select an appropriate courses to get information about different educational opportunities, to develop good study habits and social connections. The students should be helped to be acquainted with the vocational implications of various school subjects.

At Tertiary Level Educational guidance must give directions to students about the purpose and scope of higher studies and help them to choose the better option in studies which should be appropriate as per their abilities. Thus, in order to assist students, each higher-level institution must have a guidance unit with due provision of guidance services.

Thus, we can say that, educational guidance is concerned with the assistance given to pupils in their choices and adjustments with relations to schools, curriculum courses and school life.

Vocational Guidance

It is a process of providing assistance to students in choosing and preparing for a suitable occupation or vocation. It helps an individual to choose an occupation, prepare for it, enter upon it and progress in it. It is concerned primarily with helping individuals, to make decisions and choices involved in planning a future and building a career.

Objectives of Vocational Guidance

- To help the people for choosing an occupation according to their potentialities, capabilities & interests.
- To give assistance during school years, so that the individual will be able to adjust on the job work conditions and with the others.
- To help individuals, to develop an attitude towards work that will dignify whatever type of occupation they may wish to enter.
- To provide the knowledge about the different career options and institutions where the facility of training is available.
- To give information about the working conditions and future prospects of different occupations.
- To bring the excellence in the job performance by accepting the particular occupation as a vocational for an individual.
- To provide assistance as per the need of the individuals by considering the individual differences.
- To plan such a strategy which may help physically challenged persons to get the best career option in life without any hurdles.

Thus, it helps a person to choose vocation as per his/her choice and suitability. It starts at school and college level where students need this at the time to choose a suitable career.

Personal Guidance

It refers to the help, given to individuals towards a better adjustment in the development of attitudes and behaviours in all areas of life. It helps people to adjust with psychological and social environment. Its aim is to solve the emotional and psychological problems. Educational and vocational guidance can also be called personal guidance.

Personal guidance may be defined as the assistance offered to the individuals to solve their emotional, social, ethical, and moral as well as health problems. Thus, personal guidance deals with all those problems of life which are not covered under educational and vocational guidance.

Objectives of Personal Guidance

- To help an individual in analysing and understanding the personal problems of individuals.
- To make individuals sensitive about their environment.
- To assist the individuals in solving their problems related to different spheres of their life like family, school, vocation and adjustment in the society.
- To enhance the adjustability of individuals.
- To understand the personal complexity and causes in order to find out the best solution.
- To help in developing good relations with family members, relatives and society members to remove mal-adjustment and performing the role in a better way.
- To develop understanding and insight into the various life situations, so that individuals may bring excellence and adjustment in new situations.

Thus, we can say that personal guidance is the process which helps a person to understand all spheres of his/her life and solve problems related to these spheres.

Health Guidance

Health is regarded as the wealth. Health guidance is the guidance which is given about the overall health care to an individual or group of individuals. Total health is the goal of health guidance. The health guidance may be a cooperative effort of principal, doctors, counsellor/ psychologist, teachers, students and parents. They all work together to achieve the aim of health guidance.

To promote preventive care, the conditions of school hostel, canteen needs to be checked. Similarly, health education through formal classes is also essential in school education. In the present day, the concern of health guidance also pertains to give guidance in HIV/AIDS which is necessary for students to know without any delay.

Objectives of Health Guidance

- To give education about good and healthy habits.
- To help individuals, to encourage them to develop personal hygiene concept.
- To provide adequate time-table to follow, to be healthy in life.
- To create awareness about the healthy food habits, life-style, workouts, and so on, to be both physically and mentally healthy.
- To provide information that where to get proper treatment of any disorder or illness.
- To educate people, about different types of diseases and also the ways to keep oneself healthy.

Thus, health guidance plays a vital role to keep ourselves healthy and protective from different types of diseases and disorders.

Social Guidance

We are social animals. Thus, we need to adjust in a society where we have to follow some set of rules and to act accordingly. Educational institution is a miniature society and the class is an example of multi-cultural and multi-lingual space, where students come from different socio-economic status, linguistic and socio-cultural backgrounds to study. But sometimes, social relationships constitute a problem area for most of the students where they find difficulty in adjustment.

It is very important that the students, to be helped in acquiring the feeling of security and being accepted by the group, in developing social relationship and in becoming tolerant towards others. This is the task of social guidance. Formally, social guidance can be given by educational institutions, whereas informal guidance may be provided by family, religious institutions, media, etc.

Objectives of Social Guidance

- To adjust oneself in the society and to attain maturity.
- To prepare oneself for livelihood.
- To achieve economic independence and self-reliance.
- To understand the family and marital relations and related responsibilities.
- To sensitise about gender issues and make people able to respect each other.
- To develop healthy relations with peers and society members.

Thus, we can see that social guidance provides meaning to life by providing guidance at such place where it is needed the most.

Counselling

Counselling is the process of assisting and guiding clients, especially by a trained person on a professional basis, to resolve, personal, social or psychological problems and difficulties.

In a real sense, it is a consultation, mutual interchange of opinions. It aims at helping the clients to understand and to accept themselves as they are. It is a process which is done between two individuals *i.e.* one is the **counsellor**, who listens and gives an appropriate advice and on the other is a **counselee** (client) who is given counselling.

It takes place within a professional setting. It is initiated and maintained as a means of facilitating changes in the behaviour of the client. It is a professional task for professionally trained people who are master in their respective field.

Definitions of Counselling

According to **Wren** "Counselling is a dynamic and purposeful relationship between two people who approach a mutually defined problem, with mutual consideration of each other to the end that the younger or less mature or more troubled of the two is aided to a self-determined resolution to his problem".

According to **Shertzer and Stone** "Counselling is an interaction process which facilitates meaningful understanding of self and environment and results in the establishment or clarification of goals and values for future behaviours".

According to **Merle M Ohlse** "Counselling is an accepting, trusting and safe relationship in which clients learns to discuss openly what worries and upsets them, to define precise behaviour goals, to acquire the essential social skills and to develop the courage and self-confidence to implement desired new behaviour".

According to **Edwin Lewis** "Counselling is a process by which a troubled person (client) is helped to tell and behave in a more personally satisfying manner through interaction with an uninvolved person (counsellor) who provides information and reactions, which stimulate the client to develop behaviour, which enable him to deal more effectively with himself and his environment".

Thus, from the above definitions we can say that, counselling is a two-way process which involves two individuals. There are mutual relationships between the two individuals. It helps an individual to gain self-understanding, self-acceptance and self-realisation. It also helps an individual to become happy, more creative and better adjusted after having an effective counselling.

Nature of Counselling

- It is a process by which a person is assisted to behave in a more rewarding manner.
- It aims to promote healing, comfort, clarification, and reconciliation to the counselee.
- The three basic elements of counselling are the **counselee** *i.e.* a person in pain desiring to be healed, the **counsellor** *i.e.* the helper who listens and provides help, and the **negative experience** *i.e.* the cause of pain and distress.
- In the counselling process, the counselee identifies the negative experience and is helped to choose a path that is more satisfactory with the help of a counsellor.
- Its function is to produce changes in the individual that will enable him to extricate himself from his difficulties.
- The nature of counselling is to assist individuals through a helping relationship to alleviate current negative responses to a challenging situation.

Objectives of Counselling

- To enable an individual, to become oriented to the educational environment.
- To provide information, about different aspects of life.
- To help, to recognise problems with learning and to develop coping skills.
- To help to identify and express positive feelings and behaviours needed for successful learning
- To demonstrate how effort and persistence affect learning.
- To encourage and develop special abilities and right attitudes.
- To achieve academic goals and to apply study skills necessary for academic success at each grade level.
- To develop mutual understanding between a counsellor and a counselee.
- To help to make plans as per the educational qualifications, requirements and desire of success of the counselee.
- To develop skills and social adjustment techniques in the counselee.

Characteristics of Counselling

- It is a process which involves two individuals; one seeking help and the other, a professionally trained person, who can help the first.
- In counselling, there should be a relationship of mutual respect between the two.
- The counsellor should be friendly and cooperative and the counselee (client) should have trust and confidence in the counsellor.
- It is important to help a student, to take a decision, make a choice and to seek a direction.
- It helps a counselee to acquire independence and develop a sense of responsibility, explore and utilise his potentialities.
- It is more than just giving advice. The progress comes through the thinking that a person with a problem does for himself, rather than through solutions offered by the counsellor.
- It produces changes in the individual that will enable him to extricate himself from his difficulties.
- It involves a face-to-face relationship between two persons.

Principles of Counselling

Principle of Acceptance According to this principle, each client must the accepted as an individual and dealt with as such. The counsellor should give, due regard to the rights of the client.

Principle of Permissiveness Counselling is such a relationship which develops optimism and the environment shapes according to the person. All the thoughts accept the relative relationship of counselling.

Principle of Respect for the Individual All the schools of thoughts of counselling advocate for the respect of the individual *i.e.* respecting an individual's feelings must be an integral part of counselling process.

Principle of Thinking with the Individual Counselling emphasizes thinking with the individual. It is essential to differentiate think for whom? And 'why to think'? It is the role of the counselor to think about all the forces around the client to join client's thought process and to work collectively with the client regarding his problem.

Principle of Learning All the assumptions of counselling accept the presence of learning-elements in the counselling process.

Principle of Consistency with Ideals of Democracy All the principles are associated with ideals of democracy. The ideals of democracy desire to accept a person and want to respect the rights of others. The process of counselling is based upon the ideals of a person's respect. It is a process which accepts individual differences.

Types of Counselling

There are different types of counselling, which are important in human life. *These are given below*

Directive Counselling

It is a counselling, in which a professional plays an active role in a client's decision making by offering advice, guidance, and recommendations. It is counsellor-centered, which gives complete importance to the counsellor. Its chief exponent was **BG Williamson**. Its major goal is to replace the emotional behaviour of an individual with deliberately, rational behaviour. Under this process, the counsellor plans the counselling process, his work is to analyse the problem, identify the exact nature of the problem and to provide various options.

Williamson stated that **directive counselling** is good to address the problems relating to educational and vocational adjustment. It is a concept, where educational and vocational guidance relates to the personality dynamics and inter-personal relationships.

It is more useful where the individual wants information and advice for choice of a career. This approach does not focus its attention on personality development as such. Here, the problem is the focal point of the counselling and not the counselee. The counselee is under the counsellor and is not equal to him.

Here, a counsellor can look at the counselee directly. It is useful due to its limited time which saves a lot of time. It gives happiness to the counselee, as he gets a solution to the problem.

Steps of Directive Counselling

There are six steps of directive counselling which have been given by Williamson

Synthesis It includes collection of information about the individual through structured interviews, psychological case history methods, interaction with family members, friends, etc.

Analysis After collection of data, the information is organised in the logical manner to analyse the individual in terms of his qualifications, assets potentials, liability adjustment, cultural background, habits, etc.

Diagnosis The diagnosis consists of the interpretation of the data in relation to the nature and problem, the causes of problems and so on.

Prognosis Under this step, a prediction is made about the future development of the problem.

Counselling Here, the counselling is to bring about adjustment and re-adjustment to an individual in relation to his/her problem.

Follow-up It is extremely important among all the given steps. An individual may be able to solve immediate problems through counselling but new problems may occur or the original problem may re-occur. Thus, follow-up with the counselee is extremely necessary. The role of counsellor is important as he/she has to make the individual understanding and accept his/her strength, weakness and faults.

Limitations of Directive Counselling

- It kills the initiative.
- It makes a counselee helpless.
- It does not guide counselee to be efficient and confident.
- It is undemocratic.
- It makes the counselee dependent on the counsellor.

Non-Directive Counselling

It is counselee-oriented. Its chief exponent was **Carl Rogers**. In this counselling, the counselee is allowed for free expression. The role of counsellor is to only direct and guide. Counsellor asks a few questions, so as to think about the solution of the problem. Counselee takes an active part, gains insight into the problem with the help of the counsellor and arrives at the decision and action to be taken.

Here, the role of counsellor is passive. Here, goal is independent and integration of the counselee rather than the solution.The main role of the counsellor is to create an environment in which the counselee can work out with his own understanding. In this type of counselling, emotional aspect of a counselee is more emphasised, rather than the intellectual aspect. The main emphasis is to establish a warm, permissive and accepting environment, which helps the counselee to express his self-structure.

In this type of counselling, the counselee is free to choose the objectives of his life. Through this counselling, a counselee becomes able to take decisions in a limited period of time.

Steps of Non-Directive Counselling

There are five steps of non-directive counselling which have been given by Carl Rogers

Defining the Problematic Situation At first, the counsellor defines the problematic situation.

Free Expression of Feelings In the second step, the counsellor provides such situation where the client can express his emotions freely.

Development of Insight As the counselee starts to have self-realisation, a counsellor keeps on explaining his emotions so that a counselee can develop a proper insight.

Classification of Positive and Negative Feelings In this step, the counsellor identifies the negative and positive feelings of the counselee and classifies them.

Termination of Counselling Situation In the end, the counsellor looks for a point where he can terminate the counselling situation after all the above steps. This step can be taken by anyone either the client or the counsellor.

Limitations of Non-Directive Counselling

- It is a time-consuming process.
- In this counselling, wisdom and judgement of the client cannot be relied upon.
- In this counselling, all the problems cannot be sorted out through talking.
- This type of counselling cannot be utilised in institutions, such as school.
- Due to passivity of a counsellor, sometimes, a counselee hesitates to speak out freely.

Eclectic Counselling

The combination of directive and non-directive counselling depending upon the situational factors is known as **Eclectic Counselling**. Its chief exponent was **Bordin** (Thorne).

In this type of counselling, the counsellor is neither fully active nor fully passive, rather he studies different aspects of a counselee's personalities and selects certain useful techniques for him. Under this process, the counsellor can begin his work from the directive counselling and then starts to use non-directive counselling method, keeping in with the time and place. In this, counselee and counsellor are active and together finds the solution. The major techniques of this type of counselling are compilation of data, assurance, case history, examination, and so on. In this type of counselling, objectives and integrative methods are used.

Steps of Eclectic Counselling

- Take initial interview, to collect the relevant data about the counselee.
- Selection of appropriate techniques, keeping in mind the needs of the counselee.
- Use of techniques under specific circumstances as per the desire and need of the counselee.
- In this step, evaluation of the effect is done of the used techniques.
- In this step, due preparation is made, for giving counselling and guidance to a counselee.
- Under the final step, the advice is sought out from the counselee and other related individuals regarding the topics of its programs and other aims.

Limitations of Eclectic Counselling

- It has no set of rules, as it is not clearly defined by the scholars, which makes this type of counselling unclear.
- It is very difficult to present a synthesised form of directive and non-directive counselling, because these two are like poles apart.
- There is no definite rule as to how much freedom should be given to a counselee.

Difference Between Guidance and Counselling

Guidance	Counselling
Guidance is a process of helping young persons learn to adjust to self, to others and to circumstances.	Counselling means consultation, mutual interchanging of options deliberating together.
Guidance is a wider process.	Councelling has a narrower meaning
Guidance includes counselling.	Counselling is a part of guidance.
Guidance may be individual as well as in group.	Counselling is individual.
Guidance is related with personal, educational, vocational and other problems.	Counselling is mainly related with mental health and emotional problems.
Guidance can be given by any person. Training is not required for guidance Psychologist.	Pre-training is must for counsellor.
Guidance may be provided through books or magazines.	In counselling, mutual discussion, consultation and interchange of opinions plays a significant role.

Approaches to Counselling

There are various ways to take and provide counselling. In counselling, there are different situations of counsellor and counselee and their contribution is also different from each other. Thus, this can be known as different approaches to counselling where situations are different. *These approaches are as follows* :

Cognitive-Behavioural Counselling (Albert Ellis-REBT)

Under Cognitive-Behavioural counselling, counselling is given by keeping in view of thinking, presumption, evaluation, etc.

In this regard, Rational Emotive Behavioural Therapy (REBT) is more important which belongs to the behavioural school of therapy. REBT is the pioneering form of Cognitive Behavioural Therapy which was devised by **Albert Ellis**, an American Psychologist in 1950s. It is an active-directive therapy, based on challenging faulty beliefs, to resolve emotional and behavioural problems.

REBT is based on the ABCD technique, which was formulated in the year 1950.

Such as

- Action (For example, a person crashes his car)
- Belief (This leads him to believe that he is a bad driver)
- Consequence (He stops driving because he fears that he will have another accident)
- Dispute (The counsellor disputes that he is a bad driver, and points out that most people have at least one accident in their driving career).

The goal of REBT and ABCD technique is to help counselee replace irrational thinking with rational thinking.

Albert Ellis, published REBT in his first book, in the year 1962. As per REBT, humans have both logical and irrational behaviours by birth. REBT believes that humans deliberately create emotional problems like, self-blame, self-pity, anger, crime, shame, depression and anxiety and human turns back in behaviours like procrastination, compulsion, avoidance and addiction.

It is an Action-Oriented approach to manage cognitive, emotional, and behavioural disturbances. It is a practical approach to assist individuals in coping with and overcoming adversity as well as achieving goals. It is considered as an educational process in which a therapist often deals in an active and direct form that how to identify the illogical and self-defeated opinions and how to solve and change these situations with positive ones. **Ellis**, suggested that rather than simply being warm and supportive, the therapist needs to be blunt, honest, and logical in order to push people towards changing their thoughts and behaviours in positive way.

Humanistic Counselling

This type of approach has originated from the Existentialist Humanist Philosophy. It gives emphasis on to understand the counselee effectively.

This recognises the uniqueness of every individual. **Camp** (1971), **Rogers** (1975), **Baruth and Hubar** (1985) are the supporters of this type of approach. They all believed that human interaction is the main focus for the effective counsellor.

Humanistic approach assumes that everyone has an innate capacity to grow emotionally and psychologically towards the goals of self-actualisation and personal fulfilment.

Humanistic counsellors believes that problems are not caused by life events themselves, but how we experience them. Thus, our experience affects and be affected by how we feel about ourselves and also influence our self-esteem and confidence, Therefore, this approach encourages the counselee to learn to understand how negative responses can lead to psychological discomfort. It aims at self-acceptance of both negative and positive aspects of our characters and personalities.

The main goal of humanistic counsellors is to help counselees to explore their own thoughts and feelings and to work out their own solutions to their problems.

This is very similar to the approach used in coaching, except those coaches that are more focused on the present, and less on the past.

But, coaching aims to address the issue of 'how', and counselling looks more at 'why'. Thus, we can conclude that Humanistic approach has three general characteristics, one is the **existentialist concept**, second is the **client-centred approach** and third is the **holistic approach**.

Person-Centered Counselling (Carl Rogers)

The Person-Centred Approach to Counselling belongs to the humanistic school of therapy. It was devised by **Carl Rogers**, an American Psychologist in 1940s. It is also known as **'Client-Centred Therapy'** and **'Rogerian Therapy'**, which is a non-directive form of **Talk Therapy**.

This approach deals with the ways in which individuals perceive themselves consciously, rather than how a counsellor can interpret their Unconscious thoughts or ideas. Ultimately, this approach sees human beings as having an innate tendency to develop towards their full potential. But, sometimes this ability can be blocked or distorted by certain life experiences, particularly those experiences which affect our sense of value.

In this approach, therapist works to understand an individual's experience from their perspective. Thus, therapist must positively value the counselee to as a person in all aspects of his experiences. This approach emphasises that it is vital in helping the counselees to feel accepted, and better able to understand their own feelings.

This approach can help the counselee to reconnect with their inner values and sense of self-worth, thus, enabling them to find their own way to move forward and progress.

This approach focuses on the belief that the counselees (clients), and not the counsellor, is the expert of their own thoughts, feelings, experiences and problems. It clearly mentions that the counselee is the person, who is most capable of finding an appropriate solutions. The counsellor does not suggest any course of action, make recommendations, ask questions or try to interpret anything, the counselee says, rather the responsibility for working out problems rests wholly with the counselee. When the counsellor gives response, his aim is to reflect and clarify what the counselee has been saying. The only work of an expert and trained client-centred counsellor is to show empathy, warmth and genuineness, which he believes will enable the counselee's self-understanding and psychological growth.

***Carl Rogers** identified three basic principles of the Person-Centred Approach, such as*

Congruence The therapist is congruent with the client such as honest.

Unconditional Positive Regard The therapist provides the counselee with unconditional positive regard. Such as warm, positive feelings, regardless of the counselee's behaviour.This refers to the therapist's deep and genuine caring for the counselee.

Empathy The therapist shows empathy to understand the counselee. It means the ability to imagine oneself in another person's position.

Thus, we can say that in this Person-Centred approach, the counsellor has a very positive and optimistic view of human nature who gains trust of the counselee at the end.

Theories of Counselling

There are many different theories of counselling which are briefly explained

Behaviouristic Theory

Its main focus is to analyse the behaviour of the counselee. In other words, behaviourists are more interested to know and understand about the behavioural characteristics of the counselee rather than his past experiences.

The insight of the level of emotions or awareness for the behavioural counsellor is not enough. He accepts the acts or behaviour of the counselee rather than speech.

The behaviourist stresses more on the symptoms of the person who is facing some problem. These problems are related to the counselee, who fails to deal with the situation, due to his inappropriate behaviour. Thus, the behaviourist counsellor stresses more on the activity of a counselee.

Rational Theory

It accepts that cognition and perception are two most effective determinants. A person acts according to his thought. It is mainly based on analysis of work. It accepts that understanding of behaviour depends on the belief that all the people can learn to believe in themselves. People can think or act for themselves. They can take decisions for themselves and express their feelings.

***Ellis**, represented the general hypothesis of Rational Theory in the following ways*

- I am good, you are also good- this is the significance of a healthy mind.
- I am not good; you are also not good- this indicates the unhealthy mind of people who have pessimistic approach.
- I am good, you are not good-this is the condition of the mind of that person, who blames others for his problems.
- I am not good, you are good-this is the general condition of people who think themselves weak as compared to others.

In this theory, the counsellor helps the counselee to reconstruct his lost ego trait. He also helps to develop his ego trait in timely manner, so that he can develop positive attitude towards life, boost his self-confidence, and solve his problems for which he used to blame others.

Emotive and Reality Theory

The main characteristic of this theory is that counselling is arranged in different steps. As per the steps, various stages of counselling have been accepted in this theory. All these stages are considered connected to each other and interactive. This is the basis of this theory and the founder of the specific method of counselling.

The stages are as follows

- First stage- Investigation of problem
- Second stage- Defining of binary problem
- Third stage- Identification of the alternatives
- Fourth stage- Planning
- Fifth stage- Taking action
- Sixth stage- Evaluation and feedback

In this theory, special significance is given to the emotional aspect as well as real or actual circumstances. Therefore, counselling should be done as per the practical, self-centred and emotional situations, in order to suit the real conditions and to enable a person, to imagine such a system where he can create an appropriate environment for his contemporary world along with the development.

EXAM BASED QUESTIONS

1 Which of the following is important to develop the identity of a person?

(a) Guidance (b) Counselling
(c) Motivation (d) Both a and b

2 When a person needs guidance ?

(a) When he faces difficult situation.
(b) When he wants to change his environment.
(c) When he wants help to achieve his goals.
(d) All of the above

3 Through which process' a person gets an appropriate help to achieve the desirable aim of life?

(a) Motivation (b) Reinforcement
(c) Counselling (d) Guidance

4 Who stated that, "Guidance is an assistance given to an individual in making intelligence choices and adjustments"?

(a) Chisholm (b) AJ Jones
(c) Dunsmoor and Miller (d) Merle M. Ohese

5 Guidance can be given in the field of

(a) education (b) vocational
(c) personal (d) in any field

6 Guidance is considered as a

(a) concept (b) process
(c) theory (d) Both a and b

7 Guidance is a

(a) self oriented activity (b) problem-solving activity
(c) multi-faceted activity (d) All of these

8 Guidance includes a person of

(a) any age (b) any interest
(c) any nature (d) All of these

9 Which of the following, best describes the principle(s) of guidance?

(a) An organised activity
(b) A life long process
(c) Guidance for all
(d) All of the above

10 Which of the following, develops self-determination in an individual?

(a) Guidance (b) Counselling
(c) Motivation (d) All of these

11 Guidance emphasises on

(a) code of conduct (b) flexibility
(c) personality (d) All of these

12 Guidance helps in

(a) curriculum development
(b) a person to achieve his/her goal
(c) a student to complete his/her education
(d) All of the above

13 Which of the following is included in the types of guidance?

(a) Educational (b) Vocational
(c) Health (d) All of these

14 Which type of guidance, identifies and takes care of student's problems?

(a) Vocational (b) Educational
(c) Health (d) Social

15 Which type of guidance, has the aim to develop the ability of coordinating with the school environment in the students, to create necessary awareness, so that they may select themselves proper learning objectives and situations?

(a) Vocational (b) Health
(c) Educational (d) Social

16 The aim of educational guidance involves

(a) to monitor the academic progress of students.
(b) to identify the gifted, creative, backward categories of special learners.
(c) To help students to make an educational place.
(d) All of the above

17 Vocational education is given stressed, on which of the following level of education?

(a) Primary level (b) Secondary level
(c) Higher level (d) University level

18 Which type of guidance is concerned with the assistance given to pupils in their choices and adjustments with relations to schools, curriculum courses and school life?

(a) Social guidance (b) Personal guidance
(c) Educational guidance (d) Health guidance

19 Which type of guidance, helps students in choosing and preparing for a suitable occupation?

(a) Educational (b) Vocational
(c) Personal (d) Health

20 The aim of vocational guidance is

(a) to give information about the working conditions and future prospects of different occupations.
(b) to bring the excellence in the job performance by accepting the particular occupation as a vocational for an individual.
(c) to provide assistance as per the need of the individuals by considering the individual differences.
(d) All of the above

21 Which of the following guidances refers to the help given to individuals towards a better adjustment in the development of attitudes and behaviours in all areas of life?

(a) Personal (b) Health
(c) Vocational (d) Educational

22 Which of the following aspects, is/are included in the personal guidance?

(a) Moral (b) Religious

(c) Emotional (d) All of these

23 The objectives of personal guidance is/are

(a) to understand the personal complexity and causes, in order to find out best solution.

(b) to help, in developing good relations with family, relatives and society to remove maladjustment and performing the role in a better way.

(c) to develop understanding and insight into the various life situations, so that individuals may bring excellence and adjustment in new situations.

(d) All of the above

24 Which of the following guidance is extremely important in the distorted form of human's lifestyle?

(a) Personal guidance (b) Health guidance

(c) Educational guidance (d) Social guidance

25 The goal of health guidance is/are

(a) to achieve total health

(b) to develop good relations

(c) understand personal complexity

(d) All of the above

26 The health guidance is a cooperative work of

(a) Principal

(b) Doctor

(c) Counsellor/Psychologist

(d) All of the above

27 The task of social guidance, especially for students, is

(a) to help them in acquiring feeling of security

(b) to make them able by being accepted by the group

(c) to develop social relationship

(d) All of the above

28 How many types of social guidance are there?

(a) Two (b) Three

(c) Four (d) None of these

29 The source of formal social guidance is

(a) Media

(b) Family

(c) Educational institutions

(d) Religious institutions

30 A guidance programme is to be established in a new public school that has just opened in an expanding school district. The first step in developing the guidance programme is to

(a) clarify the school district's unique instructional goals

(b) devise behavioural objectives for classroom management

(c) gather an appropriate counselling and guidance materials such as tests and occupational information

(d) survey the guidance and counselling needs of the student

31 Which of the following components is the least important in a comprehensive guidance programme?

(a) Student outcomes and competencies.

(b) Direct delivery of counselling on a demand basis placement.

(c) Placement follow-up and follow through activities.

(d) Accurate counts of the frequency of student initiated contact with the school's counsellors.

32 Which of the following helps to find out the unhealthy reason which affects a person to take decision?

(a) Counselling (b) Motivation

(c) Punishment (d) Reinforcement

33 Counselling is

(a) a consultation

(b) a mutual interchange of opinions

(c) Both a and b

(d) None of the above

34 Which of the following is not included in the process of counselling?

(a) Counsellor

(b) Counselee

(c) Aim of counselling

(d) Assumption of counselling

35 Counselling is a .... process involving individuals.

(a) one-way (b) two-way

(c) three-way (d) None of these

36 The aim of counselling is to promote

(a) healing (b) comfort

(c) clarification (d) All of these

37 Which of the following is an important element of counselling?

(a) Counselee

(b) Counsellor

(c) The negative experience

(d) All of the above

38 The objectives of counselling are

(a) to demonstrate how effort and persistence affects learning.

(b) To encourage and develop special abilities and right attitudes.

(c) To develop mutual understanding between counsellor and counselee.

(d) All of the above

39 A school counsellor is working with a group of fourth grade students, to develop the socio-emotional skills, needed to negotiate peer interactions. Which of the following guidance activities, would be most appropriate for a session designed to help the students to develop their ability to understand the point of view of others?

(a) A biblio counselling activity, in which students are asked to comment on the thoughts and feelings of characters in a story.
(b) A play media activity, in which students are encouraged to express their feelings about one another.
(c) A classroom guidance activity, in which students listen to a presentation on social skills by the school psychologist.
(d) A verbally based guidance activity, in which students are asked to analyse cause and effect relationships in their own behaviour.

40 When providing counselling to a student, a school counsellor is most likely to use a system approach to
(a) identify the support mechanisms that may be necessary to help the student to achieve his or her goals.
(b) understand how the student's behaviour patterns are affected by family relationships.
(c) organise the counselling sessions, to follow a particular sequence of steps.
(d) determine how the student's physical health is affecting their mental health

41 After several sessions, with the school counsellor Jamal, a 9th grade student, has identified five occupations that match reasonably well with his interests and abilities. The school counsellor can best help Jamal further, to narrow his choices among these career alternatives by
(a) visiting workplaces, where people are employed in one or more of the occupations, he has identified.
(b) identifying ways in which the five occupations he has identified, differ from forms of employment that he finds less desirable.
(c) gathering information on the history of job availability in the five occupations, he has identified.
(d) preparing a list of the advantages and disadvantages of the five occupations, he has identified.

42 Tara is a High School senior, who did very poorly in most classes, prior to her previous year, when her academic performance showed marked improvement. She now wants to attend college and has asked the school counsellor, whether she should attempt, to explain her earlier difficulties on college application forms. Which of the following would be the most appropriate strategy for the counsellor to recommend?
(a) Tara should find a place somewhere on the application, to offer a detailed explanation of her earlier difficulties.
(b) Tara should forget her earlier difficulties and should makes no mention, of them, on the application form.
(c) Tara should include a separate sheet of paper, presenting her earlier difficulties as symptoms of special needs.
(d) Tara should explain in the personal essay, how overcoming her earlier difficulties, made her a better person.

43 The counsellor's behaviour during the interview suggests that his objective is probably to facilitate
(a) the student's understanding that he has not made as much progress as his father expects.
(b) the father's understanding that the student's progress has been as much as can reasonably be expected.
(c) the student's ability to listen more attentively and follows directions more carefully.
(d) more direct and constructive communication between the student and his father.

44 In consulting with a teacher about disciplinary problems in her daily interactions with her students, a High School counsellor demonstrates keen interest in the teacher's various concerns by listening and empathising with her. By doing this, the counsellor is assuming the role of
(a) a supervisor (b) an expert
(c) a collaborator (d) a helper

45 When should the counsellor informs a student about conditions that may require the provision of more than routine counselling?
(a) At a time, half-way through the counselling relationship.
(b) Only, by when an ethical issue arises during the counselling relationship.
(c) Only, by giving student advice, on which the counsellor expects the student to act.
(d) At or before the time, the student enters the counselling relationship.

46 The best way for a counsellor, to address the problem of a student's monopolising group counselling time is to
(a) tell the student that group participation will be terminated, if the behaviour does not change.
(b) have the group, to examine the student's behaviour in a productive and non-threatening manner.
(c) ask the student, politely to allow the other group members to speak more frequently.
(d) discuss the student's monopolising behaviour with the student outside of group time.

47 When working with students with disabilities, it is important for the school counsellor to communicate with outside doctors and therapists to enhance school based services. By doing so, the guidance counsellor is taking the role of
(a) an investigator
(b) a collaborator
(c) an enabler
(d) a school psychologist

48 A High School counsellor meets with a student, who is having difficulty deciding what college to attend in the fall. The counsellor discloses his own personal reflections on decisions he made relating to college choice. As the counsellor reflects on his past decisions, he describes regrets. The counsellor's comments are

(a) appropriate because they help the student to understand that he is not alone in his dilemma about choosing a college.
(b) appropriate because they allow the student to feel close to his High School counsellor.
(c) inappropriate because the counsellor does not understand contemporary issues related to choosing a college.
(d) inappropriate because they focus more on the counsellor's experience rather than on the student's current dilemma.

49 Which of the following is a type of counselling?
(a) Eclectic (b) Directive
(c) Non-directive (d) All of these

50 Which of the following counselling is counsellor centred?
(a) Non-directive (b) Directive
(c) Eclectic (d) None of these

51 In which type of counselling, the counselee is under the counsellor and is not equal to him?
(a) Eclectic counselling (b) Directive counselling
(c) Non-directive counselling (d) None of these

52 Which type of counselling is counselee-oriented?
(a) Eclectic (b) Non-directive
(c) Directive (d) None of these

53 Which type of counselling cannot be utilised in institutions, such as school?
(a) Directive (b) Non-directive
(c) Eclectic (d) None of these

54 Who was the chief exponent of non-directive counselling?
(a) Bordin (b) Carl Rogers
(c) BG Williamson (d) None of these

55 Who was the chief exponent of eclectic counselling?
(a) Bordin (b) Carl Rogers
(c) Williamson (d) Crow and Crow

56 The term 'REBT' was devised by whom, among the following?
(a) Crow and Crow (b) Bordin
(c) Carl Rogers (d) Albert Ellis

57 Which of the following approaches of counselling is action-oriented?
(a) Cognitive Behavioural counselling
(b) Person-Centered counselling
(c) Humanistic counselling
(d) None of the above

58 Camp, Rogers, Baruth and Hubar are the supporters of which approach of counselling?
(a) Humanistic (b) Person-Centered
(c) REBT (d) None of these

59 Which approach of counselling is also known as Rogerian Therapy?
(a) Humanistic (b) Person-Centered
(c) REBT (d) None of these

60 According to Carl Rogers, a congruent counsellor is one
(a) whose actions are not at odds with his or her feelings and thoughts.
(b) whose expression reflects what the client is presenting.
(c) whose choice of techniques and interventions remains constant throughout the counselling relationship.
(d) who gets a client, to do what the counsellor thinks he or she should be doing.

61 The main focus of which theory of counselling is to analyse the behaviours of the counselee?
(a) Behaviouristic theory
(b) Rational theory
(c) Emotive and Reality theory
(d) None of the above

62 Which theory of counselling accepts that cognition and perception are two most effective determinants?
(a) Behaviouristic theory
(b) Rational theory
(c) Emotive and Reality theory
(d) None of the above

63 In which theory, counselling is arranged in different stages?
(a) Behaviouristic theory
(b) Emotive and Reality theory
(c) Rational theory
(d) None of the above

64 Match the following

List I (Steps)	List II (Types of Counselling)
A. Analysis	1. Directive
B. Termination of counselling situation	2. Non-Directive
C. Take initial Interview	3. Eclectic

Codes

	A	B	C		A	B	C
(a)	1	2	3	(b)	3	2	1
(c)	1	3	2	(d)	2	1	3

65 Match the following

List I (Stages of Emotive and Reality Theory)	List II (Explanation)
A. First stage	1. Investigation of problem
B. Second stage	2. Defining binary problem
C. Third stage	3. Identification of the alternatives
D. Fourth stage	4. Planning

Codes

	A	B	C	D
(a)	1	2	3	4
(b)	2	3	1	4
(c)	2	1	3	4
(d)	4	3	2	1

66 Who said "Guidance seeks to help each individual become familiar with a wide range of information about himself, his abilities, this previous development in the various areas of living and his plans or ambitions for the future"?

(a) Chisholm (b) AJ Jones
(c) Dunsmoor and Miller (d) Crow and Crow

67 According to whom "Guidance is a means of helping individuals to understand and use wisely the educational, vocational and personal opportunities, they have or can develop and as a form of systematic assistance, whereby students are aided in achieving satisfactory adjustment to school and to life"?

(a) Dunsmoor and Miller
(b) Crow and Crow
(c) AJ Jones
(d) Chisholm

68 Who said "Guidance is not giving directions. It is not the imposition of one person's point of view upon another person. It is not making decisions for an individual, which he should make for himself. It is not carrying the burdens of another life"?

(a) Crow and Crow (b) AJ Jones
(c) Chisholm (d) None of these

69 Which of the following, best describes the nature of guidance?

1. Guidance is a helping service, whether it is given to an individual or a group. Its aim is to provide assistance to individuals.
2. Guidance is a self-oriented, problem-solving and multi-faceted activity.
3. Guidance can be given to any individual who needs that. The scope of guidance is very wide, which includes individuals of any age, any interest, and of any nature.
4. Guidance cannot be given by any person. It is a work of experts. In the field of psychology, it is work of techniques, which needs expert guides, career experts, psychologists and counsellors.

Codes
(a) Only 1 (b) 2 and 3
(c) 3 and 4 (d) All of these

70 Which of the following is true in terms of guidance?

1. Guidance helps a person to adjust in the environment, where he lives and also adjust with oneself and others.
2. Guidance develops self-determination in an individual. It helps to develop self-dependence in the person, to solve his difficulties and problems by himself.
3. Guidance cannot be used as counselling.

Codes
(a) Only 1 (b) Only 3
(c) 1 and 2 (d) All of these

71 Which of the following is/are the principles of guidance?

1. A life long activity
2. Based on cooperation
3. Emphasis on personality
4. Flexibility

Codes
(a) Only 1 (b) 2 and 3
(c) Only 4 (d) All of these

72 Which of the following is true about need of guidance?

1. Guidance helps a person, to develop his/her capabilities and prepares him/her to cope with different situations.
2. There are many examples of individual differences among people who face difficulties in performing in different situations. Some are shy, social, kind, etc., by nature. Thus, guidance helps individuals to adjust in his / her environment and act accordingly.
3. Guidance helps students to choose which stream and career is best for them. This situation usually, arises at the time of career selection and after board exams. Thus, guidance plays a very important role at this time and helps youths, to opt best career plan, which gives meaning to their life.

Codes
(a) Only 1 (b) 3 and 4
(c) Only 2 (d) All of these

73 Educational guidance focuses on which of the following problems of students?

1. Failure in examinations
2. Poor standards
3. Unsatisfactory involvement in the academic work by students

Codes
(a) Only 1 (b) Only 2
(c) Only 3 (d) All of these

74 Which of the following is true about the objectives of educational guidance?

1. To help students to, adjust with the school's environment, its rules and regulations, and social life, connected with it.
2. To help students, to participate in the educational activities, in which they can develop leadership, etiquettes and other social qualities.
3. To help students, to make educational plans, consist of their abilities, interests and goals.

Codes
(a) Only 1 (b) Only 2
(c) 2 and 3 (d) All of these

75 What should be the aim(s) of educational guidance at the elementary level?

1. To help the students, to make good beginning.
2. To plan intelligently.
3. To get the best out of the student's education and prepare them for secondary level.

Codes

(a) Only 1 (b) Only 2 (c) 2 and 3 (d) All of these

76 What should be the aim(s) of educational guidance at the secondary level?

1. To help students, to understand themselves better.
2. To understand different areas of education.
3. To select an appropriate courses, to get information about different educational opportunities.

Codes

(a) Only 1 (b) Only 2 (c) Only 3 (d) All of these

77 Which of the following is true about the aim of vocational guidance?

1. To help the people, for choosing an occupation according to their potentialities, capabilities and interests.
2. To give assistance, during school years so that the individual will be able to adjust on the job work conditions and with others.
3. To help individuals, for developing an attitude towards work that will dignify whatever type of occupation they may wish to enter.
4. To provide the knowledge about the different career options and institutions, where the facility of training is available.

Codes

(a) Only 1 (b) 2 and 3
(c) 1 and 4 (d) All of these

78 Which of the following statements is/are correct about the objectives of personal guidance?

1. To help an individual, in analysing and understanding the personal problems of individuals.
2. To make individuals, sensitive about their environment.
3. To assist the individuals, in solving their problems, related to different spheres of their life like family, school, vocation and adjustment in the society.
4. To enhance the adjustability of individuals.

Codes

(a) Only 1 (b) 2 and 3 (c) 3 and 4 (d) All of these

79 Which of the following statements is/are correct, about the objectives of health guidance?

1. To help individuals, to encourage them to develop personal hygiene concept.
2. To provide an adequate time-table, to follow, to be healthy life.
3. To create awareness about the healthy food habits, life style, workouts, and so on to be both physically and mentally healthy.

Codes

(a) Only 1 (b) Only 2
(c) 2 and 3 (d) All of these

80 Which of the following statements is/are correct? about the aim of social guidance

1. To ajdust oneself in the society and to attain maturity
2. to prepare oneself for livelihood.
3. To achieve economic independence and self-reliance.
4. To understand the family and marital relations and related responsibilities.

Codes

(a) Only 1 (b) Only 2
(c) 3 and 4 (d) All of these

81 Consider the following statement.
"To sensitise people about gender issues and make people able to respect each other".
The above statement is associated with which of the following guidance?

(a) Educational guidance
(b) Health guidance
(c) Social guidance
(d) Vocational guidance

82 Who said "Counselling is a dynamic and purposeful relationship between two people, who approachs to a mutually defined problem, with mutual consideration of each other, to the end that the younger or less mature or more troubled of the two is aided to a self-determined resolution to his problem"?

(a) Shertzer and Stone (b) Wren
(c) Edwin Lewis (d) None of these

83 According to whom "Counselling is an interaction process that facilitates meaningful understanding of self and environment and results in the establishment and clarification of goals and values for future behaviours"?

(a) Wren
(b) Shertzer and Stone
(c) Edwin Lewis
(d) None of the above

84 Which of the following statements is/are not correct, about counselling?

1. In the counselling process, the counselee identifies the negative experience and is helped to choose a path that is more satisfactory with the help of counsellor.
2. The main goal of the counsellor is carefully listening and help the counselees to sort out his/her pain.
3. In this whole process, the counsellor provides an atmosphere of acceptance and genuine caring to facilitate the counselling.

Codes

(a) Only 1 (b) Only 2
(c) Only 3 (d) None of these

85 Find out the correct statement

(a) Guidance is provided when required
(b) Counselling is a continuous process
(c) Guidance and counselling do not require reliable data
(d) Guidauce and counselling are age-specific

86 Which of the following statements is/are correct about objectives of counselling?

1. To enable an individual to become oriented to the educational environment.
2. To provide information about different aspects of life.
3. Helps to recognise problems with learning and develops coping skills.
4. Helps to identify and express positive feelings and behaviours needed for successful learning.

Codes

(a) 1 and 2
(b) 2 and 3
(c) 3 and 4
(d) All of the above

87 Which of the following statements best defines the characteristic(s) of counselling?

1. Counselling is a process, which involves two individuals, one seeing help and the other, is a professionally trained person, who can help the first.
2. In counselling, there should be a relationship of mutual respect between the two.
3. The counsellor should be friendly and cooperative and the counselee (client) should have trust and confidence on the counsellor.
4. Counselling is important to help a student, to take a decision, to make a choice or to seek a direction.

Codes

(a) 1 and 2 (b) 2 and 3
(c) 3 and 4 (d) All of these

88 Which of the following is/are the principles of counselling?

1. Counselling is emotional rather than purely intellectual attitude.
2. Counselling is more than advice giving, which prepares the counselee to cope up with future situations.
3. In the process of counselling, progress comes through the thinking that a person with a problem does for himself.
4. The process of counselling involves solution of immediate problem as well as the future decision of the individual.

Codes

(a) Only 1 (b) 2 and 3
(c) 3 and 4 (d) All of these

89 Which of the following is true about the limitations of the directive counselling?

1. It makes a counselee helpless.
2. It does not guides counsellee to be efficient and confident.
3. It is undemocratic.
4. It makes the counselee dependent on the counsellor.

Codes

(a) Only 1 (b) Only 2
(c) 3 and 4 (d) All of these

Directions (Q. Nos. 90-97) *In each of the questions given below, there are two statements marked as Assertion (A) and Reason (R). Mark your answer as per the codes given below.*

Codes

(a) Both A and R are true and R is the correct explanation of A.
(b) Both A and R are true but R is not the correct explanation of A.
(c) A is true but R is false.
(d) A is false but R is true.

90 **Assertion** (A) Human needs to adjust in a society, where he has to follow some set of rules and act properly.

Reason (R) Human is a social animal.

91 **Assertion** (A) Social guidance improves human personality.

Reason (R) Educational institutions are the main sources of social guidance.

92 **Assertion** (A) Social guidance provides meaning to life.

Reason (R) Social guidance develops healthy relations with peers and society members.

93 **Assertion** (A) Counselling is a two way process.

Reason (R) Counselling includes counsellor and counselee (client).

94 **Assertion** (A) Counselling helps to recognise problems with learning.

Reason (R) Counselling develops coping skills.

95 **Assertion** (A) The function of counselling is to produce changes in an individual.

Reason (R) This change enables an individual to extricate himself from his difficulties.

96 **Assertion** (A) Counselling is more than just giving advice.

Reason (R) The progress of counselling, comes through the thinking that a person with problem does for himself rather than through solutions offered by the counsellor.

97 **Assertion** (A) In non–directive counselling, counselee takes active part, gains insight into the problem with the help of the counsellor and arrives at the decision and action to be taken.

Reason (R) In non–directive counselling, the role of counsellor is passive.

98 Arrange the steps of directive counselling in sequential order.

1. Synthesis 2. Analysis
3. Prognosis 4. Diagnosis
5. Counselling 6. Follow-up

Codes

(a) 1, 2, 3, 4, 5, 6 (b) 2, 1, 4, 3, 5, 6
(c) 3, 2, 4, 1, 5, 6 (d) 2, 4, 3, 1, 5, 6

99 Arrange the steps of non-directive counselling in sequential order.
1. Free expression of feelings
2. Development of insight
3. Classification of positive & negative feelings
4. Termination of counselling situation
5. Defining the problematic situation

Codes
(a) 1, 2, 3, 5, 4 (b) 5, 1, 2, 3, 4
(c) 4, 3, 2, 1, 5 (d) 1, 2, 3, 4, 5

100 Arrange the ABCD technique, used in REBT counselling, in sequential order.
1. Dispute 2. Consequence
3. Belief 4. Action

Codes
(a) 4, 3, 2, 1 (b) 1, 2, 3, 4
(c) 4, 2, 3, 1 (d) 2, 1, 4, 3

101 Arrange the different stages of counselling, given by the Emotive Reality theory in sequential order.
1. Investigation of problem
2. Defining binary problem
3. Identification of the alternatives
4. Planning
5. Taking action
6. Evaluation and feedback

Codes
(a) 2, 3, 4, 5, 6, 1 (b) 1, 2, 3, 4, 5, 6
(c) 6, 5, 4, 3, 2, 1 (d) 4, 2, 1, 3, 5, 4

PREVIOUS YEARS' QUESTIONS

July 2018

1 A teacher discusses in depth the problems and challenges being faced by a student with a view to help him/her to arrive at a decison. Which of the following modality of guidance will designate this situation appropriately?
(a) Counselling type
(b) Vocational guidance type
(c) Educational guidance type
(d) Information, exploration technique type

2 Which of the following tools at a guidance centre can be used for ascertaining prospective success in a chosen occupation?
(a) Achievement test (b) Interest inventory
(c) Differential aptitude test (d) Personality inventory

3 For an effective non-directive counselling session, which one of the following will be most essential?
(a) Training of the counsellor
(b) Establishing a rapport with the client
(c) Expertise in using tests
(d) Conversational fluency

4 Which of the following set of statements is correct in the context of guidance?
1. guidance is a personal help.
2. Guidance leads to self-regulation.
3. Guidance focuses on problems, rather than on individual.
4. Guidance considers individual differences as a basic starting point.
5. Guidance service can be organised with various time lags.
6. Guidance is panacea for all ills.

Codes
(a) 1, 2 and 3 (b) 3, 4 and 5
(c) 2, 4 and 5 (d) 1), 2 and 4

5 Match the following.

List I (Guidance Services)	List II (Roles / Functions)
A. Occupational information service	1. Gives information about the characteristics i.e. strengths and weaknesses of a person.
B. Placement service	2. Provides information about world of work.
C. Follow-up-service	3. Provides suitable engagement as per the vocational preparedness.
D. Individual inventory service	4. Takes up a view of how things are going on, after entring into the specific job.
	5. Provides an opportunity for understanding oneself in a realistic way.

Codes

	A	B	C	D		A	B	C	D
(a)	2	3	4	1	(b)	3	2	4	5
(c)	1	3	5	2	(d)	2	4	5	1

November 2017

6 Below given are few items needed as a support to guidance personnels. Which of them is scarce in Indian context? Select your answers from the codes given below.
1. Availability of lists and inventories.
2. Physical facilities and infrastructural support.
3. Academic resources available in schools and colleges.
4. Courses in guidance and career counselling.
5. Professional training facilities.
6. Components of guidance and counselling courses in teacher education programme.

Codes
(a) 2, 3, 4, 6 (b) 1, 2, 4, 5
(c) 3, 4, 5, 6 (d) 4, 5, 3, 6

7 A high school student, soon after passing the examination, intends to choose subjects for future professional placement. Which of the following will be useful in this regard ?

(a) Career counselling
(b) Educational guidance
(b) Vocational guidance
(b) Personal guidance

8 To bring about the attitudinal changes in the students, which of the following guidance techniques will be helpful ?

(a) Group guidance
(b) Directive counselling
(c) Non-directive counselling
(d) Individual guidance

9 For making guidance and counselling an effective programme in Indian context, which of the following is the major constraint?

(a) Scarcity of funds
(b) Educational policy
(c) Mind set of functionaries at various levels of education
(d) Apathy of parents

10 Below given are few strategies, for making guidance and counselling programme effective in the Indian context. Choose the most appropriate strategies for disadvantaged section of society.

1. Making follow-up, an integral part of guidance and counselling programme.
2. Orientation of teachers in guidance and counselling.
3. Providing need based counselling opportunities.
4. Conducting training programmes for teachers, for learning techniques of guidance.
5. Changing the mind set of parents.
6. Linking guidance activities with curriculum.

Codes

(a) 2, 1, 3, 4 (b) 5, 6, 4, 3
(c) 1, 2, 3, 6 (d) 4, 2, 5, 6

January 2017

11 Match the following.

List I (Tools of Guidance)	List II (Associated Functions)
A. Testing	1. Tracking whether students are doing well in their profession.
B. Counselling	2. Details reflecting particular events/ episodes related to student.
C. Follow up	3. Organising face to face interaction, to solve the problems.
D. Anecdotal record	4. Diagnosing the ability of students.

Codes

	A	B	C	D		A	B	C	D
(a)	1	4	2	3	(b)	4	3	1	2
(c)	3	1	4	2	(d)	2	4	3	1

12 Guidance is a process, which enables each individual to

1. understand one's abilities
2. develop a realistic picture of one's own self
3. sharpen one's understanding about life goals
4. procure information about the role of community
5. help in achieving a state of mature self-guidance

Codes

(a) 1, 4, 3, 2 (b) 3, 1, 4, 3 (c) 3, 4, 1, 3 (d) 1, 2, 3, 4

13 Educational guidance to the students may be provided through

1. organising interactive sessions
2. engaging students in co-curricular activities in a meaningful way
3. promoting sensitivity to others
4. aquenting students with available vocational opportunities
5. introducing students to group life situations

Codes

(a) 1, 2, 4, 5 (b) 5, 3, 2, 4
(c) 3, 2, 5, 1 (d) 5, 4, 1, 3

14 Match the following.

List I (Techniques)	List II (Procedural concerns)
A. Group guidance	1. Giving students, a scope for personal inquiries
B. Directive counselling	2. Conducting need based intimate discussion sessions
C. Group counselling	3. Advising students about do's and don'ts
D. Eclectic counselling	4. Conducting discussions in a group

Codes

	A	B	C	D		A	B	C	D
(a)	1	3	2	4	(b)	2	1	3	4
(c)	4	3	1	2	(d)	3	1	2	4

July 2016

15 Which of the following is correct in the context of eclectic counselling ?

(a) Role of Counsellor is conspicuous.
(b) Role of Counselee is relatively more visible.
(c) Depending upon the context the role of the counsellor and the counselee may undergo a change.
(d) Counsellor's role is of a minor nature.

16 Which of the following types of counselling is also known as 'client centered' counselling ?

(a) Directive (b) Non-directive
(c) Eclectic (d) Group counselling

17 Establishment of rapport in the context of counselling means

(a) Keeping report of the individual's academic record
(b) Availability of records to the counsellor
(c) Trusting relationship between the counsellor and counselee
(d) Trusting relationship between the counsellor and school staff

18 The emphasis of guidance programme is relatively more on
(a) individual (b) problem
(c) Both a and b (d) Neither a nor b

19 Match the following.

List I	List II
A. Placement service	1. To ascertain, whether students placed in job, are going ahead satisfactorily or not.
B. Follow-up service	2. To help an individual student in solving his/her problem, through face to face interaction.
C. Counselling service	3. To help the students in getting part time/ summer/full time job.
D. Occupational information service	4. To provide an information about world of work.

Codes

	A	B	C	D
(a)	1	4	2	3
(b)	3	2	4	1
(c)	3	1	2	4
(d)	2	1	3	4

December 2015

20 A teacher holds discussion with a student and enables him/her to select appropriate choice of subject at higher secondary stage. This type of guidance is called
(a) Personal guidance (b) Vocational guidance
(c) Educational guidance (d) Psychological guidance

21 In a school, a class teacher daily talks to his/her students in respect of how to make better use of reading room and laboratory and improve performance in the subjects. His/her engagement in this way will be called
(a) Personal guidance (b) Educational guidance
(c) Directive counselling (d) Information service

22 Which of the following guidance services in India is on the weakest footing in so far as vocational courses are concerned ?
(a) Individual guidance service
(b) Counselling service
(c) Placement service
(d) Follow-up service

23 The focus of vocational guidance has to be on
(a) providing job to the client
(b) helping the client to seek an appropriate job
(c) enabling the system of education to become job - oriented
(d) helping the client to select an appropriate job

24 An effective counselling is one which provides help to the client in understanding his/her
(a) potential ability and temperament
(b) strength and weakness in respect of exercising his/her choices
(c) possibility of success in a job
(d) friends and foes with whom relationship should be developed

25 Match the following.

List I	List II
A. Non-directive counselling	1. Where an individual is helped to become adjusted to his/her circumstance.
B. Group guidance	2. A list of occupations with job descriptions.
C. Testing service	3. Clients are given help in respect of their problems collectively.
D. Occupational inventory	4. Where the counsellor does not impose his/her views on the client.
E. Personal guidance	5. Where a client receives assistance to get an exact idea about his qualities/abilities.
	6. Where the teacher assumes the role of a counsellor.

Codes

	A	B	C	D	E
(a)	4	3	5	2	1
(b)	1	2	3	6	4
(c)	6	5	4	3	2
(d)	5	4	3	2	1

June 2015

26 For effective guidance, which of the following is most important?
(a) Need assessment of the client
(b) Case history of the client
(c) Attitude of the client
(d) Relationship with the client

27 In counselling, the first step should be to create
(a) a need in the counsellee
(b) rapport with the counsellee
(c) a situation for self-analysis
(d) free and frank discussions of the problems

28 Which one of the following guidance services is on the weak footing in India?
(a) Information service (b) Inventory service
(c) Counselling service (d) Follow-up service

29 In the Indian context, counselling services at all the levels of education, have not proved to be effective owing to the
(a) apathy of the parents
(b) policies of the government
(c) non-cooperation of teachers
(d) inadequate school - community linkages

December 2014

30 For organising eclectic counselling, which of the following is most important?
(a) Study of needs and personality characteristics
(b) Selection of techniques
(c) Preparation for counselling
(d) Seeking the opinion of the client and other related people

31 The kinds of services required for organising a School Guidance Programme are
(a) personal, professional, placement, follow-up
(b) information, testing, counselling, follow-up
(c) information, guidance, counselling, follow-up
(d) information, testing, counselling, placement

32 Which of the following will not be acceptable as a rationale of group guidance?
(a) Acquainting the client group about their assumptions and beliefs
(b) Developing inter-personal relations
(c) Promoting a democratic climate during guidance
(d) Encouraging mental understanding and cooperation

33 Which one of the following is considered central service in guidance programme?
(a) Information service (b) Self-inventory service
(c) Placement service (d) Counselling service

34 Non-directive counselling is mainly meant for
(a) analysis of client data (b) diagnosis of relevant factors
(c) emotional release (d) placement service

June 2014

35 The Psychotherapeutic Method of Guidance involves in
(a) emphasising the use of the cumulative record
(b) supporting the giving of advice to the counsel
(c) placing confidence in the pupils ability to solve his/her own problems
(d) the destructive method of counselling pupils

36 In counselling with pupil, a teacher should
(a) plan to do most of the talking
(b) establish rapport with the pupil
(c) refrain from giving him information
(d) assumes responsibilities for solving his problems

ANSWERS

Exam Based

1 *(d)*	2 *(d)*	3 *(d)*	4 *(b)*	5 *(d)*	6 *(d)*	7 *(d)*	8 *(d)*	9 *(d)*	10 *(d)*
11 *(d)*	12 *(d)*	13 *(d)*	14 *(b)*	15 *(c)*	16 *(d)*	17 *(b)*	18 *(c)*	19 *(b)*	20 *(d)*
21 *(a)*	22 *(d)*	23 *(d)*	24 *(b)*	25 *(a)*	26 *(d)*	27 *(d)*	28 *(a)*	29 *(c)*	30 *(d)*
31 *(d)*	32 *(a)*	33 *(c)*	34 *(d)*	35 *(d)*	36 *(d)*	37 *(d)*	38 *(d)*	39 *(a)*	40 *(b)*
41 *(d)*	42 *(d)*	43 *(d)*	44 *(d)*	45 *(d)*	46 *(b)*	47 *(b)*	48 *(d)*	49 *(d)*	50 *(b)*
51 *(b)*	52 *(b)*	53 *(b)*	54 *(b)*	55 *(a)*	56 *(d)*	57 *(a)*	58 *(a)*	59 *(b)*	60 *(a)*
61 *(a)*	62 *(b)*	63 *(b)*	64 *(a)*	65 *(a)*	66 *(a)*	67 *(a)*	68 *(a)*	69 *(d)*	70 *(d)*
71 *(d)*	72 *(d)*	73 *(d)*	74 *(d)*	75 *(d)*	76 *(d)*	77 *(d)*	78 *(d)*	79 *(d)*	80 *(d)*
81 *(c)*	82 *(b)*	83 *(b)*	84 *(d)*	85 *(d)*	86 *(d)*	87 *(d)*	88 *(d)*	89 *(d)*	90 *(a)*
91 *(a)*	92 *(a)*	93 *(a)*	94 *(b)*	95 *(a)*	96 *(a)*	97 *(a)*	98 *(b)*	99 *(b)*	100 *(a)*
101 *(b)*									

Previous Years' Questions

1 *(a)*	2 *(c)*	3 *(b)*	4 *(d)*	5 *(a)*	6 *(b)*	7 *(a)*	8 *(a)*	9 *(c)*	10 *(c)*
11 *(b)*	12 *(d)*	13 *(a)*	14 *(c)*	15 *(c)*	16 *(c)*	17 *(c)*	18 *(a)*	19 *(c)*	20 *(c)*
21 *(b)*	22 *(d)*	23 *(d)*	24 *(b)*	25 *(a)*	26 *(a)*	27 *(b)*	28 *(d)*	29 *(d)*	30 *(a)*
31 *(b)*	32 *(b)*	33 *(d)*	34 *(c)*	35 *(c)*	36 *(b)*				

CHAPTER 13

Teacher Education

Teacher education is a programme that is related to the development of teacher proficiency and competency that would enable and empower the teacher to meet the requirements of the profession.

Meaning of Teacher Education

Teachers are significant pillars of societal development. There was a time when teacher education meant that any person who knows the subject matter could be a teacher. These people will take a short course in mechanics of classroom management, record keeping, reciting communication and become teachers.

Now a days, a sound teacher must have knowledge about, pedagogy, attitude, traits, personality and exceptionality of children. Thus, teacher education is the professional preparation of a person into a teacher.

The quality and the extent of learner's achievement are determined by the competence of teacher and the motivation provided by him. It is the formal program that have been established for the preparation of teachers at the elementary and secondary school levels. It refers to the policies and procedures designed to equip teachers with the knowledge, attitudes, behaviours and skills require to perform their tasks effectively in the school and classroom.

Teacher education helps in development of teacher's proficiency and competency. This would enable the teachers to meet the requirement of the profession.

Between 1906-1956, teacher education was called 'teacher training'. But, it was not a broad subject and prepared the teacher as mechanics or technicians. The focus was on skill training, only.

According to **NCTE**, teacher education is defined as "A programme of an education, research and training of persons to teach from pre-primary to higher education level".

Elements of Teacher Education

Teacher education consists of teaching skills, sound pedagogical theory and professional skills. *These are as follows*

Teaching Skills It includes giving out training and practice for the field of teaching. That may encompass techniques, approaches and strategies. This would help teachers to plan and impart instruction and conduct effective assessment. This can be done through classroom management skill. That also includes preparation and use of an instructional material.

In this Chapter

Pedagogical Theory For teaching in a classroom, this enables teacher with philosophical, sociological and psychological skills. The theory differs from place to place. It is dependent upon the participants.

Professional Skills Various techniques, strategies and approaches are employed by teachers to grow in the profession. This also facilitates the growth of profession. They include skills like counselling skills, inter-personal skills, computer skills, information retrieving and management skills.

These aspects provide a Holistic approach towards teacher education.

Objectives of Teacher Education

School system has emerged and puts pressure on teacher education, making it sensitive. *Thus, now the teacher have to be prepared for the following roles*

- Teacher needs to be encouraging, supportive and human. They need to encourage the learners, help them to discover their talents. This leads to the realisation of their physical and intellectual potential to the fullest. Thus, developing a character with desirable, social and human value.
- Teachers are also meant to be an active participant, who contributes to renewal of school curriculum. They should update it, according to the recent developments, and keep it relevant to the learners. It should be guided by the past experiences and changing national development goals.

These factors show that a teacher needs to be responsive and sensitive to the context of education. *To meet these expectations, teacher education should be comprised of the following objectives*

Adequate Knowledge of Subject Matter It is expected to the teacher to know the subject given to him.

Equiping the Teacher with Required Pedagogical skill The teacher should be able to create an emotional atmosphere. He or she should be equipped enough to stimulate an experience under artificially created emotional atmosphere.

Enabling the Teacher to Acquire Child Psychology Skill The teacher should be able to understand child psychology. As such he/she may know the difficulties faced by child and help to overcome it.

Development of Teaching Attitude To maximise the potential of material and human resources, a teacher should have proper attitude.

Developing Self-Confidence of the Teacher Teacher education helps the teacher in self care by

- adjusting to physical conditions.
- fruitful adjustment with social environment.
- self-adjustment to get an emotional satisfaction.

Enabling Teachers to Make Use of Instructional Facilities The teacher should be available to expand school resources by improvising an instructional facilities.

Enabling Teacher to Understand Individual Differences of Child and Optimise their Development Teacher education tries to solve the difference within individual. Thus, the teacher can treat his learner as his peer.

Development of Abilities to Give Direct Satisfaction to Parents Proper habits of children is developed by the teacher. It includes taking care of oneself, progress in the class and positive attitude. This is specially important for teachers in an elementary school.

Nature of Teacher Education

- Teacher education is a life-long process. It consists of pre-service, induction, and in-service stages. The three stages constitutes the continuous process of learning.
- 'Teachers are made not born.' Teaching is both a science and an art. The teacher cannot only rely on an education itself. He/she has to learn the tricks of trade and adapt according to situations.
- Teacher education is very broad. Apart form pre-service and in-service programmes, a teacher is expected to participate in various other programmes as well. This may include community programmes and extention activities like literacy and development activities of the society.
- Teacher education is constantly evolving. So, in order to prepare teachers with recent times, teacher education needs to be updated on a regular basis.
- The core of teacher education lies on its curriculum, design, structure, organisation and transaction modes.
- The curriculum for the teacher education is sensitive to field application. It comprises of blending of theoretical knowledge with several other disciplines. It is a sum part.
- Teacher education is divided into different levels. It includes elementary, pre-primary, primary, secondary, higher secondary and tertiary level. The student and teacher will be given out knowledge, accordingly to respective level. Thus, the curriculum is designed as such that the knowledge is divided between the levels.
- In teacher education, there is input of learner, the process of learning that the student and teacher goes through and there is output in the form of new students.

Scope of Teacher Education

Scope of teacher education means an opportunity and application of the subject. *Scope of teacher education can be understood in the following ways*

Teacher Education at Different Levels of Education

All the levels of an education, *i.e.* pre-primary, primary, elementary, secondary, higher secondary and tertiary, requires teachers. The knowledge required by teacher at each level varies. Thus, stage and level specific education is needed. Teacher education is also needed for teaching student to be a teacher. This is done in professional institutes. Here, the teacher requires specific training to deal with the students.

Thus, where there are teachers, there will be a teacher education.

Triangular Basis of Teacher Education

Creating a knowledge base for teachers requires a lot of academic and an intellectual understanding. This involves selection of theoretical knowledge from disciplines cognate to education, namely, psychology, sociology and philosophy and converting it into forms suitable for teacher education. These discipline provides the base for better understanding and application of teacher education.

Philosphical basis provides the students, teachers with various schools of philosophy, an ancient and the modern philosophical thoughts, educational thoughts of philosophical thinker. **Sociological basis** helps the student to understand the role of society and its dynamics in the country. **Psychological basis** helps the teacher to understand student's psychology. This benefits both the student and the future learners.

Aspects of Teacher Education

Teacher education is guided by aspects of teacher education, student teacher, content and teaching strategy.

Teacher education is dependent on the quality of teacher educator. The use of pedagogical inputs in teacher education and their utilisation to help future teacher is dependent on the teacher education. The main scope of teacher education is to provide student teacher with relevant knowledge, attitude and skills. Thus, the student teacher needs to be fully equipped with conceptual and theoretical framework, so that they can know the minute details of the profession. This enables them to carry on the function of being a teacher efficiently.

Types of Teacher Education Programs

Teacher education program can be of various types, *but it is divided broadly into following three categories*

Pre-Service Training

Pre-service training of a teacher starts before their teaching job. After completing the pre-service training, a student teacher becomes the teacher. The main need to pre-service training is that the student teacher must understand the role of teacher. This equips the student teacher with necessary skills and competencies to become a teacher.

It imparts an inclusive education as well. This may comprises of school visits, classroom observations and practical assignments. Inclusive education is a big part of pre-service training.

Objectives of Pre-Service Training

- To provide teacher with proper understanding regarding the aims and objectives of education.
- To promote in prospective teachers a proper understanding of the basic principles of child growth, development and process by which pupil learn.
- To enable them to plan and present subject-matter in a manner which will promote the interest, sense of purpose and an understanding process of pupil's growth.
- To develop communication and psychomotor skills and abilities conductive to human relations for interacting with children in order to promote learning in them, both inside and outside the classroom.
- To develop understanding, interest, attitude and skill which would enable him/her to promote all round development of children under his/her care.

In-Service Training

It is basically for teachers who are already working. *The training can be done in many forms like*

- two weeks intensive training.
- weekly/monthly session over a period of time.
- several intensive training sessions during a longer period.

It can be done by group of teachers from different schools or whole team of teachers in one school.

Objectives of In- Service Training

- To provide professional training and qualification to untrained working teachers. Though, most of the working teachers have background training, some may lack it. For them, in-service training is important.
- To upgrade the qualification of currently serving teacher. The teacher education gets updated and renewed continuously. So, in-service training should help in this matter.
- To arrange refresher courses to familiarise teachers with modern practices being encouraged in school. The teacher should be able to handle modern teaching material like audio-visual aids.
- To improve the quality of teacher education, there is growing emphasis on the need for continuous training of teacher education themselves.

Distance Learning/Self-Study

Distance learning of teacher education is for the teacher who cannot attend training events. There is a flexibility of time and place which is a win-win situation for working adults.

There is a separation between the teacher and learner in case of distance education. This separation is fused with the help of DVDs, podcasts and online lectures.

Distance learning has its benefits, only if

- apropriate methods are used.
- regular teacher-learner interaction is there.
- the learners are provided with valuable feedback.

Objectives of Distance Learning

- To provide an effective alternative path to wider opportunities in education of especially in higher education.
- To provide an efficient and less expensive education.
- To provide education facilities to all qualified and willing person, who can't join regular university and other courses for various reasons.
- To provide an opportunity of an academic pursuit to educated citizens, who are willing to improve their knowledge.

Pros and Cons of Pre-Service Training, In-Service Training and Distance Learning

	Pros	Cons
Pre-Service Training	• Student are already trained and are pro towards inclusive education. • Approach of teaching can be influenced of student teacher. • Less resistant towards new ideas.	• The student teacher have little or no experience. • Student teachers are not being given adequate preparation at present in this area of competence. • They lack in cooperation, once they start working.
In-Service Training	• The teachers are able to practice what they have learnt. • Learners have lot of experience that can be related to.	• Some resistant must be there as the learner can be stringent teacher.
Distance Learning	• Learner can learn at their own place. • The time duration and the location of the course taken is not fixed.	• Requirement of an electronic media or an internet, which is not always present. • Basic computer skills are needed. • Required feedback is not frequent. • Lack of human contract may result in demotivation.

Structure and Vision of Teacher Education Curriculum

The structure of teacher education is the foundation on which teacher education programmes are formed. The design, enactment and assessment of teacher education unavoidably reflect the structural anatomy on which programmes are built. According to NCERT, "The structure and vision of teacher education curriculum must provide an understanding of issues relating to children's learning, the nature of knowledge and the school as an institution. NCERT is an apex educational body strives to achieve the aim of enhancing school education and teacher education. Another statutory council *i.e.* National Council for Teacher Education (NCTE) by an Act of Parliament in 1993 is committed to initiate suitable measures to make teacher education responsive to various levels of development and change. The agenda of NCTE is to remove and minimize the existing deficiences of teacher education and to meet the demand of new challenges before it.

The recent effort to modify teacher education curricula to meet contemporary requirements has been initiated by the NCERT in the context of the recommendation of the committee appointed by it to review teacher education programmes offered in RIEs (Govinda committee). The committee highlighted the inter-disciplinary nature of education and recommended that, a systematic exercise needs to be undertaken to identify fundamental concepts with a view to

- highlighting connectivity among these concepts linked to teaching-learning processes and practices.
- focusing on distinct nature of education as an area of study with its emerging and evolving inter-disciplinary knowledge base and its epistemology.

Teacher education curricula should therefore, allow space to the teachers to introspect, reflect on their own practices and become agents of change. Inspite of the thrust of various curricular reform efforts to evolve stage-specific curricula for school education, there is a considerable mismatch in practice.

Vision for Teacher Education

- According to **NCTE**, teacher education must become more sensitive to the emerging demands from the school system.
- For this, it has to prepare teachers for the role of being an encouraging, supportive and humane facilitator in teaching-learning situations to enable learners to discover their talents and realise their physical and intellectual potentialities to the fullest.
- Teacher education must engage with theory along with field experiences to help trainees to view knowledge not as external to the learner but as something that is actively constructed during learning. Teacher education should integrate academic knowledge and professional learning into a meaningful whole.
- Teacher education should engage teachers with the curriculum, syllabi and textbooks to critically examine them, rather than taking them as 'given' and accepted without question.
- Teachers need to be trained in organizing learner-centered, activity based, participatory learning experiences, play projects, discussion, dialogue, observation, visits and integrating academic learning with productive work.
- Teacher education programmes need to broaden the curriculum (both school and teacher education) to include different traditions of knowledge, educate teachers to connect school knowledge with community knowledge and life outside the school.

Teacher Education at Elementary Stage

Vision for teacher education at elementary stage includes

- Teacher must possess knowledge of the first and second language, maths and the topics related to social and natural science.
- Teacher must have the ability to identify, select and organise learning experiences related to subjects mentioned.
- Teacher must have theoretical and practical knowledge of child health, physical and creational activities, games, creative art, and music.
- Teacher must know major psychological principles related to growth and development of children under his/her care.
- Teacher must possess theoretical and practical knowledge in respect of childhood education.
- Teacher must know major principles of learning in terms of formal and informal situation.
- Teacher must understand the role of school, the peer groups and community, in shaping personality of the child.
- Teacher must know the role of school teacher in changing society.
- Teacher must be aware of the nature, purpose, problems of an elementary education.
- Teacher should understand the nature and maturity of the children. This is important to impart education and ensure many sided development.
- Teacher must develop holistic approach to understand and solve the problems of life.

Teacher Education at Secondary Stage

Teacher education at secondary stage consists of teaching specialised subjects. *Teachers after completing their teacher education must have following traits*

- Depth of understanding to the concept of specific discipline.
- Know the ways through the adolescent learn.
- Understand the concept of work and experience.
- Possess the skill to teach.
- Able to develop understanding, skill, interest and attitude which will help the all around growth of the child.
- Understands the concept of personality and personality development.
- Possess communication, mental and social skills to interact with the pupils.
- Know the structure and functioning of various body system.
- Know the role of physical education, games, recreational activities for the betterment of adolescent health.
- Shows interest in the development of child.
- Develop skills in guiding and counselling the learner in academic and vocational subjects as well as in academic and personal problems.

Teacher Education at Higher Secondary Stage

Vision for the teacher after completing teacher education for higher secondary stage includes :

- Development of perspective for specific stream among the teachers.
- Able to guide the learner and prepare them for self-study, independent learning, critical thinking and self-evaluation.
- Make the student aware of the philosophy, purpose and teaching-learning strategies of the subject they have to teach.
- To be able to communicate abstract and complex ideas in simple terms.
- Develop the patriotism and national consciousnss among the learner.
- Sensitise the student about HIV/AIDS, and bring attitudinal change in understanding numerous problems related to healthy life.

Components of Pre-Service Teacher Education

Pre-service teacher education means education of teacher before entering into the service as teacher.

- In India the requirement for what qualifications are needed vary from state to state and can vary again depending on whether their plan is to be primary or secondary school teacher. While the composition of pre-service programmes may differ, they generally share common components.
- Subject-content knowledge.
- Pedagogic content knowledge (teaching methodology and assessing learning).
- Understanding how children learn (cognitive and social development).
- Teaching practice (opportunities to practice teaching usually under some form of supervision from a senior).
- Teachers often value their pre-service training as it can instill confidence, raise their awareness of what is involved in being a teacher and give them a new discourse with which to successfully enter the teaching profession.

Organization of Components of Pre-Service Teacher Education

Organization is a means to bring the plan into existence. It is directly connected with planning and efforts of the people. It is a medium through which, teaching goals and objectives are achieved.

Components of pre-service teacher education should be organized in the following manner

Determining Objectives First of all, the teacher determines the teaching objectives according to the psychology of pupils and needs of school and society. Teacher tries to understand how children learn as per their cognitive and social development.

Subject Content Knowledge Subject knowledge has a very important role to play because high-quality teaching rests on teacher understanding, the subjects they are teaching, knowing the structure and sequencing of concepts, developing factual knowledge essential to each subject and guiding the students in different ways.

Pedagogic Content Knowledge Teacher use their subject knowledge base for decision-making and what they are going to do. Sound teacher subject content knowledge positively affects decisions to change pedagogical strategies on assessment, implementation of curriculum and curriculum development.

Teaching Practice It is an opportunity for aspiring teachers to experience working with students in actual classrooms and acquiring professional competence. It is a practical experience for the pupil-teacher to meet the requirement of degree in education.

Transactional Approach

In this process, a situation is created, where student can interact with the material to be learnt in order to construct knowledge. In this policy, constructivism is related. The knowledge is not spoofed but instead, it is built by student as they connect experience with new knowledge.

As the student's past experience is different so is the interpretation. Teachers assist the learner in construction of knowledge rather than pouring the knowledge.

For foundation courses, three kinds of transactional approach *i.e. Expository method, collaborative learning and experimental learning*

Expository Method

In this method, a comprehensive topic or subject matter is explained or interpreted. The teacher leads the discussion, and guides the lesson. He/she can asks the questions from the student. It is more popular because it is more efficient and takes less time than discovery learning.

Applications of Expository Method

- When an important information is needed to make the class understand.
- When previous knowledge of the learner is lacking, time can be saved by teacher telling the part.
- An idea or the principle can be learned only by explaining.
- Induction may take too much time and its difficulty may out weigh its value.

Steps of Conducting

Expository teaching includes various steps and they are as follows

- Expository teaching begins with an introduction and overview of the topic before providing more specific information in detail.
- The teacher focuses the student's attention on the key points of the subject and may use graphics, diagrams or other representations to elaborate on the subject.
- It moves from general to specific and allows students to understand the increasingly detailed explanations of the information and link those explanations to information that was presented previously as a part of general overview.
- Teacher instructional strategy is designed to assist students in the acquisition of relatively factual material. This technique is facilitated by the use of pre-instructional verbal statements and the sequencing of the content.

Tools for Exposition

To make exposition clear, following tools can be used

- Analogies and stories
- Illustrations
- Models
- Diagrams
- Demonstrations
- Outlines and summaries

Collaborative Learning

As the name suggests, the teaching and learning process, which involves small group of learner working together to solve a specific problem. In this, learners are working in a group of two or more, collecting useful material and knowledge.

Active learning is the superset of collaborative learning; which involves talking, listening, writing and reading with individual involvement in the learning pedagogy. The concept of collaborative learning evolved from 'virtual classroom, where people having similar interest and similar area to research, share their ideas and knowledge.

Objectives of Collaborative Learning

- In collaborative learning, learner can reach each other to solve problem, can share knowledge and resources, can build team skill and lead toward, deeper understanding.
- Collaborative learning environment let the member to solve many complex problems and sharing expensive resources.
- It increases the productivity towards the common goal in terms of improving learning skills and generating knowledge in a group.

Approaches for Collaborative Learning

- Integrate the information and relate this and generate new knowledge.
- Identify the needs of the peer, process it and produce information which is needed by peers.
- Making healthy discussion as the team may comprise of different background members.

Advantages of Collaborative Learning

- Promotes critical thinking skill.
- Building and give away of knowledge.
- Exchanging, debating and negotiating ideas.
- Active thinking process of the learner.
- More achievements and greater productivity.
- Develops social interaction skills.
- Highly communicative and discussion skills.
- Multi-dimensional problem-solving skills.
- On demand interaction and support.

Experiential Learning

When learning is facilitated by experience, then it is known as experiential learning.

The concept of experiential learning was first explored by John Dewey and Jean Piaget, among others. It was made popular by education theorist David A Kolb, who along with Ron Fry developed the Experiential Learning theory, which is based on the idea that learning is a process, whereby knowledge is created through the transformation of experience.

Experiential Learning theory is a learning theory developed by **David A Kolb**, who published his model in 1984. His theory works on two levels *i.e.* a four stage cycle of learning and four separate learning styles. Kolb's theory has a holistic perspectives which includes experience, perception, cognition and behaviour. The learning cycle basically involves four stages *i.e.* concrete learning, reflective observation, abstract conceptualization and active experimentation. While, Kolb's learning styles include diverging, assimilating, converging and accomodating styles of learning.

Experiential Learning Cycle

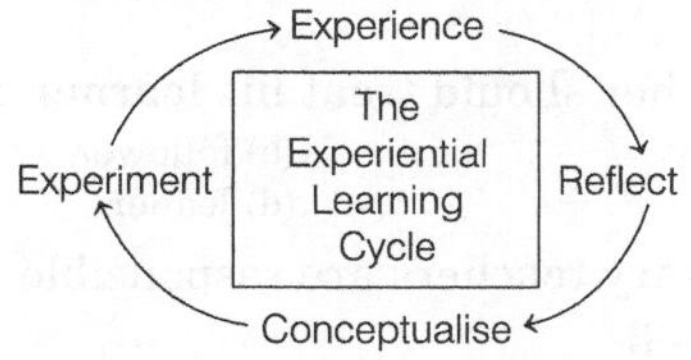

Concrete Experience It is the personal experience that learner already possesses. This experience could be anything from learners life which can be used to help the studying process.

Reflective Observation Next step is to put learners experience to use, the learner needs to reflect on the experience. Learner ponder over their experience.

Abstract Conceptualisation Once the learner has reflected on the experience, he/she needs to know what can be done differently. This makes it easy to learn as the learner is taking clues from his/her own experience.

Active Experimentation This is where learner put an idea into use. This is an application based process and shows how well the student has learnt.

Importance of Experiential Learning

Makes Learning Relatable to Participants Participants build on what they already know and are provided with opportunities to make connections between new concepts and existing ones.

Increases the Effectiveness of Learning Participants engage in critical thinking, acquire problem-solving skills and engage in decision-making.

Links Theory to Practice Participants have the chance to engage in the experience and practice what they have learned, see the application of the theoretical concepts in practice, process that application and make generalizations.

Assists in Memory Retention By building strong relationships between feelings and thinking processes, participants have the capacity to learn successfully when the information is associated with values and feelings.

Leads to Development of Skills for Lifelong Learning By assisting in the acquisition of essential skills and encovraging participants to reflect, conceptualize and plan for next steps.

Methods of Experiential Learning

Field Trips It is a brief observational activity that occurs outside the classroom doors. This offers a real oppurtunity of experience.

Narratives Specific and sensory details provided by author to get the reader involved into the story.

Experiments Proving a hypothesis correct or wrong by trial and error method. Experiments tells the learner about cause and its effect.

Simulation The teacher controls an artificial world to achieve desired result.

Games It provides children to work out their feelings while playing. It builds social skill.

Story-Telling Conveying events in words and capturing the moment to immortalise it.

Focussed Imaging Imaging exercises, nurture and develop students creative potential. The student relaxes and experiences the situation first hand.

Role Playing Student act as a character in a pre-defined situation. This helps the student to understand the concerns and values of other people.

Model Building It involves creation of models, either from kits or from component from a builder.

Surveys It is a method of gathering information and interpreting it.

EXAM BASED QUESTIONS

1 Teachers are significant pillars of
(a) societal culture (b) societal development
(c) societal diplomacy (d) societal construct

2 'Education' is derived from which Latin word?
(a) Edumust (b) Educare
(c) Eduformation (d) Eduation

3 Teacher education helps in the development of teacher's
(a) practicality (b) accountability
(c) proficiency (d) motivation

4 Teacher education was called teacher training in
(a) 1906-1956 (b) 1905-1958
(c) 1910-1966 (d) 1902-1945

5 Teacher education consists of teaching skill, professional skill and
(a) pedagogical skill
(b) teacher initiative
(c) teaching method
(d) Pedagogical theory

6 Teaching skill helps the teacher to
(a) plan and impart instruction
(b) conduct fullproof assessment
(c) promote classroom management
(d) all of the above

7 Counselling skill, inter-personal skill, computer skill, management skill are all part of
(a) personal development
(b) professional skills
(c) intra-personal skills
(d) duality control

8 What are the qualities of teacher?
(a) Encouraging (b) Supportive
(c) Humane (d) All of these

9 What should be updated by teacher on regular basis?
(a) School Anthem (b) Dress code
(c) School curriculum (d) Lesson plan

10 What kind of atmosphere should a teacher be able to create?
(a) Aggressive (b) Strict
(c) Emotional (d) All of these

11 For maximum output, the teacher should
(a) have adequate knowledge of subject matter
(b) know about child psychology
(c) have self-confidence
(d) All of the above

12 The teacher should treat his learner as a
(a) student (b) follower
(c) peer (d) leader

13 Elementary teachers are responsible for developing
(a) proper habits
(b) friendship between learner
(c) dressing sense
(d) All of the above

14 Which stage does teacher education involves?
(a) Pre-service (b) Induction
(c) In-service (d) All of these

15 In which extra programme, the teacher should participate in?
(a) T.V. Programme
(b) Community Programme
(c) Media Programme
(d) None of the above

16 The core of teacher education lies in
(a) curriculum (b) design
(c) transactional mode (d) All of these

17 In teacher education, knowledge is divided according to
(a) institutions (b) levels
(c) persons (d) None of these

18 Teacher education involves ....
(a) input of learner
(b) process of learning
(c) output of learner
(d) All of the above

19 Triangular basis of teacher education involves which discipline?
(a) Cognate (b) Education
(c) Science (d) None of these

20 Cognate discipline in teacher education involves
(a) psychology (b) sociology
(c) philosophy (d) All of these

21 Sociological basis helps the student to understand the role of
(a) person (b) psychology
(c) society (d) philosophy

22 Which apex educational body emphasized on an Integrated Model for Teacher Education?
(a) NCTE (b) NCERT
(c) AICTE (d) UGC

23 Pre-service teaching starts.........the teaching job.
(a) during (b) after
(c) simultaneously (d) before

24 An inclusive education may involve
(a) school visit
(b) classroom observation
(c) practical assignment
(d) All of the above

25 Professional competencies include
(a) finding out ways to compete with peer groups
(b) being punctual and setting examples
(c) employing interactive learning strategies.
(d) All of the above

26 Student in pre-service training develops
(a) only teaching based knowledge
(b) positive attitude and aesthetic interest
(c) subject based knowledge
(d) None of the above

27 Short-term training courses are meant for
(a) pre-service teacher (b) in-service teacher
(c) Both a and b (d) an administration

28 In-service teacher education is for
(a) new teacher (b) teacher in service
(c) retired teacher (d) student-teacher

29 Why distance education is a win-win situation?
(a) Flexiblity of time and place
(b) Less syllabus
(c) Unavailiblity of teacher
(d) Variety of courses to choose from

30 Distance learning is supported by
(a) DVD's (b) Podcast's
(c) Online lectures (d) All of these

31 The first National Policy of Education was drafted in
(a) 1978 (b) 1958
(c) 1988 (d) 1968

32 When did NCTE became a statutory council?
(a) 1994 (b) 1993
(c) 1995 (d) 1996

33 Teacher education must engage with theory, along with ....
(a) field experiences
(b) demonstration
(c) training
(d) None of the above

34 Teacher education should engage teachers with the curriculum, ... and .... to critically examine them.
(a) syllabi, textbook
(b) online lecture, textbook
(c) counselling, syllabi
(d) All of the above

35 How the teachers need to be trained?
(a) By activity-based learning
(b) By participatory learning
(c) By discussion
(d) All of the above

36 Aim of NCTE is to check
(a) process and procedure of Indian Education System
(b) background of students, being enrolled
(c) infrastructure of institutes
(d) None of the above

37 Functions of NCTE includes
(a) coordinate and monitor teacher's education.
(b) putting up guidelines for various happening related to teacher's education.
(c) Both a and b
(d) None of the above

38 What is the duration of B.Ed Programme?
(a) 4 Years (b) 5 Years
(c) 2 years (d) 3 years

39 How many working days are there, per year in B.Ed Programme?
(a) 200 (b) 250
(c) 290 (d) 270

40 B.Ed Programme provides sustained engagement with
(a) self (b) child
(c) community (d) All of these

41 20-30% of marks must be assigned to
(a) practical paper (b) theoretical paper
(c) internal assessment (d) external evaluation

42 An elementary school teacher
(a) must know major psychological principles
(b) must have theoretical and practical knowledge of child's health
(c) must possess the knowledge of first and second language
(d) All of the above

43 Pre-Primary Teacher Training is also called
(a) Training for Nursery
(b) Junior Teacher Training
(c) Prepatory Training
(d) Nursery Teacher Training

44 Junior Basic Training is a
(a) degree course (b) diploma
(c) certificate course (d) post graduate course

45 Which language courses are preferred in India?
(a) Hindi (b) Punjabi
(c) Sanskrit (d) Foreign

46 Secondary teacher imparts knowledge to
(a) primary classes
(b) middle or higher secondary classes
(c) colleges
(d) pre-primary classes

47 **In Transactional Approach, knowledge is based on**
(a) past experience of student
(b) past experience of teacher
(c) lesson plan
(d) extra-curricular activities

48 **In Expository Method, who guides the lesson ?**
(a) Student (b) Facilitator
(c) Teacher (d) None of these

49 **Which of the following are tools of exposition ?**
(a) Illustration
(b) Diagrams
(c) Demonstration
(d) All of the above

50 **In collaborative learning, the student learns**
(a) in groups (b) from teachers
(c) alone (d) from family

51 **"Knowledge results from the combination of grasping experience and transforming it", was said by**
(a) Kolt (b) Koll
(c) Kolb (d) Kolk

52 **In experiential learning cycle, when does the learner puts an idea into use?**
(a) Concrete experience
(b) Reflective observation
(c) Abstract conceptualisation
(d) Active experimentation

53 **Functions of NCERT includes**
1. monitoring of regional college of education
2. dictating lesson plan to the teacher
3. developing curriculum
4. carrying out research in all branches of education
Codes
(a) 3 and 4 (b) 1 and 2
(c) 1, 3 and 4 (d) Only 2

54 **Match the following**

List I	List II
A. NCTE	1. Conducted in a group
B. Experiential learning	2. Checks standard, procedure and process of an Indian education
C. Expository Method	3. Learning facilitated by experience
D. Calloboratory learning	4. Teacher leads the lesson

Codes

	A	B	C	D
(a)	4	3	1	2
(b)	1	4	3	2
(c)	2	3	4	1
(d)	1	3	2	4

55 **Which of the following statement is not correct about collaborative learning?**
1. It promotes critical thinking skill.
2. It develops social interaction skills.
3. This concept was first explored by John Dewey and Jean Piaget.
4. It brings more achievements and greater productivity.
Codes
(a) 1 and 2 (b) 3 and 4
(c) Only 3 (d) Only 4

56 **Vision for the teacher after completing teacher education for higher secondary stage includes**
1. development of perspective for specific stream among the teacher.
2. learn and trying to mould the psychology of the student.
3. learn to work in other than teaching role.
4. develop patriotism and national consciousness among the learner.
(a) 1 and 4 (b) 2 and 3
(c) 1 and 2 (d) 3 and 4

57 **Match the following**

List I	List II
A. Concrete experience	1. Learner decides what can be done differently.
B. Reflective observation	2. Learner already poses the experience.
C. Abstract conceptualisation	3. Learner ponder over the experience.
D. Active experimentation	4. an application of an idea

Codes

	A	B	C	D		A	B	C	D
(a)	2	3	1	4	(b)	1	3	2	4
(c)	2	1	3	4	(d)	4	3	2	1

58 **Scope of education can be understood by which of the following ways?**
1. Teacher education at different levels of education
2. An aspects of teacher education
3. Triangular basis of teacher education
Codes
(a) 1 and 2 (b) 3 and 1
(c) 2 and 3 (d) 1, 2 and 3

59 **Choose the incorrect pairing.**
(a) Simulation : Artificial world
(b) Field trip : Outside the classroom
(c) Story telling : Computer knowledge
(d) Role playing : Character in pre-defined situation

60 Choose the correct option.
Aspect of teacher education includes

1. teacher education
2. student teacher
3. teaching strategy
4. administration

Codes
(a) 1, 2, 3 and 4
(b) 1, 2, and 3
(c) 1 and 2
(d) 2 and 4

Directions (Q. Nos. 61- 65) *Given below are two statements, one labelled as Assertion (A) and the other labelled as Reason (R). Following are the codes given below. Choose the correct option.*

Codes
(a) Both A and R are true
(b) Both A and R are false
(c) A is true but R is false
(d) A is false but R is true

61 **Assertion** (A) Distance learning is for student who wish to stay in hostel and complete their study.
Reasoning (R) Distance learning is time and place flexible.

62 **Assertion** (A) Teacher education consists of teaching skills, Pedagogical Theory and professional skills.
Reason (R) Teacher education is about how a student teacher perform as learner.

63 **Assertion** (A) In Expository method, the teacher guides the lesson.
Reason (R) Expository method is used used when past knowledge of learner is lacking.

64 **Assertion** (A) Teacher education at secondary stage consists of teaching specialised subjects.
Reason (R) Teacher at this level develops under standing, skill, interest and attitude to help the child grow.

65 **Assertion** (A) Pedagogical skill is not required by the teacher.
Reason (R) Teacher has nothing to do with child's psychological development.

PREVIOUS YEARS' QUESTIONS

July 2018

1 Which of the following statement is relevant for describing teaching as profession?

1. Teaching profession has an organised body of knowledge
2. Teaching profession implies a set of attitudes.
3. Duration of Teacher Training Programme is not a professional pre-requisite.
4. Teaching profession has its own code of moral ethics.

Codes
(a) 2, 3, 4
(b) 1, 3, 4
(c) 1, 2, 4
(d) 1, 2, 3

2 Which one of the following combination gives a correct reason for including philosophy of education in teacher education curriculum?

1. Philosophy is an oldest discipline.
2. Philosophy helps in understanding educational concepts in a holistic way.
3. Philosophy and education are the two sides of the same coin.
4. Philosophy helps in developing a better personality of prospective teachers.
5. Philosphical Analysis of educational concepts helps in developing a rational view-point.

Codes
(a) 1, 2, 3 and 4
(b) 2, 3 and 3
(c) 2, 3, 4 and 5
(d) 1, 2, 3 and 4

November 2017

3 Practicum in teacher education courses should be implemented with the focus on
(a) theory courses
(b) social problems
(c) value orientation
(d) professional competencies

4 Which of the following step(s) have been taken by NCTE for the systematic improvement in teacher education?

1. Rationalisation in the demand and supply situation in the country.
2. Curriculum of teacher education at various levels has been updated.
3. Enhancement of academic support in the form of various resources.
4. Periodic monitoring of teacher education.
5. Emphasis on reflective practices.

Codes
(a) 1, 2, 4 5
(b) 2, 3, 5, 1
(c) 4, 5, 3, 4
(d) 3, 1, 2, 5

5 An effective programme of teacher education aims at developing teacher proficiency and competence that will consequently empower the teacher with which of the following?

1. Skill in designing the teaching-learning situations.
2. Eagerness for upgradation of knowledge.
3. Ability to minimise the wastage of resources.

4. Understanding of inter-personal relations in a class.
5. Competencies in making quality decisions about managing, monitoring and evaluating learning behaviours.

Codes

(a) 2, 3, 4, 1 (b) 3, 4, 2, 1 (c) 1, 2, 4, 5 (d) 4, 5, 3, 1

January 2017

6 Orientation and refresher courses are the devices for competency building in

(a) pre-service teacher education
(b) in-service teacher education
(c) distance education programmes for teachers
(d) faculty improvement programme for teacher education

7 Which of the following statement(s) describe(s) the current problems of teacher education?

1. Launching of integrated programmes without adequate preparation on the part of sponsers.
2. Apathy and competency level of teacher educators.
3. Enhanced duration of courses without attention on time intensive transactional strategies.
4. Inadequate or no dialogue between teacher's education institutions and the practising schools.
5. Internship programmes as an integral part of teacher's education courses.
6. No space for faculty improvement programme for teacher educators.

Codes

(a) 1, 4, 3, 5 and 6 (b) 4, 3, 2, 5 and 6
(c) 1, 4, 3, 2 and 6 (d) 1, 2, 3, 4 and 5

8 Match the following.

List I (Levels of Teacher Education)	List II (Objectives)
A. Pre-Primary level	1. Updating, advancing content knowledge and providing orientation in teaching, evaluating, and curriculum design.
B. Primary level	2. Sharpening and enhancing professional competencies and content mastery.
C. Secondary level	3. Developing proactive, open, amiable disposition and excellent emotional management skills.
D. College level	4. Promoting competencies for addressing diverse learner's needs, a sense of national identity and regard for environment.

Codes

	A	B	C	D		A	B	C	D
(a)	1	2	3	4	(b)	2	3	4	1
(c)	3	4	2	1	(d)	1	4	3	2

July 2016

9 Match the following

List I (Types of Teacher Education Programmes)	List II (Functions)
A. In-Service Teacher Education	1. To sharpen and deepen the subject knowledge
B. Pre-Service Teacher Education	2. To being refinement upgradation in teaching skills
C. Distance education	3. To prepare teachers in terms of the requirements of demand-supply analysis
D. Refresher courses	4. To help the disadvantaged society
	5. To meet the large scale shortage of teachers in rural areas
	6. To prepare teacher with an eye on the shortage of teachers in the for flung areas

Codes

	A	B	C	D
(a)	1	3	6	2
(b)	2	1	5	6
(c)	1	5	4	3
(d)	2	3	4	5

10 Which of the following statement(s) reflects the concerns of National Curriculum Framework (NCF), 2005?

1. A commitment to democracy and values of equality, justice, freedom, secularism and respect for human dignity and rights.
2. Burdening children with information resulting from an erroneous ratio of knowledge.
3. A capacity to learn and willingness to unlearn and relearn as means of responding to new situations in a flexible and creative manner.
4. Appreciation of beauty and art, being an integral part of human life.

Codes

(a) 1, 2, 4 (b) 2, 3, 4
(c) 1, 2, 3 (d) 2, 4, 3

December 2015

11 Which of the following statement(s) is/are related to teacher as a formal authority?

(a) Teacher is a member of the community also
(b) Teachers and students may, in various ways be bound together within the process of socialization
(c) Teacher is an agent not only of instructions but of control and evaluation
(d) Teacher has certain rights and and duties which flow from his/her position in the larger system

12 Which of the following is/are related to pre-service teacher education?
(a) Revision of school education syllabus by State Institute of Education/SCERT
(b) Orientation and refresher courses
(c) Proper screening of teaching aspirants through teaching aptitude tests
(d) Crash course for mathematics teachers

13 Implementation of curriculum of teacher education is the direct responsibility of
(a) NCERT
(b) UGC
(c) NCTE
(d) Teacher Education Institutions

June 2015

14 India has taken a move to ensure that there would be no untrained teacher at elementary school level by the end of August, 2015. This is in the wake of
(a) Verdict of Supreme Court
(b) Right to Education Act (2009)
(c) Rule made by NCTE
(d) Recommendation of NPE (1986)

December 2014

15 The purpose of estabilishing NCTE is to
(a) universalisation of Education
(b) improve the quality of teacher's education
(c) empower teachers in India
(d) encourage educational research

16 Faculty Improvement Programme is meant for
(a) Primary school teachers
(b) Pre-primary teachers
(c) Secondary school teachers
(d) College and university teachers

June 2014

17 Accreditation of Teacher Education Institutions is done by
(a) NCERT (b) NCTE
(c) NAAC (d) NUEPA

18 Integrated Teacher Education Programmes are offered by
(a) Self-Financing Colleges of Education
(b) Open Universities of India
(c) State Institutes of Education
(d) Regional Institutes of Education

19 The most important factor of success for a teacher in the beginning of teaching career is
(a) personality and ability to adjust to classroom
(b) positive attitude and outlook towards life
(c) verbal fluency and organizational ability
(d) competence and professional ethics

ANSWERS

Exam Based Questions

1 (b)	2 (b)	3 (c)	4 (a)	5 (d)	6 (d)	7 (b)	8 (c)	9 (c)	10 (c)
11 (d)	12 (c)	13 (a)	14 (d)	15 (b)	16 (d)	17 (b)	18 (d)	19 (a)	20 (d)
21 (c)	22 (b)	23 (d)	24 (d)	25 (c)	26 (b)	27 (b)	28 (b)	29 (a)	30 (d)
31 (d)	32 (b)	33 (a)	34 (a)	35 (d)	36 (a)	37 (c)	38 (c)	39 (a)	40 (d)
41 (c)	42 (d)	43 (d)	44 (b)	45 (d)	46 (b)	47 (b)	48 (c)	49 (d)	50 (a)
51 (c)	52 (d)	53 (c)	54 (c)	55 (c)	56 (a)	57 (a)	58 (d)	59 (c)	60 (b)
61 (d)	62 (c)	63 (a)	64 (a)	65 (b)					

Previous Years' Questions

1 (c)	2 (b)	3 (d)	4 (b)	5 (c)	6 (b)	7 (c)	8 (c)	9 (a)	10 (a)
11 (c)	12 (c)	13 (d)	14 (b)	15 (b)	16 (d)	17 (c)	18 (d)	19 (a)	

CHAPTER

14

Models of Teacher Education

Models of teacher education deal with the ways in which learning environment and instructional environment can be constructed, sequenced and delivered. The Behaviouristic, Competency Based and Inquiry Oriented Models of Teacher Education are discussed for better understanding.

Teacher Knowledge

Every profession has a body of knowledge that set it apart from others and makes people who master such skills considered suitable professionals to exercise the profession. Interestingly, for the profession that educates all other, the teachers, there is no consensus about the body of knowledge necessary to be a teacher, even about its existence. Common sense is that a teacher just knows some specific content. Consequently, the widespread idea that other skills are not needed beyond the specific content to be a teacher. This situation makes the teacher profession often a temporary one and shows inconsistency between the social and economic depreciation of the profession with the responsibility and training required. Although, knowledge of the specific content is the primary task of being a teacher, your domain is only part of the story, since specific skills for teaching are long recognised as necessary.

Conceptualising teacher knowledge is a complex issue that involves understanding key underlying phenomena such as the process of teaching and learning, the concept of knowledge, as well as the way teacher's knowledge is put into action in the classroom. The conceptualisation of knowledge base was restricted to the attainment of the basic skills required for teaching, the competency of educators in their subject matter area, and the use of pedagogical strategies. However, there are other variables that are critical in teaching, *i.e.* the classroom context, the physical and psychological characteristics of the learners, the personal and practical experiences of teachers, their reflective practices and research skills.

An effective teacher needs to master at least two types of basic knowledge, *i.e.* content knowledge and pedagogical knowledge. The former refers to the knowledge that a teacher should possess in the subject itself, while the latter refers to the teaching and learning of subjects and their curriculum.

In this Chapter

- *Teacher Knowledge*
- *Knowledge Base of Teacher Education*
- *Reflective Teaching*
- *Models of Teacher Education*

Knowledge Base of Teacher Education

A knowledge base is a technology used to store complex information, by the use of computer system. Generally, it is a centralised database, more like a public library.

In teacher education, it is linked to profession, related to insight, relevant for teaching profession. This knowledge is required for teacher's activities. Thus, it is said that teacher's practical knowledge should be added to knowledge base, along with formal knowledge. Teacher knowledge may be different, due to their different life experiences. But some elements are shared by all. Thus, teacher's knowledge can be used to make educational innovation and improve teacher's education.

Let us discuss about the knowledge base of teacher education from the viewpoint of Schulman, Habermas and Deng and Luke.

Schulman

Lee S Schulman is an American Educational Psychologist. He has made notable contributions to the study of teaching, assessment of teaching, and the fields of medicine, science and mathematics. He is credited with popularising the phrase 'pedagogical content knowledge' that includes pedagogical knowledge and 'content knowledge'. He had a long and deep association with professional education. With collaboration from **Arthur Elstein**, a colleague in medical school, he conducted a study of medical decision-making. Here, he studied the thinking of medical diagnosticians as they performed clinical diagnostics.

In 1986, **Schulman and Sykes** defined the knowledge base for teaching as "The body of understanding and skills, device and values, character and performance, that together constitutes the ability to teach".

They listed eight categories involving this base and they are

- General liberal education, including basic skills for reading, math, writing and reasoning.
- Content knowledge in the domains in which teaching will occur
- Content-specific pedagogical knowledge.
- General knowledge of pedagogical principles and practices.
- Curriculum knowledge.
- Understanding of student diversity and individual differences.
- Performance skills.
- Foundation of professional understanding (including history and policy, philosophy and psychology, cultural and cross-cultural factors and professional ethics).

In the same year, **Schulman** (1986) also proposed three categories of content knowledge for teachers, saying that "The content has different facts to the teacher who has to consider content knowledge itself, the pedagogical content knowledge and curricular knowledge". And so the Pedagogical Content Knowledge (PCK) expression was launched by Schulman and apparently came to mean a special kind of knowledge of teachers who had not previously served by any name.

According to **Schulman** (1986), "Content knowledge includes knowledge of concepts, theories, ideas, proofs and evidences as well as practices and approaches to develop this knowledge. While, the pedagogical knowledge includes the educational purposes, the methods of teaching and learning, that is knowledge about techniques or methods used in the classroom, the nature of the target audience and strategies for assessing student's knowledge". In general, pedagogical knowledge encompasses educational purposes and values and in addition, requires a Cognitive, Social and Developmental Theory of Learning and how they apply within the classroom.

Ideology/Knowledge Base According to Schulman

Schulman (1987) outlines the categories of teacher knowledge to promote understanding among its students. *He considers seven types of basic knowledge that a teacher must have and they are*

- Content knowledge
- General pedagogical knowledge
- Curricular knowledge
- Pedagogical Content Knowledge (PCK)
- Knowledge of learners and their characteristics
- Knowledge of educational contexts
- Knowledge of purpose, educational purpose and educational values and their philosophical and historical base.

Pedagogical Content Knowledge (PCK)

Schulman (1987) says that the PCK is that special amalgam of content and pedagogy that is uniquely the province of teacher, their own special form of professional understanding.

Pedagogical Knowledge General knowledge about pedagogy is known as pedagogical knowledge. This includes Teaching Approach, how student learn, methods of assessment and knowledge of different theories about learning.

Content Knowledge It is about the knowledge of the subject matter, without consideration about teaching the subject matter.

Pedagogical Content Knowledge (PCK) It is a combination of both content and pedagogical knowledge. It is understanding, what makes learning of some topics easy or difficult on the basis of students' age and background. He had special interest in PCK as it involves different bodies of knowledge for teaching. It tries to understand how particular topic, problem or issue are organised and adopted to the diverse interest and ability of learner and presented for instruction.

According to Schulman, PCK is

- the most regularly taught topic in one's subject area.
- the most useful form of representation of ideas.
- the most powerful analogies, illustration examples, explanations and demonstrations.
- the way of representing and formulating the subjects, that makes it comprehensible to others.

Deng And Luke

Zongyi Deng is an associate professor at National Institute of Education, Nanyang Technological University, **Singapore**. He is also an editor of Journal of Curriculum Studies. He has interest in curriculum content or subject matter, Curriculum Theory, didactics, comparitive and international education and Chinese education.

Allan Luke is an educator, author, activist, international researcher and policy change agent in all Australian states and New Zealand, Singapore and Hongkong. He has written or edited over 15 books and more than 200 articles and book's chapters.

Deng and **Luke** (2008) proposed three conceptions of knowledge based on their examination of several disciplinary and epistemological knowledge classification schemes.

They are :

- The **disciplinary conception of knowledge**, describes canonical knowledge in the established disciplines.
- The **practical conception of knowledge**, represented by procedural knowledge, derives from the wisdom of practice.
- The form of knowledge is the **experiential conception of knowledge** based on Dewey's (1916) notion, that knowledge is located in and based on human experience.

While, there are other ways of knowing, for example, scientific or aesthetic ways of knowing. These three different ways of knowing, provides a useful interpretive framework to conceptualise secondary school teacher's sources of knowledge. Deng and Luke's (2008) conceptions of knowledge and what it means for teachers 'to know' something raises broader questions of the purpose of this knowledge and what kind of knowledge is important in terms of student's engagement.

Habermas

Jurgen Habermas is a German Philosopher and Sociologist in the tradition of Critical theory and pragmatism. He works for whole society, not only for one aspect of it. His work is used internationally in philosophy, political science, sociology and education.

He has theorised history, in a way that it may resonate with teachers. Though, not referred much, Habermas's work is still use in pre-service training.

Habermas (1971) studied the nature of knowledge that human beings adopts or generates (*i.e.* knowledge is constitutive interests of human beings) and the use of reflection, as one of the process that human beings adopt in the generation of particular form of knowledge.

The knowledge constitutive interests are of three types, *i.e.* technical/instrumental knowledge constitutive interest, knowledge constitutive interests in hermeneutic disciplines, and emancipatory knowledge constitutive interests. In social science, both Interpretive Process of Enquiry (which is the basic method) and Critical/ Evaluative Process of Enquiry (which provides critique so necessary for self-understanding and critique of the process) are adopted for knowledge generation and interpretation.

The evaluative enquiry is equated to reflection, and the Critical Theory of Social Science uses questioning and understanding to serve the emancipatory interest. While, reflection may not play any role in physical science, it is important in case of Interpretive Enquiry of Social Science and for emancipatory interests and reflection should be used, both at stages of interpretive enquiry and empowerment and emancipation. While applying to the context of teaching.

Van Manen (1991) *suggests the applications of reflection at four levels, and they are*

- Day-to-day application in thinking and acting.
- Reflecting on specific events or incidents.
- Reflection on personal experiences and experiences of others and developing understanding through interpretation (*i.e.* Interpretive Enquiry of Habermas).
- Reflecting on reflection, *i.e.* understanding the nature of knowledge and possible emancipation (*i.e.* Emancipatory Interests of Habermas).

Ideology/Knowledge Base According to Habermas

Habermas *classifies three forms of knowledge as*

Technical Knowledge It refers to those form of knowledge, related to manipulation of the environment, controlling the natural object and event.

Practical Knowledge It concerns with 'hermeneutic' task of extending understanding in inter-subject relation. By this, we achieve consensus, community and mutuality.

Emancipatory Knowledge It is more about abstract level. It involves liberating people from their socio-historic constraints. This is achieved through self-reflection.

Technical knowledge and practical knowledge are primary. While emancipatory knowledge is derivatory, in the sense it is dependent upon some actions like exploitation, distorted communication and so on.

Reflective Teaching

Reflective teaching is a process where teachers thinks over their teaching practices, analysing how something was taught and how the practice might be improved or changed for better learning outcomes.

It is a process of self-observation and self-evaluation. It involves examining oneself in the class, thinking of what he/she does and if it works or not. By collecting what goes in the classroom and by evaluating it, the teacher identifies and explores our own practices and underlying beliefs.

It is a personal tool. The teacher can utilise this tool to observe and evaluate the way they behave in the classroom. It can be both private or something that can be discussed with colleagues. In the process of reflective teaching, not only the teacher figures out what works and what didn't, but they also build self-awareness that is a good tool for a teacher.

Definitions of Reflective Teaching

According to **Richards** "Reflective teaching is a move beyond the ordinary to a higher level of awareness of how teaching takes place".

According to **Bailey**, "Reflective teaching is about a skilled teaching of knowing what to do".

According to **Tyce**, "Reflective teaching means looking at what one does in the classroom, thinking about way one does it and thinking about if it works a process of self- observation and self-evaluation".

According to **Lockhant**, "A reflective approach to teaching is one in which teachers and students teachers collect data about teaching, examine their attitude, belief, assumptions and teaching practices and use the information obtained as a basis for critical reflection about teaching".

Importance of Reflective Teaching

- The teacher collects a variety of different aspects of their lessons. They know how to present the lesson to his/her student. This includes methods, like organisation of lesson, teacher's time management, student's performance on task, teacher's questions and student's answers, classroom interaction, etc.
- It implies a systematic method of collecting, recording and analysing the thoughts and observations. The teacher does not jump into conclusion, by considering the response of louder student, instead analyse the overall class.
- It helps to evaluate and improve the quality of teaching.
- It gives freedom to teachers to impose their own methodology enhancing rational thinking.
- It develops critical thinking and promotes experiential learning.
- Reflective teaching practice can be a beneficial form of professional development of both the pre-service and in-service levels of teaching.

Approaches of Reflective Teaching

The approaches of reflective teaching are as follows

External Assessment

(i) **Peer Observation** It allows the teacher to know each other's teaching style. They can gain some insights from it and gets an opportunity to reflect on own's teaching.

Peer observation can be carried out by

- Participants observing each others classes.
- Pre-determination of what will be taught and how it will be taught.

- Observer will observe the class, on the basis of set parameters.
- After the observation is over, the teacher will meet and discuss the result.

(ii) **Student Evaluation** Instructors can consider student evaluation as one data source in their instruction. They can seek out other ways to assess their practices to accompany student evaluation data before taking steps to modify the instruction.

Written Account of Experience

Written account can be a helpful way of engaging in reflective teaching.

Different kinds of written account can be

(i) **Self-reporting** It involves completing a checklist in which the teacher indicates, which technique was used for given lesson. Self-reporting is a way to note down regularly the where abouts of the classroom.

(ii) **Journal Writing** It is a very famous way to reflect on the lesson plans. It is an important cause for the teacher that can track his/her self-development process. Teacher can record his/her experience in a personal and dynamic way.

(iii) **Recording Lesson** Recording audio or video can be a useful tool in reflective teaching. Diaries and self-reporting may be a good way but some things may not be noticed by the teacher's mind and be forgotten. Thus, diary and reporting should be complemented by recording.

Self-Assessment

This approach mainly consists of

(i) **Teaching Inventories** A number of inventories have been developed to help instructors to assess their teaching approaches. Inventories are usually designed to assess the extent to which particular pedagogies are employed.

(ii) **Teaching Portfolio** It allows instructors to pull the various components of their teaching into a cohesive whole. The portfolio does not capture classroom practices very well, but provides an opportunity from instructors to see their teaching in a big framework.

Strategies for Promoting Reflective Teaching

The **first** step towards the process of reflection is to gather information about what happens in the class followed by analysis of the data. *Some of the strategies used by the teachers are :*

Reflective Journal This is the easiest way to begin a process of refection since it is purely personal. Student teachers encounter many issues in classroom settings. They can describe about their own reactions and feelings and these things which happened during each session.

Collaborative Learning Brook field maintains the importance of continual dialogue with peers about teaching in the mutually cooperative environment rather than a competitive one. Collaboration with peer members increases the probability that students teachers will be successfully reflective and more confident in their professional development.

Recording Lessons Video or audio recordings of lessons can provide very useful information for reflection. A classroom video can vividly picture the whole process of teaching. It can trigger teachers reflective thinking, reflect on their weaknesses and help them get some inspiration and ideas for their teaching improvement.

Teacher Education Feedback The feedback from the teacher educator can help the student teacher to reflect upon their lesson or any activity conducted in the institution.

Peer Observation Observation is the most basic research technique that student teachers employ in classrooms. The student teacher invites a peer member to observe his/her class to collect information about the lesson.

This may be with simple observation task or through note taking. The observer should not be involved in evaluating a student teacher's lesson. Therefore, observation is a good way for their professional development.

Student Feedback The student teacher can ask their students about what goes on in the classroom. Their opinions and perceptions can add a different and valuable perspective. This can be done with simple questionnaires.

Action Research It is also a kind of reflective practice. It is a reflective process of progressive problem-solving led by teachers to understand their practice and improve the way they address issues and solve problems. It helps student teachers to become aware of what's happening in the classroom by identifying common problems and hypothesising about possible causes and solutions and attempting to apply an action plan.

Advantages of Reflective Teaching

- It develops the quality of education through continuous improvement.
- It helps the teacher to reflect and assess their own teaching.
- It enables teachers to bring in new ideas, methods, approaches and materials.
- It gives an opportunity to assess how effective new approaches are.

Disadvantages of Reflective Teaching

- It may not be adequate to resolve educational problems through reflective practice.
- It is not suitable for small children at the lower level of teaching.
- It could be time consuming process.
- At this level, the study material is neither organised nor pre-planned. Therefore, students cannot acquire systematic and organised knowledge of their study courses.

Models of Teacher Education

Models of teacher education deals with the ways in which learning environment and instructional environment can be constructed, sequenced and delivered. There are literally, hundreds of models of teaching and learning, so that the teachers don't have to worry about which new model to follow.

Model of teacher education helps the teacher to

- grow highly tuned and more varied professional stock.
- reach large number of students effectively.
- create uniform or varied instructional event, guided by target subject content or process.
- understands the focus of curriculum better.
- gains insight, on why all the models don't work with all the students.
- modify existing methods of teaching and instructional delivery, so that they can meet the needs of today's students.

Behaviouristic Model

Behaviour is reaction and movement that an organism does in a given situation. It normally consists of what appears on the outside. Behaviourists claim that learning can be conducted by noticing the behaviour to a particular stimuli. Also, the behaviour can be changed by reinforcement.

Behaviourists believe that people are not good or bad from birth. Experience and environment changes the person. A human brain is compared to **black box**. One doesn't need to know, what is inside of it. Only thing that matters is what goes in the black box (input) and what comes out of it (output). Output is objective, observable and measurable. Inputs and outputs can be arranged, adjusted and controlled.

Basic Concept of Behaviouristic Model

According to behaviouristic model, conditioning is the base of all human behaviour. It is against the concept that says mental process are under mind and conscious.

The basic concepts of behaviourist approach are

Conditioning

Behaviouristic approach says that learning takes place through conditioning. Conditioning occurs in a way that organism matches certain stimuli with certain reaction.

When a reaction is obtained from certain stimuli, the organism is said to be condition.

Conditioning can be of two types

(i) **Classical Conditioning** It says that neutral stimulus is matched with unconditioned reaction.

(ii) **Operant Conditioning** It is a learning process through which the strength of a behaviour is modified by reinforcement or punishment.

Organism

Behaviourists used more general term, **'organism'** instead of **'human'** or **'individual'**. The term **'organism'** signifies both **people and animal**.

Reaction

Behavourist's psychologists are also called **S-R theorist**. In this theory, reaction is a behaviour by an organism against a stimulus.

Stimulus

It is composed of change in the internal and external states that moves the organism. Behaviouristic Approach mainly deals with external changes of state rather than internal changes.

Reinforcement and Punishment

Reinforcement constitutes of increasing the possiblity of an organism to display behaviour to a certain stimulus. The stimulus in this process is called **reinforcer**.

The response to an organism's behaviour can be of three kinds :

- Reinforcement
- Punishment
- Not reinforcing

While **reinforcement**, increases the possibility of behaviour displayed once more, **punishment** results in chances of not displaying the behaviour. **Not reinforcing** means, not giving any response and decrease in chances of behaviour being repeated.

Scholar's View Point about Behaviouristic Model

Ivan Pavlov

Ivan Pavlov was a nobel prize winner and a Russian scientist. In 1927, he conducted a famous experiment with dogs. Pavlov, taught the dogs to salivate when they heard bell, a signal of their feeding time. Later, he did not feed them but still rang the bell. But, the dogs still salivated. Thus, learned behaviour was a result of event experienced, rather than conscious thought process. This is termed as classical conditioning.

It can be helpful for behaviours of man and animal alike. So, it can be used to shape the behaviour of children as well.

John B Watson

Behaviourism is closely related to Pavlov's experiment but it was Watson, who established Behaviourism in 1913 with his article. He is best known for taking his theory of behaviourism and applying it to child's development. He strongly believed that child's environment contributes more than genetic makeup in forming the child's behaviour. He believed that one can expose the child to certain environmental forces and over time the child is conditioned to become any kind of person.

BF Skinner

Skinner's primary contribution in Behavioural Philosophy is operant conditioning and reinforcement schedules. An operant is a behaviour that acts on the surrounding environment to produce a consequence. The operant is said to be reinforced, if the consequence increases the probability of behaviour's occurrence.

He believed the goal psychology should be able to find ways to make education enjoyable. His Learning Theory is based on an assumption that best way to modify behaviour is to modify environment. He is pioneer in suggesting the use of modern days method of teaching. This includes scaffold instruction, small units repetition and review of instruction and immediate feedback.

Skinner did not advocate for punishment, he found punishment to be futile. He believed in frequent use of reinforcement to modify and influence student's behaviour.

Competency Based Model

Competency Based model is an approach to education that focuses on the student's demonstration of desired learning outcome as central to the learning process of teacher education.

It is concerned with student's progression through curriculum at their own pace, depth, etc. There is no course or module, every individual has own skill or learning outcome which is known as competency.

Learner works on one competency, which is like a small component of large learning goal. Students are evaluated on individual's competency and can move to other competency, only if they have mastered the previous competency.

Characteristics of Competency Based Model

- An important characteristic of competency based learning is its focus on mastery. In other learning method, students are exposed to content overtime and success is measured summatively. In competency based learning, students are supposed to continue and demonstrate mastery in the choosen competency.
- Competency based programs tend to be reality oriented, the students spend a great deal of time in the school interacting with children and many of their competencies are evaluated in that setting.
- The flexibility of competency based program allows students a choice of goals and objectives within the framework of specified education goals. This increases their chances of becoming independent, self-directed and continuing learners.

Advantages of Competency Based Model

- Participants will achieve competencies required in the performance of their job.
- Participants get confident as they succeed in mastering specific competencies.
- Training time is used more effectively as the trainer is facillator of learning rather than just a provider of information.
- More time is spent with learners as opposed to presenting lectures.
- More time is devoted to evaluate each learner's ability to perform a specific skill.
- Providing framework for identifying learning options to meet organisational needs.

Disadvantages of Competency Based Model

- Teachers are mostly ill-equipped to implement Competency Based model, unless they themselves were a product of it.
- The leck of awareness about the need as well as the required know, how and about benchmarking of assessment was one of the main obstacles to effective implementation of Competency Based model.

Inquiry Oriented Model

Inquiry based learning is a form of learning that starts with posing questions, problems and scenario. Inquiry based learning is often assisted with facilitator, rather than a lecturer.

Richard Schuman is an originator of Inquiry Teaching Programme. He said that it is a natural way of learning, when the individual is left alone.

Characteristics of Inquiry Oriented Model

- It focuses on constructive ideas of teacher education knowledge, generally, built in a step-wise manner.
- In a group, the learning is much better. Teacher does not begin with a statement rather with a question.
- Giving question to tackle is an effective method of instruction in many areas. This helps the students to learn of its own with teacher's guidance.
- The topics, problems and methods are used to answer the problems that are determined by the student and not the teacher.

Phases of Inquiry Oriented Model

Phases of inquiry oriented model includes :

Interaction The first step in Inquiry Oriented model is interaction.

Different kinds of interaction are as follows :

(i) **Student to Material** Material is obtained through both formal and informal means.

(ii) **Student to Peer** Due to need of information and perspective, this interaction is choosen.

(iii) **Student to Expert** There is a need of experts within relevant fields at accessible levels.

(iv) **Student to Media** This allows the students to actively engage themselves with learning with the help of media.

Clarification Clarification of a subject that occurs by analysing data, identifying and clearing out misconceptions.

After reading, watching and interacting with media, this process is for the learners to clarify their thinking.

Thinking is both outward and inward. Thus, students can reflect both on their knowledge and can identify the best way to proceed further.

Questioning Questioning phase is the most important phase. Both student and teacher should trust the nature and the pattern of inquiry that is often repititive. Often, they move back and forth in phases to make any kind of progress. But, Inquiry Oriented Model is more about the process, tone and instincts of learning, rather than other academic forms.

Advantages of Inquiry Oriented Model

- Its emphasis is on the process of gathering and processing more information.
- The approach involves some degrees of freedom that leads to initiative and divergent thinking.
- A deep sense of responsibility is developed, when the learners are left to manage their own learning.
- The facts and concepts that learners develops themselves becomes a part of permanent memory.
- Experiencing success in this approach boosts up the confidence of learners.
- Participating in inquiry activities strengthens learner's intellectual capabilities.

Disadvantages of Inquiry Oriented Model

- This model requires total student engagement, but it could be challenging for those students who do not think quickly or suffering from learning disabilities.
- If teachers do not completely understand this concept at a deeper level then it creates a disconnect, which in turn leaves the students unprepared.
- This model will standardise and effectively limit the levels of achievement to those that have already been decided by the teacher.
- When teachers are unsure of how to manage this process, they may default to asking closed, content-specific questions and the rigour of authentic inquiry is lost.

EXAM BASED QUESTIONS

1 Knowledge constitutes of
(a) power and persistence (b) emotional intelligence
(c) experience and education (d) achievement

2 Knowledge base is a
(a) centralise database (b) well developed map
(c) hotspot of information (d) collection of database

3 Teacher's .... knowledge should be added with formal knowledge in knowledge base.
(a) theoretical (b) practical
(c) general (d) teaching

4 Which of the following is/are not in the Schulman's basic knowledge that a teacher must have?
(a) Content Knowledge
(b) Curricular Knowledge
(c) Administrative Knowledge
(d) Pedagogical Content Knowledge

5 What is the name of Schulman's colleague, who helped him in the study of medical decision-making?
(a) Arthur Elstein (b) Albert Elstein
(c) Arthur Einstein (d) Robert Elstein

6 What did Lee S Schulman studied on medical diagnosticians?
(a) Their preparation before diagnostic
(b) Their thinking as they performed
(c) Their procedure of diagnostic
(d) Their diagnosis

7 In which year, did Lee S Schulman identified different types of knowledge that a teacher should possess?
(a) 1997 (b) 1987 (c) 1957 (d) 1967

8 Schulman had a long association with
(a) personal development
(b) research
(c) finance
(d) professional education

9 PCK stands for
(a) Principle Content Knowledge
(b) Pedagogical Content Knowledge
(c) Pedagogical Creative Knowledge
(d) Principle Creative Knowledge

10 Which of the following was listed by Schulman and Sykes?
(a) Content specific pedagogical knowledge
(b) Curriculum knowledge
(c) Performance skill
(d) All of the above

11 What is/are the main component(s) of Schulman's view about education?
(a) Change in learning method
(b) Pedagogical content knowledge
(c) Curriculum oriented learning
(d) Past experience based learning

12 Content knowledge is
(a) teaching of subject matter
(b) preparing subject matter
(c) dissipating subject matter
(d) knowledge of subject matter

13 In PCK theory, learning is said to be affected by
(a) teacher's experience
(b) student's age and background
(c) use of teaching aids
(d) interest of student

14 Which is the most useful form of representation of ideas?
(a) PCK (b) PKS
(c) PDF (d) PKC

15 Zongyi Deng is a professor at
(a) School of Education, Singapore
(b) Technological University, Singapore
(c) Technological University, Indonesia
(d) School of Education, Indonesia

16 Allan Luke is an educator, author, activist, a researcher and a ......
(a) doctor (b) political leader
(c) policy change agent (d) educator

17 How many conceptions of knowledge did Deng and Luke proposed?
(a) four (b) two
(c) five (d) three

18 Disciplinary conception of knowledge describes
(a) canonical knowledge (b) biblical knowledge
(c) technical knowledge (d) IT knowledge

19 Knowledge in experiential conception of knowledge is based on
(a) Dewen's Notion (b) Dewey's Principle
(c) Dewen's Principle (d) Dewey's Notion

20 Jurgen Habermas is a German...
(a) Idealist and Philosopher
(b) Marxist
(c) Philosopher and Sociologist
(d) Sociologist

21 Which subject has Habermas theorised?
(a) History (b) Teacher Education
(c) Politics (d) Science

22 Manipulation of environment is a part of which form of knowledge?
(a) Practical (b) Technical
(c) Emancipatory (d) Theoretical

23 Practical knowledge concerns with understanding of
(a) self-reflection (b) philosophy in teaching
(c) teacher's training (d) inter-subject relation

24 Emancipatory knowledge is achieved through
(a) teacher-training (b) psycomotor re-framing
(c) self-reflection (d) philosophy

25 Technical and practical knowledge are primary and emancipatory knowledge is
(a) secondary (b) repititive (c) derivatory (d) evolved

26 Reflective teaching is a process involving examination of
(a) one's own self (b) student
(c) students in group (d) peer group

27 How does the teacher identifies and explores own's practices and underlying beliefs?
(a) Get feedback from the students.
(b) Asking questions from the students.
(c) Collecting happening of classroom and evaluating it.
(d) Discussing their plan with their colleague.

28 How do teachers evaluates the way, they behave in the classroom?
(a) Through observation (b) By self-awareness
(c) Evaluate themselves (d) All of these

29 Reflective teaching helps the teacher to figure out
(a) their capabilities
(b) how lesson went
(c) what works and what doesn't works
(d) All of the above

30 Lesson can be presented to students in which of the following ways?
(a) Teacher's questions and student's answers
(b) Student's performance on task
(c) Organisation of lesson
(d) All of the above

31 Reflective teaching consists of systematic collection, recording and analysing of
(a) thoughts and observations
(b) teaching habits
(c) student's behaviour
(d) All of the above

32 In peer observation, the teaching gets insight from
(a) student (b) fellow teacher
(c) principle (d) one-self

33 In peer observation, the teacher comes to know
(a) each other's teaching style
(b) gains insight
(c) reflects on own teaching
(d) All of the above

34 Peer observation is carried out by
(a) determining the lesson to be taught
(b) observer observing the class on the basis of set parameter
(c) Discussion of result, after observing
(d) All of the above

35 What are the different approaches of reflective teaching?
(a) Peer observation (b) Recording
(c) Writing (d) All of these

36 Written account consists of
(a) self-reporting and journal writing
(b) diary entry
(c) on the spot note-making
(d) drawing conclusion

37 Self-reporting involves completing
(a) notes (b) checklist
(c) conclusion (d) puzzles

38 Self-reporting is done
(a) monthly (b) weekly
(c) hourly (d) regularly

39 Journal writing is useful for
(a) reflecting on lesson plan
(b) tracking of self-development
(c) recording the experience
(d) All of the above

40 A lesson can be recorded through
(a) audio only (b) video only
(c) Both a and b (d) None of these

41 Advantage of reflective teaching includes
(a) development of quality of education
(b) reflection and assessment of own's work by teacher
(c) None of the above
(d) All of the above

42 Reflective teaching helps to bring new
(a) ideas (b) methods
(c) approaches (d) All of these

43 Strategies used by reflective teachers includes
(a) journalising and utilising self-assessment forms
(b) recording classroom work
(c) taking student's feedback
(d) All of the above

44 Group of teachers, keeping and sharing diary is known as
(a) contributive journal writing
(b) journal writing
(c) competitive journal writing
(d) collaborative journal writing

45 Different models of teaching, helps the teachers to
(a) reach a large number of students
(b) understand the focus of curriculum better
(c) modify existing method of teaching, so that it meets every student's need
(d) All of the above

46 What is behaviour?
(a) Physical appearance of an organism
(b) Reaction of an organism
(c) Social ability of an organism
(d) Preference of an organism

47 What can be conducted by noticing behaviour to particular stimuli?
(a) Study (b) Talking (c) Learning (d) Thinking

48 According to behaviourists, what changes a person?
(a) Friends and peers
(b) Conditioning by school
(c) Parents and siblings
(d) Experience and environment

49 Behaviourists compare the mind with a
(a) black box (b) black bird
(c) blind box (d) blind bird

50 What matters in Behaviourist theory?
(a) Inside of brain (b) Process
(c) Input and output (d) Teachers

51 According to Behavioristic theory, outputs are
(a) objective (b) observable
(c) measurable (d) All of these

52 What is the base of all human behaviour, according to Behaviouristic theory?
(a) Listening (b) Learning
(c) Talking (d) Conditioning

53 Conditioning occurs when
(a) certain reaction is repeated to specific stimuli
(b) certain stimuli is matched with certain reaction
(c) different related stimuli gives out same reaction
(d) All of the above

54 Behaviourists used which term to denote human or animals in general?
(a) Living-being (b) Organism
(c) Mankind (d) Animal kingdom

55 Behaviourist's psychologists are also called
(a) Behavioural theorists (b) R-S theorists
(c) S-R theorists (d) R-S psychologists

56 Response of organism behaviour can be
(a) punishment (b) reinforcement
(c) not reinforcing (d) All of these

57 Pavlov worked on
(a) Classical Conditioning
(b) Operant Conditioning
(c) Knowledge Based Behaviour
(d) Knowledge Based Conditioning

58 Who utilised behaviourism and applied it to child's development?
(a) Skinner (b) Pavlov (c) Watson (d) None of these

59 In which behaviour, the surrounding is acted upon?
(a) Classical conditioning (b) Close behaviour
(c) Open conditioning (d) Operant conditioning

60 Skinner believes goal of psychology should be to make education
(a) accessible (b) permissible
(c) enjoyable (d) strictable

61 Which learning model, focuses on progressing according to student's speed?
(a) Behaviouristic Model
(b) Competency Based Model
(c) Inquiry Oriented Model
(d) All of the above

62 Important characteristic of Competency Based model is
(a) focus (b) mastery
(c) coverage (d) precision

63 Disadvantage of CBT model includes
(a) CBT teachers may slip back into traditional mode of teaching.
(b) if the essential skills are not identified, the training course is likely to be ineffective.
(c) CBT is course material dependent.
(d) All of the above

64 Inquiry Oriented model starts with posing
(a) questions (b) expectations
(c) commands (d) inspection

65 Who was the originator of Inquiry Oriented Model?
(a) Richard Schul (b) Henry Schuman
(c) Richard Schuman (d) Henry Schull

66 Interaction in Inquiry Oriented model could be between
(a) student to peer
(b) student to expert of relevent field
(c) student to material
(d) All of the above

67 Clarification of subject in Inquiry Oriented model could be
(a) reflective (b) outward
(c) inward (d) Both b and c

68 Facts and concepts that learner develops in Inquiry Oriented Model become a part of
(a) common sense (b) permanent memory
(c) temporary memory (d) All of these

69 Match the following.

	List I	List II
A.	PCK	1. Pavlov
B.	Classical Conditioning	2. Skinner
C.	Enquiry Based Teacher Education	3. Lee Schulman
D.	Operant Conditioning	4. Richard Schulman

Codes

	A	B	C	D
(a)	1	2	3	4
(b)	4	3	2	1
(c)	3	1	4	2
(d)	4	3	1	2

70 What are the different models of teacher education?
1. Behaviouristic model
2. Collaborative model
3. Competency Based model
4. Inquiry Oriented model

Codes
(a) 1, 3 and 4 (b) 1, 2 and 3
(c) All of these (d) None of these

71 Pedagogical Content Knowledge is a combination of both content and pedagogical knowledge.
1. It is the most regularly taught topic in one's subject area.
2. It is to make the class to understand the curriculum.
3. It is the way of representing and formulating subject, that make it comprehensive to others.
4. Change the behaviour of student by conditioning.

Codes
(a) 1, 2 and 3 (b) 2 and 4
(c) 1 and 4 (d) 1 and 3

72 Match the following.

	List I		List II
A.	Habermas	1.	Australia
B.	Schulman	2.	Germany
C.	Deng	3.	America
D.	Luke	4.	Singapore

Codes

	A	B	C	D		A	B	C	D
(a)	2	3	4	1	(b)	4	2	3	1
(c)	3	1	2	4	(d)	1	3	4	2

73 Arrange the Scholar's Model, in accordance to occurance in history.
1. Skinner 2. Watson 3. Pavlov

Codes
(a) 2, 3, 1 (b) 3, 2, 1
(c) 1, 2, 3 (d) 1, 3, 2

74 Reflective teaching is significant because
1. it is a systematic way of collecting inputs from class.
2. it involves observation and self-evaluation.
3. it does not involves student's view point.
4. it is more about teacher than student.

Codes
(a) 3 and 4 (b) 2, 3 and 4
(c) 1 and 4 (d) 1 and 2

75 Find the correct pair.
(a) Schulman - Competency Based model
(b) Skinner - Operant conditioning
(c) Deng - PCK
(d) Watson - Reflective teaching

76 Phases of Inquiry Oriented model includes
1. Interaction 2. Clarification
3. Questioning

Codes
(a) Only 1 (b) 1, 2 and 3
(c) 1 and 2 (d) Only 3

77 According to Deng and Luke, conceptions of knowledge are
1. objective knowledge where the focus of the study is to prepare for lesson.
2. disciplinary conception of knowledge describes canonical knowledge in the established discipline.
3. psyhological knowledge impacting the student's knowledge.
4. practical knowledge is represented by procedural knowledge.

Codes
(a) 2 and 3 (b) 2 and 4 (c) 1, 3 and 4 (d) 1 and 2

78 Match the following.

	List I		List II
A.	Competency Based Model	1.	Judging the teacher by one's ownself.
B.	Behaviouristic Model	2.	Student's learning is dependent on themselves.
C.	Reflective Teaching	3.	Lesson starts with a question.
D.	Inquiry Oriented Model	4.	Conditioning is the base of all learning.

Codes

	A	B	C	D		A	B	C	D
(a)	1	3	4	2	(b)	3	1	2	4
(c)	4	3	1	2	(d)	2	4	1	3

79 Choose the correct statement(s).
1. Habermas work is still used in pre-service education.
2. Habermas is from Italy.
3. Habermas classified three forms of knowledge.
4. Habermas has Behaviouristic Approach.

Codes
(a) 2 and 3 (b) 1 and 3
(c) 1 and 4 (d) 2, 3 and 4

80 For a maximum reinforcement effect, a given reward should be
1. applied immediately upon the response
2. applied immediately proceeding the response
3. applied simultaneously with the response
4. follow the response only after substantial delay

Codes
(a) Only 1 (b) 4 and 1 (c) Only 4 (d) 2 and 3

81 Negative reinforcement means
(a) not presenting any stimulus
(b) presenting an unpleasant stimuli
(c) punishment
(d) terminating an unpleasant stimulus

Directions (Q. Nos. 82-87) *Given below are two statements, one labelled as Assertion (A) and the other labelled as Reason (R). Following are the codes given below. Choose the correct code.*

Codes
(a) Both A and R are true
(b) Both A and R are false
(c) A is true, but R is false
(d) A is false, but R is true

82 Assertion (A) Behaviourists believe that people are not good or bad from birth.
Reason (R) Experience and environment influence the person.

83 Assertion (A) Technical knowledge refers to those forms of knowledge that relates to manipulation of the environment.
Reason (R) Technical knowledge is derivatory.

84 Assertion (A) In Inquiry Oriented Model, the students enquires the teacher about the lesson.
Reason (R) The Inquiry Oriented Model starts with questioning.

85 Assertion (A) PCK is a combination of both content and pedagogical knowledge.
Reason (R) PCK involves conditioning of a child.

86 Assertion (A) Deng and Luke believes in Behaviouristic Model.
Reason (R) They conducted experiment in the field of behaviourism.

87 Assertion (A) Pleasure or displeasure, resulting from learning experiences, decides the degree of its effectiveness.
Reason (R) All pleasant experiences have a lasting influence and are remembered for a long time, while unpleasant one are soon forgotten.

PREVIOUS YEARS' QUESTIONS

January 2017

1 Which one of the following themes may be appropriate for areas of action research in the field of teacher education?
1. Improving teaching skills of student teacher.
2. Identifying suitable criteria for admissions.
3. Modification of teaching behaviour of trainees.
4. Revisiting teacher education curriculum.
5. Enhancing professional competencies of both trainees and teacher educators.
6. Preparing teachers for special schools.

Codes
(a) 1, 3 and 5 (b) 2, 4 and 6
(c) 1, 2 and 3 (d) 2, 3 and 4

June 2015

2 How is reflective level teaching different from understanding level teaching?
(a) On the basis of developing strong grip over facts of information
(b) In terms of raising the level critical understanding and interaction
(c) On the basis of command over the teaching-learning materials in their use
(d) In terms of teacher-learner involvement

ANSWERS

Exam Based Questions

1 (c)	2 (a)	3 (b)	4 (c)	5 (a)	6 (b)	7 (b)	8 (d)	9 (b)	10 (d)
11 (b)	12 (d)	13 (b)	14 (a)	15 (b)	16 (c)	17 (d)	18 (a)	19 (d)	20 (c)
21 (a)	22 (b)	23 (d)	24 (c)	25 (c)	26 (a)	27 (c)	28 (d)	29 (d)	30 (d)
31 (a)	32 (b)	33 (d)	34 (d)	35 (d)	36 (a)	37 (b)	38 (d)	39 (d)	40 (c)
41 (d)	42 (d)	43 (d)	44 (d)	45 (d)	46 (b)	47 (c)	48 (d)	49 (a)	50 (c)
51 (d)	52 (d)	53 (b)	54 (b)	55 (c)	56 (d)	57 (a)	58 (c)	59 (d)	60 (c)
61 (b)	62 (b)	63 (d)	64 (a)	65 (c)	66 (d)	67 (d)	68 (b)	69 (c)	70 (c)
71 (d)	72 (a)	73 (b)	74 (d)	75 (b)	76 (b)	77 (b)	78 (d)	79 (b)	80 (a)
81 (c)	82 (a)	83 (c)	84 (d)	85 (c)	86 (b)	87 (a)			

Previous Years' Questions

1 (a)	2 (b)

CHAPTER 15

In-Service Teacher Education

In-service teacher education provides the teacher with opportunities to learn specific skills, techniques and new instructional approaches that they can inculcate in their own teaching.

Concept of In-Service Teacher Education

In-service teacher education is provided by an organisation to an employee. It is a learning experience for an employee, who has already completed his/her education. These kinds of learning experiences are provided to make an employee more skilled for the current or upcoming position.

Education system's performance depends upon the performance of a teacher. In-service teacher education helps the teacher to progress and know more about the subject area. The teacher is updated with the latest knowledge. This makes them capable to serve in any kind of environment.

In-service teacher education can be defined as relevant course and an activity in which an employed teacher participates to upgrade their professional knowledge and skills. Therefore, it constitutes all kinds of education and training, given to a teacher, who is already serving.

It is a way of staff development, which is a necessary and continous process. It provides the teacher with essential knowledge, to meet the needs of school. Thus, the school/institute gains more from in-service teacher education as it develops the teacher.

Teacher plays a vital role in an education development. In-service teacher education is concerned with activities and courses which helps the teacher to upgrade his/her knowledge and interest. As such, in-service teacher education fills the gap of professional inadequacies.

It also refers to as continuing education. This includes re-training, re-skilling and updating the knowledge. Continuing an education helps the teacher to develop their abilities, enrich their knowledge and improve their qualification.

In this Chapter

Definitions of In-Service Teacher Education

Bolam (1982) has defined in-service teacher education as "The education and training activities engaged by primary and secondary school teachers and principals, following their initial professional certification and intended mainly or exclusively to improve their professional knowledge, skills and attitudes, in order, that they can educate children more effectively".

MB Buch, a former director of the department of field services, defined in-service teacher education as "A programme of activities aiming at the continuing growth of teachers and educational personnel in-service".

Cane (1969) defined in-service teacher education as "It is primarily meant for regular serving teachers. It subjects the serving teachers to such activities, which may enhance their professional knowledge, interest and attitude, so that they are able to maximise, their pupil's learning and in turn derive maximum inner satisfaction and sense of achievement".

***Cane** summed up the following significant components of the in-service teacher education programme*

- Professional knowledge
- Skills
- Attitude towards profession
- A code of conduct or ethics of profession
- Professional skills
- Interest towards teaching profession
- Activities such as seminars, symposiums, workshops, discussions, brain storming, etc, helps in development of professional knowledge.

Therefore, in-service teacher education can be defined as all those activities and courses, which aims at enhancing and strengthening the professional knowledge, interest and skills of serving teachers.

Nature of In-Service Teacher Education

- It's activities are based on real and specific problems of workers.
- It involves all the personnel in planning.
- The in-services teacher educator has developed insight and taking abilities in all the participating members.
- The learning principles are utilized and learning growth takes place in a climate, favouring the development of new participations, that can be translated into actual practice.
- It is an integral part of a working programme, and time and money etc, are provided for its proper functioning.
- There is a participation and cooperation with the community, and educational facilities are included in the activities.
- The activities of the programme are evaluated continuously and intelligently.

Needs of In-Service Teacher Education

In-service teacher education provides the teacher with opportunities to learn specific skills, techniques and new instructional approaches, that they can inculcate in their own teaching.

Following are the needs of in-service teacher education

- To suggest remedies for inadequacies of an existing Teacher Training Programme (TTP).
- To provide a chance to update teacher's knowledge in development of science and technology applications.
- Helps to get improved understanding of pedagogical techniques and equitable teaching practices.
- Practice new teaching techniques and share the experience with other teachers.
- To upgrade the knowledge of teaching techniques.
- To provide an exposure to new techniques and development in IT sector.

Scope of In-Service Teacher Education

- Maintenance of familiarity, with updated knowledge and subject matter.
- Increase in the skills of participants.
- Improved attitude towards peer as in-service teacher education training takes place in groups.
- Improved skills in utilization of a community resources by the teacher.
- Teacher develops common values and goals.

Purpose of In-Service Teacher Education

According to Asian Programme of Educational Innovation for Development (APEID), 1978, *following are the purposes of in-service teacher education in developing countries*

- To provide an adequate professional training, so as to make teaching and learning effective.
- To keep the teacher abreast of new developments in curricular subjects and pedagogy.
- To upgrade an academic qualification of teachers.

- To develop the skills and attitudes, responsive to emerging national development goals and programmes.
- To make the teachers aware to the problems of the community and to develop the necessary skills and attitudes, enabling them to be an effective change agents in the community.

Objectives of In-Service Teacher Education

On the basis of various reports on in-service teacher education, submitted in various international conferences and workshops organised by Common Wealth Secretariat, **UNESCO** and its **APEID**, six objectives of in-service teacher education in developing countries of Asia including India have been developed. These objectives are directly related to in-service teacher education needs of schools and teachers.

The objectives are :

- Providing professional training and qualifications to untrained working teachers. Although, majority of teachers are inducted after obtaining a specified initial teacher training, still there are some teachers in certain states, who were appointed without any prior training for teaching. For them, there is a need for providing a first level in-service teacher education training.
- Upgrading the qualifications of serving teachers, whose original qualification may have been rendered out of date, due to the changes and reforms. The process of improvement and change in teacher preparation programmes is continuous and therefore, in-service teacher education programmes should focus on this objective.
- Arranging refresher courses to familiarise teachers with modern practices, being encouraged in schools. Improvement in competence of teachers in their subjects and in practical teaching skills is important for every school. The need to update teachers, in production of teaching materials, use of audio-visual aids and applications of evaluation techniques.
- Disseminating specific educational innovations such as curriculum change, population education, children from deprived section of society, etc.
- Ensuring quality management of an educational administration at all levels is an important goal of in-service teacher education. This may involves retraining teachers to enable them to take up new responsibilities outside the classroom for which their earlier training or experience may not have prepared them.
- Improving the quality of teacher education. There is growing emphasis on the needs for continuing training of the teacher educators themselves.

Advantages of In-Service Teacher Education

- The serving professional teachers get an ample of opportunities for updating their knowledge and skills towards betterment of performance and advancement in schools, without resigning from their position.
- The school's system can retain the services of trained and qualified teachers while in in-service teacher education programme.
- Greater degree of opportunities for increasing the number of trained and qualified teachers at all levels of education.
- Reducing the financial burden of employers of teachers, as the money they had to pay as allowances on full-time to their teachers on their education programme was saved.
- Providing additional sources of revenue generation for teacher education institutions in which the in-service teacher education programmes are based.
- The staff members who are participating, gets additional source of income.
- The teacher education institutions provide service in essential areas of national development, especially, by putting their facilities and staff into use during the long vacations.

Disadvantages of In-Service Teacher Education

- In-service teacher education programme is an expensive and most of participants are self-sponsored.
- As a result, many of the teachers cannot cope with high training fees and other incidental expenses for textbooks and personal upkeeps.
- The time factor is a major constraint, as designated hours for lectures and examinations are inadequate. Therefore, an effectiveness and scope of an instruction is in doubt.
- There are lot of discrepancies in the approaches and techniques, adopted by the different institutions involved in the in-service teacher education programmes, which implies lack of uniformity in course content and methodology.
- There is a problem of poor planning and organization, whereby available activities for participants are impersonal and unrelated to their job settings in the classroom.
- There is a problem of an inadequate facilities in terms of classrooms, laboratories and boarding facilities to accommodate the size of an enrollment.

Organisation and Modes of In-Service Teacher Education

In-service teacher education programmes can be of various pattern including single or many schools. The format depends from informally arranged programme to highly structured programme. Organisation of the modes in the in-service teacher education is necessary as it will help the teachers to deepen their knowledge of teaching methods and educational theories.

Depending on the instructional need, given are some of the different modes of in-service teacher education

Seminar

A seminar is generally used as one of the common devices to impart information regarding specific topic to develop higher cognitive abilities *i.e.* analysis, synthesis, evaluation and observation and to develop cooperation and toleration among the participants. It is a small group discussion in a formal setting with a clear agenda. A speaker presents a theme or a set of papers and it is discussed by all those who participates.

The chairperson guides, directs, coordinates and organises the discussion in a systematic way in order to optimise time, resources and get more benefits. A seminar may either take the form of a small group discussion, followed by the presentation of a paper of a lead lecture, or a short course or conference of a number of sessions with a full participation and discussion between experts and participants. Such discussion not only provides the participants with required knowledge and insight but also an opportunity for clarification of doubts. Moreover, the participants make queries for classification of any point and the paper presentation is required to meet these queries with an adequate facts and figures.

Workshop

As an essential technique of in-service teacher education training, workshop is organised with a group of 10 to 25 persons having shared problems in order to develop the psychomotor aspect of the teachers regarding practices and innovations in the area of education. It was first introduced in 1936, by the Progressive Educational Association at Ohio University.

Now, this technique has been accepted as one of the best to solve the problems of teaching profession, to meet the instruction-based needs of the in-service teachers, to develop skills to perform a task independently, to use teaching strategies effectively, to provide training of new practices in teacher education.

Since, it is skill-based, it is organised to develop certain skills in teachers. For example, teachers could be provided knowledge about computer language for which they would be able to develop some simple computer software. They could be trained in new laboratory skills, developing a question bank, analyzing questions for different examinations and suggesting reforms.

Panel Discussion

Herry A Ober Street was the first person to use panel discussion technique in 1929 to highlight the certain topics, which attracted the attention of an audience. As a good device, panel discussion is used for the training of teachers on job.

A panel of experts with sound knowledge and experience in the subject-concerned, first presents their own angle of thinking on selected aspects of a problem to be followed by questions from the audience and responses by the panelists.

The panel members interact with each other in an atmosphere of freedom and spontaneity. One of the panel member acts as a chairperson, to see that discussion is kept on smooth sailing and all members participates more or less equally and freely. The essence of the discussion is the joint effort, to solve problems through group thinking and active involvement.

Symposium

Symposium as an instructional technique, is a meeting of persons, to discuss a problem or theme in which views are presented in a sequence. It comprises field experts who focuses on the specific aspect of the theme. It is organised, to discuss different significant issues in a short period, to bring the main thoughts into foucs. It serves as an excellent device for informing the audience, crystallizing opinion and preparing them to understand and arrive at decisions, policies, values, judgements or understanding.

Conference

A conference is a meeting of individuals called together to engage in discussion with the aim of accomplishing a limited task in a limited time. It is organised to discuss current problems with a view to provide a workable solution. It is generally organised by organisation having permanence as an attribute.

Conference is organised to achieve the following objectives at cognitive and affective level

- Development of analysis, synthesis, evaluation, reasoning and critical abilities, abilities of expressing one's own feelings and observations, sensitive towards the problems and abilities to study the facts, concepts, problems in depth are of the former category.

- Development of toleration and respect for anti-ideas, feeling of co-operation and freedom of thoughts, development of emotional maturity and balance are of the later objective domain. In brief, behavioural skills and mannerism are nurtured among the participants who are trained to present the ideas and put questions and seeks clarification.

Auto-Instructional Methods

Reading of professional literature can contribute to the growth of professionalism of teachers. Much of the information, understanding and skills required of a teacher could be picked up through self-directed activities such as reading books and articles on education. Professional materials should be consulted as sufficient resources to improve teaching skills. These do have tremendous influence upon the teaching profession.

Summer and Winter Institutes

These are very effective means of promoting professional growth of teachers. Through these institutes, teachers can refresh and update their knowledge, learn new methods of teaching and meet emerging challenges of education. In brief, these institutes helps in the growth of professionalism of teachers on job.

Refresher Courses

These are important techniques of professional growth of teachers. They can help in updating the knowledge and experience of teachers.

These courses can be used for

- giving training to teachers in connection with latest developments in teaching and education.
- giving them an understanding of educational plans and schemes introduced by government and other agencies from time to time.

Orientation Training

It is essential for ensuring quality in an education. It provides adequate knowledge, skills, values, etc, to teachers with a view to improving their styles of teaching. It helps in updating their knowledge. Thus, it helps in promotion of professionalism in teachers on job.

Agencies and Institutions of In-Service Teacher Education

The agencies of in-service teacher education are at the district, state and national level. At the district level, the different agencies are DIET, SSA. At the state level, the different agencies are, SIE, SCERT, SBTE and UDE. At the national level, the different agencies are UGC, NUEPA, NCTE and NCERT. The goals and objectives of these agencies are different, but they have one important goal, which is focused upon leading to improvements in the quality of education.

The teachers are considered to render an indispensable contribution in leading to improvement in the overall system of education as well as in encouraging growth and development of the students.

Explosion of knowledge in India has lead to a change in educational needs. A teacher is supposed to face this change, with the help of training. Such training needs are satisfied by different agencies at different levels.

Agencies at District Level

Following are the agencies of in-service teacher education at district level

DIET

District Institute for Education and Training (DIET) are district-level educational institutes which has been established in each district of India by the Government of India.

They help in coordinating and implementing governmental policies at district level. Continuous in-service education of teacher is necessary to keep the teachers at par, with changes taking place in their professional environment. In-service teacher education also develops their skills and attitudes in the light of their changing roles. Latest approaches and methodologies should be followed in the training. Action research and experimentation, needs to be conducted, to tackle specific problems. This field experience should be used in different in-service teacher education programmes.

Objectives of DIET

- To conduct effective training in pre-service and in-service training, including the latest developments in the teaching-learning process.
- To enable the teachers, to aware and develop new techniques and strategies in education.
- To give support to schools and teachers for improving the quality of primary education.
- To organize seminars, debates, etc, on different areas related to school education such as integrated education for the disabled, National Curriculum Framework, research seminars, etc.

Functions of DIET

- Training and orientation of following target groups.
  - (i) Elementary school teachers (both pre-service and in-service).
  - (ii) Head masters, heads of school complexes and officers of educational department upto block level.
  - (iii) Development of locally relevant materials, teaching aids, evaluation tools, etc.
- To provide training and guidance for implementation of programmes like activity based and joyful learning for creating willingness to go to school.
- To undertake research and experimentation, keeping in mind, problems of the educational area and to solve them.
- To provide guidance and evaluation techniques, to ensure success for activity based education.

SSA

Sarva Shiksha Abhiyan (SSA) is a Government of India's flagship programme for achievement of universalization of elementary education in a time bound manner. This is in accordance with 86th amendment of the Constitution of India, making free and compulsory education to the children of 6 to 14 years age group, a fundamental right. In-service teacher education is understood as professional development or sometimes as part of wider professional development or growth.

In-Service Teacher Education Guidelines by SSA

- It takes into account the Constructivist Approach as laid down in NCF, 2005. This means that the teacher should act as a **facilitator** and work towards creating a variety of learning experiences in and out of the classroom that enable a children to construct knowledge from activities and experiences in day to day life.
- This approach requires being reflective, *i.e.* teachers need to become mindful enquires into their own experiences, to guide children meaningfully.
- The guidelines advocate a **Split Up Model** of in-service training, in which 6 to 8 days training is provided at the DIET level and 2 days training through actual observation of the classroom's situation.
- In keeping with NCF 2005, the guidelines recommend training of teachers in areas such as art and heritage crafts, health and physical education, work education and education for peace, besides training in basic subjects like language, EVS and Mathematics.
- The guidelines stress identification of training needs and development of appropriate training modules through SRG'S/DRG'S. It is also recommended that the training design should emphasize local contextuality and specificities in the teaching-learning situation.
- A list of suggested readings, educational audio and video programmes for teachers have also been provided in the guidelines.

Agencies at State Level

Following are the agencies of in-service teacher education at state level

SCERT

State Council for Educational Research and Training (SCERT) is a leading body responsible for quality education in the state. It is an autonomous body entrusted with planning implementation and evaluation of all academic programmes from pre-school to higher secondary level.

SCERT has been organizing in-service teacher education for teachers in small groups of 50 teachers in each group.

The methodology of training in a small group includes

Activity The participant is expected to perform an activity either individually or in group of 5.

Workshop Workshop is organised to consider intensive practical problems of classroom's teaching like lesson planning, curriculum construction, etc.

Training Various kinds of training are provided to teachers, to face the challenges of teaching better. This may include training on adult health education, ICT training, pre-primary training, etc.

Programmes These are long term courses, carried out to make a teacher professionally fit for the course. The programmes may include guidance and counselling, comprehensive teacher transformation programme, language courses, etc.

Objectives of SCERT

- To conduct teacher education courses as per National Curriculum Framework on teacher education.
- To conduct short-term training programmes for teachers and teacher educators development.
- To conduct and promote educational research and surveys for qualitative improvement of school education and teacher's education scenario of the state.
- To organize seminars and conferences on emerging issues, related to school and teacher's education of the state.

Functions of SCERT

- To assist. the Government of State in formulating academic policies, planning for quality improvement of school and teacher's education.
- To design pre-service and in-service teacher education course as per guideline of NCTE from time to time.
- To promote applications of ICTs in educational programmes.
- To perform any other duties and responsiblities to be assigned by the government, from time to time on academic matter.
- To impart in-service training to the teachers from pre-primary to higher secondary schools.
- To prepare training aids for educational institutions.

RMSA

Rashtriya Madhyamik Shiksha Abhiyan (RMSA) is the most recent initiative of Government of India, to achieve the goal of universalisation of secondary education. It is aimed at expanding and improving the quality of secondary education from classes IX to X.

Under RMSA, NCERT wishes to strengthen in-service teacher professional development programmes at secondary stage. Professional devlopment is the enrichment training, provided to teacher, over a period of time. Professional devlopment promotes the development in all aspects of context and pedagogy.

In the last few years, major in-service professional development programme has been conceptualised and implemented. RMSA have brought in the possibility of continuous capacity building exercise for teachers.

Objectives of RMSA

- Establishing secondary school within a radius of 5 km.
- Achieving 75% access by 2012-13 and 100% access by 2017-18.
- Achieving 100% retention by 2020.
- Providing necessary physical facilities, teaching and non-teaching staff for every secondary school.
- To see that no student shall be deprived of secondary education because of gender disparity, socio-economic reasons, disability or any other reasons.

Functions of RMSA

- Coordination with different departments of NCERT and outside agencies to support the implementation of RMSA in the country with special reference to quality embedded with equity.
- Initiating and promoting dialogue with various stakeholders on quality issues and concerns related to secondary education under RMSA.
- Strengthening ICT enabled secondary education for quality improvement in all curricular areas.
- Capacity building of various stakeholders including teachers and teacher-educators for the effective implementation of quality aspects such as curriculum reform, continuous and comprehensive evaluation, examination reforms, etc.
- Promoting research studies on quality aspects in secondary education.
- Strengthening coordination mechanism and collaboration with different agencies at various levels line within NIE department, SCERTs, School Education Board, etc and develop feedback mechanism for the effective functioning of these institutions.

Agencies at National Level

Following are the agencies of in-service teacher education at national level

NCERT

The **National Council of Educational Research and Training** (NCERT), is an autonomous body financed by the Government of India, was established on **1st September, 1961**.

The council operates through its six constituent units. They are

- NIE (National Institute of Education)
- Four RCEs (Regional Colleges of Education)
- CIET (Central Institute of Educational Technology)

Objectives of NCERT

- Undertake, aid, promote and coordinate research in areas related to school education.
- Prepare and publish model textbooks, supplementary material, newsletters, journals and other related literature.
- Organise pre-service and in-service training of teachers.
- Develop and disseminate innovative educational techniques and practices.
- Collaborate and network with state educational departments, universities, N90s and other educational institutions.
- Act as a clearing house for ideas and information in matters related to school education.
- Act as a **nodal agency** for achieving goals of universalisation of elementary education.

Functions of NCERT

- Develops curriculum, instructional materials, methods of teaching, techniques of evaluation, teaching aids, kits and equipments, learning resources, etc.
- Organises pre-service and in-service training of teachers, teacher educators and other educational personnel.
- Conducts and promotes educational research and innovation.
- Disseminates improved educational techniques and practices and research findings.
- Acts as a clearing house for ideas and information on all matters related to school education.
- Assists and advices the MHRD in formulating and implementing policies and programmes concerning with school education.

NCERT plays an important role in training secondary teachers, elementary and pre-school teacher educators and key personnel connected with school education. NIE, RCE and CIET organise training programmes, seminars and workshops for teachers, teacher educators and educational administrators and also undertake research and extension activities in the field of school education. The NIE has conducted many short term in-service programmes in different vocational courses.

It also conducts in-service training courses and orientation programmes in educational and vocational guidance for teachers, teacher educators, educational administrators and guidance personnel. Along with this, NCERT has also been taking interest in a number of innovative projects including use of computers in education, value education, creating awareness in children, about unplanned population growth. It also develops materials and methods in these areas and shows interest in the educational development of the deprived sections of the society. To pursue this programme, the council has initiated a scheme of opening **Regional Resource Centres** (RRCs) at selected universities. Two RRC's are operating at **Aligarh Muslim University** and **Jamia Millia Islamia.**

Four Regional Colleges of Education (RCEs), are located at **Ajmer**, **Bhopal**, **Bhubaneshwar** and **Mysore**. The RCE's are primarily engaged in providing innovative pre-service and in-service education. Regular in-service training programmes for secondary school teachers, elementary and secondary teachers educators and others. These colleges also arranged for extension of work. A special summer school cum correspondence course is offered in all the four colleges.

NCTE

Kothari Commission Report (1964-1966) criticized teacher education programme being convention rigid and far off from reality. In face of these criticisms, **National Council of Teacher Education**, (NCTE) was establised in **1973**. It has got **independent constitutional status** on **21 May, 1973**.

A Programme of Action (POA) for in-service teacher education, started taking shape from 1988. Currently, it comprises approximately a total of 750 institutions including DIETs, CTEs, IASEs. In addition, a sole district structure namely BRC and CRC has been established in every block under DPEP and SSA to provide in-service teacher education. Recurrent and continuing programmes are organised through seminars, workshops, orientation courses as per the professional requirement.

Objectives of NCTE

- To work especially, towards planned and coordinated development of teacher-education.
- To improve the standard and functioning of teacher educators.

Functions of NCTE

- Undertake survey and studies relating to various aspects of teacher-education and publish the results.
- Making recommendations to the central and state government universities. The UGC and other institutions in the preparation of plans and programmmes in the field of teacher education.
- Coordinating and monitoring teacher education and its development in the country.
- Preparing a guideline with regard to minimum qualifications for the candidates to be employed as teacher educators at different levels.
- Developing norms for any specified category of courses or training in teacher education, including minimum eligibility criteria for admission.
- Preparing a guideline and specified requirements for starting new courses and programmes under teacher's education.
- Developing a guideline for general teacher education programme.
- To advise central government on matters like teacher education (in building pre-service and in-service training), evaluation of the curricula for teacher education and periodical review with respect to revision of curricula.
- To review the progress of plan of teacher's education submitted by central/state governments.
- To advise the government on ensuring adequate standards in teacher's education.

- To give approval to teacher education institutions.
- To lay down norms for maintaining standards of teachers education.
- Supervising the teacher's education programmes and providing financial assistance.

UGC

University Grant Commission (UGC) was established on 28 December, 1953 at New Delhi. It was given autonomy, by Government of India in 1956.

The UGC, in persuance of NPE (1986) had set up 66 academic staff colleges (ASCs) in different Universities/institutions in the country. These academic staff colleges conduct specially designed orientation programmes for newly appointed lecturer and refresher courses for in-service teacher.

The orientation programme is intended to inculcate in the young lecturers, the quality of self-reliance through awareness of the social, intellectual and moral environment as well as to discover self-potential and confidence.

The orientation programme leads to teacher, the awareness of the problem of Indian society and the role of education, higher education leader and educator in the resolution of these problems. This will help in achieving positive goals of national development.

The refresher courses provides opportunities for employed teacher, to exchange experiences with their peers and mutually learn from each other. It will also be a place to known about latest advances in the subjects, technological spin off, etc.

Objectives of UGC

- Coordination, determination and maintenance of standards of university education.
- It provides recognition to universities in India and disburses funds to such recognized universities and colleges.

Functions of UGC

- To upgrade the standard of education with regards to the teacher's education.
- It provides awareness of new innovations and research in teacher's education.
- The national fellowship and teacher fellowship are granted for the encouragement of research and teaching work.
- It provides travel grants to the university lecturers for attending international conferences and seminars, visiting professors are appointed from among the university professors for interchange programmes and delivering lectures.
- Residential accommodation are also provided for the university and college teachers and research associates are appointed for the post doctoral research studies.
- Grants are given by the UGC to the university teachers, for conducting their own researches.

Planning of In-Service Teacher Education Programme

Planning is an important aspect for conducting a successful In-Service Teacher Education Programme.

Effective planning can be broken down to the following steps:

Purpose The reason, why the in-service teacher education is being conducted, is a major factor in deciding the later step. The purpose could be to upgrade teacher's knowledge about

- curriculum
- technology
- way of teaching

As the purpose is decided, the way to conduct the in-service teacher education can be mapped out by:

Formulating In this process, formulation of plans for proper execution of In-Service Teacher Education Programme is emphasised.

Determining the Course of Action During this process it is being determined that how the teaching objectives, will be completed in a certain time. This is done through mapping out various factors.

Duration Depending upon the purpose, the in-service teacher education can be for few days, week or a month long. Duration plays an important role as it helps the teacher to decide whether they will be available for particular period of time or not.

Resources This involves assessing of the all available resources for conducting the programme. Human and financial resources are of particular importance.

Budget The budget will depend upon the kind of programme being conducted and seminar will definitely have less budget than a training programme.

EXAM BASED QUESTIONS

1 In-service teacher education is
(a) provided by an organisation
(b) undergone by an employee
(c) Both a and b
(d) None of the above

2 In-service teacher education is provided to make the teacher
(a) lively (b) skilled
(c) smart (d) enigmatic

3 In-service teacher education makes the teacher
(a) skilled
(b) updated with latest knowledge
(c) capable to serve any kind of environment
(d) All of the above

4 Why does the original qualification of teacher needs an upgrade?
(a) Change in students' attitude
(b) Change in school policies
(c) Change in the curriculum
(d) Change in peer group's attitude

5 Refresher course in in-service teacher education includes
(a) revision of teaching material
(b) production of audio- visual material
(c) applications of new evaluation techniques
(d) All of the above

6 What is a way for staff development?
(a) Technological advancement
(b) New evaluation process
(c) In-service teacher education
(d) Pre-service teacher education

7 In-service teacher education fills the gap of
(a) personal problems
(b) professional inadequacies
(c) teacher-student communication
(d) All of the above

8 In-service teacher education is also known as
(a) distance education
(b) opportunity learning
(c) collaborative learning
(d) continuing education

9 Under continuing education, in-service teacher education involves
(a) re-training
(b) re-skilling
(c) updating knowledge
(d) All of the above

10 In-service teacher education helps the teacher to know about latest .... technology.
(a) science (b) new teaching
(c) Both a and b (d) None of these

11 What are the needs of in-service teacher education?
(a) Understanding of pedagogical techniques
(b) Practice new teaching techniques
(c) Provides exposure to new technique and development in IT sector
(d) All of the above

12 Scope of in-service teacher education includes
(a) increase in the skill of participant
(b) development of common values and goals
(c) Both a and b
(d) None of the above

13 What is the full form of APEID?
(a) Asian Policy of Education Innovation for Development
(b) Asian Programme of Education Innovation for Development
(c) Asian Programme of Education Intelligence for Development
(d) Asian Policy of Education Intelligence for Development

14 What is the purpose of in-service teacher education in developing countries?
(a) Upgrades academic qualification of teacher
(b) Compete teachers against one another
(c) Rejuvinate teachers from the repetitive lessons
(d) All of the above

15 In-service teacher education makes the teacher aware of ....problems.
(a) school (b) life
(c) community (d) None of these

16 In-service teacher education programme may includes
(a) single school (b) many school
(c) Both a and b (d) None of these

17 What quality does seminar helps in achieving?
(a) Analysis (b) Synthesis
(c) Evaluation (d) All of these

18 What kind of group discussion happens in seminar?
(a) Small (b) Formal
(c) Both a and b (d) None of these

19 What does the speaker presents in seminar?
(a) Lecture (b) Set of papers
(c) Lesson (d) Research

20 Who guides and directs the seminar?
(a) Chairperson (b) Teacher
(c) Head master (d) Faciliator

21 Discussion in seminar provides
(a) required knowledge (b) insight
(c) clarification of doubts (d) All of these

22 Workshop aims to develop a teacher's ....
(a) pedagogical knowledge (b) psychology
(c) competency (d) psychomotor

23 Workshops were first introduced by
(a) California University
(b) Ohic University
(c) University College of London
(d) Oxford University

24 Workshops are
(a) talent based (b) technological based
(c) skill based (d) None of these

25 Who was the first person to use panel discussion?
(a) Henry Osborn (b) Herry A Ober Street
(c) Henry A Ober (d) Herry A Ober

26 Panel discussion involves
(a) presentation of thinking about the subject
(b) question about the presentation
(c) responses from the panelist
(d) All of the above

27 Panel members interact with each other in the atmosphere of
(a) freedom (b) spontaneity
(c) Both a and b (d) None of these

28 Symposium is a .... technique
(a) instructional (b) industrial
(c) lively (d) All of these

29 What conference aims to do?
(a) Make the teacher go on an evaluation
(b) Present the topic in a sequence-wise manner
(c) Engage in discussion to accomplish limited task in limited time.
(d) None of the above

30 What are the objectives of a conference?
(a) Development of analysis, synthesis, evaluation, reasoning and critical abilities.
(b) Abilities of expressing one's own feeling and observation, sensitivity towards the problems.
(c) Development of toleration and respect for anti-ideas.
(d) All of the above.

31 In Auto-Instructional Method, what is the way of learning?
(a) Self-learning (b) Computer based learning
(c) Both a and b (d) None of these

32 What are the different agencies of in-service teacher education at national level?
(a) NCERT (b) NCTE
(c) UGC (d) All of these

33 How many constituent units do NCERT have?
(a) 5 (b) 4 (c) 6 (d) 3

34 Name the constituent units of NCERT.
(a) Regional College of Education
(b) National Institute of Technology
(c) Both a and b
(d) None of the above

35 CIET stands for
(a) Controlled Institute of Educational Technology
(b) Central Institute of Educational Training
(c) Central Institute of Educational Technology
(d) None of the above

36 NCERT trains teachers for
(a) secondary level
(b) elementary level
(c) pre-school level
(d) All of the above

37 NIE has conducted many short term in-service programme in different .... courses.
(a) language (b) technical
(c) regional (d) vocational

38 Apart from teacher, for whom does NCERT conducts in-service training course?
(a) Administrator (b) Teacher educator
(c) Guidance personnel (d) All of these

39 What was Kothari Comission's view on Teacher's Education Programme?
(a) Criticism (b) Acceptance
(c) Both a and b (d) None of these

40 When was NCTE established?
(a) 1972 (b) 1973
(c) 1982 (d) 1983

41 How many institutes have been established under NCTE?
(a) 710 (b) 780 (c) 750 (d) 720

42 Name of the institute to provide in-service teacher education, established by NCTE is
(a) DIET (b) BRC
(c) Both a and b (d) None of these

43 What has UGC set up for in-service teacher education?
(a) Academic staff colleges
(b) Staff colleges
(c) Teacher's association
(d) Teaching institute for teachers

44 How many ASC are there?
(a) 58 (b) 66 (c) 78 (d) 42

45 What does academic staff colleges conduct?
(a) Orientation programmes
(b) Refresher courses
(c) Both a and b
(d) None of the above

46 Orientation programme tries to inculcate quality of .... in young lecturer.
(a) self-reliance (b) leadership
(c) Both a and b (d) None of these

47 Methodology of in-service teacher education under SCERT includes
(a) training (b) activities
(c) programmes (d) All of these

48 What are different kinds of training, that is given under in-service teacher education conducted by SCERT?
(a) Adult health education
(b) Physical education
(c) First aid
(d) All of the above

49 What is the goal of RMSA?
(a) Free education to all
(b) Universalisation of secondary education
(c) Mid-day meal upto secondary level
(d) None of the above

50 Professional development promotes development in all aspects of........... .
(a) pedagogy (b) content
(c) Both a and b (d) None of these

51 What are the different agencies providing in-service teacher education programme at district level?
(a) DIET and SSA (b) DIET and RMSA
(c) SCERT and RMSA (d) SSA and RMSA

52 What does SSA plans to do?
(a) Provide free books to secondary level student
(b) Provide free education upto elementary level
(c) Both a and b
(d) None of the above

53 What can be the purpose, to plan an In-Service Teacher Education Programme?
(a) Curriculum change (b) Upgraded technology
(c) Teaching methodology (d) All of these

54 Match the following

List I (Agencies)	List II (Function)
A. SCERT	1. Assits and advices MHRD
B. UGC	2. Coordinating teacher education
C. NCERT	3. Provides grants for research
D. NCTE	4. Prepare training aids

Codes

	A	B	C	D		A	B	C	D
(a)	4	3	1	2	(b)	1	2	3	4
(c)	1	4	3	2	(d)	3	2	1	4

55 Match the following

List I (Agencies)	List II (Programmes)
A. RMSA	1. UEE
B. UGC	2. USE
C. SSA	3. RCE
D. NCERT	4. ASC

Codes

	A	B	C	D		A	B	C	D
(a)	1	3	2	4	(b)	2	1	4	3
(c)	4	1	3	2	(d)	3	4	1	3

56 Match the following

List I (Modes of INSET)	List II (Techniques)
A. Seminar	1. Giving education in accordance to latest development
B. Workshop	2. Training one ownself
C. Auto-instructional	3. Speaker presents a theme.
D. Refresher course	4. Organised to develop certain skill in teacher

Codes

	A	B	C	D		A	B	C	D
(a)	3	4	2	1	(b)	2	3	1	4
(c)	1	2	4	3	(d)	4	1	2	3

57 Find out the incorrect pairing.
1. National agency – UGC
2. National agency – DIET
3. State agency – SCERT
4. District agency – SSA

Codes
(a) 1 (b) 2 (c) 3 (d) 4

58 Choose the correct pairing.
1. NCERT – 1995
2. NCTE – 1964
3. UGC – 1953
4. SCERT – 1981

Codes
(a) 1 (b) 2 (c) 3 (d) 4

59 The purpose of in-service teacher education is to
1. upgrade academic qualification of teachers
2. provide professional training
3. keep the teacher updated
4. make the teacher feel less qualified

Codes
(a) 1 and 2 (b) Only 4 (c) 1, 2 and 3 (d) 1 and 4

60 What is DIET?
1. It is a district level institute
2. It arranges BRC and DRC
3. It organises orientation programme for new teachers
4. It helps in coordinating and implementing governmental policy

Codes
(a) 1 and 2 (b) 1 and 4 (c) 1, 3 and 4 (d) Only 4

61 Choose the correct statement.
1. Symposium includes teacher presenting a theme
2. Auto-Instructional Method includes teacher teaching oneselves
3. Summer and winter institutes are for students.
4. Refresher course trains the teacher in latest technology.

Codes
(a) 1 and 2 (b) 3 and 4
(c) 1, 2 and 4 (d) 1, 3 and 4

62 Choose the correct statement.
1. UGC was established in 1983.
2. UGC has set up 66 academic staff colleges.
3. UGC provides free secondary education to all.
4. UGC conducts orientation and refresher courses.

Codes
(a) 2 and 4 (b) 1 and 4 (c) Only 2 (d) Only 4

63 Choose the correct statement.
1. In-service teacher education is a way of staff development.
2. In-service teacher education upgrades the knowledge of teacher.
3. In-service teacher education provides education to those who can't be available at study centre.
4. In-service teacher education referred to as continuing education.

Codes
(a) 1 and 2 (b) 3 and 4 (c) 2, 3 and 4 (d) 1, 2 and 4

Direction (Q. Nos. 64 to 70) *given below are two statements, one labelled as Assertion (A) and other labelled as Reason (R). Following are the codes given below. Choose the correct code for each.*

Codes
(a) Both A and R are true (b) Both A and R are False
(c) A is true, But R is false (d) A is false, But R is true

64 **Assertion** (A) SSA's main aim is universalization of elementary education.
Reason (R) SSA works at a state level.

65 **Assertion** (A) Purpose of in-service teacher education is to keep the teacher abreast of new development in curricular subjects and pedagogy.
Reason (R) In-service teacher education's main aim is to upgrade academic qualification of teacher.

66 **Assertion** (A) Budget of In-Service Teacher Education Programme is always fixed and same.
Reason (R) Duration of In-Service Teacher education Programme depends upon the purpose of programme.

67 **Assertion** (A) Self-directed professional development include the teacher sharing his/her views with peer.
Reason (R) The peer group guides the teacher.

68 **Assertion** (A) NCERT is an autonomous body financed by Government of India.
Reason (R) NCERT has six constituent units.

69 **Assertion** (A) The refresher courses provide opportunities for employed teacher.
Reason (R) It helps the teacher to exchange experiences and mutually learn from each other.

70 **Assertion** (A) NCERT plays an important role in training of teachers.
Reason (R) It conducts and promotes educational research and innovation.

PREVIOUS YEARS' QUESTIONS

July 2018

1 Below are given a few programmes for enhancing teacher's quality. Which of them are specially related to in-service teacher education? Select the correct code to indicate your answer.
1. Induction training
2. Skill development training
3. Pedagogy courses in specific subjects.
4. Foundation courses in teacher's education.
5. Micro-simulation for particular competencies.

Codes
(a) 1, 3, 4 (b) 1, 2, 5 (c) 3, 4, 5 (d) 2, 3, 5

November 2017

2 Which of the following step(s) have been taken by NCTE for the systematic improvement in teacher's education?
1. Rationalization in the demand and supply situation of the country.
2. Curriculum of teacher's education at various levels has been updated.
3. Enhancement of academic support in the form of various resources.
4. Periodic monitoring of teacher's education.
5. Emphasis on reflective practices.

Codes
(a) 1, 2, 4, 5 (b) 2, 3, 5, 1
(c) 4, 5, 3, 2 (d) 3, 4, 2, 5

January 2017

3 Which of the following institution(s) is/are the apex body for contracting, guiding and monitoring the activities and programmes of DIETS and other centrally sponsored schemes of teacher's education?
(a) National Council for Teacher Education (NCTE)
(b) National Council for Educational Research and Training (NCERT)
(c) University Grants Commission (UGC)
(d) State Council of Educational Research and Training (SCERT)

4 **Which of the following institutions is the apex body for controlling, guiding and monitoring the activities and programmes of DIETs and other centrally sponsored schemes for teacher's education?**

(a) NCTE (b) NCERT (c) UGC (d) SCERT

July 2016

5 **Establishment of DIETs was the result of one of the recommendations of**

(a) Indian Education Commission (1882)
(b) University Education Commission (1948-49)
(c) Secondary Education Commission (1952-53)
(d) National Policy of Education (1986)

6 **Match the following.**

List I (Teacher Education Programme)	List II (Functions)
A. In-Service Teacher Education	1. To sharpen and deepen the subject knowledge
B. Pre-Service Teacher Education	2. To bring refinement and upgradation in teaching skills
C. Distance Education	3. To prepare teachers in terms of requirements of demand-supply analysis
D. Refresher Courses	4. To help the disadvantaged society
	5. To meet the large scale shortage of teachers in rural areas
	6. To prepare teachers with an eye on the shortage of teachers in the far flung areas

Codes

	A	B	C	D		A	B	C	D
(a)	1	3	6	2	(b)	2	1	5	6
(c)	1	5	4	3	(d)	2	3	4	5

June 2015

7 **Distance Institutes of Education and Training (DIETs) were created in pursuance of the recommendation of**

(a) National Policy of Education (1968)
(b) National Policy of Education (1986)
(c) Kothari Commission (1964-66)
(d) 42nd Constitutional Amendment Act (1976)

8 **Which of the following statement is not related to In-Service Teacher Education Programme?**

(a) There is an urgent need to develop comprehensive programmes for continuing professional development of secondary school teachers
(b) Aspirants to join teaching profession be screened carefully for their aptitude of teaching
(c) A teacher should continue her/his education to attain competency in teaching methodology
(d) Faculty development programmes for teacher educators should be institutionalised

December 2014

9 **Identify the pair of institution, which is not directly responsible for the professional growth of education in India.**

(a) NCERT and SCERT (b) DIET and IASE
(b) NCTE and UGC (d) CSIR and ICSSR

ANSWERS

Exam Based Questions

1 (a)	2 (b)	3 (d)	4 (c)	5 (d)	6 (c)	7 (b)	8 (d)	9 (d)	10 (c)
11 (d)	12 (c)	13 (b)	14 (a)	15 (c)	16 (c)	17 (d)	18 (c)	19 (b)	20 (a)
21 (d)	22 (d)	23 (b)	24 (c)	25 (b)	26 (d)	27 (c)	28 (a)	29 (c)	30 (d)
31 (a)	32 (d)	33 (c)	34 (a)	35 (c)	36 (d)	37 (d)	38 (d)	39 (a)	40 (b)
41 (c)	42 (c)	43 (a)	44 (b)	45 (c)	46 (a)	47 (d)	48 (a)	49 (b)	50 (c)
51 (a)	52 (b)	53 (d)	54 (a)	55 (d)	56 (a)	57 (b)	58 (c)	59 (c)	60 (b)
61 (c)	62 (a)	63 (d)	64 (c)	65 (a)	66 (d)	67 (b)	68 (a)	69 (a)	70 (a)

Previous Years' Questions

1 (b)	2 (b)	3 (d)	4 (d)	5 (d)	6 (a)	7 (b)	8 (b)	9 (d)

CHAPTER
16

Teaching as a Profession

Teaching as a profession provides highly specialised intellectual services. It is based on long specialised, intellectual training representing a high degree of creative thought and contributing to the development of a wide range of research specialist.

Introduction

A teacher is one of the highly valued personality in society. As such, teaching is considered to be the most sacred and distinctive profession. History is full of evidence about nation where education has brought significant progress. With the change in demands, the profession of teaching has become demanding. Many factors have been at work for years in bringing the change in the attitude towards teaching. Thus, now it is a learned profession. Global emphasis on literacy through programme like Education For All (EFA) and Right To Education (RTE) shows the world's concern for the teacher's role in the development of the society.

Concept of Profession

We often use the term 'profession' in a generic sort of way referring to what is your trade/vocation. Profession is derived from the word 'profiteor' means 'to profess'. Here, the connotation is that a professional is a person who possesses knowledge of something and has a commitment to a particular set of values both of which are generally well accepted characteristics of professions. History records the early professions of the priesthood, law, medical/physicians and university teaching. As time progressed, dentistry, engineering, accountants and architects were ascribed 'professional' status. The key characteristics that define an occupation as a profession are an assessment process for entry into the profession, a common body of knowledge, a code of ethics and a professional association.

In this Chapter

- *Concept of Profession*
  - *Concept of Professionalism*
  - *Teaching as a Profession*
  - *Professional Ethics of Teachers*
  - *Factors Affecting Teacher's Development*
- *ICT Integration*
- *Quality Enhancement of Teacher Education*
- *Innovation in Teacher Education*

Definitions of Profession

According to **Webster's New World Dictionary of American Language**, "Profession is a vocation or occupation requiring advanced training in some liberal art or science, and usually involves mental, rather than manual work as teaching, engineering, writing, etc".

According to **Obidi**, "Profession is an occupation that claims the exclusive technical competence and which also adheres to the service ideals and allows ethics of professional conduct".

According to **Hoyle and Megarry**, "Profession is an occupation that asserts an exclusive monopoly of knowledge, having definite standards and possesses the ability to convince the generality of the public that its services are unique".

According to **Falade**, "Profession contains essential characteristics such as an occupation, that carries with it great responsibility and that members of a profession possess special skills and competencies based upon a long period of theoretical and practical training".

According to **William**, "Profession usually exercises a system of control or a code of ethics over practice through professional societies, associations and institutions or sometimes by law".

According to **Saunder and Wilson**, "Profession is an application of intellectual technique to the ordinary business of life acquired as a result of prolonged and specialised training".

According to **Douley**, "Profession is a type of higher grade non-manual occupation, with both subjectively recognised occupational status, possessing a well defined area of study or concern and providing a definite service after advanced training and education".

Characteristics of Profession

- It must satisfy an indispensable social need and be based upon well established and socially acceptable scientific principles.
- It demands continuous in-service training of its membes.
- It must give evidence of needed skills, which general public does not possess, i.e. skills that are partly native and partly acquired.
- It must have developed a scientific technique that is the result of tested experience.
- It must require the exercise of discreation and judgement according to the time and manner of the performance of duty.
- It must be a type of beneficial work, the result of which is not subject to standardisation in terms of unit performance or time element.
- There is a clear requirement for ethical constraints in the professions.
- It must have sufficient self-impelling power to retain its members throughout life.
- It must not be used for a mere stepping stone to other occupations.
- It must recognise its obligations to society by insisting that its members live up to an established and accepted codes of ethics.

Concept of Professionalism

Professionalism is the conduct, behaviour and attitude of someone in a work or business environment. It is defined as "an ideal to which individuals and occupational groups aspire, in order to distinguish themselves from other workers". It leads to workplace success, a strong professional reputation and a high level of work ethic and excellence.

The **Merriam-Webster Dictionary** defines professionalism as "The conduct, aim, or qualities that characterises or marks a profession or a professional person".

Attributes of Professionalism

Specialised Knowledge Professionals have a deep personal commitment to develop and improve their skills, hence, they possess specialised knowledge. All the business areas do not have a stable core of knowledge, they neither demand extensive knowledge nor do they have professionals with top degrees. But, the professionals works in serious, thoughtful and sustained way to master the specialised knowledge that they need to succeed in their field and that they keep this knowledge up to date, so that they can continue to deliver the best work as possible.

Competency Professionals know how to get the job done. They are reliable and they stick to their promises. In any case, they can't deliver their promise, they manage expectations and do their best to make the situation right. Professionals do not make excuses but focus on finding solutions.

Honesty and Integrity Professionals exhibit qualities such as honesty and integrity. They keep their word and can be trusted, because of that, they never compromise their value and will do the right thing even when it means taking the harder road.

Accountability Professionals holds themselves accountable for their thoughts, words and actions especially when they have made mistake. This personal accountability is linked to honesty and integrity and it is a vital element of professionalism.

Self-Regulation Professionals remain professional under pressure as well. A customer service employee will remain calm even facing an angry irritated customer. Genuine professionals show respect for people around them, no matter what.

Teaching as a Profession

To some, the essence of a profession is advanced training. Hence, the best way to professionalise teaching and upgrade teacher knowledge and skills is through professional development.

Other thinks that the essence of profession lies in the attitude now individual practitioners visionise their work. In this view, the best way to professionalise teaching is to instill ethos of public service and high standard and a sense of professionalism among teachers. Even for others, the focus is on the organisational conditions, under which teachers work. In this view, the best way to professionalise teaching is to improve teacher's working condition.

Teachers work in an environment characterised by change and uncertainty, where it might be said that change is paradoxically, one of the few constant. It is quite possible that teachers came in the profession for different reasons in different country contexts, in different economical circumstances and with varying expectations of the rewards and challenges of the role. However, common to all, there is a need for an appreciation, autonomy and affiliation.

Their places within a hierarchy of needs varies country by country depending on an essential infrastructure of safety, security, working conditions, resourcing and an adequate remuneration. Therefore, it can be said that "Teaching is a profession that lies at the heart of both learning of children and young people and their social, cultural and economical development. It is crucial to transmit and implant social values, such as democracy, equality, tolerance, cultural understanding and respect for each person's fundamental freedom".

Teaching as a profession can be described as an occupation, which provides highly specialised intellectual services. It is a body of erudite knowledge, a set of attitude and a technique, which is applied to the service of mankind through an educated group. It needs a long period of training and certification.

Thus, teaching profession is based on long specialised, intellectual training representing a high degree of creative thought and contributing to the development of a wide range of research specialist. Teaching as a profession, also fullfills certain conditions which supports it as a profession, like teachers are organised at local, state and national levels. Teaching requires careful skills and understanding. Teachers are required by law to complete certain requirements for certification and entrance into the profession.

Professionalisation in Teaching

Following are the indicators that are used to define profession and professionals in refrence to teachers and schools

Credentials

The most important quality of distinguishing profession from other kinds of occupations is the degree of expertise and complexity involved in the work itself. Professional work involves highly complex set of skills, intellectual functioning and knowledge that are not acquired easily and not widely used.

For this reason, professions are often referred to as the knowledge based occupations. Entry into profession requires credentials. These credentials serve as screening or gate keeping devices. Their rationale is protection of the interest of the public by assuring that practitioners hold as agreed upon level of knowledge and skill.

Giving importance of credentials to profession helps in upgrading the licensing requirements for new teachers has been important issue in teaching (licenses for teachers are known as teaching certificates issued by the central or state government). Also it has been source of contention. Entry in teaching should be made highly restricted, as in traditional professions. It helps in upgrading the quality and qualification of teaching and teachers.

Induction

In addition to initial, formal training and preparation, professional work typically requires extensive training for new practitioners upon entry. Such training is designed, to give the feel of an environment.

While, credentials and examinations in many professions are usually designed to assure that new entrants have a minimum or basic level of knowledge and skills. Induction programmes are designed to augment the basic level of knowledge and skills. As a result, entry to professions involves both formal and informal mechanism of induction i.e. internships or mentoring programmes. Sometimes, these periods of induction can be prolonged and intensive.

The objective of such programmes and practices is to aid new practitioners in adjusting to the environment, to familiarise them with concrete realities of their jobs and also to provide second opportunity to filter out those with sub-standard levels of skills and knowledge. In teaching, mentoring and induction programmes have been a subject of much discussion. It is the best way to increase the efficacy and retention of the new teachers, by assisting them in coping with the practicalities of teaching of managing groups of students and of adjusting to the schools environment.

Authority

Professionals are considered experts in whom, substantial authority is vested and professions are marked by a large degree of self-governance. The rationale behind professional authority is to place substantial levels of control in the hands of the experts. Professionals exerts substantial control over the curriculum, admissions and accreditation of professional training schools. It also sets and enforces behavioural and ethical standards for practitioners. Sometimes, this control is exerted through professional organisations.

At some other time, this control is exerted directly in work places. The distribution of power, authority and control in schools, is one of the most important issue in contemporary education research and policy. Autonomy of teachers are always in question. Some researchers says that the schools are decentralised organisations, in which teachers have autonomy and discretion. Other says that, schools are overly centralised, in which teachers have to give little influence over school's operations.

Professional Development

Beyond both, pre-service training and mentoring for beginners, professionals also requires ongoing in-service growth and development, throughout their career.

The underlying assumption is that to achieve a professional level mastery and complex skills and knowledge is a prolonged and continuous process. Also, it is important for professionals to update their skills and knowledge. As a result, professionals take up conferences, workshops and also joins associations to update their knowledge. Professional development has been one of the most important reforms in the field of teaching. Most of the schools and colleges, both public and private, provides professional development to their teachers. Teachers participates in workshops or activities for professional development.

Specialisation

Professionals are not generalists, amateurs, they possess expertise over a specific body of knowledge and skill. The importance of expertise to professions, is that it follows the most important attribute of profession, *i.e.* specialisation. In profession, the great deal of skill, training, expertise, specialisation is considered necessary and good.

In contrast to non-professions, semi or low skill occupation requires far less training and expertise than professions. Professionalisation of teachers argues that there is a need of reform in teachers specialisation, specially at the elementary school level, because it does not address the needs of the whole child, which leads to alienation of students. Also, teachers are assigned to teach subjects, which do not match their fields of speciality and training.

Compensation and Prestige

Professionals are well compensated and are provided with relatively high salary and benefits levels throughout their career span. The lengthy training and complexity of knowledge and skills requires high levels of compensation, to recruit and retain capable and motivated individuals. Also, professions are high status and high prestige occupations. They are respected and envied. Attitude, public perceptions of other occupations are less prestigious. Teaching is a female dominated profession and is rated in middle. The status of teaching is increasing in today's time.

Professional Ethics of Teachers

Every profession has its own professional ethics that are different from general ethics. The word 'ethics' adds the professional obligation for an individual, that he/she has to fulfil. Institutions have code of conduct, but not professional ethics.

A code of conduct is a sophisticated version of do's and dont's. On the other hand, professional ethics give certain sets of broad principles, derived from deep values and reflection on the nature and role of profession in the society. The main aim of education is to develop citizens, who will safeguard, strengthen and improve democracy and maintain national ideals. The quality of education reflects the ideals, motives and conduct of the members of teaching profession. The members of teaching profession has the obligation to conduct himself/herself in accordance to the code and ethics of the profession. Code of professional ethics are adopted as a guide by teachers. They apply to all the persons engaged in the professional aspects of education at elementary, secondary and college level.

The teaching profession has slowly evolved a code of conduct and professional ethics. These code of ethics are established to protect the society from the incompetent practitioner. The codes formulated in the teaching profession, prohibits its member from engaging in undesirable behaviour that can bring profession to trouble. Code of professional ethics are adopted as a guide by teachers. They apply to all the persons engaged in the professional and college level.

The teachers as professionals are accountable to teaching, society, students and parents.

Ethics Towards Students

Effective teaching is the main aim of teaching and it occurs with the feeling of mutual respect between teachers and students. As a teacher, he/she should understands them, be just and courteous, promotes a spirit of enquiry, fellowship and joy in the students.

The interest of the teachers should lie in the welfare of students. Youngsters need support and appreciation from the adults and specially from teachers. It helps in the development of the self-confidence. So, the teacher should inspire students and works with them to create and maintain a pleasant and attractive learning environment. And while working with students, the teacher should be friendly and empathetic.

Also, the teacher should recognise the difference among students and seeks to meet their individual needs. And to encourage students, to formulate and work for high individual goals in the development of their physical, intellectual, creative and spiritual endowments.

Ethics Towards Parents

There should be a mutual cooperation between home and school environment. The establishment of a desirable learning environment in the classroom requires working together on the part of student and teacher and providing the child with the guidance he/she needs with the mutual coordination of parents and teachers.

The teacher should make friendly and informative contacts with the parents. Parents and teachers can help each other in understanding the personality of the child. Their combined knowledge can help in the overall development of the child. Therefore, the teacher keeps the parents informed, about the progress of their child and also discrete the information received from the parents.

Ethics Towards Society

Apart from parents and students, it is important for the teacher to develop favourable and useful relationships within the community. Education is the most effective way to make these relationships friendly and cooperative. The teaching profession occupies a position of trust of the society. Thus, the teacher should set an example in citizenship, by performing the duties and participating in community activities and also to promote the public good and uphold dignity of the society.

Ethics Towards Administration

A teacher also establishes an agreeable relationship with school supervisors, administrators and the Board of Education. The teacher should perform his/her duties and support school policies and also interpret them intelligently. The teacher should cooperate with school's officials in an effort to improve learning opportunities.

Factors Affecting Teacher's Development

The personal and contextual factors affecting teacher's development are as follows

Psychological Factors

Interest The teacher should be able to make the lesson interesting, so that the students are eager to learn.

Intelligence The teacher should be intelligent enough to know how to maneuvar the class.

Attitude The teacher should have the right and positive attitude towards teaching. If the attitude is positive, teacher can create love for education, hope, good ideas and development.

Feelings Teacher should have positive feelings and emotions. He/she has to eradicate the feelings of fear and anger from the mind of young learner.

Aptitude Teachers should know how to deal with students, having no aptitude for the subject.

Mental health It is a state of well being, in which every individual realises his or her own potential, can cope with the normal stresses of life, can work productively and fruitfully.

Ability Teachers should get to know their student and then they can help them to learn the lesson content by teaching to their strengths.

Biological Factors

Maturity A teacher should be mature enough to know the student's unmet needs. Meeting certain needs, can also act as motivator and significantly enhancing learning.

Physical Health It is one of the most important aspect of teacher development. The teacher should be able to take care of themselves as well as the students.

Self-Concept Teachers can incorporate activities into the learning environment for their students and for developing their self-concept.

Proper Sleep A good and proper sleep makes the teacher fresh, active, competent and ready for working and learning.

Social Factors

Social Expectation It is an internalised norm for individuals and organisation and for society, as a whole. Teachers should abide by there norms.

Cultural Demand Cultural values include particular religious belief often shape the way of living for a teacher.

Achievement Teacher should use a variety of instructional technique appealing to different interest and learning orientation, to make sure that every student has a taste of achievement.

ICT Integration

ICT integration is defined as the use of ICT to introduce, reinforce, supplement and extend skills (Pisapia, 1994).

According to **Kennewell**, "Integration of ICT in teaching requires understanding at a deeper level to facilitate the development of strategies and process to identify opportunities, solve problems and evaluate solution".

According to **Bruniges**, "ICT integration is a strategy to integrate Information and Communication Technology into all facts of education and training, including the administrative functions and e-business models required to support learning".

Over the last few decades, the rapid growth of ICT has become one of the most important topic discussed by the scholars in education. This is due to the capability of ICT to provide a dyanamic and proactive teaching and learning environment. In line with current digital era, teachers are required to integrate ICT in their daily teaching and replace their traditional methods with modern tools and facilities.

It's integration has been attracting a great deal of interest among researchers in professional development communities and human-computer interaction circles. At the same time, ICT integration has been fueling contentions amongst stakeholders and administrators of ICT in institutes of higher learning, schools and corporate training environments. Adoption issues surrounding ICT integration is contested at every level, all aimed at preventing failure and maximising return on investment.

Schools use a diverse set of ICT tools to communicate, create, disseminate, store, and manage information. In some contexts, ICT has also become an integral to the teaching-learning interaction, through such approaches as replacing chalkboards with interactive digital whiteboards, using student's own smart phones or other devices for learning during class time, and the **Flipped Classroom Model**, where students watch lectures at home on the computer and use classroom time for more interactive exercises.

When teachers are digitally literate and trained to use ICT, these approaches can lead to higher order thinking skills that will provide creative and individualized options for students to express their understandings, and leave students better prepared to deal with ongoing technological change in society and the workplace.

The purpose of integrating ICT is to improve and increase the quality, accessibility and cost-efficiency of the delivery of education, while taking advantage of the benefits of networking learning communities, together to equip them to face the challenges of global competition.

ICT Integration in Education

ICTs have become the most basic building block of modern industrial society in a very short time. Mastering information technology, understanding basic skills and concept of ICT are now highly regarded by many countries. ICT has been used at amazing rate for instruction among teachers.

ICT can work in a number of ways as follows

- It can be used to train students in skills, which they will need for further education and as an ongoing learning process throughout the rest of their lives and for future jobs.
- It can provide access information and communication outside the classroom via internet.
- It can be used to support teacher's development via external networks.
- It can support and potentially transforms the teaching and learning process.

Both student and teacher need to learn to trust the technology. Teachers needs to be confident enough in using various ICT tools to build their trust in technology. Without teacher's competency, ICT cannot be put to a good use for instructional delivery. In this regard, a teacher should be able to use various ICT tools including chat rooms, word processing skills, web pages authoring, File Transfer Protocol (FTP), compress and decompress a file and so on.

Quality Enhancement of Teacher Education

Teacher education is a global profession that needs to be understood properly. If teacher education is professionalised, it would produce teachers with professional outlook and professional work ethics. Effective professional development practice promotes collegiality and collaboration; it encourages risk taking and experimentation. It also involves teacher educators in decision-making on the basis of their experiences and it helps them to reflect on as well as put into practice what they learn. Professionally, powerful teaching is very important and is increasing in our contemporary society. Due to the developments in these field, quality of teacher's education is better in 21st century than in 20th century. The professional development of teachers have received a great deal of attention in all countries, including India.

According to **NCTE**, "Teacher is the most important element in any educational program. He plays a central role in implementation of education processes at any stage. The level of achievement of learner is determined by teacher competence".

So, the quality of education is basically depends on the quality of teachers.

Developing Professionalism for Teacher Educator

Teacher professionalism contains three essential characteristics

Competence

It is important in an educator's pursuit of excellence. Generally, it focuses on three important ideas *i.e.* preparation, knowledge of subject area and defined pedagogy. Preparation prepares the professional for the adversity of the classroom. From language and cultural barriers to socio-economic differences, all educators face deterrents in the classroom that must be broken down by individualised techniques. Decision-making by well-trained professionals allow individual student's needs to be met more precisely and promotes improvement in overall learning. Thus, by bridging these barriers, the educator will be better prepared for classroom management and create an effective learning environment.

Furthermore, by doing this, the professional teacher leads students by his or her example *i.e.* one who is prepared for difficulties will be able to overcome them. A professional educator must have a **strong knowledge of his / her subject** area. Then, he/she has the opportunity to concern himself/herself with preparing innovative techniques to teach material rather than spending significant amount of time in studying the material.

With the advantage of knowing one's curriculum material well, the educator has more confidence in their teachings, having already placed significant thought on the material being taught. Thus, a professional is able to dwell on how to relate subject matter to the students and their cultures in an original method. The final portion of competence is discovering and assuming a defined pedagogy.

A professional teacher who has a defined pedagogy has already journeyed through several trials to discover which pedagogical techniques are more effective. Although, this may take years to fine-tune, a professional is willing to self-evaluate his/her pedagogy as he/she develops it, and apply one's ideas to a practical situation.

Furthermore, by acquiring a **defined pedagogy**, a professional creates more autonomy for himself/herself, allowing a partial release from the constraints created by the administration, school board or parents.

Performance

It is the ability to effectively teach the concepts of a curriculum. However, this is performance defined at its most fundamental level. As individuals, professionals have the right to perform their work as they see fit, based on knowledge acquired through specialised training. As such, performance is derived from both pre-meditated and improvisational techniques.

A professional teacher educates, so that students learn concepts and apply them to their lives. Although, this undermines the school's emphasis on state test results, a quality educator prepares for the tests through this unique style of applying to his/her student's lives. Thus, the application of these concepts must be inside the bounds of student's lives. Furthermore, an educator who has a high standard of performance is reliable and dedicated. This type of educator becomes an active teacher rather than a passive teacher, showing the students a genuine interest in their progress as a student.

Conduct

It is the manner in which an educator carries himself/ herself is a reflection on one's classroom, school, community and educational system.

It is a representation of how well one takes care of himself/ herself, from aesthetics to language and behaviour. However, these are minor qualities of conduct. It also includes one's ability to initiate and to maintain quality communication with all the people involved in education *i.e.* students, fellow teachers, school board, administration, and parents. It is through energetic communication by a professional that initiates understanding, whether it is a student grasping to their potential or the professional voicing their displeasure on a newly implemented regulation.

A professional teacher desires to locate effective communicative skills to achieve preferred educational goals. In conclusion, a completed definition of teacher professionalism far exceeds the simple notion that a teacher be prepared in a certain manner. A professional is trained to handle all situations, as most episodes in the classroom requires quick thinking. Also, teacher professionalism extends beyond one's ability to understand content, the educator must discover, if the students are being reached in an effective way.

With the role of teacher becoming more autonomous, an educator must be competent in their studies, perform well under the eye of the administration and parents, while maintaining good conduct to facilitate quality communication.

Qualities of a Good Teacher

Good education system needs a good quality professional teacher.

Following are the qualities that the teacher must possess

- Sufficient knowledge of subject matter to be able to teach with confidence.
- Knowledge and skills in a range of appropriate and varied teaching methodologies.
- Fluency in the language of instruction.
- Knowledge of sensitivity and interest in young learners.
- Ability to reflect on teaching practices and children's responses.
- Ability to modify teaching/learning approaches as a result of reflection.
- Ability to create and sustain an effective learning environment.
- Understanding of the curriculum and its purposes, particularly when reform programs and new paradigms of teaching and learning are introduced.
- General professionalism, good morale, and dedication to the goals of teaching.
- Ability to communicate effectively.
- Ability to communicate enthusiasm, for learning to students.
- Interest in students as individuals, sense of caring and responsibility for helping them learn and become good people, and a sense of compassion.
- Good character, sense of ethics, and personal discipline.
- Ability to work with others and to build good relationships with the educational institutions and communities.

Innovation in Teacher Education

Education is the foundation of our economy. What and how we learn in school determines that what we will become as individuals and our success throughout our life. It informs how we will solve problems, how we will work with others, and how we will look at the world around us. In today's world, innovation, economy and education becomes even more important for developing the next generation of innovators and creative thinkers.

The word 'innovation' is derived from latin word 'innovate' which means 'to change something into something new'. It is a promotion of new ideas and practices in education and training. Innovations should be done in each and every aspect of teacher education, like methodology, curriculum, research and evaluation. Many countries are using different kinds of innovative approaches, such as school clusters, field based trainings, school self-review and development, distance learning methods and visiting advisors".

Innovative Programs in Teacher Education

Various innovative programs in teacher education have been initiated from time to time to bring quality improvement in the system. These attempts were successful but due to some challenges fulfilment of all objectives was not witnessed.

Some of these programs are as follows

- Master of Educational Technology (Computer Applications) by SNDT, University, Mumbai.
- M.Tech (Educational Technology) by Kurukshetra University, Kurukshetra.
- Four years, Integrated Program of Teacher Education, Kurukshetra University, Kurukshetra (1955).
- Four years, Integrated Program of Teacher Education, RIE, NCERT (1963).
- HSPT Training Teachers, Eklavya, MP (1982).
- B.Sc. in Teaching Technology by Sikkim Manipal University.
- Activity Based Teacher Education Program, DAVV, Indore (1991).
- Personalized Teacher Education Program, Lucknow University, Lucknow (1996).

- Comprehensive Teacher Education Program, Gandhi Shikshan Bhavan College of Education, Mumbai University, Mumbai (2000).
- Early Faculty Induction Program (EFIP), under QIP by AICTE, New Delhi.
- University of Teacher Education, Chennai, Tamil Nadu (2008).
- IGNOU Insitute of Professional Competency Advancement of Teachers (IIPCAT, 2009), IGNOU, India.
- Indian Institute of Teacher Education, Gujarat (Bill 4, 2010).
- Two years, B.Ed Program of Secondary Teacher Education by NCTE (2014).
- The central government and NCTE have planned to change the present two years B.Ed Program into four years course in a phased manner. Further, changing curriculum and introducing some more innovating things will definitely be a welcoming move to improve the quality of teachers.

Aspects Given by NCTE

Innovations have been done in pre-service education, like introduction of ICT/technology in teacher education, professional development of teacher educators, Public Private Partnership (PPP) in teacher education and improving monitoring mechanism. There is an urgent need for creating an innovative learning environment for teachers in making to explore technology and device creative and meaningful approaches to integrate technology into their future classrooms (Beaudin and Madden, 2002).

The following aspects were emphasized by NCTE in teacher education

- **School Based Teacher Education** Observation and practice teaching are no longer undertaken in the laboratory schools of the colleges of education and teacher training colleges. They occur in the government or private school for longer duration at least for six months and in two phases.
- **Practicum Based Teacher Education** Practical aspect is more emphasized in B.Ed. course. The curriculum involves a structured program in which the pupil teachers work with students and the community. There is integration of theory and practice through additional field based experiences.
- Teacher educators are highly qualified and well trained in latest technology to fulfil the need of course.
- Evaluation includes continuous assessment, tests and exams.
- More emphasis is given on strategy, instructional technology, human development and linking school knowledge with community life.
- There is a provision of comprehensive curriculum which includes various subjects, like lifelong education, ICT, yoga and gender education and community education.
- Modern technologies, like e-mail, blog, web based learning, video conferencing, virtual and online learning play an important role in enhancing learner's capacity to investigate and draw conclusion.

Teachers should know about how to use best technology for preparing lesson in order to achieve pedagogical goals. They can use ICT to explore and learn new courses and skills, participate in community and group activities and discussions to understand newer perspective. Though many reforms or innovative practices are implemented in teacher education, but some resisting factor prevent it to be successful.

Barriers to Innovation

- Many insitutions are suffering from paucity of funds and physical facilities, like infrastructure, laboratories, equipment and man power. They are not able to put things into actions.
- Teacher educators are not able to imply innovations in their institutions as there is no support from the management and administration. No facilities are provided to them.
- Many teacher educators are not aware of modern trends in their field as they are not allowed to attend any refersher/ orientation courses, workshops and conferences to avoid any disturbance in their rigid routine work.
- Sometimes teacher educators are not willing to practice new ideas as there is no motivation for this. They have not yet developed any research aptitude as well as attitude.
- There is no flexibility in curriculum and examination system of teacher training institutions. They work in a rigid framework which is the biggest stumbling block in practicing innovative ideas.
- Professional rivalries, lack of cooperation among teacher educators and lack of expertise are some important factors in preventing innovations in institutions.
- Pupil teachers are not having required aptitude as well as attitude to give desirable output. They entered the system just to have degrees.

EXAM BASED QUESTIONS

1 Teaching professional ethics are related to
(a) profession (b) society
(c) values (d) All of these

2 Global emphasis on literacy is done through which programme?
(a) Education For All (EFA)
(b) Right To Education (RTE)
(c) Both a and b
(d) None of the above

3 Who defined "profession as an occupation that claims the exclusive technical competencies and also adheres to service ideals and allows ethics of professional conduct"?
(a) William (b) Wilson
(c) Obidi (d) Falade

4 Who used the word 'exclusive monopoly of knowledge' in regards with profession?
(a) Saunder and Wilson (b) Falade and William
(c) Obidi (d) Hoyle and Megarry

5 What is/are the characteristic(s) of profession?
(a) It must demand an adequate professional and cultural training
(b) It must develop scientific technique that is a result of tested experiment
(c) It must have sufficient self-impelling power to retain its member throughout the life
(d) All of the above

6 Which attribute(s) define(s) a 'professional'?
(a) Specialised knowledge (b) Accountability
(c) Self-regulation (d) All of these

7 Professionals have deep personal commitment to
(a) improve their skill
(b) build a strong peer group
(c) behave professionally
(d) develop a good behaviour

8 Professionals are competent. It means they are
(a) honest (b) reliable
(c) competitive (d) self-made

9 What is the vital element of professionalism?
(a) Reliability (b) Self-regulation
(c) Accountability (d) Sincerity

10 In the last decade of 20th century, what had changed?
(a) Teaching as a sake of employment
(b) Teaching the poor children
(c) Both a and b
(d) None of the above

11 Teacher's professionalism means
(a) the extent to which a teacher subscribes to a professional code.
(b) a teacher has to teach for the sake of getting salary.
(c) a teacher must have completed professional teacher training course before his appointment.
(d) All of the above

12 Which one of the following is true for a professional teacher?
(a) Creates problems in school administration
(b) Is friendly and predictable
(c) Have good knowledge
(d) Is lazy

13 Credentials are also known as
(a) automatic startup
(b) gate keeping devices
(c) professional doorways
(d) All of the above

14 Extensive training for new practitioner is known as
(a) in-service training (b) initial learning
(c) induction (d) screening

15 Professional exert a substantial control over the
(a) curriculum
(b) admission
(c) accreditation of professional training school
(d) All of the above

16 Professional development means
(a) updating skills and knowledge
(b) undergoing workshops and conferences
(c) taking part in in-service training
(d) All of the above

17 How the professionals are compensated?
(a) Meagre salary
(b) High salary and benefits
(c) Gifts
(d) All of the above

18 What qualities does a teacher should possess?
(a) Understanding the students
(b) Be just and courteous
(c) Promotes a spirit of enquring
(d) All of the above

19 What is the role of teacher in society?
(a) Performing duties
(b) Participating in community's activities
(c) Both a and b
(d) None of the above

20 Which of the following factor(s) affect(s) teacher's development?
(a) Psychological factor (b) Biological factor
(c) Environmental factor (d) All of these

21 What kind of attitude should the teacher have?
(a) Positive attitude (b) Laid back attitude
(c) Modern attitude (d) Negative attitude

22 What does the teacher need, to eradicate from the mind of young learner?
(a) Doubts (b) Laziness
(c) Fear and anger (d) Over confidence

23 In case of mental well being, an individual can
(a) cope with normal stresses of life
(b) work fruitfully and productively
(c) Both a and b
(d) None of the above

24 A teacher should be mature enough to know student's ....
(a) behaviour (b) likes and dislikes
(c) unmet needs (d) None of these

25 What is/are the environmental factor(s), affecting personal and contextual development?
(a) Social expectation (b) Cultural demand
(c) Achievement (d) All of these

26 Meaning of computer education is
(a) hardware knowledge (b) software knowledge
(c) Both a and b (d) None of these

27 Why is ICT used?
(a) To support information delivery
(b) To enhance information delivery
(c) To optimise information delivery
(d) All of the above

28 ICT has become basic building block of modern .... society.
(a) domestic (b) urban
(c) industrial (d) None of these

29 ICT has been used, at a amazing rate for instructions, among the ....
(a) teachers (b) students
(c) nurses (d) industrialists

30 In what ways, ICT can work?
(a) To develop student's skills
(b) To access to information and communication
(c) To support and transform the teaching and learning process
(d) All of the above

31 For using ICT, the teacher and student should trust
(a) each other (b) system
(c) technology (d) administration

32 For using ICT, the teacher needs to be
(a) funny (b) competent
(c) lively (d) None of these

33 What are the various ICT's tools that the teacher should know?
(a) Chat rooms
(b) File Transfer Protocol (FTP)
(c) Word processing skills
(d) All of the above

34 Teaching is a .... profession.
(a) global (b) loving
(c) lazy (d) monetary

35 Professionally, powerful .... is very important, in our contemporary society.
(a) learning (b) knowledge
(c) living (d) teaching

36 Professionalism of teaching should have
(a) competence (b) performance
(c) conduct (d) All of these

37 What does competence focuses on?
(a) Preparation
(b) Knowledge of subject area
(c) Defined pedagogy
(d) All of the above

38 What kind of barrier, does a professional faces in the classroom?
(a) Cultural barrier
(b) Socio-economic difference
(c) Both a and b
(d) None of these

39 If a teacher has good knowledge of his subject matter, then he can spend his extra time in ......
(a) preparing innovative techniques
(b) evaluating students
(c) discussing topics with peer group
(d) solving teacher's doubt

40 A good performance of teacher is derived from
(a) pre-mediated (b) improvisation
(c) Both a and b (d) None of these

41 Who is an active teacher?
(a) One, who can dance well.
(b) One, who has high performing rate.
(c) Both a and b
(d) None of the above

42 On which aspect professionals conduct depends on?
(a) aesthetic (b) language
(c) behaviour (d) All of these

43 A professional teacher must have good
(a) communication skills
(b) adventure training
(c) personality
(d) None of the above

44 Good education system, needs a good quality ....
(a) learner (b) curriculum
(c) professional teacher (d) All of these

45 Qualities that a teacher should possess includes
(a) knowledge of subject matter
(b) fluency in the language of instruction
(c) ability to create, learn and sustain
(d) All of the above

46 Innovation is derived from the word
(a) innovative (b) innovate
(c) innove (d) None of these

47 What is/are the way(s) of an innovative teaching?
(a) Collaborative/cooperative learning process
(b) Reflective teaching
(c) Constructivism and blended learning
(d) All of the above

48 What happens in cooperative learning?
(a) Each individual learns what is taught.
(b) Individual helps fellow classmate in learning.
(c) Both a and b
(d) None of the above

49 Constructivism evolves from
(a) pedagogy (b) self-contentment
(c) cognitive psychology (d) student's psychology

50 Blended learning involves traditional teaching and ....
(a) ICT
(b) resource management
(c) evaluation and assessment
(d) All of the above

51 Who stated that "the existing system of teacher education needs to be overhauled or revamped"?
(a) NCTE (b) UGC
(c) Kothari Commission (d) NPE

52 Choose the correct statement.
1. Psychological factors do not affect teacher's development.
2. Interest, intelligence, aptitude and mental health are all part of psychological factors.
3. Teachers should ignore the fact that some students do not have aptitude for learning.
4. Teachers should have positive feelings and emotions.

Codes
(a) 2 and 4 (b) 1 and 3
(c) Only 1 (d) 2, 3 and 4

53 Choose the correct statement.
1. Teacher must examine their belief, assumptions, and basis regarding teaching.
2. Reflective teaching is a natural process.
3. In reflective teaching, the learner's point of view is important.
4. Reflective teaching is a method of assessing the learner.

Codes
(a) 1 and 2 (b) 1, 2 and 3
(c) 1 and 4 (d) 2 and 4

54 Match the following

List I	List II
A. Job	1. Which occupies time
B. Profession	2. Specific task
C. Occupation	3. Liesure time
	4. Requires advanced training

Codes

	A	B	C		A	B	C
(a)	1	2	3	(b)	4	2	3
(c)	2	4	1	(d)	3	2	1

55 Match the following

List I (Programmes)	List II (Years)
A. Activity Based Teacher Education Programme	1. 1996
B. Personalized Teacher Education Programme	2. 2000
C. Comprehensive Teacher Education Programme	3. 2014
D. Two years, B.Ed Programme	4. 1991

Codes

	A	B	C	D		A	B	C	D
(a)	1	3	2	4	(b)	3	2	1	4
(c)	2	1	3	4	(d)	4	1	2	3

56 Match the following

List I	List II
A. NPE	1. 1995
B. NCTE	2. 1986-1990
C. PMOST	3. 1986
D. SOPT	4. 1993-94

Codes

	A	B	C	D		A	B	C	D
(a)	1	2	4	3	(b)	2	3	4	1
(c)	3	1	2	4	(d)	4	2	1	3

57 Match the following

List I	List II
A. Douley	1. Profession contains essential characteristic such as an occupation, that carries with it great responsibility.
B. William	2. Profession is the application of intellectual technique to the ordinary business of life, acquired as a result of prolonged and specialised training.
C. Falade	3. Profession usually exercises a system of control or a code of ethics, over practice through professional societies, associations and institutions or sometimes by laws.
D. Saunder & Wilson	4. Profession is a type of higher grade non-mannual occupation, with both subjectively recognised occupational status, possessing a well defined area of study and providing definite service after advanced training.

Codes

	A	B	C	D		A	B	C	D
(a)	2	3	4	1	(b)	4	1	3	2
(c)	1	3	2	4	(d)	4	3	1	2

58 Choose the correct statement.
1. Profession demands an adequate professional and cultural training.
2. A person in profession, can behave rudely.
3. One profession can be a stepping stone for other profession.
4. Profession must satisfy an indispensable social need.

Codes
(a) 1 and 4 (b) 2 and 3 (c) 1, 3 and 4 (d) 2, 3 and 4

59 What does youngsters need from a teacher?
1. Support 2. Appreciation
3. Criticism 4. Inspiration

Codes
(a) 1 and 4 (b) 2 and 4
(c) 1, 3 and 4 (d) 1, 2 and 4

60 Attributes of professionalism includes
1. competency
2. self-regulation
3. efficiency
4. accountability

Codes
(a) 1 and 2 (b) 3 and 4 (c) 1, 2 and 4 (d) 1 and 4

61 In the ethical code of conduct, teacher has relationship with
1. pupil 2. politician
3. parents 4. community

Codes
(a) 1 and 3 (b) 1, 3 and 4
(c) 1 and 4 (d) Only 2

62 Find out the incorrect pairing.
1. Biological factor – Physical health
2. Environmental factor – Cultural demand
3. Competence – Defined pedagogy
4. ICT – Traditional learning

Codes
(a) 1 (b) 2 (c) 3 (d) 4

63 Choose the correct statement.
1. A teacher should not care about student's unmet needs.
2. Sleep doesn't plays as an important biological factor.
3. Teacher should design a lesson as such that each student can learn something.
4. Teacher should not care about the social expectations.

Codes
(a) 1 and 4 (b) Only 3 (c) 1 and 2 (d) 3 and 4

64 Choose the correct statement.
1. ICT can be used to complete evaluation.
2. ICT is used to train students in technological skills.
3. ICT can provide access to information, outside the classroom.
4. ICT helps various school teachers to connect.

Codes
(a) 2 and 3 (b) 1 and 4
(c) Only 4 (d) 1 and 2

65 What is/are the qualit(y)(ies) of a good teacher?
1. Ability to communicate
2. Knowledge of subject matter
3. Keep check on the peer
4. Sensitive to young learners

Codes
(a) 2 and 4 (b) 3 and 2
(c) Only 1 (d) 1, 2 and 4

Directions (Q. Nos. 66-71) *Given below are two statements, one labelled as Assertion (A) and other labelled as Reason (R). Following are the codes given below. Choose the correct code.*

Codes
(a) Both A and R are true (b) Both A and R are false
(c) A is true, but R is false (d) A is false, but R is true

66 **Assertion** (A) Constructivism has evolved from conditioned pedagogy.
Reason (R) Students construct their own knowledge by testing ideas and approaches.

67 **Assertion** (A) Competence focuses on defined pedagogy as well.
Reason (R) A teacher having defined pedagogy already knows which techniques are more effective.

68 **Assertion** (A) ICT can provide dyanamic and pro-active teaching and learning environment.
Reason (R) ICT is a tool which can be used by anyone.

69 **Assertion** (A) Substantial authority is vested upon professionals.
Reason (R) Professionals control the curriculum, and admission.

70 **Assertion** (A) There is no need of mutual cooperation between home and school environment.
Reason (A) Guidance should be only given by teacher, parents have no role to play.

71 **Assertion** (A) Initiative steps in innovation of teacher's education was started by NPE.
Reason (R) NPE established NCTE in 1995.

PREVIOUS YEARS' QUESTIONS

July 2018

1 Which of the following has relatively greater promise for professionalisation of teacher's education in India?

(a) Forming teacher's associations
(b) Developing teacher code for transaction of teaching-learning system
(c) Special packages offered to teachers
(d) Enhancing the period of Pre-Service Teacher Education Programme

November 2017

2 An effective programme of teacher education aims at developing teacher proficiency and competence that will consequently empower the teacher with of the following?

1. Skill in designing the teaching-learning situations.
2. Eagerness for upgradation of knowledge.
3. Ability to minimise the wastage of resources.
4. Understanding of interpersonal relations in a class.
5. Competencies in making quality decisions about managing, monitoring and evaluating learning behaviour.

Codes

(a) 2, 3, 1 and 4 (b) 3, 4, 2 and 1
(c) 1, 2, 4 and 5 (d) 4, 5, 3 and 1

December 2015

3 Continuing professional development and updating a teacher is an essential requirement to ensure that

(a) teacher should remains in active touch with the changes in the content.
(b) teacher should remains a thinking practitioner of ideas and practices.
(c) teacher should be motivated to secure more promotional avenues.
(d) teacher should play an active part in the process of qualitative improvement of education.

June 2015

4 Which of the following is not a characteristic of a profession?

(a) Membership of a professional organisation
(b) Long duration of pre-service training
(c) Working with service motive
(d) Promoting activism for attractive emoluments

June 2014

5 When the children become mischievous and disobedient in the classroom, the teacher should examine

(a) home background of the students
(b) influence of outside elements in class
(c) teaching methods and subject knowledge
(d) co-curricular and other attractions in the school

ANSWERS

Exam Based Questions

1 *(d)*	2 *(c)*	3 *(c)*	4 *(d)*	5 *(d)*	6 *(d)*	7 *(a)*	8 *(b)*	9 *(c)*	10 *(a)*
11 *(a)*	12 *(c)*	13 *(b)*	14 *(c)*	15 *(d)*	16 *(d)*	17 *(b)*	18 *(d)*	19 *(c)*	20 *(d)*
21 *(a)*	22 *(c)*	23 *(c)*	24 *(c)*	25 *(d)*	26 *(c)*	27 *(d)*	28 *(c)*	29 *(a)*	30 *(d)*
31 *(c)*	32 *(b)*	33 *(d)*	34 *(a)*	35 *(d)*	36 *(d)*	37 *(d)*	38 *(c)*	39 *(a)*	40 *(c)*
41 *(b)*	42 *(d)*	43 *(a)*	44 *(c)*	45 *(d)*	46 *(b)*	47 *(d)*	48 *(c)*	49 *(c)*	50 *(a)*
51 *(d)*	52 *(a)*	53 *(a)*	54 *(c)*	55 *(d)*	56 *(c)*	57 *(d)*	58 *(a)*	59 *(d)*	60 *(c)*
61 *(b)*	62 *(d)*	63 *(b)*	64 *(a)*	65 *(d)*	66 *(d)*	67 *(a)*	68 *(c)*	69 *(a)*	70 *(b)*
71 *(a)*									

Previous Years' Questions

1 *(b)*	2 *(c)*	3 *(d)*	4 *(d)*	5 *(c)*

CHAPTER 17

Curriculum and Its Principles

The curriculum is the totality of experiences that the child gains through the multifarious activities in school. A well designed curriculum helps the learner in gaining knowledge, developing concepts and inculcating skills, attitude, values and habits which are conducive for the all round development of their personality.

Meaning and Definitions of Curriculum

A curriculum can be called as a plan for learning, which contains assumptions about the purpose of an education in our society. It also has a definite structure through which the vision of the planner can be translated into learning experiences of the learner. Hence, any curriculum comprises of two major dimensions *i.e.* a vision and a structure.

According to the **Modern Concept of Curriculum**, it does not mean only the academic subjects, traditionally taught in schools but it includes the sum total of experiences that pupil receives through the manifold activities that go on in the school, classroom, library, laboratory, workshop, playgrounds and in the numerous informal contacts between teachers and pupil. In this sense, curriculum touches the life of the students at all points and helps in the evolution of a balanced personality.

Thus, a curriculum is a systematic arrangement of the sum total of selected learning experiences planned by a school for a defined group of students to attain the aim of particular educational programme. It is commonly formed as a Programme of Studies.

It is intimately related with an education. While an education is a process, curriculum is a means of the process. While an education is learning, curriculum signifies situation for learning.

In this Chapter

According to **Tanner and Tanner**, "Curriculum is the reconstruction of knowledge and experience systematically developed under the auspices of the school (or university), to enable the learner to increase his or her control of knowledge and experience".

According to **Coles**, "Curriculum is the sum of all the activities, experiences and learning opportunities for which an institution takes responsibility either deliberately or by default".

Characteristics of Curriculum

- It must be continuously evolving from one period to another, to the present. For a curriculum to be an effective, it must have continuous monitoring and an evaluation. It must adapt its educational activities and services to meet the needs of modern and dynamic community.
- It is based on the needs of the people. It should be in proper sequence in order to meet the challenges of time and to make an education more responsive.
- It comprises of complex details as it includes guidance and counselling, health services, projects and also provides the proper instructional equipments that are often most conductive to learning.
- It complements and cooperates with other programs of the community. So, curriculum is responsive to the needs of the community.
- Each curriculum objective should constitute learning i.e.
  - (i) Durable–will be useful to the student for a considerable period of his/her lifetime.
  - (ii) Significant–will have a major effect upon how the student will function.
  - (iii) Transferable–will be useful in meeting needs in other educational programmes or the student's personal life.

Each outcome assessment and evaluation should be accompanied by both the criteria by which the learning will be judged and the standards of quality which will apply.

Principles of Curriculum

The success of curriculum depends on certain principles which needs to be developed in mind, while framing a curriculum. *These are as follows*

Principle of Child-Centeredness It means that what is to be given to children in the form of learning experiences at a particular age and grade should properly suit their age, abilities, capacities, interests, mental development and previous experiences. Therefore, in all circumstances it should fulfil the needs and requirements of the developing children.

Principle of Comprehensiveness Curriculum must have necessary details because merely a list of topics will not serve the purpose either of the teacher or the student. Material aids, techniques, life situations, related activities, possibilities of correlation, etc, should be listed in the curriculum, so, that these can serve as a guide to the teachers and authors of textbooks.

Principle of Correlation The curriculum should be such that all subjects are related to each other. Teaching all subjects separately would be unpsychological, so it must be kept in mind that the subject matter of various subjects has some affinity with each other so that they can help the child eventually.

Principle of Utility According to this principle, only those topics, subject materials and learning experiences should be included in the curriculum, which are found to possess any utility to the students.

Principle of Forward Looking The principle of forward looking, asks for an inclusion of those topics, contents and learning experiences that may prove helpful to the students in leading their future life in a proper way. Therefore, attempts should always be made to include the topics and learning experiences.

Principle of Environmental Centeredness The curriculum is developed keeping in view the physical and social environment of the students. Therefore, the selection of subject material and learning experiences should be based on or link with an events, the problems and situations prevalent in their physical and social environment.

Curriculum Development

Curriculum development refers to the actual implementation of the results of the decisions reached during curriculum planning. This means that when decision have been made in respect to the nature, organization and orientation of the curriculum, it becomes the place of curriculum development to build a curriculum based on the decisions.

According to **Nicholls and Nicholls**, "the planning of learning opportunities intended to bring about certain changes in pupils and the assessment of the extent to which these changes have taken place in what is meant by curriculum development".

So, curriculum development and planning has been visualized as a continuous and dynamic process.

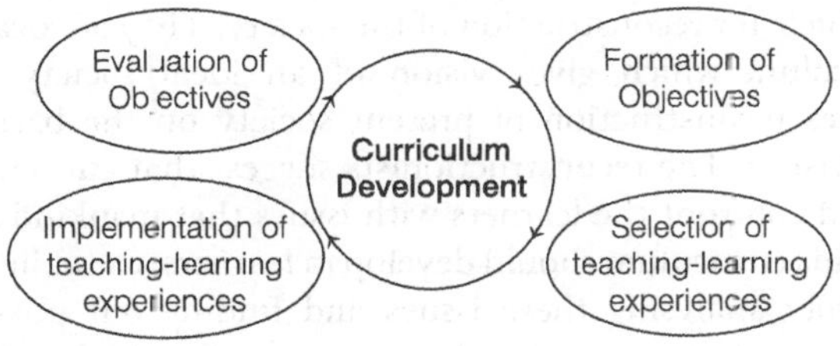

Strategies of Curriculum Development

There are few strategies that plays a significant role in the curriculum development and they are discussed below

Problem Identification Firstlly, while developing a curriculum, the problem areas is need to be identified to meet the needs of the curriculum as it will help to improvise the content formation. It is an important strategy in curriculum development as it highlights the issues of relevance that needs modification for an effective curriculum.

Needs Assessment of Learners Curriculum development should be viewed as a process by which meeting student's needs lead to improvement of student's learning. It should include the desired outcomes or expectations of a high quality program, the role of an assessment, the current status of student's achievements and actual program content. An effective curriculum development process usually entails a structured needs assessment to gather information and to guide the curriculum development process.

Goals and Objectives Curriculum goals are general and broad statements that lead towards long-term outcomes. Specifically, goals are always for reaching the objectives and are usually based on the ideas that they lead students towards being better able to be productive members of the society.

Educational Strategies and Implementation An educational strategies must be clear as per the requirement of the curriculum. An innovative and productive approach will help the students to gather relevant information from the sources provided by their teacher Proper implementation of an educational strategies will fetch maximum output in the process of curriculum development.

Feedback and Evaluation The curriculum development cycle ends and then begins again with a careful evaluation of the effectiveness and impact of the program. The detailed review and analysis of quantitative and qualitative information of the programmes, impact and on people's perceptions of its strengths and weaknesses forms the foundation for the next round of curriculum development and improvement. Feedback helps the teacher to improve and modify the framework of curriculum as it provides an interpretation of performance.

Stages of Curriculum Development

There are four stages in the process of curriculum development that are discussed below

Planning The curriculum planning considers the vision, mission and goals. It also includes the philosophy of strong education belief of the school. All of these will eventually, be translated to classrooms desired learning outcomes for the learners. The planning stage lays the foundation for all of the curriculum development steps that are identifying the needs according to the curriculum and need to conduct assessment and analysis.

Curriculum Designing It is the way in which curriculum is conceptualized to include the selection and organization of the content, the selection and organization of learning experiences as well as the selection of an assessment procedure to measure achieved learning outcomes. A curriculum design will also include the resources to be utilized and the statement of the intended learning outcomes.

Curriculum Implementing It means putting into action the plan which is based on the curriculum design in the learning environment. The teacher is the facilitator of learning and together with the learners uses the curriculum as to design to what will transpire in the classroom with the end in view of achieving the intended learning outcomes. Implementing the curriculum is where action takes place.

Evaluation It determines the extent to which the desired outcomes have been achieved. This procedure is ongoing in finding out the progress of learning. Along the way, an evaluation will determine the factors that have supported the implementation. It will help in making improvements and taking corrective measures. The result of an evaluation is very important for curriculum planners and implementors.

Foundations of Curriculum Planning

The foundation of curriculum sets an external boundaries of the knowledge of curriculum and defines what constitutes valid source of information from which are accepted theories, principles and an ideas relevant in the field of curriculum.

The foundations of curriculum are considered usually from philosophical, sociological and psychological point of view as discussed below

Philosophical Foundation of Curriculum

It helps to determine the driving purpose of education as well as the roles of various participants. While, all foundations propose to set goals of curriculum, philosophy presents the manner of thinking from which those goals are created. Philosophies vary in perception of truth ranging from absolute to relative and from moralistic to scientific.

In essence, the philosophy of education influences to a large extent that determines our educational decisions and alternatives. Those who are responsible for curricular decisions, therefore, should be clear about what they believe.

There are four major philosophical positions that have influenced curriculum development and they are

- Idealism
- Realism
- Pragmatism
- Existentialism

Idealism and Curriculum The idealists approach the problem of curriculum from the domain of ideas and ideals. Idealistic curriculum provides for the training and cultivation of the intellectual, moral and aesthetic activities. For the intellectual development of the child, languages, literature, sciences, social studies and mathematics are included in the curriculum. For the aesthetic and method of development fine arts, poetry-ethies and religion are provided.

Realism and Curriculum Realism centred the education field as a protest against the narrowness of the bookish, sophisticated and abstruse curricula. Realism holds that education should be closely related with the actual realities of life in all conceivable aspects.

Pragmatism and Curriculum Pragmatism is a practical and utilitarian school of philosophy, it has influenced the educational curriculum to the maximum extent. It enable the child to solve his daily problems and also lead a better and happier life by creating new values.

Sociological Foundation of Curriculum

Education is the process that takes place in society, for society and by society. The changing nature of the cultural aspect has its impact on education. Education has to adjust itself to the changing situations. So, curriculum should be designed according to the changes and should promote desirable changes in learners also.

The social reconstructionists are dissatisfied with the social, political and economic order of society and take curriculum as vehicle for reconstruction of the society. They advocate a curriculum which gives vision of an ideal society and ensures reconstruction of present society on the basis of that vision. The reconstructionists suggest that curriculum should confront the learners with issues that mankind face and this curriculum should develop in learners, the ability of critically analysing these issues and finding out possible solutions. Consequently, the learners will develop deep understanding of the society and they will strive for better social order.

Psychological Foundation of Curriculum

It consists of the accumulated knowledge which guides the learning process and allows the teacher, who is executing the curriculum to make intelligent decisions regarding the behaviour of the learner.

Selection of curriculum content and its organization are based on various theories of Psychology such as laws of learning, theories of interest and attention, transfer of learning, growth and development of physique and mental intelligence, creativity and personality development. It is agreed by all that curriculum should be organised on theories of learning and motivation and on the aptitude and ability of the learner. *It is based on certain theories of learning that comprised of :*

Behaviourist Theories They deals with an aspect of stimulus *i.e.* response and reinforcement scheme.

Cognitive Theories They view the learner in relationship with total environment.

Phenomenology Theories They emphasizes an affective domain of learning.

Benchmarking

It is a tool for improving performance by comparing the performance or standards or both with those of its peers. It can be strategic (addressing priority issues) or cyclical (addressing a number of areas on a regular basis) or adhoc (taking advantage of an opportunity).

The strategy of benchmarking is important both conceptually and practically and it is being used for improving an administrative processes as well as an instructional models at colleges and universities by examining processes and models at other schools and adopting their techniques or approaches.

The goal of benchmarking is to provide key personnel, incharge of processes, with an external standards for measuring the quality and cost of internal activities and helps to identify where an opportunities for improvement may reside.

Benchmarking with appropriate partners, at a national or international level, enables the University to compare and evaluate its performance in doing so, monitor standards, compare good practice and make quality improvements.

According to **Kempner**, "Benchmarking is an ongoing, systematic process for measuring and comparing the work process of an organisation to those of another, by bringing an external focus to internal activities, functions or operations".

According to **Leibfried and Mcnair**, "Benchmarking is an analogous to the human learning process and it has been described as a method of teaching an institution how to improve".

Types of Benchmarking

Benchmarking as a process, is both complex and comprehensive in terms of what type and for what purpose it can be used. In the past, it was commonly used as a way to compare data only. However, it is used as a more investigative, research informed process, is gaining momentum in the higher education sector and adds rigour to decision-making processes at an institutional level.

The university employs a number of different types of benchmarking to support its goal of continuous improvement. These are internal, competitive, functional and genetic benchmarking.

It can also be characterised as

Quantitative Where the focus is on quantifiable outputs of data.

Qualitative Which looks at the systems and processes that delivers the result where benchmarks are generally attributes of good practices.

The different types of benchmarking are

Internal The work processes are compared between departments, divisions or other internal university segments. Advantages of such benchmarking includes the ease of data collection and the definition of areas for future external investigation. The primary disadvantage of an internal benchmarking is a lower probability that will yield significant process improvement breakthrough.

Competitive An organisation's performance is measured against its peers or competitors. In competitive benchmarking, a third party rather than an organisation itself, often collects and analyses the data because of its proprietary nature.

Functional This type of benchmarking is an opportunity for breakthrough improvements by analyzing high performing processes across a variety of students.

Generic This type of benchmarking makes the broadest use of data collection from different kinds of organizations.

Role of National Level Statutory Bodies

There are several national level statutory bodies in India for higher education and they are as follows

University Grants Commission (UGC)

According to the recommendation of the **University Education Commission**, the Government of India established **University Grants Commission** in **1953**. Later, it was made a statutory body under the **University Grants Commission Act** of **1956**. It prescribes standards for infra structural facilities, curricula and qualification of teachers, salary of teachers and other factors required for maintaining the quality of higher education.

The commission inspects universities with a view to evaluate the above aspects and give recognition to the deserving institutions. It provides financial assistance to the recognised universities in the form of grants and conducts periodical evaluation to ensure the standards are maintained without lapse.

Role of UGC in Curriculum Development

The University Grant Commission plays an important role in the development of curriculum, as explained below

- It reviews and updates curriculum which is the essential ingredient of its academic system.
- It works in coordination with other related bodies towards curriculum development like NCTE.
- It also cooperates in curriculum creation programme with international level organisations.
- For the development of curriculum, the committees for each subject is constituted.
- It upgrades/reframe the curricula in various subjects at the UG/PG levels.
- It organises training programmes, workshops, seminars and conferences.
- It advises the central government and state governments on the measures for the improvement of university education.

- It allows to provide fellowships and scholarships to students.
- It monitors its 24 hour's educational channel **Vyas** through which it imparts education to students from various streams.
- It monitors an educational curriculum and scrutinises the proposals from universities for new courses and grants.

So, UGC plays a significant role in the curriculum development process. Irrespective of this, it collects an information on university's education system in India and compares the same with the education system in other countries.

National Council for Teacher Education (NCTE)

Since **1973**, the National Council for Teacher Education was an advisory body for the central and state governments, on all matters pertaining to teacher education, with its secretariat in the Department of Teacher Education of the National Council of Educational Research and Training (NCERT). The NCTE as a statutory body came into existence in pursuance of the National Council for Teacher Education Act, 1993 on 17th August, 1995. It has it's headquarters at New Delhi and four regional committees at Bangalore, Bhopal, Bhubaneshwar and Jaipur.

The NCTE in Delhi as well as its four regional committees have administrative and academic wings to deal respectively, with finance, establishment and legal matters with research, policy planning, monitoring, curriculum, innovations, coordination, library and documentation in service programmes. It's headquarter is headed by the chairperson, while each regional committee is headed by regional director.

Role of NCTE in Curriculum Development

It lays down norms for any specified category of courses or training in teacher education including course content and mode of curriculum. It makes recommendations to the central and state governments, universities, UGC and its recognised institutes in matters of preparing plans and programmes for teacher education.

From time to time, NCTE brings about necessary changes in curriculum. It prepared National Curriculum Framework For Teacher Education (2009). This curriculum has given a systematic and comprehending framework for teacher education and also highlights the strategies to implement it. In this curriculum framework almost every aspect of teacher education got preference. The NCFTE (2009) paved the way for implementing of curricular areas by giving practical and reasonable strategies.

It's main role is to achieve planned and coordinated development of teacher education system throughout the country which is important part of curriculum development process. It aims at training an individuals for equipping them to teach pre-primary, primary, secondary and senior secondary stages in schools, non-formal and part-time education.

It also promotes and conduct innovation research in various areas of teacher education.

It has revised the regulations in 2014 that includes

- establishment of teacher education in composite institutions that consists of multi-disciplinary education programmes.
- each programme curriculum gives importance to yoga education, ICT, inclusive education, etc.
- open and distance learning has developed and improved the performance due to inbuilt quality assurance mechanisms.

University in Curriculum Development

University plays an important role in implementing the curriculum and ***its responsibilities are discussed below***

- It facilitates the collaboration with community colleges, to ensure that the materials are suitable for college's student population and methods of instructions.
- It ensures materials can be accessed electronically by students, allowing their use for distance learning.
- It works with an industry and employee groups to ensure that the material will prepare the students to meet emerging workforce needs.
- It collaborates with the community college's members in each region to support the discrimination and use of these materials.

Thus, university plays a significant role in curriculum development process and tries to ensure that it can provide proper guidance to the learners.

Conclusion

Curriculum is an instructional and educative programme, by following which the pupils achieve their goals, ideals and aspirations of life. The curriculum should integrate cognitive, affective and psychomotor objectives and abilities.

Curriculum development have to satisfy the different foundations of curriculum and thereby they could be adopted in multi-cultural classroom settings. Hence, great effort should be taken to frame such a curriculum before executing the process of teaching at all levels of education.

EXAM BASED QUESTIONS

1 Curriculum in education is a
(a) plan for learning
(b) plan for growth and development
(c) control of knowledge
(d) None of the above

2 An important factor of curriculum is to help to achieve the
(a) education (b) objectives (c) values (d) job

3 Which of the following is the nature of curriculum?
(a) Critical (b) Creative
(c) Conservative (d) All of these

4 Curriculum provides guidance for
(a) schools (b) teachers (c) students (d) parents

5 Syllabus is a part of
(a) curriculum (b) classroom (c) activities (d) society

6 Curriculum presents an instructional material, is stated by
(a) Elizhalh Maccis (b) Jack Kerr
(c) W Teller (d) Smith

7 Who said that "curriculum is the sum of all the activities, experiences and learning opportunities for which an institution takes responsibility either deliberately or by default"?
(a) John Dewey (b) Coles
(c) Tanner (d) Smith

8 Curriculum comprises of two major dimensions i.e.
(a) vision and control (b) structure and activities
(c) vision and structure (d) All of the above

9 Curriculum in a fixed programme of courses is a ____ of curriculum.
(a) old concept (b) contemporary concept
(c) logical concept (d) All of these

10 Modern concept of curriculum is helping in the evolution of
(a) average personality (b) balanced personality
(c) extrovert personality (d) reserved personality

11 Psychological foundation plays its role in development of curriculum in view of the
(a) student's needs (b) student's interests
(c) student's capabilities (d) All of these

12 Major concern of curriculum is
(a) change in an individual's behaviour
(b) preparation for service
(c) personal satisfaction
(d) None of the above

13 The importance of curriculum in the system of education is just like a
(a) preparation of students for service
(b) constitution in a country
(c) provision of latest knowledge
(d) None of the above

14 The curriculum is supposed to
(a) be organized (b) achieve an objective
(c) both (a) and (b) (d) None of these

15 Curriculum reflects the culture of
(a) college (b) home (c) area (d) society

16 An effective curriculum is based on the principle of
(a) continuous monitoring (b) continuous evaluation
(c) both (a) and (b) (d) None of the above

17 A curriculum is the blueprint of an institution that includes experiences for the
(a) expert (b) teacher
(c) learner (d) curriculum planner

18 The Principle of Forward Looking is necessary because
(a) it will be helpful for the students
(b) it will be helpful for teachers
(c) it will solve the problems
(d) All of the above

19 The curriculum development refers to the total process of curriculum
(a) implementation (b) evaluation
(c) designing (d) All of these

20 Balanced curriculum is also known as
(a) integrated curriculum
(b) experienced curriculum
(c) activity centered curriculum
(d) core curriculum

21 An effectiveness of curriculum is determined by
(a) evaluation (b) objective (c) method (d) design

22 When, what, why and how, to teach is the main task of
(a) Educational Psychology (b) Educational Philosophy
(c) Economics (d) History

23 The forces that effect the development of curriculum are called
(a) curriculum design (b) curriculum evaluation
(c) elements of curriculum (d) foundation of curriculum

24 Philosophical foundation of the curriculum is concerned with
(a) ideas (b) History (c) Economy (d) contents

25 Student's needs and interests are important in
(a) sociological foundation (b) psychological foundation
(c) economical foundation (d) historical foundation

26 Psychological foundation of curriculum helps curriculum developers to understand the nature of
(a) content (b) learner
(c) teacher (d) ideas

27 The sources of information for Psychological foundation are
(a) learning process (b) teaching method
(c) student's characteristics (d) All of these

28 The curriculum based on thinking of John Dewey is
(a) learner centered curriculum
(b) activity centered curriculum
(c) subject centered curriculum
(d) None of the above

29 The factor effecting curriculum development is/are
(a) sociological factor (b) economical factor
(c) scientific factor (d) All of these

30 Making value judgement about curriculum is
(a) curriculum development (b) curriculum evaluation
(c) curriculum elements (d) curriculum design

31 Curriculum effectiveness is determined by
(a) community cooperation (b) teacher's competence
(c) student's interest (d) quality of supervision

32 The Sociology of Education is
(a) a branch of Anthropology
(b) a study of the society
(c) an analysis of sociological processes involved in an institutions of an education
(d) a science which studies primitive societies

33 Curriculum improvement should be a....... process.
(a) initial (b) last (c) continuous (d) internal

34 The implementer for curriculum is
(a) curriculum bureau b) curriculum wing
(c) textbook board (d) educational institutions

35 Curriculum decision is affected by
(a) aims of an education
(b) the structure of knowledge
(c) the worth whiteners of knowledge
(d) All of the above

36 The most important factor which resists the curriculum change is
(a) aristocratic class of the society
(b) political leaders
(c) teachers
(d) parents

37 The process in which strengths and weaknesses of the curriculum are identified is called
(a) content selection (b) content organisation
(c) teaching methodology (d) evaluation

38 The foundation(s) of the curriculum is/are
(a) philosophical (b) psychological
(c) sociological (d) All of these

39 The theory helps to determine the driving purpose of education as well as roles of various partners is known as ....
(a) Philosophical (b) Psychological
(c) Sociological (d) Humanism

40 Curriculum construction in Indian education is mostly influenced by
(a) child's psychology (b) teacher's personality
(c) family structure (d) constitutional provisions

41 Psychological foundation is based on
(a) behaviour of the learner (b) environment
(c) mental intelligence (d) None of these

42 Which is the second stage of curriculum development?
(a) Planning (b) Evaluation
(c) Curriculum implementing (d) Curriculum designing

43 .... is the stage of curriculum development which determines the extent to which the desired outcomes are achieved.
(a) Planning (b) Evaluation
(c) Designing (d) Implementing

44 It is the strategy that highlights the issues of relevance for an effective curriculum
(a) feedback (b) goals and objectives
(c) problem identification (d) educational strategies

45 An effective curriculum development process usually entails
(a) need based assessment (b) feedback
(c) structured objectives (d) None of these

46 The strategy which fetch maximum output in the process of curriculum development is
(a) evaluation (b) problem identification
(c) implementation (d) None of these

47 The strategy which helps the teacher to improve and modify the framework of curriculum is
(a) needs assessment (b) feedback and evaluation
(c) implementation (d) All of these

48 It is a tool for improving performance.
(a) evaluation (b) feedback
(c) objectives (d) benchmarking

49 Benchmarking can be conducted by using
(a) Case Study approach (b) performance indicators
(c) Both a and b (d) None of these

50 Who said that "Benchmarking is an ongoing, systematic process for measuring and comparing the work processes of an organization, by bringing an external focus to an internal activities, functions or operations"?
(a) Kempher (b) Leibfried (c) Menair (d) None of these

51 Benchmarking can be broadly categorised on the basis of
(a) quantitative basis (b) qualitative basis
(c) Both a and b (d) None of these

52 UGC was established in
(a) 1953 (b) 1956 (c) 1954 (d) 1955

53 When was UGC made a statutory body?
(a) 1957 (b) 1956 (c) 1954 (d) 1958

54 Under which act, UGC was made a statutory body?
(a) University Grants Commission Act of 1956
(b) University Grants Commission Act of 1955
(c) University Grants Commission Act of 1954
(d) None of the above

55 What is the name of channel through which UGC imparts an education to its students, 24 hours?
(a) Exam Fear (b) Vyas
(c) Tutor Vista (d) Unacademy

56 NCTE has revised its regulations on teacher education in
(a) 2009 (b) 2014
(c) 2015 (d) None of these

57 NCTE became a statutory body on
(a) 17th August, 1994 (b) 17th August, 1993
(c) 17th August, 1996 (d) 17th August, 1995

58 Under which act, NCTE was made a statutory body?
(a) National Council for Teacher Education Act, 1993
(b) National Council of Educational Research and Training Act, 1993
(c) Both (a) and (b)
(d) None of the above

59 NCTE's headquarter is located in
(a) Raipur (b) New Delhi
(c) Assam (d) Mumbai

60 Four regional committee offices of NCTE are in
(a) Bhopal, Mumbai, Jaipur and Bangalore
(b) Bhopal, Jaipur, Jammu and Kashmir, Bangalore
(c) Bhubaneshwar, Bhopal, Jaipur, Bangalore
(d) Orissa, Bhopal, Jaipur, Bangalore

61 The NCTE's headquarter is headed by
(a) chairman (b) chairperson
(c) director (d) officer

62 Each regional committee of NCTE is headed by
(a) regional officer (b) regional head
(c) regional director (d) None of these

63 Which of the following is the apex body in the area of teacher education in India?
(a) UGC (b) MHRD (c) NCTE (d) NCERT

64 Consider the following statements about the role of NCTE.

Statement I It's main role is to achieve planned and coordinated developed of teacher education throughout the country.

Statement II It aims at training individual to teach at pre-primary, primary and secondary level.

Codes
(a) Only Statement I is true
(b) Only Statement II is true
(c) Both statements, I and II are true
(d) Neither Statement I nor Statement II is true

65 Match the following

	List I	List II
A.	UGC	1. Initiating innovations in teacher's education
B.	NCERT	2. Provides fellowships and scholarships
C.	NCTE	3. Educational research body

Codes

	A	B	C		A	B	C
(a)	2	3	1	(b)	3	2	1
(c)	1	2	3	(d)	None of these		

66 Match the following

	List I	List II
A.	Principle of Environment Centeredness	1. Related to other disciplines also
B.	Principle of Correlation	2. Must have necessary details
C.	Principle of Utility	3. Possess relevant utility
D.	Principle of Comprehensiveness	4. Related to physical and social aspects

Codes

	A	B	C	D		A	B	C	D
(a)	1	2	3	4	(b)	3	2	4	1
(c)	4	1	3	2	(d)	1	4	2	3

67 Match the following

	List I	List II
A.	Philosophical basis	1. Vision of an ideal society
B.	Psychological basis	2. Influenced from an idealism, realism, pragmatism and an existentialism
C.	Sociological basis	3. Based on Behaviourist and Cognitive theories

Codes

	A	B	C		A	B	C
(a)	1	2	3	(b)	3	1	2
(c)	2	3	1	(d)	None of these		

Direction (Q. No. 68 to 74) *Given below are two statements, one labelled as Assertion (A) and other labelled as Reason (R). In the context of the given statements, select the correct code(s) given below.*

Codes
(a) Both A and R are true
(b) Both A and R are false
(c) A is true, but R is false
(d) A is false, but R is true

68 **Assertion** (A) Philosophy helps in determining aims of education.
Reason (R) Education depends mostly on Philosophy.

69 **Assertion** (A) Traditional curriculum includes only the academic aspects.
Reason (R) Traditional curriculum touches the life of the students at all points.

70 **Assertion** (A) Curriculum is intimately related with an education in every aspect.
Reason (R) Education is a process and curriculum is a means to the process.

71 **Assertion** (A) Effective curriculum is a continuously evolving in nature.
Reason (R) It meet the needs of modern and dynamic community.

72 **Assertion** (A) Democratic curriculum is based on new learning in a collaborative way.
Reason (R) It is for the students to discover knowledge.

73 **Assertion** (A) Benchmarking is an ongoing and systematic process which helps in an improvement.
Reason (R) It leads to comparative analysis by examining processes and models.

74 **Assertion** (A) Education promotes peace and harmony.
Reason (R) Democratic curriculum is practiced in the classrooms.

75 The child centered education means
1. education liked by children
2. education liked both by children and teachers.
3. education geared to child's needs and aspirations.
4. education is considered worthwhile and desirable.

Codes
(a) Both 1 and 2 (b) Only 3
(c) Both 3 and 4 (d) Only 4

76 What are the determinates of 'objectives' in the development of curriculum?
1. Socio-psychological needs of an individuals of the level concerned.
2. Economical needs of the society.
3. Thrust areas at the time of curriculum development.
4. National aims of secondary education.

Codes
(a) 1, 2 and 4 (b) 2, 3 and 4
(c) 1 and 2 (d) 1, 2 and 3

77 The stage(s) of curriculum development is/are
1. planning
2. designing
3. implementing and evaluation
4. improvement and progress

Codes
(a) 1, 2 and 4 (b) 1, 3 and 4
(c) 1, 2 and 3 (d) Only 4

78 In universities, which different types of benchmarking are used?
1. international and discipline specific
2. sector and process based
3. internal and external
4. value based

Codes
(a) 1, 2 and 3 (b) 1, 2 and 4
(c) 1, 3 and 4 (d) 1 and 2

Directions (Q. Nos. 79 to 82) *Read the given passage and answer the following questions.*

The aim of the curriculum is to enable the student to learn with a lot of ease and have the ability to comprehend and solve problems, adequately. Also there are some valuable advices to the teachers on how they can handle students based on the quality of training they got. An educational curriculum has proved to be a powerful base of knowledge for any nation in advance. It provides an effective method to accomplish an educational policies with a lot of integration, by employing new technologies. Its innovation is highly complex and requires further research and investigation. It is common for curriculum innovations to change with little noticeable impact on the classroom work and more so in the field work i.e. practical.

79 The aim of curriculum is to
(a) solve the problems of an educational institution.
(b) enable the students to learn effectively.
(c) provide and fulfil philosophical aspects.
(d) None of the above

80 Educational curriculum provides
(a) Effective Method (b) Innovative Approach
(c) Both (a) and (b) (d) None of the above

81 An innovation in educational curriculum requires
(a) research and investigation
(b) new educational policy
(c) high goals
(d) All of the above

82 Curriculum innovations should have
(a) high impact on classroom work
(b) little impact on classroom work
(c) Both (a) and (b)
(d) None of the above

Directions (Q. Nos. 83 to 86) *Read the given passage and answer the following questions.*

Curriculum development is a dynamic process. It changes according to the need of the society and the stakeholders of an education system. The curriculum development process includes several stages such as planning, preparing, designing, developing, implementing, evaluating, revising and improving. Traditionally, curriculum has been seen as the planning for a sustained process of teaching and learning in a formal institutional setting. Curriculum development is a systematic and dynamic process, sensitive to time and place in which preparation, development, implementation and evaluation steps are evaluated. There are varieties of challenges facing by curriculum development, but in general they are classified into three types *i.e.* global (external), internal challenges of an educational system and challenges specific nal to region.

83 Curriculum changes as per the
(a) needs of the society
(b) stakeholders of an education system
(c) Both a and b
(d) None of the above

84 Which stage is not a part of curriculum development?
(a) Planning (b) Evaluating
(c) Implementing (d) Modelling

85 The varieties of challenges are faced by curriculum development including
(a) global challenges (b) internal challenges
(c) regional challenges (d) All of these

86 The curriculum development process is sensitive to
(a) time and place (b) behaviour and time
(c) Both a and b (d) None of these

Directions (Q. Nos. 87 to 89) *Read the given passage and answer the following questions.*

Curriculum effectiveness is defined as an extent to which a curriculum and its implementation produce positive and curricularly valid outcomes for students, in relation to multiple measures of student's proficiency, disaggregated by content strands and the extent to which these effects can be convincingly or casually attributed to the curricular intervention through an evaluation studies using well conceived research designs. Describing curricular effectiveness involves the identification and description of a curriculum and its Programmatic theory and stated objectives. Its relationship to local, state or national standards, subsequent scrutiny of its program content for comprehensiveness, accuracy and depth, balance, engagement and timeliness and support for diversity and an examination of the quality, fidelity and character of its implementation components.

87 What is the need of an effective curriculum?
(a) It will make a potential impact on students
(b) Provides coherent learning experiences
(c) Both a and b
(d) None of the above

88 The qualities of a good curriculum are
(a) it allows flexibility
(b) based on well conceived research designs.
(c) promotes the value of overall development of child
(d) All of the above

89 The important components of implementing curriculum are
(a) subsequent security of content
(b) comprehensiveness, accuracy and depth
(c) limitless
(d) Both a and b

90 Evaluation means
(a) process of collecting an information by reviewing the student's work or testing.
(b) process of using information that is collected through assessment.
(c) process of arriving at a logical conclusion from a body of evidence.
(d) None of the above

91 Stages of curriculum development are
1. curriculum implementing
2. evaluation
3. designing
4. planning

Codes
(a) 2, 3, 1, 4 (b) 4, 3, 2, 1
(c) 3, 2, 1, 4 (d) 1, 2, 3, 4

PREVIOUS YEARS' QUESTIONS

July 2018

1 Which one of the following combinations gives a correct reason for including philosophy of education in Teacher Educaiton Curriculum?
1. Philosophy is an oldest discipline.
2. Philosophy helps in understanding educational concepts in a holistic way.
3. Philosophy and education are two sides of the same coin.
4. Philosophy helps in developing a better personality of prospective teachers.
5. Philosophical analysis of educational concepts helps in developing a rational view point

Codes
(a) 1, 2, 3 and 5 (b) 2, 3 and 5
(c) 2, 3, 4 and 5 (d) 1, 2, 3 and 4

2 The concept of formative evaluation implies that
(a) benchmarking data should be considered essential
(b) learning should be assessed at terminal stages
(c) learning should be managed and monitored continuously
(d) there should be emphasis on gradation of students in terms of learning outcome

3 In which of the following approaches to curriculum design constructivist orientation will be manifest?

(a) Job analysis of learning tasks
(b) Evaluation approach to curriculum design
(c) Concept map as a tool for curricular choice
(d) Input emphasis on curriculum

November 2017

4 Curriculum is regarded as the sum total of experiences acquired by the learner in a school. Which combination of the following set of experiences will be deemed congruent in this regard?

1. Planned and known experiences.
2. Unplanned and known experiences.
3. Experience gained during co-curricular activities.
4. Lived experiences which promote creative outlook.

Codes

(a) 1, 2, 3 and 4
(b) 1, 2 and 3
(c) 1, 3 and 4
(d) 1 and 3

July 2016

5 Which of the following do lay foundations for curriculum?

(a) Societal priorities, government and resources
(b) Philosophy, Sociology and Psychology
(c) Study material, training facilities and societal needs
(d) Psychological base of education

December 2015

6 The curriculum for refresher courses in Academic Staff Colleges can be made more effective by

(a) Microteaching
(b) Teacher Competency Development Programmes
(c) Internship
(d) Team Teaching

December 2014

7 The most appropriate approach for implementing an administrative model of curriculum is to focus on

(a) Hierarchy of staff (b) Democratic values
(c) Participative Values (d) Horizontal coordination

8 National Curriculum Framework for Teacher Education in India 2009 was developed by

(a) NCERT (b) NUEPA (c) NCTE (d) NAAC

June 2014

9 The core curriculum does not emphasise

(a) democratic procedures
(b) problem solving
(c) total experiences in the school
(d) unit and lesson plans prepared by the teachers

10 A curriculum maker is interested in designing a functional curriculum would need an understanding of

(a) Educational philosophy
(b) Psychological principles
(c) Pedagogical procedures
(d) All of the above

ANSWERS

Exam Based Questions

1 *(a)*	2 *(b)*	3 *(d)*	4 *(c)*	5 *(a)*	6 *(d)*	7 *(b)*	8 *(c)*	9 *(a)*	10 *(b)*
11 *(d)*	12 *(a)*	13 *(c)*	14 *(c)*	15 *(d)*	16 *(c)*	17 *(c)*	18 *(a)*	19 *(d)*	20 *(d)*
21 *(a)*	22 *(a)*	23 *(d)*	24 *(a)*	25 *(b)*	26 *(b)*	27 *(d)*	28 *(b)*	29 *(d)*	30 *(b)*
31 *(c)*	32 *(c)*	33 *(c)*	34 *(d)*	35 *(d)*	36 *(c)*	37 *(d)*	38 *(d)*	39 *(a)*	40 *(d)*
41 *(a)*	42 *(d)*	43 *(b)*	44 *(c)*	45 *(a)*	46 *(c)*	47 *(b)*	48 *(d)*	49 *(c)*	50 *(a)*
51 *(c)*	52 *(a)*	53 *(b)*	54 *(a)*	55 *(b)*	56 *(b)*	57 *(d)*	58 *(a)*	59 *(b)*	60 *(c)*
61 *(b)*	62 *(c)*	63 *(c)*	64 *(c)*	65 *(a)*	66 *(c)*	67 *(c)*	68 *(a)*	69 *(c)*	70 *(a)*
71 *(a)*	72 *(a)*	73 *(a)*	74 *(a)*	75 *(b)*	76 *(c)*	77 *(c)*	78 *(d)*	79 *(b)*	80 *(c)*
81 *(a)*	82 *(b)*	83 *(c)*	84 *(d)*	85 *(d)*	86 *(a)*	87 *(c)*	88 *(d)*	89 *(d)*	90 *(b)*
91 *(b)*									

Previous Years' Questions

1 *(b)*	2 *(c)*	3 *(c)*	4 *(b)*	5 *(d)*	6 *(d)*	7 *(a)*	8 *(c)*	9 *(b)*	10 *(d)*

CHAPTER 18

Models of Curriculum Design

Curriculum design is a complex but systematic process. The curriculum designing is conducted stage by stage. Generally, all models stress the importance of considering a variety of factors that influence curriculum. It involves issues based on three basic ideas *i.e.* theoretical, philosophical and practical.

Curriculum Design

The term 'curriculum design' is used to describe the purposeful, deliberate, and systematic organisation of curriculum (instructional blocks) within a class or course. In other words, it is a way for teachers to plan instruction. When teachers design curriculum, they identify what will be done, who will do it, and what schedule to follow. It refers to the arrangement of the components or elements of a curriculum.

It is a very important part of creating a contextually relevant and responsive teaching and learning environment for both teachers and students. It is a process of critical questioning to frame learning and teaching. The main purpose of the process is to translate broad statements of intent into specific plans and actions.

According to **Saylor and Alexander**, curriculum design means "The pattern or framework or structural organisation used in selecting, planning and carrying forward educational experiences in the school".

Johnson *identified three notions of curriculum design as*

- an arrangement of selected and ordered learning outcomes intended to be achieved through instruction.
- an arrangement of selected and ordered learning experiences to be provided in an instructional situation.
- a scheme for planning and providing learning experiences.

While designing the curriculum following factors should be considered

- The design should facilitate and encourage all types of learning experiences essential for the achievement of the desired outcomes.

In this Chapter

- Curriculum Design
- Curriculum Design Models
  - – Traditional Model
  - – Contemporary Model
  - – Competency Based Model
  - – Academic/Discipline Based Model
  - – Activity Model
  - – Social Reconstruction Model
  - – Social Function Model
  - – Individual's Needs and Interest Model
  - – Outcome Based Integrative Model
  - – Intervention Model
  - – Stufflebeam's Context, Input, Process, Product Model/CIPP Model

- The design should permit teachers to utilise principles of learning for guiding learning activities.
- The design should enable the teachers to develop those experiences that are most meaningful to a particular group of learners.
- The design should be in accordance to the developmental needs of the students.
- The design should be in such a way that there should be continuous flow of learning experiences.
- The design should be realistic, feasible, cost effective, accessible and widely acceptable.

Thus, designing curriculum means planning which the teachers follow for providing learning activities in the class and the school.

Curriculum Design Tips

The following curriculum design tips can help educators to manage each stage of the curriculum design process

Identify the Needs of Stakeholders (i.e. students) early on in the curriculum design process. This can be done through needs analysis, which involves the collection and analysis of data related to the learner. This data might include what learners already know and what they need to know to be proficient in a particular area or skill. It may also include information about learner's perceptions, strengths and weaknesses.

Create a Clear List of Learning Goals and Outcomes This will help to focus on the intended purpose of the curriculum and allow to plan instruction that can achieve the desired results. Learning goals are the things teachers want students to achieve in the course. Learning outcomes are the measurable knowledge, skills and attitudes that students should have achieved in the course.

Identify Constraints That will impact curriculum design. For example, time is a common constraint that must be considered. There are so many hours, days, weeks and months in the term. If there isn't enough time to deliver all of the instructions that has been planned, it will impact learning outcomes.

Identify the Instructional Methods That will be used throughout the course and consider how they will work with student's learning styles.

Establish Evaluation Methods That will be used at the end and during the year to assess learners, instructors and the curriculum, which will determine the success and failure of curriculum.

Types of Curriculum Design

There are three basic types of curriculum design and they are

Subject-Centered

It revolves around a particular subject matter or discipline. It tends to focus on the subject rather than the individual. It describes what needs to be studied and how it should be studied.

Core curriculum is an example of a subject-centred curriculum design, which can be standardised across schools, states and the country as a whole. In standardised core curricula, teachers are provided a pre-determined list of things that they need to teach their students, along with specific examples of how these things should be taught.

The primary **drawback** of subject-centered curriculum design is that it is not **student-centered**. In particular, this form of curriculum design is constructed without taking into account the specific learning styles of the students. This can cause problems with student's engagement and motivation and may even cause students to fall behind in class.

Learner-Centered

In this the centre of the interest is the learner. The students are given more importance. In this the teachers role is not that of a task master but that of a guide. In this, the child is treated as plant, the teacher as gardener and the school as garden. It gives several options to the students. Students are actively involved in planning and evaluation of the options in general and for themselves in particular. Learner-centered curriculum points out that "the more experience in life a child has the more eager he will be to learn". Thus, the learner-centred broadly encompasses methods of teachers that shift the focus of instruction from the teacher to the student.

Problem-Centered

It focus on teaching students how to look at a problem and come up with a solution to the problem. Thus, students are exposed to real-life issues, which helps them to develop skills that are transferable to the real world.

It increases the relevance of the curriculum and allows students to be creative and innovate as they are learning. The **drawback** of problem-centered curriculum design is that it does not always takes learning styles into consideration.

Dimensions of Curriculum Design

The curriculum design is a statement, reflecting the relationships between the curricular components. It has to be developed on the basis of certain dimensions like scope, integration, sequence, continuity, articulation and balance. These considerations will determine the shape of the curriculum and the kinds of learning experiences, it will provide.

The various dimensions of curriculum design are

Scope According to **Saylor,** scope is defined as "The breath, variety and types of educational experiences that are to be provided to pupil as they progress through the school programme. It represents the latitudinal axis for selecting curriculum experiences". It determines the depth to which the subject matter has to be dealt with, the type of learning activities to be provided and decisions about the arrangement of curricular components.

Integration Learning becomes meaningful when content from one field is inter-related with content from another. The major task confronting a curriculum design is to integrate learning experiences of the learner at a particular level of the curriculum. "It is an attempt to inter-relate content with learning experiences and activities to ensure that students' needs are met".

Sequence While arranging the components of curriculum, a vertical sequence should be followed, i.e there should be a vertical relationship between the curricular elements so as to enable continuous learning. Based on well accepted learning principles, **Smith, Stanley** and **Shores** (1957) have given four basis for sequencing content. *These are*

(i) **Simple to Complex Learning** For instance, teaching two-digit addition to five-digit addition.

(ii) **Part to Whole** Like teaching digestive system to the entire human body system.

(iii) **Whole to Part** Teaching the concept of animal and then giving an example of types of animal.

(iv) **Chronological Learning** Chronological occurrence of historical events.

Continuity It implies the repetition of such skills of ideas in the curriculum, about which the learners should have indepth knowledge.

Articulation and Balance It refers to inter-relatedness of concepts of a curriculum. The relation can be either horizontal or vertical. Vertical articulation occurs when certain topics, lessons or courses are related to those occurring later in the curriculum sequence. Horizontal articulation occurs between curricular components, simultaneously.

Curriculum designers are also concerned about an appropriate weightage to be given to every aspect of curriculum, so that a balanced curriculum emerges. A balanced curriculum is one, that helps the learners to gain knowledge and utilise it, to achieve their goals.

Curriculum Design Models

The concept of curriculum design refers to the arrangement of elements of curriculum into a holistic plans. It is a complex but systematic process. Here, are discussed variety of models of curriculum design in order to make this complex activity understandable and manageable.

Traditional Model

Ralph Tyler was the first to layout the **Traditional Model** in **1949**, in his influential book, 'Basic Principles of Curriculum and Instruction'. In general, his method is thought of to be the principal way to form a concept of curriculum development. Because of its wide use in schools, throughout the world, many teachers and students find it a familiar concept. The approach has a 'subject-centered' orientation, i.e. a set of experts, pre-determine subject matters that are mastered by students. The curriculum is structured around content's units and the sequence of what is taught follows the logic of the subject matter (Knowles, 1984).

The systemised ideologies, demonstrated in the introduction of Tyler's book, categorise the school as the controller of power in deciding what is taught.

- "What educational purposes should the school seeks to attain?
- How can learning experiences be selected, which are likely to be useful in attaining these objectives?
- How can learning experiences be organised, for effective instruction?
- How can the effectiveness of learning experiences be evaluated?"(Tyler, 1971)

According to **Tyler**, "Curriculum is a growing process, over the course of the schooling years, educational experiences accumulate to exert profound changes in the learner, in the way water dripping upon a stone wear it away (Tyler, 1971)". He expresses that knowledge and skills cannot be photocopied, but instead, are taught in a sequence over time. A Spiral approach, in which learners return to topics, in more complexity over time, can also be considered a Traditional approach. Skills based or competency based instruction, common in adult basic education, often draws upon a Traditionalist approach to curriculum, with students mastering a given set of skills or procedures in a reasonable instructional cycle.

Advantages

- The main advantage of this model is that students easily adapt to various methods of teaching.
- Another advantage is that learning distinct skills in a systematic fashion provides itself to traditional testing. Test scores can be easily calculated, and explained to funders as program results.
- Program administrators can use the results of traditional tests to defend their program's achievements. Students, tutors and teachers can direct to confirmed progress, and that is undoubtedly motivating.
- Where resources are limited, the traditional model is much more competent.

Disadvantages

- The traditional approach to syllabus design, lacks integration.
- It focuses on one particular subject, without the students being able to understand how one subject implements another.
- It includes passivity and authority. Student within the traditional curriculum often becomes passive learners.

Contemporary Model

It indicates a close relationship between curriculum, planning goals, learning objectives and implementation. It is based on Learner-Centered Approach. It places the child at the centre of education. It begins with understanding the educational contexts from which a child comes. The curriculum is constructed based on the needs, interests, purposes and abilities of the learners.

Teacher tries to maximise student's productivity, knowledge acquisition, skills argumentation and development of personal and professional abilities. Teachers may use variety of instructional tools and methods, as well as flexible arrangement of time and place.

The major difference between the two models is that, in the **Contemporary Model** the curriculum is a combined effort of teachers and learners, since learners are very much involved in the decision-making, regarding the content of the curriculum and the manner it is delivered. Whereas in **Traditional Model**, the teacher has most, if not all authority when comes to decisions.

Advantages

- Learning comes to be seen as a process of gradually reaching achievable goals.
- Students develop greater sensitivity to their role as learners, and their vague notions of what it is to be a learner can become much sharper.
- Self-evaluation becomes more feasible.
- Classroom's activities can be seen to relate to the learner's real-life needs.
- Greater emphasis on the student's needs.

Disadvantages

- Most of the outcomes rely on teacher's ability to create material, appropriate to the learner's needs.
- It requires a skilled teacher, time and resources.
- Teacher finds it difficult to strike a balance between among the competing needs and interests of the child.

Competency Based Model

According to **Anshari R Sastrawinata**, "Competence is a statement which describes the appearance of a certain ability unanimously that a blend of knowledge and skills that can be observed and measured". **Elza Mylona** said that competency is about integration and applications of learned facts, skills and effective qualities, needed to serve the patient, the community and the profession.

It refers to system of instructions, assessments, grading, and academic reporting that are based on students, demonstrating that they have learned the knowledge and skills that they are expected to learn as they progress through their education.

In other definition he says that "Competency Based concept is a focus on student's mastery of performance and learning outcomes through a set of pre-defined learning objectives".

It is a design, based on specific competencies characterised by specific, sequential, and demonstrable learning of the tasks, activities, or skills, which constitutes the act to be learned and performed by students.

It is a model that emphasises the complex outcomes of a learning process (*i.e.* knowledge, skills and attitude to be applied by learners) rather than mainly focusing on what learners are expected to learn about in terms of traditionally defined subject content. In principle such a curriculum is learner-centered and adaptive to the changing needs of students, teachers and society. It implies that learning activities and environment are choosen, so that learners can acquire and apply the knowledge, skills and attitude to situations, they encounter in everyday life. They are usually designed around a set of key competencies/competencies that can be cross-curricular and/or subject- bound.

There are some aspects that describe the concept are

- Knowledge
- Skill
- Attitude
- Understanding
- Value
- Interest

Characteristics of Competency Based Model

***Jobelle B Salvador** wrote the characteristics of competency based model and they are*

- Learning is measured according to how well the learner performs in relation to competencies (objectives).
- Instructional system in which performance based learning process is used.
- Focuses on the outcome of the learning.
- Addresses, what the learners are expected to do rather than on what they are expected to learn about.
- Allows the student to learn at their own pace.
- Student's progress by demonstrating competence, which means they have to prove that they mastered the knowlecge and skills required for a particular course.

Advantages

- The learning centres on real world skills and competency development programs.
- Participants build confidence as they succeed in mastering specific competencies.
- Students learning is enhanced because of the specification of expected outcomes and continuous feedback.
- The quality of assessment and teaching is improved.

Disadvantages

- It works well with same learning environment and less well with others.
- It focuses on immediate needs and is less focused on preparing learners with the flexibility needed for much uncertain future.
- It takes an objectivist approach to learning.
- It does not suit all kinds of learners.

Academic/Discipline Based Model

It is model of curriculum in which content is divided into separate and distinct subjects or disciplines, such as language, science, mathematics, and social studies. The term 'discipline based' or 'subject based' covers the full range of distinct subjects or fields of study, including the more traditional usage in areas such as mathematics or physics, in areas of study with a strong professional focus such as molecular biology and in newer areas of study such as media education.

Learners must have frequent and recurring opportunities to practice their disciplinary skills throughout their fields of study, in a way that allows later courses to build on the work of earlier ones.

The instructional emphasis of it tends to be on specific, current, and factual information and skills, as it emerges from the discipline experts. Its approach characterises teaching practice within one subject and encourages teachers for specialisation, depth of content knowledge, and integrity to the conventions of their disciplines.

The problem with it is that they are likely to ignore the knowledge and skills that lie between and among various disciplines, but which may be central in the lives or future of the students. For example, students needs to learn the relationship between science, technology and culture, these relationships are ignored by the science, itself. Activities must be centered not on a given discipline but on a broad field including several disciplines.

Activity Model

It is a format for curriculum design developed to meet unique needs, contexts and purposes. In order to address these goals, curriculum developers design, reconfigure or rearrange one or more key curriculum components. Activity is the natural urge of the child. It is used as a media or means for imparting knowledge and skills. In this model, activity is the greatest motivation, provided to the child to enjoy the freedom of expressing himself fully. Its core premises include the requirement that learning should be based on doing some hands on experiments and activities. In short, it is anything that students do in a classroom other than merely passively listening to an instructor's lecture. According to **Tanner and Tanner**, "Activity Model is an attempt to treat learning as an active process".

It discards the boundaries and the model was centered largely on areas of child's interest. It's objective was child growth through experience. According to **Beans**, "the major premise of activity movement was that learner ought to be an active rather than a passive participant in learning". However the title 'activity curriculum' did not come into general use before 1920. In 1944, **David Horsburgh** started his school **Neel Bagh** in India. It was based on an innovative idea of **Horsburgh**. It was known for its creative methods in teaching and well-planned learning materials. Later, this initiative of Horshburgh was proved to be one of the pioneer and milestones in Activity Based model.

Requirement of Activity Model

School must have proper infrastructure, ample facilities or displays and decorations, well lighted and there must be separate ground for gardening.

Training of teachers, classroom equipments, activity rooms, transportation facilities, students grouping and flexibility in administrative arrangements.

Advantages

- It revolves around those childrens who are either not an academically talented or have not shown interest in school. It tends to stimulate these type of students into participating and eventually absorbing information.
- It makes the teaching, fun.
- Students feel a sense of accomplishment, when the task is completed.
- Students are able to transfer that experience easier to other learning situations.
- Students who are involved in activities are empowered in their own learning experiences.

Disadvantages

- A radical departure from traditional ways of learning and teaching.
- It has not assurance of learning cultural heritage.
- The facts and principles that are learned, are not permanently retained.
- Teachers are not prepared to carry on an activity program.
- Schools are also not equipped completely.
- There is no adequate provision for logical organisation.

Social Reconstruction Model

Social reconstructionists are interested in the relationship between curriculum and the social, political and economic development of society. They are convinced that education can affect social change, curriculum, for example, literacy campaigns that have contributed to successful political revolutions.

Aspects of reconstructionism, appeared in American curriculum thought in the 1920s and 1930s.

Rugg's textbooks, teachings and professional leadership had one over riding quality i.e. the spirit of social criticism. He wanted learners to use newly emerging concepts from social science and aesthetics to identify and to solve current problems.

The reconstructionists seek a curriculum that emphasises cultural pluralism, equality and futurism. They critically examines the cultural heritage of a society as well as entire civilisation. It is deliberately committed to bring about social and constructive change. It cultivates future planning attitude that considers the realities of the world. It enlists students and teachers in a definite program to enhance cultural renewal and inter-culturalism.

It strengthens the control of the schools by and for goal seeking interests of the overwhelming majority of mankind. For reconstructionism analysis, interpretation and evaluation of problems are insufficient, commitment and action by students and teachers are needed. The teacher should measure up to their social responsibilities. The reconstructionist design provides students, with learning requisite for altering social, economical and political realities. The curriculum should foster social action, aimed at reconstructing society. It encourages industrial and political changes. The students should be involved in creating a more equitable society.

It would include bringing students into their community. Ideally, students would spend half of their time in the classroom and other half, outside of the curriculum in different settings. It would encourage students to directly apply, what they are learning through social activism, reforms and change. As part of this model, curriculum would use service learning and discussion group to teach, while also bringing the world into the classroom and the students out into their community.

In early **1950s**, **Theodore Brameld** outlined the distinctive features of social reconstructionism model.

They are

First, he believed in a commitment to building a new culture. He was infused with the conviction that people are in the midst of a revolutionary period from which the common people will emerge as controllers of the industrial system, public services, and of cultural and natural resources.

Second, he felt that the working people should control all principal institutions and resources if the world is to become genuinely democratic. Teachers should ally themselves with the organised working people. A way should be found to enlist, the majority of people of all races and religions into a great democratic body with power to enforce its policies.

Third, he believed that the school should help an individual, not only to develop socially, but to learn how to participate in social planning as well.

There are many premises of social reconstruction and the different directions taken by different social re-constructionist such as revolution, critical inquiry, and futurism. A distinction is also made between a curriculum of reconstruction, which attempts to change the social order, and a curriculum of social adaptation, which helps students to fit into a world they never made.

Social Function Model

It focuses heavily on society. Social processes, functions or problems become the centre for the design of the curriculum. One way to look at this approach is to see it as using social studies to become the general background of the entire curriculum.

The curriculum is structured around the various aspects of problems and processes of community life with the subject areas subservient to the problem. This design is more subjective than is either the subject-centered or broad field. Cooperative planning occurs more frequently. The curriculum is more flexible.

The curriculum developed through this model creates an awareness among the learners regarding social problems and enables them to solve the problems.

Individual's Needs and Interest Model

It takes each individual's needs, interests and goals into consideration. In other words, it acknowledges that students are not uniform and adjusts to those student's needs. It is meant to empower learners that allows them to shape their education through choices.

The instructional plans in this model are differentiated, giving students the opportunity to choose assignments, learning experiences and activities. This can motivate the students and helps them to stay engaged in the material that they are learning.

The drawback of it is that it is labour intensive. Developing differentiated instruction, puts pressure on the teacher to create instruction or to find materials that are conducive to each student's learning needs. Teachers may not have the time or may lack the experience or skills to create such plans.

It requires that teachers balance student's wants and interests with student's needs and required outcomes, which is not an easy balance to obtain.

Outcome Based Integrative Model

It was designed to help students to develop a deep understanding of organised bodies of knowledge while simultaneously developing critical thinking skills. It is closely related to Inductive Model and based on the work of **Hilda Taba** (1965-67). It uses organised bodies of knowledge that combine facts, concepts, generalisations and the relationships among them.

It has two learning objectives

- Deep and thorough understanding of organised bodies of knowledge.
- Use of critical thinking skills.

In this model, the teacher facilitates student's analysis of information about a topic in an organised way. This model relies on formal strategies that teach students how to analyse and interpret information. The model supports student's learning across the academic subject area while also empower them to become independent learner. This model is one of the best model for teaching conceptual knowledge, the interrelationship of facts, concepts and generalisation. Thus, the model is equally effective addressing learning goals related to students development and critical thinking skills required to understand information presented in organised bodies of knowledge.

Implementing Lessons with Outcome Based Integrative Model

Phase 1: The Open ended Phase In this phase, learners describe, compare and search for patterns in data. It promotes involvement and ensures success. The teacher starts with one cell of information and moves to other cells. Teacher records student's observations or comparisons on the board.

Phase 2 : The Casual Phase In this phase, students explain similarities and differences, using data to justify conclusions (documenting assertions). In this, students develop perception of competence.

Phase 3 : Hypothetical Phase In this phase, learners hypothesise outcomes for different conditions (as suggested by teacher). It facilitates transfer and student's self-efficacy increases as they learn to respond successfully.

Phase 4 : Closure and Application Phase In this phase, students generalise to form broad relationships which summarises the content.

Intervention Model

It is designed to meet the complex needs of children with mild disabilities. The interventions developed through this are called the **Strategies Interventions Model**. They can be grouped into three major **categories according** to **Deshler** and **Schumaker**. The **first category** of interventions, called **learning strategy interventions** were developed because many students with disabilities are ineffective rearer, who lack information processing skills to cope with wide range of content and complexity of tasks, they encounter in secondary classes.

The critical features of successful strategy instruction includes

- daily and sustained instruction.
- multiple opportunites to practice the strategy of variety of situations.
- individualised feedback and
- required mastery of the strategy.

The second category of interventions called content enhancement routines, are instructional routines use to enhance their delivery of content information and improve their student's understanding and recall of the content. Many cognitively and emotionally challenged students have difficulty in organising, understanding, storing, and remembering of information, presented during large group instruction, in general education classroom.

The third category of intervention called empowerment interventions, which are geared towards empowering students to perform at their best and to create positive relationships with others, in the school setting. For instance, several social and motivational strategies have been developed to enable students to interact in a positive way with peers and teachers as well as to engage in self-advocacy.

Stufflebeam's Context, Input, Process, Product Model/CIPP Model

The weaknesses in the Tyler's Model led several evaluation experts in the late 1960s and early 1970s to attack the Tyler's Model and to offer their own alternatives.

The alternative that had the greatest impact was that developed by a **Phi Delta Kappa Committee, chaired by Daniel Stufflebeam** (1971). This model seemed to appeal to educational leaders because it emphasised the importance of producing evaluative data for decision-making. Infact, decision-making was the sole justification for evaluation, in the view of the **Phi Delta Kappa Committee**.

To serve the needs of decision makers, the **Stufflebeam's** model provides a means for generating data relating to four stages of program; operation, which continuously assesses needs; problems in the context to help decision makers to determine goals and objectives; input evaluation, which assesses alternative means for achieving those goals to help decision makers to choose optimal means; process evaluation, which monitors the processes, both to ensure that the means are actually being implemented and to make the necessary modifications; and product evaluation, which compares actual ends with intended ends and leads to a series of recycling decisions.

During each of these four stages, specific steps are been taken and they are :

- Kind of decisions are identified.
- Kinds of data needed to make those decisions, are identified.
- That data was collected.
- Criteria for determining quality were established.
- Data was analysed on the basis of those criteria.
- Needed information was provided to decision makers (as cited in Glatthorn 1987, pp. 273-274).

Stufflebeam's CIPP model is described below in detail

Context According to this the curriculum evaluator is engaged in studying the environment (context) in which the curriculum is transacted. It provides the rationale for selection of objectives. Content evaluation is not a one time activity. It is a continuous process for furnishing baseline information for the operation of the total system.

Input The purpose of input evaluation is to get information for how to utilise resources optimally to meet the objectives of the curriculum. It includes evaluation of some sort of physical and non-physical inputs such as availability of physical and human resources, time and budget. It also includes previous achievements, education and aspiration of pupil.

Process It is the most critical component of the overall model. Quality of the product largely depends on it. It addresses the curriculum implementation decisions.

Stufflebeam presents the three strategies for process evaluation and they are

(i) To detect or predict defects in the procedural design or it's implementation during the diffusion stage. In dealing with or curriculum defects one should identify and monitor continually the potential sources for the failure of the curriculum.

(ii) To provide information for curriculum decisions. Here the decisions should be regarding test development prior to the actual implementation of the curriculum.

(iii) To maintain a record of procedures as they occur. It addresses the main features of the project design. For example, the content selected, the instruction strategies planned or the time allotted to the planning for such activities.

Product It helps to determine whether the curriculum objectives have been achieved or not. On the basis of collected data, we can decide whether to continue, modify, change or terminate or curriculum.

It has several features for those interested in curriculum evaluation. Its emphasises on decision making, seems appropriate for administrators concerned with improving curricula. It concerns for the formative aspects of evaluation remedies, a serious deficiency in the Tyler's model. Finally, the detailed guidelines and forms created by the committee provides step by step guidance for users.

However, it has some serious drawbacks also that are associated with it. It's main weakness seems to be it's failure, to recognise the complexity of the decision-making process in organisations. It assumes more rationality than exists in such situations and ignores the political factors that plays a large part in these decisions. Also, as **Cuba and Lincoln** (1981) noted, it seems difficult to implement and expensive to maintain.

EXAM BASED QUESTIONS

1 Curriculum design is a way for teachers to
(a) plan instruction (b) plan evaluation
(c) plan content (d) None of these

2 Which is not a dimension of curriculum design?
(a) Integration (b) Continuity
(c) Articulation (d) None of these

3 Articulation refers to
(a) repetition of skills
(b) inter-relatedness of concepts of curriculum
(c) types of education experiences
(d) helps to gain knowledge

4 Balanced curriculum is also known as
(a) integrated curriculum
(b) experienced curriculum
(c) activity-centred curriculum
(d) core curriculum

5 The Traditional Model of Curriculum, developed in
(a) 1950 (b) 1949
(c) 1959 (d) 1969

6 Traditional Model is based on........... orientation.
(a) learner-centred (b) subject-centred
(c) problem-centred (d) None of these

7 When resources are limited, which model is more competent?
(a) Traditional Model
(b) Contemporary Model
(c) Problem-Centred Model
(d) All of the above

8 Contemporary Model is based on ....Approach.
(a) Learner-Centred
(b) Subject-Centred
(c) Problem-Centred
(d) None of the above

9 The curriculum was constructed in the Contemporary Model on the basis of
(a) needs and interests
(b) purpose
(c) abilities of the students
(d) All of the above

10 Which is not an advantage of Contemporary Model of Curriculum Design?
(a) Self-evaluation becomes more feasible.
(b) It focuses on one particular subject.
(c) Greater emphasis on the student's needs.
(d) Students develops greater sensitivity to their role as learners.

11 Competency based curriculum is a design, based on ....
(a) activities (b) skills
(c) specific competencies (d) All of these

12 A discipline based curriculum emphasised upon ....
(a) factual information (b) specific skills
(c) Both (a) and (b) (d) None of these

13 Who defined that "activity curriculum is an attempt to treat learning as an active process"?
(a) Tanner and Tanner (b) John Dewey
(c) Ralph Tyler (d) None of these

14 Which is not a feature of successful strategy instruction?
(a) Daily and sustained instruction
(b) Individualised feedback
(c) Required mastery of the strategy
(d) Learner's hypothesis outcomes

15 Who held that curriculum is a gearing process?
(a) Ralph Tyler (b) Daniel Stufflebeam
(c) Theodore Brameld (d) Harold Rugg

16 Competency based instruction is common in
(a) primary education
(b) adult basic education
(c) pre-primary education
(d) None of the above

17 Which of the following is not a Curricular Model?
(a) CIPP Model
(b) Competency Based Model
(c) Intervention Model
(d) None of the above

18 Who has written the characteristics of Competency Based Model?
(a) Harold Rugg (b) Jobelle B Salvador
(c) Theodore Brameld (d) David Horsburgh

19 What is the problem that lies in the discipline-centred curriculum?
(a) It ignores the knowledge and skills among various disciplines.
(b) Content is divided into separate disciplines.
(c) Learners must have frequent opportunities.
(d) All of the above

20 What is the greatest motivation, provided to the child in teaching-learning process?
(a) Assessment (b) Activities
(c) Learning (d) Evaluation

21 Which curriculum is creative in its approach and uses well planned learning materials?
(a) Integrative curriculum
(b) Activity-centred curriculum
(c) Balanced curriculum
(d) None of the above

22 What is the objective of Activity Curriculum model?
(a) Child growth through motivation
(b) Child growth through experience
(c) Child growth through assessment
(d) All of the above

23 In which year, Activity model was emerged?
(a) 1933 (b) 1920
(c) 1944 (d) 1955

24 Who started the 'Neel Bagh' in India?
(a) David Horsburgh
(b) John Dewey
(c) Daniel Stufflebeam
(d) Ralph Tyler

25 Which is not an advantage of Activity model?
(a) It makes teaching fun.
(b) Students feel a sense of accomplishment.
(c) Students experience learning through activities.
(d) Schools are not equipped completely.

26 What are the requirements of Activity model?
(a) Classroom equipments (b) Activity rooms
(c) Teacher's training (d) All of these

27 Which model cultivates future planning attitude?
(a) CIPP model
(b) Social Reconstruction model
(c) Activity model
(d) Competency Based model

28 Why the students are involved in Social Reconstruction model?
(a) To create a more equitable society
(b) To reform the curriculum
(c) To provide students, with learning requisite
(d) Both a and c

29 Who was concerned about social reconstructionism?
(a) David Horsburgh (b) Harold Rugg
(c) Daniel Stufflebeam (d) John Dewey

30 In the early 1950s, who has outlined the distinctive features of social reconstructionism?
(a) Harold Rugg (b) Daniel Stufflebeam
(c) Theodore Brameld (d) David Horsburgh

31 In which model of curriculum design, the instructional plans are differentiated?
(a) Activity model
(b) Individual's Needs and Interest model
(c) Social Reconstruction model
(d) Intervention model

32 Which model is related to Inductive Model and based on the work of Hilda Taba?
(a) Activity model
(b) CIPP model
(c) Outcome Based Integrative model
(d) Social Reconstruction model

33 How the school plays a significant role in implementing Social Reconstruction model?
(a) School should helps an individual.
(b) Develops an individual, socially.
(c) Helps them to learn that how to participate in social planning.
(d) All of the above

34 Which curriculum design model, empowers learners to shape their education through choices?
(a) Social Reconstruction model
(b) Individual Needs and Interest model
(c) CIPP model
(d) Intervention model

35 What is the drawback of Social Reconstruction model?
(a) Developing differentiated instruction, puts pressure on a teacher.
(b) Acknowledges students
(c) Adjusts to student's needs
(d) Empower the learners

36 Outcome Based Integrative model was designed to help the students to develop.
(a) deep understanding
(b) critical thinking
(c) acknowledges that students are not uniform
(d) Both a and b

37 The open ended phase in Outcome Based Integrative model promotes.
(a) involvement of students
(b) ensures success of students
(c) observations are recorded
(d) Both a and b

38 Which model is designed to meet the complex needs of children with mild disabilities?
(a) Outcome Based Integrative model
(b) Intervention model
(c) CIPP model
(d) Activity model

39 What is the requirement of Individual Needs and Interest model?
(a) Teacher must balance student's needs and interests.
(b) Teacher should be motivated.
(c) Teacher should use Teacher-Centered Learning approach.
(d) None of the above

40 How teachers help to develop critical thinking skill among students?
(a) Through practice (b) Identifying topics
(c) Specifying objectives (d) All of these

41 Which instructional routine, enhances the delivery or content information?
(a) Learner's strategy intervention
(b) Content enhancement routine
(c) Empowerment intervention
(d) None of the above

42 Who propagated the CIPP model?
(a) John Dewey
(b) Ralph Tyler
(c) Daniel Stufflebeam
(d) Harold Rugg

43 CIPP model emphasised upon
(a) producing evaluative data for decision-making
(b) repetition of skills
(c) content enhancement
(d) None of the above

44 Context evaluation assesses the
(a) alternative means for achieving goals
(b) needs and problems in the context, to help decision makers to choose optimal means.
(c) compares actual ends
(d) monitors the processes

45 What is the attractive feature of CIPP model?
(a) Appropriate for administrators concerned for improving curricula.
(b) Failure to recognise complexity of the decision-making process.
(c) Ignores political factors
(d) None of the above

Directions (Q. Nos. 46-55) *Two statements are given below, one labelled as Assertion (A) and other labelled as Reason (R). Choose the correct code for your answer.*

Codes
(a) Both A and R are true and R is the correct explanation of A
(b) Both A and R are true, but R is not the correct explanation of A
(c) Both A and R are false
(d) A is false, but R is true

46 **Assertion** (A) Curriculum design is a process of critical questioning.
Reason (R) Content needs to be designed in a structured combination.

47 **Assertion** (A) Curriculum design has to be developed on the basis of certain dimensions.
Reason (R) It's dimensions are scope, integration, sequence, continuity, articulation and balance.

48 **Assertion** (A) Scope or curriculum design determines the depth to which the subject matter has to be dealt with.
Reason (R) The major task or curriculum design is to integrate learning experiences of the learner.

49 **Assertion** (A) A balanced curriculum is one that helps the learners, to gain knowledge and utilise it.
Reason (R) It emerges when every aspect of curriculum is given equal weightage.

50 **Assertion** (A) The Traditional model to syllabus design lacks integration.
Reason (R) It focuses on one particular subject without the subject being able to understand, how one subject implements another.

51 **Assertion** (A) Contemporary model is based on Learner-Centered approach.
Reason (R) It places the child at the centre of education.

52 **Assertion** (A) Classroom activities can be seen to relate to the learner's real life needs.
Reason (R) Learning comes to be seen as process of gradually reaching achieveable goals.

53 **Assertion** (A) Activity model curriculum discards the boundaries and centered largely on areas of child's interest.
Reason (R) The objective was child's growth through experience.

54 **Assertion** (A) The curriculum should foster social actions, aims at reconstructing society.
Reason (R) Social Reconstructionists would encourage students to directly apply, what they are learning through social activism.

55 **Assertion** (A) Developing critical thinking skills, requires practice in forming explanations.
Reason (R) It is encouraged in Outcome Based Integrative model.

56 Match the following

List I	List II
A. CIPP model	1. Activity-centered
B. Traditional model	2. Learner-centered
C. Contemporary model	3. Decision-making
D. Activity model	4. Subject-centered

Codes

	A	B	C	D
(a)	3	4	2	1
(b)	1	2	3	4
(c)	2	1	3	4
(d)	4	1	2	3

57 Which of the following statement(s) is/are incorrect?

1. Activity model is developed to meet unique needs.
2. Learning should be based on hands-on experiments and activities.
3. It is one of the creative method in teaching.
4. It is based on hypothetical approach.

Codes

(a) Both 1 and 2 (b) Only 2
(c) Both 3 and 4 (d) Only 4

58 Which of the following statement(s) is/are incorrect?

1. Contemporary model is constructed, based on needs, interest and abilities of the learners.
2. Teacher trys to maximise student's productivity.
3. Teacher has the authority, when comes to decisions.
4. Self-evaluation becomes more feasible.

Codes

(a) Both 1 and 2 (b) Only 3
(c) Both 2 and 3 (d) Only 4

59 Which of the following statement(s) is/are correct?

1. Competency based curriculum emphasises complex outcomes of learning process.
2. It is usually designed around a set of competencies.
3. It is leaner-centered and adaptive to the changing needs of the students.
4. It focuses on learning outcomes, through a set of pre-defined learning objectives.

Codes

(a) Only 1 (b) Both 1 and 2
(c) Both 3 and 4 (d) All of these

Directions (Q. Nos. 60-62) *Read the given passage and answer the following questions.*

In essence, the main purpose and objective of a curriculum reflecting traditional education is to prepare the young for future responsibilities and for success in life through an education of instruction and discipline. These pedagogic methods of instruction and discipline employed in traditional education system, utilises large bodies of organised knowledge and prepared forms of skill (Dewey, 1938, p. 15).

He makes this clear, by explaining a popular method used throughout the traditional schools, subject matters and standard of conduct, are passed on from the past, via the teachers and textbooks that are in a sense organs and agents in making sure, this knowledge is communicated and the rules of conduct enforced (Dewey, 1938 p. 16). This suggests to authoritative figures, only capable to dictating what is right and what is wrong, while the student is a passive learner, who accepts this body of knowledge without question. This narrow attitude to reality and in particular, progressive education is greatly detrimental to the learner, if does not acknowledge an open and contextualised world view as argue by Dewey (Dewey, 1938, p. 16).

60 What is the main objective of curriculum?

(a) To prepare the youngsters for future
(b) To help the youngsters to understand content
(c) To communicate effective teaching
(d) None of the above

61 Who are the sources in traditional curriculum?

(a) Teachers (b) Textbooks
(c) Both a and b (d) None of these

62 Progressive education is detrimental to

(a) subject (b) teacher
(c) learner (d) All of these

PREVIOUS YEARS' QUESTIONS

July 2018

1 Which one of the following is an essential part of the curricular design process?

(a) Demographic features of the community
(b) Development index of the parents
(c) Consideration of inputs, process and output of instruction
(d) Affiliation of the school to a particular school board

2 There is a maximum scope of change in curricular contents by the State Boards of School Education in

(a) Demonstration Model (b) Administrative Model
(c) System Analysis Model (d) Grassroot Model

3 In which curricular model, a school teacher enjoys maximum autonomy?

(a) Demonstration model
(b) Administrative model
(c) System Analysis model
(d) Grassroot model

4 In which of the following approaches to curriculum design, constructivist orientation will be manifest?

(a) Job analysis of learning task
(b) Evaluation approach to curriculum design
(c) Concept mapping as a tool for curricular choice
(d) Input process emphasis on curriculum

November 2017

5 Which of the following model(s) of curriculum has minimum scope for democratic decision-making?
(a) Demonstration model
(b) Grassroot model
(c) System Analysis model
(d) Administrative model

6 Which of the following combination(s) describe(s) the characteristic(s) of System Analysis Model of Curriculum?
1. The system has it's sub-systems.
2. System and it's sub-systems interacts with each other.
3. There is inherent coordination in it's various sub-systems.
4. Over a period of time, the system's output decreases.
5. The quality of output depends on the quality of input.

Codes
(a) 1, 2, 3 and 5 (b) 2, 3, 4 and 5
(c) 1, 3, 4 and 5 (d) 1, 2, 3 and 5

January 2017

7 Which of the following will be more benefited by the diversified curriculums?
(a) Tribal girls (b) Scheduled tribes
(c) Scheduled castes (d) Slum dwellers

July 2016

8 Which one of the following is not a curricular model?
(a) Administrative Line Staff model
(b) System Analysis model
(c) Jurisprudence Inquiry model
(d) Demonstration model

9 Who makes decisions in Grassroot Model of Curriculum Development?
(a) Community
(b) Students
(c) District inspector of schools
(d) Teacher

10 Which combination is related to curriculum development?
1. Hilda Taba
2. Taylor
3. Alexander and Saylor
4. Hilgard

Codes
(a) 1, 2 and 4 (b) 1, 3 and 4
(c) 2, 3 and 4 (d) 1, 2 and 3

11 Which of the following combination(s) of statement(s) reflects the concerns of National Curriculum Framework (NCF), 2005?
1. A commitment to democracy and values of equality, justice, freedom, secularism, respect for human dignity and rights.
2. Burdening children with information, resulting from an erroneous notion of knowledge.
3. A capacity to learn and willingness to unlearn and relearn as means of responding to new situation in a flexible and creative manner.
4. Appreciation of beauty and are being and integral part of human life.

Codes
(a) 1, 3, 4 (b) 2, 3, 4
(c) 1, 2, 3 (d) 2, 4, 3

December 2015

12 In which curriculum model, the least authoritative character is visualised?
(a) Demonstration model
(b) Administrative model
(c) Grassroot model
(d) System Analysis model

13 Which of the following curriculum model involves a hierarchy of educational officers for its implementation?
(a) System Analysis model (b) Administrative model
(c) Demonstration model (d) Grassroot model

14 Select the most appropriate combination(s) for System Analysis Model of Curriculum.
1. Instrumentation and Logistics.
2. Coordination and Processing
3. Identifying teaching and learning operations
4. Input and Output

Codes
(a) 1, 2 and 3 (b) 2, 3 and 1
(c) 1, 2, 3 and 4 (d) 2, 3 and 4

June 2015

15 In a remote tribal area of Madhya Pradesh, some tribal teachers devised a unique way of curriculum transaction. Everyone praised it and after through examination, the curriculum was implemented by the government in the whole of the state. This is an example of
(a) Grassroot model
(b) Administrative model
(c) System Analysis model
(d) Demonstration model

December 2014

16 In Grassroot Model of Curriculum, directly accountable functionary for curriculum implementation is
(a) learner (b) teacher
(c) headmaster (d) parents

17 The most appropriate approach for implementing an Administrative Model of Curriculum is to focus on
(a) hierarchy of staff (b) democrative values
(c) participative culture (d) horizontal coordination

18 The ultimate purpose of Demonstration Model of Curriculum is
(a) employing strategies by teachers in curriculum develpment
(b) maximising activity approach for curriculum transaction
(c) getting feedback for implementing at a larger scale
(d) demonstrating the feasibility of the model

June 2014

19 The core curriculum does not emphasise
(a) democratic procedures
(b) problem-solving
(c) a well defined body of subject matter
(d) integration of different subject matters

20 The core curriculum consist of the
(a) subject matter, children must learn in school
(b) subject offered by the school authorities
(c) total experience in the school programme
(d) unit and lesson plans preparation by the teachers

21 A curriculum maker, interested in designing a functional curriculum would need an understanding of
(a) Educational Philosophy
(b) Psychological Principles
(c) Pedagogical Procedures
(d) All of the above

ANSWERS

Exam Based Questions

1 (a)	2 (d)	3 (b)	4 (a)	5 (b)	6 (b)	7 (a)	8 (a)	9 (d)	10 (b)
11 (c)	12 (c)	13 (a)	14 (d)	15 (a)	16 (b)	17 (d)	18 (b)	19 (a)	20 (b)
21 (b)	22 (b)	23 (c)	24 (a)	25 (d)	26 (d)	27 (b)	28 (d)	29 (b)	30 (c)
31 (b)	32 (c)	33 (d)	34 (b)	35 (a)	36 (d)	37 (d)	38 (b)	39 (a)	40 (d)
41 (b)	42 (c)	43 (a)	44 (b)	45 (a)	46 (b)	47 (a)	48 (b)	49 (a)	50 (b)
51 (a)	52 (b)	53 (a)	54 (b)	55 (b)	56 (a)	57 (d)	58 (b)	59 (d)	60 (a)
61 (c)	62 (c)								

Previous Years' Questions

1 (a)	2 (b)	3 (d)	4 (c)	5 (d)	6 (a)	7 (a)	8 (c)	9 (d)	10 (d)
11 (a)	12 (c)	13 (b)	14 (d)	15 (d)	16 (b)	17 (a)	18 (d)	19 (b)	20 (c)
21 (d)									

CHAPTER 19

Curriculum and Instruction

Curriculum and instruction is a field within education which seeks to develop and implement curriculum changes that increases student's achievement within and outside the school. In this chapter, we will discuss various approaches to curriculum and instruction.

Curriculum Transaction

It is an effective and desired implementation of the curriculum contents, on the basis of aims and objectives listed in the curriculum. It incorporates effective planning for providing learning experiences for its learners, organisation of planning, administration of the organised planning and evaluation of the implementations by the implementer and the experts in the relevant field.

Curriculum transaction or curriculum management is the process of planning and organising the curriculum in a particular subject area for different levels of education and continuously monitoring it while being implemented.

With changing time, curriculum should also change reflecting the needs and aspirations of the people. There cannot be a uniform curriculum for all countries, because education is related to social, economical and political changes in the country. Its content should be based on current information and not on the past information that has been proved to be outdated and unusable. Therefore, there is a need for constantly changing and updating the curriculum's content.

Need and Importance of Curriculum Transaction

Curriculum is a systematic and intended packaging of competencies (*i.e.* knowledge, skills and attitudes that are underpinned by values) that learners should acquire through organised learning experiences, both in formal and non-formal settings. A noble curriculum plays an important role to the development of thinking skill and acquisition of relevant knowledge that learners needs to apply in context of their studies, daily life and careers.

Major emphasis should be given on effective transaction of curriculum in any educational program. The main responsibility of curriculum transaction lies on the teachers and trainers who may use different types of pedagogies, so that students can be benefitted in gaining knowledge and developing skills.

In this Chapter

- Curriculum Transaction
  - Techniques to Enhance Curriculum Transaction
- Approaches to Curriculum and Instruction
- Curriculum Evaluation
  - Models of Curriculum Evaluation

Curriculum is implemented by teachers and moreover, depends on the quality of teaching and learning strategies, learning materials and assessment. The set of teaching techniques strongly depends on instructional form of education.

Transaction of curriculum is a much difficulut task because it is based on theoretical and practical aspects as well. Two basic considerations needs to be covered while planning transaction processes. One is the context, in which transaction is carried out in terms of physical and social characteristics of the setting. Second, relates to teachers who actually are to transact the curriculum *i.e.* their capabilities and attitudinal dispositions. These adaptations by teachers to the changing demands of the physical and social settings, where the curriculum is transacted as well as their own proficiency in various methods of transaction becomes a pre-requisite for making the process of curriculum transaction effective and meaningful.

Instructional System

Students in the educational system are subjected to many situations to learn various things. These situations are developed deliberately by the teacher. Even before thinking about the topic to be learned and how the students will learn, the teachers think as to what will be the objectives that should be attended by the students. Then, only the teacher may think as to what should be the topic/learning experiences to be organised.

To make the students learn, the teachers scientifically selects the methods and approaches to teach different material needed for interacting and manipulating by students and teachers. Teacher also thinks about the sequencing of the materials and methods to make the student learn in a scientific process. This **scientific process** is also known as the **instructional system.**

Techniques to Enhance Curriculum Transaction

The techniques to enhance curriculum transaction are instructional media, instructional system, instructional techniques and instructional material.

They are discussed below

Instructional Media

According to **Romiszowski** (1988), "It refers to devices and materials employed in teaching and learning. It includes hardware like blackboards, radio, television, tape recorders, video tapes, recorders and projectors, models, maps, etc".

Similarly, **Scanean** indicates that "instructional media encompasses all the materials and physical means an instructor might use to implement instruction and facilitates student's achievements of instructional objectives. This may include traditional materials such as chalkboards, handouts, charts, slides, real objects and video tapes as well as newer materials and methods such as computers, DVDs, CD-Rom(s), internet and interactive video conferencing. It plays a key role in the design and use of systematic instruction".

Advantages of Instructional Media

In general, the advantages of instructional media is to facilitate interaction between teachers and students, so that learning activities can become more effective and efficient.

Advantages of instructional media are :

- The delivery of learning materials can be standardised with the help of instructional media, different interpretations among teachers can be avoided and can reduce the information gap between students, wherever located.
- The learning process becomes more clear and interesting. It can display information through sound, image, movement and colour, either naturally or manipulatively, thus helping teachers to create a learning atmosphere becomes more lively, is not monotonous and tedious.
- Improving the quality of student's learning outcomes. It can help students to absorb the material and learn more mandalam intact. By listening verbal information from the teacher only, students do not understand the lesson, but if enriched with activities to see, touch, feel and experience themselves through the media, student understanding will be better.
- It enables the learning process that can be done anywhere and at anytime. It can be stimulated in such a way that students can make learning activities more freely anywhere and at anytime, without depending on a Guru. We need to realise that time is very limited to study in school and infact, the most time is being spent outside the school environment.
- It can foster positive attitude towards students and learning materials. The learning process becomes more attractive that encourages students to love science and love to find their own sources of knowledge.
- It helps the teachers to teach more effectively and enable the students to learn more readily.

Instructional Techniques

They are an integral component of any instructional system. An instructional system is designed to achieve one or multiple objectives. These objectives are achieved through a combination of various methods or techniques which includes the use of media. A combination of these techniques and materials, employed to achieve a pre-stated objective, is what we call **teaching-learning strategies.**

Broadly, there are four kinds of instructional techniques which are discussed below

Learner-Centered Techniques

In a learner-centered system, the focus is on the individual learner, and the various system's components are geared to help the learner to achieve his/her learning objectives. *In general, learner-centred system has the following important learner-centred teaching-learning techinques*

Personalised System of Instruction In the late 1960's, **F.S. keller** developed a personlised system of instruction, called the **Keller's Plan.** In his plan, the course materials consist of a number of units. Each unit has its own learning objectives and the learner is supplied with a study guide that suggests a number of means to achieve the stipulated unit's objectives. The units supplied to the learner are self-instructional in nature. So, the Personalised System of Instruction (PSI) is based on the principles of independent study, individualised learning and self-pacing.

Flexi Study It is another significant and popular student-centered technique of instruction. It combines both correspondence and tutorial support in an institution. A learner takes on the individualised learning materials through correspondence and attends the counselling/ tutorial sessions as per his/her convenience.

Distance Education In the early stages of distance education, only print materials were used, but now it utilises multi-media learning strategies. The use of Multi-Media Approach enables the system to provide as much support as possible, even to isolated distance learners. These innovations have provided opportunities to the socially disadvantaged population, to further their access to higher education.

Programmed Learning It refers to a procedure of self-instruction, which uses an instructional sequence in which the content to be learned is presented in a series of small steps, arranged in a logical sequence. To facilitate self-learning, programmed instruction materials are designed as to give various kinds of intellectual, emotional and psycho-motor experiences to the learners in a controlled situation, through a variety of devices like booklet, teacher, etc.

Computer Assisted Learning In computer assisted learning, the computer helps a learner by indicating whether or not a response given by him/her is correct. Besides this, it can make learning more individualised by taking into account the needs, characteristics, skills, aptitudes and pace of an individual learner. It provides a two way communication and such interaction mainly consists of monitoring and providing feedback for individualised learning.

Group Learning Techniques

Under this, care is taken to stimulate group discussions and other activities within a group to achieve the stipulated educational objectives. They are more suitable than individualised learning techniques for achieving objectives concerned with the development of inter-personal skills, problem-solving skills, oral-communication skills, critical thinking skills, etc.

Various group learning techniques are

Tutorial It provides students with a chance to express their individual learning difficulties and help the teacher to pay attention to each learner, individually. The teacher selects the topic and puts it for discussion in the group.

Seminar In a seminar, occasionally, one of the student of a group presents a written essay or talks. The techniques used in the seminar may differ from subject to subject and from one level of education to another. The contents of the presentation are discussed by the group within the frame of their pre-determined learning transactions.

Group Discussion In a group discussion, the students are free to ask questions and contribute to the discussion through their comments. Such discussions are used in case of large groups. It is usually used to reinforce the content of the course, already taught through the formal classroom lecture.

Group Project In a group project, a small group is assigned to the task of selecting a problem and conducting a study on it, while carrying out a group project work, skills for group work, group communication and personal development within the group are given emphasis. The interaction in a group teaches the learner, the basic principles behind adjustment in a societal framework.

Experiential Learning Techniques

It can be defined as learning that occurs outside the classroom. It is generally bringing knowledge from society to classroom rather than from classroom to society. Experiential learning implies that learning is highly individualistic and the condition under which knowledge or competency is acquired very widely.

Various experiential learning techniques are

Discovery Learning It refers to those situations in which the learner achieves the instructional objectives with little or no guidance from the teacher. The effectiveness of discovery learning as a method, infact requires the individual learner to find out the solution to a problem. By implication, the learners themselves arrives at various possibilities independently by applying their skills and then find out the solution. The application of the discovery technique as a method of learning leads to individual capabilities of various kind.

Simulation Technique Simulation means the replication of reality in order to make it easily accessible to the learner. In teaching-learning situation, simulation technique is used in order to make reality, easily accessible to the learner. Thus, in simulated situation, learner deals with simulated problems through action. The essence of simulation is the involvement of participants (learners) and observers in a specially created situation.

Case Study Technique It is a way of organising and analysing the data for the purpose of studying a social unit. In other words, it is a research technique that attempts to examine contemporary phenomena in a real life situation. In distance education, case studies are important mechanism to obtain feedback from various functionaries and learner to strengthen the teaching-learning system.

Teacher-Centered Techniques

These techniques are largely applied in the conventional face to face classroom setup, where the major part of the instructional transaction is carried out by the teacher, who usually acts as a philosopher and guides to impart knowledge, develops attitude and skills.

In the teacher-centeered techniques, two methods are quite often used are they are

(i) **Lecture Method** It generally involves one-way communication, where a supposedly learned person explains the subject's complexities to a supposedly motivated audience. It is extensively used in conventional educational situations. In this method, there is a very limited scope for individualised learning.

(ii) **Demonstration Method** It is used mainly to develop the psychomotor and manipulation skills of the students. The teacher demonstrator has to handle the sessions carefully so as to provide an adequate individual's attention to each student.

Instructional Materials

Instructional materials are also know as Teaching Learning Materials (TLM), are any collection of materials including animate and inanimate objects and human and non-human resources that a teacher may use in teaching and learning situations to help achieve desired learning objectives. They may aid a student in concretizing a learning experience so as to make learning more exciting, interesting and interactive. They are tools used in instructional activities, which include active learning and assessment. They encompasses all the materials and physical means, an instructor might use to implement instruction and facilitate student's achievement of instructional objectives.

They act as support to teachers by providing the language input that they could use in the classroom, to expose their learners to the language. They also supply to the teacher, the exercises and activities to give to their students for them to engage in as practice material that will lead them to learn the language. They take on the responsibility of providing material for teaching which will realise the syllabus or objectives of teaching prescribed for the specific level.

They provide the core information that students will experience, learn and apply during a course. They hold the power to either engage or demotivate students. This is especially true for online courses, which rely on a thoughtful and complete collection of instructional materials that students will access, explore, absorb and reference as they proceed in a course.

Therefore, such materials must be carefully planned, selected, organised, refined and used in a course for the maximum effect. The planning and selection of instructional materials should take into consideration, both the breadth and depth of content so that student's learning is optimized.

The instruction materials can broadly be classified as follows

- Projected audio and visual aids.
- Non-projected visual aids.

The **first** category consists of chalk boards, white boards, wall charts, models, flip-charts, handouts, etc, which do not need the use of an optical or electronic projector. The effective use of these tools depends largely on the skills of the teacher.

Wall charts consist of maps, photographs, diagrams, graphs, cartoons, etc. are especially helpful to motivate the students, to initiate a discussion, or to substitute for information storage memory. **Flip charts** are used during a lecture to reveal key points as and when these are required. **Models** are especially useful to present the various dimensions of an object or an event, but these can be used only with a small group of learners because of the fact that these are indistinguishable to a large audience, sitting far away from the teacher's desk. **Handouts** may contain printed diagrams, tables, notes, etc. that can be supplied to students to concentrate more on what was said during the lecture.

Curriculum transactions, film strips, projectors, slides and slide projectors, overhead projectors, etc. that might have either front or back projection, belongs to the **second**

category. The audio-visual aids are prepared and very often integrated with the lecture. To make them effective, a lecturer/teacher needs to learn how to prepare and handle them.

For the learners, it is a chance to get relief from the straight forward lecture, and interaction with other media, motivates them as well as increases the effectiveness of learning. The functions of audio aids like tape recorders and record players are similar ones.

In learner-centered systems, self-instructional materials play an important role in providing mediated teaching to the learner, while the teacher only manages and supports the learning process. Varieties of hardware and software like textual materials, audio-visual self-instructional materials, computer based self-instructional materials, etc. are used to individualise learning.

These materials and their roles in individualised instruction/learning are discussed below

Textual Materials It includes books, structured notes and textual programmed materials. Books may not generally be self-instructional in their design, but with the help of a study guide a learner may be advised how he/she should go about learning. In the case of subject areas, textbooks may form an integral part of such learning, provided they are appropriate in so far as their level and treatment of the subject matter are concerned.

Audio-Visual Self-Instructional Materials It consists of audio-visual learning programmes, language laboratories, and broadcast media. In a multi-media instructional programme, such as you in distance learning, besides print, or non-print, self-instructional electronic media are put to use. The multi-media non-print package may include slides, audio and video cassettes, practical kit, etc. These materials aims at achieving the cognitive objective of mastery of a knowledge base, the psychomotor objective of skill acquirement, and the affective objective of attitudinal change.

In essence, we can assume, and to a certain extent ensures a high degree of student's involvement in the teaching/ learning activity.

Computer-Based Self-Instructional Materials Computer-assisted learning and interactive video can be cited as examples of this type of materials. As far as computer assisted learning is concerned, two modes (namely, the tutorial and the laboratory) of individualised learning are important. In the tutorial mode, the computer plays the role of an instructional device.

Programmed materials are used to react to the responses of the learner and in the laboratory model, the computer can be used to simulate a laboratory situation, to set problem-solving exercises, and to model's experiments. Computer-assisted learning is a highly stimulating and interactive learning device so far, as individualised learning is concerned.

Interactive video combines computer and video recorder to provide interactive teaching-learning in individualised learning situations. The computer provides the programme, and the video recorder provides, sound and visual displays. The combination and procedure results in rich self-learning materials to meet individual's learning needs. A later development in this area includes the combination of the video disk with the micro-computer to provide better access and individualisation for the learner.

Approaches to Curriculum and Instruction

An approach expresses a view-point about the development and design of the curriculum,the role of the teacher, learner and curriculum specialists in planning the curriculum, the goals and objectives of the curriculum studies and the important issues that needs to be examined.

The two significant approaches are

Academic Approach

It is sometimes referred as the traditional, synoptic, intellectual or knowledge oriented approach. It tries to analyse and synthesise major positions, trends, and concepts of the curriculum. It tends to be historical or philosophical or to a lesser extent social in nature. In this approach, the discussion of curriculum making is usually scholarly and theoretic, (not practical, and concerned with many broad concepts or aspects of schooling) and the treatment of curriculum as an intellectual thought are reflected in a good deal of background information and a broad overview of events and people.

It is rooted in the philosophical works of John Dewey, Henry Morrison and Bonoyd Bode. It became popular in the 1930's and 1950's.

During this period, new topics related to curriculum expanded the boundaries of the field to include a good number of trends and issues and the integration of various instructional, teaching, learning, guidance, evaluation, supervision and administrative procedures. However, after the 1950's, the Academic approach losts some of its glamour among curricularists. This is when, its major interest in curriculum centred on the structure of the discipline and qualitative methods.

Advantages of Academic Approach

- Logical arrangement of educational content in there in this approach.
- It mainly focus on the academic subjects and use of qualitative methods.

Disadvantages of Academic Approach

- It lacks tools of teaching.
- Curriculum is not practical in nature.

Competency Based Approach

It is an approach to education that focuses on the student's demonstration of desired learning outcomes as central to the learning process. It is concerned chiefly with a student's progression though curriculum at their own pace, depth, etc. As competencies are proven, students continues to progress. It is similar to mastery based learning, with the primary difference being that competency based learning often focuses on observable skills or competencies, while mastery based learning may be academic as likely to focus on concepts and skills.

In this approach, students are not allowed to continue until they have demonstrated mastery of identified competencies (*i.e.* desired learning outcomes to be demonstrated). It's strength lies in it's flexibility, as learners are able to move at their own pace. This supports students with diverse knowledge backgrounds, literary levels and other related aptitudes. It can be an effective model as it is potentially reducing inefficiency and increasing pedagogical precision and student's achievement.

So, a competency based curriculum emphasises the complex outcomes of a learning process (*i.e.* knowledge, skills and attitude to be applied by learners) rather than mainly focusing on what learners are expected to learn about, in terms of traditionally defined subject's content. In principle such a curriculum is learner-centred and adaptative to the changing needs of students, teachers and society.

The advantages of competency based is that in this the emphasis is not placed upon the learner's accumulation of memorised knowledge or behaviour, but instead on their proficiency in a particular realm. It has certain disadvantages too, it works well with some learning environment and less with others. It does not suit subject areas where it is difficult to prescribe specific competencies or where new skills and new knowledge need to be rapidly accommodated. It ignores the importance of social learning. It does not fit with preferred learning styles of many students.

Curriculum Evaluation

Curriculum is a system of learning experiences, deliberately designed and transacted for realising certain goals. On the other hand, **evaluation** is a systematic process of determining and appraising the proficiency level of a system or a practice. When evaluation is applied to curriculum, it focuses on discovering whether the curriculum as designed, developed and implemented, is producing or can produce the desired results. Evaluation serves to identify the strengths and weaknesses or the curriculum before implementation and the effectiveness of it's delivery after implementation.

Evaluation of curriculum is an integral and essential part of the whole process of curriculum development. It is a continuous activity and not a 'tail end process'.

It refers to an ongoing process of collecting, analysing, synthesising and interpreting information to aid in understanding what students know and can do. It refers to the full range of information gathered in the school district to evaluate (make judgements about) student's learning and program effectiveness in each content area. It must be based on information gathered from a comprehensive assessment system that is designed for accountability and committed to the concept that all students will achieve at high levels, is standard based and informs decisions which impact significant and sustainable improvements in teaching and student's learning.

Bruce Tuckman (1979) has defined curriculum evaluation as "The means for determining whether the programme is meeting its goals *i.e.* whether the measures/outcomes for a given set of instructional inputs matches the intended or pre-specified outcomes".

So, evaluation enables educators to identify alternative curricular actions and determine various combinations of curriculum to ensure maximum student's learning in the light of overall programme's goals.

Approaches to Curriculum Evaluation

Evaluation may be considered as a broad and continuous effort to find out the effects of implementing content and procedures to achieve pre-set goals. It is not content specific but it is a methodological process.

Approaches to curriculum evaluation are

Scientistic and Humanistic Approaches

Cronbach (1982) has identified two approaches to evaluation *i.e.* the Scientistic Ideals Approach and the Humanistic Ideals Approach. He has presented these two approaches at the two ends of evaluation. The **scientistic** end advocates **experimentation** and **humanistic end** does not have faith in **experimentation**.

Scientistic approach, in scientistic approach all efforts are focused on the learners. Student's achievements in different situations are compared by the way of test scores. Quantitative measures are adopted for data collection and statistical tools are employed for data analysis.

Humanistic approach would study a program already in place, not one imposed by the evaluator. Analysis of data, collected through this approach differs significantly from that collected through Scientistic Approach. It is more qualitative and the techniques employed are basically observation, interviews, personal meetings and discussions with participants.

Intrinsic and Pay-Off Evaluation

Intrinsic evaluation of curricula implies that evaluators study the content, it's sequence, organisation, accuracy, learning experiences provided, etc. They believe that with an accurate content and organisation student's learning would be stimulated. Most of the time, evaluators tend to neglect the concept of intrinsic evaluation.

According to **Scriven**, pay-off evaluation occurs when the effects of the delivered curriculum are examined and it's worth has been established. The effects of the curriculum on learners can be determined since this evaluation involves judgements based on pre-test, post test, scores or experimental group tests and other parameters.

Formative and Summative Evaluation

Formative evaluation aims to improve an existing programme based on the feedback obtained from the evaluation. Hence, programme developer must be frequently provided with detailed and specific information, to guide them in the developmental phase. On this basis, evaluators can revise the programme while it is being developed, before it can be implemented on a large scale. **Formative evaluation** can occur at several stages during the curriculum development process. At any stage, the validity of the content can be checked, *i.e.* whether students are achieving the stated goal, if not, then that content could be modified.

Summative evaluation assesses the effect of a complete programme. It is carried out at the end of an educational programme. This type of evaluation is based on the evidence about summed effects of various components in the curriculum. The people involved in the curriculum process can conclude, how successfully the curriculum has worked. It uses formal tools for gathering data. One of the main purpose of summative evaluation is to select from several completing curricular programmes, the one, which should be accepted, and those which should be discontinued.

Models of Curriculum Evaluation

Tyler's Objectives-Centered Model

One of the earliest curriculum evaluation model, which continues to influence many assessment projects, was that proposed by **Ralph Tyler** (1950) in his monograph **Basic Principles of Curriculum and Instruction**. Tyler's approach moved rationally and systematicly through several related steps. *They are*

- Begin with the behavioural objectives that have been previously determined. Those objectives should specify both the content of learning and the student behaviour expected i.e. demonstrate familiarity with dependable sources of information on questions relating to nutrition.
- Identify the situations that will give the student the opportunity to express the behaviour embodied in the objective and that evoke or encourage this behaviour. Thus, if you wish to assess oral language use, identify situations that evoke oral language.
- Select, modify or construct suitable evaluation instruments and check the instruments for objectivity, reliability, and validity.
- Use the instruments to obtain summarised or appraised results.
- Compare the results obtained from several instruments before and after given periods in order to estimate the amount of change, taking place.
- Analyse the results, in order to determine strengths and weaknesses of the curriculum and to identify possible explanations about the reason, for this particular pattern of strengths and weaknesses.
- Use the results to make the necessary modifications in the curriculum.

He maintains that evaluation is a reocurring process and that evaluation feedback should be used to reformulate or redefine objectives. In other words, information gatherd could be ploughed into the system, to modify the objectives and the programme, which is being evaluated. This recycling process keeps the evaluation system, dynamic.

Advantages of Tyler's Model

- It is relatively easy to understand and apply.
- It is rational and systematic.
- It focuses attention on curricular strengths and weaknesses, rather than being concerned solely with the performance of individual student.
- It also emphasises the importance of a continuing cycle of assessment, analysis and improvement.

Disadvantages of Tyler's Model

As **Guba and Lincoln** (1981) pointed out, however, it suffers from several deficiencies. *They are*

- It does not suggests, how the objectives themselves should be evaluated.
- It does not provides standards or suggests how standards should be developed.
- Its emphasis on the prior statement of objectives may restrict creativity in curriculum development and it seems to place undue emphasis on the pre-assessment and post assessment, ignoring completely the need for formative assessment.

Similarly, **Baron and Boschee** (1995) in their **book Authentic Assessment**, the key to unlocking student's success states that "We are encountering fundamental changes in the way we view and conducts assessment in American schools and sixty years have been passed since we experienced such a deep-seated and thoughtful re-evaluation of our assessment methods".

Scriven's Goal Free Model

Scriven was the first to introduce the concept of **Goal Free Evaluation Model**. It is not a comprehensive stand along evaluation model rather it is considered either a perspective or position concerning an evaluator's goal orientation throughout an evaluation or a technique or tool for evaluating without referencing goals. According to **Scriven**, Goal Free Evaluation Model is methodologically neutral which means that it can be used or adopted for use with various other evaluation approaches, models and methods as long as the other approaches do not mandate goal orientation.

In conducting a goal free evaluation, the evaluator functions as an unbiased observer, who begins by generating a profile of needs for the group served by a given program. (Scriven is somewhat vague as to how this needs profile is to be derived). Then, by using methods that are primarily qualitative in nature, the evaluator assesses the actual effects of the program. If a program has an effect that is responsive to one of the identified needs, then the program is perceived as useful. Obviously. His main contribution was to redirect the attention of evaluators and administrators to the importance of unintended effects i.e. a redirection that seems especially useful in education.

If a mathematics program achieves it's objectives of improving computational skills but has the unintended effect of diminishing interest in mathematics, then it cannot be judged completely successful. He emphasis on qualitative methods, also seemed to come at an opportune moment, when there was increasing dissatisfaction in the research community with the dominance of quantitative methodologies.

However, he himself notes, goal-free evaluation should be used to complement, not supplant goal based assessments. Used alone, it cannot provides sufficient information for the decision maker. Some critics have faulted him for not providing more explicit directions for developing and implementing the Goal Free Model, as a consequence, it probably can be used only by experts who do not require explicit guidance in assessing needs and detecting effects.

It has certain **advantages** and **disadvantages**. The goal free model allows evaluators to be attentive to a wider range of program's outcomes rather than just link for the program's results that are stuck to the program aims/goals. It can be used to supplement goal based evaluation. The goal free model has a long history, it has remained conceptually abstract and highly theoretical with very few practitioners. Goal Free Evaluation model has been criticised for the lack of operation by which to conduct it.

Stake's Responsive Model

Robert E. Stake in **1970** created a system for carrying out evaluation in education. It was then developed with the name Stake's Responsive model. In Responsive Model, the evaluator is a full subjective partner in the educational program who is really involved and interactive. The evaluator's role is to provide an avenue for continued communication and feedback during the evaluation process. According to **Stake**, there is no single true value to anything, but the value is in the eye of beholder. This means that there are may be many valid interpretations of the same events based on person's point of view, interest and belief. The duty of the evaluator is of collecting the views, opinions of people in and around the program.

Stake *recommends an interactive and recursive evaluation process that embodies these steps*

- The evaluator meets with clients, staff, and audiences to gain a sense of their perspectives on and intentions regarding the evaluation.
- The evaluator draws on such discussions and the analysis of any documents, to determine the scope of the evaluation project.
- The evaluator observes the program closely, to get a sense of its operation and to note any unintended deviations from announced intents.
- The evaluator discovers the states and real purposes of the project and the concerns that various audiences have about it and the evaluation.

- The evaluator identifies the issues and problems with which the evaluation should be concerned. For each issue and problem, the evaluator develops an evaluation design, specifying the kinds of data needed.
- The evaluator selects the means, needed to acquire the desired data. Most often, the means will be human observers or judges.
- The evaluator implements the data collection procedures.
- The evaluator organises the information into themes and prepares portrayals that communicates in natural ways, the thematic reports. The portrayals may involve video tapes, artifacts, case studies, or other faithful representations.
- By again being sensitive to the concerns of the stakeholders, the evaluator decides which audiences require which reports and chooses formats, most appropriate for given audiences (as cited by Galtthorn, 1987, pp. 275-276).

Clearly, the chief **advantage** of the Responsive Model is it's sensitivity to clients, by identifying their concerns and being sensitive to their values, by involving them closely throughout the evaluation, and by adapting the form of reports to meet their needs.

The model, if effectively used, should results in evaluation of high utility to clients. It also has the virtue of flexibility. The evaluator is able to choose from a variety of methodologies, once client concerns have been identified. Its chief **disadvantage** would seems to be its susceptability to manipulation by clients, who in expressing their concerns might attempt to draw attention away from weaknesses that they did not want to exposed.

Kirkpatrick's Model

It was develcped by **Dr Donald Kirkpatrick** (1924-2014) in the 1950's. It can be implemented before, throughout the following training to show the value of training to the business. As outlined by this system, evaluation needs to start with **level 1**, after which as time and resources will allow, should proceed in order through **level 2**, **3** and **4**. Data from all of the previous levels can be used as a foundation for the following levels analysis. As a result, each subsequent level provides an even more accurate measurement of the usefulness of the training course, yet simultaneously, cause for a significantly more time consuming and demanding evaluation. It has been used for over 30 years by many different types of companies as the major system for training evaluation. It is evident that Kirkpatrick's vision has made a positive impact to the overall practice of training evaluation.

The four levels of Kirkpatrick's model are

Level 1 : Evaluation-Reaction

The objective for this level is **straight forward,** it evaluates how individuals react to the Training Model, by asking questions that establishes the trainee's thoughts. As outlined by **Kirkpatrick,** each program needs to be assessed at this level, to help, improve the model for future use. On the top of that, participants' responses are essential for determining how invested, they will be in learning the next level. Even though, an optimistic reaction does not ensures learning, an unfavourable one, definitely makes if less likely that the uses will pay attention to the training.

Level 2 : Evaluation-Learning

Evaluating at this level, means to gauge the level participants have developed in expertise, knowledge or mind set. Exploration at this level is far more challenging and time-consuming as compared to level one techniques vary from informal to formal tests and self-assessment of at all possible, individuals take the test or evaluation prior to the training, the following training (post test) to figure out how much the participant comprehended.

Examples of tools and procedures, at level 2 are

- observations by peers and instructors.
- strategies for assessment should be relevant to the goals of the training program.
- a distinct clear scoring process needs to be determined, in order to reduce the possibility of inconsistent evaluation reports.

Level 3 : Evaluation-Transfer

It analyses the differences in the participant's behaviour at work, after completing the program. Assessing the change, makes it possible to figure out if the knowledge, mindset or skills, the program taught are being used at the work place.

For the majority or individual, this level offers the truest evaluation of a program's usefulness. Testing at this level is challenging, since it is impossible to anticipate when a person will start to properly utilise what they have learned from the program, making it more difficult to determine when, how often and exactly how it evaluates a participant's post assessment. It starts within 3 to 6 months after training.

Examples of assessment resources and techniques for level 3 are

- It can be carried out through observations and interviews.
- Observations should be made to minimise opinion based views of the interviewer, as this factor is too variable which can affect consistency and dependability of assessments.

Level 4 : Evaluation-Result

Commonly regarded as the primary goal of the program, it determines the overall success of the Training model by measuring factors such as lowered spending, improved and higher quality of products.

Advantages of Kirkpatrick's Model

- It is probably the best known model for analysing and evaluating the results of training and educational programmes.
- It takes into account any style of training, both formal and informal to determine aptitude based on four level criteria.
- It provides opportunity to learner to demonstrate learning transfer.
- It provides more objective feedback.
- It is relatively simple to understand.
- It presents a useful taxanomy for considering the impact of training programmes at different organisational levels.
- The model provides a logical structure and process to measure learning.

However, the model has certain disadvantage too that it does not consider the wide range of individual, organisational and training design.

EXAM BASED QUESTIONS

1 Curriculum transaction generally incorporates
(a) effective and desired implementation of curriculum
(b) planning for providing learning experiences
(c) a written plan that drives instruction
(d) Both a and b

2 Curriculum transaction is also known as
(a) Curriculum planning
(b) Curriculum management
(c) Curriculum instruction
(d) None of the above

3 Curriculum content should be based on
(a) current information (b) past information
(c) outdated information (d) None of these

4 Who is mainly responsible for curriculum transaction?
(a) Student (b) Teacher
(c) Administrator (d) School

5 Instructional media is defined as
(a) devices and materials employed in teaching and learning.
(b) materials for distance learners
(c) self-instructional aids and materials
(d) None of the above

6 Which of the following is/are not an advantage(s) of instructional media?
(a) The learning process becomes complex and less interesting.
(b) The learning process becomes more interactive.
(c) The delivery of learning materials can be standardised.
(d) Improves the quality of student's learning outcomes.

7 Instructional system is a .... process.
(a) pragmatic
(b) scientific
(c) logical
(d) deliberate

8 Which technique focuses on the individual learner?
(a) Group learning technique
(b) Experiential learning technique
(c) Learner-centred technique
(d) Teacher-centred technique

9 Personalised system of instruction was developed in ....
(a) 1940's (b) 1950's (c) 1960's (d) 1970's

10 The personalised system of instruction is based on the principles of independent study, self-pacing and ....
(a) group learning
(b) individualised learning
(c) counselling
(d) None of the above

11 Which technique combines both correspondence and tutorial support in an institution?
(a) Flexi study
(b) Programmed learning
(c) Distance education
(d) Computer assisted learning

12 Which innovation has facilitated the distance learners?
(a) Use of multi-media (b) Tutorial support
(c) Counselling sessions (d) None of these

13 It is also called a procedure of self-instruction.
(a) Personalised system of learning
(b) Programmed learning
(c) Computer assisted learning
(d) Personalised System of Instruction

14 Which type of learning provides a two-way communication?
(a) Persoanlised system of learning
(b) Programmed learning
(c) Simulation technique
(d) Computer assisted learning

15 Which technique is used in large groups?
(a) Seminar (b) Group discussion
(c) Tutorial (d) None of these

16 Which method provides student with a chance to express their individual learning?
(a) Seminar (b) Tutorial
(c) Group project (d) Group discussion

17 Which type of learning occurs outside the classroom?
(a) Teacher-centred learning
(b) Group learning
(c) Experiential learning
(d) Learner-centred learning

18 In which situation of learning, learner achieves the instructional objectives with little guidance from the teacher?
(a) Simulation technique (b) Discovery learning
(c) Case study technique (d) None of these

19 Programmed learning involves
(a) a graded series of audio tapes
(b) an ordered sequence of stimulus items
(c) a well planned lesson material, used for continuing education.
(d) collection of slides and film strips on the lesson

20 Which technique is used in order to make reality easily accessible to the learner?
(a) Case study technique (b) Discovery learning
(c) Simulation technique (d) Group discussion

21 Which of the following technique helps to obtain feedback from learners?
(a) Case study (b) Group discussion
(c) Simulation technique (d) Discovery learning

22 Which of the following involves one-way communication?
(a) Lecture method (b) Seminar
(c) Group project (d) Group discussion

23 A method used to develop the psychomotor and manipulation skills of the students is
(a) Lecture method
(b) Demonstration method
(c) Aids and Materials method
(d) None of the above

24 The non-projected visual aids consist of
(a) Flip charts (b) video recorder
(c) Graphs (d) Both a and c

25 Which tool depends largely on the skills of the teacher?
(a) Projected visual aids (b) Non-projected visual aids
(c) Textual material (d) None of these

26 Which form of learning is highly stimulating ?
(a) Tutorial
(b) Textual material
(c) Computer assisted learning
(d) Audio based materials

27 Which approach is referred as the Traditional or Knowledge Oriented Approach?
(a) Historical approach
(b) Competency based approach
(c) Academic approach.
(d) None of the above

28 Academic Approach is rooted in the philosophical works of
(a) John Dewey (b) Henry Morrison
(c) Boyd Bode (d) All of these

29 Academic Approach became popular during
(a) 1930s and 1950s (b) 1940s and 1960s
(c) 1920s and 1930s (d) 1970s and 1980s

30 It supports students with diverse knowledge backgrounds, literacy levels and other related aptitudes. Which approach is this?
(a) Competency vased approach
(b) Academic approach
(c) Historical approach
(d) None of the above

31 It serves to identify the strengths and weaknesses of the curriculum. Here 'it' stands for
(a) curriculum transaction (b) curriculum development
(c) curriculum design (d) curriculum evaluation

32 Who defined curriculum evaluation in 1979?
(a) John Dewey (b) Bruce Tuckman
(c) Henery Morrison (d) Boyd Bode

33 In which approach, quantitative measures are adopted for data collection and statistical tools are employed for data analysis?
(a) Humanistic approach (b) Formative approach
(c) Scientistic approach (d) Intrinsic approach

34 Techniques employed are basically observations, interviews, personal meetings and discussions with participants. The method of approach is__.
(a) formative (b) intrinsic
(c) humanistic (d) pay-off

35 Which evaluation of curricula believes that with an accurate content and organisation, student learning would be stimulated?
(a) Formative (b) Intrinsic
(c) Summative (d) Pay-off

36 In which evaluation effects of the delivered curriculum are examined and its worth has been established?
(a) Pay-off (b) Intrinsic
(c) Formative (d) Summative

37 Which type of evaluation can occur at several stages, during the curriculum development process?
(a) Pay-off (b) Summative
(c) Formative (d) Intrinsic

38 Which of the following is/are the advantage(s) of Tyler's model?
(a) It is rational and systematic
(b) It is difficult to understand
(c) It emphasis the importance of continuing cycle of assessment, analysis and improvement
(d) Both a and c

39 Tyler's Model is also known as .... Model.
(a) Goal Free (b) Responsive
(c) Objectives-Centred (d) None of these

40 Basic principles of curriculum and instruction was written by ....
(a) Robert Stake (b) Ralph Tyler
(c) Michael Scriven (d) Donald Kirkpatrick

41 In 1981, which thinkers pointed out the deficiencies in Tyler's Objective-Centered Model?
(a) Baron and Baschee
(b) Guba and Lincoln
(c) Robert Stake and Michael Scriven
(b) None of the above

42 Who was the first to question the assumption, that goals are crucial in the evaluation process?
(a) Robert Stake (b) Ralph Tyler
(c) Michael Scriven (d) Donald Kirkpatrick

43 In which model of evaluation, the evaluator functions as an unbiased observer ?
(a) Responsive model
(b) Goal Free model
(c) Objective-Centered model
(d) All of the above

44 Which model recommends an interactive and recursive evaluation process?
(a) Objective-Centred (b) Goal Free
(c) Responsive (d) None of these

45 Kirkpatrick's model was developed in ....
(a) 1940s (b)1950s
(c) 1960s (d) 1970s

46 Kirkpatrick's Model is based on .... levels.
(a) two (b) three (c) four (d) five

47 The Kirkpatrick's Model has been used for .... years.
(a) twenty (b) thirty
(c) ten (d) fifty

48 Observations by peers and instructors as a procedure is used at level ....
(a) 1 (b) 3
(c) 2 (d) 4

49 Which level offers the truest evaluation of a program's usefulness?
(a) Level 1 (b) Level 2
(c) Level 3 (d) Level 4

50 Level 2 of evaluation is based on ....
(a) reaction (b) learning
(c) transfer (d) results

51 Which level is commonly regarded as the primary goal of the program?
(a) Results (b) Learning
(c) Reaction (d) Transfer

52 Match the following

List I (Methods)	List II (Techniques)
A. Personalised System of Learning	1. Teacher-centred technique
B. Seminar	2. Learner-centred technique
C. Demonstration Method	3. Group learning technique
D. Simulation	4. Experiential learning technique

Codes

	A	B	C	D
(a)	2	3	1	4
(b)	1	2	3	4
(c)	3	2	1	4
(d)	4	3	2	1

53 Match the following

List I (Approaches)	List II (Characteristics)
A. Scientistic Approach	1. Knowledge oriented
B. Humanistic Approach	2. Faith in experimentation
C. Academic Approach	3. Does not have faith in experimentation
D. Competency Based Approach	4. Flexible approach

Codes

	A	B	C	D
(a)	3	2	1	4
(b)	4	2	3	1
(c)	3	4	1	2
(d)	1	2	3	4

54 Match the following.

List I (Evaluations)	List II (Characteristics)
A. Pay-off evaluation	1. Improves existing programmes
B. Intrinsic evaluation	2. Changes the curriculum
C. Summative evaluation	3. Based on accuracy
D. Formative evaluation	4. Based on pre-test or scores

Codes

	A	B	C	D
(a)	1	3	4	2
(b)	4	3	2	1
(c)	2	3	4	1
(d)	3	2	1	4

55 Match the following

List I (Models)	List II (Researchers)
A. Objective-Centred Model	1. Robert Stake
B. Responsive Model	2. Michael Scriven
C. Goal Free Model	3. Donald Kirkpatrick
D. Level Based Model	4. Ralph Tyler

Codes

	A	B	C	D		A	B	C	D
(a)	1	2	3	4	(b)	2	3	1	4
(c)	3	1	2	4	(d)	4	1	2	3

56 Which of the following statement(s) is/are incorrect.

1. Learner-centred system focus on the individual learner.
2. Personalised system of instruction was developed by FS Keller.
3. Flexi study is a teacher-centered technique.
4. Group discussion is not beneficial for learners.

Codes
(a) Both 1 and 2 (b) Only 2
(c) Only 3 (d) Both 3 and 4

57 Which of the following statement(s) is/are correct?

1. Simulation means replication of reality.
2. Essence of simulation is involvement of participants and observers.
3. It does not makes reality accessible to the learner.
4. In simulated situation, learners deal with simulated problems through actions.

Codes
(a) Both 1 and 2 (b) Only 2
(c) 1, 2 and 4 (d) Only 4

58 Which of the following statement(s) is/are correct?

1. Teacher-centered techniques are largely applied in the conventional classrooms.
2. Teacher-Centred Approach is quite often used.
3. It is based on Lecture and Demonstration Method.
4. There is a limited scope for individualised learning.

Codes
(a) Only 1 (b) Both 2 and 3
(c) Only 3 (d) All of these

59 Which of the following statement(s) is/are incorrect?

1. Evaluation serves to identify the strengths and weaknesses of the curriculum.
2. Evaluation is a systematic process.
3. Evaluation is a narrow concept.
4. Student's learning is an important aspect of the overall programme goals.

Codes
(a) Only 1 (b) Only 2
(c) Only 3 (d) Both 3 and 4

60 Which of the following statement(s) is/are incorrect?

1. Curriculum is a written plan that drives instruction.
2. Curriculum transaction does not incorporate planning.
3. Curriculum should change with change in time.
4. A noble curriculum plays an important role to the development of thinking skills.

Codes
(a) Both 1 and 2 (b) Only 2
(c) Only 3 (d) Only 4

Directions (Q. Nos. 61-71) *Below given are two statements, one labelled as Assertion (A) and other labelled as Reason (R). Choose the correct code for the following.*

Codes
(a) Both A and R are true and R is the correct explanation of A
(b) Both A and R are true, but R is not the correct explanation of A
(c) Both A and R are false
(d) A is false, but R is true

61 **Assertion** (A) Curriculum is generally understood as the courses offered by an educational institution.
Reason (R) It delineates the skills and concepts taught and evaluated to enhance student's achievement.

62 **Assertion** (A) The main responsibility of curriculum transaction lies on the teachers.
Reason (R) Teachers use different types of pedagogies, so that students can be benefitted in gaining knowledge.

63 **Assertion** (A) Transaction of curriculum is a difficult task .
Reason (R) As, it is based on theoretical and practical aspects as well.

64 **Assertion** (A) Instructional media encompasses all the materials and physical means.
Reason (R) It includes traditional as well as newer materials.

65 **Assertion** (A) An instructional system is designed to achieve one or multiple objectives.
Reason (R) There are four kinds of instructional techniques in teaching-learning process.

66 Assertion (A) The personalised system of instruction is based on the principles of independent study.
Reason (R) It was developed in 1960's and also known as Keller's Plan.

67 Assertion (A) Learner-centred system is based on group-learner methodology.
Reason (R) It is composed of personalised system of instruction, flexi study, programmed learning, etc.

68 Assertion (A) Earlier, only print materials were used by distance learners.
Reason (R) The innovation of Multi-Media Approach is beneficial for disadvantaged people.

69 Assertion (A) Experiential learning occurs outside the classroom.
Reason (R) It brings knowledge from society to classroom.

70 Assertion (A) Case Study Method is a research technique.
Reason (R) It attempts to examine, contemporary phenomena in a real-life situation.

71 Assertion (A) Tyler' Model is relatively easy to understand and apply.
Reason (R) It focuses attention of curricular strengths and weaknesses.

Directions (Q. Nos. 72-76) *Read the passage and answer the following questions.*

According to Allan Olson (2004), President and Executive Director of North-West Evaluation Association, schools in the future will not be grouped by age but by instructional needs and it will be done electronically. Students will not be assigned, only one teacher and will not be in a closed door classroom, but rather, will have multiple teachers and be in a more open and collaborative environment. Students will be matched with teachers, who have the skills and proficiency to best instruct them. To arrive at this future, schools must use cutting edge evaluation tools such as adaptive electronic testing that provides a comprehensive assessment of a student's needs.

The ultimate indicator of an effective school is the measure of academic growth of it's students. Without sufficient data, school cannot fine-tune programs or respond to student's individual needs, quickly enough to meet local, state, or federal guidelines. This is a major problem with the states and the federal government mandating that schools, attains a high proficiency rate of student's achievement.

New development in technology are allowing schools to use internet and enable assessment tools that adjusts in difficulty to the individual student's ability. Because electronic tests are customised on demand, each student is engaged and the results are more accurate. Electronic results are also instantaneous. This allow teachers to see quickly whether students are succeeding or falling behind.

Curriculum and instruction can then be modified to address the results. Electronic adaptive tests can be given at any time *i.e.* winter or spring. Tests can be tailored to meet federal, state and district mandates. Unlike conventional evaluative tests, computerised adaptive tests measures achievement status and academic growth for every child.

Schools and curriculum leaders can assess a program's effectiveness for children with different instructional needs. Timely, accurate data provides school leaders with information to adjust instruction and/or programs as needed during the school year to ensure individual learning and to improve program effectiveness. Using up to date internet enabled assessments, curriculum leaders and teachers will have a chance to shape tomorrow's schools, today.

72 Schools in the future will be grouped by ....
(a) instructional needs
(b) instructional objectives
(c) instructional techniques
(d) None of the above

73 Which evaluation tool(s) will be used to provide(s) a comprehensive assessment?
(a) Textual material
(b) Adaptive electronic testing
(c) Whiteboard
(d) All of the above

74 Through which assessment, results are more accurate?
(a) Formative
(b) Summative
(c) Internet abled
(d) Computer based

75 Programme's effectiveness can be judged through ....
(a) role of a teacher
(b) student's achievement
(c) teaching goals
(d) teaching techniques

76 Instructions and curriculum must be adjusted
(a) as per the need of the schools
(b) as per the need of curriculum leaders
(c) as per the requirement of teachers
(d) as per the needs of students

Directions (Q. Nos. 77-80) *Read the given passage and answer the following questions.*

In the words of Munroe, "Curriculum embodies all the experiences which are utilised by the school to attain the aims of education". Thus, the various subjects included for study in a curriculum, are not intended merely for study or rate learning but to convey experiences of various kind". The concept has been defined in more or less, the same terms in the report of the Secondary Education Commission in these words that curriculum does not mean only the academic subject traditionally taught in the school, but it includes the totality of experiences that a pupil receives through the main fold activities that go on in the school, classroom, library, laboratory, workshop, playground and in the numerous informal definition of curriculum as experience is provided by Crow and Crow, "The curriculum includes are the learner's experiences in or outside the school that are included in a programme which has been devised to help them to develop mentally, physically, socially, spiritually and morally".

77 In which report, curriculum has been defined.
(a) Secondary Education Commission
(b) UGC
(c) NCERT
(d) SCERT

78 Curriculum includes ....
(a) learner's experience (b) guidance of teachers
(c) instructional techniques (d) All of these

79 Curriculum is intended for ......
(a) rote learning (b) conveying experiences
(c) Both a and b (d) None of these

80 Curriculum has been devised to help the children, to develop them
(a) mentally and morally (b) physically and socially
(c) spiritually (d) All of these

PREVIOUS YEAR'S QUESTIONS

January 2017

1 Summative evaluation implies
(a) use of daily quizzes
(b) monitoring of learning through homework
(c) terminal tests
(d) weekly grading of students

2 Which of the following is a case of formative evaluation of curriculum?
(a) Conducting an evaluation of the curriculum concerned before the course is completed
(b) Evaluating the curriculum concerned getting it appraised by students and teachers
(c) Evaluating the curriculum concerned, in the middle of the course, collecting the views of students and parents and providing feedback
(d) Evaluating the curriculum concerned by teachers based on the performance by students

ANSWERS

Exam Based Questions

1 (d)	2 (b)	3 (a)	4 (b)	5 (a)	6 (a)	7 (b)	8 (c)	9 (c)	10 (b)
11 (a)	12 (a)	13 (b)	14 (d)	15 (b)	16 (b)	17 (c)	18 (b)	19 (b)	20 (c)
21 (a)	22 (a)	23 (b)	24 (d)	25 (b)	26 (c)	27 (c)	28 (d)	29 (a)	30 (a)
31 (d)	32 (b)	33 (c)	34 (c)	35 (b)	36 (a)	37 (c)	38 (b)	39 (d)	40 (b)
41 (b)	42 (c)	43 (b)	44 (c)	45 (b)	46 (c)	47 (b)	48 (c)	49 (c)	50 (b)
51 (a)	52 (a)	53 (a)	54 (b)	55 (d)	56 (d)	57 (c)	58 (d)	59 (c)	60 (c)
61 (b)	62 (a)	63 (a)	64 (a)	65 (b)	66 (a)	67 (d)	68 (b)	69 (a)	70 (a)
71 (a)	72 (a)	73 (b)	74 (c)	75 (b)	76 (d)	77 (a)	78 (d)	79 (c)	80 (d)

Previous Years' Questions

1 (c)	2 (c)

CHAPTER

20

Approaches to Curriculum Change

Curriculum approach is a way of dealing with curriculum, a way of doing, creating, designing and thinking about the curriculum. There are various approaches to curriculum change namely, Bottom-Up approach, Systematic and Panic approach and Appreciative Inquiry approach. In curriculum change, the teachers, students and educational administrators play a very important role.

Curriculum Change

Curriculum change means making the curriculum different in some way, to give it a new position or direction. This often means alteration to its philosophy by way of its aims and objectives, reviewing the content included, revising its methods and rethinking it's evaluatory procedures. Change in terms of curriculum involves adapting a new educational method. When change is made in the classroom, it can enhance the social skills of students and focus on unique methods for teaching historical, technological, organisational and political lessons. An innovative curriculum relies on students to make discoveries with an instructor, present to serve as a mentor or guide instead of taking the role of the expert who controls the learning.

Suarez Orozco (2007) suggests that "Teachers should recognise the opportunity to enhance the contemporary relevance of their curriculum. The curriculum planners and teachers could attempt to infuse problem based learning and critical thinking in the school curriculum".

Some of the suggested ways to reform the curriculum and teaching are discussed below

- A student-centered approach that stressed the active acquisition of knowledge through experience. Inquiry based learning and problem-solving activities of students should be used in designing the curriculum.
- Curriculum and pedagogy should be capable of developing high order thinking skills and other capacities that are pertinent to the life long process of learning.
- Curriculum should be developed with a process approach, which uses the experience and interest of students as the basis for content selection.
- An inter-disciplinary approach should be adopted to integrate knowledge into all disciplines.
- Multi-cultural issues, differences in gender, intelligencies and other kinds of diversity in the classroom must be considered.

In this Chapter

- Constructivist pedagogy, such as knowledge building through computer networks must be encouraged.

Thus, the process of curriculum change is defined as "permissiveness and support in accordance with a helpful improvement in a curriculum with adequate use of resources".

Types of Curriculum Change

There are broadly **two** types of curriculum change and *they are classified as below*

(i) **Hardware Change** This change is generally composed of introduction of new classrooms, books, educational equipments, overall structure, etc.

(ii) **Software Change** This change affects the content of the curriculum and it is related to the methods of delivery of curriculum. *There are several categories of curriculum change that are discussed below*

- **Substitution** The current curriculum will be replaced or substituted by a new one. New textbooks, equipments, replacement of teachers and administrators.
- **Alteration** Minor changes to the current or existing curriculum rather than complete replacement of the whole curriculum, syllabus or course of study.
- **Restructuring** It is building a new structures that would mean major modifications in the school system, degree program or educational system. Sharing of resources among a group of schools or institutions.
- **Addition** Introduction of new components without changing the old elements. *e.g.* audio-visual aids.
- **Value Orientation** A type of curriculum change that was classified to respond to shift in the emphasis that the teacher provides which are not within the mission or vision of the school or vice-versa.

Factors Affecting Curriculum Change

There are various factors that affects curriculum change as discussed below

Political Factors

Politics influences curriculum design and development starts with funding. Both private and public educational institutions rely on funding for hiring personnel, building and maintaining facilities. Politics has tremendous influence on the education system as it determines and defines the goals, content, learning experiences and evaluation strategies in education. Curriculum materials and their implementation are usually influenced by political considerations.

Technological Factors

The intention is to equip the learners with the requisite computer skills and knowledge. In addition to computers, other forms of electronic media are being used in teaching. Technological multi-media influences educational goals and learning experiences among students. So, change in technology also leads to curriculum change.

Social Factors

To fulfil the societal needs as society has it's own expectations about the aims and objectives that should be considered while designing the curriculum. Developing relevant curriculum takes into account society's expectations, accomodating group traditions and promoting equality.

Economic Factors

Curriculum planner should try to establish a closer relationship between education and economic development, which are to a larger extent inter-dependent on each other. An industrial country like England gives emphasis on technical and industrial education because the economy of that country is based on industrial production. So, depending upon the demand for certain skills in the market and technology available to the people, curriculum could be used to prepare children for the work force of the future. For instance, many schools have decided to phase out workshop programs in favour of the more modern technology programs because the local economies had little demand for those type of skills.

General Factors

It includes the following

- Student limitations to understand the content.
- Professional accreditation needs.
- University or government requirement.

Approaches to Curriculum Change

Approaches to curriculum change are as follows

Bottom-Up Approach

This approach is seemingly more favoured in the emerging paradigm of curriculum. The term **bottom-up** is also referred to as **Grassroots Approach**. It suggests that the process of curriculum receives its initial momentum from the bottom/root of the structure of educational institutions, at the level of teachers and learners. The seed for development emerges from the actual site of action, the classroom. The pressure comes from the teachers and the learners who have immediate experiential access to the day to day factors influencing the effectiveness of the existing curriculum. In this case, the curriculum can be seen as the consequence of a deliberate collaborative enterprise involving the teachers, learners, subject-matter and the situational context or environment. The teachers and learners are recognised as the actual creator of the curriculum.

Bottom-Up approach gave more consideration to the needs of the learners and curriculum based on this approach is dynamic, emergent, rich, self-organised, open and existentially realised by the participants.

Beale (2002) reminds us that in the process of designing change, "it is important to avoid imposing a foreign teaching method, without consideration of the existing cultural characteristics and constraints within which it must be applied". It was hoped that the introduction of more communicative methods into a curriculum would create a balanced approach.

Systematic and Panic Approach

A systematic way of reviewing a curriculum involves needs assessment, planning, design, teacher's training, material's preparation, modification, implementation, monitoring, feedback and evaluation.

Tyler offers a systematic way of developing curricula and instruction. He uses four questions that seeks to determine objectives, work out learning experiences, select and organise learning experiences so as to attain specified outcomes and provides a program to evaluate outcomes.

The **Panic approach** according to **UNESCO-IBE** (1999) is caused by a situation where local or international pressures cause rapid decisions to be made to structured planning.

From the above descriptions of the Panic Approach, it seems that the approach is reactive rather than proactive, that it is preferred where curriculum decision makers are under pressure to provide instant solutions to educational problems or situations that unlike the Systematic Approach. It minimises the tasks like wide consultation, situational analysis and thorough preparation for implementation.

Appreciative Inquiry Approach

The term **appreciative inquiry** was first coined by **David Cooperrider** and **Suresh Srivastava**. It is a powerful approach that builds on the positive core of organisation in both action planning and transformational change. It helps people to create vision for a system based on people's personal experiences, expertise, knowledge and skills.

According to this approach, curriculum change will come about as a result of a highly interactive process that brings people from all levels of institution together to learn from one another and with another, building relationships and expanding collective wisdom. Through this approach, during the curriculum design phase academic staff identifies key facts of institutional systems and structures that will be needed to support the realisation of their collectively generated new or revised curricula. Appreciative Inquiry approach creates transformative learning experiences for both educators and students.

Role of Teachers in Curriculum Change

The role of teacher in the process of curriculum change is that of an expert from the discipline. Their knowledge has to be updated to support and assess the students in new authentic tasks. It is widely acknowledged that the teachers are key actors in curriculum innovation. Curriculum innovation usually requires a change in teacher's practice.

However, experienced teachers do not tend to change their current practice easily because it is rooted in their beliefs and in the practical knowledge, they have accumulated during their years of teaching. To accomplish change in teaching practice, teachers should not only implement innovation, but they should also become actively involved in the development of innovation. In general, it is assumed that the teachers develop co-ownership of new curriculum when they are actively involved in it's development.

Role of Students in Curriculum Change

Students have their own knowledge and skills, which they have constructed through learning experiences. The issue of getting students involved in curriculum planning is not new. It can be traced far back to the idea of **Kilpatrick** and **Rugg**, child-centred culturalists who outlined the role and concepts of curriculum, making that involves students in planning themes, units, lesson's plans and school's projects that allowed for considerable student's input. **Ornstein** and **Hunkins** further consider students as a most important source for curriculum development.

They contend that students should have a voice in curriculum development and change. Their input is important in it's own right, but allowing them to participate in curriculum development also empowers them and encourages them to take responsibility for matters that concern them. So, change in curriculum equips students for challenging world of 21st century, needs to ensure that students are supposed to take increasing responsibility of their own learning.

Role of Educational Administrators in Curriculum Change

Successful educational administrators value high standards, clarity in communication and transparency in authentic professional relationships to implement and sustain curriculum change and improve student's development and achievement. They play a significant and direct role to influence on student's learning.They supervise and monitor teaching and learning in the school, facilitate the development of successful goals and build culture dedicated to continuous improvement of teaching and learning.

Curriculum Research

Curriculum research is a systematic attempt to gain a better understanding of all components of curriculum.

The research attempts to understand the current state of curricular thinking in schools and universities. It tries to find out that substance of education i.e. knowledge, skills and progression and more important aspects in designing a qualitative curriculum. Educators must review the curriculum on timely basis and make intelligent use of assessment in curriculum designing and planning.

The research design is based on two main core principles

- Developing a valid research model of the quality of education, covering the intention, implementation and impact of the curriculum.
- Designing an approach that focused on the collection of first hand evidence in the quality of education.

Scope of Curriculum Research

Research in curriculum is difficult primarily because the term curriculum refers to everything of importance in education but specifies very little in particular. Research is an indepth inquiry into a problem which needs an amicable solution. Curriculum research requires a lot of expertise with respect to its planning, designing implementing and processing.

The scope of curriculum research is very broad in nature as it involves invention of new teaching methods, curriculum transaction strategies, effective use of teaching aids, building new knowledge, regarding the methodology. Specifically, scope refers to the breadth of the curriculum, the organising threads that constitute the skills and content that teachers are expected to include in their instruction.

Types of Research in Curriculum Studies

Following are the types of research in curriculum studies

Experimental Research

Experimental research is a method used by researchers through manipulating one variable and control the rest of the variables. The process, treatment and program in this type of research are also introduced and the conclusion is observed. The aim of experimental research is to predict phenomena. In most cases, an experiment is constructed so that some kinds of causation can be explained.

Experimental research is helpful for society as it helps to improve everyday life. Here, the problems are identified and accordingly the problem is resolved with regard to the curriculum. Under this research, the changes in the curriculum are made so that in the teaching-learning activity the basic problems of the students are resolved. In this research, the emphasis is laid on experimentation. In this research, the basic changes can be made in the curriculum.

Fundamental Research

Fundamental research can be stated as pure research. It's purpose is to develop theories by discovering broad generalisation and principles. It has little to do with the application of findings. This type of research has interested the doctoral candidates, and only a small portion of teachers who have been casual rather than active consumers are participants in the research.

In this type of research, teacher studies various aspects and then incorporate them accordingly. Under fundamental research, the curriculum is made learner-centered so that the students could understand the topics easily. In the development of curriculum the role of teacher is of utmost importance. Under fundamental research, the problems are identified first then it is analysed and accordingly the problems are resolved.

Action Research

It was initiated in the early 1940s by **Kurt Lewin**. Underlying the Action Research Approach, one finds important assumptions about the nature of research and of knowledge itself. The investigators are not passive observers whose sole interest is to collect data, they look for causes and make generalisations which can be converted into recommendations.

Objectives of Action Research

- To improve the practices going on in the schools.
- To make teachers and educational administrators research minded.
- To make the environment of the school more conducive for effective teaching and learning.

In action research, the changes in curriculum are made 'on the spot' or 'of the spot'. While conducting such research the interest of students and teachers are considered. The action research is a process where teacher analysis his teaching and tries to improve his teaching methods. Through action research the curriculum is made qualitative and effective.

Search Conference

It is a method of participatory planning which enables a group of people to identify and discuss problems and plan future action. As a planning technique, a search conference reverses the traditional planning approaches by encouraging democratic participation of the entire group. It has been used within success in curriculum development.

Questionnaire Surveys

The questionnaire technique involves collecting primary data through the selection of an appropriate sample from the population and entails the development of structured sets of questions on specific issues. A thorough search of secondary sources is required to ensure that all existing data has been discovered prior to developing a questionnaire. It is a flexible method of obtaining information. So, data can be collected in the form of questions from the teachers as well as learners and that will help to improvise the curriculum.

Conclusion

To conclude, we can say that curriculum change is a process of restructuring for both the teachers as well as students. It is a necessary perspective as it helps in including new areas and concepts which were not taken into account. Curriculum should be comprehensive in it's approach so that it will serve as a guideline for school improvement. Essential reforms and changes in the curriculum will help both the educators and learners to enrich and achieve their goals.

EXAM BASED QUESTIONS

1 Curriculum change is a

(a) learning process (b) evolutionary process
(c) serious process (d) All of these

2 Necessary conditions for curriculum change and practice are

(a) re-conceptualising curriculum
(b) sophisticated implementations strategies
(c) change in teaching methods
(d) All of the above

3 Which approach is used by curriculum reformers?

(a) Pragmatic approach
(b) Over-Simplistic approach
(c) Diffused approach
(d) None of the above

4 Need of curriculum change is emphasised for

(a) sustainable improvement
(b) belief's systems
(c) increasing the capacity of teachers
(d) increasing the capacity of learners

5 Which change affects the content of the curriculum and is related to the methods of delivery of curriculum.

(a) Hardware change (b) Software change
(c) Substitution (d) Value orientation

6 The ways in which curriculum is implemented depends on

(a) selection of content
(b) organisation of content
(c) what are over perspective of the curriculum
(d) principles of curriculum

7 Technical procedure of curriculum does not include which of the following?

(a) Formulation of objectives
(b) Selection of content
(c) Organisation of learning experiences
(d) Successful implementation of curriculum

8 The moral purpose of change is

(a) raising the quality and closing the gap in student's achievement.
(b) raising the quantity of content
(c) raising Value Based Learning Theories
(d) None of the above

9 For sustainable implementation of curriculum reforms, we must have understanding of

(a) complexity and internal dynamics of change process
(b) culture of school
(c) perspective of teachers and students
(d) All of the above

10 "It is a powerful approach that builds on the positive core of an organisation in both action planning and tranformational change". Which is the approach of curriculum change?
(a) Bottom-Up Approach
(b) Systematic and Panic Approach
(c) Grassroot Approach
(d) Appreciative Inquiry Approach

11 Education's leaders must be
(a) facilitator
(b) productive and sustainable
(c) disciplined
(d) None of the above

12 What is the missing link of today's education system?
(a) Hidden capacities of schools and teachers
(b) Need of understanding
(c) Potential of students
(d) None of the above

13 Broadly, there are two types of curriculum change and they are
(a) hardware and software change
(b) need and assessment based change
(c) evaluation and organised change
(d) traditional and contemporary change

14 Substitution means
(a) building a new structure
(b) current curriculum will be replaced or substituted.
(c) introducing new components
(d) All of the above

15 Alteration basically means
(a) major modifications in the school's system
(b) minor changes to current curriculum
(c) complete replacement of existing curriculum
(d) None of the above

16 Which of this is not a factor of curriculum change?
(a) Political factor
(b) Environmental factor
(c) Technological factor
(d) Societal needs factor

17 Which of this is not an approach of curriculum change?
(a) Bottom-Up approach (b) Systematic approach
(c) Panic approach (d) Traditional approach

18 Bottom-Up Approach emphasises on
(a) promoting changes at grassroot level
(b) promoting changes at the top level
(c) promoting foreign teaching methods
(d) None the above

19 Which method would create a balanced approach in curriculum change?
(a) Traditional Approach Method
(b) Communicative Method
(c) Contemporary Method
(d) All of the above

20 Teacher-centred curriculum is presented in
(a) Communicative Method
(b) Contemporary Method
(c) Traditional Approach Method
(d) All of the above

21 Which educationist thinker offers a systematic way of curriculum and instruction?
(a) Tyler (b) Westerly
(c) Richard (d) Bobbit

22 Panic Approach is caused by
(a) preparation of curriculum
(b) planning and designing of curriculum
(c) rapid decision-making
(d) wide consultation

23 Panic Approach minimises the task of
(a) wide consultation and situational analysis
(b) improvement
(c) Pragmatic and Broad Based Approach
(d) None of the above

24 Who are the key actors in curriculum innovation?
(a) Students (b) teachers
(c) Administrators (d) None of these

25 Who considers that students are important source for curriculum development?
(a) Kilpatrick (b) Ralph Tyler
(c) Ornstein and Hunkins (d) Rugg

26 What is the role of educational administrators in curriculum change?
(a) To implement and sustain curriculum change
(b) To challenge the curriculum
(c) To build the curriculum
(d) All of the above

27 The feasibility of research study should be considered in the light of
(a) potential ethical concerns
(b) skills required for the researcher
(c) cost and time required to conduct the research
(d) All of the above

28 Curriculum research does not involves
(a) invention on new teaching methods
(b) curriculum transaction strategies
(c) effective use of teaching aids
(d) None of the above

29 Few research methods of curriculum change includes
(a) scientific research and action research
(b) search conference and questionnaires
(c) Both a and b
(d) None of the above

30 Who initiated the Action Research Method in early 1940's?
(a) Kurt Lewin (b) Ralph Tyler
(c) Bobbitt (d) None of these

31 Questionnaire research is based on
(a) participatory planning
(b) assumptions
(c) scientific principles
(d) structured sets of questions

32 Curriculum innovation refers to
(a) it may occur in response to external events.
(b) it is always planned.
(c) ideas and practices that are new and different.
(d) Both (b) and (c)

33 Curriculum change and innovation are necessitated by
(a) political, social and economical factors
(b) psychological factors
(c) cultural and technological factors
(d) Both a and c

34 **Statement I** The role of teacher in the process of curriculum change is that of an expert.
Statement II They are the key in curriculum innovation.
(a) Both statements I and II are correct
(b) Only statement I is correct
(c) Only statement II is correct
(d) Neither b nor c

35 Tanner and Tanner emphasises three principle models of curriculum change in the year
(a) 1979 (b) 1980 (c) 1981 (d) 1986

36 Which model stresses the importance of inter-personal networks of information, leadership and personal contact?
(a) Social Interaction Model
(b) Problem-Solving Model
(c) Diffusion Model
(d) Research and Development Model

37 The seminal work of Raipu Tyler was published in
(a) 1949 (b) 1959 (c) 1948 (d) 1957

38 Name the title of the book that made a lasting impression on curriculum theories and practices.
(a) The Curriculum
(b) Curriculum Implementation
(c) Basic Principles of Curriculum and Instruction
(d) None of the above

39 Match the following

	List I		List II
A.	Political factors	1.	Use of ICT
B.	Technological factors	2.	Promotion of equality
C.	Societal influence	3.	Funding & building infrastructure

Codes

	A	B	C		A	B	C
(a)	2	1	3	(b)	3	1	2
(c)	1	2	3	(d)	None of these		

40 Match the following

	List I (Approaches)		List II (Characteristics)
A.	Bottom-Up Approach	1.	Reactive Approach
B.	Panic Approach	2.	Attains specified outcomes
C.	Systematic Approach	3.	Alleviate problems, linked to Top-Down Approach

Codes

	A	B	C		A	B	C
(a)	3	2	1	(b)	1	2	3
(c)	2	3	1	(d)	None of these		

41 Match the following

	List I (Books)		List II (Author)
A.	Curriculum Implementation	1.	Ralph Tyler
B.	Basic Principles of Curriculum	2.	Tanner & Tanner
C.	The Curriculum	3.	Bobbit

Codes

	A	B	C		A	B	C
(a)	1	2	3	(b)	2	1	3
(c)	3	2	1	(d)	None of these		

42 Match the following

	List I (Models)		List II (Features)
A.	Problem-Solving Model	1.	Determines the problem
B.	Research and Development Model	2.	Discovers and produces
C.	Social Interaction Model	3.	Awareness of innovation

Codes

	A	B	C		A	B	C
(a)	2	1	3	(b)	1	2	3
(c)	3	1	2	(d)	Data inadequat		

Directions (Q.Nos. 43 to 46) *Below there are two statements. One labelled as Reason (R) and other as Assertion (A). Based on the following options choose the correct answer.*

Codes
(a) Both A and R are true
(b) Both A and R are false
(c) A is true, but R is false
(d) A is false, but R is true

43 **Assertion** (A) The role of teacher in the process of curriculum change is of an expert from the discipline.
Reason (R) Experienced teachers do not tend to change their current practice easily.

44 Assertion (A) Panic Approach is reactive rather than proactive.
Reason (R) It minimises that tasks of wide consultation.

45 Assertion (A) Students are the important source of curriculum development process.
Reason (R) Students have gained knowledge through their learning experiences.

46 Assertions (A) Change in curriculum, equips the students to challenge the world.
Reason (R) Students are supposed to take increasing responsibility of their own learning.

47 Curriculum research requires a lot of expertise with respect to

1. planning
2. designing
3. implementing
4. processing
5. evaluating

Codes
(a) 1, 2, 3, 5 (b) 2, 3, 4, 5
(c) 1, 2, 3, 4 (d) All of these

48 Principles of successful curriculum is composed of

1. capacity building
2. developing cultures of learning
3. understanding change process
4. discussing in the classroom

Codes
(a) 1, 2 and 3 (b) 1 and 3
(c) Only 4 (d) Only 3

Directions (Q. Nos. 49 to 53) *Read the passage given below and answer the following questions.*

Change is learning.Undermining this characteristic of change or learning has led many education developers in general and curriculum reformers to adopt over simplistic approaches in trying to change the existing practices and modes of thinking in schools. Curriculum change efforts are typically labelled as implementation or transmission of intended curriculum into classroom's practice in schools. A common means of this transmission is the diffusion of information to raise the awareness of reform, in-service training of teachers, to improve their knowledge and relevant skills and dissemination of support materials, such as teacher's guides and educational pamphlets to parents, to backup the intended change.

49 Change is needed because
(a) to improvise learning and teaching
(b) to stabilise learning
(c) to label learning and teaching
(d) None of the above

50 Curriculum developers use approaches to
(a) change the existing practices
(b) modes of curriculum
(c) change the pattern of curriculum
(d) None of the above

51 The most important part of curriculum change is
(a) designing (b) processing
(c) implementing (d) evaluating

52 In-service training of teachers helps in
(a) improving knowledge and relevant skills
(b) designing of teaching methodology
(c) helps in building teaching aids
(d) None of the above

53 Educational pamphlets are useful for
(a) parents (b) teachers
(c) students (d) None of these

Directions (Q.Nos. 54 to 56) *Read the passage given below and answer the following questions.*

The curriculum's principles are expected to be the foundation of curriculum's decision-making at each school. When they are used well the principles put students at the centre of teaching and learning by fostering the design of a curriculum that includes, engages, and challenges them.

When the principles are not fully enacted, students do not have opportunities to experience a broad and deep curriculum that caters for their interests, strengths and learning needs, and promotes their independence, self-responsibility and engagement. It is unlikely that learners from diverse cultures or those that needs additional support will accelerate their progress in schools that are focused on the principles of curriculum development. The curriculum supports and empowers all students to learn and achieve personal excellence, regardless of their circumstances.

54 Which is not a part of curriculum's decision-making?
(a) Principles of curriculum
(b) Foundation of curriculum
(c) Challenges of curriculum
(d) None of the above

55 When the principles of curriculum are not properly enacted, it will lead to
(a) strengthen the learning needs
(b) will not affect the teaching-learning process
(c) students will lack opportunities
(d) None of the above

56 Curriculum supports and empowers students
(a) to learn and achieve personal excellence
(b) to be outdated
(c) to lack opportunities
(d) All of the above

57 **Factors responsible for curriculum change are**
1. societal factors
2. economical Factors
3. political factors
4. technological factors

Codes
(a) 2, 3, 1, 4
(b) 1, 4, 2, 3
(c) 2, 1, 3, 4
(d) 1, 2, 3, 4

58 **Match the following**

List I	List II
A. Based on survey	1. Action research
B. Pure research	2. Questionnaire
C. Creates artificial conditions	3. Fundamental research

Codes

	A	B	C
(a)	3	1	2
(b)	2	3	1
(c)	1	2	3

(d) Data inadequate

59 **Which of the following statement(s) is/are incorrect in context of curriculum change?**
1. Curriculum should be capable of developing high order thinking skills.
2. Curriculum should be developed with a process approach.
3. Curriculum must be teacher-oriented.
4. Workshop programs should be introduced.

Codes
(a) Only 1 is incorrect
(b) Only 2 is incorrect
(c) Only 3 is incorrect
(d) None of the above

60 **Which statement is correct about curriculum research?**
1. Curriculum research doesn't understands the current state of curricular thinking in schools and universities.
2. Curriculum research helps in designing a qualitative curriculum.
3. Educators must review the curriculum on timely basis with the help of research.
4. Research in curriculum is not mandatory.

Codes
(a) Only 1 is correct
(b) Only 2 is correct
(c) Both 2 and 3 are correct
(d) Only 4 is correct

ANSWERS

1 (a)	2 (d)	3 (b)	4 (a)	5 (b)	6 (c)	7 (d)	8 (a)	9 (a)	10 (d)
11 (b)	12 (a)	13 (a)	14 (b)	15 (b)	16 (b)	17 (d)	18 (a)	19 (b)	20 (c)
21 (a)	22 (c)	23 (a)	24 (b)	25 (c)	26 (a)	27 (d)	28 (d)	29 (c)	30 (a)
31 (d)	32 (d)	33 (d)	34 (a)	35 (b)	36 (a)	37 (a)	38 (c)	39 (b)	40 (a)
41 (b)	42 (b)	43 (a)	44 (a)	45 (a)	46 (d)	47 (c)	48 (a)	49 (a)	50 (a)
51 (c)	52 (a)	53 (a)	54 (c)	55 (c)	56 (a)	57 (c)	58 (b)	59 (c)	60 (c)

CHAPTER 21

Educational Research

Research is an art of scientific investigation. It is regarded as a systematic effort to gain new knowledge, so the educational research is the way in which one acquires dependable and useful information about the educational process. Educational research is an application of Scientific method to the study of educational problems.

Research

Research is the voyage of discovery. It is the quest for answers to unsolved problems. Research may be defined as the application of the scientific method in the study of problems. The terms 'Research' and 'Scientific Method' are sometime used interchangeably. Research is considered to be more structured and systematic process of carrying on a Scientific Method of Analysis that is directed towards discovery and development of an organised body of knowledge. The only difference which lies between research and Scientific Method is that it is possible to employ Scientific method without research, but it is not possible to conduct any research without employing Scientific method.

Concept and Definitions of Research

The term 'research' is a combination of two words 're' and 'search'. 'Re means again and again' and 'search' refers 'to explore something new'. Research is a process of observing the phenomenon (*i.e.* event, anything and process, etc) again and again. Collecting the data and drawing scientific conclusion on the basis of those data. Research is a search for knowledge. It is a systematic effort to gain new knowledge in any kind of discipline.

According to **Advanced Learner's Dictionary of Current English** (1952), "Research is a careful investigation or inquiry specially through search for new facts in any branch of knowledge".

According to **Redman and Morey**, "Research is a systematised effort to gain knowledge".

Research is an objective, impartial, empirical, logical analysis and recording of controlled observations that may lead to the development of generalisations, principles or theories, resulting to some extent in prediction and control of events that may be consequences or causes of specific phenomena.

Research is required in any field to come up with new theories or modify, accept or nullify the existing theory, but when it seeks a solution of any educational problems it leads to educational research.

In this Chapter

Educational Research

Educational research refers to a systematic attempt to gain a better understanding of the educational process, generally with a view in improving its efficiency. It is an application of Scientific Method to the study of educational problems. The main concerns of educational research are to understand, explain, predict and control human behaviour in individual and social situations, so that events or situations can be improved further.

Educational research primarily aims at conceptualisation and theorisation of the processes and practices so as to understand the educational events and phenomena. In education, growth in knowledge by experience is very slow and accidental. We need solutions based on research, so that the coming generation is not left with ignorance and prejudice.

"Educational research represents an activity directed towards the development of an organised body of scientific knowledge about the events with which the educators are concerned of central importance are the behaviour patterns of pupils and particularly those to be learned through educational process. A scientific body of knowledge about education should enable the educators to determine just what teaching and other learning conditions provide in order to produce desired aspects of learned behaviour among young people who attend school (Travers, 1985)".

Definitions of Educational Research

According to **Mouly**, "Educational research is the systematic application of Scientific Method for solving educational problems".

According to **Whitney**, "Educational research aims at finding out solution of educational problems by using Scientific Philosophical Method".

Monroe states that "The final purpose of educational research is to ascertain principles and develops procedure in the field of education".

Since, education is a behavioural science, the main aim of educational research is to solve educational problems in systematic and scientific manner, to understand, explain, predict and control human behaviour in educational settings. It is a process of development of organised and useful body of scientific knowledge with which the academicians are concerned with. It tries to gather facts about child's personality, learning process, emotional development, social adjustment and skills. It also tries to study child's stage of growth and development and the factors influencing these with the aim of improving teaching-learning process in the classroom.

Characteristics of Educational Research

- It is highly purposeful.
- It attempts to solve educational problem.
- It is based upon observable experience or empirical evidence.
- It involves gathering new data from primary to first hand source or using existing data for new purposes.
- It attempts to organise data quantitatively and qualitatively to arrive at statistical inferences.
- It deals with educational problems regarding students and teachers as well.
- It emphasis the development of generalisation, principles or theories which will help in understanding, prediction and control.
- It demands subjective interpretation and deductive reasoning in some cases.
- It generally employs carefully designed procedures and rigorous analysis.
- It discovers new facts in new perspective i.e. it generates new knowledge.

Need and Importance of Educational Research

The importance and need for research in education was acknowledged for the first time in the **Government Resolution of the Indian Educational Policy** in **1913**, but it was only after independence in 1947 that a planned and systematic effort was made to promote educational and/or classroom research by establishing national and state organisations for the development of elementary and secondary education, research in the development of curriculum and textbooks and evaluation procedures.

Research in education is essential for providing useful and dependable knowledge through which the process of education can be made more effective.

Education is considered as much a science as an art. As a science, it has a corpus of knowledge which concerns the nature of human mind, its growth and development, theories of administration and supervision, educational programmes, curricula and practices. Since education depends on a corpus of knowledge, there is need to add new knowledge which has to be scientific, to enrich and improve education with different dimensions.

Research helps in clarification and re-interpretation of existing knowledge which is also necessary in education. Education has strong roots in the field like philosophy, history, economics, psychology and sociology. It is through an intensive process of scientific inquiry about the philosophical, historical, economical, psychological and sociological impact on various aspects of education that sound educational theories can be established. There is need for educational research because of the changing conception of education.

The International Commission on the Development of Education in its report 'Learning Be'.

UNESCO (1972) emphasises education from now can no longer be defined in related to a fixed content, which has to be assimilated but must be conceived of as a process in the human being. They can learn to express themselves to communicate and to question the world, through his/her various experiences and increasingly all the time try to fulfil himself through constant learning. So, the limits of educational research have to be extended from the formal and conventional modes of education to the non-formal and innovative systems based on ecological and cybernetics models.

Purpose of Educational Research

The purpose of educational research is to develop new knowledge about the teaching-learning situation, to imporve the educational practice.

Research in education are conducted for fulfiling different purposes, which are

- To solve the immediate local problems in education.
- To asertain principles and develop procedures for use in the field of education, to determine to what extent we should go in educating children and adults.
- To answer the questions related to education through reflective thinking.
- To discover new application of principles and laws in the field of education.

***Creswell** (2002) stated the following reasons, describing the various purposes of educational research*

Improve Practice Research can suggest ways of improving practice that have been verified with many applications and by many different types of people which is difficult for practitioners

Expand Knowledge Research can allow us to extend what we know in ways we never convinced.

Address Gaps in Knowledge Research can address areas in which we know little, such as the effect of online versus traditional classroom teaching.

Replicate Knowledge Research can act as a test to verify previous findings.

Add Voices of Individuals to Knowledge Research can add important perspectives for different learning types. Much of educational research prior to 80s was based on middle to upper class males. This is certainly not reflective of our increasingly heterogeneous students and research helps revise theory and practice to reflect different student's needs.

Scope of Educational Research

The field of educational research can be classified into the following categories

Educational Psychology

Research in this field, help the teacher to understand the child in the classroom in order to improve teaching-learning process.

This research provides the following information

- Relative effectiveness of socio-cultural forces on the development of children.
- Usefulness of learning theories in various educational settings.
- Identification of factors conclusive to learning.
- Role of physical/intellectual efficiencies and defects in learning.
- Role of teachers and textbooks in removing delinquency in adults and so on.
- Conditions conducive to effective learning, factors helpful in promoting memory and concept formation.
- Cognitive and non-cognitive factors, like intelligence, aptitudes, attitudes, creativity, interest, motivation, personality traits, needs and adjustment of pupils provide a promising field of research in educational psychology.

Philosophy of Education

- Role of logic in various areas of education from concept formation to theory development.
- Role of knowledge, beliefs and values in developing educational theories.
- Role of ideologies and religion for improving educational practices.
- Development of a practical philosophy in Indian context.
- Finding new implications of ancient Indian philosophies in the present scenario.
- Re-organisation of social structure and educational system in India.
- Determining the contribution of different philosophers and their implications.

Sociology of Education

- Effects of changes in the demographic structure on education.
- Effects of New Education Policy (1986), on expansion of education and employment.
- Role of educational institutions in bringing about social change and vice-versa.
- Role of social and cultural factors in bringing about social change and vice-versa.
- Role of teachers as agents of social change, modernisation and social equity.
- Minorities and their problems.
- Reservation policy.

Comparative Education

- Administrative and educational policies of different countries and their impact on the society as a whole.
- Impact of various systems of education in the world on one another.
- Comparison of educational progress in various countries of the world.
- Impact of economic progress on education.
- Allocation of budget on education in different countries and its impact on educational progress and so on.

Guidance and Counselling

- Role of family and neighbourhood in making the children adjusted in the society.
- Construction of tools for diagnosing adjustment problems of students.
- Methodology of vocational guidance for children belonging to different strata of society.
- Adaptation of foreign tests and inventories to Indian situations.

Educational Technology

- Development of new teaching strategies by action researches.
- Role of technology in teaching-learning process.
- Application of psychology to solve teaching problems.
- Development of new audio-visual aids and so on.
- Applications of technological equipments and laws in education.

Educational Management and Administration

- Problems of educational administration in India and its impact on performance.
- Impact of educational planning and legislation on performance.
- Techniques to improve the efficiency of school organisation and inspection system.
- Role of teachers and principals in enhancing performance of students.
- Supervision and performance.
- Contribution of NGOs to education.

Inclusive Education

The inclusive classroom relies on the simultaneous use of differentiated instruction and assessment techniques for maximizing a student's learning potential by tailoring and teaching to every student. Although many educational innovations take shape and undergo testing in the classroom, research is necessary to substantiate these new techniques beyond anecdotal evidence. This helps broaden their exposure, boost their inclusion in professional development programmes for teachers and encourages widespread implementation.

Curriculum Development

- Structure of the curriculum in India from the primary to higher level.
- Analysis and organisation of curriculum in various subjects.
- Analysis of textbooks at different stages of learning.
- Modernisation of curriculum in relation to changing needs.
- Inculcation of national values through curriculum development.

Scientific Methods

Karl Pearson held that "The Scientific method is one and same in the branches (of science) and that method is the method of all logically trained minds ..... the unity of all sciences consists alone in its methods, not its material the man who classifies facts of any kind, who sees their mutual relation and describes their sequences, is applying the scientific method and is a man of science." This method is the pursuit of truth as determined by logical considerations.

The ideal of science is to achieve a systematic interrelation of facts. Scientific method attempts to achieve the ideal by experimentation, observation, logical arguments from accepted postulates and combination of these three in varying proportions. This method encourages a rigorous, method wherein the researcher is guided by the rules of logical reasoning, a method wherein a investigation proceeds in an orderly manner and a method that implies internal consistency.

Educational research is the application of Scientific method to the study of educational problems. The Scientific method has acquired highly specific meaning in modern science.

Scientific method stands for systematic and acceptable set of procedures, used for generating new knowledge, the validity of which is self-evident because of the logical constructs implied in their ordering. To be termed scientific, a method of inquiry is commonly based on empirical or accessible evidence subject to specific principles of reasoning.

Scientific methods operate primarily at the empirical level of research *i.e.* how to make observations, analyse and interpret observations. Very little of this method is directly pertinent to the theoretical level, which is really the more challenging part of scientific research.

According to **GA Lundburg**, "Scientific method consists of systematic observation, classification and interpretation of data".

According to **Barry F Anderson**, "Scientific method is a set of rules, comprising operational definition generally controlled observation, repeated observation, confirmation and consistency".

Characteristics of Scientific Method

Replicability It means research must be replicable or repeated. The research is replicable when an independent group of researcher can copy the same process and arrive at the same results as the original study. When a study cannot be replicated it suggests that our current understanding of the study or our methods of testing are insufficient.

Precision It refers to theoretical concepts, which are often hard to measure, these must be defined with such precision that others can use those definitions to measure those concepts and test that theory.

Falsifiability It means a theory must be stated in a way that it can be disproven. Theories that cannot be tested or falsified are not scientific theories, any such knowledge is not scientific knowledge. A theory that is specified in imprecise terms or whose concepts are not accurately measurable cannot be tested and is therefore not scientific.

Parsimony When there are numerous explanations of a phenomena, scientist must always accept the simplest or logically most economic explanation. This concept is called parsimony Parsimony prevents from pursuing overly complex theories with endless number of concepts and relationship that may explain a little bit of everything but nothing in particular.

Steps of Scientific Method

Identification and Definition of the Problem A scientific inquirer starts with the identification of a problem that is in need of solution. The problem identified must be defined in such a manner that observation or experimentation in the natural world can provide a solution.

Formulation of a Hypothesis Once the problem is defined, the next step is to formulate the hypothesis, which provides an intelligent guess for the solution of the problem. It requires a critical review of the knowledge or information related to the problem.

Implication of Hypothesis through Deductive Reasoning The next step after the formulation of a hypothesis is to deduce the implications of the suggested hypothesis *i.e.* what would be observed if the hypothesis is true.

Collection and Analysis of Evidence The deduced implications of the hypothesis are tested by collecting relevant evidence related to them through observation, testing and experimentation.

Verification, Rejection or Modification of Hypothesis Once the evidence has been collected and analysed, the results are analysed in order to verify whether the evidence supports the hypothesis. It may be noted that the characteristic of Scientific method is not to prove the hypothesis in terms of absolute truth but to conclude that the evidence does or does not support the hypothesis.

Types of Scientific Method

Exploratory

Exploratory research method is defined as a research, used to investigate a problem which is not clearly defined. It is conducted to have a better understanding of the existing problem, but will not provide conclusive results. In this, a researcher starts with a general idea and uses this research as a medium to identify issues that can be the focus for future research. Such a research is usually carried out when the problem is at preliminary stage. It is often referred to as Grounded Theory Approach or interpretive research, as it used to answer questions what, why and how. The exploratory studies are also conducted to develop, refine and/or test measurement tools and procedures.

This type of research is applied when there are number of factors studied within time constraints and it is possible to define each problem, then this type of research is required. In 1994, exploratory research means "to get a clear knowledge of seeking new approaches, new ideas and assess in innovative manner".

The objective of the exploratory research is to define the problems accurately, clarify concepts, collect details and discarded informal and unnecessary ideas after the framing of the hypothesis of the study. Literature, survey, focus group and case studies are usually used to carry out exploratory research. An exploratory research may develop hypothesis, but it does not seeks to test them (Darabi, 2007).

Explanatory

This research method has been used by many researchers in explaining the theoretical explanations. The researcher is interested in this approach in giving real explanations, predicting the results, controlling the phenomena and searching the causes for the happenings. This approach depicts the relationship between cause and effect variables. This approach focuses on the changes in one variable affects the change in other variable.

This research is conducted in order to help us find the problem that was not studied before in depth. It is actually a type of research design which focuses on explaining the aspect of your study in detailed manner. Explanatory research is conducted in order to help us find the problem that was not studied before in depth. The explanatory research is not used to give us some conclusive evidence but helps us in understanding the problem more efficiently. Research allows the researcher to tackle such problems where no or less research has been done.

The purpose of the explanatory research method is to increase the understanding of a researcher on certain subject. It gives flexibility of sources, means published literature or data are commonly used in explanatory type of research. The explanatory research design includes popular methods, such as literature searches, indepth survey of every single problem, focus group research and case analysis research.

Explanatory research is such type of research which is pillar of the other type of researches.

Descriptive

Descriptive research method is a research used to describe a situation subject, behaviour or phenomena. This research is used extensively in social science, psychology and educational research. It is used to answer questions of who, what, when, where and how associated with a particular research question or problem. Descriptive studies are often described as studies that our concerned with finding out 'what is'. This research is sometimes referred to as non-experimental or correlational research. It studies the relationship among non-manipulated variables only.

In descriptive research, the investigator selects the relevant variables from the events/conditions that have already occured or exist at present and analysis their relationship without introducing any manipulation to the variables.

It's purpose in education is to study the present problem of the students, teachers, administration, curriculum, teaching, learning process and the like and to suggest some solutions to the problems. For example, **Frederic Jones** (1979) conducted a descriptive research on classroom discipline and used the collected information to formulate a system of discipline which now has been used by many teachers in their classroom to maintain discipline among students.

Descriptive research is important as the research studies describe the current and present educational phenomena, problems and/or opinions possessed by the teachers, students, etc, about their educational environment/scenario. This method of research is easy and direct, so it is very popular and widely used. Descriptive research not only describes the current problems but also many times suggests valuable solutions to the educational problems. This type of research is also very useful and helpful in developing the data collection tools, such as questionnaires, schedules, checklist, etc.

Aims of Research as a Scientific Activity

Research is often described as a problem-solving activity and as a result, descriptions of problems and solutions are an essential part of the scientific discourse, used to describe research activity. The problem solving activity helps a learner in constructing new scientific knowledge. The problem-solving activity helps students in developing decision-making skills, critical thinking, autonomy communication, negotiations, team building and personal responsibility for learning.

Problem-solving can be used for improving research skills, increasing the knowledge base, developing divergent, creative, inventive thinking, developing convergent critical thinking, fostering innovative solutions and presentation skills. The theory building as a discipline can be considered rich on the basis of scientific theories it has.

We must understand that the theories upon which scientific knowledge is based are only explanations of a particular phenomena as suggested by scientist. As such, there may be a good or poor explanations, depending on the extent to which those explanations fit well with reality and consequently, there may be good or poor theories. The progress of science is marked by our progression, over time from poorer theories to better theories through better observations using more accurate instrument and more informed logical reasoning.

We arrive at a scientific laws or theories through a process of logic and evidence. Logic (theory) and evidence (observations) are the two and only two pillars upon which scientific knowledge is based. Theories provide meaning and significance to what we observe and observations help to validate or refine existing theory or construct a new theory. A theory describes the relationship among key variables for purposes of explaining a current state or predicting future occurrences.

The researchers make predictions about various phenomena. In developing descriptions, researchers make predictions. Predictions are sometimes made in the form of hypothesis, which are tentative, testable predictions concerning the relationship between or among variables. Hypothesis are frequently derived from theories or interrelated sets of concepts that explain a body of data and make predictions.

Types of Research

Research are classified into three types on the basis of objectives or purposes, the researchers intend to accomplish. *These are:*

Basic or Fundamental Research

Basic research is primarily concerned with the formulation of a theory or contribution to the existing body of knowledge. The major aim is to obtain and use the empirical data and evidence to formulate, expand or evaluate theory.

The purpose of basic research is generation of new knowledge for knowledge's sake.

Some have termed this research **pure** or **fundamental**, are often used synonymously. Basic research draws its pattern and spirit from the physical sciences. It represents a rigorous and structured type of analysis. It employs careful sampling procedures, in order to extend the findings beyond the group or situation and thus develops theories by discovering proved generalisations or principles.

It ultimately leads to a clearer and sharper definitions of laws, which govern the nature and also the understanding of natural phenomena. Basic research is not directed towards the solution of immediate practical problems.

According to **Menon** (1982), Basic research by definition is at the frontier of our knowledge and the quality of work and achievements have to be judged by the entire international scientific community. It is characterised by high quality research designs and sophisticated techniques, involving originality, imagination and inventiveness.

Basic research or pure research does not usually generate findings that have immediate applications in practical level. Fundamental research is driven by curiosity and the desire to expand knowledge in specific research area. This type of research makes a specific contribution to the academic body of knowledge in the research area. Basic or fundamental research draws its pattern and spirit from the physical sciences.

It represents a rigorous and structured type of analysis. It employs careful sampling procedures, in order to extend findings beyond the group or situation and thus develops theories by discovering proved generalisations or principles. It ultimately leads to a clearer and sharper definition of laws, which govern the nature and also the understanding of natural phenomena.

Fundamental research tends to contribute the pool of fundamental knowledge in the research area. Basic research rarely helps the practitioners, directly with their everyday concerns, nevertheless it stimulates new ways of thinking that have the potential to revolutionise and dramatically improve how practitioners deal with a problem in the future.

Basic research is essentially positive. It explains the phenomena as they are and as not they should be. It may verify or establish new one. Its aim is to obtain empirical data and evidence to formulate expand.

In the field of education, it involves concepts, such as motivation, reinforcement formation in learning and results into fundamental type of research. The best example in pure or basic research is in psychology, sociology and philosophy.

Thus, the fundamental research focuses on one discipline. It involves a descriptive study of the research problem. In this type of research, reporting is done in technical language. It is concerned with generalisations and formulating theories. It aims to solve general problems.

Applied Research

It is directed towards the solution of immediate, specific and practical problems. It is performed in relation to actual problems and under the conditions in which they are found in practice. The goal of applied research in terms of adding scientific knowledge, acquires only secondary position.

The applied research also uses the Scientific Method of Inquiry. It has most of the characteristics of basic research. Its methodology, however is not as rigorous as the basic research. Moreover, its findings are to be evaluated in terms of local applicability and not in terms of universal validity. It has very definite practical objectives.

It is not the degree of creative process, involving originality, imagination and inventiveness that distinguishes basic from applied research, but at the clear practical direction of applied research. Most educational research is applied research, to develop generalisations about teaching-learning processes, instructional materials, the behaviour of children and way to modify it and so on.

Steps in Applied Research

- A growing concern is studied and points of weaknesses in the system are isolated.
- Some of these weaknesses are selected for investigation.
- Investigation is followed by solution, either in the laboratory or in the field.
- Solution is modified and installed, so that it may work in practice.
- Solution must be maintained by planning it in the organisation, so that it may become a permanent part of the system.

Action Research

The field of education has shown great interest in action research since 1930s. In **1926**, **Buckingham** used the concept of action research in education for the first time in his book **Research for Teachers**, but the credit goes to **Stephen M. Corey** for using the concept (action research) for the first time in the field of studying and solving educational problems.

Action Research is a method of systematic enquiry that teachers undertake as researchers of their own practice.

In the field of educational research, it is an applied research that the teachers, instructors and school administrators conduct to tackle and deal with classroom problems and improving their classroom practices.

According to **Corey**, "Action research is the process by which practitioners attempt to study their problems, scientifically in order to guide, correct and evaluate their decision and action. He further states that "action research is a process for studying problems by practitioners, scientifically to take decisions for improving their current practices".

According to **Wallace**, "action research is done by systematically collecting data on your everyday practice and analysing it in order to come to some decisions about what your future practice should be".

Best and Kahn write the purpose of action research, is to improve school practices and at the same time to improve those who try to improve the practices to combine the research process, habits of thinking, ability to work harmoniously with others and professional spirit.

In India, the action research was palpable in 60s and 70s. However, the boost to research action came up with the establishment of **District Institute** of **Education** and **Training** (DIET). It is worth noting that action research is a research conducted through direct action and is primarily focused on immediate application, not on the development of broad theories or generalisations or on general applications. It studies the problems from the point of view of here and now in one's local setting and its findings are evaluated in terms of local applicability, not in terms of universal applicability and validity.

Characteristics of Action Research

- In action research, teachers and the classroom practitioners feel and solve the problem. A practitioner undertakes both the function of diagnosis and therapeutic treatment.
- It is a scientific process for studying and solving the current practical problems of education.
- It tries to heighten self-awareness, self-criticality and analytical abilities of teachers and teacher educators.
- It tries to inject innovative approaches to teaching.
- It focuses on immediate application, not on the development of theory or on general application. Its findings are to be evaluated in terms of local applicability and not universal validity.
- It focuses on improving and modifying current practices.
- It is small scale and narrowly focused research, undertaken by teachers in given context.
- It has also been referred to as "Research into practice by practitioners, for practitioners".

Objectives of Action Research

- To identify problem areas and improve the working conditions of a school.
- To develop scientific attitude among teachers, students, principals and administrators, for studying, understanding and solving their current academic problems.
- To bring potential of excellence in school functionaries.
- To raise the performance and aspiration level of the students, by generating a healthy environment for learning.

Areas of Action Research

The areas of action research can fall under the following categories

Related to Learner It can be on motivation, learning style, attention plan, concentration, etc.

Related to Teacher It can be on level of competencies, commitment, teaching style, attitude towards weak students, attitude towards notoriously inquisitive students, motivation, etc.

Related to Methodology It can be on activity based teaching, child-centered learning, play way approach, project approach, mediated learning, etc.

Related to Evaluation It can be on criterion reference testing, diagnostic testing, formative testing, achievement testing, objective type testing, etc.

Related to Curriculum It can be on mechanism of curriculum design, mechanism of curriculum construction, teacher's role in curriculum design and development, intended, transacted and hidden curriculum.

Steps in Action Research

Action research applies scientific thinking and methods to solve real life problems of immediate concern using following systematic steps

Identification of a Problem For action research, problem emerges out of perceived dissatisfaction with the existing situation and also with the need for bringing out improvement in the situation.

Defining, Analysing and Explaining the Problem Once the problem is identified, it needs to be defined, analysed and explained in operational terms. It requires the understanding of various issues that surround the perceived problem.

Listing and Stating the Probable Causes This step involves the identification and stating of probable causes in unambiguous terms. Here, the practitioner also needs to spell out the possible strategies with which the problems can be solved in a best possible manner.

Development of Propositions/Formulation of Hypothesis After stating the probable causes, it is necessary to develop a conceptual and functional relationship which tentatively aims to explain a given situation in the form of hypothesis. This facilitates the process of conducting action research.

Planning, Development, Implementation and Evaluation of Action Research Plan This step involves planning and development of a suitable intervention programme, its implementation and examining its effectiveness. The duration of the intervention and modality of its implementation with respect to remediation measures, etc, need to be carefully planned.

Drawing Conclusions and Taking Decisions The impact of intervention programme is judged on the basis of the conclusions, which are helpful in taking decisions.

Sharing of Results After the completion of the study, it is beneficial to share the results and findings with the colleagues, administrators and other functionaries. The sharing can be done through presentation in seminars, conferences and also publication in journals, newspapers etc.

Approaches to Educational Research

Educational research can take a wide variety of forms and serve many different purposes. Sometimes, it is located within social science disciplines, especially psychology and sociology and sometimes quite closely linked to educational practice, these include laboratory and classroom experiments, large scale surveys of the behaviour, attitudes, aptitudes, etc. of teachers, children's heads and others. Analysis of published and unpublished texts, both qualitative and quantitative and small scale investigations of particular institutions.

The quantitative and qualitative research approaches in education have arisen from different research needs. The **quantitative research approach** endlessly pursues facts, whereas the **qualitative research approach** recognises that the researcher's viewpoint is central. The quantitative research approach is used when the researcher desires to obtain entire trends or statistical truth in the research, while the qualitative research approach is used if the researcher wants to observe in detail by his/her own research view point.

Qualitative Research Approaches

The **qualitative paradigm** of research is based on the methods and techniques, developed in the humanities and social sciences, whereas the **quantitative paradigm** is developed on the methods used in the natural sciences. Qualitative approaches seek to obtain qualitative information and thick descriptions of complex and dynamic processes, using holistic, naturalistic and non-manipulative methods.

The term 'qualitative approach' covers a variety of research methods, which have some common characteristics.

The four features of qualitative research identified by ***Bogdam and Biklen*** *(1982) are*

(i) "Qualitative research has the natural setting as the direct source of data and the researcher is the key instrument". As the setting influences human behaviour in which it occurs, researchers spend considerable time in the setting and study it in its entirety.

(ii) "Qualitative research is descriptive". It collects soft data consisting of rich descriptions, which cannot always be reduced to numbers and analysed statistically.

(iii) "Qualitative researchers are concerned with process, rather than simply with outcomes or products".

(iv) "Qualitative researchers tend to analyse their data inductively". They do not begin with specific questions to answer or hypothesis to test and then collect data, rather on the basis of the data collected and analysed, explanatory concepts or abstractions are built.

Quantitative Research Approaches

Quantitative research consists of those studies in which the data concerned can be analysed in terms of numbers. An example of quantitative research might be a study comparing two methods of teaching-reading to first-grade children, because the data used to determine which method is more successful and will be a test score. The average score of the children receiving one method will be compared to the average score of children receiving the other method.

Research can also be qualitative *i.e.* it can describe events, persons and so forth scientifically, without the use of numerical data. A study consisting of interviews of mothers of handicapped infants, to determine how child is an example of qualitative research. Such a study, would carefully and logically analyse the responses of the mothers and report those responses that are consistent as well as areas of disagreement.

The quantitative research is based on logical positive paradigm which utilises experimental method and quantitative measures to test specific hypothetical generalisations with narrow angle lens. The quantitative research uses scientific method with 'hard science trappings'. In this the researcher treats their subject of study as having an existence independent of themselves and without any intrinsic meaning.

Quantitative research is deductive in that it test theories which have already been proposed. It aims at analysing of representative and validated quantitative data, through the use of sophisticated statistical methods and software packages. In quantitative research the findings are based on identified statistical relationships and generalisable fundings. Using the principles of probability, quantitative research makes predictions representative of a large population.

Quantitative research uses deductive approach. Here, the researcher formulates and uses hypothesis and theory with data. Thus, the quantitative research involves sucessive phases of hypothesis formulation, data collection, analysis and interpretation. Using deductive approach, it seeks to establish facts, make predictions and test hypothesis that have already been stated.

In quantitative research, the experimenter has carefully planned the study including the tests or other data collection instruments, to be used. Each subject is studied in an identical manner and there is little room for human bias to create problems with the data.

Quantitative research is based more directly on its original plans and its results are more readily analysed and interpreted.

Designs in Educational Research

Research design is needed because it facilitates the smooth sailing of various research operations, thereby making research as efficient as possible, yielding maximal information with minimal expenditure of effort, time and money.

Research design is the arrangement of conditions for collection and analysis of data in a manner that aims to combine relevance to the research purpose with economy in procedure. Research design is the conceptual structure, within which research is conducted, it constituents the blueprint for the collection, measurement and analysis of data. As such, the design includes an outline of what the researcher will do from writing the hypothesis and its operational implications to the final analysis of data.

Research design, infact has a great bearing on the reliability of the results, arrived at and as such constitutes the firm foundation of the edifice of the research work.

Here, a research design related to historical descriptive and experimental are discussed as follows

Historical Research

Historical research design analyse the past events and develops concept and conclusion. It analyses the previous information or events minutely and testing their validity. The purpose of historical research design is to collect, verify and synthesise evidence from the past to establish facts that defends or refute a hypothesis. It describe what occurred in the past. The historical research design depends upon data observed by other rather than investigator.

It uses secondary sources and a variety of primary documentary evidences, such as diaries, official records, archives and non-textual information (maps, pictures, audio and visual recordings). The limitation is that the sources must be both authentic and valid. The historical research design is unobtrusive, the act of research does not affect the results of the study. The historical approach is well suited for trend analysis. Historical records can add important contextual background, required to more fully understand and interpret a research problem. There is often no possibility of researcher-subject interaction that could affect the findings. Historical sources can be used over and over to study different research problems or to replicate a previous study.

It shares a great deal with qualitative research in education even though it may make use of quantitative material like other forms of quantitative research, the concern is with natural behaviour in a real situation and the focus is on interpretation of what it means in the context. Unlike other forms of educational research, the historical research does not creates data. Rather, the historian attempts to discover data that exists already in some form.

Historical research attempts to establish facts, so as to arrive at conclusions concerning past events. This is usually accompanied by an interpretation of these events and of their relevance to present circumstances and what might happen in the future. The main purpose of historical research, therefore is to arrive at an accurate account of the past, so as to gain a clearer perspective of the present. This knowledge enables us atleast partially to predict and control our future existence.

Historical research includes the delimitation of a problem, formulating research questions or tentative generalisations, gathering and analysing data and arriving at conclusions or generalisations based upon deductive-inductive reasoning. However, the historian faces greater difficulty than researchers in any other field. Historical datas are closed class of data, located along a fixed temporal locus and historian has no choice of sampling his data and he is supposed to include every type of data that comes his way. Historical research is not based upon experimentation, but upon reports of observation, which cannot be repeated. The historian handles unique type of data which cannot be repeated. They are mainly traces of past events. The historian must depend upon the reported observations of others, often witnesses of doubtful competence and sometimes of doubtful objectivity.

Types of Historical Research

Various types of historical researchs are

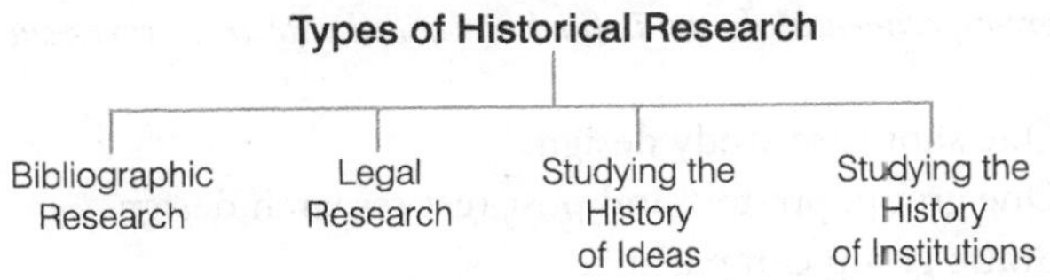

Bibliographic Research It aims at determining and presenting truthfully, the important facts about the life, character and achievement of important educators.

Legal Research It is of immense value and interest to educational administrators. It aims to study the legal basis of educational institutions, run by different religions and castes and relation between central and state governments, with regard to education, legal status of teachers, etc.

Studying the History of Ideas It involves the tracing of major philosophical or scientific thoughts from their origins through their different stages of development. It also aims at tracing of changes in popular thoughts and attitudes over a given period of time.

Studying the History of Institutions Studying the history of some prominent schools, universities and other educational institutions also provide numerous opportunities for significant historical research. When studying such history, the same general method applied as for the study of an educator's life.

Steps of Historical Research

The steps involved in undertaking a historical research are not different from other forms of research, but the nature of the subject matter presents a researcher some peculiar problems and requires him to apply some special standards and techniques.

In general, historical research involves the following steps

Selection of the Problem A researcher may select a problem, pertaining to the history of individuals, institutions, organisations, laws, curriculum, administration, textbooks, teacher education, equipment, important concepts and thoughts that have influenced education during a specific period of time in a given culture or sub-culture, determined by religion, caste, sex, age or work.

Formulation of Hypothesis The hypothesis that the researcher constructs for historical research are useful in explaining events, conditions or phenomenas of the historical period in question. **Best** and **Kahn** have also remarked that, although hypothesis are not always explicitly stated in historical investigations, they are usually implied. The historian gathers evidence and carefully evaluates its trust worthiness. If the evidence is compatible with the consequences of hypothesis, it is confined.

Collection of Data After formulation of hypothesis, the researcher collects the data through primary and secondary sources. It involves comprehensive gathering of data.

Interpretation of Data After the data have been collected and criticised, the researcher turns himself to the task of inerpretation of these data in the light of this problem. As historical data has unique nature, the task of interpretation becomes complicated and acquires special significance. It requires greatest ingenuity and imagination on the part of the researcher.

The researcher in the historical type of investigation must be very cautious while dealing with cause and effect relationship. Here, his position is entirely different from a researcher of physical sciences, who deals with very simple isolated laboratory phenomena. The researcher in the historical types of investigation should not only establish facts, but also determine trends which the data may suggest and to draw inferences from the data. His goal should be one of synthesis and interpretation rather than mere summation.

Value of Historical Research

Knight *(1934),* ***Scates*** *(1941) and* ***Good*** *has given the following analysis of the value of historical research*

- A knowledge of the history of schools and other educational agencies is an important part of the professional training of the teacher or the school administrator.
- Much of the work of the school is traditional. The nature of the work of the teacher and the school administrator is restrictive and tends to foster prejudices in favour of familiar methods. The history of education is the sovereign solvent of educational prejudices.
- The history of education enables the educational worker to detect fads and frills in whatever form, they may appear and it serves as a necessary preliminary to educational reform.
- Only in the light of their origin and growth, can the numerous educational problems of the present be viewed sympathetically and without bias by the teacher, the school administrator or the public.
- The history of education shows how the functions of social institutions shift and support and control of education have changed from very simple and local arrangements to those that are now somewhat centralised and complex.
- It inspires respect for sound scholarship and reverence for great teachers.
- The history of education is an ally in the scientific study of education rather than a competition. It serves to present the educational ideals and standards of other times and it enables social workers to avoid mistakes of the past.

Experimental Research

In descriptive research, a researcher may analyse the data, he has collected and discovers that different variables are related. The relationships between the variables can be interpreted in several ways. Experimental research on the other hand, provides for such control and therefore, establishes a systematic and logical association between manipulated factors and observed effects.

The researcher defines a problem and proposes a tentative answer or hypothesis. He tests the hypothesis and accepts or rejects it.

John Stuart Mill (1846) defined law of the single variable in his work methods of experimental inquiry.

He stated the following five canons or rules of experimental research

- The Method of Agreement
- The Method of Difference
- The Joint Method
- The Method of Residues
- The Method of Concomitant Variations

These rules served as guides in the design of early experiments and are now used chiefly as guides in planning of experiments.

Types of Experimental Research Designs

There are various types of experimental research designs. They vary in complexity and adequacy. The selection of a particular design depends upon such factors, as the nature and purpose of the experiment, the type of the variables to be manipulated, the nature of the data, the facilities or the conditions for carrying out the experiment and the competence of the experimenter. Although, the designs can be combined into various ways.

They are broadly classified as under

- Pre-experimental designs
- True experimental designs
- Quasi experimental designs

These designs resemble one another from the point of view of purposes and their adherence to the principles of experimentation. They differ in the degree of accuracy with which they attack the problem or meet the essential criteria of control, manipulation, observations and replication.

Pre-Experimental Research Design It is the simplest form of experimental research design. In this design, a group or various groups are kept under observation, after factors are considered for cause and effect. It is generally conducted to understand whether further investigation needs to be carried out on the target group(s) due to which it is considered to be cost effective.

The pre-experimental design is further divided into three types such as

- One shot case study design.
- One group, pre-test and post test research design.
- Static group comparison.

True Experimental Research Designs This design is the most accurate form of experimental research design as it relies on statistical analysis to prove or disprove a hypothesis. It is the only type of experimental design that can establish a cause effect relationship, within groups. In a true experiment, there are three factors which needs to be satisfied.

They are

- **Control group** (group of participants for research that are familiar to the experimental group, but experimental rules do not apply to them) and **experiment group** (research participants on whom the experimental research rules do apply).
- **Variables** which can be manipulated by the researcher.
- Random distribution.

These designs are mostly used for experimental research in education because they seek to control the main effects of history, maturation, testing, measuring instruments, statistical regression, differential selection and mortality.

Quasi Experimental Research Design The word 'quasi' indicates 'resemblance'. A quasi experimental research design is similar to experimental research, but is not exactly that. The difference between the two is the assignment of a control group. In quasi experimental research design, an independent variable is manipulated but the participants of a group are not randomly assigned as per conditions. The independent variable is manipulated before calculating the dependent variable and so directionally the problem is eliminated. Quasi research is used in field settings, where random assignment is either irrelevant or not required.

Characteristics of Experimental Research

- The experimental researcher randomly assigns participants to group or other units.
- They provide control over extraneous variables, to isolate the effects of the independent variable on the outcomes.
- They physically manipulate the treatment conditions for one or more groups.
- They then measure the outcomes for the groups to determine if the experimental treatment had a different effect than the non-experimental treatment.
- The researcher design an experiment to reduce the threats to internal and external validity.

Thus, the experimental research designs are concerned with examination of the effect of independent variable on the dependent variable, where the independent variable is manipulated through treatment or intervention(s) and the effect of those interventions is observed on the dependent variable.

Value of Experimental Research

It is used to determine and evaluate the adequacy and effectiveness of the educational and instructional objectives, through the measurement of their outcomes. After evaluating the efficacy of objectives, the suggestions are made for the formulation, execution and modification of educational programmes and classroom practices. The experimental research is not considered a precise method of research in the field of education because of the complex nature of the human beings and problems of controlling the extraneous variables. However, inspite of all such difficulties, experimentation has been put to various uses in solving educational problems.

Descriptive Research Design

Descriptive research studies are those studies, which are concerned with describing the characteristics of a particular individual or of a group and studies concerned with specific prediction, with narration of facts and characteristics concerning individual or group of situations are all examples of descriptive research studies. Most of the social researchs come under this category.

From the point of view of the research design in descriptive studies, the researcher must be able to define clearly, what he wants to measure and must find adequate methods for measuring it along with a clear cut definition of 'population' he wants to study. Since, the aim is to obtain complete and accurate information in the said studies, the procedure to be used must be carefully planned. The research design must make enough provision for protection against bias and maximum reliability, with due concern for the economical completion of the research study. The design in such studies must be rigid and not flexible.

Descriptive research design aims to observe, describe and document aspects of a situation as it naturally occurs without any manipulation or control. Descriptive studies are designed to gain more information about characteristics with a select or a particular field of study. These studies provide a picture of a situation as it occurs in a natural setting.

The descriptive design does not involve manipulation of variables. Variables are studies as they exist in the natural world. Descriptive research designs are used to develop theories, identify problems with current practices, makes judgements and determine alternative solutions for the existing practices.

In case of descriptive studies, bias is prevented through operational definitions of variables, by choosing a large sample size, by using random sampling techniques. By means of using valid and reliable tools of measurement and formal data collection procedures. Thus, through descriptive designs, description of variables leads to an interpretation of the theoretical meaning of the findings and development of hypothesis. The descriptive research design is a Scientific Method, which involves observing and describing the behaviour of a subject without influencing it in any way.

Descriptive research design is a valid method for researching specific subjects and as a pre-cursor to more quantitative studies. It is the most widely used research design. The means of obtaining information, include the use of the questionnaries and personal interviews with the aid of study guide or interview schedule and observation either participatory or not.

Descriptive study determines and reports the way things are. It has no control over what is and it can only measure what already exists.

The descriptive research has undoubtedly been the most popular and widely used research method in education. It helps to explain educational phenomena in terms of the conditions or relationships that exist held by students, teachers, parents and experts processes that are going on effects that are evident or tends that are developing. Because of the apparent ease and directness of this method, a researcher can gather information in terms of individual's opinion about some issue by a simple questionnaire.

Descriptive studies are closely associated with observational studies, but they are not limited with Observation Data Collection Method. Case studies and surveys can also be specified as popular data collection methods, used with descriptive studies. Descriptive researchs are of great importance in solving problems about children, school organisation, supervision and administration, curriculum, teaching methods and evaluation.

Thus, it can be said that the descriptive research design is a Scientific Method which involves observing and describing the behaviour of a subject, without influencing it in any way.

EXAM BASED QUESTIONS

1 A research is

(a) a goal directed activity
(b) a solution to the problem local or universal
(c) an effort to formulate new laws and principles of their applications
(d) All of the above

2 A good piece of research is the product of

(a) collective scholarship
(b) a good research library
(c) penetrating and analytical mind
(d) a touch of genius

3 The quality of research is judged by

(a) relevance of research
(b) methodology followed in conducting the research
(c) depth of the research
(d) experiences of the researcher

4 What is the aim of educational research?

(a) Identifying major problems needed to be solved
(b) Searching for the new facts and principles underlying the process of education
(c) Identifying the aims of education
(d) Identifying the values that needed to be included in the pupils

5 Criteria of good research is written by

(a) James Harold Fox
(b) PV Young
(c) Karl Popper
(d) Delta Kappan

6 Research is an organised and systematic enquiry, is defined by

(a) Kerlinger (b) Marshall
(c) Emroy (d) PV Young

7 Research is not considered ethical if it

(a) is not of a very high standard
(b) tries to prove a particular point
(c) does not investigate the data, scientifically
(d) does not ensure privacy and anonymity of the respondent

8 Which of the following statements regarding the meaning of research are correct?

1. Research refers to a series of systematic activity or activities undertaken to find out the solution of a problem.
2. Process wherein verification of hypothesis, data analysis, interpretation and formation of principles can be done.
3. It is an intellectual enquiry or quest towards truth.
4. It leads to enhancement of knowledge.

Codes

(a) 1, 2 and 3 (b) 2, 3 and 4
(c) 1, 3 and 4 (d) 1, 2, 3 and 4

9 Arrange the following steps of research in correct sequence.

1. Identification of research problem
2. Listing of research objectives
3. Collection of data
4. Methodology
5. Data analysis
6. Results and discussions

Codes

(a) 1, 2, 3, 4, 5 and 6 (b) 1, 2, 4, 3, 5 and 6
(c) 2, 1, 3, 4, 5 and 6 (d) 2, 1, 4, 3, 5 and 6

10 "Research is an honest, exhaustive and intelligent searching for facts and implications with reference to a given problem". Who said this?
(a) JW Best (b) PM Cook
(c) M Fair Child (d) Dewey

11 Which of the following is not the reason, underlying the importance of research in education?
(a) It is tool for verifying, testing and validating knowledge
(b) It is a potent means of creating new knowledge
(c) It has moved to the centre of the behavioural science
(d) It provides answers to many problems, faced by the educators

12 Research means
(a) searching again and again
(b) finding solution to any problem
(c) scientific approach to new truth
(d) conducting experiment

13 Which of the following is not the characteristic of a researcher?
(a) He is specialist, rather than a generalist
(b) He is industrious and persistent on the trial of discovery
(c) He is not an inspirational to his choosen field, but accepts the reality
(d) He is not versatile in his interest and even in his native abilities

14 The main purpose of pilot study in educational research is
(a) to improve the research plan
(b) to try the research tool
(c) to train the research team
(d) to collect preliminary data

15 Research is a 'scientific undertaking' opined by
(a) Young (b) Kothari
(c) Emroy (d) Kerlinger

16 Which of the following is not a criterion for the statement of a good research problem?
(a) Expression of relationship between/among variables
(b) Clarity and unambiguousness
(c) Possibility of empirical testing
(d) Possibility of use of statistical analysis

17 **Statement I** Research should always be focussed on discovering new facts.
Statement II Research should always validate results in a new setting.
Codes
(a) Only statement I is true
(b) Only statement II is true
(c) Both the statements I and II are true
(d) None of the above

18 The main purpose of research in education is to
(a) help in the personal growth of an individual
(b) help the candidate become an eminent educationist
(c) increase job prospects of an individual
(d) increase social status of an individual

19 The essential qualit(y) (ies) of a researcher is/are
(a) spirit of free inquiry
(b) reliance on observation and evidence
(c) systematisation or theorising of knowledge
(d) All of the above

20 Which of the following is not a characteristic feature of a research process?
(a) Empirical approach (b) Systematic endeavour
(c) Uncontrolled condition (d) Critical analysis

21 Who among the following gave the statement "research is an honest effort carried out through ensight"?
(a) Cook (b) Crick
(c) Watson (d) None of these

22 Generally the data of the research is
(a) quantitative only (b) qualitative only
(c) Both a and b (d) None of these

23 Which of the following statement is not true about research?
(a) One research gives birth to another research
(b) Good researcher is a humble person
(c) The researcher is expected to be well-behaved person
(d) All researchs contribute to the existing knowledge

24 Consider the following statement(s) is/are correct with regard to the purpose of educational research.
Statement I It solve the immediate local problems in education.
Statement II It ascertain principles and develop procedure for use in the field of education.
(a) Statement I is correct
(b) Statement II is correct
(c) Both statement are correct
(d) Neither a nor b

25 The scope of educational research can be classified as
(a) educational psychology (b) comparative education
(c) educational technology (d) All of these

26 One of the main aim of scientific method in research is to
(a) confirm triangulation
(b) introduce new variables
(c) improve data interpretation
(d) eliminate spurious relations

27 Which of the following is not the goal of scientific method of acquiring knowledge?
(a) Explanation (b) Fact's finding
(c) Control (d) Prediction

28 An example of scientific knowledge is
(a) social traditions and customs
(b) authority of the prophet and great men
(c) religious scriptures
(d) laboratory and field experiment

29 In scientific research
(a) there are assumptions, which can easily be verified experimentally
(b) there are no assumptions at all
(c) there are assumptions, but experiments cannot verify them
(d) experiments can only refute assumptions

30 What is the basis of Scientific method?
(a) To test hypothesis in condition that are conducive to its success
(b) To formulate a research problem and disprove the hypothesis
(c) To formulate a research problem and test the hypothesis in carefully controlled conditions that challenge the hypothesis
(d) To test hypothesis and if they are disproved, they should be abandoned completely

31 Who said that "Scientific method consists of systematic observation, classification and interpretation of data"?
(a) Barry F Anderson (b) GA Lundberg
(c) Kerlinger (d) Emroy

32 When there are numerous explanations of a phenomena, scientist accepts the simplest or logically most economic explanation it is known as.......
(a) parsimony (b) falsifiability
(c) precision (d) replicability

33 Tge steps of scientific method involves
(a) identification and definition of the problem
(b) formulation of a hypothesis
(c) implication of hypothesis through deductive reasoning
(d) All of the above

34 Who said that "Action research is done by systematically collecting data on your everyday practice and analysing it in order to come to some decisions about what your future practice should be"?
(a) Emroy (b) Kerlinger
(c) Wallace (d) Corey

35 .... refers to theoretical concepts which are often hard to measure.
(a) Replicability (b) Falsifiability
(c) Presision (d) Parsimony

36 What is the purpose of theory building?
(a) Survey research (b) Applied research
(c) Action research (d) Fundamental research

37 Which of the following statement is/are correct with regard to problem-solving activity?
Statement I Problem-solving activity help the learner in constructing new scientific knowledge.
Statement II It can be used for improving research skills, critical thinking autonomy, negotiations team building and personal responsibility for learning.
(a) Only statement I is correct
(b) Only statement II is correct
(c) Both statement are correct
(d) Neither a nor b

38 Which of the following statements about the fundamental research is/are correct?
(a) It does not usually generate findings that have immediate application in practical level
(b) It explains the phenomena as they are and as not they should be
(c) It is concerned with the formulation of a theory or contribution to the existing body of knowledge
(d) All of the above

39 Fundamental research reflects the ability to
(a) expound new principles
(b) synthesise new ideals
(c) evaluate the existing material concerning research
(d) study the existing literature, regarding various topics

40 The principles of fundamental research are used in
(a) action research (b) applied research
(c) historical research (d) philosophical research

41 Match the following

List I (Types of Researhes)	List II (Characteristics)
A. Fundamental research	1. Finding out the extent of preceived impact of an intervention
B. Applied research	2. Developing an effective explanation through theory building
C. Action research	3. Imbronro a
D. Evaluative research	4. Exploring the possibility of a theory for use in various situations

Codes

	A	B	C	D
(a)	1	2	4	3
(b)	2	1	3	4
(c)	4	3	2	1
(d)	1	2	3	4

42 Match the following

List I	List II
A. Researcher by the user for the user	1. Fundamental research
B. Research for applicability	2. Action research
C. Research for general abstract knowledge	3. Applied research

Codes

	A	B	C
(a)	1	2	3
(b)	3	2	1
(c)	2	3	1
(d)	2	1	3

43 Consider the following statements about field study.
1. A field study is conducted in a real life setting.
2. It effectively uses scientific method.

Select the correct answer using the codes given below.
(a) Only 1 (b) Only 2
(c) Both 1 and 2 (d) None of these

44 The development of a solid foundation of reliable knowledge, typically is built from which type of research?
(a) Basic research (b) Action research
(c) Evaluation research (d) Orientational research

45 Which of the following is/are the characteristics of applied research?
(a) It is directed towards the solution of immediate, specific and practical problems
(b) It uses scientific method of inquiry
(c) It draws its pattern and spirit from physical sciences
(d) Both a and b

46 Who said that "Action research is done by systematically collecting data on your everyday practice and analysing it in order to come up to some decisions about what your future practice should be"?
(a) Best and Kaln (b) Wallace
(c) Corey (d) B F Anderson

47 The name of Stephen M Corey is associated with
(a) fundamental research (b) action research
(c) applied research (d) sociometric research

48 Which one of the following purpose demands action research?
(a) Developing theory
(b) Writing a thesis
(c) Solving a classroom problem
(d) Testing a theory

49 In qualitative research paradigm, which of the following feature may be considered critical?
(a) Data collection with standardised research tools
(b) Data collection with bottom-up empirical evidence
(c) Sampling design with probability sample techniques
(d) Data gathering to take up top-down systematic evidence

50 Which of the following is a method of qualitative research?
(a) Experimental research
(b) Normative survey
(c) Ethenomethodology
(d) Ex-post factor research

51 Procedures determining what two issues are rarely used in quantitative research?
(a) Objectivity and subjectivity
(b) Reliability and validity
(c) Accessibility and reliability
(d) Quality and quantity

52 Which of the following is a weakness of quantitative research?
(a) Provides precise and numerical data
(b) The researcher's categories that are used might not reflect local constituencies understanding
(c) Testing hypothesis that are constructed before the data are collected
(d) Can study large number of people

53 Historical research design is
(a) Unobtrusive, the act of research does not affect the results of the study
(b) Well-suited for trend analysis
(c) Uses secondary sources and variety of primary documentary evidences
(d) All of the above

54 Historical research is interpretative.
(a) True
(b) False
(c) Just a statement
(d) None of the above

55 The historical research is different from experimental research in the process of
(a) replication
(b) the formulation of the hypothesis
(c) the hypothesis testing
(d) All of the above

56 The process not needed in experimental research is
(a) controlling
(b) observation
(c) Reference collection
(d) manipulation and replication

57 The process not needed in experimental research is
(a) observation
(b) controlling
(c) manipulation and replication
(d) reference collection

58 What is the key defining characteristic of experimental research?
(a) Extraneous variables are never present
(b) A positive correlation usually exists
(c) A negative correlation usually exists
(d) Manipulation of the independent variables

59 Exploratory research addresses which one of the following type of question?
(a) why (b) how
(c) what (d) All of these

60 Match the following

List I (Researches)	List II (Features)
A. Experimental research	1. Observations
B. Historical research	2. Independent variables
C. Survey research	3. Criticism

Codes

	A	B	C		A	B	C
(a)	1	2	3	(b)	2	3	1
(c)	2	1	3	(d)	3	1	2

61 Which of the following study does not need hypothesis?
(a) Survey study (b) Normative study
(c) Experimental study (d) Historical study

62 The process not needed in experimental research is
(a) observation (b) manipulation
(c) controlling (d) content analysis

63 Which of the following statement is incorrect with respect to "an experimental design is a set of procedures specifying"?
(a) How the extraneous variables are to be controlled?
(b) What dependent variables are to be measured?
(c) How the test units (subjects) are to be divided into homogeneous sub-samples?
(d) What independent variables or treatments are to be measured?

64 Why causal comparative research is not considered a kind of experimental research?
(a) It studies cause effect relationship between the variables.
(b) It is just a correlation type of study
(c) Its method is comparative and analytical
(d) It neither controls extraneous variables nor does it manipulate independent variables

65 A Phd scholar conducted a study with a view to address the language problems of tribal children at the elementary level. This study can be categorised as
(a) action research (b) applied research
(c) basic research (d) None of these

66 Determining the relationship between two or more variables occurs in
(a) correlational research
(b) action research
(c) naturalistic observation
(d) survey research

67 The status quo of a situation in research can be studied through
(a) experimental research
(b) survey research
(c) historical research
(d) phenomenological research

68 The government of India conducts census after every ten years. The method of research used in this is
(a) case study (b) developmental
(c) survey (d) experimental

69 If the purpose of the research is to discover the relative incidence, distribution and inter-relationship of sociological and psychological variables, this should be classified as
(a) experimental research
(b) survey research
(c) ex-post facto research
(d) field experiment

70 To explain, predict and/or control phenomena are the goal of
(a) tradition (b) inductive logic
(c) deductive logic (d) scientific method

71 The step of experimental method is
(a) selection and definition of a problem
(b) survey of the related literature
(c) experimental design
(d) All of the above

72 What does the descriptive research include according to Van Dalen?
(a) Survey studies
(b) Inter-relationship studies
(c) Developmental studies
(d) All of the above

73 What is/are the type(s) of descriptive research?
(a) Survey test (b) Questionnaire survey
(c) Interview survey (d) All of these

74 The research antagonistic to expost facto research is
(a) normative research (b) library research
(c) experimental research (d) None of the above

75 If a researcher is studying the effect of using laptops in the classroom to ascertain their merit and worth, he is likely conducting which type of research?
(a) Basic (b) Evaluation
(c) Applied (d) Experimental

76 ……… is a way to systematically solve the research problem.
(a) Technique (b) Research process
(c) Research methodology (d) Operation

77 Major drawback of research in India is
(a) lack of sufficient funds
(b) lack of scientific training in research
(c) lack of sufficient number of universities
(d) lack of scientific training in research

78 Converting a question into a researchable problem is called
(a) solution (b) problem-solving
(c) examination (d) problem formulation

79 Research conducted to find solution for an immediate problem is
(a) survey (b) analytical research
(c) action research (d) long term research

80 Research related to abstract ideas or concepts is
(a) empirical research (b) quantitative research
(c) qualitative research (d) conceptual research

81 Research concerned with the derivation of generalisation of broad applicability and only secondarily with any practical value is called
(a) applied research (b) fundamental research
(c) action research (d) practical research

82 How can the objectivity of the research be enhanced?
(a) Through its validity (b) Through its reliability
(c) Through its impartiality (d) All of these

83 The research, which is exploring new facts through the study of the past is called
(a) content analysis (b) historical research
(c) mythological research (d) philosophical research

84 If a researcher conducts a research on finding out which administrative style contributes more to institutional effectiveness. This will be an example of
(a) applied research (b) action research
(c) basic research (d) None of these

85 Jean Piaget gave a theory of cognitive development of humans on the basis of his
(a) action research (b) evaluation research
(c) applied research (d) fundamental research

86 Which of the following is not a characteristic of a good theory or explanation?
(a) It is parsimonious
(b) It is testable
(c) It is general enough to apply more than one place, situation and person
(d) All of the above

87 Which of the following best describes quantitative research?
(a) The collection of non-numerical data
(b) An attempt to confirm the researcher's hypothesis
(c) Research that is exploratory
(d) A research that attempts to generate a new theory

88 Research in which the researcher uses both qualitative and quantitative research within a stage or across two of the stages in the research process is known as
(a) action research (b) basic research
(c) mixed model research (d) mixed method research

89 If a researcher was studying the use of various instructional approaches to the multiple intelligences of his students, he is likely to be conducting which type of research?
(a) Basic (b) Grounded Theory
(c) Evaluation (d) Applied

90 The research antagonistic to ex-post facto research is
(a) normative research (b) library research
(c) experimental studies (d) None of the above

91 Which of the following statement is most correct?
(a) Applied research adds to an organised body of scientific knowledge, but action research does not do that.
(b) The findings of applied research have practical implications for educational practices, but action research is not concerned with that.
(c) Applied research and action research, both are undertaken to solve immediate practical problems, but in action research the researcher is the same person as the practitioner who will use the findings of the research.
(d) The difference between them is that of nomenclature only, otherwise they are the same.

92 A study aimed at finding out the feasibility of a new method of teaching may be classified as
(a) action research (b) descriptive research
(c) experimental research (d) survey research

93 If the finding of a research have practical implications for improving educational practices, this should be classified as
(a) pure research
(b) applied research
(c) descriptive research
(d) experimental research

94 Which of the following is not an approach of analysis of qualitative data?
(a) Logical analysis (b) Criterion analysis
(c) Content analysis (d) Inductive analysis

95 What is the purpose of reviewing the related literature for conducting an action research?
(a) To determine the contribution of the study to scientific literature
(b) To clarify the design of the study
(c) To identify effective ideas and practices
(d) To ascertain whether the study is of qualitative or quantitative in nature

96 Which of the following best describes quantitative research?
(a) Research that is exploratory
(b) An attempt to confirm the researcher's hypothesis
(c) A research that attempts to generate a new theory
(d) The collection of non-numerical data

97 Match the following.

List I		List II
A.	Test theories and explains relation in behavioural science	1 Applied research
B.	Test usefulness of scientific theories in a given field	2. Basic research
C.	Establishes an accepted body of research based knowledge	3. Evaluation research
D.	Assesses the merit and worth of a particular practice at a given site	

Codes

	A	B	C	D		A	B	C	D
(a)	2	1	3	2	(b)	1	2	2	3
(c)	3	1	2	2	(d)	3	1	2	3

98 Arrange the following steps in historical research.
1. Collection of data.
2. Selection of the problem.
3. Formulation of hypothesis.
4. Primary and secondary sources.
5. Criticism of data.

Codes
(a) 1 2 3 4 and 5 (b) 2 3 1 4 and 5
(c) 5 4 3 1 and 2 (d) 2 1 4 3 and 5

99 Which of the following statement is true of a theory?

(a) It mostly means explanation
(b) It answers 'why' and 'how' of questions
(c) It can be a well developed explanatory system
(d) All of the above

100 If the findings of a research, have practical implications for improving educational pattern it is called

(a) pure research
(b) descriptive research
(c) applied research
(d) experimental research

101 Which one of the following is an example of qualitative research?

(a) Descriptive survey
(b) Experimental study
(c) Ex-post facto study
(d) Case study

102 Four essential characteristics of experimental research are

(a) control, regression, manipulation and variable
(b) variable, external validity, observation and control
(c) control, manipulation, observation and replication
(d) replication, control, variable and regression

Directions (Q. Nos. 103-114) *Given below are two statements. One labelled as Assertion (A) and other labelled as Reason (R). Select the correct code for the following.*

(a) Both A and R are true and R is the correct explanation of A
(b) Both A and R are true, but R is not the correct explanation of A
(c) Both A and R is true
(d) A is false, but R is true

103 **Assertion** (A) Research is a process of observing phenomena again and again.

Reason (R) It is a systematic effort to gain new knowledge in any kind of discipline.

104 **Assertion** (A) Educational research is an application of scientific method to the study of educational research.

Reason (R) It demands subjective interpretation and deductive reasoning in some cases.

105 **Assertion** (A) The philosophy of education is related to reorganisation of social structure and educational system in India.

Reason (R) It is also related to supervision and performance.

106 **Assertion** (A) Exploratory method are used to investigate a problem which is not clearly defined.

Reason (R) It depicts relationship between cause and effect variables.

107 **Assertion** (A) Descriptive method is easy and direct so it is very popular and widely used.

Reason (R) This method is useful in developing the data collection tools.

108 **Assertion** (A) Basic or fundamental research draws its pattern and spirit from the physical sciences.

Reason (R) This research is not directed towards the solution of immediate, specific and practical problems.

109 **Assertion** (A) In applied research solution is modified and installed, so that it may work in practice.

Reason (R) In applied research some of the weaknesses are selected for investigation.

110 **Assertion** (A) Action research is a method of systematic enquiry that teachers undertake as researchers of their own practice.

Reason (R) The boost to action research did not came up with the establishment of National Council of Educational Research and Training during 70's.

111 **Assertion** (A) Action research tries to inject innovative approaches to teaching.

Reason (R) It does focuses an development of theory or on the general application.

112 **Assertion** (A) In quantitative research the researcher carefully planned the study including the tests or other data collection instruments.

Reason (R) In quantitative research the data can be analysed in terms of numbers.

113 **Assertion** (A) Historical research design analyses the past events and develops the present concepts and conclusions.

Reason (R) It describes data observed by other rather than investigator.

114 **Assertion** (A) Descriptive research design aims to observe, describe and document aspects of a situation as it naturally occurs without any manipulation or control.

Reason (R) The design in such study must be rigid and not flexible.

PREVIOUS YEARS' QUESTIONS

July 2018

1 Match the following.

List I (Attribute Based Scientific Criterias)	List II (Descriptions)
A. Parsimony	1. Knowledge should remain open to revision
B. Empiricism	2. Interpretation of research should not reflect personal basis
C. Precision	3. Knowledge should be as simple as possible
D. Objectivity	4. Explanations should be as simple as possible
	5. Research statement should be based on accurate measurements

Codes

	A	B	C	D		A	B	C	D
(a)	2	4	3	5	(b)	4	3	5	2
(c)	3	5	2	4	(d)	1	2	4	5

November 2017

2 An investigator uses two matched groups to compare effectiveness of two methods of teaching science. This study would come in the ambit of

(a) experimental study
(b) causal comparative study
(c) descriptive survey study
(d) phenomenological study

3 Which of the following type is most useful for the government in planning policies?

(a) Correlational studies (b) Descriptive studies
(c) Experimental studies (d) Historical studies

4 Match the following.

List I (Types of Researches)	List II (Intended Uses of Researches)
A. Fundamental research	1. Exploring applicability of research based knowledge in a given field
B. Applied research	2. Advances scientific knowledge with addition of basic laws and principles
C. Evaluation research	3. Attempts to establish universal generalisation
	4. Explores research based knowledge about a specific practice

Codes

	A	B	C		A	B	C
(a)	1	2	4	(b)	2	1	4
(c)	3	2	1	(d)	4	1	2

January 2017

5 In educational research, case study method given importance.

(a) Prediction (b) Causal connections
(c) Generalisation (d) Unique characteristics

July 2016

6 In the formation of research problems for educational studies using quantitative paradigms, a sequence of logical steps has to be followed usually in a particular order.
From the list given below, select an appropriate sequence from the code.

1. Deciding the specific problem.
2. Determining the field of study.
3. Identifying the variables involved.
4. Evaluating on the basis of personal and academic suitability of the problem.

Codes

(a) 1, 2, 4, 3 (b) 3, 4, 2, 1
(c) 2, 4, 3, 1 (d) 2, 1, 3, 4

7 For conducting action research, reviewing of related literature is done to

(a) classify the design of the study
(b) ascertain the quantitative or qualitative nature of the situation
(c) ensure the contribution of the study to existing literature
(d) identify the effective ideas and practices

December 2015

8 Importance of the subject, feasibility and time needed for the study, have essentially be kept in mind at the time of

(a) collection of data (b) selection of the problem
(c) analysis of data (d) writing the report

9 Questions like what data is to be collected?, what characteristics of data are relevant and needed to be studied? and what techniques are to be used for the purpose? can be answered, it

(a) related literature is studied adequately
(b) problem is defined properly
(c) tools are constructed properly
(d) data are organised properly

10 A researcher is studying the effect of reinforcement on student's achievement with appropriate controls imposed in practical situation. What is the type of research in this situation?

(a) Fundamental research (b) Applied research
(c) Action research (d) Both (b) and (c)

June 2015

11 A teacher is studying the impact of his personal association with students on students' discipline in his/her class. This type of research may be called

(a) fundamental and action research
(b) action and applied research
(c) descriptive and fundamental research
(d) analytical and action research

12 In a study, the effect of peer's learning is being studied in relation to students' achievement and motivation. What type of research label will be acceptable for this study?

(a) Fundamental research
(b) Evaluative research
(c) Applied research
(d) Descriptive research

13 A systematic, objective and deliberate effort at answering meaningful questions, pertaining to a field of enquiry or about phenomena is called

(a) problem-solving (b) research
(c) theorising (d) invention

14 Which one is not a valid argument for conducting research in education?

(a) For advancement of Educational Theory
(b) For improvement of educational practices
(c) For improving social awareness of teachers
(d) For developing sound educational policies

15 Which type of research aims at explanation of the status and conditions exist at present?

(a) Applied research
(b) Analytical research
(c) Descriptive research
(d) Fundamental research

December 2014

16 Some usual steps in conducting research are given below, identify the code which gives acceptable rational sequence.

1. Formulating hypothesis
2. Collecting data and its analysis
3. Identifying the research problem
4. Testing the hypothesis

Codes

(a) 1 3 2 and 4 (b) 1 2 4 and 3
(c) 3 1 2 and 4 (d) 2 1 4 and 3

June 2014

17 Which one of the following may be considered as the best source for the formulation of a research problem?

(a) Consulting the research supervisor
(b) Holding a discussion with librarian
(c) Reflecting on research articles, reported in a journal
(d) Reflecting on the problems of education

ANSWERS

Exam Based Questions

1 (a)	2 (c)	3 (a)	4 (b)	5 (a)	6 (c)	7 (d)	8 (d)	9 (b)	10 (b)
11 (c)	12 (c)	13 (b)	14 (d)	15 (a)	16 (d)	17 (b)	18 (b)	19 (d)	20 (c)
21 (d)	22 (c)	23 (d)	24 (c)	25 (d)	26 (d)	27 (c)	28 (d)	29 (d)	30 (c)
31 (b)	32 (a)	33 (d)	34 (b)	35 (c)	36 (d)	37 (c)	38 (d)	39 (a)	40 (b)
41 (a)	42 (d)	43 (a)	44 (a)	45 (d)	46 (b)	47 (b)	48 (c)	49 (b)	50 (c)
51 (b)	52 (b)	53 (d)	54 (a)	55 (d)	56 (b)	57 (d)	58 (d)	59 (d)	60 (b)
61 (a)	62 (b)	63 (d)	64 (d)	65 (b)	66 (a)	67 (b)	68 (c)	69 (b)	70 (d)
71 (d)	72 (d)	73 (c)	74 (c)	75 (d)	76 (c)	77 (d)	78 (d)	79 (c)	80 (d)
81 (b)	82 (d)	83 (b)	84 (a)	85 (d)	86 (d)	87 (b)	88 (c)	89 (c)	90 (c)
91 (c)	92 (b)	93 (b)	94 (b)	95 (c)	96 (b)	97 (a)	98 (b)	99 (d)	100 (c)
101 (d)	102 (c)	103 (a)	104 (a)	105 (b)	106 (b)	107 (a)	108 (d)	109 (a)	110 (b)
111 (d)	112 (a)	113 (a)	114 (b)						

Previous Years' Questions

1 (b)	2 (a)	3 (b)	4 (b)	5 (d)	6 (d)	7 (d)	8 (b)	9 (b)	10 (b)
11 (b)	12 (c)	13 (b)	14 (c)	15 (c)	16 (c)	17 (c)			

CHAPTER 22

Research : Variables and Hypothesis

In the research process, while formulating the problem, the variables must be eminent and easily identifiable while hypothesis should accompany each research problem. As the variable represents a quality that can exhibit differences in values usually magnitude or strength. The hypothesis enables the researcher to develop a specific direction as well as better understanding about the subject matter under study.

In this Chapter

- Concept
- Construct
- Variables
- Hypothesis

Concept

The terms **concept** and **construct** have similar meanings. Yet, there is an important distinction. A concept may be defined as any describable regularity of real or imagined events or objects. A concept is a set of features connected by some rule. Concepts are building block of thinking. They allow us to organise knowledge in systematic ways. Concept represents objectives of activities, ideas or living organism. Concepts also represent properties, abstraction and relations between the features. For example, achievement. It is an abstraction formed from the observation of certain behaviours of children. These behaviours are associated pictures and so on. The various observed behaviours are put together and expressed in a word achievement. Intelligence, aggressiveness, conformity and honesty are all concepts, used to express varieties of human behaviour of interest to behavioural scientists.

Categories of Concepts

Concepts are divided into two categories *i.e.* concepts by postulation and concept by intuition. The concepts following in the first category have meaning except from the specific theory. When these concepts are used in two different theories these communicate two different meanings, sometimes even different and opposite from each other. On the other hand, concept by intuition denotes something which is easily apprehended.

Types of Concepts

Concrete Concepts Symbolise material objects which can be seen, touched and fret. *e.g.* book and table.

Abstract Concepts refer to properties or characteristics of objects. *e.g.* weight and height.

Characteristics of Concepts

- Concepts are symbols which we attach to the bundle of meanings we hold.
- Concepts represent only one part of reality.
- Different people hold different concepts of the same thing.
- Concepts also represent various degrees of abstraction.
- A concept is thus an abstract symbol, representing an object, a property of object or a certain phenomena.

Construct

The word 'construct' means focussed abstract idea on something inferred from an observable phenomena.

Researcher often invents or constructs new concepts for special scientific purposes, such concepts are called constructs. Thus, you may well explain construct as concept. It has the added meaning *i.e.* invented or adopted for a special scientific purpose. For example, Intelligence is a concept, an abstraction from intelligent and non-intelligent behaviours. But, as a scientific construct, intelligence means both more and less than a concept.

It means that scientists consciously and systematically use it in two ways. **One**, it enters into theoretical schemes and related in various ways to other constructs. In this sense, school's achievement may also be in part, a function of intelligence and motivation. **Two**, intelligence is so defined and specified that it can be observed and measured. We can make observations of the intelligence of children by administering X intelligence test to them, or we can ask teachers to tell us the relative degrees of intelligence of their pupils.

Constructs are created and used for a wide variety of reasons, but generally have two common characteristics. **First**, the construct is a part of a theoretical framework and is related in various ways to other constructs. **Second**, a construct usually, operationally defined so as to allow its observation and measurement.

An example of a commonly employed psychological constructs, such as drive, motivation, association, habit and strength. Further reinforcement may be operationally defined as any stimulus or event which increases the probability of the occurrence of a (desired) response. A construct is a concept, used for scientific purpose and it is a part of theoretical framework. It has an added meaning and it is adopted for a special scientific purpose.

Types of Construct

Intervening Variables An intervening variable is a construct which is utilised for a group of other construct. It has no meaning apart from context in which it is utilised. It is a term which is internal and directly, unobservable psychological processes that, in turn, inferred from behaviour.

Hypothetical Constructs A hypothetical construct is a theoretical term which is employed to describe something 'real'. It is an intermeditary which has tangible characteristics.

Variables

A variable is any entity that can take on different values, this means anything that can vary can be considered a variable. A variable is a concept or abstract idea that can be described in measurable terms. In research, this term refers to the measurable characteristics, qualities, traits or attributes of a particular individual, object or situation being studied. For instance, age can be considered a variable because age can take different values for different people or for the same person at different times.

It is a value that can be manipulated, measured, described or controlled. Value after giving a name becomes variable *e.g.* height, weight, IQ, personality, performance level, income, age, etc.

Etymologically, speaking a variable is a quantity that can vary. In scientific research, a variable is a quantity measurable representation of an abstract construct. Every variable has atleast two possible values in order to vary. Thus, the variables are the conditions or characteristics that the experimenter manipulates, controls or observe.

Variable is defined by many scholars in different ways i.e.

According to **Kerlinger**, "Variable is defined as a property that takes on different values".

According to **Black and Champion**, "Variable as a rational units of analysis that can assume any one of a number of designated set of values".

Types of Variables

Independent Variable or Experimental Variable

The independent variables are the conditions or characteristics that the experimenter manipulates or controls in his or her attempt to ascertain their relationship to observed phenomena. In educational research, an independent variable may be a particular teaching method, a type of teaching material, a reward of a period of exposure to a particular condition or an attribute such as sex or level of intelligence.

There are two types of independent variables and they are:

Treatment Variables The treatment variables are those factors that the experimenter manipulates and to which he/she assigns subjects.

Attribute Variables The attribute variables are those characteristics that cannot be altered by the experimenter. Such independent variables like sex, age, race and intelligence level have already been determined, but the experimenter can decide to include them or remove them as variables to be studied.

Dependent Variables or Criterion Variables

The dependent variables are the conditions or characteristics that appear, disappear or change as the experimenter introduces, removes or changes independent variables. The dependent variable may be a test score, the number of errors or measured speed in performing a task. So, the dependent variables are the measured changes in pupil's performance, attributable to the influence of the independent variables.

Extraneous Variables

Extraneous variables are those uncontrolled variables that may have a significant influence upon the results of the study. Suppose, the researcher wants to test the hypothesis that there is a relationship between children's gain in social studies achievement and their self-concept. Here, self is independent variable and achievement in social study is dependent variable. Intelligence may as well affect the social studies achievement, but since it is not related to the purpose of the study undertaken by the researcher, it will be termed as extraneous variable. Whatever effect is noticed on dependent variable as a result of extraneous variable is technically described as an experimental error.

A study must always be so designed that the effect upon the dependent variable is attributed to the independent variables and not to some extraneous variable. When the dependent variable is not free from the influence of extraneous variable, the relationship between the dependent and independent variable is said to be confounded by an extraneous variable. Extraneous variable can be controlled by removing variables causing distraction. It may be eliminated by selecting cases with uniform characteristics and through randomisation.

Intervening Variable

An intervening variable is that factor which theoretically affects the observed phenomenon, but cannot be seen measured or manipulated, its effect must be inferred from the effect of the independent and moderator variables on the observed phenomenon. For example, in a classroom language experiment, a researcher is interested in determining the effect of the immediate reinforcement upon learning the parts of speech. He/She suspects that certain factor or variable, other than the one being studied immediate reinforcement may be influencing the results, even though they cannot be observed directly. These factors anxiety, fatigue, motivation may be intervening variables. They are difficult to define in operational and observable terms, but they cannot be ignored. Rather, they must be controlled as much as is feasible through the use of appropriate designs.

The intervening variable, however always refers to conceptual variable that which is being affected by the independent, moderator and control variables and in turn affects dependent variable.

Moderator Variables

The term moderator variable describes a special type of independent variable, a secondary independent variable selected for the study to determine if it affects the relationship between the primary independent variable and the dependent variable. The moderator variable is defined as that factor which is measured, manipulated or selected by the experimenter to discover whether it modifies the relationship of the independent variable to an observed phenomena.

The word moderator acknowledges the reason that this secondary independent variable has been singled out for study. If the experimenter is interested in studying the effect of independent variable 'X' on dependent variable 'Y', but suspects that the nature of relationship between 'X' and 'Y' is altered by the level of third factor 'Z' then 'Z' can be in the analysis as a moderator variable.

Hypothesis

The word 'hypothesis' consists of two words 'hypo' + 'thesis'. 'Hypo' means tentative or subject to the verification. Thesis means statement about solution of the problem. Thus, the literal meaning of the term 'hypothesis' is a tentative statement about the solution of the problem. Hypothesis offers a solution of the problem that is to be verified empirically and based on some rationale.

Again 'hypo' means composition of two or more variables which are to be verified and 'thesis' means position of these variables in the specific frame of reference. The 'hypothesis' is a powerful tool in research process to achieve dependable knowledge. It helps the researcher to relate theory to observation and observation to theory.

Few important definitions are as follows

- A statement temporarily accepted as true in the light of what is known about the concerned phenomenon at the commencement of the study. **(Barr and Scates)**
- A proposition which can be put to test in order to determine its validity **(Goode and Hatt)**.
- A tentative proposition or provisional guess which seems to explain the situation under observation (Creighton).
- A tentative generalisation, the validity of which remains to be tested **(Lundberg)**.
- An informed guess or inference with a reasonable chance of being right, formulated and tentatively adopted to explain observed facts or conditions and to guide in further investigation **(Goode)**.
- An assumption or proposition whose testability is to be tested on the basis of the compatibility of its implications with evidence and with previous knowledge **(Mouly)**.

Hence, the above definitions help us to obtain better understanding of the concept. It is a scientifically deduced proposition that is to be put to test in an experiment. Expressed differently, it is a statement which is tentatively accepted as the solution to a problem under investigation. It is based on all the available knowledge about the phenomena (theories, research findings, personal experience, etc.) and hence the possibility of it coming out true is very great. However, there is no guarantee that this deduction will prove to be valid. The validity of the deduction will be decided on the basis of an experiment. If it is found true on the basis of an experimentation, the deduction is discarded from the body of scientific knowledge.

Sources of Hypothesis

Theory This is one of the main source of hypothesis. It gives direction to research by stating what is known. Logical deduction from theory leads to new hypothesis.

Observation Hypothesis can be derived from observation. For example, from observation of price behaviour in a market, the relationship between price and demand of an article can be hypothesised.

Analogies Analogies are another sources of hypothesis. Julian Hexley has pointed out that causal observation in nature or in the framework of another science may be a fertile source of Hypothesis.

Intuition and Personal Experiences Intuition and personal experiences may also contribute to the formulation of hypothesis. Personal life and experience of person determine their perception and conception. These may in term direct a person to certain hypothesis more quickly. The stories, Newton and falling apple and the flash of wisdom to Shree Buddha, under banyan tree illustrate this accidental process.

Findings and Studies Hypothesis may be developed out of the findings of other studies in order to repeat the test.

Culture Another source of hypothesis is the culture in which the researcher is nurtured. For example, sociology as an academic discipline originated from western culture. Over the past decade, a large part of the hypothesis on American society examined by researchers were connected with violence. Indian society is caste ridden. It is riddled with inequalities and privileges.

Types of Hypothesis

Types of hypothesis are explained below

Research Hypothesis

When a prediction or a hypothesised relationship is to be tested by scientific method, it is termed as research hypothesis. The research hypothesis a predictive statement that relates an independent variable to a dependent variable. Generally, a research hypothesis must contain, at least one independent and one dependent variable. Predictive statements which are not to be objectively verified or the relationship that are assumed but not to be tested are not termed as research hypothesis.

Directional Hypothesis

It explains and predicts the direction and existence of a specific relationship. The predicted relationship will be either positive or negative. A directional hypothesis is more specific than non-directional hypothesis. It is also known as the cause and effect hypothesis, For example, it is hypothesised that the co-educated students are more interactive and smarter than the non-co-educated students.

Key words that distinguish a directional hypothesis are higher, lower, more, less, increase, decrease, positive and negative. A researcher develops a directional hypothesis from research questions and uses statistical methods to check the validity of the hypothesis.

The following are other examples of directional hypothesis

There is a positive relationship between the number of books read by children and a children's score on reading test.

Teenagers who attend tutoring sessions will make higher achievement test scores than comparable teenagers who do not attend tutoring sessions.

Non-Directional Hypothesis

It predicts a change, relationship or difference between two variables but does not specifically designate the change, relationship or difference as being positive or negative.

The examples of non-directional hypothesis are

- There is a relationship between the number of books read by children and the children's scores on a reading test.
- Teenager who attends tutoring sessions will have achievement test scores that are significantly different from the scores of comparable teenagers who do not attend tutoring sessions.
- There is no significant difference between 9th class boys and girl's abilities of learning moral values.

Null Hypothesis

Null means zero. When a hypothesis is stated negatively, it is called null hypothesis. The object of this hypothesis is to avoid the personal bias of the investigator. In the matter of collection of data, a null hypothesis is used to collect additional support for known hypothesis.

The statistical tests are not designated to test a directional hypothesis or non-directional hypothesis, but rather a null hypothesis. A null hypothesis is a prediction that there will be no change, relationship or difference between two variables. A null hypothesis is designated by 'Ho'.

The following are the examples of null hypothesis

- There is no relationship between the number of books read by children and the children's scores on a reading test.
- Teenagers who attend tutoring session will make achievement test scores that are equivalent to those of comparable teenagers, who do not attend tutoring session.

Formulation of a Hypothesis

How we form a hypothesis? Does it just come to the mind of the investigator the way poet gets a sudden inspiration for writing a poem? Or is it a product of long and sustained thinking and argument? A very important fact we have to keep in mind is that a scientific hypothesis is the result of a focused mental activity. The investigator surveys the whole field of research and studying different theories relating to the area of investigation.

He may also recall his personal experience in this regard. All these things combined and logical are made from the total body of available knowledge. The hypothesis is partly based on known facts and explanations and partly conceptual. There are no precise rules for formulating hypothesis and deducing consequences from them that can be empirically verified. However, there are certain necessary conditions that are conducive to their formulation.

Steps in Formulating Hypothesis

Choosing a Topic A researcher must familiarise himself while choosing a topic for research. Topic should be researchable in an interdisciplinary sense that means there must be sufficient published material on the topic.

Richness of Background Knowledge Hypothesis must be formulated correctly by person who have rich experience and academic background. Due to this, a researcher will arrive at a conclusion, a theory or understanding that will be useful or applicable beyond the research itself.

Level of Hypothesis Hypothesis msut involve an issue or question that cannot be answered exclusively by the discipline of law. It is best to choose a hypothesis where a researcher already have some level of familiarity with the disciplines that are most relevant to the topic.

Versatility of Intellect A researcher must possess a versatile intellect to understand a theory to deduce a hypothesis from theories, to be able to spot very quickly the contributing variables in a study, to creatively imagine the output or solution to the problem. All of this depends upon considerable time and effort along with the persistence of the researcher.

Analogies and Other Practices A researcher must use analogies for the formulation of hypothesis and finding out solutions to the problem. Reasoning by analogy is based on similarities and differences between two situations in which a similar or the same phenomenon or event takes place.

Criteria of Formulating a Hypothesis

- Hypothesis must be stated in clear and precise terms. General terms, such as personality, intelligence, etc, should not be used here. It means the terms used in the hypothesis should not create any confusion in the minds of others.
- Hypothesis should be testable on the basis of data collected. Conclusion is drawn only after testing the hypothesis. If data collected are in accordance with the hypothesis, then it is accepted otherwise rejected.
- Tools must be available to measure the variables mentioned in the hypothesis. If such tools are not available, they have to be constructed by the researcher himself.
- Hypothesis should defines variables operationally, not conceptually.
- Hypothesis should be limited in scope. Hypothesis of global significance are not usable because they are not specific and hence, they cannot be tested.
- Hypothesis should be consistent with most known facts. They should be grouped on well established theories. If hypothesis is from known facts, nothing will come out by research.

Characteristics of a Good Hypothesis

- One of the valuable attribute of a good hypothesis is to predict for future. It not only clears the present problematic situation but also predict for the future that what would be happened in the coming time. So, hypothesis is a best guide of research activity due to power of prediction.
- A hypothesis must have close contact with observable things. It does not believe on air castles but it is based on observation. Those things and objects which we cannot observe, for that hypothesis cannot be formulated. The verification of a hypothesis is based on observable things.
- A hypothesis should be so dabble to every layman, PV Young says, "A hypothesis would be simple, if a researcher has more in sight towards the problem". W-ocean stated that, "A hypothesis should be as sharp as razor's blade". So, a good hypothesis must be simple and have no complexity.
- A hypothesis must be conceptually clear. It should be clear from ambiguous information's. The terminology used in it must be clear and acceptable to everyone.
- A good hypothesis should be tested empirically. It should be stated and formulated after verification and deep observation. Thus test ability is the primary feature of a good hypothesis.
- If a hypothesis is relevant to a particular problem, it would be considered as good one. A hypothesis is guidance for the identification and solution of the problem, so it must be accordance to the problem.
- It should be formulated for a particular and specific problem. It should not include generalisation. If generalisation exists, then a hypothesis cannot reach to the correct conclusions.
- Hypothesis must be relevant to the techniques which is available for testing. A researcher must know about the workable techniques which is available for testing. A researcher must know about the workable techniques before formulating a hypothesis.
- It should be able to provide new suggestions and ways of knowledge. It must create new discoveries of knowledge **JS Mill**, one of the eminent researcher says that "Hypothesis is the best source of new knowledge it creates new ways of discoveries".
- Harmony and consistency is a major characteristic of good hypothesis. It should be out of contradictions and conflicts. There must be a close relationship between variables with one is dependent on other.

EXAM BASED QUESTIONS

1 The variable that the researcher changes or manipulates is called

(a) control variable (b) dependent variable
(c) independent variable (d) responding variable

2 The changes in dependent variable is caused by

(a) control variable (b) dependent variable
(c) independent variable (d) responding variable

3 Variables, whose measurements are done in terms of weight, height and length are

(a) continuous variables (b) measuring variables
(c) flow chart variables (d) discrete variables

4 What is meant by a 'spurious' relation between two variables?

(a) One that is ridiculously illogical, it cannot possibly be true
(b) An apparent relationship that is so curious, it demands further attention
(c) A relationship that appears to be true because each variable is related to a third one
(d) One that produces a perfect negative correlation on a scatter diagram

5 What is the opposite of a variable?

(a) A constant
(b) An extraneous variable
(c) A dependent variable
(d) A data set

6 Which of the following is a discrete variable?

(a) Age (b) Nationality
(c) Test score (d) Income

7 The best way to control for extraneous variables in research studies is

(a) randomisation
(b) valid and reliable instrumentation
(c) avoiding all threats to external validity
(d) using intact groups

8 Which of the following variance is not controlled or manipulated in a research design?

(a) Variance of independent variable
(b) Variance of dependent variable
(c) Variance of extraneous variables
(d) Error Variance

9 Which of the following variable is continuous?
(a) Attitude towards school
(b) Family size in a locality
(c) Marital status of college students
(d) Religious affiliation of workers

10 Two variables X and Y are correlated. This means that the two variables
(a) cause variation in each other
(b) measure the same trait
(c) vary together
(d) vary independently

11 The variable which impacts the relationship between independent variable and dependent variable is
(a) antecedent variable (b) precedent variable
(c) predictor variable (d) control variable

12 Which schedule of reinforcement in operant conditioning is likely to produce steadiness in acquired behaviour?
(a) Continuous schedule of reinforcement
(b) Fixed interval schedule of reinforcement
(c) Variable interval schedule
(d) Variable ratio schedule of reinforcement

13 A researcher wants to study whether discovery learning procedure has an impact on the motivation of students. In this situation, the variable motivation will be labelled as
(a) intervening variable (b) independent variable
(c) dependent variable (d) extraneous variable

14 In labelling research variables, the designations of variables from one research to other, have to be
(a) identical (b) different
(c) sometimes identical (d) sometimes different

15 While conducting experimental research, a researcher should control the
(a) independent variables (b) dependent variables
(c) no variables (d) extraneous variables

16 Which of the following variance is not controlled or manipulated in a research design?
(a) Variance of independent variable
(b) Variance of dependent variable
(c) Variance of extraneous variable
(d) Error variance

17 Two variables X and Y are correlated. This means that the two variables
(a) cause variation in each other
(b) measure the same trait
(c) vary together
(d) vary independently

18 Two variables X and Y are significantly correlated. This means that
(a) X causes variation in Y
(b) Y causes variation in X
(c) X and Y vary together
(d) No such conclusion may be drawn

19 Attributes of objects, events or things, which can be measured are called
(a) data (b) qualitative measures
(c) variables (d) None of these

20 Independent variables are not manipulated in
(a) ex-post facto research
(b) normative research
(c) Both a and b
(d) None of the above

21 The other name of independent variable for an experimental research is
(a) experimental variable (b) treatment variable
(c) manipulated variable (d) All of these

22 Which of the following is not an extraneously variable?
(a) History (b) Statistical regression
(c) Sex (d) Pre-testing

23 In research, something that vary is called a
(a) variable (b) method
(c) constant (d) control group

24 The variables which are unrated to the study, but may affect the dependent variables are
(a) background variables (b) extraneous variables
(c) internal variables (d) antecedent variables

25 What is the name of an unknown variable that correlates with the independent variable and explain the outcome of the experiment in the same way as the specified independent variable does?
(a) Controlled variable (b) Extraneous variable
(c) Confounded variable (d) Implicit variable

26 What does defining the terms, concepts and variables used in the title of the research problem operationally mean?
(a) Defining them in such a way that everyone understands them well
(b) Defining them in the way as others have defined them
(c) Defining them in behavioural terms as they are going to be measured in the study
(d) Defining them in standard ways as defined in the literature, dictionaries, encyclopaedias, etc

27 Which of the following is not common to experimental and ex-post facto designs of research?
(a) Cause and effect relationship
(b) Manipulation of independent variable
(c) Controlling extraneous variable
(d) Observation of dependent variable

28 The internal validity of an experimental research is related to
(a) variation in the dependent variable
(b) effective control of intervening variable
(c) variation in the independent variable
(d) accuracy of measurement methods

29 Which of the following statement is not correct?
(a) Extraneous variables are controlled by randomisation
(b) Extraneous variables are controlled by matching
(c) Extraneous variables are controlled external validity
(d) Extraneous variables are controlled by analysis of variance

30 **Statement I** It predicts a change, relationship between two variables.
Statement II It does not specifically designate the change, relationship or difference as being positive or negative.
(a) Statement I is correct
(b) Both statements are correct
(c) Statement II is correct
(d) Neither a nor c

31 Attribute variable is a category of
(a) independent variable (b) dependent variable
(c) confounding variable (d) extraneous variable

32 In experimental research, the variable manipulated by the experimenter is
(a) dependent variable (b) independent variable
(c) extraneous variable (d) confounding variable

33 By the term, independent variable in conducting any educational research we mean
(a) the condition which the experiments cannot manipulate or change
(b) the freedom and independence of the experiments in formulating his approach
(c) the factors that are beyond to reach the experiments for conducting a research
(d) the conditions or situations, which the experiments can be manipulate or change

34 If a researcher wants to study achievement in a school subject with respect to the intelligence than he has to take
(a) one variable in nominal scale and other in interval scale
(b) both the variables in interval scale
(c) both the variables in ratio scales
(d) one variable in interval scale and other in ratio scale

35 Which of the following statement is true in the context of the testing of a hypothesis?
(a) It is only the alternative hypothesis that can be tested
(b) It is the only null hypothesis that can be tested
(c) Both a and b
(d) Neither a nor b

36 Which is not correct about hypothesis?
(a) It is essential in studies where cause effect relationship are to be discovered
(b) It is less crucial in studies in which the task is one of determining the status of a given phenomenon
(c) Its absence, essentially, means no research or poor research
(d) Even in case of status studies, the investigator is likely to need some tentative hypothesis to guide him

37 A hypothesis in educational research need not be
(a) compatible with well attested theories and models
(b) logically consistent and pertinent to the question under consideration
(c) capable of establishing generalisations that can be applied in many areas of education or other fields
(d) precise and plausible

38 Which of the following statement does not goes with the other three?
(a) A hypothesis must be based directly on existing data
(b) A hypothesis must explain existing data in simpler terms than any competing hypothesis
(c) A hypothesis must be stated as simply and concisely as the complexity of the concepts involved will allow
(d) A hypothesis must be such or it can be confirmed easily

39 The view that a hypothesis is never proved, it is merely sustained or rejected only tentatively is
(a) a misconception
(b) a correct and valid statement
(c) a wrong assumption about hypothesis
(d) a fact not accepted by all

40 Which of the following form, a research hypothesis cannot take
(a) declarative form (b) problem form
(c) question form (d) null from

41 Which of the following alternative is most correct about the necessary condition that are conducive to the formulation of hypothesis?
(a) Richness of researcher's background knowledge
(b) Researcher's creative imagination
(c) Analogy and consultation with experts and the guide
(d) All of the above

42 Which of the following is irrelevant in the context of the criteria of acceptable hypothesis?
(a) A hypothesis should be clearly and precisely stated
(b) A hypothesis should state the expected relationship between the variables
(c) A hypothesis should be such that it can be proved
(d) A hypothesis should be testable

43 A good or adequate hypothesis should
(a) be limited in scope
(b) not be a bunch of relationships
(c) be consistent with known theories and facts
(d) have all the above characteristics

44 Deductive reasoning helps in
(a) sample selection (b) hypothesis generation
(c) problem identification (d) None of these

45 What is the meaning of null hypothesis?
(a) Difference between two parametric means is zero
(b) The difference is due to error in sampling
(c) Both a and b
(d) None of the above

46 Hypothesis test may also be called as
(a) informal test (b) significance test
(c) moderating test (d) T-test

47 Formulation of hypothesis may not be required in
(a) survey method (b) historical studies
(c) normative studies (d) experimental studies

48 What determines, whether a researcher should use 0.05 or 0.01 level of significance for testing the hypothesis?
(a) How important are the findings?
(b) How much risk is involved in incorrect finding?
(c) How much precision is required?
(d) All of the above

49 In experimental research hypothesis are formulated
(a) before the experiment (b) during the experiment
(c) after the experiment (d) None of these

50 Type-I error, in the testing of a null hypothesis, occurs when the researcher
(a) rejects it when it is true (b) accepts it when it is false
(c) Both a and b (d) Neither a nor b

51 Hypothesis can be formulated using
(a) the established theories
(b) the findings of previous research
(c) experience of the researcher
(d) the result of the same study

52 "Those who enroll themselves in an exploratory vocational programme will contribute more to the development of society than those not enrolled in the programme". Which one of the important characteristics of a good hypothesis is violated in the above hypothesis?
(a) A hypothesis should be logically acceptable
(b) A hypothesis should be concise
(c) A hypothesis should be defined in operational terms
(d) A hypothesis should be testable

53 "Hypothesis is a tentative supposition or provisional guess which sees and explains the situation under observation". Who defined hypothesis?
(a) James E Greetari (b) John W Best
(c) Emroy (d) Kerlinger

54 Why is it essential to convert the research hypothesis into null hypothesis?
(a) Because it does not express the relationship existing between the dependent and the independent variable
(b) It is not a scientific statement
(c) It cannot be tested statistically
(d) It is a very general statement and does not indicates the specified direction of research

55 What is irrelevant in the context of the criteria of acceptable hypothesis?
(a) A hypothesis should be clearly and precisely stated
(b) A hypothesis should state the expected relationship between the variables
(c) A hypothesis should be such that it can be proved
(d) A hypothesis should be testable

56 Which one of the following assumption cannot be tested through a research hypothesis?
(a) Growth of intellect does not depend on age and training of any child
(b) Prejudiced people develop negative attitude towards on object they dislike
(c) Academic aptitude is contributory function of academic achievement
(d) Learning is facilitated by advance organizers

57 Null, prediction, declaration, question are
(a) forms of hypothesis
(b) types of hypothesis
(c) variations
(d) None of the above

58 A research hypothesis is generally converted into null hypothesis because
(a) it is safer
(b) it cannot be tested statistically
(c) it is a general statement
(d) it is a vague statement

59 Some usual steps in conducting research are given below, identify the code which gives acceptable rational sequence.
1. Formulating hypothesis
2. Collecting data and its analysis
3. Identifying the research problem
4. Testing the hypothesis
Codes
(a) 1, 3, 2 and 4
(b) 1, 2, 4 and 3
(c) 3, 1, 2 and 4
(d) 2, 1, 4 and 3

60 Match the following.

List I (Variables)	List II (Characteristics)
A. Independent	1. These are controlled variables that may have a significant influence upon the results.
B. Dependent	2. Affects the observed phenomena but cannot be seen or manipulated.
C. Extraneous	3. They are the conditions or characteristics that appear or disappear as the experiments introduces or changes independent variables.
D. Intervening	4. They the conditions or characteristics that the experiments manipulates or control in his/her attempts to ascertain their relationship to observed phenomena.

Codes

	A	B	C	D		A	B	C	D
(a)	4	3	1	2	(b)	1	2	3	4
(c)	2	4	1	3	(d)	4	2	1	3

Directions (Q. Nos. 61-69) *Below given are two statements, one labelled as Assertion (A) and other labelled as Reason (R). Choose the correct code for the following.*

Codes

(a) Both A and R are true and R is the correct explanation of A
(b) Both A and R are true, but R is not the correct explanation of A
(c) Both A and R is true
(d) A is false, but R is true

61 **Assertion** (A) In ex-post facto research, the researcher does not have control on independent variables.

Reason (R) Manifestation of independent variables have already occurred.

62 **Assertion** (A) Concept is a set of features connected by some rule.

Reason (R) Concepts are building blocks of thinking.

63 **Assertion** (A) The treatment variables are those factors that the experiments manipulates.

Reason (R) These variables are theoretically affects the observed phenomenon but cannot be seen, measured or manipulated.

64 **Assertion** (A) A variable is any entity that can take on different values.

Reason (R) Age can be considered a variable as age can take different values.

65 **Assertion** (A) This explains and predicts the direction and existence of specific relationship.

Reason (R) The object of this hypothesis is to avoid the personal bias of the investigator.

66 **Assertion** (A) The research hypothesis is a predictive statement that relates that related an independent variable to a dependent variable.

Reason (R) These hypothesis must contain atleast one independent variable and one dependent variable.

67 **Assertion** (A) A good hypothesis is clear and precise.

Reason (R) It should be amenable to testing within a reasonable time.

68 **Assertion** (A) A null hypothesis challenges the assertions of a declarative hypothesis and denies it altogether.

Reason (R) It states that even where it seems to hold good it is due to mere chance.

69 **Assertion** (A) Intution is often considered a reasonable source of research hypothesis.

Reason (R) It is the intution of a well-known researcher or theoretician who knowns what is known.

PREVIOUS YEARS' QUESTIONS

July 2018

1 If two variables X and Y have significant negative correlation, which of the following statement is true?

(a) X causes variation in Y
(b) Y causes variation in X
(c) X and Y vary together
(d) X and Y cause each other to vary

2 Two variables X and Y have a negative correlation coefficient of –.48. The proportion of variance common to both the variables will be

(a) 0.23 (b) 0.27
(c) 0.48 (d) 0.52

July 2017

3 The hypothesis in research usually formulated on the basis of

(a) setting up relationships between two or more than two variables
(b) identification of variables and their nature
(c) reading research articles
(d) holding conversations with senior researchers

January 2017

4 **Assertion** (A) The research hypothesis, being the alternative hypothesis (H_1) has to be kept in the domain of acceptability.

Reason (R) The null hypothesis (H_0) has been rejected at high alpha (significance) level, thereby rendering the possibility of Type I error quite insubstantial.

Codes

(a) Both A and R are true and R is the correct explanation of A
(b) Both A and R are true, but R is not the correct explanation of A
(c) A is true, but R is false
(d) A is false, but R is true

December 2015

5 In the process of classroom teaching and learning, which of the following schedule of reinforcement may not be usually found?
(a) Variable ratio schedule
(b) Continuous schedule
(c) Interval schedule
(d) Fixed interval schedule

6 Hypothesis making is basically a
(a) creative process
(b) logical process
(c) scientific process
(d) epistemological process

June 2015

7 In order to ensure that the impact on dependent variables is only due to independent variable, which of the following method will be more appropriate?
(a) Descriptive method (b) Experimental method
(c) Field study (d) Ex-post facto research

8 In a positive correlation, the increase in X (one variable) is followed by
(a) decrease in Y
(b) increase in Y
(c) Neither a nor b
(d) decrease/increase in Y is by chance

December 2014

9 A researcher wants to study whether discovery learning procedure has an impact on the motivation of students. In this situation, the variable motivation will be labelled as
(a) intervening variable
(b) independent variable
(c) dependent variable
(d) extraneous variable

10 In labelling research variables, the designations of variables from one research to the other have to be
(a) identical
(b) different
(c) sometimes identical
(d) sometimes different

June 2014

11 Which of the following variable is discrete?
(a) Achievement
(b) Intelligence
(c) Aptitude
(d) Attribute

ANSWERS

Exam Based Questions

1 (c)	2 (c)	3 (c)	4 (c)	5 (a)	6 (b)	7 (a)	8 (b)	9 (a)	10 (c)
11 (d)	12 (b)	13 (b)	14 (b)	15 (b)	16 (b)	17 (c)	18 (c)	19 (c)	20 (c)
21 (d)	22 (c)	23 (a)	24 (c)	25 (c)	26 (c)	27 (b)	28 (a)	29 (b)	30 (b)
31 (b)	32 (d)	33 (d)	34 (c)	35 (b)	36 (c)	37 (c)	38 (d)	39 (b)	40 (b)
41 (b)	42 (c)	43 (b)	44 (b)	45 (d)	46 (b)	47 (b)	48 (d)	49 (a)	50 (a)
51 (d)	52 (d)	53 (a)	54 (c)	55 (c)	56 (a)	57 (a)	58 (b)	59 (b)	60 (a)
61 (b)	62 (a)	63 (b)	64 (c)	65 (b)	66 (a)	67 (b)	68 (a)	69 (a)	

Previous Years' Questions

1 (c)	2 (a)	3 (a)	4 (c)	5 (b)	6 (a)	7 (b)	8 (b)	9 (c)	10 (b)
11 (d)									

CHAPTER
23

Research : Tools, Sampling and Writing Proposal

The collection of data is of paramount importance in the conduct of research. The sampling is the act, process or technique of selecting suitable sample or representative part of a population for the purpose of determining parameters or characteristics of the whole population.

Tools of Data Collection

The instruments that are employed to collect new facts or to explore new fields are called tools. It is of vital importance to select suitable instruments and tools. As for any research study, the researcher has to collect data and on the basis of that data, he draws conclusions and arrives at generalisations. These conclusions and generalisations will be correct and valid, if the data is methodically collected. For collecting reliable and valid data, one needs reliable and valid tools and techniques of data collection. The researcher has to select tools and techniques of data collection, carefully and judiciously. He/she might make use of standardised readymade tools or may develop his/her own tools, ensuring that the tools developed are reliable and valid, so that the data obtained through these tools are also reliable and valid.

Data collection tools are very helpful because they provide a picture of your class/work environment. The goal for using tools is to help the researcher to clarify information, process knowledge and identify opportunities for continuous improvement. These are the instruments used to collect information, for use in performance assessment, self-evaluation and external evaluation.

Tools of data collection are instruments, like rating scale, checklist, questionnaire attitude scale, etc. Whereas, the techniques of data collection are the processes, through which data are obtained such as interviews, observations, etc. Each research tool is appropriate in a given situation, to accomplish a specific purpose. These tools should be used together or in combination, as they supplement the work of each other. **J W Best**, an author of **Research in Education** commented that like the tools in the carpenter box, each is appropriate in a given situation, to accomplish a particular purpose. Each data collecting device has both merits and demerits. However, for effective result, each tool has its own significance. It must be used according to the situation.

In this Chapter

- *Tools of Data Collection*
- *Techniques of Research*
- *Universe*
- *Sample*
- *Research Proposal*

Criteria of a Good Tool

Following are the criteria of a good tool

Validity

Each tool of evaluation has specific purposes. Therefore, the foremost consideration one must look for, while choosing a tool is the purpose for which it is being used, that is the tool being used, should be valid. Thus, a tool is valid, if it serves the purpose for which it is designed.

According to Stanley and Hopkings, "The validity of a measures how well it fulfils the function, for which it is being used and the degree to which it is capable of achieving certain aims".

Therefore, the concept of validity of a test is chiefly a concern for the basic honesty of the test honesty, in the sense of doing, what are promises to do.

Validity can be divided into five categories and they are :

(i) **Content Validity** A systematic evaluation of the test content, to determine whether it covers a representative sample of the behaviour domain or not to be measure.

(ii) **Criterion Related Validity** This approach entails detecting the presence of one or more criteria, considered to represent traits or construct of interest.

(iii) **Construct Validity** It refers to the limit to which operationalisations of a construct, do actually measure what the theory says to do.

(iv) **Face Validity** It refers to an estimate of the operationalisation and to see whether or not on its face, it seems like a good translation of the construct.

(v) **Factorial Validity** It refers to the validity of the instrument's factor structure, most frequently assessed by factor analysis.

Reliability

It is concerned with the question of 'accuracy' with which the 'what' is measured. It refers to the results obtained with an evaluation instrument and not to the instrument itself. An evaluation tool may have a large number of different reliabilities, depending on the groups of subjects and situations of use. Reliability is a necessary, but not a sufficient condition for validity.

Objectivity

It is an important criteria of a good evaluation tool. A tool is objective if it makes for the elimination of the scorer's personal opinion *i.e.* bias or judgement. It is an honest opinion based on facts, evidences, without influence of extraneous considerations, the evaluator's personal judgement may also be accepted.

A tool is objective, if it gives the same score even when different scorers score the item. Thus, objectivity in scoring may be considered as consistency, in scoring by different scorers.

Types of Tools

According to **J C Agrawal**, who has authored many books on education and research, the tools of research has been classified into following types:

Different types of tools are

(i) Inquiry forms
- Rating scale
- Questionnaire
- Attitude scale

(ii) Psychological tests and inventories
- Achievement test
- Aptitude test
- Inventory

Inquiry Forms

It is one of the most important tool of data collection that seeks to extract information and a price of knowledge from the targeted audience. Various types of inquiry forms are administered for assessing people's opinion, attitude, belief and other dimensions of question.

It includes

Rating Scale

It refers to a scale, with a set of points that describe varying degrees of the dimension of attribute, being observed.

Classification of Rating Scale

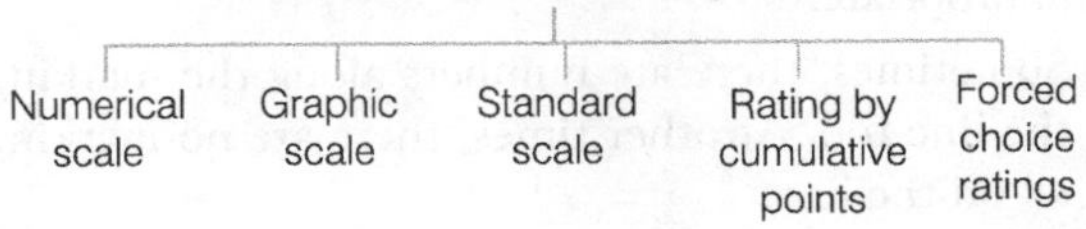

It is a set of categories, designed to elicit information about a quantitative or a qualitative attribute. In social science, common examples are **Likert scale** and **1-10 rating scale,** in which a person select the number, which is considered to reflect the perceived quality of a product.

Thus, rating scale is a method that requires to assign a value, sometimes numeric to the rated object as a measure of some rated attribute.

It is broadly classified into five categories and they are

(i) **Numerical Scale** In a numerical scale, a sequence of definite numbers is supplied to the rater or to the observer. The observer assigns to each stimulus to be rated, an appropriate number in line with those definitions or descriptions.

The following scales may be used in obtaining ratings of the affective values of colours on a point scale, which may consists of different points.

Point Scale	Rating
Most pleasant	9
Extremely pleasant	8
Moderately pleasant	7
Mildly pleasant	6
Indifferent	5
Mildly unpleasant	4
Moderately unpleasant	3
Extremely unpleasant	2
Most unpleasant	1

Instead of **9** point scale, we can draw **3** point, **5** point or **7** point scales too. It is always useful to have an odd number of points in a scale line like 3, 5 and 7, so that there could be a middle point *i.e.* a favourable one and an unfavourable one. This scale is easiest to construct and to apply. They are also the simplest in terms of handling the results.

(ii) **Graphic Scale** It is the most popular and widely used type of rating scale. In this scale, a straight line is shown vertically or horizontally with various clues to help the rater. The line is either segmented into units or is continuous. If the line is segmented, the number of segments can vary from case to case.

It is also known as 'continuous rating scale'. The ends of the continuous are sometimes labelled with opposite values. Respondents are required to make a mark, at any point on the scale that they find appropriate.

Sometimes, there are numbers along the markings of the line too. At other times, there are no markings at all on the line.

(iii) **Standard Scale** In standard scale, a set of standards is presented to the rater. Usually, the standards are objects of the same kind, to be rated with pre-established scale values. This type of scale is like that of the scale for judging the quality of hand writing. The scale of hand writing provides several standard specimens that have previously been spread over on a common scale, by some standardised procedure, like equal appearing intervals.

The 'man-to-man' scale and the 'portrait matching' scale are the other two forms that conform more or less to the principles of standard scales.

(iv) **Rating by Cumulative Points** The unique and distinctive feature of rating by cumulative points is its immense and easily utility of scoring. The rating score for an attribute, object or individual is the sum or average of the weighted or unweighted points. The 'checklist method' and the 'guess', technique belongs to this category of rating.

(v) **Forced Choice Ratings** They are those ratings, which are biased or influenced by some external factors.

Advantages of Rating Scale

- Rating scales are less time consuming to develop.
- It can be used with a large number of stimuli.
- They also allow for quantitative comparison.
- Rating scale is quite interesting to the raters, especially if graphic methods are used.
- Best rating can be obtained by presenting one stimulus to a rater at a time.
- Rating can be used with ratees who have very little training for the purpose.
- Rating scales have much wider range of application and can be used for teacher ratings, personality ratings, school appraisal, sociological survey, etc.

Disadvantages of Rating Scale

Limited Reliability Rating scale method has limited reliability.

Ease of Use Rating scale can be used by unqualified users.

Sophisticated Treatment Planning Rating scale is not suitable for sophisticated treatment planning.

Error of Central Tendency Most of the raters hesitate to rate the individuals on the extremes of the scale, instead they tend to rate the individual on the middle of the scale. Hence, the results get distorted.

Substantial Variations Rating scale may be substantial variations among informants.

Halo Effect It is an error, which obscures the clusters of traits within an individual. The raters form a general opinion about the person's merit and his ratings on specific traits are greatly influenced by this general impression.

Contrast Error It is due to a tendency of a rater to rate others in the opposite direction (contrasting) from himself in a trait.

Questionnaire

A questionnaire is a research instrument consisting of a series of questions and other prompts for the purpose of gathering information from respondents. Although, they are often designed for statistical analysis of the responses, this is not always the case. The questionnaire was invented by **Sir Francis Galton**.

It is a self-report data collection instrument that each research's participant fills out as part of a research study. Researchers use questionnaire to obtain information about the thoughts, feelings, attitudes, beliefs, values, perceptions, personality and behavioural intentions of research participants.

According to **John W. Best**, "a questionnaire is used when factual information is desired, when opinion rather than facts are desired and an opinionnaire or attitude scale is used".

They have advantages over some other types of surveys in that they are cheap, do not require as much efforts from the questioner as verbal or telephone surveys and often have standardised answers that make it simple to compile data.

Basic rules for preparation of questionnaire are:

- Use statements which are interpreted in the same way by members of different sub-populations of the population of interest.
- Use statements where persons that have different opinions or traits will give different answers.
- Think of having an open answer category, after a list of possible answers.
- Use only one aspect of the construct you are interested in per item.
- Use positive statements and avoid negatives or double negatives.
- Do not make assumptions about the respondent.
- Use clear and comprehensible wording, easily understandable for all educational levels.
- Use correct spelling, grammar and punctuation.
- Avoid items that contain more than one question per item (*e.g.* Do you like apples and tomato?).

Types of Questionnaire

Questionnaire means a set of questions prepared for drawing the responses from the subjects for research work. Every researcher uses this technique in their survey research. Researchers have classified questionnaire into the following groups:

According to **P V Young**, *questionnaire is of two types and they are :*

- Structured questionnaire
- Non-structured questionnaire

(i) **Structured Questionnaire** In structured questionnaire, definite concrete and pre-ordinated questions are used for two purposes.

They are :

Accurate Communication It is justified when the respondents understand the survey objectives.

Accurate Response It is obtained when the replies contain the information sought and at the same time fulfil the demands of tabulation plans and analytical programmes.

(ii) **Non-Structured Questionnaire** It is known as interview guide. It contains definite subject matter areas. The interviewer is free to arrange the form and timing of enquiry.

Advantages of Questionnaire

Giving Way to Put Forward The questionnaire as a tool of educational research has a great importance in its form. It helps the researcher to put forward his project.

Summarising A questionnaire summarises the ideas of the respondent.

Written Form Questionnaire in written form will enable the researcher to get more responses. Because the respondent feels more free while expressing his views regarding a question in written form.

Helps in Collecting Information Sometimes, the researchers are unable to move the geographical areas, on which they have taken their study. Thus, this helps them to collect information.

Less Pressure on the Subject to Respond A questionnaire places less pressure on the subjects to respond immediately. It gives a lot of time to fill it up. Before filling up the questions, he thinks more about the suitable answer of the question.

To the Point Answers Questionnaire does not require the unnecessary materials. What actually, the question wants the respondent answers to the point only.

Helps in Minimising the Expenses Questionnaires help in minimising the expenses, both in terms of money and effort. Whenever the researcher is enable to go to collect information of a school, he collects information through his mates and also teachers concerned of the particular school.

Validity of the Project Information collected in a lot will give a greater validity of the project.

Disadvantages of Questionnaire

Rigid and Complicated Questionnaire A rigid and complicated questionnaire does not draw accurate responses from the subject.

Without Holding True Answer Sometimes, respondents do not give true answer of their questions. Some respondents play mischievous with the researcher.

Confusion About Actual Meaning Some subjects are confused to understand the actual meaning of the questions.

Lost Mail A questionnaire sent by mail is sometimes not found.

Incomplete Answers Sometimes, the respondents give incomplete answers. This makes the researcher confused in drawing the accurate answers.

Not a Matter of Interest Many times, the questionnaire sent to the subjects are neglected and overlooked due to lack of interest. Even after a few nudges, the subject may not reveal true answers.

Attitude Scale

It is a form of appraisal procedure, which is designed to measure attitude of a subject of group of a subjects towards issues, institutions and group of people.

Attitude is a special type of questionnaire, designed to produce scores, indicating the intensity and direction of a person's feeling or opinion about an object or event. This scale provides a quantitative measurement of attitudes, opinions or values by summarising numerical scores given by researchers to people's responses to a set of statements exploring dimensions of an underlying theme.

The term attitude is defined in many ways. But, all definitions conclude it as an established way of thinking or feeling reflected in a person's behaviour towards others. Sometimes, opinion and attitude are used in a synonymous manner, but there is a thin line of difference between the two. An opinion may not lead to a kind of activity in a particular direction. But, attitude compels one to act favourably or unfavourably, depending upon the perception.

The most common types of attitude scales are discussed below:

(i) **Likert Scale** It is a psychometric response scale, primarily used in questionnaires to obtain participant's preferences in terms of degree of agreement to a statement or set of statements.

Variations are most commonly seen as a 5 point scale ranging from 'strongly disagree' on one end to 'strongly agree' on the other with 'neither agree nor disagree' in the middle. However, some practitioners advocate the use of 7 and 9 point scales, which add additional granularity. Sometimes, a 4 point scale (or other even-numbered) is used to produce an **ipsative** (forced choice) measure, where no indifferent option is available. Each level on the scale is assigned a numeric value or coding, usually starting at 1 and incremented by one for each level.

For example:

①	②	③	④	⑤
Strongly agree	Agree	Neither	Disagree	Strongly disagree

Sample Scale Used in Likert Scale Questions

(ii) **Guttman Scale** It is based on the idea that items can be arranged along a continum in such a way that a person, who agrees with an item or finds an item acceptable will also agree with or finds acceptable all other items, expressing a less extreme position. This scale presents a number of items to which the person is supposed to either agree or disagree, which is typically done in a 'Yes/No' dichotomous format.

(iii) **Thurstone Scale** It is also known as equal appearing interval scale. It is used to measure the attitude towards a given concept or construct. For this, a large number of statements are collected that relate to the construct in consideration. The judges rate these statements, along on 11 category scale, in which each of the categories have fixed level of propensenties towards the concept.

(iv) **Semantic Differential Scale** This method requires respondents to choose in the questionnaire between two opposite positions, using qualifies to bridge gap between them. One must decide the two extremely opposite terms, related to a particular dimension and create a rating sheet.

It measures an individual's reaction to stimulus words and concepts in terms of ratings on bi-polar adjectives at each end.

For example, enjoyable and unenjoyable, funny and not funny, relatable and non-relatable, etc.

A typical question with semantic differential scale would be as follows :

	Very much	Some what	Neither	Some what	Very much	
Enjoyable		×				Unenjoyable
Funny			×			Not funny
Relatable					×	Unrelatable

Advantages of Attitude Scale

- An attitude is a learned tendency, so it can be learnt.
- It is a point or object of reference.
- It includes certain aspects of personality as interests, appreciations and social conduct.

Disadvantages of Attitude Scale

- Attitude is a complex affair which can't be wholly described by any single numerical complex.
- Attitude is subject to change. So what is measured today about a student's attitude may not indicate his future attitude towards the subject or occupation.
- Students sometimes give vague responses to items on an attitude scale. It is not always and in all cases possible to get real attitude of a student.

- Generally, pupils or students are trained to give tick marks on the middle of the scale. So their responses don't reveal the true dimension of their attitudes.
- Discrepancy is noticed in student's expressed attitude and tested attitude. Hence tested attitude isn't always dependable.

Psychological Tests and Inventories

Achievement Test

These tests attempt to measure the present level of performance of a group or an individual. It is commonly used in schools and colleges. They are helpful in determining individual or group status in academic learning. Also, they are used in diagnosing strengths and weaknesses and as a basis of awarding degrees, prizes or scholarships.

Advantages of Achievement Tests

- Achievement tests allow for data to be collected about student achievement and learning that helps to inform educators, curriculum planners and the state officials who can help to determine the budget for a school.
- It also helps to point out instructional leaders who are falling short of their duties and whose standards are performing below standards.
- These tests are non-discriminatory because the content evaluated on the tests has been presented to all students. It helps to create educational equity in the schools.

Disadvantages of Achievement Test

- Tests do not help student achievement in any meaningful way and the increase in positive scores that are seen on the test is merely a reflection of curriculum that is designed to help students score high but perhaps less quantifiable learning that should be taking place in the classroom.
- Students lack critical thinking skills and due to these tests they are being focussed predominantly on rote memorisation.
- These tests are not indicative of strong instructional leadership in the classroom nor an academically rigorous classroom. Critics also held that these tests posed challenges for children with learning disabilities whom the stress of test or structure of questions may affect negatively.

Aptitude Tests

These tests attempt to predict the capacities or the degree of achievement that may be expected from a group or an individual in a particular activity. Like achievement tests, they also measure past learning. They attempt to predict group or individual's capacity to acquire improved performance with additional training. It helps to check one's knowledge and filters the good candidates. The ability of creativity and intelligence is proved by the aptitude test.

Advantages of Aptitude Test

- Aptitude tests attempt to predict the capacities or the degree of achievement that may be expected from individuals in a particular activity.
- Aptitude is a means by which one can find the relative knowledge of a person in terms of his intelligence and also his knowledge in general.
- They are excellent predictors of future scholastic achievement. They provide ways for comparison of a child's performance with other in a same situation. They provide a profile of strength and weaknesses. They asses difference among individuals.
- Aptitude tests are valuable in making programme and curricula decisions.

Disadvantages of Aptitude Test

- The physical, social and emotional environment of the pupil is often different from the actual environment in the job or in college. This reduces the predictive value of aptitude test.
- An aptitude test gives us a prediction of the probability only. There is never any certainty that predictions will always come true. It is noticed that brilliant students sometimes fail to top the list while an average student who was initially not doing well may top the list.

Inventory

It is a list, record or catalogue containing list of traits, preferences, attitudes, interests or abilities, used to evaluate personal characteristics or skills. The purpose of inventory is to list a specific trait, activity or programme and to check to what extent the presence of that ability.

There are two types of inventories and they are

(i) **Interest Inventory** They attempt to yield the measure of the types of activities that an individual has a tendency to like or choose. They are self-report instruments, in which the individuals note their own likes and dislikes. They are the standardised interviews, in which the subject gives an introspective report of his/her feelings about certain situation and phenomena, which is then interpreted in terms of interests. The use of interest inventories is most frequent in the areas of educational, vocational guidance, and case studies.

(ii) **Personality Inventory** These are the self-report instruments. These instruments yield scores that are assumed or have been shown to measure certain personality traits or tendencies.

Techniques of Research

Observation

The cause effect relationship and study of event in original is known as **observation**. According to **C A Mourse**, "Observation employs relatively more visual senses than audio or video organs". In this method of data collection, it involves something that we do most of our working hours i.e. observe things. Researchers are also observers of things in the world.

Classification of Observation

- **On the Basis of Form of Observation**
  - Formal observation
  - Informal observation
- **On the Basis of Control of Observation**
  - Controlled observation
  - Uncontrolled observation
- **On the Basis of Planning of Observation**
  - Planned observation
  - Unplanned observation
- **On the Basis of Direction of Observation**
  - Direct observation
  - Indirect observation
- **On the Basis of Information of Observation**
  - Qualitative observation
  - Quantitative observation
  - Qualitative and quantitative observation
- **On the Basis of Interview's Observation**
  - Individual observation
  - Group observation
- **On the Basis of Person's Observation**
  - Self-observation
  - Outsiders observation

In research, observation is defined as the watching of behavioural patterns of people in certain situations to obtain information about the phenomenon of interest. It is an important way of collecting information about people because people do not always do what they say they do. It is a maxim in the social and behavioural sciences that attitudes and behaviour are not always congruent.

Modes of Collecting Observational Data

Modes of collecting observational data are

(i) **Laboratory Observation** It is carried out in settings that are setup by the researcher and inside the confines of a research lab. An example would be a researcher observing the behaviour of children through a one way window in the researcher's laboratory.

(ii) **Naturalistic Oobservation** It is carried out in the real world. Observing the behaviour of children in their classrooms is an example of naturalistic observation.

(iii) **Quantitative Observation** Quantitative or structured observation involves the standardisation of all observational procedures in order to obtain reliable research data.

It often involves the standardisation of each of the following

Who is observed? (*e.g.* What kinds of people are to be studied, such as teachers or students).

What is observed? (What variables are to be observed by the researcher, such as time on tasks or out of seat behaviour).

When the observations are to be take place? (during morning hour or during break time).

Where the observations are to be carried out? (In the laboratory, in the classroom, in the lunchroom, in the library or on the playground).

How the observations are to be done? Usually, quantitative observation results in quantitative data, such a counts or frequencies and percentages. It might also involves observational sampling techniques. One technique is called **time interval sampling,** which involves checking for events during time interval, specified in advance of the actual data collection.

Another technique is called **event sampling,** which involves making observations only after a specific event has occurred.

(iv) **Qualitative Observation** It involves observing all relevant phenomenas and taking extensive field notes without specifying in advance, exactly what is to be observed.

Usually, it is done for exploratory purposes. It is usually done in natural setting. It is usually carried out by qualitative researchers.

The four main roles that a researcher can take during qualitative observation are as follows

(i) **Complete Participant Observer** Essentially, the observer takes on the role of an insider, becoming a member of the group being studied and spending a great deal of time with the group and does not tell members they are being studied.

(ii) **Participant as Observer** Researcher spends extended time with the group as an insider and tells members they are being studied.

(iii) **Observer as Participant** Researcher spends limited amount of time observing group members and tells members they are being studied.

(iv) **Complete Observer** Researcher observers as an outsider and does not tell the people they are being observed.

Features of Observation

- In an accurate sense, observation involves the use of the eyes rather than the use of the ears and the voice. An experienced worker never believes in hear say. He only trusts if he has observed that with his own eyes.
- Observations which act on scientific grounds are brought in use by the scientists or the researchers with some or the other aim to achieve something. Such scientists make their observations in a very minute and a detailed manner, which helps them in achieving specific goals.
- The value of an observation in an operation is only if it is done properly in a planned manner, but if it is done in a careless sense then the chance of making such an observation again may come or not. Hence, observation should be carried out in a very phased and a planned manner in order to get indepth understanding of an activity.
- Observation should be based on standardised tools of research, which makes an observation exact in its nature of working.
- Observation is a very vital scientific method that helps a lot in the collection of the primary information that is reliable in nature, in which direct study of the situation is involved.
- Observation is a scientific method, in which we make hypothesis of explain observation.
- The various operations that we perform and the results that we obtain should be rememberd, but a known fact is that memory is very deceptive in nature. With the passage of time, things tend to get out of mind, so it is very important to keep a record of such activities.
- Sense organs have a very critical role to play in observation process. During the observation, researcher or an investigator has to use his sense organs for seeing and hearing things and then has to keep in mind the whole set of observations for an indepth analysis of the matter later on.

Advantages of Observation

- Personality is better assessed by observation of behaviour, than by reporting which may hide facts.
- The tool does not need any communication medium. Thus, it can be used for collecting data regarding infants and illiterates or people who don't understand the observer's language.
- The main strength of observation is that it provides direct access to the social phenomena, under consideration.
- Observation can take diverse forms, from informal and unstructured approaches through to tightly structured and standardised procedures and can yield associated diverse types of data, both qualitative and quantitative observation, therefore, it is applicable in a wide range of contexts.
- All observations entail some form of recording means is that it provides a permanent record of such events or behaviour, thus, allowing further analysis or subsequent comparisons across time or location to be carried out.
- The behaviour can be observed in natural setting and hence, the inferences can have applicability to ordinary life situations as well. This is called 'external validity' i.e. applicability beyond the observed situation.
- Using more than one technique of data collection through a process of triangulation is seen as highly desirable as an over arching research strategy. Therefore, another strength of observation is that it can effectively complement other approaches and thus, enhance the quality of evidence available to the researcher.

Disadvantages of Observation

- One of the main disadvantage of observation is that it can be very much time consuming and resource intensive. It may be a very desirable strategy to explore certain research questions, but it may simply not be feasible for the researcher with limited time and resources to carry out the observation and therefore, alternative strategies would have to be pursued.
- Covert behaviour and traits cannot be observed.
- The behaviour of grown up adult people turns artificial, when they become conscious of the observe.
- Even though, the inferences have applicability to ordinary life situation, still the internal validity of the inferences may be low in uncontrolled situations and natural setting without any experimental controls as the data collected may not be really reliable and valid. The observation may get prejudiced and coloured by the subjectivity or feelings of the observer and suffer in reliability.

- Another potential weakness of observation is the so called **observer effect**, which refers to the way in which the presence of an observer in some way influences the behaviour of those being observed. In order to avoid or minimise this, methods of observation sometimes attempt to be as unobtrusive as possible.
- A fundamental potential weakness of all observation is that it is susceptible to observer bias, subjective bias on the part of the observer, thus, undermining the reliability and hence, the validity of the data gathered. This can be because the observer records not what actually happened, but what they either wanted to see, expected to see or merely thought they saw.

Types of Observations

- Structured to unstructured
- Disguised or undisguised
- Natural or contrived
- Non-participant to participant
- Personal
- Mechanical

Sometimes, observation process is treated casually, but is a method that needs to be treated as rigorously as any others.

Observation should includes:

- planning
- reflecting
- survey design
- recording
- authenticating

Interview

It is one-to-one direct communication between researcher and subject for collection of data. It is a series of questions to be asked in an interview. It is a great process for generating information on a number of questions or issues at once. It balances participation and requires an active involvement and critical thinking skills.

The interview design works well with a group of 12 or more people and requires time between 75 to 90 minutes. This is a multi-step process, where each participant first collects information (ideas, opinions or experiences related to the topic) through interviewing at least four other participants. Interview questions should be generated in advance. Persons with like questions are then grouped for the purpose of analysing the responses in depth. In the final step, each group depicts their response in the form of a graphic display that is shared with the whole group in debriefing the group process.

Types of Interviews

According to ***Goode and Hatt*** *various types of interviews are as*

Clinical Interview In clinical work, social workers and psychiatrists use interview to secure information about an individual's problem his past history, job or family adjustment. In such situations, the major purpose of interview are diagnosis and treatment. This type of interview is called clinical interview.

Research Interview The investigator attempts to collect relative information for solving his problem of historical, experimental, surveys or clinical type.

Group Interview A group interview is one which consists of some sociable, intellectual and educated persons from whom effective information can be collected.

Direct Interview It is a structured interview. It is a set of closed type questions is prepared for the purpose.

Non-Directive Interview It includes the questions of the open end form and the researcher talks freely about the problem under study.

Focused Interview It aims at active responses from the respondents on a specific events.

Generally, **Goode** and **Hatt** point out the interview conducted by a researcher may be of different in its structure, but its sole aim is to collect information from the respondents for the project taken for study.

Advantages of Interview

An interview is a conversation between two or more people, when questions are asked by the interviewer to elicit facts or statements from the interviewer. Although, interview is a standard part of journalism and media reporting, the focus of this piece is on how interviews can be used as a tool of psychological research.

Interview can be used as a tool in psychological research in following ways:

- In a questionnaire, only the answer to the question is required. Sometimes, the respondent is unable to answer due to problem in understanding the matter. But, in interview, if the respondent is not able to answer a particular question, the researcher also asks other questions, relating to the asked question for its answer. Thus, through interview he gets more response.
- An interviewer can try his best to establish good rapport with the interviewer.
- An interview can be used to collect facts. *e.g.* information about people's place of work, age, etc, but such questions are usually not more than opening items, which precede the main substance.
- The bulk of interview questions seeks to elicit information about attitudes and opinions and perspectives and meanings, the very stuff of much of both psychology and sociology.
- Interviews are available in a range of style.
- There is a half-way house, where the researcher designs a set of key questions to be raised before the interview takes place, but builds in considerable flexibility about how and when these issues are raised and allows for a considerable amount of additional topics to be built in response to the dynamics of conversational exchange.

Disadvantages of Interview

- Hesitation to express.
- Vague and unclear questions.
- Time restrictions.
- Less time for thinking.
- Subjective in nature.
- Researcher's influence necessary.
- Consciousness required.
- Manipulated/socially accepted responses may be preferred.
- Psychological, social and educational hindrances.
- More expense in time and money.
- Requires high level of expertise.

Conducting of an Interview

- Interview schedule should be as per objectives.
- Planning of time duration, place and mode of recording.
- Follow formalities.
- Use of an appropriate language.
- Positive body language.
- Directing the interview.
- Questioning proper stress and tone and use of sub-questions if required.
- Researcher must be sociable and also should be faithful to the respondents. So, the respondents can express their answers more clearly and freely.
- Listen to the opinions of the subject patiently.
- Questions prepared for the hypothesis must be clear in its meaning.
- No irrelevant conversation should be organised at the time of interview.

Usage of Forms of Interview

A great deal of qualitative material comes from talking with people whether it be through formal interviews or causal conversation. If interviews are going to tap into depths of reality of the situation and discover subjects's meanings and understandings, it is essential for the researcher to develop empathy with interviewees and win their confidence to be unobtrusive, in order not to impose one's own influence on the interviewee.

The best technique for this is the **unstructured interview**. Here, the researcher has some general ideas about the topics of the interview and may have an aid memory of points that might arise in discussion for use as prompts, if necessary. But, the hope is that those points will come up in the natural course of the discussion as the interviewee talks.

As with observation, it may be that the researcher begins with a more focused study and wishes to know certain things. In these cases, a **structured interview** might be more appropriate. Here, the researcher decides the structure of the interview and sets out with pre-determined questions.

These tests are the useful and most frequently employed tools of educational research. They are used to describe and measure a sample of certain aspects of human behaviour or inner qualities. They provide the data for most experimental and descriptive studies of education. They yield objectives and standardised descriptions of some psychological aspects of an individual's personality and translate them in quantitative terms. There are various kinds of psychological tests.

Projective Techniques

This technique of data collection has been developed by the psychologists to use projections of respondents for inferring about underlying motives, urges or intentions, which are such that the respondent either resist to reveal them or is unable to figure out himself. In projective techniques, the respondent in supplying information tend unconsciously to project his/her own attitude or feelings on the subject under study.

Projective techniques play a significant role in motivational researchers or in attitude surveys. The use of these techniques require intensive specialised training. In such techniques, the individual's responses to the stimulus situation are not taken at their face value. The stimuli may arouse different kinds of reactions. The nature of the stimuli and the way they are presented under these techniques do not clearly show the way in which the responses is to be interpreted. The stimulus may be a photograph, a picture, an inkblot and so on. Responses to these stimuli are interpreted as indicating the individual's own view, his personality structure, needs, tensions, etc, in the context of some pre-established psychological conceptualisation of what the individual's response to the stimulus mean. Projective techniques may be used in qualitative as well as quantitative techniques and they are useful in both.

The **Oxford University Press Dictionary of Psychology** (Colman, 2001) defines projective techniques as "Any of a variety of personality test in which the respondents give free responses to a series of stimuli, such as an inkblots, pictures or an incomplete sentence. Such tests are based on the psychoanalytic concept of projection,the assumption being that the respondents project unconscious aspect of their personality into the test items and reveal them in their responses".

The use of projective device is particularly helpful in counteracting the tendency of subject to try to appear in their best light, to respond as the believe they should.

The projections may be accomplished through a number of techniques such as

Association The respondent is asked to indicate what he/she feels or thinks when presented with a picture, carbon, inkblot, word or phrases. The thematic apperception test, the Rorschach's inkblot test and various word association tests.

Completion The respondent is asked to complete an incomplete sentence or task.

A sentence completion instrument may include following items:

- My greatest ambition is
- My greatest fear is
- I mostly enjoy
- I dream a greatful deal about
- I get angry when
- If I could do anything I wanted it would be to

Role Playing Here, the subjects are asked to improvise or act out a situation in which they have been assigned various roles. The researcher may observe such traits as hostility, frustration, dominance, sympathy, insecurity, prejudice or the absence of such traits.

Creative or Constructive Permitting subjects to model clay, figure paint, play with dolls, play with toys or draw or write imaginative stories about assigned situations may be revealing. The choice of colour, form, words, the sense of orderliness, evidence of tensions and other reactions may provide opportunities to infer deep seated feelings.

Universe

The universe consist of all survey elements that qualify for inclusion in the research study. The precise definition of the universe for a particular study is set by the research question. The universe may be individuals, group of people, organisations or even objects. The population or universe represents the entire group of units. Universe is the set of all experimental units from which a sample is to be drawn. From a statistical point of view, the term 'Universe' refers to the total of the items or units in any field of inquiry. Universe can be finite or infinite. It is said to be finite if it consists of a fixed number of elements so that it is possible to enumerate it in its totality. Whereas in infinite aspect is theoretically impossible to observe all the elements. We cannot have any idea about the total number of items.

Sample

The representative proportion of the population is called a **sample**. To obtain a representative sample, the researcher selects each unit in a specified way under controlled conditions.

Usually, four steps are involved in the process

- Defining the population
- Listing the population
- Selecting a representative sample
- Obtaining an adequate sample

After defining a population and listing all the units, a researcher selects a sample of units from the sampling frame. The process of such a selection is called **sampling**. In order to serve a useful purpose, sampling should be unbiased or representative.

A good sample must be as nearly representative to the entire population as possible and ideally, it must provide the whole of the information about the population from which of the sample has been drawn.

The logic of the theory of sampling is the theory of induction, that is we proceed from particular, to general and all the results are expressed in terms of probability.

Garrett (1962) has pointed out that if the size of the sample is less than 25, there is often little reason for believing such a small group of units to be adequately descriptive of any population. If a greater precision of results in an investigation is needed, the sample should be larger. Greater precision is sometimes needed when one is dealing in areas where differences are likely to be small. The adequacy of the sample depends upon our knowledge of the population as well as upon the method used in drawing the sample.

A true representative sample can exactly be defined by the researcher through given steps

- Listing the population with comprehensive and accurate list.
- Selecting a representative sample by pairing a list and sample is selected from the frame.
- Obtaining an adequate sample, which depends upon the method used in drawing the sample.

Characteristics of Good Sample

- The sample must be representative of the population.
- The sample size must be selected, depending upon the research objectives.
- Sample should be flexible, so that it can be modified depending upon the prevailing circumstances.
- Sample should reflect all the members of the population of data.

- Sample should be large enough to give sufficient precision.
- Sample should be unbiased by the sampling procedure or equipment.
- Sample should be choosen in a systematically random way so that chance or the operation of probability is utilised.

Techniques of Sampling

Techniques of sampling are given below

Probability Sampling

In probability sampling, the units of the population are not selected at the discretion of the researcher, but by the means of certain procedures, which ensure that every unit of a population has one fixed probability of being included in the sample. This method is also called as **random sampling.**

Randomisation has two important applications in research, which are as follows

- Selecting a group of individuals for observation, who are representative of the population about which the researcher wishes to generalise.
- Equating experimental and control groups in an experiment. Assigning individuals by random assignment (each individual in the sample has an equal and independent chance of being assigned to each of the groups) is the best method of providing for their equivalence.

Characteristics of Probability Sampling

*According to **Good** (1966), probability sample have the following characteristics*

- Each unit in the sample has some known probability of entering the sample.
- Weights appropriate to the probabilities are used in the analysis of the sample.
- The process of sampling is automatic in one or more steps of selection of units in the sample.

Advantages of Probability Sampling

- It helps the researcher to know the size of the sample needed to achieve any desired level of accuracy.
- The researchers also may be able to specify the chance of each unit being selected.
- This method also helps to estimate the magnitude of error due to sampling.

Disadvantages of Probability Sampling

- It depends upon how good a sampling frame is made, although this remains a limitation in complete enumeration studies.
- In this process, only a portion of the sampling frame is examined and so specific information on every sampling unit (people, account, inventory, etc) are ignored.
- In small areas or rare sub-population, sampling error may be high.
- Representative of the frame may be questionable and controversial.

Types of Probability Sampling

There are different methods of selecting a probability sample, which have their own advantages and limitations.

Types of probability samplings are as follows

(i) **Simple or Unrestricted Random Sampling** In simple or unrestricted random sampling, each unit of the population is given an equal chance of being selected. The selection of units from the population is done in such a manner that every unit in the population has an equal chance of being choosen and the selection of anyone. Unit is in no way tied to the selection of any other. The law of chance is allowed to operate freely in the selection of such a sample and carefully controlled conditions are created to ensure that each unit in the population has an equal chance of being included in the sample.

Several devices are used here to draw samples from population:

Lottery Method In this case, researcher will use a set of N tickets, if there are N units in the population, with numbers I to N written on the tickets. The tickets will be thoroughly mixed up and then N tickets will be drawn one by one, if the sample of size N is required. The units which have the serial numbers occurring on these N tickets will be considered as selected.

Use of Random Table In this, consecutive numbers are assigned to the units of the population, the investigator starts at any point on the table of random numbers and consecutive numbers in any direction. Researcher reads the number on the table and picks up that very number of unit one by one and in this way, the required number of units are selected.

(ii) **Stratified Random Sampling** This method is used to overcome the four problems related to simple random sampling. Here, the researcher first divide his whole population into different strata on the basis of certain characteristics and random sample is drawn from each stratum.

Such stratification of the population makes different small homogenous groups of the population and simple random sampling technique can be applied to each group to select required number of sample.

A population can be stratified on many grounds, such as age, sex, grade, economic condition, place of residing, occupation, caste, etc. The efficiency of stratified random sample depends on the allocation of sample size to strata. Percentage Method is the best method of allocating sample size among strata.

Stratified random sampling ensures that specific groups are represented, even proportionally, in the sample(s) (*e.g.* by gender), by selecting individuals from strata test.

(iii) **Systematic Sampling** When a frame of a population is available or when a population can be accurately listed and is finite, a method of systematic selection will provide a sample which approximates a random sample. Here, all the units of the population are listed in an alphabetical order first. Then if 100 units, out of 1000 units of a population has to be selected, one may keep interval of 10 units of a population, throughout the population.

(iv) **Cluster Sampling** This is a variation of simple random sampling.

This method is used when

- population is infinite.
- list of all units of population is not available.
- population is scattered over a wide geographical area.
- individuals have to be studied as a group.

In this method, different clusters of whole population are formed due to large area of the population. That is why, it is also called area sampling. The individuals in these clusters have almost all the same characteristics of their respective groups. The final result is generalised to the whole state.

(v) **Multi-Stage Sampling** This is used in large scale surveys for making the study more comprehensive. Sampling here is done in two, three or four stages. Multi-stage sampling is comparatively convenient, less time consuming and less expensive method of sampling. However, an element of sample bias gets introduced because of the unequal size of some of the selected sub-samples. This method is recommended only when it would be impracticable to draw random sample.

Non-Probability Sampling

In non-probability sampling, the units are selected at the discretion of the researcher. Such samples use human judgement in selecting units and have no theoretical basis for estimating population characteristics. While selecting the sample, the researcher only thinks where he will get the required data to serve his purpose. That is why, it is also called **purposive sample**.

The non-probability sampling methods are very convenient in the situations, when the sample to be selected is very small and the researcher wants to get some idea of the population characteristics in a short time.

Such samples are used in the situations, where the researcher does not want a representative sample, but to gain insight into the problem by selecting only informed person, who can provide him the maximum degree of insight into his problem with comprehensive information.

Types of Non-Probability Samplings

Types of non-probability samples are as follows

Quota or Chunk Sample In this method, quota of sample from different units of the population is fixed and thus, total sample is selected.

Incidental/Volunteer/Convenient Sampling In this method, whosoever is available to cooperate for providing information is selected and thus, the required number of sample is obtained.

Snowball Sampling It is used to find subjects of interest from those, who are most likely to be able to identify them. In this technique, the researcher uses few subjects to identify the other individuals who might be appropriate for the study. This continues with the new subjects, until the researcher has a sufficient sample size.

Advantages of Non-Probability Sampling

- They are quicker, cost effective and more convenient than probability samples.
- Non-probability samples do not require a sampling frame.
- The sample size and quota requirements are usually achieved.

Disadvantages of Non-Probability Sampling

- Less confidence is placed in the data obtained from samples and thus, results obtained cannot be generalised for the entire population.
- Sampling based on convenience affects the variance within groups as well as between groups.
- Sampling errors of these samples cannot be determined.
- They depend exclusively on uncontrolled factors and researcher's insight and there is no statistical method to determine the margin of sampling errors.
- Sometimes, such samples are based on absolute frame, which does not adequately cover the population.
- There is considerable scope for bias in the selection of units to be included in the sample.

Research Proposal

According to **Koul**, "The research proposal is a systematic plan, which brings to focus the preliminary planning that will be needed to accomplish the purpose of the proposed study".

The preparation of a research proposal is an important step in the process of research. There is no universally accepted format for preparing research proposal. Most of the institutions and funding agencies require the researcher to submit their research proposal as per the specific format of that agency.

Before submitting a proposal for funding, follow the particular format that is specified by the funding agencies. However, almost all the formats ask for certain specifications of the plan to appear in research proposal. These specifications provide sufficient information about the researcher's planning and for evaluation of the research proposal. There are certain specifications, which are common to all type of research proposal and are included in all types of format.

Steps for Writing Research Proposal

A research proposal should be framed on the basis of the following steps/guidelines

Title of the Project

The title of the research proposal is just the name of the topic and suggest the theme of the work to be done. While selecting the title of the project, the researcher should take care that instead of using flowery words, professional language and terms should be used in an easy and understandable manner. Also the title should be brief, concise and specific. Specific in the sense that it should claim for the study what it going to actually deliver. Thus, a good title is that which provides sufficient information about the nature of the proposed project.

The Statement of the Problem

The statement of the problem may be presented either as declarative statement or in question form. This attempt to focus on a stated goal, gives direction to the research process. It must be limited enough in scope to make a definite conclusion possible. The major statement may be followed by minor statement. A problem suggests a specific answer or conclusion. Usually, a controversy or a difference of opinion exists. A cause and effect relationship may be suggested upon the basis of theory or previous research findings.

Personal observation and experience may be the basis of a problem. *Some examples of the problem statements are*

- Children who have kindergarten experience might demonstrate greater academic achievement in the first grade than those who have not had this experience.
- Knowledge of participation in an experiment may have a stimulating effect upon the reading achievement of the participants.
- The significance of the problem is important for both the researcher and the evaluator of research proposal. The researcher must show how his/her research work is going to contribute to the existing knowledge or influence the Educational Theory and/or practice. He/she must focus on the significance and relevance of his/her study. And in order to maintain the quality of educational research, the evaluator must critically examine the significance and relevance of the submitted proposal.

Assumptions, Limitations and Delimitations

The researcher should define all unusual terms that others could misinterpret. These definitions help to establish the frame of reference with which the researcher approaches the problem. The operational definitions of the variables should be given in research proposal. Such expressions as academic achievement and intelligence are useful concept, but they connot be used as criteria, unless they are defined as observable samples of behaviour or score on standardised intelligence test is an operational definition of intelligence.

Assumptions These are those statements, which are assumed to be the facts but can't be verified without testing. The researcher should give sufficient details and basis of these assumptions in his/her research proposal.

Limitations These are those conditions beyond the control of the researcher that may place restrictions on the conclusion of the study and their application to other situations. The limitations such as inability to select sample randomly or inability to use validated test for data collection should be properly reported in research proposal.

Delimitations These are the boundaries of the study. A study may focus on the achievement motivation in relation to the socio-economic status of the 9th grade students. Here, the conclusions can't be extended beyond this population sampled studied. We should give sufficient space to these various delimitations, also in our research proposal.

Review of Related Literature

The review of literature by any researcher shows how up to date he/she in the area of research. Any new research is built upon or adds to what is known up to that point of time. The review should provide evidence of the investigators knowledge of the field of investigation and also help him/her evolving new insight and build new approaches to the problem under investigation.

It is usual to review all relevant theories, writings and studies bearing on the theme depending upon the specific needs of the study. Only those studies that are plainly relevant, competently executed and clearly reported should be included.

The reviews must be classified in the most appropriate and meaningful form. The reviews should also point out the inadequacies in existing studies (methodological, conceptual, etc), research areas which have been left out, areas requiring cross cultural confirmation, studies which need updating, etc.

Hypothesis

Hypothesis is a tentative solution to our problem, which is tested on the basis of the analysis of the collected data. In research proposal, researcher should specify one major hypothesis and several minor hypothesis as the case and the need may be. Hypothesis are not just guess work rather depend upon logic and previous knowledge.

These give direction to data gathering and research process. The hypothesis should always be reasonable and consistent with previously known facts/theories. Also, we must state it in such a way that we can test it and find it to be either probably true or probably false. The formulation of the hypothesis in advance of the data gathering process is necessary for an unbiased investigation. It is not appropriate to formulate additional hypothesis after data are collected, but they should be tested on the basis of new data and not on the old data that suggested them.

Methods

In this part of the research proposal, we usually specify the nature of the subjects, selected through sampling procedures tools to be used and procedures and data analysis.

Subjects The subject section details the population from which the researcher plans to select the sample. The most frequently studied variables are the subjects, age, gender, race, caste, religion, socio-economic status, educational level, IQ, etc. In this section, we also have to describe the size of the sample (the number of the subjects to be studied) and the sampling procedures (how the sample will be selected from the population).

Tools The researcher in the research proposal, should fully describe the tool(s) to be used, the reliability and the validity of the tools(s) and the reason for the selection of that particular tool or tools for data collection. If the researcher is going to develop his/her own tool, then he should outline the procedure he is going to follow in test development and standardisation. So, the use of any reliable and valid tool is inevitable for the collection of evidence or data for the research study.

Procedures This section outlines the research plan. It describes in detail what will be done, how it will done, what data will be needed and what data gathering devices will be used. There is no single universal procedure which can be followed in all types of research studies, rather it highly depends on our particular research objectives. For example, the procedure of using mail questionnaire will be totally different from using interview technique or observation technique.

Data Analysis There are mainly two types of data *i.e.* qualitative and quantitative. Both the types of data are to be analysed differently. Mostly there are different types of statistical techniques to analyse these two different types of data. What particular is to be used and how the data are to be analysed, depend on our particular study.

If the data are to be processed through computer this should be explained in research proposal. We should completely describe our complete data analysis procedure in our proposal, so that the readers may get the clear idea of research plan.

Summary and Conclusion

This provide the reader a quick review of what has been done to obtain the results. It is the most utilised part of the report. This chapter usually commences with a re-statement of the problem and brief description of the procedures followed by the principal fundings which are presented as suggestions.

References/Bibliography

This provides information regarding the literature materials and the sources used for conducting the study. In our research proposal, we should list all the references that were cited in the text. We should cite in the research proposal, the material that have helped in the preparation of research proposal.

In this case, we should prepare and present bibliography in which all the relevant references, whether cited or not are included. This list to be prepared alphabetically and according to the set pattern of writing the references.

Time Schedule

In the research proposal, the researcher should also indicates a realistic time schedule to complete the study/project. It is very helpful for the researcher in terms of both, using time systematically and minimising the natural tendency of procastination.

Budget Schedule

Conducting research, requires a lot of money also. The researcher while preparing research proposal should estimate the cost of the project, considering the required persons, months and facilities. This budget along with research proposal should be submitted to either government, private or any other agency for financial assistance. In our research proposal, the researcher should justify the allocation of money for various heads of the budget estimate because the funding agency evaluates very carefully.

Types of Research Proposals

On the basis of the type and purpose of the research study, *research proposal can broadly be categorised into the following categories*

Research Proposal for Degree

This common type of proposal is prepared and presented by those researchers who are required to conduct a research study for the fulfilment of their **Master's degree** or Doctoral Degree in Education.

Most universities require the beginner researchers to submit the research proposal, that is then evaluated by a committee of experienced experts. These experts determine the significance, utility and feasibility of the proposed study and may suggest some modifications in the research proposal.

Research Proposal for Financial Assistance

Many times conducting a particular research seems to go beyond the budget of the researcher for which he/she requires some financial assistance. He/she then submits the research proposal to a government or private agency, requesting for financial assistance. Such an agency then asks empanelled experts for comments and/or recommendations, after evaluating the proposal and the agency then decides to provide (or not to provide) the financial assistance on the basis of these comments and/or recommendations.

Research Proposal for Grants by Government

Since, various research organisations, such as universities, the UGC, the NCERT and the ICSSR are ear marking more and more funds at present for a specific purpose of promoting research. More and more colleges and university teachers are becoming motivated to conduct research in their respective areas of concern at school, college or university level. They are also required to submit their research proposal for evaluation and are provided grants if experts recommend so after evaluation of the research proposal.

EXAM BASED QUESTIONS

1 An instrument used in method is called
(a) sample (b) technique (c) tool (d) survey

2 Which one of the following is a research tool?
(a) Graph (b) Illustration
(c) Questionnaire (d) Diagram

3 Which of the following is the correct explanation about a test?
(a) Reliability is sufficient
(b) Validity is sufficient
(c) Reliability and validity are not essential
(d) Reliability is essential but not sufficient

4 Which of the following term is related to an idea of validity of a test?
(a) Errors of measurement (b) True score variance
(c) Common score variance (d) Random errors

5 One of the tools that can be used for indepth data collection is
(a) test (b) interview
(c) rating scale (d) observation

6 How many points does your text recommended for rating scales?
(a) Always 4
(b) Sometimes from 4 to 11 points
(c) Always 10
(d) Always 5

7 Which method should be used for establishing reliability of the questionnaire?
(a) Test-Retest method
(b) Split Half method
(c) Parallel Form method
(d) Rationale Equivalence method

8 A summated rating scale is also known as
(a) event sampling (b) Likert scale
(c) interview protocol (d) ranking

9 An example of non-personal method of data collection is
(a) interview (b) group interview
(c) schedule (d) telephonic interview

10 Who among the following gave a classification for the tools of research?
(a) Francis Galton (b) Stanley and Hopkins
(c) J C Agarwal (d) John W. Best

11 Which is not true about the validity of the questionnaire?
(a) It is the validity of the items, than that of the total instrument which should be considered important.
(b) The questionnaire must have a unity and validity of its own with respect to the topic under investigation.
(c) The validation of a questionnaire utilises the same principles and procedures as the validation of any other instrument.
(d) The question of validity in the case of the questionnaire does not arise.

12 Which of the following tool of collecting psychological information about pupils is the most objective?
(a) Rating scale (b) Interview
(c) Standardised test (d) Projective devices

13 Which of the following is not a method of data collection?
(a) Questionnaires (b) Focus groups
(c) Correlational Method (d) Secondary data

14 For any study, one should question the validity and reliability of
(a) the interviewing process
(b) the questionnaire
(c) the sampling procedure
(d) All of the above

15 Match the following.

List I	List II
A. Rating by cumulated points	1. Man-to-man scale
B. Standard scale	2. Checklist method
C. Graphical scale	3. Point scale
D. Numerical scale	4. Continuous rating scale

Codes

	A	B	C	D		A	B	C	D
(a)	1	2	3	4	(b)	4	3	2	1
(c)	2	1	4	3	(d)	1	2	4	3

16 Which technique is mostly used in educational research?
(a) Questionnaire (b) Interview
(c) Observation (d) Sociometry

17 A researcher is interested in studying the prospects of a particular political party in an urban area. What tool should he prefer for the study?
(a) Rating scale (b) Interview
(c) Questionnaire (d) Schedule

18 Which of the following steps are required to design a questionnaire?
1. Writing primary and secondary aims of the study
2. Review of current literature
3. Prepare a draft of questionnaire
4. Revision of the draft

Codes
(a) 1, 2 and 3 (b) 1, 3 and 4
(c) 2, 3 and 4 (d) All of these

19 Sending questionnaire to a respondent with a request to complete and return by post is called
(a) mail survey (b) interview
(c) observation (d) panel

20 Questions which allow only a few alternative way of answering is called
(a) open-ended questions
(b) unstructured questions
(c) structured questions
(d) dichotomous questions

21 How many types of questionnaire have been defined by P V Young?
(a) Three types (b) Four types
(c) Two types (d) None of these

22 Which of the following is/are principle(s) of questionnaire construction?
(a) Always pilot test your questionnaire
(b) Do not use leading or loaded questions
(c) Both b and c
(d) All of the above

23 What is the most suitable placement of a demographic question in a questionnaire as suggested by most of the writers?
(a) In the middle
(b) At the end
(c) Random placement should be used
(d) At the beginning

24 Which of the following is an advantage of an Interview Method of Data Collection versus a questionnaire?
(a) Data are less expensive to obtain
(b) Data collectors do not need to be trained
(c) Data may be collected more easily from a wide spread geographical area
(d) Data collectors may assess/enhance validity of responses

25 The questionnaire was invented by
(a) John W. Best (b) Francis Galton
(c) J C Agarwal (d) Stanley and Hopkins

26 **Which of the following is not included in open ended questions?**
(a) High exploratory nature (b) Less depth in questions
(c) Analysis in detail (d) Speed of completion

27 **What is undesirable in a questionnaire?**
(a) Asking for unnecessary information that lengthens the questionnaire
(b) Avoiding ambiguity in questions
(c) Simplest possible wording and suitable vocabulary
(d) Avoiding questions, which the subject will not answer or will not answer truthfully

28 **What is desirable in a questionnaire?**
(a) Emotionally toned questions
(b) Too broad questions
(c) Two ideas in one question
(d) Questions, which will elicit valid and reliable answers

29 **The face validity of a questionnaire does not involve**
(a) relating each question to the topic under investigation
(b) checking the responses, which the questionnaire elicits against an external criterion
(c) seeing that there is an adequate coverage of the overall topic
(d) seeing that questions are clear and ambiguousness

30 **A test conducted by a classroom teacher for the purpose of identifying the strength and weaknesses of students in a specified content area is technically called**
(a) aptitude test (b) prognostic test
(c) diagnostic test (d) placement test

31 **Generally, "questionnaire refers to a device for securing answers to questions, by using a form which the respondent fills by himself". Who has defined questionnaire in these words?**
(a) Goode and Hatt (b) Goode and Scates
(c) Barr, Davis and Johnson (d) John W. Best

32 **Which of the following is typically used to plan a questionnaire?**
(a) Gantt chart (b) Flow chart
(c) Pie chart (d) Polar diagram

33 **Which of the following is an unstructured tool?**
(a) Attitude scale (b) Objective test
(c) Intelligence test (d) Essay test

34 **Researcher intends to ascertain the attitude of adolescents toward modernisation. Which one of the following tool is an appropriate one?**
(a) Projective technique (b) Interview
(c) Likert scale (d) Sociometry

35 **Which of the following is not assessed by using essay type questions?**
(a) Thinking skills
(b) Knowledge of wide content area
(c) Supplying suitable arguments
(d) Detailed description of an event

36 **...... has/have a direct impact on research tools and techniques.**
(a) Processes (b) Knowledge
(c) Aspirations (d) Concepts

37 **The qualitative research interview is typically**
(a) unstructured
(b) structured
(c) similar to survey interview
(d) Both a and b

38 **Man to man scale and portrait matching are examples of**
(a) graphic scale
(b) forced choice rating
(c) standard scale
(d) rating by cumulated points

39 **A purpose of observational research is to**
(a) determine cognitive behaviours
(b) determine affective behaviours
(c) determine psychomotor behaviours
(d) All of the above

40 **Which of the following is not a type of validity?**
(a) Content validity
(b) Criterion related validity
(c) Construct validity
(d) Cumulative validity

41 **Which of the following is not a demerit of interview schedule?**
(a) Time restrictions
(b) Objective in nature
(c) Consciousness required
(d) Less time for thinking

42 **Who said "Observation employs relatively more visual senses than audio or video organs"?**
(a) JW Best (b) CA Mourse
(c) Stanley and Hopkins (d) Francis Galton

43 **Which of the following type of interview aims at active responses, from the respondents on a specific event?**
(a) Focused interview (b) Diagnostic interview
(c) Clinical interview (d) Reserve interview

44 **In which of the following, researcher observes as an outsider and does not tell the people that they are being observed?**
(a) Complete observer (b) Participant as observer
(c) Observer as participant (d) All of these

45 **Descriptive rating scale, standard scale and forced choice scale are examples of which of the following scale?**
(a) Thurstone scale (b) Attitude scale
(c) Likert scale (d) Interval scale

46 **Accurate communication and response are features of which of the following interview?**
(a) Focused interview (b) Direct interview
(c) Non-directive interview (d) Group interview

47 **Which of the following type of interview schedule requires research?**
(a) Semi-structured
(b) Focused schedule
(c) Structured schedule
(d) Non-directive schedule

48 **Which of the following tool of research gives most precise measurement?**
(a) Questionnaire (b) Observation schedule
(c) Rating scale (d) Information schedule

49 **A well defined aggregate, from which a researcher selects some representative units for study purpose is called**
(a) sample (b) universe
(c) population (d) representation portion

50 **The structured interview is**
(a) used to derive more precise generalizations, in the early stages of investigation
(b) such as it calls for less versatility and on the spot adaptability on the part of the interviews
(c) most useful, when insight into a particular situation in the early stages of investigation is called for
(d) more flexible than the unstructured interview

51 **Which is not a correct statement?**
(a) A test can be reliable, without being valid
(b) A test cannot be valid, without being reliable
(c) A test can be both reliable and valid
(d) A test can be valid, without being reliable

52 **Identifying a factor to be measured, placing units or categories on a scale, to differentiate varying degrees of that factor and describing these units in some manner is known as**
(a) a checklist (b) a schedule
(c) a test (d) a rating scale

53 **Which of the following is a projective test?**
(a) Edward Personal Preference Schedule (EPPS)
(b) Alport Vernon-Liendzey, a study of values
(c) Rorschach test
(d) Minnesotta Multi-phasic Personality Inventory (MMPI)

54 **Projective technique is used for measuring**
(a) individual's need for self-actualisation
(b) individual's inventoried interests
(c) individual's dominant feelings, emotions, conflicts and need, which are generally repressed by the individual and are stored up in the unconscious mind
(d) individual's value system

55 **Which is not measured by TAT test?**
(a) Personality needs
(b) Emotions
(c) Personality adjustment
(d) Personality ability

56 **The method of summated ratings for measuring attitudes was developed by**
(a) Chove in 1920 (b) Thurstone in 1932
(c) Likert (d) Both a and b

57 **Projective tests are of great value because**
(a) they alone reveal deeper layers of personality, such as repressed feelings, emotions, conflicts, etc
(b) they are highly reliable and valid
(c) they are indirect methods of knowing about what an individual is
(d) they are non-verbal and can be used even in case of an illiterate person

58 **An attitude is**
(a) a special mental ability
(b) an emotionalised mental state about some issue
(c) a kind of feeling, free floating and unattached to anything
(d) an aptitude in other words

59 **The most objective psychological tool is**
(a) thematic apperception test
(b) Rorschach test
(c) interview
(d) intelligence test

60 **Which of the following is not correctly matched?**
(a) Achievement test – Content validity
(b) Aptitude test – Predictive validity
(c) Reasoning test – Content validity
(d) Personality test – Concurrent validity

61 **Rearrange the following points of Likert type attitude scale.**
1. Strongly agree
2. Strongly disagree
3. Agree
4. Disagree
5. Undecided
Choose the correct option.
(a) 1, 3, 4, 5, 2 (b) 2, 4, 5, 3, 1
(c) 1, 2, 5, 3, 4 (d) 1, 3, 4, 2, 5

62 **Rearrange the following activities, related to test standardisation.**
1. Preparing of test items
2. Planning the test
3. Assessment of reliability and validity
4. Try out of the test
Choose the correct option.
(a) 2, 1, 4, 3 (b) 3, 4, 1, 2
(c) 4, 1, 2, 3 (d) 1, 4, 3, 2

63 **Asking each member of the group, with whom he/she would like to or would not like to engage in some relevant activity is known as**
(a) a social distance measuring technique
(b) a personality measuring technique
(c) a socio-emotional climate measuring technique
(d) a sociometric technique

64 **If content and material, gathered for certain number of students by different interviews to be compared in a piece of research, the best format to use would be**
(a) projective (b) structured
(c) unstructured (d) analytical

65 Which of the following tool of research gives most precise measurement?
(a) Questionnaire (b) Observation schedule
(c) Rating scale (d) Information schedule

66 Which of the following is/are classification(s) of observation, on the basis of person's observation?
(a) Self-observation (b) Outsider's observation
(c) Both a and b (d) Group observation

67 Which is a focus group technique?
(a) It is a method of research, involving the observations of a small group
(b) It is a quantitative research method, involving structured interview, using closed questions in a large group of people
(c) It is a method of interviewing, which involves more than one and usually four interviews
(d) None of the above

68 Which of the following is/are feature(s) of close-ended questions?
(a) Speed of completion is fast
(b) Low exploratory nature
(c) Easy to prepare
(d) Both a and b

69 Which is the best technique of measuring the internal feelings of a student?
(a) Questionnaire (b) Interview
(c) Projective technique (d) Sociometry

70 A question during an interview, such as why do you feel that way? It is known as
(a) probe (b) filter question
(c) response (d) pilot

71 Researchers used both, open ended and closed-ended questions to collect data. Which of the following statement(s) is/are true in context of the above statement?
(a) Open-ended questions directly provide quantitative data, based on the researcher's pre-determined response categories
(b) Closed-ended questions provide quantitative data in the participant's own words
(c) Open-ended questions provide qualitative data in the participant's own words
(d) Closed-ended questions directly provide qualitative data in the participant's own words

72 Camera, tape recorder, video tapes, etc, are ...... devices of observation.
(a) casual (b) mechanical
(c) technical (d) manual

73 The question by which its content, structure or wordings lead the respondent in the direction of a certain answer is called
(a) factual question (b) opinion question
(c) leading question (d) structural question

74 Which of the following statement(s) is/are correct about the advantages of observation?
(a) The tool does not need any communication medium
(b) It provides direct access to social phenomena under consideration
(c) It can effectively complement other approaches and enhance the quality of evidence available to the researcher
(d) All of the above

75 For what is the Thematic Apperception Test (TAT) most useful?
(a) Differential diagnosis
(b) Predicting suitability for psychotherapy
(c) Assessment of intellectual level
(d) Assessment of motivational variables

76 Technique that allows several members of a hiring company to interview a job candidate at the same time is
(a) self-administered interview
(b) mail interview
(c) panel interview
(d) electronic interview

77 A census taker often collects data through which of the following?
(a) Standardised test (b) Interview
(c) Secondary data (d) Observation

78 An unguided interview of psycho-analytical nature, permitting the subject to talk freely with a view to obtain insight into hidden motive is called
(a) a focused interview
(b) a non-directive depth interview
(c) a directive interview
(d) a structured interview

79 What best describes the Likert's technique of attitude measurement?
(a) Subjects indicate whether they agree with each of a series of attitude statements, which are equally spaced along an attitude continuum.
(b) Subjects indicate on five point scales, the extent of their agreement with a set of attitude statements.
(c) Subjects judge a particular concept on a series of bi-polar semantic scale.
(d) Subjects response to an open-ended interview are coded by content analyst.

80 .... measures the extent of students learning, in a given content area.
(a) Achievement test (b) Aptitude test
(c) Diagnostic test (d) Readiness test

81 Match the following.

List I	List II
A. Form of observation	1. Qualitative observation
B. Control of observation	2. Direct observation
C. Direction of observation	3. Controlled observation
D. Information of observation	4. Informal observation

Codes

	A	B	C	D
(a)	1	2	3	4
(b)	1	2	4	3
(c)	4	3	2	1
(d)	4	3	1	2

82 Match the following.

List I (Research Methods)	List II (Data Collection Tools)
A. Experimental Method	1. Using primary and secondary sources
B. Ex-Post Facto Method	2. Questionnaire
C. Descriptive Survey Method	3. Standardised tests
D. Historical Method	4. Typical characteristics tests

Codes

	A	B	C	D
(a)	2	1	3	4
(b)	3	4	2	1
(c)	2	3	1	4
(d)	2	4	3	1

83 Match the following.

List I (Interviews)	List II (Meanings)
A. Structured Interview	1. Greater flexibility approach
B. Unstructured Interview	2. Attention on the questions, to be answered
C. Focussed Interview	3. Individual life experience
D. Clinical Interview	4. Pre-determined questions
	5. Non-directive

Codes

	A	B	C	D
(a)	4	1	2	3
(b)	2	4	1	3
(c)	5	2	4	1
(d)	1	3	5	4

84 Match the following.

List I (Interviews)	List II (Meanings)
A. Structured interview	1. In depth task on issue
B. Semi-structure interview	2. Free task on issue
C. Non -directive	3. Flexible but structured
D. Focused interview schedule	4. Research

Codes

	A	B	C	D
(a)	1	2	3	4
(b)	2	1	4	3
(c)	4	3	2	1
(d)	1	2	4	3

85 Arrange the following steps of research in correct sequence.

1. Identification of research problem
2. Listing of research objectives
3. Collection of data
4. Methodology
5. Data analysis
6. Results and discussions

Codes

(a) 1, 2, 3, 4, 5, 6 (b) 1, 2, 4, 3, 5, 6
(c) 2, 1, 3, 4, 5, 6 (d) 2, 1, 4, 3, 5, 6

86 Sampling frame' means

(a) identification of target and accessible population
(b) defining sample unit and selecting units
(c) preparing a complete list of the units of a finite population for drawing a sample
(d) fixing the sample size and drawing a sample

87 Who said that "The problem is proposed question for solution"?

(a) John C Torensand (b) J E Almak
(c) Fred N Kerlinger (d) John W Best

88 Which one of the following cannot be considered a quality of good hypothesis?

(a) Clarity (b) Modifiability
(c) Plausiability (d) Verifiability

89 Ben has defined hypothesis as

(a) it is a temporary solution
(b) it is an expected happening
(c) it is a forward thinking
(d) it is a thoughtful statement

90 Which of the following is not a common element of a research proposal and research report?

(a) Objectives and hypothesis
(b) Implications for further research
(c) References to previous research
(d) Sources of information

91 What is irrelevant in the context of the feasibility consideration of research problem?

(a) Researcher's competencies
(b) Researcher's interest and enthusiasm
(c) Supervisor's willingness, if he is required to guide the research work
(d) Researcher's financial, time and energy resources

92 What is/are the characteristic(s) of a good sample?

(a) Economy of time (b) Economy of money
(c) Knowledge of more truth (d) All of these

93 The characteristic of a sample is

(a) isolation from population (b) different from population
(c) subjectivity (d) Both band c

94 Match the following.

List I (Samples)	List II (Meanings)
A. Random sampling	1. The unit of sampling cannot be selected directly
B. Purposive sampling	2. The population is homogeneous and frame is available
C. Multi-stage sampling	3. The frame is not available
D. Stratified sampling	4. The population is heterogeneous and geographically widespread

Codes

	A	B	C	D
(a)	3	1	5	2
(b)	1	2	3	4
(c)	2	3	1	4
(d)	5	3	2	1

95 Every individual has an equal chance of being selected by the method of
(a) quota sampling
(b) purposive sampling
(c) non-probability sampling
(d) probability sampling

96 When a researcher includes in his sample, those individuals who are willing and are readily available, the sampling technique is called
(a) simple random sampling (b) quota sampling
(c) snowball sampling (d) incidental sampling

97 Multi-stage sampling is recommended in a large scale survey because
(a) it is convenient
(b) it is less time consuming
(c) we may overcome the problem of non-response, here
(d) All of the above

98 A researcher studying the development of self-esteem, among primary school children can interview only 35 students in each grade. Which one of the following approach to sampling is most appropriate?
(a) Systematic sampling
(b) Stratified sampling
(c) Non-proportionate random sampling
(d) Quota sampling

99 The size of a population is 100 and every 5th person is selected to form a sample. This technique of sampling is known as
(a) random (b) stratified
(c) cluster (d) systematic

100 What is the main method of selecting sample?
(a) Systematic sample (b) Stratified sample
(c) Multiple sample (d) All of these

101 Sampling is preferred to entire population because
(a) sample may have the same characteristics of the population
(b) it is possible to control a sample as compared to the entire population
(c) Both (a) and (b)
(d) None of the above

102 Which one of the following method of study will need a very small sample?
(a) Clinical sample (b) Fixed experiment
(c) Surveys (d) All of these

103 The main type(s) of probability sampling is/are
(a) double sampling (b) random sampling
(c) model sampling (d) All of these

104 In the probability sampling, the unit population is selected on the basis of
(a) chance (b) bias
(c) subjectivity (d) Both b and c

105 Stratified sampling is adopted when
(a) when the universe is homogeneous
(b) the universe is heterogeneous
(c) selected group needed to be studied
(d) data about the universe is not available

106 Which of the following approach to sampling seems to be most appropriate, when a researcher wishes to obtain a sample that will sustain accurate generalisation about gender and ethnic differences in scores on a standardised test?
(a) Systematic sampling
(b) Proportionate stratified sampling
(c) Incidental sampling
(d) Extreme case sampling

107 Cluster sampling, stratified sampling and systematic sampling are the types of
(a) direct sampling (b) indirect sampling
(c) random sampling (d) non-random sampling

108 A researcher divides the population into P.G., graduates and 10 + 2 students, using the random digit table, he selects some of them from each. This is technically called
(a) stratified sampling
(b) stratified random sampling
(c) representative sampling
(d) None of the above

109 Which one of the following is a non-probability sampling?
(a) A simple random (b) Purposive
(c) Systematic (d) Stratified

110 Which of the following sample method is not based on probability?
(a) Simple random sampling (b) Stratified sampling
(c) Quota sampling (d) Cluster sampling

111 When two or more successive foot notes refer to the same work, which one of the following expression is used?
(a) Ibid (b) Et.al
(c) Op.cit (d) Loc.cit

112 Suppose you want to investigate the work efficiency of nationalised Bank in India, which one of the following would you follow?
(a) Area sampling (b) Multi-stage sampling
(c) Sequential sampling (d) Quota sampling

113 Which technique is generally followed when the population is finite?
(a) Area sampling technique
(b) Purposive sampling technique
(c) Systematic sampling technique
(d) None of the above

114 A researcher selects a probability sample of 100 out of the total population. It is a
(a) cluster sampling (b) random sampling
(c) systematic sampling (d) stratified sampling

115 Sampling case means
(a) sampling using a sample frame
(b) identifying people who are suitable for research
(c) literally the researcher's brief case
(d) sampling of people, newspapers, television programme, etc

116 Sampling is qualitative research is similar to .... sampling in quantitative research.
(a) simple random (b) systematic
(c) quota (d) purposive

117 Which one of the following is the main problem with using non-probability sampling?
(a) The expenses
(b) The results are never representative
(c) Human judgement error
(d) Informants can refuse to participate

118 Systematic sampling procedure is a kind of
(a) purposive sampling (b) quota sampling
(c) random sampling (d) non-probability sampling

119 Define the correct sequence in the stage of sampling.
(a) Population definition, sampling frame development, sampling unit specification, sampling method selection, sample size determination
(b) Sampling method selection, sampling unit specification, sample size determination, population definition, sampling frame development
(c) Sample size determination, population definition, sampling frame development, sampling unit specification, sampling method selection
(d) Sampling method selection, population definition, Sampling frame development, sampling unit specification, sample size determination

120 Which of the following is not an example of a non-random sampling technique?
(a) Cluster (b) Purposive (c) Convenience (d) Quota

121 Match the following.

List I (Types of Samplings)	List II (Purposes Served)
A. Dimensional sampling	1. Choosing the nearest individuals to serve as respondents
B. Cluster sampling	2. Hand pick the cause to be included on the basis of their typical characteristics
C. Purposive sampling	3. Selecting a specific group of individuals from a widely dispersed population
D. Convenience sampling	4. Identifying various factors of interest in a population and obtaining at least one respondent of every combination
	5. Sampling in stage wise

Codes

	A	B	C	D		A	B	C	D
(a)	3	2	5	4	(b)	4	3	2	1
(c)	2	3	1	4	(d)	5	2	3	4

122 The delimitation(s) of sample is/are
(a) possibilities of bias
(b) needs of trained persons
(c) inconsistency of sample units
(d) All of the above

123 Which of the following include(s) example(s) of quantitative variables?
(a) Age, temperature, income and height
(b) Grade point average, anxiety level and reading performance
(c) Gender, religion and ethnic group
(d) Both a and b

124 The method by which sample is choosen.
(a) unit (b) census
(c) design (d) random

125 Read the following statements about a laboratory experiment.
1. It has relatively complete control of extraneous variables.
2. Its results are applicable to real life situations.

Choose the correct option.
(a) Both 1 and 2 are correct
(b) 1 is incorrect but 2 is correct
(c) Neither 1 nor 2 is correct
(d) only 1 is correct

126 An investigator wants to study the vocational aspirations of visually challenged children in a wide geographical area. He should select his sample by using
(a) sample random sample (b) stratified sampling
(c) purposive sampling (d) convenient sampling

127 Identify the non-probability sampling technique(s).
1. Stratified random sampling
2. Systematic sampling
3. Snowball sampling
4. Incidental sampling

Codes
(a) 1 and 2 (b) 2 and 3
(c) 3 and 4 (d) 1 and 4

128 A researcher is interested in studying the flood victims. Which one of the following is a suitable sample selection method?
(a) Random sampling (b) Stratified sampling
(c) Systematic sampling (d) Purposive sampling

129 Which of the following is not a common element of a research proposal and a research report?
(a) Objectives and hypothesis
(b) Implications for further research
(c) References to previous research
(d) Sources of information/data

130 .... is compared to Mariner's compass in sea voyage.
(a) Research problem (b) Data collection
(c) Sampling (d) Research design

131 Who has called sample 'an element of facts'?
(a) W G Kokaran (b) John W Best
(c) George J. Mouly (d) W S Travers

132 Which of the following statement is wrong about research?
(a) The research has been carried out for ornamental degree
(b) The research has been carried out for name and fame
(c) The research has been carried out for invention
(d) None of the above

133 Which of the following is not the relevant to analysis of the research problem?
(a) Isolating the variables that are involved in the problem and clarifying their relationship
(b) Accumulating the facts that might be related to the problem
(c) Attending seminar on research methodology
(d) Proposing various relevant explanations (hypothesis for the cause of the difficulty)

134 The advantage of research report writing in a scientific manner is
(a) global standardisation
(b) global communication
(c) global awakening
(d) global welfare

135 The basic principle(s) of problem selection is/are
(a) novelty of a problem
(b) practicality of a problem
(c) future orientation of a problem
(d) All of the above

136 The best quality of a researcher is
(a) curious (b) active imagination
(c) ability (d) All of these

137 In relics, the researcher includes
(a) building furniture and equipment
(b) library facilities
(c) photographs and records
(d) degree, diploma and all of the above

138 The research guide require(s) which of the following essential quality (ies)?
(a) Subject matter expertise
(b) Methodological experience
(c) Inter-disciplinary experience
(d) All of the above

139 Severally, in all researches, an abstract of each article has been prepared, which focuses upon
(a) the central theme of the research paper
(b) the research innovation employed in research paper
(c) the effective conclusion of the research paper
(d) All of the above

140 A good research always begins with
(a) an original idea
(b) preparation of plan and design for study
(c) study of relevant research methodology
(d) review of literature

141 According to Good Barr and Scates, one of the following is not the source of problem.
(a) Analysis of the field of knowledge
(b) Specific studies
(c) Different areas under study
(d) Suggestion of an intelligent person

142 Which one of the following is treated as basis of evaluation for the proposed problem of research?
(a) Nobility of the problem
(b) Presence of problem-solving potentiality
(c) Possibilities of data collection from the sample
(d) All of the above

143 Which of the following statements is/are correct?
(a) Research objectives can be worded in question form
(b) Research objectives can be worded in statement form
(c) Objectives are to be stated in chapter 1 of the thesis
(d) All of the above

144 In finalising a thesis writing format, which of the following would form part of supplementary pages?
(a) List of tables and figures
(b) Table of contents
(c) Conclusion of the study
(d) Bibliography and appendices

145 Which sequence of research steps is logical in the list given below?
(a) Problem formulation, analysis, development of research design, hypothesis making, collection of data, arriving at generalisations and conclusions
(b) Development of research design, hypothesis making, problem formulation, data analysis, arriving at conclusions and data collection
(c) Problem formulation, hypothesis making, development of research designs, collection of data, data analysis and formulation of generalisation and conclusion
(d) Problem formulation, deciding about the sample and data collection tools, formulation of hypothesis collection and interpretation of research evidence

146 A good thesis writing should involve
1. reduction of punctuation and grammatical error to a minimum.
2. careful checking of references.
3. consistency in the way the thesis is written.
4. a clear and well written abstract.

Codes
(a) 1, 2, 3 and 4 (b) 1, 2 and 3
(c) 1, 2 and 4 (d) 2, 3 and 4

147 A thesis statement is
(a) an observation (b) a fact
(c) an assertion (d) a discussion

148 Which is the main objective of research?
(a) To review the literature
(b) To summarise what is already known
(c) To get an academic degree
(d) To discover new facts or to make fresh interpretation of known facts

149 Arrange the following steps of research in correct sequence.
1. Identification of research problem.
2. Listing of research objectives.
3. Collection of data.
4. Methodology.
5. Data analysis.
6. Results and discussions.

Choose the correct option.

(a) 1, 2, 3, 4, 5, 6 (b) 1, 2, 4, 3, 5, 6
(c) 2, 1, 3, 4, 5, 6 (d) 2, 1, 4, 3, 5, 6

Directions (Q.Nos. 150-157) *Below given are two statements, one labelled as Assertion (A) and other labelled as Reason (R). Choose the correct code from the following.*

Codes

(a) A is true, but R is false (b) Both A and R are true
(c) A is false, but R is true (d) Both A and R are false

150 **Assertion** (A) Longer tests are more reliable than shorter one.

Reason (R) Each item adds to test reliability.

151 **Assertion** (A) A questionnaire places less pressure on the subjects, to respond immediately.

Reason (R) It gives a lot of time to fill it up. Before filling up the questions, the subjects think more about suitable answers of questions.

152 **Assertion** (A) Questionnaire have advantages, over some other types of surveys.

Reason (R) They are cheap, do not require as much efforts from the questionnaire, as verbal or telephonic surveys.

153 **Assertion** (A) Graphic scale is the most popular and widely used type of rating scale.

Reason (R) In this scale, a straight line is shown vertically or horizontally with various clues to help the rater.

154 **Assertion** (A) In structured questionnaire a definite concrete and preordinated questions are used for two purposes.

Reason (R) A questionnaire is a research instrument consisting of series of questions and other prompts for the purpose of gathering information from respondents.

155 **Assertion** (A) Personality inventory are self-report instruments.

Reason (R) These instruments yield scores that are assumed or have been shown to measure certain personality traits or tendencies.

156 **Assertion** (A) Projective techniques plays an important role in motivational researchers or in attitude surveys.

Reason (R) These technique may be used in qualitative as well as quantitative techniques.

157 **Assertion** (A) A good sample must be as nearly representative to the entire population as possible and ideally it must provide whole information about the population from which sample has been drawn.

Reason (R) Sample should be unbiased, it should reflect all the members of the population of data.

PREVIOUS YEARS' QUESTIONS

July 2018

1 Which of the following tools at a guidance centre can be used for ascertaining prospective success in a choosen occupation?

(a) Achievement test
(b) Interest inventory
(c) Differential aptitude test
(d) Personality inventory

2 An investigator wants to conduct a study to ascertain the progress of implementation of RTE Act-2009. Which of the following research tools would be most suitable for this purpose?

(a) Rating scale (b) Questionnaire
(c) Observation (d) Sociometry

3 Match the following.

List I (Approaches to Sampling in Qualitative Research)	List II (Characteristics)
A. Extreme case sampling	1. Seeks cases that are typical
B. Purposive sampling	2. Seeks cases that are highly similar to each other
C. Snowball sampling	3. Seeks cases that are unusual
	4. Seeks help from participants to identify additional participants
	5. Seeks cases according to his/her judgement about the appropriateness

Codes

	A	B	C		A	B	C
(a)	1	4	3	(b)	2	4	1
(c)	3	5	4	(d)	4	2	3

4 Which of the following decisions will tend to decrease sampling error?

(a) Obtaining representative sample
(b) Decreasing the sample size
(c) Homogeneous grouping of individuals
(d) Possibility of reduction of the sample size

5 A method of sampling that ensures proportional representation of all sections of a population is technically called

(a) Quota sampling (b) Systematic sampling
(c) Snow-ball sampling (d) Stratified sampling

6 When you read a research article published in a journal which is not peer reviewed, what aspect of the report should you be most concerned about?

(a) author's sincerity and skill in writing
(b) rigour reflected in reporting the research
(c) length of the report
(d) practical importance of the research question

7 Match the following.

List I (Categories of Test)	List II (Description)
A. Standardised test	1. developed by teachers for local purposes to measure achievement
B. Norm referenced test	2. used for comparing individuals in terms of their relative position
C. Diagnostic test	3. analysis of strength and weakness of students for further help
D. Criterion referenced test	4. developed by experts, administered and scored by using an objective procedure
	5. ray scores are compared with some pre-determined standard

Codes

	A	B	C	D		A	B	C	D
(a)	3	5	1	4	(b)	4	2	3	5
(c)	2	3	4	1	(d)	4	5	3	2

November 2017

8 Match the following.

List I (Techniques of Sampling)	List II (Characteristics of Procedure)
A. Purposive sampling	1. Dividing the population into subgroups and taking one or more groups at random
B. Multistage sampling	2. Researcher relies on his or her own judgement when choosing members from the population
C. Systematic sampling	3. Obtaining K 'interval' through N/n and using it for constituting the sample
D. Stratified sampling	4. Researcher divides the entire population into homogeneous subgroups and randomly selects the final sample

Codes

	A	B	C	D		A	B	C	D
(a)	1	3	4	2	(b)	2	1	3	4
(c)	4	2	1	3	(d)	3	1	4	2

9 A test conducted by a classroom teacher for the purpose of identifying the strengths and weaknesses of students in a specified content area is technically called

(a) Aptitude Test
(b) Prognostic Test
(c) Diagnostic Test
(d) Placement Test

10 Match the following.

List I (Item Types)	List II (Characteristics)
A. Short Answer items	1. Require students to demonstrate skills by actually engaging in the task
B. Interpretive exercises	2. Measure exclusively the recall of memorised information
C. Performance based tests	3. Assess a large amount of related factual material in a relatively short time
D. Matching exercises	4. More flexible to measure a variety of learning outcomes
	5. Provide scope to measure a large number of factual information in a given field

Codes

	A	B	C	D
(a)	2	5	1	3
(b)	1	2	3	5
(c)	3	4	1	2
(d)	5	1	3	4

January 2017

11 A student wants to know whether he will perform well in a particular job. Which of the following tools will predict this?

(a) Attitude test
(b) Aptitude test
(c) Intelligence test
(d) Interest test

12 For collecting data in respect of attitude of school teachers towards the new curriculum, which of the following scales, will use summated rating scores as an indicator?

(a) Thurstone scale (b) Guttman scale
(c) Likert scale (d) Osgood scale

13 Which of the following sampling techniques belongs to probability sampling?

(a) Convenience sampling
(b) Snowball sampling
(c) Quota sampling
(d) Random sampling

July 2016

14 A good research tool is identified on the basis of
(a) Availability in the market
(b) Ease of administration and handling
(c) Reliability index coupled with its validity
(d) The kinds of data it is going to provide

15 Which research tool is befitting for phenomenological researches?
(a) Questionnaire (b) Interview
(c) Conversations (d) Self-report

16 Mention the non-probability counterpart of stratified random sampling.
(a) Stage sampling (b) Purposive sampling
(c) Snowball sampling (d) Quota sampling

December 2015

17 Which of the following technique cannot specifiy the probability of each unit to be included in the sample?
(a) Stratified sampling (b) Systematic sampling
(c) Quota sampling (d) Cluster sampling

18 In a study on tribal community the researcher finds that there are several groups in which the members exist. As an advise to the researcher for the choice of sample which method from among the following you will recommend?
(a) Stratified sampling (b) Simple random sampling
(c) Quto sampling (d) Cluster sampling

19 In a case study of truant children in a school a few cases have to be identified to compose the sample. Which of the following sampling procedures will you recommend for the sample of the case study?
(a) Simple random sampling
(b) Cluster sampling
(c) Snowball sampling
(d) Quota sampling

20 A researcher wants to conduct a large scale survey regarding the effectiveness of mid-day-meal scheme. For this purpose which tool will be suitable?
(a) Observation schedule (b) Questionnaire
(c) Sociometric technique (d) Interview

21 The dimensional sampling procedure is the same as
(a) a further reinforcement of quota sampling
(b) Stage sampling
(c) Cluster sampling
(d) Purposive sampling

22 Interview is considered as the best tool in analysing the problem of a client because
(a) it is very easy to conduct
(b) it will give first-hand information
(c) it will help for counselling
(d) it can be recorded easily

June 2015

23 A well defined aggregate from which a researcher selects some representative units for study purpose is called ....
(a) sample (b) universe
(c) population (d) representative portion

24 Quality of testing and information services dependent mostly on the
(a) availability of valid and reliable tools
(b) infrastructural support
(c) suitable personnel to handle them
(d) attitude of clients

25 When the population is homogenous, which of the following sampling techniques will be more appropriate?
(a) Random sampling (b) Convenience sampling
(c) Snowball sampling (d) Stratified sampling

December 2014

26 For collecting information under Right to Information Act from five different states, the better research tool will be
(a) observation schedule (b) rating scale
(c) questionnaire (d) checklist

27 The procedure of sampling which provides equal and independent chance to each unit while being selected in a sample is called
(a) purposive sampling
(b) convenient sampling
(c) snowball sampling
(d) random sampling

28 Which of the following research tools/technique will be appropriate for an in-depth understanding of cultural and social aspects of a tribe?
(a) Questionnaire
(b) Participant observation
(c) Sociometric technique
(d) Rating scale

29 Match the following.

List I		List II	
A.	Achievement test	1.	Predictive validity
B.	Aptitude test	2.	Content validity
C.	Personality test	3.	Criterion related validity
D.	Performance test	4.	Concurrent validity
		5.	Construct validity

Codes

	A	B	C	D
(a)	2	3	4	1
(b)	1	2	5	3
(c)	2	1	5	4
(d)	4	2	3	5

June 2014

30 Which of the following types of tools is most appropriate to assess one's interest in a particular phenomenon?

(a) Questionnaire (b) Scale
(c) Test (d) Inventory

31 Which of the following is not related to item analysis?

(a) Item difficulty index
(b) Item discrimination index
(c) Reliability co-efficient
(d) Sensitivity of item to instructional effects

32 Miss Reema obtained grades in the subjects as follows in a 5 point scales : English-A; Mathematics-B; Science-D and Social Science-A. Her Grade Point Average (GPA) will be

(a) 5 (b) 3
(c) 4 (d) 3.5

33 Teacher Eligibility Test conducted for selection of candidates for admission into teacher education institution is an example of

(a) placement test (b) aptitude test
(c) attitude test (d) achievement test

34 For conducting research in group dynamics, which of the following techniques can be used?

(a) Anthropometry (b) Biometry
(c) Geometry (d) Sociometry

35 An experimenter administered a pretest on both experimental and control groups and found that the pre-test mean scores of the groups differ. Which of the following statistical techniques can address this difference in studying the impacts of independent variable?

(a) Analysis of variance (b) T-test
(c) Regression analysis (d) Analysis of co-variance

36 Sampling error cannot be estimated when the researcher employs

(a) simple random sampling
(b) stratified random sampling
(c) systematic sampling
(d) quota sampling

37 Which of the following is not a non-probability sampling technique?

(a) snowball sampling
(b) stratified random sampling
(c) incidental sampling
(d) purposive sampling

ANSWERS

Exam Based Questions

1 (c)	2 (c)	3 (b)	4 (c)	5 (b)	6 (b)	7 (a)	8 (b)	9 (d)	10 (c)
11 (d)	12 (c)	13 (c)	14 (d)	15 (c)	16 (c)	17 (c)	18 (a)	19 (a)	20 (c)
21 (c)	22 (d)	23 (c)	24 (d)	25 (b)	26 (b)	27 (a)	28 (a)	29 (d)	30 (c)
31 (b)	32 (b)	33 (d)	34 (c)	35 (b)	36 (d)	37 (d)	38 (c)	39 (d)	40 (d)
41 (b)	42 (b)	43 (a)	44 (a)	45 (d)	46 (c)	47 (c)	48 (a)	49 (c)	50 (a)
51 (b)	52 (d)	53 (c)	54 (c)	55 (d)	56 (c)	57 (a)	58 (c)	59 (d)	60 (c)
61 (b)	62 (a)	63 (d)	64 (b)	65 (a)	66 (c)	67 (c)	68 (d)	69 (b)	70 (a)
71 (c)	72 (b)	73 (c)	74 (d)	75 (d)	76 (c)	77 (b)	78 (b)	79 (b)	80 (a)
81 (c)	82 (b)	83 (a)	84 (c)	85 (b)	86 (c)	87 (a)	88 (b)	89 (d)	90 (b)
91 (c)	92 (c)	93 (c)	94 (c)	95 (b)	96 (d)	97 (d)	98 (d)	99 (d)	100 (d)
101 (d)	102 (d)	103 (c)	104 (a)	105 (d)	106 (a)	107 (b)	108 (b)	109 (c)	110 (b)
111 (b)	112 (c)	113 (a)	114 (b)	115 (c)	116 (b)	117 (d)	118 (b)	119 (c)	120 (c)
121 (a)	122 (a)	123 (b)	124 (d)	125 (b)	126 (b)	127 (d)	128 (c)	129 (c)	130 (d)
131 (b)	132 (d)	133 (c)	134 (b)	135 (d)	136 (d)	137 (d)	138 (d)	139 (d)	140 (d)
141 (d)	142 (d)	143 (d)	144 (a)	145 (c)	146 (a)	147 (c)	148 (d)	149 (d)	150 (a)
151 (b)	152 (b)	153 (a)	154 (b)	155 (a)	156 (a)	157 (b)			

Previous Years' Questions

1 (c)	2 (b)	3 (c)	4 (a)	5 (d)	6 (b)	7 (b)	8 (b)	9 (c)	10 (a)
11 (b)	12 (c)	13 (d)	14 (c)	15 (d)	16 (d)	17 (c)	18 (d)	19 (c)	20 (b)
21 (a)	22 (b)	23 (c)	24 (a)	25 (a)	26 (c)	27 (d)	28 (b)	29 (c)	30 (d)
31 (c)	32 (c)	33 (b)	34 (d)	35 (b)	36 (b)	37 (b)			

CHAPTER

24

Analysis of Data

Statistics is a numerical representation of information. Whenever, we quantify or apply number to data, in order to organise, summarise or better understand the information in which statistical methods are used. Data analysis is done for inspecting, cleaning, transforming and presenting data with the goal of discovering useful information.

Data Analysis

The credibility of findings and conclusions significantly depends on the quality of the research design, data collection, data management and data analysis. Data analysis is the process of systematically applying statistical and/or logical techniques to describe and illustrate, condense and recap and evaluate data.

According to **Koul** (1997), "the analysis of the qualitative data means studying the organised material, in order to discover inherent facts. These data are to be studied from many angles as possible, either to explore new facts or to interpret already existing known facts".

There are many different data analysis methods, depending on the type of research. But the data may be classified into two broad categories *i.e.* quantitative and qualitative.

In **quantitative data analysis**, one is expected to turn raw numbers into meaningful data, through the application of rational and critical thinking. It may include the calculation of frequencies of variables and differences between variables. A quantitative approach is usually associated with finding evidences to either support or reject hypothesis, which the researchers have formulated at the earlier stages of research process.

Qualitative data analysis is the range of processes and procedures, whereby we move from the qualitative data that have been collected into some form of explanation, understanding or interpretation of the people and situations we are investigating.

In this Chapter

Levels of Measurement

The level of measurement refers to the relationship among the values that are assigned to the attributes for a variable. It is important to understand the level of measurement as it helps you to decide how to interpret the data from the variable concerned. Second, knowing the level of measurement helps you to decide which statistical techniques of data analysis are appropriate for the numerical values that were assigned to the variables. The scale of measurement refers to ways in which variables numbers are defined and categorised. Each scale of measurement has certain properties which in turn determine the appropriateness for use in certain statistical analysis.

Types of Measurement Scales

Before a researcher begins his/her analysis he/she must identify the level of measurement, associated with the quantitative data. The level of measurement can influence the type of analysis, one can use.

There are four levels of measurement scale and they are

Nominal Scale

Simply, it is a system of assigning number symbols to an event, in order to label them. For example, the assignment of numbers of basketball players, in order to identify them. Such numbers cannot be considered to be associated with an ordered scale, for their order is of no consequence, the numbers are just convenient labels for the particular class of events and as such, have no quantitative value. Nominal scales provide convenient ways of keeping track of people, objects and events. One cannot do much with the numbers involved. For example, one cannot usefully average the number on the back of a group of football players and come up with a meaningful value.

Neither can one usefully compare the numbers assigned to one group, with the numbers assigned to another. The counting of members in each group is the only possible arithmetic operation, when a nominal scale is employed. Accordingly, we are restricted to use mode as the measure of central tendency. Generally, there is no used measure of dispersion for nominal scales. Chi-square test is the most common test of statistical significance that can be utilised, and for the measures of correlation, the contingency coefficient can be work out.

It is the least powerful level of measurement. It indicates no order or distance relationship and has no arithmetic origin. It simply describes difference between things, by assigning them to categories. The scale wastes any information that we may have about varying degrees of attitude, skill understandings, etc. Inspite of all this, nominal scales are still very useful and are wide used in surveys and other ex-post facto research, when data is being classified by major sub-groups of the population. Thus, nominal data is counted data.

Ordinal Scale

The lowest level of the ordered scale that is commonly used is the ordinal scale. It places events in order, but there is no attempt to make the interval of the scale equal, in terms of some rules. Rank orders represent ordinal scales and a frequently used in research relating to qualitative phenomena. A student's rank in graduation class involves the use of an ordinal scale. One has to be very careful in making statement about scores based on an ordinal scale. For instance, if Ram's position in his class is 10 and Mohan's position is 40, it cannot be said that Ram's position is four times as go as that of Mohan. The statement would make no sense at all. Ordinal scales only permit ranking of items, from highest to lowest. Ordinal measures have no absolute values and real differences between adjacent ranks, may not be equal. All that can be said is that person is higher or lower on the scale than another, but more precise comparisons can be made.

Thus, the use of an ordinal scale implies a statement of greater than or less than (equality statement is also acceptable) without our being able to state how much greater or less. The real difference between ranks I and 2 may be more or less, than the difference between ranks 5 and 6. Since, the numbers of this scale have only a rank meaning appropriate measure of central tendency is the median. A percentile or quartile measure can used for measuring dispersion. Correlations are restricted to various rank order methods, whereas measures of statistical significance are restricted to the non-parametric methods.

Interval Scale

In interval scale, the intervals are adjusted in terms of rule that have been established as a basis for making the units, equal. The units are only in so far as one accepts the assumptions, on which the rule is based. It can have an arbitrary zero, but it is not possible to determine for them, what may be called an absolute zero or the unique origin. The primary limitation of the interval scale is the lack of true zero; it does not have the capacity to measure the complete absence of a trait or characteristic.

The **Fahrenheit scale** is an example of an interval scale and shows similarities in what one can and cannot do with it. One can say that an increase in temperature from 10° to 40° involves the same increase in temperature as an increase from 60° to 70°, but one cannot say that the temperature of 60° is twice as warm as the temperature of 30° because both numbers are dependent on the fact that the zero on the scale is set arbitrarily, at the temperature of the freezing point of water. The ratio of the two temperatures *i.e.* 30° and 60°, means nothing because zero is an arbitrary point.

It provides more powerful measurement than ordinal scales, for interval scale also incorporates the concept of equality of interval. As such, more powerful statistical measures can be used with interval scales. Mean is an appropriate measure of central tendency, while standard deviation is the most widely used measure of dispersion. Product moment correlation techniques are appropriate and the generally used tests for statistical significance are the T-test and F-test.

Ratio Scale

Ratio scale have an absolute or true zero of measurement. The term **absolute zero** is not as precise as it was once believed to be. We can conceive of an absolute zero of length and similarly we can conceive of an absolute zero of time. For example, the zero point on a centimeter scale indicates the complete absence of length or height. But an absolute zero of temperature is theoretically unobtainable and it remains a concept, existing only in the scientist's mind.

The number of minor traffic rule violations and the number of incorrect letters in a page of type script, represents scores on ratio scales. Both these scales have absolute zeros and as such, all minor traffic violations and all typing errors can be assumed to be equal in significance. With ratio scales involved one can make statement like Jyoti's typing performance was twice as good as that of Reetu. The ratio involved does have significance and facilitates a kind of comparison, which is not possible in case of an interval scale.

It represents an actual amount of variables. Examples are measures of physical dimensions, such as weight, height, distance, etc. Generally, all statistical techniques are usable with ratio scales and all manipulations that one can carry out with real numbers, can also be carried out with ratio scale values. Multiplication and division can be used with this scale, but not with other scales mentioned above. Geometric and harmonic means can be used as measures of central tendency and coefficients of variation may also be calculated.

Thus, proceeding from the nominal scale (the least precise type of scale) to ratio scale (the most precise), relevant information is obtained, increasingly. If the nature of the variables permits, the researcher should use the scale that provides the most precise description. Researchers in physical sciences have an advantage to describe variables in ratio scale form, but the behavioural sciences are generally limited to describe variables in interval scale form, a less precise type of measurement.

Quantitative Data Analysis

Statistics is a numerical representation of information. Whenever, we quantify or apply numbers to data, in order to organise, summarise or better understand the information, in which statistical methods are used. These methods can range from somewhat simple computations, such as determining the mean of a distribution to very complex computations, such as determining factors or interaction, effects within a complex data set, etc.

Descriptive Data Analysis

There are two major branches of statistics, each with specific formulas. The first, descriptive statistics refers to the analysis of data of an entire population.

In other words, descriptive statistics is merely using numbers, to describe a known data set. The term population means we are using the entire set of possible subjects as opposed to just a sample of these subjects. It is a summary of information and the data presented is easily understood.

- It is used to describe basic features of the data, in the study.
- It is used to present quantitative descriptions, in a manageable form.
- It includes the construction of graphs, charts and tables.

The following statistical measures of descriptive analysis are used to computer further statistical testing

Measures of Central Tendency

Mean, **Median** and **Mode** are three most commonly used measures of central tendency.

They can be explained as below

Mean

The mean of a distribution is commonly understood as the **arithmetic average.** Its perhaps the most familiar, most frequently used and well understood average. The mean of a set of observations or scores is obtained by dividing the sum of all the values by the total number of values. It is used to describe the middle of a set of data that does not have an **outlier.**

Arithmetic Mean (AM) The arithmetic mean (or simple mean) of a sample $x_1, x_2, \ldots, x_n$ is the sum of the sampled values, divided by the number of items in the sample.

It can be represented as :

$$\bar{x} = \frac{x_1 + x_2 + \ldots + x_n}{n}$$

Geometric Mean (GM) It is an average that is useful for sets of positive numbers that are interpreted, according to their product and not their sum (as in the case with the arithmetic mean) *e.g.* rates of growth.

$$\bar{x} = \left(\prod_{i=1}^{n} x_1\right)^{\frac{1}{n}}$$

Harmonic Mean (HM) It is an average, which is useful for sets of numbers, which are defined in relation to some unit, *e.g.* speed (distance per unit of time).

$$\bar{x} = n.\left(\sum_{i=1}^{n} \frac{1}{x_i}\right)^{-1}$$

Advantages

- Most popular measure in fields of business, engineering and computer science.
- It is unique, there is only one answer.
- Useful, when comparing sets of data.

Disadvantages

- It is affected by extreme values (outliers).
- It is not often used for analysing business problems.
- The calculation of HM involves complicated calculations.

Relationship Between AM, GM and HM

AM, GM and HM satisfy these inequalities:

$$AM \geq GM \geq HM$$

Equality holds, only when all the elements of the given samples are equal.

Median

It is a point in an array, above and below, where one half of the scores fall. It is a measure of position, rather than of magnitude.

Use the median to describe the middle of a set of data that does have an outlier.

Median for Grouped Data In case of grouped data, we first prepare a cumulative frequency distribution.

It can be represented as :

$$\text{Median} = l + \frac{N/2 - fc}{fm} \times i$$

where,

l = Limit of lower median class

$N/2$ = Half of the sum of total frequencies

fc = Preceding middle class of cumulative frequency

fm = Frequency of median class

i = Size of the class interval

Median for Ungrouped Data If the scores are ungrouped and their number is small, then

(a) For number of scores, if they are **even**

$$\text{Median} = \frac{\text{Sum of mid two scores}}{2}$$

(b) For number of scores, if they are **odd**

Median = Mid score

Advantages

- Extreme values (outliers) do not affect the median as strongly as they do the mean.
- Useful when comparing sets of data.
- It is unique, there is only one answer.

Disadvantages

- Not as popular as mean.
- Takes a long time, to calculate for a very large set of data.

Mode

It is defined as the most frequently occurring score in a distribution. If there is only one value, which occurs a maximum number of times, then the distribution is said to have one **mode**.

It is used when the data is non-numeric or when asked to choose the most popular item.

It can be represented as:

$$M_0 = L + \left(\frac{f_1 - f_0}{2f_1 - f_0 - f_2}\right) \times h$$

where,

L = Lower limit of the modal class

f_0 = Frequency before the frequency of modal class

f_1 = Frequency of the modal class

f_2 = Frequency after the frequency of modal class

h = Class size of the modal class

Advantages

- It is easy to understand and simple to calculate.
- It can be located, graphically.
- It is not affected by extreme large or small values.
- It can be useful for qualitative data.

Disadvantages

- It is not used more frequently, as compared to mean and median.
- Not necessarily unique, may be more than one answer.
- When no values repeat in the data set, the mode is every value and is useless.
- When there is more than one mode, it is difficult to interpret and/or compare.

Relationship Between Mean, Median and Mode

In can be represented as:

Mode = 3 Median – 2 Mean

or $M_o = 3M_d - 2M_n$

Statistical Parameter

- A **statistical parameter** is a parameter that indexes a family of probability distribution.
- It can be regarded as a numerical characteristic of a population or a model.
- In statistical inference, parameters are something taken to be unobservable.

Measures of Variability

The measures of variability are also called the **measure of spread or dispersion.**

There are several measures of variability :

- Limit Method
- Average of Deviation

Limit Method

There are four ways of variability measurement:

Range

The range is the most general and simplest measures of variability. It is defined as the difference between the most extreme scores in a distribution.

It can be represented as:

R = L – S

where, R = Range, L = Largest value
S = Lowest value

Applications

- When the data are too scant or scattered to justify, the computation of a more precise measure of variability.
- When a knowledge of extreme scores or of total spread is all that is wanted.

Disadvantages

- The value of range is based on only two extreme scores in the total distribution, which means that it does not give any idea of the variation of other scores of distribution.
- It is not a stable statistic, because its values can differ from sample to sample, drawn from same population.

Quartile Deviation

Quartile deviation is also known as **measure of dispersion.** The quartile deviation is one half of the middle 50% of the cases. It is one half of the scale, distance between the third and first quartile. First quartile Q_1 is a point below, which lies 25% of the scores or the scale. The third quartile Q_3, the point below which lies 75% of the scores on the score scale.

It can be represented as:

$$Q = \frac{Q_3 - Q_1}{2}$$

$$Q_3 = l_3 + \frac{3N/4 - fc}{fm} \times i$$

$$Q_1 = l_1 + \frac{N/4 - fc}{fm} \times i$$

$$Q_2 = Q_1 + Q_D, Q_3 - Q_D$$

Applications

- When the median is the measure of central tendency.
- When there are scattered or extreme scores, which would influence the SD.
- When the concentration around the median is the middle 50% of case, which is of primary interest.

Percentile Range

It is used as a measure of dispersion. It is difference between 90th and 10th percentile.

It can be represented as:

Percentile range = p90–p10

Inter-Quartile Range

In descriptive statistics, the **Inter-Quartile Range** (IQR), also called the **midspread** or **middle fifty** is a measure of statistical dispersion, being equal to the difference between the upper and lower quartiles. It is a trimmed estimator, defined as the 25% trimmed mid range and is the most significant basic robust measure of scale. It is the third quartile of a box plot minus the first quartile.

It can be represented as:

$$IQR = Q_3 - Q_1$$

Average of Deviation

Two types of average of deviation methods are

Average Deviation

The Average Deviation (AD) is the mean of the deviations of all of the separate scores in a series, taken from their mean. In averaging deviations to find the AD, no account is taken of signs and all deviations, whether plus or minus are treated as **positive**.

- When scores are **ungrouped** $AD = \frac{\Sigma|x|}{N}$ $x = x - \bar{x}$
- When scores are **grouped** $AD = \frac{\Sigma|fx|}{N}$

Applications

- When it is desired to weight all deviations from the mean, according to their size.
- When extreme deviations would influence standard deviation unduely.

Standard Deviation

The average of the square deviations of the measures or scores from their mean is known as the variance and positive square root of variance is known as **standard deviation.**

This is a most stable index of variability. In this, we avoid the difficulty of signs by squaring the separate deviations. The squared deviations used in computing the SD, are always taken from the mean, never from the median and mode.

Standard deviation is denoted by σ.

Standard Deviation for **ungrouped data**

$$\sigma = \sqrt{\frac{\Sigma x^2}{N}}$$

Standard Deviation for **grouped data**

(a) In case of **actual mean** $\sigma = \sqrt{\frac{\Sigma fx^2}{N}}$

(b) In case of **assumed mean**

$$\sigma = i\sqrt{\frac{\Sigma fx^2}{N} - c^2} \Rightarrow c = \text{Correction factor}$$

$$\sigma = i\sqrt{\frac{\Sigma fx^2}{N} - \left(\frac{\Sigma fx}{N}\right)^2}$$

Applications

- When the statistic having the greater stability is sought.
- When extreme deviations should exercise a proportionally greater effect upon the variability.
- When coefficients of correlation and other statistics are subsequently to be computed.

Fudiciary Limits

These indicate the interval (or the fiduciary limits) within which the mean of the population will lie at 0.95 or 0.99 levels of confidence. The fiduciary limits or the confidence interval of the population mean is estimated based on the sample mean. The sample mean is known as the **statistic** and the population mean is known as the **parameter**. The computation of population mean requires the use of standard error of the mean. Similarly, fiduciary limits or the confidence interval of the population standard deviation is also computed.

Graphical Presentation of Data

This includes bar diagrams, pie charts and line graph. The line graph is usually used to represent the distribution of the scores obtained on a variable with the objective of indicating the shape of the distribution. The bar diagrams are used for making comparisons of mean scores on the variable being studied in various sub-groups, such as boys v/s girls, urban v/s rural, private aided v/s private unaided v/s municipal schools, SSC v/s CBSE v/s ICSE v/s IGCSE schools and so on. Pie charts are used to indicate proportion of different sub-groups in the sample or the variance of specific variable associated with another variable.

Graphic presentation is another way of the presentation of data and information. The graphic presentation offers a quick and simple way of understanding the features and drawing comparisons. It is an effective analytical tool. Graphical presentation is used in situations, when we observe some functional relationship between the values of two variables.

Graphs help to understand the data easily. All statistical packages, MS Excel, and OpenOffice.org offer a wide range of graphs. In case of qualitative data (or categorised data), most common graphs are bar charts and pie-charts.

Bar Chart

A bar chart consists of a series of rectangles (or bars). The height of each rectangle is determined by the frequency of that category. Suppose that the sales of a popular soft drink in the year 2018-19, in five geographical regions, denoted as A, B, C, D and E, are 15245, 23762, 9231, 14980, and 12387, respectively, measured in 10,000 USD.

A bar chart of this data is as below:

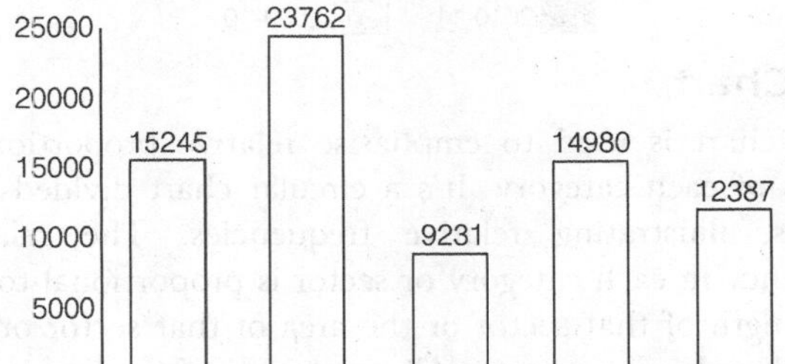

A line chart can also be plotted in this data by connecting the midpoints of each rectangle as below

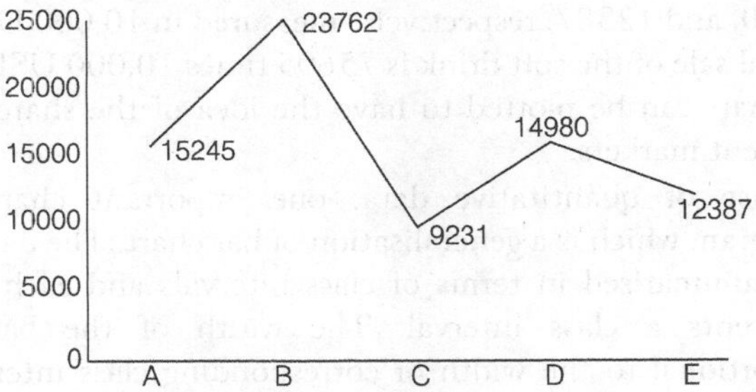

Line charts are useful when we wish to compare to data sets as we can overlap to line charts. For example, the sales data of the same soft drink in the same geographical regions in the year 2017-18 were 1975, 5686, 10652, 15199 and 726, respectively, measured in 10,000 USD.

The line chart showing the data for both the years is

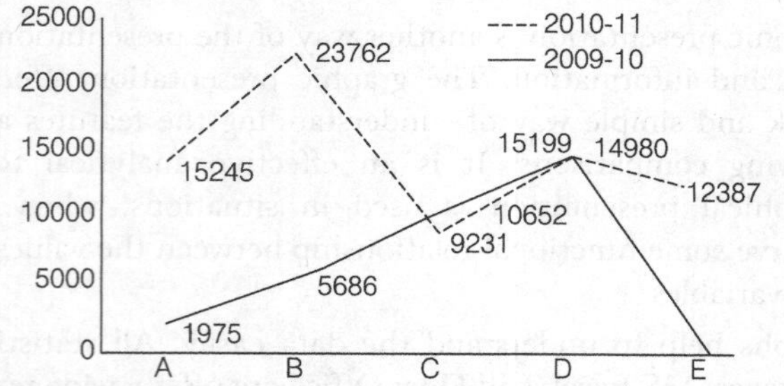

Another graphical representation of the same data is using multiple bars as below:

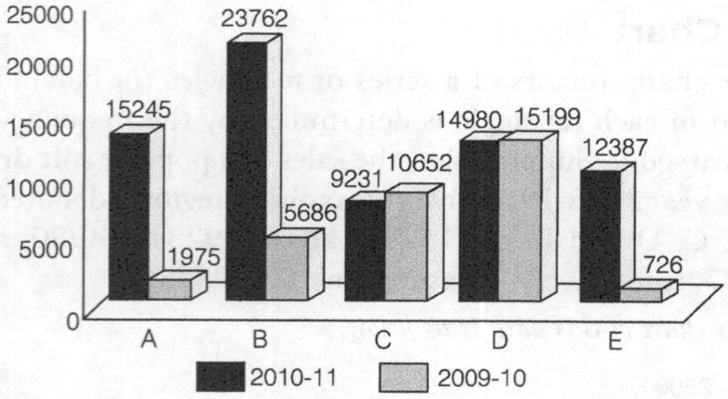

Pie-Chart

A pie-chart is used to emphasise relative proportion or shares of each category. It's a circular chart divided into sectors, illustrating relative frequencies. The relative frequency in each category or sector is proportional to the arc, length of that sector or the area of that sector or the central angle of that sector. Given above in the example, the soft drink has its market only in the five geographical regions, denoted as A, B, C, D and E. For the year 2018-19, the sales data in these regions are 15245, 23762, 9231, 14980, and 12387, respectively, measured in 10,000 USD. A total sale of the soft drink is 75605 times 10,000 USD. A pie-chart can be plotted to have the idea of the shares of different markets.

In case of quantitative data, one important chart is histogram which is a generalisation of bar chart. The data is first summarised in terms of class intervals and each bar represents a class interval. The width of the bar is proportional to the width of corresponding class interval. The area of the bar is proportional to the frequency of corresponding class interval. After making the class intervals in a quantitative data set, a pie-chart can also be used to read the share of each class interval.

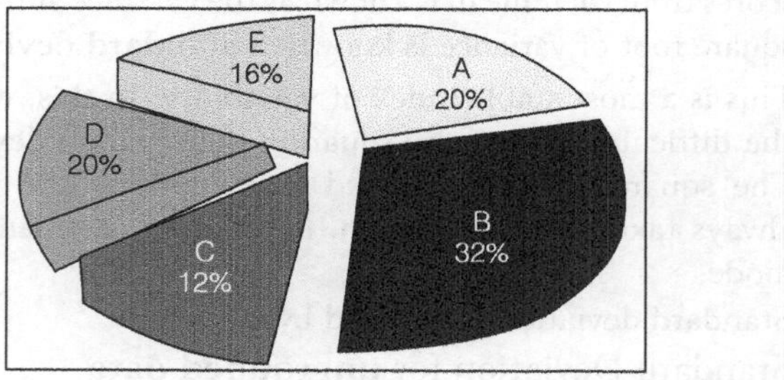

Principles of Hypothesis Testing

Hypothesis testing is a systematic way to select samples from a group of population with the intent of making a determination about the expected behaviour of entire group. Hypothesis testing is also known as significance testing. Hypothesis testing is used to infer the result of the hypothesis performed on a sample from a larger population. Hypothesis testing attempts to validate or disprove preconceived ideas.

Hypothesis testing works by collecting data and measuring how likely the particular set of data is assuming the null hypothesis is true. If the data set is very unlikely, defined as being part of a class of sets of data that only rarely will be observed, the experimenter rejects the null hypothesis concluding it (probably) is false. This class of data set is usually specified via a test static, which is designated to measure the extent of apparent departure from the null hypothesis. The procedure works by assessing whether the observed departure measured by the test statistic is larger than a value defined, so that the probability of occurrence of a more extreme value is small under the null hypothesis. If the data does not contradict the null hypothesis, then only a weak conclusion can be made, namely the observed data set provides no strong evidence against the null hypothesis. As the null hypothesis could be true or false, in this case, in some cases this is interpreted as meaning that the data give insufficient evidence to make any conclusion on others. It means that there is no evidence to support changing from a currently useful regime to a different one.

Example

Given the test scores of two random samples of men and women, does one group differ from the other? A possible null hypothesis is that the mean male score is the same as the mean female score.

$$H_0 : \mu_1 = \mu_2$$

Where,

H_0 = The null hypothesis

μ_1 = The mean of population 1

μ_2 = The mean of population 2

A stronger null hypothesis is that the two samples are drawn from the same population, such that the variance and shape of the distributions are also equal.

Introduction of Error

The word **error** entails different meanings. The concrete meaning of the Latin word **error** is **wandering** or **straying**.

In statistics, an error is not a mistake but rather a difference between a computed, estimated or measured value and the accepted true, specified or theoretically correct value. A statistical error is the amount, by which an observation differs from its expected value. The statistical error is based on the whole population from which the statistical unit was choosen randomly.

The error of an observed value is the deviation of the observed from true function value, while the residual of an observed value is the difference between the observed value and the estimated function.

Types of Error

While testing a hypothesis, there are some wrong decisions can be noticed, *which are*

- The researcher decides, based on the statistical findings, to reject the null hypothesis when it is false (Method A ≠ B). Correct decision.
- The researcher decides, based on the statistical findings, to not reject the null hypothesis when it is true (Method A = Method B). Correct decision.
- The researcher decides, based on the statistical findings, to reject the null hypothesis when it is true (Method A = Method B). Wrong decision.
- The researcher decides, based on the statistical findings, to not reject the null hypothesis when it is false (Method A ≠ B). Wrong decision.

In these cases, two types of errors can be seen i.e.

- Hypothesis is true, but our test rejects (Type I error)
- Hypothesis is false, but our test accepts it. (Type II error)

There is always a possibility that the researcher will make a mistake regarding the relationship between the two variables.

There are two possible mistakes or errors i.e.

Type I Error

It is committed by rejecting the null hypothesis when it is true. This occurs when the researcher assumes that a relationship exists when infact the evidence is that it does not. In a Type I error, the researcher should accept the null hypothesis and reject the null hypothesis, but opposite occurs. The probability of committing a Type I error is called **alpha**.

i.e. α = Prob (Type I error)

Type II Error

Type II error occurs when the researcher assumes that a relationship exists when infact the evidence is that it does. In a type II error, the researcher should reject the null hypothesis and accept the research hypothesis, but the opposite occurs. The probability of committing a Type II error is called **beta**.

i.e, β = Prob (Type II error)

While testing hypothesis, a researcher reduces these two types of errors. But due to fixed sample size, it is not possible to control both errors simultaneously. Generally, reducing the possibility of committing a Type I error increases the possibility of committing Type II error and vice-versa reducing the possibility of committing a Type II error increases the possibility of committing a Type I error.

Researchers generally try to minimise Type I error because when a researcher assumes a relationship exists when one really does not, things may be worse off than before. In Type II error, the researcher misses an opportunity to confirm that a relationship exists, but is no worse off than before.

Three Kinds of Error

In **1948**, **Mosteller** (1916-2006) argued that a third kind error was required to describe circumstances.

He observed:

Type I error rejecting the null hypothesis when it is true.

Type II error accepting the null hypothesis when it is false.

Type III error correctly rejecting the hypothesis for the wrong reason.

Mitroff (1974) argued type III error as either the error of having solved the wrong problem when one should have solved the right problem or the error of choosing the wrong problem representation.

Level of Significance

The level of significance is defined as the probability of rejecting a null hypothesis by the test when it is really true, which is denoted as α *i.e.* P (Type I error) = α. Confidence level: The level of significance 0.05 is related to the 95% confidence level.

The rejection or acceptance of a null hypothesis is based on some level of significance as a criterion.

- Rejecting a null hypothesis at the 0.05 level indicates that a difference in means as large as that found between the experimental and control groups would have resulted from sampling error is less than 5 out of 100 replications of the experiment. This suggests a 95% probability that the difference was due to the experimental treatment rather than to sampling error.

- A more rigorous test of significance is the 1% (0.01) level. Rejecting a null hypothesis at the .01 level would suggest that a difference in means as large as that found between the experimental and control groups would have resulted from sampling error is less that 1 in 100 replications of the experiment.

Example

The reading experiment has found the data and test the null hypothesis that there was no significant difference between the mean, reading achievement of the initial teaching alphabet, experimental group and the traditional alphabet control group.

Experimental ITA Group	Control Traditional Alphabet Group
$N_1 = 32$	$N_2 = 34$
$\overline{X}_1 = 87.43$	$\overline{X}_2 = 82.58$
$S_1^2 = 39.40$	$S_2^2 = 40.80$
$t = \dfrac{\overline{X}_1 - \overline{X}_2}{\sqrt{\dfrac{S_1^2}{N_1} + \dfrac{S_2^2}{N_2}}}$	$= \dfrac{87.43 - 82.58}{\sqrt{\dfrac{39.40}{32} + \dfrac{40.80}{34}}}$
$= \dfrac{4.85}{\sqrt{1.23 + 1.20}}$	$= \dfrac{4.85}{\sqrt{2.43}} = \dfrac{4.85}{1.56} t = 3.11$

Because the *t* value of 3.11 exceeds 2.58, the null hypothesis may be rejected at the .01 level of significance. If this experiment was replicated with random samples from the same population, the probability is that a difference between mean performance as great as that observed would result from sampling error in fewer than 1 out of 100 replications. This test would indicate rather strong evidence that the treatment would probably make a difference in the teaching of reading, when applied to similar populations of pupils.

Procedures Used to Test the Significance

Whenever, a significance test is performed, it involves comparing a test value that have calculated to some critical value for the statistics. It doesn't matter that what type of statistic we are calculating, the procedure to test for significance is the same.

- Decide on the critical alpha level (*i.e.* the error rate which researcher is willing to accept).
- Conduct the research.
- Calculate the statistic.
- Compare the statistic to a critical value obtained from a table.

If statistic is higher than the critical value

- Findings will be significant.
- Null hypothesis will be rejected.
- Probability is small than the difference or relationship happened by chance and P is less than the critical alpha level (P < alpha).

If statistic is lower than the critical value

- Finding will not be significant.
- Null hypothesis will be failed to reject.
- The probability is high that the difference or relationship happened by chance and P is greater than the critical alpha level (P > alpha).

Power of a Statistical Test and Effect Size

The power of a statistical test gives the likelihood of rejecting the null hypothesis when the null hypothesis is false. Just as the significance level (alpha) of a test gives the probability that the null hypothesis will be rejected when it is actually true (a wrong decision), power quantifies the chance that the null hypothesis will be rejected when it is actually false (a correct decision). Thus, power is the ability of a test to correctly reject the null hypothesis.

The effect size tells us something about how relevant the relationship between two variables is in practice. There are two types of effect sizes *i.e.* effect size based on the proportion of explained variance and the proportion of explained variance is often indicated by one of the following terms *i.e.* R^2 or eta squared, partial eta squared or omega squared.

Techniques Used for Testing Hypothesis

There are two types of statistical techniques which are used for testing of hypothesis. They are parametric and non-parametric techniques.

Parametric Techniques

It can be applied for the purpose of testing the hypothesis if the following conditions are satisfied.

- When the sample is randomly selected.
- When the variance of the various groups are equal or near equal.
- When the data is in the form of interval scale or ratio scale.
- When the observations are independent.
- When the data follows a normal distribution.

Non-Parametric Techniques

The techniques which enable us to compare samples and make inference or tests of significance without having to assume normality in the population are known as non-parametric techniques. Some of the non-parametric techniques are the Chi square test, the rank difference correlation coefficient, sign test, median test and sum of ranks test. These tests are less able to detect a true difference and it should not be used when other more exact tests are applicable.

Inferential Data Analysis

Inferential statistics has two goals and they are :

- To determine what might be happening in a population, based on a sample of the population.
- To determine what might happen in the future.
  Thus, inferential statistics are to estimate and/or to predict. To use inferential statistics, only a sample of the population is needed.

These are much more detailed and are used to draw conclusions about hypothesis and to determine probabilities of an outcome.

- It comprise the use of statistics to make inferences, concerning some known aspects of population.
- It draws inferences beyond data, obtained from sample.
- It includes T-test, analysis of variance, Pearson's correlation, linear regression and multiple regression.

Statistical

T-test

The T-test assesses whether the means of two groups are statistically different from each other. This analysis is appropriate, whenever you want to compare the means of two groups and especially appropriate as the analysis for the post test, only two, groups randomised experimental design.

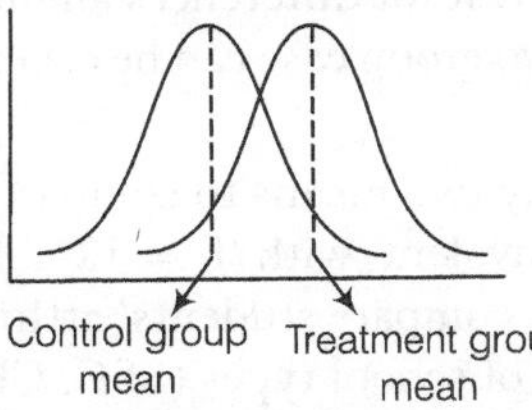

Idealised Distributions for Treated and Comparison Group Post Test Values

The figure shows the distribution for the treated and control groups in a study. In reference to this graph, we can consider the three possible situations. The first thing to notice about the three situations is that the difference between their means is the same in all three.

- **First** case shows a moderate variability of scores within each group.
- **Second** situation shows the high variability case.
- **Third** shows the case with low variability.

Representations of all the three cases are given below:

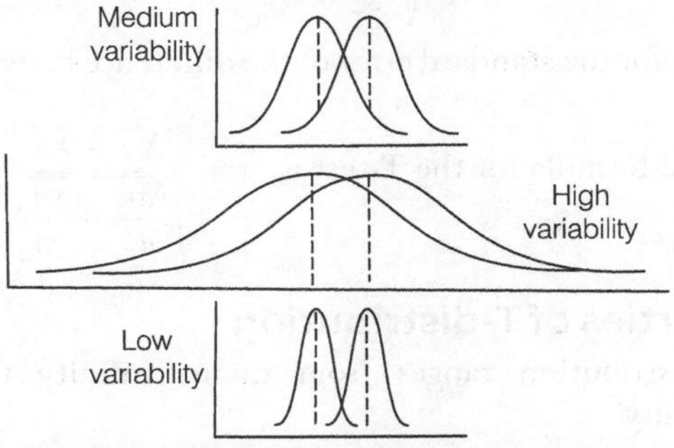

Three Scenarios for Differences Between Means

This leads to a very important conclusion. When we are looking at the differences between scores for two groups, we have to judge the difference between their means relative to the spread or variability of their scores. The T-test does just this.

William Sealy Gosset

- Gosset devised the T-test in 1908, as a cheap way to monitor the quality of stout.
- Gosset was known as statistician and the editor.
- He worked for the **Guiness Brewery** in Dublin, Ireland.
- The T-test work was submitted to and accept in the journal **Biometrika**.

Statistical Analysis of the T-test

The formula for the T-test is a ratio. The top part of the ratio is just the difference between the two means or averages. The bottom part is a measure of the variability or dispersion of the scores.

$$= \frac{\text{difference between group means}}{\text{variability of groups}}$$

$$= \frac{X_T - X_C}{SE(X_T - X_C)}$$

= **T-value**

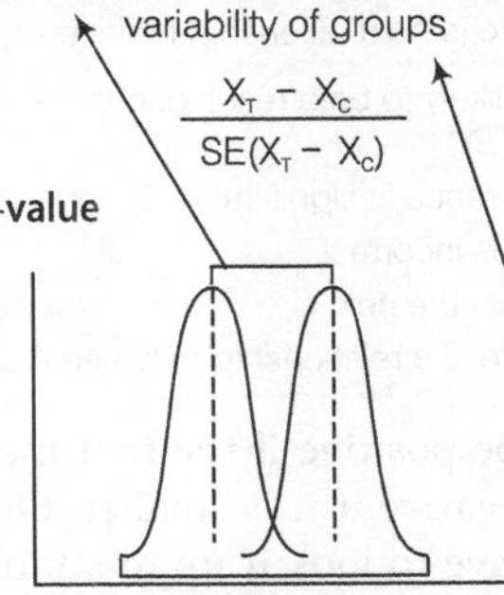

Formula for the T-Test

Figure shows the formula for the T-test and how the numerator and denominator are related to the distributions. The top part of the formula is easy to compute. The bottom part is called the standard error of the difference. To compute it, we take the variance for each group and divided by the number of people in that group. Variance is simply the square of the standard deviation.

$$SE(\overline{X}_T - \overline{X}_C) = \sqrt{\frac{var_T}{n_T} + \frac{var_C}{n_C}}$$

Formula for the standard error of the difference between the means.

The final formula for the T-test is, $t = \dfrac{\overline{X}_T - \overline{X}_C}{\sqrt{\dfrac{var_T}{n_T} + \dfrac{var_C}{n_C}}}$

Properties of T-distribution

- T-distribution ranges from minus infinity to plus infinity.
- Constant C actually a function of V, the distribution of $f(t)$ is completely specified. Thus, $f(t)$ is a family of functions, one for each value of V.
- Like the standard normal distribution, the T distribution is symmetrical and has a mean zero.

Assumptions of T- test

- Each group is considered to be a sample from a distinct population.
- The responses in each group are independent of those in the other group.
- The distributions of the variable of interest are normal.
- At least ordinal measures.
- Representative sample.
- Normal distributions for population.

Interpretation of T-test Results

If this sign	It means all these things
$p \geq .05$ or .01	Likely to be a result of chance (same as saying $A = B$) Difference is not significant Null is correct Fail to reject the null There is no relationship between A and B
$p \leq .05$ or .01	Not likely to be a result of chance (same as saying $A \neq B$) Difference is significant Null is incorrect Reject the null There is a relationship between A and B

The T value will be positive if the first mean is larger than the second and negative if it is smaller. Once you compute the T value you have to look it up in a table of significance to test whether the ratio is large enough to say that the difference between the groups is not likely to have been a chance finding. To test the significance, researcher needs to set a risk level. Researcher also need to determine the degree of freedom in the T-test.

Advantages of T-test

- We test the significance of difference between two means of the two groups. We can thus, find out whether there is really a difference between means or it is due to chance factors.
- We can easily find out the effectiveness of a treatment, given to two different groups or to a single group.
- We can also find out the mean of the population from which the sample is drawn.
- T-test can be applied to even large samples and we will get very dependable results.

ANOVA

Prof. R A Fisher was the first man to use the term 'variance' and infact it was he who developed a very detailed theory concerning ANOVA explaining its usefulness in practical field. ANOVA is essentially a procedure for testing the difference among different groups of data for homogeneity. The essence of ANOVA is that the total variation in a set of data is broken down into two types that amount which can attributed to chance and that amount which can be attributed to specific causes ANOVA consists in splitting the variance for analytical purposes. It is a method of analysing variance to which response is subject into various components corresponding various sources of variation. Through ANOVA one can investigate any number of factors which are hypothesised or said to influence the dependent variable.

Types of ANOVA

These are as follows

One Way ANOVA

It is used to test for differences among two or more independent groups. Typically, however, the one way ANOVA is used to test for differences two or more independent groups. Typically, however, the one way ANOVA is used to test for differences among three or more groups, since the two group case can be covered by student's T-test.

When there are only two means to compare, the T-test and the F-test are equivalent with F = t2 . For example, a researcher wants to compare students' attitude towards the school on the basis of school types (SSC, CBSE and ICSE). In this case, there is one dependent variable, namely attitude towards the school and three groups, namely SSC, CBSE and ICSE schools. Here, the one way ANOVA is used to test for differences in students' attitude towards the school among the three groups.

One way ANOVA for repeated measures is used when the subjects are subjected to repeated measures. This means that the same subjects are used for each treatment. Note that this method can be subject to carry over effects. This technique is often used in experimental research in which we want to compare three or more groups on one dependent variable which is measured twice *i.e.* as pre-test and post test.

Two Way ANOVA

It is used when the researcher wants to study the effects of two or more independent or treatment variables. It is also known as **factorial ANOVA**. The most commonly used type of factorial ANOVA is the 2×2 (read as two by two, as you would a matrix) design, where there are two independent variables and each variable has two levels or distinct values.

Two way ANOVA can also be multi-level such as 3×3, etc or higher order such as $2 \times 2 \times 2$, etc, but analyses with higher numbers of factors are rarely done by hand because the calculations are lengthy. However, since the introduction of data analytic software, the utilization of higher order designs and analyses has become quite common.

For example, a researcher wants to compare students' attitude towards the school on the basis of school types (SSC,CBSE and ICSE) and gender. In this case, there is one dependent variable, namely attitude towards the school and two independent variables *viz* school types, including three levels, namely SSC, CBSE and ICSE schools and gender including two levels, namely boys and girls.

Here, the two way ANOVA is used to test for differences in students' attitude towards the school on the basis of school types and gender. This is an example of 3×2 two way ANOVA as there are three levels of school types, namely SSC, CBSE and ICSE schools and two levels of gender, namely boys and girls. It is known as **two way ANOVA** as it involves comparing one dependent variable (attitude towards the school) on the basis of two independent variables, *viz* school type and gender.

MANOVA

When one wants to compare two or more independent groups in which the sample is subjected to repeated measures, such as pre-test and post test in an experimental study, one may perform a factorial mixed design ANOVA *i.e.* Multivariate Analysis of Variance or MANOVA in which one factor is a between subject's variable and the other is within subject's variable. This is a type of Mixed Effect model. It is used when there is more than one dependent variable.

ANCOVA

While comparing two groups on a dependent variable, if it is found that they differ on some other variable, such as their 10, SES or pre-test, it is necessary to remove these initial differences.

Assumptions of Using ANOVA

- Independence of cases.
- Normality of the distributions in each of the groups.
- Equality or homogeneity of variances, known as homoscedasticity *i.e.* the variance of data in groups should be the same. Levene's test for homogeneity of variances is typically used to confirm homoscedasticity. The Kolmogorov-Smirnov or the Shpiaro-Wilk test may be used to confirm normality.

According to **Lindman**, F-test is unreliable if there are deviations from normality whereas **Ferguson** and **Takane** claim that the F-test is robust. The **Kruskal-Wallis'** test is a non-parametric alternative which does not rely on an assumption of normality.

Chi-Square (Equal Probability and Normal Probability Hypothesis)

A chi-square test (also chi-squared or $\chi 2$ test) is any statistical test in which the test statistic has a chi-squared distribution when the null hypothesis is true or any distribution in which the probability distribution of the test statistic (assuming the null hypothesis is true) can be made to approximate a chi-square distribution as closely as desired by making the sample size large enough. Chi-square is a statistical test commonly used to compare observed data with data we would expect to obtain, according to a specific hypothesis. For example, if a researcher expects parents' attitude towards sex education to be provided in schools to be normally distributed, then he might want to know about the **goodness to fit** between the observed and expected results *i.e.* whether the deviations (differences between observed and expected) the result of chance or whether they are due to other factors. The chi-square test tests the null hypothesis, which states that there is no significant difference between the expected and observed result.

If it is assumed that the expected frequencies are equally distributed in all the cells, the chi-square test is known as **equal distribution hypothesis**. On the other hand, if it is assumed that the frequencies are expected to be distributed normally, the chi-square test is known as **normal distribution hypothesis**. The chi-square (χ^2) test measures the alignment between two sets of frequency measures.

These must be categorical counts and not percentages or ratios measures. Thus, $\chi^2 = \Sigma$ (fo-fe) 2/ fe, where fo = observed frequency and fe = expected frequency. It may be noted that the expected values may need to be scaled to be comparable to the observed values.

A simple test is that the total frequency/count should be the same for observed and expected values. In a table, the expected frequency, if not known, may be estimated as fe = (row total) x (column total) / N, where N is the total number of all the rows (or columns). The obtained chi square is compared with that given in the chi square table to determine whether the comparison shows significance.

In a table, the degrees of freedom are computed as follows

$$df = (R - 1) \times (C - 1)$$

Where, R = number of rows

C = number of columns

Chi-square indicates whether there is a significant association between variables, but it does not indicate just how significant and important this is.

Chi-square (χ^2) test is undoubtedly the most important and most used member of the non-parametric family of statistical tests. Chi-square is employed to test the difference between an actual sample and another hypothetical or previously established distribution, such as that which may be expected due to chance or probability.

There are many situations, in which it is not possible to make any rigid assumption about the distribution of the population, from which samples are drawn, *i.e.* the distribution is not definitely said to be normal. Chi-square test is one of them.

The reasons why such tests are used so popularly are given below

- These tests are distribution free *i.e.* they can be used with any shape of population distributions.
- They can be easily computed, handled and understood.
- They can be used with those types of measurements that prohibit the use of parametric test.

x^2 test was first used by **Karl Pearson in 1890**. Chi-square can also be used to test differences between two or more actual samples.

Steps in the Calculation of χ^2

- Expected frequencies (E) are calculated first by using the following formula $\frac{RT \times CT}{N}$

  RT = The row total for the row containing the cell.

  CT = The column total for the column containing the cell.
- Get the difference between observed and expected frequencies and then find the value of $(O - E)^2$.
- Divide this value by E and then find the sum total. The value of χ^2 ranges from zero to infinity. Zero χ^2 means observed and expected frequencies completely coincide. Greater the discrepancy between O and E, greater will be the value of χ^2.

Basic Computational Equation

$$\chi^2 = \Sigma \frac{(\text{Observed frequency} - \text{Expected frequency})^2}{\text{Expected frequency}}$$

$$\text{or } \chi^2 = \Sigma \frac{(\text{Observed frequencies} - \text{Expected fr} \quad 2}{\text{Expected frequencies}}$$

$$= \Sigma \frac{(F_o - F_e)^2}{F_e}$$

	A	U	D
Observed responses (Fo)	8	8	14
Expected responses (Fe)	(10)	(10)	(10)
Fo – Fe	– 2	– 2	4
$(F_o - F_e)^2$	4	4	16
$\frac{(F_o - F_e)^2}{F_e}$	.4	.4	1.6
$\Sigma \frac{(F_o - F_e)^2}{F_e}$		2.4	

Degrees of freedom – (number of levels – 1) = 2

$$x^2 .05 = 5.991 2.4 < 5.991$$

Therefore, accept null hypothesis.

When there is only one degree of freedom, an adjustment known as **Yates**. Correction for continuity must be employed. To use this correction, a value of 0.5 is subtracted from the absolute value (irrespective of algebraic sign) of the numerator contribution of each cell to the above basic computational formula. The basic chi-square computational formula then becomes

$$x^2 = \Sigma \frac{(\text{Observed frequency} - \text{Expected frequency} | - 0.5 |)^2}{\text{Expected frequency}}$$

Some Points Related to χ^2

- In χ^2, sum of the observed and expected frequencies is always zero *i.e.*

  $$\Sigma = (O - E) = N - N = O$$

  This equation provides a check on the computation of χ^2.
- χ^2 depends upon only the set of observed and expected frequencies and degree of freedom. It is a distribution free test.
- χ^2 distribution is a limiting approximation of the multi-nominal distribution. Yet, χ^2 test can be applied to discrete random variables whose frequencies can be counted and tabulated.

Level of Significance

The calculated value of χ^2 is compared with the table value of χ^2 for given degree of freedom at a certain specified level of significance. Generally, 5% level of significance is selected for this purpose. If the value of $\chi^2 >$ table value of χ^2, the distribution between theory and observation is considered to be significant. The value of χ^2 is a random variable, which takes on different values from sample to sample and its value will always be positive. Besides, χ^2 is derived from observation, so it is a statistic not a parameter.

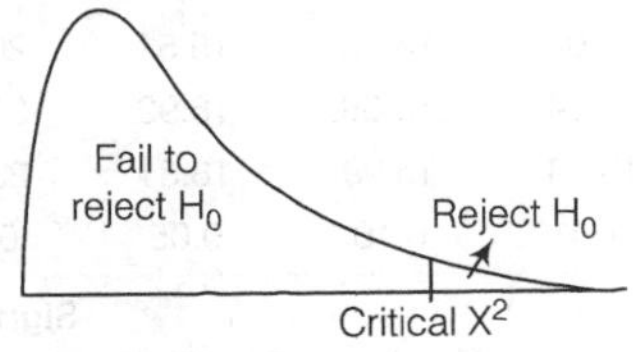

df	.05	.025	.010	.005	.001
4	9.49	11.14	13.28	14.86	18.47

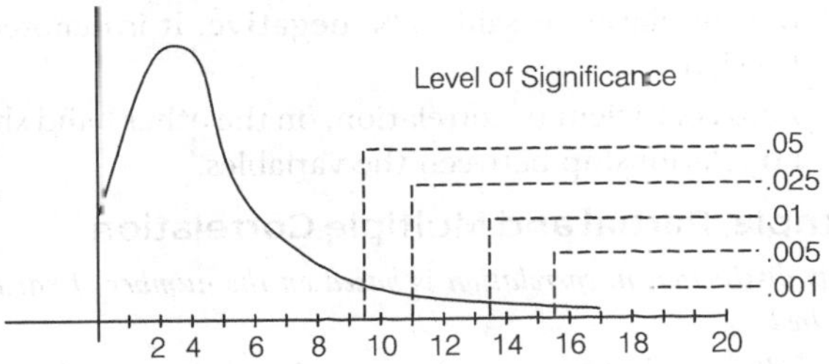

Above table is representing a graph given for degree of freedom, which is 4 at different levels of significance.

Uses of χ^2 Test

χ^2 Test as the Test of Independence

With the help of χ^2 test, we can find out whether two or more attributes are associated or not. In order to test whether the attributes are related or not we take the null hypothesis that there is no association in the attributes under study.

If the value of χ^2 is less than the table value at a certain level of significance (5% level) we say that the results of the experiment provide no evidence for doubting the hypothesis *i.e.* attributes are not related. On the other hand, if value of χ^2 > table value, null hypothesis will be rejected *i.e.* attributes are related.

χ^2 Test as a Test of Goodness of Fit

It enables us to ascertain how appropriately the theoretical distribution fit empirical distribution. When an ideal frequency curve is fitted to the data, χ^2 test find out how well this curve fits with the observed facts.

χ^2 Test as a Test of Homogeneity

Tests of homogeneity are designated to determine whether two or more independent random samples are drawn from the same population or from different populations.

Example Suppose, that we flip a coin 20 times and record the frequency of occurrence of heads and tails. We know from the laws of probability that we should expect 10 heads and 10 tails. We also know that because of sampling error, we could easily come up with 9 heads and 11 tails or 12 heads and 8 tails.

Let us suppose, our coin flipping experiment yielded 12 heads and 8 tails. We would enter our expected frequencies (10- 10) and our observed frequencies (12 – 8) in a table.

	Observed	Expected	(Fo-Fe-0.5)	$(Fo\text{-}Fe\text{-}0.5)^2$	$\frac{(Fo-Fe-0.5)^2}{Fe}$
Heads	12	10	1.5	2.25	0.225
Tails	8	10	– 1.5	2.25	0.225
	20	20			0.450

The calculation of x in a one way classification (Yates' correction) is very straight forward. The expected frequency in a category (heads) is subtracted from the observed frequency and since Yates' correction is being used, 0.5 is subtracted from the absolute value of Fo - Fe, the difference is squared and the square is divided by its expected frequency. This is repeated for the remaining categories and as the formula for χ^2 indicates, these results are summed for all categories.

How does a calculated χ^2 of 0.450 tell us if our observed results of 12 heads and 8 tails represent a significant deviation from an expected 10-10 split? The shape of the chi-square sampling distribution depends upon the number of degrees of freedom. The degrees of freedom for a one way classification χ^2 is r - 1, where r is the number of levels.

In our problem above, r = 2, so there would obviously be 1 degree of freedom. From our statistical reference tables, a χ^2 of 3.84 or greater is needed for χ^2 to be significant at the .05 level, so we conclude that our χ^2 of 0.450 in the coin flipping experiment could have happened by sampling error and the deviations between the observed and expected frequencies are not significant.

We would expect any data set yielding a calculated χ^2 value less than 3.84 with 1 degree of freedom at least 5% of the time due to chance alone. Therefore, the observed difference is not statistically significant at the .05 level.

Different Levels of Significance

Degrees of Freedom (df)	χ^2 value[14]										
1.	0.004	0.02	0.06	0.15	0.46	1.07	1.64	2.71	3.84	6.64	10.83
2.	0.10	0.21	0.45	0.71	1.39	2.41	3.22	4.60	5.99	9.21	13.82
3.	0.35	0.58	1.01	1.42	2.37	3.66	4.64	6.25	7.82	11.34	16.27
4.	0.71	1.06	1.65	2.20	3.36	4.88	5.99	7.78	9.49	13.28	18.47
5.	1.14	1.61	2.34	3.00	4.35	6.06	7.29	9.24	11.07	15.09	20.52
6.	1.63	2.20	3.07	3.83	5.35	7.23	8.56	10.64	12.59	16.81	22.46
7.	2.17	2.83	3.82	4.67	6.35	8.38	9.80	12.02	14.07	18.48	24.32
8.	2.73	3.49	4.59	5.53	7.34	9.52	11.03	13.36	15.51	20.09	26.12
9.	3.32	4.17	5.38	6.39	8.34	10.66	12.24	14.68	16.92	21.67	27.88
10.	3.94	4.86	6.18	7.27	9.34	11.78	13.44	15.99	18.31	23.21	29.59
P value (Probability)	0.95	0.90	0.80	0.70	0.50	0.30	0.20	0.10	0.05	0.01	0.001
	Non-significant (df) and their χ^2 Values								**Significant**		

Correlation

Statistically, correlation refers to a quantifiable relationship between two variables. Furthermore, it is a measure of the strength and direction of that relationship. Two measures for every subject in the group are required. If two quantities vary in such a way that movements in the other, these quantities are said to be correlated.

- How much the two variables are correlated is determined by the degree of correlation.
- The degree of relationship is measured through the correlation analysis. This is called correlation coefficient.
- Two independent variables are never correlated because they will have nothing for interpretation.
- The degree of correlation will always vary from −1 to + 1 *i.e.* from perfectly negative to perfectly positive and zero degree means no correlation at all.

There are four things, which could be determined by correlation

- Whether a relationship exists between variables *i.e.* measurement of relation.
- Whether correlation is positive or negative.
- Whether the degree of correlation is significant or not.
- Establishment of cause and effect relationships between variables.

Types of Correlation

There are different types of correlation and they are

Positive and Negative Correlation

- If both the variables are varying in the same direction *i.e.* if intelligence is high, adjustability is also high and vice-versa, the correlation is said to be **positive**, which is denoted by (+) sign.
- On the other hand, if values of two variables move in different directions, so that with the increase in the value of one, the other value decreases and vice-versa, the correlation is said to be **negative**. It is denoted by (−) sign.
- Zero coefficient of correlation, on the other hand shows no relationship between the variables.

Simple, Partial and Multiple Correlation

This distinction in correlation is based on the number of variables studied

- When only two variables are taken into consideration, it is simple correlation.
- In partial correlation, more than two variables are considered with only two variables to be influencing each other. Here, the effects of other variables are kept constant.
- In multiple correlation, three or more variables are studied simultaneously.

Linear and Non-Linear Correlation

When the variations in the values of two variables are in a constant ratio, correlation is said to be **linear**. Here, relationship will be maintained at a constant rate till the end.

Example

Variable X	2	4	6	8	10
Variable Y	5	10	15	20	25

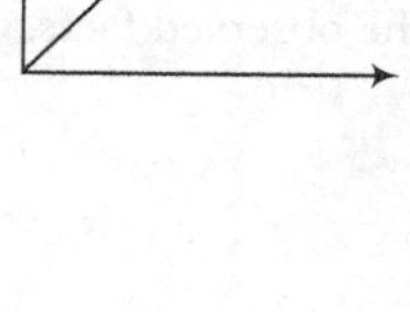

On the other hand, if percentage change in X and Y are not constant all the time, it is further fluctuating, the relationship is said to be **non-linear** or **curvi-linear**.

Example

Variable X	2	4	6	8	10
Variable Y	5	8	12	17	24

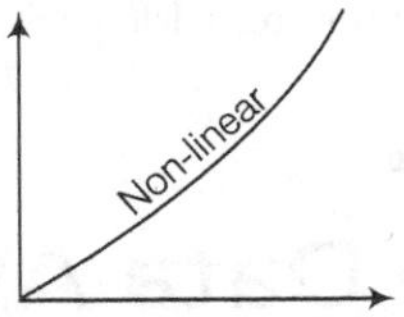

Methods of Studying Correlation

These are:

- Scatter Diagram
- Correlation Graph
- Product Moment Coefficient of Correlation
- Rank Difference Correlation Method
- Coefficient of Concurrent Deviation
- Method of Least Square.

Uses of Correlation

- To evaluate the degree of reliability and validity of psychological tests and inventories.
- In the technique of factor analysis.
- To make predictions.
- In the technique of path analysis

Two Methods of Correlation

Product Moment Method of Coefficient

Pearson's coefficient is denoted as Y.

- It is used where relation between two variable is linear.
- In some situations, the data for two variables X and Y are expressed in interval or ratio level of measurement and the distribution is linear.

Product moment means that the mean of the product of the mean adjusted random variables, hence the modifier product moment in the name. It is a measure of the strength and direction of the linear relationship between two variables that is defined as the (sample) co-variance of the variables, divided by product of their standard deviations.

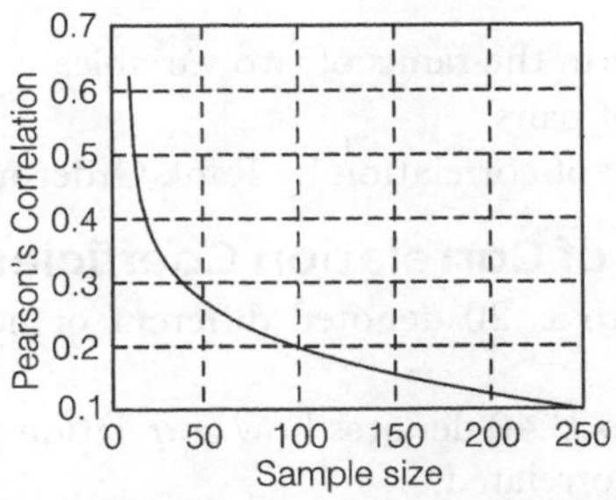

A graph showing the minimum of Pearson's correlation coefficient that is significantly different from zero at the 0.05 level, for given sample size

There are two methods of Pearson's coefficient of correlation, which are

- Long Method (Actual Mean Method)
- Short Method (Assumed Mean Method)

For **Actual Mean Method,**

$$\gamma = \frac{\Sigma xy}{\sqrt{\Sigma x^2 . \Sigma y^2}}$$

For **Assume Mean Method,**

$$\gamma = \frac{\frac{\Sigma xy}{N} - C_x C_y}{\sigma_x . \sigma_y}$$

In this, $C_x = M_x - AM_x$

$C_y = M_y - AM_y$ and $\sigma_x = \sqrt{\frac{\Sigma x^2}{N} - C_x^2}$

$$\sigma_y = \sqrt{\frac{\Sigma y^2}{N} - C_y^2}$$

Points which should be taken care:

- From the above examples, we see that if value of Σxy is very high in relation to $\Sigma x^2 . \Sigma y^2$, then correlation will be high and vice-versa. Moreover, if value of Σxy is in negative, negative coefficient of correlation will be there.
- Degree of γ only shows the degree of variations on the two series.

Rank Order Coefficient of Correlation

It is used when we do not have data in the form of score, where rank of the individual is given. Nominal or cardinal range of scale, it is used if relationship of two variables are differ and then relation between the variable is found with the help of rho (ρ). There are problems, in which the relationship among the measurement made is non-linear and cannot be described by product moment coefficient of correlation. In this case, rank order method is used.

$$\rho = \frac{1 - 6\,\Sigma D^2}{N\sqrt{N^2 - 1}}$$

Where,

D = Difference in the ranks of two variables

N = Number of pairs

ρ = Coefficient of correlation by Rank Order method

Significance of Correlation Coefficient

- From ± .00 to ± .20 denoted different or negligible relationship.
- From ± .20 to ± .40 denotes how correlation present, but slightly correlated.
- From ± .40 to ± .70 denotes substantial or marked relationship.
- From ± .70 to 1 .00 denotes high to very high relationship.

Z-Test

A Z-test is a type of hypothesis test. Hypothesis testing is just a way for you to figure out if results from a test are valid or repeatable. For example, if someone said they had found a new drug that cures cancer, you would want to be sure it was probably true. A hypothesis test will tell you if it's probably true or probably not true. A Z-test is used when data is approximately **normally distributed.**

You would use a Z-test if:

- Your sample size is greater than 30. Otherwise, use a T-test.
- Data points should be independent from each other. In other words, one data point is not related or does not affect another data point.
- Your data should be normally distributed. However, for large sample sizes (over 30) this does not always matter.
- Your data should be randomly selected from a population, where each item has an equal chance of being selected.
- Sample sizes should be equal if at all possible.

One Sample Z-Test Example

For example, assume an investor wishes to test whether the average daily return of a stock is greater than 1%. A simple random sample of 50 returns is calculated and has an average of 2%. Assume the standard deviation of the returns is 2.50%. Therefore, the null hypothesis is when the average or mean is equal to 3%.

Conversely, the alternative hypothesis is whether the mean return is greater than 3%. Assume an alpha of 0.05% is selected with a two tailed test. Consequently, there is 0.025% of the samples in each tail and the alpha has a critical value of 1.96 or -1.96. If the value of z is greater than 1.96 or less than -1.96, the null hypothesis is rejected.

The value for z is calculated by subtracting the value of the average daily return, selected for the test or 1% in this case, from the observed average of the samples. Next, divide the resulting value by the standard deviation, divided by the square root of the number of observed values.

Therefore, the test statistic is calculated to be 2.83 or (0.02-0.01)/(0.025 / (50) (1/2)). The investor rejects the null hypothesis since Z is greater than 1.96 and concludes that the average daily return is greater than 1%.

Qualitative Data Analysis

Qualitative data are verbal or other symbolic materials. The detailed description of observed behaviours, people, situations and events. The analysis of qualitative data means studying the organised material in order to discover inherent facts. The data are studied from as many angle as possible either to explore new facts or to reinterpret already existing known facts.

The types of qualitative data analysis are:

Data Reduction

Data reduction refers to the process of selecting, focusing, simplifying, abstracting and transforming the data that appear in writing up field notes or transcriptions. **First**, the mass of data has to be organized and somehow meaningfully reduced or reconfigured. These data are condensed so as to make them more manageable. They are also transformed so that they can be made intelligible in terms of the issues being addressed. Data reduction often forces choices about which aspects of the accumulated data should be emphasised, reduced or set aside completely for the purposes of the topic at hand.

Data in themselves do not reveal anything and hence, it is not necessary to present a large amount of unassimilated and uncategorized data for the reader's consumption in order to show that you are perfectly objective. In qualitative analysis, the researcher uses the Principle of Selectivity to determine which data are to be singled out for description. This usually involves some combination of deductive and inductive analysis. While, initial categorizations are shaped by pre-established research questions, the qualitative researcher should remain open to inducing new meanings from the data available. Data reduction should be guided primarily by the need to address the salient question(s) in a research.

In data reduction, the coding of data should be done as per topics of disussion or guide or checklist of observation or semi-structured interviews.

Classification

Classification is a way of knowing the attributes of things to be able to group them (Tesch, 1990). Infact in the early days, science was considered largely a way of developing classification systems. For some scholarly fields, classification is still a major objective. Botanical classification schemes and the periodic table of elements are well known examples of classification schemes.

The qualitative analyst, using classification as a tool for analysis, then looks for convergence in the data that have been categorised using typologies. Such activity leads to a classification system of data. **Guba** (1978) suggested several steps for converting field notes and interview transcripts into systematic categories for the purpose of analysis. The analyst begins by looking for reocurring regularities in the data. These regularities represent patterns that can be sorted into categories. Categories should then by judged by two criteria *i.e.* internal homogeneity and external heterogeneity. The **first** criterion concerns the extent to which the data that belong to a certain category hold together in a meaningful way. The **second** criterion concerns the extent to which differences among categories are bold and clear.

The existence of a large number of unassignable or overlapping data items is good evidence of some basic fault in the category system. The analyst then works back and forth between the data and classification system to verify the meaningfulness and accuracy of the categories and the placement of data in categories.

Several different classification systems have been developed, some priorities must be established to determine which category systems are more important than others. Prioritising is done, according to the salience, credibility, uniqueness, feasibility and materiality of the classification schemes. Finally, the category system or class of categories are tested for completeness.

The completeness can be tested by examining the categories internally or externally. **Internal examination** means the individual categories should appear to be consistent. **External examination** means the class of categories should seem to comprise a whole picture. The steps and procedures suggested by Guba for categorising and classifying the qualitative data are not mechanical and rigid. It involves both technical and creative dimensions. No infallable procedure exists for performing it.

To sum up, we can say that the basic requirements for classification are to identify, generate and develop categories using anyone typology or both. Judge the categories for internal homogeneity and external heterogeneity. Arrange or sort out the data as per the developed categories. There might be possibility of some data remaining out of the categories. Check, recheck and verify the meaningfulness and accuracy of the categories and the placement of data in categories. Prioritise the categories, according to salience, crediability and uniqueness of the classification schemes. Test the categories for completeness, both internal and external. Label the categories with some identification mark that will represent a class.

Analytical Induction

Analytical induction is a way of building explanations in qualitative analysis by constructing and testing a set of causal links between events, actions, etc, in one case and the iterative extension of this to further cases. It is research logic, used to collect, develop analysis and organise the presentation of research findings. It refers to a systematic and exhaustive examination of a limited number of cases in order to provide generalisations and identify similarities between various social phenomena, in order to develop contacts or ideas. Its formal objective is causal explanation. It has its origin in the theory of symbolic interaction which stipulates that a person's actions are built up and evolve over time through processes of learning, trial and error and adjustment to responses by others.

This helps in searching for broad categories, followed by development of sub-categories. If no relevant similarities can be identified, then either the data needs to be re-evaluated and the definition of similarities changed or the category is too wide and heterogeneous and should be narrowed down.

In analytical induction, definitions of terms are not identified/determined at the beginning of research. They are rather considered hypothesis to be tested, using inductive reasoning. It allows for modification of concepts and relationships between concepts, aimed at representing reality of the situation most accurately.

According to **Katz**, "Analytic Induction (AI) is a research logic used to collect data, develop analysis and organize the presentation of research findings". AI calls for the progressive redefinition of the phenomenon to be explained (the explanandum) and of explanatory factors (the explanans), such that a perfect (sometimes called universal) relationship is maintained. Initial cases are inspected to locate common factors and provisional explanations. As new cases are examined and initial hypothesis are contradicted, the explanation is reworked in one or both of two ways.

According to Cressey, the steps of analytical induction process are as follows

- A phenomenon is defined in a tentative manner.
- A hypothesis is developed about it.

- A single instance is considered to determine if the hypothesis is confirmed.
- If the hypothesis fails to be confirmed, either the phenomenon is redefined or the hypothesis is revised so as to include the instance examine.
- Additional cases are examined and if the new hypothesis is repeatedly confirmed, some degree of certainty about the hypothesis is ensured.
- Each negative case requires that the hypothesis be reformulated until there are no exceptions.

Constant Comparison

Constant comparison is used for analysing qualitative data, in order to develop a theory of deep and is considered synonymous with Grounded Theory approach used by most scientists. The constant comparison allows the researcher to think and compare the analysis of different levels and angles so that the similarities and differences in data acquisition can establish a pattern.

Many writers suggest about the ways of approaching your data so that you can do the coding of the data with an open mind and recognize noteworthy patterns in the data. This could be done through constant comparison method. This requires that every time you select a passage of text (or its equivalent in video, etc) and code it, you should compare it with all those passages you have already coded that way, perhaps in other cases.

This ensures that your coding is consistent and allows you to consider the possibility either that some of the passages coded that way do not fit as well and could therefore be better codes as something else or that there are dimensions or phenomenas in the passages that might well be coded another way as well. But, the potential for comparisons does not stop there. You can compare the passage with those codes in similar or related ways or even compare them with cases and examples from outside your data set altogether. Previously coded text also needs to be checked to see if the new codes created are relevant.

Constant comparison in newly gathered data are continually compared with previously collected data and their coding is done in order to refine the development of theoretical categories. The purpose is to test emerging ideas that might take the research in new and fruitful directions.

According to Strauss and Corbin (1990), they suggest following components of constant comparison

Word Repetitions Look for commonly used words and words whose close repetition may indicated emotions.

Indigenous Categories (what the grounded theorists refer to as in vivo codes) It refers to terms used by respondents with a particular meaning and significance in their setting.

Key Words in Context Look for the range of uses of key terms in the phrases and sentences in which they occur.

Compare and Contrast It is essentially the Grounded theory idea of constant comparison. Ask, what is this about? and how does it differ from the preceeding or following statements?

Social Science Queries Introduce social science explanations and theories, for example, to explain the conditions, actions, interactions and consequences of phenomenas.

Searching for Missing Information It is essential to try to get an idea of consequences of phenomena. Searching for missing information, it is essential to try to get an idea of what is not being done or talked out, but which you would have expected to find.

Metaphors and Analogies People often use metaphor to indicate something about their key and central beliefs about things and these may indicate the way they feel about things too.

Transitions One of the discursive elements in speech which includes turn taking in conversation as well as the more poetic and narrative use of story structures.

Pawing It refers to marking the text and eye balling or scanning the text. Circle words, underline, use coloured high lighters, run coloured lines down the margins to indicate different meanings and coding. Then look for patterns and significance.

Cutting and Sorting It refers to the traditional technique of cutting up transcripts and collecting all those coded the same way into piles, envelopes or folders or pasting them onto cards. Laying out all these scraps and re-reading them, together, is an essential part of the process of analysis.

Triangulation

Triangulation means using more than one method to collect data on the same topic. Triangulation facilitates validation of data through cross verification from more than two sources. It tests the consistency of fundings obtained through different instruments and increases the chance to control or atleast assess, some of the threats or multiple causes influencing results. Triangulation is not just about validation but about deepening and widening one's understanding. It can be used to produce innovation in conceptual framing. Triangulation is the use of two or more methods of data collection in the study of some aspect of human behaviour.

According to **Berg** and **Berg**, "Triangulation is a term originally associated with surveying activities, map making, navigation and military practices".

The word 'triangulation' was first used in the social science as metaphor, describing a form of multiple operationalisation or convergent validation. **Camp Bell** and **Fiske** were the first to apply the navigational term 'triangulation to research'.

They used the term triangulation to describe multiple data collection strategies for measuring a single concept. This is known as **data triangulation**. According to them, triangulation is a powerful way of demonstrating concurrent validity, particularly in qualitative research.

The purpose of triangulation is not restricted to combining different kinds of data but to relate them so as enhance the validity of the findings.

Triangulation is an approach to research that uses a combination of more than one research strategy in a single investigation. Triangulation can be a useful tool for qualitative as well as quantitative researches.

Types of Triangulation

- Data Triangulation : Time, space and person
- Method Triangulation : Design and data collection
- Investigator Triangulation
- Theory Triangulation
- Multiple Triangulation : It uses a combination of two or more triangulation techniques in one study.

Each of these are described in detail in the following paragraphs.

Data Triangulation

*According to **Denzin** (1989), there are three types of data triangulation i.e.*

Time Triangulation Here, the researchers collect data about a phenomenon at different points in time. However, studies based on longitudinal designs are not considered examples of data triangulation for time because they are intended to document changes over time. Triangulations of data analysis in cross sectional and longitudinal research is an example of time triangulation.

Space Triangulation It consists of collecting data at more than one site. At the outset, the researcher must identify how time or space relate to the study and make an argument, supporting the use of different time or space and collection points in the study. By collecting data at different points in time and in different spaces, the researcher gains a clearer and more complete description of decision-making and is able to differentiate characteristics that span time periods and spaces from characteristics, specific to certain time and space.

Person Triangulation According to **Denzin**, person triangulation has three levels *i.e.* aggregate, interactive and collective. It is also known as combined levels of triangulation. Here, researchers collect data from more than one level of person i.e. a set of individuals, groups or collectives. Researchers might also discover data that are dissimilar among levels. In such a case, researchers would collect additional data to resolve the incongruence.

According to Smith, there are seven levels of person triangulation as follows

(i) Individual level.

(ii) **Group Analysis** The interaction patterns of individuals and groups.

(iii) **Organisational Units of Analysis** Units which have qualities not possessed by the individuals making them up.

(iv) **Institutional Analysis** Relationships within and across the legal (For example, court and school), political (For example, government), economic (For example, business)and familial (For example, Marriage) institutions of the society.

(v) **Ecological Analysis** Concerned with spatial explanation.

(vi) **Cultural Analysis** Concerned with the norms, values, practices, traditions and ideologies of a culture.

(vii) **Societal Analysis** Concerned with gross factors such as urbanisation, industrialisation, education, wealth, etc.

Methods Triangulation

Methods triangulation can occur at the level of design or data collection.

Design Level Triangulation Methods triangulation at the design level has also been called between method triangulation. Design methods triangulation most often uses quantitative methods combined with qualitative methods in the study design. There is simultaneous and sequential implementation of both quantitative and qualitative methods.

Data Collection Triangulation Methods triangulation at the data collection level has been called within method triangulation. Using methods triangulation at the level of data collection, researchers use two different techniques of data collection, but each technique is within the same research tradition. The purpose of combining the data collection methods is to provide a more holistic and better understanding of the phenomenon under study. It is not an easy task to use method triangulation, it is often more time consuming and expensive to complete a study using methods triangulation.

Investigator Triangulation

Investigator triangulation occurs when two or more researchers with divergent backgrounds and expertise work together on the same study. To achieve investigator triangulation, multiple investigators, each must have prominent roles in the study and their areas of expertise must be complementary.

Theory Triangulation

A fourth kind of triangulation involves using different theoretical perspectives to look at the same data. Thus, it can be said that triangulation is a strategy that enhances the quality of the research, thereby ensuring that the findings are reliable, dependable and valid. It helps to unveil the complexities of phenomena under study and understand them in depth rather than generalising the findings. In qualitative research, more than one theoretical explanation emerges from the data. Researchers investigate the utility and power of these emerging theories by cycling between data generation and data analysis, until they reach a conclusion.

Multiple Triangulation

A multiple triangulation approach as described by Denzin is to incorporate multiple methods of data collection, multiple sources of data and multiple investigators with multiple areas of expertise. The multi-site and multi-method design facilitated the identification and validation of relevant issues.

Denzin states that multiple research methods are desirable because each method reveals a different aspect of reality. This idea has since been developed to include triangulation as a metaphor for strength, trustworthiness and comprehensiveness. Guba argues that trustworthiness through triangulation enhances the credibility, dependability and 'confirmability' in qualitative studies.

EXAM BASED QUESTIONS

1 **What is the scale on which the distance between scale positions are equal?**

(a) Ordinal scale (b) Nominal scale
(c) Ratio scale (d) Interval scale

2 **Interval scales have**

(a) no statistical value (b) no mathematical design
(c) equal appearing units (d) no equal appearing units

3 **Which scale is the simplest form of measurement?**

(a) Interval scale (b) Nominal scale
(c) Ordinal scale (d) Ratio scale

4 **Match the following.**

List I	List II
A. Nominal scale	1. Geometric Mean
B. Ordinal scale	2. Frequency distribution
C. Interval scale	3. Median and rank correlation
D. Ratio scale	4. Mean, SD and correlation

Codes

	A	B	C	D		A	B	C	D
(a)	4	3	2	1	(b)	1	3	2	4
(c)	2	3	4	1	(d)	1	4	3	2

5 **What is ordinal data?**

(a) Ranked data (b) Well-behaved data
(c) Numbers (d) Ordinary data

6 **Which one of these is not a way of measuring central tendency?**

(a) Measuring the middle value or mid-point after the data have been ranked (median)
(b) Measuring the value that occurs most frequently (mode)
(c) Regression analysis
(d) Measuring the value often known as the average, that includes all data values in its calculation (mean)

7 **By breaking the scale on X and Y axis in a graphical representation, we will be creating**

(a) line graph (b) false baseline
(c) bar diagram (d) None of these

8 **The following measure of central tendency cannot be represented graphically.**

(a) Arithmetic Mean (b) Mode
(c) Median (d) Quartile

9 **Frequency is not taken into consideration in**

(a) individual observation
(b) discrete series
(c) continuous series
(d) None of these

10 **If null hypothesis is rejected, when it is true, it indicates**

(a) sampling error (b) Type II error
(c) standard error (d) Type I error

11 The process of grouping of related facts into classes is called
(a) tabulation (b) classification
(c) pie-diagram (d) None of these

12 Which of the following is a non-parametric test?
(a) Analysis of co-variance (b) Analysis of variance
(c) Median test (d) Critical ratio

13 The value which cannot be determined graphically is
(a) median (b) mean
(c) frequency table (d) None of these

14 "Statistics is called sound of counting" is said by
(a) Cowden (b) Bowley
(c) Pearson (d) Karl Marx

15 Parametric and non-parametric are
(a) terms used in medical practice
(b) general tests of statistical relevance
(c) two main groups of statistical significance tests
(d) alternative to standard deviation test

16 Power of the test of significance means probability of what?
(a) Incorrect rejection of the null hypothesis
(b) correct rejection of the null hypothesis
(c) Incorrect acceptance of the null hypothesis
(d) Correct acceptance of null hypothesis

17 Who have given the following suggestions about the analysis of data?
1. Thinking over data through meaning table.
2. Carefully examining the problem statements.
3. Thinking over the problem like an ordinary person.
4. Using various ordinary statistical analysis.

Choose the correct option.
(a) Goode, Barr and Scales
(b) George J Mouly
(c) W S Munroe
(d) John W Best

18 Which test are used in explanation of results?
(a) Parametric tests (b) Non-parametric tests
(c) Both a and b (d) None of these

19 A researcher commits Type I error, when he
(a) accepts null hypothesis, when it is false
(b) rejects null hypothesis, when it is false
(c) accepts null hypothesis, when it is true
(d) rejects the null hypothesis, when it is true

20 When a non-directional hypothesis is stated, the test of significance would be
(a) One tailed (b) Two tailed
(c) Both a and b (d) None of these

21 Statistical hypothesis is derived from
(a) frame (b) data
(c) sample (d) facts

22 In rejecting a null hypothesis (H_0), a researcher is likely to commit which type of error?
(a) Type I error (b) Type II error
(c) Both a and b (d) Neither a nor b

23 Graphically, mode can be estimated from
(a) Ogive (b) bar diagram
(c) histogram (d) historigram

24 Why do we use inferential statistics?
(a) Inferential statistics are used to help us to show the difference between the sample and the whole population
(b) Inferential statistics are used to help us to compare the 1 sample to the whole population
(c) Inferential statistics are used to help us to generalise from the sample to the whole population
(d) All of the above

25 Which combination of the following points is true of non-parametric methods?
1. Do not demand assumption about population.
2. Actual scores are used in combination.
3. Generalisation do not seem to be realistic.
4. They are also called distribution free method.

Select the correct option.
(a) 1, 2 and 2 (b) 1, 3 and 4
(c) 2, 3 and 4 (d) 2, 3 and 1

26 The choice of statistical test to be used in the analysis of the data of the qualitative research is determined by
(a) the power of the test
(b) the kind of sampling used
(c) nature of the population
(d) All of the above

27 Qualitative analysis is not at all used in
(a) descriptive research (b) ethnographical research
(c) experimental research (d) historical research

28 The sum of the derivations of the items from mean is always
(a) 1 (b) 0 (c) 2 (d) 6

29 If both the variables are varying in the same direction, it is called
(a) positive correlation (b) multiple correlation
(c) negative correlation (d) None of these

30 Which average is affected most by extreme observations?
(a) Median (b) Mode
(c) Arithmetic Mean (d) Geometric Mean

31 Karl Pearson's coefficient of skewness
(a) is always negative (b) is always positive
(c) cannot be zero (d) Both a and b

32 The nature of relationship is studied through
(a) correlation (b) regression
(c) progression (d) None of these

33 **Which of the following would not allow you to calculate a correlation?**
(a) A negative relationship between X and Y
(b) A positive relationship between X and Y
(c) A curvi-linear relationship between X and Y
(d) A linear relationship between X and Y

34 **The coefficient value of correlation lies between**
(a) 0 to 1 (b) 0 to −1
(c) −1 to 1 (d) 1 to −10

35 **The coefficient of variation is always a**
(a) ratio (b) percentage
(c) average (d) None of these

36 **Testing the probability of relationship between variables occurring by chance alone, if there really was no difference in the population, from which that sample has been drawn is known as**
(a) Multiple Regression Analysis
(b) Correlation coefficients
(c) Chi-square tests
(d) Significance testing

37 **The way in which this significance is tested, using both parametric and non-parametric statistics can be thought of as answering one from a series of questions. Which one of the question given below is the odd one out?**
(a) Are the predicted values statistically significant?
(b) Does it look statistically significant on the face of it?
(c) Are the difference statistically significant?
(d) What is the strength of the relationship and is it statistically significant?

38 **ANOVA is**
(a) a one way analysis of variance
(b) a government body which collects social statistics
(c) the name of a statistical software package
(d) a two way analysis of variance

39 **What determines, whether a researcher should used .05 or .01 level of significance for testing the hypothesis?**
(a) How important are the findings?
(b) How much risk is involved in incorrect finding?
(c) How much precision is required?
(d) All of the above

40 **What determines the choice of statistical test to be used in the analysis of the data of the qualitative research?**
(a) The power of test (b) Kind of sampling used
(c) Nature of population (d) All of these

41 **What do correlation studies reveal?**
(a) Whether there is relationship between the variables or not.
(b) How much relationship is there and of what kind between the variables?
(c) All of the above
(d) None of the above

42 **What is the importance of the correlation coefficient?**
(a) The fact that there is linear relationship between the correlated variables
(b) The fact that it is one of the most valid measures of education
(c) The fact that it allows one to determine the degree or strength of the association between two variables
(d) The fact that it is Non-Parametric Method of Statistical Analysis

43 **What type of correlation are used in educational research?**
(a) Coefficient correlation
(b) Partial correlation
(c) Multiple cummulative correlation
(d) All of the above

44 **In case of ANOVA, what is the variance caused by treatment?**
(a) $SS_{A\times B}$ (b) SS_T (c) SS_A (d) SS_W

45 **When, the achievement and degeneration of one group is to be tested in T-test, the test used is**
(a) two tailed test (b) one tailed test
(c) analysis of variance (d) All of these

46 **What is the nature of the statement that experimental generalisations are statistical inferences, they can only attain a degree of probability, somewhere along a continum between truth and falsity?**
(a) Not wholly true (b) Wholly true
(c) Incorrect entirely (d) None of these

47 **When is Type I error increased?**
(a) When alpha level decreases
(b) When alpha level increases
(c) When the sample size increases
(d) When the sample size decreases

48 **Which of the following is a measure of location?**
(a) Mode (b) Mean
(c) Percentile (d) Standard Deviation

49 **Which of the following gives a more accurate measure of relationship than the other three?**
(a) Spearman's Rho
(b) Biserial Correlation
(c) Kendall's Tau
(d) Product Moment Method

50 **The difference between a statistical average based on the entire population and the one based on a sample is known as**
(a) standard error (b) mean difference
(c) sampling error (d) Mean Deviation

51 **One of the appropriate statistics that can be used for Solomon's four experimental design is**
(a) correlation analysis (b) one way ANOVA
(c) chi-square (d) median test

52 **Which one of the following is the stable measure of dispersion?**
(a) Range (b) Quartile Deviation
(c) Average Deviation (d) Standard Deviation

53 **Chi-square test is an example of**
(a) parametric test (b) non-parametric test
(c) descriptive test (d) survey test

54 **The square root of variance is**
(a) standard error (b) error variance
(c) Standard Deviation (d) deviation quotient

55 **Summarising a raw data and displaying them on compact statistical tables for analysis is**
(a) tabulation (b) coding (c) transcription (d) editing

56 **Coefficient of variation is given by**
(a) $\frac{A-Z}{\sigma}$ (b) $\frac{\sigma}{X}$ (c) $\frac{Q_3 - Q_1}{Q_3 + Q_1}$ (d) None of these

57 **Which will be the most appropriate method of statistical analysis, if a researcher wants to know how much contribution a JRF test makes to the overall success of the candidates?**
(a) F-test
(b) Linear Regression Method
(c) T-test
(d) Product moment correlation

58 **The measure which divides a distribution in ten equal parts is known as**
(a) percentile (b) deviation
(c) decile (d) quartile

59 **Given the following series 6, 3, 2, 8, 4, 7, 9, 1, 10, 11, 12, 13, the value of mode is**
(a) not defined (b) 13 (c) 9 (d) 12

60 **The Arithmetic Mean of the direct 100 natural number is**
(a) 55.2 (b) 50.5 (c) 25.7 (d) 60.1

61 **Which statistical tool comes under bivariate analysis?**
(a) Linear regression analysis
(b) Association of Attributes
(c) Two way ANOVA
(d) All of the above

62 **In which situation, χ^2 (Chi-square) test can be used?**
(a) K = 2, but some expected frequencies are less than 5
(b) df is greater than 1, but more than 20% of frequencies are smaller than 5
(c) Any expected frequency is smaller than 1
(d) None of the above

63 **...... is the Standard Deviation of a sampling distribution.**
(a) Standard error
(b) Sample Standard Deviation
(c) Replication error
(d) Meta error

64 **Coefficient of variation is given by**
(a) (A-Z) Sigma
(b) Sigma X
(c) (Q.3 + Q.1) (Q.3 + Q.1)
(d) (Q.3-Q.1) (Q.3 + Q.1)

65 **Which of the following is a graph or chart suitable for correlation analysis?**
(a) Bar chart (b) Histogram
(c) Frequency polygon (d) Scatter graph

66 **The idea that the more times a research finding is shown with different sets of peoples, the more confidence we can place in the finding and in generalising beyond the original participant is known as**
(a) data triangulation
(b) methods generalisation
(c) naturalistic generalisation
(d) replication logic

67 **The average age of 10 students in a class is 17 years. If one of them who is 26 years old leaves the school, the average will be**
(a) 15 years (b) 18 years
(c) 16 years (d) 17 years

68 **Which of the following is the incorrect pair?**
(a) Rank Correlation - Spearman
(b) Product Moment Correlation - Pearson
(c) Split Half Correlation - Kuder Richardson
(d) Contingency Correlation - Cramer

69 **Statement I** Correlation coefficient may be negative as well as positive.
Statement II Reliability of a test can be negative.
Codes
(a) I is false but II is true
(b) Both I and II are true
(c) I is true but II is false
(d) Both I and II are false

70 **Which of the following is not correctly matched?**
(a) Test Retest-Stability
(b) Split Half-Internal consistency
(c) KR 20-Stability
(d) Parallel form-Equivalence

71 **A distribution of scores was negatively skewed. It can be stated that**
(a) mean and median are coincide
(b) mean is more than the median
(c) mean is less than the median
(d) no such relationship exists

72 **What are the parametric test in the following list?**
1. F-test 2. T-test
3. Sign test 4. Median test
Choose the corrent option.
(a) 1 and 2 (b) 3 and 4
(c) 1 and 4 (d) 2 and 3

73 Multiple correlation studies

(a) comparison of beta, weighs and regression coefficients
(b) use of many independent variables
(c) comparison of R and beta weighs
(d) use of many dependent variables

74 Which of the following is not related to analysis of qualitative data?

(a) Axial coding (b) Meta analysis
(c) Rich thick description (d) Writing memos

75 In plotting a frequency polygon, it is important to see that

(a) each class interval is represented by a separate rectangle
(b) midpoint of all class intervals are joined together
(c) the midpoint of an interval is always taken to represent the entire interval
(d) None of the above

76 Bowley's coefficient of skewness is given by

(a) $\frac{Q_3 - Q_1 + 2}{Q_3 + Q}$ (b) $\frac{Q_3 + Q_1 - 2}{Q_3 - Q_c}$
(c) $\frac{Q_3 + Q_1 + 2}{Q_3 + Q_1}$ (d) $\frac{Q_3 + Q_1 + 2}{Q_3 - Q_1}$

77 The formula for calculation of the mode is

(a) Mode = 3 Mean – 2 Median
(b) Mode = 2 Median – 2 Mean
(c) Mode = 3 Median – 2 Mean
(d) Mode = 4 Median – 3 Mean

78 T formula has been given by

(a) Fisher (b) Best
(c) Karl Pearson (d) None of these

79 A researcher has decided to test his one tail hypothesis at 0.1 level of significance. The critical value expected for rejection of null hypothesis would be a value equivalent .... level of significance for a two tailed hypothesis.

(a) 0.1 (b) 0.2 (c) 0.05 (d) None of these

80 Match the following.

List I (Terminologies)	List II (Concepts)
A. Standard Deviation	1. Difference between mean and a score
B. Quartile Deviation	2. Difference between highest score and lowest score
C. Score Deviation	3. Average of all the deviations
D. Mean Deviation	4. Root mean square deviation
	5. Semi-interquartile range

Codes

	A	B	C	D		A	B	C	D
(a)	2	4	1	3	(b)	3	1	5	2
(c)	5	3	4	1	(d)	4	5	1	3

81 Logic of induction is very close to

(a) the logic of sampling
(b) the logic of the controlled variables
(c) the logic of observation
(d) None of the above

82 Partial correlation is calculated when

(a) we want to nullify the effect of the third variable on other two variables
(b) we want to know the partial relationship between two variables
(c) Both a and b
(d) None of the above

83 1.96 level of significance for a large sample means

(a) 2.5% on each side of the normal curve out of range of the investigation
(b) 5% chance is there that the result obtained will not match the population mean
(c) Both a and b
(d) None of the above

84 Significance of contingency coefficient is calculated by the formula

(a) $C = \sqrt{\frac{X^2}{N + X^2}}$ (b) $C = \frac{X^2}{N + X}$
(c) $C = \frac{\sqrt{X^2}}{N + X^2}$ (d) None of these

85 I $\beta_3 > 3$ the curve is called

(a) mesokurtic (b) lepotokurtic
(c) positively skewed (d) platykurtic

86 The quartile deviation is a frequency distribution is

(a) the distance between the 70th and 30th percentage
(b) half of the distance between the 75th and 25th percentiles
(c) half of the distance between the 70th and 30th percentiles
(d) the distance between the 75th and 25th percentiles

87 A symmetrical distribution is one where

(a) mean = median
(b) median = mode
(d) mean = median = mode
(d) mean = mode

88 Which of the following situation calls for the use of ratio scale?

(a) A researcher waits to assert that the two persons X and Y differ in their attitudes towards natioalisation of education
(b) He wishes to state that the attitude of one person X is more favourable than that of Y
(c) He wishes to make a statement that as compared to Y, X is much more in favour of nationalisation than he is as compared to 2
(d) He wants to show that X is twice as much in favour of nationalisation as Y

89 The limitation of ANOVA would be its inability to indicate

(a) interaction among variables, under study
(b) effects of different variables, under study
(c) interaction among the variables
(d) All of the above

90 In order to ensure maximum acceptability of data analysis and its interpretation, the help should be taken from
(a) statistics
(b) graphs and diagrams
(c) computer floppy
(d) appreciable typing

91 What should we do, if we want to reduce both the Type I and Type II error?
(a) Reduce the size of the sample
(b) Decrease the size level of significance
(c) Increase the size of the sample
(d) Increase the level of significance

92 In the formula, $t = \frac{MD}{SE_{MD}} \cdot SE_{MD}$ is
(a) a standard error of mean difference
(b) standard error of mean deviation
(c) Both (a) and (b)
(d) None of the above

93 Match the following.

List I (Types of Correlations)	Type II (Nature of Variables)
A. Biserial correlation	1. Continuous Vs Continuous
B. Pie-coefficient	2. Continuous Vs Dichotomous
C. Point biserial correlation	3. Dichotomous Vs Dichotomous
D. Tetra-choric correlation	4. Dichotomised Vs Dichotomised
	5. Continuous Vs Dichotomised

Codes

	A	B	C	D		A	B	C	D
(a)	4	1	5	2	(b)	5	3	2	4
(c)	3	2	5	1	(d)	5	4	2	1

94 Match the following.

List I (Types of ANOVA)	List II (Characteristics)
A. One way ANOVA for repeated measures	1. Used comparing two groups on a dependent variable
B. Two way ANOVA	2. Used when one wants to compare two or more independent groups in which sample is subjected to repeated measures
C. MANOVA	3. Used when the researcher wants to study the effects of two or more independent or treatment variables
D. ANCOVA	4. It is used when subjects are subjected to repeated measures

Codes

	A	B	C	D
(a)	2	4	1	3
(b)	1	2	3	4
(c)	4	3	2	1
(d)	1	4	3	2

95 Match the following.

List I (Qualitative Research Analysis)	List II (Characteristics)
A. Data reduction	1. It is a way of building explanations in qualitative analysis by constructing and testing of causal links between events, action, etc.
B. Analytical induction	2. Refers to process of selecting focussing, simplifying and transforming the data.
C. Classification	3. It is a powerful way of demonstrating concurrent validity in qualitative research.
D. Triangulation	4. In

Codes

	A	B	C	D		A	B	C	D
(a)	2	1	4	3	(b)	1	4	3	2
(c)	1	2	3	4	(d)	2	4	1	3

Directions (Q. Nos. 96-100) *Below are two statements, one labelled as Assertion (A) and other labelled as Reason (R). In the context of the two statements, which one of the following is correct?*

Codes
(a) Both A and R are true and R is the correct explanation of A
(b) Both A and R are true, but R is not the correct explanation of A
(c) A is true, but R is false
(d) A is false, but R is true

96 **Assertion** (A) In interval scale, the intervals are adjusted in terms of rule that have been established as a basis for making the units.
Reason (R) The primary limitation of interval is the lack of true zero, it does not have the capacity to measure the complete absence of trait or characteristics.

97 **Assertion** (A) A Z-test is a type of hypothesis test.
Reason (R) Z-test is used when the data is approximately normally distributed.

98 **Assertion** (A) In quantitative data analysis, researcher turns raw numbers into meaning data.
Reason (R) It is done through the application of rational and critical thinking.

99 **Assertion** (A) Triangulation is an approach to research that uses a combination of more than one research strategy in a single investigation.
Reason (R) Triangulation is a useful tool for qualitative as well as quantitative research.

100 **Assertion** (A) Graphical presentation is another way of the presentation data and information.
Reason (R) Graphs helps to understand the data easily.

PREVIOUS YEARS' QUESTIONS

July 2018

1 A researcher used t-test to compare two means based on independent and found the t-value to be significant at .05 level. This means that
(a) chances are 5 out of 100 that the difference between means has occurred due to sampling errors
(b) chances are 95 out of 100 that the difference between means has occurred due to sampling errors
(c) if experiment is repeated 100 times, it would give the obtained result only 5 times
(d) if the experiment is repeated 5 times, it would give the same result every time

2 A researcher uses both t-test and F-test on the same data obtained from two groups. The functional relationship between values of t and F, if calculate would be
(a) $t = F$ (b) $t^2 = F$
(c) $t = F^2$ (d) $t^2 = F^2$

3 Match the following.

List I (Parametric Tests)	List II (Non-Parametric Tests)
A. Independent T-test	1. Chi-square test
B. Dependent T-test	2. Kruskal Wallis' H-test
C. ANOVA F-test	3. Mann Whitney's U-test
	4. Willeoxon's T-test

Codes

	A	B	C		A	B	C
(a)	2	1	4	(b)	3	1	2
(c)	3	4	2	(d)	2	1	3

4 In a normal distribution of scores, the percentile rank of a students scoring at $-1Z$ is
(a) 16 (b) 34 (c) 48 (d) 68

5 In a sample distribution, with N = 300, M = 60 and SD = 12, the number of cases falling above the score 48 will be
(a) 252 (b) 204 (c) 184 (d) 48

6 Match the following.

List I (Scales)	List II (Characteristics)
A. Nominal scale	1. Superior performance in musical events
B. Ordinal scale	2. Performance scores on a spelling test
C. Interval scale	3. Listing students, according to participation in co-curricular activities
D. Ratio scale	4. Speed of students in writing words per minute

Codes

	A	B	C	D		A	B	C	D
(a)	3	1	2	4	(b)	1	3	2	4
(c)	2	1	4	3	(d)	4	2	3	1

7 Given, Mean = 100, SD = 20 and N = 100. Which one of the following will be the **correct** statement for indicating the possibility of population mean at 0.01 level of confidence?
(a) Population mean falls between 93 to 107
(b) Population mean falls between 96.08 to 103.9
(c) Population mean falls between 97.2 to 102
(d) Population mean falls between 94.8 to 105.2

8 A multiple choice test consists of 50 test items. The difficulty values of items vary in a narrow range with an average value of 0.48. The test gave a students. The reliability coefficient of the test would be
(a) 0.91 (b) 0.86 (c) 0.78 (d) 0.67

November 2017

9 The mean and Standard Deviation of a set of scores are 50 and 10, respectively. If each raw score is increased by 3, the new mean and Standard Deviation would be
(a) 53, 13 (b) 50, 13 (c) 53, 10 (d) 50, 10

January 2017

10 In a study, the significance of difference between means was tested through use of a T-test for a large group. The value of 't' being 2.10, what will be the decision warranted in respect of H_O (Null hypothesis)?
(a) The H_O will be retained
(b) The H_O will be rejected at 0.01 level of significance
(c) The H_O will be rejected at 0.05 level of significance only
(d) The H_O will be rejected at both the levels of significance

11 For use of a non-parametric test, like the chi-square, which of the following assumptions has to be satisfied?
(a) The data should arise from interval measures
(b) The distribution has to be normal
(c) No assumption about nature of distribution is required
(d) The variables under reference must be dichotomous

12 A researcher finds out the relationship between three variables, such as academic achievement, intelligence and socio-economic status of children using Pearson's product moment γ. As per objective of his/her study, the relationship between academic achievement and intelligence is also to be estimated by controlling the influence of socio-economic status. Which statistical technique will be appropriate in this context?
(a) Finding out multiple correlation?
(b) Finding out correlation ratio
(c) Estimating contingence coefficient via chi-square
(d) Finding out partial correlation

13 For computation of F value in one way ANOVA, what is the final procedural step?
(a) Finding out the within sum of squares
(b) Finding out the between sum of squares
(c) Finding out the ratio of within and between sum of squares
(d) Finding out the ratio of between and within variance

14 Percentile scores assume a scale of measurement called
(a) nominal scale (b) ordinal scale
(c) interval scale (d) ratio scale

15 The purpose of methodology section of qualitative studies is to
(a) show how researcher inter-relations will be made
(b) present the focus of the study
(c) provide general background of the study
(d) describe the overall design of the study

16 Internal reliability in qualitative research design, refers to
(a) information selection
(b) inter-observer reliability
(c) extent to which the results approximate the reality
(d) accuracy of measures

July 2016

17 On a test, with a mean of 80 and a Standard Deviation of 20, an individual with a score of 60 will have a Z-score of
(a) 0.1 (b) 1.0
(c) –0.1 (d) –1.0

18 Match the following.

List I (Variables)	List II (Scales of Measurement)
A. Intelligence scores on a verbal test	1. Ratio scale
B. Ranks of the students in a musical test	2. Interval scale
C. Number of children in tribal families	3. Ordinal scale
D. Length and breadth of classroom	4. Nominal scale

Codes

	A	B	C	D		A	B	C	D
(a)	2	3	4	1	(b)	2	4	3	1
(c)	1	2	3	4	(d)	4	3	1	2

19 In using inferential statistics, which one of the following will be considered as relevant information?
(a) Information about the tool of research
(b) Information about the research design
(c) Nature of the aggregate (population)
(d) Sampling procedure used

20 In calculating F value from a research data, which of the following is required at the end of operation?
(a) Finding out the total sum of squares
(b) Finding out the ratio of total sum of squares and between sum of squares
(c) Finding out the ratio of between sum of squares and within sum of squares
(d) Finding out the ratio of within sum of squares and total sum of squares

December 2015

21 For estimating coefficient of correlation, in which of the following techniques, characteristics of both the variables and assumed to be essentially on a nominal scale with genuine dicthotomy?
(a) Biserial coefficient (b) Point Biserial coefficient
(c) Tetra-choric coefficient (d) Pie-coefficient

22 An educational researcher wants to study the relationship between academic performance and motivation, by keeping the effect of a third variable, such as socio-economic status neutral. Which of the following technique of correlation will be appropriate in such a situation?
(a) Contingency coefficient (b) Eta coefficient
(c) Multiple correlation (d) Partial correlation

23 In a research, undertaken by a school teacher in respect of critical understanding of the students of his/her school, the following results were obtained.
Mean = 50, $\sigma = 10$, N = 100
Indicate the range of scores at alpha level 0.05 for finding the value of true mean for the population of such students in the whole district.
(a) From 50.1 to 52.2 (b) From 48.04 to 51.96
(c) From 47.42 to 52.58 (d) From 48.11 to 53.0

24 In a normal distribution, what is the position of the three measures of central tendency?
(a) Mean is higher than median
(b) Median is lower than mode
(c) Both mean and median are higher than mode
(d) All the three measures coincide

25 Which of the following statements is not correct?
(a) Correlation indicates causation or cause and effect relationship
(b) In a negatively skewed curve, the value of mean will be pulled towards the lower end of the scale
(c) Chi-square test is a distribution free test
(d) For computing Pearson's γ, the relationship between two variables have to be rectilinear

June 2015

26 If there is true dichotomy present in two variables, which of the following correlational techniques will be suitable?
(a) Point biserial correlation
(b) Biserial correlation
(c) Product moment correlation
(d) Rank difference correlation

December 2014

27 Match the following.

List I	List II
A. Product moment correlation	1. Both variables expressed in an ordinal scale
B. Rank order correlation	2. Both variables are in an interval scale
C. Biserial correlation	3. One variable is continuous and the other is truly dichotomous
D. Point biserial correlation	4. Both variables are true dichotomy
	5. One variable is continuous and the other is artificially dichotomous

Codes

	A	B	C	D
(a)	1	3	2	5
(b)	2	1	5	3
(c)	2	3	5	1
(d)	1	2	5	3

28 In the process of standardistation of a multiple choice test, the researcher while doing item analysis wants to test the hypothesis for each item response. The most appropriate statistics, the researcher may use will be

(a) T-test (b) F-test
(c) Chi-square test (d) Sign test

29 The association among variables in a scientific study is indicated quantitatively as

(a) coefficient (b) ratio
(c) percentile (d) variance

30 If the computed values are used only to explain the properties of a particular sample taken for the study, the statistics used is called

(a) descriptive statistics (b) inferential statistics
(c) Both a and b (d) Neither a nor b

31 Which of the following research tools/techniques will be appropriate for an indepth understanding of cultural and social aspects of a tribe?

(a) Questionnarie
(b) Participant's observation
(c) Sociometric technique
(d) Rating scale

32 In research situations, non-parametric statistics is used for

(a) nominal data (b) ordinal data
(c) interval data (d) ratio data

June 2014

33 Which of the following is a non-parametric test?

(a) T-test (b) F-test (c) χ^2 test (d) Z-test

34 The range of coefficient of correlation between two variables is

(a) 0 to +1 (b) +1 to −1
(c) 0 to −1 (d) None of these

35 The most stable measure of variability is

(a) range (b) mean deviation
(c) standard deviation (d) quartile deviation

36 Which of the following falls under inferential statistics?

(a) Arithmetic Mean (b) Standard Deviation
(c) Harmonic Mean (d) Analysis of variance

ANSWERS

Exam Based Questions

1 (d)	2 (c)	3 (b)	4 (c)	5 (a)	6 (c)	7 (b)	8 (a)	9 (a)	10 (d)
11 (b)	12 (c)	13 (a)	14 (b)	15 (c)	16 (d)	17 (a)	18 (c)	19 (d)	20 (b)
21 (b)	22 (a)	23 (c)	24 (c)	25 (b)	26 (d)	27 (c)	28 (b)	29 (a)	30 (c)
31 (d)	32 (b)	33 (c)	34 (a)	35 (b)	36 (d)	37 (b)	38 (a)	39 (d)	40 (d)
41 (b)	42 (c)	43 (d)	44 (c)	45 (b)	46 (b)	47 (a)	48 (c)	49 (d)	50 (b)
51 (b)	52 (d)	53 (b)	54 (c)	55 (a)	56 (b)	57 (b)	58 (c)	59 (a)	60 (b)
61 (d)	62 (d)	63 (a)	64 (b)	65 (d)	66 (d)	67 (c)	68 (d)	69 (c)	70 (c)
71 (b)	72 (a)	73 (b)	74 (b)	75 (b)	76 (b)	77 (c)	78 (a)	79 (c)	80 (d)
81 (c)	82 (a)	83 (c)	84 (a)	85 (b)	86 (b)	87 (c)	88 (d)	89 (d)	90 (a)
91 (c)	92 (a)	93 (c)	94 (c)	95 (a)	96 (b)	97 (b)	98 (a)	99 (b)	100 (b)

Previous Years' Questions

1 (a)	2 (b)	3 (c)	4 (a)	5 (a)	6 (a)	7 (d)	8 (b)	9 (c)	10 (c)
11 (c)	12 (d)	13 (d)	14 (b)	15 (d)	16 (b)	17 (d)	18 (a)	19 (c)	20 (c)
21 (d)	22 (d)	23 (b)	24 (d)	25 (a)	26 (a)	27 (b)	28 (c)	29 (a)	30 (a)
31 (b)	32 (a)	33 (c)	34 (b)	35 (c)	36 (a)				

CHAPTER 25

Qualitative Research Design

Qualitative research design is research method used extensively by researcher to study human behaviour, opinions. Here, we will study about the major types of qualitative research design used commonly *viz*, grounded theory research, narrative research, case study, ethnography, mixed method, triangulation, exploratory and explanatory.

Qualitative Research

Qualitative research is a process of naturalist inquiry that seeks indepth understanding of social phenomena within their natural setting. It focuses on 'why' rather than 'what' of social phenomena and relies on the direct experience of human beings rather than by logical and statistical procedure, qualitative researchers use multiple system of inquiry for the study of human phenomena including case study, ethnography, grounded theory, etc. In qualitative research, researcher typically gather multiple forms of data such as interviews, observations and documents rather than relying on a single data source. The research process for qualitative research is emergent design.

Qualitative Research Designs

The design of qualitative research is probably the most flexible of the different experimental techniques encompassing a variety of accepted methods and structures. The qualitative research design not only account for what is said or done but also the manner in which something spoken or carried out by a participant. The design is generally based on social constructivism perspectives. Sample size can be as small as one. Though there is no standardised structure, this type of study still needs to be carefully constructed and designed. The qualitative research methods are not as dependent upon sample size as quantitative methods. Case studies for example can generate results with just a small group.

In this Chapter

- Qualitative Research
- Grounded Theory Designs
- Narrative Research Designs
- Case Study
- Ethnographic Research
- Mixed Method Research Designs

Grounded Theory Designs

Grounded Theory is a well known methodology employed in many research studies. Its disciplinary origin is sociology. Grounded Theory refers to a set of systematic and inductive methods for conducting qualitative research, aimed towards theory development. The term Grounded Theory denotes dual referents *i.e.* a method consisting of flexible methodological strategies and the products of this type of inquiry.

Ground Theory is introduced as an inductive and comparative methodology that provides systematic guidelines for gathering, synthesising, analysing and conceptualising qualitative data for the purpose of theory construction. The founders of Grounded Theory, Barner, G. Glaser and Anselm L. Strauss, offered the first explicit codified statement of how to analyse qualitative data.

The focus of Grounded Theory approach is on the development of 'Inductive Bottom-Up Theory' that is 'grounded' directly in the empirical data. The fundamental question in Grounded theory is what theory or explanation emerges from an analysis of data collected about the phenomenon. This approach is generally used to generate theories which tells us 'how' and 'why' something operates as it does, theories provide explanation about the phenomenon.

Characteristics of Grounded Theory

The Grounded Theory provides explicit and sequential guidelines for conducting qualitative research.

- It offers specific strategies for handling the analytical phases of inquiry.
- It streamlines and integrates data collection and analysis.
- It advances conceptual analysis of qualitative data.
- It legitimises qualitative research as scientific inquiry. Grounded Theory is a well known methodology, employed in many research studies.
- Qualitative and quantitative data generation techniques can be used in a Grounded Theory study.
- Creswell (2012) viewed Grounded Theory as a powerful tool when a researcher needs a broad theory or explanation of a natural phenomenon.
- In Grounded Theory, analytical and interpretative procedures are used for analysing and conceptualising data through coding, non-statistical sampling, writing memos, diagraming of conceptual relationships, written and verbal reports.

Types of Grounded Theory

There are several main types of Grounded Theory, namely Classical Grounded Theory, Strauss and Corbin's Grounded Theory, Constructivist Grounded Theory and Feminist Grounded Theory.

They can be explained as given below

Classical Grounded Theory

This theory is based on the Glaser and Strauss (1967) book, **The Discovery of the Grounded Theory** in which it is envisaged more as a theory generation methodology, rather than just an Analytical Approach. The idea is that one examine data and discover it in a new theory and new ways of explaining the world. In this, everything is data and you (researcher) should include field work notes and other literature in your process. Here, the common coding types are substantial and theoretical creating an iterative.

Strauss and Corbin's Grounded Theory

This type of Grounded Theory probably links closest to Strauss and Corbin (1990), interpretation of Grounded Theory, which is probably more systematic and concerned with coding and structuring qualitative data. It traditionally proposes a three (or sometimes two) stage Iterative Coding Approach, **first** creating open codes (inductive), **then** grouping them with axial coding and **finally** a process of selective coding. In this approach, you may consider a literature review to be restrictive process, binding you to prejudices from existing theory. The Straussian's methodology has proven too difficult for most researchers to follow and most revert back to the less perspective CGT Approach (Partinton, 2000).

Constructivist Grounded Theory

The seminal work on constructivism is from Charmaz (2000) and its about the way researcher create their own interpretations of theory from the data. It aims to challenge the idea that theory can be discovered from the data as if it was just lying there, neutral and waiting to be unearthed. Instead, it tries to recognise that theory will always be biased by the way researchers and participants create their own understanding of society and reality. The engagement between participants and researcher is often cited as a key part of Constructivist Approach.

Feminist Grounded Theory

This theory was developed initially for nurses in recognition of the andocentric bias and to ensure that women's voices were heard in the research community (Wuest 1955). Wuest overlays Feminist Theory onto the CGT, the Straussian and the Constructivist Grounded Theory, advocating that Grounded Theory is consistent with the post modern feminist epistemology in the recognition of multiple explanations of reality. The Feminist Grounded Theory has been widely accepted as a method of research, ideally suited to the nursing profession and Grounded Theory is enriched by taking a feministic perspective when the research is based on women (Plummer and Young).

The Feminist Grounded theory and other Grounded theory approach can be most appropriate in the efforts to theoretically advance the field of adult and continuing education.

Research Designs in Grounded Theory

Systematic Design

This type of Grounded Theory design is broadly applied in educational research. A systematic Grounded Theory design is composed of **three** stages of coding, namely open coding, axial coding and selective coding. In the **first** stage, **open coding**, the grounded theorist forms initial categories of information about the phenomenon being studied by segmenting information.

The researcher basis categories on all data collected such as interviews, observations and researcher's memos or notes. In open coding the data are divided into segments and then scrutinised for communalities that reflect categories or themes. After data are categorised, they are further examined for properties that charaterises each category. In general, open coding is the process of reducing the data to a small set of themes that appear to describe the phenomenon under investigation. In short, open coding is the initial stage of forming Emergent Theory or conceptualisation.

Axial coding comes **second** after the open coding. In this stage, the grounded theorist selects one open coding category, position it at the centre of the process being explored and relates other categories to it. These other categories are the causal conditions, strategies, contextual and intervening conditions and consequences. This stage involves drawing a diagram, called a coding paradigm. In this coding stage, hypothetical relationships between the major categories and their corresponding sub-categories are built. **Strauss** and **Corbin** refers to this phase as axial coding, reflecting the idea of clustering the open codes around specific axis or points of intersection. So, this step is to group the discrete codes, according to conceptual categories that reflect the communalities among codes.

The **selective coding** is the **third** stage of coding. In selective coding, the grounded theorist writes a theory from inter-relationships of the categories in the Axial Coding Model. At a basic level, this theory provides an abstract explanation for the process being studied in the research. It is the process of integrating and refining the theory through such techniques as, writing out storyline that inter-connects the categories and sorting through personal memos about theoretical ideas. At this stage, the researcher treats the various code cluster in a selective fashion, deciding how they relate to each other and what stories they tell. Thus, the analyst construct a set of relational statements that can be used to explain, in a general sense what is going on. Use of these three coding procedures means that grounded theorists use set procedures to develop their theory.

Emerging Design

The emerging design was in many ways a reaction to systematic design. **Glaser** has issues with systematic design, he considered it too rigid and strict with the emphasis on rules and procedures. In response to this, he developed the emerging design. Glaser proposed to allow the theory to emerge from the data rather than forcing the data into pre-conceived categories. Glaser was also focused on Iterative Approach. This means that data was compared to data, data was compared to category and category compared to category. Glaser viewed Grounded Theory as the process of abstracting to higher and higher level rather than only describing a process. The Generate Theory should appropriately fit the data, should actually work, be relevant and changeable.

Researcher constructs a theory by discussing the inter-relationships among the emerged categories, without referring to a diagram (Creswell).

The emergent design refers to the ability to adapt to new ideas, concepts or findings that arise while conducting qualitative research. An emergent design welcomes unanticipated information, often adding to the richness of the data. Emergent design is not limited to the data collection and analysis.

An Emergent Approach to qualitative research is embedded within every stage from conceptualisation to publication. The researcher takes clues from the data, process or conclusion and the whole study is a reflection of varying levels of emergent characteristics within that research process.

Constructivist Design

It is the youngest of the three Grounded Theory designs. This design was developed by **Kathy Charmaz**. The design advocator **Charmaz** viewed that the constructivist design has advantages in addressing 'why' questions and preserving the complexity of social life . Charmaz paid more attention to individual's principles, opinions, beliefs, sensations, expectations and philosophy, rather than truth and explaining acts (cited in Creswell, 2012). In other words, constructivist design emphasises the values and beliefs of the researcher. According to **Guba**, **Lincoln** and **Schwandt** (1994), a constructivist design aims to explain participants' meanings towards a process in reality. The Constructivist Ground Theory uses an Inductive Approach to generating a new theory from the data gathered through participant, interview and focus group.

Steps in Conducting a Grounded Theory Research

To conduct the Ground Theory research, the researcher is required to take following steps into consideration

First, As a researcher, decide if a Grounded theory design best addresses the research problem. A Grounded theory design is appropriate, when you (researcher) wants to develop or modify a theory, explain a process and develops a general abstraction of the interaction and action of the people.

Second, You need to identify early tentative process to examine Ground theory study because the intent of the Ground theory research is to explain a process.This process should naturally follows from the research problems and questions that have to answer. It needs to involve people who are acting or interacting with identifiable steps or sequence in their interactions.

Third, As a researcher seeks approval and access it means that you need to obtain approval from the institution. You also need access to individuals who can provide insight into the process that you plan to study. This step involves seeking approval to collect data, appraising individuals of the purpose of the study and guaranteeing protection of the site and participants as you conduct inquiry.

Fourth, Conduct theoretical sampling, means that in Grounded Theory data collection is to gather information that can assist in developing a theory. A characteristic of Grounded Theory research is that the inquirer collects data more than once and keeps returning to data sources for more information throughout a study, until the categories are saturated and the theory is fully developed.

Fifth, In this step, you code the data as the the process of coding data occurs during data collection so that you can determine what data to collect next. It begins with the identification of open coding categories and using Constant Comparison Approach for saturation by comparing data with incident and incident with category.

Sixth, Use selective coding and develop the theory. This procedure includes inter-relating the categories in the coding paradigm. It may involve refining axial coding paradigm and presenting it as a model or theory of the process. It may include writing prepositions that provide testable ideas for further research. This stage may involve writing a story or a narrative that describes inter-relationships among categories.

Seventh, In Grounded theory research, validation is an active part of the process of research. After developing a theory, the ground theorist validates the process by comparing it with existing processes found in the literature.

Eight, In this step, the researcher write Grounded Theory research report. The structure of the Grounded Theory report vary from flexible structure in the emerging and constructivist design to a more quantitatively oriented structure in the systematic design. All Ground Theory projects, however end with the theory generated by the researcher reporting his/her abstraction of the process under examination.

Advantages of Grounded Theory

- An effective approach to build new theories and understand new phenomenon.
- High quality of the emergent theory.
- Emergent research design reflects the idiosyncratic nature of the study.
- Findings and methods are always refined and negotiated.
- Requires detailed and systematic procedures for data collection, analysis and theorising.
- The resulting theory and hypothesis help generate future investigation into the phenomenon.
- Requires the researcher to be open-minded and able to look at the data through many lenses.
- Data collection occurs over time and at many levels, helping to ensure meaningful results.

Disadvantages of Grounded Theory

- Huge volume of data.
- Time consuming and pain takingly precise process of data collection / analysis.
- Prescribed application required for the data gathering process.
- There are tensions between the evolving and inductive style of a flexible study and the Systematic Approach of Grounded Theory.
- It may be difficult in practice to decide when the categories are saturated or when the theory is sufficiently developed.
- It is not possible to start a research study without some pre-existing theoretical ideas and asumptions.
- Requires high level of experience, patience and acumen on the part of the researcher.

Narrative Research Design

The term 'narrative' comes from the verb 'to narrate' or 'to tell' (as a story) in detail. It is a literary form of qualitative research with strong ties to literature and it provides a Qualitative Approach in which one can write in a persuasive literary form. In narrative research design, researchers describe the lives of individuals, collect and tell stories about people's lives and write narrative of individual experiences.

As a distinct form of qualitative research, a narrative typically focuses on studying a single person, gathering data through collection of stories, reporting individual experiences and discussing the meaning of those experiences for the individuals It focuses on micro-analytic picture and individual stories rather than the broader picture of cultural norms as in ethnography or abstract theories as in Grounded Theory research.

For educators, looking for personal experiences in actual school settings, narrative research offers practical and specific insights. By conductive narrative studies, researcher establishes a close bond with the participants. This may help reduce a commonly held perception by practitioners in the field that research is distinct from practice and has little direct application.

Additionally, for participants in a study, sharing their stories may make them feel that their stories are important and they are heard. When they tell a story, it helps them understand topics that they need to process. Telling stories is a natural part of life and all individuals have stories about their experiences to tell others.

In this way, narrative research captures an everyday normal form of data that is familiar to individuals.

Characteristics of Narrative Research Design

- Narrative research places the data in chronological order. This is one main characteristic that makes narrative research different from other forms of research. The sequencing of events helps in creating a picture for the reader to appreciate the experiences of the individual.
- Narrative research allows restorying which helps the researcher to develop a sequence of events while establishing cause and effect. The researcher needs to be sensitive to the interaction of characters in the narrative, continuity of text and the setting of experience.
- Narrative research includes coding. Benefit of coding is that it is one way in which to summarise information and make it understandable to readers.
- In narrative research, collaboration involves including the participants in the interpretation and results of the project. There is an active discussion about the presentation and meaning of the data.

Steps in Conducting Narrative Research

There are many everyday examples that employ narrative design, including autobiographies, biographies, narrative interviews, oral histories and personal accounts. But, there are commonly used steps during a narrative study.

These are as follows

- Identify an issue of concern, provides the purpose for a study and enables the researcher to understand personal or social experiences of an individual.
- Select an individual who can provide an understanding of the issue. Carefully select this persons based on their experiences.
- Collect the story from that participant. It means that besides the participants verbally sharing their story through conversation or interviews, field texts also provide information about the participant. For example, journal or diary entries, letters sent by the individual, photographs, memory boxes and stories acquired through friends or family members.
- Restory or retell the individual's story.
- Collaborate with participant story teller.
- Write a story about participant's experience. It is a biggest step in narrative research. The participants' life experiences are written into a story by the researcher.
- Validate the accuracy of the report, as an accurate report is essential to preserving the story.

Case Study

Case study research refers to an indepth and detailed study of an individuals or a small group of individuals. Such studies are typically qualitative in nature, resulting in a narrative description of behaviour or experience. Case study research is not used to determine cause and effect, nor it is used to discover generalisable truths or make prediction. Rather, the stress in case study research is placed on exploration and description of a phenomenon.

Characteristics of Case Study

- The main characteristics of case study research are that it is narrowly focused, provides a high level of detail and is able to combine both objective and subjective data to achieve an indepth understanding.
- It is highly data based and strives for the same degree of reliability and validity as any good research.
- The case study strives towards a holistic understanding of cultural system of action. (Cultural system of actions refer to sets of inter-related activities engaged in by the action in a social situation). The case studies must always have boundaries.
- Case study research is not a sampling research. However, selecting cases must be done so as to maximise what can be learned in the period of time available for the study.
- Case study tends to be selective, focusing on one or two issues that are fundamental to understanding the system being examined.
- Case studies are multi-perspective analysis. This means that the researcher considers not just the voice and perspective of the action but also of the relevant groups of actors and the interaction between them.
- The case study is undertaken to examine a social unit as a whole . The unit may be a person, a social group, a family, a social institution or a community.
- The basic question in a case study is what are the characteristics of this single case or of these comparison cases? The case study are used to answer the question of how or why.
- They are commonly used to collect indepth data in a natural setting, where the researcher has little or no control over the events and there is a real life context. Often times, the goal of a case study is to provide information that may research in the formulation of hypothesis for future research.
- Case studies are commonly used in social science research and educational settings. For example, case study may be used to study psychological problems, such as the development of a child raised by a single, deaf parent or the effects on a child who had been isolated, abused and neglected until the age of 12 years. In the educational context, case studies may be used to study typical individuals, such as juvenile delinquents, school dropouts, gifted children, etc. Institutions such as school showing poor performance.

Components of Case Study Research Design

Components of case study research design are as follows

Study Questions

It means the form of question in terms of 'who', 'what' 'where' 'how' and 'why' provides an important clue regarding the most relevant research strategy to be used. The case study strategy is most likely to be appropriate for 'how' and 'why' questions, so your initial task is to clarify precisely the nature of your study questions in this regard.

Study Propositions

As for the second component, each proposition directs attention to something that should be examined within the scope of the study. For instance, the research on the topic of inter-organisational partnerships began with the questions how and why do organisations collaborate with one another to provide joint services.

These how and why questions, capturing what you are really interested in answering, led you to the case study as the appropriate strategy in the first place.

Study Unit of Analysis

This component is related to the fundamental problem of defining 'what the case' is a problem that has plagued many investigators at the outset of the case studies. The case studies of clinical patients, of exemplary students or of certain type of leaders. In each situation, an individual person is the case being studied and the individual is the primary unit of analysis.

Information about each relevant individual would be collected and several such individuals or cases might be included in a multiple case study.

The fourth and fifth component is the logical linking of data to prepositions and criteria for interpreting the finding have been the least well developed in case studies. These components represent the data analysis steps in case study research and a research design should lay the foundations for this analysis.

Types of Case Study Designs

There are several types of case study methods. The methods selected depend upon the nature of the questions being asked and the goals of the researcher.

Following are the different types of case study designs

Illustrative This is used to illustrate or describe an event or situation in such a way that people can become more familiar with the topic in question and perhaps become acquainted with the terminology associated with the topic.

Exploratory This is a condensed case study and the purpose is to gather basic and initial data that could be used to identify a particular question for a larger study. This study is not designed to produce detailed data from which any conclusions could be drawn. It is simply exploratory in nature.

Cumulative The cumulative design is designed to pull together information for several events/situations and aggregate it in such a way that it allows for greater generalisation. It has the advantage of saving time and money by not creating new and repetitive studies.

Critical Instance These studies are used to examine situations of unique interest or to challenge a universal or generalised belief. Such studies are not to create new generalisations, rather several situations or events may be examined to raise questions or challenge previously held assertions.

Once the question has been identified and the basic type of case study method has been selected, the researcher will need to begin designing their Case Study Approach. In order to obtain a full and detailed picture of the participant or small group, the researcher can use a variety of approaches and methods to collect data. These methods may include interviews, field studies, protocol or transcript analysis, direct participant observations, a review of documents and archived records and an exploration of artifacts. Researchers may choose to use one of these methods to collect data (Single Method Approach) or they may use several methods (Multi-Model Approach).

After the researcher has determined the data collection methods and what type of data will be used and recorded in the study, he/she will need to decide upon a strategy for analysing the data.

Case study researchers typically interpret their data either holistically or through coding procedures. A Holistic Approach reviews all of the data as a whole and attempts to draw conclusions based on the data in its entirety. This is an appropriate approach when the question being studied is more general in nature and the data provides an overview. Sometimes, it may be more useful to break the data into smaller pieces. This usually involves searching the data to identify and categorise specific actions or characteristics. These categories can be assigned a numeric code that allows the data to be analysed using statistical and quantitative methods.

In the design of a case study, it is important to plan and design how you are going to address the study and make sure that all data collected is relevant. Unlike scientific report, there is no strict set of rules, so the most important part is making sure that the study is focused and concise. Otherwise, you will end up having to wade through a lot of information.

It is best make short list of 4 to 5 bullet points and you are going to try and address during the study. With a case study, even more than a questionnaire or survey. It is important to be passive in your research, you are much more of an observer than an experimenter. Even in multi-subject cases, each case must be treated individually and then cross case conclusions can be drawn.

The final report of the case study is a rich (vivid and detailed) and holistic (describes the whole and its parts) description of a case/cases. It is the detailed discussion of the themes and issues concerning the case/cases along with their implications.

Steps of Conducting Case Study Research

Following are the steps of conducting case study research

Step 1 : Determine and Define the Research Questions

The first step in case study research is to estabilish a firm research, focus to which the researcher can refer over the course of study of a complex phenomenon or object. The researcher establishes the focus of the study by forming questions about the situation or problem to be studied and determining a purpose for the study. The research object in a case study is often a program, an entity, a person or a group of people. Each object is likely to be intricately connected to political, social, historical and personal issues, providing wide ranging possibilities for questions and adding complexity to the case study. The researcher investigates the object of the case study in depth, using a variety of data gathering methods to produce evidence that leads to understanding of the case and answers the research questions. The study's questions are most likely to be 'how' and 'why' questions and their definition is the first task of the researcher. To assist in targeting and formulating the questions, researcher conduct a literature review.

This review estabilishes what research has been previously conducted and leads to refined and insightful questions about the problem. Careful definition of the questions at the start, pin points where to look for evidence and helps determine the methods of analysis to be used in the study.

Step 2 : Select the Cases and Determine Data Gathering and Analysis Techniques

During the design phase of case study research, the researcher determines what approaches to use in selecting single or multiple real life cases to examine in depth and which instruments and data gatering approaches to use.

When using multiple cases, each case is treated as a single case. Each case's conclusion can then be used as information contributing to the whole study, but each case remains a single case. Exemplary case studies carefully select cases and carefully examine the choices available from among many research tools, available in order to increase the validity of the study. Careful discrimination at the point of selection also helps erect boundaries around the case.

The researcher must determine whether to study cases, which are unique in some way or cases which are considered typical and may also select cases to represent a variety of geographic regions, a variety of size parameters or other parameters. A useful step in the selection process is to repeatedly refer back to the purpose of the study, in order to focus attention on where to look for cases and evidence that will satisfy the purpose of the study and answer the research questions posed. Selecting multiple or single cases is a key element, but a case study can include more than one unit of embedded analysis.

A key strength of the case study method involves using multiple sources and techniques in the data gathering process. The researcher determines in advance, what evidence to gather and what analysis techniques to use with the data to answer the research questions. Data gathered is normally largely qualitative, but is may also be quantitative. Tools to collect data can include surveys, interviews, documentation review, observation and even the collection of physical artifacts.

Step 3 : Prepare to Collect the Data

Because case study research generates a large amount of data from multiple sources, systematic organization of the data is important to prevent the researcher from becoming overwhelmed by the amount of data and to prevent the researcher from loosing sight of the original research purpose and questions. Advance preparation assists in handling large amount of data in a documented and systematic fashion. Researchers prepare databases to assist with categorizing, sorting, storing and retrieving data for analysis.

Step 4 : Collect Data in the Field

The researcher must collect and store multiple sources of evidence, comprehensively and systematically that can be referenced and sorted so that converging lines of inquiry and patterns can be uncovered. Researchers carefully observe the object of the case study and identify causal factors associated with the observed phenomenon. Renegotiation of arrangements with the objects of the study or addition of questions to interviews may be necessary as the study progresses. Case study research is flexible, but when changes are made they are documented systematically.

Good case studies use filed notes and databases to categorize and reference data so that it is readily available for subsequent reinterpretation. Field notes, record feelings and intuitive hunches, pose questions and document the work in progress. They record testimonies, stories and illustrations which can be used in later reports.

Step 5 : Evaluate and Analyse the Evidence

This aspect of the case study methodology is the least developed. As a result, some researchers have suggested that if the studies were made conducive to statistical analysis, the process would be easier and more acceptable. This quantitative approach would be appealing to some of the critics of the case study methodology. **Miles** and **Huberman** suggested analytic techniques, such as rearranging the arrays, placing the evidence in a matrix of categories, creating flowharts or data displays, tabulating the frequency of different events, using means, variance and cross tabulations to examine the relationship between variables and other such techniques to facilitate analysis.

Step 6 : Prepare the Report

Case studies do not have the uniform outline as do other research reports. It is essential to plan this report as the case develops, to avoid problems at the end.

Advantages of Case Study

- Case studies are more flexible than any other type of research and allow the researcher to discover and explore as the research develops.
- Case studies emphasise indepth content. The researcher is able to develop deep and use a variety of data sources to get a complete picture.
- The data is collected in a natural setting and context.
- Often leads to the creation of new hypothesis that can be tested later.
- Case studies often shed new light on an Established Theory that results in future exploration.
- Researchers are able to study and analyse situations, events and behaviours that could be created in a laboratory setting.

Disadvantages of Case Study

- The uniqueness of the data usually means that it is not able to be replicated.
- Case studies have some level of subjectivity and researcher bias may be a problem.
- Due to indepth nature of the data, it is not possible to conduct the research on a large scale.
- There are concerns about the reliability, validity and generalisability of the results.

Ethnographic Research

Ethnography is a qualitative research, sometimes known as **cultural anthropology** or more recently as **naturalist inquiry**. Its disciplinary origin is **anthropology**. This research study looks at the social interaction of users in a given environment. It provides an indepth insight into the user's views and actions along with the sights and sounds they encounter during the day. Ethnography deals with the discovery and description of the culture of a group.

Since, the concept of culture is of central importance, it seeks answer to the question that what are the cultural characteristics of this group of people or of this cultural scene? Culture is the system of shared beliefs, values, practices, languages, customs, norms, rituals and material things that group members use to understand their world.

In its early application, ethnography was used to study the cultural characteristics of African, South Sea Island and American-Indian primitive tribes, who were geographically and culturally isolated, with little specialisation in economics, technology and social function. Here, observation was used as the main technique to gather information in respect of cultural features. Since, the researcher used to spend too little time with the primitive tribal groups and did'nt know their language they had to depend on the information gathered by the poorly trained informants.

Later, researchers made their studies more reliable and valid by spending more time among the tribes during observation. They also learnt the native language of tribal groups so as to interpret observations in terms of tribes concepts, feelings, norms and values.

The informants were given training in systematically recording field data in their own language and cultural perspective. The ethnographic methods are of recent origin in the field of education.

The ethnographic methods include direct observation, diary studies, video recordings, photography and artifact analysis, such as devices that a person uses throughout the day. Ethnographic study uses participant's observation as the primary data collection technique, along with the interviews with the members of group or community.

The participant's observation may extend from one month to a year, depending upon the nature of the problem as well as the research questions formulated for probing the cultural characteristics of a group of people or describing the cultural scenes.

This research involves intensive data collection on many variables, over an extended period of time in a naturalistic situation. The variables are studied where they naturally occur and as they occur without any control of the researcher on the environment or experimental conditions. The concern in ethnographic research is the context and therefore, the researcher goes there and participates in it. As during observation, the main objective of the researcher is to observe, listen and converse with the participants in as free and natural atmosphere as possible.

Characteristics of Ethnographic Research

- People's behaviour is studied in everyday contexts.
- It is conducted in a natural setting.
- Its goal is more likely to be exploratory than evaluative.
- It is aimed at discovering the local person's or native's point of view, wherein, the native may be a consumer or an end user.
- Data is gathered from a wide range of sources, but observation and/or relatively informal conversations are usually the principle ones.
- The approach to data collection is unstructured in that it does not involve following through a pre-determined detailed plan setup at the beginning of the study, nor does it determines the categories that will be used for analysing and interpreting the soft data obtained. This does not mean that the research is unsystematic. It simply means that initially the data is collected as raw form and a wide amount as feasible.
- The focus is usually a single setting or group of a relatively small size. In life history research, the focus may even be a single individual.
- The analysis of the data involves interpretation of the meanings and functions of human actions and mainly takes the form of verbal descriptions and explanations, with quantification and statistical analysis playing a subordinate's role at most.
- It is cyclic in nature, concering data collection and analysis. It is open to change and refinement throughout the process as new learning shapes future observations. As one type of data provides new information, this information may stimulate the researcher to look at another type of data or to elicit confirmation of an interpreation from another person, who is part of the culture being studied.

Assumptions in Ethnographic Research

- Ethnography assumes that the principal research interest is primarily affected by community cultural understandings. The methodology virtually assures that common cultural understandings will be identified for the research interest at hand. Interpretation is apt to place great emphasis on the causal importance of such cultural understandings. There is a possibility that an ethnographic focus will overestimate the role of cultural perceptions and underestimate the causal roles of objective forces.
- Ethnography assumes an ability to identify the relevant community of interest. In some settings, this can be difficult. Community, formal organisation, informal group and individual level perceptions may all play a causal role in the subject, under study and the importance of these may vary by time, place and issue. There is a possibility that an ethnographic focus may overestimate the role of community and culture and underestimate the causal role of individual psychological or of sub-community (or for that matter, extra community) forces.
- Ethnography assumes that the researcher is capable of understanding the cultural mores of the population under study, has mastered the language or technical jargon of the culture and has based findings on comprehensive knowledge of the culture. There is a danger that the researcher may introduce bias towards perspectives of his/her own culture.
- While not inherent to the method, cross cultural ethnographic research runs the risk of falsely assuming that given measures have the same meaning across cultures.

Steps of Conducting Ethnographic Research

The following steps are involved in conducting ethnographic research

Identify Research Question

Here, you (researcher) determines what problem you are seeking to better understand? Develop a problem statement that raises questions, you seek to know more about. The problem or question may be about nearly any topic that addresses people in a designated environment.

Determine Location(s) for Research

Identify the best place to conduct the participatory research. You may choose more than one location, if the research question or problem warrants. Select a location that will provide the best opportunity to observe, participate, take field notes and understand how the people in that environment act, communicate and think.

Formulate Presentation Method

Consider the most effective way(s) to obtain objective information. For example, will you be adopting a role of a person in the community or organisation you are observing?, Will you be covert or will others know you are conducting a research? If as a researcher they don't know you then consider the most ethical way to observe and collect data.

Acquire Permission

As ethnographic research can be a bit intrusive, it usually necessary to obtain permission for access into the location you plan to research. Always obtain permission in writing.

Observe and Participate

Ethnography requires more than just observation. To research, effectively determine the types of things you are looking for in regards to your question and problem. Determine the most effective way to collect notes. Be as objective as possible, as a researcher when observing and participating write running descriptions, things you remember, impressions and feelings, ideas that come to your mind, etc.

Interview

To increase your understanding of behaviours and actions, interviews may be necessary. You may do these interviews immediately after witnessing something, at the end of a designated observation period, at the end of the day or even at the end of the entire research period.

Collect Archival Data

It means that many organisations, communities and cultures have other artifacts and information that you can use to assist in your data collection. For example, reviewing things like papers, physical artifacts, phone conversations and other information rich sources.

Code and Analyse Data

As a researcher, code your data in a way that makes the most sense for your observations. Code and label things you saw and heard, sort for patterns, identify outliers, compare with theories and take notes of reflective remarks.

Writing an Ethnographic Account

In this type of research, the report is not attempted until the field notes have been analysed and the major conclusions have been formulated in the mind.

Following are the steps followed in writing the ethnographic account:

Questionnaire Formation Doing research for ethnography means that when you are physically present in the community or society under investigation, you need to design a questionnaire. Through this questionnaire, you need to ask a series of questions from the specific people of that community, centering on how they perceive their culture and lifestyle. Questionnaires make the ground work for most anthropological studies.

Research for a Questionnaire It should be based on your personal and theoretical observations. This would help in drafting real-time questions leading to viable conclusion.

Introduction Now, when you have collected the data through questionnaire, you need to construct an introduction.

The introduction must communicate two things to the readers i.e.

- What are you studying?
- How are you studying?

Once you succeeded in providing justified answers for these two points, include a brief background of the culture you intend to study as well as the areas you want to probe.

Methodology In this explanation to the readers, how you went about gathering information for your study. Support by giving reference to the conversations you had with community folks and their response. You can also mention the difficulties and limitations you faced in collecting data.

It includes:

Data Analysis Present a thorough analysis of the data, collected through observation and questionnaire. Here, you can also give a brief account of your personal opinions and experiences during the cultural study. You can also include learning from the study.

Conclusion Sum up your cultural research in the conclusion focusing on your methodology and learning. Restate the main points of your study. The ethnography must convince the readers that your findings have contributed a lot in the overall study of that community/ culture.

Advantages of Ethnographic Research

- It provides a comprehensive perspective.
- Ethnographic research observes behaviours in their natural environments.
- It accounts for the complexity of group behaviours, reveal interrelationships among multifaceted dimensions of group interactions and provide context for behaviours.

Disadvantages of Ethnographic Research

- This research is dependent on the researcher's observations and interpretations.
- It is difficult to check the validity of the researcher's conclusion.
- Observer bias in almost impossible to eliminate.
- It may lack transferability.
- Ethnographic research is time consuming and requires a well-trained researcher.

Mixed Method Research Designs

The term 'mixed method' refers to an emergent methodology of research that advances the systematic integration or mixing of quantitative and qualitative data within a single investigation or sustained program inquiry. The basic premise of this methodology is that such integration permits a more complete and synergistic utilization of data than do separate quantitative and qualitative data collection and analysis. It also encourages the collection of more comprehensive evidence for study problems, help answer questions that quantitative or qualitative methods alone cannot answer.

Mixed method research is important today because of the complexity of problems that need to be addressed, the rise of interest in qualitative research and the practical need to gather multiple forms of data for diverse people/audience. **Johnson Onw Uegbuzie** and **Turner** defind "Mixed Method research is the type of research in which a researcher or a team of researchers combine elements of quantitative and qualitative approaches (*e.g.* use of qualitative and quantitative view points, data collection analysis and inference techniques) for the purpose of breadth and depth of understanding and collaboration".

The Mixed Method research involves both collecting and analysing quantitative and qualitative data. Quantitative data includes closed-ended information, such as that found on attitude, behaviour or performance instruments. The analysis consists of statistically analysing scores collected on instruments, checklist or public documents to answer research questions or to test hypothesis.

On the other hand, qualitative data consists of open ended information that researcher gathers through interviews with participants. Qualitative data may be collected by observing participants. The analysis of qualitative data (word or text, images) follows the path of aggregating the words or images into categories of information and presenting the diversity of ideas gathered during data collection.

Characteristics of Mixed Method Research Designs

- The analysis of both qualitative and quantitative data.
- The collection of both open and closed-ended data (qualitative and quantitative data) in response to research questions.
- Persuasive and rigorous procedures for the qualitative and quantitative methods are used.
- The use of specific mixed method design that involves a concurrent or sequential integration.

Types of Mixed Method Research Designs

Triangulation Design

It is the most common and well known approach. According to **Creswell, Plano Clark** and **et.al**, (2003), the purpose of this design is to obtain different but complementary data on the same topic. **Morse**, (1991) says that to best understand the research problem, the intent in using this design is to bring together the differing advantages and non-overlapping disadvantages of quantitative methods (large sample size, trends, generalisations, etc.) with those of qualitative methods (small N, details indepth, etc).

This design is used when a researcher wants to directly compare and contrast quantitative statistical results with qualitative findings or to validate or expanad quantitative results with qualitative data. It is an efficient design in which both types of data are collected during one phase of research at roughly the same time. In this design, each type of data can be collected and analysed separately and independently using the technique, traditionally associated with each data type.

Explanatory Design

It is a two phased mixed method design. The overall purpose of this design is that qualitative data helps explain or build upon initial quantitative results. For instance, this design is well suited to a study in which a researchar needs qualitative data to explain significant (or non-significant) results or surprising results. This design can also be used when a researcher wants to form group based on quantitative results and follow-up with the groups through subsequent qualitative research (Morgan, Tasha Kkori and Teddlie, 1998).

This design starts with the collection and analysis of qualitative data. There are two variants of the explanatory design *i.e.* the Follow-Up Explanation model and the Participant Selection model. The explanatory design is considered the most straight forward of mixed method designs. Its two phase structure makes it straight forward to implement because the researcher conducts the two methods in separate phase and collects only one type of data at a time. This means that single researcher can conduct this design, a researcher team is not required to carry out the design.The final report can be written in two phases, making it straight forward to write and provide clear delineation for readers. This design lends itself to multi-phase investigations as well as single mixed method studies. This design appeals to quantitative researcher because it often begins with a strong quantitative orientation.

Exploratory Design

This design is based on the premise that an exploration is needed for one of several reasons. Measures or instruments are not available, the variables are unknown or there is no guiding framework or theory because this design begins qualitatively, it is best suited for exploring a phenomenon. This design is mainly useful when a researcher needs to develop and test an instrument because one is not available or identify important variables to study quantitatively. When the variables are unknown. It is also appropriate when a researcher wants to generalise results to different groups, to test aspects of an Emergent Theory or classification or to explore a phenomenon indepth and then measure its prevalence.

Researcher using this design, builds on the results of the qualitative phase by developing an instruments, identifying variables or stating propositions for testing based on an Emergent theory or framework. In this design, the researcher first qualitatively explores the research topic with the few participants. The qualitative finding then guide the development of items and scales for a quantitative survey instrument. In the second data collection phase, the researcher implements and validates this instrument quantitatively. In this design, the qualitative and quantitative methods are connected through the development of the instrument items.

Due to its two phase structure and the fact that only one type of data is collected at a time, the exploratory design shares many of the same advantages as the explanatory designs. This design typically emphasizes the qualitative aspect, the inclusion of a quantitative component can make the qualitative approach more acceptable to quantitative based audience. This design is applied to multi-phase research studies in addition to single studies.

Steps in Conducting MM Research Designs

- Be proficient in MM research by keeping up to data with latest techniques, software, textbooks and manuals.
- Consider other data analytic approaches that are not used in your field.
- Choose the research design that best the hypothesis and know the assumptions and limitations of that design.
- Incorporate figures and tables into your qualitative codebook to deepen the conceptualisations for the codes and provide a few examples of already coded data in order to provide thorough instructions.
- Create and use summary statements for each participants to help with the abstract portion of the analysis. Summary statement should be in a few sentences that describes the participants' statements and provide an overall gist of the available qualitative information.

Advantages of Mixed Method Research Designs

- It can be used to increase the generalising of the results.
- Researcher can provide strong evidence for a conclusion through convergence and collaboration of findings.
- Researcher can answer a broader and more complete range of research question because he is not confined to single method or approach.
- Words, pictures and narratives can be used to add meaning to numbers and numbers can be used to add precision to words and narrative.
- Researcher can add insights and understanding that might be missed, only a single method is used.
- It provides the strength of both qualitative and quantitative researchs.
- The qualitative and quantitative research used together to produce more complete knowledge, necessary to inform theory and practice.

Disadvantages of Mixed Method Research Designs

- Researcher has to learn about multiple methods and approaches and understand how to mix them appropriately.
- It can be difficult for a single researcher to carry out both qualitative and quantitative research, especially if two or more approaches are expected to be used concurrently, it may require a research team.
- It may be more time consuming and require additional finding.
- Methodological pursuits contend that one should always work with either a qualitative or a quantitative paradigm.

EXAM BASED QUESTIONS

1 Which of the following does not apply to qualitative research?
(a) Data are often words and pictures
(b) Uses the Inductive and Scientific Method
(c) Ends with a statistical report
(d) Involves direct and personal contact with participants

2 What is a research design?
(a) A way of conducting research that is not grounded in theory.
(b) The choice between qualitative and quantitative methods.
(c) The style in which you present your research finding, e.g. a graph.
(d) A framework for every stage of the collection and analysis of data.

3 Qualitative research design involves
(a) emergent design (b) co-relative design
(c) experimental design (d) cohort design

4 The Grounded Theory approach was developed by
(a) Heidegger (b) Glaser and Strauss
(c) Husserl (d) Denzin

5 Which of the following is not a tool of Grounded Theory?
(a) Theoretical sampling (b) Coding
(c) External validity (d) Constant comparison

6 ... is a general methodology for developing theory that is based on data, systematically gathered and analysed.
(a) Theory confirmation (b) Grounded theory
(c) Theory deduction (d) All of these

7 **The final stage in Grounded Theory Data Analysis is called**
(a) theoretical saturation
(b) axial coding
(c) Constant and Comparative Method
(d) selective coding

8 **The grounded theorist is finished analysing data when theoretical saturation occurs**
(a) true (b) false
(c) neither (a) nor (b) (d) None of these

9 **Which research strategy is described here? Theory is developed from data generated by a series of observations or interviews principley involving an Inductive approach.**
(a) Grounded theory (b) Action research
(c) Ethnography (d) Experiment

10 **Which of the following statement(s) is/are incorrect with regard to constructivist design?**
(a) It is the youngest of the three Grounded Theory designs.
(b) Constructivist design emphasises the values and beliefs of the researcher.
(c) This type of design is not limited to the data collection and analysis.
(d) The Constructivist Design Theory was developed by Kathy Charmaz.

11 **Match the following.**

List I (Designs)	List II (Characteristics)
A. Systematic design	1. Theory to emerge from the data, rather than forcing the data into pre-conceived categories
B. Emergent design	2. Emphasises the values and beliefs of the researcher
C. Constructivist design	3. Developed initially for nurses
D. Feminist Grounded Theory	4. It is composed of three stages open, axial and selective coding

Codes

	A	B	C	D		A	B	C	D
(a)	4	1	2	3	(b)	2	3	4	1
(c)	4	2	3	1	(d)	1	2	3	4

12 **In .... coding, the data is divided into segments and then scrutinised for communalities that reflect categories or themes.**
(a) axial coding (b) open coding
(c) selective coding (d) Only a

13 **Statement I** Classical Grounded Theory is based on the Glaser and Strauss (1967) book 'The Discovery of the Grounded Theory'.
Statement II In this the common coding types are substantial and theoretical.
Codes
(a) Statement I is true
(b) Both statements, I and II are false
(c) Statement II is true
(d) Both statements, I and II are true

14 **In .... designs, the researcher describes the lives of individuals, collect and tell stories about people's lives.**
(a) Grounded Theory Research
(b) Ethnography research
(c) Narrative research
(d) Case study

15 **In data analysis of the Grounded theory approach, the step which focuses on the main idea, developing the story line and finalising the theory is called ....**
(a) theoretical saturation (b) axial coding
(c) selective coding (d) open coding

16 **...... theory provides an explicit and sequential guidelines for conducting qualitative research.**
(a) Ethnographic (b) Case study
(c) Grounded (d) Narrative

17 **A distinct form of qualitative research, typically focuses on studying a single person gathering data through collection of stories, reporting individual experiences and discussing meaning of those experiences for the individuals is a .... research.**
(a) ethnographic (b) grounded
(c) narrative (d) phenomenological

18 **What do advocates of narrative analysis prefer to study?**
(a) The extent to which analytic induction can be value free.
(b) The iterative process of Grounded Theory.
(c) The ethical implications of conducting secondary analysis of qualitative data.
(d) The ways in which people use stories to make sense of events in their lives.

19 **What is narrative analysis?**
(a) A literary approach to documents.
(b) An approach that is sensitive to question that concern how people choose to sequence and represent people and events.
(c) A form of thematic analysis.
(d) A method of improving the quality of interview material.

20 **The case study is the study of a**
(a) single group.
(b) single individual.
(c) single community or family.
(d) single unit done intensively to bring out the processes and dynamics underlying its problems and functioning.

21 **Which of the following method of data collection is not discussed in the case study?**
(a) Interviews (b) Mail surveys
(c) Questionnaires (d) Observations

22 **A research which follows case method is called**
(a) clinical or diagnostic (b) causal
(c) analytical (d) qualitative

23 **The contribution of case study is**
(a) in study and data collection of a case related to caste age, sex, religion, problems, intellectual level and socioeconomic status.
(b) in evaluation of historical facts related with person or case.
(c) in study of institutionalised groups and families.
(d) All of the above.

24 **Case study collects data from the following sources.**
(a) From individual
(b) From ancedotal records
(c) From government documents
(d) All of the above

25 **Which of the following is similar to case study?**
(a) Longitudinal studies (b) Social surveys
(c) Follow - up studies (d) Horizontal studies

26 **The Government of India conducts census after every 10 years. The method of research under study in this process is ....**
(a) case study (b) developmental
(c) survey (d) None of these

27 **The main types of case study are**
(a) four (b) five (c) six (d) None of these

28 **Which of the following involves the study of multiple cases in one research study?**
(a) Intrinsic case study
(b) Single case study
(c) Instrumental case study
(d) Collective case study

29 **Which of the following is not an advantage of studying multiple cases?**
(a) Multiple cases can be compared to similarities and differences.
(b) Multiple cases can more effectively test, a theory than a single case.
(c) Generalisations about population are usually better when based on multiple cases.
(d) Cost is lower and depth of analysis is easier, when you study multiple cases in a single research study.

30 **Which of the following is the basic purpose to pre-test interview in this case study?**
(a) To develop the questionnaire
(b) To use agency representative
(c) To identify the potential problem
(d) To know the sample size

31 **Statement I** Case study research refers to an indepth detailed study of an individual or a small group of individuals.
Statement II It looks at the social interaction of users in a given statement.
Codes
(a) Both statements, I and II are ture
(b) Statement I is true, but II is false
(c) Both statements, I and II are false
(d) Statement II is true

32 **Match the following.**

List I (Studies)	List II (Features)
A. Illustrative	1. These studies are used to examine situations of unique interest or to challenge a universal or generalised belief
B. Exploratory	2. It is used to illustrate or describe an event or situation in such a way that people can become more familiar with the topic
C. Cumulative	3. It is a condensed case study and the purpose is to gather basic and initial data that could be used to identify a particular question for a large study
D. Critical instance	4. It is designed to pull together information for several events / situations and aggregate in such a way that it allows for greater generalisation

Codes

	A	B	C	D		A	B	C	D
(a)	2	3	4	1	(b)	3	2	4	1
(c)	4	3	2	1	(d)	1	4	3	2

33 **Which of the following statement(s) is/are true with regard to the case study strength?**
(a) Case studies emphasise indepth content.
(b) Case studies are more flexible than any other type of research and allows the researcher to discover and explore as the research develops.
(c) It often to the creation of new hypothesis that can be tested later on.
(d) All of the above

34 **In case study, the executive summary is placed**
(a) with the recommendations
(b) at the beginning
(c) at the end
(d) as part of the introduction

35 **All case studies involve documentation of the process of**
(a) exploring alternative choice (b) evaluating a problem
(c) strategic decision-making (d) story telling

36 **Which research strategy is described here? The researcher is involved in the acts under study, she/he causes changes and monitors the outcomes.**
(a) Case study (b) Grounded Theory
(c) Survey (d) Action research

37 **Who was pioneer in using case study methods in the field of psychiatry to treat his psychoneurotic patient?**
(a) Dewey (b) Sigmund Freuel
(c) Van Dalen (d) Best and Kahn

38 **The components of case study research design can be categorised into**
(a) two (b) four (c) five (d) three

39 **The case study is undertaken to examine a .... unit as a whole. The unit may be a person, a social group, a family, a social institution or community.**
(a) social (b) psychological
(c) educational (d) philosophical

40 **One strength of ethnography is that**
(a) the influence of the specific variables can be controlled by the investigator.
(b) it usually generates richer and more indepth information than other methods.
(c) it is essential when the study is primarily historical or has a historical dimension.
(d) it can only be used relatively small groups or communities.

41 **What is the name of the role adopted by an ethnographer, who joins in with the group's activities but admits to being a researcher?**
(a) Complete participant
(b) Participant as observer
(c) Observer as participant
(d) Complete observer

42 **What are the two main types of data that can be used in visual ethnography?**
(a) Positivist and interpretivist
(b) Qualitative and quantitative
(c) Nominal and ordinal
(d) Extant and research driven

43 **Why is an ethnographic study unlikely to use a probability sample?**
(a) Because the aim of understanding is more important than that of generalisation.
(b) Because the researcher cannot control who is willing to talk to them.
(c) Because it is difficult to identify a sampling frame.
(d) All of the above

44 **What is the name of the role adopted by an ethnographer, who joins in with the group's activities but admits to being a researcher?**
(a) Complete participant (b) Participant as observer
(c) Observer as participant (d) Complete observer

45 **Which of the following is a component of ethnographic research?**
(a) Being immersed in a social group or setting.
(b) Participant observation, interviews, and/or documentary analysis.
(c) A written account of an ethnographic study.
(d) All of the above

46 **What is one of the main disadvantage of using the covert role in ethnography?**
(a) It can be hard to gain access to the social group.
(b) It is difficult to take notes without arousing suspicion.
(c) The problem of reactivity, people may change their behaviour if they know they are being observed.
(d) It is usually too time consuming and expensive to be a realistic option.

47 **The Primary Data Analysis Approach in ethnography is**
(a) open, axial and selective coding
(b) holistic description and search for cultural themes
(c) cross case analysis
(d) Identifying essences of a phenomenon

48 **In which Qualitative Research Approach is the primary goal to gain access to individual's inner worlds of experience?**
(a) Phenomenology (b) Ethnography
(c) Grounded theory (d) Case study

49 **You want to study a Native American Group in New Mexico for a six month period to learn all you can about them, so you can write a book about that particular tribe. You want the book to be accurate and authentic as well as informative and inspiring. What type of research will you likely be conducting when you get to New Mexico?**
(a) Ethnography (b) Phenomenology
(c) Grounded Theory (d) Collective case study

50 **........ is used to describe cultural scenes or the cultural characteristics of a group of people.**
(a) Phenomenology (b) Ethnography
(c) Grounded theory (d) Instrumental case study

51 **Arrange the following steps of ethnography researches.**
1. Data collection
2. Identification of subjects
3. Hypothesis generation
4. Identification of the phenomenon
5. Drawing conclusions

Choose the correct option.
(a) 4, 2, 3, 1, 5 (b) 2, 3, 1, 5, 4
(c) 4, 2, 1, 3, 5 (d) 5, 2, 3, 1, 4

52 **What are two types of validity in ethnography researches?**
1. Extraneous validity 2. Exernal validity
3. Population validity 4. Internal validity

Choose the correct option.
(a) 1 and 2 (b) 2 and 3 (c) 2 and 4 (d) 1 and 3

53 **Triangulation helps in enhancing**
(a) reliability (b) validity
(c) variability (d) None of these

54 **The ethnographic studies in educational settings are characterised by**
(a) integrating very close interpersonal notes
(b) copious field notes
(c) participant's observations
(d) conservation and participant's observation

55 **Participant's observation method is used in**
(a) experimental research (b) ethnographic studies
(c) historical research (d) ex-post facto research

56 **Which of the following statement regarding the role of ethnographic research is correct?**
(a) It is heavily context dependent, which is suitable for educational research.
(b) Focus on how things are and how they get that way.
(c) Extensive description provides good context for theoretical contributions.
(d) All of the above

57 .... uses inductive logic and formulate their hypothesis on the basis of their observations. These hypothesis are re-evaluated periodically in the light of new observation and modified when appear to be inconsistent with the evidence.

(a) Grounded Theory (b) Case study
(c) Ethnography (d) Mixed Method

58 Here is a mixed design, using notation 'QUAL --> quan'. What type of mixed research is this?

(a) Specific Method (b) Mixed Model
(c) Specific Model (d) Mixed Method

59 Which of the following cannot be a purpose or rationale for a mixed research design?

(a) Triangulation (b) Complementarily
(c) Development (d) All of these

60 Research in which the researcher uses qualitative paradigm of one phase and the quantitative paradigm for another phase is known as

(a) action research (b) quantitative research
(c) basic research (d) Mixed Method research

61 Which of the following is a disadvantage of mixed research?

(a) Words, pictures and narratives can be used to add meaning to numbers.
(b) Researcher can generate and test a Grounded Theory.
(c) Numbers can be used to add precision to word, pictures and narratives.
(d) It is more time consuming and expensive.

62 What would this method design be called 'Qual + QUAN'?

(a) Equal status concurrent design
(b) Dominant status sequential design
(c) Equal status sequential design
(d) Dominant status concurrent design

63 .... is a Two Phased Mixed Method design. The overall purpose of this design is that qualitative data helps explain or build upon initial qualitative results.

(a) The triangulation design
(b) The explanatory design
(c) Exploratory design
(d) Equal status concurrent design

64 Which of the following is an incorrect statement about the disadvantage of MM research?

(a) It is time consuming and requires additional funding.
(b) Researcher can add insight and understanding that might be missed.
(c) Research has to learn multiple methods and approaches and understand how to mix them appropriately.
(d) It can be difficult for a single researcher to carry out both qualitative and quantitative researchs.

65 The idea that the more times a research finding is shown with different sets of people, the more confidence we can place in the finding and in generalising beyond the original participants is known as

(a) data triangulation (b) methods generalisation
(c) naturalistic generalisation (d) replication logic

66 In Mixed Method research, qualitative and quantitative findings should be

(a) integrated
(b) contained in separate sections
(c) listed in order of importance
(d) shown fully in appendices

67 Which sequence do Creswell and Planko Clark (2011) recommended for an article writing up mixed method research?

(a) Introduction, methods, results, discussion
(b) Introduction, background, methods, findings, discussion, conclusion
(c) Introduction, literature review, data collection
(d) Introduction, theory, data collection, measurement, methods and models, results, conclusion

68 What is triangulation?

(a) Using three quantitative or qualitative methods in a project.
(b) Cross check the results found by different research strategies.
(c) Allow theoretical data to emerge from the data.
(d) Drawing a triangular diagram to represent the relations between three concepts.

69 Which of the following statement(s) is/are **true** in the context of participatory research?

(a) It recognises knowledge as power
(b) It emphasises on people as expert
(c) It is a collective process of inquiry
(d) Its soul purpose is production of knowledge

70 Which of the following is a disadvantage of qualitative interviewing relative to participant observation?

(a) It has a more specific focus.
(b) It is more ethically dubious, in terms of obtaining informed consent.
(c) It may not provide access to deviant or hidden activities.
(d) It does not allow participants to reconstruct their life events.

71 The qualitative research strategy places a value on

(a) using numbers, measurements and statistical techniques.
(b) generating theories through inductive research, about social meanings.
(c) conducting research that is of a very high quality.
(d) All of the above

72 The term used to describe suspending pre-conceptions and learned feelings about a phenomenon is called

(a) axial coding (b) design flexibility
(c) bracketing (d) ethnography

73 Which major characteristic of qualitative research refers to studying real world situations as they unfold naturally?

(a) Holistic perspective (b) Naturalistic inquiry
(c) Dynamic system (d) Inductive analysis

74 The strongest evidence for causality comes from which of the following research methods?

(a) Experimental (b) Causal comparative
(c) Correlation (d) Ethonography

75 When more than one observer engaged in research setting is known as
(a) triangulation
(b) space triangulation
(c) investigator triangulation
(d) combined triangulation

Directions (Q. Nos. 76-80) *Below given are two statements, one labelled as Assertion (A) and other labelled as Reason (R) select the correct code for the following.*

Codes
(a) Both A and R are true and R is the correct explanation of A
(b) Both A and R are true, but R is not the correct explanation of A
(c) Both A and R are false
(d) A is true, but R is false

76 **Assertion** (A) Qualitative research in India has a long way to go to reach international standards.
Reason (R) Because the funding agencies do not support qualitative research in academic institutions.

77 **Assertion** (A) Grounded theory provides explicit and sequential guidelines for conducting qualitative research.
Reason (R) It advances conceptual analysis of qualitative data.

78 **Assertion** (A) Case study research refer to an indepth study of an individual or a small group.
Reason (R) The case studies are typically qualitative in nature.

79 **Assertion** (A) Enthnographic research is conducted in natural setting.
Reason (R) People's behaviour is not studied in everyday context.

80 **Assertion** (A) Mixed method research uses both quantitative and qualitative data.
Reason (R) It presents a thorough analysis of data collected through observation.

81 Match the following.

List I (Type of Research)	List II (Characteristics)
A. Grounded Theory	1. It is undertaken to examine a social unit as a whole
B. Case Study	2. Focuses on studying a single person gathering data through collection of stories
C. Narrative	3. It is conducted in natural setting
D. Ethnography	4. A set of systematic and inductive method for conducting research

Codes

	A	B	C	D		A	B	C	D
(a)	4	1	2	3	(b)	1	2	3	4
(c)	3	2	1	4	(d)	4	3	2	1

82 Match the following.

List I (Designs of Research)	List II (Characteristics)
A. Systematic Design	1. Used when researcher wants to compare and contrast quantitative statistical results with qualitative fundings
B. Triangulation Design	2. It is composed of three stages-coding, axial coding and selective coding
C. Constructivist Design	3. Explain aims of participant towards a process of reality
D. Exploratory	4. Is based on the premise that an exploration is needed for one of several reasons

Codes

	A	B	C	D		A	B	C	D
(a)	1	2	3	4	(b)	2	1	3	4
(c)	4	3	2	1	(d)	2	4	1	3

PREVIOUS YEARS' QUESTIONS

July 2018

1 While assessing the attitude of administrators towards a 'women empowerment programme', a researcher had no pre-conceived notions about what she might discover and she continued interviewing until key themes emerge. Indicate the paradigm of research being followed.
(a) Ethnographic Study Approach
(b) Grounded Theory Approach
(c) Phenomenological Study Approach
(d) Case Study Approach

November 2017

2 Match the following.

List I (Types of Researchs)	List II (Descriptions)
A. Naturalistic inquiry	1. Analytical description of social group, related to the shared beliefs, practices and behaviours
B. Phenomenological research	2. Sophisticated analysis, which links participant's perception
C. Ethnographic research	3. Desinged to aid and assess the merit and worth of a specific practice in terms of the values

List I (Types of Researchs)	List II (Descriptions)
D. Grounded Theory research	4. Analysis of qualitative data to provide an understanding of a concept from the participant's perspective
	5. Prefer inductive reasoning from grassroot's observation and discovery with an emergent design

Codes

	A	B	C	D
(a)	3	1	5	2
(b)	2	3	1	5
(c)	1	4	5	2
(d)	5	4	1	2

January 2017

3 Which one of the following theme may be appropriate for areas of action research in the field of teacher education?

1. Improving teaching skills of student teacher.
2. Identifying suitable criteria for admissions.
3. Modification of teaching behaviour of trainees.
4. Revisiting teacher education curriculum.
5. Enhancing professional competencies of both trainees and teacher educators.
6. Preparing teachers for special schools.

Codes

(a) 1, 3 and 5 (b) 2, 4 and 6
(c) 1, 2 and 3 (d) 2, 3 and 4

4 Which of the following is/are not a characteristic(s) of narrative research?

1. Collecting individual stories.
2. Collaborating with participants.
3. Chronology of the experience.
4. Association of variables for group of participants.
5. Data collection at one point of time from a sample.

Codes

(a) 2 and 3 (b) 1 and 5
(c) 4 and 5 (d) 2 and 4

July 2016

5 Which of the following methods of data collection can be considered as ....an attempt to map out or explain the richness and complexity of human behaviour by studying it from more than one standpoint, using both quantitative and qualitative data?

(a) non-participant observation
(b) triangulation
(c) indepth interview
(d) participant's observation

6 Which of the following type of research can be called as .... a small scale intervention in the functioning of the real world with an intent of a close examination of the effects of such intervention?

(a) case study (b) naturalistic research
(c) action research (d) historical research

December 2015

7 Match the following.

List I (Types of researches)	List II (Characteristics)
A. Case study	1. Field research using spontaneous and uninterrupted data collection techniques
B. Phenomenological research	2. Research investigating the implised cause-effect relationship, already evident
C. Ex-post facto research	3. An analysis, the results of which are not generalisable
D. Naturalistic inquiry	4. Application of analytical methodology to the study of the past
	5. Analysis to provide understanding of a concept from the participant's perspectives
	6. Direct manipulation of at least one independent variable

Codes

	A	B	C	D
(a)	5	3	1	4
(b)	1	6	4	5
(c)	3	5	2	1
(d)	2	4	3	6

June 2015

8 Match the following.

List I (Study)	List II (Description)
A. Analysis of historical records	1. Collection of data for indepth study in a vertical or horizontal or both manner
B. Non-participant's observation	2. Uses open ended and closed questions
C. Participant's observation	3. Recording notes from documents, listening to tapes and watching available films
D. Case study	4. Observation scales, use of score cards, etc.
	5. Interaction, formal and informal, possible use of tape and video recording

Codes

	A	B	C	D
(a)	1	3	5	4
(b)	3	4	5	2
(c)	2	4	3	5
(d)	3	4	5	1

9 For conducting a study to understand the social customs in a tribal society, which of the following technique will be most appropriate?
(a) Interview
(b) Participant's observation
(c) Self-reporting
(d) Testing

10 A researcher reports a study in respect of prevailing class control procedures, used by the public schools of Uttar Pradesh. As an expert in research methodology, what will be your intelligent guess in respect of the methodology of research indicated below?
(a) Historical (b) Descriptive
(c) Case study (d) Experimental

11 Internal criticism of data is considered important in which of the following researches?
(a) Philosophical (b) Case study
(c) Descriptive (d) Experimental

12 In which of the following form of enquiry, research design functions as a specific and precise guidance?
(a) Experimental research (b) Philosophical research
(c) Ethnographic studies (d) Case studies

December 2014

13 In which research design, sampling is least necessary?
(a) Comparative analysis (b) Experimental study
(c) Case study (d) Correlational study

14 Research for exploring the applicability of a theory or law formulated in a specific situation in the field of education is termed as
(a) pure research (b) action research
(c) applied research (d) theoretical research

June 2014

15 A non-government organisation conducted a study in a Gram Panchayat to see the impacts of campaign approach on enrollment and retention of rural elementary school children. This is an example of
(a) descriptive study (b) field experiment
(c) ex-post facto research (d) historical research

16 Match the following.

List I (Type of Research)	List II (Characteristics)
A. Experimental	1. Criticism
B. Historical	2. Control
C. Case study	3. Interpretative
D. Ethnography	4. Intensive
	5. Intuitive

Codes

	A	B	C	D
(a)	2	3	4	5
(b)	1	2	5	3
(c)	3	1	4	5
(d)	2	1	4	3

17 Research conducted by classroom teacher to improve spelling among students in English language is categorised as
(a) pure research (b) qualitative research
(c) quantitative research (d) active research

18 A study of the causes and consequences of India's freedom struggle movement falls under which of the following type of research?
(a) Ex-post facto research
(b) Historical research
(c) Correlational research
(d) Phenomenological research

ANSWERS

Exam Based Questions

1 (c)	2 (d)	3 (a)	4 (b)	5 (c)	6 (b)	7 (d)	8 (a)	9 (a)	10 (d)
11 (a)	12 (b)	13 (d)	14 (c)	15 (c)	16 (c)	17 (c)	18 (d)	19 (b)	20 (d)
21 (d)	22 (a)	23 (d)	24 (d)	25 (c)	26 (c)	27 (c)	28 (d)	29 (d)	30 (c)
31 (a)	32 (a)	33 (d)	34 (c)	35 (c)	36 (d)	37 (b)	38 (c)	39 (a)	40 (b)
41 (b)	42 (d)	43 (d)	44 (b)	45 (d)	46 (b)	47 (b)	48 (a)	49 (a)	50 (b)
51 (a)	52 (c)	53 (a)	54 (c)	55 (a)	56 (d)	57 (c)	58 (d)	59 (d)	60 (d)
61 (d)	62 (d)	63 (b)	64 (b)	65 (d)	66 (a)	67 (a)	68 (d)	69 (d)	70 (c)
71 (b)	72 (b)	73 (b)	74 (a)	75 (c)	76 (d)	77 (b)	78 (a)	79 (d)	80 (d)
81 (a)	82 (b)								

Previous Years' Questions

1 (c)	2 (d)	3 (a)	4 (c)	5 (b)	6 (c)	7 (c)	8 (d)	9 (b)	10 (b)
11 (a)	12 (a)	13 (c)	14 (c)	15 (b)	16 (d)	17 (d)	18 (b)		

CHAPTER 26

Concept of Pedagogy and Andragogy

Pedagogy is authority focused, where teacher has a complete control over a child's learning experience, whereas andragogy is focused on the learning experiences of adults and the methods which work best in adult's education.

Pedagogy

Broadly, it refers to the theory and practice of education and how it influences the growth of learners. It is taken as an academic discipline, which is the study of how knowledge and skills are imparted in an educational context. It considers the interaction, that takes place during learning.

Literally, pedagogy is both an art and a science of teaching children. The word 'Pedagogy' comes from ancient Greek word 'paidagogos', a compound comprised of 'paidos' (child) and 'agogos' (leader) means 'to lead a child'.

- It was considered a form of art in the beginning. The art of teaching of leading children to knowledge.
- With the advent of scientific fields, like sociology and psychology, pedagogy was counted as true science. Thus, the function of pedagogy was to guide the process of teaching and learning.
- It is now accepted as applied science. It is a discipline that is geared towards the practical applications of acquired knowledge.

Simply, it is the method and practice of teaching. It includes different types of teaching styles, feedbacks, assessments and teacher's theory. When people talk about the pedagogy of teaching, they refer to the way in which teacher delivers the content of the curriculum to the class.

Definitions of Pedagogy

According to **Watkins** and **Mortimore**, "Pedagogy is any conscious activity, by one person designed to enhance learning in another".

According to **Bernstein**, "Pedagogy is a sustained process where by somebody acquires new forms or develops existing forms of conduct, knowledge, practice and criteria from somebody or something deemed to be an appropriate provider and evaluator".

In this Chapter

- *Pedagogy*
- *Levels of Teaching*
- *Andragogy*
- *Self-Directed Learning*

According to **Durkheim**, "Pedagogy is a practical theory, focused on the attainment of the educational phenomenon, counter-pointed to the Scientific Theory, which is focused on the knowledge of the educational fact, a task which is up to the sociology of education to undertake".

According to **Givanni Genovesi**, "Pedagogy is an autonomous science because it has its own language and is aware of how to use it, according to its own methods and its own ends and by this language, pedagogy generates a body of knowledge and a series of experiments, without which any construction of education models would be impossible".

Principles of Pedagogy

- It equips learner for life in its broader sense.
- It engages with valued forms of knowledge.
- It recognises the importance of prior experience and learning.
- It requires learning to be scaffolded.
- It needs assessment to be in harmony with learning.
- It promotes the active engagement of the learner.
- It fosters both individual and social processes and outcomes.
- It recognises the significance of informal learning.
- It depends on the learning of all those who support the learning of others.
- It demands consistent policy frameworks with support for learning as their primary focus.

Pedagogical Analysis

It means the logical and systematical breaking of the curriculum from the point of view of a pedagogue for the purpose of its effective transaction. Pedagogical Analysis is selection of an appropriate objectives and strategies in various instructional situations to access the level of actual teaching at the end. It involves various logical steps to arrive at logical inference and it also helps the students to understand the concepts, principles and phenomenas.

Stages of Pedagogical Analysis

Stage 1 Divide the content of the selected unit into suitable sub-unit and arrange the selected sub-units into number of required periods.

Stage 2 Briefly write the essence of the content of the selected sub-unit.

Stage 3 Write an appropriate previous knowledge, required for the sub-unit.

Stage 4 Write an appropriate instructional objective, to be selected for the sub-unit.

Stage 5 Select an appropriate teaching strategies for the sub-unit, according to the given instruction.

- Write the name of the methods applied.
- Mention the teaching aids required.
- Briefly illustrate the necessary demonstration and/or experimentation required.
- Mention the necessary board work required.
- Write probing questions related to the sub-unit and provide answer for them.
- Prepare a worksheet for the sub-unit.

Stage 6 Give suitable examples/illustrations/analogies for the sub-unit.

Stage 7 Prepare a table of specification, for the sub-unit. Write at least six criterion refrenced test items, each with specific criteria for the sub-unit.

Critical Pedagogy

Critical Pedagogy is a philosophy of education and social movement that combines education with critical theory. First described by **Paulo Freire**, it has since been developed by **Henry Giroux** and other praxis oriented, "Educational movement guided by passion and principle, to help students to develop consciousness of freedom, recognise authoritarian tendencies and connect knowledge to power and the ability to take constructive actions".

According to **Ira Shor**, "Critical pedagogy as habits of throught, reading, writing and speaking which go beneath surface meaning, first impressions, dominant myths, official pronouncements, received wisdom and mere opinions, to understand the deep meaning, social context, ideology and personal consequences of any action, event, object, process, organization, subject matter or discourse".

Need of Critical Pedagogy

- It advocates the necessity for 'skilled critical questioning' for teaching practitioners and learners.
- It believes that it is essential to develop in the learners, the ability to see through the beliefs and practices in a society either for appreciating and accepting them.
- By adopting this approach, students from different sections can be equipped with the knowledge and skills required to effectively encounter the challenges posed by the hidden curriculum.

Characteristics of Critical Pedagogy

- It centers its practice on community and collaboration.
- Must remain open to diverse voices and thus requires invention to reimagine the ways that communication and collaboration happen across cultural and political boundaries.
- The objective of this pedagogy is to empower students and help them to help themselves.
- Promotes emancipation and intellectual growth.
- The aim is to liberate students from oppression.

Implications of Critical Pedagogy in Teacher Education

Attention to Traditional and Indigenous Context of Society It is necessary to include rural population in education planning, in order to uplift the country. It has been observed that education plans are based on higher class of the society. The designer of educational content should include the minorities as well.

Coaches and Student's Mutual Participants in Educational Plan Development Elite and senior managers are not the only officers of educational plan development. But the professors, experts, parents, teachers, local groups and learners should contribute in educational planning.

Attention to the Political Position of Education in Curriculum Planning Important characteristic of critical pedagogy is its attention towards political aspect of education. Critical pedagogy believes that education is a political activity and its mission is to analyse the social relations.

Role of Cultural Segment From critical pedagogical perspective, literacy helps in bridging the cultural barriers. Cultural segment plays an important role in teaching-learning process.

The Importance of Adult Education Many comprehensive plans can be formulated to teach the adults. The adults need to understand the lesson and critically analyse it.

Levels of Teaching

Teacher can organize the content at three levels that are discussed below

- Memory level of teaching.
- Understanding level of teaching.
- Reflective level of teaching.

Memory Level of Teaching

At this level, the situation of thoughtlessness is found. It is concerned with memory or mental ability that exists in all living beings. Teaching at memory level is considered to be the lowest level of the teaching. *At this level,*

- the thinking ability doesn't play a role.
- students only cram the facts, information, formulas and laws that are taught to them.
- teaching is nothing, but learning the subject matter by rote.
- the role of the teacher is prominent and the student is secondary.
- the study material is organised and pre-planned. The teacher presents the study material in a sequential order.

Memory level teaching lacks insight. Psychologically, it is cognitive level of teaching.

Herbartian Model of Memory Level of Teaching

Herbart was the exponent of memory level teaching.

***Herbart** described the following steps for presenting the Model of Memory Level of Teaching*

- Focus
- Social system
- Syntax
- support system

Focus

It emphasises on cramming of facts and development of following capacities i.e.

- Training of mental aspects
- Providing knowledge of facts
- Retaining the learnt facts
- Recalling and representing the learnt facts

Syntax

Preparation The pupils are prepared to acquire new knowledge by testing their previous knowledge.

Statement of Aim Topic is made clear to the pupils and teacher writes the topic on the blackboard.

Presentation The pupils are provided with opportunities for self-learning. Teacher tries to derive most of the information from the pupils, so that a relationship may be established between the new and the previous knowledge.

Comparison of Association Teacher establishes a relationship between two subjects i.e. facts and events of the same subject. By comparison, the new knowledge may be clarified and made permanent in the minds of the pupils.

Generalisation After explaining the basics of lesson, the pupils are given an opportunities to think on that lesson. Pupils formulate some principles and laws which can be used in the future life situations.

Application Observe, whether these new learnt knowledge can be used in new situations or not. This is verified through questioning or new opportunities, to make use of learnt knowledge. It makes the knowledge permanent and laws can be verified.

Social System

The process of teaching is both social and professional. Pupils and teachers are members of this social system. The teacher occupies the **primary** phase and the students occupies the **secondary** phase.

Thus, the function of the teacher includes :

- Presenting the content
- Controlling the student's activities
- Providing motivation

Support System

- More emphasis is laid on the power of learning by rote.
- To evaluate the pupil, both oral and written tests are conducted.
- In this, essay type test is more useful.
- Recall and recognition are used successfully, through the objective type examination.

Understanding Level of Teaching

Understanding is something to perceive the meaning, grasp the idea and comprehend the meaning.

In the field of education and psychology, the meaning of understanding can be classified as

- Seeing the total use of facts
- Seeing relationship
- A generalised insight

The teaching at the understanding level is of a higher quality than the one at the memory level. It is more useful and thoughtful from the view point of mental capabilities. At this level of teaching, the teacher explains the student about the relationship between principles and facts.

Teachers teach them, how these principles can be applied. Memory level teaching barrier is essential to be crossed for this level of teaching. As compared to memory level teaching, the understanding level teaching has greater merit. This enable students to have complete command over subject material. In the understanding level, role of the teacher is more active.

At this level also, students are secondary. At this level, no cramming is encouraged. The new knowledge acquired at this level is related to the earlier knowledge gained. A generalisation is made on the basis of facts and the facts are used in the new situations.

Morrison's Model of Understanding Level of Teaching

Morrison very clearly stated that understanding is not simply being able to recall something, it is not a mere generalization deduced from specific facts, it is insight into how it may be used in future situations. Morrison asserted that the outcome of all teaching is 'mastery' and not memorization of facts. He proposed a unit plan, each unit representing an insight which is relatively in itself.

Morrison described the following steps for presenting the Model of Understanding Level of Teaching

Focus

The pupil should achieve the mastery of the concept. Teacher stresses upon the mastery of the content, so that a desirable change may occur in the personality of the pupils.

Syntax

Syntax is divided into five following steps

Exploration Previous knowledge is tested by questioning. After analysing the content, the elements are arranged in a logical sequence from psychological point of view. Then, it is determined by how the units of content or new knowledge should be presented.

Presentation Teacher remains more active. *He forms the following activities for the presentation of the contents*

- Presents the content in small units, maintain the sequence of these units and a relationship with the pupil's establishers.
- Teacher diagnosis whether the content have been understood by the pupils or not.
- Teacher repeats the content, until most of the pupil does not acquire the knowledge.

Assimilation Teacher provides opportunities to pupils for assimilation.

Assimilation has the following characteristics

- Pupils are provided with occasions for generation, through assimilation.
- Opportunities are provided, in order to stress upon the depth of the content.
- At the time of assimilation, every pupil studies in accordance with his requirement.
- In assimilation, the pupils work themselves in laboratories and libraries.
- Supervised study occurs.
- Both pupils and teachers remains active.
- The pupils perform individual activities and teachers guides them according to their need, during supervision.
- During assimilation period, the teacher tests whether the pupils have achieved mastery over the content or not.

Organisation Pupils are provided with the occasions for representation, all the pupil write contents in their own language. The teacher comes to the conclusion, whether the pupils can write the content without anybody's help or not. The representation in the subjects, like mathematics, grammar and arithmetic has no importance.

Recitation This is the last step of understanding level of teaching. The pupils present the contents orally in front of the teacher and his mates.

Social System By providing motivation, the teacher controls the behaviour of the pupils. Both intrinsic and extrinsic motivation is used. Thus, the teacher imparts instructions to the pupils and works with full involvement.

Support System It does not remains constant, it keeps on changing. In assimilation, the pupils have to pass the exam to enter into organisation and recitation. At the end of organisation period, written test takes place. Then after recitation, oral test takes place. Both oral and written tests occur during various steps of understanding level of teaching.

Reflective Level of Teaching

This level is also known as **introspective level**. Reflecting on something means giving a careful thought to something, over a period of time. It also means thinking deeply about a particular thing.

Reflective level of teaching is significant due to the following reasons

- It is considered to be the highest level of teaching.
- It is highly thoughtful and useful.
- A student can attain this level, only after going through previous levels.
- Teaching at the reflective level, enables the students to solve the real problems of life.
- At this level, the student is made to face a real problematic situation.The student by understanding the situation and using his critical abilities, succeeds in solving the problem.
- At this level, emphasis is laid on identifying the problem, defining it and finding a solution to it. The student's original thinking and creative abilities develops at this level.
- The role of teacher at this level of teaching is democratic. He does not force knowledge on the students, but develops their talents and capabilities.
- The role of the student is quite active.
- It is problem-centered and the student is busy in an original imagination.

For development of reflective level of teaching, the credit goes to **Hunt** and **Biggie**. Thus, the level is also known as **Biggie** and **Hunt's Teaching model**.

Biggie and Hunt's Teaching Model of Reflective Level of Teaching

M Biggie held that "Reflective level of teaching tends to develop the classroom atmosphere, which is more exciting and active, more critical and penetrating and more open to fresh and open thinking". Furthermore, the type of enquiry pursued by a reflective class tends to be more rigorous and work producing then pursued at an understanding learning level. Thus, this level of teaching develops the thinking ability of students, so that they can solve the real life related problems by reasoning, logic and imagination.

M Biggie and Hunt described the following steps in their model of reflective teaching :

- Focus
- Social system
- Syntax
- Support system

Focus

- To develop problem-solving competency among the pupils.
- To develop critical and constructive thinking among pupils.
- To devlop independent and original thinking power among the pupils.

Syntax

Following the individual and social nature, syntax of reflective level teaching can be defined in following four steps

- The teacher presents a problematic situation before the pupils.
- Pupils formulate hypothesis for testing.
- Pupils collect data to verify the hypothesis.
- Hypothesis are tested. Results are derived on the basis of the test, which are original ideals of the pupils.

Social System

- The classroom environment is open and independent.
- Pupils occupy primary and teacher occupies secondary place.
- Discussion and seminar are used during teaching.
- All the pupils become active and sensitive for solving the problem.

Support System

Objective type test does not use essay type test, for evaluation.

Following things are being evaluated

- Attitude and belief of pupils.
- Involvement in the learning activities.
- Development of critical and creative competencies of the pupils.

Andragogy

It means the understanding of the science and practice of adult learning. The word 'andragogy' comes from the Greek word 'andr' meaning 'man' and 'agogos' meaning leader of. In the Greek, andragogy means 'man-leading'.

Two primary understandings of andragogy are

- The science of understanding (theory) and supporting, (practice) lifelong education of adults.
- In the tradition of **Malcolm Knowles**, it is a specific theoretical and practical approach. It is based on a humanistic conception of self-directed and autonomous learner as well as teachers as facilitator of learning.

Definitions of Andragogy

According to **Cooper and Henschke**, "Andragogy is a theory that guides the scope of both research and practice on how adults learn, how they need to be taught and elements to be considered when adults learn in various situations and contexts".

According to **Malcolm Knowles**, "Andragogy is an art and science of adults learning, thus, it refers to any form of adult's learning".

Characteristics of Andragogy

- Adults have many experiences and are knowledgeable. Their backgrounds provide a rich resource for learning.
- Adults have various values, beliefs and opinions.
- They are responsible for their own learning.
- Adult's self-concept is self-direction.
- They often approach learning as problem- centered, rather than content oriented.

Principles of Andragogy

In 1984, **Knowles** suggested four principles that are applied to adult learning. *They are*

- Adults need to be involved in the planning and evaluation of their instruction.
- Experience (including mistakes) provides the basis for the learning activities.
- Adults are most interested in learning subjects, that have an immediate relevance and impact to their job or personal life.
- Adult learning is problem-centered, rather than content oriented.

Theory of Andragogy

Malcolm S Knowles' Theory of Andragogy is a learning theory that is developed on the specific needs of the adults. In contrast to pedagogy or learning in childhood, Knowles emphasized that adutls are self-directed and expect to take responsibility for decisions. Adult learning programs must accomodate this fundamental aspect. He has discussed characteristics, principles and essential assumptions related to andragogy in his Theory of Andragogy.

Assumptions Underlying Andragogy

It is an attempt to develop a theory, specifically for adults learning. He emphasises on that adults are self-directed and expects to take responsibilities for decision. Adults learning programme must accommodate this fundamental aspect.

It is based on following six assumptions

Self-Concept Adults at development stage, are more secure for themselves than childrens. This allows them to take part in directing their own learning.

Past Learning Experience An adult is a mature being. He/she accumulates a growing reservoir of experience that becomes an increasing resource for learning.

Readiness to Learn Many adults reach a point in which they see the value of education and are ready to be serious about and focused on learning.

Practical Reasons to Learn Adults are looking for practical, problem-centred approaches to learning. Many adults return to continuing education for specific practical reasons, such as entering in new field.

Internal Motivation While many children are driven by external motivation, adults are more internally motivated.

Problem-Centered Focus Adults need to see an immediate application of learning. Therefore, they seek learning opportunities that will enable them to solve problems.

Critiques of Knowles' Theory

The critiques were of the opinion that Knowles' andragogy suffered from a weak or non-existent empirical basis and that consequently, andragogy could not be caused "a theory of adult learning". This particularly applied to Knowles' assumptions about adult learners.

Among others, Jarvis (1984) and Davenport (1987) pointed out these assumptions lacked empirical basis.

Sandlin (2005) claimed that by considering the learning process and the individual to be separated from the social, political, economical and historical context, Knowles ignored the relationship between the individual and society.

Difference Between Pedagogy and Andragogy

Basis	Pedagogy	Andragogy
The learner	• The learner is dependent upon the instructor for all learning. • The teacher/instructor assumes full responsibility for what is taught and how it is learned. • The teacher/instructor evaluates learning.	• The learner is self-directed. • The learner is responsible for his/her own learning. • Self-evaluation is a characteristic of this approach.
Role of the learner's experience	• The learner comes to the activity with little experience that could be tapped as a resource for learning. • The experience of the instructor is most influential.	• The learner brings a greater volume and quality of experience. • Adults are rich resource for one another. • Different experiences assure diversity in groups of adults. • Experience becomes the source of self-identify.
Readiness to learn	• Students are told, what they have to learn in order to advance to the next level of mastery.	• Any change is likely to trigger a readiness to learn. • They need to know, in order to perform more effectively, in some aspect of one's life is important. • Ability to assess gaps between where one is now and where one wants and needs to be.
Orientation to learning	• Learning is a process of acquiring prescribed subject matter. • Content's units are sequenced according to the logic of the subject matter.	• Learners want to perform a task, solve a problem and live in a more satisfying way. • Learning must have relevance to real life tasks. • Learning is organized around life/work situations rather than subject matter's units.
Motivation for learning	• Primarily motivated by externed pressures, competition for grades and the consequences of failure.	• Internal motivators i.e. self-esteem, recognition, better quality of life, self-confidence and self-actualization.

Self-Directed Learning

It is a process in which learner assumes primary responsibilities for planning, implementing and evaluating a learning project. The learner chooses, what to learn, how to learn and also decides when to continue and when to end the learning project.

According to **Malcolm Knowles**, "Self-directed learning describes a process in which individuals take the initiative, with or without the help of others, in diagnosing their learning needs, formulating learning goals, identifying human and material resources for learning, choosing and implementing appropriate learning strategies and evaluating learning outcomes".

Competencies of Self-Directed Learning

- To plan and participate in one's own learning activities.
- To develop the capacity of learning and thinking of learner.
- To develop the sense of independence by enhancing free learning.
- To develop problem-solving approaches.
- To develop time management skills.
- To develop decision-making skills.

Key Assumptions of Self-Directed Learning

Knowles states five key assumptions which underlie self-directed learning

- Self-directed learning assumes that the human being grows in capacity and needs to be self-directing as an essential component in maturing.
- Self-directed learning assumes that the learners' experiences become an increasingly rich resource for learning that should be exploited along with the resources of experts.
- It assumes that individuals become ready to learn what is required to perform their evolving life task or to cope more adequately with their life problems.
- It also assumes that the natural orientation of inclividuals is task or problem-centered.
- Self-directed learning assumes that learners are motivated by internal incentives such as the need for self-esteem.

Characteristics of Self-Directed Learner

According to Winne, the self-directed learners have following characteristics

- Set goals for extending their knowledge and sustaining their motivation.
- Learners can manage their emotions well.
- They can periodically monitor their progress towards the goals.
- Revise their strategies to fine tune their progress towards goal.
- They can evaluate obstacles that may arise and take necessary adaptations.

Dynamic Model of Learner's Autonomy

The Dynamic Model of Learner's Autonomy is a tool designed, in order to support the self-assessment and evaluation of learning competencies and to help both learners and advisors to focus on relevant aspects of learning process. The Dynamic model accounts for cognitive, metacognitive, action oriented and affective components of learner's autonomy and provides descriptors of learner's attitudes, competencies and behaviours. It is dynamic in order to allow learners to focus on their own needs and goals. The three dimensions in the Dynamic model are a predominantly action oriented dimensions (planning, choosing materials and methods, completing tasks, monitoring, evaluating, cooperating, managing my own learning), a predominantly affective and motivational dimension (dealing with my feelings, motivating myself) and a predominantly cognitive and metacognitive dimension (structuring knowledge). In addition, a social dimension (cooperating) is integrated into each component. In learning and teaching, all these aspects are closely interrelated.

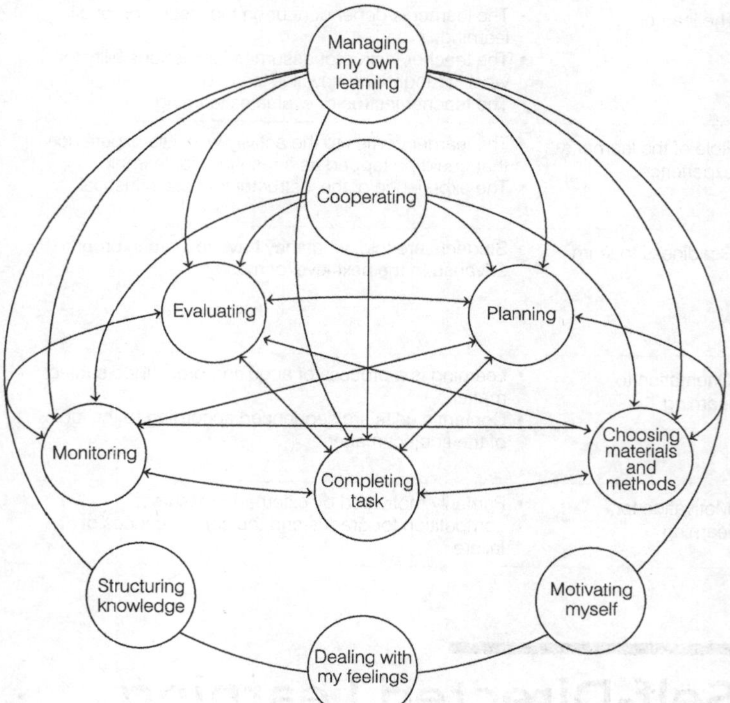

Dynamic Model of Learner's Autonomy

The Dynamic Model of Learner's Autonomy sums up these components in terms of learner's competencies, skills, choices and decision-making processes and accounts for mutual relationship.

There is no hierarchy among these components, except for 'managing my own learning' which summarises all other components and super-ordinates them. This model is structurally and functionally, dynamic. It is structurally dynamic because each component is directly related to all the others. It is functionally dynamic, because learner can decide to enter the model from any component and move freely from one component to other without following a given path, according to their need and purpose.

EXAM BASED QUESTIONS

1 Pedagogy is defined as the .... of teaching.
(a) method (b) practice
(c) both (a) and (b) (d) None of these

2 What is meant by pedagogy of teaching?
(a) How the teacher interact with the parents.
(b) The way teacher delivers the content of curriculum.
(c) The way administration responds to the needs of students.
(d) None of the above

3 Pedagogy influences the growth of
(a) teacher (b) administrater
(c) learner (d) educator

4 Pedagogy is a/an .... of teaching children.
(a) art (b) science
(c) Both (a) and (b) (d) None of these

5 The word 'pedagogy' comes from Greek word
(a) pedagogue (b) pedagog
(c) pedagogos (d) paidagogos

6 Pedagogy is now accepted as ....
(a) applied science
(b) sociology
(c) applied maths
(d) applied social science

7 What are the key principles of Pedagogy?
(a) Pedagogy equips learner for life.
(b) Pedagogy promotes active engagement of learner.
(c) Pedagogy demands consistent policy framework, with support for learning as their primary focus.
(d) All of the above

8 What is the first step of pedagogical analysis?
(a) Divide the unit into sub-unit
(b) Choosing easy subject to work with
(c) Both (a) and (b)
(d) None of the above

9 What teaching strategies are used in teaching sub-unit?
(a) Writing the name of method applied
(b) Illustrating the necessary demonstration and experiments to be performed
(c) Writing of related question from sub-unit
(d) All of the above

10 Critical pedagogy combines education with
(a) Marxism (b) Realism
(c) Critical theory (d) None of these

11 Who first described the Critical theory?
(a) Paulo Freire (b) Henry Giroux
(c) Paulo Giroux (d) Henry Freire

12 Critical pedagogy firmly believes that
(a) the learner need not reason independently.
(b) what children learn, out of the school is irrelevant.
(c) the experience and perception of learners are important
(d) the teacher should always lead the classroom's instructions

13 Which of these is/are the need(s) of critical pedagogy?
(a) To include the excluded
(b) Identifying the source of power and recognition of student's position in relation to power
(c) allowing the students to gain necessary social skills
(d) All of the above

14 Which of the following is not a characteristic of critical pedagogy?
(a) Indigenous knowledge
(b) Justice and equality in education
(c) Role of vacation in education
(d) Promotes emancipation and an intellectual growth

15 In order to uplift the country, we must include .... in education planning.
(a) student (b) urban population
(c) rural population (d) None of these

16 What does critical pedagogies believe?
(a) Education is a political activity.
(b) Education should be pursued by urban people.
(c) Both (a) and (b)
(d) None of the above

17 .... helps in bridging the cultural barrier.
(a) War (b) Lecture (c) Workshop (d) Literacy

18 Memory level of teaching is also a .... level of teaching.
(a) first (b) thoughtless
(c) Both (a) and (b) (d) None of these

19 In memory level of teaching, what students do?
(a) Learn the fact (b) Cram the fact
(c) Experiment (d) Discuss the fact

20 Herbart's model focuses on
(a) training of mental aspects
(b) providing knowledge of facts
(c) retaining the learnt facts
(d) All of the above

21 In Herbart's model, relationship is established between
(a) new and pervious knowledge
(b) inside and outside the environment
(c) student and teacher
(d) All of the above

22 **Function of a teacher does not includes**
(a) presenting the content
(b) controlling the pupil's activities
(c) get angry on pupil and scold them
(d) providing motivation

23 **What kind of test(s) is/are used in Herbat's model?**
(a) Oral (b) Written
(c) Both (a) and (b) (d) None of these

24 **The meaning of 'understanding' can be classified as**
(a) seeing the total use of facts
(b) seeing relationship
(c) a generalised insight
(d) All of the above

25 **In understanding level, which relationship is established?**
(a) Knowledge and facts (b) Principles and facts
(c) Life and death (d) Teaching and education

26 **The focus of Morrison's model is to achieve mastery on**
(a) theory (b) experiment
(c) exercise (d) concept

27 **How does the teacher controls the behaviour of pupils?**
(a) By providing motivation
(b) By giving speech
(c) By giving incentives
(d) None of these

28 **Under support system of Morrison's Model, the pupils have to pass the examination to enter into a/an**
(a) organisation (b) recitation
(c) Both (a) and (b) (d) None of these

29 **Which level is also known as introspective level?**
(a) Understanding level (b) Memory level
(c) Reflective level (d) None of these

30 **What is/are the feature(s) of reflective level of teaching?**
(a) It is highly thoughtful and useful.
(b) Enables student to solve the real life problems.
(c) Teacher does not force knowledge on students.
(d) All of the above

31 **Which of the following aim(s) does not comes under Biggie and Hunt's model?**
(a) To develop problem-solving competencies, among the pupils
(b) To develop critical and constructive thinking among the pupils
(c) To make pupil good, in extra curricular activities
(d) To make the pupil independent and encourage original thinking

32 **Who formulates the hypothesis in Biggie and Hunt's model?**
(a) Teacher (b) Student
(c) Both (a) and (b) (d) None of these

33 **What is the feature of classroom's environment, in social system of Biggie and Hunt's model?**
(a) Open (b) Independent
(c) Both (a) and (b) (d) None of these

34 **What is evaluated in support system of Biggie and Hunt's Model?**
(a) Attitude and belief of people
(b) Involvement in learning activities
(c) Development of critical and creative competencies of pupils
(d) All of the above

35 **What is meant by andragogy?**
(a) Adult learning (b) Student learning
(c) Children learning (d) All of these

36 **What does 'andragogy' means in Greek?**
(a) Adult learning (b) Man leading
(c) Man learning (d) Adult leading

37 **Andragogy is a science of .... education of adult.**
(a) late (b) new
(c) life long (d) higher

38 **What is the status of learner in andragogy?**
(a) Self-directed learning
(b) Autonomous learning
(c) Both (a) and (b)
(d) None of the above

39 **Which one is the principle of adult learning?**
(a) Teacher teaches the adults and plans lesson.
(b) Adults are interested in learning relevant subjects.
(c) Experience creates a problem in learning activities.
(d) Adult learning is content oriented rather than problem-centered.

40 **Which is/are the competency (ies) of self-directed learning?**
(a) To plan and participate in one's own learning activities.
(b) To develop the sense of independence.
(c) To develop problem-solving approaches.
(d) All of the above

41 **According to Knowles, adults are**
(a) self-directed
(b) responsible for their decision
(c) Both (a) and (b)
(d) None of the above

42 **Adults have great reservoir of**
(a) experience (b) laziness
(c) sadness (d) None of these

43 **What is/are the assumption(s), listed by Malcolm Knowles?**
(a) Self-concept (b) Readiness to learn
(c) Internal motivation (d) All of the above

44 **How adults are motivated?**
(a) Internally (b) Externally
(c) Both (a) and (b) (d) None of these

45 Essential components of learner's autonomy does not includes
(a) affective and motivational components
(b) action oriented components
(c) social components
(d) reflective components

46 What is included in cognitive and meta-cognitive components?
(a) Awareness, learner's belief
(b) Psychology
(c) Pedagogy
(d) All of the above

47 What is/are the characteristic(s) of Dynamic model?
(a) Action oriented
(b) Process oriented
(c) Both (a) and (b)
(d) None of these

48 Choose the correct statement(s).
1. Pedagogy is a form of art and science.
2. Pedagogy involves adult education as well.
3. Pedagogy equips learners for life.
4. Pedagogy includes self-learning as well.

Codes
(a) 1, 2 and 4
(b) 1 and 2
(c) 1 and 4
(d) 3 and 4

49 Choose the correct statement(s).
1. Components of Dynamic Model are expressed in verbs.
2. There is a hierarchy, among the components.
3. The model of learner's autonomy is structurally dynamic.
4. In learner's autonomy, learners take control of their learning process.

Codes
(a) 1 and 4
(b) 2 and 4
(c) 3 and 1
(d) 1, 2 and 4

50 Choose the correct statement(s).
1. Self-directed learning is taught by teacher.
2. The teacher makes the lesson plan in self-directed learning.
3. Learner develops a sense of independence in self-directed learning.

Codes
(a) Only 1 (b) Only 2 (c) Only 3 (d) 1 and 3

51 Choose the correct statement(s).
1. In understanding level, the learner learns himself.
2. Understanding level of teaching is of higher quality than one in memory level.
3. Cramming/rote learning is not encouraged in understanding level.
4. Morrison gave a model for understanding level.

Codes
(a) 1, 2 and 3
(b) 2 and 4
(c) 1 and 4
(d) 2, 3 and 4

52 Find the incorrect pairing.
(a) Understanding level – Morrison
(b) Memory level – Herbartian
(c) Reflective level – Biggie and Hunt
(d) Pedagogy – Malcolm Knowles

Directions (From Q.Nos. 53-60) *Given below are two statements, one labelled as Assertion (A) and the other labelled as Reason (R). Following are the codes given below. Choose the correct code.*

Codes
(a) Both A and R are true
(b) Both A and R are false
(c) A is true, but R is false
(d) A is false, but R is true

53 **Assertion** (A) Andragogy means the understanding of science and practice of adults learning.
Reason (B) In Greek, andragogy means 'man leading'.

54 **Assertion** (A) The learner chooses what to learn and how to learn in self-directed learning.
Reason (R) Lesson plan is decided by teacher in self directed-learning.

55 **Assertion** (A) In critical pedagogy, students aim to criticise a political leader.
Reason (B) Critical pedagogy was first discovered by Paulo Freire.

56 **Assertion** (A) Malcolm Knowles gave theory for pedagogy.
Reason (R) Malcolm gave seven assumptions under his theory.

57 **Assertion** (A) Reflective level is the thoughtful level of teaching.
Reason (R) Model for reflective level of teaching was given by Biggie and Hunt.

58 **Assertion** (A) Pedagogy is a method and a practice of teaching.
Reason (R) Pedagogy considers the interaction, that takes place during learning.

59 **Assertion** (A) Characteristic of critical pedagogy includes awareness of political nature of education.
Reason (R) Critical Pedagogy is to build bridges across the diverse cultural segment.

60 **Assertion** (A) Memory level of learning is a thoughtful way of learning.
Reason (R) In Herbartian model, pupils acquire new knowledge by utilising their previous knowledge.

Directions (From Q.Nos. 61-63) ***Read the given passage and answer the following questions.***

Pedagogy is dealing with ideation and techniques of teaching. The main concern of pedagogy lies in setting up an environment, where the needs and dreams of a student are being understood by the teacher. Johann Herbert was the first to establish the relationship between pedagogy and its effect on society. Education was the basic step for transformation and pedagogy were learning the techniques to imply it. He emphasized how five key factors of this concept *i.e.* preparation, presentation, association, generalization and application can turn a normal citizen into the most productive asset for economy and society. Over a time, a new term was being introduced known as critical pedagogy.

61 Who was the first to establish the relationship between pedagogy and its effect on society?
(a) John Dewey
(b) Johann Herbert
(c) Malcolm Knowles
(d) None of the above

62 What was the basic step, for transformation in learning?
(a) Education
(b) Techniques
(c) Pedagogy
(d) All of the above

63 Which new term was introduced over a time?
(a) Presentation
(b) Critical pedagogy
(c) Association
(d) Application

64 Match the following.

List I	List II
A. Memory Level model	1. Macolm Knowles
B. Understanding Level model	2. Herbart
C. Reflective Level model	3. Morrison
D. Theory of Andragogy	4. M.Biggie and Hunt

Codes

	A	B	C	D		A	B	C	D
(a)	1	2	3	4	(b)	2	3	4	1
(c)	4	3	2	1	(d)	3	4	1	2

65 Match the following.

List I	List II
A. Introspective level	1. Understanding level
B. Lowest level	2. Reflective level
C. Generalised Insight level	3. Memory level
D. Structurally and functionally dynamic	4. Dynamic model

Codes

	A	B	C	D		A	B	C	D
(a)	3	4	2	1	(b)	1	2	3	4
(c)	2	3	1	4	(d)	4	3	2	1

66 Arrange the steps of Morrison's model in correct order.
1. Recitation
2. Assimilation
3. Presentation
4. Organisation
5. Exploration

Select the correct code.
(a) 5, 3, 2, 4, 1
(b) 2, 3, 4, 5, 1
(c) 1, 2, 3, 5, 4
(d) 4, 5, 1, 2, 3

ANSWERS

1	(c)	2	(b)	3	(c)	4	(c)	5	(d)	6	(a)	7	(d)	8	(a)	9	(d)	10	(c)
11	(a)	12	(c)	13	(d)	14	(c)	15	(c)	16	(a)	17	(d)	18	(c)	19	(b)	20	(d)
21	(a)	22	(c)	23	(c)	24	(d)	25	(b)	26	(d)	27	(a)	28	(c)	29	(c)	30	(d)
31	(c)	32	(b)	33	(c)	34	(d)	35	(a)	36	(b)	37	(c)	38	(c)	39	(b)	40	(d)
41	(c)	42	(a)	43	(d)	44	(a)	45	(d)	46	(a)	47	(c)	48	(b)	49	(a)	50	(c)
51	(d)	52	(d)	53	(a)	54	(c)	55	(d)	56	(b)	57	(a)	58	(a)	59	(c)	60	(d)
61	(b)	62	(a)	63	(b)	64	(b)	65	(c)	66	(a)								

CHAPTER

27

Concept of Assessment

Assessment is the systematic process of documenting and using empirical data on the knowledge, skill, attitude and belief to refine programs and improve student's learning. Assessment can focus on the individual learner, the learning community, a course, an academic program, the institution or the educational system as a whole.

Assessment

The word 'assessment' has been widely used by educator to evaluate, measure and document the academic readiness, learning progress and skill acquisition of students, throughout their learning in life. It is the process of gathering information, systematically as a part of an evaluation.

It is carried out to see what children and young people know, understand and are able to do It is very important for tracking progress, planning next steps, reporting and involving parents , children and young people in learning.

It is a process by which information is obtained, relative to some known objective or goal. It is a broad term that includes testing. Tests are assessments that are made deliberately, so that they can be administered. In other words, all tests are assessments, but all assessments are not tests. Teachers assess progress at the end of a school year through testing.

Definitions of Assessment

According to **Allen** (2004), "It involves the use of empirical data on student learning, to refine programs and to improve student's learning".

According to **Huba and Freed** (2000), "It is the process of gathering and discussing information from multiple and diverse sources, in order to develop a deep understanding of what students know, understand and can do with their knowledge as a result of their educational experiences, the process culminates when assessment's results are used to improve subsequent learning".

According to **Erwin** (1991), "It is the systematic basis for making inferences about the learning and development of students. It is the process of defining, selecting, designing, collecting, analysing, interpreting and using information to increase student's learning and development".

In this Chapter

- *Assessment*
- *Relationship Between Objective and Outcome*
- *Three Domains of Learning*

According to **Palomba and Banta** (1999), ''Assessment is the systematic collection, review and use of information about educational programs, undertaken for the purpose of improving student's learning and development".

Nature of Assessment

It is embedded in the learning process. It is tightly inter-connected with curriculum and mode of instruction. As teachers and students work towards the achievement of curriculum outcomes, assessment plays a crucial role in informing instruction, guiding the students to next steps and checking progress and achievement.

Therefore, the nature of assessment is enumerated in following points

- It involves students and teachers in continuous monitoring of student's learning.
- It has a great impact on the self- esteem of pupils, which will have critical influence on learning.
- It helps in collection of frequent feedback on student's learning and how they respond to particular teaching approaches.
- It provides an opportunity for close observation of students in the process of learning.
- It gives students a measure of their progress as learners.

Functions of Assessment

- Monitoring the progress of students.
- Helps in decision-making skills.
- Screening of the students.
- Placement of students in remedial courses.
- Instructional planning helps to create adaptive learning strategies.
- Evaluation of instructional programme.
- Feedback helps in developing lifelong learning skills.
- Student motivation is necessary for quality education.

Importance of Assessment

Assessment is a common tool used in education. When a teacher creates instruction (lesson material) for the students, it becomes important to evaluate those instructions. The teacher set goals to achieve at the end of each chapter or/and at the end of instruction. Assessment determines whether or not the goals of education are being met.

Continuous questions that come to a teacher's mind, when taking assessment are "Are we teaching, what we are supposed to be teaching"?, "Are we reaching the goals we set for the instruction"?, "Is there a way to improve your instructions and promote better learning"? These questions don't have to be asked at a certain stage of developing instruction, but rather these questions are to be asked throughout the whole instruction and even after its implementation.

Therefore, assessment affects decisions on different domains, grades, advancement, instructional needs, placement and curriculum.

Perspectives of Assessment

Perspectives of assessment are discussed below

Assessment for Learning

It is the process of seeking and interpreting evidences for learners and for their teachers, to decide that where the learners are in their learning, where they need to go and how best to get there.

It's strategies are :

Strategic Use of Questioning Questioning is used not only as a pedagogical tool, but also as a deliberate way for the teacher to find out what students know, understand and are able to do.

Effective Teacher's Feedback It focuses on established success criteria and tells the students, what they have achieved and where they need to improve. Importantly, the feedback provides specific suggestions about how that improvement might be achieved.

Peer's Feedback It occurs when a student uses established success criteria to tell another student what they have achieved and where improvement is necessary. Again, the feedback provides specific suggestions in achieving improvement.

Student's Self-Assessment It encourages students to take responsibility for their own learning. It incorporates self-monitoring, self-assessment and self-evaluation.

Assessment of Learning

It refers to strategies, designed to confirm what students know, demonstrates and whether or not, they have met curriculum outcomes or the goals of their individualised programs, or to certify proficiency and makes decisions about student's future programs or placements.

It is designed to provide evidence of achievement to parents, other educators, the students themselves and sometimes to outside groups (*e.g.* employers, other educational institutions). Assessment of learning is the assessment that becomes public and results in statements or symbols about how well students are learning. It often contributes pivotal decisions that will affect student's future. It is important to know that the underlying logics and measurements of assessment of learning must be credible and defensible. As the consequences of assessment of learning are often far reaching and seriously affects students, teachers have the responsibility of reporting student's learning accurately and fairly, based on evidence obtained from a variety of contexts and applications.

Effective assessment of learning requires that teachers provide

- a rationale for undertaking a particular assessment of learning at a particular point of time.
- clear descriptions of the intended learning.
- processes that makes it possible for students to demonstrate their competencies and skills.
- a range of alternative mechanisms for assessing the same outcomes.
- public and defensible reference points for making judgements.

Assessment as Learning

Assessment as learning occurs when students are their own assessors. Students monitor their own learning, ask questions and use a range of strategies to decide what they know and can do and how to use assessment information for new learning.

Assessment as learning :

- encourages students to take responsibility for their own learning.
- requires students to ask questions about their learning.
- involves teachers and students, creating learning goals to encourage growth and development.
- provides ways for students to use formal and informal feedback and self-assessment to help them understand the next steps in learning.
- encourages peer assessment, self-assessment and reflection.

Types of Assessment

It is a process of gathering information. More specifically, assessment is the way, instructors gather data about their teaching and their student's learning. As a continuous process, assessment establishes measurable and clear student's learning outcomes for learning, provisioning a sufficient amount of learning oppurtunities to achieve these outcomes. Teacher uses the collected information to inform improvement in student's learning.

*There are **four** different types of assessments and they are*

- Placement
- Formative
- Summative
- Diagnostic

Placement Assessment

It is used to place students, according to their prior achievements or personal characteristics, at the most appropriate point in an instructional sequence, in a unique instructional strategy, or with a suitable teacher, conducted through placement testing i.e. the tests that colleges and universities use to assess college's readiness and place students into their initial classes. Placement evaluation is also referred to as pre-assessment is conducted prior to instruction. This is done to establish a base line from which individual student's growth can be measured. This type of particular assessment is used to know the student's skills level about the subject. It helps the teacher to explain the material more efficiently. These assessment are not graded.

Formative Assessment

It is generally carried out, throughout a course or project. It provides feedback and information during the course or project, while the learning is occurring. It measures student's progress as well as teachers own progress as an instructor. For example, when implementing a new activity in class, teacher can observe students and determine if the activity should be used again or not.

A primary focus of **formative assessment** is to identify areas that may need improvement. These assessments are not graded and act as a gauge to student's learning progress and determines teacher's effectiveness.

Types of Formative Assessment

- Observation during in-class activities and non-verbal feedback during lecture.
- Homework exercises as review for exams and class discussion.
- Reflection journals that are reviewed periodically, during the semesters.
- Question and answer sessions, both formal planned and informal spontaneous.
- Conferences between the instructor and student at various points in the semester.
- In-class activities, where students informally present their results.

Summative Assessment

Generally, it is carried out at the end of course or project. It provides information and feedback that sums up the teaching and learning process. They are evaluative. They are made to summarise what students have learnt and to determine, whether they understand the subject matter well or not.

This type of assessment is typically graded and can take form of tests, exams or projects. Typically, no more formal learning takes place at this stage.

Types of Summative Assessment

- Examination
- Term paper
- Projects
- Portfolio
- Performances
- Student's evaluation of the course
- Instructor's self-evaluation

Diagnostic Assessment

It helps the teacher to identify student's present knowledge of a subject, their skill sets and capabilities, to clarify misconception before the teaching takes place. Knowledge of student's strength and weakness can help the teacher to plan better on what to teach and how to teach.

Types of Diagnostic Assessments

- Pre-test (on content and abilities)
- Self-assessment (identifying skills and competencies)
- Discussion board responses (on content's specific prompts)
- Interviews (brief, private, 10 minutes interview of each student)

Relationship Between Objective and Outcome

These terms are often used interchangeably and they are all related to the teaching and learning that is expected to take place in the classroom. However, the difference between objectives and outcomes lies in the emphasis on who will be performing the activities. Learning objectives generally describe what an instructor or program aims to do whereas, a learning outcome describes in observable and measurable terms what a student is able to do as a result of completing a course.

Objective

- It describes the goals and intentions of the professor who teaches the subject of particular course.
- It often termed as the input in the course, state the purpose and goals of the course.
- It focuses on content and skills, important within the classroom or program.
- It describes what the staff and faculty will do.
- It can often be numerous, specific, and detailed. Assessing and reporting on each objective, for each student may be impossible.

Outcome

- It catalogues the overarching of **products** of the course and are the evidence that the goals or objectives were achieved.
- They are statements that describes or lists measurable and essential mastered content knowledge, reflecting skills, competencies and knowledge that students have achieved and can demonstrate upon successfully, after completing a course.
- They express higher level thinking skills that integrate course content and activities and can be observed as a behaviour, skill or discrete usable knowledge upon completing the course.
- They are exactly what assessments are intended to show specifically, what the students will be able to do upon completing the course.
- An assessable outcome can be displayed or observed and evaluated against criteria. Outcomes are clear and measurable criteria for guiding the teaching, learning, and assessment process in the course.

Three Domains of Learning

Bloom's Taxonomy was created by **Benjamin Bloom** in 1956, published as kind of classification of learning outcomes and objectives that have been used for everything from framing digital tasks and evaluating applications to write questions and assessments.

Bloom's Taxonomy is hierarchical ordering of cognitive skills that help teachers teach and students learn. It is a set of three hierarchical models used to classify educational learning objectives into levels of complexity and specificity. The three lists cover the learning objectives in cognitive, affective and psychomotor domains. All teachers should know about them and use them to construct lessons.

Each domain has a taxonomy associated with it. **Taxonomy** is simply a word for **classification**.

Three domains are :

- Cognitive (Thinking)
- Affective (Feeling)
- Psychomotor (Physical)

Cognitive Domain

Of the three learning domains, the cognitive domain is assessed more commonly.

Cognitive domain is divided into six categories by ***Anderson*** *and* ***Krathwohl*** *as*

Remembering It is recognising or recalling knowledge from the memory. It is implemented when memory is used to produce or retrieve definition, facts or lists or to recite previously learned information.

Understanding Constructing meaning from different types of functions, be they written or graphic messages or activities like interpreting, exemplifying, classifying, summarising, inferring, comparing or explaining.

Applying Carrying out or using a procedure through executing or implementing. Applying relates to or refers to situations where learned material is used through products like models, presentations, interviews or simulations.

Analysing Breaking materials or concepts into parts, determining how the parts relate to one another or how they inter-relate or how the parts relate to an overall structure or purpose. Mental actions included in this function are differentiating, organising and attributing as well as being able to distinguish between the components or parts. When one is analysing, he/she can illustrate this mental function by creating spreadsheets, surveys, charts, diagrams or graphic representations.

Evaluating Making judgements based on criteria and standards through checking and critiquing. Critiques, recommendations and reports are some of the products that can be created to demonstrate the processes of evaluation. In the newer taxonomy, evaluating comes before creating as it is often a necessary part of the pre-cursory behaviour before one creates something.

Creating Putting elements together to form a coherent or functional whole, reorganising elements into a new pattern or structure through generating, planning or producing. It requires users to put parts together in a new way or synthesise parts into something new and different, thus, creating a new form or product. This process is the most difficult mental function in the new taxonomy.

Assessing Cognitive Learning

The commonly used methodology in assessment that teachers used to measure learning in the cognitive domain are **objective tests** and **essay tests.**

Objective Test

An objective type test is one which is free from any subjective bias either from the tester or the marker. It refers to any written test that requires the examinee to select the correct answer from among one or more of several alternatives or supply a word or two and that demands an objective judgement when it is scored.

Types of Objective Tests

(i) **Selection Type** It generally consists of question, an incomplete statement or simply a direction followed by a number of response options from which examinees must select one or more alternatives. *For e.g.*
- Multiple Choice Item
- Alternate Response Item
- Matching Item
- Computer Adaptive Testing

(ii) **Short Answer Type** It generally consists of a question, an incomplete statement or a direction to which the examinee must forward a response. Standard types of short answer includes the direct question, completion, identification and directed exercise.

Essay Tests

An essay question is a topic or brief statement to which an examinee must construct an extended response. An essay question can be used to measure a person's ability to make comparisons, apply principle to new situations, organise information, communicate ideas, be creative, conduct a critical study make judgement, draw interference, integrate knowledge and applications, summarise information and demonstrate indepth knowledge. The key to essay questions is used to measure any or all of these abilities is the fact that examinees must produce their own extended responses, in their own words.

Affective Domain

Krathwohl's affective domain taxonomy is perhaps the best known of any of the affective taxonomies. The affective taxonomy includes the manner in which we deal with things, emotionally such as feelings, values, appreciation, enthusiasm, motivation and attitude.

Following are the taxonomy in the affective domain

Receiving It describes the stage of being aware of or sensitive to the existence of certain ideas, material or phenomena and being willing to tolerate them. For *e.g.* to differentiate, to accept, to listen (for), to respond, etc.

Responding It describes the second stage of the taxonomy and refers to a commitment in some small measures to the ideas, materials or phenomena involved by actively responding to them. For *e.g.* to comply with, to follow, to commend, to volunteer, to spend leisure time in, to acclaim, etc.

Valuing It means being willing to be perceived by others as valuing certain ideas, materials or phenomena. For *e.g.* to increase measured proficiency into relinquish, to subsidise, to support, to debate, etc.

Organisation It is the fourth stage of Krathwohl's taxonomy and involves, relating the new values to those one who already holds it and bringing it into a harmonious and internally consistent philosophy. For *e.g.* to discuss, to theorise, to formulate, to balance, to examine, etc.

Characterisation By value or value set means acting consistently in accordance with the values, an individual has internalised. For *e.g.* to revise, to require, being rated high in the value, to avoid, resisting, managing, to resolve, etc.

Affective Assessment Tools

Various assessment tools that can be used to measure affective learning are discussed below

Self-Report Most commonly used measurement tool in the affective domain. It essentially requires an individual to provide an account of his attitude or feelings toward a concept or an idea or people. It is also known as **written reflection.**

Rating Scale It refers to a set of categories designed to elicit information about a quantitative attribute.

Semantic Differential Scale It tries to assess an individual's reaction to specific words, ideas or concepts in terms of ratings, on bi-polar scales, defined with contrasting adjectives at each end.

Example : Good 2 1 0 1 2 Bad

(2- extreme; 0- neutral)

Thurstone Scale Louise Thurstone is considered to be the father of attitude measurement. He addressed the issue on, how favourable an individual is with regards to given issue. He developed an attitude, continuum to determine the position of favourability on the issue.

Likert Scale In 1932, **Rensis Likert** developed the method of summated ratings (or Likert scale) which is widely used. This requires an individual to tick on a box, to report whether they 'strongly agree', 'agree', 'undecided', 'disagree' or strongly disagree in response to a large number of items, concerning attitude, objects or stimulus.

Checklist The most common and perhaps the easiest instrument in the affective domain is to construct the check list.

Psychomotor Domain

The psychomotor domain includes physical movement, coordination and use of motor skill areas. It has been revised over the years by Dave (1970), Harrow (1972) and Simpson (1972).

Dave's Psychomotor Domain It is the simplest domain and easiest to apply. Dave's 5 levels of motor skills represent different degrees of competence in performing a skill.

The five levels are :

Imitate The ability to observe and to pattern your behaviour after someone else. At this level, you will simply copy someone else or replicates someone's actions following observations.

Manipulate The ability to perform certain actions by memory or following instructions. At this level, you can perform a task from written or verbal instructions.

Precision The ability to perform certain actions with some level of expertise and without help or intervention from others. At this level, you are able to perform a skill with a high degree of precision and accuracy and with few errors.

Articulation The ability to adapt and integrate multiple actions to develop methods to meet varying and novel requirements. At this level, your skills are so well developed that you can modify movement to fit special requirements or to meet a problematic situation.

Naturalisation It is the ability to perform actions in an automatic, intuitive or unconscious way. At this level, your performance is automatic with little physical or mental exertion. Your performance will become second nature or natural, without any need to think much about it.

Tools to Assess Psychomotor Domain

Observational Tools Observation provides insights so that planning can be done to meet individual needs and evaluates the learning that takes place. With the help of observational tools, teachers can focus on student's performance during a single activity or during routine classroom activities.

Types of observation tools are

1. **Checklist** It is basically a method of recording, whether a characteristic is present or absent, or whether an action have or have not taken place. It provides a simple yes/no judgement.

Advantages

- It is adapted to most of the subject matter's areas.
- It is useful in evaluating those learning.
- It is useful in evaluating those learning activities that involves a procedure.
- Process record observations.
- It objectively evaluates traits and characteristics.

Disadvantages

- It does not indicate quality of performance.
- It is a close ended method.
- It does not give a context for the information.
- It may miss important information not included in the checklist.

2. **Rating Scale** Rating scale is a standardised method of recording and interpretation of behaviour. With this technique, students/ individuals can be rated on a scale from low to high, with respect to particular trait.

Advantages

- Technically, it is a standard device for recording qualitative and quantitative judgements about observed performance.
- It specified outcomes and objectives.
- It evaluates personal social development.
- It helps teachers to rate their students periodically, on various characteristics, like honesty, cooperativeness, consideration of others and other personality traits.
- A student can use it to rate himself.
- It can be used with a large number of students.

Disadvantages

- There is a lack of uniformity, with which terms are interpreted by evaluation.
- Ratings are subjective and raters may give biased responses.
- This method exmine only specific behavioural traits and may overlook important behaviours.

3. **Anecdotal Records** They are factual description of the meaningful incidents and events that the teacher has observed in the pupils lives. Each incident should be written down shortly, after incident happens. The descriptions may be recorded on separate card or as running accounts, one for each pupil on separate pages in a notebook.

Advantages

- It records incidents of spontaneous behaviour on natural settings.
- It directs the teacher's attention to a single student.
- It provides cumulative records of growth and development.
- It can be used as a supplement to quantitative data.
- The new members may use these records and can acquaint themselves with the students.

Disadvantages

- They are time consuming.
- When incidents are noted and recorded, out of context, they may lose their meaning.
- The teacher should have practice and training in making observational and writing anecdotal records.
- It is less reliable than other observational tools.

4. **Critical Incident Technique** Critical incident is a method of assessing the student's analytical and problem-solving competencies. In this, student's performance can be recorded and performance can be evaluated, according to the stated criteria. Use of the critical incident technique as a data gathering mechanism, could be similar to that of the anecdotal record.

Advantages

- Flexible method that can be used to improve when there are multiple tasks.
- It identifies even rare events that might be missed by other methods which only focus on common and everyday events.
- It is a technique which provides rich information.
- It can be applied using questionnaires or interviews.
- This method is easy to understand.

Disadvantages

- It is a time consuming method.
- Through critical incident analysis no hard qualified data is produced.
- The techniques aim is to produce dense material, but to make most out of this rich material a concise analysis structure is highly needed.

EXAM BASED QUESTIONS

1 The word ___ has been used by educator to evaluate, measure and document the academic progress.
(a) assessment
(b) evaluation
(c) documentation
(d) measurement

2 Assessment is very important for
(a) tracking progress
(b) planning, next step of education
(c) involving parents in learning
(d) All of the above

3 Assessment is a broad term that includes
(a) acting (b) testing
(c) playing (d) None of these

4 Who said that "assessment involves the use of empirical data on student's learning, to refine programs and to improve student's learning"?
(a) Allen
(b) Huba and Freed
(c) Palomba and Banta
(d) Erwin

5 Assessment plays a crucial role in
(a) informing instruction
(b) guiding the student's successive steps
(c) checking progress
(d) All of the above

6 Which is not included in nature of assessment?
(a) Monitoring student's learning
(b) Profound impact on self-esteem of pupils
(c) Outdoor activities are monitored
(d) Measures student's progress as a learner

7 Function of assessment includes
(a) screening of the student
(b) evaluation of instructional programme
(c) Both (a) and (b)
(d) None of the above

8 Assessment for learning is the process of .... for used by teachers and learners.
(a) seeking and interpreting evidences
(b) checking out teacher's pedagogical skills.
(c) Both (a) and (b)
(d) None of the above

9 Assessment for learning, strategies are
(a) strategic use of questioning
(b) peer's feedback
(c) student's self-assessment
(d) All of the above

10 Assessment of learning is
(a) self-oriented (b) public
(c) exciting (d) of no use

11 For an effective assessment of learning, the teacher doesn't needs to provide
(a) clear description of the intended learning.
(b) range of alternative mechanism for assessing the same outcome.
(c) processes that make it possible for students, to demonstrate their competencies and skills.
(d) taking notes on how the administration is performing.

12 On what basis, students are placed in placement assessment?
(a) Prior achievements
(b) Personal characteristics
(c) Both (a) and (b)
(d) None of these

13 What colleges and universities use, to assess college's readiness?
(a) Placement assessment
(b) Placement testing
(c) College's placement
(d) All of these

14 When is formative assessment carried out ?
(a) Throughout the year (b) End of the year
(c) Mid of the year (d) Twice a semester

15 What is the primary focus of formative assessment?
(a) To identify areas that need improvement
(b) To strengthen teacher and student's bond
(c) To check administrative staff
(d) None of the above

16 What are the types of formative assessment?
(a) Observation of in-class activities
(b) Homework exercises
(c) Conferences between instructor and student
(d) All of the above

17 When is summative assessment carried out?
(a) Mid of the year (b) End of the year
(c) Throughout the year (d) Thrice a semester

18 Summative assessment can take from of
(a) tests and exam (b) project
(c) Both (a) and (b) (d) None of these

19 Which of the following is a type of summative assessment?
(a) Portfolio (b) Term paper
(c) Performances (d) All of these

20 What does diagnostic assessment wants to know?
(a) Student's strength and weakness
(b) Health of student
(c) Student's hobbies
(d) None of the above

21 Which is not a type of diagnostic assessment?
(a) Pre-test
(b) Discussion
(c) Evaluation of course, learnt
(d) Interviews

22 What is meant by outcome?
(a) Expectation kept by the student
(b) Expectation kept by the teacher
(c) Expection kept by the staff member
(d) All of the above

23 What does objective do?
(a) States the purpose (b) Gives the goals
(c) Both (a) and (b) (d) None of these

24 Learning outcome describes measurable mastered ....
(a) content knowledge (b) pedagogical knowledge
(c) psychological knowledge (d) All of these

25 How many domains of learning are there?
(a) Two (b) Three
(c) Five (d) Four

26 What do you mean by cognitive domain?
(a) Feeling (b) Thinking
(c) Physical (d) None of these

27 Who divided the cognitive domain?
(a) Krathwohl (b) Anderson
(c) Both (a) and (b) (d) None of these

28 Which is not the category of cognitive domain?
(a) Remembering (b) Applying
(c) Analysing (d) Participating

29 How is the cognitive learning assessed?
(a) Through objective questions
(b) Through essay tests
(c) Both (a) and (b)
(d) None of the above

30 What are the different types of questions in selective type objective test?
(a) Multiple Choice Questions
(b) Matching Items
(c) Alternate Response Items
(d) All of the above

31 A short answer item consists of ....
(a) a question
(b) an incomplete statement
(c) Both (a) and (b)
(d) None of these

32 Standard type of short answer item includes
(a) direct questions (b) completion
(c) identification (d) All of these

33 What kind of answers are expected in essay test?
(a) MCQ (b) One liner
(c) Extended answer (d) None of these

34 What are the applications of essay questions?
(a) Check person's ability to make comparison
(b) Apply principles to new situations
(c) Communication of ideas
(d) All of the above

35 Affective taxonomy includes the manner, in which we deal with things ....
(a) emotionally (b) physically
(c) psychologically (d) liberally

36 What are the various divisions of affective domain?
(a) Receiving (b) Valuing
(c) Characterisation (d) All of these

37 .... requires individual to provide an account of his feelings.
(a) Life study (b) Self-reporting
(c) Both (a) and (b) (d) None of these

38 Bi-polar scale is used in
(a) semantic differential scale
(b) rating scale
(c) Thurstone scale
(d) Likert scale

39 Who is the father of attitude measurement?
(a) Rensis Likert (b) Rensis Thurstone
(c) Louise Thurstone (d) Louise Likert

40 The term 'summated rating' is used in
(a) Thurstone scale
(b) Likert scale
(c) Rating scale
(d) Semantic differential scale

41 What is the most common tool of assessment of affective learning?
(a) Checklist (b) Rating scale
(c) Self-reporting (d) Likert scale

42 Psychomotor domain includes
(a) physical functions
(b) reflexive actions
(c) interpretive movements
(d) All of the above

43 How many levels of motor skill did Dave gave?
(a) Three (b) Five
(c) Six (d) Seven

44 Which is not included in the Dave's psychomotor skills?
(a) Imitate (b) Manipulate
(c) Organisation (d) Precision

45 Which of the following are types of observational tool(s) to assess psychomotor domain?
(a) Checklist (b) Rating scale
(c) Anecdotal record (d) All of these

46 Which is not an advantage of checklist?
(a) Checklist is adapted to most subject matter's areas.
(b) Checklist is useful in evaluating those learning.
(c) Checklist does not indicates quality of performance.
(d) Process, record observation.

47 Which is/are the type(s) of rating scale ?
(a) Numerical Rating Scale
(b) Graphic Rating Scale
(c) Both (a) and (b)
(d) None of the above

48 Rating scale is a standard device for
(a) recording
(b) qualitative judgement
(c) quantitative judgement
(d) All of these

49 What are anecdotal report?
(a) Factual description from pupil's life
(b) Self-reporting by learner
(c) Reflecting of oneself by teacher
(d) None of the above

50 Critical incident is a method of assessing the student's ....
(a) analytical capabilities
(b) problem-solving competencies
(c) Both (a) and (b)
(d) None of the above

51 Choose the correct statement.
1. Rating scale uses bi-polar scale.
2. Rating scale measures specified outcomes and objectives.
3. Rating scale records spontaneous behaviour.
4. Rating scale can be used by student on himself.

Codes
(a) 1 and 2 (b) 2 and 4
(c) 1 and 4 (d) Only 4

52 Choose the correct statement.
1. Placement assessment occurs after the student has completed the course.
2. Formative assessment is carried out throughout the course.
3. Summative assessment occurs at the end of course.
4. Diagnostic Assessment helps the teacher, to identify student's current knowledge and skill.

Codes
(a) 1 and 2 (b) 1 and 3
(c) 2, 3 and 4 (d) 1, 3 and 4

53 Choose the correct statement.
1. Classroom assessment involves students and teachers in continuous monitoring of student's learning.
2. Assessment includes only tests.
3. Assessment gives students a measure of their progress as learners.
4. Assessment is equal to evaluation.

Codes
(a) 1 and 2 (b) 2 and 4
(c) 3 and 4 (d) 1 and 3

54 In cognitive domain
1. remembering is when memory is used to produce definitions, facts or lists.
2. applying is carrying out a procedure, through executing or implementing.
3. understanding is making the staff understand, the value of learning.

Codes
(a) 1 and 2 (b) 2 and 3
(c) 1, 2 and 3 (d) 1 and 3

55 Match the following.

List I	List II
A. Allen	1. Assessment is a systematic base for making inference, about learning and development of student.
B. Huba and Freed	2. Assessment is the systematic collection, review and use of information about education programs, undertaken for the purpose of student's learning and development.
C. Erwin	3. Assessment involves the use of empirical data on student's learning to refine programs.
D. Palomba and Banta	4. Assessment is a process of gathering and discussing information from multiple and diverse sources, in order to develop understanding of what student knows.

Codes

	A	B	C	D
(a)	1	2	3	4
(b)	4	3	2	1
(c)	1	3	4	2
(d)	3	4	1	2

Direction (From Q.No. 56-60) *Given below are two statements, one labelled as Assertion (A) and the other labelled as Reason (R). Following are the codes given below, choose the correct code.*

Codes
(a) Both A and R are true and R is the correct explanation of A
(b) Both A and R are true, but R is not the correct explanation of A
(c) Both A and R are false
(d) A is false, but R is true

56 **Assertion** (A) Assessment helps in decision-making skill.
Reason (R) Assessment is done in once a year.

57 **Assertion** (A) Student's self-assessment encourages student to take responsiblity for their own learning.
Reason (R) Questioning is used not only as a pedagogical tool, but also as a deliberate way for the teacher, to find out what student knows and understands.

58 Assertion (A) Formative assessment measures teacher's progress.

Reasoning (R) When implementing a new activity in class, teacher can observes students and determines, if the activity is successful or not.

59 Assertion (A) Summative assessments are not graded.

Reason (R) Summative assessments are not evaluative.

60 Assertion (A) An assessment's outcome can be displayed or observed and can be evaluated against criteria.

Reason (R) Outcomes express higher level thinking skill that integrates course of content and activities.

Directions (From Q.Nos. 61-63) *Read the following passage carefully and answer the following questions.*

The assessments best suited to guide improvements in student's learning are quizzes, tests, writing assignments and other assessments that teacher administers on a regular basis in their classrooms. Teachers trust the results from these assessments because of their direct relation to classroom instructional goals. Results are immediate and easy to analyze at the individual student level. To use classroom assessments to make improvements, however, teachers must change both their view of assessments and their interpretation of results. Specifically, they need to see their assessments as an integral part of the instruction process and as crucial for helping students learn. Teachers must follow their assessments with instructional alternatives that present those concepts in new ways and engage students in different and more appropriate learning experiences.

61 What are the types of assessments helpful in student's learning?

(a) Quiz (b) Test
(c) Assignment (d) All of these

62 Why teachers trust the results from the assessments?

(a) Due to direct relation with classroom instructional goals
(b) To analyze individual student level
(c) As an integral process
(d) None of the above

63 Teachers must follow their assessments with ..... objectives.

(a) instructional (b) learning
(c) teaching (d) All of these

ANSWERS

1 (a)	2 (d)	3 (b)	4 (a)	5 (d)	6 (c)	7 (c)	8 (a)	9 (d)	10 (b)
11 (d)	12 (c)	13 (b)	14 (a)	15 (a)	16 (d)	17 (b)	18 (c)	19 (d)	20 (a)
21 (c)	22 (b)	23 (c)	24 (a)	25 (b)	26 (b)	27 (c)	28 (d)	29 (c)	30 (d)
31 (c)	32 (d)	33 (c)	34 (d)	35 (a)	36 (d)	37 (b)	38 (a)	39 (c)	40 (b)
41 (a)	42 (d)	43 (b)	44 (c)	45 (d)	46 (c)	47 (c)	48 (d)	49 (a)	50 (c)
51 (b)	52 (c)	53 (d)	54 (a)	55 (d)	56 (c)	57 (a)	58 (d)	59 (b)	60 (a)
61 (d)	62 (a)	63 (a)							

CHAPTER 28

Assessment in Pedagogy of Education

Pedagogy constitutes a broad range of elements in curriculum, assessment and instruction that teachers use to promote student´s learning. So in pedagogy, instruction is one component of an interrelated set of curricula and assessment strategies that teachers use in the service of learning.

Pedagogical Assessment

Teachers play a crucial role in engaging students in the process of learning. Effective teaching is about what students learn and not simply what students do. The pedagogical dimension is one of the formula that teacher needs to take into account. Assessing learners can be a meaningful activity for both teacher and learner. For the teacher, it gives an indication of how well the teacher has taught and for learner, how well the learner has learnt. It is through pedagogical assessment in the form of feedback, evaluation and ICT resources that teacher becomes more organised and responsive observer of learning.

Feedback Devices

Feedback devices are used in teaching for controlling, reinforcing, modifying and improving the performance and behaviour of teachers. Feedback devices are quite effective for bringing desirable changes and improvement in the teaching behaviour of the individual teacher or group of teachers whether in service or under training.

Feedback device is a process or mechanism with the help of which an individual or a system receives information (Feedback) about its working in terms of its strength and weakness in order to bring desirable improvement. The teacher can teach well and a strategy can work well with the help of an appropriate feedback devices simply because it is able to receive timely and appropriate knowledge of the strength and weaknesses of its working.

Types of Feedback Devices

There are various devices which are used for making the student-teacher competent and the main task done by these devices is to create a situation for the student-teacher to bring the desirable change in his teaching competence.

In this Chapter

The various feedback devices are as follows

Simulated Social Skill Training (SSST) It means the teaching performed and training received through simulation. It conveys the use of simulation technique. Basically, it is a learning or training technique for helping the learner to bring desirable changes in his behaviour through some systematic and organised learning experiences in simulated conditions. It was developed by Cruick Shunk in 1968. This technique induce certain behaviours in artificial situations. Simulated social skill training can be defined as a mechanism of feedback device to induce desirable competence among student-teachers by playing the role of teacher in their own group as an artificial situation of classroom teaching.

Interaction Analysis It is a technique for analysing and observing the classroom behaviour. It is developed by Ned A Flender in 1959. It provides the structure, components and flow of behaviour of classroom activities. It is used as a mechanism of feedback device for the modification of student-teachers teaching competence, as the competence of a student-teacher can be adjusted through the degree of effectiveness of his teaching, which in turn can be assessed through his classroom behaviour or interaction. In this way, a systematic or objective analysis of the teacher's classroom behaviour or interaction provide a reliable assessment of what goes on inside the classroom in terms of teaching and learning. Such type of analysis of classroom behaviour and interaction is known as Interaction Analysis.

Micro-Teaching Micro teaching is a technique or device of imparting training to the inexperienced or experienced teachers for learning the art of teaching by practicing specific skills through "Scaled down teaching encounter". Micro teaching is a training concept, as it provides teachers with a practice setting in which the normal complexities of classroom are reduced and in which the teacher gets feedback on his performance. The feedback devices are used to create the situation for the student-teacher to bring desirable change in his teaching. The chief objective of micro-teaching is the development of teaching skills in student-teachers.

Criteria of Feedback Devices

Feedback devices should target individual needs, be linked to specific assessment criteria and be received by a student in time to benefit subsequent work.

Effective feedback devices

- guide students to adapt and adjust their learning strategies.
- guide teachers to adapt and adjust their teaching to accommodate student's learning needs.
- guide students to become independent and self-reflective learners for better critics of their own work.
- stimulate reflection, interaction and dialogue about learning improvement.
- are constructive, so that students feel encouraged and motivated to improve.
- have consequences, so that it engages students by requiring them to attend to the feedback as part of the assessment.
- are efficient, so that staff can manage it effectively.

Guidance as a Feedback Device

Guidance can speed up the learning process and provide feedback as well. Feedback exerts a strong influence on learning and achievement. However, the type of feedback provided and the way instructors deliver it results in varying degrees of effectiveness. Teacher's feedback is a powerful pedagogical tool for promoting interaction in educational guidance between teachers and students. Guidance as a feedback device generally has positive effect in classroom interventions, as it focus on ways to improve the performance.

Assessment of Portfolio

Portfolios are personalised long-term documentation of student mastery of course material. An essential element of portfolios are student's reflections on their own learning and progression towards the mastery of the material documented in the portfolio. As such portfolios are windows of the meta-cognitive process of students.

A portfolio is a purposeful collection of selective and significant samples of student's work accompanied by clear criteria for performance, which evidence student's efforts, progress and achievements. They exhibit students progress and achievements in several areas. Portfolio assessment have been used for large scale accountability and purposes of schools to work in transition and for the purposes of certification.

Need for Assessment of Portfolio

Teachers and administrators have been making a move from traditional paper and pencil type test to alternate forms of assessment. Teacher's observation, projects and essays are more creative ways of evaluating student's achievement have gained a large following within the classroom.

Although, its use has declined by one type of tool that can be used effectively is **portfolio**. It remains quite popular in education, coursework and with administrators evaluating senior teachers. It is seen that so many class teachers forgot the use of portfolio assessment as a tool. The reason might be that portfolio is very subjective form of assessment.

It provides both formative and summative assessment opportunities for monitoring progress towards reaching an identified outcome. By setting criteria for content and outcomes, portfolios can communicate concrete information about what is expected from students in terms of the content and quality of performance in specific curriculum areas, while also providing a way of assessing their progress along the way. Depending on content and criteria, portfolios can provide teachers and researchers with information relevant to the cognitive processes that students use to achieve academic outcomes. Thus, the portfolio provides the necessary mechanism for housing all the information available about student's learning. It offers a holistic approach for student's learning.

Assessing Performance Through Portfolios

The assessment of portfolio will help to define what the student knows and can do and will facilitate the planning of further learning. Even when a portfolio is used for a short three week class, it is possible for the student and the teacher to see the growth in learning that has been made in relation to the course or module objectives. It provides more authentic and valid assessment of students' achievement and comprehensive views of students' performances in contexts and encourages students to develop independent and self-directed learners and enhances communication among teacher, student and parents. It can provide learners' opportunities to demonstrate his/her weakness and strengths and for teachers to direct their teaching. It also can encourage students to take responsibility for their own learning and enhance student-teacher communication.

Characteristics of Portfolio

There are several characteristics that are essential for the development of any type of portfolio that can be used for assessment. *According to Barton and Collins (1997), portfolio should be :*

Multi-sourced It means allowing for the opportunity to evaluate a variety of specific evidence. Multiple data includes both people (statements of participants, teachers or programme staff, parents and community members) and artifacts (anything from test scores of photos, drawings, journals and audio or video tape performances).

Authentic In this, the context and evidence are directly linked. Here, the items selected or produced for evidence should be related to programme activities as well as the goals and criterias. If portfolio is assessing the effect of a programme on participants of the communities then the evidence should reflect the activities of the programme rather than skills that were gained elsewhere.

Explicit The students or programme participants should know in advance what is expected of them, so that they can take responsibility for developing their evidence.

Integrated The evidence should establish a correspondence between programme activities and life experiences.

Multi-purposed A well designed portfolio assessment process evaluates the effectiveness of intervention at the same time, that it evaluates the growth of individuals or communities. It also serves as a communication tool, when shared with family, other staff and community members. In school setting, it can be passed on the other teachers or staff, as the child moves from one grade level to another.

Reflective Journal

A reflective journal is a means of recording ideas, personal thoughts and experiences as well as reflections and insights, a student have in the learning process of a course. In addition to the demands of a typical written assignment, reflective journal requires the students to think more deeply to challenge their old ideas with new incoming information and to synthesise the course materials they have learnt into their personal thoughts and philosophy and also to integrate it into their daily experiences and future actions.

A reflective journal often called a 'learning journal' as it is a steadily growing document that the learner writes to record the progress of his learning. It a powerful tool promote autonomy and improve student's learning.

Reflective journals allow students to practice their writing skills in an open-ended format that encourages the same thought process that is used in analytical writing. Zemelman, Daniels and Hyde believe that the most powerful learning happens when students self-monitor or reflect.

Structure of Reflective Journal

Basically, there are two standard forms of reflective journals. *They are*

Structured Journals Students are given a specific question, target or set of guidelines to base their writing on.

Unstructured Journals Students are required to record thoughts and feelings with minimal direction.

Designing a Good Reflective Journal Assessment

To design a good reflective journal assessment, following points should be considered :

- Consider the types of reflective journals that fits into your course. Suppose, if the students are inexperienced with reflective journals, the structure form would be more student friendly because specific questions and guidelines are available.
- Make sure that there are clear ideas about expectations and assessment criteria given to the students. For example, what can students put in their journals?, What is the definition of reflection? What is the approximate length of each journal entry? etc.
- Try to make students understand the purpose and benefit of reflective journal from the very beginning.
- Make sure that the teachers have explained and discussed the policies concerning privacy and confidentiality of information with students.
- Decide the regularity of journal entry.
- Provide timely feedback to students.

Possible Questions for a Reflective Journal

Some of the possible questions that can be framed for the reflective journal are as follows

- What was the most interesting thing that I read for this lesson?
- What were the three main things that I learned from this lesson?
- What I previously think was true, but now known to be wrong?
- What we do not cover that is expected we should?
- What was new or surprising to me?
- What have I changed my mind about, as a result of this lesson?
- What are the issues that interested me a lot, and that I would like to study in more detail?

Advantages of Reflective Journal

Active Learning The process of reflection encourages the students to take the initiative to be active, self-driven allows an individual learner to explore concepts and ideas in relation to their thoughts and feelings from various perspectives.

Understanding the Progress of Students Reflective journal provides opportunities for teachers to gain better understanding about how the students think and feel about the course and the learning progress of the students throughout the course which will eventually enhance the student's learning process.

Improving Writing Skills Writing reflective journals can involve students in a new form of writing, which they may not have a chance to experience in the past.

Freely Expressing Personal Views and Criticising the One Self Reflective journal assignments provides the platform for students to freely express, what they think and feel about the course and their learning to process and also promotes their expression of ideas, personal experiences and opinions.

Enhance Critical Thinking and Creativity The process of self-reflection enhances the development of critical thinking skills, among students when they relate their knowledge to real world issues. It can help students to develop their creativity and a questioning attitude towards different issues and problems.

Disadvantages of Reflective Journal

Difficult for Objective Marking Due to the subjective nature of reflective assignments, it is rather difficult for assessors to be objective and have consistent grading.

Different assessors when marking, may have quite a large discrepancy in their judgement of different types of work.

Time Consuming for Grading The context of reflective writing can be very wide, and involves a wide range of concepts, issues and perspectives. As a result, it often takes considerable amount of time for assessors to read and grade student's work.

Confidentiality As students have to disclose their personal and private views and information in their reflection, some of them may be unwilling to honestly disclose their real perspectives. They may be concerned that what they wrote will significantly affect the grade, they receive.

Clear Guidelines Needed Many students may not be familiar with the procedure of writing reflective assignments and may feel very lost when working on it for the first time. Teachers have to give clear guidelines to students about what should be included in the reflective journals, what can be learnt from writing it, as well as how they will be graded.

Rubrics

Rubrics means a scoring guide used to evaluate the quality of students' constructed responses. It is a scoring tool that explicitly describes the instructor's performance expectations for an assignment or piece of work. It can be used for making assignments, class participation or overall grades.

There are two types of rubrics that are **Holistic** and **Analytical**. Holistic rubrics group several assessment criteria and classify them together under achievement levels. Whereas analytic rubrics separate different assessment criteria and address them comprehensively.

It is a great tool for teachers because it is a simple way to set up a grading criteria for assignments. This tool is also useful for both teacher and student. A rubric defines in writing what is expected of the student, to get a particular grade on an assignment.

Heidi Goodrich Andrade, a rubrics expert defines rubrics as "a scoring tool that lists the criteria for a piece of work or what counts".

Field Engagement using Rubrics

A rubric is an assessment tool that clearly indicates achievement criteria across all the components of any kind of student work, from written to oral to visual.

Rubrics can be excellent tool to use when assessing student's work for several reasons as given below

- No re-writing of same comments on several different student's assignments.
- No wasting of time on writing up comments.
- No repeated questions about the assignment requirement, even after handing back the marked assignment.
- Addressing the specific components of marking scheme for student and instructor, prior to assignment submission.
- Grading equally the beginning, middle and end of grading session.

Importance of Rubrics

Rubrics are important due to the following reasons

As an Assessment Tool The main purpose of a rubric is it's ability to assess student's performance or work. Rubrics can be adapted to each assignment or to the course to better assess the learning objectives.

Improve Learning Using a rubric is an active and engaging form of learning. When rubrics are used by both student and teacher alike a rubric creates a feed forward mechanism which means a rubric should allow the students to reflect on their work and focus on how to improve in the future.

As a Communication Tool Rubrics can be seen as a communication tool between student and teacher as it aligns expectations and outlines learning objectives for the assignment between student and teacher. Rubrics define clear learning objectives by which teachers can quickly and effectively monitor students progress.

Involving Students in Rubric

Understanding a Rubric

Arranging the students into groups of four or more and given them the rubric, that teacher will be using for that particular task. Tell the student to discuss the task that teacher have given to them and create quick sample of papers which would receive marks in each of the categories. Then, the group will present their result to the whole class.

Creating a Rubric

It is a good idea to involve students in creating their own rubrics for classroom assignments. A student who can write the rubric for math problem knows the whole process inside and out and he/she can apply the knowledge and skills learned from the process to future assignment.

How to Make a Rubric

- Decide what criteria or essential elements must be present in the student's work, to ensure that it is high in quality. At this stage, teacher might even consider selecting samples of exemplary student's work that can be shown to students when setting assignments.
- Decide how many levels of achievement teacher will include in the rubric and how they will relate to your institution's definition of grades as well as own grading scheme.
- For each criterion, component, or essential element of quality, describe in detail, what the performance at each achievement level looks like.
- Leave space for additional, tailored comments or overall impressions and a final grade.

Usage of Rubric Effectively

Develop a Different Rubric for Each Assignment Although, this takes time in the beginning, you'll find that rubrics can be changed slightly or re-used, later. Whether you develop your own or use an existing rubric, practice with any other graders in your course to achieve inter-rater reliability.

Be Transparent Give students a copy of the rubric when you assign the performance task. These are not meant to surprise criteria. Hand the rubric back with the assignment.

Integrate Rubrics into Assignments Require students to attach the rubric to the assignment, when they hand in it. Some instructors ask students to self-assess or give peer's feedback, using the rubric prior to handing in the work.

Leverage Rubrics to Manage Your Time When you mark the assignment, circle or highlight the achieved level of performance, for each criterion on the rubric. This is where you will save a great deal of time, as no comments are required.

Include any additional specific or overall comments, that do not fit within the rubric's criteria.

Be Prepared to Revise Your Rubrics Decide upon a final grade for the assignment based on the rubric. If you find, as some do, that presented work meets criteria on the rubric, but nevertheless seems to have exceeded or not met the overall qualities you are seeking, revise the rubric accordingly for the next time you teach the course. If the work achieves highly in some areas of the rubric but not in others, decide in advance how the assignment grade is actually derived. Some uses a formula or multiplier, to give different weightings to various components, be explicit about this right on the rubric.

Consider Developing Online Rubrics If an assignment is being submitted to an electronic drop box, you may be able to develop and use an online rubric. The scores from these rubrics are automatically entered in the online grade book, in the course management system.

Competency Based Evaluation

It is the process of collecting evidences and establishing conclusions on the character and scope of the learner's progress, towards professional standards. Competence goes beyond mere mastery of information, but is an expectation to skillfully organise factual knowledge within the framework, comprised of communications skills, clinical reasoning, professional ethics, social engagement, interpersonal conduct and cross-cultural awareness.

Assessments are on the actual skills and knowledge, the learner can demonstrate in the education setting.

The general features are

Criterion Based on standard of practice.

Evidence Based accumulation of informal verbal/written assessment/feedback, assignment log, critique and self-assessment.

Participatory Based learner is involved in the process and consults with the assessor.

Assessment Tools in Competency Based Evaluation

It may include a wide range of assessment tools and activities, such as feedback, competency sampling, observation, 360 degree review, presentations and papers. No matter what method or tool utilised, four paramount features must be incorporated *i.e.* validity, reliability, fairness and flexibility.

Feedback

- It justify to students how their marks or grade was derived.
- It identify and reward specific qualities in student's work.
- It guide students on what steps to be taken for their improvement.
- It motivate them to act on their assessment.
- It develop their capability to monitor, evaluate and regulate their own learning.

Competency Sampling

- Sample of work for assessment.
- Follows learning period/schedule.
- Reflects competency in practice.
- Permits the inclusion of patient feedback (as in patient management assessment).
- Clearly identify which units will be utilised in the assessment.

Observation

- Focused on behavioural markers i.e. What are you looking for?, How will you know when you see it?
- Conduct the observation and utilise the observations, personally and/or utilise the observation of colleagues that have had training. Reliability of rating from colleague to colleague must be consistent and acceptable.

360° Review

- Multiple informants.
- Evaluation from the perspectives of the clinical educator, mentor, team members, other students, administrators and from the learner themselves.
- Best method as a survey format via anonymous respondents.

Presentation and Papers

- Some student's benefit from the opportunity to present at a lunch and learn, rounds, etc.
- Encourage students to include their own experiences from the viewpoint of a student.
- Ensure relevancy.

ICT Resources

ICT resources offer the possibility of acquiring knowledge, attitudes and procedures during the teaching process. It also offers various forms of work with content and activities. An integrated design of learning resources is an important part of the instructional process that helps to achieve the expected learning outcomes. There is a growing body of evidence that says use of ICT in the classroom can enhance learning. Thus, it is essential that the contemporary teacher has good ICT skills and is able to integrate ICT into the teaching and the learning processes. *Following are the ICT resources, that can help the teacher to get started*

- Basic knowledge of computer
- Basic computer task
- Basic knowledge of using different types of productivity software
- Using electronical forms of communication
- Internet skills

Assessment of Teacher Prepared ICT Resources

ICT can act as a tool to help teacher and to create a 'learner centric' environment. Thus, a teacher needs to be trained to be able to use ICT resources. The assessment of the ICT resources being used by teacher and its result is very important.

Assessment of teacher ICT resources are as follows

- Learn about integration of ICT and developing ICT capability.
- Planning and identifying opportunity for assessment.
- Determining the progression.
- Unlock barriers to assess ICT capabilities.
- Establishing a relevant and meaningful learning environment.
- Gathering strong empirical evidences of attainment.

EXAM BASED QUESTIONS

1 Who described feedback as "most powerful single moderator that enhances achievement"?

(a) Betty (b) Hattie
(c) Hetty (d) Helly

2 Feedback devices are effective for

(a) bringing desirable changes
(b) improvement in teaching behaviour
(c) Both (a) and (b)
(d) None of the above

3 Who developed Simulated Social Skill Training?

(a) Cruick Shunk
(b) Ned A Flander
(c) John Dewey
(d) None of the above

4 Interaction analysis was developed in

(a) 1968 (b) 1959
(c) 1978 (d) 1960

5 Which device impart training to the experienced or inexperienced teachers learning the art of teaching?

(a) Interaction Analysis
(b) Simulated Social Skill Training
(c) Micro Teaching
(d) All of the above

6 To help students reach autonomy, teacher can

(a) explicitly identify, share and clarify learning goals and success criteria.
(b) model the application of criteria using samples
(c) allow time for self feedback/reflection
(d) All of the above

7 Criteria of feedback devices does not includes

(a) guidance to students to adapt and adjust the learning strategies.
(b) leaving the school without permission
(c) students feel encouraged and motivated to improve
(d) staff management

8 Which of the following is not true about portfolio assessment?

(a) Usually, the student is involved in selecting material to be included.
(b) Its sample tasks regularly performed in a natural setting.
(c) Raw and summary data are usually included
(d) All of the above

9 Which of the following is the first decision that needs to be made, when developing a portfolio?

(a) What goes in it?
(b) How and when are the entries selected?
(c) What should it look like?
(d) How is the portfolio evaluated?

10 In portfolio assessment, a benchmark is used to
(a) increase the validity of the rubric
(b) increase the reliability of the rubric
(c) increase the length of the rubric
(d) increase the number of criteria of a rubric

11 The content of a portfolio is largely based on
(a) the goal and purpose of the portfolio
(b) the characteristics of the student evaluated
(c) the length of the portfolio
(d) None of the above

12 Which of the following is considered to be an advantage of portfolio assessment?
(a) Time required to collect the processes and products
(b) Logistics of collecting and maintaining student's portfolios
(c) Ability to involve students
(d) Ability to score objectively

13 Portfolio assessment serves as a .... tool
(a) communication (b) interaction
(c) multi-purpose (d) All of these

14 Which of the following characteristic(s) is/are essential for the development of portfolio, used for assessment?
(a) It should be authentic
(b) It should be explicit
(c) It should be multi-purposed
(d) All of these

15 What are portfolio assessments?
(a) Collection of student's work, used to evaluate students for a specific purpose.
(b) Methods teachers uses to help students, reflects upon their classwork.
(c) Collection of student's work, to determine high school readiness.
(d) Methods that teachers uses to help students make sense of content.

16 Portfolio assessment can provide
(a) only formative opportunities
(b) only summative opportunities
(c) Both (a) and (b)
(d) None of the above

17 Product portfolio includes
(a) find evidence (b) internal information
(c) Both (a) and (b) (d) None of these

18 Portfolio assessment grew in popularity in the .... in the 1990s, as part of a widespread interest in alternative assessment.
(a) United kingdom (b) United states
(c) India (d) Greece

19 .... type of portfolios focused on documenting the achievement of mastery of specific course goals/objectives, set by the course instructor.
(a) All inclusive portfolies (b) Showcase portfolios
(c) Selection portfolios (d) Progress portfolios

20 .... is a means of recording ideas, personal thoughts and experiences.
(a) Feedback Devices
(b) Reflective Journals
(c) Portfolio Assessment
(d) All of these

21 A reflective journal is often called a .... journal, is a steadily growing document that the learner writes to record the progress of their learning.
(a) learning (b) question
(c) meta-cognitive (d) visualisation

22 The process of self-reflection enhances the development of .... skills.
(a) writing (b) assessment
(c) critical-thinking (d) All of these

23 Which of the following is not considered to be an advantage of reflective journal?
(a) It provides good opportunities for teachers, to gain better understanding about how the students think and feel about the course.
(b) It can involve students in a new form of writing, which they may have a chance to experience in the past.
(c) Reflective journal assignments provides the platform for students to freely express, what they think and feel about the course and learning experiences.
(d) It can help students to develop their creativity and a questioning attitude towards different issues and problems.

24 Which of the following statement(s) is/are true?
(a) Reflective writing can be done formally as well as informally.
(b) Reflective writing is always an easy task.
(c) Reflective writing involves using mirrors.
(d) Reflective writing always has specific limits and rules.

25 In .... journal students are required to record thoughts and feelings with minimal direction.
(a) structured (b) unstructured
(c) reflective (d) learning

26 A good reflective journal assessment involves
(a) clear ideas about expectations and assessment criteria, given to the students.
(b) students understand the purpose and benefits, at the initial stage.
(c) decides the regularity of journal assessment.
(d) All of the above

27 Which of the following is/are the advantage (s) of the reflective journal?
(a) Time consuming for grading.
(b) Difficult for objective marking.
(c) Active learning.
(d) Clear guidelines needed, as to what should be included in the reflective journal.

28 A reflective journal is not ....
(a) simply a summary of course material
(b) a learning log
(c) on a learning log, you might write down the times and days when you read something
(d) All of the above

29 .... allows students to practice their writing skills in an open-ended format that encourages the same thought processes, that is used in analytical writing.
(a) Portfolio assessment (b) Reflective journal
(c) Rubrics (d) Working portfolio

30 The characteristic(s) regarding entries in reflective journal can include.
(a) Points that you found specially, interesting in your reading and would like to follow up in more detail.
(b) Questions that came up in your mind because of points made in the material, you read in the topic.
(c) Both (a) and (b)
(d) None of the above

31 The possible questions for reflective journals should include
(a) What was new or surprising to me?
(b) What were the three main things that I learned from the lesson?
(c) What did we not cover that I expected we should?
(d) All of the above

32 Which of the following will be a simple way, to setup grading criteria for assignments?
(a) Proposals (b) Rubrics
(c) Reflective journals (d) All of these

33 Name rubric expert
(a) Heidi Goodrich Andrade (b) Henry Goodrich Andrade
(c) Henry Goodrich Andre (d) Heiri Goodrich Andrade

34 Rubric is a .... tool.
(a) life saving tool (b) measurement tool
(c) assessment tool (d) interactive tool

35 Why do teachers use rubrics?
(a) No re-writing of same comments, on several different student's assignment.
(b) Grading equally in the beginning, middle and end of the grading system.
(c) Both (a) and (b)
(d) None of the above

36 Who can prepare a rubric?
(a) Teacher (b) Student
(c) Both (a) and (b) (d) None of these

37 Which steps are included in the process of making rubrics?
(a) Decision on what criteria must be present in the student's work.
(b) Decision on how many levels to be included in rubrics.
(c) Description of what the performance in each level look like.
(d) All of the above

38 Which is not a way to use rubrics effectively?
(a) Being transparent
(b) Regular revision of rubric
(c) Not using rubric after failed attempt
(d) Develop different rubric for each assignment

39 Competency based evaluation is the process of...... .
(a) collecting evidences
(b) establishing conclusion of the character
(c) Both (a) and (b)
(d) None of the above

40 General feature(s) of competency based evaluation includes
(a) criterion based knowledge
(b) evidence based knowledge
(c) participatory based knowledge
(d) All of the above

41 Which is not an assessment tool, used under competency based evaluation?
(a) 360° review (b) Presentation and paper
(c) Term paper/exam (d) Observation

42 How do we survey 360° review?
(a) Anonymous respondent (b) Known person
(c) Both (a) and (b) (d) None of these

43 Use of ICT at classroom can enhance ....
(a) learning (b) teaching skill
(c) Both (a) and (b) (d) None of these

44 Which of the following is/are the part(s) of ICT resources?
(a) Basic computer task
(b) Using productive software
(c) Internet skill
(d) All of the above

45 What kind of environment do ICT create?
(a) Learner centric (b) Teacher centric
(c) Toxic (d) None of these

46 How is assessment of teacher prepared ICT resources can be used in class?
(a) Learning about integrating ICT and developing ICT Capabilities.
(b) Determining the progression
(c) Both (a) and (b)
(d) None of the above

47 What is the need of teacher professional development?
(a) It is critical for successful utilisation of ICTs in education
(b) One time training is not effective
(c) Optimise the teacher's use of ICTs
(d) All of the above

48 What amount of teacher have expertise in using ICT?
(a) Few (b) Large number
(c) Half (d) None of these

49 Choose the correct statement.
1. Feedback is an important part of assessment.
2. It helps learner to maximise their potential.
3. Feedback is only used in hospitality services.

Codes

(a) 1 and 2 (b) 2 and 3 (c) 3 and 1 (d) Only 3

50 Choose the correct statement.
1. ICT can be used without proper training.
2. Changes must be implemented to optimise teacher use of ICT.
3. Teachers can be trained in one go.
4. ICT can provide access to better education content.

Codes

(a) 1 and 2 (b) 2 and 4 (c) 2 and 3 (d) 1, 2 and 4

51 Choose the correct statement.
1. Rubrics combine game and studies.
2. Student cannot prepare rubric.
3. Rubric is an assessment tool.
4. Rubric is good for topper student only.

Codes

(a) 2 and 4 (b) 1 and 4
(c) 2 and 3 (d) Only 3

52 In competency based evaluation
1. feedback includes, informal, formative and summative feedback.
2. competency sampling follows learning period/schedule.
3. observation of teacher by student.
4. students present their experience.

Choose the correct option.

(a) 1 and 3 (b) 2 and 4
(c) 1, 2 and 4 (d) 2, 3 and 4

53 Choose the correct statement.
1. Contemporary teachers have good ICT skills.
2. ICT does not require any resources.
3. ICT creates 'teacher centric' environment.
4. Use of ICT can enhance learning.

Codes

(a) 1 and 4 (b) 2 and 3 (c) Only 4 (d) Only 3

Directions (Q. Nos. 54-63) *Given below are the statements, one labelled as Assertion (A) and the other labelled as Reason (R). Following are the codes given below. Choose the correct option.*

Codes

(a) Both A and R are true and R is the correct explanation of A
(b) Both A and R are true, but R is not the correct explanation of A
(c) Both A and R are false
(d) A is false, but R is true

54 **Assertion** (A) Assessment of teacher. prepared ICT resources includes determining the progression of student.

Reason (R) It also establishes a relevant and meaningful learning environment.

55 **Assertion** (A) Assessing learner can be a meaningful activity.

Reason (R) Pedagogy does'nt play an important part in assessment.

56 **Assertion** (A) Oral feedback occurs after a task.

Reason (B) Oral feedback is a very formal task.

57 **Assertion** (A) Written feedback does not guide students, where the improvement is needed.

Reason (R) Written feedback needs to be timely.

58 **Assertion** (A) In peer feedback, students provide feedback to each other.

Reason (B) Teachers teach the students, how to provide effective feedback to each other.

59 **Assertion** (A) Rubric is a tool that requires special training.

Reason (R) One can consider rhodes, if looking for per-existing rubrics.

60 **Assertion** (A) Rubrics are not meant to be a surprise.

Reason (R) Students should not have a copy of rubrics, to be used.

61 **Assertion** (A) Reflective journal provides a channel of inner communication that connects beliefs, feelings and actions, which allows students to develop their knowledge and understanding of course content.

Reason (R) It creates effective learning conditions that results in self-discovery.

62 **Assertion** (A) Reflective journals open the windows of a student's mind and they also allow teachers to look in.

Reason (R) This creates an effective learning conditions that results in self-discovery.

63 **Assertion** (A) Portfolio provides the necessary mechanism for housing all the information, available about a student's learning.

Reason (R) Portfolio assessments have been used for large scale assessment and accountability purposes.

64 Statement I Portfolio can provide teachers and researchers with information relevant to the cognitive process.

Statement II Engaging students more deeply in instructional and assessment process, portfolio benefits student's learning.

(a) Statement I and II are false.
(b) Statement I is true
(c) Statement II is false
(d) Both the statements, I and II are true

65 Match the following.

List I	List II
A. Simulated Social Skill Training	1. Development of Teaching Skills
B. Micro Teaching	2. Analyse Classroom Behaviour
C. Interaction Analysis	3. Use of Simulation Technique

Codes

	A	B	C		A	B	C
(a)	1	2	3	(b)	2	1	3
(c)	3	2	1	(d) None of these			

66 Match the following.

List I (Types of Portfolios)	List II (Characteristics)
A. Showcase portfolio	1. Contains a complete record of all work done by a student in a course or programme.
B. Working portfolio	2. Contains multiple examples of the same type of work, done overtime and are used to assess progress.
C. Progress portfolio	3. Exhibit the best of student's performance.
D. All inclusive portfolio	4. contains drafts that students and teachers reflects on process.

Codes

	A	B	C	D		A	B	C	D
(a)	4	4	3	1	(b)	3	4	2	1
(c)	1	2	3	4	(d)	4	3	2	1

Directions (Q. Nos. 67-70) *Read the passage given below and answer the following questions.*

Portfolio assessment is an alternative method of evaluating student's performance. Portfolios provide an opportunity for students to display a broader range of abilities when compared to traditional testing techniques. Students assume a more active role in the learning process when developing a portfolio because they must create, analyze and evaluate their own work. The role of the faculty member also changes from providing information to facilitating the learning process and empowering the learner. Administrators and faculty members should consider incorporating portfolio assessment techniques into their evaluation of student's performance. Portfolio assessment is an evaluation technique that emerged in the 1980s as an alternative for or companion to traditional testing. Portfolio assessment has been identified as one of the top three curriculum trends of 90s.

67 Portfolios provide an opportunity for students to display a .... range of abilities.

(a) broader
(b) less
(c) few
(d) None of the above

68 Portfolio assessment is an .... technique.

(a) curriculum
(b) evaluation
(c) alternative
(d) All of the above

69 Portfolio assessment emerged in the .... as an alternative to traditional testing.

(a) 1970s (b) 1990s
(c) 1980s (d) 1960s

70 When did portfolio assessment has been identified as one of the top three curriculum trends?

(a) 1970s (b) 1980s
(c) 1990s (d) 1960s

ANSWERS

1 (b)	2 (c)	3 (a)	4 (b)	5 (c)	6 (d)	7 (b)	8 (d)	9 (c)	10 (b)
11 (a)	12 (c)	13 (a)	14 (a)	15 (a)	16 (c)	17 (a)	18 (b)	19 (c)	20 (b)
21 (a)	22 (c)	23 (b)	24 (d)	25 (b)	26 (d)	27 (c)	28 (d)	29 (b)	30 (c)
31 (d)	32 (b)	33 (d)	34 (c)	35 (c)	36 (c)	37 (d)	38 (c)	39 (c)	40 (d)
41 (c)	42 (a)	43 (c)	44 (d)	45 (a)	46 (c)	47 (d)	48 (b)	49 (a)	50 (b)
51 (d)	52 (c)	53 (a)	54 (a)	55 (b)	56 (c)	57 (d)	58 (a)	59 (d)	60 (b)
61 (b)	62 (d)	63 (d)	64 (c)	65 (c)	66 (a)	67 (a)	68 (b)	69 (c)	70 (c)

CHAPTER 29

Assessment in Andragogy of Education

Assessment is the systematic collection, interpretation and use of information, about learning. The assessment in andragogy is important for assessing the educational activities of the learners. The andragogical approach has changed the teaching philosophy of educators, around the world. Assessment is central to successful teaching and learning.

Introduction

Assessment has always had a special place in programs for adults. The adults have different styles of learning, which can either enhance or deter their learning. Educators use a number of strategies to assess adult learning. However, assessment is a perpetual challenge for educators because of concerns of assessment, validity and fairness to learners. Assessment can be a useful tool to help learners, to determine gaps in their knowledge or help to instructors determine if they need to make changes to their teaching strategies. The adult learners are self-directed, autonomous and independent. Thus, the andragogical process is an excellent preparation for lifetime learning.

In assessment, the system of interaction analysis can be used to study the relationship between teaching style and pupil achievement.

Interaction Analysis

It is a process of encoding and decoding the study pattern of teaching and learning. In the encoding process, categories of classifying statements are established, a code symbol is assigned to each category and a trained observer records by jotting down code symbols.

In the decoding step, a trained analyst interprets the display of coded data and reconstructs the original events on the basis of the encoded data, even though he may not have been present, when the data were collected. Although, there are many systems for coding spontaneous verbal communication in classroom.

A typical system for interaction analysis will usually includes

- A set of categories, each defined clearly.
- A procedure for observation and a set of ground rules, which govern the coding process.

In this Chapter

- *Interaction Analysis*
  - *Flander's Interaction Analysis*
  - *Galloway's System of Interaction Analysis*
- *Criteria for Teacher's Evaluation*
- *Rubrics*

- Steps for tabulating data, in order to arrange a display.
- Suggestions, which can be followed in some of the more common applications.

Classroom Interaction Analysis

It is a specialised research procedure that provides information, about only a few of the many aspects of teaching. It is an analysis of spontaneous communication between teacher and pupils, that it is of no value, if no one is talking or if teacher talks continuously, or if student reads from a book. Unless, additional records are kept, the following kinds of information will be ignored i.e. right or wrong, good or bad content information, whatever is being discussed, the variety of instructional material being used, the various class information during learning activities, the preparation of the teacher as received by lesson plan and anything else, not directly revealed by verbal communication.

Its **Teaching Interaction Analysis**, which applies only to the content free characteristics of verbal communication. The entire process of communication analysis becomes a measure of teacher influence because it makes an assumption that most of teacher's influence is expressed through verbal statements and most of non-verbal influence is positively co-related with verbal. Those who have worked upon this technique, are disposed to accept this assumption.

So far as the communication is concerned, the ***three*** *conditions are taken as:*

- Teacher's talk
- Pupil's talk
- Silence or confusion

These three conditions are said to exhaust all possibilities. It is an objective and systematic technique for evaluating the classroom's performance of a teacher. Interaction Analysis is nothing more and nothing less than an observational technique, which can be used to obtain a fairly reliable record of spontaneous verbal statements and to determination.

Flander's Interaction Analysis is concerned primarily with verbal behaviour. This can be observed with high reliability than non-verbal behaviour. An assumption is made that verbal behaviour of the teacher is an adequate sample of his/her total behaviour in the classroom, we must assume that the verbal statements of the teacher are consistent with his/her non-verbal gestures, infact, his/her total behaviour. This assumption cannot be easily tested, since it will take too long a period, to develop a reliable measure of a non-verbal behaviour.

Basic Theoretical Assumptions of Interaction Analysis

The various theoretical assumptions, which are basic to the idea of Interaction Analysis are as follows

According to **Flander's** (1965), in a normal classroom situation, it is verbal communication, which is pre-dominant.

According to **Flander's** (1966), we can normally assume that verbal statements of a teacher are consistent with his non-verbal gestures and infact, his total behaviour. This assumption was sustained in terms of experience in minnesotu studies.

According to **Anderson** (1946), the teacher exerts a great deal of influence on the pupils. Pupil's behaviour is affected to a great extent, by this type of teacher's behaviour, exhibited.

According to **Haggerty** (1932), the relation between students and teacher is a crucial factor in the teaching process and must be considered an important aspect of methodology.

According to **Lewin** (1939), it has been established that social climate is related to productivity and to the quality of inter-personal relations. It has been proved that democratic atmosphere tends to keep work of a relatively high, even in the absence of the teacher.

According to **HV Perkins** (1950), children tend to be conscious of a warm acceptance by the teacher and to express greatest fondness for the democratic teacher.

According to **Perkins** (1956), the role of classroom climate is crucial for the learning process.

According to **Flanders** (1963 and 1966), modification of teacher's classroom behaviour through feedback is possible, though how much can change occur and more knowledge relating to the performance of these changes will require further research.

According to **Raths**, teacher influence is expressed primarily through verbal statements. Now, verbal acts of influence do occur, but are not recorded through Interaction Analysis. The reasonableness of this assumption rests upon the assertion that the quality of the non-verbal acts is similar to the verbal acts, to assess verbal influence, therefore, it is adequately a simple of all influences.

These assumptions focus the attention on the verbal communication, participation of teachers and students in teaching process.

Flander's Interaction Analysis

The development of interaction analysis was primarily the work of Ned Flanders in the year 1959. Indeed, the system is often referred to as Flander's System of Interaction Analysis an innovation which make possible significant insights into the analysis and improvement of instruction. It involves categorisation of all the sets of possible verbal behaviours of a teacher in the classroom, while interacting with his students.

Flander's Interaction Analysis Categories

In total, there are **ten** categories of verbal behaviour in this system, which are grouped into **three** major sections.

They are

- Teacher's talk
- Student's talk
- Silence or confusion.

Teacher's Talk It consists of seven categories. The first four categorie belongs to an indirect influence and the later three to direct influence. The category of indirect influence covers those verbal behaviours of the teacher, which gives the sutdents, a greater opportunity to respond or to maximise their freedom of action. In contrary, the category of direct influence exhibits those verbal behaviours of the teacher, which tend to restrict or minimise the student's freedom of action.

Pupil's Talk It is divided into two categories. The third section, silence/confusion, includes all those behaviours that are not covered in the first and second sections. These sections and their ten categories with underlying component behaviours are summarised in table.

Silence or Confusion Pauses, short periods of confusion in which communication cannot be understood by the observer.

Flander's Interaction Analysis Categories

Teacher's Talk	
(i) Indirect Influence	• Accepts feelings
	• Praises or encourages
	• Accepts or uses pupil's ideas
	• Asks questions
(ii) Direct Influence	• Lecturing
	• Giving directions
	• Criticising or justifying authority
Pupil's Talk	
(i) Response	• Pupil's talk response
(ii) Initiation	• Pupil's talk initiation
Silence/Confusion	• Silence or confusion

All categories are mutually exclusive, but subsume all types of verbal behaviour. The categories or verbal interactions are based upon the following **two** major activities i.e. initiation and response of both. The interchange between initiation and response, forms the classroom verbal interacation. The non-verbal interaction takes place through on task and off-task activities, caused by teacher or students.

Usage of Flander's Interaction Analysis

This system involves ***three*** *major steps, which are as follows*

Observation or Recording of Classroom's Events

The observer is required to select an appropriate position in the classroom, to listen and watch the events as smoothly as possible, without disturbing or interfering with the spontaneous activities. He is also required to train himself for the proper recording (referred to as encoding in the language of Interaction Analysis). For this purpose, he must memorise the code numbers (the category number) in relation to the component behaviours, represented by the different categories.

The next thing he has to do is to note down within every three seconds, the code or category number, which best represents the interaction event, just observed. For instance, when the teacher is praising, he should put 2; when he is lecturing, he should write 5; when he is asking questions, he should write 4; and again if he praises, he should write 2 on his datasheet.

The procedure of recording or encoding of the classroom events may go on at the rate of 20 to 25 observations per minute. Here, the observer, in a sense, acts as an automatic device, highly discriminating and objective in observing each and every aspect of the classroom events and recording it in terms of the code or category number. These numbers are recorded in a sequence in a column. Therefore, at the end of his observation, he may get a long series of numbers, written from top to bottom, so that the original sequence of events is preserved. Besides, he may write down marginal notes for explaining the unusual class' events.

Ground Rules

The task of observation, recording and encoding is quite complex and needs sufficient training, practice and care on the part of the observer. For maintaining objectivity and reliability of the process, there are certain ground rules, which have to be kept in mind.

They are:

Rule 1 When not certain, to which two or more categories a statement belongs. Choose the category that is numerically farthest from category 5; *e.g.* for choosing between 3 and 4, choose 3 and for 8 and 9, choose 9.

Rule 2 If the primary tone of teacher's behaviour has been consistenly direct or indirect, do not shift to the opposite classification, unless a clear indication of the shift is given.

Rule 3 The observer must not be concerned with his own basis or teacher's intent.

Rule 4 If more than one category occurs during the three seconds interval, all categories used in that interval are recorded; therefore, record each change in category. If no change occurs within three seconds, repeat that category number.

Rule 5 For silence, longer than three seconds, record 10 for every three seconds.

Rule 6 A teacher's joke, which is made at the expense of children is recorded as 7.

Rule 7 It is recorded as 8, if a student gives a specific predictable answer to a narrow question, or a number of students, respond collectively.

Construction of Interaction Matrix

After recording or encoding the classroom events into ten categories, the next task is concerned with the construction of an interaction or observation matrix table. The matrix table consists of 10 rows and columns. The category numbers of the record sheet are tabulated in the table. Each number is entered in the form of sequence pairs, being used twice, **firstly** as the first number and **secondly** as second number. It's rows represent the first number in the pair and the column, the second. Each pair of numbers, overlaps with the previous pair and such over-lapping pairs of observation are entered in appropriate cells of the matrix.

In the matrix construction, one is to make sure that the entire series begins and ends with the same number. It is customary to add a 10 to the beginning and end of the series if is not already present. Let us illustrate the process of matrix construction with an example.

Suppose that an observer has recorded or encoded the category numbers as 5, 4, 3, 10, 6, 2, 6, 1, 8 and 2. Let us add 10 in the beginning and 10 at the end of this series and try to form pairs. *The result may be represented as:*

Original Series	Series for Pairing	Pairing
5	10	
4	5	I Pair (10, 5)
3	4	II Pair (5, 4)
10	3	III Pair (4, 3)
6	10	IV Pair (3, 10)
2	6	V Pair (10, 6)
6	2	VI Pair (6, 2)
1	6	VII Pair (2, 6)
8	1	VIII Pair (6, 1)
2	8	IX Pair (1, 8)
	2	X Pair (8, 2)
	10	XI Pair (2, 10)

The pairs may be now entered in the matrix.

The **first** sequence pair (10, 5) has been tallied in the cell located at the intersection of 10th row and 5th column. The **next** pair (5, 4) is being tallied in the cell located at the intersection of the 5th row and the 4th column. Similarly, all the remaining pairs have been tallied in their respective cells.

For exercising a check in the construction of the matrix, the total number of observations 'N' will always be tabulated by N – 1 tallies, in the matrix. In the present example, there are

Interaction Matrix Table

Category	1	2	3	4	5	6	7	8	9	10	Total
1								/			1
2										/	2
3										/	1
4			/								1
5				/							1
6	/	/									2
7											0
8		/									1
9											0
10					/	/					2
Total	1	2	1	1	1	2	0	1	0	2	11

12 category numbers (including the extra 10), which have produced a total of 11 tallies in the matrix.

Interpretation of Interaction Matrix

The process of interpretation of interaction or observation data is often called as **decoding**. It may help in knowing what was going on inside the classroom, in terms of teacher's behaviour and classroom's interaction for communication. It has two broad aspects.

They are

- Quantitative
- Qualitative.

Quantitative Analysis of Teacher Behaviour *It may be based on the following aspects*

- Interaction categories
- Areas of interaction
- Behaviour ratios
- Interaction variables

The classroom teaching or classroom communication has two types of interactions and they are

- Verbal interaction
- Non-verbal interaction

There are several techniques, which have been devised to study and analyse the classroom's verbal interaction. Number of studies have been conducted to analyse the classroom's verbal behaviour of teachers, even the norms have been developed for the verbal interaction of teaching at different levels. **Flander** has developed Interaction Model of Teaching and seven models of verbal interaction, but non-verbal interaction has not been investigated, so intensively and a very few techniques have been developed so far as the agents of classroom's teaching.

Qualitative Analysis of Teacher Behaviour *It is based on the following methods*

- Clockwise flow diagrams.
- Box-flow diagrams.
- Interaction models of critical teaching behaviour.

Method of Clockwise Flow Diagrams It provides a visual display of the chain of classroom interaction which may prove more acceptable for understanding the nature and structure of classroom verbal behaviour. Flow diagrams help in clarifying the sequence of events and making the matrix to be more understandable.

Method of Box-Flow Diagrams In place of clockwise flow diagrams, Flanders suggested to draw box-like diagrams, which look little less complicated and help more in understanding the nature and structure of verbal behaviour of the teacher.

Method of Interaction Models of Critical Teaching Behaviours It has been defined by Flanders as a pattern of acts or interaction models that:

- are logically related to certain educational outcomes.
- follow a certain sequence with measurable probability.
- seem crucial in terms of a theory of teacher influence verified by past research.

He has developed seven interaction models of critical thinking behaviour and they are

- High content emphasis under close-teacher direction.
- Teacher-directed quick drill.
- Drill combined with lecture demonstration.
- Teacher gives directions with some clarification.
- Stimulating independent student thought.
- Attending to student feelings.
- Teacher transitions from affective to an intellectual emphasis.

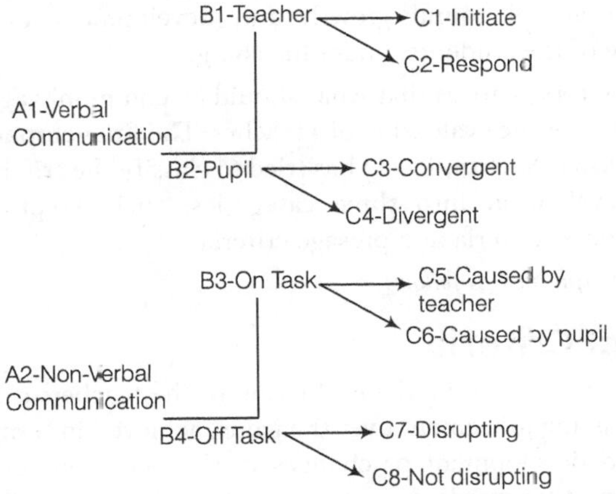

Verbal and Non-verbal Classroom Interaction Analysis

Galloway's System of Interaction Analysis

The system of Interaction Analysis was developed by Charles Galloway in the form of teachers' training technique. It is basically a category type system involving categorisation of all sets of possible verbal and non-verbal behaviour of teacher in the classroom while interacting with students. If teachers are to become more effective in the classroom, they need to become attentive, not only to what they communicating, but also to how are they communicating. They need to know the importance of verbal and non-verbal, in their classroom. The non-verbal behaviour often reflects their real feelings and students, but most of the teachers are not aware of what are they communicating, non-verbally.

Galloway has developed the categories for non-verbal communication by incorporating **Flander's Ten Category System**. Thus, his system of observation is the combination of both verbal and non-verbal or classroom's communication as a whole.

*He has classified the classroom interaction into **four** components as*

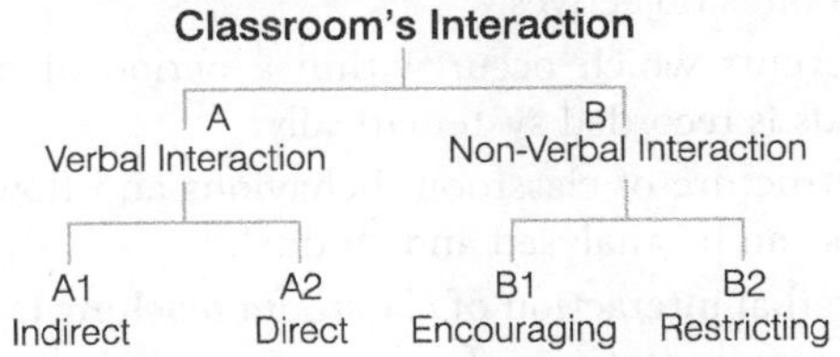

Charles Galloway has used direct-indirect and encourging-restricting components. The observer encodes the teacher-pupil's verbal and non-verbal behaviour.

This system of classroom observation involves the following categories

Galloway's System of Observation

Direct-Indirect (Verbal)	Encouraging-Restricting (Non-Verbal)
Accepts student's feelings	Acceptance or indifference
Praises or encourages	Congruent or incongruent
Uses student's ideas	Implement or perfunctory
Asks questions	Personal and impersonal
Lecturing gives information	Responsive and unresponsive
Giving directions	Involve or dismiss
Criticising or justifying authority	Receptive or attentive
Student's talk (Response)	Receptive or inattentive
Student's talk (Initation)	Firm of harsh
Silence or confusion	Comfort or distress

Assumptions of Galloway's System

- Non-verbal communication of a teacher do, has a significant role in classroom interaction.
- As one cannot see when he/she behaves, so a feedback is necessary for the behaviour.
- The non-verbal cues are important, as they can reinforce and can motivate a student.
- Non-verbal communication can be more effective during interaction in the classroom.
- Becoming aware of his non-verbal events occurring around us, one can achieve a better understanding of himself.
- Training of teachers enhances the aspect of non-verbal communication in teachers.
- The system is based upon the theory of modification of the teacher's behaviour.

Characteristics of Interaction Analysis Techniques

- It is an objective and scientific technique of classroom's objectives.
- The events which occur within a period of of 3 seconds is recorded systematically.
- The structure of classroom behaviour and flow of events can be analysed and studied.
- The verbal interaction of classroom teaching is the true representative of classroom, verbal and non-verbal behaviour.
- It can be used as an observation technique for classroom's teaching in teaching education programme. It is employed as a research tool for analysing and studying teaching.
- With the help of normative expectations of behaviour, it can also be used as an evaluatory device, though it is an exploratory device.
- The Interaction Analysis is used as a mechanism of feedback and device, for the modification of teacher's behaviour.
- It is also employed as a supplementary device, with other mechanism of feedback devices. For example, micro-teaching and simulated social skill teaching for the modification of teacher's behaviour.
- The technique may be helpful for developing theory of teaching, because Interaction Model of Teaching is most popular.
- It functions as measuring instrument for classroom's teaching and serves prognostic and diagnostic functions.

Disadvantages of Interaction Analysis Technique

- The Interaction Analysis technique is used for observing verbal behaviour of classroom's teaching, while non-verbal behaviour is equally important.
- All the classroom's teaching activities encoded forcely into ten categories. Thus, it narrows the structures of teaching behaviour.
- It has several categories for teachers and two categories for pupil, out of ten categories. Hence, there is no balance in the teachers and pupil's categories.
- This technique does not provide any information about the quality of content. It is content free technique of observation. It confines only to verbal communication of teaching.
- It encodes and occurrence of a particular activity, but does not consider its intensity. Teaching effectiveness concerns with force and intensity of teaching events.
- It records the actions of teacher and pupil, but does not encode their reactions.

Criteria for Teacher's Evaluation

The term evaluation, as reflected through it's naming, stands for the evaluation of teachers, in terms of the quality of their roles, played as a teacher. It means the extent to which they may be adjudged as good or poor in fulfiling their duties and obligations. The term teacher's evaluation can be defined as a process of helping the evaluators, to draw inferences or pass judgement over the effectiveness of a teacher, in terms of his teacher, like behaviour and abilities demonstrable through his perfomance, leading to an all round growth and development of the personality of the students, under his charge.

Now, the question arises that what should be commonly agreed upon criteria for the evaluation of a teacher. The **Encyclopaedia of Education** (Deightn, 1971) has tried to classify the criteria of teacher's evaluation into three categories, such as product criteria, process criteria and presage criteria.

They can be explained as follows

Product Criteria

According to this criteria, the evaluation of the teachers can be made by passing judgement over the gains, achieved in terms of growth and development or changes in the behaviour of the students. In other words, from the extent to which a teacher is able to help his/her students in the realisation of the set teaching-learning objectives, he is said to be a competent or effective teacher.

Under the product criteria, the evaluation of teacher's work must be made through the nature of the end results of his effort, it means the gains achieved in terms of the pupil's growth and development or the desirable changes in their behaviour.

Process Criteria

Under this criteria, a teacher needs to be evaluated in terms of the nature of the quality of his efforts, made for the realisation of the set teaching-learning objectives, irrespective of the products i.e. student's gains, student's growth and student's changes.

This criteria rests on the very assumption that the process choosen or the efforts made are more substantial and important than the outcomes achieved. Therefore, what goes at the time of ongoing teaching-learning process, in terms of the typical situations, involving classroom's conditions and interaction of students and teachers and the teaching competencies and skills demonstrated by the teacher, thus, may be adjudged as various criteria for teacher's evaluation.

It can be said that when teacher's evaluation is based upon classroom's behaviour, either the teacher's behaviour, his student's behaviour or the interplay of teacher-student's behaviour, the judge is using process criteria.

Presage Criteria

This criteria neither tries to evaluate the ends of the teaching-learning process, like product criteria, nor lay emphasis on the nature of the means, like process criteria, for the evaluation of the teachers. On the other hand, the presage criteria tries to focus on the evaluation of the total nature, qualities and characteristics of that very source (the teacher) responsible for carrying out, both the means and the ends, through his efforts.

It may involve the personality attributes of the teachers, the number of years of the experience, academic and professional qualification, aptitude for teaching interest, attitude towards teaching, personal and professional adjustment, knowledge of the subject, growth in basic skills of student taught, job satisfaction, etc. These criteria are at best indirect measure of a teacher's effectiveness and are normally choosen, because they are related to and therefore, predict, either process or product criteria.

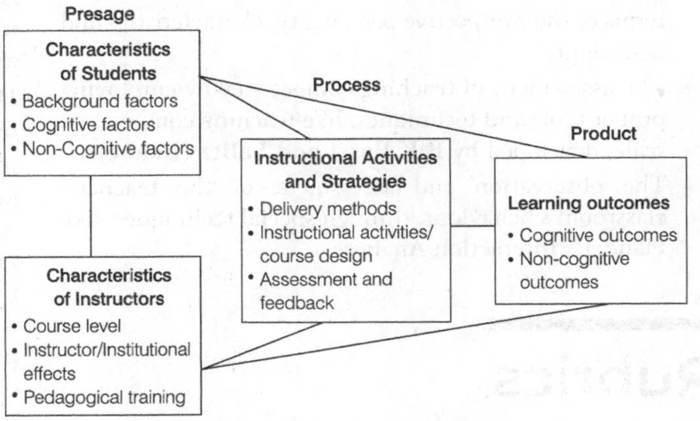

Criteria for Teacher's Evaluation

The product, process and presage criteria, forms the backbone of taking decisions, about the methods and techniques to be employed for the evaluation of teachers. Each of these criteria has it's own merits and limitations for being used as a yardstick for the assessment of the goodness and effectiveness of a teacher, working at any stage of the school or higher education. It is useful to employ an Integrated Approach of evaluation. *Let us see, how far we can integrate these criteria.*

- The results of the house tests, monthly, terminal and annual examinations of the school, board and other accreditation agencies, showing academic achievements of the students, taught by the teachers.
- The results of the performance shown by the students in sports, constructive and creative activities, curricular and other fields attributable to the efforts made by the teachers.
- The change in attitude, interests, philosophy of life and overall growth and development in the personality of the students, measured through special means and devices in terms of behavioural changes, brought about by the efforts and influences of particular teachers.
- The use of the properly constructed rating scales, for rating the overall performance, teacher's behaviour and personality characteristics of the teacher by the teachers, themselves, their colleagues, head of the institutions, supervisors, students, etc.
- The use of the questionnaire, inventory, etc., for collecting information about the product, process and presage variables of teacher effectiveness from teachers themselves, their colleagues, students, heads of the institutions, supervisors, etc.
- The information received through self-assessment or appraisal performa filled in by the teachers, themselves.
- The record of the inspection committee and other day to day supervision work.

- The overall impressions, likings and dislikings, expressed by the students, about their teachers, in terms of their respective personality, characteristics and behaviour.
- The assessment of teaching competency by employing proper tools and techniques, like teaching competency scale, developed by **B K Passi and Lalita** (Indore).
- The observation and assessment of the teacher's classroom's behaviour, through special techniques, like Flander's Interaction Analysis.

Rubrics

In education terminology, **Rubric** means a scoring guide, used to evaluate the quality of student's constructed responses. Usually, rubrics contain evaluative criteria, quality definition for those criteria at particular levels of achievement and a scoring strategy. They are often presented in table format and can be used by teachers, when marking and by students, when planning their work. The main purpose of rubrics is to assess performance. The genius of rubrics is that they are descriptive and not evaluative. Rubrics give structure to observations. Matching the observations of a student's work to the descriptions in the rubric averts the rush to judgement that can occur in classroom evaluation situations. Effective rubrics have appropriate criteria and well-written description of performance.

Wiggins said that a rubric contains a scale of possible points, to be assigned in scoring on a continum of quality. High numbers are usually assigned to the best performances. Moreover, a rubric provides descriptors, for each level of performance, to enable more reliable and unbiased scoring. Rubric's assessment is itself valid and reliable, when proper descriptors are formulated because descriptors contain criteria, which often refer to standards.

According to **Arthur and McTighe**, "Rubric is a set of general criteria, used to evaluate a student's performance, in a given outcome area". Rubrics consist of fixed measurment scale and list of criteria that describes the characteristics of product and performance for each score point.

Types of Rubrics

Rubrics for scoring constructed responses have **two** general categories *i.e.* analytic scoring rubrics and holistic scoring rubrics.

They can be explained as follows:

Analytic Scoring Rubric It requires that the teacher identifies the important aspect of a good solution and then assign points to each aspect.

Holistic Scoring Rubric It requires that the teachers must determine the overall quality of the constructed response.

According to **Nikto** (1996), the holistic scoring rubric could be extended to include comments and this creates another rubric type as annotated holistic rubric. The holistic rubric rates or scores the product or the process as a whole, without first scoring parts or components, separately. The analytic rubric rate or score separate parts or characteristics of the product or the process first and then sum these part scores to obtain a total score.

In an annotated holistic scoring rubric, rater uses a holistic rating first and then they rate or describe as few characteristics that are strengths and weaknesses, to support their holistic ratings. Using an analytic scoring rubric is more time consuming task, since the rater has to look for and separately rate each component of a performance.

Rubrics can also help teachers, analyse and describe student's responses to complex tasks and determine student's level of proficiency. Rubrics give students more specific criteria detailing, what is expected and what constitutes a complete response.

According to **Meier** (2006), in a study reported by him, in which a rubric for self-assess and peer-assess, mathematical problem-solving, where middle school teachers used rubrics on 8th grade students, to score non-traditional mathematical tasks. The teachers used analytic scoring rubrics that outlined three categories *i.e.* mathematical knowledge, strategic knowledge and explanation. Using rubrics, have some benefits for providing feedback, grading or assessing, namely rubrics create a focus on instruction and learning. It improves the clarity of the feedback, provided to students, students get clear description of their strengths and weaknesses.

Rubric characterises the desired results/products of student's work, objectively. They give students, clear instruction about the instructor's expectations for an assignment. Students can use rubrics to assess their own work, they can have a better idea about whether they are meeting expectations, before they submit their work for formal evaluation or thus, rubrics develop competence in self-evaluation. It engages students in the learning process, when students can describe exactly what is expected of them, they may be more strongly motivated to work to meet the expectations.

Steps for Constructing Rubrics

A good rubric needs to be designed with care and precision, in order to truly help teachers, distribute and receive the expected work. The following six steps will help you, when you decide to use a rubric for assessing an essay, a project, group work, or any other task that does not have a clear right or wrong answer.

They are

Step 1 : Define Your Goal

Before you can create a rubric, you need to decide the type of rubric you would like to use, and that will largely be determined by your goals for the assessment.

Ask yourself the following questions

- How detailed do I want my feedback to be?
- How will I break down my expectations for this project?
- Are all of the tasks equally important?
- How do I want to assess performance?
- What standards must the students hit, in order to achieve acceptable or exceptional performance?
- Do I want to give one final grade on the project or a cluster of smaller grades, based on several criterias?
- Am I grading, based on the work or on participation? or Am I grading on both?
- Once you've figured out, how detailed you'd like the rubric to be and the goals you are trying to reach, you can choose a type of rubric.

Step 2 : Choose a Rubric Type

Although, there are many variations of rubrics, it can be helpful to at least have a standard set to help you decide where to start. Here are two types of rubrics, that are widely used in teaching as defined by DePaul, University's Graduate in Educational Department.

The **analytic rubric** is the standard grid rubric that many teachers routinely use to assess students' work. This is the optimal rubric for providing clear and detailed feedback. With an analytic rubric, criteria for the students' work is listed in the left column and performance levels are listed across the top. The squares inside the grid will typically contain the specs for each level.

A rubric for an essay, for example, might contain criteria like organisation, support, and focus and may contain performance levels like exceptional, satisfactory, developing and unsatisfactory. The performance levels are typically, given percentage points or letter grades and a final grade is typically calculated at the end. The scoring rubrics for the ACT and SAT are designed this way, although when students take them, they will receive a holistic score.

The holistic rubric is much easier to create, but much more difficult to use accurately. Typically, a teacher provides a series of letter grades or a range of numbers (1-4 or 1-6, for example) and then assigns expectations for each of those scores. When grading, the teacher matches the student's work in it's entirely to a single description on the scale. This is useful for grading multiple essays, but it does not leave room for detailed feedback on student's work.

Step 3 : Determine Your Criteria

This is where the learning objectives for your unit or course come into play. Here, you'll need to brainstorm a list of knowledge and skills, you would like to assess for the project. Group them, according to similarities and get rid of anything that is not absolutely critical. A rubric with too much criteria is difficult to use. Try to stick with 4-7 specific subjects, for which you'll be able to create an unambiguous, measurable expectations in the performance levels. You'll want to be able to spot the criteria, quickly while grading and be able to explain them, quickly when instructing your students. In an analytic rubric, the criteria are typically listed along the left column.

Step 4 : Create Your Performance Levels

Once you have determined the broad levels you would like students to demonstrate mastery of, you will need to figure out what type of scores you will assign based on each level of mastery. Most rating scales include between three and five levels. Some teachers use a combination of numbers and labels like (4) Exceptional, (3) Satisfactory, etc, while other teachers simply assign numbers, percentages, letter grades or any combination of the three for each level. You can arrange them from highest to lowest or lowest to highest as long as your levels are organised and easy to understand.

Step 5 : Write Descriptors for Each Level of Your Rubric

This is probably your most difficult step in creating a rubric. Here, you will need to write short statements of your expectations, underneath each performance level for every single criteria. The descriptions should be specific and measurable. The language should be parallel to help with student's comprehension and the degree to which the standards are met should be explained.

Step 6 : Revise Your Rubric

After creating the descriptive language for all of the levels (making sure it is parallel, specific and measurable), you need to go back through and limit your rubric to a single page. Too many parameters will be difficult to assess at once, and may an ineffective way to assess students' mastery of a specific standard.

Consider the effectiveness of the rubric, asking for student's understanding and co-teacher's feedback, before moving forward. Do not be afraid to revise as necessary. It may even be helpful to grade a sample project, in order to gauge the effectiveness of your rubric. You can always adjust the rubric, if need before handing it out, but once it is distributed, it will difficult to retract.

Before creating the rubric grid, a tester needs to

- build a full range of skills and knowledge with clear indication of each level of performance.
- plan them in a grid.
- share the rubric with students.
- make it visible at all times on a bulletin board or distributed in a handout, to direct attention to the key concepts and standards, students must meet.
- finally, apply it and consider if any revision or modification is required to apply to more activities.

EXAM BASED QUESTIONS

1 Interaction Analysis category system in education, for increasing the teacher's effectiveness, was developed by

(a) Amindon and Semon
(b) Flander
(c) Rayon
(d) Richard Over

2 Flander's Interaction Analysis technique is used for modifying and improving

(a) non-verbal behaviour
(b) verbal behaviour
(c) Both (a) and (b)
(d) None of these

3 While using the Flander's Interaction Analysis, the focus is on

(a) Class climate (b) Learner's behaviour
(c) Teacher's behaviour (d) Class interaction

4 The technique for improving teachers' efficiency in classroom teaching is

(a) simulation technique (b) micro-teaching
(c) interaction analysis (d) action research

5 Which of the following statement(s) is/are not true?

(a) Method of the behaviour ratios, provides qualitative analysis of teacher's behaviour.
(b) Method of interpretation categories, provides qualitative analysis of teacher behaviour.
(c) For the recording of the classroom events, the observer must memorise the category number, in relation to the compare behaviour.
(d) Silence or confusion is given the category or code number 10, for the recording of classrooms events in Flander's system.

6 In Flander's Interaction Analysis, if there is shifting from one category to another are found frequently, it represents

(a) verbal and non-verbal communication is more flexible
(b) confusion is more in the classroom
(c) students are more active
(d) teacher is inactive in the class

7 Flander's Interaction Analysis System was developed by

(a) Ned (b) Lewin and others
(c) Perkins (d) Haggerty

8 In FIAS system, the entire classroom's interaction is put into how many categories?

(a) One (b) Two (c) Three (d) Four

9 The use of Flander's Interaction Analysis is beneficial in terms of ....

(a) time (b) labour (c) money (d) All of these

10 "Modification of teacher's classroom's behaviour through feedback is possible, though how much can change occur and more knowledge relating to the permanence of these changes will require further research". Who said this?

(a) Keith Davis (b) Flanders
(c) Lewin (d) Perkins

11 Which of the following statement(s), regarding FIAS is/are incorrect?

(a) It supplements the training techniques, like micro and team teachers.
(b) It helps to determine classroom climate.
(c) It hardly takes into consideration, classroom's interaction, in the form of student-student interaction.
(d) It is used as an observation technique, in teacher education programme.

12 .... consist of seven categories, the first four categories belongs to indirect influence and the latter three to direct influence.

(a) Pupil's talk (b) Silence/confusion
(c) Teacher's talk (d) Pupil's talk initiation

13 Who among the following has developed the categories for non-verbal communication, by incorporating ten category system?

(a) Flander (b) Galloway
(c) Anderson (d) Keith Davis

14 Flander's Instruction Analysis is not concerned primarily with

(a) verbal behaviour
(b) non-verbal behaviour
(c) direct behaviour
(d) Both (b) and (c)

15 Indirect influence is sub-divided into

(a) accepting feeling
(b) accepting and using ideas
(c) asking questions and praising or encouraging
(d) All of the above

16 In Galloway's System of Observation, the encouraging and restricting are the part of

(a) direct interaction (b) verbal interaction
(c) indirect interaction (d) non-verbal interaction

17 Charles M Galloway has used which of the following components?

(a) Formal and informal
(b) Direct and indirect
(c) Encouraging and restricting
(d) Both (a) and (c)

18 Through which of the following means, we express our feelings, pain, pleasure, joy, sorrow, anger, pity and other emotions?

(a) Verbal communication
(b) Written communication
(c) Oral communication
(d) Non-verbal communication

19 Appearance, facial expressions and voice inflection are part of

(a) verbal communication
(b) written communication
(c) non-verbal communication
(d) telephone communication

20 Which of the following is not classified under class interaction by Galloway?

(a) Indirect (b) Direct
(c) Encouraging (d) Informal

21 .... developed the categories for non-verbal communication, by incorporating Flander's Ten Category System.

(a) H.V. Perkins (b) Galloway
(c) Raths (d) Anderson

22 Galloway's verbal interaction involves which of the following categories.

(a) uses student's ideas
(b) criticising or justifying authority
(c) receptive or inattentive
(d) accept student's feelings

23 The matrix table consists of

(a) 5 rows and 5 columns
(b) 10 rows and 10 columns
(c) 9 rows and 9 columns
(d) 12 rows and 12 columns

24 "Statements intended to change pupil's behaviour, from non-acceptable pattern, pointing someone out stating, why the teacher is doing and what he is doing". This statement falls under which category of Flander's Interaction Analysis?

(a) Lecturing
(b) Pupil's talk response
(c) Criticising or justifying authority
(d) Pupil's talk initiation

25 Which of the following comes between encoding and decoding?

(a) Channel (b) Feedback
(c) Message (d) Both (a) and (b)

26 Which of the following does not falls under verbal category, according to Galloway's System of Classroom's Observation?

(a) Acceptance or indifference
(b) Silence or confusion
(c) Student's talk (Response)
(d) Student's talk (Initiation)

27 .... a teacher needs to be evaluated in terms of the nature of the quality of his efforts made, for the realisation of the set teaching learning objectives.

(a) Product criteria
(b) Process criteria
(c) Presage criteria
(d) None of the above

28 When it can be said that, the judge is using process criteria?

(a) When the teacher's evaluation is based upon classroom's behaviour, either the teachers' behaviour, his student's behaviour or the inter-play of teacher-student's behaviour.
(b) Under this, the evaluation of teacher's work must be made through the nature of the end results of his efforts.
(c) It tries to focus on the evaluation of the total makeup, nature, qualities and characteristics, of that very source (the teacher) responsible for carrying not both the means and the ends through his efforts.
(d) All of the above

29 .... criteri as are at best, indirect measure of teacher's effectiveness and are normally choosen because they are related to and therefore, predict either process or product criteria.
(a) Presage
(b) Norm referenced
(c) Product
(d) Process

30 The word 'rubric' is derived from .... word for 'red'.
(a) Greek
(b) Latin
(c) Both (a) and (b)
(d) Hebrew

31 A .... rubric is an attempt to communicate expectations of quality around a task.
(a) scoring (b) grading
(c) essay (d) holistic

32 An analytic rubric is used when
(a) you want detailed feedback.
(b) you want to assess complicated skills and products.
(c) you want to see relative strength and weakness.
(d) All of the above

33 Match the following.

Column I (Types of Rubric)	Column II (Advantages)
A. Holistic	1. More reliable assessment of performance on the task.
B. Analytic	2. Can use same rubric across different tasks.
C. Task specific	3. Given more detailed feedback.
D. General	4. Quick scoring provides an overview of student's achievement.

Codes

	A	B	C	D
(a)	4	3	1	2
(b)	1	2	3	4
(c)	4	2	1	3
(d)	3	4	2	1

34 A holistic rating scale assesses
(a) several dimensions together.
(b) views the final product as a set of inter-related tasks, contributing to the whole.
(c) one score provides an overall impression of ability on any given product.
(d) All of the above

35 A carefully designed rubric benefits to
(a) help instructors more clearly, in identifying strengths and weaknesses, across an entire class and adjust their instruction appropriately.
(b) helps to ensure consistency, across time and grades.
(c) reduce the uncertainty, which can accompany grading.
(d) All of the above

36 Which of the following statement(s) is/are incorrect with regard to the advantage(s) of rubric?
(a) It helps in communicating between faculty and students.
(b) Students can understand better, the rationale and the reason for grades.
(c) Defining the correct set of criteria, to define performance can be complex.
(d) Helps to improve student's performance because they know what to focus on.

37 Rubrics are sometimes called
(a) criteria sheets (b) grading schemes
(c) scoring guides (d) All of these

38 Which of the following statement(s), regarding limitations of Interaction Analysis technique, is correct?
(a) There is no balance in the teacher and pupil's categories.
(b) It records action of teachers and pupil, but does not encode their reactions.
(c) Teaching effectiveness is concerned with force and intensity of teaching events.
(d) All of the above

39 Galloway's classroom interaction can be classified into .... components.
(a) five (b) two (c) four (d) seven

40 A rubric is used for assessing ....
(a) an essay (b) a project
(c) group work (d) All of these

41 Before creating the rubric grid, the tester needs to
(a) build a full range of skills and knowledge with clear indication of each level of performance.
(b) plan them is a grid.
(c) share the rubric with students.
(d) All of the above

42 **Statement I** Rubrics engage students into learning process.
Statement II Students can use a rubric to assess their own work.
Choose the correct option.
(a) Both the statements, I and II are correct
(b) Both the statements, I and II are incorrect
(c) Only statement I is true
(d) Only statement II is true

43 **Statement I** In matrix construction, one is to make sure that the entries begin and end with same number.
Statement II It is customary to add 10 to the beginning and the end of the series, it is not already present.
Choose the correct option.
(a) Statement I is correct.
(b) Both statements, I and II are correct.
(c) Statement II is incorrect.
(d) Both statements, I and II are incorrect.

44 **Statement I** The criteria neither trys to evaluate, nor the ends of teaching-learning process.

Statement II Under this criteria, the evaluation of the teacher can be made by passing judgement over the gains achieved, in terms of growth and development.

Choose the correct option.

(a) Both statements, I and II are correct
(b) Statement I is incorrect
(c) Statement, I is correct
(d) Both statements I and II are incorrect

45 **Statement I** Give diagnostic information to teacher.

Statement II Give formative feedback to students.

Choose the correct option.

(a) Only statement I is correct
(b) Both the statements, I and II are correct
(c) Both the statements, I and II are incorrect
(d) Only statement II is correct

Directions (Q. Nos. 46-50) *Two statements are given below, one labelled as Assertion (A) and other labelled as Reason (R). Choose the correct code from the following.*

Codes

(a) Both A and R are true and R is the correct explanation of A
(b) Both A and R are true, but R is not the correct explanation of A
(c) A is true, but R is false
(d) A is false, but R is true

46 **Assertion** (A) Interaction analysis technique does not provide any information about the quality of content.

Reason (R) It is content free technique of observation. It confines only to verbal communication of teaching.

47 **Assertion** (A) Galloway has developed the categories for non-verbal communication, by incorporating Flander's Ten Category System.

Reason (R) His system of observation is the combination of both verbal and non-verbal or class room communication, as a whole.

48 **Assertion** (A) Galloway has used direct-indirect and encouraging-restricting components.

Reason (R) His system of classroom's observation involves verbal and non-verbal interaction.

49 **Assertion** (A) A good rubric must have a list of specific criteria to be related.

Reason (R) The rubric should be unidimensional, so that students and raters know exactly what the expectations are.

50 **Assertion** (A) Rubrics help elementary school teachers so much, because they can be targeted to meet young children's needs.

Reason (R) They can also improve student's interests and performances.

51 Arrange the following steps for constructing rubrics in a sequential order:

1. Choose a Rubric type.
2. Define your goal.
3. Revise your rubric.
4. Determine your criteria.
5. Create your performance levels.
6. Descriptors for each level of your rubric.

Codes

(a) 1, 2, 3, 5, 4, 6 (b) 2, 1, 4, 5, 6, 3
(c) 3, 2, 4, 5, 1, 6 (d) 6, 5, 4, 3, 2, 1

ANSWERS

1 *(b)*	2 *(b)*	3 *(c)*	4 *(c)*	5 *(b)*	6 *(a)*	7 *(a)*	8 *(c)*	9 *(d)*	10 *(b)*
11 *(c)*	12 *(c)*	13 *(a)*	14 *(b)*	15 *(b)*	16 *(b)*	17 *(d)*	18 *(a)*	19 *(d)*	20 *(d)*
21 *(c)*	22 *(c)*	23 *(b)*	24 *(c)*	25 *(d)*	26 *(a)*	27 *(b)*	28 *(a)*	29 *(a)*	30 *(b)*
31 *(a)*	32 *(d)*	33 *(a)*	34 *(d)*	35 *(d)*	36 *(c)*	37 *(d)*	38 *(d)*	39 *(c)*	40 *(d)*
41 *(d)*	42 *(a)*	43 *(b)*	44 *(a)*	45 *(b)*	46 *(a)*	47 *(a)*	48 *(c)*	49 *(b)*	50 *(c)*
51 *(b)*									

CHAPTER 30

Educational Technology (ET) as a Discipline

Educational Technology is a systematic approach to designing and evaluating learning and teaching methods and methodologies. It includes informal technology, communication technology and instructional technology.

Origin of Educational Technology

The term 'Educational Technology' is used to describe the technological enhancement and advancement in the education sector. The subject deals with identifying the most suitable, appropriate and developed technology for serving the educational needs and purposes of the students. There has been a continuous shift with the usage of technology for improving the processes and products of education in different periods of human history and civilisation. *The process can be summarised as follows:*

Early Period In the early period, when writing was unknown, the method of teaching was used that of verbal presentation where students used to memorise. The oral teaching tradition was prevalent at that time, maintained by the ancient sages in the 'Gurukuls' of our country that may be cited as a testimony for the use of technology in the field of teaching and learning.

Medieval Period The next breakthrough in the field of teaching and learning was the advent of writing as the means of learning and communication. Different writing technology started emerging like writing on the leaves and tree-trunks, engraving on the metals and rocks, and then the use of some type of paper and ink. This all provided a great impetus in the field of teaching and learning.

Modern Period Then the production and use of the instructional material like chalks, blackboards, pictures, charts, models, maps, diagrams and other graphic materials came into existence and took its next leap in helping the cause of teaching and learning. The use of printing technology also came under this phase.

After Industrialisation Then, with the development of industries, various scientific instruments, mass media and educational materials were used. This led to

In this Chapter

the usage of hardware and software such as radio, television, tape recorder, films, transparency, etc. in the field of education.

Present Scenario Later on, the existence of system approach, micro-teaching, interaction analysis and computer assisted instruction added another dimension to the meaning and concept of an educational technology.

Meaning and Definitions of Educational Technology

It is the systematic application of science and technology which utilises all human and non-human resources to achieve an educational objectives. It plays an effective role in communication between teachers and students. It provides technical guidance and solution to the problems of education and efficiency in teaching and learning.

According to **Shiv K Mitra**, "Educational Technology can be conceived as a science of techniques and methods by which educational goals could be realised".

According to **D Unwin**, "Educational Technology is concerned with applications of modern skills and techniques to fulfill the requirements of education and training. This includes the facilitation of learning by manipulation of media and methods, and the control of environment in so far, as this reflects on learning".

According to **I K Davies**, "Educational Technology is concerned with the problems of an education and training context and it is characterised by the disciplined and systematic approach to an organisation of resources for learning".

According to **Scottish Council for Educational Technology**, "Educational Technology is a systematic approach for designing and evaluating learning and teaching methods and methodologies and to the application and exploitation of media and the current knowledge of communication techniques in an education, both formal and informal".

Thus, the main role of Educational Technology is to enhance the teaching and learning process. Today's educational technology is the result of the integration of the technological devices with the newly explored psychological principles of learning and teaching.

Characteristics of Educational Technology

- It is the systematic application of scientific principles.
- It emphasises on the continuous development of methods and techniques for effective teaching.
- It uses audio-visual aids for direct teaching and learning.
- It involves the use of equipments and electronics such as projectors, tape-recorders, radio and television, hardware and software.
- It includes informal technology, communication technology and instructional technology.

Objectives of Educational Technology

- To identify an educational needs and aspirations of the community.
- To gauge the aim, structure and strategies of an education.
- To develop a curriculum with correspondence to science, art and human values.
- To develop methods to improve the process of teaching and learning.
- To identify the major issues with an educational system and means and ways to tackle those.
- To help the neglected section of the community to come under the preview of an education.
- To analyse educational needs of the students.
- To plan teaching strategies.
- To evaluate the effectiveness of the classroom teaching.
- To provide feedback to the teachers and students to bring any modification in the education process.

Significance of Educational Technology

- It sets the educational goals and objectives by identification of educational needs and aspirations of the community.
- It helps in the development of curriculum by describing the ways and means for selecting a suitable learning experience.
- It tries to develop teaching and learning material like programmed learning material, computed assisted software and instructional material like programmed learning material, computer assisted learning material, mass media instructional material, etc.
- It describes the ways and means of discovering, selecting and developing tactics of teaching.
- It is also concerned with the development, selection and use of the appropriate audio-visual aids.
- It considers education as a system, operating in a systematic and scientific way as it incluces topics dealing with the theory and principles of system approach.
- It provides appropriate feedback to the learners as well as teachers for bringing necessary improvements. Educational technology discuses the means and ways for a suitable evaluation technique.

Scope of Educational Technology

Educational Technology is a wide concept. It not only includes the optimum utilisation of all human and non-human resources but also *includes the below mentioned technologies*

Information Technology It is the use of systems (computers and telecommunications) as a medium for achieving educational objectives.

Communication Technology It is the transfer of information that must be understood from one person to another.

Information and Communication Technology It is defined as the diverse set of technological tools and resources used to communicate and to create, disseminate store and to manage information.

Instructional Technology It implies a network of techniques or knowledge of instructions to accomplish certain set of learning objectives.

Educational Technology as a Discipline

The term 'Educational Technology' involves many disciplines and demands specialisation and understanding of the planning, processing and products of education. The scope of educational technology is conceived by different individuals differently, for example, persons dealing with audio-visual aids, educational technology is confined to the use of audio-visual aids, while who are working in mass media emphasise the importance of hardware, software and communication technology. Educational Technology exists in a fragmented ways not only in India but also globally, there is a significant diversification in terms of objectives, topics and coverage of contents. However, a uniform concept and meaning of Educational Technology is being developed at the global level.

Let us discuss various disciplines of Educational Technology in detail

Information Technology

Information Technology refers to the process of generating information with the use of machines and technologies. It includes gathering, organising, storing, publishing and using the information in the form of sound, picture, graphic text, number through the use of computer. It deals with the use of electronic computers and computer softwares to convert, store, protect, process, transmit and securely retrieve an information.

In the field of teaching and learning, these new and emerging technologies challenge the traditional method of teaching. Information technology, while an important area of study in its own, is having a major impact accross all the educational curriculum.

According to **Attaran**, "It is defined as the capabilities offered to organisations by computers, software applications, and telecommunications to deliver data, information and knowledge to an individuals and processes".

According to **Information Technology Association of America** (ITAA), "It is defined as the study, design, development, implementation, support or management of computer-based information systems, particularly software applications and computer hardware".

According to **Tan et al**, "It is defined as the information and communication technologies tools including computer network, software and hardware required for internet connection".

Communication Technology

It refers to the process of communicating information with the help of different equipments, programs and hardware and software systems.

It involves computer capabilities that facilitates exchange of information between an individuals. It plays an important role in education. It helps in an immediate decision making and can be reached in any part of the world. In the process of teaching and learning, communicational technology has made many advances and it is emerging with new technologies and inventions.

According to **Oxford Dictionary**, "The technology associated with data communication refers to communication technology".

Information and Communication Technology

Information and Communication Technologies (ICT) are those technologies which enable us to create, collect, consolidate, communicate, manage and process information in multimedia and various digital formats by using telecommunication techniques. It consists of hardware, software, network media, computers, internet, broadcasting technologies, etc.

In an education sector, it has resulted in enormous benefits for students as well as teachers, the teaching-learning process has become more meaningful and productive. It has enhanced the whole teaching and learning environment.

According to **UNESCO**, it is defined as "The scientific, technological and engineering disciplines and the management techniques used to handle transmit information with men and machines".

According to **Digital Video Technical Glossary**, "It is the computing and communications facilities and features that supports teaching, learning and a range of activities in education".

According to **UK National Curriculum**, "It is used as the technology to handle information and aid communication".

According to **IBM Glossary**, "It is the use of computer based information systems and communication system to process, transmit and store data and information".

According to **Bruer**, "It is defined as learners must rise above the rote, factual level to begin to think critically and creatively".

Origin and Growth of ICT

The process of collecting information and communicating it, is as old as the human civilisation itself. During early times, the information was stored in the memory and transmitted orally. The invention of paper and ink must be regarded as the first revolution in the field of Information and Communication Technology.

As it can be traced back when humans started to use objects to communicate and deliver their message to one another.

So, the history of Information and Communication Technology can be divided into four phases

Phase I (1450 BCE - 1450 CE)

- The pictograms and words curved in rocks were used as a mean of communication during this time. e.g. Sumerian Pictogram (dated back 3100 BCE).
- Paper from papyrus plants, writing on the leaves and tree trunks was widely used.
- These papers were then combined to gather to make books and eventually, the storage place of these books came up as library.
- China-Abacus was created in this period in 500 BC.
- Printed book in 1438, by German inventor Johannes Gutenberg, movable type, the 'forty-two-line' Bible was created.

Phase II (1450 to 1840)

- This phase marked as a link between the last and the first phase.
- The interest in automating and speeding up numerical calculations grew during this time.
- Pascaline in 1645 (calculator), by Blaise Pascal.
- Telegraph is 1837, by SFB Morse of USA.
- Computer concept (father of computer) in 1837, by Charles Babbage.

Phase III (1840-1940)

- The use of electricity for information handling and transfer emerged.
- Photography in 1849, by a Frenchman LGM Daguerre and an Englishman WHF Talbot.
- Telephone was invented in 1876, by Alexander Graham Bell of Scotland.
- Radio by G Marconi of Italy in 1895.
- Photostat in 1900, by Abbe Rene Graftin of France.
- Xerography in 1938, by Chester F Carlson of USA.
- Micrography in 1940, by JBD Ancer and Frenchman Rene Dagran.
- Television in 1925, by J.L. Baird.

Phase IV (1940 - Present)

- This phase came up with the advent of electronic devices.
- Development of communication satellites (Sputnik was the first satellite launched by USSR on 4th October, 1957) and Facsimile (Fax) technology in 20th century.
- Laser technology in 1960, by Theodore Maiman of USA.
- Magnetic video camera, video disc and computer developed in 20th century.
- Electronic Numerical Integrator and Computer (ENIAC), an electronic general purpose computer, developed in 1945.

The applications of Information and Communication Technology did not remain limited to certain fields of science and industry, but gradually got broadened to other fields such as banking, management, offices, police and military establishment and education. As a result, we use it in teaching and learning and also in other forms of an education. Thus, utilising its power as an effective medium for formal and non-formal education.

Information and Communication Technology in Education (Channels and Medium)

In an education it is used as a combination of hardware and software, media and delivery systems. *Some of the medium through which an education can be transmitted are mentioned below*

- Audio-visual hardware (radio, television, slide projector, tape recorder and teaching machine).
- Digital video camera.
- Multi-media Personal Computer (PC), laptop and notebook.
- Application softwares such as word processing spreadsheets, power point simulation and speed recognition.
- Multi-media projector (LCD or DLP) to communicate to larger group.

- Local Area Network (LAN), Metropolitan Area Network (MAN) and Wide Area Network (WAN).
- Multi-media PC/laptop with video card and web camera or digital video camera.
- Computer data base and data processing mechanism, CD ROM and DVD.
- Digital libraries.
- E-mail, internet and World Wide Web (WWW).
- Hypermedia and hypertext resources.
- Video text, tele-text, interactive video text, Interactive Video Disk (IVD) and Interactive Remote Instruction (IRI)
- Computer mediated conferencing video and audio conferencing.
- Virtual classroom and virtual reality.

Advantages of ICT

Advantages of ICT are described below

For Students

- It offers student centered learning.
- Provides greater opportunity for personal communication and collaboration with teachers.
- Creates enthusiasm and motivation for learning.
- Provides online educational materials to distant learners.
- Provides learners with additional resources.
- Easy access to quality educational material for learners.
- It encourages independent and active learning.
- It satisfies their urge of curiosity, inventiveness, etc.
- It brings precision, speed and accuracy in receiving, transforming and communicating the required information.
- Students become acquainted and trained for handling electronic appliances, software and techniques.

For Teachers

- Provides teachers with new source of information and knowledge.
- It helps them in their task of teaching.
- They are able to acquire teaching material and techniques in the form of audio-visual material, equipment and electronic and telecommunication media.
- It provides them relief as their students use various ICT's resources for self-learning, for example, programmed learning material, self-learning modules, teaching machines and computers.

Disadvantages of ICT

- Most of the schools do not possess the required facility and infrastructure for the implementation of ICT as they are not in a position to afford the purchase, maintenance and other expenditure involved in its use.
- Various head of institutions and teachers tend to ignore the, applications and advantages of ICT's.
- The teachers offer fear of losing their dominance over the teaching and learning activities.
- The teachers want to stick over the broadcast model of teaching rather than the interactive model (use of ICT).
- Many students are not in favour of this transition due to fear of cumbersome processes involved in independent or interactive learning methods.
- There is a lack of knowledge, skills, attitude and interest on the part of teachers for the utilisation of ICT.
- The school authorities and administrative department is also resistant to adopt the ICT in school education.

Instructional Technology

It is defined as a sub-system of educational technology which helps the instructor or the learner himself as a part of his self-learning or auto instruction by determining the media, methods and material for the realisation of the stipulated instructional objectives in a given teaching and learning situation.

Thus, in simple terms, it is a type of technology meant for bringing improvement in the instructional process. The term 'instruction' stands for a certain type of command meant for getting some specific information, knowledge and understanding about a thing, system or process.

It makes the learner independent in his learning task and it provides an appropriate stimuli to the learner to produce certain type of responses for making learning more effective. It determines the media, methods and materials required for attaining instructional objectives.

According to **Smalding, L Lowther & Rusell**, "It is defined as the integration of teacher and student use and knowledge of tools and techniques to improve student learning".

Instructional Technology in Education (Channels and Medium)

- Attendance sheets
- Handouts and presentations
- Media/Technology (videos, podcasts, computer, software tools)
- Graphic organisers
- Posters
- Charts/Flip chart
- Instructional guides

- Checklists and case studies
- Quizzes
- Pictures, graphs, bulletin boards, diagrams
- Models, slides

Advantages of Instructional Technology

- It helps students to clarify their concepts and relationships.
- It encourages the application of knowledge and skills.
- It helps tc stimulate learner's interest.
- It engages learners with relevent content (visual, test, audio, etc).
- It brings out attention, relevance, confidence and satisfactions among students.

Limitations of Instructional Technology

- The use of technology requires skill, knowledge, coordination, management and organisational expertise which the educational bureaucracies have been unable to commit.
- Technology costs too much and part of this cost is the high level of expertise needed to apply it.
- The Hardware and Software have not yet reached the required level of perfection.
- High technology substitutes machines for humans.

Applications of ET in Education System

Educational Technology can be applied in the education system in the following manner

Formal Education

Formal education is basically full time institutional activity that is uniform and subject oriented in a hierarchal structure. It is often carried for certificate, degree or diploma.

It has following characteristics :

- It gives technical and professional training.
- It works on full time education.
- It includes a variety of specialised programmes.
- It runs from primary schools to universities.
- It is a sequential graded education system.

Applications of Educational Technology in the Formal Education

In present scenario, teachers are actively engaged in the usage of technology to display information, charts and to monitor and engage students. In order to be a part in this competitive world, students must have access to technology.

Visual Technology Classrooms are equiped with smart boards. This interactive whiteboards allow different media (photos, documents, etc.) to be displayed by projector which enhances teaching and learning experience. It enables learners an opportunity to share and participate in the instructional process. It also gives access to online information.

Computer Technology using computers in education brings significant change in teaching and learning process. Learners can access global libraries and internet. It helps in huge and organised storage of information, quick communication, typing and publishing papers with help of word processing. Internet Technology The internet technology can provide infinite amount of useful and relevant information. Learners can have an easy access to quality education and fast update of any information.

Technology Used

Projectors A projector is an output device that takes images generated by a computer and reproduce them by projection on to a screen, wall or another surface. In a classroom, projector is hooked up to teacher's laptop and projects the screen from the laptop to the white board of the classroom. A word document, powerpoint presention, educational videos can be projected.

Different types of technologies used are as follows

SMART Technologies SMART technologies are now being widely used for the teacher learner interaction in the classroom using computers. SMART boards is an interactive white board that allows the teacher to display any image from a laptop and digitally draws on that image as well. Graphs and tables are available templates in SMART boards. It can store lessons as well. It has immense benefits in the field of education.

Mimio Boards They are similar to white boards. It allows the teachers to manipulate computer functions on the white board in front of the room. The teacher uses a special pen that acts like a mouse which helps him/her to search through websites, graphs and other lessons.

Classroom PCs Some learners are lucky to have an individual PCs in the classroom. If every student has his/her own laptop, a teacher can allow them to research and explore on their own. PCs can store student's work efficiently rather carrying bulky encyclopedias and dictionaries, they can access the internet on their own. A paperless world in the classroom can be organised as well as environmental friendly.

SMART Classroom Smart classrooms are technology enhanced classrooms that foster opportunities for teaching and learning by integrating learning technology such as computers, softwares, audience responses, assistive listening devices, networking and audio-visual capabilities.

Non-Formal Education

Non-formal education is outside scope of formal system for providing education. It includes flexible curriculum, methodology which adapts according to the needs and interests of the students. Time is not a constraint here. It includes two processes, namely '**open learning**' and '**distance learning**'.

It has following characteristics

- It is flexible and works according to student's choice.
- It is fully learner oriented.
- It is non-authoritarian.
- It is built on learner-participation.
- It enhances human potential.

Applications of Educational Technology in the Non-Formal Education

Non-formal education includes open and distance learning where both give a broad access to education. In this type of education, either the lessons are broadcast or lessons are conducted by correspondence without the student needs to attend a school or college. The usage of an educational technology, thus, hold an immense importance in the effectively working of the non-formal educational system.

Computer Assisted Learning (CAL) It aims to provide interactive instruction with wide range of computer-based packages. CAL runs from a CD or floppy disk or over a local network, so the constraint of the internet may not apply. It offers more advanced, interactive, multimedia learning experience. CAL has been an integral part of the curriculum till date.

Internet Technologies The arrival of the internet has made communication between machines easier. E-mail and the world wide web are the forerunner. Web pages provides authoring access to anybody. Internet technology covers a wide range of resources such as video conferencing, virtual learning environments and e-learning technologies, etc.

Technology Used

Digital Learning Resources It means placing word document or powerpoint presentations on the web for students to download and print.

Computer Mediated Communication (CMC) It is defined as any means in which individuals can talk to each other.

It can be of two types

Synchronous It is a mode of online delivery where exchange takes place in 'real time'. It requires a timetable to be organised. It includes telephone, video conferencing, web conferencing, audio conferencing, internet chat.

Asynchronous In this mode, messages are posted up at any time and read and responded to, by others at a time which suits them. It includes audio cassette, e-mail, message board forums, print materials, voice mail/fax, videocassette, broadcast video, radio, CD-ROM.

Computer Assissted Assessment (CAA) It is the process of utilising computing technologies for accessing student's work. It includes accessing and providing feedback of teacher's lesson. It is an opportunity to provide timely response to student progress. The use of CAA for self-diagnosis and self assessment is quick to set up and if it is used wisely, it can provide valuable feedback.

Virtual Learning Environment (VLE) It is a set of teaching and learning tools designed to enhance a student's learning experience with the use of computer and internet. It includes curricular mapping, student tracking, online support for both teacher and student, electronic communication and internet links. The users of VLE are assigned a teacher ID or a student ID.

e-learning It refers to a course, program or degree delivered online. The term 'e-learning' is also used to describe 'distance learning', where a learner enjoys an interactive session where he/she can communicate with teachers, professors or students in the class. It can also be delivered live. E-learning has become a successful method of the training and education.

Informal Education

Informal education covers every aspect of learning that doesn't take place in a normal school setting. It is truly a lifelong process whereby every individual acquires attitudes, values and skills and knowledge from daily experiences or resources in his/her environment *i.e.* family, neighbours, from work and play, from technology, etc.

It has following characteristics

- It is determined by an individual.
- There is no existence of mentor, coach or teacher.
- It is an unstructured activity.
- The learner learns from real-world experiences.
- Its objectives are more meaningful.
- It is a life long process.

Applications of Educational Technology in the Informal Education

The usage of technology in the informal education system has emerged as very crucial. If a learner wants to seek education outside of a structured curriculum, he/she can attain the knowledge through various sources like listening to radio, broadcasting or watching TV programmes on an educational theme. Students can also download e-books or visits educational video channel or download applications on mobile. Learners can also enroll in various online courses and communicate with other learners.

Technology Used

- Videos and podcasts
- Wikis, blogs and forums
- World Wide Web
- Applications
- Learning and knowledge portals
- e-books
- Social network

Inclusive Education

It is defined as "a learning environment that promotes the full personal, academic and professional development of all learners irrespective of race, class, colour, gender, disability, sexual preference, learning styles and language". All students attend and are welcomed by their neighbourhood schools to learn, contribute and participate in all aspects of the life of school.

It has following characteristics

- It provides right to education for all.
- It develops social consciousness among students.
- The student's views are listened to and taken seriously.
- It demands the participation of all students, teachers, parents and community members.
- It helps in restructuring the culture, policies and practices in schools to respond to the diversity of learners within their locality.

Applications of Educational Technology in the Inclusive Education

Technology is present in every other sphere of an educational system, it has also emerged greatly in the field of special education.

Technology is a growing epedemic in the classroom and it helps students with disabilities to work more quickly, easily and independentlly. Students in special education use i-pads to learn concepts such as counting and spelling. The technology helps students with visual problems to see the text easily.

Alternative Input Devices It allows students with disabilities to use computer and other technology easily. It includes touch screens, modified keyboards, joysticks and on-screen keyboards, etc.

Speech to Text Options It provides a learning advantage for students who have mobility problems, or those who are blind. It allows students to speak their thoughts without typing and even navigate the internet. It also consists of 'talk-back' option to let them know the potential errors.

Sensory Enhancers Some children with disabilities may need to learn differently than their peers. Instead of learning ABC and numbers, a child with language hindrance may benefit form bright pictures or colors to learn new concepts. It includes voice analysers, speech synthesisers, etc.

Screen Readers It reads out the text on the screen loudly. A student who is blind or struggling to see what is on the screen can benefit from the audio interface screen readers provides.

Technology Used

- I-pads
- Computers
- Smart Boards
- Scanners
- Wand and joysticks
- Sip and puff system
- Digital book
- Voice recognition software
- Braille embossers and refreshable Braille displays
- Screen magnifiers
- Text To Speech (TTS)
- Alternative keyboards
- Light signals
- Touch screens

Learning Theories

Learning theories explain how individuals acquire, organise and deploy skills and knowledge. *Three basic categories of learning theories are*

- Behaviourist
- Cognitive
- Constructive

Behaviourist Learning Theory

According to **Ertmer & Newby**, "Behaviourism focuses on the importance of consequences of the performances and contends that responses that are followed by reinforcement are more likely to occur in the future."

According to **Good & Brophy**, "The theory of Behaviourism concentrates on the study of overt behaviours that can be observed and measured".

It is a learning process which is a conditioned response to a stimulus. It emphasises changes in behaviour that results from stimulus response associations made by the learner.

Thus, Behaviourism uses a system in which the instructor provides a stimulus (material to be learned) and learners provide a response (evidence of learning). The knowledge exists outside the learner, *e.g.* take the maths equation $8 + 8 = ?$ The learner replies 16. The equations is the stimulus, and answer is the response.

BF Skinner introduced the 'Theory of Operant Conditioning' in Behaviourism Learning theory. It is a method of learning that occurs through rewards and punishments for behaviour.

BF Skinner

The eminent psychologist **BF Skinner** propounded the theory of operant conditioning. According to this theory, learning is based on the consequences of the responses. He emphasises on the stimulus response (S-R) behaviour.

Skinner highlighted that if an individual behaves in someway, does something or in technical sense 'Operates' on an environment, in return, environment also responds of such behaviour by rewarding or punishing it.

Skinner's research was centered around the Skinner box. A Skinner box is an experiment space that contains one or more operands, such as lever, that may be pressed by a cat. The box also contained various sources of stimuli. When a particular S-R pattern is reinforced (rewarded), an individual is conditioned to respond.

Principles and Mechanisms of Skinner's Operant Conditioning

Positive Reinforcement Behaviours that is positively reinforced will reoccur, intermittant reinforcement Vs particularly effective. For example, a verbal praise a good grade or feeling of satisfaction.

Negative Reinforcement Responses that allows escape from painful or undesirable situations are likely to be repeated. A negative reinforcement is any stimulus that results in the increased frequency of a response when it is withdrawn. It results in reduced response.

Punishment The responses that brings painful or undesirable consequences will be suppressed, but may reappear if reinforcement contingencies change.

Non-Reinforcement The responses that are not reinforced are not likely to be repeated.

So, the 'operant teaching model' focuses on the modification of one's behaviour by making use of the principles of operant conditioning.

It aims to control and manage the learning environment in such a way as to provide proper reinforcement for the shaping of a new or desired behaviour.

Cognitive Learning Theories

According to **Shelly**, "The cognitive theory's, activities like thinking and remembering seems like a behaviour, thus providing an avenue to use behaviour analysis to measure their effect on learning".

According to **Ertmer & Newby**, "Acquisition of knowledge is processed through mental structure changes, rather than through responses and stimuli. The mind is used as reference tool to process past information and to create new knowledge."

Thus, they stress on the acquisition of knowledge and skills, processing of information and beliefs. Here, cognitivist educators try to transfer new knowledge to students and helps them to organise, integrate, and retrieve it, knowledge so that exists outside the learner. It is very useful when learners face introductory courses or courses in which a variety of learning styles can be accommodated.

Major theorists associated with Cognitive Learning theory are Jean Piaget, David Ausubel and J Bruner.

Jean Piaget

The cognitive development model is the outcome of the Philosophy and views expressed by Jean Piaget, a Swiss psychologist, about the intellectual development of the children right from the period of their birth.

Given below are some essential theoretical notations and ideas related to Piaget's theory

- One's cognitive development at any stage of his/her life is the joint product of his hereditary potential and interaction with his/her physical and social environment.
- The key to child's cognitive development lies in his constant interaction with the physical and social environment. The process of such interaction is carried through assimilation (incorporation of new experiences) and accommodation (modification of existing experiences).
- The child's cognitive structure and its functioning, always remains in a state of constant change and development as a result of the process of assimilation and accommodation for bringing desired equilibration between his self and the environment.

Piaget model involves around four stages of intellectual development as shown below :

Piaget's Stages of Cognitive Development

Stages	Nature of Cognitive Development
Sensory Motor Stage (0-2 years)	(i) Thinking is based on sensory and motor exploration.
	(ii) Child learns that he is separate from his environment.
	(iii) He acquires the concept of object durability.
Pre-operational Stage (2-7 years)	(i) Use of language and symbols to build thought process.
	(ii) Mode of thinking is illogical, imaginative and intuitive.

Stages	Nature of Cognitive Development
Concrete Operational Stage (7-11 years)	(i) Child is able to recognise concepts of number, classification, conservation, and reversibility. (ii) Logical thinking started emerging using inductive and deductive approaches but is able to do so only in terms of concrete objects and events.
Formal Operational Stage (11-16 years)	(i) Child is able to think abstractly, deals with imaginary and hypothetical problems. (ii) He acquires the ability of scientific thinking and problem solving and tries to reach at the peak of his cognitive development.

Piaget advocated stage-linked characteristics of cognitive development. Therefore, any scheme of education or teaching learning process must be planned well in time with the nature of the cognitive development of the children belonging to a particular age and grade level. Thus, Cognitive Development Model stands for organising the teaching-learning environment and activities for development of stage-relevant cognitive abilities and learning experiences to the children of a particular age group and testing the nature of their cognitive development.

David Ausubel

David Ausubel, psychologist gave the 'meaningful learning theory'. He was influenced by the work of Piaget. His theory was concerned with how students learn large amount of meaningful material form verbal/textual presentations. Learning, under this theory, is based on the representation , subordinate and combinational process that occur during the learning process. A primary process in meaningful learning is a formation in which new material is related to relevant ideas in the existing cognitive structure on the basis of previous knowledge. It is the result of linking new information in the learner's own cognitive structure.

Ausubel proposed the following four processes

(i) **Derivative Subsumption** Situation in which the new information that pupil learns is an instance or example of a concept that they have already learned.

(ii) **Correlative Subsumption** It's enriches the higher-level concept.

(iii) **Super-ordinate Learning** A lot of examples of a concept are known but the concept is unknown until it is taught to pupils.

(iv) **Combinational Learning** A process in which new idea is derived from another idea on the basis of previous knowledge. Relevance to student's cognitive structures happens when we pay attention to early knowledge of the concepts that preceded the concept to be learned. For Ausubel, meaningful learning is a process that is related to new information relevant to the concepts contained in a person's cognitive structure. It enables students to associate their early knowledge and with the new knowledge which will allow students to build knowledge in discovering learning activities.

Jerome Bruner Theory

J.Bruner was a cognitive and educational psychologist. He believes that classroom learning should take place indicatively (specific to generalisation). He argued that schools wastes time to match the complexity of subject material to a child's cognitive stage of development. He believed that complex ideas first should be taught at a simplified level and then the level of subject should increase gradually.

The modes of representations of Bruner theory are

Enactive Stage (Birth to 3 years)

The child learns through movement or action. It is also known as **concrete stage**. It involves encoding action based information and storing it in memory. It can be in the form of muscle memory where a body might remember the action of shaking a rattle. Example, usage of coin or paper for maths education.

Iconic Stage (3 to 8 years)

This stage is also known as 'pictorial stage' or 'photographic memory'. It involves images or other visuals to retain memory. It is represented by image of objects on paper or to picture them in one's head. *e.g.* use of shapes, diagrams and graphs.

Symbolic Stage (From 8 years)

Under this stage, child learns through abstract symbols. It takes the images from the second stage and represents them using words and symbols. It helps student to recognise information in the mind by relating concepts together. Example, variables (*x* and *y*), mathematical symbols (+, –, /) or words (addition, infinite, subtraction) and use of language and words.

Constructive Learning Theories

According to **Moscolol & Fischer**, "Constructivism is the philosophical and scientific position that knowledge arises through a process of active construction".

According to **Brooks**, "As long as there were people asking each other questions, we have had constructivist classrooms. Constructivism, the study of learning, is about how we all make sense to our world, and that call hasn't changed".

The learning under this theory occurs through interaction. The information is received through the guidance of a peer or instructor and the learner creates knowledge through the exchange of the knowledge with his peers.

Thus, constructivism helps learners to build knowledge by integrating prior learning, context, and experiences. Knowledge exists within the learner. The **Lev Vygotsky**, a psychologist, proposed the 'Socio-cultural theory', under 'Constructive Learning theory'.

Lev Vygotsky's Socio-Cultural Theory

The Social Cultural theory of **Lev Vygotsky** was made on the belief that parents, care givers, peers and the culture at large were responsible for developing high order skills.

He also suggested that human development is a result of interaction between individuals and society. Through this interaction, children learn from parents and teachers.

Vygotsky's theory emphasises an active role of students in the learning process.

The four basic principles underlying the Vygotskyian framework are

(i) Language plays an important role in the mental development.
(ii) Development cannot be seperated from its social concept.
(iii) Learning can lead to development.
(iv) Children construct their knowledge.

According to **Vygotsky**, "The zone of proximity is the distance between the actual development level as determined by independent problem-solving and the level of potential development as determined through problem-solving under guidance or in collaboration with more capable peers".

The zone of proximity development contains two features

(i) **Scaffolding** requires that an instructor shows by examples how to solve a problem, while controlling the learning environment, so that student can take things step by step by expanding their base of knowledge without excessive frustration.
(ii) **Reciprocal Teaching** It provides an environment of open dialogue between student and teacher which goes beyond a simple question and answer session.

He believed that the child can gain knowledge through the help of others. However, the knowledge must be appropriate for the child's level of comprehension. Anything that is too complicated for the child to learn or that is not in their Zone of Proximity Development (ZPD) cannot be learnt until there is a shift in the ZPD.

He emphasised on the role of teacher in constructive development, and the need to have support from More Knowledgeable than Others or MKO (coach, teacher). The ZPD differentiates between a learner's current development and their potential development being taught from MKO.

Relationship Between Learning Theories and Instructional Strategies

'Learning theories' are described as a collection of learning theory and models and 'instructional design', is a collection of instructional strategies that are designed with the help of learning theories.

Influential behaviourist like the Skinner and cognitivist like Piaget, Ausubel and Bruner and constructivists like Vygotsky, have designed learning theories as a means to educate learners. The applications of these theories were presented in the 1950s through the advent of Skinner's teaching machines and many more. The machines were designed, so that the learner can complete each task in order to move forward. The machines were inventive and based on obtaining a positive response from the learner in the form of behaviour.

These machines led to the development of programmed instructions which follows a systematic approach to problem solving. It was marked as a birth of system design or instructional design approach to an education. Various lessons like guides, tasks, practice and feedback, contents are laid out for students.

The learning results in the development of a skill and practising that skill will result in a response to a stimulus. The focus of learning theories resides in the use of reinforcement to drive learning, instructional strategies as a means to trained learners to complete instructional objectives. The teaching machines and programmed instructions are small contributions to the field of an education but have paved the way to instructional designers to shape the learning environment to result in more effective strategies. Many instructional strategies includes the use of feedback to the learner as it helps in the development of positive behaviour that result from instruction.

With the advent of Cognitive Learning Theory, instructional design expanded its scope of practice to include solutions to focus on the learner in the design process. It uses the information about the learners as well as environment to develop instructional solutions. The instructional strategy use various assessment tools to test the transferred acquired knowledge of the learner. Instructional strategy shifted in the presence of cognitivism and includes a more system, like design approach with the focus on learners.

The Constructive Theory has expanded in the way that instructional solutions can be developed. New opportunities for learning has generated with the addition of social aspect in learning. Collective learning groups and the use of peer review are widely used in the learning process. Thus, learners can interpret various learning theories to improve their understanding. Instructional strategies have influenced learning theories like behaviourism, cognitivism and constructivism which acts as a pillar of successful approaches.

As each of these theories include different learning strategies, either by behavioural response or knowledge acquisition, they have largely contributed in the learning processes and are responsible for how the field of instructional strategy has evolved over time.

Let us discuss the methods necessary for learning and effective instructional strategies in the classroom

Small Group Methods

For certain objectives, small-group methods are the techniques of choice. In other instances, they are valuable options that can provide an educational system with needed flexibility. When used properly, the methods are invaluable for increasing student motivation through greater involvement and participation. Under certain conditions, they even make it possible to ease the loads of overburdened instructors by reducing the time required to prepare formal presentations.

In general, it is feasible to use small-group methods in courses to

- Increase understanding and grasp of course content.
- Enhance motivation and generate greater student involvement.
- Develop positive attitudes toward later use of presented material.
- Develop problem-solving skills specific to the course content.
- Provide practice in the application of concepts and information to practical problems.
- Generate ideas among students concerning ways of applying acquired knowledge.
- Develop student commitment to recommended ways of handling problems.
- Emphasise an important issue.
- Proceed with instruction when content experts are scarce or not available.

Large Group Teaching

Large group teaching if carefully organised and implemented can cause more active learning in students. With a large group setting, active learning can be encouraged in

- Individual or pairs of students in a large lecture
- Groups of students in a large group.

One technique for managing large classes is to sub-divide the class into more manageable groups, using peer-assisted mentoring. In peer-assisted learning, there is an educational gain for both the mentoring students and the mentees, both group of students are given modular credit for their respective roles in the educational arrangement.

The examples of the use of technology in large class settings to improve engagement and student assessment are-student response system and virtual laboratories. The student response systems are educational technologies most often used for the purpose of making face-to-face lectures interactive by engaging students in real-time activities. On the other hand, virtual laboratories can go some way to bridge the gap between the demand and capacity to deliver laboratory-based practicals. It enhance the educational experience of students.

Formal Group Learning

Formal learning groups last from one class period to several weeks, whatever it takes to complete to a specific task or assignment. The purpose is to use the group to accomplish shared goals to capitalise on different talents and knowledge of the group, and to maximise the learning of everyone in the group.

Examples of formal learning groups are

Group Projects Assignments complex enough or large and time sensitive enough to require the effort of a group. Some work may be done outside of class.

Collaborative Learning Classroom activities, projects or assignments designed so that the group succeeds when every individual succeeds.

Non-Formal Group Learning

It is free from rigidity with regard to curriculum, learning materials, methodology, venue, duration or the length an individual takes to complete a particular instructional session. There are number of methods and instructional media found effective in non-formal education which are projected media, display boards, graphic media, multimedia mix, etc.

EXAM BASED QUESTIONS

1 Which method of teaching and learning was used in early period?
(a) Writing on the leaves
(b) Verbal presentations
(c) Engraving on rocks
(d) Chalk or black board

2 Which period marked the use of radio for the purpose of an education?
(a) After industrialisation
(b) After civilisation
(c) After independence
(d) In medieval period

3 Which of the following were used as the tools for imparting an education?
(a) Micro-teaching (b) Computers
(c) Interaction analysis (d) All of these

4 As per 'Shiv K Mitra', an Educational Technology is a/an ....
(a) art (b) art and science
(c) science (d) philosophy

5 The definition of 'J.K. Davies' was concerned with the
(a) problem of education
(b) disciplined approach to learning
(c) manipulation of media
(d) to realise educational goals

6 How educational technology achieves its objectives?
(a) By communicating
(b) By providing guidance
(c) Through effective teaching
(d) Through application of science and technology

7 Which of the following is not an equipment used for education?
(a) Tape-recorder (b) Television
(c) Black board (d) Hardware and software

8 What is the objective of educational technology?
(a) To teach moral value to students
(b) To develop teaching and learning methods
(c) To help neglected community for food and shelter
(d) To identify the potential learners

9 How can we bring modifications in the education process?
(a) Through notice board
(b) Providing feedback
(c) Introducing technologies
(d) Through planning of strategies

10 Which method helps the teacher to evaluate the applied technique?
(a) Educational technology
(b) Systems approach
(c) Audio-visual aids
(d) Computed assisted software

11 Which of the following technologies are a part of educational technology?
(a) Information technology
(b) Instructional technology
(c) Communication technology
(d) All of the above

12 Why educational technology is diversified globally?
(a) Because of its non-utilisation
(b) Because of diversification of objectives
(c) Because of vast contents
(d) Both (b) and (c)

13 The 'Attaran' defined the term 'information technology' as the use of
(a) computer and software
(b) information and knowledge
(c) experience
(d) radio and television

14 Which of the following would help in the process of communication excercise?
(a) Programs and equipments
(b) Technologies and inventions
(c) Hardware and software systems
(d) Both (a) and (c)

15 According to the definition given by 'UNESCO', Information and Communication Technology (ICT) includes
(a) information technology
(b) enhancement in technology
(c) management techniques
(d) communication technology

16 Which technology of teaching is achieved through telecommunication and multimedia technique?
(a) Instructional Technology
(b) Information and Communication Technology
(c) Educational Technology
(d) Communication Technology

17 Which of the following inventions can be termed as the first revolution in the field of Information and Communication Technology?
(a) Paper and ink (b) Computer softwares
(c) Metals and rocks (d) Photography

18 When did the phase II started in the history of Information and Communication Technology?
(a) 1840 (b) 1451
(c) 1450 (b) 1940

19 Which of the following was the first pictogram which was dated 3100 BCE?
(a) Indus scripts (b) Paprus
(c) Kadamba alphabet (d) Sumerian

20 When was 'China Abacus' invented?
(a) 500 AC (b) 500 BC
(c) 3100 BC (d) 1500 BC

21 Which phase acted as a bridge between the modern time of electronic media and the early phase?
(a) Phase II (b) Phase III
(c) Phase IV (b) Phase I

22 Who invented xerography?
(a) G Marconi (b) Alexander Graham Bell
(c) Chester F Carlson (d) Rene Dagran

23 .... was invented by J L Baird.
(a) Photostat (b) Television
(c) Radio (d) Micrography

24 When was the USSR satellite 'Sputnik' launched?
(a) 1957 (b) 1975
(c) 1999 (d) 1960

25 Which of the following are the ways through which education can be transmitted?
(a) Connecting to a Local Area Network
(b) Accessing to digital libraries
(c) Communicating through multi-media projector
(d) All of the above

26 What benefit does student gets through applications of Information and Communication Technology in an education?
(a) Good marks and grades
(b) Independent and active learning
(c) Access to educational resources
(d) Both (b) and (c)

27 What are the various Information and Communication Technology resources for self-learning?
(a) Audio-visual aids
(b) An electronic appliances
(c) Self-learning modules
(d) Hardware and software

28 Who tends to be ignorant to an applications of Information and Communication Technology in schools?
(a) Parents and guardians
(b) Heads and teachers
(c) Students and learners
(d) None of the above

29 What does 'interactive model of teaching' stands for?
(a) The use of Information and Communication Technology
(b) Acquiring knowledge and skills
(c) Through interaction and communication
(d) Both (a) and (c)

30 .... is a sub-system of an educational technology.
(a) Formal education system
(b) Information technology
(c) Non-formal educational system
(d) Instructional technology

31 How can the learner attains instructional objectives with the help of instructional technology?
(a) By following a system or process
(b) By producing responses
(c) By determining media and material
(d) Data inadequate

32 Which of the following is not a channel for imparting instructional technology?
(a) Attendance sheet (b) Digital library
(c) Graphic organisers (d) Instructional guides

33 Which of the following is a characteristic of formal education?
(a) Its runs from high school to university
(b) It is part-time education
(c) It deals with a specific programme
(d) It runs from primary to university

34 The Visual technology as a means of formal education includes ....
(a) smart boards (b) internet network
(c) projectors (d) Both (a) and (c)

35 What are the different types of projectors?
(a) Video projectors (b) Slide projectors
(c) LCD/DLP projectors (d) All of these

36 .... helps the teacher to search through websites, graphs and lessons.
(a) White board
(b) Mimio boards
(c) Classroom PCs
(d) SMART technologies

37 Which of the following is not a characteristic of non-formal education?
(a) It works according to student's choice
(b) It is non-authoritarian
(c) It is built on learner's participation
(d) It is rigid

38 What are the platforms through which computer assisted learning runs?
(a) CD (b) Floppy disk
(c) Both (a) and (b) (d) None of these

39 The 'Message Board Forms' is a part of which of the following technology?
(a) Digital learning resources
(b) Asynchronous computer mediated communication
(c) Synchronous computer mediated communication
(d) Computer assisted assessment

40 How does virtual learning environment enhance a student's learning experience?
(a) By the use of internet
(b) By the use of LAN network
(c) By utilising the computer technologies
(d) By electronic gadgets

41 Which of the following is not a characteristic of informal education?
(a) It is a structured activity
(b) It is determined by an individual
(c) There is no existence of a teacher
(d) It is a life long process

42 What are the technologies used in informal education system?
(a) Mimio boards (b) SMART classrooms
(c) Blogs and forums (d) None of these

43 Which education system promotes the development of all learners, irrespective of their race, gender, etc?
(a) Formal education
(b) Inclusive education
(c) Non-formal education
(d) Informal education

44 Which of the following is an application of educational system in inclusive education?
(a) Speech to text option (b) Sensory enhancer
(c) Screen readers (d) All of these

45 According to the 'Gwod & Brophy', behaviourism is the study of
(a) overt behaviour
(b) performance
(c) learning teaching process
(d) response of stimuli

46 Operant conditioning is associated with
(a) Vygotsky (b) Pavlov
(c) Thorndike (d) Skinner

47 Under operant conditioning theory, if a response allows escape from and undesirable situation, then it is knows as
(a) positive response
(b) negative reinforcement
(c) positive reinforcement
(d) non-reinforcement

48 Who emphasised on the development of children form birth?
(a) Bruner (b) Skinner
(c) Piaget (d) Ausubel

49 Which of the following are the stages of cognitive development as explained by Piaget?
(a) Pre-operational stage (b) Iconic stage
(c) Formal operational stage (d) Both (a) and (c)

50 Who gave the theory of 'meaningful learning'?
(a) Ausubel (b) Piaget
(c) Vygotsky (d) Bruner

51 What do you understand by 'combinatorial learning'?
(a) Learning of unknown concepts
(b) Process of deriving to a new idea
(c) Learning higher level concepts
(d) None of the above

52 The importance of motivation and reciprocity was brought out in the learning theories by
(a) Skinner (b) Piaget (c) Bruner (d) Ausubel

53 Under the theory of Bruner, which age was marked as the symbolic stage?
(a) 3 to 8 years (b) Birth to 3 years
(c) 5 to 10 years (d) From 8 years

54 Who gave the theory of 'zone of proximal development'?
(a) Vygotsky (b) Bruner
(c) Skinner (d) Both (a) and (b)

55 For 'teaching', Vygotsky, used the term ....
(a) maintaining (b) scaffolding
(c) Both (a) and (b) (d) None of these

56 Whom does 'More Knowledgeable Other' or MKO refers to?
(a) Coach (b) Parents
(c) Teacher (d) Both (a) and (c)

57 Match the following.

List I (Procedures of operant conditioning)	List II (The forms of reinforcement, cue and response)
A. Reward training	1. Positive reinforcement with making of a response in the absence of cue.
B. Escape training	2. Negative reinforcement with holding of response in the presence of cue.
C. Discrimination training	3. Positive reinforcement with making of response in the presence of a cue.
D. Active-avoidance training	4. Negative reinforcement with making of a response in the presence of a cue.
	5. Negative reinforcement with making of a response in the absence of a cue.

Codes

	A	B	C	D
(a)	1	5	3	4
(b)	5	1	2	3
(c)	1	3	5	4
(d)	3	5	4	2

58 Match the following.

List I (Stages of Development)	List II (Characteristics Associated)
A. Sensory motor stage	1. Transductive reasoning
B. Pre. operational stage	2. Reversibility
C. Concrete operational stage	3. Object permanence
D. Formal operational stage	4. Repetitive acts
	5. Intense self-awareness
	6. Concept formulation

Codes

	A	B	C	D		A	B	C	D
(a)	5	3	1	2	(b)	4	5	1	2
(c)	3	1	2	5	(d)	1	2	3	4

59 Match the following.

List I	List II
A. Audio-visual aids	1. Response to stimulus
B. Behavioural technology	2. Hardware
C. Programmed instruction	3. Learning experience from learners
D. Training psychology	4. System analysis
	5. Internet

Codes

	A	B	C	D		A	B	C	D
(a)	2	3	4	1	(b)	1	4	3	2
(c)	4	3	2	1	(d)	2	1	4	3

60 Match the following.

List I	List II
A. Constructivism	1. Paradigm for technology based learning.
B. Scaffolding	2. Real world is not like studying in school.
C. Situated learning	3. That allows the students to grow in independence as a learner.
D. Anchored Instruction	4. A view that emphasises the active role of the learner in building, understanding and making sense of information.
	5. Learner learns the cognitive strategies and meta cognitive skills.

Codes

	A	B	C	D		A	B	C	D
(a)	4	2	3	5	(b)	4	3	2	1
(c)	2	3	1	4	(d)	1	2	3	4

61 Match the following.

List I (Theories)	List II (Theorists)
A. Classical conditioning	1. Hull
B. Socio-cultural theory	2. Tolman
C. Operant conditioning	3. Pavlov
D. Drive reduction	4. Vygotsky
	5. Skinner

Codes

	A	B	C	D		A	B	C	D
(a)	1	3	5	2	(b)	3	4	5	1
(c)	2	1	5	3	(d)	5	3	1	2

62 Match the following.

List I (Theorists)	List II (Characteristics)
A. Vygotsky	1. Meaningful learning theory
B. Piaget	2. Operant conditioning
C. Ausubel	3. Zone of proximity
D. Bruner	4. Emphasis on classroom learning
	5. Intellectual development of child

Codes

	A	B	C	D		A	B	C	D
(a)	1	2	4	5	(b)	3	1	5	4
(c)	1	5	4	3	(d)	3	5	1	4

63 Match the following.

List I (Forms of Education)	List II (Features)
A. Formal education	1. Learners oriented
B. Inclusive education	2. No existence of a mentor
C. Non-formal education	3. Subsytem of education technology
D. Informal education	4. Full time education
	5. Education for all

Codes

	A	B	C	D		A	B	C	D
(a)	1	2	4	3	(b)	2	1	4	5
(c)	4	5	1	2	(d)	4	5	2	1

64 According to Piaget, at what stage does abstract thinking began to develop?

(a) Sensory motor
(b) Pre-operational
(c) Concrete operational
(d) Formal operational

65 The main source of informal education is ....

(a) home (b) society
(c) radio and TV (d) newspaper

66 What provides access to excellent resources to explore and discover?

(a) Language lab (b) Interactive board
(c) LCD projector (d) Internet

67 Curriculum written as part of formal instruction of school experience, is known as .... curriculum.

(a) explicit (b) societal
(c) spiral (d) hidden

68 .... is a collection of electronic evidence assembled and managed by a user demonstrating his/her abilities and platforms for self reflection.

(a) Wikipedia (b) e-portfolio
(c) Programmed learning (d) e-mail

69 .... is an example of Learning Management theory.
(a) Noodle
(b) MOOC
(c) Blackboard
(d) Edmodo

70 "Information and Communication Technologies tools, including computer network, software and hardware required for internet connection". This definition is given by ....
(a) Inford
(b) Tanetal
(c) UNESCO
(d) Attaran

71 Which theory contributed to the development of cooperative learning strategies?
(a) Behaviourism
(b) Connectivism
(c) Cognitivism
(d) Constructivism

72 Which of the following computer-based instructional materials can be used to learn new concepts?
(a) Drill and practice
(b) Games
(c) Tutorials
(d) Simulation

73 According to Piaget, in .... stage of development, the child shows attainment of concept of reversibility as a cognitive capacity.
(a) Sensory motor
(b) Pre-operational
(c) Concrete operational
(d) Formal operational

74 Arrange the process of information technology according to their chronology.
1. Process
2. Store
3. Transmit
4. Protect

Codes
(a) 3, 4, 2, 1
(b) 4, 3, 2, 1
(c) 2, 4, 1, 3
(d) 2, 4, 3, 1

75 Arrange the following according to their occurrence in history.
1. Satellite
2. Telephone
3. Pictograms
4. Pascaline

Codes
(a) 2, 4, 3, 1
(b) 3, 2, 1, 4
(c) 1, 4, 3, 2
(d) 3, 4, 2, 1

76 Arrange the following stages of cognitive development in chronology.
1. Concrete operational stage.
2. Formal operational stage.
3. Pre-operational stage.
4. Sensory motor stage.

Codes
(a) 2, 3, 4, 1
(b) 4, 3, 1, 2
(c) 1, 2, 3, 4
(d) 4, 2, 1, 3

77 Rearrange the following processes of meaningful learning theory in chronology.
1. Correlative learning
2. Combinational learning
3. Derivative subsumption
4. Subordinate learning

Codes
(a) 4, 1, 2, 3
(b) 1, 3, 4, 2
(c) 3, 4, 2, 1
(d) 3, 1, 4, 2

78 Arrange the following representation of Bruner theory in chronology.
1. Symbolic stage
2. Inactive stage
3. Iconic stage

Codes
(a) 2, 3, 1
(b) 1, 2, 3
(c) 3, 2, 1
(d) 1, 3, 2

79 The concept of distance education implies
1. imparting quality education through mitigating the negative effects of distance in education.
2. imparting education form distance.
3. using mass media and computer in class.
4. broadcasting the lessons.

Codes
(a) Both 2 and 3
(b) Both 1 and 4
(c) Only 2
(d) Only 1

80 What is the purpose and effect of Educational Technology (ET)?
1. ET is used with the intent of making instructions attractive.
2. Multimedia approach in ET ensures catering to diversity of learner characteristics.
3. ET is a supplement rather than a substitute of teacher.
4. ET should lay more emphasis on software rather than hardware.

Codes
(a) Only 4
(b) Both 1 and 2
(c) Both 2 and 3
(d) Only 2

81 Information Technology is defined as
1. generating information with the use of machines.
2. a field of science and an art.
3. process of communicating information.
4. a subsystem of educational technology.

Codes
(a) Both 2 and 4
(b) Only 1
(c) Both 1 and 2
(d) Only 2

82 How instructional technology helps students?
1. It is student's centered teaching.
2. It provides opportunity for personal communication.
3. To stimulate learner's interest.
4. To bring attention and satisfaction among students.

Codes
(a) Both 3 and 4
(b) Both 1 and 3
(c) Only 2
(d) Only 3

83 Which of the following is not a characteristic of formal education?
1. It is flexible.
2. Lessons are conducted by correspondence.
3. It is a full time education.
4. It is a sequential grading system.

Codes
(a) Both 2 and 4 (b) Both 1 and 2
(c) Only 4 (d) Only 2

84 Which of the following technologies are used in non-formal education system?
1. Learning and knowledge portals.
2. Computed mediated communication.
3. e-books and social networks.
4. Computed assissted assessment.

Codes
(a) 1 and 2 (b) Only 1 (c) 2 and 4 (d) Only 4

85 What do you understand by constructive learning theories?
1. The learning which occurs through interaction.
2. It stresses on the acquisition of knowledge.
3. It includes the guidance of instructor.
4. It helps in the intellectual development of a learner.

Codes
(a) Both 2 and 4 (b) Both 1 and 3
(c) Only 1 (d) All of these

Directions (Q. Nos. 86-90) *Given below are two statements, one labelled as Assertion (A) and the other labelled as Reason (R). Following are the codes given below, choose the correct option.*

Codes
(a) A and R is true and R is the correct explanation of A
(b) A and R is true, but R is not the correct explanation of A
(c) A is true, but R is false
(d) A is false, but R is true

86 **Assertion** (A) Education is the key that unlocks the door to modernisation.
Reason (R) Development of technology facilitates interaction among people.

87 **Assertion** (A) For an effective classroom communication at times it is desirable to use the projection technology.
Reason (R) The projection technology does not facilitates coverage of course contents.

88 **Assertion** (A) Inclusive education ensures education for all.
Reason (R) It focuses on providing infrastructure for the needs of the students.

89 **Assertion** (A) Large group teaching leads to active learning.
Reason (R) It generate ideas among students concerning ways of applying acquired knowledge.

90 **Assertion** (A) Lev Vygotsky proposed the 'Socio-cultural theory'.
Reason (R) His theory was made on the belief that parents, peer and culture at large were responsible for developing high order skills.

PREVIOUS YEARS' QUESTIONS

July 2018

1 From the list of statements given below, which of them indicate the meaning, purpose and scope of Educational Technology. Give your answer by selecting from the codes.
1. ET optimises learning outcomes.
2. ET reduces the cost of education.
3. ET is user friendly.
4. ET ensures effectiveness of learning outcomes.
5. ET has a tremendous role in rendering teaching-learning system effort effective.
6. ET is the outcome of communication's network.

Codes
(a) 1, 2, 3 (b) 4, 5, 6
(c) 2, 3, 6 (d) 1, 4, 5

November 2017

2 From the list of statements given below identity those which most appropriately explain the purpose and effects of Educational Technology (ET). Choose your answer from the codes given below
1. ET is a supplement rather than a substitute of a teacher.
2. ET is used with the intent of making instructions attractive.
3. The purpose of ET is to optimise learning outcomes.
4. Multi-media approach in ET ensures catering to diversity of learner characteristics.
5. Use of ET at pre active and post active stages is a kind of superimposition.

6. ET should lay more emphasis on software rather than hardware.

Codes

(a) 1, 2, 3 (b) 2, 3, 5
(c) 1, 3, 4 (d) 4, 5, 6

July 2016

3 Which of the following sets of statements relate more appropriately to the meaning and scope of Educational Technology? For your answer, select the correct alternative set from the codes given under the list of statements.

1. Hardware in ET is the modality of presentation whereas software is the content or massage which is presented.
2. ET caters to memory level teaching only.
3. Interactive stage of teaching is outside the scope of ET.
4. ET aims at optimising learning outcomes.
5. ET is restricted to only conditioning and training modalities.
6. System's approach in ET followed hardware and software approaches.
7. The purpose of multimedia is confined to making engagement in learning sustained for a long time.
8. Simple cognitive interchanges in teacher and learner form part of reflective level teaching.

Codes

(a) 1, 2, 3, 4
(b) 6, 7, 8, 2
(c) 1, 4, 6, 8
(d) 2, 3, 4, 6

June 2015

4 Which one of the following will be the most appropriate description of 'Educational Technology'?

(a) Educational Technology is an effective use of hardware for optimising learning outcomes in a school.
(b) Educational Technology is a network of various techniques to ensure and optimise learning outcomes effectively.
(c) Educational Technology is efficient use software for optimising learning outcomes.
(d) Educational Technology is an effective use of multi-media in a classroom context.

ANSWERS

Exam Based Questions

1 (b)	2 (a)	3 (d)	4 (c)	5 (a)	6 (d)	7 (c)	8 (b)	9 (b)	10 (a)
11 (d)	12 (d)	13 (a)	14 (d)	15 (c)	16 (b)	17 (a)	18 (c)	19 (d)	20 (b)
21 (a)	22 (c)	23 (b)	24 (a)	25 (d)	26 (d)	27 (c)	28 (b)	29 (a)	30 (d)
31 (c)	32 (b)	33 (d)	34 (d)	35 (d)	36 (b)	37 (d)	38 (c)	39 (b)	40 (a)
41 (a)	42 (c)	43 (b)	44 (d)	45 (a)	46 (d)	47 (b)	48 (c)	49 (d)	50 (a)
51 (b)	52 (c)	53 (d)	54 (a)	55 (b)	56 (d)	57 (a)	58 (b)	59 (d)	60 (c)
61 (b)	62 (d)	63 (c)	64 (c)	65 (a)	66 (d)	67 (a)	68 (b)	69 (c)	70 (b)
71 (d)	72 (c)	73 (b)	74 (c)	75 (d)	76 (b)	77 (d)	78 (a)	79 (b)	80 (c)
81 (b)	82 (a)	83 (b)	84 (c)	85 (b)	86 (b)	87 (c)	88 (d)	89 (b)	90 (a)

Previous Years' Questions

1 (d)	2 (c)	3 (c)	4 (b)

CHAPTER 31

Systems Approach to Instructional Design

The concept of System approach is a part in the field of education to manage its affairs. It has been introduced in education to improve, manage and control its process and products. Let us understand, what is System approach and its application to instructional design.

Systems Approach

The term **System approach** has been formed by two words **system** and **approach**. By system is meant the entirely or wholeness, in which all elements, factors, organs or components are mutually related, knit together and self - controlled. The System approach believes in the entirely . It is a method to arrive at solutions to problems and it helps to carry forward and develop the teaching and training system as per new changes.

It indicates systematic thinking, step by step problem-solving and considering many variables of a problem as interacting with each other. In other words, studying the phenomenon or process as a whole and not in bits and pieces. In this approach, a problem is taken into account in its totality and *attempts are made to solve it, in the context of the*

- pre-determined objectives,
- functioning of its interrelated parts and the whole system under the given environmental constraints.

It advocates the exercise of a reasonable control, over the organisation, process and product of a system meaning and creates a reasonable balance among input, process, output and the environment constraints for achieving the specified objectives. If a system meets the requirements of the system's objectives, it is maintained. If it does not, then it is modified. Thus, the term **System approach**, refers to the use of a system in identification, execution and evaluation of goals in any given situation.

In general, the System approach includes the following steps

- Analysis of the given situation.
- Setting up relevant objectives or goals.
- Evaluation of all the modes before adoption.
- Devising the most appropriate ways and means to achieve the specified objectives or goals, keeping in mind various factors, like resources, human finance, machinery, environment.

In this Chapter

- Devising monitoring tools to evaluate the achievement of specified goals and thus, the effectiveness of the system.
- Planning alternative solution, in case of failure of the solution.

Definitions of System Approach

According to **Twelkier**, "System approach is a management tool that allows individuals to examine all aspects of the organisation, to inter-relate the effects of one set of decisions to another and to optimally use all the resources at hand, to solve the problem".

According to **Keshow** and **Michean**, "System approach is one of the techniques which aims at finding the most efficient and economically intelligent methods for solving the problems of education, scientifically".

Importance of System Approach in Education

- Framework for planning, decision-making, controlling and problem-solving.
- Throws light on dynamic nature of management.
- Provides a unified focus to institutional efforts.
- Helps to look at institution as a whole and not as a part.
- Helps the manager to identify the critical sub-systems and their interaction with each other.
- Helps in improving institution.
- Helps in bringing efficiency in school's administration and management.
- Helps in systematic educational planning.
- Maximum utilisation of resources.
- Helps in improving examination and evaluation system.
- Maintaining, controlling and improving the guidance services.
- Designing, controlling and improving non-formal and adult education system.
- Helps in improving quality of education.
- Helps in improving the teacher's training programmes, in-service as well as pre-service.

Instructional Design

An instructional designer is somewhat like an engineer. It is the process by which educational products are designed, developed and delivered. These products include online courses, manuals, tutorials, etc. So, instructional design is the analysis of learning needs and then systematic development of instruction. Instructional technology is often used by the instructional designers.

According to **Smith, Patricia L and Tillman J Ragan**, "The term instructional design refers to the systematic and reflective process of translating principles of learning and instruction into plans for instructional materials, activities, information resources and evaluation".

Thus, it is the entire process of analysis of educational needs and goals to meet those objectives. It includes development of a delivery system and instructional materials and activities to meet the learning needs.

System Approach to Instructional Design

System Approach to instructional design is known as common sense by designing a systematic way of analysing a problem and solving it. It helps in understanding, controlling and improving the structure and functioning of the system, to fully realise the instructional objectives.

Jalaluddin in 1981, marked six major phases in the approach to the instructional design as mentioned below.

They are:

Formation of Objectives It includes the specification of instructional objectives in terms of the expected outcomes.

Pre-Assessment of Student's Entering Behaviour It includes the assessment of student's initial performance, with the help of certain criterion.

Designing and Development of the System In this process, an instructional system is developed, with the help of planned and designed inputs.

It consists of the following process:

- Analysing of the task.
- Devising teaching strategies.
- Selection of media and material.
- Selection and organisation of appropriate contents (learning experiences).
- Assigning roles to the elements, involved in the instructional system.

Operation or Implementation Phase Under this process, the actual operation or implementation of the instructional system takes place. All the elements of the instructional systems are integrated, for achieving the desired instructional objectives.

Evaluation of Outcomes The students' achievement is evaluated according to the stipulated instructional objectives, on the basis of the post test scores.

Improvement of the System This process deals with the improvement of the system, on the basis of feedback from evaluation results. It aims to improve effectiveness as per the specified objectives.

Thus, the goals of the education system can be obtained through the technique of System approach in the most economical and scientific way. It provides the scope to improve and modify the system. Thus, a teacher may be able to develop a suitable instructional design based on the feedback provided by the System approach.

Models of Development of Instructional Design

Below are procedural and conceptual models based on the theory and practice of instructional design, which helps to give structure or meaning to a problem. *They are*

ADDIE

It is a framework used by training developers and instructional designers to create instruction. It represents a guideline for building effective training and performance support tools in five ways. The five phases of ADDIE are analyse, design, development, implementation and evaluation. They altogether, provide the framework for the development of training courses in a systematic and cost effective manner.

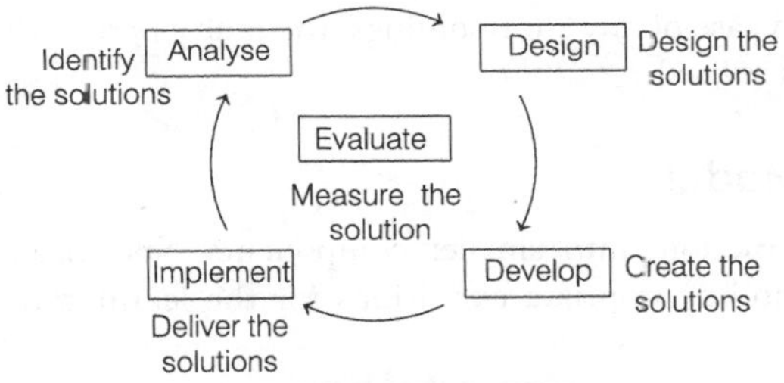

The Five Steps of ADDIE

They can be explained as below

Analyse

It establishes the instructional goals, objectives and targeted outcomes. It also makes sure that there is no duplication of knowledge and repetition, by identifying the existing knowledge and skills of the targeted audience.

At the end of this phase, a training plan with training needs analysis, should be completed for the design phase.

Design

The focus of this phase is on learning objectives, the content framework and the structure.

This phase determines

- Delivery methods
- Content's elements
- Assessment type and tools
- Duration
- Excercises and activities
- Media and visuals

Develop

In this phase, course content is developed using the plans and guidelines from the design phase. All needed assets should be created (audio, video) to support the learning delivery. The programmers should integrate and develop technologies, in the course of delivery.

Implement

This is the delivery phase, where learning services are delivered to the learners. Highly competent trainers can make poorly designed programs, work well and well-designed programs, work great.

Evaluate

The aim of this phase is to check, whether the learning goals have been met or not. It establishes the required modification, to increase the efficiency and success rate of the learning program. A feedback mechanism ensures that the course has met the learning needs of the students and they have been presented with effective and necessary tools and aids.

ASSURE

It was developed by **Robert Heinich, Michael Molenda** and **James D Russell**. This model of instructional design, focuses on planning and conducting lessons, that aims to integrate media and technology, while focusing on the learner's needs. Thus, it is a systematic approach of developing lesson's plans that help teachers to organise instructional procedures and do an authentic assessment of student's learning.

Assure Model contains ***six*** *steps and they are*

A—Analyse learners
S—State objectives
S—Select methods, media and materials
U—Utilise media and materials
R—Require learner's participation
E—Evaluate and revise

Analyse Learners

- Identify the learners, so that you may select the best medium to meet the objectives.
- Analyse the audience, in terms of general characteristics (grade, age, sex, socio-economic level, etc.) and specific characteristics (knowledge, skills and attitude).
- Identify the learning style of the students (verbal, logical, visual, musical, structured).

State Objectives

- The next step is to state the objectives, as specifically as possible.
- Include conditions and degree of acceptable performance.
- The objectives may be derived from an assessment or course syllabus, stated in a text book, taken from curriculum, guide or developed by an instructor.
- Objectives are the learning outcomes, *i.e.* what will the students get out of the lesson?

The ABCDs of writing objectives are :

A — Audience Name-The audience of learners, for whom the objective is intended.

B — Behaviour Specify-The behaviour or capability to be learned.

C — Conditions-State the conditions, under which the performance would be observed.

D — Degree-Specify the degree, to which the new skill must be mastered.

Select Methods, Media and Materials

A systematic plan for deciding an appropriate media, must be selected.

It consists of two steps and they are

- Choosing an appropriate media format.
- Selecting, modifying and designing the specific materials, within that fomat.

Utilise Media and Materials

Utilisation procedures must be followed, in order to get maximum learning impact.

Following steps are included, in efficiently utilsing of media and materials

- Preview the material
- Practice the presentation
- Prepare an environment
- Prepare an audience and present

Require Learner's Participation

- It provides an opportunity for the learner, to test the lessons, being taught.
- Participation of the learners in the learning process, enhances learning.

Evaluate and Revise

- The final step of **ASSURE model** is to sit back and look at the results of your evaluation data gathering.
- The purpose of evaluation is to measure student's achievements, to evaluate media, methods and instructional process.
- In case of any shortcomings, the faulty part of the plan is revised.

Dick and Carey Model

This model is based on the Educationist Model of breaking instruction, into smaller components. Specifically, the instruction is targeted on the skills and knowledge to be taught and appropriate conditions for the learning of these outcomes. Its goal is to improve the instructor.

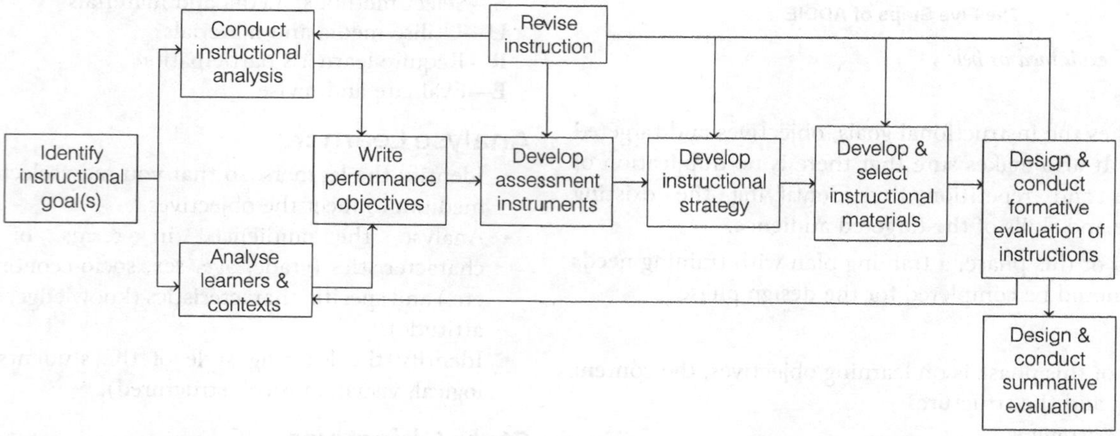

The ten steps in this model represent a set of procedures, which refers to as System Approach because it is made of interacting components. All the components are carefully linked.

This model is divided into six phases and they are :

Design Identify instructional goals and conduct Instructional Analysis.

Analysis Analyse learners and contexts.

Development Write performance objectives, develop assessment instruments, develop instructional strategies, develop and select instructional materials.

Formative Assessment Design and conduct formative evaluation of instruction.

Revision Revise instructions.

Summative Evaluation Design and conduct summative evaluation.

First Two Phases : Design and Analysis

Identify Instructional Goals Decide the goal of the instruction and what will the learners be able to perform, after they complete the training program. The goals can be derived from needs assessment, a list of smaller goals, practical experience with learning or analysis of job performance.

Conduct Instructional Analysis This process deals with the skills required by the students, to achieve desirable goals. It questions what step by step skills do students need to achieve instructional goal.

Analyse Learners and Contexts Analyse the instructional goals of the learners, the contexts in which they will learn the skills and where they will use the knowledge. Also look for learner's current skills, preferences, attitude and finally determine instructional settings.

Next Phase : Development

Write Performance Objectives Describe the skill or behaviour conditions that prevail, while carrying out task and the criteria to evaluate performance.

Develop Assessment Instruments Based on the objectives described, assessments are developed that are parallel to the learner's ability to perform. Examples of testing and measurement instrument are criterion reference tests, behaviour tests, pre-tests, post tests, practice tests, etc.

Develop Instructional Strategy Identify the strategy to be used while delivering instruction, to achieve the terminal objectives. The strategy that will emphasise components, to foster student's learning include pre-instructional activities, presentation of content, learner's participation assessment and follow through activities.

Develop and Select Instructional Material Instructional strategy is used to produce the instruction. It includes guidance for learners, instructional materials and assessments. Some of the examples are teaching guides, transparencies, computer applications, video-tapes, web pages, etc.

Final Phases : Formative Assessment, Revision and Summative Evaluation

Design and Conduct Formative Evaluation of Instruction After the completion of a draft of the instruction, a series of evaluations are conducted to collect data, to identify the need to improve instruction. The three types of **formative evaluation** are one to one evaluation, small group evaluation and field-trial evaluation.

Revise Instruction Data from the formative evaluation are summarised and interpreted to identify difficulties, experienced by learners in achieving the objectives and then specify the deficiencies in the instruction. It is used to re-examine the validity of Instructional Analysis and the assumptions about the entry behaviours and characteristics of learners. The instructional strategy is reviewed and finally, all these considerations are incorporated into revisions of the instruction, to make it a more effective instructional tool.

Design and Conduct Summative Evaluation It is an evaluation of the absolute value or worth of the instructional methods. It occurs only after the instruction has been formatively evaluated and sufficiently revised. It involves an independent evaluator.

Mason's Model

Charlotte Mason's Philosophy of Education has persisted for over a century and has regained popularity, especially among a subset of home schooling families. She believed that education should involve the whole person, not just the mind. According to **Mason**, education is "an atmosphere a discipline, a life". She advocated a high-quality, interesting curriculum for all children, not merely to 'educate' them, but also to guide them in the development of character and cultivate in them a lifelong love of learning.

In terms of home schooling, the Charlotte Mason's approach translates to

- the abundant use of narrative literature.
- plenty of time spent in outdoor's exploring.
- the development of an appreciation for art, music and nature.

The Charlotte Mason's teaching method consists of activities and attitude that help a child to learn self-discipline as well as academic subjects.

The specific steps to her method includes

(i) **Narration** An activity that consists of the child telling back a story she has heard or read. It is done orally, when the child is young and as she grows older, she begins to write out her narrations. This learning is both efficient and effective in terms of long-term retention.

(ii) **Picture Study** Teacher shows students a picture and gives the student a period of time in which to study it. When the time is up the picture is turned over and students tell back from memory what they remember about the picture.

(iii) **Nature Study** A study of living science, with a focus of observation of things seen on nature walk. This type of study is accessible to children both young and old. It relates them to the physical world while developing their powers of observation and creating in them a lifelong appreciation for the flora and fauna in the world around them.

(iv) **Living Books** Books written in an alive, engaging way by an author who had a passion for the subject. This would be in contrast to textbooks, which are often created by committees to achieve government's set school standards.

(v) **Scheduled Free Time** Mason insisted that children need "free" time" in which to pursue their interests, read, reflect and simply play. It helps children to pursue self-directed learning with their teacher close at hand to provide direction, stimulation and support.

Characteristies of Mason's Model

Short Lessons Charalotte Mason recommended starting out with short lessons and slowly increasing them as children get older. The goal is to train the child to focus fully on their work, but only for the amount of time they are developmentally capable of short lessons means that more subjects can be incorporated.

Habits Charlotte believed that the development of good habits within a child provides the foundation for early education.

Living Books Living books are the opposite of textbooks quality literature. They present inspiring stories that engage the minds of children and adults, like providing characters our children can look up to and emulate.

Dictation Dictation exercises, introduce and reinforce spelling and grammar concepts. Formal grammar study is usually delayed until age 10 or 11 in a Charlotte Mason's education.

Benefits of Mason's Education

- Keeping students engaged with their learning by keeping lessons short and manageable.
- Instilling love for literature through the use of living books.
- Teaching a child to express himself/herself clearly and articulately through narration practice.
- Reinforcing spelling and grammar concept through dictation exercises.
- Exposing students to fine arts particularly art and music.
- Infusing a student's life with an appreciation of nature and the natural world.

Gagne's Nine Events of Instruction

Robert Gagne was an educational psychologist, who created a nine step process called the **Events of Instruction**. It helps trainers, educators and instructional designers to structure their training sessions. It is a systematic process that helps them to develop strategies and create activites for instructional classes.

The nine events provide a framework for an effective learning process. Each step addresses a form of communication that supports the learning process. When each step is completed, learners are much more likely to be engaged and to retain the information or skills that they are being taught. Essentially, the steps give designers an outline or prototype to use prior to perform teaching or training activities.

He also made exceptional contributions in the field of instructional design. He propounded nine events of instruction, five E's of constructivism and nine elements of constructivist instructional design. He believed that, skills should be learned at the lowest level and mastered, before proceeding. The instructor should use positive reinforcement and repetition with each new skill, building upon previously acquired skills.

Steps of Instruction

Gain Attention The first event or step of instruction is to gain attention, to get the reception of stimuli.

Informing the Learners the Objective It is important to inform the learner, the purpose and expected outcome of the learning to provide the motivation to learners.

Stimulating Recall of Prior Learning The learners are asked to recall the existing relevant knowledge.

Presenting the Stimulus Relevant stimulus to the subject matter, should be presented.

Providing Learning Guidance It requires the instructor to make the stimulus as meaningful as possible.

Eliciting Performance The learners are asked to demonstrate the newly learned behaviour.

Providing Feedback Giving informative feedback to learner's performance is important.

Assessing Performance It consists of assessments to verify that learning has occurred.

Enhancing Retention and Transfer It refers to retaining the learned capability over a long period of time and transferring it to new situations, outside the learning environment.

Table : Nine Events of Instruction

Internal Process	Instructional Event	Action's Examples
Reception	Gaining attention	Use abrupt stimulus change
Expectancy	Informing learners of the objective	Tell learners, what they will be able to do after learning
Retrieval to working memory	Stimulating recall of prior knowledge	Ask for recall of previously learned knowledge of skills
Selective perception	Presenting the stimulus	Display the content with distinctive features
Semantic encoding	Providing learning guidance	Suggest a meaningful organisation
Responding	Eliciting performance	Ask learner to perform
Reinforcement	Providing feedback	Give informative feedback
Retrieval and reinforcement	Assessing performance	Require additional learner performance, with feedback
Retrievel and generalisation	Enhancing retention and transfer	Provides varied practices and paced reviews

Five E's of Constructivism

The **Five E's of Constructivism** was developed in 1987, by the biological sciences curriculum study, promotes collaborative and active learning in which students work together to solve problems and investigate new concepts by asking questions, observing, analysing and drawing conclusions. It is an Instructional model, based on the Constructivist approach to Learning.

Each of the Five E's of Constructivism describes a phase of learning and allows students and teachers to experience common activities, to use and build on prior knowledge and experience and to assess their understanding of a concept. Whereas, **constructivism** is a learning strategy that draws on student's existing knowledge, beliefs and skills with a Constructive approach, students synthesise new understanding from prior learning and new information.

The five E's of constructivism are

Engage This process helps to make connection between past and present learning experiences. Teachers can ask opening questions to students or task them to write down what they already know about the topic . It is also important to foster an interest of the students in the upcoming concept or skill.

Explore In this phase, students actively explore the new concept, through concrete learning experiences. They can be asked to go through the scientific method and communicate with peers to make observations. They identify and develop concepts, processes and skills.

Explain This phase helps students to synthesise new knowledge and ask questions for clarifications. For the 'explain' phase to be effective, teachers should ask students, to share what they have learned during the explore phase.

Elaborate This phase helps students to apply what they have learned. Teachers may ask students to create presentations or additional investigations to reinforce new skills. The purpose is to develop a deeper understanding and to cement their knowledge, before evaluation.

Evaluate In the last phase, teachers observe their students and check whether the students are totally familiar with the learned concepts or not. Means of evaluation are self-assessment, peer's assessment, writing assignments and exams.

Nine Elements of Constructivist Instructional Design

Gagne's approach to instructional design is considered a seminal model that has influenced many other design approaches.

The nine elements of constructivist instructional design are discussed below

Reception Voice modulations, gestures, short introductory video, handouts, etc. can be used for this purpose.

Expectancy Learners are informed about what they are about to learn so that their interest will be developed.

Retrieval Teacher must relate the new information with their prior knowledge.

Selective Perception Information should be presented in a practical and easy to understand manner depending on the needs and level of students.

Sementic Encoding Help student to learn and retain new information by use of examples, case studies, storytelling, etc.

Responding Students can demonstrate what they have learned through question-answer rounds, etc.

Reinforcement Reinforcement is given to the students in the form of feedback for helping them in retaining new information.

Retrieval Student's performance should be assessed through some tests.

Generalisation Students should apply what they have learned to new situations and conditions, then with practice they will be able to generalise it.

Applications of Computer in Education

Computer is the finest and most important gift of science and technology. It has done great miracles to the mankind. Today, there is no aspect of our life that remains untouched by the use and application of computers. In the field of education, the use of computers is of utmost importance. In **1986**, with the introduction of **New Education Policy**, our country also took initiatives for making the use of computers in teaching-learning activities.

Computer Assisted Instruction (CAI)

It is defined as the use of computers and software applications to teach concepts or skills. **IBM** developed one of the first instructional computer systems in the **1960s**, using **mini-computers**. It is an interactive instructional technique, whereby a computer is used to present the instructional material and monitor the learning that takes place. It uses a combination of text, graphics, sound and video in enhancing the learning process. It's programs use tutorials, drill and practice, simulation and problem-solving approaches to present topics and they test the student's understanding. The instructional work carried out with the help of computers is known as **CAI**. The computer is said to be ahead of the teaching machine on account of its capacity of doing more work, at the same time for an unlimited number of individual learners than the teaching machine.

Applications of CAI in Education

Hardware The computer as a machine represents the hardware. The teacher must have the knowledge to operate the computer.

Software The programmes containing instructions to the computer, in a language that it can understand are called software. The softwares used in CAI is of two types i.e. application software and system software.

Courseware It is the base of the instruction that is imparted to the learner by CAI. For example, a student of IX class wishes to learn about some topic. For this purpose, the computer machine as a hardware will need the services of software and the application and system programmes for its operation. These programmes will be prepared by the software programmer for its operation.

Advantages of CAI

- It is easy to change the instructions, practices, examples and tests.
- It is self-administered and just in time.
- Feedback can be either immediate or delayed, comprehensive or partial.
- It provides good lesson integrity.
- It is individualised and customised for users who need specific skills.
- Automatic record keeping.
- Program user interaction can after be increased, which offers more lesson control for more advanced learning that can be motivating for some users.

Disadvantages of CAI

- It promotes convergent thinking.
- Long development time and a short shelf life.
- It is more costly to develop than hiring an instructor.
- It assumes reading ability and spatialacuity.

Computer Assisted Learning (CAL)

It may be defined as any learning that is mediated by a computer and which requires no direct interaction between the user and a human instructor, in order to run. It is developed by combining knowledge from all fields of education/learning, Human Computer Interaction (HCI) and cognition. It is an interactive instruction technique, whereby a computer is used to present the instructional material for the learning-teaching process. It is useful for teachers, when to convey a vast amount of information in a very short period of time.

Types of CAL

Drill and Practice It helps the learners to practice the skills that have previously been presented and that further practice is necessary for mastery. In this technique, students learn facts and memorise them by drill method. *e.g.* MCQs.

Tutorial Under this method, computer assumes the role of a tutor, introducing content providing practice and assessing learning. Tutorials are used to introduce a new content to learners.

Problem-Solving Problem-solving software allows learners to see the results of their reactions to various events. Learners manipulate variables and feedback is provided based on these manipulations. Though, it is sometimes difficult to provide feedback based on individual choices of students without the computer.

Simulation It provides a real life scenario with the material to be learned, being applied as it would in the real world. It provides a simplified representation of a real situation, phenomenon or process. It also provides an oppurtunity for students to apply knowledge in a realistic format without time, expense or risk associated with the real thing.

Games They can create a contest for the learner. The learner can compete with the computer or other learner, while mastering the material. Usually, they are aimed at younger learners (those in the elementary grades). Games can substitute for worksheets and exercises.

Discovery It gives an opportunity to learners, to draw their own conclusions. It allows the learners to seek the answers on his own. It provides a large database of information specific to a course.

Laboratory Mode Computers are programmed to stimulate a variety of biological processes, to supplement the laboratory experiments. The learner explores various options and learns by inference.

Advantages of CAL

- CAL is individualised, that is each student is free to work at his own place, totally unaffected by the performance of any other students.
- Information is presented in a structured form. It proves useful in the study of a subject where there is hierarchy of facts and rules.
- CAL forces active participation of the part of the student, which contrasts with the more passive role in reading a book or attending a lecture.
- CAL utilises a reporting system that provides the student with a clear picture of his progress. Thus, students can identify the subject areas in which they have improved and in which they need improvement.
- By enabling students to manipulate concepts directly and explore the results of such manipulation, it reduces the time taken to comprehend difficult concepts.
- CAL offers a wide range of experiences that are otherwise not available to the student. It works as multi-media providing audio as well as visual inputs. It enables the student to understand concepts clearly with the use of stimulating techniques such as animation, blinking, graphical display, etc.
- CAL provides a lot of drilling which can prove useful for low aptitude students.
- CAL can enhance reasoning and decision-making abilities.

Disadvantages of CAL

- A CAL package may be regarded simply as a novelty, rather than an integral part of the educational process.
- Though simulation permits execution of chemical and biological experiments, hand-on experience is missing. Morever, CAL packages cannot develop manual skills, such as handling an appartus, working with a machine, etc.
- There are real costs associated with the development of CAL systems. It is expensive in terms of staff time to device and programme effective CAL.
- Content covered by a certain CAL package may become outdated. A very high cost is involved in the development of these packages. If the course is outdated, the resources involved in its development will be a waste.
- CAL packages may not fulfil expectations of teachers. Objectives and methods decided by the CAL author and of a teacher may differ.
- Motivating and training teachers to make use of computers in education is a challenging task. They may have fear of this new device. They may be unwilling to spend extra time for preparation, selection and use of CAL packages. It may also be perceived as a threat to their job.
- There are administrative problems associated with computer installation. The problems particularly related to the physical location of the computer resources, the cost of hardware maintenance and insurance and time-tabling.
- The rapid development of hardware makes it difficult to select a system before it becomes obsolete. If a new system is installed by a maximum number of institutions, that may not get courseware required for the system and courseware developed so far may become useless.

Computer Based Training (CBT)

It is an interactive training experience in which the computer provides the learning stimulus and the trainee must respond, so that the computer analyse the responses and provides feedback to the trainee. CBT and CAL are both synonym terms. So, the application of CAL (drill, practice, tutorial and simulation) can be used in CBT as well.

Applications of CBT in Education

E-learning It is associated with e-learning, which involves computers and interactive networks, simultaneously. **Web Based Learning** It is associated with learning materials delivered in a web browser. It also includes materials packed on CD-ROM or other media, like, disk.

Problem-Solving It helps to develop critical thinking skills. Learners can develop skills and follow directions through this technique. This approach often involves some type of problem, for which students have to figure out a solution.

Demo and Presentation This technique is often used to review information that has been learned. It is very useful, when a lecturer wants to present information in a lecture style format.

Advantages of CBT

- Classwork can be scheduled around work and family.
- Reduces travel time and travel cost for off campus students.
- Students may have option to select learning materials that meet their level of knowledge and interest.
- Students can study anywhere they have access to a computer and internet connection.
- Self-paced learning modules allow students to work at their own pace.

Disadvantages of CBT

- Learners with low motivation or bad study habits may fall behind.
- Without the routine structures of a traditional class, students may get lost or confused about course activities and deadlines.
- Students may feel isolated from the instructor and classmates.
- Instructor may not always be available when students are studying or need help.
- Slow internet connection or older computers may make accessing course materials frustrating.

Computer Managed Learning (CML)

It extends the scope of CAI with self-contained instructional range and testing experience for students. It is an application of computer technology for accountability and documentation of student's progress, by electronic filling, sorting and reporting of his learning outcomes.

According to **Hofmeister**, "The systematic control of instruction by the computer, characterized by testing, diagnosis, learning prescriptions and through record keeping".

According to **Hartmann**, "CML as a record keeping system or information management system is a significant improvement over manually based operations".

Applications of CML in Education

- Computerised libraries with control access and remote access, as per needs.
- Learning assessment, through administration of pre-tests and post tests.
- Design and preparation of learning prescriptions.
- Calculation analysis and storage of student's scores.

Advantages of CML

For Teachers

- CML system treats every student as an individual and helps teachers to follow their methods.
- It allows students to be extended or remediated as required.
- It makes computer software accessible and relevant.
- It gives back huge amount of time from testing and marking that is better spent on creative student's learning.
- It provides previously unknown data on which to constantly refine and improve the teaching method.

For School Principals and Management

- It provides accurate measurement and analysis for informed decision-making.
- It provides accountability and control.
- It facilitates quality control of teaching process.

Disadvantages of CML

- The volume of information can present problems for teachers, providing too much material to use in reasonable ways.
- Not enough well trained educators assure proper use of systems.
- There is too much emphasis on data and not enough emphasis on instruction.

Open and Distance Learning Material (ODLM)

According to **Gunther Dohmen**, "Distance education is a systematically organised form of self-study, in which student's counselling, the presentation of learning material and the securing and supervising of student's success are carried out by a team of teachers, each of whom has responsibilities. It is made possible, at a distance, by means of media which can cover long distances. The opposite of distance education is 'direct education' or 'face to face education', a type of education that takes place on the direct contact between lecturers and students".

According to **D Garrison and D Shale,** "Distance education implies that the majority of educational communication between teacher and students, occurs non-contiguously. It must involve two way communication between teacher and student(s), for the purpose of facilitating and supporting the education process. It uses technology to mediate the necessary two way communication".

According to **Picciano**, "Distance education uses three current and popular forms of media *i.e.* broadcast television, two way video-conferencing and a synchronous learning networks (multi-modal web based delivery of instructions that can be reviewed by the students at any time)".

In simple terms, the term **distance education** means the type of education that is organised by keeping in mind the distance factor, who imparts such education and who receives it, both are seperated by a common factor, known as distance. It is a two way interaction and communication between the teacher and the learner, through information and communication technologies with a freedom of choice related to time, space, pace, medium, access and curriculum.

Process of ODLM

The distance education has a great challenge, before its planners and organisers. One should have thorough knowledge and expertise for going through the task of the planning and organisation of the activities, concerning a distance education programme.

The processes associated with planning and management of a distance education programme are :

Pre-Assumptions and Knowledge About the Learners The planners before planning the programme must be clear about its purposes and objectives, like who may get benefit through the distance education programme?, what is their educational, social and cultural background?, what type of technologies, resources and skills are available at their end the accessing the programmes?, etc.

Distance Education requires :

- structured planning.
- well-designed courses.
- special instructional techniques.
- methods of communication, by electronic and other technologies.

Planning It is the foundation stone of quality assurance in distance education. It should be systematic and well-planned. The planning should be done on the basis of social demand, educational demand, resources and teacher's profile.

Preparation of the Programme It is the next step after doing the planning. In this stage, training objectives are prepared before implementing the programme, by assessing the training needs of the teacher. Then, suitable curriculum is designed to fulfil the objectives.

Process of Course Design It tells the dynamics of the various instructional inputs, involved in curriculum transaction. This includes mainly two components i.e. developing course materials and delivering mechanism.

Evaluation of the Course It is one of the most important component of the programme. Evaluation of the trainees, trainers, curriculum, materials, etc, should be done from time to time. Evaluation of overall programme effectiveness and achievement of training objectives, has to be done both formatively and summatively.

E-Learning

It stands for the type of learning carried out, facilitated or supported by some or the other electronic gadgets, media or resources. It is facilitated by the use of any electronic media, micro-phones and listening devices or audio and video tapes.

It is an electronically carried out learning facilitated and supported by the use of advanced learning technology of computers, networking and multi-media.

It is very much associated with the use of the internet and web technology via computers or laptops. Mobile learning may be well regarded as an extension of e-learning.

Bnooma Krishnan in his finding on the history of e-learning, mentioned four distinct stages in the evolution of the concept of e-learning, namely, multi-media era (1984-1993), web infancy (1994-1999), next generation web (2000-2005) and mobile learning. So, e-learning can be defined as a learning carried out, supported and facilitated by the advanced multi-media facilities, as well as internet and web technology delivered to the learners via computers, laptops, mobile and ICT appliances.

E-learning is defined in the **National Testing Information System** as "Any learning that is assisted by information and communication technology. This mainly includes computer- based online learning, but also covers interactive CD-ROMs, Videos, handhold computers, mobile phones, tele-conference and video-conferencing".

According to **Clark and Mayer**, "e-learning is instruction delivered on a computer by way of CD-ROM, internet or intranet".

According to **Stockley**, "e-learning as the delivery of a learning, training or education program by electronic means. e-learning involves the use of a computer or electronic device (*e.g.* mobile phone) to provide training, educational or learning material".

Advantages of E-learning

- It is a very efficient way of delivering courses, online.
- Due to its convenience and flexibility, the resources are available from anywhere and at anytime.
- Web based learning promotes active and independent learning.
- Through discussion boards and chats, people are able to interact with everyone online and also clear downs if any.
- People have access to the net, 24×7, we can train ourself anytime and from anywhere also.

Disadvantages of E-learning

- Most of the online assessments are limited to questions that are only objective in nature.
- There is also the problem of the extent of security of online learning programs.
- The authenticity of a particular student's work is also a problem as online just about anyone can do a project rather than the actual student, itself.
- The assessments that are computer marked generally have a tendency of being only knowledge based and not necessarily practicality based.

Approaches to E-learning

Any particular learning is termed as e-learning, when the mode of delivering instructions is electronic, like computers, multi-media, mobile and ICT appliances.

Different approaches to e-learning, for different modes, are discussed below

Blended Learning In this approach, a combination of traditional and ICT enhanced e-learning practice is used. The programmes and activities are designed as to present both the traditional classroom teaching practices and e-learning based instruction.

Mobile Learning The easy availability and affordability of mobile devices has created the space for mobile enabled learning. It is the acquisition of knowledge and skills, through mobile technology, anytime and anywhere.

Online Learning It refers to the use of online tools for learning. When lectures, assignments, tests are available on virtual platforms.

Offline Learning Learning activities can be carried out offline. It includes the access of well-stored information and learning packages available in the form of recorded CD-ROM, DVD, etc.

Synchronous Learning It resembles traditional classroom teaching methods, despite the participant being located, remotely. It requires a time-table to be organised, web-conferencing, video-conferencing, educational television, instructional television. Examples of synchronous technology are Direct Broadcast Satellite (DBS), internet, radio, live streaming, telephone and web based VOIP. Online meeting software such as adobe connect, has helped to facilitate meeting in distance learning courses.

Asynchronous Learning In asynchronous learning, participants access course materials flexibly on their own schedules. Students are not required to be together at the same time. Mail correspondence, which is the oldest form of distance education, is an asynchronous delivery technology, as are message board forums, e-mail, video and audio recordings, print materials, voice-mail and fax.

The last two methods can be combined. Many courses offered by the Open University use periodic sessions of residential or day teaching to supplement the remote teaching. The open university uses a blend of technologies and a blend of learning modalities (face to face, distance and hybrid) all under the rubric of 'distance learning'.

Distance learning can also use Interactive Radio Instruction (IRI), Interactive Audio Instruction (IAI), online virtual worlds, digital games, webinars and web casts.

EXAM BASED QUESTIONS

1 The concept of System approach is related to which of the following field?
(a) Systematic organisation of e-learning
(b) Instructional design
(c) Education
(d) Information Technology

2 Who defined 'system' as a system is a set of inter-related and inter-dependent elements?
(a) R L Ackoff
(b) Twelkier
(c) Crawford Robb
(d) A K Jalaluddin

3 According to Jalaluddin, in the system's process, how can we achieve pre-determined and specified objectives?
(a) By systematically organising the elements
(b) By organising inter-related elements
(c) By operating the elements
(d) None of the above

4 Which of the following step(s) is/are involved in system approach?
(a) Problem-solving
(b) Studying the problem
(c) Systematic thinking
(d) All of the above

5 According to Twelkier, how can an individual solve his problem with system approach?
(a) By managing the educational tools
(b) By examining, thoroughly
(c) Through optimal utilisation of all resources
(d) By evaluating the problem

6 Which of the following, have greatest stake in educational technology related development?
(a) Mobile learning
(b) System approach
(c) Electronic learning
(d) Instructional System

7 What is the foremost step in a simplified system approach to curriculum design?
(a) Assessing and evaluating
(b) Selecting instructional methods
(c) Considering target population
(d) Operating a course/curriculum

8 According to Tillman, an instructional designer is like a/an
(a) doctor (b) carpenter
(c) teacher (d) engineer

9 Which of the following cannot be termed as educational products?
(a) Online courses (b) Social networks
(c) Manuals (d) Tutorials

10 Which of the following is a process of instructional design?
(a) Development of delivery system
(b) Formulating objectives
(c) Estimating skills of learners
(d) None of the above

11 In which year, did Jalaluddin developed six phases in the system approach to instructional design?
(a) 1900 (b) 1891
(c) 1981 (d) 1800

12 Which of the following is the fourth phase in system approach to instructional design?
(a) Designing of the system
(b) Operation phase
(c) Formation of objectives
(d) Evaluation of outcomes

13 The process, 'evaluation of outcomes' deals with
(a) assessment of student's performance
(b) implementation of Instructional System
(c) feedback of evaluation results
(d) post test's scores by students

14 Why is system approach important in education?
(a) It helps in educational planning.
(b) It improves the institution.
(c) It improves the quality of education.
(d) All of the above

15 Which of the following is not a component of ADDIE Model?
(a) Authoritative (b) Design
(c) Development (d) Implementation

16 How do ADDIE model avoids duplication and repetition of knowledge?
(a) By estimating the targeted audience
(b) By identifying existing skills
(c) By mentioning goals and objectives, clearly
(d) None of the above

17 In which of the following phase, learning services are delivered to the learners?
(a) Evaluate (b) Design
(c) Implement (d) Analyse

18 In ADDIE model, what is the aim of the last stage?
(a) To establish targeted outcomes
(b) To develop the content framework
(c) To develop the course content, using the guidelines
(d) To check, whether learning goals have been met or not

19 Who developed the 'ASSURE model'?
(a) Robert Heinich (b) Michael Molenda
(c) James D Russell (d) All of these

20 In ASSURE model, 'U' stands for
(a) utilising and revising
(b) unorganise media and methods
(c) utilise media and materials
(d) unethical code of conduct

21 In which of the following methods, does ABCDs of writing are specified?
(a) State objectives
(b) Select methods, media and materials
(c) Require learner's participation
(d) Evaluate and revise

22 Why the evaluate and revise process is important in ASSURE model?
(a) It helps the learner to select an appropriate media.
(b) It helps the learner to practice the knowledge.
(c) It helps the learner to measure student's achievement.
(d) None of the above

23 How many steps are included in 'Dick and Carey model'?
(a) Eight (b) Nine (c) Ten (d) Eleven

24 Which of the following process, determines skills required by learners to achieve instructional objectives?
(a) Conduct Instructional Analysis
(b) Analyse learners and contexts
(c) Develop assessment's instruments
(d) Identify instructional goals

25 Which of the following step(s) is/are included in developing an instructional strategy?
(a) Presentation of content (b) Criterion reference test
(c) Pre-tests (d) Post tests

26 Which of the following is not an instructional material?
(a) Video-tapes (b) Teaching guides
(c) Web pages (d) Behaviour tests

27 The last phase of 'Dick and Carey model' includes
(a) formative assessment (b) summative evaluation
(c) revised instruction (d) All of these

28 Why revising of the instruction is an important step in Dick and Carey model?
(a) It helps to identify the correct instructional tool.
(b) It makes the instructional tool more effective.
(c) It helps to evaluate the instructions.
(d) None of the above

29 In which of the following field(s), did Gagne's work was based?
(a) To improve the instructor
(b) Medium of learning
(c) Conditions of learning
(d) Both (b) and (c)

30 According to Gagne, skills should be learned at
(a) highest level (b) horizontal level
(c) vertical level (d) lowest level

31 Which step of instruction in Gagne's Nine Events of Instruction, talks about 'reception of stimuli'?
(a) Stimulating recall of prior learning
(b) Presenting the stimulus
(c) Gain attention
(d) Eliciting performance

32 Which of the following best explains the step of 'eliciting performance'?
(a) Demonstrate the learned behaviour
(b) Giving feedback about performance
(c) Providing stimulus to the matter
(d) To recall the knowledge

33 How can an instructor assess the performance of learners?
(a) By conducting regular tests
(b) By verifying that learning has happened
(c) By evaluating the Instructional Method
(d) None of the above

34 How to retain the learned capability for a long period of time?
(a) Through behavioural tests
(b) By conducting drills and giving feedbacks
(c) Through practice and spaced reviews
(d) Both (b) and (c)

35 What is the aim of Five E's of Constructivism?
(a) To effectively analyse the instruction
(b) To grow, understanding of a concept
(c) To evaluate instructional strategy
(d) To gain new information

36 Which of the following is not included in Five E's of Constructivism?
(a) Engage (b) Evaluate (c) Elaborate (d) Evolve

37 How can a teacher, foster an interest of the students in the new learning concept?
(a) By making a connection between past and present learning
(b) To explore new concept to students
(c) By showing a tutorial, about the new concept
(d) All of the above

38 How can a teacher make the phase 'explain' more effective?
(a) By conducting pre-tests and post tests
(b) By asking students, to apply the learned knowledge
(c) By asking students, what they have learned
(d) None of the above

39 In the model, 'Five E's of Constructivism', elaborate phase includes ....

(a) reinforcement of new skills
(b) creating presentation and investigation
(c) develop a deep understanding
(d) All of the above

40 Who propounded, 'Nine Elements of Constructivist Instructional Design'?

(a) David Ausubel (b) Robert Gagne
(c) Mark Gagne (d) Skinner

41 Which of the following is the advantage of computer assisted instruction?

(a) Modular (b) Individualised
(c) Accurate (d) None of these

42 How do computer assisted instruction, helps in education?

(a) It contains programmes with instructions.
(b) It is the base of the instruction.
(c) It gives access to hardware.
(d) All of the above

43 What do you understand by computer assisted learning?

(a) Interactive instruction technique
(b) Instructional work, carried by computers
(c) Interactive training experience
(d) None of the above

44 Why computer assisted learning is beneficial for teachers?

(a) It helps them to evaluate learning performance.
(b) It helps them to convey vast information.
(c) It helps them to save time.
(d) Both (b) and (c)

45 Which of the following is not an application of computer assisted learning?

(a) Drill and practice (b) Discovery
(c) e-learning (d) Laboratory modes

46 .... is/are used, to introduce new content to learners.

(a) Drills (b) Tutorials (c) Simulation (d) Discovery

47 How does Discovery Method, helps in computed assisted learning?

(a) It provides database of information
(b) It allows learners to seek answers on their own
(c) It helps learners to draw their own conclusions
(d) All of the above

48 Which of the two can be described as synonym terms?

(a) CBT and CAL (b) CAL and CML
(c) ODLM and CAI (d) CAI and CBT

49 Which technique is used to review information of the learners that has been learned?

(a) Problem-solving (b) e-learning
(c) Web based learning (d) Demo and presentation

50 Which of the following is an application of CML in education?

(a) Calculation of student's score
(b) Pre-tests and post tests
(c) Both (a) and (b)
(d) Data inadequate

51 According to Gunther Dohmen, distance education is

(a) direct education between teachers and students
(b) systematic form of self-study
(c) non-contiguous communication between students and lecturers
(d) a two way video-conferencing

52 What is the third process in preparing ODLM?

(a) Pre-assumptions about learner
(b) Process of course design
(c) Planning
(d) Preparation of programme

53 Which of the following tool is not used for e-learning?

(a) Micro-phones (b) Electronic media
(c) Blackboards (d) Voice-mails

54 As per Bhoomo Krishnan, what was the duration of next generation web?

(a) 1984-1993 (b) 2000-2005
(c) 1994-1999 (d) 2006 to present

55 What do you understand by 'blended learning'?

(a) Combination of ICT and traditional learning
(b) Learning from mobile devices
(c) Use of online tools for learning
(d) None of the above

56 Which of the following is not an example of synchronous learning?

(a) Web based VOIP
(b) Direct Broadcast Satellite
(c) Interactive Audio Instruction
(d) Radio and live streaming

57 Match the following.

List I	List II
A. Computer assisted learning	1. Interactive instructional technique
B. Computer assisted instruction	2. Self-contained instructional range for students
C. Computer based training	3. Software based system of instruction
D. Computer managed learning	4. Interactive training technique
	5. Small step presentation, with priming and prompting

Codes

	A	B	C	D		A	B	C	D
(a)	3	1	2	5	(b)	1	3	4	2
(c)	5	4	1	2	(d)	1	3	2	4

58 Match the following.

List I	List II
A. Administrative	1. Community
B. Grassroot	2. Apex level policy's formulator
C. Demonstration	3. Textbooks' writers
D. System Analysis	4. Review committees at all levels i.e. local, state and national
	5. Students, teachers and stakeholders
	6. Students and teachers

Codes

	A	B	C	D		A	B	C	D
(a)	4	5	6	2	(b)	2	6	1	5
(c)	4	1	3	5	(d)	2	5	6	4

59 Match the following.

List I	List II
A. In-service teacher education	1. To sharpen and deepen the subject knowledge
B. Pre-service teacher education	2. To bring refinement and upgradation in teaching skills
C. Distance education	3. To prepare teachers, in terms of the requirements of Demand-Supply Analysis
D. Refresher courses	4. To help the disadvantaged society
	5. To prepare teachers with an eye on the shortage of teachers, in the far flung areas

Codes

	A	B	C	D		A	B	C	D
(a)	1	3	5	2	(b)	1	5	4	3
(c)	3	1	5	2	(d)	2	3	4	5

60 Match the following.

List I	List II
A. ADDIE	1. Reductionist Model of Breaking Instructions
B. ASSURE	2. Gain attention, to get the reception of stimuli
C. Dick and Carey	3. Analysing the audience, in terms of knowledge and skills
D. Gagne's Five E's of Constructivism	4. Development of course contents, using the plans and guidelines
	5. Explore the new concept, through concrete learning

Codes

	A	B	C	D		A	B	C	D
(a)	1	5	2	3	(b)	4	3	1	2
(c)	4	3	1	5	(d)	3	2	5	1

61 Match the following.

List I (Gagne's Nine Events of Instructions)	List II (Action's example)
A. Eliciting performance	1. Display the content with distinctive features
B. Presenting the stimulus	2. Provide varied practice and spaced reviews
C. Providing feedback	3. Suggest a meaningful organisation
D. Enhancing retention and transfer	4. Ask learner to perform
	5. Giving informative feedback

Codes

	A	B	C	D
(a)	1	3	2	5
(b)	5	4	3	1
(c)	4	2	5	3
(d)	4	1	5	2

62 Match the following.

List I	List II
A. Next generation web	1. 1970-1983
B. Mobile learning	2. 1984-1993
C. Multi-media	3. 1994-1999
D. Web infancy	4. 2000-2005
	5. 2006 to present

Codes

	A	B	C	D		A	B	C	D
(a)	4	3	5	1	(b)	1	2	5	4
(c)	4	5	2	3	(d)	3	2	5	4

63 Match the following.

List I	List II
A. Online learning	1. Adobe connect
B. Offline learning	2. Print materials
C. Synchronous	3. Mobile and ICT technology
D. Asynchronous	4. Virtual platform
	5. CD-ROM, DVD

Codes

	A	B	C	D		A	B	C	D
(a)	4	5	1	2	(b)	3	5	4	2
(c)	4	1	5	2	(d)	2	3	5	1

64 The main approach of instructional design is
(a) System Analysis
(b) training Psychology
(c) cybernetic
(d) All of the above

65 Distance education is also called as .... education.
(a) correspondence (b) home
(c) independent (d) indoor

66 Computer assisted instruction is used for
(a) instructional purpose
(b) teaching purpose
(c) individual variation
(d) All of the above

67 .... is the promotion of the development of appropriate mental mode, for solving problem.
(a) Instruction (b) Teaching
(c) Learning (d) Conditioning

68 Language laboratory is used for .... skills.
(a) teaching (b) language
(c) social (d) instructional

69 In Gagne's hierarchy of learning, which one of the following will not be included in rule learning?
(a) Concept learning
(b) Discrimination learning
(c) SR learning
(d) Problem-solving learning

70 What type of model is ADDIE best described as?
(a) Educational Technology
(b) Educational Psychology
(c) Constructivism
(d) Instructional design

71 .... can be defined as most recent and perhaps the most comprehensive technique, for solving computers' problems.
(a) System Analysis (b) System data
(c) System procedure (d) System record

72 What is something that you would assess in the analysis phase of ADDIE model?
(a) Learner's characteristics
(b) Instructor's performance
(c) Student's satisfaction
(d) Content

73 Which of the following is not the web based teaching tool?
(a) Virtual news and letters
(b) Homework hotlines
(c) Mails
(d) All of the above

74 Which of the following is not an example of real time distance learning?
(a) Tele-conferencing
(b) Web based applications
(c) Virtual tours of historic sites
(d) Closed circuit T.V. monitors

75 Which of the following could be considered to be an advantage of using e-learning?
(a) Quick to access (b) Easy to use
(c) Flexible (d) Easy to implement

76 Arrange the following phases, on system's approach in chronology.
1. Management 2. Monitoring
3. Planning 4. Analysis
Choose the correct option.
(a) 1, 2, 4, 3 (b) 2, 1, 3, 4
(c) 4, 3, 1, 2 (d) 2, 1, 4, 3

77 Arrange the steps of instruction, in Gagne's Nine Events of Instruction in chronology.
1. Stimulating recall of prior learning
2. Gain attention
3. Presenting the stimulus
4. Informing the learners, the objective
Choose the correct option.
(a) 1, 4, 3 and 2 (b) 1, 2, 4 and 3
(c) 2, 4, 1 and 3 (d) 4, 3, 1 and 2

78 Arrange the Five E's of Constructivism in chronology.
1. Engage 2. Elaborate
3. Explain 4. Explore
Choose the correct option.
(a) 1, 3, 2 and 4 (b) 1, 4, 3 and 2
(c) 4, 2, 3 and 1 (d) 2, 4, 1 and 3

79 Arrange the following phases of System approach to Instructional Design.
1. Development of the system
2. Formation of objectives
3. Operation and implementation
4. Pre-assessment of student's behaviour
Choose the correct option.
(a) 1, 3, 4 and 2 (b) 3, 2, 4 and 1
(c) 1, 2, 4 and 3 (d) 2, 4, 1 and 3

80 Arrange the following steps of ASSURE Model, in chronology.
1. Utilise materials 2. State objectives
3. Analyse the learners 4. Select media
Choose the correct option.
(a) 3, 2, 4 and 1 (b) 2, 4, 3 and 1
(c) 1, 2, 4 and 3 (d) 3, 4, 2 and 1

81 Arrange the last four phases of 'Dick and Carey Model' as and when they occur.
1. Revise instruction
2. Develop instructional material
3. Conduct formative evaluation
4. Design summative evaluation
Choose the correct option.
(a) 2, 3, 4 and 1 (b) 2, 3, 1 and 4
(c) 1, 3, 4 and 2 (d) 3, 1, 4 and 2

82 Arrange the phases of 'ADDIE model' in chronology.
1. Design 2. Development
3. Analysis 4. Implementation

Choose the correct option.
(a) 1, 2, 4 and 3 (b) 3, 4, 2 and 1
(c) 3, 1, 2 and 4 (d) 3, 2, 1 and 4

83 What are the application(s) of System Analysis, when applied to classroom's instruction as a sub-system of the curriculum?
1. It helps to design classroom instruction, differently.
2. It helps a Novel Method of reviewing classroom instruction.
3. It helps the teacher, to verify results and get feedback.
4. It helps to evaluate the process of learning.

Choose the correct option.
(a) 1 and 3 (b) 2 and 4
(c) Only 1 (d) Only 4

84 An individual learner is facilitated by
1. confirmation 2. response
3. behaviour 4. language

Choose the correct option.
(a) 3 and 4 (b) 1 and 3
(c) 1 and 2 (d) Only 1

85 Which learning, resembles traditional classroom teaching method, despite the participant being located remotely?
1. Miscellaneous learning
2. Asynchronous learning
3. Contiguous learning
4. Synchronous learning

Choose the correct option.
(a) 1 and 3 (b) 2 and 4 (c) Only 2 (d) Only 4

86 Distance education employs
1. computer 2. television
3. radio 4. smart board

Choose the correct option.
(a) 1, 2 and 3 (b) 2, 3 and 4
(c) 1 and 2 (d) Only 1

Directions (Q. Nos. 87-94) *Given below are two statements, one labelled as Assertion (A) and other labelled as Reason (R). Following are the codes given below. Choose the correct code.*

Codes
(a) Both A and R are true (b) Both A and R are false
(c) A is true, but R is false (d) A is false, but R is true

87 **Assertion** (A) Gagne made exceptional contribution in the field of instructional design.
Reason (R) Gagne has propounded 'ADDIE model'.

88 **Assertion** (A) The aim of 'develop phase' is to deliver learning services.
Reason (R) Evaluate means to develop the course content.

89 **Assertion** (A) ASSURE model was developed by Robert Michael and James.
Reason (R) ASSURE model focuses on planning and conducting lessons.

90 **Assertion** (A) The goal of Dick and Carey model is to improve the instructional Technology.
Reason (R) Dick and Carey model is based on breaking instruction, into smaller components.

91 **Assertion** (A) Constructivism is a learning strategy that draws on student's existing knowledge, beliefs and skills.
Reason (R) Constructive approach helps students synthesise new understanding from prior learning and new information.

92 **Assertion** (A) Discovery allows the learners to seek the answers on his own.
Reason (R) It provides a simplified representation of a real situation or process.

93 **Assertion** (A) Mail correspondence is an asynchronous delivery technology.
Reason (R) Students are not required to be together at the same time in asynchronous learning.

94 **Assertion** (A) The five E's of constructivism was developed in 1985.
Reason (R) It promotes collaborative and active learning in which students work together.

ANSWERS

1 (c)	2 (a)	3 (b)	4 (d)	5 (c)	6 (b)	7 (c)	8 (d)	9 (b)	10 (a)
11 (c)	12 (b)	13 (d)	14 (d)	15 (a)	16 (b)	17 (c)	18 (d)	19 (d)	20 (c)
21 (a)	22 (c)	23 (c)	24 (a)	25 (a)	26 (d)	27 (d)	28 (b)	29 (c)	30 (d)
31 (c)	32 (a)	33 (b)	34 (c)	35 (b)	36 (d)	37 (a)	38 (c)	39 (d)	40 (b)
41 (a)	42 (d)	43 (a)	44 (d)	45 (c)	46 (b)	47 (d)	48 (a)	49 (d)	50 (c)
51 (b)	52 (d)	53 (c)	54 (b)	55 (d)	56 (c)	57 (b)	58 (d)	59 (a)	60 (c)
61 (d)	62 (c)	63 (a)	64 (d)	65 (a)	66 (c)	67 (a)	68 (b)	69 (b)	70 (d)
71 (a)	72 (a)	73 (d)	74 (c)	75 (c)	76 (c)	77 (c)	78 (b)	79 (d)	80 (a)
81 (b)	82 (c)	83 (a)	84 (c)	85 (d)	86 (a)	87 (c)	88 (b)	89 (b)	90 (d)
91 (a)	92 (c)	93 (a)	94 (c)						

CHAPTER 32

Emerging Trends in E-Learning

The technological trends of e-learning are enormous and growing with a very rapid pace. Some of the emerging trends of e-learning are mobile learning, micro-learning, adaptive e-learning, Artificial Intelligence, etc. All these trends help people to get access to a world class learning experience.

E-Learning

E-learning or the electronic learning is the type of learning carried out, facilitated or supported by some or the other electronic gadgets, media or resources. It facilitates the use of electronic media, like microphones and listening devices, like audio and video tapes.

In this sense, e-learning may call for the services of the advanced electronic information and communication media like CD-ROMs, DVDs, tele-conferencing, video conferencing, computer based conferencing, e-mail, live chat, surfing on the internet and web browsing, online reference libraries, video game-style simulation, customised e-learning courses and web blogs.

According to **Rosenberg (2001)**, "e-learning refers to the use of the internet technologies to deliver a broad array of solutions to enhance knowledge and performance".

According to **Santheesh Kumar and Saggy John**, "Though computer is used for instruction and learning, the non-web technology does not come under e-learning. The entire computer based instruction, like computer assisted instruction and computer managed instruction, integrated learning systems, multi-media, interactive video, virtual reality, Artificial Intelligence, etc, are not delivered through the internet but are still used for learning and instruction that cannot be included in e-learning. However, when these techniques are delivered via internet for instruction and learning, becomes e-learning".

In this Chapter

- *E-Learning*
- *Social Learning*
- *Open Education Resources (OER)*
- *E-inclusion*
- *Ethics in E-learning*

Nature and Characteristics of E-Learning

- It is used to refer computer enhanced learning.
- It is a type of 'online learning' carried out through the internet or web-enabled technology.
- It conveys broader meaning compare to the terms computer based teaching and computer aid instruction.
- It should not be taken as synonymous to audio-visual learning. Now a days, multi-media technology and distance education programmes rests heavily on the use of the internet and web services provided through the computers, yet these are not identical but complementary.
- It is restricted to the type of e-learning carried out, facilitated or supported through web-enhanced instructions and the internet based communication, like e-mail, audio and video conferencing, mail list, live chats and telephone.

Emerging Trends in E-Learning

The technological trends of e-learning are enormous and growing with a very rapid pace. In this competitive world, daily new trends are being emerged to provide good learning techniques to the learner. It helps people to get access to a world class learning experience, when traditional learning may not be possible due to financial, personal or any other constraint.

Some of the emerging trends of e-learning are

Mobile Learning

It is the ability of an individual to obtain or provide educational content on personal pocket devices, such as PDAs, smartphones and mobile phones.

Mobile phones are considered to the best platform for e-learning because

- It has the potential to reach masses
- Carried all the time
- Easy to use
- Just in time learning

Micro-Learning

It is a way of teaching and delivering content to learners in small, very specific bursts.

The main benefits of this kind of learning are

- Accessible
- Less time consuming
- Learner-centric
- Rich media
- Just in time
- Less time consuming

Gamification

This type of e-learning is through games and it really depends on the program and the audience desires.

Some of the benefits of gamification in e-learning are

- Better learning experience
- Helps to remember for long time
- Instant feedback

Adaptive E-Learning

Adaptive e-learning uses computers as an interactive teaching devices. These methodology arrange the allocation of human and mediated resources according to the unique learning needs of each learner.

Some major benefits of this technological trend in case of e-learning are

- Very rich study resources
- Saves a lot of time of learners

Augmented Reality

This technology super imposes a computer generated image on a user view of real world. It is really a great boon technology for the students or learners in general. This technology needs device, internet and software of augmented reality.

Some benefits of augmented reality in case of e-learning can be as follows

- Easy, instant and deep learning of things
- Huge collection of information

Internet Of Things (IOT)

It refers to the ever growing network of physical things or objects around us which hold IP address for internet connectivity and the communication that occurs between these connected objects and other internet enabled devices and systems.

Some major benefits of IOT in case of e-learning are

- Learner is part of the learning system as an entity
- Continuous tracking of learner by the system
- Continuous updates to learners

Cloud Based E-Learning

This type of e-learning creates ripples in the field of education and business. These learning systems are hosted on the internet and can be easily accessed by logging into a service provider's site. Rather than installing all the software and course on user's computer, the instructional designer will simply use their internet browsers to upload course content, create new courses and communicate with learners and users directly.

Some of the advantages are

- Faster development
- Easier to maintain
- Learner oriented service request
- Cost predictability
- More storage space

Video E-Learning

This kind of e-learning helps the learner to grasp the content by watching the videos. This kind of e-learning gives a very quick idea and helps to understand the things with multi-media affects. This serves as very effective medium of e-learning.

Some benefits of video e-learning can be as follows

- Video explanation.
- More information in less time.
- Best learning experience.

Becon E-Learning

Becon e-learning is a wireless device that transmits signals or other nearby devices via low-energy bluetooth connections. This is used as on Indoor Positoning System (IPS).

Some great benefits of this technological trend are

- Better accessibility.
- More powerful communication.
- Increased intellectual discovery.
- Insightful data.
- Improved in-class experiences.

Artificial Intelligence

It is something like intelligent software which is designed to take some intelligent actions reading entire environment around it. The involvenment of artificial intelligence in e-learning helps the learner to take very wise descisions and quality resource, which in turn helps the learner to excel and make his achievements at faster pace.

Some major benefits of AI in case of e-learning are

- Provides expert tutors for learners
- Automated teaching
- Rich information

Social Learning

Social learning is learning from others. This kind of learning can occur through direct as well as indirect contact. **Direct contact** refers to face to face interactions whereas **indirect contact** refers to interactions on social media. It creates a learning setting where learners can network, share, collaborate and exchange ideas on problem-solving. It is the learning that takes place through social interaction between peers and it may or may not lead to a change in attitude or behaviour.

If learning is to be considered 'social,' then it must

- demonstrate a change in understanding that has taken place in the individuals involved. This may be at a surface level (recalling new information) or deeper levels (change in attitude, beliefs).
- go beyond the individual to become situated within wider social units or communities of practice within society.
- occur through social interactions and processes within a social network, either through direct interaction (conversation) or through other media (social media).

Thus, social learning may be defined as a change in understanding that goes beyond to the individual to become situated within wider social units or communities of practice through social interactions between actors within a social network. It includes tools, like Web 2.0, social networking sites, blogs, chats, video-conferencing and discussion forum for learning.

World Wide Web/Web 2.0

Web 2.0 is simply improved version of the first World Wide Web, characterized specifically by the change from static to dynamic user generated content and also the growth of social media. The concept behind web 2.0 refers to rich web applications, web-oriented architecture and social web. It refers to changes in the ways web pages are designed and used by the users, without any change in any technical specifications.

Web 2.0 examples include hosted services (Google Maps), web applications (Google Docs), video sharing sites (You Tube), blogs (Word Press), social networking (Facebook), microblogging (Twitter) and content hosting services and many more. It enables users to create, share, collaborate and communicate their work with others, without any need of any web design skills. These capabilities were not present in web 1.0. By using web 2.0 tools in the learning process, students have the opportunity to develop their learning skills as they learn new research methods, become independent researchers, develop skills in creative thinking, solve problems become team workers, manage their own development and education.

Web 2.0 tools support a Constructivist approach to education where students discovers and constructs knowledge as opposed to acquiring it. This enables a two-way knowledge exchange where students cannot only obtain information from the internet, but also contribute and upload knowledge to it.

Teachers and educators need to embrace this new approach in their teaching strategies, and should provide an infrastructure to support the construction rather than the transfer of knowledge. Empowering students to take charge of their learning shifts and the role of the teacher from instructor to learning partner. Learners are given greater choice by providing different ways of navigating through curriculum content. Giving students ownership of their learning promotes a deeper understanding of concepts. However, there is a need to create a balance between the freedom and creativity of developing learning experience and ensuring that some level of structure is adhered, so that effective learning can take place.

Advantages

- Vast amount of information is available on the website.
- A distant education institute helps its students around the world (apply or register to course).
- It facilitates rapid interactive communication.
- It involves low cost for initial connection.
- It has become the global media and is accessible from everywhere in the world.
- Learners can actively be involved in knowledge building.
- It provides real time discussion.

Disadvantages

- Danger of excess and worthless content.
- Net often becomes overloaded because of large number of users.
- No quality control over available data.
- There is no regulation.

Social Networking Sites

A social networking site is a platform to build social networks or social relations among people, who share the same interest, activities, backgrounds or real-life connections. Most social network sites are web based and provide a variety of ways for users to interact, such as e-mail and instant messaging services, etc. Some examples of social networking sites are Pinterest, Yahoo, Skype, Instagram, LinkedIn, YouTube, Google, Twitter, Facebook, Gmail, etc.

Advantages

For Students

- Improvement of communication skills.
- Improvement of technological skills.
- Increase in the exposure of diverse views.
- Develops a positive image.
- Increase the engagement of learning.
- Encourage students to express their own thoughts.
- Build an online learning community.

For Teachers

- Increase the access to resources.
- Collaborate with other staffs.
- Exchange information and plans lesson.
- Reach to parents who are not able to come to school.
- Form a partnership with schools in different states and countries.
- Get feedback from schools and events.
- Communicate effectively with parents.

Disadvantages

- It can lead to online bullying.
- Distraction from academic study.
- It might result in wastage of time.

Blogs

It is a term used for **web log**. It is like an online diary or journal, except they are not private, instead they are created for an audience. And just like a diary or journal, a blog makes an easy and comfortable way for students for writing. Blogs are written on all kinds of topics. Readers can usually leave comments, which lead to discussions about the blog's content. For example, a blog about flipping your classroom can lead to a discussion between novice and experienced teachers about common questions, advice, tips, and clarifications. Few examples of blogs are Kidblog, Edublog, Wordpress, etc.

Advantages

- Teachers can publish assignments, resources and keep students and parents up to date on class events, due dates and content being covered.
- Teachers can also use blogs to help students to master content and to improve their writing skills.
- Students can use blogs to publish their writing and educate others on a particular topic.
- Enhance student's communication skills and increase student's investment in learning.

Disadvantages

- It is time consuming.
- It involves lot of efforts to maintain the quality of the content on the site.
- Hard to grade and assess for educators.
- Learners can be distracted easily.
- Lack of speaking and listening skills training.

Chats

Web based chat platforms are gaining popularity as teachers look for ways to incorporate technology in the curriculum. Achieving the education goal with texting and other digital communication, well implemented electronic chats can support learner's critical thinking. It helps students to establish a direct connection with the instructor as well as classmates.

Advantages

- It promotes real time collaborations.
- It leads to deeper processing of class material.

Disadvantages

- Teachers are required to perform an intentional planning to establish online etiquettes and a process for orderly turn taking, so that every student should get a chance to participate.
- It is difficult to ensure student's safety by teachers.

Video-Conferencing

Video-conferencing is a technology that allows users in different locations to hold face to face meetings without moving to a single location together. It can also be used as a medium for conducting training, with the instructor, teaching a remote class from mostly anywhere.

It possesses wide educational applications for the best possible outcomes of the tele-conferencing system. It made easy for the students, sitting in a classroom at one location can discuss a project with students at different location. These students can see real time video image of a classroom in a distant location. The learners can type the messages on the screen in a 'chat window'.

Advantages

- Students can easily exchange information, can have conversation and can get immediate feedback.
- Learners can write and can share ideas of their own composition and can have evaluation on them.
- Students can work on a joint project by adopting the mode of tele-conferencing.
- Students can share ideas and information for better understanding and application of learned material.

Disadvantages

- There can be a short time lag between speaking and receiving a response that can disrupt the natural flow of conversation.
- It requires high internet connectivity.
- A set of high quality video-conferencing system is costly.
- It lacks personal interaction.

Discussion Forum

A discussion forum is a virtual place on the internet where conversations can take place and information can be shared more easily among a geographically dispersed group of people. Discussion forums can be public or private, depending on the forum's objective and desired level of access into the forum. It's a good idea to use discussion forum instead of direct personal e-mail whenever privacy or security concerns don't prevent it, even when the communication only involves two project members.

Learners join the discussion forum and their questions are posted and stored for everyone to read and respond. Students can have discussions with each other on course related topics.

Advantages

- Engage students in active learning.
- Promotes growth for collaborative learning communities.
- Learner's queries are posted and responded.
- Provides flexibility to students, as they can use it anywhere and anytime.

Disadvantages

- Discussions can go beyond the topic.
- It requires consistent input of teachers.
- It can be hindered by technical problems (server down or network down).
- It needs to be monitored for an inappropriate posting.

Whereas the development of Massive Open Online Courses (MOOC) is rooted in the ideals of openness in education. The knowledge should be shared freely and the desire to learn should be met without demographic, economic and geographical constraints.

Open Education Resources (OER)

Open Educational Resources are freely accessible, openly licensed text, media and other digital assets that are useful for teaching, learning and assessing as well as for research purposes. The development and promotion of open educational resources is often motivated by a desire to provide an alternate or enchanced educational paradigm.

According to **William and Flora Hewlett**, "Teaching-learning and research resources that resides in the public domain or have been released under an intellectual property license, that permits their free use and re-purposing by others. It includes full courses, course materials, modules, textbooks, streaming videos, tests, software and any other tools, materials or techniques, used to support access to knowledge".

According to **UNESCO**, "Teaching-learning and research materials in any medium, digital or that resides in the public domain or have been released under an open license that permits no-cost access, use, adoptation and redistribution by others with no or limited restrictions. Open licensing is built within the existing framework of an intellectual property rights as defined by relevant international conventions and respects the authorship of the work".

Thus, we can conclude that OERs are learning materials that can be modified and enhanced because their creators have given others permission to do so. The individual or organisations that creates OERs which include materials, like presentation, slides, podcast, syllabi images, lesson plans, lecture videos, maps, worksheets and even entire book's waive, some copyright associated with their works via legal tools, like creative commons licenses, so others can freely access, reuse, translate and modify them.

Characteristics of OER

- Clear copyright issues.
- Formatting of web and accessibility for reuse.
- Addition of descriptive meta-data.
- Published on the web.
- Available to all faculties, students and institutions.
- Shared openly and freely.

Educational resources are no longer static and scarce, but adaptable and widely available, allowing educational institutions, teachers and learners to actively participate in a global exchange of knowledge *via* Open Education Resources (OER). Creative commons provides the legal and technical infrastructure essential to the long term success of OER.

Creative Commons

It is a non-profit organisation that enables the sharing and use of creativity and knowledge through free legal tools. Creative common licenses allow content's creators to openly declare the level of sharing that is allowed with their work.

Most OER's resources use Creative Commons (CC) licences because they are well known blanket licenses that are free and easy to use. A creator only need to select a type of CC licence that they want from CC website.

It creates a 'Some Rights Reserved Model'. The copyright owner retains copyright ownership in their work, while inviting certain uses of their work by the public. Its licences create choice and options for the copyright's owner.

Thus, CC licensing is a legally valid and accepted form of licensing and is meant to work in conjunction with and to support 'All Rights Reserved Model'.

Applications of Creative Commons

CC licences types CC consist of four rights.

The four creative commons licenses are given below

Icons	Rights	Short Description
(i)	Attribution (BY)	This license lets others to distribute, remix, tweak and build upon your work, even commercially, as long as they credit you for the original creation.
($)	Non-Commercial (NC)	Licenses may copy, distribute, display and perform the work and can make derivative works based on it, only for non-commercial purposes.
(=)	No Derivative Works (NDW)	Licenses may copy, distribute, display and perform only verbatim copies of the work, not derivative works based on it.
(↺)	Share Alike (SA)	Licenses may distribute derivative works only under a license, identical to the license that governs the original work.

CC Facilitates Innovation in Education

CC licenses help educators to broaden the impact of their educational resources and the needs of their students and find relevant OER.

CC Enables Translation of Educational Resources into Different Languages When educational resources are released under a CC licence permitting adaptations, anyone interested in the subject matter may translate those resources.

CC Enables Educational Resources to Evolve and be Improved CC licensed OER are living documents that can be built upon and improved not only by authors but by students as well.

CC Enables Easier Discovery of Educational Resources on the Web CC has broadened the impact of OER by embedding each of its licenses with software code that makes the license terms machine readable *i.e.* discoverable by a search engine.

Structure of CC Licensing

Icons	Short Description
CC BY	This license lets others to distribute, remix, tweak, and build upon your work, even commercially, as long as they credit you for the original creation. This is the most accommodating of licenses offered. Recommended for maximum dissemination and use of licensed materials.
CC BY SA	This license lets others to remix, tweak and build upon your work even for commercial purposes, as long as they credit you and license their new creations under the identical terms. This license is often compared to **copyleft free** and **open source software licenses**.
CC BY ND	This license allows for redistribution, commercial and non-commercial, as long as it is passed along unchanged and in whole, with credit to you.

Icons	Short Description
CC BY NC	This license lets others ro remix, tweak and build upon your work non-commercially and although their new works must also acknow edge you and be non-commercial, they don't have to license their derivative works on the same terms.
CC BY NC SA	This license lets others to remix, tweak and build upon your work non-commercially, as long as they credit you and license you new creations, under the identical terms.
CC BY NC ND	This license is the most restrictive of the six main licenses, only allowing others to download your works and to share them with others as long as they credit you, but they can't change them in any way or use them commercially.

It is used to secure various contents over the internet. It is used to safeguard the contents on the web pages, it can be videos, documents, pictures and audios, etc.

Massive Open Online Courses (MOOC)

A MOOC is an online course aimed at unlimited participation and open access via the web. In addition to traditional course materials, such as filmed lectures, readings and problem sets, many MOOCs provide an interactive user forums to support community interactions among students and professors. They are recent and widely researched development in distance education, which were first introduced in 2008 and emerged as a popular mode of learning in 2012.

Earlier, they often emphasised open access features, such as open licensing content, structure and learning goals, to promote the reuse and remixing of resources, but later they use closed licenses for their course materials, while maintaining free access to students.

They can be seen as a term related to the scalability of an open and online education. They are courses designed for large number of participants that can be accessed by anyone and at anywhere as long as they have internet connection, open to everyone without entry qualifications and offers a free complete course experience.

Applications of MOOC

- It gives an open access to ask querries to professors.
- It contains an open courses for all interested, regardless of location, resulting in more diverse student's base.
- Students can collaborate with their peers from different parts of the world.
- It provides an opportunity for online interaction among students. Students can share work, critique and receive other's feedback.
- It helps professors to revaluate their pedagogical methods, while improving knowledge sharing.

E-Inclusion

E-inclusion refers to the degree to which information and communication technologies contribute to equalising and promoting participation in society at all levels.

According to **Hewlett Packard**, "The purpose of e-inclusion initiative is to fill the gap between the technological empowered communities and the technological excluded communities on our planet by making it profitable to do so".

It is a social movement, whose goal is to end the **digital divide**, a term used to describe the fact that the world can be divided into people, who have and who don't have access to and the capability to use modern Information Technology (IT). It has the power to close the gap between developed and less developed countries and to promote democracy and mutual understanding. It empowers disadvantaged individuals, such as poor, disabled and the unemployed.

Applications of Assistive Technology in E-learning

It is a technology used by individuals with disabilities, in order to perform functions that might be difficult or impossible for them. It includes mobility devices, such as walkers and wheelchairs, as well as hardware and software techniques that assists people with disabilities, in accessing computers or other information technologies.

For example, people with limited hand function may use a keyboard with large keys or a special mouse to operate a computer, people who are blind may use a software that reads text on the screen, people with low vision may use software that enlarges screen content, people who are deaf may use a TTY (Text Telephone) or people with speech impairments may use a device that speaks loudly as they enter text via keyboard.

It is a broad concept, covering everything that might be used to compensate for lack of certain abilities ranging from low-tech devices, like crutches or a special grip for a pen to more advanced items, like hearing aids and glasses, to high-tech devices, such as braillers and computers with specialised softwares for helping dyslectics to read.

Despite the positive impacts and advancement of AT, use of AT in inclusive education is still limited to developed countries.

Some other assistive devices for different categories of disability are discussed below

Assistive Devices for Visually Impaired Children
Computer screen magnification, descriptive video services, screen readers, Braille, scanning software, independent text reading, audio devices and Braille notetakers.

Assistive Devices for Hearing Impaired Children Personal Frequency Modulation (FM), Infrared Systems, Infrared Loop Systems, Text Telephones (TTY), Computerised Speech Recognition, Closed Captioned T.V.

Assistive Devices for Speech Impaired Children Augmentative and Alternative Communication (AAC), first words, picture exchange communication system, hand held (portable) or computer electronic speech devices.

Assistive Devices for Orthopedically Impaired Children Computer accessibility, adapted recreation equipment, daily living equipment, access to classroom or workspace science laboratory.

Assistive Devices for Children Having Learning Disabilities Abbreviation expanders, paper based computer pen, electronic math worksheets, free form database software.

Quality of E-learning

The quality of education can be defined from three perspectives that are technological, economic and pedagogical. The quality standards were associated with particular outcomes in the past. This meant that quality was evaluated on the basis of course quality and pre-defined learning outcomes. This approach has changed in the recent year due to the introduction has changed in the recent year due to the introduction of e-learning.

It must be said that e-learning is not just another way of implementation of traditional teaching, but it is a new approach to education. Quality of e-learning can be assessed by two ways *i.e.* through benchmarking or by the specification of standards. Benchmarking means the comparison of performance and results achieved by the evaluated entity against the results and performance of the entity operating under comparable conditions. When standards are defined, the performance is set by comparing them with standards. It is necessary to implement a system of quality that ensures the required minimum level of e-learning quality across the curriculum.

D & M IS Success Model

In 2003, **DeLone and McLean** introduced an update to their earlier **1992 IS model**. According to them, quality has three major dimensions *i.e.* information quality, system quality and service quality. Their model also includes intention to use and net benefits as given in below diagram.

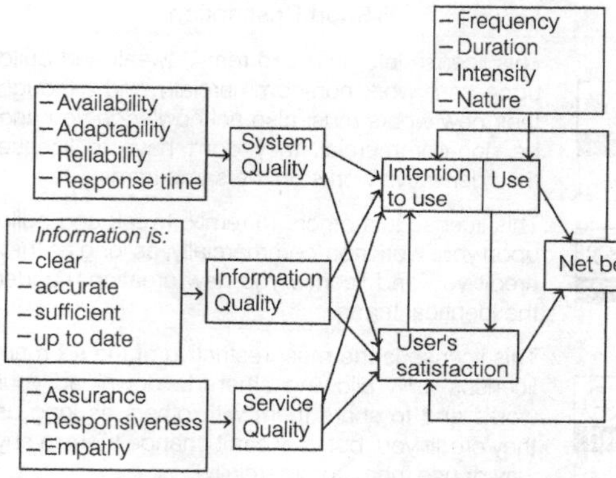

DeLone and McLean's IS Success Model

It has been widely used to gauge success. It has been modified to meet the requirements of information systems. IS aspects to e-learning systems, at the programmed level enables learning, communication, programme and course delivery and other user based activities. This model has been widely used by IS researchers for understanding and measuring the dimensions of IS success.

The dimensions of IS includes

System Quality The desirable characteristics of an information system. For example, ease of use, system's flexibility, system's reliability and ease of learning as well as system features of intuitiveness, sophastication, flexibility and response time.

Information Quality The desirable characteristics of the system outputs, that is management reports and web pages, for example, relevance, understandability, accuracy, conciseness, completeness, currency, timeliness and usability.

Service Quality The quality of the support that system's users receives from the IS department and IT support panel. For example, responsiveness, accuracy, reliability technical competence and empathy of the personal staff.

System Use The degree and manner in which staff and customers utilises the capabilities of an information system. For example, amount of use, frequency of use, nature of use, appropriateness of use, extent of use and purpose of use.

User's Satisfaction User's level of satisfaction with reports, websites, and support services, for example, the most widely multi-attribute instrument for measuring user's information satisfaction.

Net Benefits The extent to which IS is contributing to the success of individuals, groups, organisations, industries and nations. For example, improved decision-making, improved productivity, increased sales, cost reduction, improved profits, market efficiency, consumer welfare, creation of new jobs and economical development.

Thus, the DeLone and MCLean's IS Success Model is a successful model for developing comprehensive e-commerce success measures. The complex, multi-dimensional and inter-dependent nature of model requires careful attention to the definition and measurement of each dimension, of this dependent variable.

Ethics in E-learning

According to **Collin's Essential English Dictionary**, "Ethics is defined as a code of behaviour, usually that of a particular group, profession or an individual".

According to **Toprak Etal**, "In the field of education, ethics is significantly rooted in the concern with equal access to education by anyone, regardless of gender, nationality, ideological differences and physical or mental disabilities".

Need for ethics is born because of the 'psychological distance' arising from the absence of face to face interaction within an online community of e-learners. It implies that in any classroom situation, no less then virtual classroom, both learners and teachers are expected to know and to follow the acceptable ethical norms. Thereby, creating an educational atmosphere that is conducive to optimal teaching and learning, everyone knows his/her role and has the obligation to excercise it. Also, individual factors, such as differences in age, cultural, academic, political and religious backgrounds, coupled with different attitudes towards e-learning, necessitate that some ground rules should be laid down to ensure that all are on the same page of thought.

Therefore, acceptable behaviour in the traditional classroom is just as valid and needed in the virtual classroom.

E-learner and E-teacher

In an online community of e-learners and e-teachers, ethics demand that the established communication protocol should be set between all parties, while instructional ethics places this on us and on the e-teacher to comply accordingly.

The **ACM Code of Ethics and Professional Conduct** (1992), highlights the few key ethical concerns, applicable to all online users, namely, contributing to society and human well-being, avoiding harm to others, being honest and trustworthy, being fair and takes actions not to discriminate, honouring property's rights including copyrights and patents, giving proper credit for intellectual property, respecting the privacy of others and honouring confidentiality. The list reiterates the need for mutual respect, justice and goodwill in one's conduct, when engaging others to online.

Following are some of the etiquettes, most commonly required during engagement in any online teaching-learning environment

- Avoid off the topic messages, that may disturb or annoy other participant.
- Be careful of the tone of language, while writing a message.
- Do not send insulting messages (*e.g.* comments about spelling mistakes) or launch personal attacks on other participants in an online discussion.
- Do not post advertisements and commercial messages, political and religious messages and hoaxes.
- Do not send messages that may constitute invasions of privacy. For e.g. posting another person's telephone number without permission and messages that are misleading or in any way defamatory, offensive obscene and abusive or any message that promotes discrimination, violence and hatred).

Ethical Issues for the E-teacher

- The most important moral challenge for the e-teacher is maintaining the quality of the educational process.
- e-teacher must be attentive to new ways of transmitting information and assuring genuine communication.
- Providing a reliable network infrastructure with effective learning software becomes absolutely critical for the e-teacher.
- e-teacher must be attentive to educate the e-learners regarding the ethical use of internet resources.

Ethical Issues for the E-learner

- e-learners are becoming psychologically distant in their interactions with others.
- There is inappropriate assistance on examinations being provided to e-learners.
- There is lack of knowledge of curricular regulations and academic code of behaviour for the e-learner.

Research

Virtually nothing is available that applies the established principles of ethical inquiry to this new important area of moral exposure for educational institutions. Further, there is little research which is focused on the quality of learning outcomes in online education and distance education. Both of these areas represent imposing challenges for modern educational institutions and topics of significant opportunity for ethics and education scholars.

Conclusion

In the phase of technological advancement and cyber bullying, it is a challenging task to ensure integrity. Thus, it justifies the need for a code of ethics to be set in place. The ethical conduct of an online community is guided by both institutional policies and communal agreement. When all members cooperate and agree to ethically conduct themselves in their respectful roles as e-learners and e-teachers than effective learning occurs and the objective of education is attained.

EXAM BASED QUESTIONS

1 According to Rosenberg, e-learning refers to
(a) use of computer to deliver instructions
(b) use of internet
(c) use of interactive videos
(d) use of Artificial Intelligence

2 .... technology does not come under e-learning.
(a) Web based (b) Non-web
(c) Audio-visual (d) None of these

3 Which of the following is not a means of delivering education via e-learning?
(a) CD-ROMs and DVDs
(b) E-mail and tele-conferencing
(c) Live chats and web blogs
(d) Group discussions and lectures

4 The use of web services in distance education is provided through
(a) computers (b) internet
(c) WWW (d) None of these

5 What are the causes for the failure of traditional learning ?
(a) Difficulty in understanding
(b) Financial problem
(c) Personal problem
(d) Both (b) and (c)

6 Which of the following is an emerging trend of e-learning?
(a) Augmented reality (b) Adaptive learning
(c) Gamification (d) All of these

7 How social learning occurs?
(a) Through direct contact
(b) Through impersonal contact
(c) Through personal contact
(d) None of the above

8 How learning is considered as 'social'?
(a) Through participation of societies
(b) Through social interactions
(c) Through reading books
(d) Through deeper understanding of the particular subject

9 Which of the following tool(s) is/are included in social learning?
(a) Micro-learning (b) Cloud computing
(c) Chats (d) Gamification

10 Which type of e-learning trend uses computers as an interactive teaching devices?
(a) Micro-learning (b) Adaptive e-learning
(c) Mobile learning (d) Artificial Intelligence

11 Which of the following, best describes a web page?
(a) Fast growing services
(b) Large number of servers
(c) Readily available information
(d) Single unit of information

12 Which of the following cannot be considered as a benefit of Web 2.0?
(a) No regulation on the posted content
(b) Vast amount of information
(c) Interactive communication
(d) Easily accessible

13 From the list given below, which among them cannot be considered as an example of social networking site to impart education?
(a) Facebook and Twitter (b) Linkedln and Google
(c) Adobe and Photoshop (d) Skype and Wikipedia

14 How social networking sites, helps teachers in delivering e-learning?
(a) To exchange lesson's plans
(b) To develop a positive image
(c) To build an e-learning community
(d) To improve technological skills

15 What is the major disadvantage of social networking sites?
(a) They lead to online bullying
(b) They distract from studies
(c) They are time consuning
(d) All of the above

16 What is the basic purpose of creating a blog ?
(a) To give students, an access to online diary
(b) To provide students, a platform to write
(c) To form an online discussion group
(d) None of the above

17 Which of the following is a drawback of creating a blog?
(a) It is hard to assess and grade.
(b) Lack of writing skills.
(c) It takes less time to create a blog.
(d) Students publish their own writing.

18 How chats help students in teaching-learning process?
(a) In enhancing communicational skills
(b) In incorporating technology in curriculum
(c) In understanding indepth of class material
(d) All of the above

19 Which of the following is a benefit of video-conferencing?
(a) Easy exchange of information
(b) Application of learned materials
(c) Write and share ideas, instantly
(d) All of the above

20 Which of the following element(s) require(s) high internet connection?
(a) Blogs (b) Video-conferencing
(c) Chats (d) Social networking sites

21 Which among the following would be a feature of discussion forum?
(a) Outcome of tele-conferencing system
(b) Posting of questions
(c) Sharing of information
(d) Both (b) and (c)

22 Why discussion forum needs to be monitored?
(a) For an inappropriate content
(b) To prevent technical problems
(c) To provide flexibility to students
(d) None of the above

23 According to UNESCO, what is open educational resources?
(a) Released under intellectual property license
(b) Include modules and softwares
(c) Released under an open license
(d) Both (b) and (c)

24 Which of the following, can students access through an open educational resources?
(a) Lecture's videos (b) Worksheets
(c) Lesson's plans (d) All of these

25 Which is not a feature of an open education resources?
(a) Copyright issues (b) Shared secretively
(c) Available to faculties (d) Published on the web

26 Why owner of an open education resoruces, uses Creative Commons licences?
(a) Because it is easy to use (b) Because it is free to access
(c) Because it is cheap (d) Both (a) and (b)

27 What is Creative Commons?
(a) Copyright's ownership (b) Non-profit organisation
(c) Descriptive meta-data (d) Both (a) and (b)

28 CC licenses consists of how many rights?
(a) Five (b) Four (c) Six (d) Two

29 .... license copy, distribute, display and perform only verbatim copies of the work.
(a) No derivates words (b) Non-commercial
(c) Attribution (d) Share alike

30 The BYSA type of Creative Common license is defined as
(a) let others to distribute and build their work for non-commercial purpose.
(b) others to remix, tweak and build upon their work for commercial purpose.
(c) allows for redistribution to others.
(d) None of the above

31 The license, BYNCSA is used for
(a) not licensing the derivatives
(b) allowing others to download the work
(c) remix, tweak and build on non-commercial work
(d) None of the above

32 Among all the six structures of Creative Commons, which is the most restrictive licenses?
(a) BYND (b) BYNC (c) BYSANC (d) BYNCND

33 MOOC provides an interactive user forums to support community interactions among students and professors was first introduced in
(a) 2009 (b) 2012 (c) 2008 (d) 2010

34 Which of the following is a feature of MOOC?
(a) Collaboration with peers
(b) Re-evaluation of pedagogical methods
(c) Access to ask querries
(d) All of the above

35 e-inclusion empowers
(a) disadvantage students (b) rich students
(c) poor students (d) Both (a) and (c)

36 Which of the following assistive technology, can be used by a deaf person?
(a) Text telephone (b) Screen magnifier
(c) large keyboard keys (d) Walkers

37 Which high-tech device is used for assistive teaching?
(a) Wheelchairs (b) Braillers (c) Hearing aids (d) Crutches

38 What kind of modern technology is used for a visually imparied individual?
(a) Braille (b) Text readers
(c) Screen magnifier (d) All of these

39 The infrared systems are used for
(a) speech (b) visual
(c) hearing (d) None of these

40 Which of the following technology, cannot be used for an orthopedically impaired child?
(a) Access to work space
(b) Adapted recreation equipment
(c) Computer accessibility
(d) None of the above

41 When was DeLone and McLean's IS Success model introduced ?
(a) 1993 (b) 1992 (c) 2003 (d) 1990

42 What are the three dimensions of quality, according to DeLone and McLean?
(a) Information quality, service quality and system quality
(b) Information system, service quality and system quality
(c) Information quality, service quality and success quality
(d) None of the above

43 Why do researchers use the DeLone and McLean's IS Success model?
(a) To understand IS success
(b) To check whether information is clear or not
(c) To measure IS success
(d) Both (a) and (c)

44 How user's satisfaction can be achieved?
(a) By reports (b) Through support services
(c) By websites (d) All of these

45 What is the nature of IS Success model?
(a) Dependent and stress free
(b) Complex and inter-dependent
(c) Multi-dimensional canal and support
(d) Easy and inter-dependent

46 What is ethics, according to Toprak et al?
(a) Face to face interaction
(b) Code of behaviour
(c) Equal access to education
(d) None of the above

47 Why does the need of ethics arised?
(a) Violence and hatred (b) Face to face interaction
(c) Psychological distance (d) Discrimination and abuse

48 On what differences, do e-learning necessitate rules for proper conduct?
(a) Religious (b) Political
(c) Colour (d) Both (a) and (b)

49 When was ACM's code of ethics and professional conduct setup?
(a) In 1992 (b) In 1993 (c) In 1991 (d) In 2003

50 Which of the following is not highlighted in the key ethical concerns, according to ACM?
(a) Avoiding harm to others
(b) Being dishonest and untrustworthy
(c) Contributing to society
(d) Honouring property rights

51 What are some etiquettes should be followed during online teaching?
(a) Not to send insulting messages
(b) Not to post advertisements
(c) Not to spread hoaxes
(d) All of the above

52 The stakes for maintaining ethics in e-learning is higher for
(a) e-learners (b) teachers
(c) individuals (d) school's headmaster

53 What should be the desirable behaviour for an e-teacher?
(a) Modelling ethical behaviours
(b) Maintaining silence in the classrooms
(c) Guiding students in their subjects
(d) None of the above

54 What is the benefit of motivational messages from e-teacher?
(a) Exchange of ideas
(b) Giving respect to teachers
(c) Assuring and encouraging e-learners
(d) Both (a) and (c)

55 Why is it difficult to ensure integrity?
(a) Due to cyber bullying
(b) Due to non-adherence to ethical norms
(c) Due to technological advancement
(d) Both (a) and (c)

56 How do effective-learning takes place?
(a) Mutual respect of teachers and students, towards each other.
(b) Cooperation between e-learners and e-teachers.
(c) Carefully, listening online lectures.
(d) Not posting an irrelevant content on blogs.

57 Match the following.

List I (Researchers)	List II (Contribution)
A. Santheesh kumar	1. Open education resources
B. William Howlett	2. Ethics in e-learning
C. Hewlett Packard	3. Social learning
D. Toprak Etal	4. e-inclusion
	5. e-learning

Codes

	A	B	C	D		A	B	C	D
(a)	1	3	4	2	(b)	3	2	4	1
(c)	5	1	4	2	(d)	5	4	1	2

58 Match the following.

List I (Online Learning)	List II (Characteristics)
A. E-learning	1. Promotes mutual understanding
B. E-inclusion	2. Learning materials that can be modified
C. Social learning	3. Computer enhanced learning
D. Open education resources	4. Learning from and with others

Codes

	A	B	C	D		A	B	C	D
(a)	3	4	1	2	(b)	4	3	2	1
(c)	3	4	1	2	(d)	4	1	3	2

59 Match the following.

List I	List II
A. Web 2.0	1. Skype and Gmail
B. Social networking sites	2. Wordpress and Wix
C. Blogs	3. Internet and Websites

Codes

	A	B	C		A	B	C
(a)	1	3	2	(b)	3	1	2
(c)	2	1	3	(d)	1	2	3

60 Match the following.

List I (Icons)	List II (Features)
A. BY	1. It is the most restrictive, only allowing others to download your works and share them with others as long as they credit you, but they can't change them in any way or use them commercially.
B. BYND	2. It allows redistribution, commercial and non-commercial, as long as it is passed along unchanged and in whole, credits to you.
C. BYNC	3. It let others to remix, tweak, and build upon your work non-commercially, as long as they credit you and license their new creations, under an identical terms.
D. BYNCND	4. It let others to remix, tweak, and build upon your work non-commercially. Although, their new works must also acknowledge you and be non-commercial, they don't have to license their derivative works on the same terms.
	5. It let others to distribute remix, tweak and build upon your work, commercially, as long as they credits you for the original creation. This is the most accommodating licenses offered. Recommended for maximum dissemination and use of licensed materials.

Codes

	A	B	C	D
(a)	2	3	4	5
(b)	1	2	4	3
(c)	5	2	4	1
(d)	3	5	4	1

61 Match the following.

List I (Impairments)	List II (Assistive Devices)
A. Visually impaired	1. Augmentative or alternative communication
B. Hearing impaired	2. Abbreviation expanders
C. Speech impaired	3. Adapted recreation equipment
D. Orthopedically impaired	4. Braille notetakers
	5. Infrared System

Codes

	A	B	C	D
(a)	5	1	5	3
(b)	5	4	3	2
(c)	4	5	1	3
(d)	4	3	1	2

62 Tele-conferencing is used for
(a) training teachers (b) individual differences
(c) group discussions (d) social behaviours

63 Essential condition for efficiency and effectiveness support service is
(a) timeliness (b) transparency
(c) competence (d) All of these

64 Making special provisions for the promotion of education, amongst disadvantaged section of society facilitates
(a) social mobility (b) an inclusive growth
(c) social stratification (d) Both (a) and (b)

65 .... is an online course, aimed at unlimited participation and open access via web.
(a) Social learning
(b) Massive open online courses
(c) Creative common
(d) Electronic inclusion

66 Which of the following techniques is used for children, having learning disabilites?
(a) Abbreviation expanders (b) Computer accessibility
(c) Science laboratory (d) Frequency modulation

67 The adapted recreation equipments, are used for which kind of impairement?
(a) Hearing (b) Visual
(c) Orthopedical (d) Speech

68 Arrange the following dimensions of IS Success Model, according to their chronology.
1. Service quality 2. Net benefits
3. System quality 4. Information quality

Codes
(a) 3, 4, 2, 1 (b) 3, 2, 4, 1 (c) 1, 2, 4, 3 (d) 3, 4, 1, 2

69 Arrange the following influencing factors of education in the most appropriate manner.
1. Democracy 2. Religion
3. Politics 4. Modernisation

Codes
(a) 2, 3, 1, 4 (b) 3, 2, 1, 4 (c) 1, 5, 2, 3 (d) 3, 4, 2, 5

70 e-learning is defined as
1. Which is used as synonym to audio-visual learning.
2. Which occurs through direct contact.
3. Which is online-learning, carried through an internet.
4. Which consists of large number of servers.

Codes
(a) Only 3 (b) 1 and 3 (c) 3 and 4 (d) 1 and 2

71 What is the advantage of discussion forum?
1. Students can share learning materials.
2. Students can work on a joint project.
3. Easy to have conversation and to get feedback.
4. Growth for collaborative learning

Codes
(a) Only 4 (b) Only 1 (c) 1 and 4 (d) 2 and 3

72 Which of the following is/are the characteristic(s) of an open education resources?
1. Shared openly and freely 2. Available to all faculties
3. Published on the web 4. Accessible for reuse

Codes
(a) Only 4 (b) 1 and 3
(c) 1, 2 and 3 (d) All of these

73 Which of the following assistive devices are used for children, with hearing impairements?
1. Independent text reading
2. Text telephones
3. Closed captioned TV
4. Handheld speech device

Codes
(a) Only 2 (b) Only 3 (c) 1 and 4 (d) 2 and 3

Directions (Q. Nos. 74-82) *Given below are two statements, one labelled as Assertion (A) and the other labelled as Reason (R). Following are the codes given below. Choose the correct code.*

Codes
(a) Both A and R are true and R is the correct explanation of A
(b) Both A and R are true, but R is not the correct explanation of A
(c) Both A and R are false
(d) A is false, but R is true

74 **Assertion** (A) MOOC provides an interactive user forums, to support community interactions.
Reason (R) They are related to the scalability of an open and online education.

75 **Assertion** (A) Assistive technology is used by an individuals with disabilities.
Reason (R) It promotes democracy and mutual understanding.

76 **Assertion** (A) An infrared systems are used for speech impaired.
Reason (R) Scanning software is used for visually impaired.

77 **Assertion** (A) Social learning is an abbreviation of the electronic learning.

Reason (R) It includes e-learning and Artificial Intelligence.

78 **Assertion** (A) Social networking sites bring improvement in communication and technological skills.

Reason (R) It can also lead to online bullying and wastage of time.

79 **Assertion** (A) Chats help teachers, to publish assignments, resources and reports.

Reason (R) Chats can support learner's critical thinking.

80 **Assertion** (A) Video-conferencing can cause short time lags.

Reason (R) Setting a high quality video-conferencing system would be cheap.

81 **Assertion** (A) Creative Commons is an organisational setup, for the purpose of gaining profit.

Reason (R) Creative Commons created, Some Right Reserved Model.

82 **Assertion** (A) The DeLone and McLean's IS Success Model was introduced in the year, 2002.

Reason (R) It also consists of information system and service system.

Directions (Q. Nos. 83-85) *Read the passage and answer the following questions.*

Education providers have always been faced with the challenge of providing appropriate learning resources, but for the e-teacher, a whole new layer of educational infrastructure must be addressed if the e-learning environment is to be fully effective. Not only are books and learning equipment important, but providing a reliable network infrastructure with effective learning software becomes absolutely critical. With that come network security and safety issues, which have genuine ethical implications. Further, a range of duplication and copyright policies mut be in place to protect against 'softlifting' and illegal use of electronic rresources. **Miller, Kupsh** and **Jones** (1994), discussed the need to incorporate computer software ethics in the curriculum of each and every course about or utilizing computers. The computer software instruction should discuss software licensing and limited warranty agreements and should include terminology of computer software ethics.

This brings us to a broad range of ethical issues related to research. Certainly, one of the most significant new opportunities for academic fraud stems from undocumented or poorly documented use of online sources. e-teachers must be attentive to educating e-learners regarding the ethical use of internet resources. There are also a host of ethical implications regarding the use of human subjects in internet based research. Frankel and Siang (1999), have provided a basic protocol related to the ethical and legal implications of human subject research on the internet. They provide two basic principles for conducting research of human subjects on the internet *i.e.* Autonomy, all subjects are to be treated with respect as autonomous agents and beneficence, researchers are obligated to maximize the benefits of the research and minimize the harms and risks to the subjects, including informed consent and protection of privacy and confidentiality.

83 **Who has provided a basic protocol, related to the ethical and legal implications of human subject research on the internet?**

(a) Miller (b) Kupsh
(c) Frankel and Siang (d) Jones

84 **e-teachers must be attentive towards**

(a) ethical use of online sources
(b) reliable sources
(c) copyright policies
(d) None of the above

85 **Education providers have always been faced with the challenge of providing**

(a) appropriate learning resources
(b) research and development
(c) instructional objectives
(d) All of the above

ANSWERS

1 (b)	2 (b)	3 (d)	4 (a)	5 (d)	6 (d)	7 (a)	8 (b)	9 (c)	10 (b)
11 (d)	12 (a)	13 (c)	14 (a)	15 (d)	16 (b)	17 (a)	18 (c)	19 (d)	20 (b)
21 (d)	22 (a)	23 (c)	24 (d)	25 (b)	26 (d)	27 (d)	28 (b)	29 (a)	30 (b)
31 (c)	32 (d)	33 (c)	34 (d)	35 (d)	36 (a)	37 (b)	38 (d)	39 (c)	40 (d)
41 (b)	42 (a)	43 (d)	44 (d)	45 (b)	46 (c)	47 (c)	48 (d)	49 (a)	50 (b)
51 (d)	52 (b)	53 (a)	54 (c)	55 (d)	56 (b)	57 (c)	58 (a)	59 (b)	60 (c)
61 (c)	62 (c)	63 (d)	64 (d)	65 (b)	66 (a)	67 (c)	68 (d)	69 (a)	70 (b)
71 (a)	72 (d)	73 (d)	74 (a)	75 (b)	76 (d)	77 (c)	78 (a)	79 (d)	80 (b)
81 (d)	82 (c)	83 (c)	84 (a)	85 (a)					

CHAPTER 33

Uses of ICT in Evaluation, Administration and Research

ICT plays an important role in enhancing the quality of education. Its applications in education can be considered as an effective enabler to create access store, transmit and manipulate different information in audio and visual form, due to the capability of ICT in providing proactive environment.

Information and Communication Technology (ICT)

It means a variety of technological applications in the process and communication of information. It is a combination of three words i.e. 'information', 'communication' and 'technology'. 'Information' means 'knowledge', 'communication' means 'to communicate' and 'technology' means 'the use of computer'. It can be defined as "the integration of computing, networking and information processing technologies and their applications". It refers to technologies that provides access to information through tele-communications. It is similar to Information Technology (IT), but focuses primarily on communication technologies. It means a combination of computer applications and communication technology for gathering, processing, storing and disseminating of information. It is a common term, referring to the technologies used for collecting, storing, editing and communicating information in various formats. It includes the computer hardware, software, application of tele-communication technologies, projection devices, Local Area Network (LAN), Wide Area Network (WAN), digital cameras, Compact Disks (CDs), Digital Video Disks (DVDs), cell phones, satellites and fiber optic cables.

According to **Beckinsale and Ram**, "Any technology used to support information gathering, processing, distribution and use".

In this Chapter

- *Information and Communication Technology (ICT)*
- *ICT for Research*
- *Online Repositories*
- *Online Libraries*
- *Assessment Tools*

According to **OECD**, "ICT refers to the combination of manufacturing and services industries that capture, transmit and display data and information electronically".

According to **SER**, "ICT is a generic term referring to technologies, which are being used for collecting, storing, editing and passing an information in various forms".

According to **C Bwrton**, "ICT is a diverse set of technological tools and resources used to communicate and to create, disseminate, store and manage information".

Thus, the term ICT implies the technology, which consists of electronical devices and interactive materials that enables the user to experience a wide range of teaching-learning experience.

Uses of ICT

- The use of ICT offers a platform for student to question, investigate and construct new information in the process of teaching and learning.
- The use of ICT creates collaboration and interaction among students and teachers regardless of where they are.
- It helps in improving learner's teaming and commutative skills as well as their global awareness.
- ICTs improve learning by integrative approach to teaching and learning.
- It allows learners to explore and discover and it recognises many different learning pathway of knowledge.
- To exchange and share ideas among teachers for the professional growth.
- To carry out internet based research, to enhance educational process.

Use of ICT in Evaluation

Evaluation is a systematic process of collecting, analysing and interpreting information to determine the extent to which pupils are achieving instructional objectives. It is a continuous process which emphasises major objectives of an educational programme.

There are three types of evaluations and they are

Diagnostic Evaluation This type of evaluation is conducted at the beginning of teaching session, to determine the learning level of children and to group them. As per the learning levels, teachers may organise the learning experience / activities.

Formative Evaluation This type of evaluation is conducted during the course of teaching, to identify the learning performance of children. It helps children to mark out performance in learning and teacher may modify learning activities, accordingly.

Summative Evaluation This type of evaluation is conducted at the end of an instruction activity/unit course. This will help to grade learners and to judge the effectiveness of teaching. It helps in value judgement.

As mentioned above, **diagnostic evaluation** is performed before the teaching session. At this stage, teacher may ultilise ICT in place of verbal questioning. For example, Multiple Choice Questions can be prepared in computers (using application software) and children may be directed to attempt those questions. In case of **formative evaluation**, learners may be directed to attempt the questions provided in the learning management systems, like Google classroom, Moodle and Edmodo.

During summative evaluation, the possibilities of online examination could be tried out. Other techniques for evaluation can be viva or oral test, practical tests, written tests, short answer type questions, true-false type and matching type questions, rating scales, checklists, questionnaire, interview and observation.

In teaching and learning process, ICT is used for both teaching and evaluating student's performance.

Integrating ICT in evaluation of children's performance is important for the following reasons

- ICT enabled assessments, provide scope to children for engaging in individualised testing situations.
- ICT integrated assessment provides immediate feedback to the children. It also increases confidence of students as they receive instant feedbacks.
- The frequency of assessment can be increased, that would benefit children and will continuously engage them in their studies.
- It generates interest and increases motivation among learners, as they carry out various types of technological assisted tests.
- Technological assisted testing / assessment techniques are cost effective and can be easily prepared.
- It helps to develop high order thinking and digital literacy skills.
- It caters to the tastes of multiple audiences who differ in intelligence, creativity, etc.

So, ICT in teaching-learning process enables to evaluate the instructional activities and learning achievements of children. The paper and pencil tests, unit and term end examinations, oral questioning techniques, etc are some of the traditional evaluation methods. A simple example would be of recording the marks of children in excel sheet. Earlier the marks of the students were recorded in paper sheets, but today application softwares such as Microsoft Excel are used to record it.

Use of ICT in Administration

The use of Information Communication and Technology (ICT) can improve education quality, expand learning opportunities and make education accessible. ICT is very essential for the generation of quality information and management of that information which is required for effective decision-making.

- ICT assists the school administrators to meet the task of school management in the areas of curriculum and instruction, school community relationship and school business operations.
- Introduction of ICT in schools or college enhances the daily routine, programmes, evaluation as well as staff development.
- ICT can significantly influence effective planning in administration.
- The introduction of ICT tools in administration will solve the problem of poor communication in educational institutions.
- With ICT enabled administration there will be better working methodologies and re-engineered work processes.
- ICT promotes centralised storage of files and data. This enhances maintenance, reduces unnecessary efforts, minimises storage place and lessons security risks.

Internal Administration

Internal functioning of administration will become effective with the application of following devices

Wireless Devices Wireless communication devices, like cellular phones. For example, integration with wireless technology should be taken up for effective functioning of government departments.

Unified Messaging It provides users with the ability to access, receive and send different types of messages, like fax, e-mails and voice-mails through a common single interface.

e-mail It facilitates inter-employee communication and inter-department communication, as communication can be sent, received and replied accross electronically.

File Tracking Module All files moves from one section to the other and from one desk to the other in a well laid down pattern. It helps to maintain a central record of the status of the files.

Planning and Decision-Making

ICT enables planning and decision-making with the help of following applications

Geographical Information System (GIS) It can capture, store, check, integrate, analyse and display data using digitalised maps.

Management Information System (MIS) All information is smoothly exchanged among different levels and database is consolidated for planning and monitoring different schemes.

Computerisation Computerisation of all sections of the governmental departments has made the system efficient in policy-making and policy implementation.

Connectivity Connectivity among various governmental departments is provided horizontally and vertically through LAN and WAN.

Video-Conferencing It can be used for urgent matters for consultation with senior officiers, without calling them from their office.

Service Delivery

Through ICT's enabled service delivery, administration is able to provide

- qualitative and comprehensive information on departmental websites, especially in local languages.
- intergrated and seamless services to the citizens.
- a large set of conveniently located access points.
- accountability and efficiency, as they are able to dispose cases online.

Use of ICT in Research

Applications of ICT are mainly used by researchers for its ability to ease the knowledge gathering process and to enhance resource development. It helps the researcher to identify appropriate information sources, critically analyse information, research effectively, manage information, use the information to extend and communicate knowledge, across subject fields, search up to ten databases and electronic resources, simultaneously, receive results in a common format, link to individual databases for more specialised searching and select favourite resources and e-journals, save searches and records, and set up e-mail alerts.

With widespread computer networking among educational and research institutions, researchers can use e-mail to access data. They can exchange their research paper, proposals, formats and so on quickly and conveniently. Thus, e-mail keeps them in touch with professionals and experts and can enable them to access a variety of databases in almost every academic field in any part / institution of the country.

So, the various applications of ICT in the field of research are

E-mail Researchers can use e-mail to access data and to exchange with their resources through e-mail.

Video Disc It is a product of the optical disc family. It has the capacity to store information, data, visuals and voice.

Speech Recognition This feature allows a computer to recognise human speech or words. It translates the spoken words into information and makes it easier for people to do their job and learn.

E-Portfolio

Generally, the school keeps record of marks scored by the children in different subjects, also data about their family background, physical records, involvement and achievement in extra curricular activities, etc. are also recorded. All this is a part of evaluation assessment. The grades/marks represent children's performance.

The multiple data relating to a student is recorded, systematically. Portfolio's document, learning performance, activities performed, details of participation in co-curricular activities and other relevant data concerning the involvement of student throughout the session. Such record is highly useful in evaluating the student's performance during his/her schooling. But, since the augment of digitalisation, we use the term **e-portfolio**.

An e-portfolio is a digital collection of overtime work that showcases skills, abilities, values, experiences and competencies through a broad range of evidence based learning. It is the record of digital works performed by the student. The digital works include text material prepared in Microsoft Word software, PDF or other application softwares, video and audio clips, digital images, digital reports, blog entries, comments posted in discussion for a Power Point presentations, etc. It is the latest trend in teaching-learning as it is a powerful tool for evaluating student's performance. The teacher would be in a better position to gauge the student's performance easily.

To prepare the assignments, children refers to different websites, downloads images, etc. Then, they prepare it on MS Word or Power Point presentations. The assignment prepared by the student in digital format could be converted in the e-portfolio of that particular student.

There are number of tools where teachers can place the digital in formation of student's work. To create e-portfolio, the first step is to sign up in any particular website. This will generate an account on that particular website. Thereafter, start recording the digital works of children.

Some websites are

- www. rcampus. com
- www. pebblepad. co. uk
- www. portfoliogen . com
- www. mahara. org
- www. digication. com, etc.

According to **Lorenz and Ittelson**, "e-portfolio is a valuable learning and assessment tool. It is a digitised collection of artifacts including demonstrations, resources, and accomplishments that represent an individual, group, or an institution. This collection can be comprised of text based graphic, or multi-media elements archived on a website or on other electronic media, such as CD-ROM or DVD. It is more than a simple collection of data. It can also serves as an administrative tool to manage and organise work, created with different applications and to control who can see the work. It encourages personal reflection and often involve in the exchange of ideas and feedback".

Types of E-Portfolios

Generally, online portfolios function with the help of internet while other formats do not require internet.

They are classified into three categories as

(i) **Developmental E-Portfolio** It collects and records student's activities. For example, a project of two months is assigned to students as a learning activity. During this period, they have to submit short reports in every 25 days in MS Word format. Such a digital report will be stored in the database of e-portfolio. Thus, developmental e-portfolios record activities over a period of time. The primary objective of recording the progress is to communicate the progress to the students and the teachers.

(ii) **Assessment E-Portfolio** It collects and records children's activities for the entire duration of the programme or course. The primary objective is to assess and judge the competency of children in specific skills and programmes. These portfolios are submitted for assessing and evaluating the performance in a learning activity. For example, digital formats of assignments submitted during studies in primary class.

(iii) **Showcase E-Portfolio** These portfolios exhibit exceptional works and skills of an individual. This may include works in preparing reports, inserting graphics and pictures in preparing write-ups, development of quality video and audio clips and so on. These portfolios judge one's performance, selection to a job, etc. Thus, as the name indicates, showcase e-portfolios are images on an individual's persona.

ICT for Research

The application of ICT is of an immense importance and powerful in the research function. The increase in computing power has made it possible to conduct complex calculations on large data sets. Communication links make it possible for research teams to be spread accross the world instead of concentrated on a single institution. The combination of communications and digital libraries is equalising access to academic resources, greatly enriching research possibilities. Computer data processing not only free researchers from the cumbersome task of manually analysing data, but more importantly facilitates quick and accurate analysis of large amount of data from national samples or even multi-national samples, covering tens of thousands of respondents.

One more important dimension of ICT in research is the use of online full text databases and online research libraries / virtual libraries, which are the direct outcome of the growth in tele-communication's networks and technology. These databases and libraries provide researchers with online access to the contents of hundred of thousands of books from major publishing house, research reports and peer reviewed articles in electric journals.

Some examples of ICT in research are

- Online repositories
- Online libraries
- Online assessment tools
- Offline assessment tools

Online Repositories

Online or digital repositories are systems that enable the storage, discovery and retrieval of meta-data or electronic materials, stored at a local or distributed level. Learning Object Repositories (LOR) are systems that manage the access to reusable learning content. The purpose of digital repository is not only to store catalogued learning materials and distribute them, but also to allow sharing and reuse.

The material distribution and sharing circle's model categorises three main types of online learning material repositories. The **first** are **local repositories**, containing learning materials and meta-data about these materials. These repositories can be found in many institutions that develop and store learning materials for their own community. These repositories were established to serve local communities and answer specific pedagogical needs. Therefore, the learning materials they gather were developed according to learner's needs in order to improve the process of learning. They are normally designed by experts that are aware of the institution and the learner's needs. The **second** type of repository is **portals** that allow access to several online repositories, such a MAOR, MERLOT and open courseware consortium. These portals contain only the meta-data and allow a wider use of learning materials developed and stored in local repositories. These fields describe the material and the possibilities for its use, so that objects may be located using keywords, retrieved and examined to see whether it suits learner's needs or not. The **third** type is **international associations** and **consortiums** that enable the sharing of learning materials among repository networks worldwide. Consortiums such as globe, enables users to broaden their search between international repositories, according to meta-data standards via automatic content harvesting or search request as sharing of learning materials.

These consortium's features, which characterise objects and includes information fields describing materials, expand the use of learning materials by retrieving these materials via modular construction of materials and their integration into new learning processes, according to learner's needs.

Learning materials repositories provide a platform for the sharing of educational resources on the web. Many repositories are effectively created by their users and offer tools that enable users to publish their opinion and comments regarding the learning materials whether by vote, frequency of use or peer review. Using these tools, one may learn of an object's quality or receive other users recommendations of the best ways to use materials.

User's involvement and exchange of information between learners, creates a learning community that shares information of great value. The combination of different evaluated learning material offers the learner an effective and high quality learning process. Community members involvement in the repository environment increases the motivation to use the learning materials and to support the community by passing on valuable informal knowledge to other users.

Online Libraries

According to **R. Smith**, "Digital libraries are conrolled collection of information bearing objects that are in digital form and that they may be organized, accessed, evaluated and used by means of heterogeneous and extensible set of distributed services that are supported by digital technology".

A digital or online library is popularly viewed as an electronic version of a library where storage is in digital format , allowing direct communication to obtain material and copying it from a master version. It combines technology and information resources, to allow remote access and breaking down the physical barrier between resources. Now, internet is becoming an integral part of library services. Internet has empowered the libraries to develop new services and resources and provide them at a global level.

Internet based library services can be provided in the following ways

- Access to library holdings through web-OPACs (Online Public Access Catalogues) and provision of circulation services through the library website.
- Access to licensed online databases, full text journals and e-books.
- Library gateways and portals to provide access to non-library materials.
- Virtual reference and information services.

Thus, in comparison to traditional libraries, digital libraries provide efficient and qualitative services by collecting, organising, storing, disseminating, retrieving and preserving the information. It provides online access to historical and cultural documents whose existence is endangered due to physical decay.

The major areas which offer digital libraries are information retrieval, multi-media database, data mining, data warehouse, online information repositories, image processing, hypertext, World Wide Web (WWW) and Wide Area Information Service (WAIS).

Libraries have played a significant role in society and digital libraries with the promise of breaking the barriers of geographical distance, language and culture, and even have more potential to significant social roles. Digital libraries will not only change our reading and information habits, but they are also going to bring major changes in the economic models of information generation, distribution and management functions. For exploring the benefits of digital library in Indian languages there is an urgent need of tools and applications, such as OCRs and Machine Translation Systems, so that user can take benefit of reading rare classics that can be publish in any language and researchers are able to use these tools for their linguistic research.

It will boost the development of lexical and terminology databases with the combination of quantitative and qualitative analysis of text.

Text analyser is a new kind of tool which is helpful in lexicography, knowledge acquisition, language and writing variation studies. Digital libraries creation have been a good test bed for OCRs and now the world is moving towards speech to speech translation, all these tools together will help in building one for Indian languages.

Assessment Tools

Assessing student's performance is an integral part of the teaching-learning process. A lot of assessment techniques are available. Effective assessment is a continuous process and it is not simply that has to be done at the end of a unit. Evaluation is integrated into all aspects of the curriculum, thus, providing both students and teachers, useful and relevant data to gauge progress of students. Not only teachers, but also students play an important role in assessing their own learning progress.

An assessment tool is a complete set of documentation needed to assess at one or more units of competency. Each assessment tool must include two to three instruments that each support different methods of assessment (e.g. checklist, observation and questioning).

There are various tools and techniques to assess student's performance, such as

- Online assessment tools, like online surveys, instant feedback, online tests, etc.
- Offline assessment tools, like checklists, rating scales, observations, etc.

Online Assessment Tools

Online assessment tools are online tests conducted with the purpose of evaluating, measuring and documenting the academic readiness, learning progress, skill acquisition or educational needs of the test takers.

There are lot of reasons to use educational technologies for student's assessments, such as saving time, making the learning process more comprehensive and friendly, offering fast feedback, etc. The students can pre-check their assignments before submitting them, which saves teacher's time for the actual grading. Also, there will be no stacks of papers on the table, no lost tests, no need of taking all the assignments to home.

Digital assessment tools ease the lives of both teachers and learners. Due to modern technologies, students can get answer to their questions without any need to interrupt each other. All their activities can be tracked by the teacher, instantly. Also, digital testing is fun for students, which creates a better learning environment, due to which an interested audience, will makes teaching easier and more desirable for learners.

Various Online Assessment Tools

Gamifying the Answers One of the most popular tool for digital assessments is **Kahoot**. This gamification platform helps teachers to build the learning process in a form of a game by creating Multiple Choice Questions or using already existing games.

The teacher can upload media files and images to create a unique game or download readymade stuff. Though, every student needs to work on their personal computer to pass the test, but this is a great group activity, as all questions are shown on a shared screen and may be discussed if needed. Kahoot provides 100% engagement in the class, so that, students totally get plunge into the competitive atmosphere to win.

The ideal solution to get a brief and to the point feedback from a group of learners is **Answer Garden**. This simple online tool is focused on the (quick) question-answer interaction between learners and their teachers. After the teacher has shared a question in the class, students can either start forming an answer or to choose the right one from a multiple choice, provided by the teacher.

The speed of collecting data is really impressive in Answer Garden, but unfortunately it has limited online time. Therefore, this tool is not suitable for all types of questions. Teachers should avoid too long questions, as they demand even longer answers.

Giving Instant Feedback The software 'socrative' is equipped with various features that can be used by educators for many different purposes. It also includes activities, like quiz, quick questions, exit tickets, etc. Socrative has an intuitive, colourful and easy interface and apps for both students and teachers. The tool allows educators to get an immediate insight into their student's understanding in real-time, as they can create quiz in seconds and can also share them with other teachers.

Tracking Progress Plicker is another real time educational software allowing to get data for an assessment. It is a comprehensive tool that helps teachers to understand exactly whether their students are in terms of progress or not. Though, plicker is a serious tool for digital assessing, many students consider it to be a fun game, what makes the studying process even easier.

The results may be seen in two modes *i.e.* student's mode and graph mode. The graph mode allows a teacher to explore how learners make their decisions, while the students mode helps learners to track their correct and incorrect answers.

Online Survey Tools or Test Generators A widely used tool for student's assessments is Google Forms. It allows teachers to create Multiple Choice Questions in the form of a survey and enhance it with images and videos in a few minutes. They can also add collaborators to their google forms and together can work on a survey.

Mail Questionnaire According to **Lundberg,** "Fundamentally, the questionnaire is a set of stimuli, to which literate people are exposed in order to observe their verbal behaviour under these stimuli".

It is a period list of questions sent through mail to respondents and to be returned by the respondents after filling up the questionnaire.

As the name indicates, "questionnaire is a set of selected questions, whose answers, the researcher seeks from respondents in order to gain knowledge about certain specified matters". Since, the questionnaire has to be answered after reading, it is obvious that a questionnaire can be addressed only to literate people. The limitation of mail questionnaire is that it lacks personal contact and might result in incomplete responses.

Thus, there are many digital assessment tools that serve different purposes in the educational environment. Teachers have to choose the best tool which will be useful in tracking their student's progress and to provide them with more objective feedbacks and grades.

Offline Assessment Tools

Offline Assessment tools are offline tests which are conducted within the classroom. It is a systematic approach to formative evaluation used by instructors to determine how much and how well students are learning.

Some of the offline assessment tools are discussed below

Observation Assessment Tool

Observation is a very useful way to assess but as with all assessment tools, it needs to be well planned and designed. It is selective and purposeful. It gives clear instructions to both the assessor and candidate about how to 'do' the assessment.

Steps in Observation

Selection of the Topic This refers to determining the issue to be studied through observations.

Formulation of the Topic This involves fixing up categories to be observed and pointing out situations in which cases are to be observed.

Research Design This determines identification of subjects to be observed preparing observation schedule if any arranging situations to be observed.

Collection of Data This involves familiarisation with the setting, observation and recording.

Analysis of Data The researcher analyses the data, prepares tables of final report throughout the research process.

Report Writing This involves writing of the report for submission.

Portfolio Assessment Tool

Portfolio assessment can be a flexible way to collect a range of evidence. It guides the assessor on how to make the final assessment decision. There are clearly defined purpose and learning targets in this assessment. It showcase what students are capable of doing.

Three main features of portfolio assessment are

- Collection of student work must have a specific purpose.
- Students must be actively involved in the process of selecting work to be included.
- Students must actively engage in self-reflection.

Portfolios allow for direct input from students. It often require a self-evaluation component such as reflective essay that let students describe their overall experience in the class and the portfolio creation process. It helps students practice critical thinking , letting them decide how well the portfolio measures up to the course goals and standards.

Sociometry

It is a technique for describing the social relationships among individuals in a group. It attempts to describe attraction or repulsion between two individuals. In education, it is commonly used in schools.

Children are asked to name in order of preference (usually two or three) the child or children that they would invite to play, sit next to, work on a class assignment, etc. It is also common to ask children to name the children again in order of preference, that they would least like to invite to play, sit next to or work on a class assignment. It is a kind of peer rating technique. Often, sociometric choices are represented graphically on a chart known as **sociogram**.

Psychological Tests

These tests are the useful and most frequently employed tools of educational research. They are used to describe and to measure a sample of certain aspects of human behaviour or an inner qualities. They provide the data for most experimental and descriptive studies of education. They yield objective and standardised descriptions of some psychological aspects of an individual's personality and translate them in quantitative terms.

There are various kinds of psychological tests, like achievement test, aptitude test and an inventory as discussed below

(i) **Achievement Test** It is an important tool in school evaluation and has great significance in measuring instructional progress and progress of the students in the subject area. It is directly related to the pupil's growth and development in educational situations. Thorndike and Hagen held that "it is a systematic procedure for determining the amount a student has learnd through instructions". It provides basis for promotion to the next grade.

(ii) **Aptitude Test** These are assessment tools to measure the performance of an individual. It measures individual's skills, tendencies and performance achievement in a specific field. It is of great importance for the students studying in the school. The test will give them a precise result of what is the actual abilities of a person. If the students practice aptitude tests from the very beginning they will be able to solve them in a proper time.

(iii) **Inventory** A concept inventory is a test to assess students' conceptual understanding in a subject area. It consists of Multiple Choice Questions in which several items are used to evaluate understanding for each concept. It is a screening device that gives the teacher a glimpse into the ways that students think about the key concepts in a subject area and not simply a test that indicates correct and incorrect answers. Teachers can use the results to plan instruction and also monitor changes in student's understanding.

Online Survey Tools or Test Generators

In utilising an online interface, online survey tools provide a quick, easy and cost effective means of delivering surveys and analysis of the results yielded through one centralised system. It alllows the user to easily define and design the survey's questions and send web-links to prospective respondents.

A test generator is a software used to create tests for a variety of uses.

Applications of Online Survey Tools

Give Writing Prompts and Collect Responses By incorporating a login action into a survey, teacher can allow each student to sign into the assignment and be individually identified. A summary report may show how many students completed the assignment and who is lagging behind.

Give a Quiz or a Homework Most survey tools have a quiz score action which will collect responses and then grade on a percent basis.

Make Assignments Adaptive With survey logic, you can keep asking progressively more difficult questions to create your own adaptive quizzes.

Keep in Touch with Parents At the beginning of the year, teacher can collect parent's information and imports it into your survey tool's e-mail campaign.

EXAM BASED QUESTIONS

1 According to SER, ICT refers to
(a) technology for gathering information
(b) collection and passing of an information
(c) set of technological tools and resources
(d) distribution and use of information

2 Who defined ICT as a set of technological tools to store information?
(a) SER
(b) OECD
(c) C. Bwrton
(d) Beckinsale and Ram

3 Which of the following cannot be regarded as an advantage of ICT ?
(a) Process administrative data
(b) Carry internet based research
(c) To facilititate communication
(d) To use electronic toys to play

4 What is blended learning?
(a) Combination of conventional and e-learning system
(b) Broadcasting of material and resources
(c) Facilitating tele-conferencing and video-conferencing
(d) Carrying out internet based research

5 What benefits do ICT provide in evaluation of student's performance?
(a) Instant feedback of children's performance
(b) Increases motivation among learners
(c) Develop high order thinking skills
(d) All of the above

6 What are the various techniques that can be used to evaluate learner's skills?
(a) Computer assisted technology
(b) Test of art and creative skills
(c) Oral questioning
(d) None of the above

7 Which technique is used in modern period for recording the marks of the students?
(a) Excel sheet (b) Paper sheet
(c) Power Point (d) MS Word

8 Which evaluation technique is used to check the learning level of children?
(a) Formative (b) Diagnostic
(c) Summative (d) None of these

9 What do you understand by summative evaluation?
(a) It is conducted at the end of instruction
(b) It conducted at the beginning of instruction
(c) It judges the effectiveness of teaching
(d) Both (a) and (c)

10 Which technique can be used for diagnostic evaluation?
(a) Oral questioning
(b) Written test
(c) Multiple Choice Questions
(d) None of the above

11 Which method of evaluation is used for an interview?
(a) Summative (b) Formative
(c) Diagnostic (d) Data inadequate

12 What theory did A Sawhney propounded?
(a) It should process data
(b) A proper ICT architecture
(c) Effective ICT implementation
(d) None of the above

13 Why there is a need to combine various projects and initiatives in a logical manner?
(a) To evaluate learner (b) To increase performance
(c) To process data (d) To add value

14 Which of following is not a component of ICT architecture?
(a) Information (b) Application
(c) Groupware (d) Complexity

15 What does the component 'application' of ICT architecture include?
(a) Spreadsheets (b) Word processors
(c) Database (d) All of these

16 What do you understand by componentware?
(a) Collaborative software (b) Physical equipment
(c) Application software (d) Software application

17 ...... is the software layer between applications and operating system.
(a) Shared database (b) Groupware
(c) Middleware (d) Componentware

18 Which of the following is an example of network?
(a) LAN (b) PAN
(c) WAN (d) Both (a) and (c)

19 What does internal administration include?
(a) Unified messaging (b) Computerisation
(c) Connectivity (d) Video-conferencing

20 What is the benefit of an e-mail in internal administration?
(a) It helps in sending voice-mails
(b) It facilitates inter-department communication
(c) It uses devices, like cellular phones
(d) None of the above

21 **What helps to maintain a central record of the status of the files?**
(a) Groupware (b) Wireless devices
(c) Unified messaging (d) File tracking module

22 **How Geographic Information System helps in decision-making?**
(a) It moves files from one disk to another.
(b) It comprises all sections of department.
(c) It increases connectivity through LAN.
(d) It captures and displays data using digitised maps.

23 **What is the full form of MIS?**
(a) Management Informative System
(b) Management Information System
(c) Merged Information System
(d) Management Information Scope

24 **What is the main benefit derived from video-conferencing?**
(a) Quick decisions
(b) Increase connectivity
(c) Efficient working
(d) Integrating various data

25 **What are the advantages of ICT's enabled service delivery channels?**
(a) Qualitative information
(b) Seamless service to all
(c) Convenient located access points
(d) All of the above

26 **How e-mails are used in research work ?**
(a) To get in touch with professionals
(b) To access a variety of databases
(c) To establish network for tele-conferencing
(d) Both (a) and (b)

27 **How speech recognition is used by researchers ?**
(a) It helps in an effective communication
(b) It helps in understanding different languages
(c) It helps in translating spoken words
(d) None of the above

28 **What is e-portfolio, according to Lorenzo and Ittelson?**
(a) Digitised collection of artifacts
(b) It involves communication of instruction
(c) Complex collection of data
(d) It encourages impersonal reflection

29 **……… helps to assess students through academic sessions.**
(a) MS Word software
(b) e-portfolio
(c) Excel sheets
(d) CCE

30 **Which of the following technique(s) can be used to gauge student's performance?**
(a) Video and audio clips
(b) Recording performance on website
(c) Portable document format
(d) Microsoft Word software

31 **Which type of e- portfolio collects and records children's activities for the entire duration of programme?**
(a) Developmental (b) Showcase
(c) Assessment (d) Data inadequate

32 **What is showcase e-portfolio?**
(a) Collecting and recording student's activities
(b) Development of quality video-clips
(c) To judge learner's performance
(d) Both (b) and (c)

33 **What is/are the advantage(s) of computer data processing?**
(a) Quick and accurate analysis of data
(b) Online access to contents
(c) Growth in tele-communication's network
(d) They are images on an individual's persona

34 **Which of the following is not an example of ICT's research?**
(a) Online assessment tools (b) Offline assessment tools
(c) Offline libraries (d) Online repositories

35 **……… enable the storage, discovery and retrieval of electronic material at a local level.**
(a) Online libraries (b) Online repositories
(c) Online assessment tools (d) Offline assessment tools

36 **What is the second category of Material Distribution and Sharing Circles model?**
(a) Collection of learning material and meta-data
(b) Local communities and answer specific pedagogy
(c) Portals that allow access to online repositories
(d) None of the above

37 **What enable the sharing of learning materials among repository network, worldwide?**
(a) International associations
(b) National associations
(c) International consortiums
(d) Both (a) and (c)

38 **How do repositories offer tools to enable user to publish opinions and comments ?**
(a) By vote (b) By frequency of use
(c) By peer's review (d) All of these

39 **What is/are the characteristic(s) of online libraries?**
(a) Electronic version of a library
(b) Effective means of communication
(c) Establish personal contact
(d) None of the above

40 **Which of the following is not an area exploited by digital libraries?**
(a) Data warehouse
(b) World Wide Web
(c) Portable document format
(d) Hypertext

41 **Name the digital librar(y) (ies) of special materials.**
(a) IEL (b) ELINOR
(c) SETIS (d) Informedia

42 What is/are the advantage(s) of digital libraries?
(a) Break barriers of language
(b) Bring change in economical models
(c) Major significance to social role
(d) All of the above

43 Why is it important to assess student's performance?
(a) To evaluate digital techniques
(b) To gauge student's performance
(c) To teach online assessement tools
(d) None of the above

44 Which of the following cannot be considered as an online assessment tool?
(a) Test generators (b) Instant feedback
(c) Schedule (d) Gamifying

45 Give an example of online assessment tool, where there is quick question-answer interaction between a learner and a teacher.
(a) Answer Garden (b) Kahoot
(c) ACM (d) Gutenberg

46 The software 'socrative' is used for
(a) gamifying the answers
(b) tracking the progress
(c) creating Multiple Choice Questions
(d) giving instant feedback

47 Which tool can be best utilised for creating online survey tools?
(a) Socrative (b) Plicker
(c) Google Forms (d) Kahoot

48 What is the definition of mail questionnaire, according to Lundberg?
(a) Period of questions send through mail
(b) Set of stimuli expose to literate people
(c) A set of selected questions
(d) It lacks personal contact

49 Which of the following is/are the tool(s) for offline assessments?
(a) Checklist (b) Interview
(c) Inventory (d) All of these

50 What does computerised questionnaire consists of
(a) items presented on paper
(b) items presented on computer
(c) interviewer presents questions orally
(d) None of the above

51 A set of questions, formed through investigation is known as
(a) schedule (b) forum (c) checklist (d) interview

52 What is the basic example of a checklist?
(a) Reminders (b) Day to day chores
(c) To do list (d) Yes and No questions

53 According to Likert's scale, how many rating scales are there?
(a) 10 to 20 (b) 1 to 10
(c) 1 to 9 (d) 1 to 11

54 Which is not an example of attitude scale?
(a) Thurnstone (b) Semantic differential
(c) Guttman (d) Likert

55 On what basis of classification of observation, do qualitative observation comes?
(a) Planning (b) Person
(c) Information (d) Interview

56 What should be the duration of interview, to work well?
(a) 80 minutes (b) 1 hour
(c) 20 minutes (d) Half an hour

57 How do sociometry helps in assessement of student's performance?
(a) By peer pressure (b) Through following culture
(c) By peer's rating (d) None of these

58 Psychological tests are
(a) aptitude test (b) inventory test
(c) achievement test (d) All of these

59 Why modern educationists are against the use of essay test?
(a) As it is useless in evaluation of performance
(b) As it inadequately measures learner's performance
(c) As it is influenced by teacher's personal opinion
(d) All of the above

60 Who developed performance test as a tool for offline assessment ?
(a) May (b) C A Mourse
(c) Hartshore (d) Both (a) and (c)

61 Match the following.

List I	List II
A. Research for analysis	1. Fundamental research
B. Research for solution by the user	2. Applied research
C. Research for theory construction	3. Evaluative research
	4. Action research

Codes

	A	B	C		A	B	C
(a)	1	3	2	(b)	3	4	1
(c)	3	4	2	(d)	3	1	4

62 Match the following.

List I	List II
A. Form of observation	1. Qualitative observation
B. Control of observation	2. Direct observation
C. Direction of observation	3. Controlled observation
D. Information of observation	4. Informal observation

Codes

	A	B	C	D		A	B	C	D
(a)	1	2	3	4	(b)	4	3	2	1
(c)	1	2	4	3	(d)	4	3	1	2

63 Match the following.

List I	List II
A. Rating by cumulated points	1. Man to man scale
B. Standard scale	2. Checklist Method
C. Graphical scale	3. Point scale
D. Numerical scale	4. Continuous rating scale

Codes

	A	B	C	D
(a)	1	2	3	4
(b)	4	3	2	1
(c)	2	1	4	3
(d)	1	2	4	1

64 Match the following.

List I	List II
A. Structured Interview	1. In depth task on issue
B. Semi-structured interview	2. Free task on issues
C. Non-directive	3. Flexible but structured
D. Focused interview schedule	4. Research

Codes

	A	B	C	D
(a)	1	2	3	4
(b)	2	1	4	3
(c)	4	3	2	1
(d)	1	2	4	3

65 Match the following.

List I	List II
A. Vocabulary test	1. In what ways animals and plants are alike?
B. Memory test	2. Where is Tajmahal situated?
C. Information test	3. What is the meaning of the word eventually?
D. Association test	4. What is the mobile number of your teacher?
	5. Why nights are longer and days are shorter in winter ?

Codes

	A	B	C	D
(a)	3	5	4	1
(b)	4	1	5	2
(c)	1	4	2	5
(d)	3	4	2	1

66 Match the following.

List I	List II
A. Numbers and symbols	1. Ratio scale
B. order and serial	2. Nominal scale
C. Equal interval	3. Ordinal scale
D. True zero point	4. Interval scale

Codes

	A	B	C	D
(a)	1	2	3	4
(b)	2	3	4	1
(c)	4	3	1	2
(d)	2	4	1	3

67 Match the following.

List I	List II
A. Primarily prospective	1. Summative evaluation
B. Primarily retrospective	2. Formative evaluation
C. Feedback	

Codes

	A	B	C
(a)	2	1	2
(b)	2	1	1
(c)	1	2	1
(d)	1	2	2

68 Who has identified, the four distinct phases of formative evaluation?

(a) Flander (b) Varsous (c) Edron (d) Jessemer

69 .... evaluation refers to the assessment of the learning and summarises the development of learners.

(a) Assummative (b) Pre-summative
(c) Summative (d) None of these

70 Which of the following is not a key role of formative evaluation?

(a) Rapid feedback (b) Documentation
(c) Grading (d) Planning

71 Which of the following tool will provide more valid information?

(a) Interview (b) Observation
(c) Questionnaire (d) Self-report

72 Likert's method is used to prepare an

(a) Achievement test (b) Aptitude test
(c) Ability test (d) Attitude test

73 "Research is honest, exhaustive and intelligent searching for facts and implications with reference to a given problem". Who said this statement?

(a) J W Best (b) P M Cook
(c) M Fair Child (d) Dewey

74 How many types of questionnaires have been defined by P V Young?

(a) Three (b) Six (c) Two (d) Four

75 Man to man scale and portrait matching are examples of

(a) graphic scale
(b) forced choice rating scale
(c) standard scale
(d) rating by cumulated points

76 Arrange the following educational resources process in correct sequence.

1. Collection of data
2. Statement of objectives
3. Selecting the problem
4. Method/procedure

Codes

(a) 3, 2, 4, 1 (b) 1, 2, 4, 3
(c) 4, 3, 2, 1 (d) 1, 4, 2, 3

77 Arrange the following steps in correct order.

1. Sampling
2. Interference
3. Data Analysis
4. Data collection

Codes

(a) 2, 3, 1, 4 (b) 1, 4, 3, 2
(c) 3, 2, 4, 1 (d) 4, 1, 2, 3

78 Arrange the following steps of ethnographic research.

1. Data collection
2. Identification of subjects
3. Hypothesis generation
4. Identification of the phenomena

Codes

(a) 1, 2, 4, 3 (b) 4, 2, 3, 1
(c) 4, 3, 1, 2 (d) 1, 3, 4, 2

79 Arrange the four phases of formative evaluation.

1. One to one
2. Expert review
3. Small group
4. Field test

Codes

(a) 2, 3, 1, 4 (b) 2, 1, 4, 3
(c) 2, 1, 3, 4 (d) 1, 2, 4, 3

80 Survey study aims at

1. knowing facts about the existing situation.
2. comparing the present status with the standard norms.
3. criticising the existing situation.
4. identifying the means of improving the existing situation.

Codes

(a) 1, 2 (b) 1, 2, 3
(c) 1, 2, 3, 4 (d) 2, 3

81 Four main methods of survey are

1. mail survey
2. personal interview
3. internet uses
4. telephonic interview
5. internet surveys

Codes

(a) 1, 2, 3, 4 (b) 2, 3, 4, 5
(c) 1, 2, 4, 5 (d) 5, 4, 1, 3

82 The three participants in formative assessment are

1. peer
2. learner
3. principal
4. parents
5. teacher

Codes

(a) 1, 2, 5 (b) 3, 4, 5 (c) 1, 2, 3 (d) 3, 1, 5

Directions (Q. Nos. 83-87) *Given below are two statements, one labelled as Assertion (A) and the other labelled as Reason (R). Following are the codes given below. Choose the correct code.*

Codes

(a) Both A and R are true and R is the correct explanation of A
(b) Both A and R are true, but R is not the correct explanation of A
(c) Both A and R are false
(d) A is false, but R is true

83 **Assertion** (A) Laboratory experiments has relatively complete control of extraneous variables.

Reason (R) Its results are applicable to real life situations.

84 **Assertion** (A) Longer tests are more reliable than shorter ones.

Reason (R) Each item adds to test reliability.

85 **Assertion** (A) Reasearch always should be focussed on discovering new facts.

Reason (R) Research should always validate results in a new setting.

86 **Assertion** (A) Groupware includes word processor and spreadsheets.

Reason (R) Componentware is associated with physical equipment involved in data processing.

87 **Assertion** (A) Alexandria is an example of digital library used at university.

Reason (R) Guterberg is an example of digital library used at national libraries.

ANSWERS

1 (b)	2 (c)	3 (d)	4 (a)	5 (d)	6 (c)	7 (a)	8 (b)	9 (d)	10 (c)
11 (a)	12 (b)	13 (d)	14 (d)	15 (d)	16 (b)	17 (c)	18 (d)	19 (a)	20 (b)
21 (d)	22 (d)	23 (b)	24 (a)	25 (d)	26 (d)	27 (c)	28 (a)	29 (d)	30 (b)
31 (c)	32 (d)	33 (a)	34 (c)	35 (b)	36 (c)	37 (d)	38 (d)	39 (a)	40 (c)
41 (d)	42 (d)	43 (b)	44 (c)	45 (a)	46 (d)	47 (c)	48 (b)	49 (d)	50 (b)
51 (a)	52 (c)	53 (b)	54 (d)	55 (c)	56 (a)	57 (c)	58 (d)	59 (b)	60 (d)
61 (b)	62 (b)	63 (c)	64 (c)	65 (d)	66 (b)	67 (a)	68 (d)	69 (c)	70 (c)
71 (a)	72 (a)	73 (b)	74 (c)	75 (c)	76 (a)	77 (b)	78 (b)	79 (c)	80 (b)
81 (c)	82 (a)	83 (b)	84 (b)	85 (a)	86 (d)	87 (c)			

CHAPTER 34

Educational Management and Administration

In a democratic country like India, the study of educational management and administration is essential as they are not separate, both are concerned with the achievement of organisational goals. Management is a sub-set of administration. To understand its importance in the field of education, various aspects need to be studied.

Educational Management

Educational management of an institution or organisation is concerned with the objectives, targets and goals laid down by the Board of Directors of the Institutions. Educational management is concerned with the achievement of results. It is progressive, imaginative and innovative because of its emphasis on results. This result is easily measurable.

Management implies an orderly way of thinking. It describes in operational terms what is to done, how it is to be done and how we know when we have done. Management is a method of operation. Good management should result in an orderly integration of education and society.

It is a complex human enterprise in which different resources are brought together and made available to achieve and to accomplish the desire and expected goals or objectives. It implies the practical measures for ensuring the system to work for achieving the goals or objectives of educational institutions. So, it operates in educational organisations or institutions. Human resources, physical and material resources and ideational resources are different types of educational management.

Educational management in broader perspective covers the following

- Setting directions, aims and objectives of educational organisations or institutions.
- Planning for progress of the programme.
- Organising available resources *i.e.* people, time and material.
- Controlling the implementing process.
- Setting and improving organisational standards.

In this Chapter

Importance of Educational Management

- It includes the study of various theories of management which define and describe the roles and responsibilities of the educational manager and develop managerial skills.
- It includes the study of educational planning at macro level, its goals, principles, approaches and procedures. At a micro level, it helps in understanding and facilitates institutional planning and educational administration.
- It helps in decision-making, problem-solving, communication and information.
- It helps in planning of co-curricular activities, academics and preparation of time-table.
- It also helps in the maintenance of school records and evaluating students' achievements.
- Financing and budgeting of educational institutions.

Functions of Educational Management

- It helps in curriculum activity management.
- Helpful in evaluating student's achievement.
- It deals with material and institutional effectiveness.
- It improves the teaching-learning process through motivating staff and students.
- It facilitates maintenance of school records, financing and budgeting.
- It creates a healthy and conducive school climate.

Principles of Educational Management

Henry Fayol identified 14 principles of management and few of his principles can be used in education

Division of Work This principle can be used in classroom management by dividing the classroom work among the teacher and the students. This sub-division of labour would make work simpler and would result in greater efficiency. It will help students in acquiring speed along with accuracy in their performance.

Authority and Responsibility Authority and responsibility co-exist in the classroom too. Among the group of students it world refer to the right of one student to get exactness from his classmates, responsibility would entail obligation for the performance of job assigned. In classroom, this authority and responsibility can be maintained by appointing the class representative and giving him responsibility of maintaining better classroom environment in the absence of the teacher. If authority is given to a student he should always be made responsible for exercising such authority.

Unity of Direction This principle can be used for better classroom management. It should be made clear to all the students that teaching-learning process is a combined effort for the achievement of common goal and all the efforts of teacher and students are for the betterment of students and for their overall development.

Equity Equity means combination of fairness, kindness and justice. Equity is essential to create and maintain cordial relations between the teachers and students but does not always means total absence of harshness. Applying Fayol's logic, there should not be any kind of discrimination by the teacher on the basis of age, caste, gender, religion, etc in the classroom.

Discrimination free environment would create cordial relations between teacher and student. However, this relationship should always contain some elements of harshness and toughness on the part of the teacher which is necessary for improving and bringing notable positive changes in the behaviour of students.

Order This principle is concerned with proper and systematic arrangement of things and people. Likewise, order must be maintained in classroom. There should be safe, appropriate and specific place for every article, which is needed while teaching and every place has to be effectively and optimally used for teaching. Social order should be maintained with the appointments of the most deserving and suitable teachers for teaching students.

Discipline Discipline is a necessary pre-requisite for the maintenance of teaching-learning atmosphere in the classroom. There should be sincerity, obedience, respect of authority and observance of rules and regulations of the institution.

Initiative Initiative means eagerness to initiate actions without being asked to do so. In the classroom, all the students should be encouraged and motivated to take initiative in the classroom activities. Teachers should provide opportunities to students to suggest new ideas, experiences and innovative methods of teaching. It helps in developing an atmosphere of mutual understanding and trust in the classroom.

Subordination of Individual Interest to General Interest In order to achieve this attitude in the classroom situation, it is essential that students should be honest and sincere towards their school. They should be taught that the interest of the school is more important than their personal interests. They should be made ready to sacrifice their personal interest for good of the institution in times of need. A teacher can bring this attitude only when he is enjoying a permanent position in the institution.

Espirit de' corps (Union is Strength) In the classroom situation, students should be encouraged to develop informal relations among themselves and efforts should be made to create enthusiasm and keenness, so that they can work to their maximum potential. The teacher should infuse team spirit and belongingness. Highly effective students should be rewarded and those who are not upto the mark should be given a chance to improve performance. Students should be made conscious that whatever they are doing is of great importance to the society. There would be proper co-ordination of work in the class which would be a great step in better classroom management.

Educational Administration

Educational administration is a comprehensive effort to achieve some specific educational objectives. It is a complex human enterprise in which different resources are brought together and made available to achieve and to accomplish the desire and expected goals or objectives. For success of educational management, there must be adequate freedom and flexibility on the one hand and necessarily discipline and decorum on the other hand, in the educational institution.

It is concerned with both human and material resources. The human elements include children, parents, teachers and other employees. The material resources include money, building, grounds, equipments and instructional supplies. Besides these two elements, there are ideas, laws and regulations, community needs and so on. All these have a bearing on the educational process in the integration of these parts into a whole educational administration.

The major focus of administration is the harmonisation of available human and material resources in pursuit of productive activities oriented towards the achievement of the organisation's objectives. According to **Petermode**, "It refers to the process concerned with the implementation of educational programs or policies in an education enterprise".

Functions of Educational Administration

Some of the major functions of educational administration in India are planning, organisation, direction and controlling. Educational administration is a total process which provides and manages various elements of the teaching-learning situation, viz, the teachers, the learners, the curriculum and the socio-physical environment.

The different functions of administration are discussed below:

Planning It is an essential component and a useful exercise to be undertaken by the administrators. It involves systematic, organised and articulated scheme of working, thus it can be thought at the beginning.

Organisation It is an important function of good administration. The effective and efficient work of the institution depends upon the good organisation. For good organisation, the administrator should define the purpose, analyse and identify tasks required to meet these objectives.

Direction It is an important function of educational administration. It involves getting the work done through instructions and orders. It also involves exercising leadership, motivating people, determining accountability and developing guidelines for action. This step includes motivating and decision-making.

Controlling It involves measuring and monitoring performance, comparing results with plans and taking corrective actions when required. It also indicates how far the goals have been achieved and to what extent there is deviation from the real plans.

Importance of Educational Administration

- The educational administration is important for the purpose of becoming an effective leader or manager, who is incharge of educational institution.
- He needs to be familiar with the theoretical concepts and best practices, relating to educational administration.
- The administrators can perform useful functions within organisations. The knowledge and understanding of organisational behaviour, both internal and external, enable an administrator to act more effectively.
- The educational organisation and their administrations have some unique characteristics that deserve distinctive treatment. It is important to achieve some specific educational objectives.
- It ensures the efficient and effective delivery of relevant educational services as well as implementing of legislative policies through planning, decision- making and leadership.

Principles of Educational Administration

The following are the principles of educational administration

Structural Democracy

Being the first principle of educational administration in the modern era, it puts stress on democracy in structural perspective. It implies the exercise of control in democracy. The meaning of exercise of control in this light should be such that, it helps the students as future citizens in fulfiling their needs and requirements, tending to their self-realization,safeguard the democratic government and welfare of people at local, state and national levels.

In this regard, an educational administrator will be a fittest one, who can manage autocracy as and when necessary to achieve the goals of an educational programme. For actualizing, it he has to perform his duty as democratically as possible.

Operational Democracy

This principle gives priority on the practical aspects of democracy as a way of life and form of governance. To this, the essence of democracy is to give importance on the dignity of every individual and assisting him to understand his self. In this context, this principle considers democracy as a matter of spirit, way of life and a mode of behaviour. Keeping this in view, it is the task and responsibility of an educational administrator to focus on day to day happenings in relation to democratic society in educational perspective that are relevant in wider extent.

Justice

It refers to provide every individual his due in the society by honoring his individuality. This meaning of justice is the essence of democracy. As justice is one of the basic hallmark of democratic administration, it is regarded as an essential principle of educational administrating, which is democratic in form and practice.

The educational administrators for practicing justice as one of the principles of educational administration must be judicious while dealing with employees, students and public. But in practice, it is not happening as the educational administrators very often arbitrarily exercise discretionary powers and too narrowly apply uniform rules in one point.

Equality of Opportunity

One of the important social objective of education is to equalize opportunity or facility for enabling the backward or under privileged classes and individuals to use education as a means for improvement of their condition. In order to keep equality of opportunity in concrete shape in the field of education, educational administration plays a vital role. For this, greater emphasis should be given on equality of educational opportunity for the sake of accelerating the processes for building up of on egalitarian human society in which the age old social exploitation will be reduced to minimum.

The Principle of Uniformity is not to be practiced and maintained in the field of educational administration as equality does not refer to uniformity. The cause is that opportunity means to provide adequate facility or scope to every individual for his development.

Prudence

The principle, 'Prudence' is closely related to intelligent economy, which implies quality control. In order to ensure quality control in the field of education, administration has to make expenditure on education by accepting it as an investment on human resource. Because without necessary expenditure on education there will be no question of quality in it and then what about the matter of quality control?

It is evident from several studies that now in educational administration there lies a lot of wasteful expenditure for which the system of check and balance is essential. The system of check and balance is prudential in nature, which seeks to protect an educational institution or organisation, an enterprise from misbehaviours and misappropriation by an official or authority, as misuse of power and funds that creates mischief.

It is known to one and all that misuse of power and money leads to the loss of public in general. Hence, like general administration in educational administration, there is the necessity of the system of 'check and balance' to prevent such misuse. This will be done, if educational administration accepts it as its principle in real situation.

Adaptability, Flexibility and Stability

An institution must be able to adjust with changing situations, by fulfiling the developing needs and by improving its day to day dealings with persons or agencies involved. This characteristic of an institution is called **adaptability**. In the process of achieving its educational objectives, it has to deal differently with different human beings, like teachers, parents and the public at large, who are affected in one way or other by the process or its products. This tendency is called **flexibility**.

The educational institution, however must be able to achieve adaptability without creating any dislocation or disruption in its process and achievements. This property is named as **stability**. An institution must have these three characteristics in order to be able to achieve its objectives adequately and to give due regard to all persons, concerned in some way or other.

Adaptability is concerned with acts of change and flexibility to a great extent, to counteract with uniformity and stability is mainly the counterweight to adaptability. **Flexibility** is the capacity of an institution to react in variance with persons and situations affected and to warn against the dangers of uniformity.

Stability on the other hand is the capacity of an organisation to safeguard the merits of the old while it is in the process of change. Hence, all these three qualities of adaptability, flexibility and stability are complementary to each other.

Institutional Building

An educational institution, whether it is primary or secondary or higher aims at providing quality leading role in the institution building. Its success depends on their effective and efficient management.

The term 'institutional building' has been used, both in relation to the process of internal development of an institution, as well as to its capacity to promote its impact on the society. It is associated with the process of establishing or transforming an organisation into an integrated and organic part of a community in a way that helps the organisation play a proactive role in projecting new values and become an agent of change in the community (Pareek, 1981). Hence, the management of an institution must pay attention to both these aspects of institutional building. The main function of management is to make an institution more effective.

POSDCORB

American political scientist **Luther Gulick** and the British management consultant **Lyndall Urwick** elaborated **Henry Fayol's** management ideas in their paper named **Notes on Theory of Organisation** in 1937. In doing so, they built on Fayol's previous 14 management principles. They gave the idea **POSDCORB**, which stands for Planning, Organising, Staffing, Directing, Coordinating, Reporting and Budgeting. With the POSDCORB concept, **Gulick** and **Urwick** took a number of facts within organisational structure and coordination into account. This concept is applied in educational management.

Planning It refers to the establishment of a broad draft to be accomplished and the process incorporated to implement them. Planning determines the direction of the organisation.

Organising To achieve an end result, the manager needs the necessary resources, including budget, raw materials, personnel and their expertise, technology and machines. He/she will have to organise all sorts of things to achieve the end result.

Staffing Good and competent personnel is crucial for an organisation to function. It is the task of the head of the institute to first identify the expertise, skills and experiences, required for certain positions. Based on this, job profiles are drawn up and candidates can be recruited. The entire recruitment, selection and training procedure falls under this staff policy.

Directing Direction lies in the hands of the head of the institute and he maintains control over all functions. He motivates all the employees and encourages them to take challenges.

Coordinating It is the task of the head of the institute to synchronise different departments and to bring them together with the right end goal in mind.

Reporting A clear report keeps communication open throughout the entire organisation. Reporting provides insight into the progress of the organisation, problems with employees, new processes, performances, etc.

Budgeting It is very necessary for an organisation to maintain proper budget. The manager is responsible for the management, expenditure and control of the department's budget. If any error is found, the manager is responsible for the action.

Critical Path Method (CPM)

CPM is a mathematically ordered network of planning and scheduling project management. It was first used in 1957 by El Du Pontde. He developed this project management method, designed to address the challenge of crisis faced by the industry.

CPM provides a graphical view of the project. It predicts the time required to complete the project and shows which activities are critical to maintaining the schedule and which are not.

Steps in CPM Project Planning

- Specify the individual activities.
- Determine the sequence of those activities.
- Draw a network diagram.
- Estimate the completion time for each activity.
- Identify the critical path.
- Update the CPM diagram as the project progresses.

Advantages of CPM

- CPM helps in selecting, monitoring and controlling projects.
- Project manager can determine actual dates for each activity and compare what should be happening to what is taking place and react accordingly.
- The activities and outcomes can be shown as network.
- Evaluates which activities can run parallel to each other.
- It can define multiple and equally critical paths.
- CPM determines the project direction, which minimised the sum of direct and indirect costs.
- CPM helped to provide efficiency and effective management procedures in educational institutes.
- This system has streamlined all aspects of an educational project process and how management is undertaken.

Disadvantages of CPM

- It is difficult to understand for beginner.
- CPM can become ineffective and difficult to manage if it is not well defined and stable.
- If the project is far too bulky and lengthy, the CPM requires software to monitor the plan.
- The CPM takes longer to identify and monitor the critical path, when the project is of big dimension.
- It cannot effectively handle sudden changes in the implementation of the plan on ground. It is very difficult to redraw the entire CPM chart if the plan of the project sudden changes midway.
- Using CPM, identifying and determining a critical path is difficult when there are many other similar duration path in the project.
- At times, to design CPM is time consuming. It is also difficult to estimate the activity completion time in a multi-dimensional project.
- The CPM cannot form and control the schedules of the persons involved in the project.

PERT Model

The Program Evaluation and Review Technique (PERT) is a widely used method for planning and coordinating large scale projects. As **Harold Kerznes** explained in his book **Project Management**, "PERT is basically a management planning and control tool. It can be considered as a road map for a particular program or project in which all the major elements have been completely identified, together with their corresponding interrelations".

A basic element of PERT style planning is to identify critical activities on which others depend. It was developed during the 1950s. The chief feature of PERT analysis is a network diagram that provides a visual depiction of the major project activities and the sequence in which they must be completed.

There are few rules and terms to be understood in understanding the PERT model

- Each activity is represented by a single arrow sign(→)and cannot be represented more than once in the network.
- All activities precelding any activity must be completed. Thus, the network should be developed on the basis of logical dependencies between various activities of the project.
- Events marking the start of activities are called **tail events** and events making completion of an activity are known as **head events**. Suppose and activity 'A' starts from event '1' and ends at event '2'. Then, it can be shown as:

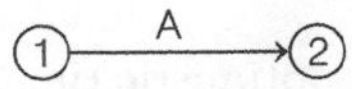

  There should not be any duplication of event numbers in a network.
- Activity can be identified as a pair of start end event number like activity A can be shown as 1-2 pair.
- An event which represents the joint completion of more than one activity is known as **merge event**. The event 4 in figure below is a merge event, showing completion of events 1,2 and 3.

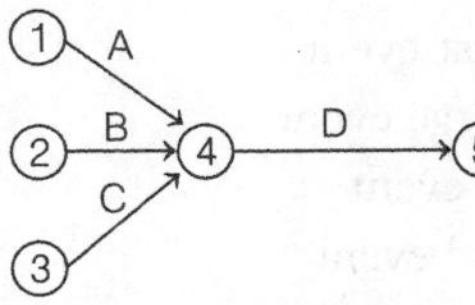

- An event which portrays the initiation of more than one activity is called the **burst event**. Just as event 2 in below figure.

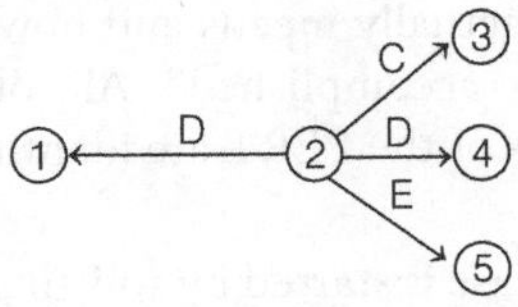

- In case, if two events are connected by two activities, A and B, then we have to make a **dummy activity**.

- In this figure, C is the dummy activity between event 2 and 3 represented by a dash line. This dummy activity is known as **identity dummy**. The dummy activities do not consume time or resources.

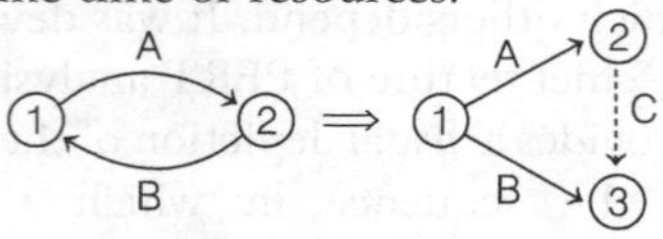

- No event is considered completed, until all the activities leading to it have been completed.
- PERT requires certain time estimates to be associated with the completion of every activity, Such time estimates are made on a three way basic optimistic time, most likely and pessimistic time.

Optimistic Time What is the least time that the activity takes, in the event that work proceeds without any problems, interferences and obstacles?

Most Likely Time How much time is required to complete the activity under normal circumstances?

Pessimistic Time Given the worst conditions, what is the time, the project is going to take?

Expected time can be calculated by formula $t_e = \frac{0 + 4m + P}{6}$

t_e = expected time, 0= optimistic time,
m = most likely time
P = pessimistic time

Structure of PERT Chart

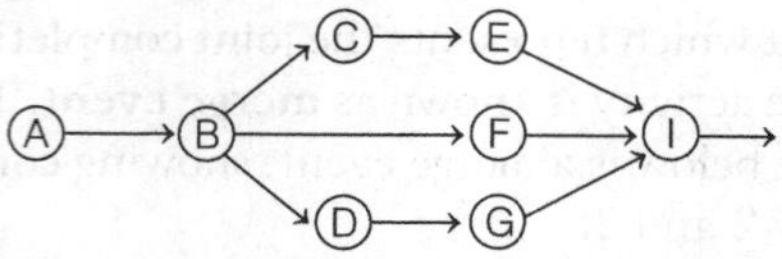

- Event B is a burst event
- Event H is a merge event
- Every A is a tail event
- Event B is a head event

Basic Steps in PERT

Defining the Objectives First, it is defined what has to be achieved, what it actually means and how can it be known that it has been accomplished? All other details and activities and steps of the PERT are identified in relation to these objectives.

Planning This phase is started by splitting the total project into small projects. These smaller projects again are divided into activities and are analysed by the relevant departments.

Scheduling It means that to prepare a time chart, showing the start and finish time for each activity as well as its relationship to other activities of the project. The schedule must suggest the critical path activities, which require special attention of the project is to be completed in time.

Allocation of Resources It is performed to achieve the desired objective. A resource is a physical variable, such as labour, finance, equipment and space, which will impose a limitation on time for the project.

Controlling The final phase in project management is controlling. Critical Path Method facilitates the application of the Principle of Management by exception to identify areas that are to the completion of the project.

Advantages of PERT

- It helps to determine the start date and end date of a particular activity, estimated project completion time and financial aspect of the project is within estimate budget or not.
- It is mathematically very simple.
- It is useful at various stages of project management.
- It provides critical path and slack time.
- It helps to determine whether the project is going as per schedule or not.
- Determine the critical path activities, having direct impact on the project completion time.
- It is useful in monitoring costs and resources.

Disadvantages of PERT

Time Focused Method The method of PERT is a time oriented method, where the time required to complete the respective activity is of higher importance. Hence, the time determination of each activity and its allocation is very much necessary. This is done, based on an assumption and within this time the work will be completed. If this is not the case, issues will arise.

Subjective Analysis The activities for a project is identified, based on the data available. This IS difficult in case of PERT as these are mostly applied for a project that is newly conducted or those without repetitive nature. The project dealt by PERT will be a fresh project data that make the collection of information to be subjective in nature. This will bring less accuracy on the time and the estimated time. There are chances to have inaccuracy and bias in the sources of data. This makes it unreliable. As this is not repetitive in nature, there is no sense in bringing the records from the past historical data.

Prediction Inaccuracy As there is no past records or assistance to bring an outline for the project, predictions take their role. The overall project may move to total loss if the predictions and the decisions are inaccurate. No trial and error method can be employed.

Expensive As this method is carried out based on predictions in overall, they find too expensive in terms of methods employed, the time consumed and the resources used.

Other Issues This method is highly labour intensive in nature. As there are chances of increase in project activities, large and complicated networks are developed as many task dependencies come into existence. If two activities share common resources, this technique won't find very apt for the project.

Difference Between CPM and PERT Methods

CPM	PERT
It is a statistical technique of project management that manages well defined activities of a project.	It is a project management teachnique, use to manage uncertain activities of a project.
It is introduced for the purpose of improving performance and advancing best practice standards for public sector managers. It is a comprehensive management development programme based upon selected set of competencies.	It is a scheduling tool that is essentially a network of project activities showing estimates of time necessary to complete each activity and the sequential relationship of activities that must be followed to complete the project.
It is deterministic in nature.	It is probabilistic in nature.
It is activity oriented.	It is event-oriented.
It shows the sequence of events and activities within a PERT network that requires longest period of time to complete.	It is a technique used for problems that occur once or relatively few times and that has a definite starting point and finishing point.

Management as a System

Management as a system is a set of policies, processes and procedures, used by an organisation to ensure that it can fulfil the tasks required to achieve its objectives. These objectives can relate to a number of different topics, including product or service quality, operational efficiency, environmental performance, health and safety in the work place and many more. The level of complexity of the system will depend on each organisation's specific context.

SWOT Analysis

SWOT is a strategic planning technique, which is used to help a person or organisation to identify strengths, weaknesses, opportunities and threats related to business competition or project planning. SWOT is described as the tried and true tool to strategic analysis. The SWOT analysis is an acronym for four parameters, the technique examines.

Strengths Characteristics of the business or project that give it an advantage over others.

Weaknesses Charateristics of the business or project that place the business or project at a disadvantage, relative to others.

Opportunities Elements in the environment that the business or project could exploit to its advantage.

Threats Elements in the environment that could cause trouble for the business or project.

A SWOT analysis is designed to facilitate a realistic, fact based, data driven look at the strengths and weaknesses of organisation or industry. It is used as a guide and technique for assessing the performance, competition, risk and potential of a business, as well no part of a business, such as a product line or division an industry or other entity.

Features of SWOT Analysis

- SWOT analysis is a strategic planning technique that provides assessment tools.
- Identifying core strengths, weaknesses, opportunities and threats lead to fact based analysis, fresh perspectives and new ideas.
- SWOT analysis works best when diverse groups or voices within an organisation are free to provide realistic data points rather than prescribed messaging.

Taylorism

Scientific Management or Taylorism is the name of the approach to management industrial and organisational psychology. It was initiated by **Frederick Winslow Taylor** in his **1911**, monograph, **'The Principles of Scientific Management'**.

It was closely associated with production methods in manufacturing factories. Taylor's own name for his approach was **Scientific Management**. This sort of task oriented optimisation of work tasks is nearly ubiquitous today in menial industries, most notably in assembly lines and fast food restaurants.

According to his observation, in general that workers in repetitive jobs work at the slowest rate that goes unpunished. The slow rate of work (which he called soldiering) was combination of the inherent laziness of people and the observation that when paid the same amount, workers will tend to do the same amount of work. He therefore, proposed that work practice that had been developed in most work environments was crafted, intentionally or unintentionally, to be very inefficient in its execution.

Taylor introduced many concepts that were not widely accepted at the time. For e.g. by observing workers, he decided that labour should include rest breaks, so that the worker has time to recover from fatigue. Today's army uses it during forced marches, the soldiers are ordered to take a break of 10 minutes for every hour of marching.

This allows for a much longer forced march than continuous walking.

***Taylor** recognised that there is a certain suitability of certain people for particular jobs, but the most important difficulties of this theory are*

- It ignores individual differences. The most efficient way of working for one person may be inefficient for another.
- It ignores the fact that the economic interests of workers and management are rarely identical, so that both the measurement processes and the re-training required by Taylor's methods would frequently be resented and sometimes sabotaged by the workforce.

Taylor's ideas can be seen as the root of a very influential series of developments in the workplace, with the goal being the eventual elimination of industry's needs for unskilled and later perhaps, even most skilled labour in any form, directly following Taylor's recipe for deconstructing a process.

Scientific Management Theory of Taylor has four principles, which are as follows

- Managers should gather information, analyse it and reduce it to rules, laws and mathematical formulas.
- Managers should scientifically select and train workers.
- Managers should ensure that the techniques developed by science are used by the workers.
- Managers should apply the work equally, between workers and themselves, where managers apply scientific management theories to planning and the workers perform the tasks pursuant to the plans.

Therefore, these four principles have been applied in education institutions, in order to create effective management and administration as the following:

Managers should scientifically select and then train, teach and develop the workers, whereas in past the workers choose his or her own work and trained himself/herself as best as he could. In this aspect, every worker is studied, then developed to bring out his or her best faculties. The worker is also trained to do higher more interesting and more profitable class for work. Actually by this point, Taylor was emphasizing the need for worker's education programmes.

Administration as a Process

Educational administration is regarded as the process of integrating the appropriate human and material resources that are made available and made effective for achieving the purposes of a programme of an educational institution. It includes a number of processes, such as planning, organising directing, coordinating, controlling and evaluating the performance.

The concept of educational administration is applicable in case of an educational organisation, which has certain purposes or goals to fulfil. Educational administration is primarily a social enterprise as it is more concerned with human resources than material resources. It is a non-profit making task. Educational administration encompasses all the levels of education i.e. pre-primary, primary, secondary, higher secondary and tertiary or higher education. Educational administration covers all forms of education i.e. formal and non-formal education, adult education, general education, vocational education, special education, teacher education, technical and professional education, etc.

Administration as a Bureaucracy

Bureaucracy is regarded as a body of non-elective government officials and an administrative policy-making group. Historically, it is a government administration, managed by departments and staffed with non-elected officials. Now, bureaucracy means administrative system governing any large institution, whether it is publicly owned or privately owned.

Educational institution as a system has goals to meet. The needs of mass administration, make it today completely indispensable. Thus, proper administrative body is needed in every institution. This body along with principles take all the vital decision about the institution which is required.

Human Relations Approach to Administration

The Human Relations Theory of Administration came into existence in 1930s, as a reaction to the classical approach. The classical thinkers, like Taylor, Fayol, Gulick, Urwick and Weber stressed the formal structure of the organisation and neglected the role of human element in the organisation. The Human Relations Theory is also known as **Humanistic theory**, **Socio-Economic theory** and **Neo-Classical theory**.

Elton Mayo, the American sociologist, is regarded as the **Father of Human Relation Theory**. He concentrated on the study of worker's behaviour and the production capacity, taking into consideration the psychological, physical, economic, social and physiological aspects.

He called this approach as **Clinical method**. He undertook the first research programme in 1923 in a textile mill, near Philadelphia and named it **The First Enquiry**.

The other writers, who contributed to the growth of Human Relations Theory include: F J Roethlisberger, William J Dickson, W Lloyd and L J Henderson.

Hawthorne Studies

The Hawthorne studies formed the basis for the rise of Human Relations Theory. These studies shook the foundations of classical approach *i.e.* concept of economic man and the role of the structure of formal organisation. These studies were conducted in the Western Electric Company at Hawthorne (near Chicago, USA) by the Harvard Business School, under the leadership of Elton Mayo.

The studies were conducted in the following four phases

Illumination Experiment (1924-27) To determine the effect of different levels of illumination on worker's productivity.

Relay Assembly Test Room Experiment (1927) To observe the effects of various changes in working conditions, on the worker's output and morale.

Mass Interviewing Programme (1928-31) To explore the employee's feelings (human attitudes and sentiments) by talking to them.

Bank Wiring Experiment (1931-32) To understand better, how the norms that controlled each members' output were established by the workers' social group (informal organisation).

The conclusion of the Hawthorne studies are

- The social and psychological factors at the workplace and not the physical conditions of work, determine the employee's morale and output.
- The organisation is a social system.
- Non-economic rewards and sanctions, significantly affect the worker's behaviour, morale and output.
- Workers are not inert or isolated, unrelated individuals, they are social animals.
- Division of labour, strictly on specialisation is not necessarily the most efficient approach.
- The workers have a tendency to form small social groups (informal organisations). The production norms and behavioural patterns are set by such groups.
- Workers react to management as members of the informal work group, rather than as individuals.
- Leadership, style of supervision, communication and participation play a central role in worker's behaviour, satisfaction and productivity.
- Thus, the finding of Hawthorne's studies were startling and revolutionised the organisational thought. They gave rise to a new theory called **Human Relations theory**.

Organisational Compliance

The word 'organisational compliance' signifies an organisation's concrete efforts to stop, detect and or else act in response suitably to unlawful behaviour linked with the activities of those individuals working on behalf of an organisation. This comprises administrators, managers, executives, employees, etc. On practical grounds, a compliance programme provides a support to the organisation's goals, recognises the limits of legal and moral activities and creates a system to make the management aware of situations when the organisation is reaching close to or to crossing a limit or approaching towards any complication that prevents the attainment of an objective.

Compliance is either a state of being in accordance with established guidelines on specifications, or the process of becoming so. The definition of compliance can also encompass efforts to ensure that organisations are abiding by both industry regulations and government legislation. In general, compliance means conforming to rule, such as a specification, policy, standard or law. Due to the increasing number of regulations and need for operational transparency, organisations are increasingly adopting the use of consolidated and harmonised sets of compliance controls.

In our country, compliance regulation takes place across three strata *viz.* central, state and local regulations. Most regulations come in the following broad categories *viz.* economic regulations, regulation in the public interest, environmental regulation, educational regulation, etc. But, India has poor record in regulatory compliance. There are mainly six types of compliance *viz.* environmental risk, workplace, health and safety, corrupt practices, social responsibility, quality and process risk.

Educational institutes must comply with laws, regulations and internal policies, designed to ensure the smooth running of their activities. For example, universities must comply with teaching regulations as set out by the University Grant Commission (UGC). They must follow the instructions of UGC, regarding their study programmes. They must ensure that they have qualified professional faculty dedicated to compliance. But today, there have been reported challenges regarding the compliance issues in most educational institutes in our country. Compliance Management System (CMS) should be an integral part of the daily routine of management and employees of any institution.

Organisational Development

Organisational development is the study of successful organisational change and performance. **Kurt Lewin** is the founding father of organisational development. Organisational development as a practice involves an on going and systematic process of implementing effective organisational change. It is both, a field of applied science focused on understanding and managing organisational change and a field of scientific study and inquiry.

Organisational development is an objective based approach to systems change within an organisation. It enables organisations to build and sustain a new desired state for the entire organisation. It can be achieved through either a changed communication process or supported by software applications.

In order to understand the organisation culture and to evaluate the positives and the negatives of the working environment, an evaluation method is required.

Colleges, universities and schools are often prime targets for organisational development. Some factors are important in education, like tradition, shared governance, etc. Both education and industry deal with people. Power, communication, culture and roles are all key factors in effectiveness. Organisational development in education is a change strategy for organisational self-development and renewal.

Organisational development in education provides some basic changes in the institutions. *These are*

- Conceptualisations of organisational change and development in the literature.
- Change methodologies flowing from practitioners experience.
- The evidential basis for effective methods of organisational change.
- The role and effectiveness of research in processes of organisational change (including the role of self-evaluation in self-improvement).

Characteristics of Organisational Development

- It is a systematic approach to the planned change. It is structured style of diagnosing organisational problems and opportunities.
- It is grounded in solid research and theory. It involves the application of our knowledge of behaviourial science to the challenge that the organisations face.
- It recognises the reciprocal relationship between individuals and organisations. It acknowledges that for organisations to change, individual must change.
- It is goal-oriented.

Steps in Organisational Development Process

Seven major steps in organisational development process explained below:

Initial Diagnosis of the Problem

In the first step, the management should try to find out an overall view of the situations to find the real problem. Top management should meet the consultants and the experts to determine the type of programme that is needed. In the first stage only, the consultants will meet various persons in the organisation and interview them to collect some information.

Data Collection

In this stage, the consultant will make the surveys to determine the climate of the organisation and the behavioural problems of the employees.

The consultant will meet groups of people away from their work environment to get some answers to the questions such as

(i) What specific job conditions contribute most to their job effectiveness?
(ii) What kind of conditions interfere with their job effectiveness?
(iii) What changes would they like to make in the working of the organisation?

Data Feedback and Confrontation

The data which has been collected in the second step will be given to the work groups, who will be assigned the job of reviewing the data. Any area of disagreement will be mediated among themselves only and priorities will be established for change.

Planning Strategy for Change

In this stage, the consultant will suggest the strategy for change. He will attempt to transform diagnosers of the problem into a proper action plan, involving the overall goals for change, determination of basic approach for attaining these goals and the sequence of detailed scheme for implementing the approach.

Intervening in the System

Intervening in the system refers to the planned programmed activities during the course of an OD programme. These planned activities bring certain changes in the system, which is the basic objective of OD. There may be various methods through which external consultant intervene in the system, such as education and laboratory training, process consultation, team development, etc.

Team Building

During the entire process, the consultant encourages the groups to examine how they work together. The consultant will educate them about the value of free communication and trust as essentials for group functioning. The consultant can have team managers and their subordinates to work together as a team in OD sessions to further encourage team building. Following the development of small groups, there may be development among larger groups comprising several teams.

Evaluation

OD is a very long process. So there is a great need for careful monitoring to get precise feedback regarding what is going on after the 00 programme starts. This will help in making suitable modifications whenever necessary. For evaluation of OD programme, the use of critique sessions, appraisal of change efforts and comparison of pre and post training behavioural patterns are quite effective.

The steps in OD are part of a whole process, so all of them need to be applied if a firm expects to get the full benefits of OD. An organisation which applies only a few steps and leaves the others will be disappointed with the results.

Organisational Climate

Organisational climate is a concept which offers the educationist a means of better understanding the operation of schools. Organisational climate is concerned with large units. It characterises properties of an entire organisation or major sub-units.

Characteristics of organisational climate are

- It is a general expression of what the organisation is?
- It is a qualitative concept, it is really difficult to explain in quantitative unit.
- It gives a distinct identity to the organisation. It explains how one organisation is different from other organisations.
- It represents a relatively enduring quality of the internal environment *i.e.* experienced by the organisational members.
- It is a multi-dimensional concept *i.e.* individual autonomy, authority structure, leadership style, pattern of communication, degree of conflicts, cooperation, etc.

Factors influencing organisational climate are

- Organisational structure
- Individual's responsibility
- Rewards
- Risk and risk taking
- Warmth and support
- Tolerance and conflict

Organisational climate influences member's behaviour and attitude. The set of internal characteristics that distinguish one school from another and influences the behaviour of members is the organisational climate of the school.

School climate may be open or closed. Same thing happens to colleges, universities and other educational institutes. **Open climate** is characterised by teacher-student relationship *i.e.* friendly, professional and healthy . The principal must be supportive and professional, does not re-strict or direct teachers with orders. **Closed climate** is characterised by teacher relations that are disengaged, distant, suspicious and not professional. The principal is directive, restrictive and not supportive here.

In healthy climate of an institution, morale is high and there is a general press for academic archievement by teachers, parents and students. In unhealthy climate, morale is poor and there is limited attention to academic matters because the teacher have given up.

To fulfil the professional goals through educational institute, some steps should be taken

- Build trust and foster authenticity in behaviour.
- Use variety of perspectives as multiple perspectives enrich analysis.
- Build a climate of openness, it enhances both the academic achievement and social emotional development of students.
- Use both climate and culture measures as part of a systematic professional development programme.
- Set professional goals for the institute.
- Enlist the teachers of the institution in the development of improvement plan as teacher plays a significant role for the improvement of the institution.

EXAM BASED QUESTIONS

1 In India, educational administration originated during
(a) ancient period (b) medieval period
(c) modern period (d) Both a and b

2 Hindu and Muslim rulers in our country spread education as a
(a) religious obligation (b) moral obligation
(c) medium of control (d) None of these

3 The Charter Act, which made the East India Company responsible for education was passed in
(a) 1800 (b) 1810 (c) 1823 (d) 1833

4 The Wood Despatch provided some new measures like
(a) promotion of English education
(b) giving formal powers to provinces
(c) Both a and b
(d) None of the above

5 Which one is not correct?
(a) The University of Calcutta (1857)
(b) The University of Madras (1857)
(c) The University of the Punjab (1880)
(d) The University of Allahabad (1887)

6 For success of educational management, there must be
(a) adequate freedom and flexibility
(b) discipline and decorum
(c) Both a and b
(d) None of the above

7 Educational administration is concerned with
(a) human resources (b) material resources
(c) Both a and b (d) None of these

8 Which principle can be used for better classroom management?
(a) Unity of direction (b) Equity
(c) Division of work (d) Discipline

9 Division of work in the management process produces
(a) increased performance (b) decreased performance
(c) improved performance (d) Both a and c

10 .... is a necessary pre-requisite for the maintenance of teaching-learning atmosphere.
(a) Initiative (b) Discipline
(c) Equity (d) Order

11 Which factor is responsible to maintain good relations between employee and management?
(a) Fair and adequate remuneration
(b) Good behaviour
(c) Developed infrastructure
(d) None of the above

12 Centralisation of power in an organisation denotes
(a) concentration of decision-making power at the top level
(b) subordinates are given a great role in management
(c) optimum utilisation of all the human resources
(d) None of the above

13 Fayol said that in case of emergency, an employee can communicate with another employee in the same rank to avoid delay in communication is known as
(a) Scalar Chain (b) Gang Plank
(c) Right Plank (d) None of these

14 What do you mean by 'Espirit De Corps'?
(a) Team spirit (b) Confidence of the player
(c) Spiritual upliftment (d) None of these

15 The major functions of educational administration in India are
(a) planning and organisation
(b) direction and controlling
(c) planning and direction
(d) Both a and b

16 Direction consists of
(a) work done through instructions and orders
(b) leadership motivating people
(c) developing guideline for action
(d) All of the above

17 .... involves measuring and monitoring performance, comparing results with plans and taking corrective action when required.
(a) Direction (b) Controlling
(c) Planning (d) Organisation

18 Institutional building is of many types
(a) government and public works
(b) healthcare
(c) education and military
(d) All of the above

19 Who gave the idea 'POSDCORB'?
(a) Henry Fayol (b) Luther Gulick
(c) Lyndal Urwick (d) Both b and c

20 The idea of POSDCORB was built on Fayol's
(a) 14 management principles
(b) 13 management principles
(c) 10 management principles
(d) None of the above

21 .... is the task of the manager, to identify the expertise, skills and experiences required for certain positions and recruit the candidates.
(a) Selection (b) Staffing
(c) Interview (d) Staff policy

22 .... is the task of the manager to synchronise different departments and to bring them together with the right end goal in mind.
(a) Organising (b) Staffing (c) Directing (d) Coordinating

23 Who is responsible in an organisation, for the management, expenditure and control of the department's budget?
(a) Accountant (b) Manager (c) Owner (d) None of these

24 .... provides insight into the progress of the organisation, problems with employees, new processes, performances, etc.
(a) Reporting (b) Budgeting
(c) Coordinating (d) Directing

25 CPM was first used in ....
(a) 1950 (b) 1952 (c) 1954 (d) 1957

26 PERT is a sophisticated mathematical technique developed by
(a) Fayol and Boos (b) Boos, Allen and Hamilton
(c) Boos and Allen (d) None of the above

27 The concept of PERT was introduced in the year
(a) 1950 (b) 1958 (c) 1968 (d) 1970

28 PERT stands for
(a) Programme Evaluation Review Technique
(b) Programme Evaluation Response Technique
(c) Progressive Evaluation Review Technique
(d) None of the above

29 An event which represents the joint completion of more than one activity is known as
(a) head event (b) merge event
(c) final event (d) None of these

30 An event which portrays the initiation of more than one activity is called the
(a) head event (b) dual event
(c) merge event (d) burst event

31 PERT requires certain time estimates to be associated, with the completion of every activity viz optimistic time, most likely time and
(a) restricted time (b) pessimistic time
(c) Both a and b (d) None of these

32 .... means that to prepare a time chart, showing the start and finish time for each activity as well as its relationship to other.
(a) Planning (b) Scheduling
(c) Controlling (d) None of these

33 A .... is a physical variable, such as labour, finance, equipment and space which will impose a limitation on time for the project.
(a) resource (b) capital (c) real object (d) None of these

34 .... is a strategic planning technique, which is used to help a person or organisation to identify strengths, weakness, opportunities and threats related to business competition.
(a) CPM (b) Coordinary (c) SWOT (d) PERT

35 SWOT analysis is an acronym for four parameters, viz, strength, weakness, opportunities and
(a) threats (b) theme
(c) theorem (d) None of these

36 Scientific Management is known as
(a) Taylorism (b) SWOT Analysis
(c) PERT (d) None of these

37 Taylorism was initiated by Frederick Winslow in
(a) 1911 (b) 1910 (c) 1992 (d) 1915

38 Which statement is not correct?
(a) Scientific Management theory of Taylor has four principles
(b) Taylor introduced many concepts that were not widely accepted at that time
(c) Taylor was the profounder of Human Relations theory
(d) Taylor held that managers should scientifically select and train workers

39 Pure Taylorism views workers simply as machines to be made efficient by
(a) removing unnecessary efforts
(b) removing wasted efforts
(c) adding special strengths
(d) Both (a) and (b)

40 The human relation movement was initiated by psychologists and employment experts in the United State in the
(a) 1930 s (b) 1920 s (c) 1940 s (d) 1950 s

41 Who is regarded as, "The Father of Human Relations Theory"?
(a) Elton Mayo (b) FW Taylor
(c) Luther Gulick (d) None of these

42 The growth of human relation theory is contributed by
(a) F J Roethlisberger (b) William J Dickson
(c) W Lloyd (d) All of these

43 Elton Mayo considered his Human Relations Theory as
(a) Social Method (b) Clinical Method
(c) Economical Method (d) None of these

44 Hawthorne studies formed the basis for the rise of
(a) Human Relation Theory
(b) SWOT Analysis
(c) PERT
(d) None of the above

45 Hawthorne studies were conducted in
(a) four phases (b) five phases
(c) six phases (d) seven phases

46 .... and sanctions significantly affect the worker's behaviour, morale and output.
(a) Non-economic rewards (b) Punishment
(c) Encouragement (d) None of these

47 There are mainly ...... types of organisational compliances.
(a) six (b) five (c) seven (d) eight

48 Who is the "Founding father of organisational development"?
(a) Kurt Lewin (b) FW Taylor
(c) Elton Mayo (d) None of these

49 Organisational climate influences
(a) the behaviour of the members
(b) the attitude of the members
(c) the work culture of the organisation
(d) All of the above

50 Management means forecasting, planning, organising, direction, coordinating and controlling. Who said this?
(a) Peter F Drucker (b) Henry Fayol
(c) Parkins (d) FW Taylor

51 Which of the following is not a part of management?
(a) Planning (b) Staffing
(c) Budgeting (d) Communication

52 "Management is an art of getting work done by others". The statement belongs to
(a) Stainley Vense (b) Peter F Druker
(c) Henry Fayol (d) Harold Koontz

53 Which of the following statement(s) is/are true?
1. Management is a thinking function of top level management.
2. Management does not ensures utilisation of available resources to achieve some objectives.
3. Management means managing men tactfully to get things done.

Select the correct answer, using the codes given below
(a) 1 and 2 (b) Only 3 (c) 1 and 3 (d) None of these

54 Father of modern management is
(a) Henri Fayol (b) Koontz and O Donnell
(c) FW Taylor (d) Stainley Vense

55 Management is concerned with
(a) legislative functions (b) administrative functions
(c) executive functions (d) All of these

56 According to Fayol, functions of management are
(a) planning and organisation
(b) direction and coordination
(c) control
(d) All of the above

57 Management is/an
(a) art (b) science (c) profession (d) All of these

58 Effective manager must be able
(a) to assess the needs of the organisation
(b) to maintain personal relations with the subordinates
(c) to work overtime
(d) None of the above

59 A good manager is
1. leader not a boss 2. psycho
3. economist and leader 4. creative
5. disciplinarian

Codes
(a) 1 and 2 (b) 2 and 3
(c) Only 1 (d) 2, 3 and 4

60 Management is pervasive in the sense that
(a) it fulfils all purposes
(b) it uses all resources, effectively
(c) it is relevant for all organisations
(d) All of the above

61 All managerial functions are settled by managers with the tool of
(a) planning (b) decision-making
(c) effective control (d) authority

62 Management provides
(a) new ideas (b) vision
(c) imagination (d) All of these

63 Which of the following statements is/are correct?
(a) Management cannot generate a favourable working environment.
(b) An ideal management takes the right decisions on all matters at the right time.
(c) Management activities need not to be result oriented.
(d) None of the above

64 Management aims at
(a) efficiency (b) effectiveness
(c) Both a and b (d) None of these

65 Management is called a process because
(a) it is applicable to the manufacturing process
(b) it is relevant for social organisation
(c) it involves a series of functions
(d) None of the above

66 Who will be the fittest one who can mange autocracy and achieve the goals of on educational programme?
(a) Educator
(b) Educational Administrator
(c) Management
(d) None of the above

67 Which statement is correct about operational democracy?
1. This principle gives priority on practical aspect of democracy as a way of life.
2. It puts stress on democracy in structural perspective.
3. It is the principle of educational administration.

Select the correct answer.
(a) 1 and 2 (b) Only 3
(c) 1 and 3 (d) 2 and 3

68 What is the social objective of education?
(a) To provide justice (b) To equalize opportunity
(c) To create disparity (d) None of these

69 .... is concerned with the acts of change and flexibility to a great extent.
(a) Stability (b) Adaptability
(c) Both a and b (d) None of these

70 Match the following

List I (Books)	List II (Years)
A. Principles of Public Administration	1. 1937
B. Papers on the Science of Administration	2. 1900
C. Politics and Administration	3. 1938
D. The Functions of the Executive	4. 1927

Codes

	A	B	C	D		A	B	C	D
(a)	3	1	4	2	(b)	4	1	2	3
(c)	4	1	3	2	(d)	3	4	1	2

71 Match the following

List I	List II
A. Executive functions	1. Administration
B. Administrative functions	2. Lower management
C. Board of Directors	3. Management
D. Research and development officer	4. Top management

Codes

	A	B	C	D		A	B	C	D
(a)	1	4	3	2	(b)	1	2	4	3
(c)	3	4	1	2	(d)	3	1	4	2

72 Arrange the following functions of a manager in an organisation in correct sequence.

1. Motivation 2. controlling
3. Organising 4. Planning

Codes
(a) 3, 4, 1, 2 (b) 3, 4, 2, 1 (c) 4, 3, 1, 2 (d) 4, 3, 2, 1

73 Match the following

List I (Concepts)	List II (Features)
A. Planning	1. Attempt in achieving coordination
B. Organising	2. Formulation of budgets
C. Staffing	3. Grouping of objectives and assignment to right people
D. Directing	4. Manpower planning or recruitment of personnel

Codes

	A	B	C	D		A	B	C	D
(a)	2	3	4	1	(b)	3	2	4	1
(c)	3	4	2	1	(d)	2	3	4	1

74 Which among the following is not one of the function performed by the government?

(a) Provide a minimum of public order
(b) Provide for the common defence and for dealing with other governments
(c) Solve problems related to private sector worker's union
(d) Provide orderly means for replacing those who rule legitimate means

75 Which among the following are the reasons for the decline of development administration?

1. Crisis of social science paradigm
2. Crisis of Development Theory
3. Crisis of Administrative theory
4. Crisis in developing countries.

Select the correct answer using the codes given below
(a) 1, 2 and 3 (b) 2, 3 and 4
(c) 1, 2 and 4 (d) 1, 3 and 4

76 Developing a vision and mission, identifying an organisation's external opportunities and threats and determining internal strengths and weakness are all ..... activities.

(a) strategy formulation (b) strategy implementation
(c) long range planning (d) short-range planning

77 Organisation structure primarily refers to

(a) how activities are coordinated and controlled
(b) how resources are allocated
(c) the location of departments and office space
(d) the policy statements, development by the firm

Directions (From Q. Nos. 78-82) *In the following questions, the Assertion (A) and Reason (R) have been put forward. Read both the statements carefully and choose the correct alternative from the following.*

Codes
(a) Both A and R are true and R is the correct explanation of A
(b) Both A and R are true, but R is not the correct explanation of A
(c) A is true, but R is false
(d) A is false, but R is true

78 **Assertion** (A) Management utilises human resources only.

Reason (R) Wastage is eliminated and efficiency is increased.

79 **Assertion** (A) Management is a continuous process, involving the integration of all functions.

Reason (R) Management first plan, then organise and finally performs the function of controlling.

80 **Assertion** (A) Management ensures high morale but does not improve discipline.

Reason (R) Management motivates people and ensures high morale by providing various monetary and non-monetary incentives to them.

81 **Assertion** (A) If organisations were to maximise effective communication and to reduce distortion, then there should be as few hierarchical layers as possible.

Reason (R) Fewer people are up and down the hierarchy.

82 **Assertion** (A) Authoritative style of decision-making comes from the top.

Reason (R) It is a joint collaboration of the leader and his subordinates.

PREVIOUS YEARS' QUESTIONS

July 2018

1 Which combination of following characteristics, correctly describes the Bureaucratic Administration?

1. Well-defined rules
2. Established hierarchy
3. Standard operating procedures
4. Good interpersonal relationships
5. Combined responsibility of completing works

Codes

(a) 1, 2 and 4 (b) 1, 2 and 5
(c) 2, 3 and 4 (d) 1, 2 and 3

2 Which of the following set of statements are relevant for describing teaching as a profession?

1. Teaching profession has an organised body of knowledge.
2. Teaching profession implies a set of attitudes.
3. Duration of Teacher Training Programme is not a professional pre-requisite.
4. Teaching profession has its own code of moral ethics.

Codes

(a) 2, 3 and 4 (b) 1, 3 and 4 (c) 1, 2 and 4 (d) 1, 2 and 3

January 2017

3 In Continuous and Comprehensive Evaluation, which of the following device will help in ensuring comprehensive nature of the evaluation?

(a) Focussing on cognitive areas of performance
(b) Including a number of evaluation tools for cognitive and non-cognitive areas
(c) Focussing on co-cognitive areas
(d) Involving a large number of expertise in test preparation

4 List the functions of educational supervision from the following.

1. Coordinating decision-making
2. Effective negotiation
3. Providing support
4. Regulating managerial tasks
5. Monitoring learning and development

Codes

(a) 1, 2, 3 and 4 (b) 1, 3, 4 and 5
(c) 2, 3, 4 and 5 (d) 1, 2, 4 and 5

5 Which one of the following is not a characteristic of perspective planning?

(a) One plan for a period of 20 or 25 years
(b) Long term planning
(c) Long range targets set in advance
(d) Reviewing the long term plan, every year

July 2016

6 In USA, higher education is controlled by

(a) the federal government
(b) respective state government
(c) private bodies and the state, both
(d) district authorities

December 2015

7 The most decentralised education system is in

(a) USA (b) UK
(c) India (d) USSR

8 Which one of the following gives the various phases of the System Approach in the correct sequence?

(a) Management, design and analysis
(b) Design, management and analysis
(c) Analysis, management and design
(d) Analysis, design and management

9 Three common approaches to educational planning are listed in four different seuqences. Identify the one which proceeds from the most crude to the most rigorous.

(a) Cost Benefit Analysis, Social Demand and Rate of Returns
(b) Rate of Returns, Social Demand and Cost Benefit Anaysis
(c) Social Demand, Rate of Returns and Cost Benefit Analysis
(d) Social Demand, Cost Benefit Analysis and Rate of Returns

10 School management and hospital management are

(a) totally different
(b) identical
(c) different but share some common features
(d) to be treated as cognates

11 Preparation of the school time table falls under the function of

(a) organising
(b) planning
(c) directing
(d) reporting

12 A school system has worked out a number of vision statements as result of SWOT analysis. What is the most obvious activity which has to follow?

(a) Meetings with teachers and parents
(b) Taking student's views
(c) Developing work plans
(d) Deciding about who, what and how of the plans

13 **The authoritative character is visualised in**
(a) Demonstrative model (b) Grassroot model
(c) Administrative model (d) System Analysis model

14 **The modern approach to management focuses on**
(a) organisational compliance
(b) organisational concerns
(c) organisational growth
(d) supervision of managers

15 **In which country's educational system, the idea of community college has been made popular ?**
(a) UK (b) Germany (c) USA (d) Australia

16 **A comparision of vocational education in India and that of USA reveals that**
(a) vocational programme in USA is taken less seriously
(b) In India, there is no coordination between the academic and vocational programmes
(c) The history and development of vocational education in India has witnessed many ups and downs in comparison to USA
(d) The vocational programme in India is very popular in comparison to USA

17 **From the point of view of educational administration, which of the following statement is correct?**
(a) Completely centralised - USA
(b) Completely decentralised - UK
(c) Partly decentralised - Ireland
(d) Partly centralised and partly decentralised - India

December 2014

18 **A school supervisor has responsibility to**
(a) help the school in its development
(b) observe the classroom teaching and suggest improvements if required
(c) develop the teaching learning material
(d) All of the above

19 **Which of the following is not the source of educational finance?**
(a) Public funds
(b) Local Bodies fund
(c) Education cess
(d) Relief fund

20 **Which of the following is not the technique of supervisor?**
(a) School visits (b) Surprise visits
(c) Annual visits (d) Excursion visits

21 **The 'Father of Scientific Management Approach' is**
(a) FW Taylor (b) Henry Fayol
(c) St Etienne (d) W Willson

22 **The most appropriate approach for implementing an Administrative Model of Curriculum is to focus on**
(a) hierarchy of staff
(b) democratic values
(c) participative culture
(d) horizontal coordination

ANSWERS

Exam Based Questions

1 *(d)*	2 *(a)*	3 *(d)*	4 *(c)*	5 *(c)*	6 *(c)*	7 *(c)*	8 *(a)*	9 *(a)*	10 *(c)*
11 *(a)*	12 *(a)*	13 *(b)*	14 *(a)*	15 *(d)*	16 *(d)*	17 *(b)*	18 *(a)*	19 *(d)*	20 *(a)*
21 *(b)*	22 *(d)*	23 *(b)*	24 *(b)*	25 *(d)*	26 *(b)*	27 *(b)*	28 *(a)*	29 *(b)*	30 *(d)*
31 *(b)*	32 *(b)*	33 *(a)*	34 *(c)*	35 *(a)*	36 *(a)*	37 *(a)*	38 *(c)*	39 *(d)*	40 *(b)*
41 *(a)*	42 *(a)*	43 *(b)*	44 *(a)*	45 *(a)*	46 *(a)*	47 *(a)*	48 *(a)*	49 *(d)*	50 *(d)*
51 *(b)*	52 *(d)*	53 *(b)*	54 *(a)*	55 *(c)*	56 *(d)*	57 *(d)*	58 *(c)*	59 *(c)*	60 *(c)*
61 *(b)*	62 *(d)*	63 *(b)*	64 *(c)*	65 *(c)*	66 *(b)*	67 *(c)*	68 *(b)*	69 *(b)*	70 *(b)*
71 *(d)*	72 *(d)*	73 *(c)*	74 *(c)*	75 *(a)*	76 *(a)*	77 *(a)*	78 *(d)*	79 *(c)*	80 *(a)*
81 *(a)*	82 *(c)*								

Previous Years' Questions

1 *(b)*	2 *(c)*	3 *(b)*	4 *(c)*	5 *(a)*	6 *(d)*	7 *(a)*	8 *(d)*	9 *(c)*	10 *(c)*
11 *(b)*	12 *(c)*	13 *(c)*	14 *(b)*	15 *(c)*	16 *(b)*	17 *(d)*	18 *(d)*	19 *(d)*	20 *(d)*
21 *(a)*	22 *(a)*								

CHAPTER

35

Leadership in Educational Administration

Different theories of leadership and models have been propounded to provide explanation on the leadership phenomenon and to help leaders influence followers toward achieving organisational goals.

Introduction

The actions of human beings in society are determined by their associations with different organisations. Every organisation has its own purposes and objectives. The achievement of objectives depends upon the cooperative efforts of individuals and the competence of the leader.

Many times organisations have failed when either their leaders have been of low calibre or there have been a lack of cooperative effort among its members and the objectives of the organisation are not essential and good for the society.

Leadership

Leadership is an art of motivating a group of people to act towards achieving a common goal. It is the ability to inspire others. Effective leadership is based upon the ideas, which inspire others to act as the leader wants them to act. In a nutshell, the leader is the inspiration and director of the action. He only is the person in the group that possesses the combination of personality and leadership skills that makes others want to follow his/her direction.

There are people who seems to be naturally endowed with more leadership abilities than others. Some people can learn to become leaders by improving particular skills. History is full of those people, having no previous leadership experience, have stepped in the crisis period and directed others to follow their suggested course of action.

Leadership is the process of influencing the behaviour of others, to work willingly and enthusiastically for achieving pre-determined goals. It is indispensable for the successful functioning of an organisation and attainment of its goals and objectives.

Leadership transforms potential into reality. It is the ultimate act, which brings to success, all the potentials that is in an organisation and its people. Achievement of organisational goals very much depend on how effectively leadership is exercised in

In this Chapter

- *Leadership*
- *Approaches to Leadership*
- *Leadership Models*

the organisation. Organisational leaders are the key figures, who can change the work climate so that all the employees are motivated to work hard with the results so that the goals can be achieved.

Definitions of Leadership

According to **Tenenbaum**, "Leadership is inter-personal influence exercised in a situation and directed through communication process, towards the attainment of a specified goal or goals".

According to **Keith Davis**, "Leadership is the ability to persuade others to seek defined objectives enthusiastically".

According to **Terry** , "Leadership is essentially a continuous process of influencing behaviour. A leader breaths life into the group and motivates it towards goals. The lukewarm desires for achievement are transformed into a burning passion for accomplishment".

Nature of Leadership

- Leadership is essential for managing. The ability to lead effectively is one of the keys to being an effective manager because she/he has to combine resources and lead a group to achieve objectives.
- Leadership and motivation are closely inter-connected. By understanding motivation, one can appreciate better, what people want and why they act as they do. A leader can encourage or dampen workers motivation by creating a favorable or unfavorable working environment in the organisation.
- The essence of leadership is followership. In other words, it is the willingness of people to follow a person that makes that person a leader. Moreover, people tend to follow those whom they see as providing a means of achieving their desires, needs and wants.
- Leadership involves an unequal distribution of power between leaders and group members. Group members are not powerless, they can shape group activities in some ways. Still, the leader will usually have more power than the group members.
- Leaders can influence the followers' behaviour in some ways. Infact, leaders can influence workers either to do ill or well for the company. The leader must be able to empower and motivate the followers to the cause.
- The leader must co-exist with the subordinates or followers and must have the clear idea about their demands and ambitions. This creates loyalty and trust in subordinates for their leader.
- Leadership is to be concerned about values. Followers learn ethics and values from their leaders. Leaders are the real teachers of ethics and they can reinforce ideas. It is very important for leaders to make positive statements of ethics if they are not hypocritical.

Characteristics of Leadership

- It is a continuous process of behaviour, it is not one shot activity.
- It may be seen in terms of relationship between a leader and his followers (individuals and/or groups), which arises out of their functioning for common goals.
- By exercising his leadership, the leader tries to influence the behaviour of individuals or group of individuals around him to achieve common goals.
- The followers work willingly and enthusiastically to achieve those goals. Thus, there is no coercive force, which induces the followers to work.
- Leadership gives an experience of help to followers, to attain common goals. It happens when the leader feels the importance of individuals, gives them recognition and conveys them about the importance of activities performed by them.
- Leadership is exercised in a particular situation, at a given point of time and under specific set of circumstances. It implies that leadership styles may be different under different situations.

Styles of Leadership

Leadership style refers to a leader's behaviour towards group members. The behavioural pattern which the leader reflects in his role as a leader is often described as the style of leadership. Leadership style is the result of the leader's philosophy, personality, value system, and experience. It also depends on the types of followers and organisational atmosphere prevailing in the enterprise.

The different types of leadership styles are

Leadership Style Based on Authority

They are of four types

(i) **Autocratic Leadership** It relies on coercion and its style is paternalism, arbitrariness, command and compliance. The autocratic leaders gives orders which must be obeyed by subordinates. He determines policies for the group without consulting them and does not give detailed information about future plans, but simply tells what immediate steps they must take.

(ii) **Democratic Leadership** Style of leadership that uses legitimate power can be classified as democratic leadership. A democratic leader usually gives instructions only after consulting with the group. He sees to it that policies are worked out in group discussion and with the acceptance of the group.

(iii) **Laisse-Faire Leadership** The leadership style which allows maximum freedom to followers may be called Laisse-Faire leadership. It gives employees a high degree of independence in their working operations. In this style, leader completely abdicates his leadership position, to give all responsibility of most of the work entrusted to him, to the group which he is supposed to lead, limiting his authority to maintain the contact of the group with persons outside the group. This is also known as the permissive style of leadership.

(iv) **Paternalistic Leadership** Under this style of leadership, the leader assumes that his function is paternal or fatherly. He works to help, guide, protect and keep his followers happily working together as members of a family. He provides them with good working conditions and employee services. This mode of leadership produces good and quick results if the followers are highly educated and have a sincere desire to go ahead and perform with responsibility.

Linkert's Four Styles of Managerial Leadership

Rensis Linkert identified four main styles of leadership, in particular around decision-making and the degree to which people are involved in the decision:

Exploitive Authoritative In this style, the leader has a low concern for people and uses such methods as threats and other fear based methods to achieve performance. Communication is almost entirely downwards and the psychologically distant concerns of people are ignored.

Benevolent Authoritative When the leader adds concern for people to an authoritative position, a 'benevolent dictatorship' is formed. The leader now uses rewards to encourage appropriate performance and listens more to concerns lower down the organization, being limited to what their subordinates think that the boss want to hear.

Consultative The upward flow of information here is still cautious, although the leader is making gemive efforts to listen carefully to ideas. Major decisions are still centrally made.

Participative At this level, the leader makes maximum use of participative methods, engaging people in decision-making of the organization. People across the organization are psychologically closer together at all levels.

Leadership Style in the Managerial Grid

The Managerial Grid model helps managers/leaders to analyze their own leadership styles through a technique known as grid training. Leaders can identify how they with respect to their concern for production and people with the Managerial Grid model.

They identified five basic leadership styles that are

- Country club style leadership
- Produce or perish leadership
- Impoverished leadership
- Middle of the road leadership
- Team leadership

Leadership Continuum

The Leadership Continuum Model of Tannebaum and Schmidt (1973) suggests that autocratic leaders are more likely to make their own decisions and not engage their subordinates, whereas a more democratic leader gives subordinates a greater degree of delegation in decision-making. In 1938, Lewin and Lippitt proposed classifications of leaders based on how much involvement leaders placed into task and relationship needs. This range of leadership behaviours was expressed along a continuum by Tannebaum and Schmidt in 1973, ranging from boss-centered (task) to subordinate-centered (relationship).

Thus, it can be said that leadership is the ability of a manager to induce the subordinates to work with confidence and zeal. Leadership is the ability to persuade others to seek defined objectives enthusiastically. It is the human factor which binds a group together and motivates it towards goals.

Approaches to Leadership

The approaches to leadership and theories of leadership evolved with greater understanding of the

- needs and expectations of people at work.
- impact of different leadership styles on followers and how the attitudes, behaviour and competence of followers impact leaders.
- effectiveness of different leadership styles in different situations.

The main approaches to leadership are discussed in detail

Trait Theory of Leadership

It is considered to be the **first** modern theory of leadership. It became popular at the end of the 20th century and remains popular till today. The theory identifies the specific personality traits that distinguish leaders from non-leaders. It is based upon the premise that **leaders are born, not made**, rather than being developed through learning. This theory focuses on the differences between leaders and followers, with the assumption that people in leadership positions would display more traits than those in subordinate position.

It is often equated to the 'Great Man Theory of Leadership'. It was first proposed by **Thomas Carlyle**. He believed that "history is shaped by extraordinary leaders and the ability to lead was something you inherited at birth and not something that could be developed". His ideas inspired researchers to look more into leadership and inheritable traits.

It seeks to determine, what makes a successful leader from the leader's own personal characteristics. From the very beginning, people have emphasised on that a particular individual was a successful leader because of his certain qualities or characteristics. It's studies were quite popular between 1930 to 1950. The method of study was to select leaders to eminence and their characteristics were studied. It was of the hypothesis that the persons having certain traits, can become successful leaders.

Various research studies have given intelligence, attitudes, personality and biological factors as ingredients for effective leaders. A review of various research studies has been presented by **Stogdill**.

According to him, various traits have been suggested and they are

- Physical and constitutional factors (height, weight, physique, energy, health and appearance)
- Intelligence
- Self-confidence
- Sociability
- Will (initiative, persistence, ambition)
- Dominance
- Surgency (talkative, cheerfulness, geniality, enthusiasm, expressiveness, alertness and originality).

But in later study, **Ghiselli** has found supervisory ability, achievement, motivation, self-actualising, intelligence, self-assurance and decisiveness as the qualities related with leadership success.

Transformational Theory of Leadership

Transformational leadership is a process that changes and transforms individuals. It is concerned with values, ethical standards and long term goals. It involves assessing follower's motives, satisfying their needs and treating them as full human being. It sub-assumes the charismatic and visionary leadership. It is an all encompassing approach that can be used to describe a wide range of leadership, from very specific attempts to influence followers on one level to very broad attempts to influence whole organisation and even entire culture.

Transformational leaders are generally energetic, enthusiastic and passionate. Not only, these leaders are concerned and involved in the process, but they are also focused on helping every member of the group to succeed as well.

Components of Transformational Leadership

There are four different components of transformational leadership and they are

Intellectual Stimulation Transformational leaders not only challenge the status quo, but they also encourage creativity among followers. They encourage followers to explore new ways of doing things and new opportunities to learn.

Individualised Consideration Transformational leadership also involves offering support and encouragement to individual followers. In order to foster supportive relationships, transformational leaders keep lines of communication open, so that followers feel free to share ideas, so that leaders can offer direct recognition of each follower's unique contributions.

Inspirational Motivation Transformational leaders have a clear vision about that they are able to articulate to followers. These leaders also help followers to experience the same passion and motivation to fulfil these goals.

Idealised Influence Transformational leaders serve as a role model for followers. Because followers trust and respect the leader, they emulate the leader and internalise his/her ideals.

Transactional Leadership

Give and take is the hallmark of transactional leadership. It is indeed modeled just like a business transaction. This theory emphasis the realisation of a desired outcome and result. The leaders motivate the followers by way of reward system *i.e.* rewarding performers and punishing the non-performers. The theory emphasises maintaining a cordial relationship with the followers and leaders and followers must work mutually to meet organisational goals. Transactional Leadership Theory suggests that leaders have to trade reward and punishment with their team in order to get the job done. Transactional leaders concern themselves with maintaining the status quo and working towards achieving today's task (Hackman et al, 2009).

Transactional leadership is not concerned with the future and does not seek to change and evolve. **Burns** (1978) noted that transactional leadership refers to a type of leadership that is based on an exchange relationship between leader and follower. Such leadership does not bring leaders and followers to pursue higher purpose. Transactional leadership involves routine activities, assigning work, evaluating performance and making decision.

The characteristic features exhibited by transactional leaders are as follows

- The leader links the goals of the organisation to rewards and clearly specifies the expectations, provides the needed resources and set SMART (Specific, Measurable, Attainable, Realistic, Timely) goals for the subordinates.
- The leader actively monitors the performance of the subordinates, watches and searches for deviations from rules and standards and take corrective actions to prevent mistakes.
- A leader intervenes only if standards are not met and even use punishments for poor performances.
- The leader gives an environment to subordinates, where they can take decisions. In this form, the leader himself abdicates from responsibilities and avoids making decisions, due to which the followers lack the direction.
- Transactional leaders are power holders by virtue of their position in the organisation. They have the capacity to influence others because of their job.
- These leaders pay attention to follower's work in order to find faults and deviations. This type of leadership is effective in crisis and emergency situations, as well as when projects needs to be carried out in specific style.

Value Based Leadership

It is an idea that leaders should draws on their own and followers values for direction and motivation. Value Based Leadership's Philosophy asserts that people are mostly motivated by values and live according to their beliefs. In other words, values are our most natural motivators. It is natural for leaders, to refer their own values in creating a vision or making decisions and equally it makes sense for leaders to connect with their follower's values, which make them more likely to act.

Richard Barrett an author of *Building a Values Driven Organisation*, defines values-based leadership as "a way of making authentic decisions that build the trust and commitment of employees and customers". As a philosophy, value based leadership assumes that an organisation, based around shared values is likely to be more flexible and productive. Leaders who apply this philosophy are likely to experience certain inner benefits.

They are

- They will make better choices, feeling more comfortable to act upon them.
- They are likely to build better, more trusting and less stressful relationships with followers.
- They are more likely to feel aligned with their 'authentic self'.

A person's values are at the core of their sense of identity. So by definition, authentic leaders will always act from their highest values.

Cultural Based Leadership

In educational approach, we can see that culture plays a vital role. The various administrative practices make way to academic governance and capacity to leadership. Any kind of leadership and decision-making affects the lifestyle and work style of people in cultural approach. The work of the person is guided by the culture, in which they tends to make their subordinates work.

The behaviour can be seen as a reward or punishment as it relates to the entire administrative system. By correcting the errors of subordinates, the efficiency of leader also improves. These culture influences various aspects of society, attaining associates spirit and objective goals. Therefore, cultural approaches prove to be important in the form of development and motivational elements of teaching, administrative system and social order.

Psychodynamic Approach to Leadership

In Psycho dynamic Leadership theory, we see that the ideal leadership style is one that takes the input into the account. These leaders encourage participation and contribution from group members and help group members to feel more relevant and committed to the decision-making process.

In this theory, the leader retains the right to allow the inputs of others. Thus, one can say that the involvement of leader in decision-making improves the understanding of the issues involved by those who must carry out the decisions.

It is believed that people are more committed to actions, where they have been involved in the relevant decision-making, that people are less competitive and more collaborative, when they are working on common goals and that several people deciding together can make better decisions than one person alone.

Charismatic Approach to Leadership

Charismatic Leadership Theory is also known as Great Man Theory, can be traced back to ancient times. **Plato's** republic and **Confucius's** analects dealt with this type of leadership. They provided some insights of leadership. Subsequent studies based on these insights have suggested that a leader is born and not made. A leader has some charisma, which acts as an influencer. **Charisma** is a Greek word meaning **gift**. Thus, charisma is a God gifted attribute in a person which makes him a leader, irrespective of the situation in which he works. Charismatic leaders are those, who inspire followers and have a major impact on their organisations through their personal vision and energy.

According to **Robert House**, "The charismatic leader has extremely high level of self-confidence, dominance and a strong conviction in the normal righteousness of his/her beliefs or atleast the ability to convince the followers that he/she possesses such confidence and conviction".

The basic assumptions and implications of charismatic leadership theory are as follows

- Leaders in general and great leaders in particular, have some exceptional inborn leadership qualities, which are bestowed upon them by the divine power.
- These inborn qualities are sufficient for a leader to be successful.
- Since, these qualities are inborn, these cannot be enhanced through education and training. Further, since these qualities are of personal nature, these cannot be shared by others.
- These leadership qualities make a leader effective and situational factors do not have any influence.

Leadership Models

Leadership models may be defined as guides that suggest specific leadership behaviour to use in a specific environment or situation. Generally, these models are in graphical forms and they help to make the mechanism more simple. A good leader must be aware about different leadership models. So far, the users and the organisation members have given positive feedback on using such leadership model. It gives an effective output for a long time. An individual of small or large scale firm can successfully perform to meet such deadlines and organise the team members properly. Usually, the team members are given the freedom, only if they are skilled and experienced in most of the leadership models.

Blake and Mouton's Managerial Grid

The Blake and Mouton's Managerial Grid also known as **Leadership Grid**.

Managerial Grid Model

The Managerial Grid Model (1964) is a behavioural leadership model, developed by **Robert Blake** and **Jane Mouton**. This model identifies five different leadership styles based on the concern for people (relationships) and concern for production (tasks). They made a grid, shown in figure below which clarifies the leadership style as exemplified by an individual. The grid read like a normal graph, wherein the first digit signifies the X-axis, while the second digit denotes the Y-axis.

- 1, 1 **Improved Management** Often referred as Laissez-Faire leadership. Leaders in this position have little concern for people or productivity, avoid taking sides and stays out of conflicts. They do just enough to get by.
- 1,9 **Country Club Management** Managers in this position have great concern for people and little concern for production. They try to avoid conflicts and concentrates on being well-liked. For them, the task is less important than good inter-personal relations. Their goal is to keep people happy.
- 9,1 **Authority Compliance** Managers in this position, have great concern for production and little concern for people. They desire tight control in order to get tasks done efficiently. They consider creativity and human relations to be necessary.
- 5,5 **Organisation Man Management** It is often termed as middle of the road leadership. Leaders in this position have medium concern for people and production. They attempt to balance their concern for both people and production, but they are not committed.
- 9,9 **Team Management** This style of leadership is considered to be an ideal leadership. Such managers have great concern for both people and production. They work to motivate employees to reach their highest level of accomplishment. They are flexible and responsive to change and they understand the need of change.

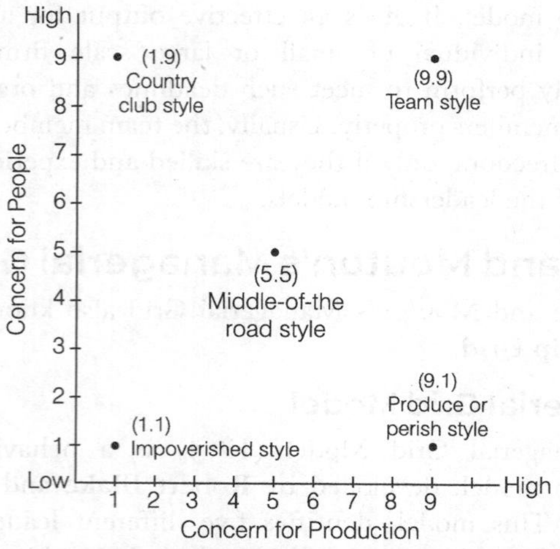

The Management Grid-A graphical representation of the Managerial Grid

Tri-Dimensional Model

Reddin (1970) has conceptualised a three-dimensional grid borrowing some of the ideas from the managerial grid. Three-dimensional axis represents task-orientation, relationship orientation and effectiveness. By adding an effectiveness dimension to the task-oriented behaviour dimensions, he has integrated the concept of leadership styles with the situational demand of a specific environment.

In his *3D Management Styles theory*, **William J Reddin** has stressed the dimensions of effectiveness. In this model, the concept of leadership style is integrated with the situational demands of a specific environment. When the style of a leader is appropriate to a given situation, it is termed as effective.

Conversely, when the style is inappropriate to a given situation, it is termed as ineffective. If the effectiveness of a leader's behaviour style depends upon the situation in which it is used, it would follow that any of the basic styles may be effective or ineffective, depending on the situation. The difference between effective and ineffective styles often lies not in the actual behaviour of the leader, but in the appropriateness of his behaviour to the environment in which it takes place. Thus, essentially the third dimension in the leader's behaviour style syndrome is the environment.

Although, effectiveness appears to be in either situation in this model, in reality it should be represented as a continuum. Any given style in a particular situation could fall somewhere in this continum from 'extremely effective' to 'extremely ineffective'. Effectiveness, therefore is a matter of degree and there could be an infinite number rather than only three facets to effective dimension. To illustrate this point, the effectiveness dimension has been divided in quartiles, ranging on the effective side from +1 to +4 and on the ineffective side from-1 to -4.

The four effective and four ineffective styles, in essence, show how appropriate a leader's basic style is in a given situation, as seen by his or her followers, superiors and associates. A model, such as the Tri-Dimensional Leader Effectiveness Model is distinctive because it does not depicts a single ideal leader's behaviour style as appropriate in all situations. For example, the high task and high relationship styles are appropriate only in certain situations.

Fiedler's Contingency Theory

In Contingency Theory of Leadership, the success of the leader is a function of various contingencies in the form of subordinate, tasks and/or group variables. This theory is a class of Behavioural Theory that contends that there is no best way of leading leadership style that may be effective in some situations, but not in others. An effect of this would be that the leaders who are very effective at one place and at time may become unsuccessful, when transplanted to another situation or when the factors around them got changed.

Fiedler's Least Preferred Co-Worker (LPC) Theory

Fiedler identified the Least Preferred Co-Worker Theory for leaders, by asking them first to think of a person with which they worked that they would like least to work with again and then to score the person on a range of scale between positive factors (friendly, helpful, cheerful, etc) and negative factors(unfriendly, unhelpful, etc).

Generally, a high LPC leader scores the other person as positive and a low LPC leader scores as negative. High LPC leader tends to have close and positive relationships and acts in a supportive way, even prioritising the relationship before the task. Low LPC leader puts the task first and will only turn to relationships, when they are satisfied with the work.

Three factors identified about the leader are as follows

Leader-Member Relations The nature of the inter-personal relationship between leader and followers may expressed in terms of good through poor, with qualifying modifiers attached as necessary. It is obvious that the leader's personality and the personalities of subordinates play an important role in the variable.

Task Structure The nature of the subordinate's task described as structured or unstructured, associated with the amount of creative freedom, allowed the subordinate to accomplish the task and how the task has been defined.

Position Power The degree to which the position itself enables the leader to get the group members to comply with and to accept his/her direction and leadership.

Hersey and Blanchard's Situational Leadership Model

It proposes that leaders choose the best course of action based upon situational variables. Different styles of leadership may be more appropriate for certain types of decision-making. Therefore, one can say that the basic assumption of this theory is that the best decision of the leader depends on a range of situational factors.

Hersey and Blanchard's Theory

The basic premise of this theory is that effective leadership requires leadership flexibility, since different situations require different leadership approaches and tactics. **Blanchard** and **Hersey** characterised leadership style in terms of the amount of direction and of support that the leader gives to his/her followers and so created a simple grid.

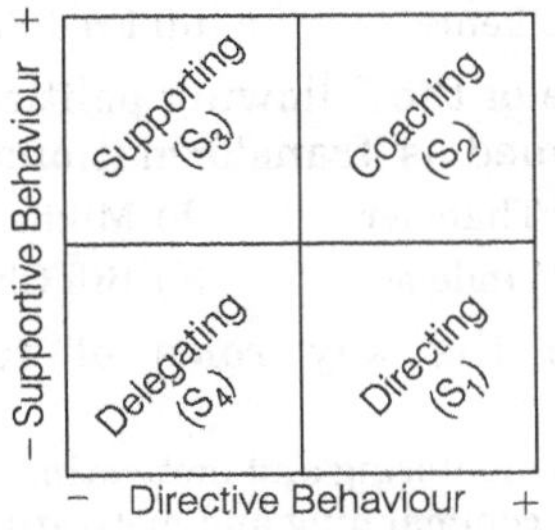

Directing Leaders Define the roles and tasks of the followers and supervise them closely. Decisions are made by the leader, so communication is largely one way.

Coaching Leaders Define roles and tasks, but seek ideas and suggestions from the followers. Decisions remain the leader's prerogative, but communication is much more two way.

Supporting Leaders Pass day-to-day decisions, such as task allocation and processes to the followers. The leader facilitates and takes part in decisions, but control is with the follower.

Delegating Leaders Are involved in decisions and problem solving, but control is with the followers. The followers decide when and how the leader will be involved.

Leader-Member Exchange Theory

Leader-Member Exchange (LMX) Theory was initially called the **Vertical Dyad Linkage theory**. The theory was introduced by **George Graen** and various colleagues in the 1970s and has been revised and refined in the years since. LMX Theory emphasises the dyadic (*i.e.* one on one) relationships between leaders and individual subordinates, instead of the traits or behaviours of leaders or situational characteristics.

The theory focuses on determining the type of leader-subordinate relationships that promote effective outcomes and the factors that determine whether leaders and subordinates will be able to develop high quality relationships.

According to **LMX theory**, leaders do not treat all subordinates in the same manner, but establish close relationships with some (the in-group) while remaining aloof from others (the out-group). Those in the in-group enjoy relationships with the leader that is marked by trust and mutual respect. They tend to be involved in important activities and decisions. Conversely, those in the out-group are excluded from important activities and decisions.

LMX theory suggests that high quality relationships between a leader-subordinate will lead to positive outcomes, such as better performance, lower turnover job satisfaction and organisation commitment. The quality of the relationship is reflected by the degree of mutual trust, loyalty, support, respect and religion.

The Leader Member Exchange Theory is rooted in the belief that and followers have a relationship that could yield advantage.

Advantages of LMX Theory

- It is an exceptional theory of leadership as unlike the other theories, it concentrates and talks about specific relationships between the leader and each subordinate.
- It focuses our attention to the significance of communication in leadership.
- It is very much valid and practical in its approach.

Disadvantages of LMX Theory

- It fails to explain the particulars of how high-quality exchanges are created.
- It objected on grounds of fairness and justice as some followers receive special attention of leaders at work place and other followers do not.

EXAM BASED QUESTIONS

1 **What is the best way to determine the actions of human beings in society?**
(a) Through knowledge
(b) Through progress of an organisation
(c) Through decentralisation of forums
(d) Through individual's achievements

2 **What do you mean by the word 'Leadership'?**
(a) Art of authority
(b) Art of motivating the group of people
(c) Art of motivating for any wrong cause
(d) None of the above

3 **Which one will be the best suitable adjective of a leader?**
(a) Inspirational (b) Motivated
(c) Authoritative (d) Dictator

4 **In leadership, what type of mistake mostly occurs?**
(a) Failure to promote talented staff
(b) Failure to listen to staff
(c) Failure to provide an adequate feedback
(d) Failure to make decisions

5 **Effective leaders are most like to**
(a) make others feel important
(b) promote a vision
(c) follow the golden rule
(d) persuade employees to admit their mistakes

6 **Is it true that through inspiration one can become a leader?**
(a) True (b) False
(c) Can't decide (d) None of these

7 **What is the characteristic of a leader?**
(a) Do according to your own will
(b) Ignore the benefit of people
(c) Transform potential into reality
(d) None of the above

8 **Who is/are the major contributor(s) in the achievement of organisational goals?**
(a) Leader (b) Social institution
(c) Peer (d) All of these

9 **Leadership, today is increasingly associated with the concept of**
(a) getting others to follow
(b) command
(c) control
(d) strategy

10 **Which of the following statement(s) is/are false about leadership?**
(a) Leadership doesn't necessarily takes palce within a hierarchical structure of organisation
(b) When people operates as leaders, their role is always clearly established and defined
(c) Not every leader is a manager
(d) All of the above

11 **What does Situational Theory of Leadership emphasise?**
(a) Personality traits (b) Events
(c) Environment (d) Political situation

12 **How can you describe the thinking and outlook of transformational leaders?**
(a) Strategic (b) Operational
(c) Functional (d) Developmental

13 **Who among the following is a leading writer on Contingency Theory of Leadership?**
(a) Rosabeth Kanter (b) Joan Woodward
(c) Remsis Likent (d) Fred Fiedler

14 **Which one of the following political leaders could not be termed as 'transformational leader'?**
(a) Margret Thatcher (b) Mikhail Gorbachov
(c) Nelson Mandela (d) Bill Clinton

15 **What are the key roles of transformational leaders?**
(a) Guiding, mentoring and motivating
(b) Guiding, commanding and motivating
(c) Guiding, demonstrating and motivating
(d) Guiding, mentoring and demonstrating

16 **Approaches to the study of leadership, which emphasise the personality of leader are termed as**
(a) Contingency Theory (b) Trait Theory
(c) Inspirational Theory (d) Group Theory

17 **The terms 'employed-centered' and 'production-centred' to describe leader's behaviour were used by**
(a) MC Gregor (b) Fielder
(c) Likert (d) Blake and MC Canse

18 **On what belief, are contingency theories of leadership based?**
(a) That there is no appropriate style of leadership
(b) That there is a single style appropriate for leadership
(c) Only a
(d) None of the above

19 **According to Fielder's scale of LPC, leaders with a low LPC score gains more satisfaction by**
(a) achieving the objectives
(b) developing a team relationship
(c) Both a and b
(d) None of the above

20 **One Contingency Model of Leadership is the Path Goal Theory. It suggests that individual's motivation is dependent on**
(a) whether path goal relationships are clarified.
(b) the necessary directions, guidance, teaching and support being provided.
(c) their effective performance.
(d) expectations that increased efforts for achieving an improved level of performance will be successful.

21 **The Situation Leadership Theory of .... and .... is based on follower's readiness to perform.**
(a) Vroom and Yetlon
(b) Hersey and Blanchard
(c) Abbot and Costello
(d) Tannenbaum and Schmidt

22 **Who is the author of the book, 'Building a Values Driven Organisation'?**
(a) Fiedler (b) Blake
(c) Richard Barrett (d) None of these

23 **Which among the following is an effective leadership?**
(a) Family (b) Peer
(c) Religion (d) Culture

24 **The capacity to influence people and to accomplish desired objectives is called**
(a) power (b) leadership
(c) authority (d) status

25 **A leadership theory that focuses on the traits of those who have assumed powers and who are considered to be an effective is called**
(a) Trait Theory (b) Behavioural Theory
(c) Contigency Theory (d) Structural Theory

26 **The recognition of task-oriented and people oriented behavioural styles are important and that people have different orientations that they bring to the management process on the result of the research of**
(a) Hersey & Blanchard (b) Fieldler
(c) Blake and M C Canne (d) None of these

27 **An approach to leadership, in which the leader's behaviour is first categorised on a scale from task orientation to people orientation and efforts are being made to find a work situation, to which that particular style is best suited is called**
(a) Hersey-Blanchard Theory
(b) Vroom-Jago Model
(c) Fielder's LPC Theory
(d) Path Goal Theory

28 **In the Hersey-Blanchard Situational Leadership Model, the authors suggested that the right mix of leadership style is best found by focusing on**
(a) intelligence (b) motivation
(c) confidence (d) maturity

29 **What is the premise that underpins behavioural models?**
(a) Leadership can be taught and hence can be learnt
(b) Leadership is about behaving correctly
(c) Leaders need to think before they act
(d) Leadership is about acting the part

30 **What does the behaviourist school promotes?**
(a) That a person can be made to lead
(b) That behaviour is acquired by conditioning
(c) A person behaves according to their own beliefs
(d) Brain washing is possible

31 **What are the two dimensions of Blake and Mouton's Managerial grid?**
(a) 'Good' and 'bad'
(b) 'Concern for outcomes' and 'concern for feelings'
(c) 'Concern for people' and 'concern for results'
(d) 'Finishing tasks' and 'liking people'

32 **The .... Theory states a manager's choice of organisational structures and control systems depend on characteristics of the external environment.**
(a) Mechanistic
(b) Management Science
(c) Organic
(d) Contigency

33 **What are the three domains of Graen's Theory?**
1. Relationships 2. Followers
3. Leaders 4. Learners
Codes
(a) 1 and 3 (b) 2 and 3
(c) 1, 3 and 4 (d) 1, 2 and 3

34 **What are the four models for leader given by Hersey and Blanchard?**
1. Supporting
2. Coaching
3. Delegating
4. Directing
Codes
(a) Only 2 (b) Only 3
(c) 1, 2 and 4 (d) All of these

35 **How any organisation achieves success?**
1. Individual effort
2. Competition with other organisations
3. Competence of the leader
4. High efficiency of employees
Codes
(a) 1 and 3 (b) 3 and 4
(c) Only 4 (d) All of these

36 What are the main reasons that lead to the failure of any organisation?

1. Low callibre of leader.
2. Lack of cooperative efforts.
3. Objective of organisation is not good.
4. No essential features in an organisation.

Codes

(a) 1 and 3 (b) 1, 2 and 4
(c) 2 and 4 (d) All of these

37 What are the characteristics of leader?

1. Great
2. Exceptional born
3. Divine power
4. Educated

Codes

(a) 1 and 4 (b) 2 and 4
(c) 1 and 3 (d) None of these

Directions (Q. Nos. 38-40) *Two statements are given below, one labelled as Assertion (A) and other labelled as Reason (R). Choose the correct code for the following.*

Codes

(a) Both A and R are true, but R is not the correct explanation of A
(b) Both A and R are true and R is the correct explanation of A
(c) Both A and R are false
(d) A is false, but R is true

38 **Assertion** (A) Transformational leader can change individuals.

Reason (R) These leaders are concerned about the values and ethical standards.

39 **Assertion** (A) In transactional leadership, leaders are powered by their position, they hold in an organisation.

Reason (R) Because they have the capacity to influence others.

40 **Assertion** (A) Leadership Model is important.

Reason (R) They guide us to formulate the specific behaviour in specific environment.

41 **Statement I** It is the first modern theory of leadership.

Statement II It is often equated to the Great Man Theory of Leadership.

Codes

(a) Only Statement I is correct
(b) Only Statement II is correct
(c) Both the statements are correct
(d) Neither a nor b

42 Trait Leadership Theory was proposed by

(a) Stogdill (b) Terry
(c) Thomas Carlyle (d) Ghiselli

43 According to this component, the transform national leaders not only challenge the status quo but they also encourage creativity among followers. Which is this component?

(a) Inspirational (b) Intellectual
(c) Idealised (d) Individualised

44 Which of the following characteristic(s) about transactional leadership is/are correct?

(a) Focuses on tactical issues
(b) Relies on human relations to lubricate human interactions
(c) Maintaining a cordial relationship with followers
(d) All of the above

45 .... defines value based leadership as "a way of making authentic decisions that build the trust and commitment of employees and customers".

(a) Richard Barret (b) Robert Blake
(c) Robert House (d) Thomas Carlyle

46 In .... Theory, the leaders retain the right the input of others. Leaders encourage participation and participators from group members.

(a) Charismatic (b) Psychodynamic
(c) Transformational (d) Transactional

47 The Managerial Grid Model was developed in ......

(a) 1961 (b) 1965
(c) 1970 (d) 1964

48 **Statement I** Charismatic Leadership theory is also known as Great Man theory.

Statement II Leaders are generally energetic, enthusiastic and passionate.

Codes

(a) Statement I is true but II is false
(b) Both the statements are true
(c) Statement II is true
(d) Both the statements are false

49 Managerial Grid Model identifies five different leadership styles based on the

(a) concern for people
(b) concern for production
(c) Both a and b
(d) Only a

50 In this type of leadership theory, the success of the leader is a function of various contingencies in the form of subordinate tasks and/or group variables. Name the theory.

(a) Hersey and Blanchard's theory
(b) Leader Member Exchange theory
(c) Fiedler's Contingency theory
(d) Blake and Mouton Grid theory

51 Leader Member Exchange theory was introduced by

(a) George Graen (b) Richard Barret
(c) Robert House (d) Plato

52 Which of the following is/are the characteristic(s) of Leader Member Exchange theory?
(a) It was initially called the Vertical Dyad Linkage Theory
(b) Leaders do not treat all subordinates in a same manner
(c) The leader and member like each other, help each other and respect each other
(d) All of the above

53 **Statement I** It is concerned with values, ethical standards and long term goals.
Statement II Leaders promote compliance of his followers, through both reward and punishment.
Codes
(a) Statement I is true
(b) Statement II is false
(c) Both the statements are correct
(d) Only statement II is correct

54 Which theory is based on the premise that 'leaders are born, not made'?
(a) Value Based Leadership
(b) Transformational Theory of Leadership
(c) Trait Theory of Leadership
(d) Transactional Theory of Leadership

55 Who said that, "Leadership is inter-personal influence, exercised in a situation and directed through communication process towards the attainment of a specified goal or goals".
(a) Terry (b) Tenebaum et al
(c) Thomas Carlyle (d) Stogdill

56 Which of the following statement holds true about transformational leadership?
(a) It focuses on tactical issues
(b) It is oriented towards long term goals
(c) It focuses more on missions and strategies
(d) Both a and b

57 .... are the approaches to the study of leadership, which emphasise the personality of the leader.
(a) Contingency theories
(b) Group theories
(c) Trait theories
(d) Inspirational theories

58 Contingency Theories of Leadership is based upon that
(a) there is no single style of leadership appropriate to all situations
(b) there is a single style of leadership appropriate to all managers
(c) there is a single style leadership appropriate to all situations
(d) None of the above

59 The capacity to influence people and accomplish desired objectives is called
(a) power (b) leadership
(c) authority (d) status

60 A transactional leader is one who
(a) inspires people and has strong interactions with them
(b) does deals with people in order to get them to do things the leader wants
(c) is the ideal form of leadership
(d) works for the long term goals of the organisation

61 Match the following

List I (Approaches to Leadership)	List II (Emphasis)
A. Transformational theory	1. Identifies specific personality traits
B. Trait theory	2. Concerned with values, ethical standards and long term goals
C. Value Based Leadership theory	3. Values are our most natural motivators
D. Culture Based Leadership theory	4. Work of a person is guided by the culture

Codes

	A	B	C	D
(a)	2	1	3	4
(b)	4	1	2	3
(c)	3	2	1	4
(d)	1	2	3	4

62 Match the following

List I (Leadership Models)	List II (Basic Premises)
A. Hersey and Blanchard's model	1. Effective Leadership requires leadership flexibility
B. Blake and Mouton's model	2. Leadership style if integrated with situational demands of specific environment
C. Fielder's Theory of Leadership	3. Leadership grid
D. Tri-Dimensional model	4. There is no best way of leading leadership style

Codes

	A	B	C	D
(a)	1	3	4	2
(b)	4	3	2	1
(c)	1	2	3	4
(d)	3	1	4	2

PREVIOUS YEARS' QUESTIONS

July 2018

1 Match the following.

List I (Leaders of Modern Concepts of Educational Administration)	List II (Specific Theory Contributed)
A. Fredrick Winslow Taylor	1. Theory X and Theory Y
B. Elton Mayo	2. Management system
C. Rensis Likert	3. Scientific Management movement
D. Douglas Mc Gregor	4. Human Relations movement
	5. SOAR Peak Performance model

Codes

	A	B	C	D
(a)	1	2	4	3
(b)	5	3	4	2
(c)	3	4	2	1
(d)	2	3	4	5

November 2017

2 For promoting effective leadership, which of the following theories has a greater potential?

(a) Great Man theory
(b) Trait theory
(c) Transactional theory
(d) Transformational theory

January 2017

3 In the long run, which leadership style is most effective?

(a) Autocratic (b) Participative
(c) Transactional (d) Transformational

July 2016

4 Which of the sets of statements gives acceptable difference between transactional and transformational leadership styles for strengthening the school system?

1. In transactional leadership style, the leader goes with his/her own vision while in transformational style, the leader creates vision in others.
2. Transactional style leader monitors while in the transformational style leader inspires.
3. Transactional style leader promotes trust while the transformational stule leader keeps strict vigil.
4. In transactional leadership style, the leaders personal traits are important while in transformational style, inter-relationships are important.
5. The transactional leader monitors while the transformational leader guides.

Codes

(a) 1, 2, 3 and 5
(b) 2, 3, 4 and 5
(c) 1, 2, 4 and 5
(d) 1, 3, 2 and 4

December 2015

5 In situational leadership style, the emphasis is on

(a) concern for task
(b) concern for relationships
(c) Both a and b
(d) Neither a nor b

ANSWERS

Exam Based Questions

1 (b)	2 (b)	3 (a)	4 (c)	5 (d)	6 (a)	7 (c)	8 (a)	9 (a)	10 (b)
11 (b)	12 (a)	13 (d)	14 (d)	15 (a)	16 (b)	17 (c)	18 (a)	19 (a)	20 (d)
21 (b)	22 (c)	23 (d)	24 (b)	25 (a)	26 (c)	27 (c)	28 (d)	29 (a)	30 (b)
31 (c)	32 (d)	33 (d)	34 (d)	35 (a)	36 (d)	37 (a)	38 (a)	39 (a)	40 (a)
41 (c)	42 (c)	43 (b)	44 (d)	45 (a)	46 (b)	47 (d)	48 (a)	49 (c)	50 (c)
51 (a)	52 (d)	53 (d)	54 (c)	55 (b)	56 (d)	57 (c)	58 (a)	59 (b)	60 (b)
61 (a)	62 (a)								

Previous Years' Questions

1 (c)	2 (d)	3 (d)	4 (c)	5 (c)

CHAPTER

36

Concept of Quality and Quality in Education

Quality is affected by various factors and insufficient focus on quality and learning contributed to global learning crises. Quality in education is associated with indicators that help in development of opportunities.

Concept of Quality

Quality is a much debated term. To some it is like 'beauty' that lies in the eye of the beholder. Those who believe in this are 'relativists', whereas those who believe quality can be specific attribute that can be identified, they are 'objectivists'. The word 'quality' comes from the Latin word 'qualis' meaning 'what kind of'. With a variety of meanings and connotations, it has been referred to as a 'slippery concept' (Pfeffer and Coote, 1991).

The British Standard Institution (BSI) defines quality as "The totality of features and characteristics of a product or service that bear on its ability to satisfy stated or implied needs" (BSI, 1991). **Green** and **Harvey** (1993) identified **five** different approaches to define quality.

They are :

- In terms of **exceptional** (exceeding high standards and passing a required standard).
- In terms of **consistency** (exhibited through 'zero defects' and 'getting right the first time', making quality a culture).
- As **fitness** for purpose (meaning the product or service meets the stated purpose, customer specifications and satisfaction).
- As value for **money** (through efficiency and effectiveness).
- As transformative (in terms of qualitative change).

Quality has a few central ideas around which the whole concept revolves i.e. quality as absolute, quality as relative, quality as a process and quality as culture.

In this Chapter

Quality in Education

High quality education is a pre-requisite for learning and human development. Quality is affected by factors, both inside and outside the classroom. Everything from the availability of a teacher and teaching aids to the child's starting point when it comes to mother tongue language or general health.

Since 2000, streneuous efforts have been made to include more children in schooling. This was the year the UN Millenium Development Goals and Six Education For All goals were adopted. Unfortunately, quality in education and in schools was not given equally high priority.

Insufficient focus on quality and learning contributed to what is non-referred to as a global learning crise. A greater number of children than ever before attend school today, but many do not learn basic skills during their schooling.

In addition to ensuring that all children are guaranteed schooling, it is vital that schools offer high quality education. This is a major challenge in many developing countries. If the parents feel that the school has little to offer that is relevant for them, their motivation for sending their children to school will be lowered.

Common challenges for the educational sector in many developing countries can be

- a shortage of qualified teachers.
- over-crowded classrooms.
- a lack of teaching materials and poor quality curricula.
- teaching in another language than the students' mother tongue.

By investing in high quality education, each individual child can be given the opportunity to learn and develop. One of the foundation of economic development and the struggle against poverty is that all children have the opportunity to attend good schools. Research also indicates that ensuring high quality education is one of the most effective instrument for ensuring democracy and good governance in a country.

Quality determines how much and how well children learn and the extent to which their education translates into a range of personal, social and developmental benefits. Education liberates the intellect, unlocks the imagination and is fundamental for self-respect. It is the key to prosperity and opens a world of opportunities, making it possible for each of us to contribute to a progressive and healthy society. Learning benefits every human being and should be available for all.

Quality in education provides the outcomes needed for individuals, communities and societies to prosper. It allows schools to align and integrate fully with their communities and access a range of services across sectors designed to support the educational development of their students.

A quality in education is supported by three key pillars *i.e.* ensuring access to quality teachers, providing use of quality learning tools, professional development and the establishment of safe and supportive quality learning environment.

Indicators of Quality in Education

The system of indicators of quality in education as well as the quality criteria associated with the indicators, help schools to point out the important areas of their own activities, their own advantages and disadvantages and development opportunities. The indicators are grouped into seven areas with specific topics.

They are

Curriculum The structure of the curriculum (programs/goals, tasks, focus on development of functional tasks, focus on students' activities, integration of programs within and between areas). It also includes courses, programmes and key competencies that students develop in the given school.

Achievements It is evaluated by external or independent agencies. The achievement quality is compared with the set goals.

Learning and Teaching Based on teacher's work, student's work and experience, meeting the needs of the students as well as monitoring and evaluating the work of students and teachers.

Student's Support It will help in student's personal, social and spiritual growth. Support in all aspects of learning, progress fetch in student's and teacher's personal development.

School Ethos It comprise of school's policy and school's atmosphere and relations. There are specific goals of each individual school.

There is always an orientation towards students', teachers' and parents' satisfaction.

Resources There is need of school resources so that teachers, professional associates can work in team with cooperation and always being open to innovation.

Management, Leadership and Quality Assurance Approaches to leadership and management must be adopted to promote quality in education.

Indian Perspective on Quality in Education

Education is one of the most important instrument for reducing poverty and inequality. Education is equally a key to enhance India's competitiveness in the global economy. Therefore, ensuring quality access to quality education for all, in particular for the poor and rural population is central to the economic and social development of India.

Some of the key challenges on quality in education are

Universalisation of Good Quality Basic Education

Almost two decades of basic education programs have expanded access to schools in India. The number of out of school children decreased from 25 million in 2003 to an estimated 8 1 million in 2009. It is due to the reason that good quality is not ensured in education. India still faces challenges in providing quality and early childhood development programs for all children.

Expanding Secondary Education and Improving Quality

- Secondary education yields social and economic benefits but constitutes the primary bottleneck in the education system, today. Access, equity, management and quality, all need major improvements.
- Curriculum and teaching practices need upgrading to impart more relevant skills, such as reasoning skills, problem-solving, learning to learn, critical and independent thinking.
- Public and private partnerships need to be expanded to tap into the potential offered by the 60% of secondary schools which are privately managed in India.

Reforming Vocational Education and Training

More and higher quality vocational education is required to adequately prepare youth for current jobs. It requires expanding vocational training in high growth sectors, to overcome existing skills' shortages and ensuring accountability and good use of resources.

Expanding and Improving Technical and Tertiary Education

India's tertiary education system is one of the largest in the world, with over 10 million students. But, still tertiary education needs to be expanded, especially among low and middle income students. This will require reforms in the governance structure of higher education, decentralisation and major investments in faculty's development.

International Perspective on Quality in Education

Education is a tool for the development and emancipation of oppressed people and it is a tool for enslavement. Education is a way to individually liberate minds and create opportunities for social, economic and cultural development and it is a way to monopolise opportunity and crush independence. Understanding international perspectives on education, requires an examination of education, both across and within systems, cultures and communities.

International perspectives on education largely take the role of comparisons, which provide a way to evaluate educational process and product. These companions are of the educational systems, conceptualising and penetrating characteristics of society and specific situations in schools and classrooms. International comparisons of education allow for the unique and sometimes useful activities of benchmarking and modelling, but they also provide a forum for unnecessary criticism as well as inadequate comparability.

Challenges in Global Education

Some of the greatest challenges in global education that the world needs to take action right now, to achieve quality education by 2030 are

Lack of Funding for Education Developing countries can't rely solely on their own financing for education, there is also a need for more foreign aid. Less than 20% of aid for education goes to low income countries, according to Global Partnership for Education (GPE). There is currently a $ 39 billion gap to providing quality education to all children by 2030.

Having No Teacher or an Untrained Teacher There are not enough teachers to achieve universal primary or secondary education and many of the teachers that are currently working are untrained. As a result, children are not receiving proper education. There are 130 million children in school who are not learning basic skills, like reading, writing and maths.

No Classroom A child cannot learn without the right environment. Children in Sub-Saharan Africa are often squeesed into over-crowded classrooms or are learning outside. In Malawi, there are an average of 130 children per classroom in grade 1.

Lack of Learning Materials Outdated and worn out textbooks are often shared by six or more students in many parts of the world. Workbooks, exercise sheets, readers and other core materials to help students learn their lessons are in short supply. Teachers also need materials to help prepare their lessons, share with their students and guide their lessons.

Hunger and Poor Nutrition Being severely malnourished impacts on the brain development. Around 151 million children under the age of five were estimated to be stunted in 2013. Stunting can affect a child's cognitive abilities as well as their focus and concentration in school. Conversely, good nutrition can be crucial preparation for good learning.

Evolution of Quality

Over the past few decades, there have been several leaders who have been instrumental to develop the concept of quality as understood today. **Joseph M. Juran** is one of these key figures. Using Eastern Philosophies learnt in Japan, he advocated the idea that quality related to 'fitness for use'. Juran believed that this definition of quality fell into two key areas.

Higher quality products had a greater number of features which fit with the requirements of the consumer and also had fewer defects.

His book, **Managerial Break Through** published in the 1960s was the first to offer a step by step sequence for improvement, while the **Juran Trilogy** published in the 1980s, produced the three definitive quality management processes i.e. quality planning, quality improvement and quality control.

Another founding father of quality, **W Edwards Deming** also took what he learnt in Japan and brought it to the west. His 14 points were presented in his work, **Out of the Crisis**, published in 1982 and had been learnt in Japan following the Second World War.

His approach led to the creation of the Theory of Total Quality Management and linked the concept of quality with efficient management. Deming said managers were required to have a system of profound knowledge, comprised of appreciation of a system, theory of knowledge, the psychology of change and knowledge about variations.

Quality has nine different dimensions. These dimensions are somewhat independent, which means that an end product can be excellent in one dimension, but poor in others (Besterfield, 1998).

Below shows these nine dimensions and their terms

- **Performance** Primary products/services' characteristics such as time, cost and workmanship aspect.
- **Features** Secondary characteristic, added consideration such as creativity in design and attractiveness.
- **Conformance** Meeting specification or industry standards, workmanship and client's requirement in contract.
- **Reliability** Consistency of performance over time, average time for the unit to fail.
- **Durability** Useful life period with less maintenance or repair.
- **Service** Resolution of problems and complaints, ease of repair.
- **Response** Human to human interface, such as efficiency during meeting, fast decision-making, effective human resource management, etc.
- **Aesthetics** Sensory characteristics in design, such as exterior finishes.
- **Reputation** Past performance, such as being ranked first in the tendering process.

In the context of evolution of quality, certain practices such as quality inspection, quality control and quality assurance are explained below

Quality Inspection

The main emphasis of inspection is on the improvement of learning and teaching activities in the school. It tends to critically examine and evaluate the school as a peace for teaching-learning enterprise. Inspection, because of its focus on monitoring and evaluation of academic performance and development in schools, is always carried out with the intention of maintaining and improving on the quality of learning of students. It tends to improve all factors that affect teaching and learning in our school system.

Osinowo said that inspection should be aimed at developing an effective learning process and provide an education which should constantly suit the changing needs of individual and the purpose for which an education has been setup.

Akpofure (1974) opines that inspection should not only encourage flexibility and initiative, but it should also attempt to provide all those connected with the school system with a constant awareness of where it is going and ways and means of getting there. He went further to say that inspection should enable the educational system fulfil its stated aims and objectives within the national system. So, we can say that the main objective of all types of inspection is the improvement of instruction (quality control) and general school's operations.

Quality Control

Quality control is the set of measures and procedures to follow in order to ensure that the quality of a product or education is maintained and improved against a set of benchmarks and that any error encountered are either eliminated or reduced. The focus of quality control is to ensure that the product and product manufacturing are not only consistent but also in line with customer's requirements.

A major aspect of quality control is the establishment of well-defined controls. These controls help standardise, both production and reactions to quality issues.

In education, quality control is an important issue as parents, students and educators want to ensure that all students receive adequate training for the future. There are many methods of quality control in education, including Standardised Testing, Teaching Review and Training.

Education quality control usually beings with the formation of school's standards. These may be institution, district, state or national guidelines that determine what a student should know by the end of each grade. Quality control standards lay out guidelines for the education requirements for teachers, such as possession of valid teaching credential. Once school standards are set, the overseeing board can implement a cycle of investigation, policy changes and additions and implementation that ensures that a school meets its standards.

Methods of Quality Control

The methods of quality control are discussed below

Standardised Testing One method of quality control in education is standardised testing. Students in each grade are given a test that measures their aptitude in required subjects, such as spelling, reading comprehension and mathematics. These tests are often administered by a third party company and do not constitute a part of the regular grading process. Standardised tests let school authorities know the level of student's education as compared to the existing standard. If an age group or grade is struggling in a particular area of the test, measures may be implemented to improve classes in that area.

Teacher's Review It is another important method of quality control in education. In many regions, teachers are periodically observed by quality control experts, colleges or school management, in order to assess their success at meeting quality standards.

In determining teacher's performance, observers may interview students, examine recent grades given and judge whether the methods used in the classroom are truly adding to education. Using many other tactics to determine teacher's performance level is often considered very important, teachers rated based on standardised testing alone may leave out important areas of learning that cannot be measured by tests.

Listening to student, teacher and parent's feedback is sometimes an important part of quality control in education. Teachers can give a clear picture of how a particular class is struggling or succeeding, while students are full of valuable information about how teachers manage a classroom and how it could be improved. Paying careful attention to feedback can help create solutions to quality control lapses.

Training It is another important method of quality control in education. It is an ongoing process to meet the standards of education. During training, quality control educators learn how a particular educational institution creates and implements testing standards, curriculum evaluation, specialised educational programmes, etc.

Quality Assurance

Quality Assurance is popularly known as **QA testing**, is defined as an activity to ensure that an organisation is providing the best possible product or service to customers. QA focuses on improving the processes to deliver quality product to the customer. An organisation has to ensure that processes are efficient and effective as per the quality standards defined for any thing specific.

Quality assurance involves the systematic review of educational processes and programmes to maintain and improve their quality, equity and efficiency. While the design of quality assurance mechanisms (tools, processes and factors) varies across national contexts, their common objective is to improve teaching and learning, with the ultimate goal to support the best outcomes for learners. Quality assurance is important for accountability as well as to support ongoing development of teaching and learning.

Quality assurance in higher education includes all policies, measures, planned process and actions through which the quality of higher education is maintained and developed. Quality of higher education can be described as the degree to which the education meets the client's needs and demands. In this respect, higher education has two different clients *i.e.* students and society.

The expectations of these clients differ depending on whether it regards academic study programmes or labour market demand driven program.

So, in short we can say that

- Quality assurance contributes to better matching of education and training supply and demand.
- Quality assurance covers the macro-level (educational system level), meso-level (level of individual educational institutions) and micro-level (level of teaching-learning process).

Features of Quality Assurance in Higher Education

Six aspects can be distinguished being the basic and common features of national quality assurance systems in higher education. *They are*

- National coordination by an independent centre/agency.
- Internal evaluation resulting in self-assessment reports.
- Intermittent evaluation by external experts, partially based on establishment and self-assessment findings.
- Publication of evaluation outcomes, including recommendations for improvement.
- Implementations of recommendations.
- Assessment of the appropriateness and effectiveness of the quality assurance methods and procedures.

The purpose of National Quality Assurance System is the maintenance and development of the quality. Since this is the major concern by definition, quality assurance is a quality driven rather than an accrediation driven process. Quality assurance systems provide for meta-evaluation mechanisms to evaluate their appropriateness. This function is often embodied in the inspectorate for higher education. The inspectorate doesn't evaluate education, but it evaluates the methodology, techniques and effectiveness of quality assurance arrangements.

Total Quality Management (TQM)

Total Quality Management (TQM) is continuous improvement in whole process of organisation for the maximum satisfaction of customers. There are 3 Cs in Total Quality Management *i.e.* **culture, commitment** and **communication.** *Where we applied the Total Quality Management on education system, the process focuses on*

- Allignment within organisation with commitment to a shared vision.
- An extended understanding of the customer driven and process oriented basis for quality.
- An organisation designed around teams, with investment made in team development and changes made on performance management systems to reflect on team work as the basis for organisations activities.
- The setting of particularity challenges goals which commit the organisation to significant increases or performance outcomes.
- The day to day systematic daily management of organisation through the use of effective tools for measurement and feedback.

Work Management

Work management is concerned with the determination of the amount of time required to perform a unit of work. e.g. preparation of time-table. It depends on the level as well as types of schools and so on. There will be a comprehensive time-table having time-table for specific levels *i.e.* time-table for pre-primary, primary, etc.

The time required for this task is commonly referred to as the **standard** or **allowed time**. Thus, work measurement is to provide a yardstick for human effort which can help in efficient manning, improved planning and control, sound and incentive schemes.

In short, we can say that work management is interested in investigating, reducing and subsequently eliminating ineffective time.

Techniques of Work Measurement

There are certain techniques of work measurement

Subjective Judgement Work management involves here the subjective judgement of the management *i.e.* experience and guess work. This is generally known as 'rule of thumb standards'. It is very difficult to apply these standards universally and in large scale organisations. Moreover, these cannot be justified on scientific grounds.

Buffer Stock Buffer stock is the quantity of stores set apart as an insurance against the variations in demand and procurement period. This quantity of the item is to be kept as an emergency for unforeseen demands. It is calculated by multiplying the difference between maximum and average consumption, rate per day with the lead time for the items.

Reorder Level This term is used to denote the stock level at which fresh order has to be placed. This is equal to the average consumption per day multiplied by lead time plus buffer stock. By ordering at the time when stock reaches the reorder level, we are fairly assured that the chances of stock out are practically absent.

Stock Turnover Another aspect of inventory control is to see that there is proper turnover of items stocked and to see that the items are used before the time, expiry of the warranty period. e.g. chemical required for science labs, medicines and other supplies required for medical room, sports items, etc are some of the items come under it. Special efforts should be made to issue items on first come first out basis. Expiry date on control sheets to keep a control against keeping out dated material on the shelf should be maintained. In case, there is no possibility of using the stocks of short life items within the expiry period, efforts should be made to deploy the stock to other institutions so that they could be issued before the expiry time. *e.g.* common chemical required under chemistry, bio-chemistry, biology laboratories could be used within the expiry date by deploying it to the laboratory is in a position to use it within that time.

Record of Past Performance These represent what is rather than what should be. Standards thus, arrived are indicators of work and time requirement and can be used for controlling the operations.

It may be calculated as follows

Staff member minutes per unit

$$= \frac{\text{Total Number of staff members considered} \times \text{Minutes in work week}}{\text{Weighted number of units completed}}$$

This method is not suitable to improve the performance of organisation as standards are measured as past performance and not what ought to be.

Lead Time It is the period that elapses between placing an order and receiving the same. These can be classified as administrative lead time, manufacturing lead time, transporting lead time and inspection lead time. Any strategy to control lead time must try to control the administrative and inspection lead time. Other, too, can be controlled to a lesser extent.

Six Sigma

In education, six sigma pertains to improving the quality of matter taught, the character generated of the pupils and the quality of study and school life. With the revolutionary usage of audio-visual devices, like projectors, video conferencing, etc, the students can also be asked to write papers on a particular subject and after the presentation of papers, a discussion can take place on the respective subject. Under this method of imparting knowledge of literacy with quality, thinking, writing and presentation skills of the students can be kindled. Six sigma can be effectively used for new and innovative projects with a web based system for assessing the extent of a student's knowledge.

Main Approach in Six Sigma Project

It is characterised as **DMAIC**, an acronym that expands to: Define, Measure, Analyse, Improve and Control.

Define This involves defining the project based on process maps, application area, desired improvement, likely benefits, etc. This phase is important in order to raise the chances of success in the later phases.

Measure Emphasis on identifying key customer's requirements, key quality and process characteristics, collecting the associated data and establishing the baseline level of quality.

Analyse This involves Data Analysis to determine the key process variables that have the greatest impact on the quality metrics of interest in the project.

Improve Through data collection on key process variables, surveys, designed experiments or other means, a systematic and thorough study is done to quantitatively model the relationships in the process, determine optimal process settings that guarantee a high level of quality and recommend (and implement) corrective and/or improvement actions.

Control Once the desired quality level is achieved, concrete measures are put in place to maintain the gains. This could be through control charts for monitoring key process and quality attributes, documentation, etc.

The following problems played the major role behind the involvement of six sigma methodology in education

- Tuition fee of many institutes were rising because of which it became difficult for many students to study in their desired institutes.
- The cycle time required fulfiling the various formalities of the institution related to the registration and admission process was quite long.
- The value of the education was decreasing.
- The students demanded a better quality in academics to excel in their fields.
- The performance of the students with respect to their grades kept on going down.

Concept Behind Six Sigma in Education

The future of any company depends on its employees and their performance, keeping in mind the needs and the demands of the customers. When six sigma's methodologies are implemented in the education sector, the teacher becomes the employee and the customers are the parents, who pay the fee for their ward.

Parents, who are paying the fee for their ward, expect a quality education to be bestowed to their wards, in return. By improving the teaching techniques and methodology, a teacher can help in increasing the performance level of the students and thus, can achieve the customer's satisfaction.

Benefits of Six Sigma in Education

- The factors delaying the admission process, registration process, information and technology process, grants administration process, certification process, sequestration, purchase orders, the repairs and maintenance process are identifiable and hence, they can be precluded with a statistical approach to the existing problem. This, in turn, reduces the cycle time of the process, lowers the cost involved in these processes and lowers the chances of defects.
- Tuition fee and the other fee involved decreases.
- The value of the education improves with improvement in quality.
- The positive changes made in the teaching methodology provide a positive result with respect to the good performance of the students.
- Apparently, the performance level of the students increases.
- A better ambience for innovation and creativity is observed.
- The reputation of the institute improves.
- With the six sigma's methodology being involved in any teaching institute, parents can expect a quality education for their ward. As a matter of fact, there is a better level of customer's satisfaction.
- With the reduction in the tuition fee, charged by any institute, more people would be able to admit their wards in the institutes and this would result into increase in literacy rate of the country increases.

Quality Gurus

The Quality Gurus, Dr. W Edwards Deming, Dr. Walter Shewhart and CK Prahalad will be discussed here. They have made a significant impact on the world through their contributions to improve not only business, but all organisations, including state and national governments, military organisations, educational institutions, healthcare organisations and many other establishments and organisations.

Dr. W Edwards Deming

Dr. Deming developed his complete Philosophy of Management, which he encapsulated into his 'fourteen points' and the 'seven deadly diseases of management'. He advanced the state of quality, originally based on work done by **Shewart** with his explanations of variation, use of control charts and his theories on knowledge, psychology and variation.

Deming greatly helped to focus the responsibility of quality on management and popularised the PDCA cycle, which led to it being referred to as the **Deming's cycle**. He gave his **System of Thought** which he called **System of Profound Knowledge.** This system includes four components or 'lenses' through which to view the world simultaneously.

They are :

- Appreciating a system.
- Understanding variation.
- Psychology.
- Epistemology, The Theory of Knowledge.

PDCA Cycle (The Deming Wheel)

Walter Shewhart originated the concept of the PDCA cycle and introduced it to **Deming**. Deming promoted the idea widely in the 1950s and it became known as the **Deming wheel** or the **Deming cycle**. The PDCA (Plan, Do, Check, Act) cycle consists of four steps or stages which must be gone through to get from 'problem faced' to 'problem solved'. *Repetition of these steps forms a cycle of continual improvement i.e.*

- **Plan** for changes to bring about improvement.
- **Do** change on a small scale first to trial them.
- **Check** to see if changes are working and to investigate selected processes.
- **Act** to get the greatest benefit from change.

Deming's 14 Points for Quality Management

Deming created 14 points which provide a framework to developing knowledge in the workplace and can be used to guide long term business plans and aims. The points constitute not so much an action plan as a philosophical code for management. They have been extensively interpreted by as many commentators on quality as on other management disciplines.

Deming's 14 Points

- **Create constancy of purpose** towards improvement of product and service, with the aim of becoming competitive, staying in business and providing jobs.
- **Adopt the new philosophy** Western management must awaken to the challenge, must learn their responsibilities and take on leadership for change.
- **Cease dependence on mass inspection** build quality into the product from the start.
- **End the practice of awarding** business on the basis of price tag alone. Instead, minimise total cost. Move

towards a single supplier for any item, based on a long-term relationship of loyalty and trust.

- **Improve constantly** and forever the system of production and service to improve quality and reduce waste.
- Institute training and re-training.
- **Institute leadership** the aim of supervision should be to lead and help people to do a better job.
- **Drive out fear** so that everyone may work effectively for the company.
- **Break down barriers between departments** people in research, design, sales and production must work as a team to foresee and solve problems of production.
- **Eliminate slogans, exhortations and targets** for the workforce as they do not necessarily achieve their aims.
- **Eliminate numerical quotas** in order to take account of quality and methods, rather than just numbers.
- **Remove barriers** to pride of workmanship.
- **Institute a vigorous program of education and re-training** for, both the management and the workforce.
- **Take action** to accomplish the transformation. Management and workforce must work together.

Deming's Seven Deadly Diseases of Management

Here, Deming describes the main barriers faced by management to improve effectiveness and continual improvement. He was referring here to US industry and their management practices.

- Lack of constancy of purpose to plan products and services that will have a market and keep the company a float.
- An emphasis on short-term profits and short-term thinking (just the opposite from constancy of purpose to stay in business), fed by fear of unfriendly takeover and by demand from bankers and owners for dividends.
- Evaluation of performance and annual reviews.
- Mobility of managers and job hoping.
- Management by use only of available data.
- High medical cost.
- High cost of liability.

Deming said that effective management and a commitment to quality were needed to combat these seven deadly diseases. He emphasised the importance of communicating quality messages to all staff and building a belief in Total Quality Management. The relevance of these principles to a wider general management application has contributed to Deming's status as a founder of the Quality Management Movement, not just quality and process control. This is why, he interests an audience that is much wider than the quality lobby.

Walter Shewart

Walter Shewart is often referred as the **Father of Quality Control.** He worked as a **process engineer** for **Western Electric** and then at **Bell Labs**. He believed that lack of information greatly hampered the efforts of control and management processes in a production environment. In order to aid a manager in making scientific, efficient and economic decisions, he developed **Statistical Process Control** (SPC) method. Many of the modern ideas regarding quality own their inspiration to Dr. Shewart.

He also developed the Shewart's cycle and Learning and Improvement cycle, combining both creative management thinking with statistical analysis. This cycle contains four continuous steps *i.e.* **Plan, Do, Study** and **Act.** These steps ultimately lead to total quality improvement. The cycle draws its structure from the notion that constant evaluation of management practices as well as the willingness of management to adopt and disregard unsupported ideas are keys to the evaluation of a successful enterprise.

Six Sigma Concept

'Sigma' is a Greek letter. It is a mathematical term which is used to denote standard deviation. It is a standard statistical unit used to measure and describe the distribution of any process about its mean. Shewhart's ideas and statistical concepts were embraced in clinical laboratories for several years. Clinical laboratories used these concepts in proficiency testing and quality control operations. Many industries have re-discovered Shewhart's methods and tools of statistical process control which is named as six sigma.

Statistical Process Control (SPC)

Statistical Process Control (SPC) is not new to industry. In 1924, a man at Bell laboratories developed the control chart and the concept that a process could be in statistical control. His name was **William A Shewart**. He eventually published a book, titled **Statistical Method from the Viewpoint of Quality Control** (1939). The SPC process gained wide usage during World War II by the military in the munitions and weapons facilities.

The demand for product had forced them to look for a better and more efficient way to monitor product quality without compromising safety. SPC filled that need. The use of SPC techniques in America faded following the war. It was then picked up by the Japanese manufacturing companies where it is still used today. In the 1970s, SPC started to gain acceptance again due to American industry feeling pressure from high quality products being imported from Japan. Today, SPC is a widely used quality tool throughout many industries.

Reducing Variation To Improve Quality

The emphasis on reducing variation to enhance quality is a great contribution to quality management. Reducing variation to improve quality resulted in manufacture of precise things. The concept was applicable in different fields, like automobiles, electronics and constructions.

Shewhart acknowledged two classes of variation, namely special cause and common cause variation. These two categories can also be termed as assignable cause and chance cause variation, respectively. A control chart was designed by him to explain these two categories of variations. Shewhart proposed new attributes and variables in his control charts. Shewhart proposed that to improve quality and reduce scrap, common cause variation should be controlled. In this way, any process can be brought under statistical control.

The objective of any industry is to develop economic methods to satisfy the human needs. This should be done by reducing the things to routines necessitating very little human effort. By making use of scientific techniques and modern statistical theories, it was possible to setup limits for the results of routine efforts economically. If the results of any routine process deviate away from the limits, it is said that the routine has broken down and will no longer be economical. The cause of trouble must be identified and eliminated in order to make the process economical.

American Society for Quality (ASQ)

ASQ of individuals who are passionate about methods of quality control. Members of ASQ contribute to industry with their ideas of quality control and experience. **Shewart** was ASQ's first honorary associate, he efficaciously brought together the principles of statistics, economics and engineering. Shewhart developed highly effective tools and specifically control charts. His contributions were widely recognised.

Shewhart always believed that Statistical Theory would serve the needs of industry. He was a man of science who worked patiently to develop ideas which made the world better. ASQ is influenced intensely by Shewhart's contributions and ideas.

Before his death, Shewhart mentioned to other members of ASQ that he was pleased by their contributions which led to extensive growth in the field of quality control. He also stated that the he was astonished by looking at the development which was beyond his expectations.

CK Pralhad

CK Pralhad (1942-2010) was determined to shake managers free of their dominant logic and deeply held assumptions. He was a proactive thinker who regularly produced starting insights that managers would never have considered. CK Pralhad is also famous for his contribution on the development of the Core Competence Model and co-creation.

CK Pralhad became particularly known for the work he conducted with **Gary Hamel**. They carried out scientific and empirical research in the area of Core Competence Model. The results of this research formed the basis for the emergence of outsourcing. His research was mainly focused on the best next practices, corporate strategies and the role of top management in multi-national organisations.

CK Pralhad's last work focused on the poor in society, four billion people who are living below the poverty line. This idea is reflected in his book, **The Fortune at the Bottom of the Pyramid** (2002), in which he explained this using the motto, eradicating poverty through profits.

The concept of The Fortune at the Bottom of the Pyramid, as described in his latest book, is based on experiences and practices in India by looking at Jaipur Foot, Jaipur Rugs, SEWA, Bombay Dabbawallas, Amul, The Aravind Eye Care System, etc. The Fortune at the Bottom of the Pyramid is a new paradigm where SIR modified and magnified the trade-offs between price, features and performance of a product and services.

SIR's core argument was that if an organisation dramatically re-engineered the product features and performance indicators, the price of the product could be kept so attractive that it can be accessed and used by a large market segment for which it was not originally intended. SIR went on to argue that designing the product and service for the economically weaker section of the society would generate more wealth as a consequence of large volume even when the margins are low. Hence, addressing The Bottom of the Pyramid is an opportunity for sustained wealth creation.

EXAM BASED QUESTIONS

1 Which among the following lies in the eyes of the beholder?
(a) Quality (b) Quantity
(c) Beauty (d) Idea

2 Who are those for whom quality can be specific attributes that can be identified?
(a) Relativist (b) Objectivist
(c) Pragmatic (d) None of these

3 What is the meaning of the word 'Qualis' in terms of quality?
(a) What it is (b) What quality it has
(c) What kind of (d) How to do

4 Who wrote the book 'Managerial Break Through'?
(a) Joseph Juran (b) Joseph green
(c) Walter Shewart (d) Edwards Deming

5 Who is marked as the founding father of quality?
(a) Edward Goseph (b) Edwards Deming
(c) Green (d) Harvey

6 What is referred as one of the major work of Edwards Deming?
(a) Crisis and upliftment
(b) Quality crisis
(c) Quality management in crisis
(d) Out of the crisis

7 How many dimensions of quality are present for the effective governance?
(a) Seven (b) Five (c) Nine (d) Eleven

8 Education liberates the intellect and unlock our
(a) experience (b) intuition
(c) imagination (d) faith

9 Mark the incorrect among the following quality education is supported by three key pillars.
(a) Ensuring good students
(b) Ensuring quality teachers
(c) Safe and supportive learning environment
(d) Quality tools and professional development

10 In which type of quality, we see that the emphasis is less on teachers that create pressure?
(a) Pedagogy (b) Syllabus
(c) Curriculum (d) None of these

11 What is the new addition to the new curriculum development in education?
(a) Curriculum based education
(b) Distance education
(c) Information and Computer Technology (ICT)
(d) Massive online open courses

12 What is said to be an instrument to National Human Resource Development?
(a) Quality (b) Reform
(c) Teachers (d) Education

13 Which among the following is not the means to determine the success of education?
(a) Number of classrooms
(b) Books in the library
(c) Playgrounds in schools
(d) Ratio of teachers

14 How can we overcome the educational crisis?
(a) Global Educational Framework
(b) New teachers
(c) Resolute political leadership
(d) Huge investment on framework

15 Who are the major contributors in education before Britishers?
(a) Mughal Education System
(b) Persian System
(c) Afgani System
(d) All of the above

16 According to Mughal, on what type of educational system does our focus be on?
(a) Formal education
(b) Informal education
(c) Neither a nor b
(d) Both a and b

17 Who plays a crucial role in spreading education during the British rule?
(a) Teachers (b) Madarsa
(c) Priests (d) None of these

18 What are the major reason for making Britishers as rulers?
(a) Lack of teachers
(b) Lack in socio-political conditions
(c) No harmony in religions
(d) No policy

19 Which indicator of quality in education is evaluated by external or independent agencies?
(a) Curriculum (b) Achievements
(c) Student's support (d) School ethos

20 There is a need of school .... so that teachers, professional associates can work in them with cooperation.
(a) management (b) leadership
(c) resources (d) assurance

21 India still faces challenges in providing quality to .... for all children.
(a) early childhood development programs
(b) basic education programs
(c) secondary education programs
(d) None of the above

22 .... and .... need upgrading to impart more relevant skills in learning.
(a) Curriculum, teaching practices
(b) Resources, management
(c) Leadership, teaching practices
(d) None of the above

23 Public-private partnerships need to be expanded to tap into the potential offered by the .... of secondary schools, which are privately managed in India.
(a) 50% (b) 60%
(c) 55% (d) 65%

24 Which statement is correct?
1. Higher quality vocational education is required to prepare youth for current jobs.
2. Vocational training does not ensures accountability.
3. Reforming vocational education and training is required in developing countries.

Codes
(a) Only 1 (b) Only 2
(c) 1 and 3 (d) Only 3

25 International perspectives on education largely take the role of comparisons, which provide a way to .... educational process and product.
(a) evaluate (b) recognize
(c) support (d) None of these

26 Less than .... of aid for education goes to low-income countries of the world.
(a) 10% (b) 15% (c) 20% (d) 25%

27 There is currently a .... gap to provide quality education to all children by 2030.
(a) $ 25 billion (b) $ 35 billion
(c) $ 39 billion (d) $ 40 billion

28 Which is the major challenge in Global education that is outdated for students and teachers?
(a) Untrained teacher
(b) No classroom
(c) Lack of learning materials
(d) Lack of funding

29 Which challenge did not help to achieve universal primary or secondary education?
(a) Untrained teachers
(b) No classroom
(c) Lack of learning material
(d) Lack of funding

30 Which statement is not correct?
(a) Emphasis of inspection is on the improvement of learning and teaching activities
(b) Inspection tends to critically examine and evaluate the school
(c) Inspection should not be aimed at developing an effective learning process
(d) It improves all factors that affect teaching and learning

31 The main objective of inspection is
(a) improvement of instruction
(b) improvement of general school operations
(c) improving quality of learning
(d) All of the above

32 Which method of quality control in education measures student's aptitude?
(a) Training
(b) Standardised testing
(c) Teaching review
(d) None of the above

33 Educational quality control begins with ....
(a) school standards
(b) national guidelines
(c) trained teachers
(d) All of the above

34 Which method is helpful, where the observers may interview students and judge the methods of teaching?
(a) Teaching review (b) Standardized testing
(c) Training (d) All of the above

35 Which commission worked for the enforcement of ICT (Information and Communication Technology)?
(a) Kothari Commission
(b) National Knowledge Commission
(c) Sadler Commission
(d) New India Commission

36 What is the important feature of quality control?
(a) Set benchmarks to attain good
(b) Making quality easy concept to deal
(c) Form new policies
(d) Make more committees

37 When a chart analyses a specific attribute of the product it is called ....
(a) production chart
(b) uni-variate chart
(c) analysis chart
(d) multi-variate chart

38 When a chart measures variances in serval product attributes, it is called ....
(a) production chart
(b) uni-variate chart
(c) analysis chart
(d) multi-variate chart

39 **What comes for looking after the good quality products and it's on time delivery?**

(a) Quality inspection
(b) Quality control
(c) Quality assurance
(d) Quality management

40 **Who among the following focuses on Total Quality Management (TQM)?**

(a) Employee (b) Customer
(c) Both a and b (d) None of these

41 **Which of the following is responsible for quality objective?**

(a) Top level management
(b) Middle level management
(c) Front line management
(d) All of the above

42 **What is the aim of fool proofing technique used for Total Quality Management?**

(a) To achieve zero defect
(b) To specify time schedules
(c) To specify targets
(d) None of the above

43 **What is ISO?**

(a) Indian Organisation for Standard
(b) Internal Organisation for Standard
(c) International Organisation for Standard
(d) None of the above

44 **What is quality assurance?**

(a) Quality assurance deals with activities which prove that products and services meet the required quality standard
(b) Quality assurance deals with activities which aim at customer's satisfaction
(c) Quality assurance deals with controlling the quality of products by inspection
(d) All of the above

45 **Which of the following statement(s) is/are false?**

1. Fault Tree Analysis Method is used to determine reliability of product
2. The goal of six sigma is to reduce number of defects to 2.4 parts per billion
3. Six sigma is represented by normal distribution curve
4. Poka Yoke is a policy which prevents occurrence of human errors

Codes

(a) Only 3 (b) 2 and 3
(c) 1, 3 and 4 (d) Only 2

46 **Which quality management program is related to the maintenance of plants and equipments?**

(a) Environmental Management System
(b) Fault Tree Analysis
(c) Failure Mode Effect Analysis
(d) Total Productive Maintenance

47 **The aim of Just In Time, manufacturing principle is to eliminate**

(a) time wastage
(b) labour wastage
(c) cost of excessive inventory
(d) All of the above

48 **Which among the following is a Pull Type Signaling System?**

(a) Just In Time (b) Kanban
(c) Both a and b (d) None of these

49 **What P, D, C, A stands for?**

(a) Plan, Do, Check, Act
(b) Plan, Do, Correct, Act
(c) Proceed, Do, Check, Act
(d) Proceed, Do, Correct, Act

50 **While setting quality objective, ... to be considered.**

(a) customer need (b) organisational need
(c) supplier need (d) worker need

51 **According to Deming, quality problems are**

(a) due to management (b) due to method
(c) due to machine (d) due to material

52 **.............. helps organisation reduce employee's turnover and absenteeism.**

(a) Job design
(b) Training and development
(c) Wage revision
(d) All of the above

53 **In the concept of quality education, on what basis the rights of the child are protested?**

1. Protection
2. Survivor
3. Participation
4. Development

Codes

(a) 1 and 2 (b) 1 and 3
(c) 1, 2 and 3 (d) 1, 2, 3 and 4

54 **What is/are the central characteristic(s) of quality?**

1. Absolute 2. Relative
3. Process 4. Culture

Codes

(a) Only 3 (b) 1 and 4
(c) 2 and 4 (d) 1, 2, 3 and 4

55 **Which among the following are the three definitive quality management processes?**

1. Quality planning
2. Quality assurance
3. Quality improvement
4. Quality control

Codes

(a) 1 and 4 (b) 3 and 4
(c) 1, 3 and 4 (d) 1, 2, 3 and 4

56 Which are the two major division of secondary education in Hunter Commission?

1. Literacy upto university
2. Vocational for commercial career
3. Literacy to poor women
4. No fee policy

Codes

(a) 1 and 2 (b) 1 and 4
(c) 2 and 3 (d) 3 and 4

57 Who play(s) an important role(s) in the transformation of education?

1. School 2. Teacher
3. Leader 4. Student
5. Society 6. Family

Codes

(a) 1 and 2 (b) 1, 2 and 4
(c) 1, 2, 3 and 4 (d) 1, 2, 3, 4, 5 and 6

58 What is the relevance of quality assurance?

1. Insuring good service
2. Improving customer's satisfaction
3. Focusing on process of delivery
4. Improving quality product

Codes

(a) 1 and 3 (b) 2 and 4
(c) 1, 2 and 4 (d) 1, 2, 3 and 4

59 Match the following

List I	List II
A. TQM promotes	1. Small change
B. Kaizen is	2. Continuous development
C. Quality circle can solve problem related to	3. Employee's participation
D. Quality circle benefit to	4. Employee

Codes

	A	B	C	D		A	B	C	D
(a)	3	1	2	4	(b)	1	3	2	4
(c)	3	1	4	2	(d)	3	2	1	4

Directions (Q. Nos. 60-65) *Two statements are given below, one labelled as Assertion (A) and other labelled as Reason (R). Choose the correct code for the following.*

Codes

(a) Both A and R are true, but R is not the correct explanation of A
(b) Both A and R are true and R is the correct explanation of A
(c) A is true, but R is false
(d) A is false, but R is true

60 **Assertion** (A) Quality education is not an easy concept to qualify.

Reason (R) Quality determines how much and how well children learn.

61 **Assertion** (A) College, principle and heads of schools have a crucial role in implementation reform.

Reason (R) Because school can be such place where children of different abilities develop, learn and grow.

62 **Assertion** (A) Result of qualitative action depends on various situations.

Reason (R) This helps in global educational goals.

63 **Assertion** (A) Decentralisation is done in Educational field so that there is increased local control in education.

Reason (R) Government handed finance for the improvement of education.

64 **Assertion** (A) British company was originally a trading company.

Reason (R) It's original purpose was to maximise profit in India.

65 **Assertion** (A) In British period, only formal education was emphasised.

Reason (R) The establishment of British education in India only favours colonial education.

ANSWERS

1 (c)	2 (b)	3 (c)	4 (a)	5 (b)	6 (d)	7 (c)	8 (c)	9 (a)	10 (a)
11 (c)	12 (a)	13 (c)	14 (c)	15 (a)	16 (b)	17 (b)	18 (c)	19 (b)	20 (c)
21 (a)	22 (a)	23 (b)	24 (c)	25 (a)	26 (c)	27 (c)	28 (c)	29 (a)	30 (c)
31 (d)	32 (b)	33 (a)	34 (a)	35 (b)	36 (a)	37 (b)	38 (d)	39 (c)	40 (c)
41 (a)	42 (a)	43 (c)	44 (a)	45 (d)	46 (a)	47 (d)	48 (c)	49 (a)	50 (b)
51 (a)	52 (b)	53 (d)	54 (d)	55 (c)	56 (a)	57 (a)	58 (d)	59 (a)	60 (a)
61 (a)	62 (b)	63 (c)	64 (a)	65 (d)					

CHAPTER 37

Change Management Process

Change management process is a wider concept dealing with goals, processes and technologies. An institution's success depends on how well it adapts to changes in a planned manner.

Change Management

Change management is a systematic approach dealing with the transition or transformation of an organisation's goals, processes and technologies. The purpose of change management is to implement strategies for effecting change, controlling change and helping people to adapt to change. Furthermore, in respect to education, it affects employees (teachers) as well as students.

Since, an organisation's success depends on how well it adapts to change, management of these situations is crucial. This is where change management comes into play. Preventing changes is not always possible, as they are inevitable sometimes.

However, it is possible to plan for changes and overcome them. The management must always strive to ensure changes happen, smoothly. The organisation and its members must not find changes too drastic.

Any kind of change in management is followed by

- Change results from the pressure of forces, which are both inside and outside the organisation.
- The whole organisation tends to be affected by change in any part of it.
- Change takes place in all parts of the organisation, but at varying rates of speed and degree of significance.

Need for Planned Change

The best hope for successful planned change occurs when teachers are participants in exchange networks that foster collaborative opportunities to work with other school leaders. Successful change requires appropriate alignment of structures and processes.

In this Chapter

- *Change Management*
- *Three Step-Model of Change*
- *Cost of Quality*
- *Cost Benefit Analysis*
  - *Cost Effective Analysis*
- *Indian and International Quality Assurance Agencies*

Strategic change is the process of managing change in a structured and thoughtful way in order to meet organizational goals, objectives and missions.

To plan change, managers must predict and diagnose the need for change. An Organisational Development theory, developed by **Larry E Greiner** is helpful in change management. **Greiner's model** shows organisation as it evolves through the **five** stages of growth, and the end of each of these stages is marked by a crisis that calls for a change.

The five stages of growth are as follows

(i) **Creativity** The founders of the organisation dominate this stage and the emphasis is on creating both a product and a market. But as the organisation grows, management problems occur that cannot be handled through informal communication. The founders find themselves burdened with unwanted management responsibilities and conflicts between the employees and management grow. It is at this point that the crisis of leadership occurs and the first revolutionary period begins.

(ii) **Direction** During this period, a strong manager, who is acceptable to the founder and who can pull the organisation together, is appointed. During this phase, the new manager and key staff take most of the responsibility for instituting direction, while lower level supervisors are treated more as functional specialists than autonomous decision-making managers. Lower level managers begin to demand more autonomy and the next revolutionary period begins.

(iii) **Delegation** This stage often possess problems for top managers, who have been successful at being directive. They may find giving up responsibility difficult. Moreover, lower level managers generally are not acustomed to making decisions for themselves. As a result, numerous organisations founder during this revolutionary period, adhering to centralised methods, while lower level employees grow disenchanted and leave the organisation.

(iv) **Control** This stage is characterised by the use of formal systems for achieving greater coordination, with top management as the watch dog. It results in the next revolutionary period, the crisis of red tape. This crisis most often occurs when the organisation has become too large and complex and is managed through formal programs and rigid systems. If the crisis of red tape is to be overcome, the organisation must move to the next evolutionary phase.

(v) **Collaboration** The last of Greiner's phases emphasise greater spontaneity in management action, through teams and the skillful confrontation of inter-personal differences. Social control and self-discipline take over from formal action. Greiner's Model shows uncertainty about what the next revolution of change will be, but anticipates that it will center on the psychological saturation of employees, who grow emotionally and physically exhausted by the intensity of teamwork and the heavy pressure for innovative solutions. To plan change, managers must predict and diagnose the need for change. Greiner's Model of Organisational Growth and Change can help managers understand, how the need for change relates to the organisational cycles.

Three Step-Model of Change

Today, the concept of change management is a familiar one in most businesses. But, how businesses manage change (and how successful they are at it) varies enormously depending on the nature of the business, the change and the people involved. And a key part of this, depends on how well people within it understand the change process.

One of the corner stone models for understanding organisational change was developed by **Kurt Lewin**, back in the 1940s and still holds true today. His model is known as **Unfreeze-Change-Refreeze**, which refers to the three stage process of change that he describes. Lewin, a physicist as well as a social scientist, explained organisational change using the analogy of changing the shape of a block of ice.

Lewin's Change Management Model

Kurt Lewin described the Freeze Model of Change, which suggests that change involves a shift from one still condition by means of a state of activity to a different still condition. If you have a large cube of ice, but realise that what you want is a cone of ice, what do you do? First, you must melt the ice to make it amenable to change (unfreeze). Then you must mould the iced water into the shape you want (change). Finally, you must solidify the new shape (refreeze). By looking at change as a process with distinct stages, you can prepare yourself for what is coming and make a plan to manage the transition, looking before you leap, so to speak. All too often, people go into change blindly, causing much unnecessary turmoil and chaos.

To begin any successful change process, you must first start by understanding, why the change must take place. As **Lewin** put it, "Motivation for change must be generated before change can occur. One must be helped to re-examine many cherished assumptions about oneself and one relations to others". This is the unfreezing stage from which change begins.

Unfreezing

This first stage of change involves preparing the organisation to accept that change is necessary. It involves breaking down the existing status quo, before you can build up a new way of operating. Key to this is developing a compelling message, showing why the existing way of doing things cannot continue. This is easiest to frame, when you can point to declining sales figures, poor financial results, worrying customer satisfaction surveys, or as such.

This shows that things have to change in a way that everyone can understand. To prepare an organisation successfully, you need to start at its core i.e. you need to challenge the beliefs, values, attitudes and behaviours that currently defines it.

Using the analogy of a building, you must examine and be prepared to change the existing foundations, as they might not support addon storeys. Unless this is done, the whole building may risk, collapse.

This first part of the change process is usually the most difficult and stressful. When you start cutting down the way things are done, you put everyone and everything off balance. You may evoke strong reactions in people and that's exactly what needs to be done.By forcing the organisation to re-examine its core, you effectively create a (controlled) crisis, which in turn can build a strong motivation to seek out a new equillibrium. Without this motivation, you won't get the buy in and participation necessary to effect any meaningful change.

Changing/ Moving

After the uncertainty created in the unfreeze stage, the moving/changing stage is where people begin to resolve their uncertainty and look for new ways to do things. People start to believe and act in ways that supports the new direction.

The transition from unfreeze to change or move does not happen overnight, people take time to embrace the new direction and participate proactively in the change. A related change model, the Change Curve, focuses on the specific issue of personal transitions in a changing environment and is useful for understanding this aspect, in more detail.

In order to accept the change and contribute to making it successful, people need to understand how it will benefit them. Not everyone will fall in line, just because the change is necessary and will benefit the company. This is a common assumption and a pit fall that should be avoided.

Time and communication are the two keys to the changes occurring, successfully. People need time to understand the changes and they also need to feel highly connected to the organisation, throughout the transition period. When you are managing change, this can require a great deal of time and effort and hands on management is usually the best approach.

Refreeze

When the changes are taking shape and people have embraced the new ways of working, the organisation is **ready to refreeze**. The outward signs of the refreeze are a stable organisation chart, consistent job descriptions and so on. The refreeze stage also needs to help people and the organisation internalise or institutionalise the changes.

This means making sure that the changes are used all the time, and that they are incorporated into everyday business. With a new sense of stability, employees feel confident and comfortable with the new ways of working.

The rationale for creating a new sense of stability in our ever changing world is often questioned. Even though, change is constant in many organisations, this refreezing stage is still important. Without it, employees get caught in a transition trap where they aren't sure how things should be done, so nothing ever gets done to full capacity. In the absence of a new frozen state, it is very difficult to tackle the next change initiative, effectively. How do you go about convincing people that something needs changing, if you haven't allowed the most recent changes to sink in? Change will be perceived as change for change's sake and the motivation required to implement new changes, simply won't be there.

As part of the refreezing process, make sure that you celebrate the success of the change. This helps people to find closure, thanks them for enduring a painful time and helps them believe that future change will be successful.

Japanese Model of Change

It is seen that with respect to any model of change, **Japanese model** is most renowned. There are **two** major kinds of Japanese model *i.e.* **Poka Yoke** and **Just-In-Time**.

They can be explained as given below

Just-In-Time

The Just-In-Time Inventory system is a management strategy that aligns raw material orders from suppliers, directly with production schedules. Companies use this inventory strategy to increase efficiency and decrease waste by receiving goods only as they need them for the production process, which reduces inventory costs. This method requires producers to forecast demand accurately.

Background and History

JIT is a Japanese Management Philosophy which has been applied in practice, since the early 1970s in many Japanese manufacturing organisations. It was first developed and perfected within the **Toyota** manufacturing plants by **Taiichi Ohno** as a means of meetting consumer demands with minimum delays. **Taiichi Ohno** is frequently referred to as the father of JIT.

Toyota was able to meet the increasing challenges for survival, through an approach that focused on people, plants and systems. He realised that JIT would only be successful, if every individual within the organisation was involved and committed to it, if the plants and processes were arranged for maximum outputs and efficiency and if quality and production programs were scheduled to meet demands, exactly.

This manufacturing has the capacity, when property adapted to the organisation, to strengthen the organisation's competitiveness in the market place, substantially by reducing wastes and improving product quality and efficiency of production. There are strong cultural aspects associated with the emergence of **Just In Time** in **Japan**. This is said to be the management philosophy and not a technique.

Originally, it referred to the production of goods to meet customer demand exactly on time, quality and quantity, whether the customer is the final purchaser of the product or another process, further along the production line.

Poka Yoke

Poka Yoke is a **Japanese** phrase that means error prevention. It is a mechanism that is put in place to prevent human error. It was developed in the 60s of the previous century by **Shigeo Shingo** from Japan. He was an engineer at the **Toyota car factory**. It is still the most famous multi-national business using, Poka Yoke today. It is used to prevent and resolve defects during the production process, eliminating the need for quality control after the process. It is a frequently used method in lean manufacturing and six sigma to ensure as little errors in a production process as possible.

A **Poka** is an inadvertent error and **Yoke** is for preventing. It forces actions to be carried out correctly, leaving no room for misunderstandings. It's about measures that prevent further errors from being made. Many solutions in it tend to be simple, cheap and effective.

They can be integrated into the product design or in one of the process steps.

The most famous examples are smartphone and SIM cards. After all, there is only one way to place the SIM card in the phone. It is impossible, to do it wrong.

In short, Poka Yoke is a continual improvement strategy that offers a way to move the QMS (Quality Management System) towards a higher level of performance.

Stages of Poka Yoke

Few stages of Poka Yoke are:

Define During this phase, the problem causing the defect is described and defined. It needs to be an objective description, that doesn't draw conclusions right away. It's possible to monitor the shop floor during the production process. This is also indicated with the word 'Gemba', which is a Japanese word for **shop floor**. The shop floor is where the process happens, and that's where the causes of problems may also be hiding. If the problem occurs at the end user, it is a good idea to define the problem objectively from this perspective.

Measure Usually, the measuring stage is applied in case of complex problems in the production process. A test is used to discover how often the problem occurs. A percentage is then calculated based on the results. The higher the percentage, the more important it is to solve the problem at its source. Apart from a production error, it may also be a case of user error. In such a case, a so called test group would be used that tests the product over a certain period. The outcome of this, determines how the problem will be dealt with and solved.

Analyse During this stage, it becomes clear whether a Poka Yoke measures can be applied. The process is analysed thoroughly and the cause of the defect is tracked down. Only when the source of the issue is clear, can the search for a solution begin.

Improve During this stage, analysis is used to deal with the cause of the problem. A solution is developed and implemented. In many cases, Poka Yoke's solutions seem obvious, but have a significant positive impact. They prevent the same mistake from being made in future.

Control During this stage, the effect of the change is measured. If the Poka Yoke measures in question, works well and the chance of further potential error is negligible. It concludes with the zero quality control and zero defects.

Types of Poka Yoke

Three types of Poka Yoke can be identified for quickly and easily delivering solutions for production problems.

They are

Visual Aids These aids are clear and show the work instructions. These may be pictograms in a user manual or a traffic sign that shows a restriction or warning.

Visual Control These refer to directing behaviour and warning in case of deviations. One example would be a traffic sign, that lights up red, when drivers are speeding and green, if they stick to the speed limit.

Fail Safes They force the user to either do or not do something. For instance, this can be road closures for motorway maintenance. Arrows on signs, force drivers to go from 3 to 2 and from 2 to 1 lanes. The arrows are followed by red Xs on the signs, until 2 of the 3 lanes are closed.

Cost of Quality

Cost of Quality is defined as a methodology, that allows an organisation to determine the extent to which its resources are used for activites, that prevent poor quality, that appraise the qaulity of the organisation's products or services and that result from internal and external failures. Having such information, allows an organisation to determine the potential savings to be gained, by implementing process improvements.

As defined by **Philip B Cosby** in his book, Quality is Fuel, the cost of quality has two main components i.e. cost of good quality (or the cost of conformance) and the cost of poor quality (or the cost of non-conformance).

- The cost of poor quality affects:
  internal and external costs, resulting from failing to meet requirements.
- The cost of good quality affects:
  (i) Cost for investing in the prevention of non-conformance to requirements.
  (ii) Costs for appraising a product or service for conformance to requirement.

The cost of quality is the cost of producing, finding, correcting and preventing defects. Quality costs are the total of the cost, incurred by investing in the prevention of non-conformances to requirements, appraising a product or service for conformance to requirements and failing to meet requirements.

Quality Cost Categories

Fegenbaum (1956) categorised quality cost into Prevention Appraisal Failure Costs (PAFC). The failure costs can be further classified into subcategories i.e. internal and external failure costs. This classification is widely used.

Prevention Cost

The cost of any action taken to investigate, prevent and reduce the risk of non-conformity or defect. Typical examples of prevention costs are quality training, quality assurance and quality planning. They are also incurred to prevent or avoid quality problems. These costs are associated with the design implementation and maintance of the quality management system. They are planned and incurred before actual operation.

They could include

Product or Service Requirements Establishment of specifications for incoming materials, processes, finished products and services.

Quality Planning Creation of plans for quality, reliability, operations, production and inspection.

Quality Assurance Creation and maintenance of the quality system.

Training Development, proparation and maintenance of programs. The cost of all activites, specifically designed to prevent poor quality of teachers and students. Examples may be cost of admission policy, review, selection process, facility induction and training policy review.

Appraisal Cost

The cost of evaluating the achievement of quality requirements including, cost of verification and control performed at any stage of the quality loop. Examples of appraisal cost are inspection, quality audits and acceptance tests. These costs are associated with the supplier's and customer's evaluation of purchased materials, processes, products and services to ensure that they conform to specifications.

They could include

Verification Checking of incoming material, process setup and products against agreed specifications.

Quality Audits Confirmation that the quality system is functioning, correctly.

Supplier Rating Assessment and approval of suppliers of products and services. The cost associated with measuring, evaluating or auditing students and teachers to assure conformance to quality standards and excellent academic performance requirements.

Failure Cost

The cost of failure is divided into two factors *i.e.* internal failure cost and external failure cost.

They can be explained as below:

Internal Failure Cost

The cost arising within an organisation, due to non-conformities or defects at any stage of the quality loop, such as cost of scrap, re-work, re-tests, re-inspection, re-design, scrap, replacement, rework and repair can be mentioned as typical examples of an internal failure.

External Failure Costs

External failure costs are incurred to remedy defects, discovered by customers. These costs occur when products or services that fail to reach design quality standards are not detected, until after transfer to the customers.

They could include:

Repairs and Servicing Both returned products and those in the field.

Warranty Claims Failed products that are replaced or services that are re-performed under a guarantee.

Complaints All work and costs associated with handling and servicing customer's complaints.

Returns Handling and investigating rejected or recalled products, including transport costs.

The cost may result from students, not confirming to the requirements of potential employers. Internal failure cost, occuring prior to the students getting out of the institution. For example, examination, testing, re-vieweing, coaching, counselling, etc. External failure cost may be the loss of institutional image, due to non-performance of the students in various organisations and blocking future prospects. An excellent education system should view itself as a learning organisation, where all employees are engaged in learning from world class research and development organisation, universities and corporate management development centres.

Cost Benefit Analysis

The term cost benefit analysis, implies a systematic comparison of the magnitude of the costs and benefits of some form of investment, in order to assess economic profitability. All forms of investment involve a sacrifice of the present consumption, in order to secure future benefits in the form of higher levels of output or income. It provides a means of appraising these future benefits in the light of the costs that must be incurred at present. The purpose of such analysis is to provide a measure of the expected yield of the investment, as a guide to the rational allocation of resources.

The importance of such analysis can be understood from its underlying assumptions, given as below

- Resources are scarce.
- These scarce resources can be used for alternative purposes.
- Decision makers want to use them in a rational way, *i.e.* where they provide the maximum benefit.
- Their costs and benefits can be measured.

It is used to address only those types of alternatives, where the outcomes can be measured in terms of their monetary values. For example, educational alternatives that are designed to raise productivity and income, such as vocational education, have outcomes that can be assessed in monetary terms and can be evaluated according to cost benefit analysis. However, most educational alternatives are dedicated to improving achievement or some other educational outcome that cannot be easily converted into monetary terms.

Cost of Education

For purposes of the cost benefit analysis of investment, it is necessary to define cost in terms of the total cost of a project, such as secondary education, *i.e.* all real resources that are used up by the project. These are called the opportunity costs, since every investment represents the sacrifice of alternative opportunities of using the resources either for present consumption or for some form of investment. There are other opportunity costs which accrue on account of the students' attending schools, instead of helping their parents in their occupations, like farming. Such opportunity costs are called foregone earnings and they are measured by what students could have earned, had they been employed. This cost item is also considered for calculating the total cost of education.

Benefits of Education

An important objective of investment in education is to identify and measure the benefits of education, which is more difficult than the measurement of costs. Just as there are private and social costs, there are also private and social benefits that accrue, *i.e.* benefits to the individual and those that accrue to the society. Further, there are also other non-economic benefits, the both to the individual and to society. If education is an investment, it contributes to future incomes by imparting skills and knowledge to the educated manpower, thus improving the productivity of labour.

If the productivity of the educated workers is higher than that of the uneducated workers, it will be reflected in a higher output and in higher earnings of the educated.

Therefore, we require an estimate of the additional life time earnings of the educated people. Ideally, these data should be collected by comparing the earnings of the educated and uneducated workers, over their whole working lives. Therefore, the usual practice is to use cross sectional data (data across various sections of earners at a particular point of time) to estimate an average age education *i.e.* earning profile for the workers of the same age with different levels of education and for workers of the same level of education with different age groups.

Cost Effective Analysis

It refers to the consideration of decision alternatives, in which both their costs and consequences are taken into account in a systematic way. It is a decision oriented tool it is designed to ascertain which means of attaining particular educational goals are most efficient. For example, there are many alternative approaches for pursuing such goals, as raising reading or mathematics achievement. These include the adoption of new materials or curriculum, teacher training, educational television, computer-assisted instruction, smaller class sizes and so on.

The cost effective solution to this challenge is to ascertain the costs and effects on reading or mathematics achievement of each alternative and to choose that alternative, which has the greatest impact on raising achievement scores, for any given resource outlay.

Purpose

The purpose of cost effective analysis in education is to ascertain which program or combination of programs, can achieve particular objectives at the lowest cost. The underlying assumption is that different alternatives are associated with different costs and different educational results. By choosing those with the least cost for a given outcome, society can use its resources more effectively.

Those resources that are saved through using more cost effective approaches, can be devoted to expanding programs or to other important educational and social endeavours.

Method

The method of doing cost effective analysis can be summarised briefly, but it is best to refer to more extensive treatments of the subject if a study is being contemplated. Cost effectiveness begins with a clear goal and a set of alternatives for reaching that goal. Comparisons can be made only for alternatives, that have similar goals, such as improvement of achievement in a particular subject or reduction in absenteeism or in dropouts.

A straight forward cost effectiveness analysis cannot compare options with different goals and objectives, any more than a standard type of evaluation could compare results in mathematics, with results in creative writing. Alternatives being assessed should be options for addressing a specific goal, where attainment of the goal can be measured by a common criterion such as an achievement test. It should be noted that a more complex, but related form of analysis and cost utility can be used to assess multiple objectives.

Educational Role

Methods of cost effectiveness analysis can assist the planner in evaluating educational programs. This concept should be broadened to include resource effectiveness analysis, which can be divided into two study areas i.e. resource analysis and analysis of effectiveness. Constructing a resource/cost model is suggested to handle the problems of resource allocation, by relating the programs to resources and costs. Defining and measuring the effectiveness of an educational program, must preceed the analysis of cost effectiveness of alternative programs. The complexity of the learning process requires the production of a set of measures or indicators.

Indian and International Quality Assurance Agencies

The National Assessment and Accreditation Council (NAAC) is India's premier higher education quality assurance agency. The NAAC quality assurance process has benefited from a thorough study of established accreditation mechanisms, worldwide. It is however, designed to meet the needs of one of the world's largest, most diverse and most complex systems of higher education, which comprises 17, 967 institutions catering to the needs of some 10.5 million students.

On international level, the International Network for Quality Assurance Agencies in Higher Education (INQAAHE) is a world wide association that is active in theory and practice of quality assurance in higher education. INQAAHE is a quality assurance community with shared interests, a common language and understanding of how things are done with regard to very specific field of work.

National Assessment Accreditation Council (NAAC)

Historical Overview of NAAC

The National Assessment and Accreditation Council (NAAC) is an autonomous body established by the University Grants Commission (UGC) of India to assess and accredit institutions of higher education in the country. It is an outcome of the recommendations of the National Policy of Education (1986) which laid special emphasis on upholding the quality of higher education in India.

To address the issues of quality, the National Policy of Education (1986) and the Programme of Action (POA, 1992) advocated the establishment of an independent national accreditation body. Consequently, the University Grants Commission established the NAAC in 1994 under its Article 12, CCC, as an autonomous body with its headquarters at Bengaluru.

NAAC as a premier quality assurance agency has always been responsive to the ever changing higher education scenario as well as stakeholder's requirements. The NAAC functions through its General Council (GC) and Executive Committee (EC) where educational administrators, policy makers and senior academicians from a cross section of the system of higher education are represented. The Chairperson of UGC is the President of GC of the NAAC, the Chairperson of the EC is an eminent academician in the area of relevance to the NAAC.

Objectives of NAAC

- Assess and accredit institutions of higher learning.
- Stimulate the academic environment and quality of teaching and research in accredited institutions.
- Generate awareness of quality in education.
- To embed self-assessment in the quality culture of the institution.
- Share information on successful quality strategies.
- Encourage innovations, self-evaluation and accountability in higher education.
- Help institutions to achieve self-actualization on institutional strengths and weaknesses.
- Focus on improvement of quality.
- Promote necessary changes, innovations and reforms in all aspects of the institutions for excellence.

Functions of NAAC

NAAC is entrusted with the primary function of assessing and accrediting higher education institutions of the country.

It entails the following

- Provide guidance to institutions for preparing their Self-Study Reports (SSRs).
- Preparing in house pre-visit documents for the perusal of assessors.
- Assessing and accrediting institutions.
- Coordinating the 'on-site' visit to its effective completion.
- Evolving appropriate instruments of accreditation and fine tuning them whenever necessary.
- Develop pre and post accreditation strategies.
- Identifying enlisting and creating a pool of efficient assessors.
- Providing appropriate training to assessors.

To supplement the functions of NAAC in addition to assessment and accreditation, it also undertakes the following functions

- Disseminates the NAAC process and quality enhancement mechanisms through relevant publications.
- Organizes seminars/workshops/conferences to share and discuss issues related to quality in higher education.
- Partner with stakeholders for promoting assessment and accreditation.
- Promotes the establishment of quality assurance units *i.e.*
  - (i) Internal Quality Assurance Cell (IQAC)
  - (ii) State Level Quality Assurance Cell (SLQAC)
- Establishes collaborations with other national and international professional agencies, involved in assessment and accreditation.

Role of NAAC

Role of NAAC in the changing scenario of higher education needs to be re-defined with respect to recognition cum accreditation, programme accreditation, national level ranking of universities, preparation of national benchmarks, national and international database, research and development centres, etc.

- Assessment and accreditation by NAAC may be made mandatory for all higher education institution of the country.
- NAAC may start programme accreditation.
- Ranking of institutions may not be very much relevant when compared to grading. All accreditation agencies, including NAAC are to be accredited once in three years.

- While NAAC could be accredited by recognized international accreditation bodies, NAAC could perform this function for all the multiple accreditation agencies getting recognized by Government of India.
- NAAC needs to continue to be an apex assessment and accreditation body for higher education institution, in the country providing vision and leadership.

Initiatives of NAAC

- Quality sustenance and promotion of sensitizing institutions to concepts, such as credit transfer, student's mobility and mutual recognition.
- Networking among accredited institutions in order to promote exchange of best practices.
- Formation of quality circle for follow-up of a accreditation outcomes.
- State-wise analysis of accreditation results for policy initiatives.
- Promoting the concept of lead colleges and cluster of colleges for quality initiatives.
- Project grants for accredited institutions for quality innovations.
- Financial support to accredited institution for conducting seminars/conferences/workshops on quality issues in higher education.
- NAAC and NCTE joint activity for self-appraised and accreditation of teacher education institutions.
- Interaction with other agencies to develop a National Qualification Framework.
- Training programmes for quality promotion and excellence in higher education.

Advantages of NAAC

- Helps the institutions to know strengths, weaknesses and opportunities, through an informed review.
- Identifies internal areas of planning and resource allocations.
- Enhances collegiality on the campus.
- The outcome of the process provides the funding agencies with objectives and systematic database for performance funding.
- Initiates institution into innovative and modern methods of pedagogy.
- Given the institution a new sense of direction and identity.
- Provides the society with reliable information on the quality of education, offered by the institution.
- Employers have access to information on standards in recruitment.
- Promotes inter-institutional and intra-institutional interactions.

Performance Indicators

They indicate what concrete actions the student should be able to perform as a result of participation in the program. Once program's outcomes have been identified, the knowledge and skills necessary for the mastery of these outcomes should be listed. This will allow the desired behaviour of the students to be described and will eliminate ambiguity concerning demonstration of expected competencies. Perfromance indicators and made up of at least two main elements *i.e.* action verb and content (referent). The expected behaviour must be specified by name, using an observable action verb, such as demonstrate, interpret, discriminate or define.

Sample performance indicators includes :

- Students will know a professional code of ethics (knowledge).
- Students will be able to describe the problem-solving process (comprehension).
- Students will solve research problems through the applications of scientific methods (applications).

Performance indicator is a type of performance measurement that helps you understand how your organization, department or institution is performing and it allows us to understand if we are headed in the right direction with our strategy.

In education, performance indicators are classified as follows

Academia or Academics

Graduation Rate It determines the number of students who completed their schooling or received a particular certificate or degree within the normal time frame.

Awards This looks at the number of awards granted to students or faculty during each academic calender year.

Research grants This examines the percentage of the grants students or faculty received versus those that were applied for.

Student's Attendance Rate Determining the number of students that have achieved say 90% attendance during a given semester or academic year is vital to track.

Finance

Percentage of Students or Aid It calculates the number of students receiving some kind of financial assistance, like scholarship, money or government aid.

Tuition Cost It examines the cost to each student in a given scholastic timeline to attend the institutiion.

Ratios

Student to Faculty Ratio Schools may want to examine this ratio to ensure that the students are receiving proper attention.

Faculty to Administration Ratio If this ratio is too low, like if you have only two administrators for 50 faculty members there may be issues with scheduling, organization and finances.

Curriculum

Proficiency Rates for Each Subject This allows us to see not just how our curriculum breaks down, but how each area of curriculum is performing.

Faculty

Number of Training Sessions Per Year Ensuring faculty members are in touch with the latest teaching methods or technologies help ensure that students receive the best educational experience.

Faculty and Staff Attendance If the institution has a low attendance rate from faculty and staff members, this can have a negative impact on the organization as a whole.

Technology

Percentage of Classes Using Technology A high percentage of classes are using technologies or online platforms that have been provided to them

Percentage of Administrators Using Technology Both teachers and administrators should be using the online or classroom based technologies they have been provided for lessons, projects or activities and the percentage will help whether that is happening or not.

Facilities

Classroom Utilization Rate It examines whether we are making the best use of campus space and keeping class as full as possible.

Quality Council of India (QCI)

Quality Council of India (QCI) was set up in 1997, as an autonomous body. It was setup jointly by the Government of India and the Indian industry, represented by the three premier industry associations *i.e.*

- Associated Chambers of Commerce and Industry of India (ASSOCHAM)
- Confederation of Indian Industry (CII)
- Federation of Indian Chambers of Commerce and Industry (FICCI)

It aims to establish and operate national accreditation structure and promote quality through National Quality Campaign.

The Department of Industrial Policy and Promotion and Ministry of Commerce and Industry, are the nodal ministries for QCI. Chairman of QCI is appointed by the Prime Minister, on recommendation of the industry to the government.

Objectives of QCI

- To establish and maintain an accreditation structure, in the country.
- To provide right and unbiased information on quality related standards.
- To spread quality movement in the country through National Quality Campaign.
- To facilitate upgradation of equipments and techniques, related to quality.
- To represent India's interest in international forums .
- To help establish brand equity of Indian products and services.

They become the world's leading national apex quality facilitation, accreditation and surveillance organisations, to continuously improve the climate, systems, processes and skills for total quality.

It also focuses on helping India achieve and sustain total quality and reliability, in all areas of life, work, environment, products and services, at individual, organisational, community and societal levels.

Roles of QCI

- To Promote quality improvement.
- To set goals and time frames.
- To make recommendations to the executive staff.
- To monitor progress, success and areas for improvement.
- To provide technical assistance with quality improvement projects.
- To promote communication about quality improvement effort throughout the organisation.
- To provide an annual written report on activities, accomplishments and future projects.

International Network for Quality Assurance Agencies in Higher Education (INQAAHE)

The International Network for Quality Assurance Agencies in Higher Education (INQAAHE) is a world-wide association of organisations that is active in the theory and practice of Quality Assurance (QA) in Higher Education (HE). The greater majority of its members are Quality Assurance Agencies (QAA) (as full members), that operate in many different ways.

However, it also welcomes other organisations (as associate members), that have an interest in QA in HE, and individuals with major interest in HE (as affiliates). Thus, INQAAHE offers its members the many benefits of being part of such an active group of workers in QA in HE.

It was established in 1991, with only 8 members. Today the total membership exceeds 300 members.

Distance education as well as vocational education have become increasingly more important, as is the need for recognition of prior learning. HE has become more global, than ever before.

Professional accreditation has become more important as more Higher Education Institutions (HEIs), delivering programs in different modes, enter the market. All these have thrust an QA agencies, into ever expanding roles.

INQAAHE is a QA community, with shared interests, a common language and an understanding of how things are done, with regard to a very specific field of work. It provides a forum for the discussion of global issues that go beyond national or regional boundaries, such as cross border education. Members have the opportunity to learn from what others are doing, both from their successes and failures and thus, have now set the ground for the development of a QA profession.

Aims of INQAAHE

The central purpose and role of INQAAHE is to promote and advance excellence in higher education, through the support of an active international community of quality assurance agencies. In order to achieve this goal, the network focuses on the development of the theory and practice of quality assurance, the exchange and understanding of the policies and actions of its members and the promotion of quality assurance for the benefit of higher education, institutions, students and society at large.

Values of INQAAHE

Fundamental to the work of the INQAAHE, the key values that support the policy and practice of quality assurance are as follows

- Recognition of the value of the collective wisdom, gathered from the practices of a diverse set of members and their ability to address the challenges of the educational and social structures, in which they operate. INQAAHE celebrates this diversity, which has also made it possible to identify and highlight commonalities and fundamental principles, that underpin good practice and guide the operation of Quality Assurance (QA) agencies.
- Belief in the primacy of academic freedom and institutional integrity and a commitment to the idea that quality and quality assurance are primarily the responsibility of higher education institutions, themselves.
- A fundamental understanding of the importance of working in partnership among members, with higher education institutions, regional, international government and non-government organisations, as well as the business sector, in order to provide member support, guidance, information and advocacy for quality assurance.

Objectives of INQAAHE

- To create, collect and disseminate information on current and developing theory and practice in the assessment, improvement and maintenance of quality in higher education.
- To undertake or commission research, in areas relevant to quality in higher education.
- To express the collective views of its members on matters relevant to quality in higher education, through contacts with international bodies and by other means.
- To promote the theory and practice of the improvement of quality in higher education.
- To provide advice and expertise, to assist existing and emerging quality assurance agencies.
- To facilitate links between quality assurance agencies and support networks of quality assurance agencies.
- To assist members, to determine the standards of institutions operating across national borders and facilitate better informed international recognition of qualifications.
- To assist in the development and use of credit transfer and credit accumulation schemes, to enhance the mobility of students between institutions (within and across national borders).
- To enable members, to be alert to improper quality assurance practices and organisations. To organise, on request, reviews of the operation of members.

EXAM BASED QUESTIONS

1 In what manner, change effects the business environment?
(a) Internal (b) External
(c) Both a and b (d) Neither a nor b

2 At what level, does change effect an individual?
(a) Leader and employer (b) Employees and students
(c) Organisational level (d) Infinite level

3 What is crucial point of management of change?
(a) When the situation is critical
(b) When there are lot of employees
(c) When people face issues
(d) When everyone is getting desired goals

4 If any kind of change is implemented in an organisation, who all will be affected by it?
(a) Some employees (b) Whole organisation
(c) Head of the organisation (d) All of these

5 What is meant by planned change?
(a) Strategy (b) Strategic change
(c) Dependent change (d) Vocational change

6 Which theory is developed by Larry E Greiner?
(a) Operational theory
(b) Organisational Protocol theory
(c) Organisational Development theory
(d) Static Formulation of Organisation theory

7 What are the five stages of growth, according to Greiner's Model of Change?
(a) Creativity, Direction, Dedication, Collaboration, Concept
(b) Create, Dictate, Delegate, Collaborate and Control
(c) Direction, Concept, Collaborate, Creativity and Delegation
(d) Collaboration, Delegation, Direction, Creativity and Control

8 Who among the following, first established the Organisational Management of Change?
(a) Edward Deming (b) Kurt Lewin
(c) Walter Shewart (d) C K Prahlad

9 What are the three steps of Lewin Model of Change?
(a) Freeze, Change and Refreeze
(b) Unfreeze, Move and Freeze
(c) Unfreeze, Change and Refreeze
(d) Refruze, Unfreeze and Movement

10 At which stage, it was realised that the change is necessary?
(a) Freezing (b) Change (c) Refreezing (d) Unfreezing

11 In change state, which among the two plays a crucial role for the success?
1. Time 2. Space
3. Organisation 4. Communication
Choose the correct option.
(a) 1 and 3 (b) 2 and 4 (c) 1, 3 and 4 (d) 1 and 4

12 Which stage is responsible for making people and the organisation, internalising change?
(a) Change (b) Refreeze
(c) Freeze (d) None of these

13 Which model of change is most renowned in the understanding of theories, related to change?
(a) Korean Model
(b) Three Line Model
(c) Japanese Model of Change
(d) Freezing Model of Change

14 What is Just-In-Time model?
(a) Strategic supply of raw material to suppliers
(b) Arrangement of raw material
(c) Production of quality products
(d) All of the above

15 What is the method required, for success of Just-In-Time model?
(a) Forecast demand, accurately
(b) Good suppliers
(c) Huge bulk, company orders
(d) High demand of products

16 Which company first implemented this model?
(a) Toyota (b) Reliance (c) Toyata (d) Huawei

17 Who is referred as a father of Just-In-Time model?
(a) Osho (b) Taiichi Ohno
(c) John Lei (d) Hua Wei

18 Explain the meaning of the word 'Poka Yoke'?
(a) Change in environment (b) Organisational change
(c) Error prevention (d) Change enhancement

19 Who developed the word 'Poka Yoke'?
(a) Shi Chang (b) Shigeo Shingo
(c) Shewart (d) Sharlin

20 What is the relevance of this model?
(a) To solve pre-production issues
(b) Looking after manufacturing defects
(c) Proper supply of law materials
(d) To resolve defects, during the production process

21 In how many stages, the Poka Yoke model can be explained?
(a) Three (b) Five (c) Four (d) Two

22 In which type of Poka Yoke, we can see the work instructions?
(a) Audio aid (b) Fail safes
(c) Visual control (d) Visual aid

23 In Just-In-Time production system, a production operation is authorised
(a) when an authorisation is obtained from downstream
(b) when the production worker is at the work station
(c) when the leader is ready
(d) when the inventory level of the work station reaches zero

24 Which of the following concept is incompatible with Just-In-Time model?
(a) Local optimisation
(b) The Economic Order Quantity Model
(c) Inspect once, at the end of the process
(d) All of the above

25 Cost incurred for defective products, after their shipment to customers is classified as
(a) prevention cost (b) external failure cost
(c) appraisal cost (d) internal failure cost

26 Which book was written by Philip B Crosby?
(a) Quality is Fuel (b) Quality and Quantity
(c) Different Quality (d) None of these

27 Incurred cost to exclude production of goods that do not meet specification, are called
(a) rework cost (b) prevention cost
(c) incremental cost (d) re-engineering cost

28 Costs that are incurred to find manufactured products,which does not meet specifications are called
(a) prevention cost (b) external failure costs
(c) appraisal costs (d) internal failure costs

29 Costs incurred for defective products, before their shipment to customers, can be categorised as
(a) prevention costs (b) external failure costs
(c) appraisal costs (d) internal failure costs

30 Costs that are incurred to prevent low quality goods production are classified as
(a) costs of quality (b) costs of learning
(c) costs of re-engineering (d) costs of spoilage inventory

31 In which analysis, both cost and consequence are considered?
(a) Cost Benefit Analysis (b) Cost Effective Analysis
(c) Cost Efficient Analysis (d) Cost Deductive Analysis

32 What can be analysed through Cost Benefit Analysis?
(a) Function of organisation (b) Raw material
(c) Output (d) Monetary importance

33 The accreditation process by National Assessment and Accreditation Council (NAAC) differs from that of National Board of Accreditation (NBA), in terms of
(a) disciplines covered by both being the same, there is duplication of efforts.
(b) one has institutional grading approach and the other has programme grading approach.
(c) once get accredited by NAAC or NBA, the institution is free from renewal of grading, which is not a progressive decision.
(d) this accreditation amounts to approval of minimum standards in the quality of education in the institution concerned.

34 NAAC is an autonomus, under the agency of
(a) ICSSR (b) CSIR (c) AICTE (d) UGC

35 Who has signed MOU, for quality education?
(a) NAAC (b) UGC (c) NCTE (d) None of these

36 Who was appointed as Director of National Assessment and Accreditation Council (NAAC)?
(a) Prof. Jagdish Kumar (b) Mr. Deepak Dantal
(c) Mr. Yogendra Alagh (d) Prof. S.C. Sharma

37 In which year, Quality Council of India was setup as an autonomous body?
(a) 1993 (b) 1998 (c) 1997 (d) 2001

38 Who appoints the Chairman of Quality Council of India?
(a) Member of QCI (b) Prime Minister
(c) President (d) ASSOCHAM Head

39 Who presents the Indian interest in international forum?
(a) Quality Bureau (b) Quality Council of India
(c) NAAC (d) FICCI

40 What is the major significance of INQAAHE?
(a) Practice quality assurance
(b) Prepare reports
(c) Look for quality check
(d) Cost beneficial parameters

41 Which organisation was established in 1991?
(a) NAAC (b) QCI (c) INQAAHE (d) FICCI

42 Who is not included in the INQAAHE?
(a) All India Council of Technical Education (AICTE)
(b) Indian Nursing Council (INC)
(c) NAAC
(d) National Metals Laboratory (NML)

43 Where is NAAC's headquarter located?
(a) New Delhi (b) Bengaluru (c) Indore (d) Ahmedabad

44 Which among the following is normally the cause of organisational change?
(a) Technological development
(b) Change in labour characteristics
(c) Mergers, acquisition, etc
(d) All of the above

45 What do you mean by the term 'strategic change'?
(a) The changes that inevitably result in organisations, as they inolve in a changing environment
(b) The proactive management of change, to achieve strategic objectives
(c) An important organisational change
(d) Planned change

46 Which of the following area is not one of the four key areas that strategic change seeks to influence?
(a) Formal organisational structures
(b) Technolgoy
(c) People
(d) Informal organisational structure

47 Which of the following is not one of the stage of Kurt Lewin's model?
(a) Unfreezing current attitudes (b) Melting resistance
(c) Refreezing attitutdes at the new level
(d) Moving to a new level

48 Which of the following will not affect the choice of strategic change programme?
(a) Leadership style (b) Nature of organisation
(c) Government policy (d) Culture

49 Which of the following is not a way of overcoming resistance to change?
(a) Bullying and harassing people into towing the line
(b) Communication and discussion
(c) Using symbols, to signify a new era
(d) Involving those, who resist in the change process
(e) Incentives

50 Which of the following is not emphasised in the learning approach?
(a) Individual learning
(b) The sharing of views and visions for the future
(c) People's skills
(d) System's thinking

51 Match the following.

List I	List II
A. Cost Effective Analysis	1. Optimisation of cost advantages
B. Quality assurance	2. Special improvement in education
C. Compulsory capital	3. Part of the quality cost
D. Evaluation money	4. Inspection and review

Codes

	A	B	C	D
(a)	2	1	3	4
(b)	3	1	2	4
(c)	1	2	4	3
(d)	1	2	3	4

52 Match the following.

List I	List II
A. Cost of failure	1. Receipt of infinite defects
B. Poka Yoke	2. The results of defective tasks
C. Just-In-Time	3. Quality measurement
D. Evaluation Cost	4. Content improvement process

Codes

	A	B	C	D
(a)	2	3	4	1
(b)	3	2	1	4
(c)	2	1	4	3
(d)	2	1	3	4

53 Match the following.

List I	List II
A. Indian Quality Council	1. Quality check
B. National Assessment Replacing Council	2. Formulated on PPP Model
C. Failure cost	3. Undefective Educational Policy
D. Quality cost	4. Dissinvestment prevention cost

Codes

	A	B	C	D
(a)	2	1	3	4
(b)	1	2	3	4
(c)	1	2	4	3
(d)	4	2	1	3

54 Match the following.

List I	List II
A. Poka Yoke	1. Shigeo Shingo
B. Quality Check	2. Figambana
C. Three Step model	3. Kurt Lewin
D. Just-In-Time model	4. Planort

Codes

	A	B	C	D
(a)	2	1	3	4
(b)	3	4	2	1
(c)	1	2	3	4
(d)	4	3	1	2

55 Just In Time Production System would not include emphasis on
1. the quality of individual output
2. producing products, as needed by the next stage
3. decentralisation of support system
4. production should be restricted

Chosse the correct option.
(a) Only 1 (b) Only 3 (c) 1 and 3 (d) 2 and 3

56 Which of the following statement(s) is/are true, with respect to Just-In-Time Model?
1. Place emphasis on simplification
2. Provide more accurate product costs than traditional system
3. Emphasise quality improvement
4. Emphasise production unit

Codes
(a) Only 1 (b) 2 and 3
(c) All of these (d) None of these

57 Which of the following core values, among the institutions of higher education are promoted by the NAAC?
1. Contributing to national development
2. Fostering global competencies, among the students
3. Inculcating values, among students and teachers
4. Promoting the optimum utilisation of the infrastructure

Choose the correct option.
(a) 2, 3 and 4 (b) 1, 2 and 3
(c) 1, 3 and 4 (d) 1, 2, 3 and 4

58 Which among them is/are the major purpose(s) of INQAAHE?
1. Create 2. Collect
3. Disseminate 4. Corporate

Codes
(a) Only 1 (b) 1 and 4 (c) 2 and 4 (d) 1, 2 and 3

59 Match the following.

List I (Institutes)	List II (Years)
A. NAAC	1. 1997
B. QCI	2. 1991
C. INQAAHE	3. 1994

Codes

	A	B	C
(a)	2	3	1
(b)	1	3	2
(c)	3	2	1
(d)	3	1	2

60 Match the following.

List I	List II
A. Unfreezing change	1. Permanent form of change
B. Moving change	2. Small scale development
C. Refreezing change	3. Dynamic change
D. Just-In-Time	4. First level of change

Codes

	A	B	C	D		A	B	C	D
(a)	3	2	4	1	(b)	4	3	1	2
(c)	4	3	2	1	(d)	1	2	3	4

Directions (Q. Nos. 61-72) *Below are two statements, one labelled as Assertion (A) and other labelled as Reason (R). In the context of the two statements, which one of the following is correct?*

Codes

(a) Both A and R are true and R is the correct explanation of A
(b) Both A and R are true, but R is not the correct explanation of A
(c) A is true, but R is false
(d) A is false, but R is true

61 **Assertion** (A) Change management is a systematic approach to organisation's goals, procedures and academic change.

Reason (R) Change management is a discipline, which provides special guidance for organisational success and good result.

62 **Assertion** (A) Change in education is based on innovation, whose good result is far sighted.

Reason (R) Globalisation contributed well to the educational society, India is far behind in attaining goal.

63 **Assertion** (A) Under the influence of privatisation, change in education world is under the planned change system.

Reason (R) System employed is considered to be fully systematic, with the change in the qualitative nature of education.

64 **Assertion** (A) The concept of cost effectiveness is applicable to planning and management of a variety of organised activities.

Reason (R) Generally, Cost Effective Analysis is expressed in the context of a ratio.

65 **Assertion** (A) Cost Benefit Analysis model was first used by Lewin.

Reason (R) He considered the first level as unfreezing change, under which the need for change is accepted.

66 **Assertion** (A) Poka Yoke is a Japanese model of one Change.

Reason (R) The Poka Yoke Model helps to do right thing, in the first place.

67 **Assertion** (A) Performance indicators are made up of two main elements.

Reason (R) Students will solve research problems through applications of scientific problems through application of scientific methods.

68 **Assertion** (A) Quality council of India promotes quality improvement.

Reason (R) It is not mandatory to promote quality improvement.

69 **Assertion** (A) INQAAHE is a quality assurance community.

Reason (R) It facilitates research into practice of quality management.

70 **Assertion** (A) Time and communication are the two keys to the change.

Reason (R) People need time to understand change with better communication.

71 **Assertion** (A) Performance indicators indicate concrete actions the student should be able to perform.

Reason (R) Students will know a professional code of ethics.

72 **Assertion** (A) Cost Benefit Analysis implies a systematic comparison of the magnitude of the costs and benefits of some form of investment.

Reason (R) The purpose of such analysis is to provide a measure of the expected yield of the investment.

ANSWERS

1 (c)	2 (b)	3 (a)	4 (b)	5 (b)	6 (c)	7 (d)	8 (b)	9 (c)	10 (d)
11 (d)	12 (b)	13 (c)	14 (a)	15 (a)	16 (c)	17 (b)	18 (c)	19 (b)	20 (d)
21 (b)	22 (d)	23 (a)	24 (d)	25 (b)	26 (a)	27 (b)	28 (c)	29 (b)	30 (a)
31 (b)	32 (d)	33 (b)	34 (d)	35 (a)	36 (d)	37 (c)	38 (b)	39 (b)	40 (a)
41 (c)	42 (c)	43 (b)	44 (d)	45 (b)	46 (b)	47 (b)	48 (c)	49 (a)	50 (a)
51 (d)	52 (c)	53 (a)	54 (c)	55 (a)	56 (c)	57 (b)	58 (d)	59 (d)	60 (b)
61 (b)	62 (c)	63 (a)	64 (b)	65 (d)	66 (a)	67 (b)	68 (c)	69 (b)	70 (a)
71 (b)	72 (a)								

CHAPTER 38

Inclusive Education

Inclusive education is a new approach towards educating the children with disability and learning difficulties with that of normal ones under the same roof. It advocates that special children with special needs have to be educated along with normal peers in the regular classrooms. India has advocated the implementation of inclusive education supported by relevant policies, legal enactments, schemes, programmes and plans.

Meaning of Inclusive Education

Inclusive education is about ensuring access to quality education for all students by effectively meeting their diverse needs in a way that is responsive, accepting, respectful and supportive. Students participate in an education program in a common learning environment with support to diminish and remove barriers and obstacles that may lead to an exclusion. Inclusive education is carried out in a common learning environment, that is educational setting where students from different backgrounds and with different abilities learn together in an inclusive environment. A common learning environment is not a place where students with intellectual disabilities or other special needs learn in isolation from their peers.

The efforts of Government of India over the last five decades have been towards providing comprehensive range of services towards education of children with disabilities. In 1974, the centrally sponsored scheme for Integrated Education for Disabled Children (IEDC) was introduced to provide equal opportunities to children with disabilities in general schools and facilitates their retention.

In almost every country, inclusive education has been emerged as one of the most dominant issue in education. With the release of the Salamanca Statement in 1994 (UNESCO), a large number of developing countries started reformulating their policies to promote inclusion of student with disabilities into mainstream schools.

The researchers show that teachers in inclusive settings collaborate more and spend more time in planning, learning new techniques from one another, participate in more professional development activities and use a wider range of creative strategies to meet student's needs.

In this Chapter

The Principle of Inclusive Education was adopted at the "World Conference of Special Needs Education : Assess and Quality" and was restated at the 'World Education Forum'. Inclusive education is defined as the process of addressing the diverse needs of all learners by reducing barriers to and within the learning environment. It is a process of strengthening the capacity of education system to reach out to all the learners.

It is a new approach towards educating the children with disability and learning difficulties with that of normal ones under the same roof. It refers to an education system that accommodates all children regardless of their physical, intellectual, social, emotional, linguistic or other conditions. The range of challenges confronting the school system while including children with diverse abilities and from diverse backgrounds have to be met by creating a child-centered pedagogy capable of successfully educating all children. Inclusive class may have amongst others, children with disability or gifted children, street or working children, children from remote or nomadic populations, children belonging to ethnic, linguistic or cultural minorities or children from other disadvantaged or marginalised groups.

Inclusive education is about restructuring the cultures, policies and practices in schools so that they respond to the diversity of students in their locality.

In recent years, the concept of inclusive education has been broadened to encompass not only students with disabilities, but also all students who may be disadvantaged.

Inclusion describes much more than the acceptance of children with disabilities/exceptionalities in the mainstream. Inclusive education programmes do not form on an accommodation of these children into a general education setting, but are focused on the reconstructing of schools to accept and provide for the needs of all students. In other words, no discrimination is made among the exceptional and non-exceptional children.

All the children in all shades of their exceptionality are welcome by making necessary arrangements and accommodations for their education in the same school and class along with their non-disabled peers.

Definitions of Inclusive Education

According to **Michael F. Giangreco**, "Inclusive education is a set of values, principles and practices that seeks more effective and meaningful education for all students, regardless of whether they have exceptionality labels or not".

In the words of **Stainback & Stainback**, "Inclusive education or setup may be defined as a place where everyone belongs, is accepted, supports and supported by his/her peers and other members of the school community in the course of having his/her educational needs met".

Nature of Inclusive Education

- It works on the Principle of Inclusion i.e. including all. So, all the students are included in this system of education in their local schools.
- Exceptional children may get unique opportunities to get education with peers in the same age group available to those without exceptionality.
- It aims to integrate and include education of the disabled children with the general system of education so that education of the disabled and non-disabled may proceed side by side by fulfiling the needs and objectives of both the groups without any differentiation.
- It tries to bring desired educational opportunities at the doorstep of exceptional children rather than expecting from them, to none and try for themselves to avail these opportunities.
- Inclusion provides a foundation for exceptional in way that are not possible in special schools and classes.

Principles of Inclusive Education

Principle of Teaching all Students Students learn in different ways, so it is important to develop the skills to teach in different ways. For example, some students learn best when introduced to an information visually, while others learn best through hearing information, working in groups or activity based projects.

Principle of Choosing Appropriate Material According to this principle, it is important to choose books and materials that reflect image of diverse people. Primary sources should be used for selecting an appropriate material, relevant to a topic.

Principle of Exploring Multiple Identities Building confidence and affirming identity for students, supports their learning.

Some ways to affirm and encourage students' identities are

- Creating activities that help students to talk about and feel pride in themselves.
- Engaging students in projects.
- Maintaining a respectful environment among the students, where they learn to respect each other's opinion.

Principle of Teaching and Learning About Cultures It is important that student learns about others' cultures and religions in a positive manner. Student should be given an opportunities to learn about the ever changing cultures of the world.

Principle of Adopting and Integrating Lessons Properly It is important for an educator to be flexible in the adaptation of all the lessons in curriculum. If a lesson is pre-designed, it is always a good starting point. It should provide meaningful opportunities for students to present their beliefs and relate it to their personal experiences.

Principle of Promoting Social Justice A teacher should promote social justice in the classroom, in terms of equality for all. In classroom, all students, should be considered equal, irrespective of their differences and they should be made to learn social justice and equality for all. Students should be encouraged to develop a sense of civic responsibility.

Characteristics of Inclusive Education

- It involves valuing all students equally.
- It increases the participation of students and reduces their exclusion from the cultures, curricula and communities of local schools/colleges.
- It acknowledges the right of students to get an education in their locality.
- It emphasises on the role of schools in community development as well as in increasing achievements.
- It provides least restrictive and most effective environment to disabled children, so that they may develop like normal children.
- It is a viable approach to attain the goals of universalization of elementary education by providing equality of education and development opportunities to the disabled who have been denied equality so far.
- It is a flexible education system that assimilates the needs of diverse range of learners and adapts itself to meet these needs.

Scope of Inclusive Education

There have been efforts internationally to include children with disabilities in educational mainstream. In order to achieve truly inclusive education, we need to think about and incorporate children with special needs into regular schools. In effective inclusive programs, teachers adapt activities to include all the students, even though their individual goals may be different. Its scope will increase when most of the students learn and perform better when exposed to the richness of the general education curriculum. Inclusion provides an opportunities to develop relationships.

Classmates of students with disabilities also experience growth in social cognition often can become more aware of the needs of others in an inclusive classroom. Inclusive education helps the disabled child to develop a sense of pride in their work because they actually feel like they have accomplished something. Educating children with disabilities, along with their non-disabled peers is considered to be one of the best way to provide education to the mass population.

Importance of Inclusive Education

- Inclusion in education involves the process of increasing the participation of students in and reducing their exclusion from the cultures, curricula and communities of local schools.
- Inclusion involves restructuring the cultures, policies and practices in schools, so that they respond to the diversity of students in their locality.
- Inclusion is concerned with the learning and participation of all students vulnerable to exclusionary pressures not only those with impairments or those who are categorised *i.e.* having special educational needs.
- Inclusion is concerned with improving schools for staff as well as for students.
- A concern with overcoming barriers to the access and participation of particular student may reveal gaps in the attempt of a school to respond to diversity more generally.
- All students have a right to education in their locality. Diversity is not viewed as a problem to be overcome, but as a rich resource to support the learning for all.
- Inclusion is concerned with fostering mutually sustaining relationship between schools and communities.
- Inclusion in education is one aspect of inclusion in the society.

Benefits of Inclusive Education

- It develops a sense of belongingness and become better prepared for life in the community.
- It encourages the involvement of parents in education of their children.
- It fosters a culture of respect and provides opportunity to learn about and accepts individual differences.
- It provides better opportunities for learning and improving the quality of education for all.
- It can help to overcome discrimination and promotes wider inclusion.

So, it helps in improving the quality of education for all, which will be beneficial for each section of the society. It will also overcome the problem of discrimination as inclusive education provides equal opportunities to both disabled and non-disabled persons.

Target Groups in Inclusive Education

Target groups are broadly understood as those whose educational needs are not significantly addressed by regular or mainstream literacy provisions. Certain children face unique circumstances that prevent them or make their attempt to realize their potential more difficultly. Those groups of children and youth suffers from societal indifferences or neglection.

Generally, learning problems we know can be due to environmental, cultural, economical deprivation, etc. They need special services to realize their potential, such as inclusive classroom setup. These groups and their families are referred by a number of different terms including educationally, culturally and socially disadvantage or deprived people.

Diverse Learners

Today's learners are more diverse than ever. A single classroom may contain students who have sensory motor, cognitive or learning disabilities, mental health or behaviour issues and differences in native language, culture and background knowledge. Studies have found that in inclusive classroom set up, the children are more compassionate, have better social skills and higher self-esteem. Children exhibit patience with slow learners and more ease with people who are disabled.

So, inclusive education is an educational concept of instructional methods, materials, activities and is evaluation of procedures is an effort to assist individuals with wide differences in their abilities to see, hear, speak, move, read, write, understand, attend, organise, engage and remember in a common classroom setup.

Marginalised Groups

The marginalised groups include women, youth and children residing in slums and bearing the greatest brunt of social inclusion. Inclusive learning programs are tailored to meet the needs of respective groups. Teacher has to play a significant role in a deeper analysis of student's background, their economical circumstances as well as their character, traits and health condition. This should be done in the initial stage, using all available resources in the coordination with other relevant school factors.

Teacher has to adjust the syllabus, activities and classroom's atmosphere towards the reduction of exclusion in the best possible manner. This will require a multi-sided approach and a lot of efforts on the side of the teacher as a classroom's mediator and negotiator and will often be directed towards the parents as well, as they may have crucial influence upon the performance of their children in many circumstances, involving marginalisation.

Learners with Disabilities

Learners with disabilities face multiple forms of discrimination which leads to their exclusion from society and school. Attitude towards children with disabilities, as well as lack of resources to accommodate them compound the challenges they face in accessing education. To ensure quality education for children with disabilities promote accessible and inclusive learning spaces. The preparation and orientation of teachers for inclusion should happen through teacher's training which besides the child-centered pedagogy will also address attitude towards children with disabilities and how to prepare/support families for them to be encouraged and keep their children in school and about their children's potential.

Children with disabilities should be educated with non-disabled children and have access to the general education curriculum. Government policies can improve the understanding and visibility of learning disabilities through explicit targeting initiatives to identify, assess and provide academic intervention and support to population learning with disabilities while offering pre-service teachers specialised training. Inclusive education to students with disabilities have shown positive results as by being included them in regular school. They tend to show more confident and display qualities of self-efficacy.

Evolution of the Philosophy Inclusive Education

The Government of India is constitutionally committed to ensures the rights of every child to basic education. In 1947, the government has created numerous policies around special education. Then in 1980s, the Ministry of Welfare realized the crucial need of an institution to monitor and regulate HRD programmes in the field of disability rehabilitation. Till 1990's, 90% of India's estimated 40 million children in the age group of 4 to 16 years with physical and mental disabilities are being excluded from the mainstream education.

In the late 90s (*i.e.* in 1997), the Philosophy of Inclusive Education is added in District Primary Education Programme (DPEP). This programme laids special emphasis on integration of children with mild to moderate disabilities and became one of the Government of India's largest flagship programmes of the time in terms of funding with 40,000 million rupees.

After this, **Sarva Shiksha Abhiyan** was launched to achieve the goal of universalization of education in 2001. Furthermore, in 2005, the Ministry of Human

Resource Development, implemented a National Action Plan for inclusion in education of children and youth with disabilities. The Government of India has demonstrated that it is committed to equalising educational opportunities for all children, including those with disabilities.

In the philosophy of education, the terms like special education, integrated education and inclusive education evolved and change with time and the prevailing learning situations. *Let us discuss these terms in detail*

Special Education

Special Education is a separate system of education for disabled children outside the mainstream education. It was based on the assumption that children with disability had some special needs, that could not be met in mainstream schools. Therefore, they need to study in a separate school with other children having similar needs. Special education in India was evolved in the 1880's and special schools are generally organized to different disabled categories. Children are taught by specialist having expertise on specific impairments, their needs may sometimes be understood better. In a special school, children grow up with their disability peers and develops a common culture.

Special education requires three elements and they are

- Trained Professionals including teachers, educationists and physiotherapists.
- Special curriculum made for students with different disabilities.
- Infrastructure facilities, like building features, study places, materials and equipments.

The major disadvantage is that it promotes separate environment because special schools are usually not available in an immediate environment. Due to these issues, another concept of integrated education, came into existence in 1986, after the recommendation of National Policy of Education.

Integrated Education

In integrated education, the child is seen as a problem and not as a system. He/she is considered to be different from others and if he/she cannot learn, it is his/her problem.

In this way, instead of subjecting the disabled students to a sort of segregation by putting them in separate special schools for their education, their integration (association) with the non-disabled population of their peers was targeted to achieve through this New Philosophy of Integration. Thus, it can be safely called a proper step in putting a disabled children into the mainstream i.e. the place and the opportunities of getting education and the training with the population of the non-disabled peers in the regular schools.

The concept of integrated education, arises as a outcome of National Policy of Education, 1986 recommended equal opportunities to all not only for access but also for success.

Integration signifies the process of interaction of disabled with normal children in the same educational setting. It inculcates affection, love and respect for disabled children among normal children.

It is less expensive and does not requires special infrastructure. Whereas, it is impossible to construct special schools with a wide selection of educational paths. But in order to ensure proper functioning of integrated education, it is necessary to establish centres for technical aids, teaching aids, etc. In many developing countries, it may be difficult or even impossible to establish this kind of services. It demands a good system of registration of the visually handicapped and an effective communication, something which is lacking in many countries.

Inclusive Education

Inclusion is a term which expresses commitment to educate each child to the maximum extent, appropriate in the school and the classroom, he/she would otherwise attend.

It involves bringing the support services to the child (rather than moving the child to the services) and requires only that the child will benefit from being in the class (rather than having to keep up with the other students). Proponents of inclusion, generally favours newer forms of education service delivery.

The era of inclusive settings i.e. educating all types of children whether exceptional or normal together in the regular classes of the mainstream schools, represents the modern era and latest development in the history of special/disability education.

Apart from dissatisfaction with continuation of special classes in the regular schools, a new way of change in the name of upholding human right providing equity and equality of educational opportunities to all children, gave birth to a strong build up in favour of inclusion *i.e.* placement of exceptional children in regular classrooms without discrimination of any sort.

The goal of inclusive education is to widen access to education and to promote full participation and opportunities for all learners to realize their potential. Use of cooperative learning and collaborative problem-solving strategies, to meet the diverse needs of all learners without labelling or categorizing them is consistent with inclusive principles.

The promotion of quality in inclusive education requires a clear stated policy. Policies that aim to promote quality in inclusive education takes account of international level policies and initiatives and are also flexible enough to reflect local level needs. To implement inclusive education, the goals of the policy should be effectively communicated to all members of an educational community. Arrangements for monitoring the implementation of policies should be agreed upon at the policy planning stage.

Legal Provisions : Policies and Legislations

National Policy of Education (1986)

The National Policy of Education (NPE) is a policy formulated by the Government of India, to promote education amongst Indian people. The policy covers an elementary education to colleges in both rural and urban India. The policy called for a special emphasis on the removal of disparities and to equalise educational opportunities, especially, for an Indian women, scheduled tribes and the scheduled castes.

The National Policy of Education, 1986 (NPE, 1986) brought the fundamental issues of equality centre-stage. It stresses the need for integrating children with disability with other groups. The objective as envisaged in the NPE, 1986 was "to integrate the physically and mentally handicapped with general community as equal partners, to prepare them for normal growth and to enable them to face life with courage and confidence".

The following measures were formulated to be taken in this regard

- Whenever possible, the education of children with motor handicaps and other mild handicaps would be common with that of others.
- Special schools with hostels would be provided, as far as possible at district headquarters, for severely handicapped children.
- Adequate arrangements would be made to give vocational training to disabled students.
- Teacher's training programmes would be reoriented in particular for teachers of primary classes, to deal with special difficulties of the handicapped children.
- Voluntary's efforts for the education of children with disability would be encouraged in every possible manner.

Programme Of Action (1992)

For the follow up and an implementation of the National Policy of Education, Plan Of Action (1992) was formulated. Looking at the magnitude of the task inolved in the care and education of about 15 million children with disabilities, the POA suggested a pragmatic principle for children with special needs. It postulated that a child with disability who can be educated in a general school should be educated, in a general school only, and not in a special school. Even those children who are initially, admitted to special schools for training in plus curriculum skills should be transferred to general schools, once they acquire daily living skills, communication skills and basic academic skills.

It emphasised on enhancing and promoting the vocationalisation of education, adult education, education for mentally and physically challenged persons, non-formal educational universities, distance learning, rural universities, early childhood care and education.

POA proposed to stipulate that education of the children with locomotor handicap and other mild handicaps should be same and common as the normal children. The objective should be to integrate the physically and mentally handicapped with the general community as equal partners, to prepare them for normal growth and enable them to face life with courage and confidence.

Following measures to be taken

- Special schools with hostels will be provided as far as possible at district headquarters, for the severely handicapped children.
- An adequate arrangements will be made to give vocational traning to the disabled.
- Teachers training programmes will be reoriented to deal with special difficulties of the handicapped children.
- Voluntary effort for the education of the disabled will be encouraged in every possible manner.

Persons With Disabilities Act (1995)

The most landmark legislation in the history of special education in India is the Person with Disabilities (equal opportunities, protection of rights and full participation) Act, 1995. The PWD Act, 1995 was comprehensive break through legislation, that was provided for education and economic rehabilitation of people with disabilities. It states that free education for children with disabilities upto the age of 18 years must be provided in an appropriate environment. This comprehensive act, covers seven disabilities, namely blindness, low vision, hearing impairment, locomotor disability, mental retardation, leprosy cured and mental illness. Chapter-5 (Section 26) of the act, which deals with education, *mentions that appropriate government and the local authorities shall*

- Endeavour to promote the integration of students with disabilties in the normal schools.
- Promote setting up of special schools in government and private sector, for those who are in need of special education, in such a manner that children with disabilities living in any part of the country have access to such schools.
- Endeavour to equip the special schools for children with disabilities with vocational training facilities.
- Transport facilities to students with disability or alternative financial incentives to the parents or guardians to enable their children with disability to attend schools.
- Removal of architectural barriers from schools, colleges or other institutions imparting vocational and professional training.
- Supply of books, uniforms and other materials to students with disability attending school.
- Grant of scholarship to the students with disability.
- Setting up of appropriate fora for the redressal of grievances of parents regarding the placement of their children with disability.
- Suitable modification in the examination system to eliminate purely mathematical questions for the benefit of blind students and stduents with low vision.
- Restructuring of curriculum for the benefit of students with disability.
- Restructuring the curriculum for the benefit of students with hearing impairment to facilitate them to take only one language as part of their curriculum.

National Policy of Disabilities (2006)

National Policy for Persons with Disabilities was formed on 10th February, 2006. This is a policy confirmed by Ministry of Social Empowerment. An intent of the policy is to realize the dream of inclusive society where each person finds equal space for oneself and the same for others. The policy reminds the privileges of equality and freedom of people in all spheres of life. It also ensures the belief that its violation is not possible at any cost.

The National Policy, 2006 recognise that persons with disabilities are valuable human resource for the country and seeks to create environment that provides them equal opportunities and complete participation in society's responsibilities to pay his duty as well as awareness to enjoy the rights equally. The National Policy for Persons with Disabilities Act, 2006, serves many of the objectives of the concerned people.

It has certain principles that deals with

- prevention of disabilities and rehabilitation measures women with disabilities.
- children with disabilities.
- barrier free environment.
- issue of disability certificate.
- promotion of NGOs.
- collection of information of disabled persons.
- social security.
- research of the situation.
- analysis of the current situation.
- cultural involvement of children with SEN *i.e.* Special Educational Needs.
- amendments to the existing acts, dealing with the children with disabilities.

National Curriculum Framework (NCF), 2005

In response to the National Policy of Education, 1986 the NCERT developed National Curriculum for Elementary and Secondary Education, a Framework in 1988. In 2000, NCERT prepared National Curriculum Framework for school education. The curriculum came into operation with the academic session 2002-2003.

In 2004, the Ministry of Human Resource Development, asked the NCERT to review the National Curriculum Framework for School Education (NCFSE), 2000 in the light of report, 'learning without burden', 1993. The 35 members of National Steering Committee, was constituted under the Chairmanship of Prof. Yashpal, former Chairman of UGC. Out of 35 members, 15 were drawn from the NCERT/Colleges of Education. A draft of National Curriculum was prepared and circulated across different sections. Consultations were held in all parts of the country. Advertisements were issued in national and regional newspapers to invite public's opinions and a large number of responses were received.

The draft of National Curriculum, was placed before the Central Advisory Board of Education, for its approval in June, 2005. Some members suggested a few changes. The draft and National Curriculum, underwent certain changes and came for approval of the CABE. The discussion took place on 6th and 7th sept, 2005. The National Curriculum was approved by the CABE on 7 September, 2005.

Chapters of NCF, 2005

- Perspective
- Learning and knowledge
- Curricular areas, school stage and assessment
- School and classroom environment
- Systematic reforms and epilogue

The NCF, 2005 proposes the following four principles for curriculum development

- Connecting knowledge to life, outside the school.
- Ensuring the learning is shifted away from rote methods.

- Enriching the curriculum to provide for overall development of children rather than remain textbook centers.
- Making examination more flexible and integral, then with classroom life.

The NCF 2005 is an excellent example of inclusive curriculum.

NCF ensures that children from different social and economical backgrounds with variations in physical, psychological and intellectual characteristics are able to learn and achieve success in school. Problems of disabled children need to be addressed directly, not only through policies and schemes, but also through the design and selection of learning tasks and pedagogic practices, right from the period of early childhood.

The major highlights of the inclusive curriculum (NCF, 2005) are

- The curriculum should provide enabling opportunities to all learners. The teaching-learning process must respond the diverse needs of the learners. Teachers must explore strategies to aid learning of all learners including children with disabilities. This could be achieved effectively if there is collaboration among teachers and even with outside organizations.
- The teachers must give individualised attention to learners and should be flexible with activities and tasks. The curriculum suggests that children and older learners must be involved in classroom planning to enrich the class proceedings. This would allow zero rejection policy, education to Children With Special Needs (CWSN) in an environment most suited to his/her needs and flexibility for planning teachers to respond to special needs of the learners.
- Schools need to upgrade their status as centers which prepare children for their adult life as well as especially the children with disabilities.
- Providing a multi-sensory learning experience to all children as their learning styles are different.
- The children with different learning abilities have to be provided learning experiences with varied options, like Sign language, Braille, etc depending on the child's needs.
- The schools must uphold quality within the landscape of cultural and socio-economic diversity.

Curriculum design must reflect the commitment to UEE (Universal Elementary Education) not only in representing cultural diversity, but also by ensuring that children from different social and economic backgrounds with variations in physical, psychological and intellectual characteristics are receiving equal educational opportunities.

Concessions and Facilities to Diverse Learners

The concessions and facilities of diverse learners are given below

Academic

Scholarships For the Challenged Persons

The Union Ministry of Welfare, since 1955 has been operating through the state governments and union territories, a scheme of scholarships awarded to challenged person for pursuing education in special schools, being run by non-government organisations. The scholarships are awarded to mentally handicapped students, subject to their being certified by clinical psychologists. The rate of scholarship is ₹ 1000/ per annum for cases hailing from the lower socio-economic status and it is renewable from year to year.

Integrated Education For Challenged Persons

This centrally scheme was launched by the Department of Social Welfare in 1974 and has been transferred to the Department of Education since 1982. The handicapped children have the benefit of receiving education in the regular schools system. Books and stationary allowance of ₹ 400 per annum, uniform allowance of ₹ 50 per annum and transport allowance of ₹ 50 per month is given to them.

Preference in Place of Posting

The Government of India makes a provision for parents in government services, having a child with mentally challenged to choose the place of posting. Government departments and ministeries have been requested to take a sympathetic view on the merits of each case and accomodate such requests for posting to the extent possible.

Reservation of Jobs

As per the Government of India, reservation of 3% in jobs has been in grade 'C' and grade 'B' posts for the physically handicapped persons.

Age Concession

As per the government order, it has been decided to extend the age concession of 10 years in favour of handicapped persons for recruitment to posts filled through employment exchange in grade 'C' and grade 'D' posts.

Financial

Fee concession

As per the order, the physically handicapped persons recruited under the posts advertised by the UPSC and SSC will be exempted from the fees payment of application forms and examination fees as prescribed by UPSC and SSC.

Conveyance Allowance

The central government employees, who are on regular establishment and who are blind or orthopedically handicapped are to be granted conveyance allowance at 5% of basic pay subject to maximum of ₹ 100 per month.

Scheme of Integrated Education

This is a centrally sponsored scheme and was launched in 1974 by Department of Social Welfare. Under this scheme, 100% assistance is provided to the states, UTs for education of children suffering from certain mild handicaps, in common schools with the help of necessary aids, incentives and specially trained teachers.

The handicapped children are provided with the following allowances and facilities

- Books and stationary allowance of ₹ 400 per annum.
- Uniform allowance of ₹ 50 per annum.
- Transport allowance of ₹ 50 per month.
- Actual cost of equipment, subject to maximum of ₹ 2000 per student for a period of five years.

Rehabilitation Council of India Act (1992)

The Rehabilitation Council of India (RCI) was set up as a registered society in 1986. On September, 1992 the RCI Act was enacted by Parliament and it became a statutory body on 22nd June, 1993. The act was amended by Parliament in 2000 to make it more broad based. The mandate given to RCI is to regulate and monitor services given to person with disability to standardise syllabi and to maintain a central rehabilitation register of all qualified profession and personal working in the field of rehabilitation and special education.

The act also prescribes punitive action against unqualified persons, delivering services to persons with disability.

Objectives of RCI

- To regulate the training policies and programmes in the field of rehabilitation of persons with disabilities.
- To bring about standardised training courses for professionals dealing with disabilities.
- To prescribe minimum standards of education and training of various categories of professionals/personal dealing with people with disabilities.
- To regulate these standards in all training institutions, uniformly throughout the country.
- To recognise institutions/organisations/universities running master's degree/bachelor's degree/P.G. diploma / Diploma/certificate courses in the field of rehabilitation of persons with disabilities.
- To recognise degree/diploma/certificate awarded by foreign universities/institutions on reciprocal basis.
- To promote research in rehabilitation and special education.
- To encourage continuing education in the field of rehabilitation and special education by way of collaboration with organisations, working in the field of disability.
- To recogniae vocational rehabilitation centers as manpower development centers.
- To register vocational instructors and other personnel working in the vocational rehabilitation centers.

Sarva Shiksha Abhiyan (SSA), 2000

Sarva Shiksha Abhiyan was introduced during the 19th plan (1997-2002) to universalise elementary education. It is an effort to universalise elementary education by community ownership of the school system.

It is response to the demand of quality basic education. It is also an attempt to provide an opportunity for improving human capabilities to all children, through provision of community owned quality education in a mission mode.

Article 21 (A) of the Constitution of India and its consequent legislation, the Right of Children to Free and Compulsory Education Act or RTE Act, 2009 became operative in the country on 1st April, 2010. This development implies that every child has a right to elementary education of satisfactory and equitable quality in formal schools which satisfies certain essential norms and standards.

Objectives of SSA

- All children to be in schools, education guarantee scheme centres, alternate schools, back to school camp by 2003.
- All children to complete 5 years of primary schooling by 2007.
- All children to complete 8 years of schooling by 2010.
- Focus on elementary education of satisfactory quality with emphasis on education for life.
- Bridge all gender and social disparities at the primary stage by 2007 and upper primary level by 2010.
- Universal retention by 2010.
- Proper measures to be taken to link education to life.

SSA realises the importance of Early Childhood Care and Education (ECCE) and looks at the 0 to 14 age as continum. All efforts to support pre-school learning in ECDs centers or special pre-school centers in non-ECDs areas will be made to supplement the efforts being made by the Department of Women and Child Development.

The program which aims to provide elementary education to all children in the 6 to 14 age group by 2010 is an effort to improve the performance of school system and provide community owner quality of elementary education in the mission mode. The SSA has a special focus on the educational needs of girls, SCs, STs and other children in difficult circumstances. The SSA envisages a close partnership of Government of India the state government, local bodies and NGOs.

It covers the following components under education for children with disability

- Early detection and identification.
- Functional and formal assessment.
- Educational placement.
- Aids and appliances.
- Support services.
- Teacher training.
- Strengthening of special schools.
- Research.
- Monitoring and evaluation.
- Extra time in exam.
- Concession in age and fees.
- Reservation in jobs.

Both SSA and inclusive education aim to bring all children in mainstream of education. Equal accers to education is a matter of right not a privilege. There is a provision of appropriate assistive devices to children with special needs by government. The establishment of resource rooms at the district level facilitates students with special equipments, learning materials and special teaching techniques.

The Zero Rejection policy states that no child should be deprived of education. SSA emphasis that children with special needs should be brought to common schools. The Individualised Education plan for children with needs to be formed by schools with consultation of experts on basis of disability.

United Nation's Convention on the Rights of Persons with Disabilities (UNCRPD)

The United Nation's Convention on the Rights of Persons with Disabilities (UNCRPD) is an international treaty of the United Nations intended to protect the rights and dignity of people with disabilities. It aims to ensure that disabled people enjoy the same human rights as everyone else and they can participate fully in society by receiving the same opportunities as others.

The convention covers a wide range of areas including

- health
- employment
- personal security
- access to information
- education
- access to justice
- independent living

Features of UNCRPD

- Reaffirming the universality, indivisibility, inter-dependence and inter-relatedness of all human rights and fundamental freedoms and the need for persons with disabilities to be guaranteed without discrimination.
- It emphasize the importance of mainstreaming disability issues as integral part of relevant strategies of sustainable development.
- It recognizes the importance of international cooperations for improving the living conditions of persons with disabilities in every country, particularly in developing countries.
- It takes appropriate measures including legislation to modify or abolish existing laws, regulations, customs and practices that constitute discrimination against persons with disabilities.

Implications of UNCRPD

The UNCRPD, along with its optional protocol was adopted on December 13, 2006 and came into force as an International Human Rights Law on May 3, 2008.

The UNCRPD seeks to protect the rights of all persons with disabilities. It treats the life of persons with disabilities as equally valuable to that of any other human being. The convention makes a paradigm shift from current approaches of disability.

The UNCRPD provides a wide range of basic rights to persons with disabilities. It recognizes inherent human dignity of all human beings. Along with equality and non-discrimination as the general principles informing the convention, Article 3, provides dignity, individual autonomy, full and active participation and inclusion, respect for difference and accessibility.

Article 5, of the convention explicity addresses the right to equality and non-discrimination. The convention also asserts the right to life, freedom from torture or cruel, inhuman or degrading treatment or punishment, freedom from exploitation, violence and abuse, protecting the integrity of persons and respect for privacy. The convention accords uni-equivocal rights to life, inherent, dignity, equality and non-discrimination to the life of persons with disabilities, the same rights are enjoyed by other human beings too.

EXAM BASED QUESTIONS

1 Inclusive education is carried out
(a) in a separate learning environment
(b) in a common learning environment
(c) where students are segregated on the basis of their disabilities
(d) None of the above

2 In which year, Government of India introduced Integrated Education for Disabled Children?
(a) 1975 (b) 1974 (c) 1976 (d) 1977

3 Integrated education for disabled children emphasizes on
(a) equal opportunities to children with disabilities in general schools and facilitates their retention
(b) special emphasize on removal of disparities
(c) provided economic rehabilitation of people with disabilities
(d) an endeavour to equip special schools for children with disabilities with vocational training facilities

4 Salamanca statement was released in
(a) 1992 (b) 1994 (c) 1993 (d) 1991

5 Inclusive education is a process of
(a) strengthening the capacity of an education system
(b) emphasize on building of special schools
(c) more time consuming
(d) None of the above

6 National Council of Educational Research and Training has joined hands with .... and launched a project of Integrated Education for Disabled Children.
(a) UNESCO (b) WTO (c) UNICEF (d) IMF

7 Who said that "Inclusive education is a set of values, principles and practices that seeks more effective and meaningful education for all students, regardless of whether they have exceptionality or not"?
(a) Stainback (b) Tim Loreman
(c) Joanne Deppeler (d) Michael F Giangreco

8 Social justice should be promoted as a Principle of Inclusive Education because
(a) it will promote equality
(b) it will help in more enrollment of students
(c) it will encourage creativity
(d) None of the above

9 Special education is defined as
(a) an integrated system of education for disabled children
(b) a separate system of education for disabled children outside the mainstream education
(c) a common learning education for disabled children
(d) None of the above

10 Special education in India was evolved in
(a) 1880s (b) 1970s
(c) 1990s (d) 1960s

11 Children are taught by .... in special schools.
(a) instructors (b) untrained professionals
(c) specialists (d) None of these

12 Special education requires three elements that are professional teachers, infrastructure facilities and ....
(a) special curriculum
(b) material based curriculum
(c) regular curriculum
(d) None of the above

13 The major disadvantage of special education is
(a) it promotes common learning environment
(b) it separates learning environment
(c) children grow up with their disability peers
(d) None of the above

14 Good environment for the development of children should have
(a) good school and good teachers
(b) family provides learning facilities
(c) love and security
(d) proper guidance

15 The concept of integrated education arises as a outcome of National Policy of Education in
(a) 1987 (b) 1985 (c) 1988 (d) 1986

16 Integrated education setup does not requires
(a) special infrastructure (b) special curriculum
(c) experts (d) None of these

17 Integrated education requires and demands
(a) special schools construction
(b) registration of visually handicapped children
(c) Both a and b
(d) None of the above

18 The goal of inclusive education is
(a) widen access to education
(b) to promote full participation and opportunities for all learners
(c) differentiate among disabled and normal children
(d) Both a and b

19 The objective of inclusive education is
(a) to uncover and minimise barriers to learning
(b) to change attitudes, behaviours, teaching methods, curricular and environment to met the needs of all children
(c) to promote constantly the local cultures and contents of various communities of the society.
(d) All of the above

20 The NPE called for a special emphasis on
(a) recruiting more teachers
(b) removal of disparities and to equalise educational opportunities
(c) development of new institutions
(d) None of the above

21 The NPE called for ...... Approach.
(a) Teacher-Centred (b) Child-Centred
(c) Both a and b (d) None of these

22 OB stands for
(a) Operation Blackboard
(b) Observation of Blackboard
(c) Operational use of Blackboard
(d) Data inadequate

23 Which of the following statement (s) is/are true about Persons with Disabilities Act, 1995?
Statement I Free education for children with disabilities up to the age of 18 years.
Statement II It recognise that person with disabilities are valuable human resource for the country.
Codes
(a) Only Statement I is true
(b) Only Statement II is true
(c) Both statements I and II are true
(d) Neither I nor II is true

24 In an integrated education
(a) curriculum and methodology are subject-centered
(b) the cost is not too high
(c) equal opportunities for participation
(d) Only a and b

25 Programme of Action was passed in
(a) 1994 (b) 1992 (c) 1993 (d) 1991

26 Persons with Disabilities Act was passed in
(a) 1992 (b) 1993 (c) 1995 (d) 1996

27 The Persons with Disabilities Act was provided for
(a) an introduction of special curriculum
(b) an education and economic rehabilitation of people with disabilities
(c) special schools for children with disabilities
(d) None of the above

28 Which section of the Persons with Disabilities Act deals with education?
(a) Section 25 (b) Section 26
(c) Section 24 (d) Section 27

29 Which act equips special schools with vocational training facilities?
(a) Persons with Disabilities Act
(b) National Policy of Disabilities
(c) National Curriculum Framework
(d) Sarva Shiksha Abhiyan

30 National Policy of Disabilities Act was formed on
(a) 10th February, 2006 (b) 10th February, 2007
(c) 10th February, 2005 (d) 10th February, 2004

31 Which act ensures social security and issues disability certificate?
(a) National Curriculum Framework
(b) Sarva Shiksha Abhiyan
(c) National Policy of Disabilities
(d) Persons with Disabilities Act

32 SEN stands for
(a) Special Enpowernment Needs
(b) Special Educational Needs
(c) Special Economical Needs
(d) None of the above

33 When did NCERT prepared National Curriculum Framework for School Education?
(a) 2005 (b) 2000 (c) 2004 (d) 2002

34 NCFSE stands for
(a) National Curriculum Forum for Special Education
(b) National Conventional Framework for School Education
(c) National Curriculum Framework for School Education
(d) National Curriculum Framework for Special Education

35 A National Steering Committee was constituted under the Chairmanship of .... in NCF Act, 2005.
(a) Prof. Yashpal (b) Prof. Satish Chandra
(c) Prof. Ved Prakash (d) Prof. D P Singh

36 CABE stands for
(a) Central Advisory Board of Education
(b) Central Approval Board of Education
(c) Curricular Advisory Board of Education
(d) Curricular Approval Board of Education

37 The NCF contains five chapters which includes
(a) Perspective, Learning and Knowledge
(b) Curricular Areas, Systematic Reforms
(c) School and Classroom Environment
(d) All of the above

38 Rehabilitation Council of India was set up as a registered society in
(a) 1985 (b) 1986 (c) 1984 (d) 1987

39 RCI was enacted by Parliament and it became a statutory body on
(a) 22 December, 1993 (b) 22 July, 1993
(c) 22 June, 1993 (d) 22 January, 1993

40 Which body regulates and monitors services to persons with disability?
(a) NCERT (b) CABE (c) UGC (d) RCI

41 Sarva Shiksha Abhiyan was introduced during the ...... plan
(a) eighth (b) seventh (c) ninth (d) fifth

42 Sarva Shiksha Abhiyan was an effort to
(a) universalize elementary education
(b) to prescribe minimum standards of education
(c) to promote research in special education
(d) delivering services to persons with disability

43 RTE Act, 2009 became operative in the country on
(a) 1st April, 2009 (b) 1st April, 2010
(c) 1st March, 2010 (d) 1st March, 2009

44 Who was the Chairman and Vice-Chairman, when SSA was constituted in November, 2000?
(a) Prime Minister and President
(b) Prime Minister and Chief Minister
(c) Prime Minister and HRD Minister
(d) President and HRD Minister

45 SSA aims to provide an elementary education to all children in the age group of
(a) 6 to 12 years (b) 6 to 13 years
(c) 6 to 14 years (d) 6 to 18 years

46 The rate of scholarship for the challenged person is
(a) ₹ 1500 per annum (b) ₹ 1000 per annum
(c) ₹ 500 per annum (d) ₹ 800 per annum

47 Integrated education, for challenged persons was launched by .... in 1974.
(a) Department of Social Welfare
(b) Department of Education
(c) Department of Human Resource
(d) None of the above

48 Department of Education is dealing with integrated education for challenged persons since ....
(a) 1983 (b) 1982 (c) 1984 (d) 1992

49 UNCRPD stands for
(a) United Nations Council on the Rights of Persons with Disabilities
(b) United Nations Convention on the Rights of Persons with Disabilities
(c) United Nations Commission on the Rights of Persons with Disabilities
(d) None of the above

50 UNCRPD along with its optional protocol was adopted on
(a) December 11, 2006 (b) December 13, 2006
(c) December 10, 2006 (d) December 12, 2006

51 Article 3 of UNCRPD provides for
(a) dignity, an individual autonomy and respect for difference and accessibility
(b) right to equality and non-discrimination
(c) right to life
(d) freedom from torture or cruel treatment

52 Article 5 of the UNCRPD deals with
(a) freedom from exploitation
(b) right to equality and discrimination
(c) protecting the integrity of persons
(d) respect for the privacy

53 Match the following.

	List I (Policies/Programmes)		List II (Years)
A.	IEDC	1.	1986
B.	SSA	2.	1992
C.	NPE	3.	2000
D.	POA	4.	1974

Codes

	A	B	C	D
(a)	4	3	1	2
(b)	3	2	1	4
(c)	1	2	3	4
(d)	2	3	1	4

54 Match the following.

	List I (Programmes)		List II (Years)
A.	RCI	1.	1995
B.	NCF	2.	1992
C.	PWD	3.	2005

Codes

	A	B	C
(a)	1	2	3
(b)	2	3	1
(c)	3	2	1

(d) Data inadequate

55 **Statement I** It came into force as a International Human Rights Law on 3rd May, 2008.
Statement II It provides wide range of basic rights to persons with disabilities.
(a) Only statement I is true
(b) Only statement II is true
(c) Both statements, I and II are true
(d) Neither a nor b

56 Tick the correct option.
It is a clear programme to universalize an elementary education in a time bound manner. Which iniative was this?
1. National Curriculum Framework
2. National Policy of Education
3. Sarva Shiksha Abhiyan
4. Programme of Action
Codes
(a) Only 2 (b) Only 3
(c) Both 1 and 2 (d) Data inadequate

57 Tick the correct statement.
1. Inclusion describes much more than acceptance of children with exceptionalities.
2. Inclusive education is carried out in a common learning environment.
3. It helps to strengthen the capacity of education system.
4. It is not an expensive method.
Codes
(a) 1 and 2 (b) 1, 2 and 3 (c) Only 4 (d) All of these

58 Tick the correct statement.
1. An integrated education is not very expensive as an inclusive education.
2. Special planning is required for an integrated education.
3. Special classrooms are designed, according to student's needs.
4. Regular curriculum is also followed by challenged students.
Codes
(a) Both 1 and 2 (b) Only 1
(c) Both 1 and 4 (d) Only 3

59 Tick the correct statement.
1. RCI was setup as a registered society in 1986.
2. RCI regulates and monitors services, given to person with disability to standardize syllabus.
3. It prescribes minimum standard of education.
4. Regulate training policies and programmes.

Codes
(a) Neither 1 nor 2 (b) Either 2 or 3
(c) Both 3 and 4 (d) All of these

Directions (Q. Nos. 60-67) *Given below are two statements, one labelled as Assertion (A) and the other labelled as Reason (R). Following are the codes given below, choose the correct code.*

Codes
(a) Both A and R are true and R is the correct explanation of A
(b) Both A and R are true, but R is not the correct explanation of A
(c) Both A and R are false
(d) A is false, but R is true

60 **Assertion** (A) Special schools are being run by the non-government organisations.
Reason (R) NGOs are funded through various private agencies to run special schools.

61 **Assertion** (A) Government of India has been working to provide comprehensive services to the disabled children.
Reason (R) Many centrally sponsored schemes and initiatives are introduced to provide equal opportunities.

62 **Assertion** (A) Inclusive education ensures quality education for all.
Reason (R) It focused on restructuring of schools for the needs of all students.

63 **Assertion** (A) Inclusive education does not promotes Principle of Social Justice.
Reason (R) Social justice perspective should be encouraged to develop a sense of civil responsibility.

64 **Assertion** (A) Classmates of students with disabilities also experience growth in social cognition.
Reason (R) They will become more aware of the needs of others in inclusive classroom.

65 **Assertion** (A) Integrated education is better than inclusive education.
Reason (R) Integrated education does not requires special curriculum.

66 **Assertion** (A) Learning takes place within a web of social relationship.
Reason (R) Specific activities ensure participation of all children (abled and disabled).

67 **Assertion** (A) The SSA has special focus on the educational needs of girls, SCs and STs.
Reason (R) It is an effort of improving the performance of school system.

Directions (Q. Nos. 68-72) *Read the given passage and answer the following questions.*

IEDC is a centrally sponsored scheme which aims to provide educational opportunities to the disabled children. It has been regarded as one of the major iniatives from the Government of India to promote integrated education. This program was initiated in 1974 by the Ministry of Welfare and central government. Under this program, children were to be provided with financial support for books, stationary, school uniforms, transportation, government's equipments and aids. The state governments were provided 50% of financial assistance to implement this program in regular schools. But, due to certain shortcomings, the program met little success. The IEDC was revised in 1992 with 100% assistance to the schools, involved in integration of students with disabilities.

68 IEDC is a .... scheme
(a) centrally sponsored (b) state sponsored
(c) people sponsored (d) None of these

69 It has been regarded as one of the major initiatives from the government to
(a) promote an inclusive education
(b) promote special education
(c) promote integrated education
(d) None of the above

70 IEDC was initiated in
(a) 1974 (b) 1973 (c) 1975 (d) 1976

71 The state government was provided with .... of assistance.
(a) 60% (b) 100% (c) 50% (d) 65%

72 IEDC was revised in ....
(a) 1993 (b) 1992 (c) 1994 (d) 1995

Directions (From Q. Nos. 73-77) *Read the given passage and answer the following questions.*

Education for the children with special needs has been a current issue not for a long time ago, but gained momentum from the late 18th and early 19th centuries. Children with disabilities were not cared for pre-historic societies. Disability of any kind in the good old days was considered the result of some kind of sin and children suffering from it, were either killed or kept isolated. Special education started with the hearing handicapped as early as 1555, when the Spanish Monk Pedro Ponce (1520-1584) taught a small number of deaf children to read, write, speak and learn academic subjects. By that time, it had not gained much attention, but originally JMG Itard, a French Physician, was the originator of instructional devices. He is also called the inventor of behaviour modification techniques. It is also noteworthy, that first school for education of the deaf was established by Thomas Gallandet in 1817. The first college for the deaf was started in 1859 in Columbia.

73 Special education, gained momentum during
(a) late 18th and early 19th centuries
(b) late 16th and early 17th centuries
(c) early 18th and late 19th centuries
(d) None of the above

74 Disability was considered a
(a) deformity (b) kind of sin
(c) major issue (d) None of these

75 Special education was started in
(a) 1555 (b) 1556
(c) 1554 (d) 1557

76 Who was the originator of instructional devices?
(a) Pedro Ponce (b) JMG Itard
(c) Thomas Gallandet (d) None of these

77 The first college for the deaf was started in
(a) 1856 (b) 1858
(c) 1859 (d) 1857

78 Rearrange the national policies, according to their chronology.
1. National Curriculum Framework
2. Sarva Shiksha Abhiyan
3. National Policy of Disabilities
4. Persons with Disabilities Act

Codes
(a) 4, 3, 2, 1 (b) 4, 1, 2, 3
(c) 4, 2, 1, 3 (d) 3, 2, 1, 4

79 Who said "Inclusive education or setup may be defined as a place where everyone belongs, is accepted, supports and supported by his/her peers and other members of the school community in the course of having his/her educational needs met"?
(a) Michael F. Giangreco
(b) Nichole Eredics
(c) Stain Back and Stain Back
(d) Daniel

80 Consider the following statement(s) about the nature of inclusive education is/are correct.
Statement I Inclusive education in India was evolved in the 1880s with the assumption that children with disability could not be met in mainstream schools.
Statement II It provides a foundation for exceptional children in a way that are not possible in special schools.

Codes
(a) Statement I is correct
(b) Statement II is correct
(c) Both the statements, I and II are correct
(d) Neither a nor b

81 Which of the following element(s) special education require(s)?
(a) It requires trained professionals including teachers, educationists and physiotherapists
(b) It requires special curriculum made for students with different disabilities
(c) It does not requires expensive and special infrastructure
(d) Both a and b

82 Disability is a social responsibility
(a) accept it (b) reject it
(c) avoid it (d) None of the above

83 Which of the following component(s) does SSA cover(s) under education for children with disability?
(a) Functional and formal assessment
(b) Support services
(c) Early detection and identification
(d) All of the above

84 The centrally sponsored Sarva Siksha Abhiyan programme is
(a) a partnership between the central, state and local governments
(b) a national mission in November, 2000.
(c) an effort to establish national unity and an integration
(d) All of the above

85 Tick the correct statement(s).
1. The United Nation's Conventions on the Rights of Person with Disabilities is an international treaty.
2. It seeks to protect the rights of all persons with disabilities.
3. UNCRPD came into force as an International Human Rights Law on May 3, 2008.
4. The UNCRPD provides a wide range of basic rights to person with disabilities.

Codes
(a) 1 and 2 (b) 2 and 3
(c) 1, 2 and 4 (d) 1 and 3

86 Building confidence and affirming identity for students, is related to which principle of inclusive education of teaching?
(a) Principle of Choosing Appropriate Material
(b) Principle of Exploring Multiple Identities
(c) Principle of Teaching and Learning about Culture
(d) Principle of Promoting Social Justice

87 Special education courses are controlled by
(a) Special Education Council of India
(b) National Council for Teacher's Education
(c) Rehabilitation Council of India
(d) Medical Council of India

88 .... scheme was launched by the Department of Social Welfare in 1974.
(a) Scholarship for the Challenged Person

(b) Integrated Education for Challenged Person
(c) Scheme for Integrated Education
(d) Reservation of Jobs

89 **Consider the following statement(s) about the United Nation's Convention on the Rights of Persons with Disabilities.**

Statement I Provides wide range of basic rights to persons with disabilities.

Statement II Recognises degree/diploma/ certificate, awarded by foreign universities/ institutions on reciprocal basis.

Codes
(a) Only I is true
(b) Only II is true
(c) Both statements, I and II are correct
(d) Neither I nor II are correct

90 **Which of the following is/are the principle(s) of the National Policy of Disabilities (2006)?**
(a) Barrier free environment
(b) Promotion of NGOs
(c) Cultural involvement of children with SEN i.e. Special Educational Needs
(d) All of the above

PREVIOUS YEARS' QUESTIONS

July 2018

1 **Which of the following statement is correct in the context of students with learning disabilities?**
(a) They show perceptual impairment affecting perceptual skills, such as thinking and reasoning
(b) They learn in the same way as efficiently as their classmates
(c) They display academic performance higher than expected
(d) They have the emotional problem which is one of the primary cause of their leaning disabilities

2 **Match the following.**

List-I (Terms Denoting Nature of Deviations)	List-II (Resultant Impairments)
A. Cerebral palsy	1. Problems re ated to reading words and letter.
B. Congenital cytomegalovirus	2. Characterised by rapid, involuntary movements of eyes which make it difficult to focus on objects and causes dizziness.
C. Dyslexia	3. Disorder related to movements and posture.
D. Nystagmus	4. Herpes related viral infection causes hearing loss.
	5. Disorder related to far sightedness.

Codes

	A	B	C	D
(a)	2	3	1	4
(b)	4	2	3	1
(c)	3	1	2	4
(d)	1	3	4	2

January 2017

3 **Match the following.**

List-I (Years of Enactment)	List-II (Captions of the Statutes/Provisions)
A. 1987	1. Persons With Disabilities Act (PWD Act)
B. 1992	2. The Mental Health Act
C. 1995	3. Rehabilitation Council of India Act
D. 1999	4. National Trust for Welfare of Persons with Autism, Cerebral palsy, Mental Retardation and Multiple Disabilities Act
	5. National Association for the Blind Act

Codes

	A	B	C	D		A	B	C	D
(a)	2	3	1	4	(b)	4	2	3	1
(c)	3	1	2	4	(d)	1	3	4	2

July 2016

4 **Anoxia is one of the cause of**
(a) mental retardation due to deprivation of oxygen at birth
(b) physical disability due to weakness
(c) jard of hearing due to bacterial infection
(d) speech impairment due to psychological cause

5 **According to legal perspective, a person with which of the following visual acuity will be called partially sighted?**
(a) Upto 20/200 or less
(b) Between 20/70 and 20/200
(c) Between 20/100 and 20/70
(d) Upto 20/60 or less

6 **Which of the following is not characteristic of the intellectually challenged child?**
(a) He/she tends to be retarded in his/her physical development
(b) He/she is above average in sensory motor and artistic aptitude

(c) He/she is lacking in ability to conceptualise and generalise
(d) He/she tends to display socially undesirable traits very often

December 2015

7 Which of the following is not the best addressing the needs of gifted children?
(a) Skipping grades (b) Enrichment programmes
(c) Special classes (d) Brain-storming sessions

8 Which of the following is not a method of C, identifying low vision children?
(a) Performance tests
(b) Classroom's observation
(c) Opthalmological examination
(d) Visual screening

9 A mildly deaf child has a hearing loss of
(a) 25-54 decibels (b) 55-59 decibels
(c) 70-85 decibels (d) 90 or more decibels

10 Which one of the following is not a characteristic of children with disability?
(a) Delayed spoken language development
(b) Poor spatial orientation
(c) Low intelligence quotient
(d) Difficulty in judging relationships

11 The causes of juvenile delinquency include
1. poor home environment
2. company of antisocial groups
3. genetic disorder
4. poverty
Codes
(a) 1 and 4 (b) 2 and 3 (c) 1 and 3 (d) 1 and 2

June 2015

12 Who established the first school to educate the mentally retarded children?
(a) Terman (b) Seguin
(c) Gardner (d) Binet

13 Ability of a child to perceive a total picture or object when actually a part is displayed/shown is called
(a) form constancy (b) visual closure
(c) visual scanning (d) visual tracking

14 At which decibel level, exposure for a prolonged period of time is risky for human hearing ability?
(a) 85 (b) 45
(c) 70 (d) 60

15 Which one of the following statement is correct?
(a) A gifted child may be creative also
(b) Creativity implies giftedness
(c) Giftedness and creativity are related concepts
(d) Creativity has nothing to do with giftedness

16 **Assertion** (A) Delinquency is intimately connected with juvenile stage.

Reason (R) Delinquency is caused by genetic factors only.

Codes
(a) Both A and R are true (b) Both A and R are false
(c) A is true, but R is false (d) A is false, but R is true

December 2014

17 Education intervention for hearing impaired children involves
(a) language development (b) curriculum adaptation
(c) concept development (d) All of these

18 Oralism is
(a) oral speech
(b) multi-sensory cueing
(c) oral mode of auditory training
(d) ability to talk comfortably

19. When an individual with multiple cognitive disabilities has extraordinary proficiency in one isolated skill, this is known as
(a) reunman syndrome (b) asperger ability
(c) intellectual isolation (d) savant syndrome

ANSWERS

Exam Based Questions

1 (b)	2 (b)	3 (a)	4 (b)	5 (a)	6 (c)	7 (d)	8 (a)	9 (b)	10 (a)
11 (c)	12 (a)	13 (b)	14 (c)	15 (d)	16 (a)	17 (b)	18 (d)	19 (a)	20 (b)
21 (b)	22 (a)	23 (b)	24 (c)	25 (b)	26 (c)	27 (b)	28 (b)	29 (a)	30 (a)
31 (c)	32 (b)	33 (b)	34 (c)	35 (a)	36 (a)	37 (d)	38 (b)	39 (c)	40 (d)
41 (c)	42 (a)	43 (b)	44 (c)	45 (c)	46 (b)	47 (a)	48 (b)	49 (b)	50 (b)
51 (a)	52 (b)	53 (a)	54 (b)	55 (c)	56 (b)	57 (b)	58 (c)	59 (d)	60 (a)
61 (a)	62 (a)	63 (d)	64 (a)	65 (c)	66 (a)	67 (a)	68 (a)	69 (c)	70 (a)
71 (c)	72 (b)	73 (a)	74 (b)	75 (a)	76 (b)	77 (d)	78 (c)	79 (c)	80 (b)
81 (d)	82 (a)	83 (d)	84 (d)	85 (c)	86 (b)	87 (c)	88 (b)	89 (a)	90 (d)

Previous Years' Questions

1 (a)	2 ()	3 (a)	4 (a)	5 (b)	6 (b)	7 (d)	8 (a)	9 (a)	10 (c)
11 (d)	12 (b)	13 (b)	14 (a)	15 (a)	16 (b)	17 (d)	18 (c)	19 (c)	

CHAPTER

39

Disability : Concepts and Classification

The concepts of impairment, disability and handicap are not synonymous terms. These are distinct and separate terms. Impairment refers to biological forces, the disability refers to how culture deals with impairment and the handicap refers to how the individual deals with physical impairment. In this context, the ICF model have been developed which provides a standard language and conceptual basis for the definition and the measurement of health and disability. It integrates various models of disability.

In this Chapter

- Classification of Disability
- Classification of Disabilities Based on ICF Model
- School Readiness
- Models of Inclusion
  - Prevalence
  - Educational Needs of Diverse Learners
  - Causes of Disability
  - Prevention of Disabilities

Classification of Disability

There is probably no society in which the disabled have not been discriminated against positively or negatively in one or more areas. Such persons often are the targets of prejudicial attitudes and discriminatory practices. In many instances they hamper their chance of becoming fully functioning members of the society. It is seen that in the last decade of the 20th century many changes have taken place for the growth and development of the disabled people.

For the appropriate use of these terms, The **World Health Organisation** (WHO), *provided the following definitions in their International Classification of Impairment, Disability and Handicap (1980)*

Impairment Any loss or abnormality of psychological, physiological or an anatomical structure of function.

Disability Any restriction or lack of ability to perform an activity in the manner or within the range, considered normal for a human being.

Handicap The result when an individual with impairment, cannot fulfil a normal life role.

Impairment

It refers to the loss or reduced functioning of a particular body part or organ. *e.g.* a missing limb. Identifying impairments that contributes to disabilities is a functional problem for a patient and a key factor for a health professional to determine an appropriate treatment. Significantly, the impact of impairment on learning will vary, according to the nature and extent of impairment.

Types of Impairment

The various types of impairment are

Physical/Orthopaedic Impairment

By virtue of its definition, it may be understood as a certain type of dysfunctions or disturbances in the body, resulting into its malfunctioning and thereby making one physically disabled or handicapped, on one account or the other.

In this way, physical impairment represents a condition of such a child who is physically impaired that interferes with his/her ability, to participate in many activities like daily routine school, home or community activities.

Generally, it constitutes as one of the most common or prevalent physical impairments in human beings.

According to **Hunt & Marshall (2002)**, "It refers to a condition that incapacitates the skeletal, muscular or neurological system of the body to some degree".

Visual Impairment

Senses are said to be the gateway of knowledge but from five sense organs, the sense of sight possesses the most unique place of providing knowledge and information of the environment suffering us in a most comprehensive and stable way that is why the knowledge gained through a picture of the object, person or an event is said to be 100 times better, than its mere description in words.

It as an umbrella term, includes all levels of vision and thus, may represents a continum from individuals with poor vision, to individuals who can see light but not shapes, to individuals who have no perception of light at all. We can use a number of terms interchangeably, to describe children to visual impairment such as visually impaired, visually disabled, visually handicapped, partially sighted children, legally blind and totally blind, etc. Visually impaired children are those children who have such marked visual difficulties that even with the best medical and optical care, they cannot see well enough to profit by the education facilities that provided for children with normal vision.

According the **Barraga (1983)**, "A visually impaired child is one whose visual impairment interferes with his optimal learning and achievement, unless adaptations are made in the methods of presenting learning experiences, the nature of materials used or in the learning environment".

Hearing Impairment

Hearing is the ability to perceive sound. A person suffering from hearing impairment, has difficulty in perceiving or identifying sound clearly due to auditory problems. Hearing impairment refers to a defect or damage in the hearing mechanism. This damage or defect may occur in any part of the ear i.e. outer or the middle or the inner ear. It leads to hearing loss.

Hearing disability or hearing loss may range in severity from mild to moderate to profound. A person may become deaf or hard of hearing, depending upon the nature of impairment and the degree of hearing loss.

A child may be born with some impairment in the hearing mechanism or the impairment may occur after birth, due to some infection and obstruction or damage due to an accident.

According to **Brill (1986)**, "Hearing impairment is a generic term used for indicating a hearing disability, which may range from mild to profound".

Central Deafness

When the sound vibrations reach the inner ear, the inner ear transforms these vibrations and sends them to auditory centre in the brain. Meaningfully, the brain perceives these sounds and understands the message, if there is any defect in the auditory centre of the brain, we cannot hear anything. This type of hearing is known as **central deafness**.

Disability

The World Health Organisation (2012) defines disability as, "Disabilities is an umbrella term, covering impariments, activity limitations and participation restrictions. Impairment is a problem in body function or structure. An activity limitation is a difficulty encountered by an individual in executing a task or action; while a participation restriction is a problem experienced by an individual in involvement in life situations. Thus, disability is a complex phenomenon, reflecting an interaction between features of a person's body and features of the society in which he or she lives".

Historically, people with disabilities subjected to prejudice and discrimination, have suffered exclusion and a significantly reduced quality of life. Societies where 'normalcy' and 'functionality', have been defined rather narrowly, persons with disabilities have little access to social, political and economic structures. Such a state of art with felt exclusion and discrimination makes the challenged more vulnerable and alienated from the mainstream.

Disability is an impairment that may be cognitive, developmental, intellectual, mental, physical, etc. It may be present in an individual from birth or occur during one's lifetime. Disability conditions can cause educational barriers in student's learning process.

Disability is a human right issue because people with disabilities are subject to violations of dignity. For example, when they are subjected to violence, abuse and prejudice because of their disability. Some people with disability are denied autonomy. As regards disability, the National Policy for Persons with Disabilities (2006) stressed the need for mainstreaming of persons with disabilities in the general education system through inclusive education, identification of children with disabilities through regular surveys, enrollment in appropriate and disabled friendly schools till successful completion of education.

There are several conceptual models of disability that suggests significant changes in the way disability is explained. There are four models of disability *i.e.* Moral model, Charity model, Medical model and Social model. (Bowe, 1978).

They can be understood as follows

- The **Moral model** refers to the attitude that people are responsible for their own diability, which is often seen as a result of bad actions of parents if congenital, or as a result of practicing witchcraft if the disability is not congenital. This attitude can be seen as a religious fundamentalist off shoot of the original animal roots of human beings, to a time when humans killed any baby that could not survive on its own in the wild.
- The **Charity model** depicts disabled people as victims of circumstance, deserving of pity and compassion. This and Medical model are probably the ones most used by non-disabled people to define and explain disability.
- The **Medical model** of disability looks at the disabled person as the problem. It addresses disability as a problem of the person, directly caused by disease, trauma, or other health condition which therefore requires sustained medical care provided in the form of individual treatment by professionals.
- The **Social model** upholds that the disabled people regardless of their particular impairments are subjected to a common oppression by the non-disabled world. As a disabled person, one is often made to feel his/her own fault that he/she is different. In this model, disability is not an attribute of an individual, but rather a complex collection of conditions, many of which are created by the social environment.

Hence, the management of the problem requires social action and it is the collective responsibility of the society at large to make environmental modifications, necessary for the full participation of people with disability in all areas of social life. Therefore, issue is attitudinal or ideological one which requires social change, which at the political level becomes a question of human rights.

Types of Disabilities

They can be explained in the following ways

Blindness It refers to a condition where a person suffers from any of the following conditions, *i.e.*

- total absence of sight, or
- visual acuity, not exceeding 6160 or 201200 (snellen) in the better eye with correcting lenses, or
- limitation of the field or vision subtending an angle of 20 degree or worse.

Person with Low Vision It means a person with an impairment of visual functioning, even after treatment or standard refractive correction, but who uses or is potentially capable of using vision for the planning or execution of a task with an appropriate assistive device.

Leprosy Cured Person It means any person who has been cured of leprosy, but is suffering from:

- loss of sensation in hands or feet, as well as loss of sensation and paresis in the eye and eye lid, but with no manifest deformity.
- manifest deformity and paresis, but having sufficient mobility in their hands and feet, to enable them to engage in normal economical activities.
- extreme physical deformity as well as advanced age, which prevents him/her from undertaking any gainful occupation and the expression 'leprosy cured' shall be construed accordingly.

Hearing Impairment It means loss of 60 decibels or more in the better ear, in the conversational range of frequencies.

Locomotor Disability It means disability of the joints of bones and muscles, leading to substantial restriction of the movement of the limbs or any form of cerebral palsy.

Mental Illness It means any mental disorder, other than mental retardation.

Mental Retardation It means a condition of arrested or an incomplete development of mind of a person, which is characterised by sub-normality of intelligence.

Disability has also been defined in the ICF, 2001. The definitions are based on a Bio-Psycho-Social Approach that has resulted from the combination of both Medical and Social Models. The approach was adopted by the ICF, provides a coherent view of different perspectives of health from a biological, individual and social perspective. According to **ICF** (2001), "An individual's functioning in a specific domain is an interaction or a complex relationship between the health conditions and contextual factors (*i.e.* environment and personal factors). There is a dynamic interaction among these entities *i.e.* an intervention in one entity has the potential to modify one or more other entities".

Handicap

A handicapped person is one who deviates from normal health status, either physically, mentally or socially and needs special care, treatment and education.

The types of handicap are discussed below

Physically Handicapped person who have a disability of locomotor and neurological origin which constitutes a disadvantage or restriction in one or more aspects of daily living activities, including work. However, from the educational point of view, not all pupils with physical disabilities require special school provisions. There are variations in duration and severity among physical disabilities.

In other words, handicap conditions may be temporary or permanent and mild or severe. Physically handicapped children may be multiple handicapped with mental handicap, visual or hearing impairment.

Mentally Handicapped A mental handicap is an impairment in an individual's ability to function cognitively, emotionally or physically due to the presence of psychiatric conditions. This condition hinders someone's ability to perform a task or presents that person from engaging in an activity without assistance.

Socially Handicapped Person whose opportunity for a healthy personality development and full unfolding of potentialities are hampered in certain elements in his social environment, such as parental inadequacy, environmental deprivation and emotional disturbance. Socially handicapped children are orphan, neglected and delinquent children.

Effects of Handicap on Education

Mobility and Physical Fitness It may cause various degrees of weaknesses and incordination of the limbs, which may affect mobility, posture and manual dexterity. Other physical problems such as heart diseases may cause poor exercise tolerance and a low level of physical fitness. All these may directly result in pupil's difficulty to cope with an ordinary school routine and to exceed their ability in exploring and understanding the environment.

Perception and Concentration Besides the above mentioned motor problems, neurological impairment may also cause sensory deficiency or over stimulation, which may disturb perception and concentration, inducing specific learning difficulties for the pupils.

Intelligence Most common disability among physically handicapped children is **cerebral palsy**. As cited in the report of a survey that 56% of the pupils intake in schools for the physically handicapped are mentally handicapped .

Emotion It is the disadvantageous position in which physically handicapped pupils are placed may cause them some of the emotional problems i.e. low self-esteem, lack of self-confidence, fear of changes in environment, low level of aspiration, anxiety and frustration.

Classification of Disabilities Based on ICF Model

The International Classification of Functioning (ICF) is a universal model and applies to all people, irrespective of their culture, health, gender and age. Instead of making disability a distinguishing mark of a discrete minority group, the ICF describes all the domains of functioning and disability that are applicable to everyone. The International Classification of Impairments, Disabilities and Handicaps (ICIDH) was published by WHO in 1980. The original model of ICIDH included conceptual model in which diseases and disorders were linked to their possible consequences, specifically impairments, disabilities and handicaps. The model is described below.

Disease → Impairments → Disabilities → Handicaps/Disorder

As time went on, it became more clear that disability was far more complex, a new model of human functioning and disability was presented. The model is given below.

Interaction of Concepts

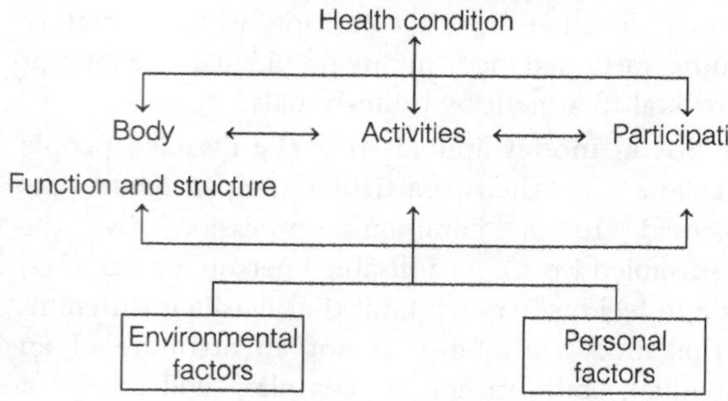

The ICF Framework consists of two parts *i.e.* functioning and disability and contextual factors.

These parts are further broken down in the following manner

Functioning and disability includes

Body Functioning and Structures It describes actual anatomy and psychology of the human body.

Activity and Participation It describes the person's functional status, including communication, mobility, inter-personal interaction, self-care, learning, applying knowledge, etc.

Contextual factor includes

Environmental Factors Factors that are not within the person's control, such as family, work, government agencies, laws and cultural beliefs.

Personal Factors It includes race, gender, age, educational level, etc. These are not specifically coded in the ICF, because of the wide variability among cultures.

The two major conceptual models of disability have been proposed

Medical Model of Disability

It views disability as a feature of the person, directly caused by disease, trauma or other health condition, which requires medical care provided in the form of individual treatment by professionals. Disability, on this model, calls for medical or other treatment or intervention, to correct the problem with the individual.

Social Model of Disability

The **Social model** of disability views disability, as a socially created problem.

For example, if the child with disability, having problem in gaining access to the school and participates in the classroom then it is not because of her disability but because of the school system that has failed to fulfil its obligation to be accessible.

According to International Classification of Functioning, Disability and Health (ICF, 2001), disability under the Social Model is not an attribute of an individual, but rather a complex collection of conditions, many of which are created by the social environment.

A better model of disability, in short, is one that synthesizes what is true in the medical and social models, without making the mistake each makes in reducing the whole, complex notion of disability to one of its aspects.

Uses of ICF

Policy Development

ICF plays an important role, whether it is devising eligibility criteria for disability pensions, developing regulations for access to assistive technology or mandating transportation policy that accomodates individuals with mobility, sensory or intellectual disability, ICF can provide a framework for comprehensive and coherent disability related social policy.

Economic Analysis

Most applications of ICF lend themselves to economic analysis. Determining whether resources are effectively used in health care and other social services requires a consistent and standard classification of health and health related outcomes that can be costed and compared internationally. We need information on the disability burden of various diseases and health conditions. ICF makes those tasks possible.

Research Uses

ICF assists in scientific research by providing a framework or structure for interdisciplinary research in disability and for making results of research comparable. Traditionally, scientists have measured the outcomes of health conditions by relying or mortality data. But recently, the international concern about health care outcomes has shifted to the assessment of functioning at level of the whole human being in day to day life. This is what ICF provides and makes possible.

Uses of Environment Factors

One of the major innovation in ICF is he presence of an environmental factor classification that makes is possible for the identification of environmental barriers and facilitators for both capacity and performance of actions and tasks in daily living. With this classification scheme, which can be used either on an individual basis or for the population wide data collection, it may be possible to create instruments that assess environments in terms of their level of facilitation for different kinds and levels of disability.

Underlying Principles

Four general principles guided the development of the ICF and are essential to its application. *They are*

Universality A classification of functioning and disability should be applicable to all people irrespective of health condition and in all physical, social and cultural contexts. The ICF achieves this and acknowledges that anyone can experience some disability. It concerns everyone's functioning and disability and was not designed, nor should be used, to label persons with disabilities as a separate social group.

Parity and Aetiological Neutrality In classifying functioning and disability, there is not an explicit or implicit distinction between different health conditions, whether mental or physical. In other words, disability is not differentiated by aetiology. By shifting the focus from health condition to functioning, it places all health conditions on an equal footing, allowing them to be compared using a common metric. Further, it clarifies that we cannot infer participation in everyday life from diagnosis alone.

Neutrality Domain definitions are worded in neutral language, wherever possible, so that the classification can be used to record both the positive and negative aspects of functioning and disability.

Environmental Influence The ICF includes environmental factors in recognition of the important role of environment in environment in people's functioning. These factors range from physical factors (such as climate, terrain and building design) to social factors (such as attitudes, institutions and laws). Interaction with environmental factors is an essential aspect of the scientific understanding of functioning and disability.

Conclusion

ICF offers an international, scientific too1 for the paradigm shift from the purely medical model to an integrated Bio-Psycho-Social Model of human functioning and disability. It is a valuable tool in research into disability, in all its dimensions i.e. impairments at the body and body part level, person level activity limitations and societal level restrictions of participation. ICF also provides the Conceptual Model and classification required for instruments to assess the social and built environment.

ICF will be an essential basis for the standardization of data concerning all aspects of human functioning and disability around the world.

ICF will be used by persons with disabilities and professionals, alike to evaluate health care settings that deal with chronic illness and disability, such as rehabilitation centres, nursing homes, psychiatric institutions and community services.

ICF will be useful for persons with all forms of disabilities, not only for identifying their health care and rehabilitative needs, but also in identifying and measuring the effect of the physical and social environment on the disadvantages that they experience in their lives.

From the viewpoint of health economics, ICF will help, monitor and explain health care and other disability costs. Measuring functioning and disabilities will make it possible to quantify the productivity loss and its impact on the lives of the people in each society. The classification will also be of great use in the evaluation of intervention programmes.

In sum, ICF is WHO's Framework for health and disability. It is the conceptual basis for the definition, measurement and policy formulations for health and disability. It is a universal classification of disability and health for use in health and health related sectors.

School Readiness

It is an interactive process and a set of relationships, in which the child, his/her family and the school interact in different ways that support the overall development of a child including physical, mental, psychological and emotional aspects. It is not easy to assess, whether a child is ready for the school or not.

It becomes more complicated, when the system of school, its operations and guidelines are put before him.

It has two separate concepts

- Readiness to learn
- Readiness for school

Readiness to learn is a level of development at which a child is able to learn. **Readiness for school** is rather different in terms of earlier one. It indicates that the child will be able to be successful in a typical school context. **School readiness** is the involvement of both concepts. It is defined as a quality that renders the child's ability to adapt the school's environment and curriculum.

Definition of School Readiness

According to the **National Educational Goals Panel**, school readiness covers three key areas *i.e.*

- Child's readiness for school.
- School's readiness for children.
- Family and community's support and services that contributes to child's readiness for school.

Factors Affecting School Readiness

Following are the factors affecting school readiness

Family Background It plays a vital role in a child's learning process. It supports child at different levels of learning. It provides a healthy and supportive environment to the child. It encourages a child at each step, whether he experiences success or failure.

Child's Health It is an important factor in school readiness. The children with mild disabilities can be sent to the school. It can affect a child's school readiness both directly and indirectly. Children learn better when they are healthy.

Socio-Economic Status of Family The socio-economic condition of a family plays a significant role in student's education and schooling. Among all students with disabilities, 50% are diagnosed with disability related problems that starts at the age of 6 years, these disabilities arise due to the poor social and economical conditions of family and lacking proper nutrition and care.

Types of Services Provided in Schools The child's readiness to school also depends upon the types of services provided in school. If quality services are provided, the child will feel like home in school. The facilities provided for special children in an inclusive school should be effective and child-centered .

Classroom Environment In an inclusive setting, it plays a major role in school readiness of a child. If the classroom environment is supportive, the school readiness will be high. It becomes the duty of teacher to generate conductive environment in classroom.

Role of Teacher in School Readiness

School readiness is a state, when the child responds appropriately to the environment of the school. Child's readiness for school is made of multiple components and shaped by various factors. Teachers may need to make few adaptations to the classroom environment. The teacher plays a significant role in creating a conducive and friendly environment in class. *The following points highlights the role of teacher, in school readiness :*

- By promoting the adjustment of the child in the educational setting.
- By enhancing the participation of child in classroom activities.
- By making the classroom environment least restrictive for the children with disabilities.
- By organising different types of activities in the classroom, to enhance learning of the children.
- Attitude and friendly gestures of teacher also motivates the children, to be ready for school.
- By empowering family as an equal partner in school readiness of the child.

Models of Inclusion

Models are instructional designs or teaching strategies which guide the teacher in planning, implementing and evaluating educational activities. In other words, a teaching model is a plan, specimen or guideline which helps teacher in creating and managing educational activities and environment to achieve goals of education. Some models are necessary to ensure the success of proper inclusion in education.

These are as follows

Strategies Intervention Model

It was developed at the University of Kansas, center for research on learning. This benefits that instruction in strategy intervention does indeed, improves the chances of success of special education in general educational classes. It is also based on that all students should develop their potential, independently. Their domain may be social or motivational.

It has three step strategy intervention curriculum. It serves in the transition of the students with disabilities into the general education environment. This transition is a directional process in which combined assistance of general education teacher and special education teacher is required.

They are

- **First**, while responding to the expectations and demands, the students are made to learn properly the steps and strategies for getting, storing and expressing the things having particular aims. This also enables a student to copy the content matter and prepare a ground to meet the special needs.
- The **second** step is aimed at enhancing the teaching routine in general education classroom. It is done on the basis of aids i.e. the teaching aids which are related to the previous knowledge of the students.
- The **third** step to the strategy intervention is designed to teach the special social skills and motivational techniques. Here, an environment is created for the purpose of developing shared behaviour, which signifies commoness in behaviour of all. It helps easy involvement in team meetings and conferences. This model is widely appreciated. It needs criteria for its implementation.

Some terms of criteria centered to the teachers are as under

- The teachers must have time to plan and think about the needs of diverse learners.
- They should apply the teaching strategies, which must be incorporated into instructional program.
- They must collaborate with special education teachers, for performance assessment of all aspects of the students with SEN.
- They must be committed to meet the needs of the students in the general classroom.

Team Teaching Model

It is a model, in which two teaching polarities are joined together. The special education teacher and the regular classroom teacher work together and teach the students in one classroom. The students must be include in one single classroom, in order to reduce the higher level of stress.

For making teaching effective, the teachers have to work together in collaboration with one another. They will have to work in team and consider the others equal.

By working together in team, they are required to meet the goals and to complete the class's tasks. For this, an effective planning and systematic working is required i.e., when the plan and the system is formulated, the implementation begins which needs a well-defined support of the team.

The team works in the following manner

- The teachers must be willing to teach together. The teaching tasks should be divided among all team members. For example, regular teacher may teach content while special teacher may provide student information, possible instructional strategies and modification ideas for assignments, tests, etc. There should be no communication gap among the team members.
- Inclusion needs a great deal of various types of elements. They may differ to each other. But, the important point is that all these elements should lay focus on teaching. It includes all issues related with the development of learners. It requires support, conducive leadership, spirit of cooperation, etc.

Team Teaching model helps in building self-esteem, self-confidence and self-reliance among children with disabilities. They start considering themselves, equal to their peers without disabilities. They get motivation and inspiration to develop their potentials. They feel new energy in themselves and learn various skills. On the other hand, teachers also get satisfaction and a feeling of dutifulness in a real sense.

Full Inclusion Model

It is also known as **Push In model**. It is the most worthy model in an inclusive education, when the teacher enters into the classroom for instructional purpose, he supports the children. He uses the material which he has already arranged to make the instruction process effective. He uses all relevant methods, materials and assistive technologies in his teaching. In this model, the special teacher/special education staff provides support to the general teacher by team teaching or collaboration. Support in discovering the comprehensive curriculum is also provided to students through accommodations.

In collaborative co-teaching, there is shared responsibility between the regular and special education teacher. Teachers may organise a class into groups and teach students, simultaneously. One teacher may lead an enrichment activity while the other teacher works with a small group on difficult content areas. Students receive age appropriate academics, support services and necessary modified instruction.

Accommodation is a technique or a support that alters the academic setting or an environment to help a student to access the curriculum. It changes how students learn and the way students demonstrate what they have learned.

Special education teacher identifies the needs of students and provides accommodation, accordingly. The ultimate goal is that all students learn to make their own accommodations and become independent learners.

The following ways help a teacher to identify whether an accommodation is effective or not

- It helps the individual compensate for intellectual changes.
- It allows the students to use current skills, while promoting ways to learn new ones.
- It reduces the level of abstract information, to make content relevant for the student's current and future life.
- It creates a balance between the student's learning style and the teacher's teaching style.

Resource Model

Although, law requires that students with disabilities should be placed in least restrictive environment, it is not necessary that students shall always be in a full inclusion setting. For example, a Full Inclusion Model may be restrictive for a student that requires intense remediation in reading. It is for this reason, that a variety of services options must be made available to disabled student. The special education staff may provide instruction and support to the student on one to one basis, outside the regular education classroom for not more than 40% of the instructional day. This small group would be directed towards the student's individualised educational plan. This model is supported by the inclusion teachers to meet the academic gaps of students during regular class with normal students. The primary goal of this is to address the comprehensive curriculum. The parents must be involved in this decision. The school has the responsibility to provide inclusion opportunities for students with disabilities.

Social Mainstreaming Model

In this model, the student with disabilities is included during regular classroom instruction to provide him/her with an appropriate interaction with non-disabled peers. The disabled students may have shortened assignements. Learning material may be adopted for this. This model provides an opportunity for the disabled children to develop their social, emotional and inter-personal skills. The students are encouraged to work together. They are aware of the strengths and weaknesses of one another in the classroom.

Normal students become actively involved with disabled students and teaching in groups can develop and appreciation for optimising the abilities of children with special educational needs. Frequent meetings with parents, students and teachers and special educational professionals are held to check and evaluate the progress and needs of the students. The outcomes of the meetings may be helpful in implementing individualised educational plan for these children.

Non-Academic Model

In this model, the students with disabilities participate only in non-academic class activities, such as an art, music, physical education and other activities. It is more appropriate for our lower functioning, alternate assessment of students.

Prevalence

It means the proportion of individuals in a population having a disease or characteristic. Prevalence is a statistical concept referring to the number of cases of a disease that are present in a particular population at a given time.

In low income countries, prevalence is often recorded very low as a result of the use of weak methodologies. The World Report on Disability, 2011 finds that there are over a billion people, about 15% of the world's population, who have some form of disability.

In India, according to the census 2011, 2.2% of population had some form of disability. The prevalence of disability was found to be more in rural areas as compared to urban areas and more among males than females. The proportion of different types of disability among people with disability as reported in seeing 18.8%, hearing 18.9%, speech 7.5%, movement 20.3%, mental retardation 7.6%, mental illness 2.7%, multiple disabilities 7.9% and any other 18.4%.

The disability prevalance is likely to rise as a result of ageing populations and the higher risk of disability. In older people as well as the global, increase in chronic health conditions such as diabetes, cardio-vascular disease, cancer and mental disorders.

Types and Characteristics of Diverse Learners

The types and characteristics of diverse learners are explained below

Multiple Disabled Children

The children with multiple disabilities do not demonstrate a precise set of common characteristics. They may exhibit a range of characteristics, depending on the combination and severity of disabilities and the person's age. *However, some general characteristics are given below*

Cognitive Abilities It depends upon their particular disability and impairment, that they suffer from. For e.g. the child who has mental retardation will be very poor in cognitive skills, while a child who has an orthopaedic impairment may exhibit good cognitive abilities.

Physical Characteristics They may suffer from chronic illness, pain in any part of the body and lack of proper coordination of muscles. But, it does not mean that their whole body is weak. A person on wheelchair may be very strong, by his upper part of the body.

Communicative Abilities Many children with cerebral palsy have little language problem. If the problem of cerebral palsy is very severe, language development will be affected.

Behavioural Characteristics Generally, the children suffering from multiple disabilities show deviant behaviour. Negative social stimuli is the main cause behind their deviant nature of behaviour. Limited motor skill and self-help skill also limit social interaction of these children.

Academic Achievement Poor academic achievement of students with multiple disabilities is a common phenomenon.

The reason may be due to behaviour problem and poor school attendance, due to musculo-skeletal disorder, poor mental and physical health, etc.

Children with Autism

- Children perform obsessively repetitive activities and stereotyped movements.
- For instance, a child with autism may back and forth exhibits rhythmic head and foot movements.
- Children with autism can be self-abusive, banging their heads, slapping, poking or biting themselves.
- Some students with autism are extremely withdrawn and do not communicate at all.
- Children with autism exhibits a wide range of intellectual and behavioural differences. They may also exhibit periodic emotional outbursts.

Children with Intellectual Disability

- May initiate negative, physical or verbal contact with other students, such as poking, slapping, teasing, etc.
- Their behaviour may be due to communication issue (not being able to communicate) and cognitive issue.
- Some teenagers with intellectual disability may have a hard time controlling physical affection and people surrounding them should be sensitive and cautions towards them.

Children with Physical Disabilities

- A physical disability can hamper a student's mobility, coordination, stamina, communication and learning abilities, to such an extent that educational objectives are difficult to accomplish and special education intervention is required.

- Children with cerebral palsy typically, have deficits in gross and fine motor development skills as well as speech and communication problems.
- Some children have extremely debilitating physical conditions that result in low intellectual functioning, serious limitations in activities and multiple primary handicaps.

Educational Needs of Diverse Learners

When working with students of diverse learners, it is important to treat each student as an unique individual.

There are some educational needs of children, who may have a disability

Individualised Educational Plan (IEP)

For these learners, Individualised Educational Plan is designed to meet the unique educational needs of one child, who may have a disability as defined by federal regulations. An IEP is intended to help children, reach educational goals more easily than they otherwise would.

Inclusion Model

It allows students with special needs spend most of their time with non-disabled students. Implementation of these practices may vary. Schools most frequently use them for selected students with mild to severe special needs. The practice of inclusion is designed to have every student with a disability spend as much time in a Traditional or general classroom as possible.

Model of Educational Intervention

In assessment procedures, an IEP team must also discuss specific information about the child. *This includes*

- The child's strenghts.
- The parent's ideas of enhancing child's education.
- The results of recent evaluations and
- How the child has done on state and district-wide tests.
- Most common accommodation is to provide more time to the students with disability and other accommodations includes different test question formats, verbal tests, large print, one on one instruction, etc.
- Another aspect is creating the least restrictive environment that means quiet and engaging for children. Basically, it depends on the student's specific needs as to what environment will be beneficial to them.

Applications of Assistive Technology

In 1994, **Lahm** and **Morissette** identified areas of instruction in which assistive technology can assist students.

Six of these are described here

Organisation Software based organisation outlines functions and internet for collaboration and feedback.

Note-Taking Video-taking class sessions, translating point to voice, using potable word processing technology, to help students to learn how to note-take.

Writing Word processing software, grammar and spell checkers and word prediction software, publishing software for students to interact and to create their work.

Academic Productivity Calculations, internet, computers and instant messaging will help in increasing the academic productivity.

Access to Reference and General Educational Materials Internet, communication, images, videos, e-books and multi-media can be used for reference.

Cognitive Assistance POAs, computers and internet are helpful for assistance.

Causes of Disability

Most often international agencies and governmental and non-governmental sources, mentioned the causes of disability are heredity,birth defects, lack of care during pregnancy and child birth, insalubrious housing, natural disasters, illiteracy and the resulting lack of information available on health services, poor sanitation and hygiene, congenital diseases, malnutrition, traffic accidents, work-related accidents and illness, sports accidents, the so called diseases of civilization (cardio-vascular disease, mental and nervous disorders, the use of certain chemicals, change of diet and life style, etc), marriage between close relatives, accidents at home, respiratory diseases, metabolic diseases (diabetes, kidney failure, etc), drugs, alcohol, smoking, high blood pressure, old age, chagus disease, poliomyelitis, measles, etc.

Non-governmental sources also place particular emphasis on factors related to the environment, air and water pollution, scientific experiments, conducted without the informed consent of the victims, terrorists, violence, wars, intentional physical mutilations carried out by the authorities and other attacks on the physical and mental integrity of persons as well as violations of human rights and humanitarian law in general.

The causes of disabilities vary according to different age groups (younger, working age and older ages population), although there are differences between males and females. It is also important to note that the causes of disability differ according to the type of disability, regions and other background characteristics, a person belongs to.

Prevention of Disabilities

Prevention of disabilities are explained below

Primary Prevention

Primary prevention aims to prevent disease or injury before it ever occurs. This is done by preventing exposures to hazards that cause disease or injury, altering unhealthy or unsafe behaviours that can lead disease at injury and increasing resistance to disease or injury should exposure occur. Examples include legislation and enforcement to ban or control the use of hazardous products (*e.g.* asbestos) or to mandate safe and healthy practices (*e.g.* use of seatbelts and bike helmets), education about healthy and safe habits (e.g. eating well, exercising regularly and not smoking) and immunization against infectious diseases.

Secondary Prevention

Secondary prevention aims to reduce the impact of a disease or injury that has already occurred. This is done by detecting and treating disease or injury as soon as possible to hault or slow its progress, encouraging personal strategies to prevent reinjury or reocurrence and implementing programs to return people to their original health and function to prevent long term problems. Examples include regular exams and screening tests to detect disease in its earliest stages (*e.g.* mammograms to detect breast cancer). Daily, low dose aspirins and/or diet and exercise programs to prevent further heart attacks or strokes and suitably modified work so injured or ill workers can return safely to their jobs.

Tertiary Prevention

Tertiary prevention aims to soften the impact of an ongoing illness or injury that has lasting effects. This is done by helping people manage long term, often complex health problems and injuries (*e.g.* chronic diseases, permanent impairments) in order to improve as much as possible, their ability to function, their quality of life and their life expectancy. Examples include cardiac and stroke rehabilitation programs and chronic disease management programs (*e.g.* for diabetes, arthritis, depression, etc). Support groups that allow members to share strategies for living well-vocational rehabilitation programs to retrain workers for new jobs, when they have recovered as much as possible.

It is extremely important that the women undertakes adequate and effective preventive measures during their pregnancy and immediate postnatal period and also for their children especially during the early childhood period, in order to significantly reduce the incidence of impairment and disabilities in them.

Identification of Diverse Learners for Inclusion

The process of identifying students with disabilities and determining their eligibility for inclusive education, typically involves three steps i.e. referral, evaluation and placement.

- **Referral** is the **primary method**, through which children begin to be considered for a disability diagnosis. If both, disability diagnosis and special educational needs are confirmed, then the student has right to Individualised Education Programme (IEP), designed to improve educational performance and to expand opportunities.
- Evaluation results are used to develop an IEP that specifies the general goals and particular instructional objectives for the child, results are also used to design instruction and related services and to monitor the child's progress towards objectives and goals.
- Students must be placed as per the disability and teachers must use assistive technology and adaptative methods for the children. Reflecting the national policy, tend towards the greater integration of students with disabilities, into the least restrictive environment. Placement in the regular education classrooms increased between 1985-86 and 1989-90, for almost all disabilities and placements in resource rooms declined. Placement of children in separate classrooms, in regular school buildings remained essentially unchanged.

Educational Evaluation Methods

Shertzer and **Stone** view evaluation as necessary to provide for the effectiveness of achieving programme goals, in relation to specific standards. The effectiveness of any programme can be sustained through continuous evaluation and practitioners need to carry it out properly.

The methods of evaluation in education are discussed below

Before and After Method This is when, the programme process is checked, after a given period of time and it checks the results of specific programme activities. For example, if students are introduced to a computer awareness programme, an evaluation of how much has been covered is carried out by the end of the year.

Comparison Method This is when the groups are compared, after different techniques have been used to achieve a goal. The comparative method may be used to judge the results in groups, like checking the impact of a programme on boys and girls. It may also be used to compare the effects of teacher-pupil ratios, on the attainment of goals.

How Do We Stand Method It helps to identify desirable programme's outcomes. Various techniques are used to check how the programme has progressed in terms of goal attainment. It compares programmes with generally accepted standards and offers an opportunity to make comparisons.

Educational Evaluation Tools

It may be defined as an instrument, to collect evidences of the student's achievement. Achievement test, anecdotal record, cumulative record, checklist, rating list, questionnaire, etc, are the main tools of evaluation in education.

Achievement Test In the Evaluation Approach, the word 'achievement' has to be understood in relation to the objectives of instruction that are translated into behavioural changes. The teacher is interested in knowing the level of achievement of each student in each of the learning points and evaluates these on the basis of pre-determined instructional objectives. This is known as **achievement test**.

Anecdotal Record These are reports of informal teacher's observations, regarding his pupils. A teacher will have the opportunity to observe certain behaviours of his students during specific occasions that reveal their attitude or personality traits. It should be recorded accurately and objectively. It should have two columns, one for the description of the incident and other for the interpretation of the incidents.

Cumulative Record The progress in the developmental pattern of each student is recorded cumulatively from period to period, in a comprehensive record designed for the purpose. Such a record is known as **cumulative record**. It will have the provision, after recording the details of a variety of dimensions like physical development, health conditions, level of attainment in various subjects, participation in co-curricular activities, etc.

Checklist The checklist is a simple list types of devices, consisting of prepared list of items. It is easy to construct and use. It is a two dimensional chart, in which the traits measured are noted in one side and the names of examinees on the other side. The results can be recorded by putting tick mark against the item.

Rating Scale It simply records the presence of the particular variable. There is no provision for expressing how much that variable is found. In order to overcome this limitation, each trait can be score on any number of convenient point, each point represents a particular degree such as good, average and poor.

Questionnaire It is a flexible tool for gathering quantitative information. It is very easy to collect the responses, using questionnaire on a broad parameter. But inadequate coverage, misinterpretation of questions and individual understanding of respondence, are the major limitations of this tool.

Educational Evaluation Technique

Observation, interview, case study, sociometry, projective techniques are the major techniques of evaluation in education.

Some of them are discussed below

Observation Continuously observing an individual and thereby measuring different dimensions of his behaviour, relevant to the teacher is one of the most effective technique used for evaluation.

Interview The teacher tries to observe the child's behaviour, directly and gathers information, orally. There are several types of interviews like survey interview is used to gather information and diagnostic interview is used to understand child's problems.

Therapeutic interviews are used to plan suitable therapy and **counselling interviews** are used to solve personal, educational and vocational problems.

Case Study The most reliable method of studying a single child in the totality, leads the case study method. In this method, the teacher collects data, relating to the individual's socio-economic status, family conditions, study habits, health and mental conditions, etc. Case study attempts to synthesise and interpret the data, collected from several sources using various methods in order to study the problems of the child.

Sociometry It is a method which was developed by **J L Moreno**, for assessing social relationships among members in a social group.

Projective Techniques Abnormal cases, whose behaviours are often controlled by the unconscious mind, are especially not suspectable to such direct techniques. In such cases, what is possible, is to provide the students with some stimulus that might make them respond in such a way as to project their inner-self in an unconscious manner. Then, these responses may be interpreted. Rorscharch Ink Blot Test, Thematic Apperception Test (TAT), etc are some examples of projective techniques.

EXAM BASED QUESTIONS

1 The impact of impairment on learning will vary, according to the

(a) nature and extent of impairment
(b) condition of weakness
(c) difficulties and inabilities
(d) None of the above

2 Physical impairment is defined as

(a) that interferes with normal functioning of bones, joints and muscles
(b) weakness or defect in the power of vision
(c) disorder in the basic psychological process
(d) None of the above

3 Orthopaedic impairments are caused due to

(a) genetic
(b) oxygen deprivation
(c) nutritional deficiency
(d) All of the above

4 Symptoms of low vision are

(a) dizziness
(b) excessive sensitivity to light
(c) blurred vision
(d) All of the above

5 If the degree of hearing loss is 50-75%, then the person is of ......deafness.

(a) mild (b) moderate
(c) severe (d) profound

6 One who is born with impaired hearing is ......

(a) adventitiously deaf (b) congenitally deaf
(c) post lingual deaf (d) pre-lingual deaf

7 The combination of conducive loss and sensory neural loss

(a) conducive loss
(b) mixed loss
(c) sensory neural loss
(d) None of the above

8 The educational needs for hearing impaired children must include

(a) classroom arrangements
(b) speech reading
(c) sign language techniques
(d) All of the above

9 Difficulty in reading comprehensions and math's skills are examples of

(a) learning disability
(b) mental illness
(c) mental retardation
(d) locomotor disability

10 ...... reflects a specific problem, in processing individual speech sounds in words.

(a) Dyspraxia (b) Dyslexia
(c) Dysgraphia (d) Dyscalculia

11 A child with a math based learning disorder, may struggle with a problem of ......

(a) dyspraxia (b) dysgraphia
(c) dyscalculia (d) dyslexia

12 Learning disabilities of writing, can involve the physical act of waiting or the mental activity of comprehending and synthesising information is visible in ...

(a) dyspraxia (b) dysgraphia
(c) dyslexia (d) dysphasia

13 The learning disability based motor skill is known as

(a) dyspraxia (b) dysphasia
(c) dysgraphia (d) dyslexia

14 Difficulty in language and communication learning disabilities are caused in

(a) dyspraxia (b) dysphasia
(c) dyslexia (d) dysgraphia

15 Which of the following is not considered as a learning disability ?

(a) Dysgraphia (b) ADHD
(c) Dyscalculia (d) Dysphasia

16 Children with ...... disorder, may have trouble in communicating, reading body language, learning basic skills and making an eye contact.

(a) ADHD (b) autism
(c) depression (d) dyspraxia

17 Effects of physical problems on education are visible in the form of

(a) perception (b) concentration
(c) emotion (d) All of these

18 The World Report on Disability, 2011 finds that about ......of the world's population have some form of disability.

(a) 10% (b) 15%
(c) 20% (d) 25%

19 Which educational plan is designed for diverse learners with special needs?

(a) Individualised Education plan
(b) Special Education plan
(c) Inclusive Education plan
(d) Comprehensive Education plan

20 **Which model, allows students with special needs to spent most of their time with non-disabled children?**
(a) Special Education model (b) Integrated model
(c) Inclusive model (d) None of these

21 **Use of calculator, internet and computer will help the students in increasing their**
(a) academic productivity (b) speed
(c) reference (d) None of these

22 **Teaching model is necessary because**
(a) it helps in creating and managing educational activities
(b) it helps in achieving goals of education
(c) it creates an environment
(d) All of the above

23 **Which model is based on the three step strategy intervention curriculum?**
(a) Team Teaching model
(b) Strategies Intervention model
(c) Resources model
(d) Full Inclusion model

24 **Which model is based on two teaching polarities joined together in one classroom?**
(a) Inclusion model
(b) Team Teaching model
(c) Strategies Intervention model
(d) Resource model

25 **What is mainly required in Team Teaching Model?**
(a) Effective planning and systematic working
(b) Instructional programmes
(c) Special education for teachers
(d) Motivation

26 **Team Teaching model helps the children with disabilities, in building**
(a) self-esteem (b) self-confidence
(c) self-reliance (d) All of these

27 **Which model is also known as Push In model?**
(a) Team Teaching model
(b) Full Inclusion model
(c) Resource model
(d) Strategies Intervention model

28 **Which technique alters the academic setting to help a student, access the curriculum?**
(a) Accommodation (b) Alteration
(c) Demonstration (d) Comprehensiveness

29 **Which way helps a teacher to identify whether an accommodation is effective ?**
(a) It helps an individual to compensate for intellectual changes.
(b) It allows the students to use current skills while promoting ways to learn new ones.
(c) It reduces the level of abstract information to make content relevant for the student's life
(d) All of the above

30 **What is the primary goal of Resource model?**
(a) To address the comprehensive curriculum and involve the parents
(b) To provide shortened assignments
(c) To meet the academic gaps of students
(d) None of the above

31 **In which model of inclusion, students are encouraged to work together?**
(a) Team Teaching model
(b) Non-Academic model
(c) Social Main Stream model
(d) Resource model

32 **Which model is appropriate for lower functioning and alternate assessment of students?**
(a) Non-Academic model
(b) Team Teaching model
(c) Social Mainstream model
(d) Resource model

33 **The most important challenge for a teacher in an inclusive setup is**
(a) to maintain discipline in the classroom
(b) to make students to do their work
(c) to prepare the question bank
(d) to make teaching process, enjoyable

34 **The child having the difficulty in picking up objects is suspected to have**
(a) sight impairment
(b) lower level of intellectual functions
(c) speech impairment
(d) locomotor impairment

35 **In .... model, the students with disabilities participate only in non-academic class activities.**
(a) Team Teaching model
(b) Resource model
(c) Full Inclusion model
(d) Non-Academic model

36 **School readiness is a/an the ...... process.**
(a) social (b) interactive
(c) mental (d) emotional

37 **School readiness focuses upon the ...... of child.**
(a) mental aspects
(b) physical aspects
(c) emotional aspects
(d) All of the above

38 **Readiness to learn is a level of development at which a child is**
(a) able to learn (b) able to socialise
(c) able to recreate (d) None of these

39 **School readiness is defined as a quality that renders the child's ability to adapt the**
(a) school's environment
(b) school's curriculum
(c) Both a and b
(d) None of the above

40 Which of these is not the factor affecting school readiness ?
(a) Family background
(b) Child's health
(c) Services provided to school
(d) None of the above

41 Which factor affects a child's school readiness, both directly and indirectly?
(a) Socio-economic status of family
(b) Health of the child
(c) Family background
(d) Services provided by the school

42 50% of the children are diagnosed with disability related problems at the age of
(a) 5 (b) 6
(c) 4 (d) 10

43 The facilities provided for special children in an inclusive school, should be ......
(a) effective (b) child-centred
(c) school oriented (d) Both a and b

44 Which factor generates high school readiness?
(a) Classroom environment
(b) Family background
(c) Socio-economic status of family
(d) None of the above

45 Teacher plays a significant role in creating a conducive and friendly environment in classroom. The role of teacher in school readiness includes
(a) by promoting the adjustment of the child in the educational setting
(b) by organising different types of activities in the classroom
(c) by enhancing the participation of child in classroom's activities
(d) All of the above

46 Which method is a primary method through which children begin to be considered for a disability diagnosis?
(a) Referral (b) Evaluation
(c) Placement (d) Assessment

47 Which method(s) must be used by the teachers for the disabled children?
(a) Reflective teaching (b) Assistive technology
(c) Adaptative methods (d) Both b and c

48 Placement of regular education classroom increased during
(a) 1985-86 (b) 1989-90
(c) 1991-92 (d) Both a and b

49 The effectiveness of any programme can be sustained through
(a) continuous evaluation
(b) comprehensive assessment
(c) comparative evaluation
(d) None of the above

50 Which method is used to compare the effects of teacher-pupil ratios on the attainment of goals?
(a) Before and After Method
(b) Comparative Method
(c) How Do We Stand Method
(d) None of the above

51 Education evaluation tools are defined as
(a) techniques, to check how the programme has progressed
(b) instrument, to collect evidences of the student's achievement
(c) reports of informal teacher's observations
(d) pre-determined instructional objectives

52 Which evaluation tool has to be understood in relation to the objectives of instructions that are translated into behavioural changes ?
(a) Anecdotal record (b) Cumulative record
(c) Achievement test (d) Rating list

53 These are basically reports of informal teacher's observations regarding his pupils. Which tool of evaluation is this ?
(a) Checklist (b) Ancedotal record
(c) Cumulative record (d) Achievement test

54 ...... have the provisions for recording the details of variety of dimensions.
(a) Anecdotal record
(b) Cumulative record
(c) Checklist
(d) Achievement test

55 Which tool is easy to construct and use?
(a) Rating scale
(b) Cumulative record
(c) Questionnaire
(d) Checklist

56 This tool basically records the presence of a particular variable. Which one of the following is this ?
(a) Rating scale (b) Questionnaire
(c) Checklist (d) Cumulative record

57 Which method is used for collecting information on a broader parameter?
(a) Rating scale (b) Checklist
(c) Questionnaire (d) Achievement test

58 Which is the most effective evaluation technique in education ?
(a) Testing (b) Interview
(c) Observation (d) Case study

59 Which type of interview is helpful to understand child's problems ?
(a) Survey interview
(b) Counselling interview
(c) Diagnostic interview
(d) Therapeutic interview

60 ...... type of interview is used to plan suitable therapy for the child.
(a) Survey interview
(b) Therapeutic interview
(c) Diagnostic interview
(d) Counselling interview

61 Which type of interview is used to solve personal, educational and vocational problems of the child, by the teacher?
(a) Counselling interview
(b) Survey interview
(c) Diagnostic interview
(d) Therapeutic interview

62 Which method attempts to synthesise and interpret the data collected from several sources using various methods?
(a) Testing (b) Interview
(c) Case Study Method (d) Observation

63 Which method was developed by J L Moreno?
(a) Sociometry
(b) Observation
(c) Projective Techniques
(d) Interview

64 Rorscharch Ink Blot Test is an example of which method?
(a) Interview (b) Projective Techniques
(c) Sociometry (d) Observation

65 Which test measures the specific abilities of students that can be made the basis for predicting the future performance?
(a) Achievement test (b) Intelligence test
(c) Aptitude test (d) Rating scale

66 The main purpose of evaluation is
(a) to reduce the burden of content's evaluation
(b) to have continuous evaluation
(c) to assess the extent to which students have learnt
(d) to help students achieve more

67 What is Rorschach's projective test designed to measure?
(a) Unconscious intentions (b) Dreams
(c) Conscious desires (d) All of these

Directions (Q. Nos. 68-75) *Below two statements are given, in which one is Assertion (A) and another is Reason (R). Select the correct code.*

Codes
(a) Both A and R are true and R is the correct explanation of A.
(b) Both A and R are true, but R is not the correct explanation of A
(c) Only A is true, but R is false
(d) Only R is true, but A is false

68 **Assertion** (A) Pre-school period is crucial for language development.
Reason (R) Brain is relatively more plastic during early stages of development.

69 **Assertion** (A) Physical impairment is understood as a certain type of dysfunction of disturbances in the body.
Reason (R) It is caused due to nutritional deficiency.

70 **Assertion** (A) Hearing impairment is classified into three sub-groups.
Reason (R) Hearing loss may range in severity from mild to moderate or profound.

71 **Assertion** (A) Multi-Sensory Approach should be used for hearing impaired children.
Reason (R) Hearing impairment is caused due to hereditary and environmental factors.

72 **Assertion** (A) Leprosy cured person means an incomplete development of mind of a person.
Reason (R) Mental illness is mental disorder other than mental retardation.

73 **Assertion** (A) Difficulty in fine motor skills of the child is visible in dysgraphia.
Reason (R) The learning disorder revolves around reading, writing and maths.

74 **Assertion** (A) Children with autism disorder may have trouble in communicating.
Reason (R) They are active learners in the classroom.

75 **Assertion** (A) An associated disability among physically handicapped children is cerebral palsy.
Reason (R) A survey shows that 56% of the pupils intake in schools for the physically handicapped are mentally handicapped also.

76 Which of the following aim(s) is/are not included in educating physically handicapped children?
1. To offer them basic education in ordinary schools without justifying their needs.
2. To teach them living skills, daily for independent living.
3. To provide them a special environment as per their disability requirements.
4. To help them to realise their limitations.

Codes
(a) Both 1 and 2 (b) 1 and 3
(c) Only 3 (d) Only 4

77 Identify the correct statement from the following.

1. The children with multiple disabilities do not demonstrate a precise set of common characteristics.
2. Many disabled children participate actively within the classroom.
3. Poor academic achievement of students is a common phenomenon.
4. They have limited motor skills.

Codes

(a) 1, 2 and 3 (b) 1, 3 and 4
(c) Either 1 or 4 (d) Both 2 and 3

78 Match the following :

	List I		List II
A	Physical impairment	1.	Asking for repetition of instruction
B.	Visual impairment	2.	Lack of muscle's control
C.	Hearing impairment	3.	Blurred vision
D.	Dysgraphia	4.	Difficulty in writing

Codes

	A	B	C	D		A	B	C	D
(a)	2	3	1	4	(b)	1	2	3	4
(c)	3	1	2	4	(d)	4	1	3	2

79 Match the following.

	List I		List II
A.	Dysphapsia	1.	Difficulty in reading
B.	Dsycalculia	2.	Difficulty in fine motor skills
C.	Dyspraxia	3.	Language difficulty
D.	Dyslexia	4.	Difficulty in maths

Codes

	A	B	C	D		A	B	C	D
(a)	2	1	4	3	(b)	3	4	2	1
(c)	4	3	1	2	(d)	1	2	3	4

80 Match the following.

	List I		List II
A.	Rating scale	1.	Time to time record
B.	Checklist	2.	Representing degree of variable
C.	Cummulative record	3.	Quantitative information
D.	Questionnaire	4	Two dimensional chart

Codes

	A	B	C	D		A	B	C	D
(a)	1	2	3	4	(b)	3	2	4	1
(c)	4	2	3	1	(d)	2	4	1	3

Directions (Q. Nos. 81-84) *Read the given passage and answer the following questions.*

Teacher's training is an essential factor for children with autism, as many teachers are not aware about the spectrum and does not have the ability to deal with the children in the spectrum. In regard to teacher's training, Reid (2005) stated that "One of the key aspect of ensuring that inclusion is effective in terms of practice is to ensure that the tasks that are set for the students and objectives that have to be met, actually match the student's needs and importantly that students have the means to achieve these needs and outcomes". Further, Lewis putted three forms of educational needs *i.e.* common needs, needs that are shared by all the children, specific needs, needs of groups of students having the same characteristics, unique needs, needs of each individual which are not similar to other one.

One of the major issue that autistic students face is becoming familiar with the routine of the lesson as students with ASD require, i.e. always a specific stricter to the activities which requires that all information should be presented in a controlled manner. Reducing ambiguity is the key element to manage negative behaviour. Thus, planning in a detailed manner will allow the symptoms of ASD to be controlled, as students already know, what will come in the lesson and what is expected from them.

81 Which factor is essential for dealing with children of autism?

(a) Training teachers
(b) Indulging teachers in various aspects
(c) Recruiting new teachers
(d) None of the above

82 Which needs are shared by all the students?

(a) Specific
(b) Common
(c) Unique
(d) None of the above

83 Basically, which needs are meant for each individual?

(a) Common
(b) Specific
(c) Unique
(d) None of the above

84 What is the key element to manage negative behaviour of an autistic child?

(a) Ambiguity (b) Motivation
(c) Discipline (d) Reliance

PREVIOUS YEARS' QUESTIONS

July 2018

1 Which of the following statement(s) is/are correct in the context of students with learning disabilities?

(a) They show perceptual impairment, affecting perceptual skills such as thinking and reasoning.
(b) They learn in the same way as efficiently as their classmates.
(c) They display their academic performance higher than expected.
(d) They have emotional problem, which is one of the primary cause of their learning disabilities.

2 Match the following.

List I (Nature of Deviation)	List II (Resultant Impairments)
A. Cerebral palsy	1. Problems related to reading words and letters.
B. Congenital Cytomegalovirus	2. Characterised by rapid and an involuntary movement of eyes, which makes it difficult to focus on the objects and causes dizziness.
C. Dyslexia	3. Disorder related to movements and postures.
D. Nystagmus	4. Herpes related viral infection causes hearing loss.
	5. Disorder related to far sightedness

Codes

	A	B	C	D		A	B	C	D
(a)	3	2	1	5	(b)	2	5	1	4
(c)	4	3	1	5	(d)	3	4	1	2

3 Marfan syndrome is a kind of

(a) genetic disorder
(b) viral infection
(c) degeneration of neuro-muscular disease
(d) muscular contraction

4 Which of the following provision(s) is/are most appropriate for addressing the learning needs of the students having disabilities/impairments?

(a) Individualised Transition Programme (IIP)
(b) Pre-School Programmes for Children
(c) Individualised Education Plan (IEP)
(d) Free and Appropriate Education (FAE)

November 2017

5 A person can be considered as legally blind, if his visual activity is measured

(a) 20/70 (b) 20/200 (c) 20/40 (d) 20/30

6 Epilepsy is a kind of

(a) muscular disorder (b) communication disorder
(c) neurological impairment (d) psychiatric disorder

7 Muscular Dystrophy (MD) is a/an

(a) neural tube defect
(b) neuro-muscular disease, which involves weakening of muscles
(c) an acquired injury to brain, caused by an external physical force
(d) abnormal discharge of electrical impulse in the brain

8 Which of the following statement(s) is/are not true in the context of gifted children?

(a) Analytical understanding
(b) Synthetic insights
(c) Creative reproduction
(d) Practical application's skills

January 2017

9 Match the following.

List I (Tools of guidance)	List II (Associated functions)
A. Testing	1. Tracking, whether students are doing well in their profession or not
B. Counselling	2. Details reflecting particular events/ episodes related to students
C. Follow-up	3. Organising face to face interaction, to help solve the problems
D. Ancedotal record	4. Diagnosing the abilites of students

Codes

	A	B	C	D		A	B	C	D
(a)	1	4	2	3	(b)	4	3	1	2
(c)	3	1	4	2	(d)	2	4	3	1

10 A gifted child will tend to surpass the average child, in which of the following areas ?

(a) Physical health and well-being
(b) Social maturity and pose
(c) Academic achievements
(d) Breadth of interest and general versatility

11 In which of the following area, deaf children tends to show relative inferiority as compared to hearing children?

(a) Socio-emotional development
(b) Language development
(c) Personal and social development
(d) Academic progress

12 Multiple sclerosis is a

(a) degenerative neuro-muscular disease which is not infectious.
(b) neuro-muscular disease presenting as a weakening of the muscles.
(c) neural tube defect caused by failure of spinal column to properly seal around the spinal cord.
(d) brain injury caused by severe trauma, inside the head that results in lasting physical and cognitive impairments.

13 Autosomal disorders are those
(a) resulting from a defect with 23rd pair of chromosomes and involves a pinched X chromosome.
(b) resulting from a defect in the 22nd pair of chromosomes that are not related to gender.
(c) resulting from a defect due to chromic genetic disorder.
(d) resulting from an inherited metabolic disorder.

July 2016

14 Which of the following is/are intimately associated with the mental health?
(a) Absence of anxiety
(b) Keeping one's desires in abeyance
(c) Resources for gratifying needs
(d) Ability to defer gratification of needs

15 Anoxia is the cause of
(a) mental retardation, due to deprivation of oxygen at birth
(b) physical disability due to weakness
(c) hard of hearing due to bacterial infection
(d) Speech impairment due to psychological causes

16 Which of the following is/are not a characteristic(s) of an intellectually challenged child?
(a) He/she tends to be retarded in his/her physical development
(b) He/she is above average in sensory motor and autistic aptitude
(c) He/she is lacking in ability to conceptualise and generalise
(d) He/she tends to display socially undesirable traits

17 Which of the following could you associate to the greatest extent with the education of the mentally retarded children ?
(a) Leta Hollingworth
(b) Lewis M. Terman
(c) Nancy Bayley
(d) Christine Ingram

December 2015

18 **Assertion** (A) Distress usually accompanies abnormal behaviour patterns.
Reason (R) Behaviour disorders are reflected in the reports of distress.
Codes
(a) Both (A) and (R) are true, but (R) is not the correct reason of (A)
(b) Both (A) and (R) are true and (R) is the correct reason of A
(c) Both (A) and (R) are false
(d) (R) is true, but can not be the reason of (A)

19 A mildly deaf child has a hearing loss of
(a) 26-54 decibels
(b) 55-69 decibels
(c) 70-85 decibels
(d) 90 decibels or more decibels

20 Which one of the following is not a characteristic of children with disability ?
(a) Delayed spoken language development
(b) Poor spatial orientation
(c) Low intelligence quotient
(d) Difficulty in judging relationships

June 2015

21 Who established the first school to educate the mentally retarded children ?
(a) Terman (b) Seguin
(c) Gardner (d) Binet

22 Ability of a child to perceive a total picture or object when actually a point is displayed is called
(a) form constancy (b) visual closure
(c) visual scanning (d) visual tracking

23 At which level, exposure for a prolonged period of time is risky for human hearing ability ?
(a) 85 decibles (b) 45 decibles
(c) 70 decibles (d) 60 decibles

ANSWERS

Exam Based Questions

1 (a)	2 (a)	3 (d)	4 (d)	5 (c)	6 (b)	7 (b)	8 (d)	9 (a)	10 (b)
11 (c)	12 (b)	13 (a)	14 (b)	15 (b)	16 (b)	17 (d)	18 (b)	19 (a)	20 (c)
21 (a)	22 (d)	23 (b)	24 (b)	25 (a)	26 (d)	27 (b)	28 (a)	29 (d)	30 (a)
31 (c)	32 (a)	33 (d)	34 (d)	35 (d)	36 (b)	37 (d)	38 (a)	39 (c)	40 (d)
41 (b)	42 (b)	43 (d)	44 (a)	45 (d)	46 (a)	47 (d)	48 (d)	49 (a)	50 (b)
51 (b)	52 (c)	53 (b)	54 (b)	55 (d)	56 (a)	57 (c)	58 (c)	59 (c)	60 (b)
61 (a)	62 (c)	63 (a)	64 (b)	65 (a)	66 (d)	67 (a)	68 (a)	69 (a)	70 (d)
71 (c)	72 (d)	73 (d)	74 (c)	75 (a)	76 (b)	77 (b)	78 (a)	79 (b)	80 (d)
81 (a)	82 (b)	83 (c)	84 (a)						

Previous Years' Questions

1 (c)	2 (d)	3 (a)	4 (c)	5 (b)	6 (c)	7 (b)	8 (c)	9 (b)	10 (c)
11 (b)	12 (a)	13 (b)	14 (d)	15 (a)	16 (b)	17 (d)	18 (a)	19 (a)	20 (d)
21 (b)	22 (b)	23 (a)							

CHAPTER

40

Planning and Management of Inclusive Classroom

Planning is an important attribute of management in achieving the aims and objectives required for education. Planning is a process that determines the future course of action to be undertaken at all levels of management. Planning and management assumes significance in the context of ensuring quality education. For effective classroom, various components must be considered such as teacher professionals, restructured classrooms, adapted curriculum and individualised education plan and remedial teaching.

Inclusive Classroom

Inclusive classroom is a general education classroom in which students with and without disabilities learn together. It is essentially the opposite of a special education classroom, where students with disabilities learns with only other students with disabilities. In inclusive classroom, all students have the right to feel safe, supported and included at school and in the regular classroom. In inclusive classroom, it is important that the teacher fully understands the social, physical and learning needs of the students. The teacher plays a central role in maximizing learning potential of students with special needs. Often, the teacher nurture a relationship between a student with special need and a same age student without a special educational need.

Characteristics of Inclusive Classroom

Active Learning In inclusive classroom, the students are actively engaged. It reduces the student's passivity because there is less rote memorization of facts. There is also a stress of competition and grades.

Provides Lots of Choices and Time Children spend a lot of time in learning centres, where they make a lot of choices about what they are working on. There is lot of time for special interaction which helps in meeting curricular expectations.

Special Help to Students in General Classroom Inclusive classroom community regardless of their strength or weakness in any area, seeks to maximise the potential of all students. It brings students with diverse needs at one place. Inclusive classroom makes sure that diverse learners with disabilities, different cultures, different interests and ways of learning are exposed to different teaching strategies that help them to learn.

Varied and Supportive Role of Teacher Inclusive classroom asks teachers to provide appropriate individualized support and services to all students without any segregation or discrimination. Teachers in inclusive classroom vary their teaching style by using a variety of techniques and strategies. This helps in learning outcomes of the students.

Meet Expectations for Curriculum Children have a high level of responsibilities for creating their community. Inclusive classroom helps the students in structuring the rules, which they are expected to follow and to meet contracted hope for curriculum.

Development of Opportunities for Students Inclusive classroom provides strong leadership and opportunities for team building and group relations in students. It also makes available more options in choosing subjects to learn, to manage change, celebrate success and learn from challenges.

Components of Inclusive Classroom

Classroom Seating Arrangement

Inclusive classroom must be physically and functionally arranged. Seating arrangement is a component of treating and creating a supportive climate in all classrooms and emphasized the need for specialized seating for students with disabilities. Teacher must make the seating arrangements in a way that benefits all the students. The seating arrangement should be done in a way, to avoid injury to physically handicapped children.

Classroom's Practices

A good number of classroom's practices are a part of inclusive education.

Some important classroom practices are

- Collaborative teaching.
- Activity based learning.
- Peer-tutoring.
- Cooperative learning.
- Multi-level instructions.
- Competition between groups, etc.

Role of Teacher

A teacher uses a number of techniques and strategies in inclusive classroom. *These are*

- Involving students in solving problems.
- Organizing student's desks in groups.
- Using games designed to build community.
- Teaching students to look for ways to help each other.
- Take breaks when necessary.
- Focusing on the strength of a student with special needs.

Supportive Aids and Materials

It includes all those aids and materials which help in movement and learning of children with special needs.

Following are few examples of such aids and materials

- Braille books for blind students.
- Sign language interpreters for deaf students.
- Computers with speech softwares.
- Posters and flip chart assist students in understanding the concepts.

Planning and Management of Inclusive Classroom

Planning and management of inclusive classroom is related to the provisions and procedures necessary to establish and maintain environment in which instructions and learning can occur. It is about the establishment and maintenance of order, designing effective instructions, dealing with students as a group, responding to the needs of individual student and effectively handling the discipline and adjustment of individual student.

Today, educators are facing a difficult task in their classrooms. They are expected to continue to use the existing curriculum to teach learners because education system did not allows them to be included with their learners. **King Carreiro** (Developmental and Educational Psychologist) argues that despite the fact that educators didn't receive in-service training on inclusion, they are expected to implement more effective delivery techniques and also change instructional strategies, grouping practices and assessments, not only to accommodate student's individual needs but also to alter the conditions that led to the referal of students to special education.

The main objective of planning and management of inclusive classroom is to focus upon the overall development of learners. The planning and management of inclusive education in the classroom is immediate priority which needs to be addressed.

In order to have successful management, there are some guidelines that have to be seriously considered. *They are* :

In-Service Training of Educators

According to **Le Roux** and **Maila**, "In-Service Education and Training (INSET) refers to instructional programmes to provide for continued professional development of educational practitioners during their working years".

Mothata explains INSET as "Programmes aim at upgrading skills and qualifications and providing training in new policy directions, as the ongoing professional development of teaching practitioners".

Educators need training, concerning the background of the barriers to learning, its causes, the type of curriculum to be followed, the materials that should be used, content, teaching strategies and how to overcome these barriers that learner's experience. Without proper training, it is going to be difficult if not impossible for educators to manage an inclusive classroom.

The issues that need to be addressed during in-service training includes

- Helping educators to acknowledge and understand differences in physical attributes, learning styles and emotional responses. Educators should also learn about activities that will help non-disabled learners accept their disabled peers.
- Showing educators how to adapt instruction and assessment to meet the needs of all learners.
- Empowering educators with the attitude and skills required for collaboration practice.
- Enabling educators to promote an involvement of parents and to communicate effectively with parents.

Early Identification of Learners and Intervention

The department of education states that the lack of knowledge of educators and parents in identification of barriers to learning prevents learners from being identified timeously for intervention. It further states that the lack of identification can also compound the child's needs over an extended period of time and later, mainfest in behavioural difficulties, low self-esteem, early drop out, passiveness and a low self-concept. Educators must have skills in detecting the barriers in the children, so that they are able to assist them in a relevant way.

Teaching Strategies

Educators are expected to use a variety of teaching strategies and have to adapt the curriculum to suit the needs of all learners. Educators should understand that there are some learners who are slow in their approach to learning. Therefore, it is indispensable that educators should use different methods of teaching to embrace them and move with them, along all steps of the way to actualise their full potential. This is what, an inclusion expects from educators to do.

Educators use the following important principles in their inclusive classrooms

- Individuality
- Motivation
- Task Analysis
- Totality
- Reduction of subject's matter
- Emphasis and purposefulness

Class's Organisation

The practical organisation of learning materials of any classroom including inclusive classroom is very important. To manage the classroom in an effective way, learners should have enough space for movement, materials and other relevant equipments should be organised in such a way that they are easily reached by learners.

- Early Childhood Development (ECD) sites should ensure that the physical arrangement in the classroom and management of space for groups, paired and individual activities should provided.
- Practitioners and educators in early childhood development needs to be sensitised to the impressionable minds, while facilitating inclusion and the mutual respect for diversity.
- In this context, **Gibson** and **Blandford** warn that "Classroom organisation concerns substantially more than a furniture arrangement, display of pupil's work and the use and choice of equipment. It includes consideration of pupil's groupings and the use of teaching assistants or other helpers. Decisions about classroom's organisation, need to support inter-activity and teachers need to be conscious of the impact of different social settings on an effective learning".

Flexible Curriculum

A flexible curriculum is one which allows for differentiation with regard to lesson's objectives, outcomes and time allocated to different lessons. This curriculum has to be underpined by a Principle of Inclusivity. It should be noted that managing inclusive classroom needs a flexible curriculum, which will challenge the skills of an educator to accomodate all learners in the classrooms. Educator needs to be supported on an ongoing basis.

Content

The content that is taught in the classroom, should be that which will equip all learners with the knowledge, skills, values and attitudes needed for success in life, unlike the old traditional Subject-Centered and Teacher-Centered or Directed approach, which was often concerned with learning the content by heart in order to advance to the next class. So, the content should be relevant to the academic progress, personal issues and societal issues.

Assessment

The preferred approaches to assessment of special needs for inclusion in the regular classroom are contextual, performance oriented, holistic, interactive, multi-perspective and real world oriented. The assessment process is broad in scope and designed to provide opportunities to obtain authentic and sensitive indicators of performances in the real world setting of classroom and community. Assessments for inclusive classroom, empower teachers by giving control of assessment and planning for intervention to those who are responsible for instructions.

Infrastructure

Facilities and infrastructures play an important role in serving special needs of students in inclusive school because they will give accessibility for special needs of students. Infrastructure provided by the school should be aligned to the needs of the students. For example, students with visual impairment may need guide blocks and specific signs to indicate rooms and other facilities, students with hearing impairment need some visual signs, students with physical disabilities need ramps and spacious room in order to make them move freely. Students with attention deficit disorder may need less distraction and students with autism may need well-organised classroom.

According to **Loreman**, **Deppeler** and **Harvey**, several things should be considered related to facilities and infrastructures in an inclusive school. *They are*

- Ramps, where there are steps.
- Width and positioning of door and doorways, opening and closing speed.
- Arrangement of furniture.
- Classroom's clutters, such as games, bags, rugs, toys, sporting equipments, etc.
- Table, bench and shelf height.
- Lighting.
- Distraction.
- Access to specialised classroom's equipments.
- Access to areas of the schools, such as other building, sporting fields, playgrounds, etc.
- The visibility of hazards.

Human Resources and Instructional Practices

Qualified and trained human resources are one of the essential elements that determine the quality of education of a child receives. Successful inclusion of children with disabilities in education requires sufficient personnels (teachers headmasters, specialists, administrative staff, care takers) including special educators with adequate preparation and training. There has been a significant increase in number of children with disabilities in schools. In recent years, as a result of several programmes and interventions, use of ICT to enhance learning within inclusive classroom is necessary for effective inclusion. Human resource planning is seriously lacking as it is largely unknown what categories of educational personnel are currently working in schools.

Human resource management needs to understand the changing requirements to implement policies and practices, accordingly. Training and development area needs to be focused as it helps in retention as well as development of conducive environment within the school. Policies, programmes, mechanisms should be creatively designed and developed that fosters growth.

In inclusive classroom, there are various instructional practices used by educator, like using technology, such as interactive whiteboard is related to high student's engagement. Peer's supported learning can be very effective and engaging and take the form of pair work, cooperative grouping and students lead demonstrations.

Instructional practices are helpful for the students in inclusive classroom in the following manner

Ensure Access to Academic Curricular Content All students need opportunity to have learning experience in line, with the same learning goals. Teacher must ensure that all students should participate in large group instruction, not only will it keep students on track with the lesson as well as it will reduce the differences among the disabled and non-disabled children.

Universal Designs for Learning These are methods that are varied and support many learner's needs. They include multiple ways of representing content to students and for students to represent learning back, such as modelling objectives, graphic organisers, oral and written responses and technology.

Creating a Respectful and Productive Learning Environment Educators must use that instructional practice that creates a respectful and productive learning environment, where all students are treated equally.

Active Learning Strategies Educators must employ active learning strategies to promote, recall and understanding of new learning. This strategy allows students to reflect individually on a question, pair up with a partner to share and compare answers and finally gives the best answer.

Curriculum and Curricular Adaptation for Diverse Learners

According to **NCERT**, "Adaptation refers to adjusting assessments, materials, curriculums or classroom's environment to accommodate student's needs, so that he/she can participate in and achieve the teaching-learning goals". *Adaptation includes but are not confined to*

- audio-tapes, electronic texts or a peer helper to assist with assigned readings.
- access to computers for written assignments.

- alternatives to written assignments and demonstrates knowledge and understanding.
- extended time to complete assignments or tests.
- use of computer software which provides text to speech.

As a teacher, you will be required to adapt the curriculum and make necessary modifications to increase the student's chances of success and to meet the requirements of diverse learners or special needs of learners.

There are specific disabilities which includes

- Hearing impairment
- Learning disabilities
- Mental retardation
- Emotional disabilities
- Attention deficit/Hyper Active Disorder
- Any other special need to children

Curriculum adaptation is an ongoing process that changes the regular prescribed curriculum by modifying or adapting it in terms of the content or delivery of an instruction to meet the learning requirements of students with learning difficulties including children with disabilities.

The following principles should be considered for adapting the curriculum

- The adaptation should not change original concept of curriculum used because the objective of adaptation is to provide some learning experiences to all learners.
- Compensatory activities should be planned in such a way that the child gets a holistic picture of the concepts taught in the regular classes. The objective of instructional material should remains same for all learners.
- Modification in the instructional material should aims to facilitate maximum participation of children with learning difficulties, in such a way that it also motivates all learners in the classroom.
- By understanding the limitations and difficulty level of a student, support can be used to overcome or to reduce the difficulty to ensure maximum learning.

Assistive and Adaptive Technologies for Diverse Learners

Adaptive technology refers to special verisons of already existing technologies or tools that provides enhancement or different ways of interacting with the technology. The adaptation helps individual with a disability or impairment to accomplish a specific task. *It includes*

- Large print books
- Digitised texts
- Large monitors
- Adjustable tables
- Electronic mail, etc.

It is a broad term often used to describe both the products and services for people with special needs. It enhances the vocation, recreation, education and independence of the user. It can provide equality between visually impaired individuals and their signed peers within an emerging information society. With the aid of an appropriate technological devices, visually impaired persons can independently access, process, store and transmit the same information handled by sighted people.

Adaptive technology is a sub-category of assistive technology as it refers to something specifically designed for people with disabilities. There are many kinds of assistive and adaptive technologies that will address the different needs of people with disabilities. These includes mobility aids, technologies for visually impaired, technologies for hearing impaired, etc.

Assistive technologies are useful in creating new abilities for children and adults with disabilities including sensory, cognitive, learning and physical disabilities. Some examples of assistive technologies are touch and control devices, alternative keyboards and mouse, grammar checkers, scanners, compact disc recorders and spell checkers. It includes mobility devices such as walkers and wheelchairs, hardware and software and peripherals that assist people with disabilities in accessing computers or other information technologies.

Assistive technology is a broad concept, covering virtually anything that might be used to compensate for lack of certain abilities ranging from low tech devices, like crutches or a special grip for a pen to more advanced items, like hearing aids and glasses, to high tech devices such as Brailles and computers with software for helping dyslectics to read. Despite the positive impact and advancement of assistive technology over years, prior research on the use of assistive technology in inclusive education is few and limited to developed countries.

Some of the assistive devices for the different categories of disability are described below

Assistive Devices for Visually Impaired

Visually impaired is a condition in which the child's vision is deficit to the extent that significantly will affects its routine, functioning, optimal learning and adjustment. The visually impaired learners need assistive technology, according to the degree of impairment they suffer.

The following measures may assist the visually handicaps

Computer Screen Magnification Magnification of screen is possible by the use of special software. The user selects a portion of the screen and then enlarge that section upto 16 times of the original size. This magnification technology helps the low vision students to see the particular portion of the screen better and larger than before.

Screen Readers Generally, screen readers are a type of software. While using the screen reading software, the user can adjust the volume, pitch and speed of reading. Even, they can choose male or female's voice, according to their choice. The computer reads text passages, analyses the phonetic structure of words and attempts to reconstruct the words.

Braille Scanning Software 'Optical Braille Recognition' is a window software program that allows to read single and double sided Braille documents on a standard, A4 scanner. It scans the Braille document, analyses the dot pattern and translates it into normal text that it presents on the computer screen.

Assistive Devices for Hearing Impaired

The hearing disabled children have different degree of loss in their auditory ability and loss of audition may be complete or partial ranging from mild to severe. The children face problems at schooling because of their disability. *Thus, need the following assistive devices*

Personal Frequency Modulation These systems are like miniature radio stations, operating on special frequencies. The personal frequency modulation system consists of a transmitter and micro-phone, used by the speaker, receiver and listener. The receiver transmits the sound to your ears directly to the hearing aid.

Text Telephone It allows phone conversations to be typed and read, rather than spoken and heard.

Computerised Speech Recognition It allows a computer to change a spoken message into readable text document.

Assistive Devices for Speech Impaired Children

Speech disability is both a physical handicap and psychological problem. The defects of pitch, tone, intensity and rhythm of spoken language are included in speech impairment.

The major types of assistive devices for speech impaired children are

Augmentative or Alternative Communication (AAC) It is the use of symbols, aids, strategies and techniques to enhance the communication process. This includes sign language and various communication boards, both manual and electronic, that are used by individuals with impaired oral motor skills.

Computer Electronic Speech Devices There are computer based software programs available that can be used to help children with their speech development and verbal skills and can even synthesize speech.

Process Involved In Inclusive Classroom

The process involved in inclusive classrooms are Individualised Education plan and remedial teaching as discussed below

Individualised Education Plan

Individualised Education Plan is a written statement of an education program designed to meet the child's individual needs.

In IEP, teachers support personnel and parents work together, as a team to meet the needs of individual student who requires a range of support.

The successful inclusion is the ability of children with disabilities to attain the outcomes on their Individualised Education Plan (IEP). IEP has become the critical instrument to understand how an inclusion conducting for young children with disabilities in inclusive classroom. Nowadays, IEP has been becoming the curriculum core as it is created intentionally to help an individual student with special needs, to fulfil his or her own potential.

For effective implementation of IEP in inclusive classroom, some important aspects need to be considered

Adjusting IEP Form IEP form for current inclusive class needs to be revised to meet the practice in inclusive class i.e. concluding the strengths and weaknesses for the focus students, design the space for writing functional objectives in IEP form.

Supporting the Implementation of IEP by Teamwork The team members should discover the special needs for the children with special needs, to determine the priority of IEP goals and objectives and provides the strategies for attaining IEP's goals.

The goal of IEP is to deliver a comprehensive, free and appropriate education with the involvement of many participants. IEP is a quasi-contractual agreement to guide and to document specially designed instructions for each student with a disability based on his/her unique academic, social and behavioural needs. Planning and implementing a procedurally sound, IEP will always be a challenge, but the developers of IEP must deliver a high quality framework to help teachers to perform at their best in providing specially designed instruction for each of their students with disabilities.

Remedial Teaching

It is just effective teaching in which the learner and his/her needs occupies the focal point. It is an integral part of all good teaching. It takes the pupil at his own level and by intrinsic methods of motivation leads him to increased standards of competence. It is based upon careful diagnosis of defects and general to the needs and interest of pupils. The remedial measures should be designed to correct the pupil's individual difficulties.

Through the use of observation, interview and diagnostic testing materials, the teacher would have analysed the work of the backward children, in order to locate the specific retaining needs. An adequate amount of remedial measures must be provided, which is designed to correct the specific difficulties identified. Short term goals should be established, which the learner considers reasonable and possible to attain. By means of progress charts, praise and social recognition the child's feeling of successful accomplishment should be reinforced.

Objectives of Remedial Teaching

- To timely solve doubts of the students.
- To solve the problems arise during teaching.
- To develop good tendency among the students.
- To correct the emotional difficulties of students.
- To overcome deficiencies in work, study and skills.
- To help pupils who have fallen behind to learn to the best of their ability.
- To bring them back into the mainstream classes as far as possible.

Principles of Remedial Teaching

Remedial teaching consists of remedial activities, taking place along with the regular instruction or instruction instruction outside the regular class instruction and usually conducted by a special teacher. The type of remedial treatment given to the students depends on the character of the diagnosis made.

If physical factors are responsible, remedial attention should be provided. The results of diagnosis are significant only if, they constitute the basis for corrective teaching and for remedial procedures, which removes alleviate or compensate for causal factors in the child and his/her environment.

General backwardness in subject, is frequently due to inadequate mastery of the basic skills of reading, arithmetic, language, handwriting and spelling or inadequate command of the work, study skills, etc. Hence, corrective work in the basic skills plus improved motivation in the subject may be sufficient enough to effect improvement.

The following are the general principles of remedial teaching

- Individual consideration of the backward pupils with recognition of his mental, physical and educational characteristics.
- Thorough diagnosis with a pre-test.
- Early success for the pupils in his backward subject(s) by use of suitable methods and materials.
- Dissipation of emotional barriers through early success, praise, continuous help, sympathetic consideration of his difficulties and sustained interest.
- The need for a new orientation towards the backward subject through new methods, involving play way approaches activities and an appropriately graded materials.
- Frequent planned remedial lessons.
- Cooperation with the parents.

Strategies of Remedial Teaching

Peer's Support Programme

Remedial teachers may train up pupils who perform better in a certain subject to become 'little teachers', who will be responsible for helping schoolmates with learning difficulties in group teaching and self-study sessions as well as outside class.

Peer Support Programme helps pupils to reinforce their knowledge and to develop their communication and cooperation skills as well as good inter-personal relationships.

Reward Scheme

The reward scheme has positive effect in enhancing pupil's motivation. It aims at guiding pupils to set their own objectives and plans and positively reinforcing their good performance. It helps to cultivate an interest in learning and to gain a sense of satisfaction and achievement during the learning process.

Steps of Remedial Teaching

Curriculum Adaptation Remedial teachers should adapt the curriculum to accomodate the learning characteristics and abilities of pupils. They should set some teaching objectives which are easy to achieve and ensure that pupils may acquire the knowledge as desired after completion of each module. Teachers should make good use of all teaching materials.

Homework Policies Formulation of clear policies on homework which should be reviewed regularly. The assignments should be targeted at the teaching objectives and serve the purposes of learning. Teacher should design homework for pupils which should have clear objectives and can accomodate the levels and needs of pupils. Homework should be used as a tool of evaluation and feedback to enhance the motivation and effectiveness of learning.

Formulation of Teaching Plans Teacher should formulate practical teaching objectives that meet the learning characteristics and weaknesses of pupils, as to foster a sense of achievement.

On the other hand, teachers should decide whether the learning items should be taught in detail or in brief.

Teaching Activities Aids and Supporting Materials Teachers should design an appropriate learning activities in line with the focus of teaching. They should encourage students to participate actively during the learning process, to help to master the skills and methods of collaborative teaching. When designing and using teaching aids, teachers should first consider their practical use and assess, whether the aim of remedial teaching can be attained.

Setting of Learning Environment Well designed learning environment helps to maintain pupil's attention and interest in learning and facilitates the achievement of teaching aims. The teaching environment should be designed to support remedial teaching and group activities. Teachers may display the teaching materials of the week at prominent places, to stimulate their motivation in learning.

Development of Generic Skills Remedial teachers should help pupils, to develop good learning habits and attitudes, such as to complete the assignments tidily, be responsible and disciplined. Pupils should be helped to master basic self-learning skills and abilities. For e.g. teachers may teach them how to set an appropriate learning objectives, priorities, time management, reading skills and examination taking skills, etc.

Teachers should also train pupils, to establish good inter-personal relationship as to facilitate an effective communication and collaboration, as well as to enhance the team spirit of students.

Assessment It plays a very crucial role in teaching and learning by means of assessment, remedial teachers can known the learning process as well as strengths and weaknesses of pupils, hence, they may design different teaching activities accordingly, to help pupils to learn in an effective manner.

Parents and Professionals' Partnership

It is regarded as the context, in which an educational programming should take place. Partnership between families of children with disabilities and professionals is particularly essential because specialized knowledge for care and development of these children is often required. Families can play key roles as both recipients and providers to enrich professional development for all learners. Successful implementation of inclusive educational programmes require the involvement and the support from the parents of learning disabilities, children at all levels. Teachers should consider parental involvement in education of their children with special needs as a parental support in the child's education, linking two important contexts in child's life education *i.e.* home and school.

Role of Parents

Parents matter in inclusive education as vital partners, who contribute much to the work of educators, schools and communities. They matter as parent leaders, mentors and models of commitments to excellence in an education and they matter everyday as they influence and support their children's academic achievement.

Active parental involvement has been considered to be an important factor related to better outcomes in an education of young children with and without disabilities in an inclusive childhood's programmes. Research has shown that high levels of parental involvement correlate with improved academic performance, higher test scores, more positive attitude towards schools, fewer placements in special education, academic perservance, lower dropout rates and fewer suspensions. For children, involvement of their parents is reported to lead to improvements in attitudes, behaviours and attendance at school, as well as their mental health. Without parent's involvement in the school, disagreements may escalate leading to increased stress, costs and reducing communication and relationships between parents and school.

Mainly, there are three barriers of parental involvement and they are

- School barriers (School's rules, schedule, etc)
- Parental barriers (Time, feeling of shame, etc)
- Other barriers (distance of school from work, relationship with teacher, etc)

Role of Peers

Peer's support is a strategy that involves placing students in pairs or in small groups to participate in learning activities that support academic instruction and social skills. This instructional approach does not require additional staff or extra funding. Peer's support provides teachers with a learning tool, to enhance instructions for students with and without disabilities. *The role of peer is so beneficial for the students with disabilities, as it is discussed below*

- Boosts friendship.
- Increases social initiations, relationships and networks.
- Increases achievement of IEP's goals.
- Greater access to general curriculum.
- Enhances skill acquisition and generalisation.
- Greater opportunities for interactions.
- Higher expectations.

- Increases school-staff collaboration.
- Families are more integrated into community.

With support and encouragement from adults, young children with and without disabilities can form connections that not only provide enjoyment but help to promote their growth and development in multiple domains.

Role of Professionals

In inclusive education, an inclusion specialist professional is a certified teacher who have specialised knowledge of current principles and techniques of educating students with significant disabilities in general education classrooms. The specialist, not only provides support to students in inclusion programmes, but also assists general education teachers to ensure that students have chances to succeed in the classroom.

In addition, a specialist effectively communicates with parents, concerning all aspects of their child's educational program. They possesses extensive knowledge of disabilities from mild/moderate to severe and have experience in supporting students with a wide range of educational and support needs. Their role is to regularly attend meetings, related to special education and consult with other professionals to continuously implement the best inclusion practices for students with a range of disabilities.

Role of Teachers

Most of the teachers, who teaches in an inclusive classroom modifies their curricula to meet the needs of their special education students. Teacher's role is to communicate regularly with the school, to make sure that she is aware of the specific learning needs of special education students and the academic resources that are necessary for them to experience success in an inclusive classroom's setting.

It is also important for teachers to create a safe classroom environment that allows special needs children to learn alongside their peers, while experiencing positive socialisation. Teachers are an essential component to ensure the quality of students, inclusion in the school environment. Teachers have direct interaction with students and play a vital role in determining student's experiences in the classroom, on daily basis.

Educators are required to reconsider their roles, construct new knowledge and learn new skills to equip themselves for the change. Now, the teachers are expected to address problems and to provide solutions, posed by special needs students who may vary in their skill levels. Now, they are required to undertake initial screening of students, who are at risk and adapts instruction to make them responsive to special needs of the students, to contribute in Individualised Education Program, meeting work, collaboratively with parents and other professionals and use technology to assist students to overcome their shortfalls.

Role of School

School leadership should be transformative, systematically promoting academic achievements, family and community empowerment, democratic engagement and global citizenship. These values are always essential and even more important in the context of inclusive schools. The school should provide on the job training and mentoring to the teachers who are the part of an inclusive classroom setup. It must try to build a trusting and collaborative work environment for their staff.

According to **Thomas**, "A school performs various functions like mental training, training character, training in health and sanitation, etc. A school should aims to all round development of a child and should provides training to fulfil the aims of society and nation".

Following are the important functions or roles of school in nation's development

Development of Values An important function of school is to cultivate higher values of life in the pupils. Morality should be developed, so that students may be in a position to judge right and wrong.

All Round Development of a Child The school is meant for the all round development of a child *i.e.* physical, intellectual, emotional, social, aesthetical, moral and spiritual, through its curricular and co-curricular activities like debates, declamations, exhibitions, games and sports.

Promotion of Social Efficiency It promotes social efficiency by cultivating a balanced sense of rights and duties and by providing training for an effective participation.

Developing International Understanding Another function of the school is to develop international understanding in the mind of the pupils. It implies respect for human rights and dignity, international cooperation and to live together in peace with one another.

Training for Leadership The school should discharge the function of importing training for leadership.

This can be done by providing various types of co-curricular activities in the educational institutions and encouraging students to take part in these activities.

EXAM BASED QUESTIONS

1 Inclusive classroom is
(a) same as special education classroom
(b) a general education classroom in which students with and without disabilities learns together
(c) a special educator is appointed
(d) None of the above

2 Success of inclusive education depends on
(a) community's support
(b) attitudinal change among teachers
(c) high quality teaching-learning material
(d) high quality textbooks

3 An inclusive classroom provides strong ...... and opportunities for team building.
(a) values (b) leadership
(c) group (d) structure

4 Teacher should makes the seating arrangement, in such a way that it will benefits ....
(a) disabled students (b) non-disabled students
(c) slow learners (d) all students

5 Which is not a part of an inclusive classroom's practice?
(a) Collaborative teaching
(b) Activity based learning
(c) Peer-tutoring
(d) Differentiated instruction

6 Computers with speech software are meant for
(a) blind pupil (b) deaf pupil
(c) speech impaired (d) Both a and c

7 Posters and flip charts assist students in
(a) tracing knowledge (b) understanding concept
(c) revising concept (d) None of these

8 Sign language interpreters are for ...... students.
(a) blind (b) slow learners
(c) deaf (d) speech impaired

9 Who argues that "despite the fact that educators didn't receive in-service training on inclusion, they are expected to implement more effective delivery techniques"?
(a) King Carreiro (b) Richard A Villa
(c) Thomas. P (d) Gary Thomas

10 The main objective of planning and management of inclusive classroom is
(a) to provide effective delivery techniques
(b) to focus upon the overall development of learner's need
(c) ensuring discipline
(d) None of the above

11 Give the full form of INSET ......
(a) Instructional Education and Training
(b) In-Service Training and Education
(c) In-Service Education and Training
(d) None of the above

12 INSET refers to
(a) instructional programmes, provided for continued professional development of educational practitioners during their working years
(b) branch of education concerned with scientific study of instructional design and development
(c) a method that a teacher uses during instruction
(d) None of the above

13 Inclusive schools are required for equality of an educational opportunities among
(a) talented students
(b) backward students
(c) disabled and slow learners
(d) All of these

14 Delay in identification of barriers to learning prevents learners from ....
(a) low self-esteem (b) early drop out
(c) behavioural difficulties (d) All of the above

15 Educators are expected to use variety of teaching strategies
(a) to suit the needs of all learners
(b) to start formulating hypothesis
(c) to suit the needs of talented learners
(d) None of the above

16 Educators use important principles in inclusive classroom such as
(a) motivation
(b) Task Analysis
(c) reduction of subject's matter
(d) All of the above

17 The preferred approaches to assessment of special needs for an inclusion in the regular classrooms are
(a) contextual (b) performance oriented
(c) interactive (d) All of these

18 Class's organisation is relevant because
(a) unorganized classroom creates a sense of instability
(b) to utilize the space appropriately
(c) it creates positive learning environment
(d) All of the above

19 Decisions about classroom's organisation, needs to support
(a) interactivity (b) instability
(c) inclusivity (d) None of these

20 For an inclusive classroom, an educator needs a .... curriculum.
(a) rigid (d) flexible (c) resistant (d) inflexible

21 **Statement I** It is an ongoing process.
Statement II The adaptation should not change original concept of curriculum.
Codes
(a) Statement I is true
(b) Both the statements, I and II are true
(c) Statement II is false
(d) Both statements, I and II are false

22 Content should be .... in an inclusive setup.
(a) teacher-centered (b) subject-centered
(c) learner-centered (d) None of these

23 The preferred approaches to assessment of special needs includes
(a) Holistic approach
(b) Multi-Perspective approach
(c) Performance Oriented approach
(d) All of the above

24 Students with visual impairment need infrastructure including
(a) guide blocks and specific signs to indicate rooms and other facilities.
(b) ramps
(c) arranged furniture
(d) All of the above

25 Training and development areas need to be focused because
(a) it helps in development of conducive environment within the school
(b) it helps in talent retention
(c) it is required as per the changing needs
(d) All of the above

26 Using of technology is an ....
(a) instructional practice (b) educational reform
(c) educational strategy (d) None of these

27 UDL stands for
(a) Universal Difference for Learning
(b) Universal Design for Learning
(c) Universal Design for Learner
(d) None of the above

28 Inclusive curriculum should be planned to agree with
(a) the goals, purposes and interests of the pupils
(b) available textbooks in various subjects
(c) training and development of teachers
(d) None of the above

29 Educators must employ .... learning strategies to promote recall and understanding of new learning.
(a) formal (b) active
(c) passive (d) content based

30 Curriculum adaptation is a .... process.
(a) direct (b) absolute (c) ongoing (d) indirect

31 An objective of adaptation is to provide ....
(a) construct validity
(b) learning experiences to all learners
(c) learning experiences to few learners
(d) None of the above

32 .... activities should be planned in such a way that the child gets a holistic picture of the concepts taught in the class.
(a) Compensatory (b) Collaborative
(c) Modified (d) None of these

33 .... technologies are found useful in creating new abilities for children and adults with disabilities.
(a) Adaptive (b) Assistive
(c) Reflective (d) None of these

34 Computer screen magnification, screen readers and Braille scanning software are for
(a) low vision students
(b) visually impaired students
(c) hearing impaired students
(d) Both a and b

35 A person can enlarge a section of text upto .... times of an original size, with the help of computer screen magnification.
(a) 10 (b) 20 (c) 16 (d) 25

36 The Personal Frequency Modulation system consists of a .... used by the speaker and receiver and also used by the listener.
(a) spoken message (b) transmitter micro-phone
(c) micro-chip (d) None of the above

37 The emerging patterns of technologies in teaching for speech impaired children is as followed. Which of the following is incorrect?
(a) Assistive technologies
(b) Augmentative or alternative communication
(c) Braille scanning
(d) None of the above

38 Individualised Education Plan is created to ....
(a) help an individual student with special needs
(b) to promote active learning environment in the class
(c) help the group of students
(d) None of the above

39 The goal(s) of Individualised Education plan is/are to
(a) document specially designed instruction for each student with disability
(b) deliver a comprehensive, free and appropriate education with involvement of many participants
(c) deliver a high-quality framework
(d) All of the above

40 Remedial teaching is based upon ....
(a) careful diagnosis of defects to the needs and interest of the pupils
(b) observation only
(c) analysis of the teacher
(d) None of the above

41 To tackle with the variety of individual problems, a remedial teacher needs a rich background in
(a) inclusive education
(b) child psychology and educational diagnosis
(c) special education
(d) None of the above

42 High level of parental involvement helps in
(a) improving academic performance
(b) higher test scores
(c) positive attitude towards school
(d) All of the above

43 Peer's support is necessary, as it provides teachers with
(a) a learning tool, to enhance instruction for students with and without disabilities
(b) higher expectation from students
(c) enhance skill acquisition and generalisation
(d) greater opportunities for interactions

44 Teachers play important role in the classroom as
(a) they have direct interaction with students
(b) adapts instructions, to make them responsive to the special needs of students
(c) they use technology to assist students
(d) All of the above

45 The school should provide
(a) on the job training (b) mentoring the teachers
(c) collaborative work environment
(d) All of the above

46 Match the following.

List I	List II
A. Braille books	1. Handicapped people
B. Sign language interpreters	2. Visually impaired people
C. Ramps	3. Deaf people
D. Computer electronic speech devices	4. Speech impaired people

Codes

	A	B	C	D		A	B	C	D
(a)	2	1	3	4	(b)	2	3	1	4
(c)	1	2	3	4	(d)	3	4	2	1

47 Consider the following statements regarding the role of schools in national development.
Statement I To cultivate higher values of life in the pupils.
Statement II School should develop international understanding in the minds of pupils.
Codes
(a) Both statements, I and II are correct
(b) Only statement I is correct
(c) Only statement II is correct
(d) Neither I nor II is correct

48 Match the following.

List I	List II
A. School's rules and schedules	1. Parental barrier
B. Distance of school from work	2. School barrier
C. Feeling of shame	3. Other barrier

Codes

	A	B	C		A	B	C
(a)	2	1	3	(b)	1	2	3
(c)	2	3	1	(d)	3	2	1

Directions (Q. Nos. 49-58) *Read the given statements, one is labelled as Assertion (A) and other is labelled as Reason (R). Choose the correct code for the following statements.*

Codes
(a) Both A and R are true and R is the correct explanation of A
(b) Both A and R are true, but R is not the correct explanation of A
(c) Both A and R are false
(d) A is false, but R is true

49 **Assertion** (A) Teacher plays a central role in an inclusive classroom.
Reason (R) Teacher must understand social, physical and learning needs of students.

50 **Assertion** (A) An inclusive education brings students with diverse needs at one place.
Reason (R) It seeks to maximize the potential of all students.

51 **Assertion** (A) A variety of techniques and strategies are used in an inclusive education.
Reason (R) It helps in learning outcomes of the students.

52 **Assertion** (A) A good number of classroom practices are a part of an inclusive education.
Reason (R) Classroom practices didn't help much in implementation of an inclusive education.

53 **Assertion** (A) Educator needs training with concerning the background of the barriers to learning.
Reason (R) Training is going to be difficult if not possible for educators to manage.

54 **Assertion** (A) Content should equip learners with knowledge, skills, values and attitudes.
Reason (R) It should be based on Teacher-Centered Approach.

55 **Assertion** (A) Use of ICT, to enhance learning within an inclusive classroom is necessary for an effective inclusion.
Reason (R) An ICT will create confusions and problems for both students and teachers.

56 **Assertion** (A) Teacher has to adapt the curriculum as per the needs of students.
Reason (R) A flexible curriculum should be adopted, to benefit students.

57 **Assertion** (A) Assistive technologies are of no use, for disabled people.
Reason (R) It is used to compensate for lack of certain abilities.

58 Assertion (A) Special educators possess an extensive knowledge of disabilities.

Reason (R) They implement best methods and practices for students with disabilities.

59 Which of the following is not the characteristic(s) of an inclusive education?

1. Special help to students, in general classroom
2. Active learning atmosphere
3. Supportive role of a teacher
4. On the job training of teacher

Codes

(a) Only 2 (b) Both 1 and 3
(c) Neither 3 nor 4 (d) Only 4

60 For remedial teaching .... goals should be established

1. learner-centered 2. short term
3. subject-centered 4. teacher-centered

Codes

(a) Both 1 and 2 (b) Only 2
(c) Only 3 (d) Only 4

61 Educators use certain principles in their inclusive classrooms. From the following, which is **not** included as a principle?

1. Totality and individuality
2. Reduction of subject matter
3. Motivation
4. Task Analysis
5. Reliability

Codes

(a) Both 1 and 2 (b) Only 5
(c) Only 2 (d) Only 3

62 Teachers must adapt important classroom practices for an effective teaching. Which one of the following is based on the above activity?

1. Peer-tutoring
2. Collaborative teaching
3. Activity based learning
4. Whole class teaching
5. Cooperative learning

Codes

(a) Both 1 and 2 (b) Neither 2 nor 3
(c) Only 3 (d) Only 4

63 Rearrange the following in the correct sequence for an inclusive classroom.

1. Effective curriculum
2. Class organisation
3. Assessment
4. Content
5. Identification of learners
6. Teaching strategies

Codes

(a) 5 6 4 1 2 and 3 (b) 6 5 4 3 2 and 1
(c) 4 6 5 3 2 and 1 (d) 1 2 3 4 5 and 6

Directions (Q. Nos. 64-70) *Read the passage and answer the following questions.*

Mental retardation is a serious disability. Significantly, it refers to sub-average intellectual functioning, characterised by an inadequacy in adaptive behaviour. In other words, it is a condition in which people have below average intelligence that limits their ability to function normally. Persons who are mentally retarded may have problems with communication, taking care of themselves, daily living, social skills, community interactions, directing themselves, health and safety, school's leisures activities and work. They experience personal limitations in the social, leisure activities and work. They experience personal limitations in the social, economical and psychological spheres. They may become targets for ridicule, bullying and mockery. Sometimes, the adults of the community fail to encourage other children to be supportive and the mentally retarded have to face unpleasant encounters and cruelty from peers. There are four levels of mental retardation i.e. mild, moderate, severe and profound. On the basis of IQ scores, mentally retarded children are classified into four broad categories.

These are as follows

- Border Line or Dullers (IQ 70 to 90) - Mild
- Morons (IQ 50 to 70) - Moderate
- Imbeciles (IQ 25 to 50) - Severe
- Idiots (IQ < 25) - Profound

64 Mental retardation is a condition where people have .... intelligence.

(a) below average
(b) average
(c) above average
(d) None of the above

65 Mentally retarded persons may have problems with

(a) communication (b) daily living
(c) social skills (d) All of these

66 Mentally retarded persons, experience personal limitations in the social, psychological and .... spheres.

(a) community (b) economical
(c) political (d) personal

67 Four levels of mental retardation are

1. profound 2. moderate
3. mild 4. severe

Codes

(a) 3 2 4 and 1 (b) 1 2 4 and 3
(c) 2 3 4 and 1 (d) 4 2 3 and 1

68 Border Line or Dullers have an IQ of

(a) 50 to 70 (b) 25 to 50
(c) 70 to 90 (d) Below 25

69 Imbeciles have an IQ of
(a) 50 to 70 (b) 70 to 90
(c) 25 to 50 (d) Below 25

70 Idiots have an I Q of
(a) Below 25 (b) 25 to 50
(c) 50 to 70 (d) 70 to 90

Directions (Q. Nos. 71-75) *Read the passage and answer the following questions.*

Peer-tutoring is a mode of educational practices that involves one to one instruction. It could enhance the inclusion process in schools. This mode of tutoring involves or may involve a peer, an older student or an expert teacher in the tutoring role. Though, the subject has not received much attention in India and due attention is still pending from the side of government as well as the educationists, both in literature or in practice. It is such a system which is needed especially in Indian schools. It would be very relevant for Indian schools, where teacher shortage is one of the major systematic issue that has been impeding the efforts for universalisation of elementary education.

Many efforts have been carried out and expected results are still awaiting. From all types of tutoring, peer-tutoring is the most effective in an inclusive setting because it can be used to meet the special educational needs of children's education. It can also be a cross-age tutoring or a same age tutoring refers to instructional situation in which peer-tutor provides instruction to the younger children of lower grade. In any type of peer tutoring, the tutoring of spelling, hand-writing, arithmetic and social behaviours can be involved or used. It can be used once or twice in a week, in the last period. It helps in focusing the needs of special education children.

71 Peer-tutoring is a mode of
(a) social practice
(b) educational practice
(c) inclusive practice
(d) instructional practice

72 The major issue in Indian schools is of
(a) lack of resources
(b) increase dropouts
(c) teacher shortage
(d) lack of funding

73 Peer-tutoring is used effectively in
(a) special education
(b) an inclusive education
(c) an integrated education
(d) None of the above

74 Process of peer-tutoring can be used
(a) once in a week (b) thrice in a week
(c) daily (d) None of these

75 Peer-tutoring helps in focusing the needs of .... children.
(a) special (b) disabled
(c) non-disabled (d) None of these

76 Which of the following statement (s) is/are correct in context of an inclusive classroom education?
1. Specially designed instruction which meets special educational needs.
2. It is meant for exceptional children.
3. Special educators are required for inclusive classrooms.
4. Adopting and integrating flexible curriculum for students.

Codes
(a) 1 and 2 (b) 3 and 4
(c) Only 4 (d) None of these

77 Which of the following statement(s) is/are incorrect?
1. Inclusive education is an approach to attain the goals of universalisation of elementary education.
2. Inclusion means full inclusion of children with diverse abilities in schooling.
3. It requires special classrooms and special schools to meet the needs of all children.
4. It provides equal educational opportunities to the disabled and prepare them for independent living.

Codes
(a) Only 1 (b) Only 2
(c) Only 3 (d) All of these

78 Which of the following statement(s) is/are incorrect?
1. Instructional practices are used by educators to ensure, access to curricular content.
2. Universal design for learning should be used as instructional practice.
3. Active learning strategies must be promoted.
4. Instructional practices doesn't help the educators for inclusive classroom.

Codes
(a) Only 1 (b) Only 2
(c) Only 3 (d) All of these

79 Curriculum adaptation should be based on .... in the delivery of instruction.
1. teaching process
2. physical environment
3. content and activities
4. meet the learning requirements

Codes
(a) Only 1 (b) Only 3
(c) Only 4 (d) All of these

80 Signs of visual impairment are visible in a person when he/she faces problem of
1. blurred vision
2. complaint of dizziness
3. irregular eye movements
4. psychological effects
5. average motor skills

Codes
(a) 1 and 2 (b) 1, 2 and 3
(c) Only 4 (d) Only 5

81 Which of the following is not an assistive listening device?
(a) Audio loop
(b) Text telephone
(c) Digital alarm clock
(d) Real time translations

82 Which of the following is a type of learning disability?
(a) Reading/learning disability
(b) Mathematics/learning disability
(c) Resistant to treatment
(d) All of the above

83 A flexible curriculum allows for differentiation with regard to
(a) lesson
(b) object
(c) outcomes
(d) All of these

84 According to Loreman, Deppeler and Harvey, what facilities and infrastructures should be considered in inclusive schools?
(a) Ramps where there are steps
(b) Classroom's clutters
(c) Arrangement of furniture
(d) All of the above

85 Activities or supports that enable a child with a disability to reserve a free, appropriate public education and to benefit from special education programme are referred to as
(a) assistive technology
(b) universal design
(c) service delivery
(d) related services

86 Which of the following important principle(s) is/are used by educators in inclusive classroom?
(a) Motivation (b) Totality
(c) Task Analysis (d) All of the above

87 **Statement I** Facilities and infrastructures play an important role in serving special needs of students in an inclusive school.
Statement II An inclusive provides strong leadership and opportunities for team building.
Codes
(a) Only statement I is correct
(b) Only statement II is correct
(c) Both the statements, I and II are incorrect
(d) Both the statements, I and II are correct

88 Which of the following is/are the important function(s) of school in nation's development?
(a) Development of values
(b) All round development of the child
(c) Promotion of social efficiency
(d) All of the above

89 Consider the following statements about the role of professionals in inclusive education.
Statement I A professional is a certified teacher who have specialised knowledge of current affairs and techniques of educating students.
Statement II They have direct interaction with students and plays an important role in determining student's experiences in the classroom.
Codes
(a) Only statement I is true
(b) Both statements, I and II are true
(c) Only statement II is true
(d) Neither a nor c

90 Under the scheme of integrated education, the handicapped children are provided which of the following allowance(s) and facilit(y) (ies)?
(a) Uniform allowance for ₹ 50 per annum
(b) Transport allowance of ₹ 50 per month
(c) Books and stationary allowance of ₹ 4000 per annum
(d) All of the above

ANSWERS

1 (b)	2 (b)	3 (b)	4 (d)	5 (d)	6 (d)	7 (b)	8 (c)	9 (a)	10 (b)
11 (c)	12 (a)	13 (d)	14 (d)	15 (a)	16 (d)	17 (d)	18 (d)	19 (a)	20 (b)
21 (d)	22 (c)	23 (d)	24 (a)	25 (d)	26 (a)	27 (b)	28 (a)	29 (b)	30 (c)
31 (b)	32 (a)	33 (b)	34 (d)	35 (c)	36 (b)	37 (c)	38 (a)	39 (d)	40 (a)
41 (b)	42 (d)	43 (a)	44 (d)	45 (d)	46 (b)	47 (a)	48 (c)	49 (a)	50 (a)
51 (a)	52 (b)	53 (a)	54 (b)	55 (b)	56 (a)	57 (c)	58 (a)	59 (d)	60 (a)
61 (b)	62 (c)	63 (a)	64 (a)	65 (d)	66 (b)	67 (a)	68 (c)	69 (c)	70 (a)
71 (b)	72 (c)	73 (b)	74 (a)	75 (a)	76 (c)	77 (c)	78 (c)	79 (d)	80 (b)
81 (c)	82 (d)	83 (d)	84 (d)	85 (a)	86 (d)	87 (c)	88 (d)	89 (a)	90 (d)

CHAPTER 41

Barriers and Facilitators in Inclusive Education

The importance of inclusive education cannot be neglected, the children with special needs occupy an important category. These children with disabilities are often left out of schools due to negative attitude and non-inclusive setup. There are number of barriers that hinder proper practice of inclusive education in a country. There is a need to overcome the barriers by facilitating education to all children through inclusive education with positive attitude.

Barriers in Inclusive Education

Inclusive education is a process of strengthening the capacity of the education system, to reach out to all the learners. It involves restructuring the cultures, policies and practices in schools, so that they can respond to the diversity of students in their locality. For an inclusive school, the attitude of everyone in the school including administrators, teachers and other students, should be positive towards students with disabilities.

Although, inclusive education is a priority for Indian government and there have been legislations, programmes, etc, to make it successful, but still there are many barriers that hinders an effective implementation of inclusive educational policies in India.

Some of the main barriers are explained below

Attitudinal Barrier

The acceptance of children with special needs or intellectual disability is very low in the Indian society. Some parents finds it shameful, to introduce intellectually disabled children. Even if the parents are supportive, other family members or neighbours might not willingly accept such a child with open mind. Not only from the family system, but these children fall prey to such negative attitudes at schools too. School hardly makes any efforts to mould the curriculum or the school environment in a manner which suits the needs of the children. Due to lack of awareness or discussion programs to educate children without disabilities, regarding ways in which they can help these children to adjust to the mainstream

In this Chapter

education system or to provide them a sense of belongingness in the schools. Often, children with disabilities are bullied by their peers or kept segregated from all social activities in schools.

Financial Barrier

In a country like India, a lot of people can rarely afford the basic necessities of life, having a child with intellectual disability can only add up a financial burden on the parents. Regular visits to doctor, medication, counselling, support gears, such as wheelchairs, etc can escalate cost manifold. Also, the parents have this notion that these children have to be supported financially throughout their lifetime and thus, they try to save money for the future rather than investing on their education.

Social Barrier

A major barrier to inclusion for students with special educational needs is their difficulty in friendship formation and social interaction with students who do not have special education needs. Although inclusion in mainstream can lead to higher academic achievement for some students with SEN, there is research evidence to suggest that many of these students face social exclusion in the mainstream setting. A number of factors act as barriers to social inclusion for students with SEN. Many students with SEN have cognitive, sensory and social difficulties which hinder the processes necessary for social interaction.

Such skills like communication, understanding, memory and an ability to differentiate between playfulness and bullying do not usually come naturally to students with SEN. According to Kemp and Carter, the successful inclusion of students with intellectual disabilities depends on the students' ability to demonstrate social skills. Those who could not perform or play appropriately tended to be viewed as a burden or a responsibility.

Physical Barrier

Transportation and infrastructure play a major role in successful implementation of inclusive education in India. The school must bring about infrastructural changes, to provide a comfortable and safe environment for children with special needs. Moreover, they must arrange transportation facilities to provide barrier free access to schools.

Policy Barrier

There is a lot of ambiguity regarding education of children with special needs in India. On one hand, **Ministry of Social Justice and Empowerment** runs separate schools for special children and on the other hand, **Ministry of Human Resource Development** promotes inclusive education that creates a lot of confusion in the minds of the people.

Curriculum Barrier

In an education system, the curriculum is one of the major obstacle or tool to facilitate the development of more inclusive system. In India, curriculum is not able to meet the needs of a wide range of different learners. In developed countries, the curriculum is centrally designed and rigid, leaving little flexibility for local adaptations and for teachers to experiment and to try different approaches. As a result, the knowledge based curriculum, the examinations are also too much content oriented rather than success oriented. Usually, children with special needs, need more time to read and write their paper.

Untrained Teacher's Barrier

Teacher's training, abilities and attitudes can be major limitations for inclusive education. Adequately, the teachers are not that much trained, to teach the children with special needs. The training staff at all levels is not adequate. Presently, teacher's training is fragmented, uncoordinated and inadequate for taking place in a segregated manner i.e. one for special children and other for students with general capabilities. Thus, all teachers do not have proper skills and attitude towards learners with special needs, it is unlikely that these children will receive satisfactory education.

Organisation of the Education System

In India, education at schools is controlled by state and central boards. Often, they are centrailised and this inhibits change and initiative. Responsibility for decision tends to be located at the highest level and focus of management remains towards employee's complying with the rules, rather than ensuring quality service delivery. Those having access to private schools have higher possibility of success as compared to those who go to government schools, but high cost becomes a barrier.

Constraints of Resources

Adequate financial resources is a big challenge to inclusion. India is among the countries that have a low 'Education for all Index' (EDI) of less than 800 and it is ranked 105 among 129 countries. Countries with high EDI (above 950) has government spending ranging from 5.4% to 7.7%. For inclusion, every institution requires to make financial provisions, for providing facilities like lifts, ramps, barrier free classrooms, toilets, etc. Technology can be used in the form of motion sensors to open the doors and automatic door buttons, for easier access through doors. There is a need to create learning resources for persons with disability. This could be in the form of digital library, Braille literature and additional visual resources for students with hearing disability. Also, financial resources will be required to train and restrain faculty for teaching persons with disabilities, in an inclusive environment.

Facilitators in Inclusive Education

The facilitators for successfully incorporating students with disabilities in the inclusive education classroom emerged due to various barriers in the inclusive education.

The facilitators required for a successful inclusive setup are

Parental Involvement

It is crucial in ensuring a child's educational success. There is a need to promote increased involvement of parents of children with disabilities and the community at large, in supporting inclusive practices in schools. Parents should be encouraged to participate in the organisation involved with the public schools, including parent-teacher organisation and disability person's organisation.

Recognising and Addressing Individual's Difference

This would range from changes in existing assessment, diagnosis and evaluation process, to develop new methods for responding to the particular needs of children with disabilities, within regular education. It will improve distribution of information concerning success practices by reviewing identification and evaluation methods including regular educators in the planning process. For instance, teachers may use proactive classroom's intervention strategies aimed at meeting the needs of learners with visual impairments. Making learners with low vision to sit in front and sometimes preparing separate work for them.

Legislation, Policy and National Policies

The world report on disabilities indicates that the success of inclusive education depends largely on the country's commitment, to adopt appropriate legislation, to develop policies and plans and to provide appropriate funding for its implementation. A policy of inclusion needs to be implemented in all schools and throughout the India. Schools need to become centers that can prepare children for life and ensure that all children especially, the differently abled children must get the maximum benefit of this critical area of education. The central and state governments, as well as other social actors should recognize the importance of broadened concept of inclusive education that addresses the diverse needs of all learners.

Building Teacher's Capacity

According to the **World Disability Report,** "an appropriate training for regular teachers is crucial if they are to be confident and competent in teaching children with various educational needs". This would include curriculum adoption, behaviour management, collaborative teaching techniques, problem-solving strategies and preparation of meaningful IEP which can be used in regular classrooms.

Teacher's attitude towards inclusive education could be formed and developed in the context of an educational system, which can provide some specific conditions in order to have a good practice in this field.

In-service training programs, for duration of two to three weeks for general and special educators, in all the disabilities and in specific areas of disability should arrange to effectively teach children with disabilities. There must be periodic evaluation of the training programs and constant update, to meet the challenges of changing trends in special education should be a part of the planning of teacher's preparation.

Funding

The school funding must be decentralised, to allow budgeting to be done at local (school) level basing on enrollment and other indicators. Bringing special children into mainstream requires adjustments that schools need to make in advance.

Transport facilities should be altered, so that these children can move around with relative ease. Architecturally, there should be ramps and wheelchairs access, constructed in service areas like toilets. Student oriented components such as medical and educational assessment, books and stationary, uniform, transport allowance, support services, assistive devices, therapeutic service, etc should be provided according to the needs of the students.

Overcoming Negative Attitude

The teachers should develop positive attitude towards students with disabilities and it may be achieved through workshops on disabilities, where types and causes of various disabilities are discussed to help and to remove the fear of such condition.

Those schools that are committed to take children with special needs, the teachers must attend workshops in order to be adjusted to the child's needs. Research indicates that negative attitude towards a person with disability may lead to low expectations, which in turn can lead to reduced learning opportunities.

Development of Inclusive Education in India

The Government of India has attempted to create policies that are inclusive for people with disabilities, but their implementation efforts have not resulted in an inclusive system of education, nor they have reached their goal of 'education for all' across the country. There is a need to bridge the gap in the education system, to build a strong system of inclusive education in India.

Let us discuss the steps that have been taken by the Government of India in order to promote education in inclusive setting.

They are

- There are several articles in the Constitution that refers to measures, to be taken towards improving accessibility of education in India. For instance, Article 29 states that no citizen shall be denied to take admission and Article 45 talks of provision of free and compulsory education for all children, until they complete the age of 14 years.
- **Kothari Commission Report** (1964-66) identified mass illiteracy as one of the major problem that India was facing and gave many recommendations for increasing productivity of the citizens and strengthening social and national integration.
- **The National Policy of Education** (1968) stressed the need for promoting rapid universalisation of education as well as prevention of wastage and stagnation. In order to implement it, the **Integrated Education for Disabled Children** (IEDC) scheme was launched in december 1974, for admitting children with disabilities in regular schools.
- The **National Policy of Education** (NPE, 1986) supported universalisation of education.
- In 1992, India launched the **Programme of Action** in order to implement the **NPE** (1986) in an effective manner. Under this programme, the **Project Integrated Education for the Disabled** (PIED) launched in 1987 for encouraging schools to emend children with disabilities in their children.
- The principle of inclusion brought along a change in the attitude towards the learning abilities of children with disabilities. The difficulty that a child exhibited in learning was not to be attributed to the child, but to the school system. This attitude became the prime reason for the addition of inclusive education into the **District Primary Education Programme** in 1997.
- It drews the attention of government for the need of universalisation of education, which subsequently led to the birth of the **Sarva Shiksha Abhiyan** in 2001.
- Following a successful implementation of **Sarva Shiksha Abhiyan**, a programme to universalise secondary education has been launched, under the movement **Rashtriya Madhyamik Shiksha Abhiyan** (2009). This scheme was introduced to promote inclusive education at secondary level.
- The **Central Board of Secondary Education (CBSE)** has set up an inclusion panel for children with special needs. It says that the committee should act as a facilitator for promoting inclusive education at schools and in neighbourhoods. It also takes steps to raise public awareness for the importance of equality, overcoming discrimination and to prohibit harrassment and victimisation, for a child with special needs in school.
- The latest development in the field of education is the Right to Free and Compulsory Education Act or **Right to Education** (RTE), which was passed in the Parliament on 4th August, 2009 and came into force on 1st April, 2010.

Among, people with disabilities, the most vulnerable groups are at the risk of social exclusion. On an analysis of the general condition of the disabled population that consists almost 10% of the world's population, one realises that this population is excluded from essential services which ultimately affect their participation and eventually leading their exclusion from the society. So, to handle this problem among the disabled and disadvantaged people a society must understand accept and respect diversity.

If a society is inclusive then it, not only recognises diversity but also embodies it so that each member of the diverse society can achieve their full potential in life.

Current Status of Inclusive Education in India

The Government of India since independence has undertaken a number of initiatives to provide education to children with disabilities. However, the attempts made by the government have not any significant effect impact so far. The children with disabilities still continue to be the most excluded and remains outside the school system.

To understand the current scenario of inclusive education in India, the following points need to be considered

- All the clauses of the RTE that could have been interpreted fully for the inclusion of the child with disabilities, have remained narrow in execution and thinking.
- Infrastructure that could have been made barrier free for all children with disabilities, has been narrowed down to the ramp and rail. The commitment to provide transport to children with disabilities has not started yet, in most of the states.
- The commitment to give basic facilities like toilets, drinking water, mid-day meals, etc are not available and has not been interpreted in a way that must be accessible, to children with disabilities and the state is not expected to report on this.
- Curriculum that have the power to enrich the child for life, have become whittled down to adaptations to be made for specific impairment groups. There is a little discussion on the aims of education and the heterogeneity of pedagogies that can be used.
- Teaching and learning materials have become limited to the supply of Braille books or books in large points. Little attempt has been made, to cater to the needs of all children who communicate differently.
- For implementing inclusive education in all educational institutions, at all levels, we need strong support services. But, existing support services are scarce and inadequate.
- Schools need accommodation for truly practicing inclusive education. However, such accommodations are not there in majority of schools. Facilities such as lifts, directional cues, etc. are mostly not available in schools.
- There is insufficient and improper pre-service teacher education programmes, so modification is needed to make these programmes effective. Currently, the teacher education programmes producing special teachers are controlled by Rehabilitation Council of India. Whereas, the general teachers are controlled by National Council for Teacher Education. Thus, these two apex bodies need to collaborate and devise measures for producing skilled teachers capable of implementing inclusive education.
- The implementation of the policies framed by the government towards inclusive education is not adhered effectively.
- Despite these barriers, there is also a silver lining that must be acknowledged. Clearly, there is a growing interest in governmental institutions to understand the barriers that can affect the Right to Education, for children with disabilities and take steps to break these barriers.
- In 2013, the National Commission for the Protection of Child's Rights, organised a national level workshop on the Rights of Children with disabilities to inclusive education, under RTE Act, 2009.
- In 2014, the **UNESCO** and **UNICEF** also organised national level consultation, that address the issue and the use of information and communication technologies in education. Major civil society networks like the RTE forum, the Indian Alliance for Child Rights and others are addressing disability issues and voices of the children with disabilities and being heard in these forums.

Ethical Issues of Inclusive Education

Ethical issues are those issues, in which people struggle to figure out the right thing to do. In inclusive education, the struggle to determine what is right and wrong is very tricky, as educators often need to balance the needs and wants of different educational stakeholders, from teachers and administrators to parents and most importantly students. The values and attitudes of professional educators and the manner in which they manage the learning of these pupils can raise important issues.

In inclusive classroom, it is more about adapting an educational environment, so that the system becomes more supportive and responsive to diverse learners. Teachers need to provide students who have disabilities with more individualised instruction.

Research Trends of Inclusive Education in India

Inclusive education has been regarded as the most viable strategy, to ensure rights of children with special needs to quality education in both developed and developing countries.

In India, the following trends and practices are central towards attainment of the goals of inclusive education for children, with special needs.

They are

Cross Disability Approach It is an approach which comprehensively takes into account all different kinds of disabilities, together and promotes collective planning in inclusive classroom.

Vocationalisation of Education The scheme, **Vocationalisation of Higher Secondary Education** was approved in September, 2011 and revised after the approval of the cabinet committee on skill development on 12th February, 2014. The components of the scheme include introduction of vocational education in government schools from class IX, building capacity for existing vocational education through in-service training and induction for new vocational education teachers. Teachers need to provide students who have disabilities with more individualised instruction.

Cooperative/Team Teaching A situation in a classroom, where two teachers work together on a class may be called a cooperative teaching. This can be used in any classroom, where a general educator collaborates with a special education.

Integration of ICT in Education The recent efforts of Government of India seek to deepen the use of ICT, in almost every sphere of life. The three cardinal principles of the draft of **New National Education Policy** (2016) *viz.* access, equity and quality could be served well, by harnessing the huge potential of ICT. An ICT curriculum is a common programme for all students in school.

Activity Based Learning It is a technique adopted by teachers to emphasise their own method of teaching through activity, in which the students participate rigorously and brings about efficient learning experiences. It is a Child-Centered approach. It is a method in which the child actively participates, mentally and physically.

Co-Curricular Adaptation It facilitates the development of various domains of mind and personality, such as an intellectual development, emotional development, social development, moral development and aesthetic development. It also facilitates creativity, enthusiasm and energetic domain. They are true and practical experiences, received by students.

Adapted Physical Education Although, specific disabilities may affect the intensity, duration and frequency of exercise, individuals with disabilities can benefit from training, including improving their performances. Wheel-chairs can be adjusted or modified to improve physical activity performance. For example, athletes on wheelchairs can play basketball, tennis and many other sports.

Continuous and Comprehensive Evaluation (CCE) It refers to a system of school based evaluation, that covers all aspects of student's development. The objectives selected for evaluation, are in continuity to access learning and behavioral outcomes of each. It helps in bringing awareness of the achievement of the child, teachers and parents from time to time.

Use of Assistive Technology Many students with disabilities require assistive technology to participate and to get benefit from the educational programmes. Assistive devices and technologies are those, whose primary purpose is to maintain and improve individual's functioning and independence to facilitate participation and to enhance the overall well-being.

Universal Design for Learning It is a way of thinking about teaching and learning that gives all students equal opportunity to learn. Teacher designs learning experiences in flexible ways, to meet the needs of individual learners. It is intended to enhance and access to learning by reducing physical, cognitive, intellectual and organisational barriers and other obstacles to learning.

EXAM BASED QUESTIONS

1 Inclusive education is a process of
(a) strengthening the capacity of education system
(b) it reaches out to all the learners
(c) involves restructuring the practices in schools
(d) All of the above

2 For an inclusive school, what is required?
(a) Attitude of administrators
(b) Collaborative environment
(c) Attitude of teachers
(d) All of the above

3 Which of the following is not a barrier in the implementation of inclusive education?
(a) Attitudinal barrier
(b) Financial barrier
(c) Recognising individual difference
(d) Physical barrier

4 Attitudinal barrier arises due to
(a) lack of awareness
(b) lack of discussion programmes
(c) narrow mindedness of people
(d) All of the above

5 Attitudinal barriers can be removed with the help of
(a) discussion programmes
(b) parental support
(c) providing a sense of belongingness in the school
(d) All of the above

6 Financial barriers lead to problems of
(a) financial burden on parents
(b) negative attitude
(c) high responsibility
(d) None of the above

7 Which majorly forms a problem in successful implementation of inclusive education?
(a) Transportation (b) Infrastructure
(c) Environment (d) Both a and b

8 Which ministry runs a separate school for special children?
(a) Ministry of Social Justice and Empowerment
(b) Ministry of Human Resource Development
(c) Ministry of Home Affairs
(d) None of the above

9 Which ministry promotes inclusive education?
(a) Ministry of Home Affairs
(b) Ministry of Human Resource Development
(c) Ministry of Social Justice and Empowerment
(d) None of the above

10 Which of the following is/are the major obstacle(s) or tool(s) to facilitate the development of inclusive system?
(a) Curriculum (b) Instructions
(c) Teaching aids (d) None of these

11 Why the curriculum is unable to meet the needs of diverse learners?
(a) Curriculum is rigid (b) Content oriented
(c) Centrally designed (d) All of these

12 What is the major limitation of inclusive education?
(a) Teacher's training (b) Attitude of teachers
(c) Both a and b (d) None of these

13 What is the present situation of teacher's training for inclusive classrooms?
(a) Fragmented
(b) Uncoordinated and inadequate
(c) Improper skills of teachers
(d) All of the above

14 Which country has low EDI?
(a) Korea (b) India (c) China (d) Sri Lanka

15 What is the rank of India in EDI?
(a) 102 (b) 104 (c) 105 (d) 107

16 The countries with high government spending in education sector has an EDI of …… .
(a) below .800 (b) above .950
(c) below .950 (d) below .900

17 What is the percentage of government spending in education, in developed countries?
(a) 5.4% to 7.7% (b) More than 7.7%
(c) Less than 4% (d) Less than 5%

18 How the technology can be used for disabled children in schools?
(a) By providing barrier free classrooms
(b) By motion sensors to open doors
(c) By providing automatic door buttons
(d) Both b and c

19 Which type of learning resource would be helpful for disabled people?
(a) Digital library (b) Braille Literature
(c) Visual resources (d) All of these

20 Why there is a need of parental involvement in an inclusive education?
(a) Ensuring child's educational success
(b) To motivate the child
(c) Both a and b
(d) None of the above

21 How can an educator address the needs of learners based on their individual differences?
(a) Changing the existing assessment process
(b) Changing the existing evaluation process
(c) Developing new methods
(d) All of the above

22 Which strategy can be used for visually impaired by the teachers?
(a) Proactive classroom intervention strategies
(b) Audio-visual software strategies
(c) Both a and b
(d) None of the above

23 What did the world report suggests about the success of inclusive education?
(a) Commitment to adopt legislation and to develop policies and plans
(b) To provide an appropriate funding
(c) To address the needs of learners
(d) Both a and b

24 Why there is a need for building teacher's capacity in an inclusive education?
(a) For the maximum benefit of children
(b) To address the needs of diverse learners
(c) Both a and b
(d) None of the above

25 Why is it necessary to have periodic evaluation of the training programmes?
(a) Constantly updating
(b) Meeting the challenges of changing trends
(c) To provide specific conditions
(d) Both a and b

26 The school funding must be ......
(a) centralised
(b) decentralised
(c) Both a and b
(d) None of these

27 Which adjustment(s) is/are necessary for bringing special children into mainstream schools?
(a) Proper architectural development
(b) Student's oriented components
(c) Transport facilities should be altered
(d) All of the above

28 What should be done to overcome the negative attitude of teachers, in handling children with special needs?
(a) Teachers must attend workshops
(b) Teachers must be committed
(c) Teachers should not bother
(d) Children must be adjusted

29 Why inclusive policies are not successful in Indian education system?
(a) Lack of implementation efforts
(b) Due to policy's framework
(c) Lack of funds
(d) Attitude of teachers

30 Which effort should be done, to attain the goal of education for all ?
(a) To build a strong system of inclusive education.
(b) To bridge the gap in education system
(c) Proper implementation of policies
(d) All of the above

31 Action Plan for Children and Youth with Disabilities, came in the year
(a) 2007 (b) 2006 (c) 2005 (d) 2008

32 National Policy for People with Disabilities, came in the year
(a) 2005 (b) 2006 (c) 2007 (d) 2008

33 Why the government's policies are not perfectly inclusive?
(a) They lack in objectives
(b) They discriminate against people with severe disabilities
(c) They are not framed as per the needs
(d) None of the above

34 The inclusion panel is setup by CBSE to
(a) act as a facilitator for inclusive education
(b) take steps, to raise public awareness
(c) prohibit discrimination
(d) All of the above

35 Which Article of the Indian Constitution states that no citizen shall be denied to admission in the school?
(a) Article 14 (b) Article 29
(c) Article 45 (d) Article 26

36 Which Article of Indian Constitution states that there is a provision of free and compulsory education for all children, until they complete the age of 14 years?
(a) Article 29 (b) Article 26
(c) Article 45 (d) Article 14

37 Kothari Commission Report came during
(a) between 1964-66 (b) between 1966-68
(c) between 1968-70 (d) between 1970-72

38 The National Policy of Education came in the year
(a) 1965 (b) 1968 (c) 1967 (d) 1978

39 Integrated Education for Disabled Children scheme was launched in ......
(a) November, 1974 (b) January, 1975
(c) December, 1974 (d) December, 1975

40 Which policy supported the universalisation of education that came in 1986?
(a) National Policy on Education
(b) Project, Integrated Education for Disabled
(c) Sarva Shiksha Abhiyan
(d) Right to Education

41 The project, Integrated Education for Disabled was launched in ...
(a) 1986 (b) 1987 (c) 1992 (d) 1990

42 Which programme was implemented in 1997 for the addition of inclusive education?
(a) Sarva Shiksha Abhiyan
(b) District Primary Education
(c) Rashtriya Madhyamik Shiksha Abhiyan
(d) Right to Education

43 The Sarva Shiksha Abhiyan came in............
(a) 2000 (b) 2002
(c) 2001 (d) 2004

44 Which scheme was introduced to promote an inclusive education at secondary level?
(a) District Primary Education
(b) Sarva Shiksha Abhiyan
(c) Rashtriya Madhyamik Shiksha Abhiyan
(d) Programme of Action

45 The Right to Education was passed on
(a) 4th August, 2009 (b) 4th August, 2008
(c) 4th August, 2010 (d) 4th August, 2011

46 RTE Act came into force on
(a) 1st April, 2009 (b) 31st March, 2009
(c) 1st April, 2010 (d) 31st March, 2010

47 Which of the following is not the objective of research in an inclusive education?
(a) To identify effective practice models of special needs
(b) To provide recommendations to strengthen inclusive education
(c) To estimate the state of special needs in inclusive education
(d) None of the above

48 The scheme, Vocationalisation of Higher Secondary Education was approved in
(a) August, 2011 (b) September, 2011
(c) February, 2014 (d) August, 2014

49 Which curiculum is a common programme for all students in a school?
(a) ICT based curriculum
(b) Activity based curriculum
(c) Instruction based curriculum
(d) None of the above

50 Which method involves the child actively in participating mentally and physically?
(a) Team-teaching (b) Activity based learning
(c) Peer-tutoring (d) All of the above

51 Which learning design, gives all students equal opportunity to learn?
(a) Universal design for learning
(b) Comprehensive design for learning
(c) Adaptive design for learning
(d) None of the above

52 In which year, National Commission for the Protection of Child's Rights organised a national level workshop on the rights of children with disabilities?
(a) 2013 (b) 2011 (c) 2012 (d) 2014

Directions (Q. Nos. 53-60) *Two statements are given below, one labelled as Assertion (A) and other labelled as Reason (R). Choose the correct code for the following.*

Codes
(a) Both A and R are true, but R is not the correct explanation of A
(b) Both A and R are true and R is the correct explanation of A
(c) Both A and R are false
(d) A is false, but R is true

53 **Assertion** (A) Inclusive education strengthens the capacity of the education system.
Reason (R) It involves restructuring the culture, polices and practices in schools.

54 **Assertion** (A) Inclusive education is a priority for Indian government.
Reason (R) Inclusive policies are not successful in Indian education system, due to lack of implementation efforts.

55 **Assertion** (A) Children with disabilities are often bullied by their peers.
Reason (R) It is due to lack of awareness among the people.

56 **Assertion** (A) The school must not bring any type of infrastructual changes for special need children.
Reason (R) Infrastructural issue is a major aspect for special need children.

57 **Assertion** (A) Teachers are not trained properly, to teach the children with special needs.
Reason (R) Teacher's training and attitude can be a major limitation for inclusive education.

58 **Assertion** (A) Educational systems are often centralised.
Reason (R) Educational system inhibits change and an initiative to be taken up.

59 **Assertion** (A) Adequate financial povisions for providing facilities, must be granted to educational institutions.
Reason (R) For a successful inclusion, financial resources would be required.

60 **Assertion** (A) There is lack of academic research on inclusive education in India.
Reason (R) There is a need to fill the gap, by making a significant contribution.

61 Match the following.

	List I		List II
A.	Programme of Action	1.	2010
B.	Sarva Shiksha Abhiyan	2.	1992
C.	District Primary Education	3.	2001
D.	Right to Education	4.	1997

Codes

	A	B	C	D		A	B	C	D
(a)	2	3	4	1	(b)	3	2	1	4
(c)	1	2	3	4	(d)	4	3	2	1

62 Which statement is incorrect about social barriers to inclusive education?

1. Social barriers can be overcome through social interaction among the children.
2. Social barriers arose due to difficulty in friendship formation among the children.
3. Children face social, cognitive and sensory difficulties.
4. Social barriers enrich higher academic achivement.

Select the correct option from the following.

(a) 1 and 2 (b) 2 and 3
(c) 3 and 4 (d) Only 4

63 Which of the following statement(s) is/are incorrect?

1. ICT plays an important role in educational curriculum.
2. Government of India seeks to deepen the use of ICT in every sphere.
3. The ICT based curriculum will benefit diverse learners.
4. ICT curriculum lacks quality and access.

Select the correct option from the following.

(a) 1 and 2
(b) Neither 1 nor 2
(c) Only 3
(d) Only 4

64 Which of the following factors possess hurdle in achieving targets of universalisation of elementary education in India?

1. Materials to ensure minimum levels of learning.
2. Poverty of parents.
3. Slackness in implementing related provisions.
4. Availability of boundary walls and safe drinking water.
5. Mindset of parents and teachers.
6. Inadequacy of teachers.

Select the correct option from the following.

(a) 2 3 4 and 5 (b) 2 3 5 and 4
(c) 1 2 3 and 4 (d) 2 3 4 and 6

Directions (Q. Nos. 65-67) *Read the given passage and answer the following questions.*

Most of the school's personnels in India are not trained to design and implement educational programs for students with disabilities in regular schools. Most teacher training programs in India, do not have a unit on disability studies (Myreddi & Narayan, 2000). The majority of schools in India are poorly designed and few are equipped to meet the unique needs of students with disabilities. It is also worth noting that there are challenges, around procuring and resourcing for assitive devices. Despite various efforts of inclusive education in India, about 94% of children with disabilities didn't receive any educational services. Over and above some of these challenges that India shares with other developing countries are some distinctive features that will make the implementation of educational reform, particularly difficult. The commitment of the Government of India to Universalisation of Elementary Education (UEE) cannot be fully achieved, without taking care of special educational needs of the physically and mentally challenged children.

65 What percentage of children with disabilities didn't receive any educational services?

(a) 90% (b) 94%
(c) 95% (d) 80%

66 What is/are the barrier(s) of inclusive education?

(a) Teachers are untrained.
(b) Lack of implementation
(c) Schools are poorly designed and unequipped.
(d) All of the above

67 Why Universalisation of Elementary Education (UEE) can't be fully achieved?

(a) Due to lack of funds
(b) Special educational needs remained unfullfilled
(c) Due to policy's framework
(d) None of the above

68 **Statement I** The existing support services required for inclusive education are not sufficient.

Statement II There is improper and insufficient pre-service teacher education programs.

(a) Statement I is incorrect
(b) Statement II is correct
(c) Both statements, I and II are correct
(d) Neither statement I nor statement II is correct

ANSWERS

1	(d)	2	(d)	3	(c)	4	(d)	5	(d)	6	(a)	7	(d)	8	(a)	9	(b)	10	(a)
11	(d)	12	(c)	13	(d)	14	(b)	15	(c)	16	(b)	17	(a)	18	(d)	19	(d)	20	(c)
21	(d)	22	(a)	23	(d)	24	(c)	25	(d)	26	(b)	27	(d)	28	(a)	29	(a)	30	(d)
31	(c)	32	(b)	33	(b)	34	(d)	35	(b)	36	(c)	37	(a)	38	(b)	39	(c)	40	(a)
41	(b)	42	(b)	43	(c)	44	(c)	45	(a)	46	(c)	47	(d)	48	(b)	49	(a)	50	(b)
51	(a)	52	(a)	53	(a)	54	(b)	55	(a)	56	(d)	57	(a)	58	(a)	59	(a)	60	(b)
61	(a)	62	(d)	63	(d)	64	(b)	65	(b)	66	(d)	67	(b)	68	(c)				

UGC NET/JRF/SET

EDUCATION (Paper-2)

Model Paper-1

General Instructions

1. There are total one hundred questions in this paper. Each question carries 2 marks.
2. All questions are compulsory.

---

1 According to Jalaluddin, in the system's process, how can we achieve pre-determined and specified objectives?

(a) By systematically organising the elements
(b) By organising inter-related elements
(c) By operating the elements
(d) None of the above

2 A researcher commits Type I error, when he

(a) accepts null hypothesis, when it is false
(b) rejects null hypothesis, when it is false
(c) accepts null hypothesis, when it is true
(d) rejects the null hypothesis, when it is true

3 According to National Curriculum Framework of Teacher Education (NCFTE, 1988), what are the teacher's functions and roles?

1. Organise learning resources.
2. Evaluate outcomes of learning.
3. Plan effective curricular transaction strategies.
4. Maintain silence to proceed teaching-learning process.

Select the correct answer using the codes given below

(a) 1, 2 and 3 (b) 2, 3 and 4 (c) 2, 4 and 1 (d) 3, 4 and 2

4 The book, 'Races and Culture of India' was written by

(a) DN Majumdar (b) MN Prabhu
(c) TB Bottomore (d) KM Kapadia

5 Who was the first person to use panel discussion?

(a) Henry Osborn (b) Herry A Ober Street
(c) Henry A Ober (d) Herry A Ober

6 Which of the following statement(s) is/are incorrect with regard to constructivist design?

(a) It is the youngest of the three Grounded Theory designs.
(b) Constructivist design emphasises the values and beliefs of the researcher.
(c) This type of design is not limited to the data collection and analysis.
(d) The Constructivist Design Theory was Kathy Charmaz.

7 Which of the following is/are direction of development?

1. Cephalocaudal and Proximodistal
2. Structure precedes function
3. General to specific
4. Concrete to abstract
5. Egocentrism to perspectivism

Codes

(a) 1 and 2
(b) 2 and 3
(c) 4 and 5
(d) All of these

Directions (Q. No. 8) *Given below are two statements, one is labelled as Assertion (A) and the other is labelled as Reason (R). Read the statements and choose the correct answer using the codes given below.*

(a) Both A and R are true and R is the correct explanation of A
(b) Both A and R are true, but R is not the correct explanation of A
(c) A is true, but R is false
(d) A is false, but R is true

8 **Assertion** (A) Intelligence is the ability to learn in an abstract manner or to think or adapt to his or her environment.

Reason (R) This represents a psychometric approach of intelligence, which focuses on measuring differences in intellectual abilities.

9 Match the following

List I (Interviews)	List II (Meanings)
A. Structured Interview	1. Greater flexibility approach
B. Unstructured Interview	2. Attention on the questions to be answered
C. Focussed Interview	3. Individual life experience
D. Clinical Interview	4. Pre-determined questions
	5. Non-directive

Codes

	A	B	C	D		A	B	C	D
(a)	4	1	2	3	(b)	2	4	1	3
(c)	5	2	4	1	(d)	1	3	5	4

10 "Socialisation is a process as a result of which children take on themselves the various social roles." Who said this?

(a) Cook (b) Redcliffe
(c) Linton (d) Krober

11 Which of the following tool of collecting psychological information about pupils is the most objective?

(a) Rating scale
(b) Interview
(c) Standardised test
(d) Projective devices

12 **Statement I** No educational system can be separated from political system

Statement II Considering the societal responsibilities and objectives, education and politics are inextricably related.

Codes

(a) Both statements are true, but II is not the cause of I
(b) Statement I is true, but II is false
(c) Both statements are false
(d) Both statements are true and II is the cause of I

13 Identify the non-probability sampling technique(s).

1. Stratified random sampling
2. Systematic sampling
3. Snowball sampling
4. Incidental sampling

Codes

(a) 1 and 2 (b) 2 and 3
(c) 3 and 4 (d) 1 and 4

14 Arrange the principles given by Albert Bandura in sequential order

1. Attention 2. Retention
3. Motivation 4. Reproduction

Codes

(a) 1, 2, 4, 3 (b) 2, 3, 4, 1
(c) 1, 2, 3, 4 (d) 4, 3, 1, 2

15 Attitudinal barriers can be removed with the help of

(a) discussion programmes
(b) parental support
(c) providing a sense of belongingness in the school
(d) All of the above

16 Which of the following in not an area exploited by digital libraries?

(a) Data warehouse
(b) World Wide Web
(c) Portable document format
(d) Hypertext

17 Which is the most effective reinforcement schedule according to Operant Conditioning Theory of Learning for stable learning?

1. Continuous reinforcement
2. Fixed ratio reinforcement
3. Variable ratio reinforcement
4. Fixed interval reinforcement

Codes

(a) Only 1 (b) 1, 2 and 4
(c) Only 3 (d) All of these

18 Match the following

List I (Modes of INSET)	List II (Techniques)
A. Seminar	1. Giving education in accordance to latest development
B. Workshop	2. Training one's own self
C. Auto-instructional	3. Speaker presents a theme
D. Refresher course	4. Organised to develop certain skill in teacher

Codes

	A	B	C	D		A	B	C	D
(a)	3	4	2	1	(b)	2	3	1	4
(c)	1	2	4	3	(d)	4	1	2	3

19 Who defined ICT as a set of technological tools to store information?

(a) SER (b) OECD
(c) C Bwrton (d) Beckinsale and Ram

20 The license, BYNCSA is used for

(a) not licensing the derivatives
(b) allowing others to download the work
(c) remix, tweak and build on non-commercial work
(d) None of the above

21 The terms 'employed-centered' and 'production -centred' to describe leader's behaviour were used by

(a) MC Gregor (b) Fielder
(c) Likert (d) Blake and MC Canse

22 Choose the correct statement.

1. Profession demands an adequate professional and cultural training.
2. A person in profession can behave rudely.
3. One profession can be a stepping stone for other profession.
4. Profession must satisfy an indispensable social need.

Codes

(a) 1 and 4 (b) 2 and 3 (c) 1, 3 and 4 (d) 2,3 and 4

23 Difficulty in language and communication learning disabilities are caused in

(a) dyspraxia (b) dysphasia
(c) dyslexia (d) dysgraphia

Direction (Q. Nos. 24) *Two statements are given below, one labelled as Assertion (A) and other labelled as Reason (R). Choose the correct codes for your answer.*

Codes

(a) Both A and R are true and R is the correct explanation of A
(b) Both A and R are true, but R is not the correct explanation of A
(c) Both A and R are false
(d) A is false, but R is true

24 **Assertion** (A) Curriculum design is a process of critical questioning.

Reason (R) Content needs to be designed in a structured combination.

25 Match the following

List I (Buddhist Concept)	List II (Meaning/Example)
A. Arya Satya	1. Namrupa
B. Dwadash Nidan	2. Samadhi
C. Ashtanga Marg	3. Samyaka Vyayam
D. Nirvana	4. Controlling of breath
	5. Sorrow in life

Codes

	A	B	C	D
(a)	2	4	1	3
(b)	5	1	3	2
(c)	5	1	4	2
(d)	1	5	4	3

26 Survey study aims at

1. knowing facts about the existing situation.
2. comparing the present status with the standard norms.
3. criticising the existing situation.
4. identifying the means of improving the existing situation.

Codes

(a) 1 and 2 (b) 1, 2 and 3
(c) 1, 2, 3and 4 (d) 2 and 3

27 What are the five stages of growth, according to Greiner's Model of Change?

(a) Creativity, Direction, Dedication, Collaboration, Concept
(b) Create, Dictate, Delegate, Collaborate and Control
(c) Direction, Concept, Collaborate, Creativity and Delegation
(d) Collaboration, Delegation, Direction, Creativity and Control

28 What do you mean by 'Espirit De Crops'?

(a) Team Spirit
(b) Confidence of the player
(c) Spiritual upliftment
(d) None of the above

29 Rearrange the following statements according to their correct sequence.

1. Employers set wages for the workers.
2. Employers makes the hiring decision through analysis.
3. Employers predict productivity by using the educational qualification of the employee.
4. Employers select the candidate on the basis of the educational qualification for interview.

Codes

	A	B	C	D
(a)	4	3	2	1
(b)	4	2	3	1
(c)	3	4	2	1
(d)	1	2	3	4

Direction (Q. No. 30) *Given below are two statements one labelled as Assertion (A) and the other labelled as Reason (R). Following are the codes given below. Choose the correct option.*

Codes

(a) Both A and R are true
(b) Both A and R are false
(c) A is true but R is false
(d) A is false but R is true

30 **Assertion** (A) Distance learning is for student who wish to stay in hostel and complete their study.

Reason (R) Distance learning is time and place flexible.

31 Arrange the ABCD technique, used in REBT counselling, in sequential order.

1. Dispute 2. Consequence
3. Belief 4. Action

Codes

(a) 4, 3, 2, 1 (b) 1, 2, 3, 4
(c) 4, 2, 3, 1 (d) 2, 1, 4, 3

32 An event which portrays the initiation of more than one activity is called the

(a) Head event (b) Dual event
(c) Merge event (d) Burst event

33 According to the definition given by 'UNESCO' Information and Communication Technology (ICT) includes
(a) information technology
(b) enhancement in technology
(c) management techniques
(d) communication technology

34 Choose the correct statement
1. Placement assessment occurs after the student has completed the course.
2. Formative assessment is carried out throughout the course.
3. Summative assessment occurs at the end of course.
4. Diagnostic Assessment helps the teacher, to identify student's current knowledge and skill.

Codes
(a) 1 and 2 (b) 1 and 3
(c) 2, 3 and 4 (d) 1, 3 and 4

35 How educational technology achieves its objectives?
(a) By communicating
(b) By providing guidance
(c) Through effective teaching
(d) Through application of science and technology

36 Match the following

List I (Condition)		List II (Characteristics)
A. Dysphapsia	1.	Difficulty in reading
B. Dyscalculia	2.	Difficulty in fine motor skills
C. Dyspraxia	3.	Language difficulty
D. Dyslexia	4.	Difficulty in maths

Codes

	A	B	C	D		A	B	C	D
(a)	2	1	4	3	(b)	3	4	2	1
(c)	4	3	1	2	(d)	1	2	3	4

37 Participant's observation methods is used in
(a) experimental research (b) ethnographic studies
(c) historical research (d) ex-post facto research

Direction (*Q.Nos. 38) Given below are two statements, one labelled as Assertion (A) and other labelled as Reason (R). Following are the codes given below. Choose the correct codes.*

Codes
(a) Both A and R are true
(b) Both A and R are false
(c) A is true, but R is false
(d) A is false, but R is true

38 **Assertion** (A) Gagne made exceptional contribution in the field of instructional design.
Reason (R) Gagne has propounded 'ADDIE Model'.

39 In Galloway's System of Observation, the encouraging and restricting are the part of
(a) direct interaction
(b) verbal interaction
(c) indirect interaction
(d) non-verbal interaction

40 Which of the following gives a more accurate measure of relationship than the other three?
(a) Spearman's Rho
(b) Biserial Correlation
(c) Kendall's Tau
(d) Product Moment Method

41 In FIAS system, the entire classroom's interaction is put into how many categories?
(a) One (b) Two
(c) Three (d) Four

42 The world .... has been used by educator to evaluate, measure and document the academic progress.
(a) assessment (b) evaluation
(c) documentation (d) measurement

43 Rorscharch Ink Blot Test in an example of which method?
(a) Interview (b) Projective Techniques
(c) Sociometry (d) Observation

Direction (Q. No. 44) *Given below are two statements, one labelled as Assertion (A) and other labelled as Reason (R). Following are the codes given below.*

Choose the correct code for each.

Codes
(a) Both A and R are true
(b) Both A and R are False
(c) A is true, but R is false
(d) A is false, but R is true

44 **Assertion** (A) SSA's main aim is universalisation of elementary education.
Reason (R) SSA works at a state level.

Direction (*Q. Nos. 45) Below two statements are given in which one is Assertion (A) and another is Reason (R) Select the Correct code.*
(a) Both A and R are true and R is the correct explanation of A.
(b) Both A and R are true, but R is not the correct explanation of A
(c) Only A is true, but R is false
(d) Only R is true, but A is false

45 **Assertion** (A) An associated disability among physically handicapped children is cerebral palsy.
Reason (R) A survey shows that 56% of the pupils intake in schools for the physically handicapped are mentally handicapped also.

46 Which combination of the following points is true of non-parametric methods?

1. Do not demand assumption about population.
2. Actual scores are used in combination.
3. Generalisation do not seem to be realistic.
4. They are also called distribution free method.

Select the correct option

(a) 1, 2 and 3 (b) 1, 3 and 4
(c) 2, 3 and 4 (d) 2, 3 and 1

47 The name of Stephen M Corey is associated with

(a) fundamental research (b) action research
(c) applied research (d) sociometric research

48 What is/are the feature(s) of reflective level of teaching?

(a) It is highly thoughtful and useful
(b) Enables student to solve the real life problems
(c) Teacher does not force knowledge on students
(d) All of the above

49 Which of the following statement(s) is/are incorrect?

1. Evaluation serves to identify the strengths and weaknesses of the curriculum.
2. Evaluation is a systematic process.
3. Evaluation is a narrow concept.
4. Student's learning is an important aspect of the overall programme goals.

Codes

(a) Only 1 (b) Only 2
(c) Only 3 (d) Both 3 and 4

50 Match the following

	List I (Institutes)		List II (Years)
A.	NAAC	1.	1997
B.	QCI	2.	1991
C.	INQAAHE	3.	1994

Codes

	A	B	C		A	B	C
(a)	2	3	1	(b)	1	3	2
(c)	3	2	1	(d)	3	1	2

51 Research is a 'scientific undertaking' opined by

(a) Young (b) Kothari
(c) Emroy (d) Kerlinger

52 Which of the following form cannot be taken by a research hypothesis

(a) declarative form (b) problem form
(c) question form (d) null from

53 Critical pedagogy firmly believes that

(a) the learner need not reason independently.
(b) what children learn out of the school is irrelevant.
(c) the experience and perception of learners are important.
(d) the teacher should always lead the classroom's instructions.

54 Tick the correct statement

1. Inclusion describes much more than acceptance of children with exceptionalities.
2. Inclusive education is carried out in a common learning environment.
3. It helps to strengthen the capacity of education system.
4. It is not an expensive method.

Codes

(a) 1 and 2 (b) 1, 2 and 3
(c) Only 4 (d) All of these

55 **Statement I** Charismatic Leadership Theory is also known as Great Man theory.

Statement II Leaders are generally energetic, enthusiastic and passionate.

Codes

(a) Statement I is true but II is false
(b) Both the statements are true
(c) Statement II is true
(d) Both the statements are false

56 How teachers help to develop critical thinking skill among students?

(a) Through practice (b) Identifying topics
(c) Specifying objectives (d) All of these

57 Psychological foundation plays its role in development of curriculum in view of the

(a) student's needs (b) student's interests
(c) student's capabilities (d) All of these

58 Identify the function(s) of educational philosophy.

1. To integrate divinity into an education of man.
2. To provide theoretical basis for teacher's behaviour.
3. To generate the principles of curriculum framework.
4. To answer all ultimate 'why' questions regarding educational practices.

Select the correct answer using the codes given below.

(a) 2 and 3 (b) 1 and 4
(c) 1, 2 and 4 (d) 2, 3 and 4

59 According to Twelkier, how can an individual solve his problem with System Approach?

(a) By managing the educational tools
(b) By examining, thoroughly
(c) Through optimal utilisation of all resources
(d) By evaluating the problem

60 Which of the following is a discrete variable ?

(a) Age (b) Nationality
(c) Test Score (d) Income

61 Which of the following statements (s) is/are correct?

1. Competency based curriculum emphasises complex outcomes of learning process.
2. It is usually designed around a set of competencies.

3. It is learner-centered and adaptive to the changing needs of the students.
4. It focuses on learning outcomes, through a set of pre-defined learning objectives.

Codes

(a) Only 1 (b) 1and 2
(c) 3 and 4 (d) All of these

62 Curriculum transaction generally incorporates

(a) effective and desired implementation of curriculum
(b) planning for providing learning experiences
(c) a written plan that drives instruction
(d) Both a and b

63 Which Article of Indian Constitution states that there is a provision of free and compulsory education for all children, until they complete the age of 14 years?

(a) Article 29 (b) Article 26
(c) Article 45 (d) Article 14

Direction (Q.No. 64) *Given below are two statements, one labelled as Assertion (A) and the other labelled as Reason (R). Following are the codes given below. Choose the correct code.*

Codes

(a) Both A and R are true
(b) Both Aand R are false
(c) A is true, but R is false
(d) A is false, but R is true

64 **Assertion** (A) Andragogy means the understanding of science and practice of adult learning.

Reason (B) In Greek, andragogy means 'man leading'.

65 Match the following

List I (Types of Researches)	List II (Characteristics)
A. Fundamental research	1. Finding out the extent of preceived impact of an intervention
B. Applied research	2. Developing and effective explanation through theory building
C. Action research	3. Determining impact of social intervention
D. Evaluative research	4. Exploring the possibility of a theory for use in various situations

Codes

	A	B	C	D		A	B	C	D
(a)	1	2	4	3	(b)	2	1	3	4
(c)	4	3	2	1	(d)	1	2	3	4

66 Who defined "profession as an occupation that claims the exclusive technical competencies and also adheres to service ideals and allows ethics of professional conduct"?

(a) William (b) Wilson (c) Obidi (d) Falade

67 A snake learns to dance to the tune of a flute. Which of the following theories is applicable in this case?

(a) Skinner's Operant Conditioning
(b) Thorndike's Connectionism
(c) Kurt Lewin's Field theory
(d) Pavlov's Classical Conditioning

68 Match the following

List I (Tools)	List II (Made for)
A. Braille books	1. Handicapped people
B. Sign language interpreters	2. Visually impaired people
C. Ramps	3. Deaf People
D. Computer electronic speech devices	4. Speech impaired people

Codes

	A	B	C	D		A	B	C	D
(a)	2	1	3	4	(b)	2	3	1	4
(c)	1	2	3	4	(d)	3	4	2	1

69 Which of the following statement (s) is/are incorrect?

1. Curriculum is a written plan that drives instruction.
2. Curriculum transaction does not incorporate planning.
3. Curriculum should change with change in time.
4. A noble curriculum plays an important role to the development of thinking skills.

Codes

(a) 1and 2 (b) Only 2
(c) Only 3 (d) Only 4

70 Arrange the steps of instruction, in Gagne's Nine Events of Instruction in chronology.

1. Stimulating recall of prior learning
2. Gain attention
3. Presenting the stimulus
4. Informing the learners about the objective

Choose the correct option.

(a) 1, 4, 3, 2 (b) 2, 4, 1, 3
(c) 1, 2, 4, 3 (d) 4, 3, 1, 2

71 The strategy which helps the teacher to improve and modify the framework of curriculum is

(a) needs assessment (b) feedback and evaluation
(c) implementation (d) All of these

72 Who suggested the components of emotional intelligence?

(a) Guilford (b) Gardner
(c) Goleman (d) Cattell

73 Curriculum presents an instructional material is stated by

(a) Elizhalh Maccis (b) Jack Kerr
(c) W Teller (d) Smith

74 CIPP Model emphasised upon
(a) producing evaluative data for decision-making
(b) repetition of skills
(c) content enhancement
(d) None of the above

75 Which of the following statements regarding the meaning of research are correct?
1. Research refers to a series of systematic activity or activities undertaken to find out the solution of a problem.
2. Process wherein verification of hypothesis, data analysis, interpretation and formation of principles can be done.
3. It is an intellectual enquiry or quest towards truth.
4. It leads to enhancement of knowledge

Codes
(a) 1, 2 and 3 (b) 2,3 and 4
(c) 1, 3 and 4 (d) 1,2,3 and4

76 Find the correct pair.
(a) Schulman - Competency Based Model
(b) Skinner - Operant Conditioning
(c) Deng -PCK
(d) Watson - Reflective Teaching

77 If a child develops logical operations from simple associations and add, subtract, multiply and divide, then the stage of development he has reached is
(a) sensory motor (b) pre-operational
(c) concrete operational (d) formal operational

78 Which theory was given by Thorndike?
(a) Operant Conditioning Theory
(b) Connectionism Theory
(c) Reinforcement Theory
(d) Gestalt Theory

79 Kirkpatrick's Model was developed in..........
(a) 1940s (b) 1950s (c) 1960s (d) 1970s

80 The first four and most crucial of Freud's stages of psychosexual development are
(a) Anal, Oral, Latency and Phallic
(b) Oral, Anal, Phallic and Latency
(c) Oral, Anal, Genital and Latency
(d) Anal, Latency, Phallic and Genital

81 Arrange the steps of non-directive counselling in sequential order.
1. Free expression of feelings
2. Development of insight
3. Classification of positive and negative feelings
4. Termination of counselling situation
5. Defining the problematic situation

Codes
(a) 1, 2, 3, 5, 4 (b) 5, 1,2, 3,4
(c) 4, 3, 2, 1, 5 (d) 1, 2, 3, 4, 5

82 Education and training are investments that make individuals genuinely more productive. Name the theory which claims this.
(a) Signaling Theory
(b) Human Capital Theory
(c) Cognitive Development Theory
(d) None of the above

83 National Education Commission is popularly Known as
(a) Kothari Commission
(b) Ganguly Commission
(c) Verma Commission
(d) None of the above

84 Match the following

List (Books)	**List II** (Author)
A. Curriculum Implementation	1. Ralph Tyler
B. Basic Principles of Curriculum	2. Tanner and Tanner
C. The Curriculum	3. Bobbit

Codes

	A	B	C		A	B	C
(a)	1	2	3	(b)	3	2	1
(c)	2	1	3	(d) None of these			

85 Tanner and Tanner emphasises Three Principle Models of Curriculum Change in the year
(a) 1979 (b) 1980
(c) 1981 (d) 1986

86 Which is not an aspect of mind according to the Realist's Theory of Knowing
(a) Awareness (b) Consciousness
(c) Behaviour (d) Process of awareness

87 The enlightened disciples of the Buddha in the Thervada tradition are called
(a) Bodhidharmas (b) Bodhisattvas
(c) Arhats (d) House holders

88 Match the following.

List I (Model)	**List II** (Characteristic)
A. Competency Based Model	1. Judging the teacher by one's own self.
B. Behaviouristic Model	2. Student's learning is dependent on themselves.
C. Reflective Teaching	3. Lesson starts with a question.
D. Inquiry Oriented Model	4. Conditioning is the base of all learning.

Codes

	A	B	C	D		A	B	C	D
(a)	1	3	4	2	(b)	3	1	2	4
(c)	4	3	1	2	(d)	2	4	1	3

89 Identify the wrong statement from the following.
(a) Growth does not continue throughout life.
(b) Heredity sets the limit for development.
(c) Development proceeds from specific to general.
(d) Correlation and not compensation is the rule in development.

90 Which philosophy developed the monitorial system in classrooms?
(a) Vedic (b) Islam
(c) Vedanta (d) Buddhism

91 Famous behaviourist psychologist(s) is/are
(a) Edward Thorndike (b) JB Watson
(c) BF Skinner (d) All of these

92 Who wrote the book 'School and Society'?
(a) Auguste Comte (b) John Dewey
(c) Emile Durkheim (d) Robert Merton

Direction (Q. No. 93) *Two statements are given below, one labelled as Assertion (A) and other labelled as Reason (R). Choose the correct codes from the following.*

Codes
(a) Both A and R are true and R is the correct explanation of A
(b) Both A and R are true, but R is not the correct explanation of A
(c) A is true, but R is false
(d) A is false, but R is true

93 **Assertion** (A) Interaction Analysis technique does not provide any information about the quality of content.
Reason (R) It is content free technique of observation. It confines only to verbal communication of teaching.

94 Which among the following is considered as 'The Father of Mental Test'?
(a) Francis Galton (b) William Stern
(c) Raymond Cattell (d) Stanford Binet

95 Arrange the following theories/ concepts in a sequential order.
1. Social intelligence
2. Theory of Multiple Intelligence
3. Triarchic Theory of Intelligence
4. Mind mapping

Codes
(a) 1, 4, 2, 3 (b) 1, 2, 3, 4 (c) 2, 3, 4, 1 (d) 2, 1, 3, 4

96 Bi-polar scale is used in
(a) semantic differential scale
(b) rating scale
(c) Thurstone scale
(d) Likert scale

97 Who defined curriculum evaluation in 1979?
(a) John Dewey (b) Bruce Tuckman
(c) Henery Morrison (d) Boyd Bode

98 NCERT was estblished by Government of India in
(a) 1960 (b) 1961 (c) 1962 (d) 1965

99 Match the Following

List I (Thinker)		List II (Philosophies)	
A.	Tagore	1.	Harmonious Development of Personality
B.	Swami Vivekananda	2.	The Doctrine of Karma
C.	Mahatma Gandhi	3.	Child is more important than all Kinds Books
D.	Buddhism	4.	Yoga as a Method of Education
		5.	The Doctrine of Dharma

Codes

	A	B	C	D
(a)	5	1	2	4
(b)	3	4	1	2
(c)	3	4	2	5
(d)	4	2	1	3

Direction (*Q. No. 100) In the questions given below are two statements, labelled as Assertion (A) and Reason (R). In the context of the two statements, select the correct code.*

Codes
(a) Both A and R are true and R is the correct explanation of A
(b) Both A and R are true, but R is not the correct explanation of A
(c) A is true, but R is false
(d) A is false, but R is true

100 **Assertion** (A) Man becomes the kind of work he does.
Reason (R) The work he does, his thinking and senses becomes accordingly.

ANSWERS

1	(b)	2	(d)	3	(a)	4	(a)	5	(b)	6	(d)	7	(d)	8	(b)	9	(a)	10	(a)
11	(c)	12	(d)	13	(d)	14	(a)	15	(d)	16	(c)	17	(c)	18	(a)	19	(c)	20	(c)
21	(c)	22	(a)	23	(b)	24	(b)	25	(b)	26	(b)	27	(d)	28	(a)	29	(a)	30	(d)
31	(a)	32	(d)	33	(c)	34	(b)	35	(d)	36	(b)	37	(a)	38	(c)	39	(b)	40	(d)
41	(c)	42	(a)	43	(b)	44	(c)	45	(a)	46	(b)	47	(b)	48	(d)	49	(c)	50	(d)
51	(a)	52	(b)	53	(c)	54	(b)	55	(a)	56	(d)	57	(d)	58	(d)	59	(c)	60	(b)
61	(d)	62	(d)	63	(c)	64	(a)	65	(a)	66	(c)	67	(d)	68	(b)	69	(c)	70	(b)
71	(b)	72	(c)	73	(d)	74	(a)	75	(d)	76	(b)	77	(c)	78	(b)	79	(b)	80	(d)
81	(b)	82	(b)	83	(a)	84	(c)	85	(b)	86	(c)	87	(a)	88	(d)	89	(c)	90	(a)
91	(a)	92	(b)	93	(a)	94	(d)	95	(a)	96	(a)	97	(b)	98	(b)	99	(b)	100	(a)

UGC NET/JRF/SET

EDUCATION (Paper-2)

Model Paper-2

General Instructions

1. There are total one hundred questions in this paper. Each question carries 2 marks.
2. All questions are compulsory.

1 Assertion (A) Change management is a systematic approach to organisation's goals, procedures and academic change.

Reason (R) Change management is a discipline, which provides special guidance for organisational success and good result.

(a) Both A and R are true and R is the correct explanation of A
(b) Both A and R are true, but R is not the correct explanation of A
(c) A is true, but R is false
(d) A is false, but R is true

Direction (Q. No. 2) *In the following questions, the Assertion (A) and Reason (R) have been put forward. Read both the statements carefully and choose the correct alternative from the following.*

(a) Both A and R are true and R is the correct explanation of A
(b) Both A and R are true, but R is not the correct explanation of A
(c) A is true, but R is false
(d) A is false, but R is true

2 Assertion (A) A child who is not taught to walk will nevertheless begin to do so when strength and ability permit.

Reason (R) It is a natural consequence of human maturation.

3 Who was the first to question the assumption, that goals are crucial in the evaluation process?

(a) Robert Stake
(b) Ralph Tyler
(c) Michael Scriven
(d) Donald Kirkpatrick

4 Match the following

	List I (Stage)		List II (Goal)
A.	Sensorimotor	1.	Abstract concepts
B.	Pre-operational	2.	Operational thought
C.	Concrete operational	3.	Symbolic thought
D.	Formal operational	4.	Object permanence

Codes

	A	B	C	D
(a)	2	4	3	1
(b)	3	1	4	2
(c)	1	2	3	4
(d)	4	3	2	1

5 "It is a powerful approach that builds on the positive core of an organisation in both action planning and tranformational change." Which is the approach of curriculum change?

(a) Bottom-Up Approach
(b) Systematic and Panic Approach
(c) Grassroot Approach
(d) Appreciative Inquiry Approach

6 **Which technique combines both correspondence and tutorial support in an institution?**
(a) Flexi study
(b) Programmed learning
(c) Distance education
(d) Computer assisted learning

7 **What is the second category of Material Distribution and Sharing Circles Model?**
(a) Collection of learning material and meta-data
(b) Local communities and answer specific pedagogy
(c) Portals that allow access to online repositories
(d) None of the above

8 **Curriculum comprises of two major dimensions i.e.**
(a) vision and control (b) structure and activities
(c) vision and structure (d) All of these

9 **Social justice should be promoted as a Principle of Inclusive Education because**
(a) it will promote equality
(b) it will help in more enrollment of students
(c) it will encourage creativity
(d) None of the above

Direction (Q. No. 10) *Given below are two statements, one labelled as Assertion (A) and the other labelled as Reason (R). Following are the codes given below. Choose the correct code.*

Codes
(a) Both A and R are true
(b) Both A and R are false
(c) A is true, but R is false
(d) A is false, but R is true

10 **Assertion** (A) Behaviourists believe that people are not good or bad from birth.
Reason (R) Experience and environment influence the person.

11 **Match the following**

List I (Concepts)	List II (Features)
A. Planning	1. Attempt in achieving coordination
B. Organising	2. Formulation of budgets
C. Staffing	3. Grouping of objectives and assignment of right people
D. Directing	4. Manpower planning or recruitment of personnel

Codes

	A	B	C	D		A	B	C	D
(a)	2	3	4	1	(b)	3	2	4	1
(c)	3	4	2	1	(d)	2	3	4	1

12 **What does the descriptive research include according to Van Dalen?**
(a) Survey studies
(b) Inter-relationship studies
(c) Developmental studies
(d) All of the above

13 **Who said that, "Intelligence is an innate general cognitive ability"?**
(a) David Wechsler (b) Cyril Burt
(c) Cattell (d) Guilford

14 **Which theory of counselling accepts that cognition and perception are two most effective determinants**
(a) Behaviouristic Theory
(b) Rational Theory
(c) Emotive and Reality Theory
(d) None of the above

15 **Which method should be used for establishing reliability of the questionnaire?**
(a) Test-Retest Method
(b) Split Half Method
(c) Parallel Form Method
(d) Rationale Equivalence Method

16 **"Ideas on inherited developmental tendencies" was proposed by**
(a) Piaget (b) Binet
(c) Crown (d) Freud

17 **Rozee is 86 years old. She continues to learn phrases in new languages, she writes poetry and she enjoys going to museums to see the latest up-coming artists. These examples of her adaptive capacities demonstrates**
(a) chronological age (b) biological age
(c) psychological age (d) social age

18 **Match the following**

List I (Researchers)	List II (Contribution)
A. Santheesh Kumar	1. Open education resources
B. William Howlett	2. Ethics in e-learning
C. Hewlett Packard	3. Social learning
D. Toprak Etal	4. e-inclusion
	5. e-learning

Codes

	A	B	C	D		A	B	C	D
(a)	1	3	4	2	(b)	3	2	4	1
(c)	5	1	4	2	(d)	5	4	1	2

19 **Name the first Chairman of the Secondary Education Commission.**
(a) JC Verma (b) BN Kashyap
(c) AL Mudaliar (d) None of these

20 **Coefficient of variation is given by**
(a) $\frac{A - Z}{\sigma}$ (b) $\frac{\sigma}{X}$
(c) $\frac{Q_3 - Q_1}{Q_3 + Q_1}$ (d) None of these

21 **Which type of education, helps students to develop a sense of social responsibility, strong intellectual and practical skills?**
(a) Empirical (b) Rational
(c) Liberal (d) Moral

22 Statement I In Signaling Theory, there is always asymmetrical information with respect to worker's productivity.

Statement II Individual workers known their skill levels, but the employers often do not know.

Codes

(a) Both Statements, I and II are true and II is the cause of I
(b) Only I is true
(c) Only II is true
(d) None of the above

23 Who among the following were the advocates of Human Capital Theory?

1. Adam Smith
2. Spencer
3. Schultz
4. Mincer

Codes

(a) 1, 2 and 3 (b) 2, 3 and 4
(c) 1, 3 and 4 (d) 1, 2, 3 and 4

24 What are the main reasons that lead to the failure of any organisation?

1. Low callibre of leader.
2. Lack of cooperative efforts.
3. Objective of organisation is not good.
4. No essential features in an organisation.

Codes

(a) 1 and 3 (b) 1, 2 and 4
(c) 2 and 4 (d) All of these

25 Which statement(s) is/are true as per Buddhist philosophy?

1. Maya is root cause of all troubles.
2. Sorrow is the root cause of all troubles.
3. Birth and death are cause of troubles.
4. Getting involved in worldly pursuits, is the cause of all troubles.

Which of the statement(s) given above is/are correct?

(a) 1, 2, 3 and 4 (b) 1 and 2
(c) 2 and 3 (d) 2, 3 and 4

26 What is menat by the term 'socialisation'?

(a) Participation in social services.
(b) Teaching rural masses that how to keep their homes and streets clean.
(c) Process of interaction, among members of the society and imbibing social values.
(d) Influence exerted on the illiterate rural masses by social organisations to send their children to schools.

27 The growth of the human relation theory is contributed by

(a) FJ Roethlisberger (b) William J Dickson
(c) W Lloyd (d) All of these

28 Skinner believes goal of psychology should be to make education

(a) accessible (b) permissible
(c) enjoyable (d) strictable

29 Choose the correct statement

1. In-service teacher education is a way of staff development.
2. In-service teacher education upgrades the knowledge of teacher.
3. In-service teacher education provides education to those who can't be available at study centre.
4. In-service teacher education referred to as continuing education.

Codes

(a) 1 and 2 (b) 3 and 4
(c) 2, 3 and 4 (d) 1, 2 and 4

30 Choose the correct statement(s)

1. In understanding level, the learner learns himself.
2. Understanding level of teaching is of higher quality than one in memory level.
3. Cramming/rote learning is not encouraged in understanding level.
4. Morrison gave a model for understanding level.

Codes

(a) 1, 2 and 3 (b) 2 and 4
(c) 1 and 4 (d) 2, 3 and 4

31 Arrange the following books in the chronological order in which they appeared.

1. Education and Sociology
2. School and Society
3. Principles of Educational Sociology, an outline
4. Dynamic Sociology

Codes

(a) 4, 2, 1, 3 (b) 1, 3, 4, 2
(c) 3, 2, 4, 1 (d) 2, 1, 3, 4

32 Pedagogy is defined as the.........of teaching.

(a) method
(b) practice
(c) Both a and b
(d) None of these

33 Counselling skill inter-personal skill, computer skill, management skill are all part of

(a) personal development
(b) professional skills
(c) intra-personal skills
(d) duality control

34 Which of the following steps are required to design a questionnaire?

1. Writing primary and secondary aims of the study.
2. Review of current literature.
3. Prepare a draft of questionnaire.
4. Revision of the draft.

Codes

(a) 1, 2 and 3 (b) 1, 3 and 4
(c) 2, 3 and 4 (d) All of these

35 Which of the following is/are the component(s) of social intelligence?
1. Knowledge related to society
2. Effective listening skills
3. Word fluency and conversational skills
4. Effective in classroom management

Codes
(a) Only 1 (b) 1 and 2
(c) 3 and 4 (d) All of these

36 Match the following

List I (Research Methods)	List II (Data Collection Tools)
A. Experimental Method	1. Using primary and secondary sources
B. Ex-Post Facto Method	2. Questionnaire
C. Descriptive Survey Method	3. Standardised tests
D. Historical Method	4. Typical characteristics tests

Codes

	A	B	C	D
(a)	2	1	3	4
(b)	3	4	2	1
(c)	2	3	1	4
(d)	2	4	3	1

37 Match the following

List I (Commission)	List II (Years)
A. University Education Commission	1. 1952-53
B. Secondary Education Commission	2. 1968,1986
C. NPE	3. 1948,49
D. Education Commission	4. 1964-66

Codes

	A	B	C	D
(a)	1	2	3	4
(b)	2	3	1	4
(c)	3	2	4	1
(d)	3	1	2	4

38 Match the following

List (Types of Correlations)	Type II (Nature of Variables)
A. Biserial correlation	1. Continuous v/s Continuous
B. Pie-coefficient	2. Continuous v/s Dichotomous
C. Point biserial correlation	3. Dichotomous v/s Dichotomous
D. Tetra-choric correlation	4. Dichotomised v/s Dischotomised
	5. Continuous v/s Dichotomised

Codes

	A	B	C	D
(a)	4	1	5	2
(b)	5	3	2	4
(c)	3	2	5	1
(d)	5	4	2	1

39 When, what, why and how, to teach is the main task of
(a) Educational Psychology (b) Educational Philosophy
(c) Economics (d) History

40 Renovation and rejuvenation of higher education is the main objective of
(a) Yashpal Committee Report
(b) Justice Verma Committee Report
(c) Kothari Education Commission Report
(d) None of the above

41 Arrange the following functions of a manager in an organisation in correct sequence.
1. Motivation 2. Controlling
3. Organising 4. Planning

Codes
(a) 3, 4, 1, 2 (b) 3, 4, 2, 1 (c) 4, 3, 1, 2 (d) 4, 3, 2, 1

42 Match the following

List I (Technology)	List II (Period)
A. Next generation web	1. 1970-1983
B. Mobile learning	2. 1984-1993
C. Multi-media	3. 1994-1999
D. web infancy	4. 2000-2005
	5. 2006 to present

Codes

	A	B	C	D
(a)	4	3	5	1
(b)	1	2	5	4
(c)	4	5	2	3
(d)	3	2	5	4

43 Who was pioneer in using case study methods in the field of psychiatry to treat his psychoneurotic patient?
(a) Dewey (b) Sigmund Freud
(c) Van Dalen (d) Best and Kahn

44 What is the name of the role adopted by an ethnographer, who joins in with the group's activities but admits to being a researcher?
(a) Complete participant (b) Participant as observer
(c) Observer as participant (d) Complete observer

45 Interaction Analysis category system in education, for increasing the teacher's effectiveness, was developed by
(a) Amindon and Semon (b) Flander
(c) Rayon (d) Richard Over

46 Match the following

Column I (Type of Portfolio)	Column II (Characteristics)
A. Showcase portfolio	1. Contains a complete record of all work done by a student in a course or programme
B. Working portfolio	2. Contains multiple example of the same type of work, done overtime and are used to assess progress
C. Progress portfollo	3. Exhibit the best of student's performance
D. All inclusive portfolio	4. Contains drafts that students and teachers reflects on process

Codes

	A	B	C	D		A	B	C	D
(a)	4	2	3	1	(b)	3	4	2	1
(c)	1	2	3	4	(d)	4	3	2	1

47 Educators use certain principles in their inclusive classrooms. From the following, which is not included as a principle?

1. Totality and individuality
2. Reduction of subject matter
3. Motivation
4. Task Analysis
5. Reliability

Codes

(a) Both 1 and 2 (b) Only 5
(c) Only 2 (d) Only 3

48 Consider the following statements about the role of NCTE.

Statement I It's main role is to achieve planned and coordinated developed of teacher education throughout the country.

Statement II It aims at training individual to teach at pre-primary, primary and secondary level.

Codes

(a) Only Statement I is true
(b) Only Statement II is true
(c) Both Statements, I and II are true
(d) Neither Statement I nor Statement II is true

49 In competency based evaluation

1. feedback includes, informal, formative and summative feedback.
2. competency sampling follows learning period/schedule.
3. observation of teacher by student.
4. students present their experience.

Choose the correct option.

(a) 1 and 3 (b) 2 and 4
(c) 1, 2 and 4 (d) 2, 3 and 4

50 **Statement I** Case study research refers to an indepth detailed study of an individual or a small group of individuals.

Statement II It looks at the social interaction of users in a given statement.

Choose the correct option.

(a) Both Statements, I and II are ture
(b) Statement I is true, but II is false
(c) Both Statements, I and II are false
(d) Statement II is true

51 Arrange the following steps of research in correct sequence.

1. Identification of research problem
2. Listing of research objectives
3. Collection of data
4. Methodology
5. Data analysis
6. Results and discussions

Codes

(a) 1, 2, 3, 4, 5, 6 (b) 1, 2, 4, 3, 5, 6
(c) 2, 1, 3, 4, 5, 6 (d) 2, 1, 4, 3, 5, 6

52 Arrange in sequence the Hierarchical Step Model of Learning given by Robert Gagne.

1. Signal Learning
2. Stimulus-Response Learning
3. Psychomotor Connection
4. Verbal Association Learning

Codes

(a) 1, 2, 3, 4 (b) 2, 1, 4, 3
(c) 3, 1, 2, 4 (d) 4, 1, 2, 3

53 Arrange the steps of directive counselling in sequential order.

1. Synthesis 2. Analysis
3. Prognosis 4. Diagnosis
5. Counselling 6. Follow-up

Codes

(a) 1, 2, 3, 4, 5, 6 (b) 2, 1, 4, 3, 5, 6
(c) 3, 2, 4, 1, 5, 6 (d) 2, 4, 3, 1, 5, 6

Direction (Q.No. 54) *Below there are two statements. One as Reason (R) and other as Assertion (A). Based on the following options choose the correct answer.*

Codes

(a) Both A and R are true (b) Both Aand R are false
(c) A is true, but R is false (d) A is false, but R is true

54 **Assertion** (A) The role of teacher in the process of curriculum change is of an expert from the discipline.

Reason (R) Experienced teachers do not tend to change their current practice easily.

55 **Assertion** (A) Socialisation is a continuous process.

Reason (R) Social learning never ends.

(a) A is true, but R is false
(b) A is false, but R is true
(c) Both A and R are true, but R is not the correct explanation of A
(d) Both A and R are true and R is the correct explanation of A

56 Which of the following aim(s) is/are not included in educating physically handicapped children?

1. To offer them basic education in ordinary schools without justifying their needs.
2. To teach them living skills, daily for independent living.
3. To provide them a special environment as per their disability requirements.
4. To help them to realise their limitations.

Codes

(a) Both 1 and 2 (b) 1 and 3
(c) Only 3 (d) Only 4

57 **Match the following**

List I (Concepts)		List II (Sociologists)	
A.	Organic solidarity	1.	Herbert Spencer
B.	Religious ethics	2.	Emile Durkheim
C.	Mode of production	3.	Vifredo Parito
D.	Social evolution	4.	Karl Marx
		5.	Max Weber

Codes

	A	B	C	D		A	B	C	D
(a)	1	3	4	2	(b)	2	1	5	3
(c)	5	3	4	1	(d)	2	5	4	1

58 **Assertion** (A) **Transformational leader can change individuals.**

Reason (R) **These leaders are concerned about the values and ethical standards.**

Codes

(a) Both A and R are true, but R is, not the correct explanation of A
(b) Both A and R are true and R is the correct explanation of A
(c) Both A and R are false
(d) A is false, but R is true

59 **Assertion** (A) **Education is the key that unlocks the door to modernisation.**

Reason (R) **Development of technology facilitates interaction among people.**

(a) A and R is true and R is the correct explanation of A
(b) A and R is true, but R is not the correct explanation of A
(c) A is true, but R is false
(d) A is false, but R is true

60 **Which model is related to Inductive Model and based on the work of Hilda Taba?**

(a) Activity Model
(b) CIPP Model
(c) Outcome Based Integrative Model
(d) Social Reconstruction Model

61 **What is the requirement of individual needs and Interest Model?**

(a) Teacher must balance student's needs and interests
(b) Teacher should be motivated
(c) Teacher should use Teacher-Centred Learning Approach
(d) None of the above

62 **Who used the word 'exclusive monopoly of knowledge' in regards with profession?**

(a) Saunder and Wilson (b) Falade and William
(c) Obidi (d) Hoyle and Megarry

63 **In ASSURE Model 'U' stands for**

(a) utilising and revising
(b) unorganise media and methods
(c) utilise media and materials
(d) unethical code of conduct

64 **What are the two dimensions of Blake and Mouton's Managerial grid?**

(a) 'Good' and 'bad'
(b) 'Concern for outcomes' and 'concern for feelings'
(c) 'Concern for people' and 'concern for results'
(d) 'Finishing tasks' and 'liking people'

65 **Who was concerned about social reconstructionism?**

(a) David Horsburgh
(b) Harold Rugg
(c) Daniel Stufflebeam
(d) John Dewey

66 **A rat learns that it will be reinforced only by a red light in its cage. This is an example of**

(a) generalisation
(b) stimulus control
(c) continuous reinforcement
(d) backward conditioning

67 **Which model is designed to meet the complex needs of children with mild disabilities?**

(a) Outcome Based Integrative Model
(b) Intervention Model
(c) CIPP Model
(d) Activity Model

68 **Persons with Disabilities Act was passed in**

(a) 1992 (b) 1993
(c) 1995 (d) 1996

69 **Operant conditioning is associated with**

(a) Vygotsky (b) Pavlov
(c) Thorndike (d) Skinner

Direction (*Q. No. 70) In each of the questions given below, there are two statements marked as Assertion (A) and Reason (R). Mark your answer as per the codes given below.*

Codes

(a) Both A and R are true and R is the correct explanation of A
(b) Both A and R are true but R is not the correct explanation of A
(c) A is true, but R is false
(d) A is false, but R is true

70 **Assertion** (A) **Human needs to adjust in a society, where he has to follow some set of rules and act properly.**

Reason (R) **Human is a social animal.**

71 **Who is the father of attitude measurement?**

(a) Rensis Likert (b) Rensis Thurstone
(c) Louise Thurstone (d) Louise Linkert

72 **Which of the following variance is not controlled or manipulated in a research design?**

(a) Variance of independent variable
(b) Variance of dependent variable
(c) Variance of extraneous variable
(d) Error variance

73 How the technology can be used for disabled children in schools?
(a) By providing barrier free classrooms
(b) By motion sensors to open doors
(c) By providing automatic door buttons
(d) Both b and c

74 Inclusive education is a process of
(a) strengthening the capacity of an education system
(b) emphasise on building of special schools
(c) more time consuming
(d) None of the above

75 Who propounded, 'Nine Elements of Constructivist Instructional Design'?
(a) David Ausubel (b) Robert Gagne
(c) Mark Gagne (d) Skinner

Direction (Q. No. 76) *Below given are two statements, one labelled as Assertion (A) and other labelled as Reason (R). Choose the correct codes for the following.*

Codes
(a) Both A and R are true and R is the correct explanation of A
(b) Both A and R are true, but R is not the correct explanation of A
(c) Both A and R are false
(d) A is false, but R is true

76 **Assertion** (A) Curriculum is generally understood as the courses offered by an educational institution.
Reason (R) It delineates the skills and concepts taught and evaluated to enhance student's achievement.

77 Why is Aurobindo's educational thinking called an integral education?
(a) Because it integrates Indian and Western education
(b) Because it does not neglect any physical, psychic and spiritual dimensions
(c) Because it believes that truth is innate
(d) It teaches us to live in harmony with nature and God

78 A method used to develop the psychomotor and manipulation skills of the students is
(a) Lecture Method
(b) Demonstration Method
(c) Aids and Materials Method
(d) None of the above

79 Effective leaders are most like to
(a) make others feel important
(b) promote a vision
(c) follow the golden rule
(d) persuade employees to admit their mistakes

80 Computer screen magnification, screen readers and Braille scanning software are for
(a) low vision students
(b) visually impaired students
(c) hearing impaired students
(d) Both a and b

81 The process, 'evaluation of outcomes' deals with
(a) assessment of student's performance
(b) implementation of Instructional System
(c) feedback of evaluation results
(d) post test's scores by students

Direction (Q. No. 82) *Select the correct codes from the following.*

Codes
(a) Both A and R are true and R is the correct explanation of A
(b) Both A and R are true, but R is not the correct explanation of A
(c) A is true, but R is false
(d) A is false, but R is true

82 **Assertion** (A) By teaching craft, Gandhiji objective was to produce craftsmen.
Reason (R) He wanted that the craft should be learnt to serve as a means for intellectual work and economical self-sufficiency.

Direction (Q.No. 83) *Given below are two statements labelled as Assertion (A) and other labelled as Reason (R). Following are the codes given below. Choose the correct code.*

Codes
(a) Both A and R are true (b) Both A and R are false
(c) A is true, but R is false (d) A is false, but R is true

83 **Assertion** (A) Constructivism has evolved from conditioned pedagogy.
Reason (R) Students construct their own knowledge by testing ideas and approaches.

84 Which adjustment(s) is/are necessary for bringing special children into mainstream schools?
(a) Proper architectural development
(b) Student's oriented components
(c) Transport facilities should be altered
(d) All of the above

85 "An .enduring cultural structure that meets certain fundamental needs of the society and establishes social control" is the definition of
(a) religion
(b) economical system
(c) social institution
(d) school

86 What are the three steps of Lewin Model of Change?
(a) Freeze, Change and Refreeze
(b) Unfreeze, Move and Freeze
(c) Unfreeze, Change and Refreeze
(d) Refreeze, Unfreeze and Movement

87 Workshops were first introduced by
(a) California University
(b) Ohio University
(c) University College of London
(d) Oxford University

88 'Great athletic skill' is an example of which of the following theories?
(a) Cattell's Theory
(b) Sternberg's Theory
(c) Gardner's Theory
(d) Thorndike's Theory

89 Which is not a type of diagnostic assessment?
(a) Pre-test
(b) Discussion
(c) Evaluation of course learnt
(d) Interviews

90 Education, according to Pragmatist is
(a) wholly pupil oriented
(b) wholly society oriented
(c) wholly purposive
(d) wholly inter-disciplinary

91 Who said that "Education is man-making. It is that by which character is formed, strength of mind is increased, intellect is expanded and by which man can stand on his own feet"?
(a) Swami Vivekananda
(b) Rabindranath Tagore
(c) Dayanand Saraswati
(d) All of the above

92 Which school held the view, "The God makes all the things good, the man meddles with and they become evil"?
(a) Marxism
(b) Existentialism
(c) Naturalism
(d) Pragmatism

93 Who said that in a society, moral education is necessary?
(a) Emile Durkheim
(b) BF Skinner
(c) Pavlov
(d) Tolman

94 Bodily Kinesthetic Intelligence is one of the component of which of the following?
(a) Guildford's Structural Model of Intellectual
(b) Cattell's Theory of Fluid
(c) Triarchic Theory of Intelligence
(d) Theory of Multiple Intelligence

95 Who among the following is the founder of Nyaya ?
(a) Mahavira
(b) Gautama
(c) Kanada
(d) Jaimini

96 The term 'summated rating' is used in
(a) Thurstone scale
(b) Likert scale
(c) Rating scale
(d) Semantic differential scale

97 What does the individual aim of education imply?
(a) Education must secure for everyone, the conditions under which the individuality is most completely developed.
(b) It must contribute to the peace and happiness of the whole society.
(c) It should have more and more institutions every year.
(d) It should be by and large the concern of the private sector.

98 Which one of these is not a way of .measuring central tendency?
(a) Measuring the middle value or mid-point after the data have been ranked (median).
(b) Measuring the value that occurs most frequently (mode).
(c) Regression analysis .
(d) Measuring the value often known as the average, that includes all data values in its calculation (mean).

99 The capacity to influence people and to accomplish desired objectives is called
(a) Power
(b) Leadership
(c) Authority
(d) Status

100 Which of the following is/are the major obstacle(s) or tool(s) to facilitate the development of inclusive system?
(a) Curriculum
(b) Instructions
(c) Teaching aids
(d) None of these

ANSWERS

1	(b)	2	(a)	3	(c)	4	(d)	5	(d)	6	(a)	7	(c)	8	(c)	9	(a)	10	(a)
11	(c)	12	(d)	13	(b)	14	(b)	15	(a)	16	(a)	17	(c)	18	(c)	19	(c)	20	(b)
21	(c)	22	(a)	23	(a)	24	(d)	25	(d)	26	(c)	27	(a)	28	(c)	29	(d)	30	(d)
31	(d)	32	(c)	33	(b)	34	(a)	35	(d)	36	(b)	37	(d)	38	(c)	39	(a)	40	(a)
41	(d)	42	(c)	43	(b)	44	(b)	45	(b)	46	(a)	47	(b)	48	(c)	49	(c)	50	(a)
51	(b)	52	(a)	53	(b)	54	(a)	55	(d)	56	(b)	57	(d)	58	(a)	59	(b)	60	(c)
61	(a)	62	(d)	63	(c)	64	(c)	65	(b)	66	(b)	67	(b)	68	(c)	69	(d)	70	(a)
71	(c)	72	(b)	73	(d)	74	(a)	75	(b)	76	(b)	77	(b)	78	(b)	79	(d)	80	(d)
81	(d)	82	(d)	83	(d)	84	(d)	85	(c)	86	(c)	87	(b)	88	(c)	89	(c)	90	(c)
91	(a)	92	(c)	93	(a)	94	(d)	95	(b)	96	(b)	97	(a)	98	(c)	99	(b)	100	(a)

UGC NET/JRF/SET

EDUCATION (Paper-2)

Model Paper-3

General Instructions

1. There are total one hundred questions in this paper. Each question carries 2 marks.
2. All questions are compulsory.

1 Which model is also known as Push In Model?

(a) Team Teaching Model
(b) Full Inclusion Model
(c) Resource Model
(d) Strategies Intervention Model

2 Which educational plan is designed for diverse learners with special needs?

(a) Individualised Education Plan
(b) Special Education Plan
(d) Inclusive Education Plan
(d) Comprehensive Education Plan

3 In his sociological explanation of religion, Durkheim made certain observations that

1. religion is mental illness.
2. god is only society personified.
3. religion brings salvation for the suffering humanity.
4. the kingdom of heaven is a glorified society.

Codes

(a) 1 and 2 (b) 2 and 3 (c) 1 and 3 (d) 2 and 4

4 Arrange the following educational process in correct sequence.

1. Collection of data
2. Statement of objectives
3. Selecting the problem
4. Method/procedure

Codes

(a) 3, 2, 4, 1 (b) 1, 2, 4, 3 (c) 4, 3, 2, 1 (d) 1, 4, 2, 3

5 Match the following

	List I (Thinker)		List II (Theories)
A.	Jean Piaget	1.	Humanistic theory
B.	Sigmund Freud	2.	Trait theory
C.	Carl Rogers	3.	Cognitive development
D.	Gordon Allport	4.	Psychoanalytic theory

Codes

	A	B	C	D		A	B	C	D
(a)	3	4	1	2	(b)	1	2	3	4
(c)	2	1	4	3	(d)	4	1	2	3

6 "Research is honest, exhaustive and intelligent searching for facts and implications with reference to a given problem". Who said this statement?

(a) J W Best (b) P M Cook
(c) M Fair Child (d) Dewey

7 Programmed learning is based on the principles of

(a) Conditioned Learning Theory
(b) Cognitive Learning Theory
(c) Gestalt Learning Theory
(d) Operant Conditioning Theory

8 Which method(s) must be used by the teachers for the disabled children?

(a) Reflective teaching
(b) Assistive technology
(c) Adaptative methods
(d) Both b and c

9 Assertion (A) Management utilises human resources only.

Reason (R) Wastage is eliminated and efficiency is increased.

Codes

(a) Both A and R are true and R is the correct explanation of A
(b) Both A and R are true, but R is not the correct explanation of A
(c) A is true, but R is false
(d) A is false, but R is true

10 Which of the following statement(s) is/are incorrect?

1. Activity model is developed to meet unique needs.
2. Learning should be based on hands-on experiments and activities.
3. It is one of the creative method in teaching.
4. It is based on Hypothetical Approach.

Codes

(a) Both 1 and 2 (b) Only 2
(c) 3 and 4 (d) Only 4

11 Which method of evaluation is used for an interview?

(a) Summative (b) Formative
(c) Diagnostic (d) Data inadequate

12 Who argues that "despite the fact that educators didn't receive in-service training on inclusion, they are expected to implement more effective delivery techniques"?

(a) King Carreiro (b) Richard A Villa
(c) Thomas P (d) Gary Thomas

13 In Multi Factor Theory, range is related to

(a) general intelligence of learners
(b) number of tasks that a person can do in a limited period
(c) difficulty level of items
(d) None of the above

14 Which of the following core values, among the institutions of higher education are promoted by the NAAC?

1. Contributing to national development.
2. Fostering global competencies, among the students.
3. Inculcating values among students and teachers.
4. Promoting the optimum utilisation of infrastructure.

Choose the correct option

(a) 2,3 and 4 (b) 1, 2 and 3
(c) 1, 3 and 4 (d) 1, 2, 3 and 4

15 Which type of e-learning trend uses computers as an interactive teaching devices?

(a) Micro-learning
(b) Adaptive e-learning
(c) Mobile learning
(d) Artificial Intelligence

16 Arrange the following steps in historical research.

1. Collection of data.
2. Selection of the problem.
3. Formulation of hypothesis.
4. Primary and secondary sources.
5. Criticism of data.

Codes

(a) 1, 2, 3, 4 and 5 (b) 2, 3, 1, 4 and 5
(c) 5, 4, 3, 1 and 2 (d) 2, 1, 4, 3 and 5

17 Which of the following is not a unique feature of education, envisaged by Swami Vivekananda?

(a) Cultivation of heart and physical strength
(b) Residential Programme of Education
(c) Intelligent and productive manual labour
(d) Importance of concentration

18 Which of the following statement(s) is/are not true?

(a) Method of the behaviour ratios, provides qualitative analysis of teacher's behaviour.
(b) Method of interpretation categories, provides qualitative analysis of teacher behaviour.
(c) For the recording of the classroom events, the observer must memorise the category number, in relation to the compare behaviour.
(d) Silence or confusion is given the category or code number 10, for the recording of classrooms events in Flander's system.

19 Match the following

	List I(Designs)		List II(Characteristics)
A.	Systematic design	1.	Theory to emerge from the data, rather than forcing the data into pre-conceived categories
B.	Emergent design	2.	Emphasises the values and beliefs of the researcher
C.	Constructivist design	3.	Developed initially for nurses
D.	Feminist Grounded theory	4.	It is composed of three stages open, axial and selective coding

Codes

	A	B	C	D
(a)	4	1	2	3
(b)	2	3	4	1
(c)	4	2	3	1
(d)	1	2	3	4

Direction (Q.No. 20) *Two statements are given below, one labelled as Assertion (A) and other labelled as Reason (R). Choose the correct codes for the following.*

Codes

(a) Both A and R are true, but R is not the correct explanation of A
(b) Both A and R are true and R is the correct explanation of A
(c) A is true, but R is false
(d) A is false, but R is true

20 Assertion (A) Quality education is not an easy concept to qualify.

Reason (R) Quality determines how much and how well children learn.

21 Gabriel Almond suggested that the function of political system perform at these levels.

(a) Capability (b) Conversion (c) System (d) All of these

22 Behaviourist Psychologist are also called

(a) Behavioural Theorist (b) R-S Theorist
(c) S-R Theorist (d) R-S Psychologist

23 "Knowledge results from the combination of grasping experience and transforming it", was said by

(a) Kolt (b) Koll (c) Kolb (d) Kolk

24 Which of the following is true for the processes of growth and development?

(a) Both are natural processes.
(b) Growth is natural while development needs external intervention.
(c) If growth is satisfactory, development follows.
(d) Both the process go together without any external intervention.

25 The 'Attaran' defined the term 'information technology' as the use of

(a) computer and software
(b) information and knowledge
(c) experience
(d) radio and television

26 Arrange the different stages of counselling, given by the Emotive Reality theory in sequential order.

1. Investigation of problem
2. Defining binary problem
3. Identification of the alternatives
4. Planning
5. Taking action
6. Evaluation and feedback

Codes

(a) 2, 3, 4, 5, 6, 1 (b) 1, 2, 3, 4, 5, 6
(c) 6, 5, 4, 3, 2, 1 (d) 4, 2, 1, 3, 5, 4

27 Match the following

List I (Types of Samplings)	List II (Purposes Served)
A. Dimensional sampling	1. Choosing the nearest individuals to serve as respondents
B. Cluster sampling	2. Hand pick the cause to be included on the basis of their typical characteristics
C. Purposive sampling	3. Selecting a specific group of individuals from a widely dispersed population
D. Convenience sampling	4. Identifying various factors of interest in a population and obtaining at least one respondent of every combination
	5. Sampling in stage wise

Codes

	A	B	C	D
(a)	3	2	5	4
(b)	4	3	2	1
(c)	2	3	1	4
(d)	5	2	3	4

28 Centralisation of power in an organisation denotes

(a) Concentration of decision-making power at the top level
(b) subordinates are given a great role in management
(c) optimum utilisation of all the human resources
(d) None of the above

29 "Statements intended to change pupil's behaviour, from non-acceptable pattern, pointing someone out stating, why the teacher is doing and what he is doing". This statement falls under which category of Flander's Interaction Analysis?

(a) Lecturing
(b) Pupil's talk response
(c) Criticising or justifying authority
(d) Pupil's talk initiation

30 Arrange the following stages, which are important in budget development in schools.

1. Study the budgeting guidelines issued by the Ministry of Education.
2. Identify and list activities to be carried out in the school within the session.
3. Give an estimated cost of human and physical resources.
4. Identify and list the resources, both human and physical that will be required.
5. Using the guidelines, prepare the budget and seek approval of it by the authorities.

Codes

(a) 2, 4, 3, 1, 5
(b) 1, 3, 4, 2, 5
(c) 3, 2, 1, 5, 4
(d) 1, 2, 4, 3, 5

31 Which of the following in not an example of verbal tests?

(a) Digit span
(b) Picture arrangement
(c) Comprehension
(d) Vocabulary

32 Tick the correct statement(s).

1. The United Nation's Conventions on the Rights of Person with Disabilities is an international treaty.
2. It seeks to protect the rights of all persons with disabilities.
3. UNCRPD came into force as an International Human Rights Law on 3rd May, 2008.
4. The UNCRPD provides a wide range of basic rights to person with disabilities.

Codes

(a) 1 and 2 (b) 2 and 3
(c) 1, 2 and 4 (d) 1 and 3

33 What are the different models of teacher education?

1. Behaviouristic Model
2. Collaborative Model
3. Competency Based Model
4. Inquiry Oriented Model

Codes

(a) 1, 3 and 4 (b) 1, 2 and 3
(c) All of the above (d) None of the above

34 Which of the following commission(s) first decentralised the primary education?

(a) Hunter Commission (b) Mudaliar Commission
(c) Kothari Commission (d) Sadlar Commission

35 Which device impart training to the experienced or inexperienced teachers learning the art of teaching?

(a) Interaction Analysis
(b) Simulated Social Skill Training
(c) Micro Teaching
(d) All of the above

36 Arrange the following steps of research in correct sequence.

1. Identification of research problem.
2. Listing of research objectives.
3. Collection of data.
4. Methodology.
5. Data analysis.
6. Results and discussions.

Choose the correct option

(a) 1, 2, 3, 4, 5, 6 (b) 1, 2, 4, 3, 5, 6
(c) 2, 1, 3, 4, 5, 6 (d) 2, 1, 4, 3, 5, 6

37 The first National Policy of Education in free India was launched in the year

(a) 1947 (b) 1964 (c) 1968 (d)1986

38 In Tagore's Education System, the child learns better by

1. debates and discussions
2. reading, writing and speaking
3. dance, drama and music
4. travelling and interacting with nature

Codes

(a) 1, 2, 3 and 4 (b) 1, 3 and 4
(c) 1, 2 and 3 (d) 2, 3 and 4

39 Which of the following is the first decision that needs to be made, when developing a portfolio?

(a) What goes in it?
(b) How and when are the entries selected?
(c) What should it look like?
(d) How is the portfolio evaluated?

40 Who said that "curriculum is the sum of all the activities, experiences and learning opportunities for which an institution takes responsibility either deliberately or by default"?

(a) John Dewey (b) Coles
(c) Tanner (d) Smith

41 'Growth of Mind' is a work of

(a) Max Wertheimer
(b) Kurt Koffka
(c) Wolfgang Kohler
(d) Carl Rogers

42 Power of the test of significance means probability of what?

(a) Incorrect rejection of the null hypothesis
(b) Correct rejection of the null hypothesis
(c) Incorrect acceptance of the null hypothesis
(d) Correct acceptance of null hypothesis

43 Which of the following is an advantage of an Interview Method of Data Collection versus a questionnaire?

(a) Data are less expensive to obtain.
(b) Data collectors do not need to be trained.
(c) Data may be collected more easily from a wide spread geographical area.
(d) Data collectors may assess/enhance validity of responses.

44 'Tamso Ma Jyotirgmaya' means

(a) Bringing from darkness to light
(b) Bringing from disbelief to faith
(c) Both a and b
(d) None of the above

45 Which of the following is not a characteristic of informal education?

(a) It is a structured activity
(b) It is determined by an individual
(c) There is no existence of a teacher
(d) It is a life long process

Direction (Q. No. 46) *Given below are two statements one labelled as Assertion (A) and other laballed as Reason (R). In the context of the given statements, select the correct codes given below.*

(a) Both A and R are true
(b) Both A and R are false
(c) A is true, but R is false
(d) A is false, but R is true

46 **Assertion** (A) Philosophy helps in determining aims of education.

Reason (R) Education depends mostly on Philosophy.

47 Teacher's professionalism means

(a) the extent to which a teacher subscribes to a professional code.
(b) a teacher has to teach for the sake of getting salary.
(c) a teacher must have completed professional teacher training course before his appointment.
(d) All of the above

48 Who started the 'Neel Bagh' in India?

(a) David Horsburgh
(b) John Dewey
(c) Daniel Stufflebeam
(d) Ralph Tyler

49 Which educationist thinker offers a systematic way of curriculum and instruction?
(a) Tyler (b) Westerly
(c) Richard (d) Bobbit

50 What are the various ICT's tools that the teacher should know?
(a) Chat rooms
(b) File Transfer Protocol (FTP)
(c) Word processing skills
(d) All of the above

51 Which of the following is not a characteristic of modernisation?
(a) Religious faith (b) Participation
(c) Empath (d) Mobility

52 Which of the following is not common to experimental and ex-post facto designs of research?
(a) Cause and effect relationship
(b) Manipulation of independent variable
(c) Controlling extraneous variable
(d) Observation of dependent variable

53 Which study was performed by Robert Rosenthal and Lenore Jacobson?
(a) Blue Star Theory
(b) Landmark study
(c) Descriptive study
(d) Analytics

Direction (Q. No. 54) *In each of the questions given below, there are two statements marked as Assertion (A) and Reason (R). Mark your answer as per the codes given below.*

Codes
(a) Both A and R are true and R is the correct explanation of A
(b) Both A and R are true, but R is not the correct explanation of A
(c) A is true, but R is false
(d) A is false, but R is true

54 **Assertion** (A) Classroom instruction should involve variety of strategies.
Reason (R) There are individual styles among students.

55 Which branch of the philosophy deals with the knowledge, structure, method and validity?
(a) Logic (b) Ethics
(c) Metaphysics (d) Epistemology

56 What does Gandhiji meant by 'drawing out the best'?
(a) religion (b) truth
(c) inner-voice (d) Both b and c

57 Match the following.

List I (Meaning)	List II (Sub-Theory)
A. Control, monitor and evaluate cognitive processing	1. Contextual Sub-Theory
B. Execute strategies assembled by meta components	2. Knowledge acquisition components
C. Encode, combine and compare information	3. Performance components
D. Specifies the behaviours considered intelligent in a particular culture	4. Meta components

Codes

	A	B	C	D
(a)	1	2	3	4
(b)	1	2	4	3
(c)	4	3	2	1
(d)	4	3	1	2

58 Which of the following is/are the principles of guidance?
1. A life long activity
2. Based on cooperation
3. Emphasis on personality
4. Flexibility

Codes
(a) Only 1 (b) 2 and 3
(c) Only 4 (d) All of these

59 "It denies the existence of Ishvara (God) or any other exterior influence. It regards the universe as consisting of two realities *i.e.* Purusha and Prakriti."
The above statements belongs to
(a) Nyaya (b) Yoga
(c) Sankhya (d) Vedanta

60 Instructional media is defined as
(a) devices and materials employed in teaching and learning
(b) materials for distance learners
(c) self-instructional aids and materials
(d) None of the above

61 Articulation refers to
(a) repetition of skills
(b) inter-relatedness of concepts of curriculum
(c) types of education experiences
(d) helps to gain knowledge

62 Name the economist who started Cost Benefit Analysis (CBA) in the field of education.
(a) M Blaug (b) M Woodhall
(c) Both a and b (d) None of these

Direction (Q. No. 63) *Two statements are given below, one labelled as Assertion (A) and other labelled as Reason (R). Choose the correct codes for the following.*

Codes

(a) Both A and R are true, but R is not the correct explanation of A
(b) Both A and R are true and R is the correct explanation of A
(c) Both A and R are false
(d) A is false, but R is true

63 **Assertion** (A) Inclusive education strengthens the capacity of the education system.
Reason (R) It involves restructuring the culture, policies and practices in schools.

64 What are the key principles of Pedagogy?
(a) Pedagogy equips learner for life.
(b) Pedagogy promotes active engagement of learner.
(c) Pedagogy demands consistent policy framework, with support for learning as their primary focus.
(d) All of the above

65 The internal validity of an experimental research is related to
(a) variation in the dependent variable
(b) effective control of intervening variable
(c) variation in the independent variable
(d) accuracy of measurement methods

66 Choose the correct statement(s).
1. Components of Dynamic Model are expressed in verbs.
2. There is a hierarchy, among the components.
3. The model of learner's autonomy is structurally dynamic.
4. In learner's autonomy, learners take control of their learning process.

Codes
(a) 1 and 4 (b) 2 and 4
(c) 3 and 1 (d) 1, 2 and 4

67 What is the basic trait of social movement in education?
(a) Formal (b) Informal
(c) Materialist (d) Platonic

68 Choose the correct statement.
1. Psychological factors do not affect teacher's development.
2. Interest, intelligence, aptitude and mental health are all part of psychological factors.
3. Teachers should ignore the fact that some students do not have aptitude for learning.
4. Teachers should have positive feelings and emotions.

Codes
(a) 2 and 4 (b) 1 and 3
(c) Only 1 (d) 2, 3 and 4

69 When was DeLone and McLean's is Success Model introduced?
(a) 1993 (b) 1992 (c) 2003 (d) 1990

70 Criteria of good research is written by
(a) James Harold Fox (b) PV Young
(c) Karl Popper (d) Delta Kappan

71 Match the following

List I (Online Learning)	List II (Characteristics)
A. e-learning	1. Promotes mutual understanding
B. e-inclusion	2. Learning materials that can be modified
C. Social learning	3. Computer enhanced learning
D. Open education resources	4. Learning from and with others

Codes

	A	B	C	D		A	B	C	D
(a)	3	4	1	2	(b)	4	3	2	1
(c)	3	4	2	1	(d)	4	1	3	2

Direction (Q. No. 72) *Given below are two statements labelled as Assertion (A) and Reason (R). In the context of the two statements, which of the following is correct?*

Codes
(a) Both A and R are true (b) Both A and R are false
(c) A is true, but R is false (d) A is false, but R is true

72 **Assertion** (A) Jains are Atheist.
Reason (R) Jains reject the Vedas.

73 What is the problem that lies in the discipline-centred curriculum?
(a) It ignores the knowledge and skills among various disciplines.
(b) Content is divided into separate disciplines.
(c) Learners must have frequent opportunities.
(d) All of the above

74 Which technique is used in order to make reality easily accessible to the learner?
(a) Case study technique (b) Discovery learning
(c) Simulation technique (d) Group discussion

75 What kind of test(s) is/are used in Herbat's Model
(a) Oral (b) Written
(c) Both a and b (d) None of these

76 What is DIET?
1. It is a district level institute.
2. It arranges BRC and DRC.
3. It organises orientation programme for new teachers.
4. It helps in coordinating and implementing governmental policy.

Codes
(a) 1 and 2 (b) 1 and 4
(c) 1, 3 and 4 (d) Only 4

77 Which of the following technologies are used in Non-Formal Education System?
1. Learning and knowledge portals
2. Computed mediated communication
3. E-books and social networks
4. Computed Assissted Assessment

Codes
(a) 1 and 2 (b) Only 1
(c) 2 and 4 (d) Only 4

78 Carl Roger was a
(a) Humanistic Psychologist
(b) Cognitive Psychologist
(c) Behaviouristic Psychologist
(d) None of the above

79 The infrared systems are used for
(a) speech (b) visual
(c) hearing (d) None of these

80 The Grounded Theory Approach was developed by
(a) Heidegger (b) Glaser and Strauss
(e) Husserl (d) Denzin

81 Who held that curriculum is a gearing process?
(a) Ralph Tyler
(b) Daniel Stufflebeam
(c) Theodore Brameld
(d) Harold Rugg

82 The questionnaire was invented by
(a) John W Best
(b) Francis Galton
(c) J C Agarwal
(d) Stanley and Hopkins

Direction *(Q. No. 83) In each of the questions given below, there are two statements marked as Assertion (A) and Reason (R). Mark your answer as per the codes given below*
(a) Both A and R are true and R is the correct explanation of A
(b) Both A and R are true, but R is not the correct explanation of A
(c) A is true but R is false
(d) A is false but R is true

83 **Assertion** (A) Secondary reinforcement has important practical implications.
Reason (R) Secondary reinforcement has wide degree of generalisation.

84 Which method provides student with a chance to express their individual learning?
(a) Seminar (b) Tutorial
(c) Group project (d) Group discussion

85 NCTE became a statutory body on
(a) 17th August, 1994
(b) 17th August, 1993
(c) 17th August, 1996
(d) 17th August, 1995

86 Match the following

	List I (Models)		List II (Researchers)
A.	Objective-Centred Model	1.	Robert Stake
B.	Responsive Model	2.	Michael Scriven
C.	Goal Free Model	3.	Donald Kirkpatrick
D.	Level Based Model	4.	Ralph Tyler

Codes

	A	B	C	D		A	B	C	D
(a)	1	2	3	4	(b)	2	3	1	4
(c)	3	1	2	4	(d)	4	1	2	3

87 Who developed the word 'Poka Yoke'?
(a) Shi Chang (b) Shigeo Shingo
(c) Shewart (d) Sharlin

88 Match the following

	List I (Philosophies)		List II (Approach/ Methods)
A.	Idealism	1.	Heuristic Approach
B.	Realism	2.	Deductive Method
C.	Pragmatism	3.	Experiential Learning
D.	Naturalism	4.	Inductive Method

Codes

	A	B	C	D		A	B	C	D
(a)	3	4	1	2	(b)	4	3	1	2
(c)	2	4	3	1	(d)	2	3	4	1

89 Match the following

	List I (Scale)		List II (Associated with)
A.	Nominal scale	1.	Geometric Mean
B.	Ordinal scale	2.	Frequency distribution
C.	Interval scale	3.	Median and rank correlation
D.	Ratio scale	4.	Mean, SD and correlation

Codes

	A	B	C	D		A	B	C	D
(a)	4	3	2	1	(b)	1	3	2	4
(c)	2	3	4	1	(d)	1	4	3	2

90 Arrange in sequential order, the stages in the process of learning given by Thorndike during his experiment.
1. Fixation 2. Goal
3. Drive 4. Block
5. Random movement

Codes
(a) 3, 2, 4, 5, 1 (b) 2, 3, 4, 5, 1
(c) 1, 2, 3, 4, 5 (d) 2, 3, 4, 1, 5

91 Who was the supporter of the naturalism in education?
(a) Frobel (b) Armstrong
(c) John Locke (d) Rousseau

92 The seminal work of Raipu Tyler was published in
(a) 1949 (b) 1959
(c) 1948 (d) 1957

93 Match the following

	List I (Name of the Philosopher)		List II (Year of the Signaling Theory)
A.	Arrow	1.	1975
B.	Riley	2.	1974
C.	Spence	3.	1977
D.	Wolpin	4.	1973

Codes

	A	B	C	D
(a)	4	1	3	2
(b)	4	1	2	3
(c)	3	2	1	4
(d)	2	3	4	1

94 Article 3 of UNCRPD provides for

(a) dignity, individual autonomy and respect for difference and accessibility
(b) right to equality and non-discrimination
(c) right to life
(d) freedom from torture or cruel treatment

95 Match the following

	List I (Programmes)		List II (Year)
A.	Activity Based Teacher Education Programme	1.	1996
B.	Personalised Teacher Education Programme	2.	2000
C.	Comprehensive Teacher Education Programme	3.	2014
D.	Two Year B.ed Programme	4.	1991

Codes

	A	B	C	D
(a)	1	3	2	4
(b)	3	2	1	4
(c)	2	1	3	4
(d)	4	1	2	3

96 Match the following

	List I (Theory)		List II (Thinkers)
A.	Classical conditioning	1.	Hull
B.	Drive reduction	2.	Pavlov
C.	Sign Gestalt learning	3.	Skinner
D.	Operant conditioning	4.	Tolman

Codes

	A	B	C	D		A	B	C	D
(a)	4	2	3	1	(b)	2	1	4	3
(c)	4	2	1	3	(d)	3	2	1	4

97 Match the following

	List I (Model)		List II (Characteristics)
A.	CIPP Model	1.	Activity-centred
B.	Traditional Model	2.	Learner-centred
C.	Contemporary Model	3.	Decision-making
D.	Activity Model	4.	Subject-centred

Codes

	A	B	C	D		A	B	C	D
(a)	3	4	2	1	(b)	1	2	3	4
(c)	2	1	3	4	(d)	4	1	2	3

98 Who is mainly responsible for curriculum transaction?

(a) Student (b) Teacher
(c) Administrator (d) School

99 Who wrote the book 'Managerial Break Through'?

(a) Joseph Juran (b) Joseph Green
(c) Walter Shewart (d) Edwards Deming

100 What is referred as one of the major work of Edwards Deming?

(a) Crisis and upliftment
(b) Quality crisis
(c) Quality management in crisis
(d) Out of the crisis

ANSWERS

1 (b)	2 (a)	3 (d)	4 (a)	5 (a)	6 (b)	7 (d)	8 (d)	9 (d)	10 (d)
11 (a)	12 (a)	13 (b)	14 (b)	15 (b)	16 (b)	17 (b)	18 (b)	19 (a)	20 (a)
21 (d)	22 (c)	23 (c)	24 (b)	25 (a)	26 (b)	27 (a)	28 (a)	29 (c)	30 (a)
31 (b)	32 (c)	33 (c)	34 (a)	35 (c)	36 (d)	37 (c)	38 (b)	39 (c)	40 (b)
41 (b)	42 (d)	43 (d)	44 (a)	45 (a)	46 (a)	47 (a)	48 (a)	49 (a)	50 (d)
51 (c)	52 (b)	53 (b)	54 (a)	55 (d)	56 (d)	57 (c)	58 (d)	59 (c)	60 (a)
61 (b)	62 (c)	63 (a)	64 (d)	65 (a)	66 (a)	67 (b)	68 (a)	69 (b)	70 (a)
71 (a)	72 (a)	73 (a)	74 (c)	75 (c)	76 (b)	77 (c)	78 (a)	79 (c)	80 (b)
81 (a)	82 (b)	83 (a)	84 (b)	85 (d)	86 (d)	87 (b)	88 (c)	89 (c)	90 (a)
91 (c)	92 (a)	93 (b)	94 (a)	95 (d)	96 (b)	97 (a)	98 (b)	99 (a)	100 (d)